# Latman's
# The Copyright Law
## Sixth Edition


## William F. Patry

The Bureau of National Affairs, Inc., Washington, D.C.

**Library of Congress Cataloging-in-Publication Data**

Latman, Alan.
  Latman's The copyright law.

  Rev. ed. of: The copyright law/[Herbert Allen Howell; revised by]
Alan Latman. 5th ed. c1979.
  Includes index.
  1. Copyright—United States.   I. Patry, William F.
II. Howell, Herbert Allen.   Copyright law.
III. Title.   IV. Title: Copyright law.
KF2994.L38   1986      346.7304'82        86-17494
ISBN 0-87179-506-X    347.306482

International Standard Book Number: 0-87179-506-X
Printed in the United States of America

*For Mary Lou*

# Preface

When the fifth edition of this work was issued in November 1978, the Copyright Act of 1976 had been generally effective for only 11 months. Hopes ran high that the comprehensive yet flexible approach of the new Act would accommodate technological advances without the necessity for further legislation. Indeed, the Senate was so confident this goal had been reached that it subsequently dissolved its subcommittee on Patents, Trademarks, and Copyrights. Technology, however, quickly showed this confidence to be ill-advised, and in 1983 the Senate reconstituted its subcommittee in recognition of the increasing pressure on Congress to reinvolve itself in intellectual property matters. In the 98th Congress alone, over 50 bills concerning copyright were introduced, ranging from proposals on semiconductor chip design, home television reception of satellite signals, computer program piracy, and off-air videotaping to bills predicating favorable tariff treatment and foreign aid for developing countries on their ensuring adequate and effective protection of the intellectual property rights of Americans.

The courts have also been active, grappling with the unique blending of old and new found in the 1976 Act. The Supreme Court's decision in *Sony Corp. v. Universal City Studios, Inc.* represents just such grappling, as the Court faced the problem of fitting new technology (off-air video recording) into an ancient doctrine (fair use). Many other decisions have interpreted provisions that were new with the 1976 Act. Thus, the need for a new edition of this work, covering these decisions as well as subsequent legislative and administrative developments, was readily apparent.

This task was facilitated by Roger Zissu, Esq., of Cowan, Liebowitz & Latman and Margaret Goldstein, Esq., of Weiss, Dawid, Fross, Zelnick & Lehrman, who read the entire manuscript and made innumerable improvements in it, and by Don Farwell, Louise Goines, and Cynthia S. Baskin, my editors, who provided expert assistance. The work has also benefitted from some use of the late Professor Latman's most recent thoughts on proving infringement. His great insight, scholarship, and eloquence still pervade the treatise.

I also wish to thank Irwin Karp, Fred Koenigsberg, Carol Lee, and Charles Lieb for reading sections of the manuscript and providing many helpful suggestions. As in previous editions, the chapter on taxation is the product of Robert Halper, Esq., of Cowan, Liebowitz & Latman.

WILLIAM PATRY

*May 1986*

# Summary Contents

# Detailed Contents

# 1

# Introduction

While copyright has traditionally concerned itself with the craft of the author, composer, and artist, present-day copyright disputes are increasingly likely to involve computer programs, electronic data bases, and the transmission or reception of copyrighted works by satellite, microwave, and a host of other new technological marvels. With increasing frequency, the courts are being asked to fit these new technological uses into a copyright act which, while designed to be flexible in order to accommodate such new technologies, is nevertheless occasionally unequal to the task a mere seven years after its general effective date.

Until passage of the 1976 Copyright Act, the term "copyright" had been used in contrast to the common law right of "literary property" or "right of first publication," and implied a statutory right created by Congress in order to encourage the production and dissemination of literary, dramatic, musical, and artistic works. Copyrights are not, however, granted by any government agency. Under the 1976 Act they exist automatically from the moment of the author's creation of a work whose subject matter is covered by the Copyright Act.

Although claims to copyright are submitted to the Copyright Office, certificates of registration, unlike patent applications, are issued without any search of earlier works. Also unlike a patented work, a copyrighted work need not be novel or "nonobvious." It need only be "original," that is, be the result of independent creation and not mere copying. Additionally, while a patentee may exclude the claim of another individual who has later independently developed the same invention, a person working independently does not infringe another's copyright even though the resulting work is identical to the earlier copyrighted work. In fact, such a person can also secure a copyright for his or her work and enforce it against all others except, of course, the first copyright owner.

1

The Copyright Act of 1976 modernized an antiquated statute and struck some reasonable social compromises. One thing it did not do was simplify the learning of copyright law. While introducing a number of complex exemptions and compulsory licenses governing new technological uses of copyrighted works, Congress left intact centuries of Anglo-American case law on such fundamental concepts as originality and substantial similarity. In view of this, it will be profitable to glance at the historical background of copyright.

## Historical Background

### England and the Statute of Anne

Our law relating to literary and artistic property is essentially an inheritance from England. It seems that from the time "whereof the memory of man runneth not to the contrary," the author's right to his or her manuscript was recognized on principles of natural justice, being the product of intellectual labor and as much the author's own property as the substance on which it was written.[1] Blackstone[2] associates it with the Law of Occupancy, which involves personal labor and results in "property," something peculiarly one's own (as implied by the Latin root "proprius"). But ages before Blackstone, the Irish King Diarmed had enunciated the same principle in settling a dispute between Abbot Fennian and St. Columba over the latter's furtive copying of the Abbot's Psalter, declaring "to every cow her calf."[3]

When printing from movable type was introduced into England by William Caxton circa 1476, a new trade was created, but problems

---

[1] See *Millar v. Taylor*, 4 Burr. 2303, 2398 (1769) (Mansfield, Lord Justice):
"From what source, then, is the common law drawn, which is admitted to be so clear, in respect of the copy before publication? From this argument—because it is just, that an author should reap the pecuniary profits of his own ingenuity and labor."

[2] 2 COMMENTARIES 405. But cf. A. BIRRELL, THE LAW AND HISTORY OF COPYRIGHT 11 (1899): "Occupancy and Labour are the mythical parents of Property, but we shall be less wrong in assuming that the pedigree was invented to account for the fact of possession than in attributing the fact of possession to the virtues of the pedigree."

[3] Although the story is popularly believed to be apocryphal, Birrell relates how a copy of the Psalter in St. Columba's handwriting had been exhibited in the Museum of the Royal Irish Academy in Dublin in 1867. See BIRRELL, *supra* note 2, at 42. The nonsectarian nature of copyright is revealed in the following Venetian decree issued in 1623:
"We have agreed to the reasonable and proper request of the worthy and honored Master Salamon Rossi of Mantua (may his Rock keep and save him) who has become by his painstaking labors the first man to print Hebrew music. He has laid out a large disbursement which has not been provided for, and it is not proper that anyone should harm him by reprinting similar copies or purchasing them from a source other than himself. Therefore, having seen the license granted by His Excellence, the *Cattavero* (may his glory be exalted), we the undersigned decree by the authority of the angels and the word of the holy ones, invoking the curse of the serpent's bite, that no Israelite, wherever he may be, may print the music contained in this work in any manner, in whole or in part, without the permission of the above-mentioned author or his heirs for a period of fifteen years from this date. Nor is any Jew permitted under the terms of this decree to buy from any person, whether he be of our nation or not, any of these works without the permission of the above-mentioned author, who is to indicate by some special mark that he has consented to their sale by another party. Let every Israelite hearken and stand in fear of being entrapped by this ban and curse. And those who hearken will dwell in confidence and ease, abiding in blessing under the shelter of the Almighty. Amen."

of unauthorized reproduction were not immediately encountered owing to the small number of presses. In the following decades, publishers' efforts centered principally on preventing the importation and sale of English language books printed abroad. Books had, of course, been created and distributed prior to 1476, and as early as 1403 a guild consisting of calligraphers, illuminators, bookbinders, and booksellers had been established in London. This guild, chartered in 1557 by the Catholic Queen Mary and King Philip, was known as the "Stationer's Company."

The primary purpose of the charter was to check the spread of the Protestant Reformation by concentrating the whole printing business in the hands of the members of the Stationer's Company. As the Court of the Star Chamber had jurisdiction over the enforcement of royal decrees, the government and the church could thereby exercise effective censorship and prevent seditious or heretical works from getting into print, although this goal was not fully realized until 1566, the year of the first Star Chamber decree regulating printing.[4]

For their part, the members of the Stationer's Company as a body had no particular interest in religious or political censorship, but considerable interest in utilizing their newly granted monopolistic powers to eliminate competition. Authors *qua* authors were in no way protected. Under the charter, all published works had to be entered in the register of the Stationer's Company and in the name of some member of that company. By virtue of this entry and supported by the Star Chamber, the Stationer successfully claimed the sole right to print and publish the work for himself and his heirs and assigns *forever*.

Following the chartering of the Stationer's Company, significant Star Chamber decrees were proclaimed in 1566, 1586, and 1637. In 1641, the "Long Parliament" abolished the Star Chamber, and the power of the Stationer's Company correspondingly diminished. Two years later, however, the company succeeded in getting Parliament to pass a licensing act forbidding, among other things, the unauthorized printing of copies of books published by its members. Further licensing acts were passed in 1649, 1661, 1664, and 1665, this last act expiring in 1679 upon the dissolution of Parliament. A new act, with a seven-year term, was passed in 1685 and extended in 1692 for two additional years. In 1694, Parliament refused to renew the legislation, and the licensing acts ended. Subsequently, independent printers began to spring up and invade the sacred domain of the Stationer's Company. As a result, the company applied to Parliament for a law to protect its alleged rights in perpetuity against these "pirates." As the event turned out, the stationers got much less than they had reckoned on, for Parliament, instead of recognizing their perpetual rights, proceeded to pass a law limiting the exclusive right of publication to a set term of years.[5]

---

[4]H. HALLAM, 1 CONSTITUTIONAL HISTORY 238 (1873).
[5]E. DRONE, A TREATISE ON THE LAW OF PROPERTY IN INTELLECTUAL PRODUCTIONS 69 (1879).

This was the celebrated Statute of Anne,[6] the first statute specifically to recognize the rights of authors and the foundation of subsequent legislation on the subject of copyright both here and in many other countries.[7] Because of its historical importance in relation to the study of our own copyright laws, it is well to note some of its provisions.

So far as existing works were concerned, the statute provided that the "authors or their assigns" should have the sole right of publication for 21 years, but for new works the right was to run for 14 years, and the author, if living at the expiration of such term, was granted the privilege of renewal for 14 more years. Suitable penalties were provided for violation of the Act, but conditioned always upon entry of the title of the work in the register books of the Stationers' Hall as evidence of ownership and deposit of copies of the work itself in certain designated libraries of the Kingdom. Somewhat later, as a further security to the general public so that "none may offend through ignorance of the copyright," the provision for notice of such entry was required to appear on every copy of the published work. And in order to protect the public from monopolistic prices, individuals believing that the price of a copyrighted book was "too high and unreasonable" could petition designated officials, who were empowered to reform the price.

While the statute seemed plain enough, the stationers nevertheless still contended that their perpetual rights were not taken away but that the purpose of the Act was merely to enable them to obtain speedier relief against piracy, this being the only thing they had sought from Parliament in the first place. For more than a half a century the lower courts sustained them in this view by granting many injunctions, even after the expiration of the term fixed by the statute. But in the famous case of *Donaldson v. Becket*[8] the House of Lords ruled against them, holding that upon publication, the right persisted only for the terms fixed by the statute. This decision overruled a case decided only five years earlier by the King's Bench, *Millar v. Taylor*.[9]

The Statute of Anne expressly permitted the importation of books in foreign languages without the recognition of any rights on the part of the foreign authors; but it said nothing about importation

---

[6] 8 Anne c. 19 (1710).

[7] See H. RANSOM, THE FIRST COPYRIGHT STATUTE (1956).

[8] 4 Burr. 2408, 98 Eng. Rep. 257 (H.L. 1774). Considerable confusion over the House of Lords' judgment with respect to the existence of a common law right has been caused by the failure to distinguish between the advisory opinions of the judges of the King's Bench, Common Pleas, and Exchequer to five questions submitted them by the House of Lords, and, apparent inaccuracies in reporting the votes of the judges on these questions. This topic is thoroughly explored in Abrams, *The Historic Foundation of American Copyright Law: Exploding the Myth of Common Law Copyright*, 29 WAYNE L. REV. 1119, 1156–1171 (1983).

[9] 4 Burr. 2303, 98 Eng. Rep. 201 (K.B. 1769). For excellent discussions of *Donaldson* and *Millar*, see BIRRELL, *supra* note 2, at 111–138, and Whicher, *The Ghost of Donaldson v. Becket*, 9 BULL. COPR. SOC'Y 102, 124–141 (1961); Abrams, *supra* note 8. Interestingly, both cases involved the same work, James Thomson's *The Seasons*.

of books in English printed or reprinted abroad. Such a contingency seemed out of the question, as the printing business had not as yet become a prominent institution in the Colonies. But later on, had Benjamin Franklin chosen to enlarge his printing plant, books rather than tea might well have become the bone of contention leading to the Revolution.

### The Colonies and the Constitution

After the Revolution, all of the Colonies except Delaware passed laws to afford a measure of protection to authors, pursuant to a recommendation of the Continental Congress[10] and the entreaties of one Noah Webster. But these laws were limited in their operation to the boundaries of each state. Hence, if the author of one state wished to secure protection for his work in the other states, he was obliged to comply with a multitude of laws.[11] The same situation prevailed at that time in Europe, but on this side of the Atlantic, where all spoke the same language and read the same books, a uniform national law soon became imperative.

The framers of the Constitution, therefore, embodied in that immortal instrument a simple and direct clause empowering Congress "to promote the progress of science and useful arts, by securing for limited times to authors and inventors the exclusive right to their respective writings and discoveries."[12] It should be noted that this clause does not use the terms "copyrights" and "patents," but nevertheless covers both forms of property.[13] The selection of the terms "writings" and "authors" for copyrights was made by the committee on detail or style, and the clause was adopted by the Constitutional Convention without debate.

Some contemporaneous light on the clause is often sought from the succinct, if not enigmatic, comment of Madison in *The Federalist*:

> "The utility of this power will scarcely be questioned. The copyright of authors has been solemnly adjudged, in Great Britain, to be a right of common law. The right to useful inventions seems with equal reason to belong to the inventors. The public good fully coincides in both cases with the claims of individuals. The States cannot separately make effectual provision for either of the cases, and most of them have anticipated the decision of this point, by laws passed at the instance of Congress."[14]

---

[10]24 JOURNALS, CONTINENTAL CONGRESS 326 (1783). These statutes have been reprinted in COPYRIGHT ENACTMENTS: LAWS PASSED IN THE UNITED STATES SINCE 1783 RELATING TO COPYRIGHT (Copyright Office Bulletin No. 3, Revised 1973).

[11]See *Hudson & Goodwin v. Patten*, 1 Root 133 (Conn. 1789), for a clash of interests between the assignees of copyright in different states.

[12]U.S. CONST. art. I, §8, cl. 8.

[13]See Crawford, *Pre-Constitutional Copyright Statutes*, 23 BULL. COPR. SOC'Y 11 (1975); Fenning, *The Origin of the Patent and Copyright Clause of the Constitution*, 17 GEO. L.J. 109 (1929).

[14]THE FEDERALIST No. 43 at 279 (Mod. Lib. ed. 1941).

## The First U.S. Copyright Statute

There is no committee report on the first federal Copyright Act of May 31, 1790;[15] hence the act itself must be looked to for enlightenment as to its purpose and policy. Rather than follow the lead of France, which granted copyright protection to all authors throughout the world without the need of complying with formalities of any kind, Congress fell back upon the system of formalities and restrictions inaugurated by the Statute of Anne. In one respect, however, Congress took a distinctly American approach: unlike the Statute of Anne, which as noted above, allowed the government to reform prices believed to be too high, the U.S. Copyright Act relied solely on the marketplace.

The Act of 1790 assured protection to the author or his assigns of any "map, chart, or book" for 14 years upon:

(1) recording of the title, prior to publication, in the register book of the clerk's office of the district court where the author or proprietor resided;

(2) publication of a copy of the record so made in one or more newspapers for four weeks; and

(3) depositing of a copy of the work itself in the office of the Secretary of State within six months after publication.

The privilege of renewal of the copyright for 14 more years was granted to the author (or his assigns), provided the title was again entered and the record published. The renewal term, as in the Statute of Anne, was dependent on the survival of the author throughout the first term.

The author was given the exclusive right to "print, reprint, publish, or vend" the work. No provision was made for the vesting of copyright initially in an employer or in an individual who specially ordered or commissioned a map, chart, or book. Suits for infringement of published works were to be brought within one year after the cause of action arose by an action of debt in any court of record in the United States.[16] Following English practice, this action was *qui tam*, with half the fine (set at 50 cents per sheet found in the infringer's possession) going to the author or assignee and the other half going to the U.S. government. Unpublished manuscripts were also protected,[17] with the infringer liable for "all damages occasioned by" the

---

[15]Act of May 31, 1790, 1st Cong., 2d Sess., 1 Stat. 124.

[16]The federal trial courts were not granted original jurisdiction over copyright cases until 1819. Act of February 15, 1819, 15th Cong., 2d Sess., 3 Stat. 481. Prior to this time, unless the controversy involved more than $500 and was between citizens of different states, the suit was tried in state court.

[17]Apparently, unpublished works were entitled to perpetual protection, since the 14-year term of protection set forth in §1 of the Act applied only to published works. Unpublished works, protected under §6, contained no such limit, a surprising result in view of the Constitution's express conditioning of Congress' power to grant copyright protection for a "limited time." See further discussion in note 13, Chapter 2.

infringement. The entire amount recovered went to the copyright owner.

In the first copyright case that came before the Supreme Court, *Wheaton v. Peters*,[18] the same legal question presented in *Millar v. Taylor*[19] and *Donaldson v. Becket*[20] (viz., the effect of the act in cutting off common law rights of authors) was faced. Although the Supreme Court found, as did the House of Lords in construing the Statute of Anne, that the Copyright Act provided the exclusive mechanism for published works, it did so not on the ground that the Copyright Act had "preempted" existing common law rights, but on the ground that there was no federal common law and that, therefore, such rights "originated, if at all, under the acts of Congress."[21]

## Statutory Revision

Step by step after the 1790 statute, new copyrightable subject matter was added and the scope and term of protection enlarged. In 1802 the act was amended to include "historical and other prints"[22] and to require copyright owners to include the notice and date of deposit with the clerk of the district court on every copy of the work. At the same time, the affixing of a fraudulent notice by an individual other than the copyright owner was made punishable by a fine of $100.

In 1819 original jurisdiction over copyright and patent cases was granted to the federal courts, ending an anomaly which had prevented the federal courts from hearing such cases except where diversity of citizenship existed.[23] In 1831 the first general revision of the original act occurred.[24] Principal among the changes made by this act were the extension of protection to musical compositions (but without a right of performance), extension of the original term of copyright from 14 to 28 years, with the renewal term of 14 years being restricted to the author or his widow and/or children, and extension of the statute of limitations for actions for damages from one to two years.

In 1834 the act was amended to permit, for the first time, the recordation of assignments of copyright. Although failure to record did not result in automatic forfeiture, an assignment not recorded within 60 days of the date of execution was to be "judged fraudulent

---

[18]33 U.S. (8 Pet.) 591 (1834).

[19]4 Burr. 2303, 98 Eng. Rep. 201 (K.B. 1769).

[20]4 Burr. 2408, 98 Eng. Rep. 257 (H.L. 1774).

[21]33 U.S. (8 Pet.) at 661. The Court proceeded to examine whether common law protection existed under the law of Pennsylvania. For a discussion of the impact of *Millar* and *Donaldson* on the Court's decision, see Whicher, *The Ghost of Donaldson v. Becket*, 9 BULL. COPR. SOC'Y 102 (1961).

[22]Act of April 29, 1802, 7th Cong., 1st Sess., 2 Stat. 171.

[23]Act of February 15, 1819, 15th Cong., 2d Sess., 3 Stat. 481.

[24]Act of February 3, 1831, 21st Cong., 2d Sess., 4 Stat. 436.

and void against any subsequent purchaser or mortgagee for valuable consideration without notice."[25]

In 1846 the act was amended to require the deposit of one copy of each published work with the librarian of the Smithsonian Institution and an additional copy with the Library of Congress.[26] In 1856 the first right of public performance was granted, to dramatic compositions.[27] This right was not limited to for-profit performances. Violations of the right were to be "assessed at [a] sum not less than one hundred dollars for the first, and fifty dollars for every subsequent performance, as to the court having cognizance thereof shall appear to be just."[28]

In 1865 protection was extended to photographs.[29] At the same time, however, forfeiture of copyright was mandated for failure to comply with the requirement of deposit with the Library of Congress if the deposit copy was not provided after a request therefor had been made.

In 1870 the second general revision occurred.[30] In many respects this act was less a revision and more a consolidation, with the Library of Congress (through the Copyright Office, established under the act) assuming a central role in the administration of copyright matters. Substantively, protection was extended to paintings, drawings, chromolithographs, statues and statuaries, and "models or designs intended to be perfected as works of the fine arts." Damages for infringement of these works were set at $10 per copy.

In 1874 the notice provisions, which had required the designation "Entered according to act of Congress, in the year ____, by ____, in the office of the Librarian of Congress, at Washington," to be affixed to published copies of the work, were amended to permit as an alternative the affixing of the word "Copyright" together with the year in which the copyright was registered and the name of the copyright proprietor.[31]

About this time the general movement for international copyright began to gather momentum, and there was much agitation for it in this country as well as abroad. The result in the United States was the so-called International Copyright Act of 1891,[32] by the terms of which the copyright privilege was for the first time made available to foreigners—but only on the hard condition of their complying with the age-old requirements of entry of title, notice, and deposit, as well as that of American manufacture of "any book, photograph, chromo or lithograph." Thus, it was essentially a national rather than an in-

---

[25]Act of June 30, 1834, 33d Cong., 1st Sess., 4 Stat. 728.

[26]Act of August 10, 1846, 29th Cong., 1st Sess., 9 Stat. 106.

[27]Act of August 18, 1856, 34th Cong., 1st Sess., 11 Stat. 138. Musical compositions were granted a performance right in 1897. Act of January 6, 1897, 44th Cong., 2d Sess., 29 Stat. 481. Unlike the right found in §1(e) of the 1909 Act, this right was not limited to for-profit performances. See note 40, *infra.*

[28]See *Brady v. Daly*, 175 U.S. 148 (1899), for a decision under this provision.

[29]Act of March 3, 1865, 38th Cong., 2d Sess., 13 Stat. 540.

[30]Act of July 8, 1870, 41st Cong., 2d Sess., 16 Stat. 198.

[31]Act of June 18, 1874, 43d Cong., 1st Sess., 18 Stat. 78.

[32]Act of March 3, 1891, 51st Cong., 2d Sess., 26 Stat. 1106.

ternational measure, maintaining a good part of the century-old pattern of "encouraging learning" by granting incentives to *American* authors, while permitting pirating of most foreign works.

There may have been some cultural, if not ethical, justification for allowing freebooters to offer inexpensive foreign reprints at a time when it could be said that no one "in the four quarters of the globe * * * reads an American book."[33] But toward the end of the nineteenth century it seemed to many, especially those abroad, that more than a token international protection was needed. The result was the Berne Convention, which established an International Copyright Union in 1886, making a distinct contribution to universal law. Under this convention, as subsequently amended, protection was made automatic throughout all the countries acceding to it on behalf of the authors and artists of every country in the world, whether inside or outside the union, and without the need of complying with any formalities whatever, the sole condition being publication of the work in any union country not later than the date of publication elsewhere. The protection of unpublished works under the convention was and still is limited to citizens or residents of a union country. The initial membership of only 10 countries has now increased to over 70, including all the leading countries of the world except the United States, Russia, China, and a number of Latin-American countries. Periodic revisions of the convention have taken place at Paris (1896), Berlin (1908), Rome (1928), Brussels (1948), Stockholm (1967), and Paris (1971). See Chapter 10, *infra*; Appendix G, *infra*.

In place of a comprehensive revision of U.S. laws to enable the United States to qualify for the International Copyright Union, there followed in this country still more piecemeal domestic legislation, so that by the beginning of the twentieth century there existed a variety of miscellaneous copyright acts difficult of interpretation and full of traps for the unwary author. In 1903 the then recently appointed first Register of Copyrights, Mr. Thorvald Solberg, an outstanding champion of copyright law reform, made a special report on the whole subject of domestic legislation and recommended one consolidated act. This came to fruition in the Copyright Act of March 4, 1909,[34] which, with some minor amendments, was the law in force for the next 68 years. Its provisions in certain areas will remain at least indirectly effective for many more.

### The 1909 Act

The Copyright Act of 1909 was the outcome of several years of painstaking labor and extensive discussion on the part of every interest involved, including eminent members of the bar. Care was taken

---

[33]Statement of Sidney Smith in 1820, quoted in *United Dictionary Co. v. Merriam Co.*, 208 U.S. 260, 264 (1906).
[34]35 Stat. 1075–1088, title 17, U.S.C. (1909 *repealed* 1978).

to use in the text, as far as possible, words and phrases that had already received judicial construction. In its final form, however, the Act was very largely a compromise measure, being a composite of several tentative bills and proposals embodying different points of view and interests. Changes appear often to have been made in one place without the necessary corresponding changes in other places. This process resulted in a lack of clarity and coherence in certain sections that caused no little perplexity in the practical administration of the Act.[35] (See Appendix A, *infra*, for text of Act.)

Moreover, the subsequent development of the motion picture, the phonograph, radio, television, and other techniques of aural and visual recording, together with changes in business methods and practices, created new factors to be considered. While the courts found the terms of the Act fairly adaptable to meet the situation, there was a lack of uniformity in their application to particular cases. However, some notable improvements over the old law were achieved in 1909, among which may be mentioned the following:

(1)  broadening the subject matter of copyright to include "all the writings of an author" (this also caused problems, see pp. 20–21, *infra*);

(2)  exempting books of foreign origin in foreign languages from the need of being reprinted in the United States (this being the greatest advance from the international standpoint);

(3)  in the case of published works, dating copyright from publication of the work with a proper copyright notice, instead of from the date of filing of the title, which often took place long before the work was ready for publication;

(4)  extending the renewal term of protection by 14 years, to bring the possible maximum term of protection to 56 years;

(5)  making the certificate of registration prima facie evidence of the facts recorded in relation to any work.

Nevertheless, this substantial progress fell far short of meeting the fundamental requisites of the Berne Convention, because the formalities of notice, deposit, and registration were retained, as well as the requirement of American manufacture of English-language books and periodicals of foreign origin. Further, by excluding federal protection for unpublished works except those designed for exhibition, performance, or oral delivery, the Act took a step backward which was not rectified until the general revision of 1976.

---

[35]The relevant documents pertaining to the enactment of the 1909 law are reprinted in E. BRYLAWSKI AND A. GOLDMAN, LEGISLATIVE HISTORY OF THE 1909 ACT (1976). See also Solberg, *Copyright Law Reform*, 35 YALE L.J. 61 (1925). For an expression of judicial exasperation over the 1909 Act, see *Rohauer v. Killiam Shows, Inc.*, 551 F.2d 484, 486, 192 U.S.P.Q. 545, 546 (2d Cir.), *cert. denied*, 431 U.S. 949, 194 U.S.P.Q. 304 (1977): "As has been so often true in cases arising under the Copyright Act of 1909, neither an affirmative nor a negative answer is completely satisfactory. A court must grope to ascertain what would have been the thought of the 1909 Congress on an issue about which it almost certainly never thought at all."

### Amendments to the 1909 Act

In 1912 the Act was revised to provide in Sections 5(l) and (m), respectively, for protection of "motion picture photoplays" and "motion pictures other than photoplays." Prior to this revision (known as the Townsend Amendment), motion pictures had been registered in Class (j) as photographs, and it has been suggested that the purpose of the 1912 revision was "merely to make classification easier for the Copyright Office."[36]

In 1926[37] the manufacturing-clause provisions of Section 16 of the 1909 Act were relaxed to exclude books of foreign origin in a language other than English, as well as works printed or produced in the United States by "any other process" other than typography, lithography, or photoengraving; this latter provision was adopted apparently in response to protests by university professors that the lack of typesetting equipment during World War I had caused them to lose copyright protection.[38] A similar relaxation occurred following World War II.[39]

In 1952 nondramatic literary works were granted a right of public performance where the performance was for profit.[40] In the same year the Universal Copyright Convention was signed. This multilateral treaty, offering an alternative to the older Berne Convention for international copyright protection, gave protection in all member nations to works by a national of a member nation, as well as works first published within its borders. Domestic formalities were excused if all published copies of the work bore a prescribed notice, or if the work remained unpublished. A member could add other requirements with respect to works written by its own nationals or first published within its territory, so long as it did not discriminate against protected foreigners.

In 1954 the United States became one of the first nations to ratify this convention, amending its domestic law slightly more than necessary to comply with its treaty obligations.[41] In 1957 Section 115 of the 1909 Act was amended to provide expressly for a three-year statute of limitations on civil actions measured from the date "the

---

[36] *The Meaning of "Writings" in the Copyright Clause of the Constitution*, COPYRIGHT OFFICE STUDY No. 3, 86th Cong., 1st Sess. 76 (Comm. Print 1960).

[37] Act of July 3, 1926, 69th Cong., 1st Sess., 44 Stat. 818.

[38] See statement of Register of Copyrights in his 1925–1926 *Annual Report*, quoted in McCannon, *The Manufacturing Clause of the U.S. Copyright Law*, COPYRIGHT OFFICE STUDY No. 35 at 15 (1963).

[39] Act of June 3, 1949, Pub. L. No. 81-94, 81st Cong., 1st Sess.

[40] Act of July 17, 1952, 82d Cong., 2d Sess., 61 Stat. 653. Musical works were granted a for-profit public performance right under §1(e) of the 1909 Act. This for-profit limitation was a retrenchment from the 1897 Act, which contained no such limitation. The purpose for this retrenchment is found in the right granted in 1909 to control the mechanical reproduction of the work in phonorecords, subject to a compulsory license. See PRELIMINARY DRAFT FOR REVISED U.S. COPYRIGHT LAW AND DISCUSSIONS AND COMMENTS ON THE DRAFT, COPYRIGHT LAW REVISION pt. 3 at 46 (1964).

[41] Act of August 31, 1954, Pub. L. No. 83-743, 83d Cong., 2d Sess., 61 Stat. 655.

claim accrued."[42] Notwithstanding the 1954 amendments, the American system under the 1909 law was in direct contrast to that existing in most foreign countries; the latter have largely dispensed with formalities as a prerequisite to protection, as a result of which everything published therein is automatically protected against unauthorized copying. In the United States, however, the creators or assigns of only a small percentage of the total number of literary, informational, musical, and artistic works published have been sufficiently interested to seek and perfect by registration the privileges of a statutory monopoly. The percentage varies with different classes of works, and music has constituted the largest class of all.

## The 1976 Act

Despite the lingering argument by some that the American system had on the whole proved eminently suited to American needs, it became apparent in the years following World War II that an intensive and objective examination of the 1909 law, with a view to its general revision, was overdue.[43]

A comprehensive project along these lines was authorized by Congress in 1955. Under this authorization the Copyright Office prepared a number of legal and factual studies of the major substantive problems inherent in any revision of the law. Distribution of these studies gave rise to the healthy interchange of ideas, comments, and suggestions necessary for the development of an improved law. (In addition, they serve as valuable research tools irrespective of their original purpose.) In July 1961 Register Kaminstein submitted to Congress a detailed report of his tentative recommendations for revision with a view to the introduction, after further public comment, of a new proposed law.[44]

During the next three years a tentative draft and resulting comments led to the development and introduction in 1964 of the first revision bills.[45] In 1965 and 1966 extensive hearings followed, culminating in the first committee reports.[46] In 1967 the House, but not the Senate, passed a revision bill.[47] After a delay occasioned by politi-

---

[42]Act of September 7, 1957, Pub. L. No. 85-313, 85th Cong., 1st Sess., 71 Stat. 633. Section 115 had, however, previously provided for a three-year statute of limitations for criminal proceedings, to be measured from "the time the cause of action arose." See pp. 275–276 for a discussion of statute-of-limitation issues. Section 4968 of the 1873 Act had provided for a two-year statute of limitations "in any case of forfeiture or penalty."

[43]See, e.g., Note, *Revision of the Copyright Law*, 51 HARV. L. REV. 906 (1938).

[44]REPORT OF THE REGISTER OF COPYRIGHTS ON THE GENERAL REVISION OF THE U.S. COPYRIGHT LAW, 87th Cong., 1st Sess. (Comm. Print 1961).

[45]H.R. 11947, H.R. 12354, S. 3008, 88th Cong., 2d Sess. (1964). These bills are reprinted in COPYRIGHT LAW REVISION PART 5: 1964 REVISION BILL WITH DISCUSSION AND COMMENTS, 89th Cong., 1st Sess. 1–32 (Comm. Print 1965).

[46]H.R. REP. No. 2237, 89th Cong., 2d Sess. (1966); H.R. REP. No. 83, 90th Cong., 1st Sess. (1967). These reports are identical.

[47]H.R. 2512, 90th Cong., 1st Sess. (1967).

cal and technological issues, such as cable television and educational and library uses, the Senate passed revision bills in 1974[48] and in February 1976.[49]

Another set of extensive hearings in the House produced a House-passed version of the revision legislation in September 1976.[50] The differences between the chambers were resolved in a conference report,[51] accepted by both houses. The President approved the bill on October 19, 1976.[52] It did not, however, become generally effective until January 1, 1978. (See Appendix B, *infra*, for text of Act.)

The key provisions of the law included the following:

(1) A single federal system of protection for all "original works of authorship," published or unpublished, from the moment they are fixed in a tangible medium of expression. (Pertinent state law is expressly preempted.)

(2) A single term of protection generally measured by the life of the author(s) plus 50 years after his or her death, with a term based on publication (or creation, in the case of unpublished works) reserved only for special situations, such as works made for hire.

(3) A provision for an inalienable option in individual authors and their heirs, generally permitting termination of any transfer, but with the transferee still permitted to exploit derivative works produced under the transfer before it was terminated.

(4) A provision for notice on visually perceptible copies distributed to the public, with some flexibility as to the form and position of the notice, curative provisions for notice deficiencies, and incentives for use of a proper notice, as well as for prompt registration.

(5) Recognition of a fair use privilege (with an indication of the criteria for its applicability), as well as exemptions in favor of nonprofit, library, educational, and public broadcasting uses.

(6) Imposition of copyright liability on cable television systems and jukeboxes which use copyrighted material, but subject to compulsory license provisions and other limitations.

(7) Establishment of a Copyright Royalty Tribunal to review or establish rates under compulsory licenses and to provide for certain distributions to proprietors under such licenses.

---

[48]S. 1361, 93d Cong., 2d Sess. (1974).

[49]S. 22, 94th Cong., 2d Sess. (1976). An important piece of legislative history is embodied in the committee report accompanying this bill. S. REP. No. 94-473, 94th Cong., 1st Sess. (1975).

[50]See *Copyright Law Revision: Hearings on H.R. 2223 Before the Subcomm. on Courts, Civil Liberties, and the Administration of Justice of the House Judiciary Comm.*, 94th Cong., 1st Sess. (1975). As with the Senate, an important piece of legislative history is embodied in the committee report accompanying the House-passed bill. H.R. REP. No. 94-1476, 94th Cong., 2d Sess. (1976).

[51]H.R. REP. No. 94-1733, 94th Cong., 2d Sess. (1976).

[52]Act of October 19, 1976, Pub. L. No. 94-553, 90 Stat. 2541.

(8) Protection of unpublished works regardless of the nationality of the author, as well as contraction and scheduled deletion of the manufacturing clause.

(9) Provisions implementing divisibility of copyright ownership.

During the long process of the revision effort, three significant matters were resolved by separate legislative action. First, beginning on September 19, 1962, terms of renewal copyrights which would otherwise have expired were extended so as to maintain the existence of these copyrights and bring them under the protection of the new Act. Second, in 1971 and 1974 limited federal copyright protection was extended to recorded performances insofar as duplication of recordings was concerned, but not as to independently recorded imitation of sound or as to the performance of the recordings. Third, on December 31, 1974, a National Commission on New Technological Uses of Copyrighted Works (CONTU) was established to study new technology, such as computers and reprography, and recommend to Congress detailed provisions to replace the stopgap provisions in the 1976 Act governing these fast-moving areas.

## Amendments to the 1976 Act

In July 1978 CONTU issued a final report containing several recommended changes in the Copyright Act.[53] Brief hearings were held in the House on the CONTU recommendations in 1980;[54] and on December 12, 1980, President Carter signed into law a substitute Section 117[55] adopting as modified a number of CONTU's recommendations.

In 1982, a particularly active year for copyright legislation, Congress handed President Reagan his first veto override by extending the manufacturing clause until July 1, 1986;[56] an exemption was created for performances of nondramatic literary or musical works by nonprofit veterans' and fraternal organizations under certain circumstances;[57] and increased penalties for trafficking in counterfeit labels for phonorecords, motion pictures, or audiovisuals and for criminal infringement of these works were added.[58]

---

[53]FINAL REPORT OF THE NATIONAL COMMISSION ON NEW TECHNOLOGICAL USES OF COPYRIGHTED WORKS (1978).

[54]*Industrial Innovation and Patent and Copyright Law Amendments: Hearings on H.R. 6033 et al. Before the Subcomm. on Courts, Civil Liberties, and the Administration of Justice of the House Judiciary Comm.*, 96th Cong., 2d Sess. (1980). See also the committee report, H.R. REP. No. 96-1307 (pt. 1), 96th Cong., 2d Sess. (1980).

[55]Act of December 12, 1980, Pub. L. No. 96-517, sec. 10(b), 94 Stat. 3028.

[56]Act of July 13, 1982, Pub. L. No. 97-215, 97th Cong., 1st Sess., 96 Stat. 178 (amending 17 U.S.C. §601).

[57]Act of October 25, 1982, Pub. L. No. 97-366, 97th Cong., 1st Sess., 96 Stat. 1759 (adding a new §110(10) to title 17).

[58]Act of May 24, 1982, Pub. L. No. 97-180, 97th Cong., 1st Sess., 96 Stat. 91 (amending 18 U.S.C. §2318 and 17 U.S.C. §506(a)).

Finally, in 1984 Congress amended the so-called "first sale doctrine" by prohibiting the unauthorized rental, lease, or lending of phonorecords for direct or indirect commercial advantage.[59] Other important changes, discussed in Chapter 9, have been accomplished administratively by the Copyright Royalty Tribunal through adjustments in the compulsory license payments required of jukebox and cable television operators and those making and distributing phonorecords embodying nondramatic musical works. Copyright Office regulations and policy decisions have also had an important impact in the area of cable television.

The most significant intellectual property legislation enacted since the 1976 Copyright Act, the Semiconductor Chip Protection Act of 1984,[60] began as an amendment to the Copyright Act but ended up according *sui generis* protection to semiconductor "mask works." In crafting legislation tailored to a specific industry, Congress thus manifested a willingness to experiment with new forms of intellectual property protection, a willingness which may lead to further efforts to protect industrial designs that presently fall outside the realm of both the copyright and patent laws.

---

[59] Act of October 4, 1984, Pub. L. No. 98-450, 98 Stat. 1727 (amending 17 U.S.C. §§109 and 115).

[60] Act of November 8, 1984, Pub. L. No. 98-620, 98 Stat. 3347 (establishing new chapter 9 in title 17).

# 2

# Copyrightability

## Constitutional Basis

Let us consider for a moment the pregnant terms used in the constitutional provision upon which all U.S. copyright acts were founded, namely, Article I, Section 8, Clause 8, that Congress shall have power "*to promote* the progress of science and useful arts by *securing* for *limited times* to *authors* and inventors the *exclusive* right to their respective *writings* and discoveries." (Emphasis added.)

### "To Promote the Progress of Science and Useful Arts"

The copyright and patent clause of the Constitution, unlike most of the other grants in Article I, Section 8, links a substantive power with a specific constitutional objective. The "promote the progress" language could thus be viewed as a limitation rather than merely as a purpose. This position has, however, been rejected by the courts.[1] A

---

[1] *Schnapper v. Foley*, 667 F.2d 102, 111–112, 212 U.S.P.Q. 235, 241–242 (D.C. Cir. 1981), *cert. denied*, 455 U.S. 948, 215 U.S.P.Q. 96 (1982). Accord *Hutchinson Tel. Co. v. Fronteer Directory Co.*, 770 F.2d 128, 228 U.S.P.Q. 537 (8th Cir. 1985). Cf. *Ladd v. Law & Technology Press*, 762 F.2d 809, 226 U.S.P.Q. 774 (9th Cir. 1985). Cf. *Graham v. John Deere Co.*, 383 U.S. 1, 5 (1966) (patent case). *Law & Technology Press* and *Authors League of America, Inc. v. Oman*, 790 F.2d 220, 229 U.S.P.Q. 724 (2d Cir. 1986), held, however, that Congress may constitutionally place conditions on the exercise of copyright protection, even where those conditions are imposed only on certain classes of works. In *Law & Technology Press*, the constitutionality of the mandatory deposit requirements of §407 was upheld. In *Authors League*, the constitutionality of the "manufacturing clause" (§§601 and 603) was sustained. See also *Rodgers v. Eighty-Four Lumber Co.*, 617 F. Supp. 1021, 1022–1023, 228 U.S.P.Q. 942, 944 (W.D. Pa. 1985) (constitutionality of §110(5) upheld).

To date, only one copyright act has been held unconstitutional, and this not on grounds that it failed to promote the progress of science, but because it was held to have been enacted in violation of the religious establishment clause of the First Amendment. *United Christian Scientists v. Christian Science Bd.*, 616 F. Supp. 476, 227 U.S.P.Q. 40 (D.D.C. 1985). The law in question, Private L. No. 92-60, 85 Stat. 857 (1971), extended the term of copyright in all editions of Mary Baker Eddy's *Science and Health* for a term of 75 years from the effective date of the act or from the date of first publication, whichever was later. The edition in question was first

related question is whether individual works must "promote the progress of science." Although there were some early opinions that this was the case,[2] recent appellate decisions[3] appear to have settled the issue to the contrary by finding that it is the *system* of protecting authors which must (and does) benefit the public.

## "Writings" of "Authors"

The coverage of copyright suggested by the Constitution is of the "writings" of "authors."[4] While these two terms are, of course, closely related, "writings" may be viewed as the subject matter of copyright and "authors" as indicative of the requirement of creativity to be imparted into such subject matter. In *The Trademark Cases* the Supreme Court tied these concepts and that of "originality" together by holding that the term "writings" includes only works "such as are founded in the creative powers of the mind. The writings which are protected are the fruits of intellectual labor, embodied in

published in 1906 and, but for the bill, would have fallen into the public domain in 1981. As a result of the bill, it was scheduled to fall into the public domain in 2046. In reviewing the purposes of the bill, the court found its purpose was to "secure prospective advantage for the hierocracy of one particular religion, and to no discernible advancement of the general welfare." *Id.* at 479, 227 U.S.P.Q. at 42. An examination of the legislative history of the act fully supports the court's finding. See, e.g., *For the Relief of Clayton Bion Craig, Arthur P. Wuth, Mrs. Leonore D. Hanks, David E. Sleeper, and DeWitt John: Hearings on S. 1866 Before Subcomm. No. 3 of the House Judiciary Comm.*, 92 Cong., 1st Sess. (1971); S. REP. No. 92-280, 92d Cong., 1st Sess. (1971); 117 CONG. REC. S26822 (1971) (statement of Senator Burdick), which demonstrate that the sole motive for the bill was to suppress religious dissent within the Christian Science church. As the court wisely noted: "Heresy is no part of the business entrusted to Congress by the Constitution." 616 F. Supp. at 480, 227 U.S.P.Q. at 43.

   [2] *Martinetti v. Maguire*, 16 F. Cas. 920 (C.C.D. Cal. 1867) (No. 9,173).

   [3] *Hutchinson Tel. Co. v. Fronteer Directory Co.*, 770 F.2d 128, 130, 228 U.S.P.Q. 537, 538 (8th Cir. 1985); *Pacific & Southern Co. v. Duncan*, 744 F.2d 1490, 1498–1499, 224 U.S.P.Q. 131, 136 (11th Cir. 1984), *cert. denied*, 471 U.S. ___, *on remand*, 618 F. Supp. 469, 228 U.S.P.Q. 141 (N.D. Ga. 1985); *Jartech, Inc. v. Clancy*, 666 F.2d 403, 405–406, 213 U.S.P.Q. 1057, 1059 (9th Cir.), *cert. denied*, 459 U.S. 826 (1982); *Mitchell Bros. Film Group v. Cinema Adult Theatre*, 604 F.2d 852, 860, 203 U.S.P.Q. 1041, 1049 (5th Cir. 1979), *cert. denied*, 445 U.S. 917 (1980). There is an alternative constitutional basis for protecting works that do not promote the progress of science, or that may not be "writings," namely the Commerce Clause. This alternative source has been invoked twice to accord protection to intellectual property; first regarding trademarks (following the Supreme Court's decision in "*The Trademark Cases*," 100 U.S. 82 (1879), holding trademarks may not be considered "writings" under Article I, §8, cl. 8), and, second, regarding semiconductor chip designs ("mask works"). See 17 U.S.C. §910(a) (1984), and explanations in CONG. REC. S12918, 98th Cong., 2d Sess. (daily ed., Oct. 3, 1984); CONG. REC. E4433 (daily ed., Oct. 10, 1984); H.R. REP. No. 98-781, 98th Cong., 2d Sess. 16 n. 36 (1984) (Star Print); S. REP. No. 98-425, 98th Cong., 2d Sess. 14–15 (1984). It should be noted, however, that while there is a commerce limitation with respect to the enforcement of a mask work owner's rights, there is no such limitation on the grant of protection.

   [4] Although the question has never been definitively answered, it is believed that the Constitution paired the term "writings" with "science" and "discoveries" with "useful arts," rather than vice versa. See R. DEWOLF, AN OUTLINE OF COPYRIGHT LAW 15–16 (1925); Rich, *Principles of Patentability*, 28 GEO. WASH. L. REV. 393 (1960); H.R. REP. No. 1923, 82d Cong., 2d Sess. 4 (1952); S. REP. No. 1979, 82d Cong., 2d Sess. 3 (1952); *Bleistein v. Donaldson Lithographing Co.*, 188 U.S. 239, 249 (1903); *Graham v. John Deere Co.*, 383 U.S. 1 (1966); *Taylor Instrument Cos. v. Fawley-Brost Co.*, 139 F.2d 98, 99, 59 U.S.P.Q. 384, 386 (7th Cir. 1943), *cert. denied*, 321 U.S. 785, 60 U.S.P.Q. 579 (1944); *Great Atlantic & Pacific Tea Co. v. Supermarket Equipment Corp.*, 340 U.S. 147, 154, 87 U.S.P.Q. 303, 306 (1950) (Douglas, J., concurring).

   This issue has been recently raised in a suit for declaratory judgment of noninfringement of computer microcode, *NEC Electronics, Inc. v. Intel Corp.*, C84-20799WA (N.D. Cal. complaint filed Dec. 21, 1984) (motion for summary judgment denied August 13, 1985), where plaintiff has alleged that if the Copyright Act were construed to cover the creation in question "the Act would be unconstitutional because Intel's microcode is, if anything, the 'discovery' of an 'inven-

the form of books, prints, engravings and the like.''[5] Despite the Court's coupling of the terms "creative" and "original," it has become firmly established in the case law that the requirement of "originality" does not refer to a desired modicum of artistic merit, novelty, or "nonobviousness" (as with patents), but rather to the origination of the work, viz., that the work has been "independently" created, and not merely copied.[6] The 1976 Copyright Act, unlike the 1909 Act, makes the requirement of originality express, for Section 102(a) extends copyright protection only to *"original* works of authorship."[7]

The foregoing should not obscure the fact that both "writings" and "authors" have been construed very broadly. Thus, "writings" includes works far removed from literary productions[8] and indeed "may be interpreted to include any physical rendering of the fruits of creative intellectual or aesthetic labor."[9]

In passing the Copyright Act of 1976, Congress noted that "[t]he history of copyright law has been one of gradual expansion in the types of works accorded protection * * * . Authors are continually finding new ways of expressing themselves, but it is impossible to foresee the forms that these new expressive methods will take."[10] In response to this, Congress stated that it desired

---

tor' rather than the 'writing' of an 'author' under the United States Constitution, Article I, §8, cl. 8." The rationale for this assertion appears faulty, however, since, were the court to construe the Copyright Act to cover the microcode, it would do so based on a finding that it was an "original work of authorship" under §102(a) (and by extension, therefore, a "writing") and thus within the scope of the Constitution. If an appellate court were to disagree with this finding, the proper course would be to hold that the microcode was not "an original work of authorship" and thus not copyrightable. See *Marx v. United States,* 96 F.2d 204, 37 U.S.P.Q. 380 (9th Cir. 1938) (statutes to be construed, if possible, so as to render them constitutional). It should also be noted that §102(b) of the Copyright Act expressly denies protection to "discoveries." See *Harper & Row, Pub., Inc. v. Nation Enters.,* 723 F.2d 195, 202 n. 7, 220 U.S.P.Q. 321, 327 n. 7 (2d Cir. 1983), *rev'd on other grounds,* 471 U.S. ____, 225 U.S.P.Q. 1073 (1985); *Rubin v. Boston Magazine Co.,* 645 F.2d 80, 83, 209 U.S.P.Q. 1073, 1075 (1st Cir. 1981), for discussions of the meaning of this term.

[5]100 U.S. 82, 94 (1879).

[6]*Financial Information, Inc. v. Moody's Investors Serv., Inc.,* 751 F.2d 501, 507, 224 U.S.P.Q. 632, 635 (2d Cir. 1984); *Original Appalachian Artworks, Inc. v. Toy Loft, Inc.,* 684 F.2d 821, 215 U.S.P.Q. 745 (11th Cir. 1982). See also *Transgo, Inc. v. Ajac Transmission Parts Corp.,* 768 F.2d 1001, 1019, 227 U.S.P.Q. 598, 606 (9th Cir. 1985): "Work which results from the independent efforts of its author is copyrightable, even though identical work may already be in the public domain." Cf. Justice Douglas' dissent from the Court's denial of certiorari in *Lee v. Runge,* 404 U.S. 887, 890, 171 U.S.P.Q. 322, 323 (1971), and his dissent in *Kewanee Oil Co. v. Bicron Corp.,* 416 U.S. 470, 489 n. 4, 181 U.S.P.Q. 673, 684 n. 4 (1974), as well as Professor Nimmer's criticism of the Douglas position in *Comment on the Douglas Dissent in Lee v. Runge,* 19 BULL. COPR. SOC'Y 68 (1971).

[7]17 U.S.C. §102(a) (1978). For a review of the legislative history of this section, see Patry, *Copyright in Collections of Facts: A Reply,* 6 COMM. AND THE LAW 11, 18–25 (1984). Section 102(a) further protects only such works as are "fixed in any tangible medium of expression * * * ." See also 17 U.S.C. §101 (1978) (definition of "fixed"); H.R. REP. No. 94-1476, 94th Cong., 2d Sess. 52–53 (1976); S. REP. No. 94-473, 94th Cong., 1st Sess. 51–52 (1975).

[8]See *Mazer v. Stein,* 347 U.S. 201, 210 n. 15, 100 U.S.P.Q. 325, 330 n. 15 (1954); S. REP. No. 98-425, 98th Cong., 2d Sess. 12–14 (1984); H.R. REP. No. 98-781, 98th Cong., 2d Sess. 6 (1984) (Star Print).

[9]*Goldstein v. California,* 412 U.S. 546, 561, 178 U.S.P.Q. 129, 135 (1973). See also *Burrow-Giles Lithographic Co. v. Sarony,* 111 U.S. 53, 58 (1884).

[10]H.R. REP. No. 94-1476, 94th Cong., 2d Sess. 51 (1976); S. REP. No. 94-473, 94th Cong., 1st Sess. 50, 51 (1975). The appropriateness of these developments was aptly expressed by Judge Learned Hand, to whom a debt is owed for many illuminating opinions on the law of copyright, in *Reiss v. National Quotation Bureau, Inc.,* 276 F. 717, 719 (S.D.N.Y. 1921):
"Now it is argued that these cases are distinguishable because they arose under an act of Parliament which was not limited by any Constitution. So, indeed, they were, and if our

"[n]either to freeze the scope of copyrightable subject matter at the present stage of communications technology or to allow unlimited expansion into areas completely outside the present congressional intent. Section 102 implies neither that that subject matter is unlimited nor that new forms of expression within that general area of subject matter would necessarily be unprotected."[11]

Congress did not, however, find it necessary to provide express statutory recognition for new technological works, many of which, such as electronic music and computer programs, were regarded "as an extension of copyrightable subject matter Congress has already intended to protect, and were thus considered copyrightable from the outset without the need of new legislation."[12]

### "Securing for Limited Times * * * the Exclusive Right * * * "

In his treatise *Law of Property in Intellectual Productions*, published in 1879, Eaton S. Drone earnestly contended that the term "securing" in this clause of the Constitution meant, with respect to authors, merely the confirming of a right already existing at common law; however, regarding published works we have already noted that the courts both in England and in this country had settled this question to the effect that Parliament and Congress in passing the first Copyright Acts did not sanction an existing right but created a new one, the enjoyment and exercise of which depended upon strict compliance with the terms of the statute. This did not hold true, however, for state protection of unpublished works. Under our unique federal-state system of government, it was held that the states were free to

---

Constitution embalms inflexibly the habits of 1789, there may be something in the point. But it does not; its grants of power to Congress comprise, not only what was then known, but what the ingenuity of men should devise thereafter. Of course, the new subject matter must have some relation to the grant; but we interpret it by the general practice of civilized peoples in similar fields, for it is not a strait-jacket, but a charter for living people."
Judge Hand's remarks bear a certain similarity to the following comments made by Thomas Jefferson in a July 12, 1816, letter to Samuel Kercheval:

"I am not an advocate for frequent changes in laws and constitutions. But laws and constitutions must go hand in hand with the progress of the human mind. As that becomes developed, more enlightened, as new discoveries are made, new truths are discovered and manners and opinions change. With the change of circumstances, institutions must advance also to keep pace with the times. We might as well require a man to wear still the coat which fitted him when a boy as civilized society to remain ever under the regimen of their barbarous ancestors."

[11]H.R. REP. No. 94-1476 at 51; S. REP. No. 94-473 at 51. In one area, that of typeface designs, Congress expressly chose not to extend protection for the present. H.R. REP. No. 94-1476 at 55. See also *Eltra v. Ringer*, 579 F.2d 294, 198 U.S.P.Q. 321 (4th Cir. 1978).

[12]H.R. REP. No. 94-1476 at 51; S. REP. No. 94-473 at 50. The courts have also rejected the argument, raised prominently in Commissioner John Hersey's dissent from the recommendations of the National Commission on New Technological Uses of Copyrighted Works (see FINAL REPORT OF THE NATIONAL COMMISSION ON NEW TECHNOLOGICAL USES OF COPYRIGHTED WORKS 27-37 (1978)) that copyright protection could not be extended to the machine phase of computer programs since no communication to a human being was involved. See *Apple Computer, Inc. v. Formula Int'l, Inc.*, 725 F.2d 521, 221 U.S.P.Q. 762 (9th Cir. 1984); *Apple Computer, Inc. v. Franklin Computer Corp.*, 714 F.2d 1240, 219 U.S.P.Q. 113 (3d Cir. 1983).

In connection with the increasing use of expert systems, it has been asked whether a computer (or other machine) can be an "author." Although the question is likely to be academic since few machines can be expected to file applications for registration, the Copyright Office has taken the apparent position that computers or machines are not "authors." See COMPENDIUM II OF COPYRIGHT OFFICE PRACTICES §§202.02(b), 503.03(a).

protect such works in perpetuity, and without compliance with any formalities.[13]

The right to be secured by Congress must be "exclusive" and hence savors of monopoly, the interests of the public being served by making the work available for public enjoyment and by limiting the duration of protection. The issue arises, however, whether the congressional grant must be truly "exclusive." This question was raised originally during hearings in 1908 on a proposal to include a compulsory license provision relating to mechanical reproduction of copyrighted music, ultimately established in Section 1(e) of the 1909 Act and carried over (as revised) into Section 115 of the 1976 Act. Nathan Burkan, a pioneer of the copyright bar, argued that "a compulsory license is the antithesis of the exclusive right."[14] This argument never prevailed,[15] and indeed in the 1976 Act Congress added three compulsory licenses over and above the musical recording right, covering "jukebox" performances of nondramatic musical works (§116), cable television retransmission of copyrighted material (§111), and broadcasting and certain other uses of published nondramatic musical and artistic works by public broadcasting entities (§118). Recent developments in reprographic technology (e.g., off-air recording) have resulted in calls for compulsory licenses for such uses, as private and semiprivate duplication of copyrighted works increases. It nevertheless remains the case that our copyright law is grounded on a grant of substantially "exclusive" rights, subject to specific exemptions or compulsory licenses.

## General Characteristics of Copyrightable Subject Matter

### The Statutory Scope

In pursuance of its constitutional power, Congress has passed many statutes for the protection of authors, gradually extending and enlarging the subject matter and scope of protection as the need arose until the Copyright Act of 1909 comprehended not only books, maps, and charts but broadly "all the writings of an author." This coverage was provided in Section 4 of the 1909 law and elaborated in Sections 5 and 7. The 1976 Act deliberately avoids use of the quoted phrase, providing instead in Section 102(a) for protection of "original works of authorship fixed in any tangible medium of expression,"

---

[13]Since §23 of the 1909 Act referred to the term of protection as running 28 years from the date of first publication, a literal reading of this section left unresolved the term of protection for unpublished works deposited under §11. In *Marx v. United States*, 96 F.2d 204, 37 U.S.P.Q. 380 (9th Cir. 1938), the court held that the term was to be measured from the date of registration. See also *Patterson v. Century Prods., Inc.*, 93 F.2d 489, 35 U.S.P.Q. 471 (2d Cir. 1937), *cert. denied*, 303 U.S. 655, 37 U.S.P.Q. 844 (1938).

[14]*Hearings on S. 2328 and H.R. 10353*, 69th Cong., 1st Sess. 329 (1926).

[15]*Hearings on Revision of Copyright Laws Before the Comms. on Patents*, 60th Cong., 1st Sess. 233–237 (1908).

and enumerating seven illustrative but not exclusive categories of such works.

It is immediately apparent that the 1909 statutory phrase "writings of an author" echoes the language of the Constitution analyzed above. It was sometimes said that Congress intended in the 1909 Act to exercise its constitutional power fully and to cover all subject matter that could be protected under the Constitution. The committee report accompanying that act is somewhat cryptic on this point:

> "Section 4 is declaratory of existing law. It was suggested that the word 'works' should be substituted for the word 'writings,' in view of the broad construction given by the courts to the word 'writings,' but it was thought better to use the word 'writings,' which is the word found in the Constitution. It is not intended by the use of this word to change in any way the construction which the courts have given to it."[16]

The suggestion that a work might be a "writing" under the Constitution but not under the statute was subsequently made by Professor Chafee in a seminal article on copyright,[17] while a subsequent case involving the question of protection of recorded musical performances, *Capitol Records, Inc. v. Mercury Records Corp.*, afforded at least one example of such a work:

> "There can be no doubt that, under the Constitution, Congress could give to one who performs a public domain musical composition the exclusive right to make and vend phonograph records of that rendition. The question is whether Congress has done so."[18]

Both the majority and the dissent found that the statute did not then cover such performances.

The matter was presumably put to rest in *Goldstein v. California*, a 5–4 Supreme Court decision also in the area of recorded performances. Writing for the majority, Chief Justice Burger stated:

> "Since §4 employs the constitutional term 'writings,' it may be argued that Congress intended to exercise its authority over all works to which the constitutional provision might apply. However, in the more than 60 years which have elapsed since enactment of this provision, neither the Copyright Office, the courts, nor the Congress has so interpreted it."[19]

The removal of this term from the statute in 1976 was designed "to avoid exhausting the constitutional power of Congress to legislate in this field and to eliminate the uncertainties" arising from the "writings of an author" terminology.[20] The *Capitol Records* decision, which attracted much attention in a number of connections,[21] was one of the rare instances in which a court sharply distinguished between the constitutional and statutory bases of copyright. In most

---

[16]H.R. Rep. No. 2222, 60th Cong., 2d Sess. 10 (1909). See also *Mazer v. Stein*, 347 U.S. 201, 210 n. 18, 100 U.S.P.Q. 325, 330 n. 18 (1954).

[17]Chafee, *Reflections on the Law of Copyright*, 45 Colum. L. Rev. 719, 734–735 (1945).

[18]221 F.2d 657, 660, 105 U.S.P.Q. 163, 164 (2d Cir. 1955).

[19]412 U.S. 546, 567, 178 U.S.P.Q. 129, 137 (1973).

[20]S. Rep. No. 94-473, 94th Cong., 1st Sess. 50 (1975); H.R. Rep. No. 94-1476, 94th Cong., 2d Sess. 51 (1976).

[21]See, e.g., Kaplan, *Performer's Right and Copyright: The Capitol Records Case*, 69 Harv. L. Rev. 409 (1956).

cases, however, the discussion of copyrightability of a work under the 1909 Act was based on Sections 4, 5, and 7 of the Act with implicit, rather than express, constitutional consideration. This is particularly true of determinations of the standard of creativity required of "writings of an author" under Section 4. These determinations remain completely applicable under the 1976 Act because "the phrase 'original works of authorship,' which is purposely left undefined, is intended to incorporate without change the standard of originality established by the courts under the present [1909] copyright statute."[22]

## The Quality of Creativity

In their task of statutory construction, the courts have remained reluctant to invade the subjective area of aesthetics. This judicial attitude and the copyright concept of originality, mentioned briefly above, will now be examined in more detail.

An appropriate starting point is the oft-cited approach of Justice Holmes in the "circus poster" case, *Bleistein v. Donaldson Lithographing Co.* It was there made clear that neither the modest degree of art supposedly reflected in the circus poster nor its advertising purpose would preclude copyright. Justice Holmes also noted that the fact the poster was deemed worthy of copying offered some guide as to its merit. In any event, he observed, "it would be a dangerous undertaking for persons trained only to the law to constitute themselves final judges of the worth of pictorial illustrations."[23]

In reversing the lower courts' denial of copyright protection, Justice Holmes focused not on the skill required in producing the work but rather on the humanity involved in the act of creation:

> "The copy is the personal reaction of an individual upon nature. Personality always contains something unique. It expresses its singularity even in handwriting, and a very modest grade of art has in it something irreducible, which is one man's alone. That something he may copyright unless there is a restriction in the words of the act."[24]

---

[22]S. REP. NO. 94-473, 94th Cong., 1st Sess. 50 (1975); H.R. REP. No. 94-1476, 94th Cong., 2d Sess. 51 (1976). This position has been followed by the courts in construing originality under the 1976 Act. *Sargent v. American Greetings Corp.*, 588 F. Supp. 912, 916, 223 U.S.P.Q. 1327, 1332 (N.D. Ohio 1984); *Knickerbocker Toy Co. v. Winterbrook Corp.*, 554 F. Supp. 1309, 1316 n. 9, 216 U.S.P.Q. 621, 627 n. 9 (D.N.H. 1982). *Durham Indus., Inc. v. Tomy Corp.*, 630 F.2d 905, 909–910 n. 7, 208 U.S.P.Q. 10, 14 n. 7 (2d Cir. 1980).

[23]188 U.S. 239, 251 (1903). The *Bleistein* case would have been far-reaching if only for its direct holding, over dissent, that advertising matter was copyrightable, for such works had long been regarded as tuft-hunters in the polite society of copyrights. For more recent decisions concerning advertisements, see *Canfield v. Ponchatoula Times*, 759 F.2d 493, 226 U.S.P.Q. 112 (5th Cir. 1985); *Southern Bell Tel. & Tel. Co. v. Associated Tel. Directory Pub.*, 756 F.2d 801, 225 U.S.P.Q. 899 (11th Cir. 1985); *Fabrica Inc. v. El Dorado Corp.*, 697 F.2d 890, 894, 217 U.S.P.Q. 698, 700 (9th Cir. 1983) ("Items otherwise copyrightable will not be denied copyright simply because of their advertising purpose, but they do not gain any greater protection than non-advertising materials. They must still fall within one of the seven areas of copyrightable subject matter set forth in 17 U.S.C. §102"); *Klitzner Indus., Inc. v. H. K. James & Co.*, 535 F. Supp. 1249, 216 U.S.P.Q. 73 (E.D. Pa. 1982); *Excel Promotions Corp. v. Babylon Beacon, Inc.*, 207 U.S.P.Q. 616 (E.D.N.Y. 1979) (1909 Act).

[24]188 U.S. at 250. Typical of "restrictions in the words of the act" are those found in §102(b), which denies protection for ideas, procedures, processes, systems, methods of operation, concepts, principles, and discoveries. For examples of works denied protection on these

Efforts to require an "appreciable amount of creative authorship"[25] were rejected during the omnibus revision of the 1909 Act,
with Congress expressly stating that the test of originality "does not
include requirements of novelty, ingenuity, or aesthetic merit, and
there is no intention to enlarge the standard of copyright protection
to require them."[26] As under the 1909 Act, "original" under the 1976
Act means "little more than a prohibition of actual copying."[27]

## The Quantum of Creativity

A single verse of poetry may, of course, qualify for protection;
however, the courts have held that there must be at least a "modest"
or "minimal" quantum of creative effort,[28] a requirement which has
led the Copyright Office to deny registration for catch phrases, mot-
toes, slogans, or short advertising expressions.[29] This application of

---

grounds, see *John H. Harland Co. v. Clarke Checks, Inc.*, 711 F.2d 966, 219 U.S.P.Q. 515 (11th
Cir. 1983) (blank bank checks with detachable stubs); *Morrissey v. Procter & Gamble Co.*, 379
F.2d 675, 154 U.S.P.Q. 193 (1st Cir. 1967) (sweepstakes rules).

[25]REPORT OF THE REGISTER OF COPYRIGHTS ON THE GENERAL REVISION OF THE U.S. COPY-
RIGHT LAW 51 (1961). For a review of the legislative history of the originality requirement, see
Patry, *Electronic Audiovisual Games: Navigating the Maze of Copyright*, 31 J. COPR. SOC'Y 1,
6–16 (1983).

[26]S. REP. No. 94-473, 94th Cong., 1st Sess. 50 (1975); H.R. REP. No. 94-1476, 94th Cong., 2d
Sess. 51 (1976).

[27]*Alfred Bell & Co. v. Catalda Fine Arts*, 191 F.2d 99, 102–103, 90 U.S.P.Q. 153, 156–157
(2d Cir. 1951) (Frank, J.) Accord *Original Appalachian Artworks, Inc. v. Toy Loft, Inc.*, 684
F.2d 821, 215 U.S.P.Q. 745 (11th Cir. 1982). See also *Kamar Int'l, Inc. v. Russ Berrie & Co.*, 657
F.2d 1059, 1061, 216 U.S.P.Q. 376, 378 (9th Cir. 1981) ("Anyone can copyright anything if he
adds something original to its expression"); *Baker v. Selden*, 101 U.S. 99, 102–103 (1879) ("The
copyright of the book, if not pirated from other works, would be valid without regard to its
novelty, or want of novelty, of its subject matter").
   The importance of the originality requirement should not, however, be underestimated. The
courts have held that the requirement is a constitutional as well as a statutory one. *Durham
Indus., Inc. v. Tomy Corp.*, 630 F.2d 905, 911, 208 U.S.P.Q. 10, 15 (2d Cir. 1980) (also stating
that originality is the "*sine qua non* of copyrightability"). See also *L. Batlin & Son, Inc. v.
Snyder*, 536 F.2d 486, 489–490, 189 U.S.P.Q. 753, 756 (2d Cir.), *cert. denied*, 429 U.S. 857, 191
U.S.P.Q. 588 (1976) (" 'the one pervading element prerequisite to copyright protection regardless of the form of the work' is the requirement of originality—that the work be the original
product of the claimant").

[28]*Original Appalachian Artworks, Inc. v. Toy Loft, Inc.*, 684 F.2d 821, 824, 215 U.S.P.Q.
745, 748 (11th Cir. 1981); *Durham Indus., Inc. v. Tomy Corp.*, 630 F.2d 905, 910, 208 U.S.P.Q.
10, 14 (2d Cir. 1980). Cf. *Rockford Map Pub., Inc. v. Directory Service Co. of Colorado, Inc.*, 768
F.2d 145, 148, 226 U.S.P.Q. 1025, 1027 (7th Cir. 1985), where Judge Easterbrook wrote:
   "The copyright laws protect the work, not the amount of effort expended. A person who
produces a short new work or makes a small improvement in a few hours gets a copyright
for that contribution fully as effective as that on a novel written as a life's work. Perhaps
the smaller the effort the smaller the contribution; if so, the copyright simply bestows fewer
rights. * * *
   "The input of time is irrelevant. A photograph may be copyrighted, although it is the
work of an instant and its significance may be accidental. * * * In 14 hours Mozart could
write a piano concerto, J.S. Bach a cantata, or Dickens a week's installment of *Bleak
House.* The Laffer Curve, an economic graph prominent in political debates, appeared on
the back of a napkin after dinner, the work of a minute. All of these are copyrightable.
Dickens did not need to complete *Bleak House* before receiving a copyright; every chapter—indeed every sentence—could be protected standing alone."
See also 17 U.S.C. §101 (1978) (definition of "created") and *Financial Information, Inc. v.
Moody's Investors Serv., Inc.*, 751 F.2d 501, 224 U.S.P.Q. 632 (2d Cir. 1984) (questioning
copyrightability of individual daily bond cards).

[29]37 C.F.R. §202.1(a); COPYRIGHT OFFICE CIRCULAR R34. The courts have upheld the Copyright Office's refusal to register, on *de minimis* grounds, a T-shirt design with the words
"Puerto Rico" written above two curved lines, *Designpoint Indus., Ltd. v. Padosa America,
Inc.*, 83 Civ. 9132 (S.D.N.Y. filed Nov. 2, 1984) (unpublished bench opinion); and a logo for a
television station consisting of the words "ON-TV," *Duffey Moses Design v. Sunset Prod.*,

the doctrine of *de minimis non curat lex* pervades all types of subject matter. The phrases "hang in there" and "along the way take time to smell the flowers" have been found not copyrightable,[30] and the same result obtained with respect to the simple musical representation of the ticking of a clock[31] and the reproduction of standard fleur-de-lis.[32] The National Commission on New Technological Uses of Copyrighted Works similarly wrote that a computer program "consisting of a very few obvious steps could not be a subject of copyright."[33]

A number of courts[34] have unfortunately confused the standard of originality for newly created works with the higher standard required for derivative works, a topic to which we now turn.

## Derivative Works

In many areas of intellectual and artistic activity, the author consciously works with and upon the works of predecessors. As Professor Chafee observed:

> "Roman poetry was revolutionized by the study of Greek. Dante was influenced by Mohammendan philosophers. Shakespeare got his plots from Italian novels. English writers borrowed from French in the seventeenth century, and French writers from English in the eighteenth. British drama since Shaw is the child of Ibsen. Numberless American novels are indebted to either Proust or Freud."[35]

The Copyright Act does not, however, require that a work consist only of original materials. Section 103 of the 1976 Act (like Section 7

---

*Inc.*, 83 Civ. 5365 (C.D. Cal. filed April 23, 1985) (unpublished bench opinion). On the evening before summary judgment was granted in *Duffey Moses*, the Office did register drawings of the logo "because they had perspective, depth of field, [and] shading," 33 COPYRIGHT NOTICES 5 (June 1985).

For decisions denying protection for short expressions, see *Laskowitz v. Marie Designer, Inc.*, 119 F. Supp. 541, 542, 100 U.S.P.Q. 367, 373 (S.D. Cal. 1954) (phrase "This is Nature's most restful posture" used to advertise a chair found not to comply with "even the slight requirement of originality in the law of copyright * * * ."); *E. H. Tate Co. v. Jiffy Enters., Inc.*, 16 F.R.D. 57 (E.D. Pa. 1954) (phrase "apply hook to wall" held not protectible).

[30] *Perma Greetings, Inc. v. Russ Berrie & Co.*, 598 F. Supp. 445, 223 U.S.P.Q. 670 (E.D. Mo. 1984); *Alberto-Culver Co. v. Andrea Dumon, Inc.*, 466 F.2d 705, 175 U.S.P.Q. 194 (7th Cir. 1972) (the "ordinary" phrase "most personal sort of deodorant" held not protectible; *O'Brien v. Chappel & Co.*, 159 F. Supp. 58, 116 U.S.P.Q. 340 (S.D.N.Y. 1958) (words "night and noon" as appearing in the lyrics of a song held in and of themselves not protectible).

[31] *Smith v. George E. Muehlebach Brewing Co.*, 140 F. Supp. 729, 110 U.S.P.Q. 177 (W.D. Mo. 1956).

[32] *Forstman Woolen Co. v. J.W. Mays, Inc.*, 89 F. Supp. 964, 85 U.S.P.Q. 200 (E.D.N.Y. 1956). But cf. *Thomas Wilson & Co. v. Irving J. Dorfman Co.*, 433 F.2d 409, 167 U.S.P.Q. 417 (2d Cir.), *cert. denied*, 401 U.S. 977, 169 U.S.P.Q. 65 (1971) (court not "overwhelmed" by creativity in pansy lace design but nevertheless held it copyrightable); *Soptra Fabrics Corp. v. Stafford Knitting Mills, Inc.*, 490 F.2d 1092, 180 U.S.P.Q. 545 (2d Cir. 1974) (somewhat surprising suggestion that placement of textile design "in repeat" may justify copyright). The *Soptra* holding was expressly followed in *Kenbrooke Fabrics, Inc. v. Material Things*, 223 U.S.P.Q. 1039 (S.D.N.Y. 1984). See also *Towle Mfg. Co. v. Godinger Silver Art Co.*, 612 F. Supp. 986, 991, 226 U.S.P.Q. 599, 601 (S.D.N.Y. 1985) (crystal bottles containing glassware cuttings in common usage failed to "meet even the modicum of originality necessary for copyrightability").

[33] FINAL REPORT OF THE NATIONAL COMMISSION ON NEW TECHNOLOGICAL USES OF COPYRIGHTED WORKS 20 (1978).

[34] See, e.g., *Dollcraft Indus., Ltd. v. Well-Made Mfg. Co.*, 479 F. Supp. 1105, 201 U.S.P.Q. 708 (E.D.N.Y. 1978). Cf. Judge Mishler's well-reasoned opinion in *Arc v. S. S. Sarna, Inc.*, 621 F. Supp. 916, 920–921, 229 U.S.P.Q. 25, 27–28 (E.D.N.Y. 1985).

[35] Chafee, *Reflections on the Law of Copyright*, 45 COLUM. L. REV. 503, 506 (1945). See also *Emerson v. Davies*, 8 F. Cas. 615, 619 (C.C.D. Mass. 1845) (No. 4,436).

of the 1909 Act) recognizes that a valid copyright may subsist in what are termed "derivative works," defined as works

> "based upon one or more pre-existing works, such as a translation, musical arrangement, dramatization, fictionalization, motion picture version, sound recording, art reproduction, abridgment, condensation, or any other form in which a work may be recast, transformed, or adapted. A work consisting of editorial revisions, annotations, elaborations or other modifications which, as a whole, represent an original work of authorship, is a 'derivative work.' "[36]

The requirement of originality applies with equal force to derivative works.[37] However, in order to avoid "put[ting] a weapon for harassment in the hands of mischievous copiers intent on appropriating and monopolizing public domain work" by "extend[ing] copyrightability to miniscule variations,"[38] the courts have held that derivative works must contain some "substantial, not merely trivial, originality."[39] In music, it has been held that a valid claim may attach to any substantially new adaptation of a piece, such as an arrangement for

---

[36]17 U.S.C. §101 (1978) (definition of "derivative work"). Compilations are another type of work based on preexisting material, and are discussed in the text at pp. 62–64, *infra*. Note that §114(b) limits the right to prepare a derivative work of a sound recording to those works in which "the actual sounds are rearranged, remixed, or otherwise altered in sequence or quality."

[37]Section 103 states in relevant part: "The subject matter of copyright as specified by section 102 includes * * * derivative works * * * ." Section 102(a) expressly protects only "original works of authorship." As noted in *Durham Indus., Inc. v. Tomy Corp.*, 630 F.2d 905, 911, 208 U.S.P.Q. 10, 15 (2d Cir. 1980), the originality requirement is constitutionally mandated for all works. For a review of the legislative history of §103 as it pertains to originality, see Patry, *Copyright in Collections of Facts: A Reply*, 6 COMM. AND THE LAW 11, 18–25 (1984).

[38]*L. Batlin & Son, Inc. v. Snyder*, 536 F.2d 486, 492, 189 U.S.P.Q. 753, 758 (2d Cir.) (*en banc*), *cert. denied*, 429 U.S. 857, 191 U.S.P.Q. 588 (1976). See also *Towle Mfg. Co. v. Godinger Silver Art Co.*, 612 F. Supp. 986, 991–992, 226 U.S.P.Q. 599, 601 (S.D.N.Y. 1985) (arrangement of preexisting glassware design elements on crystal baby bottle failed to meet originality requirements). Cf. *Arc v. S. S. Sarna, Inc.*, 621 F. Supp. 916, 920–921, 229 U.S.P.Q. 25, 27–28 (E.D.N.Y. 1985) (copyrightability of derivative lead crystal figurines apparently upheld).

[39]536 F.2d at 490, 189 U.S.P.Q. at 756. The question whether a derivative work possesses the requisite originality normally presents an issue of fact to be resolved by the trier of fact. *Sargent v. American Greetings Corp.*, 588 F. Supp. 912, 223 U.S.P.Q. 1327 (N.D. Ohio 1984); *Eden Toys, Inc. v. Floralee Undergarment Co.*, 697 F.2d 27, 35, 217 U.S.P.Q. 201, 206–207 (2d Cir. 1982).

In *Durham Indus., Inc. v. Tomy Corp.*, 630 F.2d 905, 911, 208 U.S.P.Q. 10, 15 (2d Cir. 1980), the Second Circuit held that the higher standard quoted in the text also applies to derivative works based on preexisting works in which copyright still subsists, a position followed by the Seventh Circuit in *Gracen v. Bradford Exchange*, 698 F.2d 300, 217 U.S.P.Q. 1294 (7th Cir. 1983). Naturally, such derivative works, if substantially similar to the underlying copyrighted work, would infringe that work, absent authorization from the copyright owner or a successful fair use claim. See H.R. REP. NO. 94-1476, 94th Cong., 2d Sess. 58 (1976); S. REP. NO. 94-473, 94th Cong., 1st Sess. 55 (1975); *Litchfield v. Spielberg*, 736 F.2d 1352, 1357, 222 U.S.P.Q. 965, 968 (9th Cir. 1984), *cert. denied*, 470 U.S. ____ (1985) (rejecting contention that an allegedly infringing derivative work need not be substantially similar to the original in order to infringe).

Where a derivative work is substantially similar to the original, and was created without the authorization of the copyright owner, it has been held that the derivative work is not subject to copyright protection since the original would tend "to pervade the entire work." *Eden Toys, Inc. v. Floralee Undergarment Co.*, 697 F.2d 27, 34 n. 6, 217 U.S.P.Q. 201, 206 n. 6 (2d Cir. 1982); *Gracen v. Bradford Exchange*, 698 F.2d 300, 217 U.S.P.Q. 1294 (7th Cir. 1983). Two exceptions to this rule are stated in the House report accompanying the 1976 Act: (1) where the unauthorized use is a fair use under §107; and (2) where the use is lawful under "applicable foreign law * * * ." H.R. REP. NO. 94-1476, 94th Cong., 2d Sess. 58 (1976). The second of these exceptions is highly questionable, since regardless of whether the conduct is lawful under a foreign copyright act, activity committed in the United States will be judged by the copyright law of the United States. It should be noted in this regard that §602(b) provides: "In a case where the making of the copies would have constituted an infringement of copyright if this title had been applicable, their importation is prohibited." Cf. *London Film Prods., Ltd. v. Intercontinental Communications, Inc.*, 580 F. Supp. 47, 223 U.S.P.Q. 381 (S.D.N.Y. 1984) (in diversity action, copyright laws of South American countries applied).

piano of the orchestral score of an opera,[40] an arrangement of traditional public domain songs for chord organs,[41] and an improvisation from subconscious memory of an old folk song.[42] On the other hand, the addition of an alto part to well-known tunes long sung with three other parts was held not to constitute a new and original work.[43]

In a recent (and questionable) decision[44] it was held that translations of a selected group of English words into Arabic did not contain sufficient originality since plaintiff's effort was "primarily a matter of determining the dialect spoken in the area," after which apparently no further skill in selecting specific words was required.

Derivative works based on preexisting pictorial, graphic, and sculptural works have been a source of frequent litigation, principally because of disagreements over the role that skill may play in establishing originality. The premier case in this area is Judge Frank's decision in *Alfred Bell & Co. v. Catalda Fine Arts, Inc.*,[45] which upheld copyright in reproductions of old masters produced through the technique of mezzotint. In *Alva Studios, Inc. v. Winninger*[46] the court followed *Bell* and found originality in the creation of an exact scale reproduction of Rodin's famous "Hand of God" to museum specifications. *Bell* and *Alva* were distinguished, however, in *L. Batlin & Son, Inc. v. Snyder*,[47] where the Second Circuit sitting *en banc* differentiated between the "true artistic skill" involved in *Bell*, the "great skill and originality" involved in *Alva*, and the "physical skill" or "special training" required for transforming a public domain metal "Uncle Sam" penny bank into a smaller plastic version, as was the case with the work at issue in *Batlin*. The court also rejected, as unprotectible, differences such as Uncle Sam's hairline or the shape of his bow tie as "not perceptible to the casual observer."[48]

---

[40] *Edmonds v. Stern*, 248 F. 897 (2d Cir. 1918).

[41] *Plymouth Music Co. v. Magnus Organ Corp.*, 456 F. Supp. 676, 203 U.S.P.Q. 268 (S.D.N.Y. 1978).

[42] *Italian Book Co. v. Rossi*, 27 F.2d 1014 (S.D.N.Y. 1928); *Wihtol v. Wells*, 231 F.2d 550, 109 U.S.P.Q. 200 (7th Cir. 1956).

[43] *Cooper v. James*, 213 F. 871 (N.D. Ga. 1914). Cf. *McIntyre v. Double-A-Music Corp.*, 166 F. Supp. 681, 119 U.S.P.Q. 106 (S.D. Cal. 1958), *motion for new trial denied*, 179 F. Supp. 160, 124 U.S.P.Q. 27 (S.D.N.Y. 1959). The Copyright Office has stated that "[a] derivative musical work may be registrable, in the aggregate, even though the individual changes, examined separately, may not be," and has given the following example:
"A revision consisting of a change in fingering of two measures, added dynamics in four measures, and three measures of additional music could, in the aggregate, constitute a derivative musical work."
COMPENDIUM II OF COPYRIGHT OFFICE PRACTICES §408.08

[44] *Signo Trading Int'l, Ltd. v. Gordon*, 535 F. Supp. 362, 214 U.S.P.Q. 793 (N.D. Cal. 1981). Cf. *Marling v. Ellison*, 218 U.S.P.Q. 702 (S.D. Fla. 1982) (compilation and translation of foreign meals held protectible); *Williams v. Arndt*, 227 U.S.P.Q. 615, 619 (D. Mass. 1985) (rejecting defendant's argument that its source code version of plaintiff's manual was noninfringing because it represented new (and allegedly different) expression, holding: "While there may be creativity and ingenuity in devising this source code, a source code is not an entirely new, unique expression of ideas. It is simply a translation from one language to another").

[45] 191 F.2d 99, 90 U.S.P.Q. 153 (2d Cir. 1951).

[46] 177 F. Supp. 265, 123 U.S.P.Q. 487 (S.D.N.Y. 1959).

[47] 536 F.2d 486, 189 U.S.P.Q. 753 (2d Cir.) (*en banc*), *cert. denied*, 429 U.S. 857, 191 U.S.P.Q. 588 (1976). Cf. Judge Meskill's dissent, *ibid*, and his opinion for the Second Circuit panel which was reversed *en banc*. 187 U.S.P.Q. 721 (2d Cir. 1975).

[48] *Id.* at 489, 189 U.S.P.Q. at 755.

The Second Circuit returned to the issue four years later in *Durham Industries, Inc. v. Tomy Corp.*, where the court rejected copyright protection for wind-up plastic toys of Disney characters, stating

"[p]articularly important for decision of the case before us is the explicit rejection in *Batlin* of the contention that the originality requirement of copyrightability can be satisfied by the mere reproduction of a work of art in a different medium, or by the demonstration of some 'physical' as opposed to 'artistic' skill."[49]

The *Batlin* and *Durham* decisions were ostensibly followed in the Seventh Circuit in *Gracen v. Bradford Exchange*. It appears, however, that the *Gracen* court confused the standard for originality with the test for infringement, as may be seen in the following passage:

"[T]he purpose of [originality] in copyright law is to * * * assure a sufficiently gross difference between the underlying and the derivative work to avoid entangling subsequent artists depicting the underlying work in copyright problems.

" * * * The requirement of originality is significant chiefly in connection with derivative works, where if interpreted too liberally it would paradoxically inhibit rather than promote the creation of such works by giving the first creator a considerable power to interfere with the creation of subsequent derivative works from the same underlying work.

" * * * [A] derivative work must be substantially different from the underlying work to be copyrightable."[50]

The error of the *Gracen* court in this regard was presaged by the Second Circuit's decision in *Eden Toys, Inc. v. Floralee Undergarment Co.*:

"The standard for sufficient originality is whether a work contains 'some substantial, not merely trivial, originality.' * * * The standard for copyright infringement, by contrast, is whether the defendant's work is 'substantially similar' to the plaintiff's work. * * *

"The difference between these two tests is not merely academic. A work which makes non-trivial contributions to an existing one may be copyrighted as a derivative work and yet, because it retains the 'same aesthetic appeal' as the original work, render the holder liable for infringement of the original copyright if the derivative work were to be published without permission from the owner of the original copyright."[51]

---

[49]630 F.2d 905, 910, 208 U.S.P.Q. 10, 15 (2d Cir. 1980). H.R. REP. No. 94-1476, 94th Cong., 2d Sess. 57 (1976); S. REP. No. 94-473, 94th Cong., 1st Sess. 55 (1975). *Gallery House, Inc. v. Yi*, 582 F. Supp. 1294, 223 U.S.P.Q. 894 (N.D. Ill. 1984) (conversion of two-dimensional design into three-dimensional object found to lack requisite originality); *M.S.R. Imports, Inc. v. R.E. Greenspan Co.*, 574 F. Supp. 31, 225 U.S.P.Q. 585 (E.D. Pa. 1983), which upheld the copyrightability of a cast-iron coke wagon based on a public domain beer wagon; *Knickerbocker Toy Co. v. Winterbrook Corp.*, 216 U.S.P.Q. 621 (1982) (change in facial expression of Raggedy Ann and Andy dolls not insufficient as a matter of law).

[50]698 F.2d 300, 305, 217 U.S.P.Q. 1294, 1298 (7th Cir. 1983). See also criticism of *Gracen* in 1 NIMMER ON COPYRIGHT §3.03.

[51]697 F.2d 27, 34, 217 U.S.P.Q. 201, 206 (2d Cir. 1982). The Eleventh Circuit has noted the difference between the standard for originality and the test for infringement. See *Original Appalachian Artworks, Inc. v. Toy Loft, Inc.*, 684 F.2d 821, 829, 215 U.S.P.Q. 745, 752 (11th Cir. 1982). See also *Sherry Mfg. Co. v. Towel King of Florida*, 753 F.2d 1565, 225 U.S.P.Q. 1005

In determining whether a derivative work is copyrightable, care should be taken to consider only the material contributed by the would-be derivative author, since under Section 103(b) of the Act copyright in a derivative work "extends only to the material contributed by the author of such work, as distinguished from the pre-existing material employed in the work * * * ."[52]

## Noncopyrightable Material

### Blank Forms and Standardized Material

The Copyright Office has long advised the public that blank forms and similar works, designed to record rather than convey information, cannot be copyrighted,[53] and its regulations state in this regard:

> "The following are examples of works not subject to copyright and applications for registration of such works cannot be entertained:
> * * *
> "(c) Blank forms, such as time cards, graph paper, account books, diaries, bank checks, score cards, address books, report forms and the like, which are designed for recording information and do not in themselves convey information * * * ."[54]

---

(11th Cir. 1985) (beach towel based on public domain design contained only trivial variations and thus was held unprotectible); *Cosmair, Inc. v. Dynamite Enters., Inc.*, 226 U.S.P.Q. 344 (S.D. Fla. 1985) (copyrightability of designs for fragrance and cosmetic products based on underlying trademark design questioned). Cf. *SAS Institute, Inc. v. S&H Computer Systems*, 605 F. Supp. 816, 225 U.S.P.Q. 916 (M.D. Tenn. 1985) (copyright in derivative computer program based on preexisting public domain program upheld); *Synercom Technology, Inc. v. University Computing Co.*, 462 F. Supp. 1003, 199 U.S.P.Q. 537 (N.D. Tex. 1979) (same; computer program manuals); *Williams v. Arndt*, 227 U.S.P.Q. 615 (D. Mass. 1985) (corrected and edited manual for futures trading held to be protected derivative work of earlier uncorrected manual).

[52]17 U.S.C. §103(b) (1978); *Conan Properties, Inc. v. Mattel, Inc.*, 601 F. Supp. 1179, 1182, 226 U.S.P.Q. 265, 267 (S.D.N.Y. 1984); *Roy Export Co. of Vaduz v. CBS, Inc.*, 672 F.2d 1095, 215 U.S.P.Q. 289 (2d Cir.), *cert. denied*, 459 U.S. 826 (1982). See also discussion of "infection principle" in note 213, *infra*. In *Kenbrooke Fabrics, Inc. v. Material Things*, 223 U.S.P.Q. 1039 (S.D.N.Y. 1984), the court correctly noted this principle, but then failed to evaluate whether the material contributed by the derivative author was copyrightable apart from the underlying work, a proposition which appears questionable since the court found that defendant had not copied any protectible "components."
The analysis of whether a derivative work is copyrightable is the same regardless if the underlying work has also been created by the author of the derivative work. *Cooling Systems & Flexibles, Inc. v. Stuart Radiator, Inc.*, 777 F.2d 485, 490, 228 U.S.P.Q. 275, 279 (9th Cir. 1985).

[53]37 C.F.R. §202.1(c); COPYRIGHT OFFICE CIRCULAR 32. 37 C.F.R. §202.1(d) also denies registration for: "Works consisting entirely of information that is common property containing no original authorship, such as, for example: Standard calendars, height and weight charts, tape measures and rulers, schedules of sporting events, and lists or tables from public documents or other common sources." Cf. H.R. REP. No. 2237, 89th Cong., 2d Sess. 44 n. 1 (1966); H.R. REP. No. 83, 90th Cong., 1st Sess. 15 n. 1 (1967).
In *Toro Co. v. R&R Products Co.*, 600 F. Supp. 400, 401, 225 U.S.P.Q. 1167, 1168 (D. Minn. 1984), the court, citing §102(b) and 37 C.F.R. §202.1(a)'s statement that "a mere listing of ingredients or contents" is not copyrightable, held that defendant's publication of part numbers from plaintiff's equipment catalogue "is analogous to publication of a list of ingredients or contents not protectible by law." On appeal, dismissal of the complaint was affirmed on a different ground—that plaintiff's numbering system lacked originality. 787 F.2d 1208, 229 U.S.P.Q. 282 (8th Cir. 1986)

[54]37 C.F.R. §202.1. See also *Notice of Termination of Inquiry Regarding Blank Forms*, 45 Fed. Reg. 63297-63300 (Sept. 24, 1980).

A landmark decision in this area is *Baker v. Selden,* in which the Supreme Court held that "blank account books are not the subject of copyright,"[55] a holding that has been applied in numerous subsequent cases involving analogous works.[56] Other decisions, however, have extended protection where the work was found to convey a minimal amount of information, even though its primary function was recordation,[57] or where a form was "integrated" with literary material explaining a system.[58]

Protection has also been granted to forms, such as legal or insurance documents, which are inherently designed to convey information,[59] although one court aptly noted in a different context "that a work is copyrighted says little about the scope of protection."[60]

Works which consist of standard geometrical shapes (or variations thereof) such as squares, rectangles, circles, and ellipses have also been held uncopyrightable,[61] although a compilation of various

---

[55]101 U.S. 99, 107 (1879). The Court's additional holding that copyright in a book explaining a system of bookkeeping did not protect the configuration of lines necessary to operate the system is discussed on p. 30, *infra.*

[56]See, e.g., *American Nursing Care of Toledo, Inc. v. Leisure,* 609 F. Supp. 419, 432 (N.D. Ohio 1984) (franchise forms held to be unprotectible as "merely common business forms for recording generic business information indigenous to the kind of business in which [plaintiff] and many other companies are engaged"). *John H. Harland Co. v. Clarke Checks,* 711 F.2d 966, 219 U.S.P.Q. 515 (11th Cir. 1983) (blank bank checks); *Januz Marketing Communications, Inc. v. Doubleday & Co.,* 569 F. Supp. 76, 222 U.S.P.Q. 389 (S.D.N.Y. 1982) (time-keeping charts); *McAlpine v. AAMCO Automatic Transmissions, Inc.,* 202 U.S.P.Q. 575, 594 (E.D. Mich. 1978) (automotive repair forms); *Time Saver Checks, Inc. v. Deluxe Check Printers, Inc.,* 178 U.S.P.Q. 510 (N.D. Tex. 1973) (blank checks); *M.M. Business Forms Corp. v. Uuarco, Inc.,* 472 F.2d 1137, 176 U.S.P.Q. 456 (6th Cir. 1973) (forms for television repair). The decisions in *Brown Instruments Co. v. Warner,* 161 F.2d 910, 73 U.S.P.Q. 427 (D.C. Cir. 1947), and in *Taylor Instrument Cos. v. Fawley-Brost Co.,* 139 F.2d 98, 59 U.S.P.Q. 384 (7th Cir. 1943), *cert. denied,* 321 U.S. 785, 60 U.S.P.Q. 579 (1944), denying protection based on the "machine parts" doctrine, have been criticized. See *Apple Computer, Inc. v. Franklin Computer Corp.,* 714 F.2d 1240, 1251, 219 U.S.P.Q. 113, 121 (3d Cir. 1983).

[57]See, e.g., *Edwin K. Williams & Co. v. Edwin K. Williams & Co.—East,* 542 F.2d 1053, 191 U.S.P.Q. 563 (9th Cir. 1976) (gas station account books); *Norton Printing Co. v. Augustana Hospital,* 155 U.S.P.Q. 133 (N.D. Ill. 1976) (forms for recording medical laboratory tests); *Baldwin Cooke Co. v. Keith Clark, Inc.,* 383 F. Supp. 650, 183 U.S.P.Q. 209 (N.D. Ill.), *aff'd per curiam,* 505 F.2d 1250, 183 U.S.P.Q. 769 (7th Cir. 1974) (a combination calendar, appointment book, diary, and information book was deemed "much more than a mere diary"); *Harcourt, Brace & World, Inc. v. Graphic Controls Corp.,* 329 F. Supp. 517, 171 U.S.P.Q. 219 (S.D.N.Y. 1971) (answer sheets for recording responses to multiple-choice psychological test questions); *Deutsch v. Arnold,* 98 F.2d 686 (2d Cir. 1938) (chart used for analyzing handwriting).

[58]*Williams v. Arndt,* 227 U.S.P.Q. 615 (D. Mass. 1985) (manual for futures trading held copyrightable); *Cash Dividend Check Corp. v. Davis,* 247 F.2d 458, 114 U.S.P.Q. 32 (9th Cir. 1957). Cf. *Gaye v. Gillis,* 167 F. Supp. 416, 119 U.S.P.Q. 292 (D. Mass. 1958).

[59]See especially Judge Sweet's comprehensive and insightful opinion in *Merritt Forbes & Co. v. Newman Investment Securities,* 604 F. Supp. 943, 948–952, 225 U.S.P.Q. 1179, 1181–1182 (S.D.N.Y. 1985). See also *Transgo, Inc. v. Ajac Transmission Parts Corp.,* 768 F.2d 1001, 227 U.S.P.Q. 598 (9th Cir. 1985) (copyright in instruction sheet for automobile transmission kits upheld); *Professional Systems & Supplies, Inc. v. Databank Supplies & Equipment Co.,* 202 U.S.P.Q. 693 (W.D. Okla. 1979) (forms for bank promissory notes); *Continental Casualty Co. v. Beardsley,* 253 F.2d 702, 117 U.S.P.Q. 1 (2d Cir.), *cert. denied,* 358 U.S. 816, 119 U.S.P.Q. 501 (1958) (insurance forms). Cf. *Dorsey v. Old Surety Life Insurance Co.,* 98 F.2d 872, 39 U.S.P.Q. 92 (10th Cir. 1937); *Miner v. Employers Mutual Liability Insurance Co. of Wisconsin,* 229 F.2d 35, 108 U.S.P.Q. 100 (D.C. Cir. 1956). See generally Luciano, *Copyright Protection for Insurance Policies,* 19 FORUM 419 (1984).

[60]*Atari, Inc. v. North American Philips Consumer Electronics Corp.,* 672 F.2d 607, 616–617, 214 U.S.P.Q. 33, 41 (7th Cir.), *cert. denied,* 459 U.S. 880 (1982).

[61]*Tompkins Graphics, Inc. v. Zipatone, Inc.,* 222 U.S.P.Q. 49 (E.D. Pa. 1983). See also *Bailie v. Fisher,* 258 F.2d 425, 117 U.S.P.Q. 334 (D.C. Cir. 1958) (copyrightability of standard five-pointed star denied), and *Kitchens of Sara Lee, Inc. v. Nifty Foods Corp.,* 266 F.2d 541, 121 U.S.P.Q. 359 (2d Cir. 1957) (copyright in photographs used on labels for bakery products upheld, but this did not prevent copying of circular, rectangular, or octagonal shapes).

trademarks consisting of similar shapes, gathered into a directory, was found protectible in a decision by Judge Learned Hand.[62]

## Ideas and Systems

*Baker v. Selden*, as well as more recent cases discussed below, illustrates a principle even more basic than the question of blank or standardized forms. The copyright on Selden's book explaining his system of bookkeeping did not cover the system itself, but only his literary expression.[63] The distinction between nonprotectible "ideas" and their protectible "expression" is one of the most pervasive, as well as one of the most elusive, threads in copyright law.[64] It applies to all areas of copyrightable subject matter and is equally applicable to correlative questions of infringement. This principle, known as the "idea/expression dichotomy," codified in Section 102(b) of the 1976 Act, was explained as follows in the Register of Copyrights' 1961 Report concerning the revision effort:

> "Copyright does not preclude others from using the ideas or information revealed by the author's work. It pertains to the literary, musical, graphic or artistic form in which the author expresses intellectual concepts. It enables him to prevent others from reproducing his individual expression without his consent. But anyone is free to create his own ex-

---

[62]*Jewelers' Circular Pub. Co. v. Keystone Pub. Co.*, 274 F. 932 (S.D.N.Y. 1921), *aff'd*, 281 F. 83 (2d Cir.), *cert. denied*, 259 U.S. 581 (1922).
  The use of color in establishing a copyright claim was noted in early legislative reports. See H.R. Rep. No. 2237, 89th Cong., 2d Sess. 44 n. 1 (1966); H.R. Rep. No. 83, 90th Cong., 1st Sess. 15 n. 1 (1967) (suggesting that color schemes could be "clothed in or combined with copyrightable subject matter and thus achieve a degree of protection" but that "any protection for them as separate copyrightable works is not here intended and will require action by a future Congress"). This language was, however, deleted in subsequent reports. See Second Supplementary Report of the Register of Copyrights on the General Revision of the U.S. Copyright Law: 1975 Revision Bill, ch. I at 3–4, 15 (draft ed. 1975), for a discussion of the effect of this deletion on state law protection and 37 C.F.R. §202.1(a) ("'mere variations" in color not protectible). Cf. *Greff Fabrics, Inc. v. Spectrum Fabrics Corp.*, 217 U.S.P.Q. 498 (S.D.N.Y. 1981), where the court apparently held that where a work is otherwise copyrightable, the use of different colors would support separate copyrights; *Storm v. Kennington, Ltd.*, 223 U.S.P.Q. 790 (N.D. Cal. 1984) (black-and-white illustrations produced from public domain color illustrations held unprotectible); *Sargent v. American Greetings Corp.*, 588 F. Supp. 912, 223 U.S.P.Q. 1327 (N.D. Ohio 1984) (color embodied in artwork may form an element of originality where it is not inherent in the medium in which the artist is working); *Pantone, Inc. v. A.I. Freedman*, 294 F. Supp. 545, 548, 160 U.S.P.Q. 530, 533 (S.D.N.Y. 1968) (Mansfield, J.) (motion for preliminary injunction granted restraining the distribution of an allegedly infringing color-matching booklet, the court holding that "[a]lthough the mere portrayal of a series of gradations of color shades, standing alone, would present a doubtful case for copyright infringement, the arrangement here possessed [a] unique quality which apparently gained ready recognition on the part of artists in a critical profession"); *Novelty Textile Mills, Inc. v. Joan Fabrics Corp.*, 558 F.2d 1090, 195 U.S.P.Q. 1 (2d Cir. 1977) (Mansfield, J., concurring in part and dissenting in part).
  Color has also been held to be a factor in an infringement analysis. See *P. Kaufman, Inc. v. Rex Curtain Corp.*, 203 U.S.P.Q. 859, 860 (S.D.N.Y. 1978); *Design Resources, Inc. v. John Wolf Decorative Fabrics*, Copr. L. Rep. ¶25,834 (S.D.N.Y. 1985); *DeMarco of California Fabrics, Inc. v. Block's Fashion Fabrics, Inc.*, Copr. L. Rep. ¶25,416 (S.D.N.Y. 1982); *Soptra Fabrics Corp. v. Stafford Knitting Mills, Inc.*, 490 F.2d 1092, 1094, 180 U.S.P.Q. 545, 546 (2d Cir. 1974); *Coleur Int'l Ltd. v. Opulent Fabrics, Inc.*, 330 F. Supp. 152, 154 (S.D.N.Y. 1971).
  [63]But see Professor Nimmer's criticism of *Baker v. Selden*, 1 Nimmer on Copyright §2.18[B].
  [64]See Judge Learned Hand's oft-cited comment on this in *Nichols v. Universal Pictures Corp.*, 45 F.2d 119, 121, 7 U.S.P.Q. 84, 86 (2d Cir. 1930), and in *Peter Pan Fabrics, Inc. v. Martin Weiner Corp.*, 274 F.2d 487, 489, 124 U.S.P.Q. 154, 155 (2d Cir. 1960).

pression of the same concepts, or to make practical use of them, as long as he does not copy the author's form of expression."[65]

In works of fiction, including dramatic material, abstract outlines of plot or character may, depending upon the amount of detail, be treated as unprotectible themes or "ideas."[66] In a related vein, so-called *"scènes à faire,"* described as "incidents, characters, or settings which are as a practical matter indispensable, or at least standard, in the treatment of a given topic," have been held unprotectible.[67]

In the case of works of nonfiction, the underlying ideas, concepts, principles, or discoveries are denied protection.[68] A number of recent

---

[65]REPORT OF THE REGISTER OF COPYRIGHTS ON THE GENERAL REVISION OF THE U.S. COPYRIGHT LAW 3 (1961). This language is substantially repeated in the legislative reports accompanying the 1976 Act. See H.R. REP. No. 94-1476, 94th Cong., 2d Sess. 56–57 (1976); S. REP. No. 94-473, 94th Cong., 1st Sess. 54 (1975).

[66]*See v. Durang,* 711 F.2d 141, 219 U.S.P.Q. 771 (9th Cir. 1983); *Warner Bros., Inc. v. ABC,* 523 F. Supp. 611, 211 U.S.P.Q. 51 (S.D.N.Y.), *aff'd,* 654 F.2d 204, 211 U.S.P.Q. 97 (2d Cir. 1981) (on motion for preliminary injunction); 530 F. Supp. 1187, 215 U.S.P.Q. 690 (S.D.N.Y. 1982), *aff'd,* 720 F.2d 231, 222 U.S.P.Q. 101 (2d Cir. 1983) (on motion for summary judgment); *Gibson v. CBS, Inc.,* 491 F. Supp. 583, 211 U.S.P.Q. 262 (S.D.N.Y. 1980); *Sid & Marty Krofft Television Prods. v. McDonald's Corp.,* 562 F.2d 1157, 196 U.S.P.Q. 97 (9th Cir. 1977); *Nichols v. Universal Pictures Corp.,* 45 F.2d 119, 7 U.S.P.Q. 84 (2d Cir. 1930), *cert. denied,* 282 U.S. 902 (1931).
 The video game fad of the early 1980s generated a number of interesting applications of the idea–expression dichotomy. See, e.g., *Atari, Inc. v. North American Philips Consumer Electronics Corp.,* 672 F.2d 607, 615–616, 214 U.S.P.Q. 33, 40–41 (7th Cir.), *cert. denied,* 459 U.S. 880 (1982); *Stern Electronics v. Kaufman,* 669 F.2d 852, 213 U.S.P.Q. 443 (2d Cir. 1982); *Williams Electronics, Inc. v. Bally Mfg. Corp.,* 568 F. Supp. 1274, 220 U.S.P.Q. 1091 (N.D. Ill. 1983); *Atari, Inc. v. Amusement World, Inc.,* 547 F. Supp. 222, 215 U.S.P.Q. 929 (D. Md. 1981). Other examples may be seen in the endless litigation over stuffed toys. See, e.g., *Eden Toys, Inc. v. Floralee Undergarment Co.,* 697 F.2d 27, 217 U.S.P.Q. 201 (2d Cir. 1982); *Original Appalachian Artworks, Inc. v. Toy Loft, Inc.,* 684 F.2d 821, 215 U.S.P.Q. 745 (11th Cir. 1982).

[67]*Alexander v. Haley,* 460 F. Supp. 40, 45, 200 U.S.P.Q. 239, 243 (S.D.N.Y. 1978). See also *Walker v. Time-Life Films, Inc.,* 784 F.2d 44, 228 U.S.P.Q. 505 (2d Cir. 1986); *Zambito v. Paramount Pictures Corp.,* 613 F. Supp. 1107, 227 U.S.P.Q. 649 (E.D.N.Y. 1985). *Hasbro Indus., Inc. v. Hot Items, Inc.,* 473 F. Supp. 1286, 207 U.S.P.Q. 996 (S.D.N.Y. 1979) (similarities in packaging, trade dress, and textual materials accompanying children's toys found noninfringing since they were based on the same idea and in marketing children's toys "there will naturally be some similarity"). In *See v. Durang,* 711 F.2d 141, 143, 219 U.S.P.Q. 771, 772 (9th Cir. 1983), however, the Ninth Circuit wrote:
 "The [district] court's characterization of the [*scènes à faire*] doctrine as relating to unprotected 'ideas' may have been technically inaccurate, but the court properly applied the doctrine to hold unprotectible forms of expression that were either stock scenes or scenes that flowed necessarily from common unprotectible ideas. 'Common' in this context means common to the works at issue, not necessarily, as plaintiff suggests, commonly found in other artistic works."
 See also *Giangrasso v. CBS, Inc.,* 534 F. Supp. 472, 477 n. 3, 215 U.S.P.Q. 219, 223 n. 3 (E.D.N.Y. 1982); *Reyher v. Children's Television Workshop,* 533 F.2d 87, 91, 190 U.S.P.Q. 387, 390–391 (2d Cir. 1976).

[68]See also *Harper & Row, Pub., Inc. v. Nation Enters.,* 723 F.2d 195, 202 n. 7, 220 U.S.P.Q. 321, 327 n. 7 (2d Cir. 1983), *rev'd on other grounds,* 471 U.S. ____, 225 U.S.P.Q. 1073 (1985) (equating "discoveries" with "facts"); *Triangle Pub., Inc. v. Sports Eye, Inc.,* 415 F. Supp. 682, 685 n. 9, 193 U.S.P.Q. 50, 52 n. 9 (E.D. Pa. 1976) ("For purposes of copyright infringement, data and ideas are treated as equivalents"); H.R. REP. No. 94-1476, 94th Cong., 2d Sess. 56 (1976); S. REP. No. 94-473, 94th Cong., 1st Sess. 54 (1975) (including "information" with scope of §102(b)).
 In a questionable application of this principle, courts have held that one who represents his book as being factual is estopped from later claiming that the work is in part or whole fictional. See *Houts v. Universal City Studios, Inc.,* 224 U.S.P.Q. 427 (C.D. Cal. 1984); *Marshal v. Yates,* 223 U.S.P.Q. 453 (C.D. Cal. 1983); *Oliver v. St. Germain Foundation,* 41 F. Supp. 296, 51 U.S.P.Q. 20 (S.D. Cal. 1941).
 For a discussion of the difference between protectible expression and nonprotectible ideas in historical works, see Ginsburg, *Sabotaging and Reconstructing History: A Comment on the Scope of Copyright Protection in Works of History After Hoehling v. Universal City Studios,* 29 J. COPR. SOC'Y 647 (1982).

decisions in this area have, however, mistakenly applied the policy behind the free use of ideas embodied in Section 102(b) to permit a greater taking of protectible expression. In *Landsberg v. Scrabble Crossword Game Players, Inc.*, for example, the Ninth Circuit stated:

"One consequence of the policy in favor of free use of ideas is that the degree of substantial similarity required to show infringement varies according to the type of work and the ideas expressed in it. * * * Some ideas can be expressed in myriad ways, while others allow only a narrow range of expression. Fictional works generally fall into the first category. The basic idea of a fictional work might be that classic, boy meets girl. This idea can be expressed, as it has been through thousands of years of literature, with variations in setting, sequence of incident, and characterization. An author wishing to write yet another work using the 'boy meets girl' idea can choose from a wide range of materials in composing his or her expression of the idea. Therefore, a new work incorporating that idea need not be a verbatim or close paraphrase of an earlier work to infringe that work. A resemblance in details of setting, incident, or characterization that falls short of close paraphrase may be enough to establish substantial similarity and infringement * * *.

"Factual works are different. Subsequent authors wishing to express ideas contained in a factual work often can choose from only a narrow range of expression. * * * Therefore, similarity of expression may have to amount to verbatim reproduction or very close paraphrasing before a factual work will be deemed infringed."[69]

Since Section 102(b) expressly denies protection to ideas, there is no reason for the policy favoring the free use of ideas to have any bearing on "the degree of substantial similarity required to show infringement." Nor does the court support with any authority its broad statement concerning the supposedly narrow range of expression available to factual writers.

The tendency of copyrightability and infringement questions to mix in this area increases as the possible permutations of expression become fewer, and leads us to another manifestation of the idea-expression dichotomy known as "merger," which has been explained as follows:

"When the 'idea' and its 'expression' are * * * inseparable copying the 'expression' will not be barred, since protecting the 'expression' in such circumstances would confer a monopoly of the 'idea' upon the copyright owner free of the conditions and limitations imposed by the patent law."[70]

---

[69]736 F.2d 485, 488, 221 U.S.P.Q. 1140, 1142–1143 (9th Cir.), *cert. denied*, 469 U.S. 1037 (1984); Cf. *Del Madera Properties v. Rhodes and Gardner, Inc.*, 227 U.S.P.Q. 486 (N.D. Cal. 1985) (merger rejected in residential subdivision map).

[70]*Herbert Rosenthal Jewelry Corp. v. Kalpakian*, 446 F.2d 738, 742, 170 U.S.P.Q. 557, 560 (9th Cir. 1971); *Freedman v. Grolier Enters., Inc.*, 179 U.S.P.Q. 476, 478 (S.D.N.Y. 1973). But cf. *Herbert Rosenthal Jewelry Corp. v. Grossbardt*, 436 F.2d 315, 168 U.S.P.Q. 193 (2d Cir. 1970) (same work as in *Kalpakian* found infringed by verbatim copy); *Arc v. S. S. Sarna, Inc.*, 621 F. Supp. 916, 923–924, 229 U.S.P.Q. 25, 30 (E.D.N.Y. 1985) (merger rejected as applied to lead crystal figurines of animals); *Animal Fair, Inc. v. Amfesco Indus., Inc.*, 620 F. Supp. 175, 227 U.S.P.Q. 817 (D. Minn. 1985) (infringement of bear claw slippers). See also *Morrissey v. Procter & Gamble Co.*, 379 F.2d 675, 154 U.S.P.Q. 193 (1st Cir. 1967); *Universal Athletic Sales Co. v. Salkeld*, 511 F.2d 904, 907, 185 U.S.P.Q. 76, 78 (3d Cir.), *cert. denied*, 423 U.S. 863 (1975)

A number of decisions,[71] however, fail to differentiate between the type of merger of idea and expression that denies, *ab initio*, copyright protection to a work and that type of merger that does not deny copyrightability but operates as a limitation on the scope of protection; i.e., in evaluating a claim of infringement, the court will find infringement only where the defendant appropriates to a substantial degree, either quantitatively or qualitatively, nonmerged expression.

The merger doctrine is believed to have particular relevance to computer programs.[72] In the first appellate opinion on this issue, *Apple Computer, Inc. v. Franklin Computer Corp.*, the Third Circuit took what it termed a "pragmatic" approach based on keeping "the balance between competition and protection * * * ."[73] This emphasis on business practices is also seen in the court's rejection of defendant's argument that the idea–expression dichotomy had relevance to its desire to create a computer operating system program for its (competing) computer capable of "running" plaintiff Apple's applications software:

> "This claim has no pertinence to either the idea/expression dichotomy or merger. The idea which may merge with the expression, thus making the copyright unavailable, is the idea which is the subject of the expression. The idea of one of the operating system programs is, for example, how to translate source code to object code. If other methods of expressing that idea are not foreclosed as a practical matter, then there is no merger. [Defendant] may wish to achieve total compatibility with independently developed application programs written for the Apple II, but that is a commercial and competitive objective which does not enter into the

---

(stick figures in wall chart depicting methods of using weight-lifting machine); *Affiliated Hospital Prods., Inc. v. Merdel Game Mfg. Co.*, 513 F.2d 1183, 1188–1189 (2d Cir. 1975) (rule book for game); *Synercom Technology, Inc. v. University Computing Co.*, 462 F. Supp. 1003, 199 U.S.P.Q. 537 (N.D. Tex. 1979) (computer input formats); *Decorative Aides Corp. v. Staple Sewing Aides Corp.*, 497 F. Supp. 154, 210 U.S.P.Q. 657 (S.D.N.Y. 1980), aff'd mem., 657 F.2d 262 (2d Cir. 1981) (instruction sheet for drapery header); *Linden v. Dial Press*, Copr. L. Rep. ¶25,179 (S.D.N.Y. 1980) (body-and-muscle development exercises); *Cooling Systems & Flexibles, Inc. v. Stuart Radiator, Inc.*, 777 F.2d 485, 228 U.S.P.Q. 275 (9th Cir. 1985) (radiator catalogues). Cf. *Runge v. Lee*, 411 F.2d 579, 169 U.S.P.Q. 388 (9th Cir.), cert. denied, 404 U.S. 887, 171 U.S.P.Q. 322 (1971) (Douglas, J., dissenting) (copyright in and infringement of facial exercises found). Copyrights consisting of "barely copyrightable" material due to merger have been termed "thin" copyrights. *Kepner Tregoe, Inc. v. Carabio*, 203 U.S.P.Q. 124, 130 (E.D. Mich. 1979).

[71]See *Consumers Union of the United States, Inc. v. General Signal Corp.*, 724 F.2d 1044, 1049–1050, 221 U.S.P.Q. 400, 406 (2d Cir. 1983), *petition for rehearing en banc denied*, 730 F.2d 47 (2d Cir.) (Oakes, J., dissenting), cert. denied, 469 U.S. 823, 224 U.S.P.Q. 616 (1984), and *Production Contractors, Inc. v. WGN Continental Broadcasting Co.*, 622 F. Supp. 1500, 1503, 228 U.S.P.Q. 604, 605–606 (N.D. Ill. 1985), which, while noting that the idea of a Christmas parade "is a common one, relatively simple and contains no original creative authorship," failed to analyze the particular characteristics of plaintiff's work.

[72]Indeed, §102(b) was added out of fear that copyright in computer programs might mistakenly be extended to the methodology or processes, such as algorithms, adopted by the programmer, rather than to the "writing" expressing his ideas. See S. Rep. No. 93-983, 93d Cong., 2d Sess. 107 (1974); Supplementary Report of the Register of Copyrights on the General Revision of the U.S. Copyright Law: 1975 Revision Bill, ch. I at p. 2 (draft ed. 1975); S. Rep. No. 94-473, 94th Cong., 1st Sess. 54 (1975); H.R. Rep. No. 94-1476, 94th Cong., 2d Sess. 57 (1976).

[73]714 F.2d 1240, 1253, 219 U.S.P.Q. 113, 124 (3d Cir. 1983). But cf. the court's further statement: "In essence, this inquiry is no different than that made to determine whether the expression and idea have merged, which has been stated to occur when there are no or few ways of expressing a particular idea." *Id.* See also *Apple Computer, Inc. v. Formula Int'l, Inc.*, 725 F.2d 521, 525, 221 U.S.P.Q. 762, 765 (9th Cir. 1984).

somewhat metaphysical issue of whether particular ideas and expressions have merged."[74]

Up to the present, litigation over infringement of computer programs has primarily arisen in the context of virtually identical programs. As competing programs move away from such close identity it is expected that application of the idea–expression dichotomy and merger will become more difficult to determine, as issues over whether particular routines, subroutines, or other component parts of computer programs are ideas, procedures, processes, systems, methods of operation, concepts, principles, discoveries, *"scènes à faire,"* or expression are debated.

## *Ideas and §301*

While it is clear that copyright protection may not be accorded to ideas apart from their expression, the question arises whether the states may do so. The starting point for such an inquiry is Section 301 of the Copyright Act, a revolutionary provision establishing a single, preemptive federal regime for

"all legal or equitable rights that are equivalent to any of the exclusive rights within the general scope of copyright as specified by section 106 in works of authorship that are fixed in a tangible medium of expression and come within the subject matter of copyright as specified by sections 102 and 103 * * * ."[75]

State law is not preempted, however, with respect to:

"(1) subject matter that does not come within the subject matter of copyright as specified by sections 102 and 103 * * * ; or
* * *

"(3) activities violating legal or equitable rights that are not equivalent to any of the exclusive rights within the general scope of copyright as specified by section 106."[76]

Preemption thus does not occur if the work either does not come within the subject matter of copyright *or* when it does, if the activities do not violate rights equivalent to those granted in the Act. Since Section 102(b) expressly prohibits protection for ideas, it may be argued that ideas are not within the subject matter of copyright protection and that thus the states may protect them. This argument was,

---

[74]714 F.2d at 1253, 219 U.S.P.Q. at 124. The court's definitional attempt in the second sentence of the cited passage is virtually tautological and thus of little aid. See also *Whelan Associates, Inc. v. Jaslow Dental Laboratory, Inc.,* 609 F. Supp. 1307, 225 U.S.P.Q. 156 (E.D. Pa. 1985): "The 'expression of the idea' in a software computer program is the manner in which the program operates, controls and regulates the computer in receiving, assembling, calculating, retaining, correlating, and producing useful information either on a screen, printout or by audio communication." *Id.* at 1320, 225 U.S.P.Q. at 166. See also Judge Higginbotham's scholarly opinion in *Synercom Technology, Inc. v. University Computing Co.,* 462 F. Supp. 1003, 199 U.S.P.Q. 537 (N.D. Tex. 1978), and *SAS Institute, Inc. v. S & H Computer Systems, Inc.,* 605 F. Supp. 816, 225 U.S.P.Q. 916 (M.D. Tenn. 1985).
[75]17 U.S.C. §301(a) (1978).
[76]17 U.S.C. §301(b) (1978).

in fact, persuasive in two recent decisions.[77] A counterargument, based on the Supremacy Clause of the Constitution, would be that the federal exclusion of protection for ideas effectuates an important federal policy of permitting free access to and use of ideas, and that state efforts to the contrary impermissibly interfere with this policy. Professor Nimmer has also argued that "the protection of ideas *per se* by either state or federal laws 'equivalent' to copyright would constitute a violation of the First Amendment guarantee of freedom of speech."[78] The courts are split, however, over whether trade secret misappropriation, an analogous form of idea protection, is preempted.[79] This topic is covered in more detail on pp. 84–87, *infra*.

In the area of historical works, and building on the nonprotectibility of ideas, the courts have held theories regarding and interpretations of historical events to be uncopyrightable apart from their expression.[80] Commentators, while agreeing with this principle, have nevertheless strongly criticized its application in specific cases.[81]

## Utilitarian Works

In 1870 Congress extended copyright protection to "statue[s], statuar[ies], or model[s] or design[s] intended to be perfected and executed as a work of the fine arts * * * ."[82] The 1909 Act revised this category to cover, in Section 5(g), "[w]orks of art; models or designs for works of art," a change in phraseology that was "deliberately intended as a broader specification than 'works of fine arts' in the [prior] statute"[83] in order to eliminate any "[v]erbal distinctions be-

---

[77] *Bromhall v. Rorvik*, 478 F. Supp. 361, 203 U.S.P.Q. 774 (E.D. Pa. 1979); *Warrington Associates, Inc. v. Real-Time Engineering Systems, Inc.*, 522 F. Supp. 367, 216 U.S.P.Q. 1024 (N.D. Ill. 1981). See also *Landsberg v. Scrabble Crossword Game Players, Inc.*, 736 F.2d 485, 489, 221 U.S.P.Q. 1140, 1143 (9th Cir.), *cert. denied*, 469 U.S. 1037 (1984), which suggests that a compilation copyright in ideas is available.

[78] 1 NIMMER ON COPYRIGHT §1.01[B][2][C].

[79] Cf. *Videotronics, Inc. v. Bend Electronics*, 564 F. Supp. 1471, 223 U.S.P.Q. 296 (D. Nev. 1983) (preemption found); *M. Bryce & Associates, Inc. v. Gladstone*, 107 Wisc. 2d 241, 319 N.W.2d 907, 215 U.S.P.Q. 81 (Wisc. Ct. App.), *cert. denied*, 459 U.S. 944 (1982). The Supreme Court's decisions in *Kewanee Oil Co. v. Bicron Corp.*, 416 U.S. 470, 181 U.S.P.Q. 673 (1974), finding that the patent law does not preempt trade secret protection, and in *Aronson v. Quick Point Pencil*, 440 U.S. 257, 201 U.S.P.Q. 1 (1979), finding that state contract law enforcing the payment of royalties for an invention held unpatentable, may be dispositive. See also H.R. REP. No. 98-781, 98th Cong., 2d Sess. 28 (1984) (Star Print) ("As under section 301 of the Copyright Act, state trade secret law provides 'non-equivalent' rights and remedies and thus constitutes a notable example of an exception to federal preemption") (Semiconductor Chip Protection Act of 1984).

[80] *Hoehling v. Universal City Studios, Inc.*, 618 F.2d 972, 205 U.S.P.Q. 681 (2d Cir.), *cert. denied*, 449 U.S. 841, 207 U.S.P.Q. 1064 (1980); *Miller v. Universal City Studios, Inc.*, 650 F.2d 1365, 212 U.S.P.Q. 345 (5th Cir. 1981) (research not copyrightable). Scientific principles are also unprotectible. See *Ricker v. General Electric Co.*, 162 F.2d 141, 144–146, 73 U.S.P.Q. 458, 459 (2d Cir. 1947).

[81] See Ginsburg, *Sabotaging and Reconstructing History: A Comment on the Scope of Copyright Protection in Works of History After Hoehling v. Universal City Studios*, 29 J. COPR. Soc'y 647 (1982), for a comprehensive study of the issue.

[82] Act of July 8, 1870, 41st Cong., 2d Sess. 100, 16 Stat. 212. Section 71 of the Patent Act of the same year covered "any new design for a bust, statue, alto-relief, or bas-relief." 16 Stat. 209.

[83] *Mazer v. Stein*, 347 U.S. 201, 211, 100 U.S.P.Q. 325, 331 (1954).

tween purely aesthetic articles and useful works of art." Congress'
intent was narrowly interpreted in regulations issued by the Copyright Office in 1910. These regulations stated in relevant part:

> "*Works of art.*—This term includes all works belonging fairly to the so-
> called fine arts. (Paintings, drawings, and sculpture).
>
> "Productions of the industrial arts utilitarian in purpose and character
> are not subject to copyright registration, even if artistically made or
> ornamented."[84]

Despite these regulations, the Copyright Office accepted for registration a litany of "works of arts" including ashtrays, salt and pep-
per shakers, candlesticks, and door knockers,[85] while the courts
found protectible items such as a design for a cemetery monument.[86]
In 1948, in an apparent effort to distinguish between "works of art"
eligible for protection and functional or utilitarian articles not so eligible, the Copyright Office promulgated the following regulation:

> "WORKS OF ART (CLASS G)
> (a) General. This class includes published or unpublished works of artis-
> tic craftsmanship insofar as their form but not their mechanical or utili-
> tarian aspects are concerned, such as artistic jewelry, enamels, glass-
> ware, and tapestries, as well as works belonging to the fine arts such as
> paintings, drawings and sculpture."[87]

This regulation was endorsed six years later in the Supreme Court's
decision in *Mazer v. Stein*, in which a statuette of a Balinese dancing
figure, created and registered as an independent work of art (but with
the intent to reproduce and sell it as a base for table lamps), was
found copyrightable, the Court holding there was "nothing in the
copyright statute to support the argument that the intended use or
use in industry of an article eligible for copyright bars or invalidates
its registration."[88]

---

[84]Copyright Office Bull. No. 15 (1910), *reprinted in Mazer v. Stein, supra* note 83, 347
U.S. at 212 n. 23, 100 U.S.P.Q. at 330–331 n. 23.

[85]See list of such items given by Justice Douglas in his dissent in *Mazer v. Stein*, 347 U.S.
201, 219, 100 U.S.P.Q. 325, 333–334 (1954). Cf. subsequent position of the Copyright Office in
*Esquire, Inc. v. Ringer*, 591 F.2d 796, 802 n. 20, 199 U.S.P.Q. 1, 5–6 n. 20 (D.C. Cir. 1978), that
the registered candlesticks belong "to a small special category of articles * * * [whose] utilitarian function * * * has now atrophied."

[86]*Jones v. Underkoffler*, 16 F. Supp. 729 (M.D. Pa. 1936).

[87]37 C.F.R. §202.10(a) (*revoked* Jan. 1, 1978, 43 Fed. Reg. 965). In *Carol Barnhart, Inc. v.
Economy Cover Corp.*, 773 F.2d 411, 416, 228 U.S.P.Q. 385, 388 (2d Cir. 1985), the Second Circuit wrote that "[w]hile this regulation seemed to expand coverage for works of applied art, it
did not explicitly extend copyright protection to industrial design objects."

[88]347 U.S. 201, 218, 100 U.S.P.Q. 325, 332 (1954). This position is expressly adopted in the
legislative reports accompanying the 1976 Act, which in discussing §113, state:

> "This section takes as its starting point the Supreme Court's decision in *Mazer v. Stein* * * *,
> and the first sentence of subsection (a) [of §113] restates the basic principle established by
> that decision. The rule of *Mazer*, as affirmed by the bill, is that copyright in a pictorial,
> graphic, or sculptural work will not be affected if the work is employed as the design of a
> useful article, and will afford protection to the copyright owner as against the unauthorized
> reproduction in useful as well as nonuseful articles."

H.R. Rep. No. 94-1476, 94th Cong., 2d Sess. 105 (1976); S. Rep. No. 94-473, 94th Cong., 1st
Sess. 86–87 (1975).

*Mazer* did not, however, confront the more difficult question: When is a creation a copyrightable "work of art" or an uncopyrightable "utilitarian article"? Following *Mazer*, and perhaps in an attempt to limit "the Court's apparent open-ended extension of copyright protection to all aesthetically pleasing useful articles,"[89] the Copyright Office promulgated the following regulation:

> "If the sole intrinsic function of an article is its utility, the fact that the article is unique and attractively shaped will not qualify it as a work of art. However, if the shape of a utilitarian article incorporates features, such as artistic sculpture, carving, or pictorial representation, which can be identified separately and are capable of existing independently as a work of art such features will be eligible for registration."[90]

This test was, however, difficult to apply, as the courts "struggled to decide whether an article's function was solely utilitarian."[91] And lurking underneath the surface was a related question: Could a useful article possessing artistic elements that were conceptually but not physically separable be copyrightable? Two decisions confronted this issue under the 1909 Act[92] and seemingly reached opposite results; however, before consideration of those decisions, a review of changes made by the 1976 Copyright Act is necessary since these changes were influential in the courts' opinions.

Section 101 of the 1976 Act, defines "pictorial, graphic, and sculptural works" in relevant part as including:

> "works of artistic craftsmanship insofar as their form but not their mechanical or utilitarian aspects are concerned; the design of a useful article, as defined in this section, shall be considered a pictorial, graphic, or sculptural work only if, and to the extent that, such design incorporates pictorial, graphic, or sculptural features that can be identified separately from, and are capable of existing independently of, the utilitarian aspects of the article."[93]

A "useful article" is defined as

> "an article having an intrinsic utilitarian function that is not merely to portray the appearance of the article or to convey information. An arti-

---

[89] *Kieselstein-Cord v. Accessories by Pearl, Inc.*, 632 F.2d 989, 992, 208 U.S.P.Q. 1, 4 (2d Cir. 1980). See also *Fabrica Inc. v. El Dorado*, 697 F.2d 890, 892–893, 217 U.S.P.Q. 698, 699–700 (9th Cir. 1983).

[90] 37 C.F.R. §202.10(c) (*revoked* Jan. 1, 1978, 43 Fed. Reg. 965–966).

[91] *Fabrica Inc. v. El Dorado Corp.*, 697 F.2d 890, 893, 217 U.S.P.Q. 698, 700 (9th Cir. 1983).

[92] *Esquire, Inc. v. Ringer*, 591 F.2d 796, 199 U.S.P.Q. 1 (D.C. Cir. 1978); *Kieselstein-Cord v. Accessories by Pearl, Inc.*, 632 F.2d 989, 208 U.S.P.Q. 1 (2d Cir. 1980). The *Kieselstein-Cord* court actually evaluated the question under both the 1909 and 1976 Acts. For other decisions under the 1909 Act, see *Vacheron & Constantin-Le Coultre Watches, Inc. v. Benrus Watch Co.*, 155 F. Supp. 932, 115 U.S.P.Q. 115 (S.D.N.Y. 1957), *rev'd on other grounds*, 260 F.2d 637, 119 U.S.P.Q. 189 (2d Cir. 1958) (ornamental watch not protectible); *SCOA Indus., Inc. v. Famolare, Inc.*, 192 U.S.P.Q. 216 (S.D.N.Y. 1976) (representation of bicycle, but not "raised wavy lines" pattern on sole of shoe, held copyrightable). Cf. *Ted Arnold, Ltd. v. Silvercraft Co.*, 259 F. Supp. 733, 151 U.S.P.Q. 286 (S.D.N.Y. 1966) (physically separable antique telephone used as a casting for a pencil sharpener copyrightable).

[93] 17 U.S.C. §101 (1978). This definition is derived from both the Copyright Office's 1948 and post-*Mazer* regulations. See *Carol Barnhart, Inc. v. Economy Cover Corp.*, 773 F.2d 411, 417, 228 U.S.P.Q. 385, 388–389 (2d Cir. 1985).

cle that is normally a part of a useful article is considered a 'useful article.' "[94]

It will be seen that the Act's definition of "pictorial, graphic, and sculptural works" incorporates many important elements of the Copyright Office's post-*Mazer* regulation.[95] One must, however, also read into this definition the definition of "useful article," and when this is done it is discovered that the 1976 Act effected a change in the post-*Mazer* regulation, for while that regulation referred to a "*sole*

---

[94]17 U.S.C. §101 (1978). It should be noted that the Senate-passed version of the revision bill contained a separate title granting protection to ornamental designs of useful articles. This provision was, however, deleted in conference. See *Carol Barnhart, Inc. v. Economy Cover Corp., supra* note 93, 773 F.2d at 416–417, 228 U.S.P.Q. at 388–389, for a review of this and other design bills.

Protection for computer programs and data bases is not affected by the fact that they may aid or implement utilitarian articles. This issue was raised in the deliberations of the National Commission on New Technological Uses of Copyrighted Works (CONTU) and was discussed in CONTU's Final Report. See FINAL REPORT OF THE NATIONAL COMMISSION ON NEW TECHNOLOG-ICAL USES OF COPYRIGHTED WORKS 26 (1978). The commission expressly rejected the argument that such programs should not be copyrightable, writing that it "is not consistent with the design of the Act of 1976 which was clearly to protect all works of authorship from the moment of their fixation in any tangible medium of expression. Further, it does not square with copyright practice past and present, which recognizes copyright protection for a work of authorship regardless of the uses to which it may be put." *Id.* at 21. Thus, a computer program or data base for constructing typeface design would be copyrightable notwithstanding the ineligibility of the typeface design for protection.

In *Eltra v. Ringer*, 579 F.2d 294, 198 U.S.P.Q. 321 (4th Cir. 1978), a mandamus action to compel registration of typeface designs, the post-*Mazer* regulation was again at issue. Agreeing with the Register that typeface designs were not "works of art" within the meaning of 17 U.S.C. §5(g) (1909 *repealed* 1978), the court relied heavily on Congress' express refusal to grant protection to such designs in the 1976 Act. For a review of that history, see SECOND SUPPLEMENTARY REPORT OF THE REGISTER OF COPYRIGHT ON THE GENERAL REVISION OF THE U.S. COPYRIGHT LAW, Ch. VII at 15–21 (draft ed. 1975), and the testimony in *Copyright Law Revision: Hearings Before the Subcomm. on Courts, Civil Liberties, and the Administration of Justice of the House Judiciary Comm.*, 94th Cong., 1st Sess. 991–1238 (1975). For a subsequent decision denying a state unfair competition claim for copying of typeface designs, see *Leonard Storch Enters., Inc. v. Mergenthaler Linotype Co.*, 208 U.S.P.Q. 58 (E.D.N.Y. 1980). Cf. *Grove Press, Inc. v. Collectors Pub., Inc.*, 264 F. Supp. 603, 152 U.S.P.Q. 787 (C.D. Cal. 1967) (preliminary injunction granted where subsequent edition of book also contained extensive editorial revisions). For a discussion of whether states may protect typeface designs, see note 13 in Chapter 3.

Along similar lines, the Copyright Office decided not to institute rulemaking proceedings with respect to the registration of claims to copyright in the graphic elements involved in the design of books and other printed publications, 46 Fed. Reg. 30651 (June 10, 1981), concluding among other things: "That a work is distinctive, unique or pleasing in appearance, and embodies certain ideas of contrast or coloring does not necessarily afford a basis for copyright." *Id.* at 30653. But cf. *Building Officials & Code Administrators v. Code Technology, Inc.*, 210 U.S.P.Q. 289 (D. Mass. 1980) (suggesting that typeface, layout, and pagination of public domain work were copyrightable).

Protection for works of calligraphy must be distinguished from both typeface and book design. In her *Second Supplementary Report*, the Register of Copyrights stated with respect to works of calligraphy:

"The age-old 'art of beautiful writing' has not, unless accompanied by illuminated letters, ornamental borders, pictorial embossing, and the like, been considered a subject of traditional copyright. In light of the recent discussions of the Copyright Office regulations in the context of the dispute over typeface designs, we are inclined to believe that this position is wrong. We believe that the [legislative] report * * * should make clear the copyrightability of original calligraphic works as 'pictorial, graphic, or sculptural works.' "

SECOND SUPPLEMENTARY REPORT, Ch. VII at 24. Although the Register's comments evidence a clear intent that original, i.e., independently created, calligraphic designs consisting of lettering unaccompanied by pictorial elements be protectible, this intent should not be construed to reach technical exercises, mere representations of alphabets, or individual letters. See 37 C.F.R. §202.1 ("mere variations of typographic ornamentation [or] lettering" not copyrightable); *Designpoint Indus., Ltd. v. Padosa America, Inc.*, 83 Civ. 9132 (S.D.N.Y. filed Nov. 2, 1984) (unpublished bench opinion) (expression of the words "Puerto Rico" in script held not protectible, citing 37 C.F.R. §202.1).

[95]See text at note 90, *supra*, and note 93, *supra*.

intrinsic function," the 1976 Act refers to "*an* intrinsic function," thereby "narrowing the sweep"[96] of the regulation. As explained in a recent decision from the Ninth Circuit:

> "The significant change from the prior law is that the courts need no longer determine whether an article's function is *solely* utilitarian. Now, if an article has *any* intrinsic utilitarian function, it can be denied copyright protection except to the extent that its artistic features can be identified separately and are capable of existing independently as a work of art."[97]

In support of this view, the court cited a passage from the 1976 House report, which, because of its importance in the "physically and/or conceptually separable" question to be discussed immediately below, is worth quoting in full here:

> "In adopting this amendatory language, the Committee is seeking to draw as clear a line as possible between copyrightable works of applied art and uncopyrighted works of industrial design. A two-dimensional painting, drawing, or graphic work is still capable of being identified as such when it is printed on or applied to utilitarian articles such as textile fabrics, wallpaper, containers, and the like. The same is true when a statue or carving is used to embellish an industrial product, or as in the *Mazer* case, is incorporated into a product without losing its ability to exist independently as a work of art. On the other hand, although the shape of an industrial product may be aesthetically satisfying and valuable, the Committee's intention is not to offer it copyright protection under the bill. *Unless the shape* of an automobile, airplane, ladies' dress, food processor, television set, or any other industrial product *contains some element that physically or conceptually can be identified as separa-*

---

[96] *Kieselstein-Cord v. Accessories by Pearl, Inc.*, 632 F.2d 989, 993, 208 U.S.P.Q. 1, 4 (2d Cir. 1980).

[97] *Fabrica Inc. v. El Dorado Corp.*, 697 F.2d 890, 893, 217 U.S.P.Q. 698, 700 (9th Cir. 1983). Cf. *Gay Toys, Inc. v. Buddy L Corp.*, 703 F.2d 970, 973–974, 218 U.S.P.Q. 13, 15 (6th Cir. 1983) (potential change noted but not decided), and *Esquire, Inc. v. Ringer*, 591 F.2d 796, 804, 199 U.S.P.Q. 1, 7 (D.C. Cir. 1978), *cert. denied*, 440 U.S. 908 (1979) ("In deleting the modifier 'sole' from the language taken from [former 37 C.F.R.] §202.10(c), the draftsmen of the 1976 Act must have concluded that the definition of 'useful article' would be more precise without this term. Moreover, Congress may have concluded that literal application of the phrase 'sole intrinsic function' would create an unworkable standard").

Note, however, that with respect to a "work that portrays a useful article as such," 17 U.S.C. §113(b) states an intent not to accord "any greater or lesser rights with respect to the making, distribution, or display of the useful article so portrayed than those afforded to such works under the law, whether title 17 or the common law or statutes of a State, in effect on December 31, 1977, as held applicable and construed by a court in an action brought under this title." This provision addresses the question of whether copyright in a pictorial, graphic, or sculptural work that represents, portrays, or depicts a useful article in such a way that the utilitarian nature of the article can be seen, would extend to the manufacture of the article itself. Due to "the insuperable difficulty" of finding any real statutory formulation that would satisfactorily express the distinction between when an article is "useful as such" or is instead an integral artistic element of the pictorial, graphic, or sculptural work, H.R. REP. No. 94-1476, 94th Cong., 2d Sess. 105 (1976), Congress chose to leave the necessary line drawing to the courts, although it did endorse specific examples set forth in the Register of Copyrights' 1961 report, REPORT OF THE REGISTER OF COPYRIGHTS ON THE GENERAL REVISION OF THE U.S. COPYRIGHT LAW, 87th Cong., 1st Sess. 14–15 (Comm. Print 1961) (e.g., copyrighted drawings of chairs and dresses would not prohibit the unauthorized manufacture of such articles). See also *Combustion Engineering, Inc. v. Murray Tube Works, Inc.*, 222 U.S.P.Q. 239, 244 (E.D. Tenn. 1984) (copyright in a drawing of a boiler would not prohibit construction of a boiler based on that design). *Muller v. Triborough Bridge Authority*, 43 F. Supp. 298, 52 U.S.P.Q. 227 (S.D.N.Y. 1942) (copyrighted bridge design would not bar construction of bridge). Cf. *Del Madera Properties v. Rhodes and Gardner, Inc.*, 227 U.S.P.Q. 486 (N.D. Cal. 1985), which seemingly stands for the proposition that copyright in a map of a residential subdivision would prevent others from developing the subdivision according to the same plan contained therein.

*ble from the utilitarian aspects of that article*, the design would not be copyrighted under the bill. The test of separability and independence from 'the utilitarian aspects of the article' does not depend upon the nature of the design—that is, *even if the appearance of an article is determined by aesthetic (as opposed to functional) considerations*, only elements, if any, which can be identified separately from the useful article as such are copyrightable. *And, even if the three-dimensional design contains some such element* (for example, a carving on the back of a chair or a floral relief design on silver flatware), *copyright protection would extend only to that element*, and would not cover the over-all configuration of the utilitarian article as such."[98] (Emphasis added.)

This report language and its proper intent provided a focal point of conflict in *Esquire v. Ringer*,[99] a mandamus action against the Register of Copyrights to compel registration of three lighting fixtures. Relying on its post-*Mazer* regulation, the Register had refused registration on the ground that the works did not contain "elements, either alone or in combination, which are capable of independent existence as a copyrightable pictorial, graphic, or sculptural work apart from the utilitarian aspect,"[100] "no matter how aesthetically pleasing [the overall shape or configuration] may be."[101] The claimant, focusing on the regulation's use of the term "*sole* intrinsic function," argued that its intent was to create "works of modernistic form sculpture," that the works' *sole* intrinsic function was, therefore, not utilitarian, and that the shape of the works was a "feature" which could be identified separately and was capable of existing independently as a work of art."[102]

After endorsing the regulation itself and the Register's application of it to the works at bar, the court turned to the above-cited legislative history from the 1976 Act[103] and found it to be

"not entirely free from ambiguity. Esquire could arguably draw some support from the statement that a protectable element of a utilitarian article must be separable 'physically *or conceptually*' from the utilitarian aspects of the design. But any possible ambiguity raised by this isolated reference disappears when the excerpt is considered in its entirety. The underscored passages indicate unequivocally that the overall design or configuration of a utilitarian object, even if it is determined by aesthetic as well as functional considerations, is not eligible for copyright."[104]

The court's statement (which is dictum since the case was decided under the 1909 and not the 1976 Act), while apparently denying the protectibility of a work that contains only conceptually separable elements, uses the report language for an entirely different purpose,

---

[98]H.R. Rep. No. 94-1476, 94th Cong., 2d Sess. 55 (1976).

[99]591 F.2d 796, 199 U.S.P.Q. 1 (D.C. Cir. 1978), *cert. denied*, 440 U.S. 908 (1979). This decision reversed a lower court ruling granting mandamus. 414 F. Supp. 939, 194 U.S.P.Q. 30 (D.D.C. 1976).

[100]591 F.2d at 798–799, 199 U.S.P.Q. at 2.

[101]*Id*. at 800, 199 U.S.P.Q. at 3.

[102]*Ibid*.

[103]See text at note 98, *supra*.

[104]591 F.2d at 803–804, 199 U.S.P.Q. at 6–7.

that of rejecting protection for the overall design of the utilitarian object.

The conceptual separability question arose again two years later in *Kieselstein-Cord v. Accessories by Pearl, Inc.*, a case described as being "on a razor's edge of copyright law."[105] At issue were designs for two belt buckles cast in gold and silver. In addition to use as belt buckles, the designs were sometimes worn around the neck "or elsewhere on the body rather than around the waist." Contrary to the *Esquire* court, the *Kieselstein-Cord* court rejected the assertion that "copyrightability cannot adhere in the 'conceptual' separation of an artistic element," noting that the 1976 House Report specifically referred to "elements that 'physically or conceptually, can be identified as separable from the utilitarian aspects of' a useful article."[106]

The *Kieselstein-Cord* decision was subsequently followed in *Norris Industries, Inc. v. International Telephone and Telegraph Corp.*, in which the Register's refusal to register automobile wire wheel covers was upheld. After noting that "[b]oth case law and legislative history indicate that separability encompasses works of art that are either physically severable from the utilitarian article or conceptually severable,"[107] the court found that the article before it did not contain any design that could be identified apart from the article itself, and was accordingly uncopyrightable.[108]

Two other decisions, though following *Kieselstein-Cord* and *Norris* on matters of law, have nevertheless evidenced a liberal attitude toward avoiding summary judgment on the issue of an asserted lack of conceptual separability. In *Trans-World Mfg. Corp. v. Al Nyman & Sons, Inc.*,[109] the protectibility of eyeglass display cases was at issue. Since there was no physical separability, the only issue was whether conceptual separability existed. Rejecting defendant's mo-

---

[105]632 F.2d 989, 990, 208 U.S.P.Q. 1, 2 (2d Cir. 1980).

[106]632 F.2d at 993, 208 U.S.P.Q. at 3. In *Trans-World Mfg. Corp. v. Al Nyman & Sons, Inc.*, 218 U.S.P.Q. 208 (D. Del. 1982), the court noted the conflict between the *Esquire* and *Kieselstein-Cord* courts but endorsed *Kieselstein-Cord*. Accord *Animal Fair, Inc. v. Amfesco Indus., Inc.*, 620 F. Supp. 175, 186–188, 227 U.S.P.Q. 817, 825 (D. Minn. 1985). The Copyright Office has stated that: "Determinations of separability may be made on either a conceptual or physical basis." COMPENDIUM II OF COPYRIGHT OFFICE PRACTICES §505.02. Note that, unlike *Esquire*, *Kieselstein-Cord* was decided under the 1909 and 1976 Acts since one of the works was created and published before January 1, 1978 (and hence governed by the 1909 Act) and the other after that date (and hence governed by the 1976 Act).

[107]696 F.2d 918, 923, 217 U.S.P.Q. 226, 230 (11th Cir.), *cert. denied*, 464 U.S. 818, 220 U.S.P.Q. 385 (1983). See also *Carol Barnhart, Inc. v. Economy Cover Corp.*, 773 F.2d 411, 420, 228 U.S.P.Q. 385, 391 (2d Cir. 1985) (Newman, J., dissenting) ("In this Circuit it is settled, and the majority does not dispute, that 'conceptual separability' is distinct from 'physical separability' and, when present, entitles the creator of a useful article to a copyright on its design"). In *Vermont Castings, Inc. v. Evans Prod. Co.*, 215 U.S.P.Q. 758, 762–764 (D. Vt. 1981), the court held that because design features of a stove were inseparable from its overall configuration, copyright protection was unavailable but that a pendent unfair competition claim was not preempted under either §301 or the *Sears-Compco* doctrine.

[108]As did the *Kieselstein-Cord* court, the *Norris* court paid particular deference to the Copyright Office's determination, based on its experience in examining applications for registration. Four days after the *Norris* decision, the Ninth Circuit found carpet display folders uncopyrightable as useful articles lacking any artistic features separately indentifiable from the utilitarian aspects of the article. *Fabrica Inc. v. El Dorado Corp.*, 697 F.2d 890, 217 U.S.P.Q. 698 (9th Cir. 1983).

[109]218 U.S.P.Q. 208 (D. Del. 1982).

tion for summary judgment, the court, citing Justice Holmes's admonition in *Bleistein v. Donaldson Lithographing Co.* that judges should avoid making aesthetic evaluations,[110] ruled that the determination of whether there was a sculptural element conceptually separate from and capable of existing independently of the utilitarian aspects should be left to the trier of fact. In so doing, the court indicated that the intent of the designer as to the artistic merit of the work was entitled to some weight in a consideration of registrability.[111]

The same result occurred in *Poe v. Missing Persons*, which involved an article described by its creator as a "three dimensional work of art in primarily flexible clear-vinyl and covered rock media," but which from a quick glance resembled a woman's two-piece swimsuit filled with colored, crushed aquarium rocks placed in strategic spots. Following *Trans-World*, and rejecting defendant's argument that the issue of whether an article is useful must be resolved by a court as a question of law, the court of appeals remanded for trial. In so doing, the court also identified evidence it believed relevant to the trier of fact, including (1) expert testimony on functionality; (2) the designer's intent; (3) customs and usage in the art and clothing worlds; and (4) the marketability of the article as a work of art.[112]

In *Carol Barnhart, Inc. v. Economy Cover Corp.*, a divided panel of the Second Circuit, perhaps unaware of *Poe*, affirmed a district court grant of summary judgment of noncopyrightability of four life-size, anatomically correct human torso forms. Two of the forms were sculpted with shirts for displaying sweaters and jackets. The remaining two forms depicted nude male and female torsos. All of the forms were without arms, necks, or backs, and had hollow backs designed to gather excess fabric when clothes were fitted on them. Plaintiff marketed the forms for use as display mannequins.

In examining the copyrightability of plaintiff's creations, the majority, per Judge Mansfield, distinguished Judge Oakes' opinion in *Kieselstein-Cord* on the ground that the ornamented surfaces of the *Kieselstein-Cord* belt buckles "were not in any respect required by their utilitarian functions," but that with the *Barnhart* forms, "the features claimed to be aesthetic or artistic, e.g., the life-size configuration of the breasts, and the width of the shoulders, are inextricably interwined with the utilitarian function, the display of clothes."[113]

---

[110]See text at note 23, *supra*.

[111]218 U.S.P.Q. at 211.

[112]745 F.2d 1238, 1243, 223 U.S.P.Q. 1297, 1301 (9th Cir. 1984).

[113]773 F.2d 411, 419, 228 U.S.P.Q. 385, 390 (2d Cir. 1985). But cf. *Animal Fair, Inc. v. Amfesco Indus., Inc.*, 620 F. Supp. 175, 186–188, 227 U.S.P.Q. 817, 825 (D. Minn. 1985) (finding conceptual separability in plaintiff's design of slippers in the shape of a bear's foot). The Copyright Office has stated, however, that the following factors are *not* relevant to the separability test:

"1) the aesthetic value of the design; 2) the fact that the shape could be designed differently; or 3) the amount of work which went into the making of the design. Thus, the mere fact that a famous designer produces a uniquely shaped food processor does not render the design of the food processor copyrightable."

Compendium II of Copyright Office Practices §505.05.

In an illuminating opinion that provides a theoretical gold mine for future decision making and commentary on the subject, Judge Newman dissented.[114] He began with the "obvious" but nevertheless essential point that "conceptual separability" "must mean something other than 'physical separability,' " and that "[s]ince 'conceptual separability' is not the same as 'physical separability,' it should also be obvious that a design feature can be 'conceptually separable' from the utilitarian aspect of a useful article even if it cannot be separated physically." Judge Newman then surveyed several possible ways in which conceptual separability could be understood (but not necessarily found). These may be summarized as follows:

1. *Primary use as a utilitarian article.*

   Under this approach, "an article used primarily to serve its utilitarian function might be regarded as lacking 'conceptual separable' design elements even though those design elements rendered it usable secondarily as an artistic work."

   Judge Newman noted that "[t]here is danger in this approach in that it would deny copyright protection to designs of works of art displayed by a minority because they are also used by a majority as useful articles."

2. *Primary aesthetic effect of the work.*

   Under this approach, copyrightability would be found "whenever the decorative or aesthetically pleasing aspect of the article can be

---

[114]773 F.2d at 419–426, 228 U.S.P.Q. at 391–396 (Newman, J., dissenting). The applicability of the useful-article bar has also been raised in connection with toys. In *Gay Toys, Inc. v. Buddy L Corp.*, 703 F.2d 970, 974, 218 U.S.P.Q. 13, 15 (6th Cir. 1983), the Sixth Circuit refused to decide whether certain aspects of a toy airplane were individually copyrightable as separate and independent features, finding that the useful-article test applies only where the work at issue has "an intrinsic utilitarian function that is not merely to portray the appearance of the article," and that "toys do not even have an intrinsic function other than the portrayal of the real item."

The district court had found the toy to be a useful article and to possess utilitarian and functional characteristics "in that it permits a child to dream and to let his or her imagination soar," a rationale firmly rejected by the court of appeals. See also *Animal Fair, Inc. v. Amfesco Indus., Inc., supra* note 113, 620 F. Supp. at 187 n. 17, 227 U.S.P.Q. at 825 n. 17:

"Plaintiff makes a strong argument that the BEARFOOT® slipper is not a useful article within the statutory definition. The slipper is a novelty item which is primarily intended for personal adornment. The story on the hangtag, as well as the impractical aspects of the design as a piece of footwear, suggest that the essential quality of the slipper is its unique appearance rather than its use as a functional piece of clothing."

In *Durham Indus., Inc. v. Tomy Corp.*, 630 F.2d 905, 208 U.S.P.Q. 10 (2d Cir. 1980), a stand-up box game was found not to have been infringed by defendant's copying of its nondecorative elements, elements which the court found to be unprotectible since they did not possess sculptural or aesthetic features separately indentifiable from and capable of existing independently of the game. See also *Schnadig Corp. v. Gaines Mfg. Co.*, 620 F.2d 1166, 1167 n. 1, 206 U.S.P.Q. 202, 206 n. 1 (6th Cir. 1980) ("Copyright is available to protect only the form of an object, as separated from its function, and if such separation is not possible, copyright protection is unavailable").

The enactment of a *sui generis* form of intellectual property protection for semiconductor chip designs (rather than, as originally proposed, amending the Copyright Act to cover such works) was in large part due to concern that the designs were intrinsically utilitarian and did not possess separable artistic elements. See H.R. REP. No. 98-781, 98th Cong., 2d Sess. 3–4 (1984) (Star Print); *Copyright Protection for Semiconductor Chips: Hearings Before the Subcomm. on Courts, Civil Liberties, and the Administration of Justice of the House Judiciary Comm.*, 98th Cong., 1st Sess. 77, 88–92 (1983); *Semiconductor Chip Protection Act of 1983: Hearing Before the Subcomm. on Patents, Copyrights, and Trademarks of the Senate Judiciary Comm.*, 98th Cong., 1st Sess. 19, 21, 30–33 (1983); *Copyright Protection for Imprinted Design Patterns on Semiconductor Chips: Hearing Before the House Subcomm. on Courts, Civil Liberties, and the Administration of Justice of the House Judiciary Comm.*, 96th Cong., 1st Sess. 53, 58 (1979).

said to be 'primary' and the utilitarian function can be said to be 'secondary.' "

Judge Newman noted that "[t]he difficulty with this approach is that it offers little guidance to the trier of fact, or the judge endeavoring to determine whether a triable issue of fact exists, as to what is being measured by the classifications 'primary' and 'secondary.' "

3. *Marketability of the work.*
Under this approach, conceptual separability would exist "where there is any substantial likelihood that even if the article had no utilitarian use it would be marketable to some significant segment of the community simply because of its aesthetic qualities."

Judge Newman noted that this approach "risks allowing a copyright only to forms within the domain of popular art. * * * However, various sculpted forms would be recognized as works of art by many, even though those willing to purchase them for display in their homes might be few in number and not a 'significant segment of the community.' "

4. *Aesthetic appeal of the work.*
Under this approach, conceptual separability would exist "whenever the design of a form has sufficient aesthetic appeal to be appreciated for its artistic qualities."

Judge Newman noted that this approach "has plainly been rejected by Congress."

Judge Newman then proposed what may be called the "temporal displacement" test. Under this approach

"[f]or the design features to be 'conceptually separate' from the utilitarian aspects of the useful article that embodies the design, the article must stimulate in the mind of the beholder a concept that is separate from the concept evoked by its utilitarian function."

This test contains two principal components: the "beholder" and the "separateness" of the concept embodied in the work for which protection is sought. The "beholder" is the "hypothetical ordinary observer" whose likely mental impressions are to be determined by the trier of fact. The requisite "separateness" is said to exist "whenever the design creates in the mind of the ordinary observer two different concepts that are not inevitably entertained simultaneously." The test is *not* whether the ordinary observer fails to recognize the object as a utilitarian article, but "only whether the concept of the utilitarian function can be displaced in the mind by some other concept." This displacement

"need not turn on the immediate reaction of the ordinary observer but on whether visual inspection of the article and consideration of all pertinent evidence would engender in the observer's mind a separate non-utilitarian concept that can displace, at least temporarily, the utilitarian concept."

This temporal displacement may occur

"even when the utilitarian function is perceived by observation, perhaps aided by explanation, if the concept of the utilitarian function can be displaced in the observer's mind while he entertains the separate concept of some non-utilitarian function."

Judge Newman stressed that a "separate" concept should not be found merely when the design evoked *any* concept that is distinct from the concept of the article's utilitarian function. Factors to be considered by the trier of fact include whether the article has been displayed or used apart from its utilitarian function, and the extent of such use or display. Expert opinion and survey evidence "ought generally to be received."

Judge Newman's temporal displacement test is believed to offer the most persuasive approach to what is, admittedly, a perplexing issue.

## Titles

Owing to the importance given under the pre-1909 copyright regime to the filing of the title of a work, it became not uncommon for lawyers as well as laymen to speak of "copyrighting" the title of a work. But the notion that the title is in itself subject to copyright protection apart from the particular work it identifies is directly contrary to the fundamental concept of American copyright and to the uniform decisions of the courts.

Analytically, titles have a twofold function—they may be deemed an identification of a work and also a component of the work. The former function has no necessary link to copyrightable subject matter;[115] the latter invariably represents only a *de minimis* portion of the work. The traditional rule denying protection for titles may have been first enunciated in the oft-cited case of *Jollie v. Jacques*, where the plaintiff argued that the title of his piece of music "The Serious Family Polka" was original and that his prior registration entitled him to restrain the defendant from using the same title for another composition. On this point the court remarked:

> "The right secured is the property in the piece of music, the production of the mind and genius of the author and not in the mere name given to the work. * * * The title is an appendage to the book or piece of music for which the copyright is taken out."[116]

This principle has been followed ever since in a large number of cases, with respect not only to music but to books and other productions as well,[117] and is reflected in Copyright Office regulations.[118]

---

[115]See *The Trademark Cases*, 100 U.S. 82 (1879).

[116]13 F. Cas. 910 (C.C.S.D.N.Y. 1852) (No. 7,437).

[117]*Arthur Retlaw & Associates, Inc. v. Travenol Laboratories, Inc.*, 582 F. Supp. 1010, 1014, 223 U.S.P.Q. 722, 725 (N.D. Ill. 1984); *Georgia v. Harrison*, 548 F. Supp. 110, 115, 218 U.S.P.Q. 119, 123 (N.D. Ga. 1982) ("brief, descriptive language used merely to designate something may not be copyrighted"); *Alexander v. Irving Trust Co.*, 132 F. Supp. 364, 106 U.S.P.Q. 74 (S.D.N.Y.), *aff'd per curiam*, 228 F.2d 221, 108 U.S.P.Q. 24 (2d Cir. 1955), *cert. denied*, 350 U.S. 996, 108 U.S.P.Q. 456 (1956); *International Film Serv. v. Associated Producers*, 273 F. 585 (S.D.N.Y. 1921), and cases cited therein; *Arnstein v. Porter*, 154 F.2d 464, 68 U.S.P.Q. 288 (2d Cir. 1946), *cert. denied*, 330 U.S. 851, 73 U.S.P.Q. 550 (1947).

[118]37 C.F.R. §202.1(a); COPYRIGHT OFFICE CIRCULAR No. 34. See also H.R. REP. No. 2237, 89th Cong., 2d Sess. 44 (1966); H.R. REP. No. 83, 90th Cong., 1st Sess. 15 (1967).

An author or proprietor whose work has become identified in the public mind under a distinctive title is not without remedy against a person who may seek to gain advantage by appropriating it to his own use. The power of the courts may be invoked to restrain such practices under equitable principles relating to unfair competition, quite irrespective of the limitations of the copyright law.[119] This should not suggest that a copyright owner can in every case restrain the use of a title similar to that of his or her work on the ground that such use unfairly competes with exploitation of the copyrighted work.[120] The owner will generally have to show that his or her work is so widely known that the public will recognize its title and associate it with the work itself or the author.[121] Under these circumstances, the author of the "Frank Merriwell" series of books was able to prevent the use of the name in the title of a motion picture.[122]

Protection under the doctrine of unfair competition extends to titles which have come to identify the copyrighted work as a description or designation of origin within the meaning of Section 43(a) of the Lanham Act.[123] In the absence of distinctiveness or confusion over origin, however, courts may limit relief by merely conditioning the defendant's use of the title on adequate accompanying statements negating a connection with the copyrighted work.[124]

Thus, the law of unfair competition protects the title of a copyrightable work against potentially confusing usage by another, much as it does with respect to other designations of goods, services, or organizations. Under this branch of the law, the test is whether the public will assume some connection between the works designated by the same or confusingly similar titles. The problem is, however, complicated by the fact that copyrighted works enter the public domain from which they may be utilized by anyone. In the ordinary case,

---

[119]For a comprehensive review of cases on this subject, see *Johnston v. Twentieth Century Fox Film Corp.*, 76 U.S.P.Q. 131 (Cal. Dist. Ct. App. 1947). But see subsequent interpretations of *Johnston* in *Gordon v. Warner Bros. Pictures, Inc.*, 74 Cal. Rptr. 499, 161 U.S.P.Q. 316 (Cal. Dist. Ct. App. 1969), and in *Tomlin v. Walt Disney Prods.*, 18 Cal. App.3d 226, 96 Cal. Rptr. 118, 171 U.S.P.Q. 415 (Cal. Dist. Ct. App. 1971).

[120]See, e.g., *Collins v. Metro-Goldwyn Pictures Corp.*, 25 F. Supp. 781, 39 U.S.P.Q. 520 (S.D.N.Y. 1938), *rev'd on other grounds*, 106 F.2d 83, 42 U.S.P.Q. 553 (2d Cir. 1939).

[121]*Becker v. Loew's Inc.*, 133 F.2d 889, 56 U.S.P.Q. 455 (7th Cir. 1943). Cf. *Jackson v. Universal Int'l Pictures, Inc.*, 222 P.2d 433, 87 U.S.P.Q. 131 (Cal. Sup. Ct. 1950); *Caddy-Imler Creations, Inc. v. Caddy*, 299 F.2d 79, 132 U.S.P.Q. 384 (9th Cir. 1962).

[122]*Patten v. Superior Talking Pictures, Inc.*, 8 F. Supp. 196, 23 U.S.P.Q. 248 (S.D.N.Y. 1934). Accord *Paramore v. Mack Sennett, Inc.*, 9 F.2d 66 (S.D. Cal. 1925) (use of "Yukon Jake" as title of copyrighted poem prevented use for motion picture). Cf. *Edgar Rice Burroughs, Inc. v. Charlton Pub., Inc.*, 243 F. Supp. 731, 145 U.S.P.Q. 655 (S.D.N.Y. 1965) (complaint alleging wrongful use of "Tarzan" in title of novel held sufficient); *Leeds Music, Ltd. v. Robin*, 358 F. Supp. 650, 179 U.S.P.Q. 413 (S.D. Ohio 1973) (defendants enjoined from using rock opera title "Jesus Christ Superstar" for infringing film); *Gruelle v. Molley-'Es Doll Outfitters*, 94 F.2d 172, 176 (3d Cir. 1937), *cert. denied*, 304 U.S. 561 (1938) (use of names "Raggedy Ann" and "Raggedy Andy" on dolls similar to those in copyrighted books and drawings enjoined).

[123]*Rossner v. CBS, Inc.*, 612 F. Supp. 334, 226 U.S.P.Q. 593 (S.D.N.Y. 1985), and cases cited therein; *Hospital for Sick Children v. Melody Fare Dinner Theatre*, 516 F. Supp. 67, 209 U.S.P.Q. 749 (E.D. Va. 1980); *Orion Pictures Co. v. Dell Pub. Co.*, 471 F. Supp. 392, 202 U.S.P.Q. 819 (S.D.N.Y. 1979) (also discussing state law claims); *Brandon v. Regents*, 441 F. Supp. 1086, 196 U.S.P.Q. 163 (D. Mass. 1977).

[124]See *Warner Bros. Pictures, Inc. v. Majestic Pictures Corp.*, 70 F.2d 310, 21 U.S.P.Q. 405 (2d Cir. 1934).

where a work has fallen into the public domain, the title goes with it and may be freely used to refer to the public domain work.[125]

## Characters

At the outset, it may be useful to note that for most purposes it will not matter whether a character is viewed as a protectible component of a novel or pictorial work, or as a separately copyrighted work.[126] There is also no question as to the potential copyrightability of characters as part of the literary work,[127] motion picture,[128] drawing, painting, or other pictorial work[129] in which they appear. Indeed, the protection of such characters may go beyond pictorial representations to include verbal descriptions of attributes.[130] And, notwithstanding dictum in isolated cases,[131] and the refusal of the Copyright Office to register claims to pictorial characters as characters,[132] the

---

[125]*Clemens v. Belford*, 14 F. 728 (N.D. Ill. 1883); *Chamberlain v. Columbia Pictures Corp.*, 186 F.2d 923, 89 U.S.P.Q. 7 (9th Cir. 1951). In *G. & C. Merriam Co. v. Ogilvie*, 159 F. 638 (1st Cir. 1908), the defendant was permitted to use the title "Webster's Dictionary," but was required to print in large type on the title page of its public domain reprint a statement clearly differentiating it from earlier copyrighted versions by plaintiff, whose name had been associated with the famous dictionary from its inception.

[126]See generally Waldheim, *Characters—May They Be Kidnapped?* 12 BULL. COPR. SOC'Y 210 (1965).

[127]*Burroughs v. MGM, Inc.*, 519 F. Supp. 388, 391, 215 U.S.P.Q. 37, 40 (S.D.N.Y. 1981), *aff'd*, 683 F.2d 610, 215 U.S.P.Q. 495 (2d Cir. 1982); *Filmvideo Releasing Corp. v. Hastings*, 509 F. Supp. 60, 212 U.S.P.Q. 195 (S.D.N.Y.), *aff'd in part, rev'd in part*, 668 F.2d 91, 218 U.S.P.Q. 750 (2d Cir. 1981); *Dealer Advertising Dev., Inc. v. Barbara Allan Financial Advertisement, Inc.*, 209 U.S.P.Q. 1003 (W.D. Mich. 1979) (radio commercials); *Goodis v. United Artists Television, Inc.*, 425 F.2d 397, 165 U.S.P.Q. 3 (2d Cir. 1970); *Nichols v. Universal Pictures Corp.*, 45 F.2d 119, 122, 7 U.S.P.Q. 84, 86 (2d Cir. 1930), *cert. denied*, 282 U.S. 902 (1931).

[128]*Warner Bros., Inc. v. ABC*, 720 F.2d 231, 235, 222 U.S.P.Q. 101, 104 (2d Cir. 1983) (Newman, J.) ("Plaintiffs own the copyrights in various works embodying the character of Superman and have thereby acquired copyright protection for the character itself"). *Universal City Studios, Inc. v. J.A.R. Sales, Inc.*, 216 U.S.P.Q. 679 (C.D. Cal. 1982); *Universal City Studios, Inc. v. Kamar Indus., Inc.*, 217 U.S.P.Q. 1162 (S.D. Tex. 1982); *United Artists Corp. v. Ford Motor Co.*, 483 F. Supp. 89, 209 U.S.P.Q. 227 (S.D.N.Y. 1980).

[129]*DC Comics, Inc. v. Unlimited Monkey Business, Inc.*, 598 F. Supp. 110, 224 U.S.P.Q. 437 (N.D. Ga. 1984); *United Feature Syndicate, Inc. v. Sunrise Mold Co.*, 569 F. Supp. 1475 (S.D. Fla. 1983); *Atari, Inc. v. North American Philips Consumer Electronics Corp.*, 672 F.2d 607, 214 U.S.P.Q. 33 (7th Cir.), *cert. denied*, 459 U.S. 880 (1982); *Warner Bros., Inc. v. ABC*, 523 F. Supp. 611, 211 U.S.P.Q. 51 (S.D.N.Y.), *aff'd*, 654 F.2d 204, 211 U.S.P.Q. 97 (2d Cir. 1981) (on motion for preliminary injunction); 530 F. Supp. 1187, 215 U.S.P.Q. 690 (S.D.N.Y. 1982), *aff'd*, 720 F.2d 231, 222 U.S.P.Q. 101 (2d Cir. 1983) (on motion for summary judgment); *Knickerbocker Toy Co. v. Winterbrook Corp.*, 554 F. Supp. 1309, 216 U.S.P.Q. 621 (D.N.H. 1982) (derivative work); *United Feature Syndicate, Inc. v. Cornwell Indus.*, COPR. L. REP. ¶25,509 (C.D. Cal. 1981); *United Feature Syndicate, Inc. v. Powell*, COPR. L. REP. ¶25,508 (C.D. Cal. 1981).

[130]*Warner Bros., Inc. v. ABC*, 720 F.2d 231, 240–242, 222 U.S.P.Q. 101, 109 (2d Cir. 1983); *National Comics Pub., Inc. v. Fawcett Pub., Inc.*, 191 F.2d 594, 600, 90 U.S.P.Q. 274 (2d Cir. 1951); *Detective Comics, Inc. v. Bruns Pub., Inc.*, 111 F.2d 432, 45 U.S.P.Q. 291 (2d Cir. 1940).

[131]*Hospital for Sick Children v. Melody Fare Dinner Theatre*, 516 F. Supp. 67, 209 U.S.P.Q. 749 (E.D. Va. 1980).

[132]COMPENDIUM II OF COPYRIGHT OFFICE PRACTICES §202.02(1): "The copyright law does not provide for the copyright registration of characters as such. However, original works of authorship describing, depicting, or embodying a character are registrable if otherwise in order." The Office practice is to request that a new application be submitted where the nature of authorship is described as "cartoon" or "pictorial" character. It will, however, accept for registration a claim describing the nature of authorship as "cartoon drawing." See also COPYRIGHT LAW REVISION PART 6: SUPPLEMENTARY REPORT OF THE REGISTER OF COPYRIGHTS ON THE GENERAL REVISION OF THE U.S. COPYRIGHT LAW, 89th Cong., 1st Sess. 6 (Comm. Print 1965):

"Proposals have been advanced for identifying fictional characters as copyrightable works in themselves under the bill. There are undoubtedly some characters that are developed in detail and with such breadth and depth that they emerge as separately indentifiable parts

prevailing (and it is submitted correct) view is that pictorial characters are separately copyrightable.[133]

The question of whether or under what circumstances literary characters may be copyrighted is less clear. The beginning point in any analysis of this issue is with Judge Learned Hand's poetic holding in *Nichols v. Universal Pictures Corp.*:

> "If Twelfth Night were copyrighted, it is quite possible that a second comer might so closely imitate Sir Toby Belch or Malvolio as to infringe, but it would not be enough that for one of his characters he cast a riotous knight who kept wassail to the discomfort of the household, or a vain and foppish steward who became amorous of his mistress. These would be no more than Shakespeare's 'ideas' in the play, as little capable of monopoly as Einstein's Doctrine of Relativity, or Darwin's theory of the Origin of Species. It follows that the less developed the characters, the less they can be copyrighted; that is the penalty an author must bear for marking them too indistinctly."[134]

The point at which the character becomes developed enough to be separately copyrightable is then one of fact,[135] but as with other works of authorship this determination is not an aesthetic one. As Judge Augustus Hand wrote two years after *Nichols* (in a case upholding the copyrightability of the Superman character): "[I]f his production involves more than the presentation of a general type [the author] may copyright it and say of it: 'A poor thing but mine

---

of the copyrightable works in which they appear. Others, perhaps the large majority, cannot be said to represent independent creations apart from the literary or pictorial works depicting them. As is equally true in the case of detailed presentations of plot, setting, or dramatic action, we believe it would be unnecessary and misleading to specify fictional characters as a separate class of copyrightable work."
This passage does not state that characters cannot be copyrighted separately, only that it was thought undesirable to statutorily specify characters as a discrete category of protectible subject matter in §102(a). If, as the Register concedes, there *are* characters (pictorial or literary) that are "developed in detail and with such breadth and depth that they emerge as separately indentifiable," there is no statutory authority permitting refusal of registration for such characters. See §410(a) (Register *shall* register the claim where material deposited constitutes copyrightable subject matter); §408(c)(1): "The Register of Copyrights is authorized to specify by regulation the administrative classes into which works are to be placed for purposes of * * * registration * * * . This administrative classification of works has no significance with respect to the subject matter of copyright or the exclusive rights provided by this title."
   [133]*DC Comics, Inc. v. Unlimited Monkey Business, Inc.*, 598 F. Supp. 110, 224 U.S.P.Q. 437 (N.D. Ga. 1984); *Wallace Berrie & Co. v. Marsh*, COPR. L. REP. ¶25,512 (C.D. Cal. 1983); *DC Comics, Inc. v. Reel Fantasy, Inc.*, 696 F.2d 24, 217 U.S.P.Q. 307 (2d Cir. 1982); *Pillsbury Co. v. Milky Way Prods.*, 215 U.S.P.Q. 124 (N.D. Ga. 1981); *DC Comics, Inc. v. Crazy Eddie, Inc.*, 205 U.S.P.Q. 1177 (S.D.N.Y. 1979); *Warner Bros., Inc. v. ABC*, 523 F. Supp. 611, 211 U.S.P.Q. 51 (S.D.N.Y.), *aff'd*, 654 F.2d 204, 211 U.S.P.Q. 97 (2d Cir. 1981) (on motion for preliminary injunction); 530 F. Supp. 1187, 215 U.S.P.Q. 690 (S.D.N.Y. 1982), *aff'd*, 720 F.2d 231, 222 U.S.P.Q. 101 (2d Cir. 1983) (on motion for summary judgment); *Atari, Inc. v. North American Philips Consumer Electronics Corp.*, 672 F.2d 607, 214 U.S.P.Q. 33 (7th Cir.), *cert. denied*, 459 U.S. 880 (1982); *DC Comics, Inc. v. Filmation Associates*, 486 F. Supp. 1273, 206 U.S.P.Q. 112 (S.D.N.Y. 1980); *Children's Television Workshop v. Diamond*, COPR. L. REP. ¶25,014 (S.D.N.Y. 1978); *Sid & Marty Krofft Television Prods., Inc. v. McDonald's*, 562 F.2d 1157, 196 U.S.P.Q. 97 (9th Cir. 1977); *Ideal Toy Corp. v. Kenner Products Division*, 443 F. Supp. 291, 197 U.S.P.Q. 738 (S.D.N.Y. 1977); *Detective Comics, Inc. v. Fox Pub., Inc.*, 46 F. Supp. 872, 54 U.S.P.Q. 485 (S.D.N.Y. 1942); *Detective Comics, Inc. v. Bruns Pub., Inc.*, 111 F.2d 432, 45 U.S.P.Q. 291 (2d Cir. 1940); *Fleischer Studios, Inc. v. Ralph A. Freundlich, Inc.*, 73 F.2d 276, 23 U.S.P.Q. 295 (2d Cir. 1934); *King Features Syndicate, Inc. v. Fleischer*, 299 F. 533 (2d Cir. 1924); *Fisher v. Star Co.*, 231 N.Y. 414, 132 N.E. 133 (N.Y.), *cert. denied*, 257 U.S. 654 (1921); *Hill & Whalen v. Martell, Inc.*, 270 F. 359 (S.D.N.Y. 1914); *Empire City Amusement Co. v. Wilton*, 134 F. 132 (C.C.D. Mass. 1903).
   [134]45 F.2d 119, 121, 7 U.S.P.Q. 84, 86 (2d Cir. 1930), *cert. denied*, 282 U.S. 902 (1931).
   [135]See Judge Hand's "abstractions" test in *Nichols, id.* at 121, 7 U.S.P.Q. at 86.

own.' "[136] The principle of separate protection for "well-defined" literary characters has been followed in a number of cases following *Nichols*,[137] but a possibly discordant note was sounded in *Warner Bros. Pictures, Inc. v. Columbia Broadcasting System, Inc.*,[138] known as the "Sam Spade" case, which either in dictum or as an alternative holding[139] stated: "It is conceivable that the character really constitutes the story being told, but if the character is only the chessman in the game of telling the story he is not within the area of protection afforded by the copyright."[140] To the extent that this statement requires a character to "really constitute the story being told," it has been strongly criticized by other courts[141] and by commentators[142] and was arguably limited by the Ninth Circuit in a subsequent character case.[143] The better rule is that literary characters should be judged according to the same standards of originality as all other categories of copyrighted subject matter.

Even where a particular character is found to be uncopyrightable or has fallen into the public domain, protection may still be available under unfair competition[144] or antidilution[145] statutes.

---

[136] *Detective Comics, Inc. v. Bruns Pub., Inc.*, 111 F.2d 432, 45 U.S.P.Q. 291 (2d Cir. 1940). Judge Learned Hand was also a member of the three-member panel deciding this case.

[137] *Warner Bros., Inc. v. ABC*, 720 F.2d 231, 240–241, 222 U.S.P.Q. 101, 108–109 (2d Cir. 1983); *Burroughs v. MGM, Inc.*, 683 F.2d 610, 623, 215 U.S.P.Q. 495, 506 (2d Cir. 1982); *Filmvideo Releasing Corp. v. Hastings*, 668 F.2d 91, 218 U.S.P.Q. 750 (2d Cir. 1981); *Ideal Toy Corp. v. Kenner Products Division*, 443 F. Supp. 291, 197 U.S.P.Q. 738 (S.D.N.Y. 1977); *De Costa v. CBS, Inc.*, 520 F.2d 499, 186 U.S.P.Q. 305 (1st Cir. 1975), *cert. denied*, 423 U.S. 1073, 189 U.S.P.Q. 64 (1976); *Goodis v. United Artists Television, Inc.*, 425 F.2d 397, 165 U.S.P.Q. 3 (2d Cir. 1970).

[138] 216 F.2d 945, 104 U.S.P.Q. 103 (9th Cir. 1954), *cert. denied*, 348 U.S. 971, 105 U.S.P.Q. 518 (1955). For perceptive analyses of this decision (and the question of character rights in general), see Zissu, *Whither Character Rights: Some Observations*, 29 J. COPR. SOC'Y 121, 122–124 (1981), and Brylawski, *Protection of Characters—Sam Spade Revisited*, 22 BULL. COPR. SOC'Y 77 (1974). Mr. Zissu was the attorney for the author, Dashiel Hammett, in the *Warner Bros.* case.

[139] Compare *Walt Disney Prods. v. Air Pirates*, 345 F. Supp. 108, 111, 174 U.S.P.Q. 463, 465 (N.D. Cal. 1972) (interpreting the statement as an alternative holding), *aff'd*, 581 F.2d 751, 755 n. 10, 199 U.S.P.Q. 769, 773 n. 10 (9th Cir. 1978), *cert. denied*, 439 U.S. 1132 (1979) (declining to resolve the issue), with 1 NIMMER ON COPYRIGHT §2.12 n. 13 (suggesting statement may be dictum).

[140] 216 F.2d at 950, 104 U.S.P.Q. at 107.

[141] *Ideal Toy Corp. v. Kenner Prods.*, 443 F. Supp. 291, 197 U.S.P.Q. 738 (S.D.N.Y. 1977); *Goodis v. United Artists Television, Inc.*, 425 F.2d 397, 406 n. 2, 165 U.S.P.Q. 3, 5 n. 2 (2d Cir. 1970). Cf. *Hospital for Sick Children v. Melody Fare Dinner Theatre*, 516 F. Supp. 67, 73, 209 U.S.P.Q. 749, 753 (E.D. Va. 1980) (in dictum erroneously cites *Warner Bros.* for the proposition that "characters alone may not be copyrightable").

[142] Zissu, *Whither Character Rights: Some Observations*, 29 J. COPR. SOC'Y 121, 124 n. 12 (1981): "This test has been viewed, at least in the case of literary characters, as having such sweeping effect as ordinarily to debar characters from copyright protection."

[143] *Walt Disney Prods. v. Air Pirates*, 581 F.2d 751, 755, 199 U.S.P.Q. 769, 773 (9th Cir. 1978), *cert. denied*, 439 U.S. 1132 (1979).

[144] *Universal City Studios, Inc. v. Nintendo Co.*, 221 U.S.P.Q. 991, 1001 n. 4 (S.D.N.Y. 1983), *aff'd*, 746 F.2d 1121, 223 U.S.P.Q. 1000 (2d Cir. 1984); *Warner Bros., Inc. v. ABC*, 720 F.2d 231, 246, 222 U.S.P.Q. 101, 114 (2d Cir. 1983); *Frederick Warne & Co. v. Book Sales, Inc.*, 481 F. Supp. 1191, 205 U.S.P.Q. 444 (S.D.N.Y. 1979) (use of illustrations from public domain Beatrix Potter books; note court's holding that secondary meaning must be associated with publisher; association with author alone considered insufficient); *In Re Frederick Warne & Co.*, 218 U.S.P.Q. 345 (Pat. & Trademark Off. TTAB 1983) (refusal to register book cover illustrations as trademark affirmed). Unfair competition claims regarding characters under either state law or the federal Lanham Act have frequently been sustained even when the character is still subject to copyright (see *Gruelle v. Molley-'Es Doll Outfitters*, 94 F.2d 172, 176 (3d Cir. 1937), *cert. denied*, 304 U.S. 561 (1938); *Edgar Rice Burroughs, Inc. v. High Society Magazine, Inc.*, 7 MEDIA L. REP. 1863 (S.D.N.Y. 1981); *Cuillford v. CBS*, 222 U.S.P.Q. 497 (D.D.C. 1984)); and where a claim of copyright infringement has been found in the same suit. See *DC Comics*,

## Obscene or Pornographic Works

Section 2(a) of the Lanham Act precludes registration of a trademark that "[c]onsists of or comprises immoral, deceptive, or scandalous matter * * * ."[146] The Copyright Act, however, contains no comparable provision, and despite early judicial efforts to impose a governmentally defined morality through denial of copyright protection,[147] recent decisions finding that copyright is not content based and that "[t]he pursuit of creativity requires freedom to explore into the gray areas, to the cutting edge, and even beyond"[148] have correctly rejected the injection into copyright of a First Amendment doctrine "that continues to dog our judicial system and society at large."[149]

In dictum, a panel of the Second Circuit has, nevertheless, suggested that the salacious nature of a defendant's work has relevance to a fair use defense.[150] This concept has been rejected by other courts[151] and has been criticized by commentators.[152]

---

*Inc. v. Unlimited Monkey Business, Inc.*, 598 F. Supp. 110, 224 U.S.P.Q. 437 (N.D. Ga. 1984); *Eden Toys, Inc. v. Floralee Undergarment Co.*, 697 F.2d 27, 217 U.S.P.Q. 201 (2d Cir. 1982); *Midway Mfg. Co. v. Dirkschneider*, 543 F. Supp. 466, 214 U.S.P.Q. 417 (D. Neb. 1981). See also *DC Comics, Inc. v. Filmation Associates*, 486 F. Supp. 1273, 1277, 206 U.S.P.Q. 112, 114 (S.D.N.Y. 1980), where, although the court stated a belief that "plaintiff's remedy more properly lies under the Copyright Act," it nevertheless found a Lanham Act violation in defendant's creation and exhibition of substantially similar characters, rejecting an argument that plaintiff was barred from proceeding under the Lanham Act because it did not also assert a claim for copyright infringement.

[145]*DC Comics, Inc. v. Unlimited Monkey Business, Inc.*, 598 F. Supp. 110, 224 U.S.P.Q. 437 (N.D. Ga. 1984) (court found copyright infringement, Lanham Act violation, state unfair competition, and anti-dilution violations). See also *Pillsbury Co. v. Milky Way Prods.*, 215 U.S.P.Q. 124 (N.D. Ga. 1981), where the court found defendant's use of plaintiff's characters to be fair use and hence not copyright infringement, found no trademark infringement or deceptive trade practices, but did find a violation of the state anti-dilution statute.

[146]15 U.S.C. §1052(a) (1952).

[147]*Martinetti v. Maguire*, 16 F. Cas. 920 (C.C.N.D. Cal. 1867) (No. 9,173); *Richardson v. Miller*, 20 F. Cas. 722 (C.C.D. Mass. 1877) (No. 11,791); *Broder v. Zeno Mauvais Music*, 88 F. 74 (C.C.N.D. Cal. 1898).

[148]*Jartech, Inc. v. Clancy*, 666 F.2d 403, 213 U.S.P.Q. 1057 (9th Cir.), *cert. denied*, 459 U.S. 826 (1982); *Mitchell Bros. Film Group v. Cinema Adult Theater*, 604 F.2d 852, 203 U.S.P.Q. 1041 (5th Cir. 1979), *cert. denied*, 445 U.S. 917 (1980). See also *Belcher v. Tarbox*, 486 F.2d 1087, 108 U.S.P.Q. 1 (9th Cir. 1973) (upholding copyright in racing forms). In a 1958 opinion, the Attorney General concluded that while the Register of Copyrights is authorized to deny registration to obscene works, he or she is "free to decide not to attempt to refuse or deny registration or claims to copyright" in such works. 41 Op. Att'y Gen. 73 (1958). The present Copyright Office practice is not to refuse registration for obscene or pornographic works. COMPENDIUM II OF COPYRIGHT OFFICE PRACTICES §108.10.

[149]*Mitchell Bros.*, *supra* note 148, 604 F.2d at 856, 203 U.S.P.Q. at 1045.

[150]*Warner Bros., Inc. v. ABC*, 720 F.2d 231, 243 n. 8, 222 U.S.P.Q. 101, 110 n. 8 (2d Cir. 1983): "We have no occasion in this case to consider the limiting principle that arises when attempts at parody take the form of scatological humor." See also *DC Comics, Inc. v. Unlimited Monkey Business, Inc.*, 598 F. Supp. 110, 118, 224 U.S.P.Q. 437, 443 (N.D. Ga. 1984), which found a potential harm to the market for the copyrighted work from the "implicit disparagement and bawdy associations undisputably created by some of defendents' adaptions."

[151]*Pillsbury Co. v. Milky Way Prods.*, 215 U.S.P.Q. 124, 131 (N.D. Ga. 1981): "The Copyright Act does not expressly exclude pornographic materials from the parameters of the fair use defense * * * . The character of the unauthorized use is relevant, but in the court's judgment, the fact that this use is pornographic in nature does not militate against a finding of fair use." See also *Guccione v. Flynt*, COPR. L. REP. ¶25,669 (S.D.N.Y. 1984), where *Hustler* magazine's reproduction of a copyrighted photograph from *Penthouse* magazine in connection with an article criticizing *Penthouse* publisher Guccione for his practice of posing fully clothed with nude female models was held to be fair use; and Judge Mansfield's dissent in *MCA, Inc. v. Wilson*, 677 F.2d 180, 191, 211 U.S.P.Q. 577, 586 (2d Cir. 1981): "We cannot, under the guise of deciding a copyright issue, act as a board of censors outlawing X-rated performances."

[152]W. PATRY, THE FAIR USE PRIVILEGE IN COPYRIGHT LAW 169 n. 116 (BNA Books, 1985).

## Government Publications and Other Works: §105

*Federal Government*

The Printing Law of 1895, designed to centralize the printing of government documents in the Government Printing Office, also contained the first statutory prohibition upon copyright in government publications, a provision added in response to the assertion of copyright by a member of Congress in a compilation of "Messages and Papers of the Presidents of the United States" printed and distributed by the Government Printing Office.[153] Prior to that time the courts had held, on public policy grounds, that copyright was unavailable for court decisions, statutes, and related governmental edicts.[154] This prohibition did not extend, however, to headnotes, syllabi, annotations, or indices.[155] The law regarding other types of works was less clear. Thus, an artist who created drawings as a member of Commodore Perry's expedition was denied copyright, the court holding: "Congress, by ordering the * * * drawings to be published for the benefit of the public at large, has thereby given them to the public."[156] A contrary result (at least with respect to ownership of the physical manuscript) was reached in a dispute over the notes and diary of William Clark of the Lewis and Clark expedition,[157] and in *Folsom v. Marsh*,[158] where a collection of letters and other private correspondence of President Washington was also held protectible.

The first copyright statute to contain a prohibition on copyright in government works was Section 8 of the 1909 Act, which stated that "[n]o copyright shall subsist in * * * any publication of the United States government, or any reprint in whole or in part thereof * * * ." This did not mean, however, that any work published in a government document became a "publication of the United States Government" (and therefore in the public domain), for Section 8 also provided that:

> "The publication or republication by the Government, either separately or in a public document, of any material in which copyright is subsisting shall not be taken to cause any abridgment or annulment of the copy-

---

[153]28 Stat. 608 (1895), codified in 44 U.S.C. §58. See Berger, *Copyright in Government Publications*, COPYRIGHT OFFICE STUDY No. 33, 86th Cong., 2d Sess. 23 (Comm. Print 1961), and Smith, *Government Documents: Their Copyright and Ownership*, TEX. TECH. L. REV. 71 (1973), for a review of pre-1976 Act law and the genesis of the 1895 Act.

[154]*Wheaton v. Peters*, 33 U.S. (8 Pet.) 591 (1834). In an intriguing 1863 case decided by the District Court of Mobile for the Confederate States, it was held that where a general had prepared a work on infantry tactics at the direction of the Secretary of War of the United States while an officer of the Union army, and the work was published at congressional expense without a claim of copyright, the work was in the public domain both in the Union, and after secession (and the general's joining the Confederacy), in the Confederacy as well. *Goetzel v. Titcomb*, 14 C.O. BULL. 1086 (C.S.D. Mobile 1863).

[155]*Wheaton v. Peters*, 33 U.S. (8 Pet.) 591 (1834).

[156]*Heine v. Appleton*, 11 F. Cas. 1031 (C.C.S.D.N.Y. 1857) (No. 6,324).

[157]*United States v. First Trust Co. of St. Paul*, 251 F.2d 686, 116 U.S.P.Q. 172 (8th Cir. 1958).

[158]9 F. Cas. 342 (C.C.D. Mass. 1841) (No. 4, 901). "Official" writings of President Carter and all subsequent Presidents are governed by the Presidential Records Act, 44 U.S.C. §2201 *et seq.* (1978, effective 1981). See Vol. 34, REC. A.B. CITY N.Y., No. 7, 506–507 (Oct. 1979).

right or to authorize any use or appropriation of such copyright material without the consent of the copyright proprietor."

The precise meaning of the term "publication of the United States Government" was never established,[159] as disputes over the scope of Section 8 generally focused on whether the work was performed within the scope of the government employee's duties. In two decisions involving lectures prepared by military officers, copyright was found to be available,[160] while in two other decisions (involving, respectively, a sculptural work[161] and a map[162]) protection was denied.

In the process of revising the 1909 Act, Congress reexamined copyright for both works prepared by government employees as part of their official duties and works created by government contractors. An early bill that would have permitted copyright to be secured in a published work of the U.S. government in exceptional cases[163] proved controversial, and was quickly dropped.[164] Thereafter, issues surrounding government-employee-created works centered primarily[165] on differences between the definition of a "work of the United States Government" and the definition of a "work made for hire." Despite an intent not to establish any difference in meaning between the two (or to alter Section 8 of the 1909 Act), the definition of the former was at first different from that of the latter, then made the same, and finally restored to its initial (and therefore different) state. As ultimately enacted, that definition is "a work prepared by an officer or employee of the United States Government as part of that person's official duties,"[166] and since the 1976 Act now applies to both published and unpublished works, it pertains to both categories of works.

---

[159]In 1911, the Superintendent of Documents, did, however, provide such a definition for purposes of the Printing Law. See Superintendent of Documents, *Checklist of United States Public Documents, 1789–1909* vii (3d ed. 1911), *quoted in* Berger, *supra* note 153, Copyright Office Study No. 33 at 30. See also Op. Compt. Gen. of the U.S., 158 U.S.P.Q. 172 (1968), and *DuPuy v. Post Telegram Co.*, 210 F. 883 (3d Cir. 1914) (term held to include lists, bulletins, and circulars of information prepared and issued by the various bureaus, agencies, and projects maintained by the government, even if the author was not a government employee).

[160]*Sherrill v. Grieves*, 57 Wash. L. R. 286 (Sup.Ct. D.C. 1929); *Public Affairs Associates, Inc. v. Rickover*, 284 F.2d 262, 127 U.S.P.Q. 231 (D.C. Cir. 1960), *judgment vacated for lack of a sufficient record*, 369 U.S. 111, 132 U.S.P.Q. 535 (1962), *on remand*, 268 F. Supp. 444, 153 U.S.P.Q. 598 (D.D.C. 1967).

[161]*Scherr v. Universal Match Co.*, 297 F. Supp. 107, 160 U.S.P.Q. 216 (S.D.N.Y. 1967), *aff'd*, 417 F.2d 497, 164 U.S.P.Q. 225 (2d Cir. 1969), *cert. denied*, 397 U.S. 236, 164 U.S.P.Q. 545 (1970).

[162]*Sawyer v. Crowell Pub. Co.*, 46 F. Supp. 471, 54 U.S.P.Q. 225 (S.D.N.Y. 1942), *aff'd*, 142 F.2d 497, 61 U.S.P.Q. 389 (2d Cir. 1944).

[163]S. 3008, H.R. 12354, §4(c), 88th Cong., 2d Sess. (1964), *reprinted in* Copyright Law Revision Part 6: Supplementary Report of the Register of Copyrights on the General Revision of the U.S. Copyright Law: 1965 Revision Bill, 89th Cong., 1st Sess. 183 (Comm. Print 1965).

[164]Copyright Law Revision Part 6, *supra* note 163, at 10.

[165]An attempt was also made to provide for a limited copyright for publications of the National Technical Information Service. Such protection was included in the House-passed version of the 1976 Act, but it was deleted in conference. See H.R. Rep. No. 94-1733, 94th Cong., 2d Sess. 69–70 (1976) (conference report).

[166]17 U.S.C. §101 (1978). See also *id.* at §105. Section 105 does not necessarily prohibit other countries from according protection to works of the U.S. government. In a memorandum dated April 15, 1985, the Library of Congress announced a policy of requiring non-U.S. subscribers to its LC MARC tapes to enter into a licensing agreement with the Library for copying and distribution of the tapes. The tapes themselves bear the following legend: "© 1985 by the Library of Congress except within the United States." See also Ringer and Flacks, *Applicabil-*

The question of whether works created by government contractors should be subject to copyright was left up to specific legislation,
individual agency regulation, or contractual restrictions. The legislative reports state in this regard:

"As the bill is written, the Government agency concerned could determine in each case whether to allow an independent contractor or grantee
to secure copyright in works prepared in whole or in part with the use of
Government funds. The argument against allowing copyright in this situation is that the public should not be required to pay a 'double subsidy,'
and that it is inconsistent to prohibit copyright in works by Government
employees while permitting private copyrights in a growing body of
works created by persons who are paid with Government funds.

"The bill deliberately avoids making any sort of outright, unquali-
fied prohibition against copyright in works prepared under Government
contract or grant. There may well be cases where it would be in the public interest to deny copyright in the writings generated by Government
research contracts and the like; it can be assumed that, where a Government agency commissions a work for its own use merely as an alternative to having one of its own employees prepare the work, the right to
secure a private copyright would be withheld. However, there are almost
certainly many other cases where the denial of copyright protection
would be unfair or would hamper the production and publication of important works. Where, under the particular circumstances, Congress or
the agency involved finds that the need to have a work freely available
outweighs the need of the private author to secure copyright, the problem can be dealt with by specific legislation, agency regulations, or contractual restrictions."[167]

It should be noted that the reference in this passage to an assumption that, where a government agency commissions a work as
an alternative to having one of its own employees prepare the work,

---

*ity of the Universal Copyright Convention to Certain Works in the Public Domain in Their
Country of Origin*, 27 BULL. COPR. SOC'Y 157 (1980), for a further discussion of this and related
issues.
     Unlike the 1909 Act, the 1976 Act does not contain an express savings clause concerning
works created by private individuals but published in government documents. However, the
legislative reports indicate that the change in terminology from "any publication of the United
States Government" to "any work of the United States Government" was intended to have the
same result as the previous statute. H.R. REP. No. 94-1476, 94th Cong., 2d Sess. 60 (1976); S.
REP. No. 94-473, 94th Cong., 1st Sess. 57 (1975); *Building Officials & Code Administrators v.
Code Technology, Inc.*, 628 F.2d 730, 735, 207 U.S.P.Q. 81, 86 (1st Cir. 1980).
     That the work is required to be filed with a government agency does not make it a "work of
the United States Government." *Rand McNally & Co. v. Fleet Mgt. Systems, Inc.*, 591 F. Supp.
726, 734–736, 221 U.S.P.Q. 827, 837 (N.D. Ill. 1983); *WPOW, Inc. v. MRLJ Enters.*, 584 F.
Supp. 132, 222 U.S.P.Q. 502 (D.D.C. 1984) (by implication).
     Neither the Act nor the legislative reports provide any detailed guidance with respect to
the term "United States." Based on the statutory definition of "State" in §101 of the Act,
§206.2(c) and (d) of the *Compendium II of Copyright Office Practices* notes that works of the
governments of the District of Columbia and the Commonwealth of Puerto Rico are not "works
of the United States." "Works of the governments of the 'organized territories' under the jurisdiction of the U.S. Government are acceptable for registration under the rule of doubt. Works of
the governments of other territorial areas under the jurisdiction of the United States are considered to be U.S. Government works." *Id.* at §206.2(e). Particular territories are further identified. *Id.* at §1102.8(a) and (b). See also Varmer, *Copyright in Territories and Possessions of the
United States*, COPYRIGHT OFFICE STUDY No. 34, 86th Cong., 2d Sess. 47 (Comm. Print 1961).
     [167]H.R. REP. No. 94-1476, 94th Cong., 2d Sess. 59 (1976); S. REP. No. 94-473, 94th Cong.,
1st Sess. 56 (1975). The Small Business and Federal Procurement Competition Enhancement
Act of 1984, Pub. L. No. 98-577, 98 Stat. 3067, mandates the promulgation of a single system of
procurement regulations with respect to U.S. government use of copyrighted works. *Id.* at Title III. See also Gabig and McAvoy, *DOD's "Rights in Technical Data and Computer Software" Clause*, 2 COMPUTER LAW. 14 (1985).

"the right to secure a private copyright would be withheld" refers to a contractual relationship and does not provide an independent basis for a court to void such a copyright.[168] Nor should a government agency be permitted to obtain (and enforce) a copyright by requiring a contractor to assign its copyright.[169] Such subterfuge would violate Congress' intent to have works either be freely available to the public or be subject to private copyright in order to encourage private investment.

## State and Local Governments

Preliminary drafts for the 1909 Act provided that no copyright should subsist in "official acts, proceedings, laws, or ordinances of public authorities—federal, state, or municipalities * * * ."[170] Objections were made to this proposal by publishers of state reporters,[171] and the provision was subsequently dropped without explanation.[172] No mention of state or municipal copyright is made either in the 1976 Act or in the accompanying legislative reports. Works of state and municipal (as well as foreign) governments are thus outside the ambit of Section 105 and are copyrightable, subject to exceptions dictated by public policy with respect to such publications, such as statutes and judicial opinions.[173]

---

[168]*Schnapper v. Foley*, 667 F.2d 102, 109, 212 U.S.P.Q. 235, 239 (D.C. Cir. 1981), *cert. denied*, 455 U.S. 948, 215 U.S.P.Q. 96 (1982).

[169]See Note, *A Constitutional Analysis of Copyrighting Government-Commissioned Works*, 84 COLUM. L. REV. 425 (1984). The refusal of the *Schnapper* court, *supra* note 168, to "lay down a broad rule" on this point has been criticized by Professor Nimmer. 1 NIMMER ON COPYRIGHT §5.06[B][3] n. 23.1. See also *Children's Television Workshop v. Diamond*, COPR. L. REP. ¶25,014 (S.D.N.Y. 1978), which rejected an argument that a producer of children's television programs could not have a copyright in programs partly funded by the Department of Health, Education & Welfare; Louisiana Att'y Gen. Op. No. 82-630, *reprinted in* COPR. L. REP. ¶25,658 (July 27, 1982) (in absence of contractual provision to the contrary, videotape series for educating deaf adults developed with HEW grant was copyrightable by state agency). Cf. *S & H Computer Systems, Inc. v. SAS Institute, Inc.*, 568 F. Supp. 416, 222 U.S.P.Q. 715 (M.D. Tenn. 1983), which, while holding that "government funding of a project, in and of itself, does not prohibit a copyright in any developments under the project," found the copyright at bar invalid under a contract clause, which clearly stated that "no copyrights shall subsist" in any publications resulting from the funded project. *Id.* at 418, 222 U.S.P.Q. at 716.

[170]S. 6330, H.R. 19853 §15, 59th Cong., 1st Sess. (1906).

[171]*Stenographic Report of the Proceedings of the Conference on Copyright*, First Session, 119–126 (1905); Third Session, 298–299 (1906).

[172]See, however, discussion in Berger, *Copyright in Government Publications*, COPYRIGHT OFFICE STUDY No. 33, 86th Cong., 2d Sess. 31–32 (Comm. Print 1961). In *Banks v. Manchester*, 128 U.S. 244 (1888), the Supreme Court held invalid a state law that permitted the official court reporter for a state supreme court to obtain copyright in the opinions of the court. Accord *Nash v. Lathrop*, 142 Mass. 29, 6 N.E. 559 (Mass. 1886); *Davidson v. Wheelock*, 27 F. 61 (C.C.D. Minn. 1866); *Howell v. Miller*, 91 F. 129 (6th Cir. 1898). Contra *Gould v. Banks*, 53 Conn. 415, 2 A. 886 (Conn. 1886) (see, however, the subsequent opinion of the circuit court for the Northern District of New York refusing to enforce this copyright, *Connecticut v. Gould*, 34 F. 319 (C.C.N.D.N.Y. 1888)).

[173]The present Copyright Office practice in this regard is set forth in COMPENDIUM II OF COPYRIGHT OFFICE PRACTICES §206.3:

"Works (other than edicts of government) prepared by officers or employees of any government (except the U.S. Government) including State, local, or foreign governments, are subject to registration if they are otherwise copyrightable."

Protection for works of foreign governments must be considered in conjunction with the eligibility requirements set forth in §104. A special provision is made in §104(b)(3) for "works first published by the United Nations or any of its specialized agencies, or by the Organization of American States." It should be noted that this provision does not condition eligibility on one of these organizations being the author; the organization need only have first published the work.

After lying dormant for over 70 years following deletion of the above-quoted proposal, issues of copyright in state works have recently resurfaced. In *Georgia v. Harrison*,[174] a state's argument that prior decisions prohibiting individuals from copyrighting court opinions or statutes did not bar the state itself from doing so, was rejected on public policy (but not statutory) grounds. In *Building Officials & Code Administrators v. Code Technology, Inc.*, a private, nonprofit organization (BOCA) spent 28 years developing a model building code, for which it obtained copyright registration. Pursuant to a license from BOCA, the Commonwealth of Massachusetts adopted a building code based in substantial part on the BOCA code, which BOCA published and distributed for sale in book form. Thereafter an unauthorized publisher created and marketed a competing work containing the BOCA-based code (in addition to other regulations). After a preliminary injunction was granted enjoining this use, appeal was taken to the First Circuit, which reversed and remanded. Noting the inapplicability of Section 105 and this treatise's statement that works of state governments are eligible for protection "subject to exceptions dictated by public policy with respect to such publications as statutes and judicial opinions,"[175] the court of appeals found an important public policy of access to regulations such as building codes that have "the effect of the law and carry sanctions of fine and imprisonment for violations * * * ."[176] Despite the court's grave doubts that this policy could be "reconciled with the exclusivity afforded a private copyright holder," the court also found that groups such as plaintiff's served an important public function by seeing that "complex yet essential regulations are drafted, kept up to date and made available."[177] The matter was remanded for development of a fuller record.[178]

A "Youth Court Handbook and Manual" created for use by a youth court (described as a quasi-judicial court forum where youths act as judges, lawyers, and court officers) was recently found to be the copyright of the town,[179] while state attorney general opinions have stated that a medical alert flag[180] and an unspecified three-dimensional "object" could be subject to copyright by state agencies.[181]

---

[174]548 F. Supp. 110, 218 U.S.P.Q. 119 (N.D. Ga. 1982). See also Op. New York Att'y Gen., 180 U.S.P.Q. 331 (1973).

[175]628 F.2d 730, 736, 207 U.S.P.Q. 81, 86 (1st Cir. 1980). See also COMPENDIUM II OF COPYRIGHT PRACTICES §§205.08(d), 206.01. Cf. *id.* at §206.03.

[176]628 F.2d at 736, 207 U.S.P.Q. at 85.

[177]*Ibid. Building Code* was distinguished in *Del Madera Properties v. Rhodes and Gardner, Inc.*, 227 U.S.P.Q. 486 (N.D. Cal. 1985), where the court held that a private developer's map for a residential subdivision, filed with and approved by the city council, was not thereby transformed into an administrative ruling, legislative enactment, or the like.

[178]Upon remand, defendant filed a motion to dismiss, which was denied. 210 U.S.P.Q. 289 (D. Mass. 1980). Cf. *Long v. Jordan*, 29 F. Supp. 287, 290, 43 U.S.P.Q. 176, 178 (N.D. Cal. 1939) ("a copyright on any exposition of a system of government cannot prevent the use of that system as intended").

[179]*Town of Clarkstown v. Reeder*, 566 F. Supp. 137, 220 U.S.P.Q. 793 (S.D.N.Y. 1983).

[180]Louisiana Att'y Gen. Op. No. 83-621, *reprinted in* COPR. L. REP. ¶25,659 (July 27, 1983). The opinion did state, however, that one state agency could not enforce its copyright against another state agency.

[181]Oklahoma Att'y Gen. Op. No. 82-167, *reprinted in* COPR. L. REP. ¶25,453 (Sept. 10, 1982).

## Classification of Copyrightable Subject Matter

### Under the 1909 Act

The use of the word "all" in the phrase "all the writings of an author" found in Section 4 of the 1909 Act did not mean, of course, that an individual author could secure in advance a general or blanket copyright on everything he or she might subsequently produce. Each work separately published had to be treated as a separate work for which the same formalities were to be observed as if it were by a different author.

One was required to specify in his or her application for registration the appropriate designated class in Section 5 for the work in which copyright is claimed. These were

"(a)   Books, including composite and cyclopedic works, directories, gazetteers, and other complications.
"(b)   Periodicals, including newspapers.
"(c)   Lectures, sermons, addresses (prepared for oral delivery).
"(d)   Dramatic or dramatico-musical compositions.
"(e)   Musical compositions.
"(f)   Maps.
"(g)   Works of art; models or designs for works of art.
"(h)   Reproductions of a work of art.
"(i)   Drawings or plastic works of a scientific or technical character.
"(j)   Photographs.
"(k)   Prints and pictorial illustrations including prints or labels used for articles of merchandise.
"(l)   Motion picture photoplays.
"(m)   Motion pictures other than photoplays.
"(n)   Sound recordings."

The classes set forth in Section 5 were not meant to be exclusive; their breadth, however, did inhibit the courts from granting protection to writings not specifically enumerated.[182] And the second subdivision of the remedial Section 101(b) spoke of "any work enumerated in section 5 of this title," perhaps suggesting the existence of nonenumerated protected works.

The enumeration, however, was primarily an administrative provision to enable the Copyright Office to perform its task in an orderly fashion, including the publication of a Catalog of Copyright Entries in conformity with the classes mentioned. Hence this section very properly closed with a proviso that these specifications were not to be held to limit the subject matter of copyright, "nor shall any error in classification invalidate or impair the copyright protection secured under this Act." It was apparently the actual nature of the work that determined the scope of the copyright protection secured, even though the work might have been registered in the wrong class.[183]

---

[182]See *Capitol Records, Inc. v. Mercury Records Corp.*, 221 F.2d 657, 105 U.S.P.Q. 163 (2d Cir. 1955). Cf. *Bailie v. Fisher*, 258 F.2d 425, 117 U.S.P.Q. 334 (D.C. Cir. 1958).
[183]*Green v. Luby*, 177 F. 287 (C.C.S.D.N.Y. 1909). But see *Corcoran v. Montgomery Ward & Co.*, 121 F.2d 572, 574, 50 U.S.P.Q. 274, 276 (9th Cir.), *cert. denied*, 314 U.S. 687, 51 U.S.P.Q. 546 (1941).

In any event, the statute did make a number of substantive and procedural distinctions according to the nature or "class" of the work.[184] In some such instances, the pertinent subsection of Section 5 was specifically cited elsewhere in the statute to describe the work in question (e.g., §§16, 19); in other cases, the works were described without reference to the specifications in Section 5 (e.g., §§1(b), 12). Upon the nature of the work depended such things as: (1) its protection against public performance not for profit (§§1(d),(e)); (2) its protectibility in unpublished form (§12); (3) the requirement that copies of the work be manufactured in the United States (§16); and (4) the required location and form of copyright notice (§§19, 20).

## Under the 1976 Act: §102

Section 102(a) of the 1976 Act protects "original works of authorship fixed in any tangible medium of expression, now known or later developed, from which they can be perceived, reproduced, or otherwise communicated, either directly or with the aid of a machine or device." The legislative reports accompanying the Act state:

> "In using the phrase 'original works of authorship,' rather than 'all the writings of an author' now in section 4 of the statute, the committee's purpose is to avoid exhausting the constitutional power of Congress to legislate in this field, and to eliminate the uncertainties arising from the latter phrase. Since the present statutory language is substantially the same as the empowering language of the Constitution, a recurring question has been whether the statutory and the constitutional provisions are co-extensive. If so, the courts would be faced with the alternative of holding copyrightable something that Congress clearly did not intend to protect, or of holding constitutionally incapable of copyright something that Congress might one day want to protect. To avoid these equally undesirable results, the courts have indicated that 'all the writings of an author' under the present statute is narrower in scope than the 'writings' of 'authors' referred to in the Constitution. The bill avoids this dilemma by using a different phrase—'original works of authorship'—in characterizing the general subject matter of statutory copyright protection."[185]

The seven illustrative examples of such "works of authorship" are

"(1) literary works;
"(2) musical works, including any accompanying words;
"(3) dramatic works, including any accompanying music;
"(4) pantomimes and choreographic works;
"(5) pictorial, graphic, and sculptural works;
"(6) motion pictures and other audiovisual works; and
"(7) sound recordings."

Section 103, which states that "[t]he subject matter of copyright as specified by section 102 includes compilations and derivative

---

[184]See *Seltzer v. Sunbrook*, 22 F. Supp. 621, 37 U.S.P.Q. 491 (S.D. Cal. 1938).
[185]H.R. REP. No. 94-1476, 94th Cong., 2d Sess. 51 (1976); S. REP. No. 94-473, 94th Cong., 1st Sess. 50 (1975).

works * * * ,'' is designed to complement Section 102 and when "[r]ead together the two sections make plain that the criteria of copyrightable subject matter stated in section 102 apply with full force to works that are entirely original and to those containing preexisting material."[186]

As suggested above, the administrative classification of the 1909 law took on substantive dimensions. The 1976 Act does not require such double duty. The illustrative enumeration in Section 102(a) is of works *protected*; provision for administrative classification for *registration* purposes is made in Section 408(c).

The 1976 Act does continue to treat works differently in numerous respects depending on their nature. Such specialized treatment includes Section 108(h) (exclusion of musical, certain audiovisual, and pictorial, graphic, or sculptural works from the library photocopying privilege); Section 110 (various limitations on performing rights of nondramatic literary and musical works); Section 112 (exclusion of motion pictures and other audiovisual works from the ephemeral recording privilege of broadcasters); Section 113 (specification of certain rights in pictorial, graphic, and sculptural works); Sections 106(4) and 114(a) (denial of performance right in sound recordings); Sections 115 and 116 (compulsory license for recording and jukebox performance of nondramatic musical works); and Section 118 (public broadcasting compulsory license in published nondramatic musical and pictorial, graphic, and sculptural works). Accordingly, it remains appropriate, particularly with respect to certain potentially troublesome categories, to examine, at least until these categories are judicially construed, interpretations of analogous classes under the 1909 law.

## Literary Works

This remains the broadest of all categories, and includes "books" and "periodicals" (Classes A and B) under the 1909 law. Literary works are defined in Section 101 of the 1976 Act as

> "works, other than audiovisual works, expressed in words, numbers, or other verbal or numerical symbols or indicia, regardless of the nature of the material objects, such as books, periodicals, manuscripts, phonorecords, film, tapes, disks, or cards, in which they are embodied."

The "catchall" quality of this definition parallels the contours given to "books" under the prior law. It would pretty nearly hit the mark to say that whatever did not fairly belong to any of the other specified classes would be a book, if it was in fact the writing of an author.

---

[186]H.R. Rep. No. 94-1476 at 57; S. Rep. No. 94-473 at 55. Cf. *Vermont Castings, Inc. v. Evans Prod. Co.*, 215 U.S.P.Q. 758, 762 n. 2 (D. Vt. 1981) ("Although the use of the word 'include' as defined in section 101, makes clear that the categories listed in section 102 are 'illustrative and not limitative' * * * , defendants do not point us beyond the listing itself").

"It is the intellectual production of the author which the copyright protects and not the particular form which such production ultimately takes, and the word 'book' as used in the statute is not to be understood in its technical sense of a bound volume, but any species of publication which the author selects to embody his literary products."[187]

While ordinarily a book contains a composition of words in readable form, it may also consist entirely of pictorial matter, or tables or figures, or lists of symbols in cipher codes. Within this category are pamphlets, leaflets, and folders, and, subject to the *de minimis* limitations discussed above, even a single verse or brief statement separately published.[188]

*Computer Programs.* These interpretations make less surprising the Copyright Office's classification of computer programs as "books" when it determined in 1964 to grant registration of such works under its "rule of doubt."[189] One consequence of this classification was the requirement that the program be "published," a step raising intriguing questions for those seeking to maintain trade secret protection.[190] The Office also required explanation of the manner of publication, as well as deposit of a human-readable form of the program (e.g., a printout) if the program had been published only in machine-readable form.

Although no court decision had validated the Copyright Office practice of registering claims to copyright in computer programs, the Office's "doubt" in doing so has been removed by the 1976 Act, which treats computer programs (and data bases) as literary works, an intent originally manifested in the legislative reports[191] accompanying the Act, and subsequently in 1980 by providing a statutory definition of "computer program"[192] and limitations on rights with respect to such works,[193] changes made as a result of the adoption, as modified, of the recommendations of the National Commission on New Technological Uses of Copyrighted Works (CONTU).

---

[187] *Holmes v. Hurst*, 174 U.S. 82 (1899).

[188] See *Jackson v. Quickslip Co.*, 110 F.2d 731, 45 U.S.P.Q. 6 (2d Cir. 1940) (greeting card); *Sebring Pottery Co. v. Steubenville Pottery Co.*, 9 F. Supp. 383, 14 U.S.P.Q. 46 (N.D. Ohio 1932) (advertising card). See also text at notes 28–33 and note 28, *supra*.

[189] COPYRIGHT OFFICE CIRCULAR NO. 61 (1964). See Cary, *Copyright Registration and Computer Programs*, 11 BULL. COPR. SOC'Y 362 (1964).

[190] See, e.g., FINAL REPORT OF THE NATIONAL COMMISSION ON NEW TECHNOLOGICAL USES OF COPYRIGHTED WORKS 38, 44 (1978) (cited hereafter as CONTU FINAL REPORT), and *Warrington Associates, Inc. v. Real-Time Engineering Systems, Inc.*, 522 F. Supp. 367, 216 U.S.P.Q. 1024 (N.D. Ill. 1981) (declining to rule as a matter of law that deposit with Copyright Office of work containing trade secrets results in loss of such secrets).

[191] H.R. REP. No. 94-1476, 94th Cong., 2d Sess. 54 (1976) ("The term 'literary works' * * * includes computer data bases, and computer programs * * * "); S. REP. No. 94-473, 94th Cong., 1st Sess. 52 (1975) (literary works may be embodied on computer punch cards).

[192] 17 U.S.C. §101 (1980): "A 'computer program' is a set of statements or instructions to be used directly or indirectly in a computer program in order to bring about a certain result." Added by Act of December 12, 1980, Pub. L. No. 96-517, §10(b), 94 Stat. 3028. See also H.R. REP. No. 96-1307, Part 1, 96th Cong., 2d Sess. 23–24 (1980); *Industrial Innovation and Patent and Copyright Law Amendments: Hearings on H.R. 6033 et al. Before the Subcomm. on Courts, Civil Liberties, and the Administration of Justice of the House Judiciary Comm.*, 96th Cong., 2d Sess. 645, 700 (1980).

[193] 17 U.S.C. §117 (1980). See discussion of this provision in text at notes 88–105 in Chapter 7.

CONTU's recommendations were not, however, the result of a unanimous opinion among its members that all computer programs were (or should be) copyrightable. The principal dissenting voice was that of CONTU Commissioner John Hersey, who, while agreeing that the source code[194] form of applications programs[195] was a protectible form of literary work, vigorously opposed protection for the object code[196] (machine-readable form) of all programs.[197] Congress did not address these issues in the 1980 amendments.[198] When coupled with the Copyright Office's decision to register object code (but not source code) deposits only under its "rule of doubt,"[199] uncertainties were created about the protectibility of certain classes of computer programs. These uncertainties have resulted in considerable litigation in recent years over issues such as whether human-to-human communication is a prerequisite for copyright protection, whether protection for computer programs is lost once they are embodied in a "read-only-memory" computer chip (on the ground that the program thereby became a nonprotectible utilitarian article), and whether operating system programs are utilitarian articles. Little purpose would be served in repeating these arguments or their rejection by the courts, which have found that it was Congress' intent to extend copyright protection to all forms of computer programs.[200] Individ-

---

[194]COMPENDIUM II OF COPYRIGHT OFFICE PRACTICES §321.01 defines source code as "the computer program code as the programmer writes it, using a particular programming language, such as, BASIC, COBOL, or FORTRAN."

[195]Applications programs, as distinguished from systems or operating programs (viz., those that control the internal workings of the computer), are designed to perform specific types of programs, e.g., word processing.

[196]COMPENDIUM II OF COPYRIGHT OFFICE PRACTICES §321.02 defines object code as "the representation of the program in machine language (*e.g.*, binary coding using letters and numbers or hexidecimal coding using 0 to 7) which the computer executes." A program in source code must be changed into object code before a computer can execute it. The question of whether the source code and object code represent a single work has yet to be definitively resolved. The Copyright Office considers them "two representations of the same work," and states that "[f]or registration purposes, the claim is in the *computer program* rather than any particular representation of the program. Thus separate registrations are not appropriate for the source code and object code representation of the same computer program." COMPENDIUM II OF COPYRIGHT OFFICE PRACTICES §321.03. See also *GCA Corp. v. Chance*, 217 U.S.P.Q. 718, 720 (N.D. Cal. 1982) ("[b]ecause the object code is the encryption of the source code, the two are treated as one work; therefore, copyright of the source code protects the object code as well").

[197]See CONTU FINAL REPORT, *supra* note 190, at 27–37.

[198]See note 192, *supra.*

[199]Unlike the application of the rule of doubt used in 1964, which concerned the copyrightability of computer programs *per se*, the Copyright Office has made it clear that "the doubt in this instance does not concern the copyrightability of computer programs in general," but is occasioned solely "[b]ecause object code is basically unintelligible to copyright examiners, [and thus] it is not possible to examine the deposit to determine the presence of copyrightable authorship." COMPENDIUM II OF COPYRIGHT OFFICE PRACTICES §324.04. See also *Apple Computer, Inc. v. Franklin Computer Corp.*, 714 F.2d 1240, 1255 n. 9, 219 U.S.P.Q. 113, 126 n. 9 (3d Cir. 1983). Nevertheless, as regards specific programs, the effect of a rule-of-doubt registration is unclear, and it is possible that the courts will refuse to accord to such certificates of registration the prima facie status ordinarily provided for in §410(c). See, e.g., *In Re Successor in Interest to Walter Andersen*, 743 F.2d 1578, 223 U.S.P.Q. 378 (Ct. App. Fed. Cir. 1984) (holding that the presumption of patent validity under 35 U.S.C. §282 does not apply where the patent issued under a rule of doubt).

Helpful examples of copyrightable and uncopyrightable elements for registration purposes are detailed in COMPENDIUM II OF COPYRIGHT OFFICE PRACTICES §325.02(a)–(c).

[200]See, e.g., *Whelan Associates, Inc. v. Jaslow Dental Laboratory*, 609 F. Supp. 1307, 225 U.S.P.Q. 156 (E.D. Pa. 1985); *SAS Institute, Inc. v. S & H Computer Systems, Inc.*, 605 F. Supp. 816, 225 U.S.P.Q. 916 (M.D. Tenn. 1985); *Apple Computer, Inc. v. Formula Int'l, Inc.*, 725 F.2d 521, 221 U.S.P.Q. 762 (9th Cir. 1984); *Apple Computer, Inc. v. Franklin Computer*

ual programs, of course, must still meet the basic requirements of originality[201] and fixation.[202]

It is expected that litigation over computer programs will now shift away from the question of categorical copyrightability and will instead be concerned with discovering the protectible elements in individual programs (e.g., whether particular routines, subroutines, or other component parts are "ideas," scènes à faire, or expression.) The courts will thus be asked to undertake difficult tasks with respect to determining what is (unprotectible) idea and what is (protectible) expression,[203] and how to adapt the basic infringement concept of "substantial similarity" to works whose expressive content is not readily perceptible to lay persons and about which experts will no doubt differ. A related question arises with respect to determining the necessary amount or type of adaptation sufficient to make a computer program based on a preexisting work eligible for protection as a "derivative work."[204] The general principles concerning derivative works were reviewed on pp. 24–28, *supra.* The Copyright Office *Compendium II of Office Practices* contains the following discussion on this question:

> "*Derivative computer programs.* A derivative computer program is one that is based on or incorporates material from a previously published or registered or public domain program that has been revised, augmented, abridged, or otherwise modified so that the modifications, as a whole, represent an original work of authorship.
>
> "*Registrability of a derivative computer program.* Registration for a derivative computer program covers only the additions, changes, or other new material appearing in the program for the first time. Therefore, the new material itself must be original and represent copyrightable author-

---

*Corp.,* 714 F.2d 1240, 219 U.S.P.Q. 113 (3d Cir. 1983); *Hubco Data Products Corp. v. Management Assistance, Inc.,* 219 U.S.P.Q. 450 (D. Idaho 1983); *Midway Mfg. Co. v. Strohon,* 564 F. Supp. 741, 219 U.S.P.Q. 42 (N.D. Ill. 1983); *Midway Mfg. Co. v. Artic Int'l, Inc.,* 704 F.2d 1009, 218 U.S.P.Q. 791 (7th Cir.), *cert. denied,* 464 U.S. 823, 220 U.S.P.Q. 480 (1983); *Tandy Corp. v. Personal Micro Computers,* 524 F. Supp. 171, 214 U.S.P.Q. 178 (N.D. Cal. 1981). The Supreme Court has not, however, spoken on these issues, and thus it is possible that the broad pronouncements in some of these opinions may be subsequently curtailed.

[201]17 U.S.C. §102(a) (1978). See also Contu Final Report, *supra* note 190, at 20, which states that a program "consisting of a few obvious steps could not be a subject of copyright."

[202]See, e.g., H.R. Rep. No. 94-1476, 94th Cong., 2d Sess. 53 (1976): "[T]he definition of 'fixation' [sic] would exclude from the concept purely evanescent or transient reproductions such as those projected briefly on a screen, shown electronically on a television or other cathode ray tube, or captured momentarily in the 'memory' of a computer." It should also be noted that once a computer program has been "fixed," infringement of the §106(1) right to reproduce the work in "copies" similarly depends upon a fixation in a "copy," but that the §106(4) and (5) rights to, respectively, perform and display the work publicly do *not* depend on a fixation in an (allegedly) infringing copy. See H.R. Rep. No. 94-1476 at 63; S. Rep. No. 94-473, 94th Cong., 1st Sess. 60 (1975) (performance may be by "any type of electronic retrieval system").

[203]See *Apple Computer, Inc. v. Franklin Computer Corp.,* 714 F.2d 1240, 1253, 219 U.S.P.Q. 113, 124 (3d Cir. 1983) (quoted in text at note 74, *supra*); *SAS Institute, Inc. v. S & H Computer Systems, Inc.,* 605 F. Supp. 816, 225 U.S.P.Q. 916 (M.D. Tenn. 1985); *Whelan Associates, Inc. v. Jaslow Dental Laboratory,* 609 F. Supp. 1307, 1320, 225 U.S.P.Q. 156, 166 (E.D. Pa. 1985): "The expression of the idea embodied in a computer program is protected by the copyright laws even though it must be altered and refined to be made adaptable to different types of computers that have different methods of responding to common controls and therefore require different source codes." Cf. *Fishing Concepts, Inc. v. Ross,* 226 U.S.P.Q. 692, 695–696 (D. Minn. 1985) (defendant's program contained a sufficient number of differences from plaintiff's to be held noninfringing).

[204]See *SAS Institute, Inc. v. S & H Computer Systems, Inc.,* 605 F. Supp. 816, 225 U.S.P.Q. 916 (M.D. Tenn. 1985) (copyright in program based on public domain program sustained).

ship. Where only a few minor revisions or additions have been made, or where those that were made are of a rote nature predetermined by the functional considerations of the hardware, registration for the new material is not possible.

"Examples:

"1)   A derivative program would be registrable where a substantial new program code has been added to a previously published program to enable it to accomplish additional functions.

"2)   A student-programmer translates a previously published program from COBOL to FORTRAN [both are source-code programming languages]. The resulting translation would represent a copyrightable derivative work.

"3)   A previously published program is adapted to run on a different model or brand of computer. The Office will question the nature and extent of the adaptation to determine registrability. If the changes were functionally predetermined, registration will be refused.

"4)   An applicant files two applications for the same program: one specifically for the source code and the other for the object code. Since the object code version does not contain copyrightable differences, there is no basis for a separate registration for the object code. The Office will communicate with the applicant suggesting single registration for the computer programs."[205]

*Compilations and Data Bases.* Computer data bases were expressly mentioned as protectible literary works in the 1976 House Report[206] and in the CONTU Final Report,[207] and should generally be regarded as "compilations,"[208] although the difference between such a data base and a "computer program" becomes difficult if not impossible to discern when both are written in hexidecimalic code. Issues with respect to data bases have tended to focus not on their protectibility but on their appropriation.[209] Owing, however, to the current conceptual confusion over the proper theoretical basis for protecting conventional compilations, and the occasional (but unfortunate) mixing of the separate issues of protectibility and infringement, it is likely that future disputes over electronic data bases will be subject to the same uncertainties as now face their conventional counterparts.

The term "compilation" is defined in Section 101 of the Act as

"a work formed by the collection and assembling of preexisting materials or of data that are selected, coordinated, or arranged in such a way that the resulting work as a whole constitutes an original work of authorship. The term 'compilation' includes collective works."

---

[205]COMPENDIUM II OF COPYRIGHT OFFICE PRACTICES §323.

[206]H.R. REP. No. 94-1476 at 54.

[207]CONTU FINAL REPORT, *supra* note 190, at 38–43.

[208]17 U.S.C. §103 (1978). See also *ibid.*, definition of "compilation."

[209]See, e.g., *Rand McNally & Co. v. Fleet Mgt. Systems,* 591 F. Supp. 726, 221 U.S.P.Q. 827 (N.D. Ill. 1983); 600 F. Supp. 933, 223 U.S.P.Q. 1200 (N.D. Ill. 1984); 224 U.S.P.Q. 246 (N.D. Ill. 1984); *National Business Lists, Inc. v. Dun & Bradstreet, Inc.,* 552 F. Supp. 89, 215 U.S.P.Q. 595 (N.D. Ill. 1982); *West Pub. Co. v. Mead Data Central, Inc.,* 616 F. Supp. 1571, 227 U.S.P.Q. 631 (D. Minn. 1985). See also *Black's Guide, Inc. v. Real Estate Communications, Inc.,* No. CV 84-3256 (C.D. Cal. filed June 29, 1984).

Although collective works are thus subsumed within the larger genus of compilations, there is an important distinction between the two. Collective works are comprised of materials that are (or were capable of being) independently protected,[210] e.g., an anthology of poetry, a law review issue, or even a broadcast day;[211] whereas compilations in the noncollective work sense are works formed by the collection and assembling of nonprotectible material.

The basis of protectibility of compilations occasionally has been misconstrued by a disjunctive reading of the various clauses of the statutory definition. Those clauses are italicized below:

"A 'compilation' is a work formed by the collection and assembling of preexisting materials or of data *that* are selected, coordinated, or arranged in such a way *that* the resulting work as a whole constitutes an original work of authorship."[212]

---

[210]See 17 U.S.C. §101 (1978) (definition of "collective work"). Collective works do not include, however, periodicals consisting of a single contribution, "a composition consisting of words and music, a work published with illustrations or front matter, or three one-act plays, where relatively few separate elements have been brought together." H.R. REP. No. 94-1476, 94th Cong., 2d Sess. 122 (1976); S. REP. No. 94-473, 94th Cong., 1st Sess. 105 (1975). Based on this legislative history, the Copyright Office has created what may be termed the "rule of four": "Any compilation consisting of less than four selections is considered to lack original authorship." COMPENDIUM II OF COPYRIGHT OFFICE PRACTICES §307.01. See also *id.* at §625.

[211] *National Ass'n of Broadcasters v. Copyright Royalty Tribunal*, 675 F.2d 367, 377–378, 214 U.S.P.Q. 161, 168–169 (D.C. Cir. 1982); 772 F.2d 922, 931, 227 U.S.P.Q. 203, 208 (D.C. Cir. 1985). See also *Apple Barrel Prods., Inc. v. Beard*, 730 F.2d 384, 222 U.S.P.Q. 956 (5th Cir. 1984).

[212]17 U.S.C. §101 (1978) (definition of "compilation").
A most extreme misreading of this provision occurred in *West Pub. Co. v. Mead Data Central, Inc.*, 616 F. Supp. 1571, 227 U.S.P.Q. 631 (D. Minn. 1985), where the court issued a preliminary injunction prohibiting defendant from inserting in its LEXIS-computerized legal research system "jump cites" to plaintiff's legal reporters (e.g., Supreme Court Reporter, Federal Supplement). Contrary to this decision, there is no copyrightable interest in the pagination of plaintiff's reporters. The numbering of the pages is a purely mechanical process dictated entirely by the format. There is no "collection and assembling of preexisting materials or data," and there is no selection, coordination, or arrangement of any such material.
In reaching the opposite result, the court looked to the collection and selection of the legal opinions reported in plaintiff's works and to their arrangement into discrete volumes by subject matter. While such activity is sufficient to support a compilation copyright, this was *not* the activity plaintiff sought to protect. Rather, plaintiff claimed an interest in the mechanical process of assigning page numbers to the compilation *after* it was created. The court's error was undoubtedly influenced by its (unsubstantiated) finding that the taking of page numbers from a collection of cases would absolutely do away with the underlying work. Even if true, this fact is entirely irrelevant to the issue of copyrightability. (It would be highly relevant to a fair use defense, though.) As one commentator accurately remarked: "A work is either copyrightable or not: it does not become copyrightable simply because it has been substantially copied." Ginsburg, *Fact Works Revisited*, NEW YORK L.J., July 19, 1984, p. 22, col. 2.
The court stated a second ground for protection, self-indexing: "By assembling the cases as they have been arranged in sequenced volumes, a case can be indexed by following its name with a volume number, series designation, and page numbers." 616 F. Supp. at 1578, 227 U.S.P.Q. at 634. There are at least three errors in this holding. First, the court again relies on the selection of cases and not the pagination in establishing originality for the pagination. Second, the "work" referred to by the court is the full citation to a judicial opinion, e.g., 723 F.2d 195 (2d Cir. 1983), and not the jump cites to the pages within the opinion—the element plaintiff sought to prohibit defendant from copying. (It should be noted, moreover, that plaintiff conceded it was fair use to use the full citation, 616 F. Supp. at 1579, 227 U.S.P.Q. at 635. Third, the indexing function utilized by the court to support plaintiff's originality is done by *third parties*, e.g., Shepard's Citations. Plaintiff may not use the efforts of third parties compiling wholly different works to support its copyright.
While it is true that a certificate of registration covers all *copyrightable* components of the work, COMPENDIUM II OF COPYRIGHT OFFICE PRACTICES §108.04, the pagination of West's reporters is not a copyrightable component of West's works, nor did it so claim in its applications for registration.
In its understandable concern over the adverse effects of defendant's project on the plain-

There are thus three necessary *conjunctive* elements—(1) a collection and assembling of preexisting materials or data (2) that are then selected, coordinated, or arranged (3) into a work which by virtue of that selection, coordination, or arrangement may be said to be as a whole an "original work of authorship." This definition encompasses two discrete types of compilation—a compilation that consists of previously uncollected and unarranged data, and a compilation that consists of data previously collected and arranged but which involves a reselection and/or rearrangement of those data in a manner which, when considered as a whole, results in a substantially different reselection and/or rearrangement.

The definition does not, however, encompass the mere collecting and assembling of data no matter how valuable the data may be.[213] It should further be noted that the extending of copyright protection to labor *qua* labor would violate the Constitution, which declares that only "writings" may be protected.[214]

---

tiff, the court granted protection to noncopyrightable material. However, as this author has previously noted:

> "There is no violation of the Copyright Act if a second work of authorship not substantially similar to the original deprives the copyright owner of his economic incentive, nor may the courts constitutionally seek to protect that incentive under the Copyright Act under such circumstances, regardless of whether this results in the appropriation of the 'fruits of another's labor.'"

Patry, *Copyright in Collections of Facts: A Reply*, 6 J. Comm. and the Law 11, 31 (1984).

[213]Note §103(b), which states that copyright in a compilation does not give the compiler any exclusive rights in the preexisting material (absent ownership thereof); H.R. Rep. No. 94-1476, 94th Cong., 2d Sess. 57–58 (1976). Compendium II of Copyright Office Practices §204.04 contains further discussion on this point, stating that where a compilation or derivative work is based on an unauthorized use of a preexisting work: (1) "the new material may be subject to copyright protection only to the extent that it can be separated from the preexisting work"; (2) "[w]here the new matter * * * is inextricably integrated with the preexisting work * * * registration for the new matter cannot be made"; (3) "[w]here the new matter * * * is capable of existing separately, registration may be possible, even though the use may be an infringement of the copyright in the preexisting work." See also *id.* at §305.08(b), *Cooling Systems & Flexibles, Inc. v. Stuart Radiator, Inc.*, 777 F.2d 485, 490, 228 U.S.P.Q. 275, 279 (9th Cir. 1985), and *Eden Toys, Inc. v. Floralee Undergarment Co.*, 697 F.2d 27, 34 n. 6, 217 U.S.P.Q. 201, 206 n. 6 (2d Cir. 1982), and the text at note 52, *supra*.

For a more detailed discussion of the proper scope of protection for factual works, including compilations, see Patry, *Copyright in Collections of Facts: A Reply*, 6 J. Comm. and the Law 11 (1984). In *Production Contractors, Inc. v. WGN Continental Broadcasting Co.*, 622 F. Supp. 1500, 1503, 228 U.S.P.Q. 604, 605–606 (N.D. Ill. 1985), the manner of arranging the flow of a Christmas parade, the floats themselves, and certain "special items of interest developed for the parade" were rejected as forming a copyrightable compilation, the court concluding that "the idea of a Christmas parade is a common one, relatively simple and contains no creative authorship."

[214]Art. I §8, cl. 8. See also *The Trademark Cases*, 100 U.S. 82, 94 (1879) (the term "writings" includes works only "such as are original and founded on the creative powers of the mind. The writings which are protected are the fruits of intellectual labor, embodied in the form of books, prints, engravings and the like"). Compare *Rockford Map Pub., Inc. v. Directory Serv. Co. of Colorado, Inc.*, 768 F.2d 145, 148, 226 U.S.P.Q. 1025, 1027 (7th Cir. 1985) (rejecting argument that "industriousness" is a requirement of copyright and holding that "[t]he copyright laws protect the work, not the amount of effort expended"); *Financial Information, Inc. v. Moody's Investors Serv., Inc.*, 751 F.2d 501, 224 U.S.P.Q. 632 (2d Cir. 1984); *Eckes v. Card Prices Update*, 736 F.2d 859, 222 U.S.P.Q. 762 (2d Cir. 1984), with *Rand McNally & Co. v. Fleet Mgt. Systems, Inc.*, 591 F. Supp. 726, 221 U.S.P.Q. 827 (N.D. Ill. 1983); 600 F. Supp. 933, 223 U.S.P.Q. 1200 (N.D. Ill. 1984); *National Business Lists, Inc. v. Dun & Bradstreet, Inc.*, 552 F. Supp. 89, 215 U.S.P.Q. 595 (N.D. Ill. 1982).

## Musical Works, Including Any Accompanying Words

The language of Section 102(a)(2) codifies prior practice whereby musical compositions under Section 5(e) of the 1909 law included not only instrumental pieces but also songs consisting of words with musical accompaniment. Both elements were protected under one copyright, for Section 3 of the 1909 law provided that the copyright "shall protect all the copyrightable component parts of the work copyrighted," a provision which was merely declaratory of a time-honored rule of construction.[215] It was held in one case, however, that the copyright of a song secured under the pre-1909 law did not protect the words unless they were separately copyrighted as a book.[216] The court here misconstrued a rule of the Copyright Office which was only to the effect that the words of a song published in the first instance without musical accompaniment would be classified as a book. Musical selections and compilations published in book form were registrable in the music category.

The 1909 Act was interpreted as requiring a system of notation capable of being read by a human being. The pertinent Copyright Office regulations[217] considered a phonograph record insufficient as a statutory, as opposed to a constitutional, "writing" for purposes of a deposit covering the recorded musical or other composition. (This is to be distinguished from the recorded *performance*, denominated as a "sound recording.") Thus, the laborious requirement of legibly notating music persisted and frustrated statutory protection for certain forms of electronic music.

This has been changed by the 1976 Act because it is clear that a musical work embodied in a phonograph or other audio recording is "fixed in a tangible medium of expression" for the purpose of enjoying statutory protection. The statute left open the important question of whether such a recording is a proper form of *deposit* for the musical composition (see Section 408(b)(2) and Sections 407(a)(1) and (2)), but it has been made proper under certain circumstances by Copyright Office regulations issued pursuant to Section 408(c), e.g., if a phonorecord is the only form of fixation.[218]

Another change wrought by the 1976 Act is that of registration of music first published in a soundtrack. Music "published" in such a form prior to 1978 could be registered apart from the motion picture as a whole only if the motion picture contained a separate copyright notice for the music. This is no longer the case under the 1976 Act.

As with other works of authorship, there are no quantitative or qualitative standards of originality, and as with all subject matter, the *de minimis* rule applies. Thus, musical compositions consisting of

---

[215]*Harper v. Donohue*, 144 F. 491 (C.C.N.D. Ill. 1905); *Ford v. Blaney*, 148 F. 642 (C.C.S.D.N.Y. 1906).
[216]*M. Witmark & Sons v. Standard Music Co.*, 221 F. 376 (3d Cir. 1915).
[217]37 C.F.R. §202.8(b) (1973 *revoked* Jan. 1, 1978).
[218]See 43 Fed. Reg. 766 (Jan. 4, 1978); 37 C.F.R. §202.20(c)(1).

only a few musical notes such as "mi do re so, so re mi do," diatonic or chromatic scales,[219] or common chord progressions are not protectible. It should also be noted that, while an arrangement of preexisting works may be copyrightable as a derivative work, arrangements embodied in a sound recording made pursuant to the compulsory license provisions of Section 115 are not subject to protection without the consent of the copyright owner.[220]

### Dramatic Works, Including Any Accompanying Music

This language replaces the rather grandiose "dramatic or dramatico-musical compositions" of Section 5(d) of the 1909 law.[221] The categorization of a work as dramatic or nondramatic has both administrative and substantive importance. Applications for registration of dramatic works are submitted on Form PA, while nondramatic literary works not intended for performance are submitted on Form TX.[222] Examples of dramatic works are operas, choral works, song lyrics, plays prepared for stage presentation, radio, television, or motion pictures, and even poems containing directions for acting out the story.[223] Dialogue *per se* is not indispensable, for as Justice Holmes wrote in the celebrated "Ben Hur" case, *Kalem v. Harper Bros.*, "[a]ction can tell a story, display all the most vivid relations between men, and depict every kind of human emotion, without the aid of a word."[224]

There is, however, no generally accepted definition of a "dramatic work." The Copyright Office (for internal administrative purposes) has defined such a work as

"one that portrays a story by means of dialog or acting and [that] is intended to be performed. It gives directions for performance or actually

---

[219]But cf. COMPENDIUM II OF COPYRIGHT OFFICE PRACTICES §404.05: "A musical composition based on a tone row [e.g., as in the music of the "Second Viennese School"], or a quarter-tone scale * * * may be accepted for registration."

[220]See 17 U.S.C. §115(a)(2) (1978).

[221]The only holdover of this prior category is found in §110(3) of the 1976 Act, which exempts, inter alia, the performance of a "dramatico-musical work of a religious nature" in the course of services at a place of worship or other religious assembly.

[222]Section 408(c) provides that the Register of Copyrights may specify administrative classes into which works are placed for purposes of deposit and registration. However, this classification "has no significance with respect to the subject matter of copyright or the exclusive rights provided" in the Act.

[223]COMPENDIUM II OF COPYRIGHT OFFICE PRACTICES §432.02. Compare *Robert Stigwood Group Ltd. v. Sperber*, 457 F.2d 50, 173 U.S.P.Q. 258 (2d Cir. 1972) (sequential singing of all songs from *Jesus Christ Superstar* held dramatic performance since music when played in sequence told entire story), with *Corcoran v. Montgomery Ward & Co.*, 121 F.2d 572, 50 U.S.P.Q. 274 (9th Cir.), *cert. denied*, 314 U.S. 687, 51 U.S.P.Q. 546 (1941) (narrative poem possessing "action in plenty" but no dialogue or perceptible plot held not a "dramatic composition"). See also *Gershwin v. Whole Thing Co.*, 208 U.S.P.Q. 557, 560 (C.D. Cal. 1980).

[224]222 U.S. 55, 61 (1911). Cf. COMPENDIUM II OF COPYRIGHT OFFICE PRACTICES §432.05, which states that while a silent drama containing visual dramatic action or pantomime (e.g., in the Noh style) would be a "dramatic work," "a still tableau depicting a story incident does not meet this criterion." In *Frank Music Corp. v. Metro-Goldwyn-Mayer, Inc.*, 772 F.2d 505, 227 U.S.P.Q. 687 (9th Cir. 1985), the court of appeals refused to endorse a district court finding that performance in a musical revue of songs by singers dressed in costumes and using the locale, settings, scenery, and props of the musical motion picture *Kismet* in order to create the movie's atmosphere was "non-dramatic."

represents all or a substantial portion of the action as actually occurring, rather than merely being narrated or described."[225]

The substantive importance of a work being dramatic or nondramatic is embodied in numerous provisions of the Act:

1. Exemptions for performance or display of works by nonprofit or governmental entities is limited in many cases to nondramatic literary and nondramatic musical works (see §§110(2), (3), (4), (6)–(10));
2. The ephemeral recording right of Section 112(c) applies only to nondramatic musical works of a religious nature;
3. The compulsory license for the making of sound recordings under Section 115 pertains only to nondramatic musical works;
4. The exemption from the public performance right of Section 106(4) for jukeboxes covers only nondramatic musical compositions.
5. The compulsory license in Section 118(d) for performance or display of works by public broadcasting entities applies only to published nondramatic musical works (as well as to published pictorial, graphic, and sculptural works);
6. Remission of statutory damages for infringement by public broadcasting entities believing their use was fair use is limited to cases involving published nondramatic literary works (§504(c)(2)(ii));
7. The manufacturing clause applies only to works consisting preponderantly of nondramatic literary material in the English language (§601(a)); and
8. The Register of Copyrights is permitted to enter into voluntary licensing arrangements for reproduction of nondramatic literary works for use by the blind and physically handicapped (§710).

The distinction between dramatic and nondramatic works also has a practical side, performing rights societies such as ASCAP, BMI, and the Harry Fox Agency being authorized to license nondramatic works only. Dramatic rights are generally licensed directly by the copyright owner.

### Pantomimes and Choreographic Works

Pantomimes and choreographic works are enumerated specifically for the first time in the 1976 Act, though their protection had been suggested by the "Ben Hur" case.[226] Insofar as they told a story, described a character, or depicted an emotion, they were protected under the 1909 law as dramatic compositions under Section 5(d) once their fixation in notation became feasible. Such a requirement of "dramatic" content is no longer necessary.[227]

Choreography is said to represent "a related series of dance movements and patterns organized into a coherent whole."[228] Exam-

---

[225]COMPENDIUM II OF COPYRIGHT OFFICE PRACTICES §431.

[226]*Kalem v. Harper Bros.*, 222 U.S. 55 (1911).

[227]COMPENDIUM II OF COPYRIGHT OFFICE PRACTICES §451.01.

[228]*Id.* at §453.03(a). See also *id.* at §451.01. In the only known decision involving infringement of a choreographic work, *Horgan v. MacMillan, Inc.*, 621 F. Supp. 1169, 227 U.S.P.Q. 975 (S.D.N.Y. 1985), the court held that "choreography has to do with the flow of the steps in a ballet," and that defendant's book, which contained numerous photographs of a production of the ballet did not infringe plaintiff's work because "though they * * * catch dancers in various attitudes at specific instants of time; they do not, nor do they intend to, take or use the underlying choreography. The staged performance could not be recreated from them." *Id.* at 1170, 227 U.S.P.Q. at 976. On appeal, the Second Circuit reversed and remanded, holding that "the stan-

ples of nonprotectible choreography include jumping jacks and walking, social, and folk dance steps. Such elements may, however, be incorporated into an otherwise registrable work. Fixation is satisfied by embodiment in standard choreographic notational systems or narrative descriptions specific enough to indicate the detailed movements of the dancers, or by capture on film.

Pantomime has been described as "the art of imitating or acting out situations, characters, or some other events with gestures and body movement,"[229] and as differing from choreography by having fewer dance movements and greater gesturing and facial expression and by being more "representational" and synchronized.[230] As with choreography, pantomimes must contain at least a minimum of action. Stock gestures and stylized movements (e.g., imitating a mechanical doll) are not protectible. Fixation may be accomplished in a manner similar to that for choreographic works.

### Pictorial, Graphic, and Sculptural Works

Protection for the artist followed closely the grant to literary authors and mapmakers in 1790. In 1802, prints, etchings, cuts, and engravings were gathered under the statutory cloak. In 1870, three-dimensional works were added within the comprehensive grouping "painting, drawing, chromo, statue, statuary, and * * * models or designs intended to be perfected as works of the fine arts." This connection with the fine arts was reinforced four years later when Congress defined the "engraving," "cut," and "print" subject to protection as "pictorial illustrations or works connected with the fine arts."

These detailed specifications were, of course, replaced in 1909 by the broad term "writings" together with specific classifications including maps (§5(f)); scientific and technical drawings (§5(i)); photographs (§5(j)); and prints and labels (§5(k)); as well as the catchall category of "works of art" (§5(g)) and the more troublesome (due to their embodiment in useful articles) "reproductions of a work of art" (§5(h)). All these categories have now been combined into Section 102(a)(5)—"pictorial, graphic, and sculptural works," which are defined as including

> "two-dimensional and three-dimensional works of fine, graphic, and applied art, photographs, prints and art reproductions, maps, globes, charts, technical drawings, diagrams, and models. Such works shall include works of artistic craftsmanship insofar as their form but not their mechanical or utilitarian craftsmanship are concerned; the design of a useful article, as defined in this section shall be considered a pictorial, graphic, or sculptural work only if, and only to the extent that, such de-

---

dard for determining infringement is not whether the original could be recreated from the allegedly infringing copy, but whether the latter is 'substantially similar.' " 789 F.2d 157, ____, 229 U.S.P.Q. 684, 688 (2d Cir. 1986).

[229]COMPENDIUM II OF COPYRIGHT OFFICE PRACTICES at §460.01
[230]*Id.* at §462.

sign incorporates pictorial, graphic, or sculptural features that can be identified separately from, and are capable of existing independently of, the utilitarian aspects of the article."[231]

The scope of protection for pictorial, graphic, and sculptural works in relation to useful articles is further described in Section 113:

"(a) Subject to the provisions of subsections (b) and (c) of this section, the exclusive right to reproduce a copyrighted pictorial, graphic, or sculptural work in copies under section 106 includes the right to reproduce the work in or on any kind of article, whether useful or otherwise.

"(b) This title does not afford, to the owner of copyright in a work that portrays a useful article as such, any greater or lesser rights with respect to the making, distribution, or display of the useful article so portrayed than those afforded to such works under the law, whether title 17 or the common law or statutes of a State, in effect on December 31, 1977, as held applicable and construed by a court in an action brought under this title.

"(c) In the case of a work lawfully reproduced in useful articles that have been offered for sale or other distribution to the public, copyright does not include any right to prevent the making, distribution, or display of pictures or photographs of such articles in connection with advertisements or commentaries related to the distribution or display of such articles, or in connection with news reports."

Issues concerning pictorial, graphic, and sculptural works embodied in useful articles were surveyed on pp. 35–45, *supra*, and thus will not be discussed again here. A few words are in order regarding other types of material embraced within the category of pictorial, graphic, and sculptural works.

*Photographs.* Photographs were first included as copyrightable subject matter in 1865, shortly after the invention of modern photography, and the Supreme Court ruled in *Burrow-Giles Lithographic Co. v. Sarony*[232] that at least some photographs were copyrightable insofar as they embodied artistic conception on the part of the photographer; but the Court queried whether copyright could be had for "the mere mechanical reproduction of the physical features or outlines of some object, animate or inanimate, involving no originality of thought."

In *Pagano v. Bessler*,[233] the photograph of a public building was held copyrightable, the artistic conception of the photographer being found in his determining just when to take the photograph so as to bring out the proper setting with reference to light, shade, etc. Shortly thereafter, Judge Learned Hand declared in *Jewelers' Circular Pub. Co. v. Keystone Pub. Co.* that

"no photograph, however simple, can be unaffected by the personal influence of the author, and no two will be absolutely alike. Moreover, this

---

[231]17 U.S.C. §101 (1978) (definition of "pictorial, graphic and sculptural works"). See also *ibid.* (definition of "useful article") and discussion in H.R. Rep. No. 94-1476, 94th Cong., 2d Sess. 54 (1976); S. Rep. No. 94-473, 94th Cong., 1st Sess. 52-53 (1975), and note 97, *supra*.
[232]111 U.S. 53 (1884).
[233]234 F.2d 963 (S.D.N.Y. 1916).

seems to me quite beside the point, because under section 5(j) [of the
1909 Act] photographs are protected without regard to the degree of
'personality' which enters into them."[234]

Of course, anyone else would be at liberty to take a picture, for example, of the same building in the *Pagano* case and get practically
the same result, without thereby infringing the rights of the first
photographer.[235]

*Maps.* Maps have been enumerated as protectible subject matter since the original Copyright Act of 1790. Of course, certain elements of a map, such as latitudes and longitudes, are usually produced by copying from what has long been established and hence are
said to be in the public domain.[236] The same is true of the general outline of the United States or state boundaries.[237] Nor are arbitrary
signs, coloring, symbols, or keys used in delineating boundaries or
locations copyrightable.[238]

While the decisions are uniform in stating that one may copyright a map produced by an independent survey of an area, there is a
split in the circuits in cases where the cartographer has synthesized,
into a new combination, elements from existing public domain maps.
In *Amsterdam v. Triangle Publications*[239] the Third Circuit answered
this question in the negative, requiring that the cartographer obtain
at least some of the elements by the "sweat of his brow." In *United
States v. Hamilton*, the Ninth Circuit declined to follow the *Amsterdam* court, declaring that

"[e]xpression in cartography is not so different from other artistic forms
seeking to touch upon external realities that unique rules are needed to
judge whether the authorship is original. * * * We rule that elements of
compilation which amount to more than a matter of trivial selection
may, either alone or when taken into consideration with direct observation, support a finding that a map is sufficiently original to merit copyright protection."[240]

*Hamilton* would appear to follow literally the statutory definition of a
"compilation" and therefore be the correct statement of the law.

---

[234]274 F. 932 (S.D.N.Y. 1921). Accord *Time, Inc. v. Bernard Geis Associates*, 293 F. Supp.
130, 159 U.S.P.Q. 663 (S.D.N.Y. 1968). See also *Bi-Rite Enters., Inc. v. Dan Barrett, Inc.*, Copr.
L. Rep. ¶25,208 (N.D. Ill. 1978) (poster of television stars held copyrightable).

[235]But cf. *Gross v. Seligman*, 212 F. 930 (2d Cir. 1914). See also *Halbersham Plantation
Corp. v. Country Concepts*, 209 U.S.P.Q. 711 (N.D. Ga. 1980) (line drawings of copyrighted furniture photographs).

[236]*Sawyer v. Crowell Pub. Co.*, 46 F. Supp. 471, 54 U.S.P.Q. 225 (S.D.N.Y. 1942), *aff'd*, 142
F.2d 497, 61 U.S.P.Q. 389 (2d Cir.), *cert. denied*, 323 U.S. 735, 63 U.S.P.Q. 359 (1944).

[237]*United States v. Hamilton*, 583 F.2d 448, 200 U.S.P.Q. 14 (9th Cir. 1978).

[238]*Ibid*; *Perris v. Hexamer*, 99 U.S. (9 Otto) 674, 675–676 (1878).

[239]189 F.2d 104, 89 U.S.P.Q. 468 (3d Cir. 1951).

[240]583 F.2d 448, 451, 200 U.S.P.Q. 14, 16–17 (9th Cir. 1978). See also *Rockford Map Pub.,
Inc. v. Directory Serv. Co. of Colorado, Inc.*, 768 F.2d 145, 226 U.S.P.Q. 1025 (7th Cir. 1985)
(copyright in plat maps upheld; compilation of information on maps found to result in an "original" work of authorship notwithstanding small amount of work involved); *Del Madera Properties v. Rhodes and Gardner, Inc.*, 227 U.S.P.Q. 486 (N.D. Cal. 1985) (copyrightability of residential subdivision map sustained).

*Prints and Labels.* Section 5(k) of the 1909 law included prints or labels used for articles of merchandise. This class had a unique history. Registration of copyrights in such so-called "commercial prints and labels" was assigned to the Patent Office in 1874. At that time the Librarian of Congress had been successful in persuading Congress that it was neither practical nor appropriate for him to provide space for the growing accumulation of advertisements, cartons, and labels as part of the central copyright deposit system established in 1870. And, even though the grant of copyright to prints and labels under the 1874 Act was distinct from patent and trademark protection,[241] prints and labels continued to be deposited for copyright purposes in the Patent Office more than 30 years after the 1909 Copyright Act.

In 1940, the Copyright Office assumed jurisdiction over all prints and labels when these categories were assimilated into the classification scheme of Section 5 of the Copyright Act as subsection (k); this provision was amended to read "prints and pictorial illustrations including prints and labels used for articles of merchandise." The copyrightability of such labels has been upheld again in two recent decisions, *Carolina Enterprises, Inc. v. Coleco Industries, Inc.;*[242] *Chevron Chemical Co. v. Voluntary Purchasing Groups, Inc.*[243]

## Motion Pictures and Other Audiovisual Works

Neither motion pictures nor audiovisual works were among the enumerated categories of copyrightable works found in Section 5 of the 1909 Act. Prior to the Townsend Amendment of 1912,[244] which specifically listed motion pictures, such works were registered by the Copyright Office in Class (j) as photographs. After the amendment, motion pictures were covered under Class (l) as "motion picture photographs" or under Class (m) as "motion pictures other than photoplays," the latter category being for nondramatic pictures. Audiovi-

---

[241] *Higgins v. Keuffel*, 140 U.S. 428 (1891).

[242] 211 U.S.P.Q. 479 (D.N.J. 1981). The legislative reports accompanying the 1976 Act state:

"There is no intention whatever to narrow the scope of subject matter now characterized in section 5(k) [of the 1909 Act] as 'prints or labels used for articles of merchandise.' However, since this terminology suggests the material object in which a work is embodied rather than the work itself, the bill does not mention this category separately."

H.R. Rep. No. 94-1476, 94th Cong., 2d Sess. 54 (1976); S. Rep. No. 94-473, 94th Cong., 1st Sess. 53 (1975). But cf. 37 C.F.R. §202.10(c):

"A claim to copyright cannot be registered in a print or label consisting solely of trademark subject matter * * * [although the Copyright Office] will register a properly filed claim in a print or label that contains the requisite qualifications for copyright even though there is a trademark on it."

The validity of this registration was upheld in *Designpoint Indus., Ltd. v. Padosa America, Inc.*, 83 Civ. 9132 (S.D.N.Y. filed Nov. 2, 1984) (unpublished bench opinion, transcript at 154–155). See also *Clarke v. G. A. Kayser & Sons, Inc.*, 205 U.S.P.Q. 610, 612 (W.D. Pa. 1979) (drawing in patent application).

[243] 218 U.S.P.Q. 440 (N.D. Tex. 1982).

[244] Act of August 24, 1912, 37 Stat. 88.

sual works (including television films) were registered in the appropriate motion picture category.

The 1976 Act specifies "motion pictures and other audiovisual works" as a separate category of copyrightable work.[245] Motion pictures are thus treated as a type of audiovisual work. Audiovisual works are defined in Section 101 of the Act as

> "works that consist of a series of related images which are intrinsically intended to be shown by the use of machines or devices, such as projectors, viewers, or electronic equipment, together with accompanying sounds, if any, regardless of the nature of the material objects, such as films or tapes, in which the works are embodied."

Motion pictures are defined as "audiovisual works consisting of a series of related images which, when shown in succession, impart an impression of motion, together with accompanying sounds, if any,"[246] and thus, unlike the larger category of audiovisual work, must (as their very name indicates) impart an impression of motion. All audiovisual works consist of a "series of related images," though there is little in the legislative history discussing the concept. During floor debates before the House of Representatives in 1967, it was stated that

> "[a] series of related images includes any group of two or more images having some type of relationship in their subject matter which gives unity to the group as a whole. However, the fact that some or all of the individual images in the group would also constitute separate works does not prevent the group of images from being an audiovisual work."[247]

---

[245]17 U.S.C. §102(6) (1978). Holograms may be registered in this category, or as a pictorial, graphic, or sculptural work. See COMPENDIUM II OF COPYRIGHT OFFICE PRACTICES §§480.02, 508.

[246]17 U.S.C. §101 (1978) (definition of "motion pictures"). See also *ibid.* (definition of to "display" and to "perform").

The copyright status of telecasts of live events such as sports events and parades was clarified by reference to the definition of fixation:

"The bill seeks to resolve, through the definition of 'fixation' in section 101, the status of live broadcasts—sports, news coverage, live performances of music, etc.—that are reaching the public in unfixed form but that are simultaneously being recorded. When a football game is being covered by four television cameras, with a director guiding the activities of the four cameramen and choosing which of their electronic images are sent out to the public and in what order, there is little doubt that what the cameramen and the director are doing constitutes 'authorship.' The further question to be considered is whether there has been a fixation. If the images and sounds to be broadcast are first recorded (on a video tape, film, etc.) and then transmitted, the recorded work would be considered a 'motion picture' subject to statutory protection against unauthorized reproduction or retransmission of the broadcast. If the program content is transmitted live to the public while being recorded at the same time, the case would be treated the same; the copyright owner would not be forced to rely on common law rather than statutory rights in proceeding against an infringing user of the live broadcast.

"Thus, assuming it is copyrightable—as a 'motion picture' or 'sound recording,' for example—the content of a live transmission should be accorded statutory protection if it is being recorded simultaneously with its transmission."

H.R. REP. No. 94-1476, 94th Cong., 2d Sess. 52–53 (1976). See *Production Contractors, Inc. v. WGN Continental Broadcasting Co.*, 622 F. Supp. 1500, 228 U.S.P.Q. 604 (N.D. Ill. 1985) (parade); *National Football League v. McBee & Bruno's*, 228 U.S.P.Q. 11 (E.D. Mo. 1985); *ESPN, Inc. v. Edinburg Community Hotel, Inc.*, 623 F. Supp. 647 (S.D. Tex. 1985); *Baltimore Orioles, Inc. v. Major League Players Ass'n*, COPR. L. REP. ¶25,822 (N.D. Ill. 1985); *National Football League v. Cousin Hugo's*, 600 F. Supp. 84 (E.D. Mo. 1984); *National Football League v. American Embassy, Inc.*, No-83-0701 (S.D. Fla. filed March 25, 1983).

[247]113 CONG. REC. 8587 (1967) (remarks of Rep. Poff).

The question of what constitutes a series of related images has been twice addressed by the Seventh Circuit, once in a dispute over television program material encoded in the vertical blanking interval of the television signal, and again in a suit for infringement of an electronic audiovisual game. In the first case, *WGN Continental Broadcasting Co. v. United Video, Inc.*, the court found that the phrase "series of related images" should not "be interpreted to mean a rigid, predetermined sequence";[248] a position followed and amplified in the second case, *Midway Manufacturing Co. v. Artic International, Inc.*, which, echoing the 1967 House floor statement, construed the phrase as meaning "any set of images displayed as some kind of unit."[249]

Audiovisual works may, as stated in their definition, include accompanying sounds. These sounds need not be physically integrated with the "series of related images" in order to be considered accompanying sounds; e.g., a film strip with a separate audio cassette could be considered an "audiovisual work."[250] However, it is well to keep in mind that such a single work could not be registered as a sound recording accompanying a motion picture or other audiovisual work, since, as we shall see below, the definition of sound recordings expressly excludes such a possibility.

## Sound Recordings

This is one category of constitutionally copyrightable subject matter that was clearly not covered by the 1909 statute until an amendment in 1971,[251] which accorded protection to recordings "fixed, published and copyrighted on and after February 15, 1972." It cannot be emphasized too often that this class of works pertains solely to the recorded performance embodied in the recording and not to the underlying musical, dramatic, or other material being performed and recorded.

Sound recordings are defined in the 1976 Act as

"works that result from the fixation of a series of musical, spoken, or other sounds, but not including the sounds accompanying a motion picture or other audiovisual work, regardless of the nature of the material objects, such as disks, tapes, or other phonorecords in which they are embodied."[252]

---

[248]693 F.2d 622, 628, 216 U.S.P.Q. 97, 100 (7th Cir. 1982); 685 F.2d 218, 217 U.S.P.Q. 151 (7th Cir. 1982) (on petition for rehearing *en banc*).

[249]704 F.2d 1009, 1011, 218 U.S.P.Q. 791, 792 (7th Cir.), *cert. denied*, 464 U.S. 823, 220 U.S.P.Q. 480 (1983). For a discussion of the copyrightability of electronic audiovisual games, see Patry, *Electronic Audiovisual Games: Navigating the Maze of Copyright*, 31 J. COPR. SOC'Y 1 (1983).

[250]COMPENDIUM II OF COPYRIGHT OFFICE PRACTICES §473.

[251]Act of Oct. 15, 1971, Pub. L. No. 92-140, 85 Stat. 391. For a discussion of the special problems of national eligibility of sound recordings, see Chapter 10, p. 308. It should be noted that a growing number of countries, particularly those characterized as "developing countries," provide a more limited form of "neighboring rights" protection rather than copyright protection for sound recordings. This fact is perhaps partly attributable to the belief that neither the Universal Copyright Convention nor the Berne Convention for the Protection of Literary and Artistic Works requires the grant of copyright protection to sound recordings.

[252]17 U.S.C. §101 (1978).

Thus, sound recordings relate to purely aural works. They have a special form of notice (§402), and are subject to unique limitations on rights (§114(a)). A recent amendment, recognizing the harm to the market from unauthorized copies made from rented phonorecords, has generally removed them from the ambit of the so-called "first sale doctrine" (§109(a)). We shall return to the special treatment given sound recordings in Chapters 5 and 7.

# 3

# Duration of Copyright

The innovative single federal regime of automatic protection in the 1976 Act emerges from Chapter 3 of the Act, the provisions governing duration. This chapter opens with the key provision on coverage and exclusivity of rights under the statute and the corresponding preemption of equivalent state rights (§301). It then proceeds to establish formulas for computation of the terms of protection for works created on or after January 1, 1978 (§302), and for works which, on that date, were the subject of common law protection (§303), first-term statutory protection (§304(a)), or renewal-term statutory protection (§304(b)). Subsisting renewals are extended for up to 19 years and, as to such extended terms, the statute permits recapture of rights by authors and their statutory successors under a complex termination of transfers and licenses provision (§304(c)). Each of these provisions will now be examined in detail.

## Single Federal System—Preemption: §301

### Overview

Section 301(a) has been characterized as the "bedrock" of the 1976 Act. It reads as follows:

> "On and after January 1, 1978, all legal or equitable rights that are equivalent to any of the exclusive rights within the general scope of copyright as specified by section 106 in works of authorship that are fixed in a tangible medium of expression and come within the subject matter of copyright as specified by sections 102 and 103, whether created before or after that date and whether published or unpublished, are governed exclusively by this title. Thereafter, no person is entitled to any such right or equivalent right in any such work under the common law or statutes of any State."

Without doubt, there is no more significant (and probably no more troublesome) question underlying the Act than the preemptive effect of this provision. Basically, this question is: How much of the common law (or state statutory law), particularly that of unfair competition, is left standing or is permitted to develop by the new copyright law?

In the analysis of this question, several things at least are clear.

(1) The statute covers, as it constitutionally must, only works "fixed in a tangible medium of expression." This is clearly intended to be comprehensive and to cover not only things such as sound recordings, computer-readable material, and works fixed by any method "now known or later developed" but also works that fit within the general subject matter of copyright but which lack sufficient originality to qualify for protection.[1]

It has already been seen that the limitation of preemption to "subject matter of copyright as specified by sections 102 and 103" still covers a very broad area of material. Nevertheless, oral works such as improvised speeches, live jazz performances, and live demonstrations or displays by cathode rays are frequently never fixed in a tangible medium of expression. Accordingly, state remedies for copying and other copyright-type uses of such material are not preempted by the statute.[2] This result is confirmed by Section 301(b)(1) which

---

[1] *Gemveto Jewelry Co. v. Jeff Cooper, Inc.*, 613 F. Supp. 1052, 1064 n. 37, 227 U.S.P.Q. 623, 630 n. 37 (S.D.N.Y. 1985); *Mayer v. Josiah Wedgwood & Sons, Ltd.*, 601 F. Supp. 1523, 1532 n. 15, 225 U.S.P.Q. 776, 781 n. 15 (S.D.N.Y. 1985); *Durham Indus., Inc. v. Tomy Corp.*, 630 F.2d 905, 919 n. 15, 208 U.S.P.Q. 10, 22 n. 15 (2d Cir. 1980); *Synercom Technology, Inc. v. University Computing Co.*, 474 F. Supp. 37, 43–44, 204 U.S.P.Q. 29, 36 (N.D. Tex. 1979) (1909 Act) (input formats used with computers); H.R. REP. No. 94-1476, 94th Cong., 2d Sess. 131 (1976).

[2] *Falwell v. Penthouse Int'l, Ltd.*, 521 F. Supp. 1204, 1207–1208, 215 U.S.P.Q. 975, 977 (W.D. Va. 1981); H.R. REP. No. 94-1476, 94th Cong., 2d Sess. 131 (1976); S. REP. No. 94-473, 94th Cong., 1st Sess. 114 (1975) (choreography that has never been filmed or notated, extemporaneous speeches, original works of authorship communicated solely through conversations or live (and nonfixed) broadcasts, improvised dramatic sketches, or musical compositions not fixed are not subject to preemption). Cf. *Rowe v. Golden West Television Prods.*, 445 A.2d 1165, 218 U.S.P.Q. 280 (Super. Ct. App. Div. N.J. 1982) (concepts not sufficiently "fixed or frozen" for state law purposes, but since encounter session at which concepts were allegedly exposed was fixed on film, preemption was mandated). Live broadcasts simultaneously taped are considered "fixed" under §101. See *Production Contractors, Inc. v. WGN Continental Broadcasting Co.*, 622 F. Supp. 1500, 228 U.S.P.Q. 604 (N.D. Ill. 1985). Based on the second sentence of the definition of "fixed" in that section ("A work consisting of sound, images, or both that are being transmitted, is 'fixed' for purposes of this title, if a fixation of the work is being made simultaneously with its transmission"), Professor Nimmer has taken the position that the unauthorized duplication of live performances of such works that are being simultaneously fixed but not transmitted does not result in copyright liability. 1 NIMMER ON COPYRIGHT §1.08[C].

The second sentence of the definition of "fixed" does not, however, act as a limitation on the first; it merely takes express note of the unique circumstances of broadcasting, as do other sections of the Act; see, e.g., §501(c). Accordingly, a work that is being simultaneously fixed is protected under the Act without regard to whether it is being transmitted at the time of such fixation. State law attempts to provide equivalent rights for the unauthorized duplication of such a work would, therefore, be preempted. It may also be argued that even where the performer does not simultaneously fix the work, unauthorized fixation perfects the copyright for the benefit of the performer. See, e.g., WIPO GUIDE TO THE BERNE CONVENTION 18 ¶2.10 (1978) ("one school of thought believes that, if a lecture is given extempore, or a tune improvised on the piano, and another records it, the latter, by doing so, perfects the copyright in favour of the lecturer or pianist"). But cf. S. REP. No. 94-473, 94th Cong., 1st Sess. 51 (1975) ("a work would be considered 'fixed in a tangible medium of expression' if there has been an authorized embodi-

presents something of a mirror image of Section 301(a) and expressly saves state rights and remedies with respect to "subject matter that does not come within the subject matter of copyright as specified by sections 102 and 103, including works of authorship not fixed in any tangible medium of expression."

(2) Rights or remedies under other federal statutes are expressly saved from preemption by Section 301(d). The patent statute, Title 35, U.S.C., is the most obvious example of such a statute; a more recent statutory source of copyright implications is the Federal Communications Act, 47 U.S.C. §151 et seq.[3] Perhaps the most intriguing statutory exception is offered by the Lanham Act, 15 U.S.C. §1050 et seq., not only in its provision for the trademark registration of shapes and designs which might otherwise be (or are) copyrighted,[4] but also in its more open-ended unfair competition "false representation" provision, Section 43(a).[5]

(3) Section 301 expressly eliminates "publication" as the dividing line between federal protection under the statute and common law protection (the new dividing line being "creation," i.e., "fixation"). Works are protected under the statute "whether published or unpublished" and indeed whether created before or after January 1, 1978. This means, at the very least, the abolition of common law literary property, often called "common law copyright," covering the copy-

---

ment in a copy or phonorecord * * * "); *Pacific & Southern Co. v. Duncan*, 744 F.2d 1490, 1497 n. 9, 224 U.S.P.Q. 131, 135 n. 9 (11th Cir. 1984), *cert. denied*, 471 U.S. ___, *on remand*, 618 F. Supp. 469, 228 U.S.P.Q. 141 (N.D. Ga. 1985):

> "It is true that a work must be fixed under the authority of the author for the protections of copyright to take effect. 17 U.S.C. §101 (1977) [sic]. But the tape that 'fixes' a broadcast need not be the same tape that is deposited for registration."

In *Duncan*, plaintiff had deposited defendant's infringing tape as its deposit copy.

Under Article 7(1)(b) of the Rome Convention for the Protection of Performers, Producers of Phonograms and Broadcasting Organisations (to which the United States does not adhere), performers are given protection against "the fixation, without their consent, of their unfixed performance."

[3] *Home Box Office, Inc. v. Pay TV of Greater New York, Inc.*, 467 F. Supp. 525 (E.D.N.Y. 1979) (preliminary injunction); Copr. L. Rep. ¶25,089 (E.D.N.Y. 1979) (summary judgment); *California Satellite Systems, Inc. v. Nichols*, Copr. L. Rep. ¶25,831 (Cal. Ct. App. 1985) (state court may entertain private action under federal communications act; state jurisdiction over such action not preempted under Copyright Act since 17 U.S.C. §301(d) saves from preemption suits under federal *statutes* regardless of forum). Cf. *Home Box Office, Inc. v. Federal Communications Comm'n*, 567 F.2d 9 (D.C. Cir. 1977). See also *Capitol Cities Cable, Inc. v. Crisp*, 467 U.S. 691 (1984) (state regulation of cable television content preempted by Federal Communications Act and Copyright Act).

[4] *In re Morton-Norwich Prod., Inc.*, 671 F.2d 1332, 213 U.S.P.Q. 9 (C.C.P.A. 1982); *DC Comics, Inc. v. Filmation Associates*, 486 F. Supp. 1273, 206 U.S.P.Q. 112 (S.D.N.Y. 1980) (Lanham Act claim not preempted even though copyright claim regarding copyrighted characters not asserted); *Chevron Chemical Co. v. Voluntary Purchasing Groups, Inc.*, 209 U.S.P.Q. 951 (N.D. Tex. 1980).

[5] 15 U.S.C. §1125(a). See *Coca Cola Co. v. Tropicana Prods., Inc.*, 690 F.2d 312, 216 U.S.P.Q. 272 (2d Cir. 1982); *Smith v. Montoro*, 648 F.2d 602, 211 U.S.P.Q. 775 (9th Cir. 1981); *Maternally Yours, Inc. v. Your Maternity Shop*, 234 F.2d 538, 110 U.S.P.Q. 462 (2d Cir. 1976); *Follett v. Arbor House Pub. Co.*, 497 F. Supp. 304, 208 U.S.P.Q. 597 (S.D.N.Y. 1980). Cf. *Gilliam v. ABC*, 538 F.2d 14, 192 U.S.P.Q. 1 (2d Cir. 1976) (deletions from "Monty Python" television programs in violation of license held copyright infringement); *National Bank of Commerce v. Shaklee Corp.*, 503 F. Supp. 533, 207 U.S.P.Q. 1005 (W.D. Tex. 1980) (unauthorized *addition* of advertising materials in book giving false impression of sponsorship held copyright infringement).

ing of manuscripts, letters, diaries, private presentations, and other unpublished material fixed in a tangible medium of expression.[6]

## Subject Matter Test: §301(b)(1)

One of the unclear areas is the scope of the savings provision of Section 301(b)(1) for subject matter not specified by Sections 102 and 103. Three questions in particular may be posed: (1) May subject matter which Congress could have but chose not to extend copyright to be protected by the states? (2) May subject matter which Congress could not have (for constitutional reasons) extended copyright to nevertheless be protected by the states? (3) May utilitarian works which fail to meet the physical or conceptual separability standards for protection under the Act be protected by the states?

An example of subject matter which Congress chose to defer copyright protection for is typeface.[7] Since typeface is thus not within the subject matter of either Section 102 or Section 103,[8] it may be argued under a plain reading of Section 301(b)(1) that the states are free to grant copyright-like protection to such works. A counterargument would assert preemption not by virtue of Section 301(b)(1) but by the Supremacy Clause,[9] the principal thrust of the counterargument being that state law protection under such circumstances would thwart a congressional intent to permit free use of typeface. This precise question was raised in *Leonard Storch Enterprises, Inc. v. Mergenthaler Linotype Co.* Acting on a motion to dismiss, the court approved a magistrate's report which, in denying the motion, concluded that a state law claim of misappropriation regarding typeface would not conflict with any federal objective.[10] To the extent

---

[6] *Van Dusen v. Southeast First National Bank of Miami*, 478 So. 2d 82, 228 U.S.P.Q. 19 (D. Ct. App. Fla. 1985); *Holland v. Marriott Corp.*, Copr. L. Rep. ¶25,670 (D.D.C. 1984); *Klekas v. EMI Films, Inc.*, 150 Cal. App. 3d 1102, 224 U.S.P.Q. 1044 (Cal. Civ. App. 1984); *Walker v. Time-Life Films, Inc.*, Copr. L. Rep. ¶25,554 (N.Y. Sup. Ct. 1983); *Overseas Exchange Corp. v. Worth & Cromwell Fifth Avenue Ltd.*, Copr. L. Rep. ¶25,626 (N.Y. Sup. Ct. 1983). A number of cases have (correctly) found state law protection of architectural plans to be preempted. See, e.g., *Jacobs v. Westoaks Realtors, Inc.*, Copr. L. Rep. ¶25,714 (Cal. Civ. App. 1984); *Mention v. Gessell*, 714 F.2d 87, 222 U.S.P.Q. 796 (9th Cir. 1983). The statement in *Emarine v. Group Ten Press, Inc.*, 217 U.S.P.Q. 90, 91 (Bankr. Neb. 1982) that the 1976 Act preempts "all" state copyright law is overbroad.

[7] H.R. Rep. No. 94-1476, 94th Cong., 2d Sess. 55 (1976). See also citations in note 94 in Chapter 2, and *Copyright Office Typeface Hearing* (Nov. 6, 1974) (unpublished transcript on deposit in Copyright Office).

[8] *Eltra Corp. v. Ringer*, 579 F.2d 294, 198 U.S.P.Q. 321 (4th Cir. 1978).

[9] U.S. Const. art. VI cl. 2: "This constitution and the Laws of the United States which shall be made in pursuance thereof * * * shall be the Supreme Law of the Land; and the Judges in every state shall be bound thereby, anything in the Constitution or Laws of any State to the contrary notwithstanding." It may be argued, though, that §301 represents the sole preemptive provision. See note 13, *infra*.

[10] 202 U.S.P.Q. 623 (E.D.N.Y. 1979). The magistrate's report is reproduced in Copr. L. Rep. ¶25,092 and states that the motion was one for summary judgment. *Id.* at p. 15,521. Upon trial, the court dismissed the case on the ground that New York state misappropriation law did not deem "mere copying, even photographic copying" actionable absent additional elements such as palming off. Copr. L. Rep. ¶25,214 at p. 16,246 (E.D.N.Y. 1980). Although *Storch* was decided under the 1909 Act, the principles it enunciated are equally applicable to situations arising under the 1976 Act. See also *Editorial Photocolor Archives, Inc. v. Granger Collections*, 61 N.Y.2d 517 (N.Y. 1984) (copying of photographic slides preempted).

that the typeface designs were being sold (and copied) as discrete works, this position appears to be in accord with the Supreme Court's decision in *Goldstein v. California*,[11] which permitted the states to prohibit record piracy of pre-1972 sound recordings. The same would not be true, however, of a claim for misappropriation of typeface design embodied in a copyrighted (or public domain) work of authorship, such as a book. Under these circumstances, a claim of misappropriation would conflict with important federal policies and thus be preempted under the Supremacy Clause.[12]

The suggested approach is thus to allow the states to extend protection to works of authorship which Congress could have but chose not to extend copyright to, where protection of such works will not conflict with rights granted under the Copyright Act or other important federal objectives (e.g., permitting copying of works in the public domain).[13]

A more difficult issue is posed by the question of whether the states have free rein to protect matters which Congress cannot constitutionally grant copyright in, e.g., ideas, procedures, principles. One decision, *Bromhall v. Rorvik*,[14] citing Section 102(b) of the Act

---

[11]412 U.S. 546, 178 U.S.P.Q. 129 (1973).

[12]See, e.g., *G. Ricordi & Co. v. Haendler*, 194 F.2d 914 (2d Cir. 1952); *Bailey v. Logan Typographics*, 441 F.2d 47 (7th Cir. 1971); *Donald v. Uarco Business Forms*, 478 F.2d 764, 766, 176 U.S.P.Q. 513, 514 (8th Cir. 1973); *H. W. Wilson Co. v. National Library Serv. Co.*, 402 F. Supp. 456, 459, 190 U.S.P.Q. 555, 557 (S.D.N.Y. 1975); *Bepex Corp. v. Black Clawson Co.*, 208 U.S.P.Q. 109, 141 (S.D. Ohio 1980).

Decisions under the 1909 Act were divided on attempts to claim protection for editorial revisions, annotations, or related artistic embellishments. Compare *Grove Press, Inc. v. Collectors Pub. Co.*, 264 F. Supp. 603, 152 U.S.P.Q. 787 (C.D. Cal. 1967); *Shulsinger v. Grossman*, 119 F. Supp. 691 (S.D.N.Y. 1954); *Amplex Mfg. Co. v. ABC Plastic Fabricators*, 184 F. Supp. 285 (E.D. Pa. 1960), with *Descle & Cie, S.A. v. Nemmers*, 190 F. Supp. 381 (E.D. Wisc. 1961); *Hebrew Pub. Co. v. Schaufstein*, 54 U.S.P.Q. 372 (N.Y. 1942).

[13]See *Goldstein v. California*, 412 U.S. 546, 559, 178 U.S.P.Q. 129, 135 (1973):
"Where the need for free and unrestricted distribution of a writing is thought to be required by the national interest, the Copyright and Commerce Clause would allow Congress to eschew all protection. In such cases, a conflict would develop if a State attempted to protect that which Congress intended to be free."

But cf. SECOND SUPPLEMENTARY REPORT OF THE REGISTER OF COPYRIGHTS ON THE GENERAL REVISION OF THE U.S. COPYRIGHT LAW: 1975 REVISION BILL, Ch. I at 3–4, 15 (draft ed. 1975) (suggesting that federal preemption of state copyright law may be statutory and not constitutional and that a "clear-cut Congressional refusal to protect a certain type of work at all [citing, *inter alia*, typeface design] could be held to mean that the States are free to give the same kind of work unlimited protection."

[14]478 F. Supp. 361, 203 U.S.P.Q. 774 (E.D. Pa. 1979). See also *Mayer v. Josiah Wedgwood & Sons, Ltd.*, 601 F. Supp. 1523, 1532 n. 16, 225 U.S.P.Q. 776, 781–782 n. 16 (S.D.N.Y. 1985): "Federal copyright law does not protect ideas, 17 U.S.C. §102(b). * * * Thus, state laws that protect ideas as distinct from their expression, are without the subject matter of copyright and therefore are not preempted under 301."

Accord *Warrington Associates, Inc. v. Real-Time Engineering Systems, Inc.*, 522 F. Supp. 367, 368–369, 216 U.S.P.Q. 1024, 1025 (N.D. Ill. 1981); *Whitfield v. Lear*, 582 F. Supp. 1186, 1188–1189, 223 U.S.P.Q. 874, 876 (E.D.N.Y.) *rev'd on other grounds*, 751 F.2d 90, 224 U.S.P.Q. 540 (2d Cir. 1984). That such a claim is not preempted does not, of course, establish its merit as a matter of state law. *Whitfield v. Lear*, 582 F. Supp. at 1189, 223 U.S.P.Q. at 876. Some states, such as California, have held that idea claims can be supported only by proof of violation of common law claims that are not dependent upon the assertion of a property right. *Ibid.* In *Rand McNally & Co. v. Fleet Mgt. Systems*, 591 F. Supp. 726, 739, 221 U.S.P.Q. 827, 838 (N.D. Ill. 1983), the court erroneously found that since reproduction of an isolated unprotectible fact from a protected compilation was a use "outside the subject matter of copyright, " "it is outside the scope of the subject matter test of §301(a), [and] is [therefore] outside of the scope of the preemption doctrine." This decision confuses the subject matter test of §301 with the question of substantial similarity. An original compilation of individually unprotectible facts is a proper subject matter of copyright, 17 U.S.C. §103 (1978), and thus state law concerning reproduction

(which statutorily excludes such matters from copyright protection) found that a claim for unjust enrichment arising out of defendant's allegedly unauthorized use of plaintiff's experimental cell transplantation techniques (explained in an unpublished doctoral dissertation) was not preempted since such techniques were excluded from copyright protection. Although *Bromhall* has been criticized as permitting states to protect "mere ideas," a close examination of the opinion reveals that this is not the case. In any event, there appears to be no constitutional bar to states protecting ideas, procedures, processes, etc. acquired and used in the context of contractual or fiduciary relationships, or obtained by fraudulent means (as was alleged to be the case in *Bromhall*).

Where, however, the constitutionally unprotectible matter (e.g., as enumerated in Section 102(b)) is not obtained by such means, the better view is that notwithstanding its being literally outside the subject matter of Sections 102 and 103 (and thus facially not preempted by Section 301(b)(1)), state protection conflicts with important public policies with respect to "the encouragement of contributions to * * * knowledge."[15]

On pages 35–45, *supra*, we reviewed the test for protectibility of utilitarian articles, and noted that the designs of such articles are protected as pictorial, graphic, or sculptural works if and only to the extent that the designs incorporate pictorial, graphic, or sculptural features "that can be identified separately from, and are capable of existing independently of, the utilitarian aspects of the article." It may be argued that where no such features can be identified, the work should be treated like any other work that fails the originality test, viz., state law protection is preempted. On the other hand, it may also be argued that the work was, in fact, never within the subject matter of copyright and thus is not preempted. Unfortunately,

---

thereof is preempted, regardless of whether that reproduction ultimately is found to be an actionable violation of the Copyright Act. See also *United States Trotting Ass'n v. Chicago Downs Ass'n*, 665 F.2d 781, 785 n. 6 (7th Cir. 1981). The correct approach is that set forth in *Harper & Row, Pub., Inc. v. Nation Enters.*, 723 F.2d 195, 200, 220 U.S.P.Q. 321, 326 (2d Cir. 1983), *rev'd on other grounds*, 471 U.S. ____, 225 U.S.P.Q. 1073 (1985):

> "The fact that portions of the Ford memoirs may consist of uncopyrightable material, an issue discussed below, does not take the work as a whole outside the subject matter protected by the Act. * * * Were this not so, states would be free to expand the perimeters of copyright protection to their own liking, on the theory that preemption would be no bar to state protection of material not meeting federal statutory standards. That interpretation would run directly afoul of one of the Act's central purposes, to 'avoid the development of any borderline areas between State and Federal protection.' "

See also *Triangle Pub., Inc. v. Sports Eye, Inc.*, 415 F. Supp. 682, 686–687, 193 U.S.P.Q. 50, 54 (E.D. Pa. 1976) (unfair competition claim for taking of horse-racing data charts printed in copyrighted newspaper held preempted under *Sears-Compco* doctrine; 1909 Act). Cf. H.R. REP. No. 94-1476, 94th Cong., 2d Sess. 132 (1976) (indicating that "consistent pattern of unauthorized appropriation of facts (i.e., not the literary expression) constituting 'hot news', whether in the mold of *International News Serv. v. Associated Press*, 248 U.S. 215 (1918), or in the newer form of data updates from scientific, business, or financial data bases" is not preempted).

[15] *Hoehling v. Universal City Studios, Inc.*, 618 F.2d 972, 980, 205 U.S.P.Q. 681, 687 (2d Cir.), *cert. denied*, 449 U.S. 841, 207 U.S.P.Q. 1064 (1980).

the legislative history on this question is confusing, and the few decisions on point have come to conflicting conclusions.[16]

### Equivalent Rights Test: §301(b)(3)

There are two prongs in the Section 301 preemption test: the "subject matter" test of Section 301(b)(1) discussed above and the "equivalent rights" test of Section 301(b)(3). Section 301(a) preempts only rights "equivalent" to any of the exclusive rights of copyright as specified by Section 106; accordingly, Section 301(b)(3) expressly saves rights with respect to "activities violating legal or equitable rights that are *not* equivalent to any of the exclusive rights within the general scope of copyright as specified by Section 106," even regarding works admittedly within the subject matter of copyright. (Emphasis added.)

Earlier versions of Section 301(b)(3) contained examples of non-preempted claims. Thus, the 1963 preliminary draft expressly saved state remedies for "breaches of contract, breaches of trust, invasions of privacy, defamation," and "deceptive trade practices such as passing off and false representation."[17] But committee reports accompanying these bills stated that "where the cause of action involves the form of 'unfair competition' commonly referred to as misappropriation, which is nothing more than copyright protection under another name, Section 301 is intended to have preemptive effect."[18]

The language enumerating examples of non-preempted rights was gradually expanded, most notably in 1975 when the Senate ex-

---

[16]See H.R. REP. No. 94-1476, 94th Cong., 2d Sess. 131 (1976); S. REP. No. 94-473, 94th Cong., 1st Sess. 115 (1975);
  "In a general way subsection (b) of section 301 represents the obverse of subsection (a). It sets out, in broad terms and without necessarily being exhaustive, some of the principal areas of protection that preemption would not prevent the States from protecting. Its purpose is to make clear, consistent with the 1964 Supreme Court decisions in *Sears, Roebuck & Co. v. Stiffel Co.*, 376 U.S. 225, and *Compco Corp. v. Day-Brite Lighting, Inc.*, 376 U.S. 234, that preemption does not extend to causes of action, or subject matter outside the scope of the revised Federal copyright statute."
  The *Sears-Compco* decisions, however, held that state law attempts to protect creations that failed the patent and copyright standards for protection *were* preempted, thus their citation as support for non-preemption of state law protection for works that fall outside the subject matter of §§102 and 103 of the Copyright Act is confusing at best. Cf. *Vermont Castings, Inc. v. Evans Prods. Co.*, 215 U.S.P.Q. 758 (D. Vt. 1981), which found that the design features of a stove were inseparable from its overall configuration, that copyright protection was therefore unavailable, but that a common law action for unfair competition was not preempted, with *Decorative Aides Corp. v. Staple Sewing Aides*, 497 F. Supp. 154, 210 U.S.P.Q. 657 (S.D.N.Y. 1980), aff'd, 657 F.2d 262 (2d Cir. 1981), which held that a drapery header was not within the subject matter of copyright but that state law protection for its copying was preempted under the *Sears-Compco* doctrine.
  [17]COPYRIGHT LAW REVISION PART 3: PRELIMINARY DRAFT FOR REVISED U.S. COPYRIGHT LAW AND DISCUSSIONS AND COMMENTS ON THE DRAFT 18 (Comm. Print 1964).
  [18]H.R. REP. No. 2237, 89th Cong., 2d Sess. 129 (1966); H.R. REP. No. 83, 90th Cong., 1st Sess. 100 (1967). These reports adopted the position taken by the Register of Copyrights in his *1965 Supplementary Report*, a report prepared in the wake of the Supreme Court's 1964 decisions in *Sears, Roebuck & Co. v. Stiffel Co.*, 376 U.S. 225, 140 U.S.P.Q. 524 (1964), and *Compco Corp. v. Day-Brite Lighting, Inc.*, 376 U.S. 234, 140 U.S.P.Q. 528 (1964). See COPYRIGHT LAW REVISION PART 6: SUPPLEMENTARY REPORT OF THE REGISTER OF COPYRIGHTS ON THE GENERAL REVISION OF THE U.S. COPYRIGHT LAW 85 (Comm. Print 1965).

pressly preserved, *inter alia*, certain types of misappropriation, so that the subsection in the bill reaching the House floor in 1976 read as follows:

"Nothing in this title annuls or limits any rights or remedies under the common law or statutes of any State with respect to—
* * *

"(3) activities violating legal or equitable rights that are not equivalent to any of the exclusive rights within the general scope of copyright as specified by Section 106, *including rights against misappropriation not equivalent to any of such exclusive rights, breaches of contract, breaches of trust, trespass, conversion, invasion of privacy, defamation, and deceptive trade practices such as passing off and false representation.*" (Emphasis added.)

The committee report accompanying this bill states regarding this section:

"In a general way subsection (b) of section 301 represents the obverse of subsection (a). It sets out, in broad terms and without necessarily being exhaustive, some of the principal areas of protection that preemption would not prevent the States from protecting. Its purpose is to make clear, consistent with the 1964 Supreme Court decision in *Sears, Roebuck & Co. v. Stiffel Co.*, 376 U.S. 225, and *Compco Corp. v. Day-Brite Lighting, Inc.*, 376 U.S. 234, that preemption does not extend to causes of action, or subject matter outside the scope of the revised Federal copyright statute.
* * *

"The examples in clause (3), while not exhaustive, are intended to illustrate rights and remedies that are different in nature from the rights comprised in a copyright and that may continue to be protected under State common law or statute. The evolving common law rights of 'privacy,' 'publicity,' and trade secrets, and the general laws of defamation and fraud, would remain unaffected as long as the causes of action contain elements, such as an invasion of personal rights or a breach of trust or confidentiality, that are different in kind from copyright infringement. Nothing in the bill derogates from the rights of parties to contract with each other and to sue for breaches of contract; however, to the extent that the unfair competition concept known as 'interference with contract relations' is merely the equivalent of copyright protection it would be preempted.

"The last example listed in clause (3)—'deceptive trade practices such as passing off and false representation'—represents an effort to distinguish between those causes of action known as 'unfair competition' that the copyright statute is not intended to preempt and those that it is. Section 301 is not intended to preempt common law protection in cases involving activities such as false labeling, fraudulent representation, and passing off even where the subject matter involved comes within the scope of the copyright statute.

" 'Misappropriation' is not necessarily synonymous with copyright infringement, and thus a cause of action labeled as 'misappropriation' is not preempted if it is in fact based neither on a right within the general scope of copyright as specified by Section 106 nor on a right equivalent thereto. For example, state law should have the flexibility to afford a remedy (under traditional principles of equity) against a consistent pattern of unauthorized appropriation by a competitor of the facts (i.e., not the literary expression) constituting 'hot news' whether in the traditional mold of *International News Service v. Associated Press*, 248 U.S.

215 (1918), or in the newer form of data updates from scientific, business, or financial data bases.''[19]

The Justice Department, however, in a letter that has been strongly criticized for its errors of omission and commission,[20] expressed concern about this language, particularly the saving of any claims for misappropriation. As a result, Rep. Seiberling offered a floor amendment deleting *all* the examples in Section 301(b)(3) (i.e., all the italicized language quoted immediately above commencing with "including"). The amendment was accepted, but not until the following unfortunate exchange occurred on the House floor:

"Mr. Seiberling: Mr. Chairman, my amendment is intended to save the 'federal preemption' of State law section, which is section 301 of the bill, from being inadvertently nullified because of the inclusion of certain examples in the exemptions from preemption.

"This amendment would simply strike the examples listed in section 301(b)(3).

"The amendment is strongly supported by the Justice Department, which believes that it would be a serious mistake to cite as an exemption from preemption the doctrine of 'misappropriation.' The doctrine was created by the Supreme Court in 1922 and it has generally been ignored by the Supreme Court itself and by the lower courts ever since.

"Inclusion of a reference to the misappropriation doctrine in this bill, however, could easily be construed by the courts as authorizing the States to pass misappropriation laws. We should not approve such enabling legislation, because a misappropriation law could be so broad as to render the preemption section meaningless.
*　*　*
"Mr. Railsback: Mr. Chairman, may I ask the gentleman from Ohio, for the purpose of clarifying the amendment that by striking the word 'misappropriation' the gentleman in no way is attempting to change the existing state of the law, that is as it may exist in certain States that have recognized the right of recovery relating to 'misappropriation': is that correct?

"Mr. Seiberling: That is correct. All I am trying to do is prevent the citing of them as examples in a statute. We are, in effect, adopting a rather amorphous body of State law and codifying it, in effect. Rather I am trying to have this bill leave the State law alone and make it clear we are merely dealing with copyright laws, laws applicable to copyrights.

"Mr. Railsback: Mr. Chairman, I personally have no objection to the gentleman's amendment in view of that clarification and I know of no objections from this side.
*　*　*
"Mr. Kastenmeier: Mr. Chairman, I too have examined the gentleman's amendment and was familiar with the position of the Department

---

[19]H.R. REP. No. 94-1476, 94th Cong., 2d Sess. 131–132 (1976). Although the report refers to being "consistent" with the *Sears-Compco* decisions, by giving wide latitude to the states to protect nonequivalent rights, the version of the revision bill here quoted was prompted by the Supreme Court's decisions in *Kewanee Oil Co. v. Bicron Corp.*, 416 U.S. 470, 181 U.S.P.Q. 673 (1970), and *Goldstein v. California*, 412 U.S. 546, 178 U.S.P.Q. 129 (1973). For a review of the effect of these decisions on the drafting of the Act, see Fetter, *Copyright Revision and the Preemption of State "Misappropriation" Law*, 25 BULL. COPR. SOC'Y 367, 396–403 (1977); Abrams, *Copyright, Misappropriation, and Preemption*, 1983 SUP. CT. REV. 509, 537–550; and the testimony of Register of Copyrights Barbara Ringer before the House in 1975, *Copyright Law Revision: Hearings on H.R. 2223 Before the Subcomm. on Courts, Civil Liberties, and the Administration of Justice of the House Judiciary Comm.*, 94th Cong., 1st Sess. 1910 (1975).

[20]Diamond, *Preemption of State Law*, 24 BULL. COPR. SOC'Y 204, 210–211 (1976).

of Justice. Unfortunately, the Justice Department did not make its position known to the committee until the last day of markup.

"Mr. Seiberling: I understand.

"Mr. Kastenmeier: However, Mr. Chairman, I think that the amendment the gentleman is offering is consistent with the position of the Justice Department and accept it on this side as well."[21]

The question posed by this debate is whether the scope of Section 301(b)(3) has been changed by the deletion of the examples of non-preempted claims. One might argue that the history of this clause reflects the addition of examples to insure non-preemption. On the other hand, the floor debate can be cited to show that the new copyright law does not attempt "to change the existing state of the law, that is as it may exist in certain States that have recognized the right of recovery relating to 'misappropriation.' " The Senate and House reports both support this latter view,[22] but they of course were written before the House floor action. The conference report merely noted the House deletion and the acquiescence of the Senate conferees, without illuminating this question.[23]

The confusing nature of the above-quoted exchange has been noted by the courts, which have written variously that

"[b]y deleting the examples [of non-preempted state claims], Congress must have decided it was better to permit the states in the first instance through statutory or decisional law to specify or fashion 'rights or remedies' that fall within clause (3), subject, of course, to court application of the copyright law limitations of clause (3). While deleted from clause (3), those causes of action remain illustrative of 'certain types of misappropriation not preempted under section 301' "[24]

and that "the thrust of the congressional discussion was in the direction of continued state protection."[25]

The Justice Department's purpose in obtaining the deletion of the specified examples of non-preempted state causes of action from Section 301(b)(3) was to ensure that the mere unauthorized reproduction of a work would not be actionable as unjust enrichment or unfair competition. This result (which would have occurred even had the Justice Department remained silent) has been honored by the courts, which have held claims for misappropriation/unfair competition,[26] in-

---

[21]122 CONG. REC. H 10910 (daily ed. Sept. 22, 1976).

[22]H.R. REP. No. 94-1476, 94th Cong., 2d Sess. 131–132 (1976); S. REP. No. 94-473, 94th Cong., 1st Sess. 115–116 (1975).

[23]H.R. REP. No. 94-1733, 94th Cong., 2d Sess. 79 (1976).

[24]*Mitchell v. Penton/Industrial Pub. Co.*, 486 F. Supp. 22, 25, 205 U.S.P.Q. 242, 245 (N.D. Ohio 1979).

[25]*M. Bryce & Associates, Inc. v. Gladstone*, 107 Wis. 2d 241, 319 N.W.2d 907, 215 U.S.P.Q. 81 (Wis. Ct. App.), *cert. denied*, 459 U.S. 944 (1982).

[26]*Walker v. Time-Life Films, Inc.*, 784 F.2d 44, 53, 228 U.S.P.Q. 505, 511 (2d Cir. 1986); *Ehat v. Tanner*, 780 F.2d 876, 228 U.S.P.Q. 679 (10th Cir. 1985); *Ronald Litoff, Ltd. v. American Express Co.*, 621 F. Supp. 981, 985–986, 228 U.S.P.Q. 739, 741–742 (S.D.N.Y. 1985); *Mayer v. Josiah Wedgwood & Sons, Ltd.*, 601 F. Supp. 1523, 1534–1536, 225 U.S.P.Q. 776, 784 (S.D.N.Y.) (snowflake design); *Smith v. Weinstein*, 578 F. Supp. 1297, 222 U.S.P.Q. 381 (S.D.N.Y.), *aff'd mem.*, 738 F.2d 410 (2d Cir. 1984) (motion picture); *P.I.T.S. Films v. Laconis*, 588 F. Supp. 1383, 224 U.S.P.Q. 446 (E.D. Mich. 1984) (television characters); *Editorial Photocolor Archives, Inc. v. Granger Collection*, 61 N.Y.2d 517 (1984) (photographic slides); *Warner Bros., Inc. v. ABC*, 720 F.2d 231, 247, 222 U.S.P.Q. 101, 114 (2d Cir. 1983) (Newman, J.); *Men-*

terference with contractual relations,[27] prima facie tort,[28] and injury to business reputation[29] preempted, absent additional elements such as "passing off" or likelihood of confusion,[30] or breach of a fiduciary duty or an implied contract arising out of a course of dealing.[31] The additional elements must, however, be ones that result in a *qualita-*

---

*tion v. Gessell*, 714 F.2d 87, 222 U.S.P.Q. 796 (9th Cir. 1983) (common law copyright); *Sammons & Sons v. Ladd-Fab, Inc.*, 138 Cal. App. 3d 306, 221 U.S.P.Q. 737 (Cal. Ct. App. 1982) (catalogue); *Giangrasso v. CBS, Inc.*, 534 F. Supp. 472, 478, 215 U.S.P.Q. 219, 224 (E.D.N.Y. 1982); *Durham Indus., Inc. v. Tomy Corp.*, 630 F.2d 905, 918–919, 208 U.S.P.Q. 10, 22 (2d Cir. 1980); *Decorative Aides Corp. v. Staple Sewing Aides*, 497 F. Supp. 154, 160, 210 U.S.P.Q. 657, 661 (S.D.N.Y. 1980), *aff'd*, 657 F.2d 262 (2d Cir. 1981); *Leonard Storch Enters., Inc. v. Mergenthaler Linotype Corp.*, 208 U.S.P.Q. 58 (S.D.N.Y. 1980) (typeface design—1909 Act); *Dealer Advertising Dev., Inc. v. Barbara Allan Financial Advertising*, 209 U.S.P.Q. 1003 (W.D. Mich. 1979) (advertisement). See also *Gilbert v. Knoxville Int'l Energy Exposition*, COPR. L. REP. ¶25,462 (E.D. Tenn. 1982) (injury to business reputation). Cf. *Board of Trade v. Dow Jones & Co.*, 96 Ill. 2d 109, 256 N.E.2d 84 (Ill. 1983).

[27]*Meyers v. Waverly Fabrics*, 489 N.Y.S.2d 891, 227 U.S.P.Q. 55 (1985); *Harper & Row, Pub., Inc. v. Nation Enters.*, 501 F. Supp. 848, 212 U.S.P.Q. 274 (S.D.N.Y. 1980), *aff'd on this ground*, 723 F.2d 195, 220 U.S.P.Q. 321 (2d Cir. 1983), *rev'd on other grounds*, 471 U.S. ___, 225 U.S.P.Q. 1073 (1985). See also *Schuchart & Associates v. Solo Serve Corp.*, 540 F. Supp. 928, 936–938, 217 U.S.P.Q. 1227, 1237 (W.D. Tex. 1982) (no preemption); *Calloway v. Marvel Entertainment Group*, COPR. L. REP. ¶25,622 at p. 18,791 (S.D.N.Y. 1983) (no cause of action under copyright act or New York law). Cf. *Astor-Honor, Inc. v. Grosset & Dunlap, Inc.*, 441 F.2d 627, 628–629, 170 U.S.P.Q. 65, 66 (2d Cir. 1971).

[28]*Suid v. Newsweek Magazine*, 503 F. Supp. 146, 211 U.S.P.Q. 898 (D.D.C. 1980). In *Universal City Studios, Inc. v. American Invsco Mgt., Inc.*, 217 U.S.P.Q. 1076, 1080 (N.D. Ill. 1981), defendant's motion for summary judgment with respect to a claim of conspiracy to commit copyright infringement was denied on the ground that material issues of fact were present. No preemption argument was raised.

[29]*Meyers v. Waverly Fabrics*, *supra* note 27; *Gilbert v. Knoxville Int'l Energy Exposition*, COPR. L. REP. ¶25,462 (E.D. Tenn. 1982).

[30]See *Meyers v. Waverly Fabrics*, *supra* note 27 (false labeling claim not preempted); *Ronald Litoff, Ltd. v. American Express Co.*, 621 F. Supp. 981, 985–986, 228 U.S.P.Q. 739, 741–742 (S.D.N.Y. 1985) ("Although some claims for unfair competition are preempted, the 'passing off' variety asserts claims qualitatively different from those protected by copyright"); *Warner Bros., Inc. v. ABC*, 720 F.2d 231, 247–248, 222 U.S.P.Q. 101, 114 (2d Cir. 1983); *Oboler v. Goldin*, 714 F.2d 211, 213, 220 U.S.P.Q. 166, 167 (2d Cir. 1983); *George P. Ballas Buick-GMC, Inc. v. Taylor Buick, Inc.*, 5 Ohio Misc. 2d 16, 449 N.E.2d 805 (C.P. Lucas County 1981), *aff'd on other grounds*, 5 Ohio App. 3d 71, 449 N.E.2d 503 (Ohio Ct. App. 1982); *Vermont Castings, Inc. v. Evans Prod. Co.*, 215 U.S.P.Q. 758 (D. Vt. 1981); *John H. Harland Co. v. Clarke Checks, Inc.*, 207 U.S.P.Q. 664 (N.D. Ga. 1980), *aff'd in part, vac'd and rem'd in part*, 711 F.2d 966, 219 U.S.P.Q. 515 (11th Cir. 1983); *Fox v. Weiner Laces, Inc.*, 74 App. Div. 2d 549, 425 N.Y.S.2d 114 (N.Y. Civ. App. 1980); *DC Comics, Inc. v. Filmation Associates*, 486 F. Supp. 1273, 206 U.S.P.Q. 112 (S.D.N.Y. 1980); *Mitchell v. Penton/Industrial Pub. Co.*, 486 F. Supp. 22, 205 U.S.P.Q. 242 (N.D. Ohio 1979). See also *Walker v. Time-Life Films, Inc.*, 615 F. Supp. 430, 441, 227 U.S.P.Q. 698, 705 (S.D.N.Y. 1985), 784 F.2d 44, 53, 228 U.S.P.Q. 505, 511 (2d Cir. 1986) (deceptive trade practices).

[31]H.R. REP. No. 94-1476, 94th Cong., 2d Sess. 132 (1976); S. REP. No. 94-473, 94th Cong., 1st Sess. 115 (1975). *Oddo v. Ries*, 743 F.2d 630, 635, 222 U.S.P.Q. 799, 802 (9th Cir. 1984); *Ronald Litoff, Ltd. v. American Express Co.*, *supra* note 30; *Walker v. Time-Life Films, Inc.*, 784 F.2d 44, 53, 228 U.S.P.Q. 505, 511 (2d Cir. 1986); *Smith v. Weinstein*, 578 F. Supp. 1297, 1307, 222 U.S.P.Q. 381, 388–389 (S.D.N.Y.), *aff'd mem.*, 738 F.2d 410 (2d Cir. 1984); *Rand McNally & Co. v. Fleet Mgt. Systems*, 591 F. Supp. 726, 739, 221 U.S.P.Q. 827, 837–839 (N.D. Ill. 1983); *Schuchart & Associates v. Solo Serve Corp.*, 540 F. Supp. 928, 217 U.S.P.Q. 1227 (W.D. Tex. 1982); *Rowe v. Golden West Television*, 445 A.2d 1165, 1167 n. 3, 218 U.S.P.Q. 280, 282 n. 3 (Super. Ct. App. Div. N.J. 1982); *Werlin v. Reader's Digest Ass'n*, 528 F. Supp. 451, 213 U.S.P.Q. 1041 (S.D.N.Y. 1981). But see interpretation of *Werlin* in *Mayer v. Josiah Wedgwood & Sons, Ltd.*, 601 F. Supp. 1523, 1532 n. 16, 225 U.S.P.Q. 776, 781–782 n. 16 (S.D.N.Y. 1985). See also *Meyers v. Waverly Fabrics*, 489 N.Y.S.2d 891, 893, 227 U.S.P.Q. 55, 56 (1985) (action for breach of oral contract not preempted but dismissed on statute of fraud grounds).

These decisions must be distinguished from those permitting the bringing of an infringement action arising out of breach of an express agreement. See *Custom Imports, Inc. v. Hanmell Trading Co.*, 596 F. Supp. 1126 (S.D.N.Y. 1984); *Kamakazi Music Corp. v. Robbins Music Corp.*, 684 F.2d 228 (2d Cir. 1982) (claim rejected that, by agreeing to arbitrate construction of contract, plaintiff elected remedy, precluding resort to federal courts on copyright violation); *Simon & Schuster, Inc. v. Cove Vitamin & Pharmaceutical, Inc.*, 211 F. Supp. 72, 136 U.S.P.Q. 32 (S.D.N.Y. 1962); *MGM Distributing Corp. v. Bijou Theatre Co.*, 3 F. Supp. 66, 17 U.S.P.Q. 124 (D. Mass. 1933) (plaintiff may elect to sue for breach of contract or copyright infringement).

*tive* change in the nature of the claim, i.e., one that alters either the act that forms the basis of the infringement claim or the rights sought to be protected. Elements such as awareness, intent, or usurpation of time, effort, money, and expertise in a "commercially immoral" or "unfair" manner will not alone save the claim from preemption.[32]

The list of non-preempted causes of action deleted from Section 301(b)(3) also included "breaches of contract, breaches of trust, trespass, conversion, invasion of privacy, and defamation." The courts have confronted the preemption issue in connection with some of these examples. "Breach of trust," which includes violation of a trade secret obligation, is mentioned in the legislative history as a non-preempted state claim, a position that has been followed by the majority of courts.[33] Claims of conversion to vindicate possessory rights in chattels have also been upheld,[34] while failure to properly attribute

---

[32] *Mayer v. Josiah Wedgwood & Sons, Ltd.*, 601 F. Supp. 1523, 1535, 225 U.S.P.Q. 776, 784 (S.D.N.Y. 1985). Accord *Walker v. Time-Life Films, Inc.*, 784 F.2d 44, 228 U.S.P.Q. 505 (2d Cir. 1986); *Harper & Row, Pub., Inc. v. Nation Enters.*, 501 F. Supp. 848, 852, 212 U.S.P.Q. 274, 278 (S.D.N.Y. 1980), *aff'd on this point*, 723 F.2d 195, 220 U.S.P.Q. 321 (2d Cir. 1983), *rev'd on other grounds*, 471 U.S. ____, 225 U.S.P.Q. 1073 (1985) (stressing need for qualitative difference in state-created right); *Rand McNally & Co. v. Fleet Mgt. Systems*, 591 F. Supp. 726, 739, 221 U.S.P.Q. 827, 837–838 (N.D. Ill. 1983) (immorality and wrongdoing are not extra elements sufficient to prevent preemption). But cf. *Filmways Pictures, Inc. v. Marks Polarized Corp.*, 552 F. Supp. 863, 868, 220 U.S.P.Q. 870, 873 (S.D.N.Y. 1984) (commercial immorality approved as element in unfair competition claim where no copyright claim asserted).

[33] *Technicon Medical Information Systems Corp. v. Green Bay Packaging, Inc.*, 687 F.2d 1032, 1038–39, 215 U.S.P.Q. 1001, 1007 (7th Cir. 1982), *cert. denied*, 459 U.S. 1106 (1983); *M. Bryce Associates v. Gladstone*, 107 Wis. 2d 241, 319 N.W.2d 907, 215 U.S.P.Q. 81 (Wis. App.), *cert. denied*, 459 U.S. 944 (1982); *BPI Systems, Inc. v. Leith*, 532 F. Supp. 209 (W.D. Tex. 1981); *Warrington Associates, Inc. v. Real-Time Engineering*, 522 F. Supp. 367, 216 U.S.P.Q. 1024 (N.D. Ill. 1981); *Synercom Technology, Inc. v. University Computing Co.*, 462 F. Supp. 1003, 199 U.S.P.Q. 537 (N.D. Tex. 1978); 474 F. Supp. 37, 204 U.S.P.Q. 29 (N.D. Tex. 1979). See also *McAlpine v. AAMCO Transmissions, Inc.*, 202 U.S.P.Q. 575, 594–595 (E.D. Mich. 1978) (by implication). The contrary decision in *Videotronics, Inc. v. Bend Electronics*, 564 F. Supp. 1471, 223 U.S.P.Q. 296 (D. Nev. 1983), is believed to be erroneous. A similar lower court decision in Alabama was affirmed on other grounds. *Avco Corp. v. Precision Air Parts, Inc.*, 210 U.S.P.Q. 894 (M.D. Ala. 1980), *aff'd on other grounds*, 676 F.2d 494, 216 U.S.P.Q. 1086 (11th Cir.), *cert. denied*, 459 U.S. 1037 (1982). See also H.R. REP. No. 96-1307, Pt. I, 96th Cong., 2d Sess. 23–24 (1980) (stating that copyright protection for computer programs does not preempt state trade secret law). *Mayer v. Josiah Wedgwood & Sons, Ltd.*, 601 F. Supp. 1523, 1536, 225 U.S.P.Q. 776, 784–785 (S.D.N.Y. 1985), while holding that claims of breach of confidentiality are not preempted, found such claims inapplicable to works that have fallen into the public domain. Cf. *Decorative Aides Corp. v. Staple Sewing Aides Corp.*, 497 F. Supp. 154, 160, 210 U.S.P.Q. 657, 661 (S.D.N.Y. 1980), *aff'd*, 657 F.2d 262 (2d Cir. 1981).

[34] *Oddo v. Ries*, 743 F.2d 630, 222 U.S.P.Q. 799 (9th Cir. 1984); *Lone Ranger Television, Inc. v. Program Radio Corp.*, 740 F.2d 718, 223 U.S.P.Q. 112 (9th Cir. 1984); *Wildlife Int'l, Inc. v. Clements*, 591 F. Supp. 1542, 223 U.S.P.Q. 806 (S.D. Ohio 1984); *Uncle Jam Records & Tapes Int'l, Inc. v. Warner Bros. Records, Inc.*, COPR. L. REP. ¶25,580 (S.D.N.Y. 1983); *United States Trotting Ass'n v. Chicago Downs Ass'n*, 665 F.2d 781, 785 n. 6 (7th Cir. 1981); H.R. REP. No. 94-1476, 94th Cong., 2d Sess. 133 (1976); S. REP. No. 94-473, 94th Cong., 1st Sess. 116 (1975): "Nothing contained in section 301 precludes the owner of a copy or a phonorecord from enforcing a claim of conversion against one who takes possession of the copy or phonorecord without consent."

In *Harper & Row, Pub., Inc. v. Nation Enters.*, 557 F. Supp. 1067, 220 U.S.P.Q. 210 (S.D.N.Y.), *aff'd on this ground, rev'd on other grounds*, 723 F.2d 195, 220 U.S.P.Q. 321 (2d Cir. 1983), *rev'd on those other grounds*, 471 U.S. ____, 225 U.S.P.Q. 1073 (1985), the court found that defendant's use was not actionable as a matter of state law. In *Mayer v. Josiah Wedgwood & Sons, Ltd.*, 601 F. Supp. 1523, 1533, 225 U.S.P.Q. 776, 782 (S.D.N.Y. 1985), the court held that a claim of conversion was preempted on the ground that plaintiff was suing over "the deprivation of the rights flowing from the labor and expertise which she embodied in the [work]." *Mayer* also noted state court decisions that permitted "maintenance of a conversion suit where the property right taken 'includes the incorporeal right to the exclusive use of its contents,' " *id.* at 1533 n. 18, 225 U.S.P.Q. at 782 n. 18, but stated an opinion that "[i]t is quite clear from the [1976] House report that 'conversion' in the draft [bill] refers to a cause of action

one's contribution to a copyrighted work has been given conflicting treatment.[35]

While rights of privacy and publicity were also stated in the legislative reports to be not preempted,[36] and the courts have generally so found,[37] a different but related question arises with respect to performance rights in sound recordings. There is no question that Congress could constitutionally extend an exclusive right to an artist in his recorded performance and that, if such a right were granted, a state attempt to protect the same right would be preempted under Section 301(a). During the revision process leading to passage of the 1976 Act, Congress did in fact consider such a possibility, but deferred action until submission of a report by the Register of Congress.[38] This report, submitted in June 1978,[39] recommended that such a right be granted.

---

to vindicate possessory rights in chattels." *Id.* at 1533, 225 U.S.P.Q. at 782. Accord *Ronald Litoff, Ltd. v. American Express Co.*, 621 F. Supp. 981, 986, 228 U.S.P.Q. 739, 742 (S.D.N.Y. 1985). See also *Dowling v. United States*, 473 U.S. ____, ____ 226 U.S.P.Q. 529, 533 (1985):

"[T]he Government's theory here would make theft, conversion, or fraud equivalent to wrongful appropriation of statutorily protected rights in copyright. The copyright owner, however, holds no ordinary chattel. A copyright, like other intellectual property, comprises a series of carefully defined and carefully delimited interests to which the law affords correspondingly exact proportions. * * * It follows that interference with copyright does not easily equate with theft, conversion, or fraud. * * * While one may colloquially lin[k] infringement with some general notion of wrongful appropriation, infringement plainly implicates a more complex set of property interests than does run-of-the-mill theft, conversion, or fraud."

[35] *Wolfe v. United Artists Corp.*, 583 F. Supp. 52, 223 U.S.P.Q. 274 (E.D. Pa. 1984) (*"Wolfe II"*); *Wolfe v. United Artists Corp.*, 742 F.2d 1439 (2d Cir. 1983) (*"Wolfe I"*); *Suid v. Newsweek Magazine*, 503 F. Supp. 146, 149, 211 U.S.P.Q. 898, 900 (D.D.C. 1980) (decision unclear on whether claim preempted or, if not preempted, whether no such common law right was believed to exist). The failure to accord screen credit may be actionable under state law. See *Meta-Films, Associates, Inc. v. MCA, Inc.*, 586 F. Supp. 1346, 1364, 222 U.S.P.Q. 211, 223 (C.D. Cal. 1984); Cal. Bus. & Prof. Code §§17200, 17203.

[36] H.R. Rep. No. 94-1476, 94th Cong., 2d Sess. 132 (1976); S. Rep. No. 94-473, 94th Cong., 1st Sess. 115 (1975).

[37] *Bi-Rite Enters., Inc. v. Button Master*, 555 F. Supp. 1188, 217 U.S.P.Q. 910 (S.D.N.Y. 1983); *Factors, Etc. v. Pro Arts, Inc.*, 496 F. Supp. 1090, 208 U.S.P.Q. 529 (S.D.N.Y. 1980), *rev'd on other grounds*, 652 F.2d 278, 211 U.S.P.Q. 1 (2d Cir. 1981); *Lugosi v. Universal Studios, Inc.*, 215 Cal. 3d 425, 448 (1979) (Bird, C. J., dissenting). Cf. *Baltimore Orioles, Inc. v. Major League Baseball Players Ass'n*, Copr. L. Rep. ¶25,822 (N.D. Ill. 1985) (preemption found with respect to baseball players' performances during baseball games being fixed simultaneously with live transmission); and discussion in *Gee v. CBS, Inc.*, 471 F. Supp. 600, 657–662, 202 U.S.P.Q. 486, 527–531 (E.D. Pa. 1979).

[38] 17 U.S.C. §114(d) (1978). See also H.R. Rep. No. 94-1733, 94th Cong., 2d Sess. 76–77 (1976).

[39] Subcomm. on Courts, Civil Liberties, and the Administration of Justice of the House Judiciary Comm., Performance Rights in Sound Recordings (Ser. No. 15, June 1978). The International Convention for the Protection of Performers, Producers or Phonograms, and Broadcasting Organisations of 1961, known as the "Rome Convention," requires its signatory members to accord a performance right in sound recordings. The United States is not a signatory to the Rome Convention, but is a member of the Convention for the Protection of Producers of Phonograms Against Unauthorized Duplication of their Phonograms, known as the "Geneva Convention," which does not require such a right. Cf. *Baltimore Orioles, Inc. v. Major League Baseball Players Ass'n*, Copr. L. Rep. ¶25,822 (N.D. Ill. 1985), which contains the startling suggestion that a performance right in baseball players' performances during a baseball game exists. This position was seemingly rejected by Congress in 1976. See H.R. Rep. No. 94-1476, 94th Cong., 2d Sess. 50 (1976) (discussing coordination of cameras filming the game as the protectible elements); *NAB v. Copyright Royalty Tribunal*, 675 F.2d 367, 377–378, 214 U.S.P.Q. 161, 168–169 (D.C. Cir. 1982); *Copyright Law Revision: Hearings on H.R. 2223 Before the Subcomm. on Courts, Civil Liberties, and the Administration of Justice of the House Judiciary Comm.*, 94th Cong., 1st Sess. 1823 (1975) (testimony of Register of Copyrights expressing doubt that "the game itself, as a game, and activities of the participants, the players, are actually copyrightable"). Cf. *id.* at 798 (testimony of Commissioner of Baseball); 785 (testimony of NAB general counsel). See also *Ettore v. Philco Television Broadcasting Corp.*, 229 F.2d 481,

To date, however, legislation embodying the recommendations has not been enacted, and in view of earlier decisions by state courts holding that a common law right exists,[40] the question arises whether a current state action regarding a performance right in a sound recording fixed after February 15, 1972,[41] should be preempted. Since such a right cannot be asserted separately from the sound recording in which it is embodied (unlike typeface designs, which may be marketed apart from their embodiment in a book), it appears that the right must be preempted to avoid conflict with the federal policies regarding use of the sound recording.

California,[42] New York,[43] and Massachusetts[44] have recently enacted legislation extending a form of protection similar to the *droit moral* found in many European countries. Under these statutes the artist is variously given the right to claim (or disclaim) authorship, to prevent others from defacing or mutilating the work, or altering it in a manner so as to damage his reputation. Although it may be argued that certain copyright decisions have accorded *droit moral* like protection, these same decisions have stated:

> "American copyright law, as presently written, does not recognize moral rights or provide a cause of action for their violation, since the law seeks to vindicate the economic, rather than the personal, rights of authors."[45]

This being the case, it would appear that state legislation according *droit moral* should not be preempted, since such rights are not equivalent to those granted under the Copyright Act. While this

---

108 U.S.P.Q. 187 (3d Cir.), *cert. denied*, 351 U.S. 926, 109 U.S.P.Q. 517 (1956) (boxers found to have right to control video reproductions of their performances); *Pittsburgh Athletic Co. v. KQV Broadcasting Co.*, 24 F. Supp. 490, 492 (W.D. Pa. 1938). Cf. *Sinatra v. Goodyear Tire & Rubber Co.*, 435 F.2d 711, 168 U.S.P.Q. 12 (9th Cir. 1970), *cert. denied*, 402 U.S. 906, 169 U.S.P.Q. 321 (1971); *Booth v. Colgate-Palmolive Co.*, 362 F. Supp. 343, 179 U.S.P.Q. 819 (S.D.N.Y. 1973).

[40] *Waring v. WDAS Broadcasting Station, Inc.*, 327 Pa. 433, 194 A. 631, 35 U.S.P.Q. 272 (Pa. Sup. Ct. 1937); *Waring v. Dunlea*, 26 F. Supp. 338, 41 U.S.P.Q. 201 (D.N.C. 1939); *Metropolitan Opera Ass'n v. Wagner Nichols Recorder Corp.*, 199 Misc. 787, 101 N.Y.S.2d 483, 87 U.S.P.Q. 173 (N.Y. Sup. Ct. 1950). Cf. *Capitol Records, Inc. v. Mercury Records Corp.*, 221 F.2d 657, 105 U.S.P.Q. 163 (2d Cir. 1955), and discussion of *Waring, supra*, in *Gee v. CBS, Inc.*, 471 F. Supp. 600, 657–662, 202 U.S.P.Q. 486, 527–531 (E.D. Pa. 1979).

[41] See 17 U.S.C. §301(c) (1978).

[42] California Art Preservation Act, *codified in* Cal. Civ. Code §987 (1980).

[43] New York Artists' Authorship Rights Act, *codified in* N.Y. Arts and Cultural Affairs Law §§14.51–14.59. See *Newman v. Delmar Realty Co.*, Civ. No. 2955184 (N.Y. Sup. Ct., N.Y. County, filed April 26, 1984); Damich, *The New York Artists' Authorship Rights Act: A Comparative Critique*, 84 Colum. L. Rev. 1733 (1984).

In *Ronald Litoff, Ltd. v. American Express Co.*, 621 F. Supp. 981, 986, 228 U.S.P.Q. 739, 742 (S.D.N.Y. 1985), §14.03 of this law, which states that the right of reproduction of a work of art which is sold or transferred remains the property of the grantor unless the work is in the public domain or is expressly conveyed in writing, was held preempted by the Copyright Act. See 17 U.S.C. §202 (1978).

[44] Massachusetts Art Preservation Act, *codified in* Mass. G.L. art 231 §85S (effective April 8, 1985).

[45] *Gilliam v. ABC*, 538 F.2d 14, 24, 192 U.S.P.Q. 1, 8 (2d Cir. 1976). See also *Gee v. CBS, Inc.*, 471 F. Supp. 600, 659–660, 202 U.S.P.Q. 486, 528–529 (E.D. Pa. 1979), indicating that infringement would lie where alterations were done to "intentionally ridicule or humiliate" the author. Cf. *Edison v. Viva Int'l, Ltd.*, 209 U.S.P.Q. 345, 347 (N.Y. App. Div. 1979), which, while stating that "in at least a number of situations the integrity and reputation of an artistic creator have been protected by judicial pronouncements," held that "[w]here * * * the parties have entered into a contract of publication, plaintiff's so-called 'moral right' is controlled by the law of contract * * * ."

does, in fact, seem to be generally the correct result, the right to prevent alteration to a work of authorship may, in some circumstances, be considered equivalent to the right to prepare derivative works found in Section 106(2) of the Copyright Act. To the extent, though, that the state right is construed to refer to mutilation or defacement of the material object in which the work of authorship is embodied or to a change in the work that demonstrably results in an injury to the artist's reputation, the state right is not equivalent to that granted by Section 106(2) and is not, therefore, preempted. Where, however, the alteration is, in effect, no more than the preparation of a derivative work (and regardless of how much the artist may dislike the end result), the right is preempted.

In 1976, California became the first (and to date only) state to also grant its fine artists a *droit de suite*[46]—a right to share in the proceeds from the resale of the work unless the right is waived by a written contract "providing for an amount in excess of 5 percent of such sale." This right appears to be equivalent to (though narrower than) the right of distribution granted by Section 106(3) of the Copyright Act.[47] In *Morseburg v. Baylon*,[48] the Ninth Circuit, construing the California Act under the 1909 Copyright Act, reached a contrary result, finding that the California Act granted an "additional right similar to the additional protection afforded by California's anti-pirating statute upheld in *Goldstein [v. California]*."[49] The statute adjudicated in *Goldstein*, however, concerned subject matter not protected (at that time) by the Copyright Act, whereas the California *droit de suite* concerns both subject matter admittedly protected by copyright and an equivalent right concerning the disposition of that subject matter,[50] a combination that mandates preemption.

A final form of state legislation that has raised preemption arguments is the so-called "anti-blind bidding" statute, designed to prohibit a motion picture industry practice of requiring motion picture distributors to bid on films that are only partially completed, by requiring a screening of the full film. In three suits over statutes in Ohio,[51] Pennsylvania,[52] and Utah,[53] copyright owners have argued

---

[46]California Resale Royalties Act, *codified in* CAL. CIV. CODE §986 (1977 as amended 1983).

[47]The so-called "first sale" provision, 17 U.S.C. §109 (1978), manifests a congressional policy to permit the sale of a lawfully made "copy" (the definition of which includes the original, see 17 U.S.C. §101, definition of "copy") of a work without the authorization of or further obligation to the author. Since the first sale of a lawful copy is considered to exhaust the copyright owner's §106(3) distribution right with respect to that copy (see text at note 116 in Chapter 7), the *droit de suite* in effect grants an additional distribution-type right to the author.

[48]621 F.2d 972, 207 U.S.P.Q. 183 (9th Cir.), *cert. denied*, 449 U.S. 983, 208 U.S.P.Q. 464 (1980).

[49]*Id.* at 977, 207 U.S.P.Q. at 187.

[50]See also *Capitol Cities Cable, Inc. v. Crisp*, 467 U.S. 691 (1984).

[51]*Allied Artists Pictures Corp. v. Rhoades*, 496 F. Supp. 408, 207 U.S.P.Q. 630 (S.D. Ohio 1980), *aff'd in part, rev'd in part, and rem'd in part*, 679 F.2d 656, 215 U.S.P.Q. 1097 (6th Cir. 1982).

[52]*Associated Film Dist. Corp. v. Thornburgh*, 520 F. Supp. 971, 214 U.S.P.Q. 742 (E.D. Pa. 1981), *rev'd and rem'd*, 683 F.2d 808, 216 U.S.P.Q. 184 (3d Cir. 1982), *on remand*, 227 U.S.P.Q. 184 (E.D. Pa. 1985).

[53]*Warner Bros., Inc. v. Wilkinson*, 533 F. Supp. 105, 216 U.S.P.Q. 837 (D. Utah 1981). This suit did not involve the trade-screening section of the statute but rather that provision concerning guarantees of minimum payments or ticket prices. Preemption was not found; indeed, the court stated "this is [not] a copyright case." *Id.* at 108, 216 U.S.P.Q. at 838.

that the statutes are preempted as interfering with their exclusive rights to perform and distribute their works. These arguments proved unavailing in the Ohio case but were initially successful before the trial court in the Pennsylvania case. The decision in that case, granted on a motion for summary judgment, was, however, reversed on appeal on the ground that there was an insufficient record establishing as a matter of law that the Pennsylvania statute stood "as an obstacle to the accomplishment and execution of the full purposes and objectives of Congress."[54] On remand, the constitutionality of the statute was upheld, with the trial court concluding that the actual effect of the act was "miniscule compared to the competing claims that it is a salvation and damnation."

Before leaving Section 301, it is well to note the provisions of subsection (b)(2), which saves from preemption "any cause of action arising from undertakings commenced before January 1, 1978."[55] Works created before January 1, 1978, but alleged to have been infringed on or after that date are governed by the rights and remedies granted by the 1976 Act. In a 1979 case from the Southern District of New York, *Orth-O-Vision, Inc. v. Home Box Office*,[56] the court mistakenly construed Section 301(b)(2) as also referring to works *created* before January 1, 1978. This opinion has not been followed by other courts, which have correctly construed it to refer to claims arising from infringing *activities*.[57]

---

[54] *Associated Film Dist. Corp. v. Thornburgh*, 520 F. Supp. 971, 214 U.S.P.Q. 742 (E.D. Pa. 1981), *rev'd and rem'd*, 683 F.2d 808, 216 U.S.P.Q. 184, 190 (3d Cir. 1982), *on remand*, 227 U.S.P.Q. 184 (E.D. Pa. 1985).

[55] 17 U.S.C. §301(b)(2) (1978). Note that §301(c) postpones the preemptive provisions with respect to sound recordings fixed before February 15, 1972, until February 15, 2047. For an explanation of this provision, see H.R. REP. No. 94-1476, 94th Cong., 2d Sess. 133 (1976). See also note 40, *supra*.

[56] 474 F. Supp. 672, 205 U.S.P.Q. 644 (S.D.N.Y. 1979). See also *DC Comics, Inc. v. Reel Fantasy, Inc.*, 696 F.2d 24, 27–28, 217 U.S.P.Q. 307, 309 (2d Cir. 1982), which made the same error as the *Orth-O-Vision* court; *DC Comics, Inc. v. Filmation Associates*, 486 F. Supp. 1273, 1278, 206 U.S.P.Q. 112, 115 (S.D.N.Y. 1980) (suggesting 1909 Act governed where defendant began the creation of his work before January 1, 1978). See criticism of these cases in *Van Dusen v. Southeast First National Bank of Miami*, 228 U.S.P.Q. 19, 22 n. 8 (D. Ct. App. Fla. 1985).

[57] See, e.g., *Mayer v. Josiah Wedgwood & Sons, Ltd.*, 601 F. Supp. 1523, 1531–1532, 225 U.S.P.Q. 776, 781 (S.D.N.Y. 1985) (criticizing *Orth-O-Vision* as "clearly erroneous"); *Mention v. Gessell*, 714 F.2d 87, 90, 222 U.S.P.Q. 796, 799 (9th Cir. 1984); *Klekas v. EMI Films, Inc.*, 150 Cal. App. 3d 1102, 224 U.S.P.Q. 1044 (Cal. Ct. App. 1984); *Meltzer v. Zoller*, 520 F. Supp. 847, 853–854, 216 U.S.P.Q. 776, 782 (D.N.J. 1981); *Strout Realty, Inc. v. Country 22 Real Estate Corp.*, 493 F. Supp. 997, 1000, 212 U.S.P.Q. 145, 147 (W.D. Mo. 1980) (also criticizing *Orth-O-Vision*); *Burke v. NBC*, 598 F.2d 688, 691 n. 2, 202 U.S.P.Q. 531, 533 n. 2 (1st Cir.), *cert. denied*, 444 U.S. 869, 203 U.S.P.Q. 640 (1979); *Bromhall v. Rorvik*, 478 F. Supp. 361, 366, 203 U.S.P.Q. 774, 777 (E.D. Pa. 1979); *Birnbaum v. United States*, 588 F.2d 319, 326 n. 15, 201 U.S.P.Q. 623, 629 n. 15 (2d Cir. 1978).

The meaning of the term "cause of action" is extensively discussed in *Kepner-Tregnoe, Inc. v. Carabio*, 203 U.S.P.Q. 124, 136–137 (E.D. Mich. 1979). See also *Landsberg v. Scrabble Crossword Game Players, Inc.*, 736 F.2d 485, 487, 221 U.S.P.Q. 1140, 1142 (9th Cir.), *cert. denied*, 469 U.S. 1037 (1984); *DC Comics, Inc. v. Filmation Associates*, *supra* note 56. In *Van Dusen v. Southeast First National Bank of Miami*, *supra* note 56, the court held that " '[u]ndertakings' refers to the alleged infringing activities, not to the creation of the underlying work."

## Duration of Works Created On or After
## January 1, 1978: §302

With the basic term of "life-plus-fifty" provided in Section 302(a), the United States joins the rest of the international copyright community by harnessing duration irremovably to the author, rather than to the date of an event controlled by a publisher. It has been suggested that this provision, in combination with others, "may mark a fundamental shift in our copyright philosophy," through "a basic identification of copyright with the author rather than the publisher."[58]

In any event, the mechanics of computation and ascertainment of lifespans may be summarized as follows:

(1) In the case of joint works, the 50 years are computed from the survivor's death (§302(b)).

(2) The basic formula of life-plus-fifty is replaced by a fixed number of years in three situations in which it was deemed impracticable to measure individual authors' lives—(a) anonymous works, (b) pseudonymous works, and (c) works made for hire. For such works, the term is 75 years after "publication" (as defined in §101) or 100 years after "creation" (as indirectly defined also in §101), whichever is earlier (§302(c)).

Anonymous and pseudonymous works are defined, respectively, as those where no natural person is identified as the author, and where the author is identified under a fictitious name *on* the copies or phonorecords of the work. If, before the end of this alternative term, the identity of one or more authors is revealed by registration or in a special registry containing recorded statements by persons having an interest in copyrights, the life-plus-fifty term applies to such author or authors. Neither the statute nor the legislative history provides guidance in determining who a "person having an interest in the copyright" may be, as status of potential significance due to the ability of such an individual to alter the duration of the term of protection. In a proposed rulemaking initiated in 1979,[59] the Copyright Office addressed this issue. While recognizing that arguably "a potential user wishing copyright restrictions in a work to end as soon as possible has 'an interest in the copyright,'" it nevertheless stated that the use of the term "interest" in other sections of the statute (e.g., Sections 203, 204, 501(b), 602(b), 603(b)) "suggests a narrower interpretation, involving at least some right in the nature of a prop-

---

[58]Ringer, *Finding Your Way Around in the New Copyright Law*, PUBLISHERS WEEKLY, Dec. 13, 1976.

[59]44 Fed. Reg. 47550 (Aug. 14, 1979). The proposed regulation was promulgated pursuant to §302(d), which permits "[a]ny person having an interest in a copyright" to "record in the Copyright Office a statement of the date of death of the author of a copyrighted work, or a statement that the author is still living on a particular date." The statement is to comply "in form and content with requirements that the Register of Copyrights shall prescribe by regulation." Those regulations have yet to be prescribed since the proposed regulations never took effect.

erty right under the copyright." Accordingly, the Office proposed that the following persons be entitled to file statements:

(a) the author of the work; or

(b) the spouse of the author of the work; or

(c) the widow or widower or any of the children or grandchildren of the author of the work; or

(d) any legal or beneficial owner of an exclusive right under copyright in the work; or

(e) any person claiming a future, contingent, or conditional expectancy or right of ownership in the copyright in the work, under a will or trust or under the applicable laws of intestate succession; or

(f) any person who, on the date the statement is executed, is the nonexclusive licensee of any rights under copyright in the work.

The term is also changed when the author's true identity is revealed in the filing of the initial or a supplementary registration. In fact, the current Copyright Office practice of requiring the author to reveal his true identity in filling out Space 4 ("Copyright Claimant(s)") of the registration application in the cases of pseudonymous works, and in both spaces 2 ("Name of the Author") and 4 in the case of anonymous works, seemingly results in an automatic conversion of the term.

The concept of "works made for hire" has several important ramifications in the 1976 Act and is a term which developed a questionable judicial gloss under the 1909 Act. It is sufficient to note here that the term is expressly defined in Section 101 in the new Act.[60] This definition will be set forth at p. 121, *infra*. It is clearly the most important category of works with a fixed term measured from publication and creation.

(3) The Register of Copyrights is directed to maintain death records of authors (which the Copyright Office has actually been compiling since the mid-1960s).

(4) A user may in good faith rely on a presumption that the author has been dead for at least 50 years if the Copyright Office records do not reveal the contrary in the case of works published more than 75 years earlier or created more than 100 years earlier (whichever is first). For example, this presumption would shield a good-faith

---

[60]The statute does not specify the term of protection for a joint work co-authored by two persons, only one of whom created the work as an employee-for-hire. The Register of Copyrights' *1965 Supplementary Report* addresses this issue and notes that the presence of a statutory reference was believed unnecessary:

"In this situation the provisions of subsection (b) [of Section 302] would not apply; the term would be based on subsection (a) (the life of the individual plus 50 years) or subsection (c) (75 years from publication or 100 years from creation), whichever is longer. Although this situation is by no means rare, it seemed unnecessary to burden the bill with a special provision dealing with it."

COPYRIGHT LAW REVISION PART 6: SUPPLEMENTARY REPORT OF THE REGISTER OF COPYRIGHTS ON THE GENERAL REVISION OF THE U.S. COPYRIGHT LAW: 1965 REVISION BILL, 89th Cong., 1st Sess. 89–90 (1965).

user in the year 2080 who finds no pertinent Copyright Office records concerning the author of an unpublished work created before 1980.

## Duration of Works Created but Not Published or Copyrighted Before January 1, 1978: §303

These are the works formerly under common law copyright and are generally assimilated to works created after January 1, 1978, for duration purposes. But since the substitution of the limited duration of Section 302 for perpetual common law protection might result in no remaining duration (e.g., letters of authors who died before 1928) or in very little, two minima are established: Protection will last through at least December 31, 2002, but (in order to encourage publication) if published by then, through at least December 31, 2027.

## Subsisting Statutory Copyrights

### First Term: §304(a)

Congress, apparently motivated by considerations of fairness and due process, declined to change the rules in the middle of the game so as to substitute the life-plus-fifty formula for the bifurcated fixed-years system governing subsisting first-term copyrights.[61] The 1976 Act accordingly maintains for such works the precise durational scheme of the 1909 Act (repeating virtually verbatim the muddy prose of Section 24 of that Act)[62] with two significant differences: (1) Renewal terms are extended from 28 years to 47 years; rights granted prior to the effective date of the 1976 Act, insofar as they pertain to the 19-year additional period, are subject to an optional reversion in authors and certain other statutory renewal beneficiaries. (2) All terms of copyright now run to the end of the calendar year in which they would otherwise expire, thus changing the time period when renewal applications must be filed.[63]

One consequence of this decision is that the entire statutory and judicial confusion surrounding renewal remains with us well into the

---

[61]Note, however, that Transitional and Supplementary §103 provided in pertinent part: "This Act does not provide copyright protection for any work that goes into the public domain before January 1, 1978."

[62]For a review of these provisions, see Ringer, *Renewal of Copyright*, COPYRIGHT OFFICE STUDY No. 31, 86th Cong., 2d Sess. (Comm. Print 1961).

[63]Under the 1909 Act, the term of copyright for published works ran from the date of publication; renewal had to be made within one year prior to the expiration of the original term of copyright. Hence, a work first published on April 19, 1917, was eligible for renewal between April 19, 1944, and April 19, 1945. Under the 1976 Act, since the term runs to the end of the calendar year in which it would otherwise expire (and, as before, renewal must be made within one year prior to the expiration of the original term), a work first published on April 19, 1957, would be eligible for renewal only between December 31, 1984, and December 31, 1985.

twenty-first century. Not only will questions as to proper renewal claimants and procedures be prospectively pressing for 28 years, but also the same questions (as well as issues concerning rights of assignees and licensees under renewals) will be asked retrospectively for the 47 additional years of the renewal copyrights. In view of these circumstances and the notably elusive nature of the renewal provision, it becomes necessary to trace in some detail the statutory and judicial history of renewals.

## Renewal in General

The renewal of copyright has been a characteristic feature of our law from the beginning, having been taken from the English Statute of Anne (1710). Other countries, including England itself, have long since replaced it in favor of either a straight term of years or a term measured by the life of the author and a designated number of years following his or her death. This period is usually 50 years, in accordance with the Berne Convention.

While the 1909 Act used the words "renewal and extension," it did not really provide a continuing right, but rather a new grant of copyright for a second term. The grant was and is conditioned upon the filing of an appropriate application in the Copyright Office within one year before the expiration of the original copyright. Generally speaking, the right to renew is accorded to the author provided he or she survives the twenty-seventh year of copyright. This right does not follow the ordinary rules of law in the case of testacy or intestacy and pass to the author's estate if the author dies before the renewal year arrives. It is given directly by the statute to designated beneficiaries in a specified order of preference. Hence the author cannot bequeath his contingent rights to renew (but cf. p. 105, *infra*) or bind the surviving beneficiaries to renew on behalf of someone designated by him in a prior contract.

The first federal copyright act gave the renewal privilege to the author and his executors, administrators, or assigns. But all succeeding legislation, down to the present, has omitted "assigns" and, subject to exceptions, limited the privilege of renewal to the author or, if he or she did not survive, designated members of his or her family or executors. The reason for this policy is explained thus in the report accompanying the bill that became the Act of 1909:

> "It not infrequently happens that the author sells his copyright outright to a publisher for a comparatively small sum. If the work proves to be a great success and lives beyond the term of 28 years, your committee felt that it should be the exclusive right of the author to take the renewal term, and the law should be framed as is the existing law, so that he could not be deprived of that right."[64]

---

[64]H.R. REP. No. 2222, 60th Cong., 2d Sess. 14 (1909).

It was provided, however, that in the case of certain works the proprietor would be the person entitled to receive the renewal copyright also. These works include: (1) posthumous works; (2) composite works where the contributing authors are often so numerous and widely scattered that it would be difficult, if not practically impossible, to secure their cooperation in seeking renewal; (3) dictionaries and similar works involving the labors of many persons, whose identity becomes lost in the work as a whole; and (4) works made by the author in the capacity of an employee for hire.

## Registration of Renewals

Notwithstanding that a whole year is given for filing the renewal application, it is surprising how frequently applicants defer mailing it until the eleventh hour, thereby running the risk of losing the renewal term altogether if for any reason the application and fee fail to reach their destination in time. In these cases, it is advisable to send a telegram setting forth all the essential facts called for in the formal application (viz., identification of the work, date of first publication, name and address of the renewal claimant, and statutory basis of the renewal claim); the fee (currently $6) should also be transmitted by wire unless the applicant maintains a deposit account with the Copyright Office. A formal application for renewal (Form RE) must then be submitted to and received by the Copyright Office by February 1 of the following year. Deposit of additional copies of the work is not required.

Under the 1909 law and the relevant provision of the 1976 Act, works published and copyrighted in the first instance under Section 10 of the 1909 Act have a first term of protection lasting 28 years from "the date of first publication." Where, however, such a work was published with a notice containing a year date earlier than the year of actual first publication, the renewal must be made within the last year of the original term as measured from the year date contained in the notice.[65] Since the term of copyright now expires at the end of the calendar year in which it would otherwise expire, the renewal period begins on December 31 of the 27th year from the year in the notice and runs through December 31 of the 28th year from that date.

In the case of works published prior to January 1, 1978, bearing a copyright notice postdated no more than one year from the actual date of actual publication, the original term for renewal purposes is computed from the date of publication. (See pp. 150–151, *infra*, for further discussion of ante- and post-dated notices under the 1909 Act).

---

[65] 37 C.F.R. §202.17(c)(2). Notwithstanding the earlier date for renewal purposes, the actual date of publication should be given in the renewal application itself. The Copyright Office will then annotate the application by writing: "Year Date in Copyright Notice: 19___."

In the case of works which were registered in unpublished form under Section 12 of the 1909 Act, judicial statesmanship led to a reading of the statute measuring the term as beginning on the date of registration.[66] This position has now been adopted in Copyright Office regulations.[67]

There must be an original registration on file with the Copyright Office before a renewal application can be made, although as long as the necessary information, deposit copies, and fees are all received by the Copyright Office before the end of the first term, it is possible to make simultaneous original and renewal registrations.[68]

An exception to the requirement of a preexisting (or simultaneous) registration is provided in the case of works in which copyright subsists by virtue of Section 9(c) of the 1909 Act, which implemented certain provisions of the United States' adherence to the Universal Copyright Convention. After September 16, 1955 (the date the Convention came into force with respect to the United States), any work first published in another UCC country was exempted from a number of requirements of the 1909 Act.[69] Copyright Office regulations applying Section 9(c) exempt this category of work from the original-registration requirement and instead require that the application for renewal be accompanied by an affidavit identified as "Renewal Affidavit for UCC work" and containing the following information: the date and place of first publication of the work; the citizenship and domicile of the author on the date of first publication; an averment that, at the time of first publication, all authorized published copies bore the symbol © accompanied by the name of the copyright proprietor, and the year of first publication and that United States copyright subsists in the work; and an appropriate deposit copy or identifying material.[70]

It was assumed under the 1909 Act that if the claimant had duly filed a renewal application and the Copyright Office declined to register, he or she did not thereby lose the right to maintain suit for any subsequent infringements. This assumption relied on dicta in *White-Smith Music Pub. Co. v. Goff*, where the First Circuit said: "It [complainant] offered registration under the statute, and, although registration was refused, yet it fully complied with the requirements of law, and is entitled to maintain this suit if it had any statutory right to the extension."[71] Presumably, the same result should obtain under the 1976 Act, and it is possible that the courts will construe the provi-

---

[66]See *Marx v. United States*, 96 F.2d 204, 37 U.S.P.Q. 380 (9th Cir. 1938).

[67]37 C.F.R. §202.17(c). Note also that §304(a) of the 1976 Act, in one of its minor modifications of the §24 language of the 1909 Act, clarified this situation by providing for a first-term copyright of 28 years "from the date it was originally secured."

[68]COMPENDIUM II OF COPYRIGHT OFFICE PRACTICES §1309.

[69]See 17 U.S.C. §9(c) (1955 *repealed* 1978). Note that this section extended the term of protection for works protected by an *ad interim* copyright for the full term of 28 years, and thus the renewal period for such works should be adjusted accordingly.

[70]37 C.F.R. §202.17(d)(2).

[71]187 F. 247 (1st Cir. 1911). The court found, however, that the complainant had no such statutory right in the capacity merely of an "assignee" of the original copyright, and the refusal of the Copyright Office to register on that basis was therefore fully justified.

sions of Section 411(a) as also applying to renewal registrations.[72] However, since review of the Copyright Office's refusal to renew a work is available under the Administrative Procedure Act, this avenue should be pursued as a matter of first recourse wherever practicable.

### Renewal Rights in the Author

The basic rule of renewal, expressed in Section 304(a) of the 1976 Act, is that the author enjoys the renewal right, and, if he is living, the renewal application must be filed in his name, even if he is insane or incompetent[73] or if the work was published anonymously or under a pseudonym.[74]

*Contributions to Periodicals, Cyclopedic, and Composite Works.* Although Section 304(a) of the 1976 Act (patterned after the 1909 Act, as mentioned above) mentions "contributions" to periodicals, cyclopedic, or other composite works, these works were neither defined nor enumerated in the classification scheme of Section 5 of the 1909 Act.[75] As originally enacted in 1909, Section 23 (which subsequently became Section 24) limited author renewals of such contributions to situations "when such contribution has been separately registered." By amendment of this provision[76] these words were eliminated, thus saving the renewal privilege for the author, widow, etc., in the case of all contributions, whether separately registered or not. Prior to the amendment the author and statutory successors could secure control of a contribution which had not been separately registered only by assignment from the proprietor of the composite work, who was in a position, if so disposed, to exact remuneration. Very often, however, when the time for renewal arrived, the original proprietor, typically a magazine, had ceased to exist, leaving no successor in interest who could act or be found. As a consequence, many contributions having great survival value fell into the public domain. It was due mainly to this consideration that Congress saw fit to strike the above-quoted restrictive phrase.[77]

The scope of renewal rights enjoyed by the proprietor of the composite work in the component parts of the work vis-à-vis those of the contributor has been far from clear in situations where the contribution did not bear a separate notice in the contributor's name. The possibility of a concurrent renewal privilege in the copyright owner of

---

[72]Section 411(a), of course, concerns only registration as a prerequisite to a suit for infringement and not the substantive issue of registration of a renewal claim as a prerequisite to obtaining protection. Cf. §408(a).

[73]17 U.S.C. §304(a) (1978); COMPENDIUM II OF COPYRIGHT OFFICE PRACTICES §1313.01. See also 37 C.F.R. §202.17(f)(iii).

[74]COMPENDIUM II OF COPYRIGHT OFFICE PRACTICES §1313.

[75]But see definition of composite works in COMPENDIUM II OF COPYRIGHT OFFICE PRACTICES §1317.04(a).

[76]Act of March 15, 1940, 15 Stat. 51.

[77]S. REP. No. 465, 76th Cong., 1st Sess. (1939).

the composite work and the contributor author (or surviving family) has been[78] and still is criticized.[79] The Copyright Office has commented in this regard:

> "While the proprietor of a composite work may claim renewal in the work as a whole, the author of an individual contribution, or the author's beneficiaries, may also claim renewal in the contribution.
> "It is unclear whether the proprietor's claim in the entire work covers everything in the work that is not separately renewed."[80]

It is also possible under the provisions of Section 408(c)(3) of the 1976 Act for an author to make a single renewal on a single application (and for a single fee) for a group of his or her works first published as contributions to periodicals, provided: (1) the renewal claimant is the same for each of the works; (2) each of the works was first published with a separate copyright notice or under a general notice in the periodical issue as a whole; (3) registration has been made for the original term, either as a separate registration or by virtue of registration of the periodical; (4) the application identifies each work separately, including the periodical containing it and its date of first publication; and (5) the application and fee are received not more than 28 or less than 27 years after the 31st day of December of the calendar year in which all of the works were first published. This provision does not apply, however, to an employer-for-hire "author."

*Works of Multiple Authorship.* Two or more authors may create a unitary work, considered a work of joint authorship, in which case both are entitled to the renewal privilege in the entire work. If one author takes out the renewal in his own name, he holds the copyright in trust for the benefit of all the other joint authors.[81] This is to be contrasted with the production by several authors of a work, such as a story with illustrations, which can be regarded as separable; in this case, each author has been held entitled to secure separate renewal for his or her own distinct component of the work and nothing more.[82] Where the contributions are not only separable but many, as in a compilation, encyclopedia, or periodical, the proprietor enjoys the renewal rights.

The statement of these three situations, each with its distinct consequences as to renewal, does not imply that they are easily distinguishable. Moreover, the situation under the 1909 law was further confused by the expansion given to the concept of "joint works" by the Court of Appeals for the Second Circuit. See pp. 115–116, *infra.*

---

[78]2 NIMMER ON COPYRIGHT §9.03[B].

[79]Brylawski, *Renewal of Copyright in a Magazine Contribution: A Belated View*, 42 GEO. WASH. L. REV. 737, 750 (1974).

[80]COMPENDIUM II OF COPYRIGHT OFFICE PRACTICES §1317.06(b). See also discussion of the term "author" in this context in *Cadence Indus. Corp. v. Ringer*, 450 F. Supp. 59, 65, 197 U.S.P.Q. 664, 671 (S.D.N.Y. 1978).

[81]*Edward B. Marks Music Corp. v. Jerry Vogel Music Co.*, 42 F. Supp. 859, 52 U.S.P.Q. 219 (S.D.N.Y. 1942).

[82]*Harris v. Coca-Cola Co.*, 73 F.2d 370, 23 U.S.P.Q. 182 (5th Cir. 1934).

As with works made for hire, the 1976 Act definition of "joint works" differs from the Second Circuit definition of the term under the 1909 law in its requirement that the work be "prepared by two or more authors with the intention that their contributions be merged into inseparable or interdependent parts of a unitary whole." The touchstone here is the intention of integration "at the time the writing is done."[83] But the choice of the 1976 Act or the 1909 Act case law definition of such intention for renewal purposes would produce different results in certain circumstances.[84]

## Renewal Rights in Widow, Widower, and Children

If the author is no longer living at the time for renewal, it is the Copyright Act, and not state rules of testamentary or intestate succession, that governs the eligibility of classes of persons entitled to claim the renewal copyright, and, given Congress' solicitude for the dependent members of an author's family, it is understandable that the widow and children have first priority in the renewal right. It has now been established that this priority is shared, i.e., the right of a child is not contingent upon the death of a widow prior to the renewal year but rather "the widow and children of the author succeed to the right of renewal as a class, and are each entitled to share in the renewal term of the copyright,"[85] although it is not clear what the respective shares of the widow(er) and the children are in such a renewal.[86]

The Copyright Act defines the author's widow as "the author's surviving spouse under the law of the author's domicile at the time of his or her death, whether or not the spouse has later remarried."[87] A divorced spouse is not an acceptable renewal claimant.[88] The Act defines the author's children as "immediate offspring, whether legitimate or not, and any children legally adopted by that person."[89] This definition does not include stepchildren as such,[90] grandchildren, or "other descendants beyond the first degree."[91]

---

[83]H.R. REP. No. 94-1476, 94th Cong., 2d Sess. 120 (1976); S. REP. No. 94-473, 94th Cong., 1st Sess. 103 (1975).

[84]See Beckett, *The Copyright Act of 1976: When Is It Effective?* 24 BULL. COPR. SOC'Y 393, 395–396 (1977).

[85]*De Sylva v. Ballentine*, 351 U.S. 570, 580, 109 U.S.P.Q. 431, 434–435 (1956).

[86]In *Bartok v. Boosey & Hawkes, Inc.*, 523 F.2d 941, 187 U.S.P.Q. 529 (2d Cir. 1975), it was apparently assumed that the shares would be equally divided.

[87]17 U.S.C. §101 (1978). This definition thus includes common law spouses where such marriages are recognized under applicable state law. See *Hill & Range Songs, Inc. v. Fred Rose Music, Inc.*, 403 F. Supp. 420, 189 U.S.P.Q. 233 (M.D. Tenn. 1975).

[88]COMPENDIUM II OF COPYRIGHT OFFICE PRACTICES §1314.02(3). *Donaldson Pub. Co. v. Bregman, Vocco & Conn., Inc.*, 253 F. Supp. 841 (S.D.N.Y. 1965), rev'd on other grounds, 375 F.2d 639, 153 U.S.P.Q. 149 (2d Cir. 1967).

[89]17 U.S.C. §101 (1978).

[90]COMPENDIUM II OF COPYRIGHT OFFICE PRACTICES §1314.03(3).

[91]*Id.* at §1314.03(4).

## Renewal Rights in Executor

If the author dies testate before the renewal year arrives, leaving no surviving spouse or children, the right to renew is given by the statute directly to the author's executor, as opposed to the legatees, apparently in order to ensure efficient administration of the author's assets.[92] The right of an executor to claim renewal is a personal one, and thus the executor must have been named in the author's will and presumably have been qualified in probate proceedings. The renewal application must be in the name of the executor and not as "Estate of John Doe," notwithstanding the fact that the executor holds the right for the persons entitled to receive the estate according to the law of the author's domicile at the time of the author's death.

Where the author dies testate but does not name an executor (or if the person named in the will cannot or will not act as executor), a court may appoint an *administrator cum testamento annexo* ("c.t.a.") who may then file the renewal application. When the estate has been settled and the executor discharged, or when the executor is removed before the estate has been completely administered, an *administrator de bonis non cum testamento annexo* ("d.b.c.n.t.a.") appointed by the court may also file the renewal claim.

It should also be noted that there can be an "absence of a will" under the Copyright Act even where the author dies testate. This anomaly has a direct impact on succession by next of kin, since such successors take only in the absence of a will. The anomaly arises where an administrator is not in office at the time of vesting of the renewal right. This situation was explored in *Capano Music v. Myers Music, Inc.*,[93] and resulted in the defeat of an assignment made by an administrator c.t.a. (the author's surviving spouse, who had died before the right to renew vested) and a distribution made by a subsequent administrator d.b.c.n.t.a. of the author, who had given the renewal rights in accordance with the will of the administrator c.t.a.

## Renewal Rights in the Next of Kin

If the author dies intestate (or otherwise "in the absence of a will"), and without surviving spouse or children, the author's "next of kin" are entitled to the renewal right. An administrator of the intestate author's estate may not assert the claim.[94] Unfortunately, the Copyright Act does not contain a definition of "next of kin." The Copyright Office has noted as follows on this issue:

"The term 'next of kin' refers only to blood relatives of the author.
"It is not clear whether the term * * * refers only to the living rela-

---

[92]See *Miller Music Corp. v. Charlie N. Daniels, Inc.*, 362 U.S. 373, 125 U.S.P.Q. 147 (1960).
[93]*Capano Music v. Myers Music, Inc.*, 605 F. Supp. 692 (S.D.N.Y. 1985). See also *Gibran v. National Committee of Gibran*, 255 F.2d 121, 117 U.S.P.Q. 218 (2d Cir.), *cert. denied*, 358 U.S. 828, 119 U.S.P.Q. 501 (1958); *Silverman v. Sunrise Pictures Corp.*, 290 F. 804 (2d Cir.), *cert. denied*, 262 U.S. 758 (1923).
[94]COMPENDIUM II OF COPYRIGHT PRACTICES §1315.03.

tives of the nearest degree of consanguinity (defined as the quality or state of being descended from the same ancestor) or whether it also includes the descendants of dead relatives claiming on the theory of representation. The Copyright Office will register the claim of any blood relative as 'next of kin,' regardless of the degree of consanguinity."[95]

## Renewal Rights in the Proprietor

Although the "basic" rule of renewal is that the author or his or her family enjoys renewal rights, the obtuse construction of Section 304(a) of the 1976 Act (which parallels Section 24 of the 1909 Act) obscures this fact. After specifying a duration of 28 years, this section then engrafts "provisos" to the 28-year term which embody the renewal concept.

The "first proviso" in Section 304(a) states that in the case of (1) any posthumous work, (2) any periodical, cyclopedic, or other composite work upon which the copyright was originally secured by the proprietor thereof, (3) any work copyrighted by a corporate body (otherwise than as assignee or licensee of the individual author), or (4) any work copyrighted by an employer for whom such work is made for hire, "the proprietor of such copyright shall be entitled to a renewal and extension of the copyright in such work for the further term of forty-seven years when application for such renewal and extension shall have been made to the Copyright Office and duly registered therein within one year prior to the expiration of the original term of copyright." The exercise of this right is not restricted to the original proprietor but includes his successor in interest, in other words, whoever may be the proprietor at the time the renewal year arrives, so long as the claimant derives title directly or indirectly from the original copyright owner.[96]

*Posthumous Works.* It is difficult to justify including posthumous works in the first proviso, since it has the effect of depriving the author's spouse and children of the renewal privilege in case the original copyright was secured by the publisher: In principle, they should have the same right of renewal as they would have if the work were not "posthumous."

The provision was undoubtedly the result of an unfortunate historical accident, having been originally introduced when the draft of the 1909 law provided for a basic life-plus term. This latter scheme may have been deemed inappropriate for posthumous works, but then the exception was inadvertently maintained when the life-plus term was abandoned.[97]

---

[95] *Id.* at §1316.02.

[96] *Shapiro, Bernstein & Co. v. Bryan*, 27 F. Supp. 11, 41 U.S.P.Q. 134 (S.D.N.Y. 1939); 36 F. Supp. 544, 48 U.S.P.Q. 69 (S.D.N.Y. 1940), *aff'd*, 123 F.2d 697, 51 U.S.P.Q. 422 (2d Cir. 1941).

[97] See Ringer, *Renewal of Copyright*, COPYRIGHT OFFICE STUDY No. 31, 86th Cong., 2d Sess. (Comm. Print 1961).

A sharp limitation of this class of works was imposed in the first case directly construing its meaning. In *Bartok v. Boosey & Hawkes, Inc.*,[98] the court of appeals held that the basic policy behind granting renewal rights, i.e., to provide for the author and his or her family, would best be served by limiting the category of posthumous works to those not covered by an assignment or other contract for exploitation of the work made during the author's lifetime. The work in question, Bartok's "Concerto for Orchestra," not only had been the subject of such an assignment but in addition had already been performed on the radio and its score set in printer's proofs before the composer died. The court rejected the district court's definition of posthumous works as those which are technically "unpublished" under the 1909 law, that is, not generally distributed in tangible form, prior to the author's death.[99]

The drafters of the 1976 Act expressly stated their intent to inject into Section 304(a) the meaning of "posthumous" given in the final *Bartok* decision.[100] Although the term is not defined in the Act, Copyright Office regulations state:

> " 'Posthumous work' means a work that was unpublished on the date of the death of the author and with respect to which no copyright assignment or other contract for exploitation of the work occurred during the author's lifetime."[101]

Notwithstanding this definition, the regulations also provide that

> "a renewal claim may be registered in the name of the proprietor of the work, as well as in the name of the appropriate claimant under paragraph (f)(1)(ii) [e.g., widow, executor], in any case where a contract for exploitation of the work but no copyright assignment in the work has occurred during the author's lifetime. However, registration by the Copyright Office should not be interpreted as evidencing the validity of the claim."[102]

*Composite Works.* Composite works were deemed to embrace compilations, cyclopedias, periodicals, and similar collections of independent and distinct contributions by various authors brought together and published as one work.[103] Thus, a work made up of selections from the works of a single author would not be renewable as a composite work; the renewal application in such case should be made in the name of the editor or compiler as "author," save where he acted in the capacity of an employee for hire (see p. 104, below). (Compare the definition of the term "collective work" in Section 101 of the 1976 Act, which is not limited to works of different authors and expressly

---

[98]523 F.2d 941, 187 U.S.P.Q. 529 (2d Cir. 1975).
[99]See 51 N.Y.U. L. REV. 332 (1976) for a comment on this.
[100]H.R. REP. No. 94-1476, 94th Cong., 2d Sess. 139 (1976).
[101]37 C.F.R. §202.17(b).
[102]*Id.* at §202.17(f)(2).
[103]*Harris v. Coca-Cola Co.*, 1 F. Supp. 713, 16 U.S.P.Q. 222 (N.D. Ga. 1932); *Shapiro, Bernstein & Co. v. Bryan*, 123 F.2d 697, 51 U.S.P.Q. 422 (2d Cir. 1941).

covers anthologies. Although the new Act does cover questions of ownership of collective works, renewal consequences under Section 304 presumably hinge on the meaning of the 1909 Act term "composite works.") Composite works may, of course, include new matter not previously published, as well as matter already copyrighted or in the public domain.

*Any Work Copyrighted by a Corporate Body (Otherwise Than as Assignee or Licensee of the Individual Author).* It is not clear why corporate bodies were singled out for this particular blessing, nor just what kinds of works were intended to be embraced. Some light, however, is shed upon the subject in the original hearings, where it is said that the words in the parenthetical clause ("otherwise than as assignee or licensee of the individual author") "are necessary to cover the case of a personal copyright taken out by an incorporated firm of publishers."[104] A work created by an individual author, who later assigned the right to secure copyright for the first term to a "corporate body," would be subject to such a "personal" copyright; the author of such work, rather than any corporate assignee, would be entitled to renew by reason of the parenthetical exclusion from this provision. Such a work is to be contrasted to works of an "impersonal character," such as digests and dictionaries, where the identity of the individual authors is merged in the work as a whole. It is to these latter types of works that this provision seems especially applicable, composite works being already covered by the preceding clause. In a case involving the famous Hummel figurines, the court stated in this regard:

> "It may be that the term 'work copyrighted by a corporate body' should apply to 'impersonal works' such as directories, dictionaries and corporate reports developed by several people. * * * In addition, where members of a religious order have taken not merely simple vows * * * but solemn vows, so that they may not own any property at all * * * then perhaps the 'corporate body' provision may apply."[105]

This holding follows Copyright Office practice. While strongly discouraging renewal claims under this provision, the Office has indicated that it will consider such claims for the following:

> "1)  Works to which the stockholders of a corporation have contributed indistinguishable parts.
> "2)  Works written or created by members of a religious order or similar order or similar organization, when the individual authors never had a personal property right in the works.

---

[104] *Hearings on Revision of Copyright Laws Before Comms. on Patents*, 60th Cong., 1st Sess. 88 (1908).

[105] *Schmid Bros., Inc. v. W. Goebel Porzellanfabrik KG.*, 589 F. Supp. 497, 505, 223 U.S.P.Q. 859, 864 (E.D.N.Y. 1984). See also *Cadence Indus. Corp. v. Ringer*, 450 F. Supp. 59, 197 U.S.P.Q. 664 (S.D.N.Y. 1978); *Epoch Producing Corp. v. Killiam Shows, Inc.*, 522 F.2d 737, 187 U.S.P.Q. 270 (2d Cir. 1975), *cert. denied*, 424 U.S. 955, 189 U.S.P.Q. 256 (1976); *Shapiro, Bernstein & Co. v. Bryan, supra* note 103.

"3) Works written by an official or major stockholder in a corporation, when the works were written directly for the corporation and the arrangement did not amount to employment for hire.

"4) Motion pictures, when the applicant asserts that the work was produced under special circumstances and was not copyrighted by an employer for whom the work was made for hire."[106]

*Any Work Originally Copyrighted by an Employer for Whom Such Work Is Made for Hire.* Where the work was created as a work made for hire, the proper renewal claimant is the employer for hire. The question of whether a work "originally copyrighted" by someone other than the employer could be renewed by the employer was raised but not decided in *Epoch Producing Corp. v. Killiam.*[107] What was decided in *Epoch* was that the director D. W. Griffith was *not* an employee for hire for renewal purposes with respect to the 1914 film classic "The Birth of a Nation." The court refused to extend to renewal certificates the presumption of validity often granted to certificates of original registration under Section 209 of the 1909 Act. Lacking this evidentiary advantage, the renewal claimant was unable to produce proof from 1914 that would support any of the theories of employment (or other theories) establishing its right to renew.[108]

In an earlier draft of this clause, the term "for salary" was used instead of "for hire," and it seems reasonable to suppose that the substitution was made for the purpose of broadening this basis of renewal beyond employment on a regular salary. But sometimes, when the time for renewal arrives, as in *Epoch*, a difference of opinion develops between the proprietor and the author, with the latter or his or her surviving spouse or children (or their assignee) claiming that the author did not make the work in the capacity of a "hired hand" but as an independent salesperson for his or her product.[109] Of course, this problem may also arise in the case of original registration, but under those circumstances the facts are fresher. The Copyright Office does not undertake to decide the issue in such cases, but will register separately for each party on proper application, leaving it to the courts to settle the question of ownership.

The factual inquiry in the "Birth of a Nation" case was made against a legal standard of "works made for hire" which had recently been expanded within the Second Circuit. Traditionally, the concept had seemed to be rooted in works created in the regular course of employment, usually salaried, and as defined by the common law.[110] But in *Picture Music, Inc. v. Bourne, Inc.,*[111] the court of appeals ex-

---

[106]COMPENDIUM II OF COPYRIGHT OFFICE PRACTICES §1317.06(c).

[107]522 F.2d 737, 187 U.S.P.Q. 270 (2d Cir. 1975), *cert. denied,* 424 U.S. 955, 189 U.S.P.Q. 256 (1976). Cf. *Schmid. Bros., supra* note 105.

[108]Cf. *Feiner & Co. v. Crown Publishers, Inc.,* 75 Civ. 3484 (S.D.N.Y. filed Aug. 29, 1975) (long acquiescence in status of Laurel and Hardy films supported estoppel).

[109]See, e.g., *Donaldson Pub. Co. v. Bregman, Vocco & Conn., Inc.,* 375 F.2d 639, 153 U.S.P.Q. 149 (2d Cir. 1967), *cert. denied,* 389 U.S. 1036, 156 U.S.P.Q. 719 (1968).

[110]See Varmer, *Works Made for Hire and on Commission,* COPYRIGHT OFFICE STUDY No. 13, 86th Cong., 2d Sess. (Comm. Print 1960).

[111]457 F.2d 1213, 173 U.S.P.Q. 449 (2d Cir.), *cert. denied,* 409 U.S. 997, 175 U.S.P.Q. 577 (1972). See criticism of *Bourne* in 2 NIMMER ON COPYRIGHT §9.03[D].

pressly recognized the applicability of the statutory work-for-hire standard to the commissioning of an independent contractor, holding that "[t]he purpose of the statute is not to be frustrated by the conceptualistic formulations of the employment relationship."[112]

We have noted that the language of Section 304(a) which we are examining has been borrowed from Section 24 of the 1909 Act. But the 1976 Act has its own definition of "works made for hire,"[113] a definition which substantially differs from that of its predecessor. The question thus arises of which definition is to apply to renewals of works published before January 1, 1978, but submitted for renewal after that date. Under the authority of the Second Circuit's decision in *Roth v. Pritikin*,[114] holding that the work-for-hire provisions of the 1976 Act are not to be applied retroactively, it appears that such renewal questions must be determined on the basis of the 1909 Act and case law interpreting it.

*Assignments, Licenses, and Renewals.* The paternalistic objectives behind the renewal reversion concept have not, however, been fully achieved. In 1943, the Supreme Court held that the statute did *not* prevent the author from specifically agreeing to assigning the renewal rights *in futuro*, provided that the author was alive at the time the right to renew vested.[115] There is, unfortunately, no guidance on when the right vests.[116]

Regardless of when that time occurs, it is clear that the registration must be made in the name of the author,[117] who may then assign all right, title, and interest in the new term of copyright thereby secured. Of course, the fulfillment of a renewal contract is contingent upon the author's surviving into the renewal period. And, as noted above, the author cannot, by will or otherwise, cut off the right of renewal of beneficiaries named in the statute. Thus, not only do the widow(er) and children prevail over the assignee of an author who does not survive, but the same priority is also given to the other designated beneficiaries. Indeed, in a 5–4 decision, the Supreme Court held that, in the absence of a widow and children, an executor, acting on behalf of the legatees, enjoys renewal rights unaffected by earlier assignments made by the author himself who died before the renewal year. *Miller Music Corp. v. Charles N. Daniels, Inc.*[118] The author can

---

[112]See also *Brattleboro Pub. Co. v. Winmill Pub. Co.*, 369 F.2d 565, 151 U.S.P.Q. 666 (2d Cir. 1966), and discussion in Chapter 4, "Works Made for Hire."

[113]17 U.S.C. §101 (1978).

[114]710 F.2d 934, 219 U.S.P.Q. 204 (2d Cir.), *cert. denied*, 464 U.S. 961, 220 U.S.P.Q. 385 (1983).

[115]*Fred Fisher Music Co. v. M. Witmark & Sons*, 318 U.S. 643, 57 U.S.P.Q. 50 (1943). Cf. *Landon v. Twentieth Century-Fox Film Corp.*, 384 F. Supp. 450, 185 U.S.P.Q. 221 (S.D.N.Y. 1974) (acquisition of renewal rights together with original rights held not to be illegal tie-in).

[116]See *Capano Music v. Myers Music, Inc.*, 605 F. Supp. 692, 695 n. 2 (S.D.N.Y. 1985); 2 Nimmer on Copyright §9.05[C] and authorities cited therein for a discussion of possible periods.

[117]Compendium II of Copyright Practices §1319.06. See also 28 Op. Att'y Gen. 162, 170 (1910).

[118]362 U.S. 373, 125 U.S.P.Q. 147 (1960).

thus, in an indirect way, defeat by will his earlier *inter vivos* transfer of a renewal interest. It must be remembered, however, that all the author could transfer during his or her lifetime was an expectancy contingent upon survival. Where the contingency fails, as in *Miller*, the statute designates the executor as the person entitled to renewal in the absence of a surviving spouse and children.

Needless to say, a specific intent to transfer the renewal expectancy, as distinguished from the original copyright, must be present before a court will enforce such a transfer. A general transfer of "the copyright" without mention of renewal rights is insufficient,[119] but circumstances may sufficiently disclose the intent of the parties so that special words are not needed.[120]

While enforcing the alienability of renewal interests in *Fred Fisher Music Co. v. M. Witmark & Sons*, the Supreme Court issued the warning that unconscionable bargains would not be enforceable. Thus, in determining the rights of successive assignees of renewal rights, the courts have refused priority to a first assignee whose contract lacked consideration flowing to the author.[121] The courts will not, however, protect an author from imprudent bargains. It has been held that questions of adequacy of consideration and unconscionability are matters of state and not federal law.[122]

In view of the interests contingent upon the death of the author prior to the 28th year, publishers and other proprietors often seek to obtain such interests when practicable. It would certainly seem that the grants from a widow(er), children, and other contingent beneficiaries are as binding as a transfer of the author's own expectancy.[123]

It is generally recognized that a renewal copyright is "a new and independent right in the copyright, free and clear of any rights, interests or licenses attached to the copyright for the initial term."[124]

Can renewal, in cutting off a license granted during the initial term, thus prevent exploitation of a derivative work, such as a motion picture, play, or opera, created pursuant to the license? In

---

[119]*Lieber v. Bienstock*, Copr. L. Rep. ¶25,818 at pp. 19,714–19,715 (S.D.N.Y. 1985); *World Music Co. v. Adam R. Levy & Father Ent., Inc.*, 214 U.S.P.Q. 854, 855 n. 1 (S.D.N.Y. 1981); *Followay Prods., Inc. v. Maurer*, 603 F.2d 72, 203 U.S.P.Q. 76 (9th Cir. 1979); *Edward B. Marks Music Corp. v. Charles K. Harris Music Pub. Co.*, 255 F.2d 518, 117 U.S.P.Q. 308 (2d Cir. 1958). But cf. *South-Western Pub. Co. v. Simons*, 651 F.2d 653, 656, 210 U.S.P.Q. 883, 884–885 (9th Cir. 1981). Where, however, the renewal right has vested, a general transfer is permissible. *Lieber v. Bienstock, supra.*

[120]*Lieber v. Bienstock, supra* note 119; *Venus Music Corp. v. Mills Music, Inc.*, 261 F.2d 577, 119 U.S.P.Q. 360 (2d Cir. 1958).

[121]*Rossiter v. Vogel*, 148 F.2d 292, 65 U.S.P.Q. 72 (2d Cir. 1945). Cf. *Rose v. Bourne, Inc.*, 279 F.2d 79, 125 U.S.P.Q. 509 (2d Cir.), *cert. denied*, 364 U.S. 880, 127 U.S.P.Q. 555 (1960); *Carmichael v. Mills Music Co.*, 121 F. Supp. 43, 101 U.S.P.Q. 279 (S.D.N.Y. 1954).

[122]*Dolch v. United California Bank*, 702 F.2d 178, 218 U.S.P.Q. 116 (9th Cir. 1983).

[123]See *Fisher v. Edwin H. Morris & Co.*, 113 U.S.P.Q. 251 (S.D.N.Y. 1957).

[124]*Followay Prods., Inc. v. Maurer*, 603 F.2d 72, 203 U.S.P.Q. 76 (9th Cir. 1979); *Fitch v. Schubert*, 20 F. Supp. 314, 35 U.S.P.Q. 245 (S.D.N.Y. 1937). Through the application of this rule in *Fitch*, all rights which the defendants had acquired to use a play as the basis of an operetta expired by operation of the statute when the original term ended and the author's next-of-kin granted the renewal copyright to a new owner.

*G. Ricordi & Co. v. Paramount Pictures, Inc.,*[125] the opera "Madame Butterfly" was created by plaintiff under a license from the proprietors of copyright in a play and novel. Plaintiff later claimed the right to make a motion picture version of the opera. Although the copyright in the play was not renewed, the copyright in the novel was. The court construed the license to cover only the original term of copyright and held that "the plaintiff is not entitled to make general use of the novel for a motion picture version." The effect of this decision was to prevent, during the renewal period, exploitation of any picture insofar as it incorporated portions of the opera *based on the novel.* Without making any distinction between the opera and motion picture versions, most commentators had read *Ricordi* as precluding exploitation in the renewal period of any derivative work incorporating underlying material not licensed for use in the renewal period.[126]

The thrust of *Ricordi* was at least temporarily dulled by *Rohauer v. Killiam Shows,*[127] which permitted exploitation of a derivative motion picture during the renewal period of the underlying copyrighted work even though the author/licensor of that underlying work had died prior to renewal and her daughter (who had renewed) granted exclusive motion picture rights to plaintiff. The intent of the *author* to grant renewal rights in *Rohauer* and the derivative work's independent copyright status were held to distinguish *Ricordi,* even though the author's death would seem to have frustrated that intent by cutting off her contingent renewal rights. *Rohauer* was strongly criticized by commentators,[128] and has been described in a decision by a subsequent panel of the Second Circuit as involving a "minor aberration." That decision, *Filmvideo Releasing Corp. v. Hastings,*[129] concerned a licensed derivative work and the underlying copyrighted matter which it incorporated. The derivative work had fallen into the public domain for failure to renew; the original had, however, been renewed, and the question presented was whether the failure to renew the derivative work also threw the underlying original work into the public domain, a possibility raised if the *Ricordi* decision were construed to hold that the copyright owner of the derivative work had obtained a proprietary interest in the underlying copyrighted material.

---

[125]189 F.2d 469, 89 U.S.P.Q. 289 (2d Cir.), *cert. denied,* 342 U.S. 849, 91 U.S.P.Q. 382 (1951). *Ricordi* was distinguished in *Classic Film Museum, Inc. v. Warner Bros., Inc.,* 597 F.2d 13, 202 U.S.P.Q. 467 (1st Cir. 1979), as referring to situations where the underlying work is protected by statutory (as opposed to common law) copyright. See also *Grove Press, Inc. v. Greenleaf Pub. Co.,* 247 F. Supp. 518, 147 U.S.P.Q. 99 (E.D.N.Y. 1965).

[126]See, e.g., Bricker, *Renewal and Extension of Copyright,* 29 S.Cal. L. Rev. 23, 43 (1955); Ringer, *Renewal of Copyright,* Copyright Office Study No. 31, 86th Cong., 2d Sess. (Comm. Print 1961). But see Engel, *Importation and Protection of Works of American Authors Manufactured Abroad Via the UCC Exemptions From Formalities,* 12 Bull. Copr. Soc'y 83, 119–120, and n. 126 (1964).

[127]551 F.2d 484, 192 U.S.P.Q. 545 (2d Cir.), *cert. denied,* 431 U.S. 949, 194 U.S.P.Q. 304 (1977).

[128]Comment, *Derivative Copyright and the 1909 Act—New Clarity or Confusion?* 44 Brooklyn L. Rev. 905 (1978); 1 Nimmer on Copyright §3.07[A].

[129]668 F.2d 91, 218 U.S.P.Q. 750 (2d Cir. 1981).

In answering the question in the negative, the Second Circuit followed the Ninth Circuit's decision in *Russell v. Price*,[130] which had criticized *Rohauer*. The facts in *Hastings* concerned a license by Clarence Mumford, author of the Hopalong Cassidy stories, to make derivative motion pictures based on the stories. The copyrights in the motion pictures were not renewed; the copyrights in the stories were. In rejecting a claim that the expiration of the copyright in the movies threw the material incorporated therein from the movies into the public domain, the court of appeals held that "a derivative copyright is a good copyright only with regard to the original embellishments and additions it has made in the underlying work," and that "[s]ince the proprietor of a derivative copyright cannot convey away that which he does not own * * * it follows that he cannot release that which he does not own into the public domain."[131]

The concept of renewal as a "new estate" has had other ramifications. For example, it supports the conclusion that a renewal copyright may escape the claims of creditors against the author's estate. Moreover, it raises a question regarding the notice to be affixed to copies issued after renewal. There is no express provision in the Act governing this situation. Often, only the original notice is affixed. In *Fox Film Co. v. Knowles*,[132] the district court approved a notice giving only the year date of renewal and the name of the renewal claimant. But the question has not been entirely free from doubt, and it has been recommended that the original notice be included as well, for example: Copyright 1945 by John Doe. Copyright Renewed 1973 by Richard Roe.[133] Since there is no requirement that a "renewal notice" be affixed, the failure to affix such a notice has no adverse consequences on copyright protection.

A final word about renewal as a new estate. Does this concept govern where the renewal right is in the proprietor, or are such renewals merely extensions of the original copyright subject to all applicable assignments, licenses, and claims of creditors? The latter conclusion has been suggested.[134]

### Renewal Term: §304(b)

We now turn to statutory copyrights which, before January 1, 1978, were in their renewal terms, or registered for renewal. These renewal copyrights were on October 19, 1976, automatically extended to endure for a term of 75 years from the date copyright was originally secured. These can be divided into several categories. For

---

[130]612 F.2d 1123, 1126–1129, 205 U.S.P.Q. 206, 209–211 (9th Cir. 1979), *cert. denied*, 446 U.S. 952 (1980).

[131]668 F.2d at 93, 218 U.S.P.Q. at 751.

[132]274 F. 731 (E.D.N.Y. 1921), *aff'd*, 279 F. 1018 (2d Cir. 1922), *rev'd on other grounds*, 261 U.S. 326 (1923).

[133]COPYRIGHT OFFICE CIRCULAR R15.

[134]Ringer, *Renewal of Copyright*, COPYRIGHT OFFICE STUDY No. 31, 86th Cong., 2d Sess. (Comm. Print 1961).

example, copyrights renewed since September 19, 1948, simply enjoy an additional 19 years of duration, i.e., from 28 to 47 years. Copyrights renewed between September 19, 1934, and September 19, 1948, are more complicated. These were works originally copyrighted between September 19, 1906, and September 19, 1920, and enjoyed the benefit of a series of interim extension bills designed to keep renewals alive pending the enactment of a longer term through general copyright revision.[135] The effective date of such laws began on September 19, 1962, in the expectation of an early passage of the revision, with a provision that all copyrights in their renewal term would continue under such protection until December 31, 1964. A series of one- and two-year extensions maintained such renewals through December 31, 1976. These renewal copyrights have thus enjoyed up to 14 years of the longer 19-year term. Accordingly, the simplest way to compute their new term is to determine the date copyright was originally secured and to add 75 years extended to the end of the calendar year. (Works copyrighted prior to September 19, 1906, are in the public domain and are not revived by the 1976 Act.)[136]

### Termination: §304(c)

When Congress extended subsisting or expectant renewal copyrights for a total of 19 years, it decided to accord authors and others covered by the "second proviso" the potential to enjoy this extended period free and clear of preexisting grants. Accordingly, Section 304(c) gives authors and their statutory successors the option, under certain conditions and limitations, to terminate transfers or licenses insofar as the extended period is concerned. This is accomplished in a complex provision which can be summarized as follows:

(1) *Grants covered* (§304(c))
   (a) transfers *or* licenses of *renewal* rights—exclusive or non-exclusive
   (b) executed *before* January 1, 1978
   (c) by a claimant of renewal under the "second proviso"
   (d) where statutory copyright—first or renewal term—is subsisting on January 1, 1978 (former common law copyrights are not covered)
   (e) except as to:
       (i) works made for hire
       (ii) dispositions by will.
(2) *Persons who may exercise right*
   (a) as to grants by author(s):
       (i) the author(s) to extent of such author's(s') interest (§304(c)(1))

---

[135]See COPYRIGHT OFFICE CIRCULAR R15t, *Extension of Copyright Terms.*
[136]TRANS. & SUPP. §103, 90 Stat. 2599.

     (ii)  if an author is dead, by owners of more than half of author's termination interest, such interest being owned as follows:
- by surviving spouse (if no children or grandchildren)
- by children and surviving children of dead child (if no surviving spouse), *per stirpes* and by majority action or
- shared, one half by widow and one half by children and deceased child's children (§304(c)(2))

    (b)  as to grants by others—*all* surviving grantors (§304(c)(1) and (4)).

(3) *Effective date of termination*
    (a)  designated time during five-year period commencing on later of:
       (i)  beginning of fifty-seventh year of copyright or
      (ii)  January 1, 1978 (§304(c)(3))
    (b)  upon 2–10 years' notice (§304(c)(4)).

(4) *Manner of terminating*
    (a)  written and signed notice by required persons or agents to grantee or grantee's "successor in title"
    (b)  specification of effective date, within above limits
    (c)  form, content, and manner of service in accordance with Copyright Office regulation (§304(c)(4)(B)) (These have now been issued. 37 C.F.R. §201.10.)
    (d)  recordation in Copyright Office before effective date (§304(c)(4)(A))
    (e)  termination right may not be waived or contracted away in advance (§304(c)(5)).

(5) *Effect of a termination*
    (a)  of grant by author
       (i)  reversion to that author or, if dead, those owning author's termination interest (including those who did not join in signing termination notice) in proportionate shares (§304(c)(6) and (c)(6)(C))
    (b)  of grant by others—reversion to all entitled to terminate (§304(c)(6))
    (c)  in either case, future rights to revert vest upon proper service of notice of termination (§304(c)(6)(B)).

(6) *Exceptions to termination*
    (a)  utilization of derivative work prepared under grant prior to termination (no right to make another derivative work) (§304(c)(6)(A))
    (b)  rights outside federal copyright statute (§304(c)(6)(E)).

(7) *Further grants of terminated rights*
    (a)  each owner is tenant in common except that a further grant by owners of particular dead author's terminated rights must be same number and proportion of his beneficiaries as required to terminate, but then binds them all, including nonsigners, as to such rights

> (b) must be made after *termination*, except that, as to original grantee or successor in title, it may be after *notice* of termination.

Needless to say, one may foresee many mechanical and other problems which may require the talents of the trusts and estates lawyer to assist the copyright lawyer.[137] One problem that arose even before the general effective date of the 1976 Act (January 1, 1978) was whether a notice of termination under Section 304(c) could be given prior to such date. In *Burroughs v. MGM*, discussed *infra*, the district court held such a notice ineffective; however, on appeal the Second Circuit decided the case on different grounds.[138]

As noted above, the Copyright Office has issued regulations implementing the procedures for a Section 304(c) notice of termination.[139] These regulations require that the notice be served upon each "grantee" whose rights are being terminated, or "the grantee's successor in title," by personal service, or by first-class mail sent to an address "which, after a reasonable investigation, is found to be the last known address of the grantee or successor in title."[140] The regulations further provide that "a reasonable investigation" includes but is not limited to a search of the records in the Copyright Office.[141]

The Act does not, however, define the term "successor in title" nor does the legislative history provide any guidance concerning its intended meaning. In *Burroughs v. MGM* the author had transferred all his existing copyrights in the "Tarzan" books to a corporation he owned, and this corporation had in turn granted MGM a nonexclusive license to create a motion picture based on the books and a continuing right to create "remakes" of that picture. The author's heirs subsequently served a notice of termination on the family-controlled corporation but not on MGM. In the resulting litigation, the heirs and MGM offered opposing interpretations of the meaning of "successors in title." The heirs argued that it meant "transferee of some *exclusive* right." MGM argued that "successor in title" should also cover a nonexclusive licensee of an author's grantee (though suggesting without apparent support that it could exclude all the nonexclusive licensees of performing rights societies). Although the issue was not reached by the Second Circuit majority, Judge Newman, in a concurring opinion, reasoned that since the Copyright Office regulations speak of providing for a reasonable investigation of "ownership,"

[137]See Curtis, *Caveat Emptor in Copyright: A Practical Guide to the Termination of Transfers Under the New Copyright Code*, 25 BULL. COPR. SOC'Y 19 (1977); Nimmer, *Termination of Transfers Under the Copyright Act of 1976*, 125 U. PA. L. REV. 947 (1977).

[138]491 F. Supp. 1320, 1324–1326, 210 U.S.P.Q. 579, 583–585 (S.D.N.Y. 1980); 519 F. Supp. 388, 215 U.S.P.Q. 37 (S.D.N.Y. 1981), *aff'd*, 683 F.2d 610, 215 U.S.P.Q. 495 (2d Cir. 1982).

[139]37 C.F.R. §201.10.

[140]*Id.* at §201.10(d)(1).

[141]*Id.* at §201.10(d)(3). In the case of musical performing rights, a report from a performing-rights society identifying the person(s) claiming current ownership of the rights being terminated is sufficient. *Ibid.* See also discussion in *Burroughs*, 683 F.2d at 633 n. 6, 215 U.S.P.Q. at 514 n. 6, of the curious provisions of 37 C.F.R. §201.10(d)(4). Note also that the "reasonable investigation" provisions apply only to §304(c) terminations and not to those under §203 which governs terminations of grants made after January 1, 1978.

and since under Section 101 of the Act a "transfer of ownership" includes assignments and exclusive licenses but excludes nonexclusive licenses, the term "successor in title" must be construed in accordance with the Section 101 definition.[142] This reading of "successor in title" is believed to be correct. Judge Newman, nevertheless, concluded that defendant MGM, as a sublicensee of the family-owned corporation, should have been served with a termination notice because the terminating heirs knew or should have known of MGM's continuing right to create remakes of the original motion picture.

While there is no form for termination notices, the regulations specify that the notice must contain a "complete and unambiguous statement of facts * * * without incorporation by reference of information in other documents or records,"[143] and include the following:

1) the name of each grantee whose rights are being terminated and each address at which service is made;
2) the title and the name of at least one author of, and the date copyright was originally secured in, each work to which the notice applies (including if available the copyright registration number);
3) a brief statement reasonably identifying the grant being terminated;
4) the effective date of the termination;
5) the name, actual signature, and address of the person executing the termination.[144]

In the case of works consisting of a series or containing characters, special care should be taken to list separately each and every work in the series or all works in which the character appears.[145] A complete copy of the termination notice must be recorded with the Copyright Office before its effective date of termination, and such recordation must be accompanied by a statement setting forth the date on which the notice of termination was served and the manner of service (unless the information is already contained in the notice)[146] and by the prescribed fee.[147]

Another provision of Section 304(c) which should be examined is subsection (c)(6)(A), which allows a derivative work prepared under the authority of a grant to be utilized under the terms of the grant

---

[142]683 F.2d at 633–634, 215 U.S.P.Q. at 513–515.

[143]37 C.F.R. §201.10(b)(2).

[144]*Id.* at §§201.10(b)(1) and (c)(1), (4). A duly authorized agent may also sign the notice but care should be taken to clearly identify the person(s) on whose behalf the agent is acting. *Id.* at §201.10(c)(3).

[145]See *Burroughs, supra* note 138, where a notice of termination listing 35 titles (including the first "Tarzan" story), but omitting 5 sequels in which the character Tarzan appeared, was found by the majority to be ineffective to prevent the grantee's continued use of the Tarzan character. Judge Newman, concurring in the result, disagreed on the effect of not terminating the five sequels, reasoning that the right to base a motion picture on those sequels would permit uses not derived from the sequels.

[146]37 C.F.R. §201.10(f)(i), (ii).

[147]*Id.* at §201.10(f)(2).

after the grant is terminated. In *Mills Music, Inc. v. Snyder*,[148] the question of whether a grantee (in this case a music publisher) who in turn had sublicensed the making of a derivative work (in this case sound recordings of musical compositions) under the term of the grant, was entitled to continue to share in the royalties from the exploitation of the sublicensed derivative works after the effective termination of the original grant.

In a 5–4 decision reversing a comprehensive and thoughtful opinion by Judge Oakes of the Second Circuit, the Supreme Court answered this question in the affirmative, reasoning that the use of the term "grant" three times in the subsection indicated a congressional intent in the derivative work exception to termination to encompass not only the original grant from the copyright owner to the grantee, but the grantee's sublicense to the creator of the derivative work as well.

Even assuming this to be a correct reading of the statute, it does not follow that middlemen are entitled to share in the royalties from the derivative work's continued exploitation.[149] It is submitted that in its detailed examination of the language of the derivative works exception, the Supreme Court did not accord sufficient weight to the fundamental purpose of the termination provision: to benefit *authors*.[150] When this basic purpose is considered, it is evident that the statute was *not* intended to benefit grantees. It is most unlikely that Congress would have extended an additional 19 years protection to renewal terms and provided for an author's right to recapture the copyright in this extended renewal period in order to permit the terminated grantee to continue to receive its share of the revenue from its sublicensees, resulting in no increased financial benefit to the author.

It is, therefore, believed that Judge Oakes's well-reasoned decision in the *Mills Music* case should have been affirmed, and that Congress should act to correct the injustice caused by the Supreme Court's reversal of that decision.

---

[148]469 U.S. ____, 224 U.S.P.Q. 313 (1985). See generally Abrams, *Who's Sorry Now? Termination Rights and the Derivative Works Exception*, U. DET. L. REV. 181 (1985), and Cohen, *"Derivative Works" Under the Termination Provisions of the 1976 Copyright Act*, 28 BULL. COPR. SOC'Y 380 (1981).

[149]See dissent of Justice White, 469 U.S. at ____, 224 U.S.P.Q. at 324–325. Note that §304(c) speaks of "any right" under a copyright, e.g., a right to receive royalties, and that subsection (c)(5) states that a termination "may be effected notwithstanding any agreement to the contrary * * * ." See also former Register of Copyrights Barbara Ringer's criticism of the majority's opinion in *Civil and Criminal Enforcement of the Copyright Laws: Hearing Before the Subcomm. on Patents, Copyrights, and Trademarks of the Senate Judiciary Comm.*, 99th Cong., 1st Sess. 79–95 (1985); *The Copyright Holder Protection Act: Hearings on S. 1364 Before the Subcomm. on Patents, Copyrights, and Trademarks of the Senate Judiciary Comm.*, 99th Cong., 1st Sess. (1985).

[150]See H.R. REP. No. 94-1476, 94th Cong., 2d Sess. 140 (1976); S. REP. No. 94-473, 94th Cong., 1st Sess. 123 (1975):
"The arguments for granting a right of termination are even more persuasive under section 304 than they are under section 203; the extended term represents a completely new property right, and there are strong reasons for giving the author, who is the fundamental beneficiary of copyright under the Constitution, an opportunity to share in it."

# 4

# Ownership of Copyright

Chapter 2 of the 1976 Act attempts to organize, clarify, and rectify the confusing and often unfair rules of ownership which emerged from the 1909 Act. Thus, while Chapter 1 of the Act addresses itself to the tensions between copyright owners and users, Chapter 2 regulates relationships within the former group, e.g., author-publisher, conflicting licensees, etc. Aside from the economic and social balances struck, this chapter attempts to establish a businesslike framework for dealings in copyright. The result is clearly a proliferation of the production and recordation of paper. While this increase in formal requirements adds burdens, it can be justified by the greater availability and reliability of pertinent records and other forms of proof needed in copyright matters.

## Initial Ownership: The "Author(s)"

The basic principle of ownership is that "the individual author is the fountainhead of copyright protection * * * ,"[1] a principle embedded in Section 201(a), which states: "Copyright in a work protected under this title vests initially in the author or authors of the work." Although the Act does not contain a definition of "author," its recognition of such person as the initial owner of copyright includes provision for two specialized situations of authorship—joint works and works made for hire.[2]

---

[1]SECOND SUPPLEMENTARY REPORT OF THE REGISTER OF COPYRIGHTS ON THE GENERAL REVISION OF THE U.S. COPYRIGHT LAW: 1975 REVISION BILL, Ch. XI at 9 (draft ed. 1975).
[2]In vesting not only ownership but authorship in the employer in the case of works made for hire, the United States stands virtually alone in the world.

## Joint Works

A joint work is defined in Section 101 as "a work prepared by two or more authors with the intention that their contributions be merged into inseparable or interdependent parts of a unitary whole." The legislative reports accompanying the Act contain important commentary on this definition:

"Under the definition of section 101, a work is 'joint' if the authors collaborated with each other, or if each of the authors prepared his or her contribution with the knowledge and intention that it would be merged with the contributions of other authors as 'inseparable or interdependent parts of a unitary whole.' The touchstone here is the intention, at the time the writing is done, that the parts be absorbed or combined into an integrated unit, although the parts themselves may be either 'inseparable' (as in the case of a novel or painting) or 'interdependent' (as in the case of a motion picture, opera, or the words and music of a song). The definition of 'joint work' is to be contrasted with the definition of 'collective work,' also in section 101, in which the elements of merger and unity are lacking; there the key elements are assemblage or gathering of 'separate and independent works * * * into a collective whole.' "[3]

The Act's definition thus strongly emphasizes the authors' intent at the time the work is created, and in so doing represents a marked departure from opinions of the Second Circuit under the 1909 Act, which had held that where the complementary efforts were performed at different times by authors unacquainted with one another, their product was a joint work because they had a common design;[4]

---

[3]H.R. REP. No. 94-1476, 94th Cong., 2d Sess. 120 (1976); S. REP. No. 94-473, 94th Cong., 1st Sess. 103–104 (1975). See *Rodak v. Esprit Racing Team*, 227 U.S.P.Q. 239, 242–243 (S.D. Ohio 1985) (material issue of fact concerning whether certain drawings were prepared with the intention to merge them into inseparable or interdependent parts of a unitary whole found to exist. Plaintiff had created some of the drawings before he became "involved" with defendant). Where the requisite intent is not present the resulting work is considered a derivative work. *Oddo v. Ries*, 743 F.2d 630, 222 U.S.P.Q. 799 (9th Cir. 1981).

Rights in interviews occasionally pose troublesome factual issues due to a lack of an express intent between the interviewer and interviewee with respect to copyright ownership. Query whether the determinative factor here (and for all works of joint authorship) is the intent that the contributions be separately owned or, as the statute seemingly indicates, only that the contributions be merged. See *Rodak v. Esprit Racing Team*, 227 U.S.P.Q. at 242: "There is * * * evidence * * * plaintiff never contemplated that his work would form a part of a whole to which someone else would contribute."

In any event, with respect to interviews, the Copyright Office has stated:

"A work consisting of an interview often contains copyrightable authorship by the person interviewed and the interviewer. Each has the right to claim copyright in his or her own expression in the absence of an agreement to the contrary. Where an application for such a work names only the interviewee or the interviewer as the author and claimant, and where the nature of authorship is described as "entire text," it is unclear whether the claim actually extends to the entire work, or only to the text by the interviewee or interviewer. In any case where the extent of the claim is not clear, the Copyright Office must communicate with the applicant for clarification."

COMPENDIUM II OF COPYRIGHT OFFICE PRACTICES §317.

An application naming only the interviewer or interviewee as the author but listing "text" instead of "entire text" as the nature of authorship will be interpreted as asserting a claim only for the interviewer or interviewee's portion of the interview.

[4]*Edward B. Marks Music Corp. v. Jerry Vogel Music Co.*, 47 F. Supp. 490, 55 U.S.P.Q. 288 (S.D.N.Y. 1942). Cf. *Shapiro, Bernstein & Co. v. Jerry Vogel Music Co.*, 161 F.2d 406, 71 U.S.P.Q. 286 (2d Cir. 1946), *cert. denied*, 331 U.S. 820, 73 U.S.P.Q. 550 (1947) ("Melancholy Baby" held to be joint work even though lyrics were substituted for those written earlier in personal collaboration with composer).

or, even more expansively, that a joint work resulted from an assignee's decision to add words to a melody composed years earlier.[5]

In addition to the requisite intent, a putative joint author must make some genuine contribution to the work's creation, a requirement stressed in a number of cases. In *Meltzer v. Zoller*[6] and *Aitken, Hazen, Hoffman & Miller, P.C. v. Empire Construction Co.*,[7] clients' sketches for residential houses or apartments detailing some of the desired features were found to be insufficient fixations of the architect's "expression," and accordingly statutorily incapable of protection, and in the alternative to be *de minimis* contributions ineligible for joint authorship status. This principle has been followed in cases involving computer programs[8] and fabric designs.[9] Joint authorship was, however, found in another fabric design case[10] and in an artist's participation in the modelling of ceramic figurines based on her two-dimensional drawings.[11]

One open question is whether the 1976 Act's definition of joint authorship will be applied retroactively. In *Grosset & Dunlap, Inc. v. Gulf & Western Corp.*[12] the court, without discussion, applied the 1976 Act definition to works created in the 1930s. However, a different result has generally obtained in cases involving retroactive application of the work-for-hire definition.[13] In any event, where joint authorship (or ownership by virtue of an assignment or operation of law) exists, the co-owners are deemed to be tenants in common,[14] with each enjoying an undivided ownership in the entire work[15] and each having an independent right to use or license the copyright, subject only to a duty to account to the other co-owner for any profits earned

---

[5] *Shapiro, Bernstein & Co. v. Jerry Vogel Music Co.*, 221 F.2d 569, 105 U.S.P.Q. 178, *modified on rehearing*, 223 F.2d 252, 105 U.S.P.Q. 460 (2d Cir. 1955) ("Twelfth Street Rag"). This expansion of the concept of joint works within the Second Circuit was probably motivated by a desire to avoid characterizing the works at issue as "composite works," with the attendant renewal ownership vesting in the proprietor rather than the author.

[6] 520 F. Supp. 847, 216 U.S.P.Q. 776 (D.N.J. 1981). See also *Dahinden v. Byrne*, 220 U.S.P.Q. 719, 721 (D. Ore. 1982) ("To be a joint author, a person's contribution must be more than *de minimis*; it must also be one of authorship").

[7] 542 F. Supp. 252, 218 U.S.P.Q. 409 (D. Neb. 1982).

[8] *Whelan Associates, Inc. v. Jaslow Dental Laboratory, Inc.*, 609 F. Supp. 1307, 225 U.S.P.Q. 156 (E.D. Pa. 1985).

[9] *Kenbrooke Fabrics, Inc. v. Material Things*, 223 U.S.P.Q. 1039 (S.D.N.Y. 1984).

[10] *Mister B Textiles, Inc. v. Woodcrest Fabrics, Inc.*, 523 F. Supp. 21, 213 U.S.P.Q. 661 (S.D.N.Y. 1981).

[11] *Schmid Bros., Inc. v. W. Goebel Porzellanfabrik KG.*, 589 F. Supp. 497, 223 U.S.P.Q. 859 (E.D.N.Y. 1984).

[12] 534 F. Supp. 606, 215 U.S.P.Q. 991 (S.D.N.Y. 1982) (reviewing earlier oral findings of fact and conclusions of law). Accord *Lieberman v. Estate of Chafesky*, 535 F. Supp. 90, 215 U.S.P.Q. 741 (S.D.N.Y. 1982).

[13] *Roth v. Pritikin*, 710 F.2d 934, 219 U.S.P.Q. 204 (2d Cir.), *cert. denied*, 464 U.S. 961, 220 U.S.P.Q. 385 (1983). Contra *Rand McNally & Co. v. Fleet Mgt. Systems, Inc.*, 591 F. Supp. 726, 737, 221 U.S.P.Q. 827, 836–837 (N.D. Ill. 1983). Cf. *Dahinden v. Byrne*, 220 U.S.P.Q. 719, 720 n. 2 (D. Ore. 1982); *Meltzer v. Zoller*, 520 F. Supp. 847, 855 n. 19, 216 U.S.P.Q. 776, 783 n. 19 (D.N.J. 1981).

[14] H.R. REP. No. 94-1476, 94th Cong., 2d Sess. 121 (1976); S. REP. No. 94-473, 94th Cong., 1st Sess. 104 (1975). Although members of an unincorporated association can take title to a copyright as tenants-in-common under circumstances where the association has an "ascertainable" membership, this standard is difficult to meet. See *Motta v. Samuel Weiser, Inc.*, 768 F.2d 481, 226 U.S.P.Q. 934 (1st Cir. 1985).

[15] *Pye v. Mitchell*, 574 F.2d 476, 480, 198 U.S.P.Q. 264, 267 (9th Cir. 1978); *Meltzer v. Zoller*, 520 F. Supp. 847, 857 n. 23, 216 U.S.P.Q. 776, 785 n. 23 (D.N.J. 1981).

thereby.[16] One co-owner may not, however, transfer all interest in the work without the other's express (and written) authorization.[17] (See Section 204(a).)

## Works Made for Hire

### The 1909 Act

Sections 24 and 26 of the 1909 Act for the first time accorded employers potential status as "authors." Section 26 provided that "the word 'author' shall include an employer in the case of works made for hire." Section 24, which principally concerned the renewal right for posthumous works, periodicals, cyclopedias, and composite works, contained a provision declaring that in the case of "any work copyrighted * * * by an employer for whom such work is made for hire, the proprietor of such copyright shall be entitled to a renewal and extension of the copyright in such work * * * ."

Earlier drafts of the 1909 Act, at the apparent request of publishers of encyclopedias, directories, "composite," and graphic works, had contained a definition of the term "author" and included therein "[a]n employer, in the case of a work produced by an employee during the hours for which his salary is paid, subject to any agreement to the contrary."[18] This provision was criticized by both author and publisher groups, though for opposite reasons. At approximately the same time, in the section of the draft bill dealing with duration, a provision was added granting a single 50-year term of protection for "any composite or collective work, any work copyrighted by a corporate body or by the employer of the author or authors."[19] This provision was subsequently omitted and then, as reworded, inserted into the *renewal* section of the final bill.

In reviewing this history and the legislative reports accompanying the 1909 Act, former Register of Copyrights Barbara Ringer concluded that "the legislators regarded a 'work made for hire' as a species of 'composite or cyclopedic work,' and did not realize the breadth of the exception they were creating."[20]

As will be discussed in Chapter 5, under the 1909 Act statutory copyright was secured by publication with proper notice. Unpublished works were generally subject to common law protection and common law rules of ownership. Since creation must precede publica-

---

[16]*Oddo v. Ries,* 743 F.2d 630, 633, 222 U.S.P.Q. 799, 801 (9th Cir. 1984) (partners as co-owners). *Oddo* also held that the duty to account arises not from copyright principles but from "equitable doctrines relating to unjust enrichment and general principles governing the rights of co-owners," *ibid.,* and that accordingly a failure to account was a matter of state and not federal jurisdiction.

[17]*Cortner v. Israel,* 732 F.2d 267, 222 U.S.P.Q. 756 (2d Cir. 1984).

[18]See Ringer, *Renewal of Copyright,* COPYRIGHT OFFICE STUDY No. 31, 86th Cong., 2d Sess. 137 (Comm. Print 1961).

[19]*Id.* at 138.

[20]*Id.* at 139. Accord *Cadence Indus. Corp. v. Ringer,* 450 F. Supp. 59, 64, 197 U.S.P.Q. 664, 669 (S.D.N.Y. 1979) (citing quotation in text).

tion in all but the most unusual cases, these common law rules had a significant effect on ownership questions not explicitly covered by Section 26 of the federal act since the owner of common law rights was also the person entitled to secure federal statutory copyright. Two effects in particular may be noted: (a) the enforceability of oral agreements establishing ownership;[21] and (b) a general presumption that "when an employer hires an employee *or an independent contractor* to produce a work of an artistic nature, * * * in the absence of contrary proof * * * the parties expected the employer to own the copyright * * * ."[22]

Section 26 of the 1909 Act did not define "employer." In a study prepared for the Copyright Office early in the 1909 Act revision process, Borge Varmer wrote in this regard:

> "The statutory concept of employment for hire is based on a specific contractual relationship between the employer and the employee. The courts have not given a definition of that relationship which will cover all situations that come up, but all the cases have involved salaried employees who received either a fixed salary or a minimum salary plus commission. * * * Hence, it may be concluded that section 26 refers only to works made by salaried employees in the regular course of their employment."[23]

The common law presumption was thus created to cover situations outside those contemplated by Section 26, viz., specially ordered or commissioned works, and even within that category the presumption noted above was not applied to all classes of works.

## The 1976 Act

We have previously noted that Section 301 of the 1976 Act provides for a unified federal system of copyright. This resulted in the elimination of the common law rules and presumptions concerning ownership[24] and their replacement with those found in Section 201 and in Section 101's two definitions of "work made for hire." In the light of recent case law, discussed below, it is well to review the evolution of these definitions.

In 1961, following circulation of the Varmer and other studies to a panel of experts, the Register of Copyrights issued a report on the

---

[21] *Roth v. Pritikin*, 710 F.2d 934, 219 U.S.P.Q. 204 (2d Cir.), *cert. denied*, 464 U.S. 961, 220 U.S.P.Q. 385 (1983).

[22] *May v. Morganelli-Heumann & Associates*, 618 F.2d 1363, 1368, 207 U.S.P.Q. 476, 480 (9th Cir. 1980). For recent cases applying this presumption to works governed by the 1909 Act, see *Burke v. Medical Economics Co.*, 219 U.S.P.Q. 139 (D.N.J. 1982) (illustrations in magazine); *Excel Promotions Corp. v. Babylon Beacon, Inc.*, 207 U.S.P.Q. 616 (E.D.N.Y. 1979) (advertisement); *Goldman-Morgen, Inc. v. Dan Brechner & Co.*, 411 F. Supp. 382, 190 U.S.P.Q. 478 (S.D.N.Y. 1976) (child's bank). For cases in which the presumption was rebutted, see *Everts v. Arkham House Pub., Inc.*, 579 F. Supp. 145, 223 U.S.P.Q. 905 (W.D. Wis. 1984) (poetry); *Sargent v. American Greetings Corp.*, 588 F. Supp. 912, 223 U.S.P.Q. 1327 (N.D. Ohio 1984) (artwork); *Varon v. Santa Fe Reporter, Inc.*, 218 U.S.P.Q. 716 (D.N.M. 1982) (photographs).

[23] Varmer, *Works Made for Hire and on Commission*, COPYRIGHT OFFICE STUDY No. 13, 86th Cong., 2d Sess. 130 (Comm. Print 1960).

[24] See *Childers v. High Society Magazine, Inc.*, 557 F. Supp. 978, 217 U.S.P.Q. 1221; 561 F. Supp. 1374, 1375, 221 U.S.P.Q. 927 (S.D.N.Y. 1983) (rejecting claim of ownership based on "common law works for hire doctrine" on ground that §301 preempted such a claim).

proposed general revision of the 1909 Act. In this report the Register recommended that copyright should vest in the author with the following two exceptions:

> "(a) In the case of a work made for hire (defined as a work created for an employer by an employee within the regular scope of his employment) * * *.
>
> "(b) In the case of a periodical, encyclopedia, or other composite work containing the contributions of a number of authors * * *."

The second category, moreover, vested authorship in the publisher only as regards the collective work and not in the individual contributions. The report also discussed the question of independent contractors who created specially commissioned works:

> "The phrase used in the present [1909] statute—'works made for hire'— has been criticized as being inexact, because it might be thought to include works made on special commission. The courts, however, have not generally regarded commissioned works as 'made for hire.'"
> * * *
> "Instead of the phrase 'works made for hire,' it was proposed in previous revision bills to substitute 'works created by an employee within the regular scope of his employment.' We would adopt this more precise language as a definition of 'works made for hire.'"[25]

The intent of the Copyright Office to exclude specially commissioned works created by independent contractors from treatment as works made for hire and to limit works made for hire to those created in the "regular scope of employment," i.e., by salaried employees, could not be clearer. The 1963 Preliminary Draft bill, prepared by the Copyright Office, incorporated the recommendations of the 1961 report in draft Section 14(c): "In the case of a work made for hire, the employer shall, for purposes of this title, be considered the author and shall have all of the rights comprised in the copyright unless the parties have expressly agreed otherwise." "Work made for hire" was to be defined as "a work prepared by an employee within the scope of the duties of his employment, but not including a work made on special order or commission."[26]

The use of the phrase "within the scope of the duties of his employment" is in line with the belief of the Office, and that of the Varmer study, that Section 26 of the 1909 Act (to be recodified in Section 14(c) of the Preliminary Draft bill) contemplated only works produced by salaried employees, a belief echoed in the parallel provision con-

---

[25]REPORT OF THE REGISTER OF COPYRIGHTS ON THE GENERAL REVISION OF THE U.S. COPYRIGHT LAW, 87th Cong., 1st Sess. 87, 88 (Comm. Print 1961).

[26]Reprinted in COPYRIGHT LAW REVISION PART 3: PRELIMINARY DRAFT FOR REVISED U.S. COPYRIGHT LAW AND DISCUSSIONS AND COMMENTS ON THE DRAFT 15 (1964). No significance should be attached to the fact that unlike the prior revision bills, which spoke of "*regular* scope of employment," the 1963 Preliminary Draft (as well as the 1976 Act) refers only to "scope of employment." The passage quoted in the text at note 25 unmistakably indicates that the Copyright Office's intent was to adopt the principle of the earlier bills. See also COPYRIGHT LAW REVISION PART 3 at 273–275 (suggestion that definition of "work made for hire" be revised to refer to "master-servant" relationship rejected on ground that it sounded "too medieval" and not on ground that it did not accurately reflect intent of draft definition).

cerning works created by a government employee "in the course of executing the duties required of him by his office or position."[27]

As we shall see below, agreement by employers and employees that certain *rights* were to be owned by the employee referred to transfer of ownership and not to work-for-hire status, which could not be changed by an agreement that the employee was not to be treated as an employee for hire (in direct contrast to the common law presumption for specially ordered or commissioned works, which permitted such agreements).

The Preliminary Draft definition was objected to by publishers of encyclopedias and dictionaries, who believed that, as a practical matter, such works must be written on special order or commission, and by motion picture companies for similar reasons.[28] A compromise was proposed in the 1964 revision bill which provided:

> "In the case of a work made for hire, the employer or other person for whom the work was prepared is considered the author for purposes of this title, and owns all of the rights comprised in the copyright unless the parties have expressly agreed otherwise.
>
> "A 'work made for hire' is a work prepared by an employee within the scope of his employment, or a work prepared on special order or commission if the parties expressly agree in writing that it shall be considered a work made for hire."[29]

The change in this bill from that of the Preliminary Draft bill was, of course, the permitting of specially ordered or commissioned works (without regard to subject matter) to be works made for hire if a written document to that effect was signed (before the work was created). This change was, however, strongly criticized by authors.

At this point in the revision process, the fierce disputes between authors and publishers over the work-for-hire provision and a provision providing for termination of transfer rights (ultimately embodied in Sections 203 and 304(c)) seriously jeopardized hopes for

---

[27]COPYRIGHT LAW REVISION PART 3 at 3. The 1976 House report expressly states that "although the wording of the definition of 'works of the United States Government' differs somewhat from that of the definition of 'work made for hire,' the concepts are intended to be construed in the same way." H.R. REP. No. 94-1476, 94th Cong., 2d Sess. 58 (1976).

[28]COPYRIGHT LAW REVISION PART 3 at 257–275. Publishers' acknowledgment that this provision, which is for all relevant purposes identical to that contained in the first subdivision of the definition of "work made for hire" in §101 of the 1976 Act, contemplated only salaried employees is seen in a statement submitted by the American Book Publishers Council to the Register of Copyrights in November 1963. COPYRIGHT LAW REVISION PART 4: FURTHER DISCUSSIONS AND COMMENTS ON PRELIMINARY DRAFT FOR REVISED U.S. COPYRIGHT LAW, 88th Cong., 2d Sess. 250 (Comm. Print 1964): " '[W]orks for hire'—in which copyright is by law owned by the employer—would be redefined to include only work done by a salaried employee in the scope of his regular duties and would exclude works made on special order or commission."

[29]S. 3008, H.R. 11947, H.R. 12354, 88th Cong., 2d Sess. §§14, 54 (1964). An inconsistency between the two paragraphs quoted in the text should be pointed out since the relevant language was adopted in §§201(b) and 101, respectively, of the 1976 Act. The first paragraph states a presumption that in the case of a work made for hire the employer *or other person for whom the work is prepared* (i.e., a party specially ordering or commissioning a work) will be considered the author unless the parties have expressly agreed otherwise. The second paragraph, however, states that specially ordered or commissioned works will be deemed works made for hire only if the parties expressly agree they will be works made for hire.

Copyright vests automatically upon creation, 17 U.S.C. §102(a) (1978), and, therefore, absent an agreement to the contrary signed before creation, vests with the author and can be owned by a third party only by virtue of a written transfer or operation of law. See §204(a).

passage of new legislation. In April 1965, both sides came to an historic compromise, contained in a joint memorandum submitted to the Register of Copyright and Congress. For their part, publishers agreed to the inclusion of termination of transfer rights provisions. As a direct quid pro quo,[30] authors agreed to the following revision in the specially ordered or commissioned "work made for hire" definition:

> "(2) a work specially ordered or commissioned for use as a contribution to a collective work, as a part of a motion picture, as a translation, or as a supplementary work, if the parties expressly agree in writing that the work shall be considered a work made for hire."[31]

This revision thus restricted works capable of being specially ordered or commissioned works made for hire to the enumerated four categories. The Register of Copyrights' Supplementary Report accompanying the bill took pains to point out in this regard that "[o]ther works made on special order or commission would not come within this definition" and that, while employers and employees could agree that the employee could receive all or some of the rights back by *transfer*, they could not "change the status of a 'work made for hire' under the statute."[32] Thus, for those works made for hire under the first definition—by salaried employees within the scope of their employment—an express agreement that the work was not to be a work made for hire would be void. Conversely, parties could not agree that an independent contractor's creation was to be considered the work of "an employee within the scope of his employment." A fortiori, the existence of supervision and control over an independent contractor could not make the contractor's work a work made for hire.

It should also be noted that the status of a work created by an independent contractor as a specially ordered or commissioned work made for hire had nothing to do with whether the commissioning party exercised any (or complete) supervision and control over the independent contractor's work. If the work was within the enumerated subject matter categories and a written agreement was entered into before the creation of the work to the effect that the work was to be a work made for hire, it automatically became a work made for hire.

In 1966 further negotiations between the affected interests took place, and as a result the specially ordered or commissioned work category was expanded to include compilations, instructional texts,

---

[30] *Copyright Law Revision: Hearings on H.R. 4347 et al. Before the Subcomm. on Courts, Civil Liberties, and the Administration of Justice of the House Judiciary Comm.*, 89th Cong., 1st Sess. 148–149 (1965). The joint memorandum is reproduced, *id.* at 134. That the publishers understood that the first subdivision of the definition of "work made for hire," left unchanged by this compromise, referred only to salaried employees has been demonstrated in note 28, *supra.*

[31] S. 1006, H.R. 4347, H.R. 5680, H.R. 6831, H.R. 6835, 89th Cong., 1st Sess. §101 (1965) (definition of "work made for hire").

[32] See note 30, *supra.*

tests, and atlases. In 1969 the Senate added "a work specially ordered or commissioned for use * * * as a photographic or other portrait of one or more persons * * * ." This provision was objected to by Register of Copyrights Barbara Ringer:

> "The addition of portraits to the list of commissioned works that can be made into 'works made for hire' by agreement of the parties is difficult to justify. Artists and photographers are among the most vulnerable and poorly protected of all beneficiaries of the copyright law, and it seems clear that, like serious composers and choreographers, they were not intended to be treated as 'employees' under the carefully negotiated definition in section 101."[33]

The Register's recommendation that this provision be deleted was accepted, with the legislative reports noting that the definition of "work made for hire" "represents a compromise which, in effect, spells out those works that can be considered 'works made for hire' under certain circumstances."[34] By so providing, Congress adopted the Copyright Office's intent to limit the types of works created by independent contractors that could be deemed works made for hire to the specified examples given in the second subdivision of the statutory definition,[35] ensuring that, contrary to some decisions construing Section 26 of the 1909 Act, works made for hire within the meaning of the "first" definition would be limited to salaried or like employees and would *not* include independent contractors even if their work was closely supervised or controlled. The second subdivision of the "work made for hire" definition was thus intended to be the exclusive provision governing works created by independent contractors.

This intent has been followed in the majority of cases construing the work-for-hire provisions of the 1976 Act.[36] Typical of these deci-

---

[33]SECOND SUPPLEMENTARY REPORT OF THE REGISTER OF COPYRIGHTS ON THE GENERAL REVISION OF THE U.S. COPYRIGHT LAW: 1975 REVISION BILL, Ch. XI at 12–13 (draft ed. 1975).

[34]H.R. REP. No. 94-1476, 94th Cong., 2d Sess. 121 (1976); S. REP. No. 94-473, 94th Cong., 1st Sess. 105 (1975).

[35]The Copyright Office has recently reiterated this provision in a study prepared for the Secretaries of the International Labor Organisation, the United Nations Educational, Scientific and Cultural Organization, and the World International Property Organization:

> "The legislative framework of copyright ownership and works made for hire [in the 1976 Act] retained the principle developed through sixty-seven years of practice under the previous copyright law that the employer is considered the author (and thus the initial owner of copyright) in all works produced by an employee within the scope of his or her employment. But by limiting the section 101 definition of works made for hire, the new law circumscribes the classes of works, *other than those produced in the normal course of employment*, that may be considered works made for hire."

GENERAL ASPECTS OF COPYRIGHT OWNERSHIP AND ITS CONSEQUENCES BETWEEN EMPLOYERS AND EMPLOYED OR SALARIED AUTHORS IN FOUR COMMON-LAW COUNTRIES: UNITED STATES OF AMERICA, UNITED KINGDOM, CANADA AND AUSTRALIA, ILO/UNESCO/WIPO/SA/CM/3 (1982) at p. 7 (emphasis added).

[36]*Baltimore Orioles, Inc. v. Major League Players Ass'n*, COPR. L. REP. ¶25,822 (N.D. Ill. 1985) (baseball players' performances during televised, copyrighted game are works for hire); *Whelan Associates, Inc. v. Jaslow Dental Laboratory, Inc.*, 609 F. Supp. 1307, 225 U.S.P.Q. 156 (E.D. Pa. 1985) (computer program); *Brunswick Beacon, Inc. v. Schock-Hopchas Pub. Co.*, 84-40-CIV-7 (E.D.N.C. filed March 11, 1985); *Kenbrooke Fabrics, Inc. v. Material Things*, 223 U.S.P.Q. 1039 (S.D.N.Y. 1984); *Town of Clarkstown v. Reeder*, 566 F. Supp. 137, 220 U.S.P.Q. 793 (S.D.N.Y. 1984); *Childers v. High Society Magazine*, 557 F. Supp. 978, 217 U.S.P.Q. 1221; 561 F. Supp. 1374, 221 U.S.P.Q. 927 (S.D.N.Y. 1983); *Rand McNally & Co. v. Fleet Mgt. Systems*, 591 F. Supp. 726, 221 U.S.P.Q. 827 (N.D. Ill. 1983); *Freedman v. Select Information Sys-*

sions is that of the court in *Aitken, Hazen, Hoffman & Miller, P.C. v. Empire Construction Co.*, which also noted the change made in those provisions from the 1909 Act:

> "Most court decisions interpreting the work-made-for-hire doctrine under the 1909 Act viewed an independent contractor in the same light as an employee. Thus, in the absence of an express intention to the contrary, copyright ownership was presumed to vest in the employer. * * * * * *
>
> "The definitional section of the 1976 Copyright Act does not adopt this judicially created presumption but, instead, limits works made for hire by independent contractors to prescribed categories and only to those situations where the parties expressly agree in a signed written instrument that the work shall be considered a work made for hire."[37]

A number of cases have, however, incorrectly viewed the provisions of the first subdivision of the definition of work made for hire (i.e., works created within the scope of employment) as continuing the common law presumptions developed under the 1909 Act and have thereby seriously upset the carefully crafted compromises enacted by Congress in the 1976 revision legislation. In the light of the above-noted deletion of portraits and like photographic works from the category of specially commissioned works under the second subdivision of the definition of "work made for hire," it is surprising that two of these decisions (apparently unaware of the deletion) found that the photographs at issue were works made for hire under the first subdivision of the definition, in one case[38] because the customer directed the freelance photographer to take certain shots at the beginning, end, and at various times during a cocktail party; and in the second case[39] because the photographer was subject to a mere (unexercised) right of supervision.

In a third case,[40] a freelance artist's contribution to circus advertising materials was also held to be a work made for hire under the first subdivision of the definition, apparently because the hiring party made criticisms and suggestions for revisions. The hiring party

---

*tems, Inc.*, 221 U.S.P.Q. 848 (N.D. Cal. 1983); *Aitken, Hazen, Hoffman & Miller, P.C. v. Empire Construction Co.*, 542 F. Supp. 252, 218 U.S.P.Q. 409 (D. Neb. 1982); *Meltzer v. Zoller*, 520 F. Supp. 847, 216 U.S.P.Q. 776 (D.N.J. 1981); *Mister B Textiles, Inc. v. Woodcrest Fabrics, Inc.*, 523 F. Supp. 21, 213 U.S.P.Q. 661 (S.D.N.Y. 1981); *BPI Systems, Inc. v. Leith*, 532 F. Supp. 209 (W.D. Tex. 1981).

The *BPI, Freedman,* and *Whelan* cases also demonstrate the inapplicability of computer programs as specially ordered or commissioned works made for hire, a position expressly stated in the Copyright Office study referred to in note 35, *supra*, which concludes at p. 48:

> "If the computer software were developed on a special order or commission basis, it would seem clear that such a work could not be deemed a work made for hire under United States law, notwithstanding any written agreement purporting to achieve that effect. The individual author would be considered the author."

[37] 542 F. Supp. 252, 257, 218 U.S.P.Q. 409, 413 (D. Neb. 1982).

[38] *Peregrine v. Lauren Corp.*, 601 F. Supp. 828, 225 U.S.P.Q. 681 (D. Colo. 1985).

[39] *Sykee v. Ruolo*, 461 N.E. 480 (Ill. Ct. App. 1984). But cf. *Granse v. Brown Photo Co.*, 228 U.S.P.Q. 635, 644 (D. Minn. 1985); *Sygma Photo News, Inc. v. Globe Int'l, Inc.*, 616 F. Supp. 1153, 229 U.S.P.Q. 610 (S.D.N.Y. 1985); *Childers v. High Society Magazine, supra* note 36.

[40] *Sigwart v. Ringling Bros. and Barnum & Bailey Circus World, Inc.*, COPR. L. REP. ¶25,717 (C.D. Cal. 1984). *Sigwart* and *Peregrine* (see note 38, *supra*) should have been decided on different grounds. As both works were "supplementary works" within the second definition of "work made for hire," they were covered under the specially ordered or commissioned work category. As there was no written agreement indicating that the works were to be treated as works made for hire, copyright vested in the artist.

did not, however, have "any particular drawing, sketch, or other art work" "in mind" when he hired the artist.

The most important of these aberrant decisions is that of the Second Circuit in *Aldon Accessories, Ltd. v. Spiegel, Inc.*[41] There a jury charge permitted an independent contractor's creation of sculptural works to be deemed "within the scope of employment" for purposes of the first subdivision of the definition if the works were created at the hiring party's instance and expense and under its actual supervision and control. Rejecting a challenge that this charge was incorrect under the 1976 Act, the court of appeals characterized decisional law under the 1909 Act as creating a presumption that copyright in all works done by an independent contractor were to be owned by the hiring party. Apparently unaware of the legislative history reviewed above,[42] the court stated that, "[h]ad Congress intended * * * to narrow the type of employment relationships within the work for hire doctrine to include only 'regular' employees, it is unlikely there would have been no discussion of this change in the legislative history."[43] On the basis of this erroneous reading of congressional intent, the court went on to hold that independent contractors who are sufficiently supervised and directed by the hiring parties could be deemed "employees" for purposes of the first subdivision of the definition of "work made for hire."[44]

If, as in *Aldon*, the hiring party contributes significant artistic effort, that party is a joint author along with the independent contractor.[45] Where the hiring party has contributed all of the expression and the independent contractor acts as a mere amanuensis, the hiring party should be considered the sole author.[46] Where, however, the hir-

---

[41]738 F.2d 548, 222 U.S.P.Q. 951 (2d Cir.), *cert. denied*, 469 U.S. 982 (1984). The challenged instruction is reproduced, *id.* at 551, 222 U.S.P.Q. at 953. Even though there was no written agreement between the parties, the court of appeals found that the sculptures did not fall within one of the enumerated specially ordered or commissioned categories, and thus could not have been specially ordered or commissioned works made for hire had there been such an agreement.

[42]See text at notes 18–33, *supra*.

[43]738 F.2d at 552, 222 U.S.P.Q. at 954. In an otherwise well-reasoned opinion, Judge Mishler was constrained to follow *Aldon's* erroneous conclusion that the 1976 Act did not effect a change from the 1909 Act's treatment of independent contractors, and held that an independent designer of lead crystal figurines who worked closely with the contracting party was the employee for hire within the meaning of the first subdivision of the definition of "work made for hire" in §101. *Arc v. S.S. Sarna, Inc.*, 621 F. Supp. 916, 919–920, 229 U.S.P.Q. 25, 27 (E.D.N.Y. 1985).

[44]*Ibid.* Cf. *Woods Hole Oceanographic Institution v. Goldman*, 228 U.S.P.Q. 874 (S.D.N.Y. 1985), where a college student was hired under a work-study program to create a documentary film for a private oceanographic research institution. Because an employment contract expressly provided for copyright ownership by the institution and the institution's supervision of the student's work, copyright was held to vest in the institution.

[45]See *Schmid Bros., Inc. v. W. Goebel Porzellanfabrik KG.*, 589 F. Supp. 497, 223 U.S.P.Q. 859 (E.D.N.Y. 1984) (artist's contributions to the creation of figurines based on her drawings were held to be sufficient to make her a joint author); *Mister B Textiles, Inc. v. Woodcrest Fabrics, Inc.*, 523 F. Supp. 21, 213 U.S.P.Q. 661 (S.D.N.Y. 1981) (joint authorship in fabric design). In *Sygma Photo News, Inc. v. Globe Int'l, Inc.*, 616 F. Supp. 1153, 1156, 229 U.S.P.Q. 610, 612 (S.D.N.Y. 1985), the court described plaintiff in *Aldon* as the "hiring author."

[46]*M.S.R. Imports, Inc. v. R.E. Greenspan Co.*, 220 U.S.P.Q. 361; 574 F. Supp. 31, 225 U.S.P.Q. 585 (E.D. Pa. 1983); *Arthur Retlaw & Associates, Inc. v. Travenol Laboratories, Inc.*, 582 F. Supp. 1010, 223 U.S.P.Q. 722 (N.D. Ill. 1984). In *Gallery House, Inc. v. Yi*, 582 F. Supp. 1294, 223 U.S.P.Q. 894; 587 F. Supp. 1036 (N.D. Ill. 1984), the designs were created by staff

ing party contributes only ideas or generalized expression incapable of copyright protection, copyright vests in the independent contractor[47] regardless of "whether the alleged employer has the right to direct and supervise the manner in which the writer performs his work."[48] Yet the hiring party under such circumstances may still obtain a transfer of all rights from the independent contractor as a condition to the creation of the work.[49]

There are, no doubt, gray areas even in determining the "regular" scope of employment"; however, guidance may be sought from the employer's treatment of the individual for tax and related purposes.[50] One decision has also held that a material breach of an employment contract (e.g., failure to pay for services) will result in recision of the employment relationship and vesting of the copyright in the employee-author.[51]

## Contributions to Collective Works

The drafters of the 1976 Act, in their willingness to address contractual questions in the statute, expressly covered ownership in "contributions to collective works," such as articles in magazines, encyclopedias, etc. Copyright in the contributions themselves (as opposed to the collective work as a whole) vests in the respective authors of the contributions and, in the absence of an express transfer, the publisher is presumed under Section 201(c) to acquire "only the privilege of reproducing and distributing the contribution as part of that particular collective work, any revision of that collective work, and any later collective work in the same series." Although the committee reports state that "the basic presumption of section 201(c) is fully consistent with present law and practice,"[52] the presumption of a limited, rather than a general, transfer seems to represent a reversal

employees *and* freelancers working on the premises, and were subsequently sent to a contract moldmaker.

[47] *Whelan Associates, Inc. v. Jaslow Dental Laboratory, Inc.*, 609 F. Supp. 1307, 225 U.S.P.Q. 156 (E.D. Pa. 1985); *Meltzer v. Zoller*, 520 F. Supp. 847, 216 U.S.P.Q. 776 (D.N.J. 1981).

[48] 1 NIMMER ON COPYRIGHT §5.03[B][1][a]. Nor does it matter if those rights are exercised.

[49] 17 U.S.C. §§201(d), 204(a) (1978). Care should be taken to ensure that the agreement is signed by the party owning the rights being transferred. A letter from the *transferee* confirming an understanding that it owns all rights is insufficient as a matter of law. *Berger v. Computer Information Pub. Co.*, COPR. L. REP. ¶25,681 (S.D.N.Y. 1984).

[50] See CAL. LABOR CODE §3351.5; CAL. UNEMP. INS. CODE §§621, 686. Cf. RESTATEMENT (2D) OF AGENCY §§2, 220. It has been held that a volunteer may be an employee for purposes of the first subdivision of the definition of "work made for hire." *Town of Clarkstown v. Reeder*, 566 F. Supp. 137, 220 U.S.P.Q. 793 (S.D.N.Y. 1984).

[51] *Black v. Pizza Time Theatres, Inc.*, COPR. L. REP. ¶25,569 (N.D. Cal. 1983). See also *Rhoads v. Harvey Pub., Inc.*, COPR. L. REP. ¶25,349 (Ariz. Ct. App. 1981) (allegations of fraudulent representations by employer that independent contractor was an employee). The *Black* opinion does not contain sufficient facts revealing whether the dispute concerned an independent contractor or a salaried employee. Cf. *Woods Hole Oceanographic Institution v. Goldman*, 228 U.S.P.Q. 874 (S.D.N.Y. 1985) ("bald and unsupported assertion of 'failure of consideration' is clearly insufficient" to void contract of employment vesting copyright in employer for hire).

[52] H.R. REP. No. 94-1476, 94th Cong., 2d Sess. 122 (1976); S. REP. No. 94-473, 94th Cong., 1st Sess. 106 (1975).

of interpretations such as *Best Medium Publishing Co. v. National Insider, Inc.*,[53] and *Geisel v. Poynter Products, Inc.*[54]

The legislative reports further indicate that the phrase "any revision of that collective work" is to be applied restrictively, being limited to changes in the collective work itself and not to revisions of the contribution or even to republication in a "new anthology or an entirely different magazine or other collective work."[55]

## Divisibility of Ownership

The "works for hire" and collective works contribution provisions each permit alteration of the initial statutory ownership by express transfer. Such transfers, as well as all others under the Act, are governed by two superficially innocuous provisions. One requires transfers of ownership to be in writing (Section 204), and the other facilitates fragmented transfers (i.e., transfers of less than all of the "bundle" of exclusive rights comprised in a copyright) (Section 201(d)(2)). These provisions turn out to be dramatically important: the writing requirement simply because of the revolutionary expansion of the coverage of the statute, and the transfer provision because it helps lay to rest the traditional and troublesome concept of indivisibility of copyright. These will be examined in reverse order.

The indivisibility concept mandated a single owner or proprietor of copyright at any one time; all others having an interest under the copyright were deemed licensees. The ramifications of indivisibility reached such questions as notice, ownership, recordation of transfers, standing to sue, and taxes.[56] For example, it was early held that the intent, express or necessarily implied by the circumstances, to transfer the entire copyright was necessary for a grantee to be a "proprietor" and that a "mere licensee" could not secure copyright.[57] The inconveniences, if not injustices, of such an approach were many.[58]

The courts had whittled away at the doctrine, perhaps most notably in *Goodis v. United Artists Television, Inc.*,[59] where a notice nam-

---

[53]259 F. Supp. 433 , 152 U.S.P.Q. 56 (N.D. Ill. 1966), *aff'd*, 385 F.2d 384, 155 U.S.P.Q. 550 (7th Cir. 1967), *cert. denied*, 390 U.S. 955, 156 U.S.P.Q. 720 (1968).

[54]295 F. Supp. 331, 160 U.S.P.Q. 590 (S.D.N.Y. 1968).

[55]H.R. Rep. No. 94-1476, 94th Cong., 2d Sess. 122–123 (1976); S. Rep. No. 94-473, 94th Cong., 1st Sess. 106 (1975).

[56]See generally Kaminstein, *Divisibility of Copyright*, Copyright Office Study No. 11, 86th Cong., 2d Sess. (Comm. Print 1960).

[57]*Public Ledger Co. v. New York Times Co.*, 275 F. Supp. 562 (S.D.N.Y. 1921), *aff'd*, 279 F. 747 (2d. Cir.), *cert. denied*, 258 U.S. 627 (1922).

[58]See Henn, *Magazine Rights—A Division of Indivisible Copyright*, 40 Cornell L.Q. 411 (1955).

[59]425 F.2d 397, 165 U.S.P.Q. 3 (2d Cir. 1970). See also *Trust Co. Bank v. MGM/UA Entertainment Co.*, 593 F. Supp. 580, 223 U.S.P.Q. 1046 (N.D. Ga. 1984), *aff'd*, 772 F.2d 740 (11th Cir. 1985) (dispute over sequel rights to *Gone With The Wind*).

ing a periodical publisher as copyright proprietor was held to cover a story in which the publisher clearly had only a limited license. This was the logical outgrowth of holdings that under certain circumstances one authorized to secure copyright in his own name might nevertheless hold such copyright in trust for another.[60] For example, if it was agreed that a publisher would "attend to the copyrighting" for an author, the author would be the equitable owner of the copyright held by the publisher.[61] Similarly, one of three joint owners who takes out copyright in his name is a constructive trustee for the others to the extent of the latters' interests.[62]

In any event, the 1976 Act expressly contemplates a divisible copyright by providing: " 'Copyright owner' with respect to any one of the exclusive rights comprised in a copyright, refers to the owner of that particular right." Section 101. This definition underlies Section 201(d)(2) which provides that "[a]ny of the exclusive rights comprised in a copyright, including any subdivision of any of the rights specified by section 106 [the provision enumerating protected rights], may be transferred * * * and owned separately." In line with the definition quoted immediately above, this subsection then provides that "[t]he owner of any particular exclusive right is entitled, to the extent of that right, to all of the protection and remedies accorded to the copyright owner by this title."

The committee reports indicate that this provision may be taken literally. The House report states:

> "It is thus clear, for example, that a local broadcasting station holding an exclusive license to transmit a particular work within a particular geographic area and for a particular period of time, could sue, in its own name as copyright owner, someone who infringed that particular exclusive right."[63]

---

[60]See also *Filmvideo Releasing Corp. v. Hastings*, 668 F.2d 91, 92 n. 1, 218 U.S.P.Q. 750 n. 1 (2d Cir. 1981); *Manning v. Miller Music Corp.*, 174 F. Supp. 192, 121 U.S.P.Q. 600 (S.D.N.Y. 1959). Cf. *April Prods., Inc. v. G. Schirmer, Inc.*, 308 N.Y. 366, 105 U.S.P.Q. 286 (1955).

[61]*Bisel v. Ladner*, 1 F.2d 436 (3d Cir. 1924).

[62]*Maurel v. Smith*, 271 F. 211 (2d Cir. 1921).

[63]H.R. REP. No. 94-1476, 94th Cong., 2d Sess. 123 (1976). Cf. S. REP. No. 94-473, 94th Cong., 1st Sess. 107 (1975). See also 17 U.S.C. §501(c) (1978), which treats television broadcasters as legal or beneficial owners of copyright for purposes of certain secondary transmissions by cable systems within the broadcast station's local service area. This provision was added to the revision bill in 1974. Its utility has been questioned by the Register of Copyrights, SECOND SUPPLEMENTARY REPORT OF THE REGISTER OF COPYRIGHTS ON THE GENERAL REVISION OF THE U.S. COPYRIGHT LAW: 1975 REVISION BILL, Ch. V at 32 (draft ed. 1975), and by Professor Nimmer, 3 NIMMER ON COPYRIGHT §12.02. The Register and Professor Nimmer may not have appreciated that the purpose of §501(c) is to permit *non*exclusive licensees to sue.

It should also be noted that Copyright Office regulations do not permit divisibility in registration. See 37 C.F.R. §202.3(a)(3)(ii) and *id.* at 202.3(b)(6) which generally permit only one registration per work. These regulations, based both on practical and legal considerations, are designed to "make[] clear that the copyright 'claimant' for purposes of copyright registration is the author of the work for which registration is sought, or a person or organization that has obtained ownership of *all rights* under the copyright initially belonging to the author," *Interim Regulation: Part 202—Registration of Claims to Copyright*, 43 Fed. Reg. 965 (January 5, 1978) and raise the question whether the term "copyright owner," as defined in §101 and used throughout the Act (e.g., §§111(d)(4), 115(c)) has a restrictive meaning limited to ownership of an exclusive right or rights, as opposed to the term "owner of copyright" as used in §§201, 302, 303, etc., which may refer to initial ownership of the entire copyright "bundle of rights." See

This language was followed in *Hubbard Broadcasting, Inc. v. Southern Satellite Systems, Inc.*,[64] in which a local television broadcaster was found to have standing to sue under Section 501(b), the court additionally rejecting defendant's argument that the Federal Communication Commission's repeal of its syndicated exclusivity rules eliminated the broadcaster's exclusive rights for copyright purposes.

Section 204(a) states that "[a] transfer of copyright ownership, other than by operation of law, is not valid unless an instrument of conveyance, or note or memorandum of the transfer, is in writing and signed by the owner of the rights conveyed or such owner's duly authorized agent."[65] Use of the term "valid" means that compliance with Section 204(a)'s requirements is not a mere matter of enforceability; the failure to comply results in a voiding of the transfer itself. No particular form is required for such a transfer;[66] and, unlike the

---

comments of the Authors League of America, Inc. re Notice of Inquiry Concerning Copyright Registration Form (October 7, 1977) (on file in the Copyright Office).

Cf. *Wales Industrial, Inc. v. Hasbro Bradley, Inc.*, 612 F. Supp. 510, 515, 226 U.S.P.Q. 584, 586-587 (S.D.N.Y. 1985), which in response to a claim that an exclusive licensee who submitted an application for registration was not entitled to do so since its license was limited in time and scope (and it was, therefore, not the owner of "all rights") noted that the term "copyright claimant" was undefined in the statute and that "one must look to the regulations of the United States Copyright Office." Despite the clear language of those regulations, the court nevertheless held that the exclusive licensee's "error, if any, would not be jurisdictional but a technical misdescription: it should have identified [the licensor] rather than itself as the 'copyright claimant' on the registration applications it submitted. Such error could be readily corrected by [the licensee's] filing supplementary registrations with the Copyright Office."

[64]593 F. Supp. 808, 224 U.S.P.Q. 468 (D. Minn. 1984), *aff'd*, 777 F.2d 393, 228 U.S.P.Q. 102 (8th Cir. 1985); *Barris Indus., Inc. v. Worldvision Enters., Inc.*, CV 84-2722, slip opn. at 11-12 (C.D. Cal. filed Oct. 7, 1985) (television program distributor became a copyright owner by virtue of author's transferring to it an exclusive license "limited in time and place, of the right to distribute the copyrighted [work] by license with non-excluded television"); See also *Ralph C. Wilson Indus., Inc. v. Chronicle Broadcasting Co.*, 221 U.S.P.Q. 955 (N.D. Cal. 1982); *Library Pub., Inc. v. Medical Economics Co.*, 548 F. Supp. 1231, 222 U.S.P.Q. 605 (E.D. Pa. 1982), *aff'd*, 714 F.2d 123 (3d Cir. 1983) (suggesting that an exclusive license to a "newsstand dealer to distribute a given edition of a given newspaper at a designated corner on a particular afternoon * * * gives the dealer 'ownership' of that right"); *Wales Industrial, Inc. v. Hasbro Bradley, Inc.*, 612 F. Supp. 510, 514, 226 U.S.P.Q. 584, 586 (S.D.N.Y. 1985) (exclusive right to distribute and sell copyrighted work in specified territory for three years constituted "transfer of copyright," entitling transferee to sue for infringement of that right).

[65]17 U.S.C. §204(a) (1978). See also definition of "transfer of ownership," *id.* at §101. Prima facie evidence of the execution of the transfer is available if in addition to the transfer agreement itself, a certificate of acknowledgment is obtained *and*

"(1) in the case of a transfer executed in the United States, the certificate is issued by a person authorized to administer oaths within the United States; or

"(2) in the case of a transfer executed in a foreign country, the certificate is issued by a diplomatic or consular officer of the United States, or by a person authorized to administer oaths whose authority is proved by a certificate of such an officer." 17 U.S.C. §204(b) (1978).

See *S. S. Enters. v. India Sari Palace, Inc.*, COPR. L. REP. ¶25,527 (S.D.N.Y. 1983), which for want of credible assignments denied a preliminary injunction against infringement of a certain Indian film. Injunctive relief was granted concerning one film that had an assignment bearing a stamp of an Indian governmental agency. See also *Hospital for Sick Children v. Melody Fare Dinner Theatre*, 516 F. Supp. 67, 209 U.S.P.Q. 749 (E.D. Va. 1980). In *Filtron Mfg. Co. v. Fil-Coil Co.*, 215 U.S.P.Q. 866, 867 (E.D.N.Y. 1981), certificates of acknowledgment were not obtained, however authentication of the transfer was proved under Fed. R. Civ. P. 901(a) by plaintiff's president's testimony that he had purchased the copyright.

[66]See *Eden Toys, Inc. v. Floralee Undergarment Co.*, COPR. L. REP. ¶25,626 (S.D.N.Y. 1984) (telex sufficient). It is questionable whether a check endorsement would be acceptable. See *Sargent v. American Greetings Corp.*, 588 F. Supp. 912, 923, 223 U.S.P.Q. 1327, 1335-1336 (N.D. Ohio 1984); *Franklin Mint Corp. v. National Wildlife Art Exchange, Inc.*, 575 F.2d 62, 64 (3d Cir.), *cert. denied*, 439 U.S. 880 (1982). Cf. UNIFORM COMMERCIAL CODE §4-205.

rule for specially commissioned works made for hire, a written assignment by the party[67] transferring the rights that confirms an earlier oral agreement satisfies the statutory requirements.[68]

A nonexclusive license does not constitute ownership and thus may be orally granted.[69] It has been held, however, that as a matter of state law an oral, nonexclusive license that is not performable within one year is void under the statute of frauds.[70]

The transfer of separate rights or all rights under copyright may be "by any means of conveyance," including a will, or "by operation of law" (§201(d)(1)). This does not include, however, government seizure or expropriation from an unwilling author (§201(e)). This limitation was introduced in response to fears that the then recent adherence of the USSR to the Universal Copyright Convention might permit the use of copyright (expropriated and thus "owned" by the Government) as a means of suppressing dissident views in nations owing Convention obligations to enforce copyrights.[71] However, the literal sweep of this provision, denying effect broadly to "action of a governmental body," prompted the drafters to state that "traditional legal actions, such as bankruptcy proceedings and mortgage foreclosures, are not within the scope of this subsection."[72] This point was further clarified with respect to bankruptcy proceedings in the comprehensive revision of the bankruptcy act in 1978, which added to the end of Section 201(e) the language "except as provided under Title 11."[73]

## Distinction Between Ownership of Copyright and Material Object

The law has long recognized a distinction between a chattel embodying a copyrightable work and the intellectual property rights comprised in the copyright in such work. For example, it has been held that mere possession of a manuscript does not imply ownership

---

[67]See *Berger v. Computer Information Pub. Co.*, Copr. L. Rep. ¶25,681 (S.D.N.Y. 1984), which held a confirmatory letter sent by the putative transferee insufficient since the transferor did not sign.

[68]*Eden Toys, Inc. v. Floralee Undergarment Co.*, 697 F.2d 27, 36, 217 U.S.P.Q. 201, 207–208 (2d Cir. 1982), *on remand*, Copr. L. Rep. ¶25,626 at p. 18,822 (S.D.N.Y. 1984); *Wales Industrial, Inc. v. Hasbro Bradley, Inc.*, 612 F. Supp. 510, 516, 226 U.S.P.Q. 584, 587 (S.D.N.Y. 1985) (suggesting limitation of such confirmation where there is no evidence of any dispute between the owner and licensee "as to the validity of the alleged oral grant"); *Dan-Dee Imports v. Well-Made Toy Mfg.*, 524 F. Supp. 615, 217 U.S.P.Q. 1363 (E.D.N.Y. 1981).

[69]*Meyers v. Waverly Fabrics*, 489 N.Y.S.2d 891, 227 U.S.P.Q. 55 (1985); *Gracen v. Bradford Exchange*, 698 F.2d 300, 217 U.S.P.Q. 1294 (7th Cir. 1983); *Freedman v. Select Information Systems, Inc.*, 221 U.S.P.Q. 848 (N.D. Cal. 1983); *Library Pub., Inc. v. Medical Economics Co.*, 548 F. Supp. 1231, 222 U.S.P.Q. 605 (E.D. Pa. 1982), *aff'd*, 714 F.2d 123 (3d Cir. 1983).

[70]*Meyers v. Waverly Fabrics, supra* note 69; *Freedman v. Select Systems, Inc., supra* note 69; *Ginsberg v. Fairfield-Noble Corp.*, 81 A.D. 2d 318 (N.Y. App. Div. 1981).

[71]119 Cong. Rec. S9387 (1976). But cf. Levin, *Soviet International Copyright: Dream or Nightmare*, 31 J. Copr. Soc'y 127 (1983).

[72]S. Rep. No. 94-473, 94th Cong., 1st Sess. 107 (1975). Cf. H.R. Rep. No. 94-1476, 94th Cong., 2d Sess. 124 (1976).

[73]Act of Nov. 6, 1978, Pub. L. No. 95-598 §313, 92 Stat. 2676.

of any literary property therein.[74] Thus, the right to publish and copyright private letters generally belongs to the writer or his or her legal representatives and not to the recipient.[75] The distinction is sometimes blurred in the case of works of art, where the "original," which is embodied on canvas or stone, has an artistic uniqueness quite apart from its potential as a "master" for making reproductions.[76] Indeed, the court in *Pushman v. New York Graphic Society, Inc.* held, in contrast to the letter cases, that an artist selling a work of art may be presumed to transfer reproduction rights as well. This decision was, however, subsequently reversed by state statute.[77]

In any event, the distinction between chattel and copyright was embodied in the 1909 law (§27) and is expressly recognized in Section 202 and indirectly in Section 109 of the 1976 Act. Thus, Section 202 provides that "[t]ransfers of ownership of any material object, including the copy or phonorecord in which the work is *first* fixed, does not of *itself* convey any rights in the copyrighted work embodied in the object. * * * " This provision, together with the writing requirement (§204(a)) and the preemption provision (§301(a)), is considered to have reversed the common law presumption exemplified by the *Pushman* decision.[78]

Section 202 also provides that in the converse situation—transfer of copyright—no property rights in the material object are conveyed, absent an agreement to that effect.

## Termination of Transfers and Licenses: §203

It has been noted that a key innovation of the 1976 Act was the abandonment of the renewal scheme for works created on or after January 1, 1978, and for works enjoying common law copyright on that date. The reversionary feature of renewal was modified and incorporated in a provision for optional termination of transfers and licenses by authors on or after this date. We have already examined Section 304(c), which takes a similar approach with respect to certain

---

[74] *Chamberlin v. Feldman*, 300 N.Y. 135 (N.Y. 1949). It has been held, however, that in some circumstances, "evidence of the parties' treatment of the manuscript is relevant to show their intentions as to the copyright." *Van Dusen v. Southeast First National Bank of Miami*, 478 So. 2d 82, 92 n. 19 228 U.S.P.Q. 19, 26 n. 19 (D. Ct. App. Fla. 1985).

[75] *Baker v. Libbie*, 210 Mass. 599, 97 N.E. 109 (Mass. 1912); *In re McCormick*, 92 U.S.P.Q. 393 (Pa. Orphans Ct. 1952). But cf. *City of New York v. Lent*, 51 Barbour 19 (1868) (exception applied to letter from George Washington to the "Mayor, Recorder, Aldermen and Community of the City of New York"). See also earlier discussions by Justice Story in *Folsom v. Marsh*, 9 F. Cas. 342 (C.C.D. Mass. 1841) (No. 4,901).

[76] See Brenner, *A Two-Phase Approach to Copyrighting the Fine Arts*, 24 BULL. COPR. SOC'Y 85 (1976).

[77] 287 N.Y. 302, 52 U.S.P.Q. 273 (N.Y. 1942), *reversed by* N.Y. GEN. BUS. LAW §224. See also CAL. CIV. CODE §982; Ch. 824, OREGON LAWS.

[78] H.R. REP. No. 94-1476, 94th Cong., 2d Sess. 124 (1976); S. REP. No. 94-473, 94th Cong., 1st Sess. 108 (1975).

renewal grants prior to that date. (See pp. 109–113, *supra*.) Although Section 304(c) has the more immediate impact, since the potential termination periods arise in the immediate future, it will eventually phase out. The provision governing post-1977 transfers—Section 203—will not become operative for a number of years, but is an important organic feature of the 1976 Act.

Study of the 1976 law is made more difficult by the fact that these two complex provisions are similar but not identical. It may accordingly be helpful to summarize the provisions of Section 203, as was done with Section 304(c), and then to note the differences.

(1) *Grants covered* (§203(a))
    (a) transfers *or* licenses of *any* rights under copyright—exclusive or nonexclusive—
    (b) executed *on or after* January 1, 1978
    (c) by an author
    (d) as to *any* work created before or after January 1, 1978, and on that date subject to common law (§303), statutory first-term (§304(a)), renewal (§304(b)), life-plus-fifty (§302(a)), or alternative fixed-term (§302(c)) protection
    (e) except as to:
        (i)  works made for hire
        (ii) dispositions by will.
(2) *Persons who may exercise right*
    (a) the author or a majority of the authors who exercised it (§203(a)(1));
    (b) if an author is dead, his or her right may be exercised by (or if he or she was one of joint authors, his or her interest may be "voted" by) majority action of the owners of more than one half of author's termination interest, such interest being owned as follows:
        (i)  by surviving spouse (if no children or grandchildren)
        (ii) by children and surviving children of deceased child (if no surviving spouse) *per stirpes* and by majority action or
        (iii) shared, one half by widow and one half by children and deceased's child's children.
(3) *Effective date of termination* (§203(a)(3))
    (a) designated time during thirty-sixth through fortieth year after grant or
    (b) if grant covers right of publication, designated time during five-year period beginning on the earlier of the following dates:
        (i)  35 years after publication
        (ii) 40 years after grant.
(4) *Manner of terminating*
    (a) written and signed notice by required persons to "grantee or grantee's successor in title" (§203(a)(4))

    (b) specification of effective date, within above limits (§203(a)(3))

    (c) form, content, and manner of service in accordance with Copyright Office regulation (§203(a)(4)(B); 37 C.F.R. §201.10)

    (d) recordation in Copyright Office before effective date (§203(a)(4)(A))

    (e) termination right may not be waived or contracted away in advance (§203(a)(5)).

(5) *Effect of termination*

reversion to author, authors, or others owning author's termination interest (including those who did not join in signing termination notice) in proportionate shares (§203(b)).

(6) *Exceptions to termination*

    (a) utilization of derivative work made under grant prior to termination (but no right to make a new derivative work) (§203(b)(1))

    (b) rights outside federal copyright statute (§203(b)(5)).

(7) *Further grants of terminated rights* (§203(b)(3))

    (a) must be made by same number and proportion of owners required for termination, then binds all (§203(b)(3))

    (b) must be made after termination, except, as to original grantee or successor in title, may be after notice of termination (§203(b)(4)).

The key distinctions between termination rights under Section 304(c) and Section 203 may be summarized as follows:

| §304(c) | §203 |
| --- | --- |
| *Grants covered* | |
| Before January 1, 1978 | On or after January 1, 1978 |
| By author or other "second proviso" renewal beneficiary | By author |
| Of renewal right in statutory copyright | Of any right under any copyright |
| *Persons who may exercise* | |
| Author or majority interest of his statutory beneficiaries (*per stirpes*) to the extent of that author's share; or | Author or majority of granting authors or majority of their respective beneficiaries, voting as a unit for each author and *per stirpes* |
| In case of grant by others, *all* surviving grantors | |

*Beginning of five-year*
  *termination period*

| | |
|---|---|
| End of 56 years of copyright or January 1, 1978, whichever is later | End of 35 years from grant of, if covering publication right, either 35 years from publication or 40 years from grant, whichever is earlier |

*Further grants*

| | |
|---|---|
| Grantors are generally tenants in common with right to deal separately, except where dead author's rights are shared, then majority action (*per stirpes*) as to that author's share | Requires same number and proportion as required for termination |

As in the case of Section 304(c), it is impossible to foresee all problems that might be engendered by Section 203. Indeed, many of the same mechanical and substantive questions, including proper parties to serve and the appropriate scope of the "derivative works" exception, are common to both Section 203 and Section 304(c). There are several problems relating to Section 203 itself and to the interrelation of the various provisions in the statute that may be noted here.[79]

When it is perceived that Section 203 covers only post-January 1, 1978, grants and Section 304(c) covers only renewal copyrights subsisting on January 1, 1978, there emerges an apparent "termination gap": pre-January 1, 1978, grants in works protected by common law copyright before that date. (These works would also not enjoy any renewal right.) For example, a manuscript may have been created in 1976, 1977, or even earlier, made subject to a prepublication agreement, and still not be published by January 1, 1978. It would appear that no statutory termination right would be available. Accordingly, since the passage of the 1976 Act, some authors sought a contractual substitute, i.e., language in their agreement providing for a right of termination.

Section 203 also poses a conundrum in its interrelation with Section 304(a), the renewal section. Works first copyrighted as late as 1977 enjoy both a termination right and a renewal right. If the author's renewal contingency does not vest, there may be no termination right at all, since post-1977 grants by other renewal beneficiaries are not terminable under Section 203. Moreover, suppose a grant is

---

[79]The Supreme Court's decision in *Mills Music, Inc. v. Snyder*, 469 U.S. ____, 224 U.S.P.Q. 313 (1985), discussed in the text at notes 149–150 in Chapter 3, *supra*, dealt with only §304(c)(6), however, the holding of the Court is obviously applicable to §203's derivative works exception as well.

In *Freedman v. Select Information Systems, Inc.*, 221 U.S.P.Q. 848 (N.D. Cal. 1983), the provisions of §203(a) were invoked to demonstrate that a nonexclusive license had not been properly terminated.

made in 1978 by an author who later decides to terminate at the earliest possible moment. To exercise his 35-year termination right in 2013, he may give notice 10 years earlier, in 2003. Although Section 203 provides (as does Section 304(c)) that the future rights to be terminated "vest" upon the service of such notice, we still have the renewal provision to reckon with, since 2003 is only the twenty-fifth year of the first-term copyright. If the author dies shortly after serving notice of termination and his widow renews two years later, what is the effect of the author's termination notice?[80]

## Recordation of Transfers and Other Documents

The legislative reports accompanying the 1976 Act state: "The recording and priority provisions of section 205 are intended to clear up a number of uncertainties arising from sections 30 and 31 of the present [1909] law and to make them more effective and practical in operation."[81]

A key purpose of recording provisions is, of course, to protect a purchaser or mortgagee against the possibility of a conflicting preexisting grant. Accordingly, the 1909 law provisions (Sections 29–31) were similar in purpose to real-estate recording statutes and might have been even more necessary in view of the intangible nature of copyrightable property. The recordation provisions of the 1976 Act serve a number of purposes, including the giving of constructive notice of the facts stated in the recorded document, the resolution of priority between conflicting transfers, and the establishment of recordation of transfers of copyright as a prerequisite to the bringing of an infringement suit.

Section 205(a) permits recordation of "[a]ny transfer of copyright ownership or other document pertaining to a copyright * * * ." The legislative reports state that such "other documents" include "documents that on their face appear self-serving or colorable."[82] The me-

---

[80]This clash of the two provisions with the same reversionary objective is pointed out in Dreben, *Section 203 and a Call for a Hurried Review,* THE COPYRIGHT ACT OF 1976: DEALING WITH THE NEW REALITIES 229, 232–233 (N.J. Copr. Soc'y 1977).

[81]H.R. REP. No. 94-1476, 94th Cong., 2d Sess. 128 (1976); S. REP. No. 94-473, 94th Cong., 1st Sess. 112 (1975).

[82]*Ibid.* A document is considered to "pertain to a copyright" if it has a "direct or indirect relationship to the existence, scope, duration, or identification of a copyright, or to the ownership, division, allocation, licensing, transfer, or exercise of rights under a copyright. That relationship may be past, present, future, or potential." COMPENDIUM II OF COPYRIGHT OFFICE PRACTICES §16.03. The Copyright Office has issued a Policy Decision detailing the circumstances and conditions under which transfers and other documents may be processed on an expedited basis. *Policy Decision: Fixing of Fees for Special Handling of Import Statements and Documents,* 50 Fed. Reg. 46206 (Nov. 6, 1985).

Section 205 does not apply to the following: (1) notices of identity and signal carriage complement, and statements of account of cable systems (17 U.S.C. §111(d); 37 C.F.R. §§201.11, 201.17); (2) certain contracts entered into by cable systems located outside of the 48 contiguous states (17 U.S.C. §111(e); 37 C.F.R. §201.12); (3) notices of intent to obtain a compulsory license to make and distribute phonorecords of nondramatic musical works (17 U.S.C. §115(b); 37 C.F.R. §201.18); (4) license agreements negotiated between public broadcasting entities and copyright owners of published nondramatic musical works and published pictorial, graphic, and

chanics of recordation are set forth in Copyright Office regulations[83] and involve, generally, ensuring that the document to be recorded is legible, bears the actual signature of the person(s) executing it (the transferee need not sign), and is complete by its own terms. No specific form is required. Upon recordation, a microfilm copy of the original is made and the original returned along with a certificate of recordation.[84]

A recorded document will give all persons constructive notice of the facts stated therein if

> "(1) the document, or material attached to it, specifically identifies the work to which it pertains so that, after the document is indexed by the Register of Copyrights, it would be revealed by a reasonable search under the title or registration number of the work; and
>
> "(2) registration has been made for the work."[85]

Failure to comply with these provisions is not, however, a defense to one who has actual notice of the transfer.[86] Another important provision of Section 205 is the establishment of recordation as a prerequisite to the bringing of an infringement action:

> "No person claiming by virtue of a transfer to be the owner of copyright or of any exclusive right under a copyright is entitled to institute an infringement action under this title until the instrument of transfer under which such person claims has been recorded in the Copyright Office, but suit may be instituted after such recordation on a cause of action that arose before recordation."[87]

An immediate question arises as to whether "the instrument of transfer under which such person claims" should be read to cover the entire chain of title or only the immediate link in the chain on which plaintiff relies. The courts have held that only the instrument under which plaintiff claims title (i.e., the "immediate link") need be recorded.[88] A related question is whether so-called "short form" assignments may be deemed to be the instrument of transfer for Section

---

sculptural works (17 U.S.C. §118; 37 C.F.R. §201.9); (5) notification of filing and determination of infringement actions (17 U.S.C. §508; 43 Fed. Reg. 24151 (June 2, 1978), as modified, 45 Fed. Reg. 41548 (June 19, 1980)); (6) statements regarding the identity of authors of anonymous and pseudonymous works, and statements relating to the death of authors (17 U.S.C. §302).

[83] 37 C.F.R. §201.4, reproduced in the Appendix. See also COMPENDIUM II OF COPYRIGHT OFFICE PRACTICES §1600.

[84] 17 U.S.C. §205(b) (1978). While a legible photocopy may be recorded, such a photocopy must be accompanied by "a sworn certification or an official certification that the reproduction is a true copy of the signed copy"; further, the certification must be signed by at least one of the persons who executed the transfer document, or by an authorized representative of that person. 37 C.F.R. §201.4(c)(1). These steps are not required, however, for a so-called "duplicate original," i.e., a photocopy of the document containing an "original" handwritten signature. *Final Regulation: Recordation of Transfers and Other Documents*, 43 Fed. Reg. 35044 (August 8, 1978).

[85] 17 U.S.C. §205(c).

[86] *Northern Songs, Ltd. v. Distinguished Prods., Inc.*, 581 F. Supp. 638, 641, 224 U.S.P.Q. 779, 782 (S.D.N.Y. 1984).

[87] 17 U.S.C. §205(d) (1978). It has been held that the specificity requirements of §205(c) does not apply to §205(d). *Swarovski America, Ltd. v. Silver Deer Ltd.*, 537 F. Supp. 1201, 1205 n. 3, 218 U.S.P.Q. 599, 601–602 n. 3 (D. Colo. 1982); *Northern Songs, Ltd. v. Distinguished Products, Inc., supra* note 86, 581 F. Supp. at 641, 224 U.S.P.Q. at 782.

[88] *Northern Songs, Ltd. v. Distinguished Prods., supra* note 86, 581 F. Supp. at 640 n. 2, 224 U.S.P.Q. at 781 n. 2; *Swarovski America, Ltd. v. Silver Deer, Ltd., supra* note 87.

205 purposes or whether the entire contract or other instrument must be recorded. The courts have held that recordation of short-form assignments is sufficient for purposes of Section 205.[89] It has also been held that a beneficial owner of copyright not claiming copyright ownership by virtue of a transfer need not comply with the recordation requirements.[90]

Section 205(d) clearly states that no infringement claim may be *instituted* (not "maintained") until recordation has occurred. Although some cases have construed this provision literally, holding that failure to allege recordation is a fatal jurisdictional defect,[91] other courts have been more liberal, allowing the filing of an amended[92] or supplementary[93] pleading where recordation has occurred following institution of the suit, with the cause of action relating back to the date the suit was commenced. The certificate of recordation must have actually issued; the mere filing of the document for recordation is insufficient.[94]

Section 205(e) sets out the priorities between conflicting transfers. As between conflicting transfers, the one executed first will prevail: (1) if recorded under the terms of Section 205(c) within one month of its execution within the United States (two months if outside the United States); or (2) at any time if recorded "before recordation in such manner of the later transfer."[95] Even without observing these time limits, the first transferee may prevail if the subsequent transferee had notice of the earlier transfer or otherwise was not in good faith or had not taken the transfer "for valuable consideration or on the basis of a binding promise to pay royalties."[96] It has been

---

[89] *Co-Opportunities, Inc. v. NBC*, 510 F. Supp. 43, 48 (N.D. Cal. 1981).

[90] *Wildlife Internationale, Inc. v. Clements*, 591 F. Supp. 1542, 1545–1546, 223 U.S.P.Q. 806, 809 (S.D. Ohio 1984).

[91] *Fabric Confirmers North America, Ltd. v. Sassouni*, 85 Civ. 2108 (S.D.N.Y. filed March 28, 1985) (failure to record prior to hearing on motion for a preliminary injunction and on defendant's motion for summary judgment resulted in dismissal for lack of subject matter jurisdiction); *Nation's Choice Vitamin Co. v. General Mills, Inc.*, 526 F. Supp. 1014, 1017, 216 U.S.P.Q. 1017, 1019 (S.D.N.Y. 1981); *Burns v. Rockwood Distributing Co.*, 481 F. Supp. 841, 845, 209 U.S.P.Q. 713, 715 (N.D. Ill. 1979) (complaint dismissed without prejudice for failure to *plead* recordation; plaintiff given five weeks to amend complaint to cure deficiency).

[92] *Techniques, Inc. v. Rohn*, 592 F. Supp. 1195, 225 U.S.P.Q. 741 (S.D.N.Y. 1984); *Ruskin v. Sunrise Mgt., Inc.*, 506 F. Supp. 1284, 1288–1289, 212 U.S.P.Q. 475, 478 (D. Colo. 1981); *Co-Opportunities, Inc. v. NBC*, 510 F. Supp. 43, 48–49 (N.D. Cal. 1981). In *Meta-Film Associates, Inc. v. MCA, Inc.*, 586 F. Supp. 1346, 1352 n. 3, 222 U.S.P.Q. 211, 215 n. 3 (C.D. Cal. 1984), the court held that plaintiff need not file an amended or a supplementary complaint.

[93] *Northern Songs, Ltd. v. Distinguished Prods., Inc.*, 581 F. Supp. 638, 641 n. 7, 224 U.S.P.Q. 779, 782 n. 7 (S.D.N.Y. 1984); *Skor-Mor Products, Inc. v. Sears, Roebuck & Co.*, Copr. L. Rep. ¶25,397 at pp. 17,297–17,298 (S.D.N.Y. 1982); *Dahinden v. Byrne*, 220 U.S.P.Q. 719, 721 (D. Ore. 1982); *Dan-Dee Imports, Inc. v. Well-Made Mfg. Corp.*, 524 F. Supp. 615, 619–620, 217 U.S.P.Q. 1363, 1365–1366 (E.D.N.Y. 1981). See generally *Baldwin County Welcome Center v. Brown*, 466 U.S. 147 (1984).

[94] *Patch Factory, Inc. v. Broder*, 586 F. Supp. 132, 133–134, 223 U.S.P.Q. 1156, 1157–1158 (N.D. Ga. 1984). Cf. *Wales Industrial, Inc. v. Hasbro Bradley, Inc.*, 612 F. Supp. 510, 514–515, 226 U.S.P.Q. 584, 586 (S.D.N.Y. 1985) (jurisdictional requirement of recordation held satisfied where although recordation did not occur until five weeks after commencement of the action, it did occur before a hearing for a preliminary injunction); *Maxtone-Graham v. Burtchaell*, 631 F. Supp. 1432, 229 U.S.P.Q. 538 (S.D.N.Y. 1986) (recordation not required under special facts).

[95] 17 U.S.C. §205(e) (1978).

[96] This last requirement changes the result under the 1909 law. See *Rossiter v. Vogel*, 134 F.2d 908, 57 U.S.P.Q. 161 (2d Cir. 1943).

held, however, that the sufficiency of such consideration is a matter of state and not federal law.[97]

Section 205(f) tackles the difficult problem of priority between conflicting transfers and nonexclusive licenses. It will be recalled that such licenses, being excluded from the definition of a "transfer of copyright ownership," need not even be in writing, much less recorded. (Of course, they *may* be recorded.) But whether or not recorded, written, signed nonexclusive licenses prevail over conflicting transfers if the license was taken either before the transfer or in good faith before recordation of the transfer and without notice of it.

---

[97] *Dolch v. United California Bank*, 702 F.2d 178, 180–181, 218 U.S.P.Q. 116, 118 (9th Cir. 1983).

# 5

# Publication and Notice

The pivot of the 1909 law was the concept of "publication." This event was generally the dividing line between common law protection on the one hand and either statutory or no protection on the other. Thus, the traditional litany was that publication with the prescribed copyright notice secured statutory copyright, while publication without such notice placed a work in the public domain. As a corollary, the term of copyright was measured from "the date of first publication" according to Section 24 of the statute, and other ramifications of publication pervaded the statute. See, e.g., Section 1(a) (exclusive right to "publish"), Section 8 (government "publications"), and Section 9(c) (nationality of the author at time of "publication").

Because of the potentially crucial impact of publication on the existence or unavailability of protection, the courts imparted a considerable gloss to the term. Accordingly, "publication" in copyright matters has meant different things in different contexts. Its significance in dividing federal and state protection was somewhat diluted even under the 1909 law by a statutory option to register certain classes of works in unpublished form (Section 12), by the judicially created doctrine of a "limited publication" used to avoid forfeiture of copyrights disseminated without notice, and by the judicial recognition of areas of state protection for published works.[1]

In any event, the adoption in the 1976 Act of a single federal statutory copyright commencing upon creation is considered to have accomplished a "fundamental and significant change" in copyright law.[2] This by no means should suggest that publication is not important under the 1976 Act. For example, its role in determining duration for anonymous and pseudonymous works and works made for hire has already been noted.

---

[1] *Goldstein v. California*, 412 U.S. 546, 178 U.S.P.Q. 129 (1973).

[2] H.R. REP. No. 94-1476, 94th Cong., 2d Sess. 129 (1976); S. REP. No. 94-473, 94th Cong., 1st Sess. 112 (1975). For a discussion of the importance of publication, see Brylawski, *Publication: Its Role in Copyright Matters, Both Past and Present*, 31 J. COPR. SOC'Y 507 (1984).

But the significance of publication under the 1909 law also remains with us, both directly and indirectly. Its indirect significance is its precedential value in filling in interstices of the 1976 Act definition. Its direct significance is based on the underlying principle that the new law "does not provide copyright protection for any work that goes into the public domain before January 1, 1978."[3] Thus, it seems inescapable that a court reviewing an alleged infringement committed in 1986 with respect to a work arguably first "published" in 1970 will examine the statutory conditions of protection in 1970 to determine whether or not the work was in the public domain on January 1, 1978,[4] e.g., whether "publication" had taken place at all and, if so, whether publication occurred with or without a notice proper under the 1909 Act. The more liberal philosophy of the 1976 Act has, however, influenced some 1909 Act cases decided before[5] and after[6] January 1, 1978.

In any event, one would be foolhardy to approach the problem of a 1970 publication without a knowledge of the pertinent provisions and judicial construction of the 1909 Act. Thus, once again, we turn to pre-1976 Act experience in some detail. Following this, we will examine the definition and impact of publication under the main body of the 1976 Act and the notice requirements imposed by the Act, noting in the process how some of the 1909 Act's questions have been answered and how some of its learning has been applied.

## Publication Under the 1909 Act

The starting point here is Section 10 of the 1909 Act, which provides: "Any person entitled thereto by this title may secure copyright for his work by *publication* thereof with the notice of copyright required by this title * * * ." (Emphasis added.) The role of publication as the traditional requirement for statutory protection in this country resulted from the legendary bargain between the public and the author reflected in a statutory system of copyright. In order to induce the author to disclose his work to the public notwithstanding

---

[3]Trans. & Supp. §103, 90 Stat. 2559.

[4]See Nimmer, *Preface—The Old Copyright Act as a Part of the New Act*, 22 N.Y.L.S. L. Rev. 471 (1977).

[5]*Rohauer v. Killiam Shows, Inc.*, 551 F.2d 484, 494, 192 U.S.P.Q. 545, 553-554 (2d Cir.), *cert. denied*, 431 U.S. 949, 194 U.S.P.Q. 304 (1977); *Goodis v. United Artists Television, Inc.*, 425 F.2d 397, 402-403, 165 U.S.P.Q. 3, 6-7 (2d Cir. 1970).

[6]*Transgo, Inc. v. Ajac Transmission Parts Corp.*, 768 F.2d 1001, 1019, 227 U.S.P.Q. 598, 606 (9th Cir. 1985); *Jerry Vogel Music Co. v. Warner Bros., Inc.*, 535 F. Supp. 172, 219 U.S.P.Q. 58 (S.D.N.Y. 1982); *Fantastic Fakes, Inc. v. Pickwick Int'l, Inc.*, 661 F.2d 479, 486-487, 212 U.S.P.Q. 727, 733-734 (5th Cir. 1981). Cf. *Original Appalachian Artworks, Inc. v. Toy Loft, Inc.*, 684 F.2d 821, 825-827, 215 U.S.P.Q. 745, 749-750 (11th Cir. 1982). Some decisions have held that the only right an author had at common law was the right of first publication. See *Van Dusen v. Southeast First National Bank of Miami*, 478 So. 2d 82, 88, 228 U.S.P.Q. 19, 22 (D. Ct. App. Fla. 1985), and cases cited therein.

the resulting loss of his perpetual common law protection, the statute substituted new rights, albeit limited in time.[7]

It is for this reason that for many works publication was not only the appropriate requisite for statutory protection but, as noted above, also the point from which the term of protection was computed (e.g., Section 24 of the 1909 Act). What was perhaps less to be expected was that the concept of "publication" as utilized in Section 10 of the 1909 statute developed into a rather technical construct; it was not always coterminous with the general notion of "making public," nor even with the statutory notion of divestment of common law rights.

## "Divestitive" Versus "Investitive" Publication

It had long been assumed that the point at which the disclosure of a work became sufficiently extensive and unrestricted to cause forfeiture of common law rights was precisely the instant at which, assuming proper observance of the notice requirement, statutory protection might be secured. There is undeniably abstract justice in such a result. But courts are faced with specific cases, many of which present the possibility of an unintentional and irrevocable loss of all rights in a work. For example, an author innocently distributed a number of copies of his work without the proper notice. If such a distribution was considered a "publication," common law rights were extinguished and the author was found to have forfeited his right to secure statutory copyright. As a consequence "[t]he courts have treated these two concepts of publication [investitive and divestitive publication] so as to mitigate the harsh forfeiture effects of an improper publication,"[8] holding that "it takes more publication to destroy a common-law copyright than to perfect a statutory copyright."[9]

On the other hand, the perpetual rights enjoyed under the common law led a few courts to the view that commercial exploitation of a work should terminate common law protection, even if such exploitation did not amount to "publication" under Section 10.[10] Thus, in a number of different contexts to be examined below, attention should be paid to the possibility of divergent definitions of "publication."

It became generally agreed that deposit of copies of a work in the Copyright Office was not itself a publication within the meaning of

---

[7]*Data Cash Systems, Inc. v. JS&A Group, Inc.*, 628 F.2d 1038, 1043, 208 U.S.P.Q. 197, 200 (7th Cir. 1980) (citing Treatise).

[8]*American Vitagraph, Inc. v. Levy*, 659 F.2d 1023, 1027, 213 U.S.P.Q. 31, 34 (9th Cir. 1981); 1095, 1101–1102 (2d Cir.), *cert. denied*, 459 U.S. 826 (1982).

[9]*Hirshon v. United Artists Corp.*, 243 F.2d 640, 644–645, 113 U.S.P.Q. 110, 113 (D.C. Cir. 1957). See also *American Visuals Corp. v. Holland*, 239 F.2d 740, 111 U.S.P.Q. 288 (2d Cir. 1956).

[10]*Shapiro, Bernstein & Co. v. Miracle Record Co.*, 91 F. Supp. 473, 475, 85 U.S.P.Q. 39, 40, 86 U.S.P.Q. 193 (N.D. Ill. 1950). But see *Rosette v. Rainbo Record Mfg. Corp.*, 354 F. Supp. 1183, 177 U.S.P.Q. 631 (S.D.N.Y. 1973), *aff'd per curiam*, 546 F.2d 461, 192 U.S.P.Q. 673 (2d Cir. 1976).

Section 10.[11] On the other hand, deposit of copies of an unpublished work pursuant to Section 12 would divest common law rights, but statutory rights would be substituted and endure for 28 years or, if renewed, 56 years from the date of deposit.[12]

### Definition of "Publication"

The 1909 Act did not expressly define "publication." This omission was apparently based on a belief that a general statutory definition of the concept was too difficult to draft.[13] In Section 26, however, we are told that in the case of a work "of which copies are reproduced for sale or distribution,"

> "the 'date of publication' shall * * * be held to be the earliest date when copies of the first authorized edition were placed on sale, sold or publicly distributed by the proprietor of the copyright or under his authority."

As noted by the court in *Cardinal Film Co. v. Beck*,[14] the section was evidently intended to fix the date from which the term of copyright should begin to run for such a work, rather than to provide a general definition of what should constitute publication in all cases. The importance of the actual date of publication arose because, in the case of every work copyrighted in the first instance by publication with notice, the first term of 28 years began to run from that date; hence any error on the part of the applicant could have serious consequences, especially in connection with applications for renewals of copyright, which had to be made "within one year prior to the expiration of the original term of copyright." (This problem is in part avoided in the 1976 Act by having the term expire at the end of the calendar year. (See Section 305.)

Beyond providing the date from which the term of statutory copyright may be computed, Section 26 furnished an indication of certain acts which would necessarily satisfy Section 10. Thus, the public distribution of copies was the prototype of publication. This distribution generally took place through sale, lease, or circulation and did not embrace such preliminary steps as printing, advertising

---

[11]COMPENDIUM I OF COPYRIGHT OFFICE PRACTICES §3.1.1. (III)(e)(3); *Mittenthal v. Berlin*, 291 F. 714 (S.D.N.Y. 1923); *Fader v. Twentieth Century-Fox Film Corp.*, 169 F. Supp. 880, 120 U.S.P.Q. 268 (S.D.N.Y. 1959). But cf. *Brown v. Select Theatres Corp.*, 56 F. Supp. 438, 62 U.S.P.Q. 240 (D. Mass. 1944); *Tams-Witmark Music Library, Inc. v. New Opera Co.*, 81 N.E.2d 70 (N.Y. 1948). The reasons for the Copyright Office position on this point were twofold. First, as a matter of general policy the Office accepts the averments of applicants concerning publication, leaving to the courts the legal determination of whether publication occurred. Second, as a matter of administrative economy it is impractical for the Office to gather the necessary facts surrounding publication (or nonpublication) of each application. This position has been followed under the 1976 Act. COMPENDIUM II OF COPYRIGHT OFFICE PRACTICES §905.04. Deposit of a manuscript in a public library (including the Library of Congress) without restricting access was, however, deemed a publication. COMPENDIUM I OF COPYRIGHT OFFICE PRACTICES §3.1.1 (III)(e)(1). This is apparently also true under the 1976 Act. COMPENDIUM II OF COPYRIGHT OFFICE PRACTICE §905.03.

[12]*Marx v. United States*, 96 F.2d 204, 37 U.S.P.Q. 380 (9th Cir. 1938).

[13]*Hearings on S. 6330 and H.R. 198553 Before the Joint Comms. on Patents*, 59th Cong., 1st Sess. 71 (1906).

[14]248 F. 368 (S.D.N.Y. 1918).

the work, or the sale or offering for sale of the author's manuscript to a prospective publisher. But the sale or placing on sale of an edition was held sufficient, even where only a single copy was involved.[15]

## "Placed on Sale" or "Publicly Distributed"

The phrase "placed on sale" was new with the 1909 Act and does not appear to have been fully defined by the courts. This provision was construed to refer to "the date when the copyright proprietor sacrificed control of the work such that anyone who wished to view [and purchase] the work could do so, not [the date] when the public actually viewed the work."[16] While distribution to a dealer for delivery may thus have fairly placed the works on sale, the exhibition of "sample" copies by agents soliciting business was not construed as publication.[17]

Of course, material that is gratuitously distributed and not sold is still "publicly distributed" and hence published. Familiar examples are house organs, pamphlets, handbills, and similar matter left on doorsteps or sent through the mails. So also, mercantile rating books have been held to be published when copies are distributed to subscribers on a license basis but without any restriction as to who may obtain a license.[18]

## Limited Publication

It should be apparent that disclosure or communication of a work to another person does not always amount to "publication." Communication under restriction of the contents of a work is not a publication of the work.[19] Such distribution with limitation by the proprietor of the persons to whom the work is communicated or of the purpose of the disclosure was long known as a "limited" publication, which

---

[15] *Atlantic Monthly Co. v. Post Pub. Co.*, 27 F.2d 556, 558 (D. Mass. 1928).

[16] *Data Cash Systems, Inc. v. JS&A Group, Inc.*, 628 F.2d 1038, 1042, 208 U.S.P.Q. 197, 200 (7th Cir. 1980). See also *Roy Export Co. of Vaduz v. CBS*, 672 F.2d 1095, 1102 n. 14, 215 U.S.P.Q. 289, 294 n. 14 (2d Cir.), *cert. denied*, 459 U.S. 826 (1982) ("Though the cases contain much talk of publication occurring upon the sale of a 'single copy,' * * * such statements express the thought that *availability* for public sale constitutes publication even if actual sales are minimal").

[17] *Falk v. Gast*, 54 F. 890 (2d Cir. 1893). Cf. *Hub Floral Corp. v. Royal Brass Corp.*, 454 F.2d 1226, 172 U.S.P.Q. 418 (2d Cir. 1972); *Bouvé v. Twentieth Century-Fox Film Corp.*, 122 F.2d 51, 50 U.S.P.Q. 338 (D.C. Cir. 1941).

[18] *Ladd v. Oxnard*, 75 F. 703 (C.C.D. Mass. 1896); *Jewelers Merchantile Agency v. Jewelers Weekly Pub. Co.*, 155 N.Y. 241 (N.Y. Sup. Ct. 1898).

[19] *Stanley v. CBS*, 35 Cal. 2d 653, 221 P.2d 73, 86 U.S.P.Q. 520 (Cal. 1950). It was generally considered that a limited publication consisted of three elements: (1) communication to only a select group, (2) for a limited purpose, and (3) with no right of further distribution by the recipients. *White v. Kimmel*, 193 F.2d 744, 746–747, 92 U.S.P.Q. 400, 401 (9th Cir.), *cert. denied*, 343 U.S. 957, 93 U.S.P.Q. 535 (1952). See also discussion in *Van Dusen v. Southeast First National Bank of Miami*, 478 So. 2d 82, 88, 228 U.S.P.Q. 19, 22 (D. Ct. App. Fla. 1985), which held that unauthorized copying and distribution to a limited group did not result in a "publication."

"is really in the eyes of the law no publication at all."[20] The distinction between a general and a limited publication was said to depend not "upon the creator's intentions, but rather * * * upon the creator's actions."[21]

## Publication by Exhibition

Many works falling within the categories of works of art, maps, photographs, prints, and motion pictures are embodied in a number of copies and distributed much the same as books, periodicals, and music. Often, however, these works appear only in a single "original"; this is, of course, particularly true in the case of works of art. In this situation, the work was deemed published under the 1909 law by exhibition of the "original" only under circumstances where "all might see it and freely copy it." *American Tobacco Co. v. Werckmeister.*[22]

The rules of the British Royal Academy prohibiting copying were deemed in *American Tobacco* to prevent a general publication of the works exhibited there. The *American Tobacco* opinion has been applied to screenings of motion pictures by distributors, with the court holding that "publication of a motion picture does not occur until the film is in commercial distribution—when copies of a film are placed in the regional exchanges for distribution to theatre operators."[23]

The absence of restrictions, and the general freedom accorded copying by hand or camera, led to a finding that exhibition of the model of the *Chicago Picasso* sculpture amounted to a general publi-

---

[20] *Clark Equipment Co. v. Harlan Equipment Corp.*, 539 F. Supp. 561, 568, 215 U.S.P.Q. 1150, 1155 (D. Kan. 1982); *Data Cash Systems, Inc. v. JS&A Group, Inc.*, 628 F.2d 1038, 1043, 208 U.S.P.Q. 197, 201 (7th Cir. 1980) (citing Treatise); *Bepex Corp. v. Black Clawson Co.*, 208 U.S.P.Q. 109, 140 (S.D. Ohio 1980); *White v. Kimmel*, 193 F.2d 774, 92 U.S.P.Q. 400 (9th Cir.), *cert. denied*, 343 U.S. 957, 93 U.S.P.Q. 535 (1952). In *Technicon Medical Information Systems Corp. v. Green Bay Packaging*, 687 F.2d 1032, 215 U.S.P.Q. 1001 (7th Cir. 1982), *cert. denied*, 459 U.S. 1106 (1983), the court suggested the questionable result of a limited publication with notice not divesting common law rights but nevertheless beginning to run the term of statutory protection.

[21] *Clark Equipment Co. v. Harlan Equipment Corp.*, *supra* note 20, 539 F. Supp at 569, 215 U.S.P.Q. at 1156; *MacMillan Co. v. I.V.O.W. Corp.*, 209 U.S.P.Q. 739, 747 (D. Vt. 1980); *Bepex Corp. v. Black Clawson Co.*, 208 U.S.P.Q. 109, 140 n. 15 (S.D. Ohio 1980); *O'Bryan Construction Co. v. Boise Cascade Corp.*, 213 U.S.P.Q. 616, 618 (D. Vt. 1980); *Burke v. NBC*, 598 F.2d 688, 692, 202 U.S.P.Q. 531, 534 (1st Cir. 1979). But cf. *Brown v. Tabb*, 714 F.2d 1088, 220 U.S.P.Q. 21 (11th Cir. 1983); *Conner v. Mark, I, Inc.*, 509 F. Supp. 1179, 213 U.S.P.Q. 116 (N.D. Ill. 1981); *Public Affairs Associates, Inc. v. Rickover*, 284 F.2d 262, 271, 127 U.S.P.Q. 231, 238 (D.C. Cir. 1960), *judgment vacated for lack of sufficient record*, 369 U.S. 111, 132 U.S.P.Q. 535 (1962), *on remand*, 268 F. Supp. 444, 153 U.S.P.Q. 598 (D.D.C. 1967), with *King v. Mister Maestro, Inc.*, 224 F. Supp. 101, 140 U.S.P.Q. 366 (S.D.N.Y. 1963); *Hirshon v. United Artists Corp.*, 243 F.2d 640, 113 U.S.P.Q. 110 (D.C. Cir. 1957).

[22] 207 U.S. 284 (1907). Cf. *Pushman v. New York Graphic Soc'y, Inc.*, 25 N.Y.S.2d 32 (N.Y. Sup. Ct.), *aff'd*, 28 N.Y.S.2d 711 (N.Y. App. Div. 1941), *aff'd*, 287 N.Y. 302, 52 U.S.P.Q. 273 (N.Y. 1942). This rule has changed under the 1976 Act. See COMPENDIUM II OF COPYRIGHT OFFICE PRACTICES §908.03 (Example 1).

[23] *American Vitagraph, Inc. v. Levy*, 659 F.2d 1023, 1029, 213 U.S.P.Q. 31, 36 (9th Cir. 1981). See also *Paramount Pictures Corp. v. Rubinowitz*, 217 U.S.P.Q. 48 (E.D.N.Y. 1981) (distribution of videocassettes to television stations); *NBC v. Sonneborn*, COPR. L. REP. ¶25,474 (D. Conn. 1980) (television broadcast under limited licensing agreements); *Dowdey v. Phoenix Films, Inc.*, 199 U.S.P.Q. 579 (S.D.N.Y. 1978) (private exhibition of film to prospective purchasers not publication).

cation which, together with other forms of distribution without notice, placed the work in the public domain.[24]

Although availability for copying is thus the touchstone of publication in this context, copying could presumably be effectively curtailed by the presence of a copyright notice. In one literate but perplexing opinion, however, a 60-foot statue with a putative notice was held to have been so exposed to copying as to be "inconsistent with a claim to copyright."[25] This decision is perhaps justifiable because of the inadequacy of the notice actually used. The rule as to works of art and other exhibited works under the 1909 law would therefore seem to have been: Publication takes place where the work is exhibited in a way that, in the absence of a claim of copyright by means of a valid copyright notice, would make it accessible to public copying.

## Publication and Performance

It has generally been accepted that the public performance of a spoken drama does not constitute publication. This rule was established under the pre-1909 law in *Ferris v. Frohman*.[26] Although, as has been observed, the *Ferris* rule was based on outmoded concepts developed before statutory performing rights were available for plays, particularly if not printed, yet it survived the provision for such rights. Reexamination of the question "whether the oral presentation alone would or would not be a publication under the Copyright Act" was found unnecessary by the Court of Appeals for the District of Columbia in the *Rickover* case.[27] Thus the oral delivery of a speech by Martin Luther King, Jr., before 200,000 people and over radio and television did not amount to a divestitive publication.[28]

The *Ferris* rule has been applied by analogy to the public performance of a musical composition, whether for profit or not,[29] and to the oral delivery of a lecture or address,[30] all irrespective of the methods employed, including radio broadcasting.[31] Performance on television of an amateur photographer's filmed encounter between a lioness and a zebra mare was also found not to be a publication.[32]

---

[24] *Letter Edged in Black Press, Inc. v. Public Bldg. Comm'n of Chicago*, 320 F. Supp. 1303, 168 U.S.P.Q. 559 (N.D. Ill. 1970).

[25] *Carns v. Keefe Bros.*, 242 F. 745, 746 (D. Mont. 1917).

[26] 223 U.S. 424 (1912). *Ferris* is also significant for its holding that unauthorized publications do not result in forfeiture of rights.

[27] *Public Affairs Associates, Inc. v. Rickover*, 284 F.2d 262, 271, 127 U.S.P.Q. 231, 238 (D.C. Cir. 1960), *judgment vacated for lack of a sufficient record*, 369 U.S. 111, 132 U.S.P.Q. 535 (1962), *on remand*, 268 F. Supp. 444, 153 U.S.P.Q. 598 (D.D.C. 1967).

[28] *King v. Mister Maestro, Inc.*, 224 F. Supp. 101, 140 U.S.P.Q. 366 (S.D.N.Y. 1963).

[29] *McCarthy v. White*, 259 F. 364 (S.D.N.Y. 1919).

[30] *Nutt v. National Institute for the Improvement of Memory, Inc.*, 31 F.2d 236 (2d Cir. 1929).

[31] *Uproar Co. v. NBC*, 81 F.2d 373, 28 U.S.P.Q. 250 (1st Cir. 1936). Cf. *Metropolitan Opera Ass'n v. Wagner-Nichols Recorder Corp.*, 199 Misc. 787, 101 N.Y.S.2d 483, 87 U.S.P.Q. 173 (N.Y. Sup. Ct. 1950), *aff'd*, 279 App. Div. 632, 107 N.Y.S.2d 795 (N.Y. App. Div. 1951) (performance of opera).

[32] *Burke v. NBC*, 598 F.2d 688, 202 U.S.P.Q. 531 (1st Cir. 1979).

### Publication and the Distribution of Phonograph Records

The interrelation of publication and phonograph records has a particularly relevant history. Familiarity with such history is necessary in order to understand a number of distinctions which are continually made in the 1976 Act (e.g., "copy" and "phonorecord").

The history begins under the pre-1909 law, when the Supreme Court in *White-Smith Publishing Co. v. Apollo Co.*[33] held that a perforated "pianola" music roll was not a "copy" of a musical composition and therefore did not infringe the copyright in the composition. While Congress directly remedied this situation in 1909 by establishing control in Section 1(e) over mechanical reproduction of music, it did so without equating mechanical reproduction with "copy." Accordingly, for many years, it was generally accepted in a number of contexts that a recording was not a "copy" of the work recorded. For example, it was held that the distribution of phonograph recordings of a composition registered in unpublished form did not amount to reproduction of the work in copies within the meaning of the deposit provisions of Section 12.[34] This result accorded with the refusal of the Copyright Office to accept phonograph recordings for the purposes of deposit.[35] Nor did it appear under the 1909 Act that a phonograph record need bear a notice of copyright.[36]

The conclusion that a recording was not a "copy" of the work recorded led to the general (though not logically compelled) assumption that the sale of recordings did not in any sense constitute publication. Yet a current of judicial thought in the 1950s began suggesting that the sale of phonograph records *should* be considered divestitive publication. The keynote was sounded by way of dicta in *Shapiro, Bernstein & Co. v. Miracle Record Co.*:[37] "It seems to me that production and sale of a phonograph record is fully as much a publication as production and sale of sheet music." This view was shared at least in part in *Mills Music, Inc. v. Cromwell Music, Inc.*, where it was indicated that the distribution of records *after* the securing of statutory copyright would not have a divestitive effect.[38]

Despite practical problems raised by it and the furor created in many copyright circles, the *Mills Music* approach would have managed to avoid perpetual common law protection for fully exploited works. Nevertheless, the tide of history began quieting these ripples in 1955 with the Second Circuit's decision in *Capitol Records, Inc. v.*

---

[33] 209 U.S. 1 (1908).

[34] *Yacoubian v. Carroll*, 74 U.S.P.Q. 257 (S.D.N.Y. 1947).

[35] 37 C.F.R. §202.8 (1959 *repealed* January 1, 1978).

[36] *Buck v. Lester*, 24 F.2d 877 (E.D.S.C. 1928).

[37] 91 F. Supp. 473, 475, 85 U.S.P.Q. 39, 40, 86 U.S.P.Q. 193 (N.D. Ill. 1950). Cf. *Blanc v. Lantz*, 83 U.S.P.Q. 137 (Cal. Sup. Ct. 1949) (distribution of motion picture forfeited common law rights to music on sound track under California statute).

[38] *Mills Music, Inc. v. Cromwell Music, Inc.*, 126 F. Supp. 54, 69–70, 103 U.S.P.Q. 84, 95 (S.D.N.Y. 1954). See *McIntyre v. Double-A-Music Corp.*, 166 F. Supp. 681, 119 U.S.P.Q. 106 (S.D. Cal. 1958), *motion for new hearing denied*, 179 F. Supp. 160, 124 U.S.P.Q. 27 (S.D. Cal. 1959).

*Mercury Records Corp.*[39] that under New York law the sale of records does not forfeit the performer's right in his recorded performance. Judge Learned Hand there dissented on the ground that federal law should govern such a question. Professor Kaplan aptly noted that Judge Hand must have assumed that forfeiture *would* result under federal law or else he would have concurred, rather than dissented. The majority apparently operated under that assumption also; otherwise the difficult conflicts-of-law problems involved in *Capitol Records* could have been avoided.[40]

The most discursive treatment of the problem is found in *Rosette v. Rainbo Record Manufacturing Corp.*[41] Judge Gurfein there reviewed the statutory scheme, its legislative history, and the direct and indirect judicial interpretations relating to "this modern version of a scholastic dialogue" which "has intrigued the law professors"; he also examined the definition of "publication" in the Universal Copyright Convention (Art. VI) (which is limited to distribution of *visually perceptible* copies) and the circumstances surrounding its adoption. He thereupon concluded that a recording, despite its permanence, is to be equated with a performance. (Judge Gurfein then proceeded to fashion a novel condition on the enjoyment of protection in recorded music, namely, compliance with the statute so that its conditions, carefully devised by Congress, could limit the common law protection in such music otherwise available—a result deemed dictated by *Sears, Roebuck & Co. v. Stiffel Co.*[42] and *Compco Corp. v. Day-Brite Lighting, Inc.*[43]

The next pre-1976 Act chapter in this saga is the Sound Recording Amendment of 1971. In addition to providing the first federal protection covering the recorded *performance*, the amendment addressed itself to the separate question of remedies for infringement of copyright in the *underlying music* recorded without authority. Equating remedies for such infringement by recording to other types of infringement, Congress amended Section 101(e) of the 1909 law to provide that discs, tapes, etc., "shall be considered *copies* of the copyrighted musical works which they serve to reproduce mechanically *for the purposes of this section 101 and sections 106 and 109* [restrictions on importation of unauthorized copies] * * * ." (Emphasis added.) This, of course, did not make recordings "copies" for purposes of Copyright Office deposit or, presumably, for purposes of determining whether their distribution constitutes "publication."

The final link in the chain of confusion is the fact that *as to the recorded performance*, i.e., the "sound recording," the record *is* a copy of the "work." We shall return to this subject when we consider

[39]221 F.2d 657, 105 U.S.P.Q. 163 (2d Cir. 1955).

[40]Kaplan, *Performer's Right and Copyright: The Capitol Records Case*, 69 Harv. L. Rev. 409, 426, (1956).

[41]354 F. Supp. 1183, 177 U.S.P.Q. 631 (S.D.N.Y. 1973), *aff'd per curiam*, 546 F.2d 461, 192 U.S.P.Q. 673 (2d Cir. 1976). See also *Dealer Advertising Dev., Inc., v. Barbara Allen Financial Advertising*, 209 U.S.P.Q. 1003 (W.D. Mich. 1979).

[42]376 U.S. 225, 140 U.S.P.Q. 524 (1964).

[43]376 U.S. 234, 140 U.S.P.Q. 528 (1964).

the relationship under the 1976 Act between records, called "phonorecords," and the musical or other compositions recorded thereon.

## Publication of Derivative Works

Considerable uncertainty has been created as to the effect of publication of a derivative work on the status of the underlying work on which it is based.[44] This question has been most troublesome in connection with notice requirements. Presumably the answer in this context depends on whether the derivative work should be considered a "copy" of the underlying work within the meaning of the notice provisions, to which we now turn.

## Notice Under the 1909 Act

Section 10 of the 1909 Act provides: "Any person entitled thereto by this title *may* secure copyright for his work by publication thereof with the notice of copyright required by this title * * * ." (Emphasis added.)[45] The 1909 law implied an invitation to the author or proprietor to "secure" the copyright. We have seen that the word "may" is to be translated into "must" if copyright is desired. The drastic consequences of omission of notice under our laws have been unique. Unlike the laws of other countries, the 1909 law required a proprietor to claim copyright by means of a notice on pain of losing rights upon publication. Thus the omission, imperfection, or misplacement of the notice alone could be fatal to copyright protection. And there developed, in addition to a statutory savings clause in the case of accidental omission of notice from certain copies (Section 21), a noticeable judicial tolerance for what were deemed immaterial errors with regard to notice.[46] For example, the requirement that the name of the proprietor and, where applicable, the year date "accompany" the word or symbol claiming copyright was liberally construed.[47] One opinion adopted the philosophy of the Universal Copyright Convention notice provisions (later to be embodied in the 1976 Act) with regard to location of notice, under which the notice need

---

[44]Compare *Rushton v. Vitale*, 218 F.2d 434, 104 U.S.P.Q. 158 (2d Cir. 1955), with *Leigh v. Gerber*, 86 F. Supp. 320, 322, 82 U.S.P.Q. 271, 272 (S.D.N.Y. 1949). See also *Roy Export Co. of Vaduz v. CBS*, 672 F.2d 1095, 1102, 215 U.S.P.Q. 289, 294 (2d Cir.), *cert. denied*, 459 U.S. 826 (1982) ("[n]ormally publication of a collective work is also a publication of preexisting component works").

[45]These provisions also apply to works created and published before January 1, 1978, but registered after that date. *Hedaya Bros., Inc. v. Capital Plastics, Inc.*, 493 F. Supp. 1021, 1024 n. 2, 211 U.S.P.Q. 327, 330 n. 2 (S.D.N.Y. 1980).

[46]See, e.g., *Uneeda Doll Co. v. Goldfarb Novelty Co.*, 373 F.2d 851, 153 U.S.P.Q. 88 (2d Cir. 1967).

[47]*Fantastic Fakes, Inc. v. Pickwick Int'l, Inc.*, 661 F.2d 479, 487, 212 U.S.P.Q. 727, 734 (5th Cir. 1981); *Harry Alter Co. v. Graves Refrigeration, Inc.*, 101 F. Supp. 703, 705, 91 U.S.P.Q. 236, 237 (N.D. Ga. 1951).

only be affixed in such manner and location as to give reasonable notice of claim of copyright."[48]

A proper notice was indispensable not only when securing a copyright by publication of the work; preservation of copyright required
that "such notice shall be affixed to each copy thereof published or
offered for sale in the United States by authority of the copyright
proprietor * * * ." (Section 10.) To insure compliance with this provision, the proprietor was well advised to condition consent to repub-
lish upon the use of proper notice so that a publication without notice
was not "by authority of the copyright proprietor."[49]

Notice was, however, required to be placed only on "copies," a
term that was construed not to encompass three-dimensional works
reproduced in two-dimensional form.[50]

### Form of the Notice: §19

The form of the notice required by Section 10 of the 1909 Act is
found in Section 19, the first part of which reads: "The notice of copyright required by section 10 of this title *shall consist* either of the
word '*Copyright*,' the abbreviation '*Copr.*,' or the symbol ©, accompanied by the *name of the copyright proprietor*, and if the work be a
printed literary, musical, or dramatic work, the notice shall include
also the *year* in which the copyright was secured by publication."
(Emphasis added.) It necessarily seemed to follow that publication
without the required notice amounted to a dedication of the work to
the public sufficient to defeat all subsequent efforts at copyright protection.[51] While Section 19 thus seems to leave little discretion in the
matter, the courts did permit certain variations from the orthodox
prescription without fatal results.[52]

### *Copyright, Copr., or ©*

Before 1955, the symbol © was permitted in lieu of the more
cumbersome word "Copyright" or abbreviation "Copr." only with respect to works specified in Classes (f) through (k) of Section 5. Mak-

---

[48] *Glenco Refrigeration Corp. v. Raetone Commercial Corp.*, 149 F. Supp. 691, 692, 113
U.S.P.Q. 155, 156 (E.D. Pa. 1957). See Advisory Opin. No. 1, UNESCO COPYRIGHT BULLETIN,
Vol. X, No. 2 (1957). Cf. *Moger v. WHDH, Inc.*, 194 F. Supp. 605, 130 U.S.P.Q. 441 (D. Mass.
1961); *Wildman v. New York Times Co.*, 42 F. Supp. 412, 51 U.S.P.Q. 530 (S.D.N.Y. 1941).

[49] *Fantastic Fakes, Inc. v. Pickwick Int'l, Inc.*, 661 F.2d 479, 486, 212 U.S.P.Q. 727, 731–
732 (5th Cir. 1981) (noting possibility of implied condition). *National Comics Pub., Inc. v. Fawcett Pub., Inc.*, 191 F.2d 594, 90 U.S.P.Q. 274 (2d Cir. 1951). See also *Walker v. University
Books, Inc.*, 602 F.2d 859, 202 U.S.P.Q. 793 (9th Cir. 1979) (transferee's importation of copies
without notice resulted in forfeiture).

[50] *Kamar Int'l, Inc. v. Russ Berrie & Co.*, 657 F.2d 1059, 1062, 216 U.S.P.Q. 376, 379 (9th
Cir. 1981); *Rushton v. Vitale*, 218 F.2d 434, 104 U.S.P.Q. 158 (2d Cir. 1955).

[51] *Universal Film Co. v. Copperman*, 212 F. 301 (S.D.N.Y.), *aff'd*, 218 F. 577 (2d Cir. 1914).
See also *Bentley v. Tibbals*, 223 F. 247, 253 (2d Cir. 1915); *Mifflin v. R.H. White & Co.*, 190 U.S.
260, 264 (1903). Cf. *Puddu v. Buonamici Statuary, Inc.*, 450 F.2d 401, 404, 171 U.S.P.Q. 709,
711–712 (2d Cir. 1971).

[52] See, e.g., *American Greetings Corp. v. Kleinfarb Corp.*, 400 F. Supp. 228, 231–232, 188
U.S.P.Q. 297, 299 (S.D.N.Y. 1975).

ing this symbol available for all works irrespective of the nationality of the author was one of the few respects in which the United States went beyond strict treaty obligations in implementing the Universal Copyright Convention. As a result of the 1954 amendments, the symbol could properly be used on all classes of works, including works not covered by the Convention.

It is clear that at least one of the above three indications of copyright claim ("Copyright," "Copr.," or ©) *must* appear.[53] Using the word "Copyright" as well as the symbol © has the advantages of conveying more information and guarding against an indistinct or blurred © symbol. "Copyright*ed*," often used in notices, is not a material variance. "Registered" instead of "Copyright," however, is insufficient.[54]

Note carefully that the "c" is to be placed *within* the circle and not on the outside; and that, strictly speaking, the enclosure should be a *circle*, not parentheses, a square, triangle, or other geometrical figure. These variations from the prescribed circle may not pass muster in a suit for infringement, though no reported cases are found directly in point and the Copyright Office in time began construing this requirement liberally.[55]

### Name of Copyright Proprietor

The purpose of the notice was to "notif[y] the public of the existence of a claim of copyright,"[56] and thus it was held that "it is not necessary that the owner's true name be used at all so long as a name with which it is identified is used and no innocent persons are misled."[57] The test might even be satisfied by a trademark which identifies the proprietor[58] as the source of the trademarked products.[59]

### Year Date

Section 19 indicated that only in the case of "a printed literary, musical, or dramatic work" was the year date required in the notice. This category apparently embraced Classes (a) to (e) inclusive in Section 5. The word "printed" was used here to take in much more than

---

[53] *Kramer Jewelry Creations, Inc. v. Capri Jewelry, Inc.*, 143 F. Supp. 120, 111 U.S.P.Q. 151 (S.D.N.Y. 1956).

[54] *Higgins v. Keuffel*, 140 U.S. 428 (1891).

[55] COMPENDIUM I OF COPYRIGHT OFFICE PRACTICES §4.2.4. But see text at note 116, *infra*, for a decision on point under the 1976 Act.

[56] *Fantastic Fakes, Inc. v. Pickwick Int'l, Inc.*, 661 F.2d 479, 487, 212 U.S.P.Q. 727, 733 (5th Cir. 1981).

[57] *Tennessee Fabricating Co. v. Moultrie Mfg. Co.*, 421 F.2d 279, 283, 164 U.S.P.Q. 481, 484 (5th Cir. 1970). See also *Urantia Foundation v. Burton*, 210 U.S.P.Q. 217 (W.D. Mich. 1980) (misstatement as to authorship on registration application "unless made for some fraudulent purpose will not invalidate an otherwise valid copyright").

[58] Cf. *Herbert Rosenthal Jewelry Corp. v. Grossbardt*, 436 F.2d 315, 318, 168 U.S.P.Q. 193, 195 (2d Cir. 1970) (abbreviation sufficient), with *Puddu v. Buonamici Statuary, Inc.*, 450 F.2d 401, 403, 171 U.S.P.Q. 709, 712 (2d Cir. 1971) (abbreviation insufficient).

[59] See *Dan Kassoff, Inc. v. Palmer Jewelry Mfg. Co.*, 171 F. Supp. 603, 606, 120 U.S.P.Q. 445, 447 (S.D.N.Y. 1959).

printing from type set by hand or machine and included all modern methods of multiplying a work in copies, such as numerographing, photography, typewriting, and the like.[60]

The necessity of a year date went beyond Section 19. It will be recalled that the only formality upon which Universal Copyright Convention protection may be conditioned by any member nation is the requirement that all published copies bear the prescribed notice. Section 9(c) of the 1909 law, parallel to Article III of the Convention, excused all other requirements for UCC works if

> "from the time of first publication all the copies of the work published with the authority of the author or other copyright proprietor shall bear the symbol © accompanied by the name of the copyright proprietor *and the year of first publication * * * ."* (Emphasis added.)

Thus, all works seeking the advantages of the UCC in the United States (and most other countries as well) should bear the UCC notice, including the year. For a discussion of these advantages, see Chapter 10, *infra.*

The courts have been as liberal with respect to abbreviation or other variant forms of the year date as they have with respect to the name of the copyright proprietor. The year date may be abbreviated, e.g., '77. It may be in Roman numerals or spelled out in writing.[61]

*Antedated and Postdated Notices.* It sometimes happens that a publisher plans to put a work on the market toward the close of the calendar year and has it printed with a copyright notice bearing that year date, but subsequently finds it impossible or inexpedient actually to publish the work before the new year arrives. More often, the work bearing the new year date in the notice is published before the turn of the year. In neither case has the law been complied with, but the legal consequence of the variance in year date has not been the same in each case.

Where the year in the notice antedates the year of actual publication, it has been held that the copyright is not thereby lost but that the beginning of the statutory term is to be reckoned from the last day of the year which appears in the notice. If, for example, the year date in the notice is 1975 but the publication did not occur until some time in January 1976, the term is to be reckoned from December 31, 1975, and not from the date of publication. This ruling was laid down by the Supreme Court in a case arising under the pre-1909 law,[62] and was followed in cases arising under the 1909 law.[63] It is important to

---

[60] *Macmillan Co. v. King,* 223 F. 862 (D. Mass. 1914).
[61] *Stern v. Remick,* 175 F. 282 (C.C.S.D.N.Y. 1910).
[62] *Callaghan v. Myers,* 128 U.S. 617 (1888). See also COMPENDIUM I OF COPYRIGHT OFFICE PRACTICES §4.2.4 IV(b), and *id.* at Supplementary Practices 18 & 19.
[63] *Shapiro, Bernstein & Co. v. Jerry Vogel Music Co.,* 161 F.2d 406, 71 U.S.P.Q. 286 (2d Cir. 1946), *cert. denied,* 331 U.S. 820, 73 U.S.P.Q. 550 (1947); *Southern Music Pub. Co. v. Bibo-Lang, Inc.,* 10 F. Supp. 972, 26 U.S.P.Q. 321 (S.D.N.Y 1935).

bear this ruling in mind in connection with renewals, lest the application arrive in the Copyright Office too late for action.

On the other hand, if the year date in the notice is 1926 and the
publication took place some time in December 1925, the variance had,
originally, been deemed fatal to the copyright.[64] Even where the year
date need not be included in the copyright notice (Classes (f) to (k),
inclusive—maps, prints, photographs, etc.), it had been said that "if
the copyright owner elects to give the date of the copyright [publica-
tion], the date must certainly not be later than the actual date."[65]

The reason advanced by the courts for this distinction was that
in the former case the shortened term of copyright is an error in the
favor of the public, whereas in the latter case the error is tantamount
to a claim of a year longer than the law allows.

In the late 1950s the Copyright Office liberalized its policy with
regard to "postdated" notices, stating in its regulations that "if the
copyright was actually secured not more than one year earlier than
the year date in the notice, registration may be considered as a doubtful case."[66] The Office relied in part on the doubt created by *Advis-
ers, Inc. v. Weisen-Hart, Inc.*[67] This decision involved a four-month
difference between the actual date of publication and the date set
forth in the application. Both dates occurred in the same year, with
the result that the year date appearing in the notice was accurate and
the notice was not literally "postdated." The philosophy of the *Ad-
visers* case was that "useless technicalities are not to be allowed to
cut down the benefits conferred."[68]

*New Editions.* New editions of a copyrighted work always posed
special problems as to notice. If the edition was merely a reprint,
there was no basis for inserting a new year date, since this would
amount to a postdated notice.[69] Similarly, where any change or addition lacked a significant amount of authorship, it was safer to use
only the year date of publication of the original work. However,

---

[64] *Baker v. Taylor*, 2 F. Cas. 478 (C.C.S.D.N.Y. 1848); *American Code Co. v. Bensinger*, 282
F. 829 (2d Cir. 1922); *Heim v. Universal Pictures Co.*, 154 F.2d 480, 68 U.S.P.Q. 303 (2d Cir.
1946) (concurring opinion); *Wrench v. Universal Pictures Co.*, 104 F. Supp. 374, 92 U.S.P.Q. 350
(S.D.N.Y. 1952).

[65] *Basevi v. O'Toole Co.*, 26 F. Supp. 41, 40 U.S.P.Q. 333 (S.D.N.Y. 1939).

[66] 37 C.F.R. §202.2(b)(6) (1959, *repealed* January 1, 1978). See also COMPENDIUM I OF COPY-
RIGHT OFFICE PRACTICES §4.2.4. IV(a). Unlike the cited cases in note 67, *infra*, this regulation
did not involve an evaluation of good faith.

[67] 238 F.2d 706, 111 U.S.P.Q. 318 (6th Cir. 1956), *cert. denied*, 353 U.S. 949, 113 U.S.P.Q.
550 (1957). See also *Davis v. E.I. duPont de Nemours & Co.*, 240 F. Supp. 612, 620, 145 U.S.P.Q.
258, 267 (S.D.N.Y. 1965); *First American Artificial Flowers, Inc. v. Joseph Markovits, Inc.*, 342
F. Supp. 178, 175 U.S.P.Q. 201 (S.D.N.Y. 1972); *Newton v. Voris*, 364 F. Supp. 562, 180
U.S.P.Q. 262 (D. Ore. 1973); *L & L White Metal Casting Corp. v. Cornel Metal Specialties Corp.*,
175 U.S.P.Q. 464 n. 2 (E.D.N.Y. 1972), *aff'd*, 177 U.S.P.Q. 673 (2d Cir. 1973), and Cary, *Proposed New Copyright Office Regulations*, 6 BULL. COPR. SOC'Y 213 (1959). These cases required
that the error be an innocent one and that "the proprietor has substantially, and in good faith,
complied with the statutory requirements * * * ." *Davis v. E.I. duPont de Nemours & Co.*,
*supra*, 240 F. Supp. at 620, 145 U.S.P.Q. at 268.

[68] 238 F.2d at 708, 111 U.S.P.Q. at 319.

[69] *Wrench v. Universal Pictures Co.*, 104 F. Supp. 374, 92 U.S.P.Q. 350 (S.D.N.Y. 1952).

where "new matter" was contained in the new edition, use of the original year date only would not be satisfactory for the proprietor who sought full protection for the new edition. In order to take advantage of the provision of Section 7 whereby "works republished with new matter" were to be regarded as "new works" for the purposes of the Act, the year date of publication of the new edition should have been used.

## Alternative Form of Notice

We have already noted that the provisions of Section 19 (but not the provisions of Section 9 implementing the Universal Copyright Convention) required a year date *only* in the case of a "printed literary, musical, or dramatic work." Section 19 proceeded to afford additional latitude in the case of certain works falling outside this description by providing in its second sentence:

> "In the case, however, of copies of works specified in subsections (f) to (k), inclusive, of section 5 of this title, the notice may consist of the letter C enclosed within a circle, thus ©, accompanied by the initials, monogram, mark or symbol of the copyright proprietor; *Provided*, That on some accessible portion of such copies or of the margin, back, permanent base, or pedestal, or of the substance on which such copies shall be mounted, his name shall appear."

The word "may" implied that the section allows an alternative form of notice for the works specified. The permissive use of the symbol © was originally a concession to artists and lithographers who complained that the customary notice tended to disfigure works of art.[70]

The works for which the optional form of notice might be used as specified in Section 5, Classes (f) through (k), of the 1909 law were maps, works of art or reproductions thereof, drawings or plastic works of a scientific or technical character, photographs, and prints and pictorial illustrations, including commercial prints and labels. It was possible for a work to fall outside Classes (f) through (k) and still not be deemed "a printed literary, musical, or dramatic work" requiring a year date. This was true of a picture book having no continuity of story.[71]

Motion pictures were added as separate classes, (l) and (m), by the amendatory Act of 1912. Before that time, they could be registered as a unit in the category of photographs, Class (j), as under the prior law, and were entitled to carry the alternative form of notice. Having been legislated out of the "preferred" class by the amendatory Act, they were thereafter required to carry the longer form of notice, al-

---

[70] *Hearings on S. 6330 and H.R. 19853 Before the Joint Comms. on Patents*, 59th Cong., 1st Sess. 97–100 (1906).

[71] *Fleischer Studios, Inc. v. Ralph A. Freundlich, Inc.*, 73 F.2d 276, 23 U.S.P.Q. 295 (2d Cir. 1934).

though the Copyright Office accepted motion pictures without a year date under its rule of doubt.[72]

### Position of the Notice: §20

The notice of copyright under the 1909 Act not only had to be substantially in the prescribed form but, to be effective for certain classes, had to appear in the prescribed *place.*

With respect to books and other printed publications, periodicals, and musical compositions, Section 20 governed the position of the notice. It provided that:

> "The notice of copyright shall be applied, in the case of a book or other printed publication, upon its title page or the page immediately following, or if a periodical either upon the title page or upon the first page of text of each separate number or under the title heading, or if a musical work either upon its title page or the first page of music * * * ."

The page "immediately following" the title page would be the other side or "verso" of the title page, since each side of a leaf of a book constitutes a page.[73] The term "other printed publication" would seem to cover everything published with a title page or its equivalent, including printed dramas, lectures, pamphlets, and leaflets. But apparently it was not meant to include periodicals (except perhaps the unorthodox type) or musical works, for these were specially provided for in the clauses immediately following.

The language quoted above indicates that "the page immediately following" the title page was not the proper place for notice in periodicals, as it was in the case of works coming within the first category. It was apparently assumed that "under the title heading" included the masthead which is frequently found on the editorial page. In any event, notice was to be placed so that it could be readily discovered without examining every page of the periodical.

There was no specific provision in the 1909 law as to where the notice was to be placed for works other than books or other printed publications, periodicals, and musical works. In providing for the alternative form of notice for works in Classes (f) to (k), Section 19 required that the name of the proprietor appear "on some accessible portion of such copies or of the margin, back, permanent base, or pedestal, or of the substance on which such copies shall be mounted * * * ."[74]

Problems as to placement of notice on works in Classes (g) and (h) became more acute as a result of the expanding coverage of these

---

[72]COMPENDIUM I OF COPYRIGHT OFFICE PRACTICES §4.2.4.

[73]*Krafft v. Cohen*, 32 F. Supp. 821, 44 U.S.P.Q. 678 (E.D. Pa. 1940), *rev'd on other grounds*, 117 F.2d 579, 48 U.S.P.Q. 401 (3d Cir. 1941). See also COMPENDIUM I OF COPYRIGHT OFFICE PRACTICES §4.3.1.

[74]*Coventry Ware, Inc. v. Reliance Picture Frame Co.*, 288 F.2d 193, 129 U.S.P.Q. 83 (2d Cir.), *cert. denied*, 368 U.S. 818, 131 U.S.P.Q. 498 (1961) (notice on the back of a wall plaque approved).

classes discussed in Chapter 2, *supra*. But the position of the notice on textile fabrics and commercial designs presented one of the most serious problems.[75]

There was no specific provision for the position of the notice on motion pictures. The courts, following the Copyright Office's *Compendium of Office Practices*, were liberal on the issue of placement, permitting a notice to appear either in the opening frames containing the title and credits or at the end of the film.[76] Similarly, the position of the notice for articles first published as a contribution to a periodical was provided for only in the *Compendium*, which stated: "The notice on a contribution to a periodical must be in a form appropriate to the character of the contribution as a separate work."[77]

## Omission of Notice

It has been observed that a notice defective in form or position has, at times, been deemed the equivalent of no notice at all. In addition, there are instances where notice is altogether omitted from a published work. The general rule in this situation was loss, forfeiture, or "abandonment" of property rights in the work. More euphemistically, the work has been held to have been "dedicated" to the public.[78]

Many contributions to collective works do not carry a separate notice in the name of the contributor, a deficiency which in some cases resulted in forfeiture of protection.[79] In *Goodis v. United Artists Television, Inc.*,[80] the Second Circuit took a more liberal position, construing a magazine's copyright notice as covering the individual contribution "where a magazine has purchased the right of first publication under circumstances which show that the author has no intention to donate the work to the public * * *."

---

[75]See *Original Appalachian Artworks, Inc. v. Toy Loft, Inc.*, 684 F.2d 821, 215 U.S.P.Q. 745 (11th Cir. 1982); *Goldsmith v. Max*, 213 U.S.P.Q. 1008 (S.D.N.Y. 1981) (pillow); *Peter Pan Fabrics, Inc. v. Martin Weiner Corp.*, 274 F.2d 487, 124 U.S.P.Q. 154 (2d Cir. 1960); *Peter Pan Fabrics, Inc. v. Dixon Textile Corp.*, 188 F. Supp. 235, 127 U.S.P.Q. 329 (S.D.N.Y. 1960); *Scarves by Vera, Inc. v. United Merchants & Manufacturers, Inc.*, 173 F. Supp. 625, 121 U.S.P.Q. 578 (S.D.N.Y. 1959). See also discussion in *Animal Fair, Inc. v. Amfesco Indus., Inc.*, 620 F. Supp. 175, 185–186, 227 U.S.P.Q. 817, 823–824 (D. Minn. 1985) (1976 Act).

[76]*Twentieth Century-Fox Film Corp. v. Dunnahoo*, 637 F.2d 1338, 209 U.S.P.Q. 193 (9th Cir. 1981).

[77]COMPENDIUM I OF COPYRIGHT OFFICE PRACTICES §4.2.1 IV. For cases concerning advertisements, see *Excel Promotions Corp. v. Babylon Beacon, Inc.*, 207 U.S.P.Q. 616 (E.D.N.Y. 1979); *Deward & Rich, Inc. v. Bristol Savings & Loan Corp.*, 34 F. Supp. 345, 47 U.S.P.Q. 128 (W.D. Va. 1940), *aff'd*, 120 F.2d 537, 50 U.S.P.Q. 1 (4th Cir. 1941).

[78]*Public Affairs Associates, Inc. v. Rickover*, 284 F.2d 262, 269 n. 26, 127 U.S.P.Q. 231, 237 n. 26 (D.C. Cir. 1960), *judgment vacated for lack of a sufficient record*, 369 U.S. 111, 132 U.S.P.Q. 535 (1962), *on remand*, 268 F. Supp. 444, 153 U.S.P.Q. 598 (D.D.C. 1967). For a discussion of the distinction between abandonment and forfeiture, see *Bell v. Combined Registry Co.*, 188 U.S.P.Q. 707 (N.D. Ill. 1975), *aff'd*, 536 F.2d 164, 168, 191 U.S.P.Q. 493, 496 (7th Cir.), *cert. denied*, 429 U.S. 1001, 192 U.S.P.Q. 121 (1976).

[79]*Moger v. WHDH, Inc.*, 194 F. Supp. 605, 130 U.S.P.Q. 441 (D. Mass. 1961); *Mifflin v. R.H. White & Co.*, 190 U.S. 260 (1903). COMPENDIUM I OF COPYRIGHT OFFICE PRACTICES §4.3.1 V stated that for separate registration of individual contributions, a separate notice should appear on the title page of the contribution. A cautionary letter would be sent if a notice referring to the individual was contained only on the title page of the periodical.

[80]425 F.2d 397, 399, 165 U.S.P.Q. 3,4 (2d Cir. 1970). Cf. *Goldsmith v. Max*, 213 U.S.P.Q. 1008 (S.D.N.Y. 1981).

Notice cannot be said to be present where the letters are so Lilliputian as to require a magnifying glass to be seen,[81] or are so blurred as not to be recognizable.[82]

The statute was not absolutely relentless in requiring notice on *all* copies. Section 21 contained a savings clause which read in part as follows:

> "Where the copyright proprietor has sought to comply with the provisions of this title with respect to notice, the omission by accident or mistake of the prescribed notice from a particular copy or copies shall not invalidate the copyright * * * but shall prevent the recovery of damages against an innocent infringer who has been misled by the omission of the notice * * *."

This applied not only to cases where the notice was altogether omitted but also to instances where the notice, though good in form, was misplaced or illegible, or where it was defective; but the section dealt only with instances in which a particular copy or copies are involved.[83] It would seem that to enable the proprietor to invoke the savings clause successfully, the copyright must have been actually secured by publication with the prescribed notice on the bulk of the edition; otherwise, as observed by the court in *United Thrift Plan, Inc. v. National Thrift Plan, Inc.*,[84] Sections 10, 19, and 20 of the Act would have to be construed as optional instead of mandatory. The section did not apply if the notice was omitted through "neglect or oversight,"[85] or even a mistake of law.[86]

## Notice With Respect to Works First Published Abroad

In the original draft of Section 9 (later Section 10) of the 1909 Act, it was provided that "any person entitled thereto by this Act may secure copyright for his work by publication thereof *in the United States* with the notice of copyright required by this Act"; but in the final draft the italicized words were transferred to the next clause: "and such notice shall be affixed to each copy thereof published or offered for sale *in the United States* by authority of the copyright proprietor * * * ." (Emphasis added.) This change makes it

---

[81] *Smith v. Wilkinson*, 19 F. Supp. 841, 35 U.S.P.Q. 113 (D.N.H. 1937), *aff'd*, 97 F.2d 506, 38 U.S.P.Q. 1 (1st Cir. 1938) ("Where the work itself required magnification for its ordinary use (e.g., a microfilm, microcard, or motion picture film), a notice which will be readable when so magnified may be accepted"); 37 C.F.R. §202(b)(8) (contained in current regulations).

[82] *Smith v. Bartlett*, 18 F. Supp. 35, 32 U.S.P.Q. 287 (D. Me. 1937). But cf. *Ted Arnold Ltd. v. Silvercraft Co.*, 259 F. Supp. 733, 151 U.S.P.Q. 286 (S.D.N.Y. 1966). Copyright Office regulations also rejected "a notice permanently covered so that it cannot be seen without tearing the work apart." 37 C.F.R. §202.2(b)(7) (continued in current regulations).

[83] See, e.g., *Herbert Rosenthal Jewelry Corp. v. Grossbardt*, 428 F.2d 551, 166 U.S.P.Q. 65 (2d Cir. 1970) (omission of notice on 5 out of 300 copies did not result in forfeiture); Cf. *Data Cash Systems, Inc. v. JS&A Group, Inc.*, 628 F.2d 1038, 208 U.S.P.Q. 197 (7th Cir. 1980) (omission of notice from all copies of computer program embodied in Read-Only-Memory chip resulted in forfeiture).

[84] 34 F.2d 300, 2 U.S.P.Q. 345 (E.D.N.Y. 1929).

[85] *Sieff v. Continental Auto Supply, Inc.*, 39 F. Supp. 683, 50 U.S.P.Q. 19 (D. Minn. 1941).

[86] *Wildman v. New York Times Co.*, 42 F. Supp. 412, 51 U.S.P.Q. 530 (S.D.N.Y. 1941).

clear that a work duly copyrighted in the United States did not lose
such copyright merely because there might be an edition published
abroad at a later time without notice of copyright and sold only for
use abroad. The Supreme Court had already ruled to the same effect
in *Merriam Co. v. United Dictionary Co.*[87]

As a matter of fact, most foreign countries have long since dispensed with the necessity of any notice of copyright as a condition for
full protection, this being in accordance with the fundamental principles of the Berne Convention, to which they have subscribed. Consequently, the editions of works intended solely for use in the countries
of the Berne Copyright Union may not bear any notice of copyright.
The Universal Copyright Convention has begun to alter this practice.

But let us suppose that a foreigner whose country has established copyright relations with the United States had already published a work abroad without having taken steps to secure copyright
in this country. Could he or she still secure copyright protection here
by subsequently publishing an edition in the United States with the
prescribed notice?

In *Italian Book Co. v. Cardilli*,[88] Judge Hough decided that the
1913 publication in Italy of a song, duly copyrighted in Italy (without
a notice), did not prevent a subsequent American copyright for an
authorized edition of the identical song published in the United
States four years later with copyright notice containing the original
year date of publication in Italy (1913). He reached this conclusion
"with considerable doubt," and said that "the principle is important
and should be decided authoritatively."

Judge Woolsey of the same district disagreed with this ruling in
*Basevi v. O'Toole Co., Inc.*,[89] expressing the view that *Cardilli* must
be regarded as having been overruled by the circuit court of appeals'
subsequent opinion in *American Code Co. v. Bensinger.*[90]

In *Heim v. Universal Pictures Co., Inc.*,[91] the court disapproved
Judge Woolsey's ruling and expressed the novel view, in extended
dicta, that American copyright can be secured by mere publication
abroad (in a "proclaimed" country, see Chapter 10, *infra*) even without the prescribed notice of copyright admittedly required for publication in the United States. This result obtained as long as the work
was not in the public domain in the foreign country. This view relied
on the second part of Section 10 of the Act, which provides that
"such notice shall be affixed to each copy thereof published or offered
for sale *in the United States* by authority of the copyright proprietor
* * * ." (Emphasis added.) But, as pointed out by Judge Clark in his
concurring opinion, that provision deals only with preserving the

---

[87]208 U.S. 260 (1908), *aff'g* 146 F. 354 (7th Cir. 1906).
[88]273 F. 619 (S.D.N.Y. 1918).
[89]26 F. Supp. 41, 40 U.S.P.Q. 333 (S.D.N.Y. 1939).
[90]282 F. 829 (2d Cir. 1922) (copyright has no extraterritorial effect).
[91]154 F.2d 480, 68 U.S.P.Q. 303 (2d Cir. 1946). See also *Midway Mfg. Co. v. Artic Int'l, Inc.*,
704 F.2d 1009, 218 U.S.P.Q. 791 (7th Cir.), *cert. denied*, 464 U.S. 823, 220 U.S.P.Q. 480 (1983),
which excused omission of notice on copies first distributed overseas where the notice was put
on all copies distributed in the United States, and cases cited in note 140, *infra*.

copyright after it has been secured by the original publication with proper notice, as provided in the first part of Section 10, namely, that the person entitled thereto "may secure copyright for his work by publication thereof with the notice of copyright required by this title * * * ." And Section 13 provided that "[a]*fter* copyright has been secured by publication of the work *with the notice of copyright* * * * , there shall be promptly deposited in the Copyright Office * * * if the work is by an author who is a citizen or subject of a foreign state or nation * * * one complete copy of the best edition then *published in such foreign country* * * * ." (Emphasis added.)

In view of these conflicting opinions, the Copyright Office for a number of years registered claims in works first published abroad without notice. It was apparent even then, however, that a foreign author or publisher desiring copyright protection in the United States would do well to print the required notice on the copies at the time of first publication abroad and to see to it that such notice appeared on all copies published or offered for sale in the United States. The Office then changed its position,[92] on the ground that Congress in 1954 covered the question of publication abroad in the implementation of the Universal Copyright Convention. It came to the view that the *Heim* doctrine conflicted with the policy that foreign works first published abroad, to enjoy full protection in the United States, should bear the "UCC notice."[93]

These regulations were attacked in *Ross Products, Inc. v. New York Merchandise Co.*,[94] as inappropriately according extraterritorial effect to U.S. notice requirement. Although the parties crossmoved for summary judgment, the court declined to decide the question, finding the existence of genuine issue of fact.

## "Publication" Under the 1976 Act

### The Contexts of Publication

When one hears the overstatement that the 1976 Act "does away with" the publication concept, one should consider at least the following contexts in which the concept of publication is significant:

• Section 104—*national origin:* Unpublished works are protected irrespective of the nationality of the author, while with respect to *published* works such nationality at the time of first publication is relevant.

• Section 108—*library photocopying:* Archival reproduction of *unpublished* works is permitted under Subsection (b), while other privileges restricted to *published* works are provided in Subsection (c).

---

[92]37 C.F.R. §202(a)(3) (1959, continued in current regulations).
[93]Cary, *Proposed New Copyright Office Regulations,* 6 BULL. COPR. SOC'Y 213 (1959).
[94]242 F. Supp. 878, 146 U.S.P.Q. 107 (S.D.N.Y. 1965).

• Section 110(9)—*performance rights exemptions:* Certain privileged performances for handicapped persons are permitted with respect to certain works *published* at least 10 years earlier.

• Sections 118 and 504(c)(2)(ii)—*public broadcasting compulsory license:* This is applicable only with respect to *published* nondramatic musical and pictorial, graphic, and sculptural works. Certain limitations on remedies for infringement with respect to *published* nondramatic literary works are found in Section 504(c)(2)(ii).

• Section 302(c) and (e)—*duration:* Duration of protection for anonymous and pseudonymous works and works made for hire and presumptions regarding the date of an author's death are measured from *publication* or creation under the formula already discussed at pp. 00–00, *supra.*

• Section 303—*unpublished works:* This section provides for the duration of protection for *unpublished* material protected by the common law or state statutory law. *Publication* can extend such duration for 25 years.

• Section 401(a) and (b)—*notice:* Works *published* in visually perceptible copies must contain a notice that includes the year of first publication.

• Section 407 *et seq.*—*deposit and registration:* Deposit for Library of Congress is mandatory for *published* works. Section 407. Whether or not a work is *published* will also have ramifications on the details of Copyright Office registration and the remedies for infringement. See Sections 408(b) and 412.

• Section 410(c)—*certificate of registration:* A certificate of registration constitutes prima facie evidence of the validity of the copyright only if issued before or within five years of the date of first *publication.*

• Section 601—*manufacturing clause:* Relief from the provisions of this clause is granted individual authors under certain limitations linked to the question of *publication.*

### The Statutory Definition

Section 101 defines publication as

"the distribution of copies or phonorecords of a work to the public by sale or other transfer of ownership, or by rental, lease, or lending. The offering to distribute copies of phonorecords to a group of persons for purposes of further distribution, public performance, or public display, constitutes publication. A public performance or display of a work does not of itself constitute a publication."

Against the backdrop reviewed above, this definition is noteworthy in a number of respects:

• It purports to *be* a definition, i.e., to state what publication *is,* not what is "included" (cf. definition of "pictorial, graphic, or sculptural works"). This is not to say that it resolves all definitional questions; indeed, new ones are created. For example, while the statute uses "copies" and "phonorecords" in the plural, Section 101 defines "copies" as including the material object (other than a phonorecord) in which the work is first fixed, and the committee reports state that under the definition of "publication" a work is " 'published' if *one or more* copies of phonorecords embodying it are distributed to the public."[95] But Chairman Kastenmeier of the House Subcommittee on Courts, Civil Liberties, and the Administration of Justice stated on the House floor that

> "in the case of a work of art, such as a painting or statue, that exists in only one copy * * * [i]t is not the committee's intention that such a work should be regarded as 'published' when the single existing copy is sold or offered for sale in the traditional way—for example, through an art dealer, gallery, or auction house."[96]

These various interpretations of the term "publication" may not be in conflict if construed to mean that, while sale or other disposition of a work that exists only in its original fixation will not result in a publication, the sale or other disposition of a single copy of a work that exists in multiple copies will.[97]

• The definition is further muddied by the second sentence, dealing with the offering to distribute for purposes of further distribution or public performance or display. This may simply be an example of an act which "constitutes" publication or an attempt to resolve the uncertainties surrounding motion picture and videotape distribution and exhibition suggested above. At least three new questions have been raised by this sentence: (1) Why is this example apparently limited to the "offering" to distribute? It would certainly seem that actual distribution with a view to redistribution should even more clearly be publication. (2) Why is it limited to distribution to "a group"? Although "distribution" to an individual may be conceptually impossible, it would seem that redistribution is the key. Accordingly, why should not delivery to one person—a nationwide distributor—be the significant step?[98] (3) Perhaps most important, "further distribution," although vague, seems to dilute the essential ingredient of the definition—distribution *to the public*.[99] Thus distribution to a "group" of three for further distribution to a fourth seems literally to come within the definition of publication, whereas "distribution" to one agency for nationwide redistribution does not. Such results would seem neither intended nor sensible. The Copyright Of-

---

[95]H.R. REP. No. 94-1476, 94th Cong., 2d Sess. 138 (1976); S. REP. No. 94-473, 94th Cong., 1st Sess. 121 (1975).

[96]122 CONG. REC. H10875 (Sept. 22, 1976). Accord COMPENDIUM II OF COPYRIGHT OFFICE PRACTICES §905.01. Cf. *NBC v. Sonneborn*, COPR. L. REP. ¶25,474 (D. Conn. 1980) (dictum).

[97]See COMPENDIUM II OF COPYRIGHT OFFICE PRACTICES §906.01.

[98]Cf. *Berger v. Computer Information Pub., Inc.*, COPR. L. REP. ¶25,681 (S.D.N.Y. 1984), which excused the lack of notice on a manuscript sent to the editor of a magazine. Since, however, the mere act of sending a manuscript to a publisher is not a publication, no notice is required. *Van Dusen v. Southeast First National Bank of Miami*, 228 U.S.P.Q. 19 (D. Ct. App. Fla. 1985).

[99]COMPENDIUM II OF COPYRIGHT OFFICE PRACTICES §§906.01; 485.01. This same result has been statutorily adopted in the Semiconductor Chip Protection Act of 1984, 17 U.S.C. §901(a)(5) (1984) (definition of to "commercially exploit").

fice has put an additional gloss on this section of the definition by stating that "[t]he offering to distribute copies or phonorecords before any are available in a form ready for distribution does not constitute publication."[100]

• Implicit in the definition and related provisions of the Act (see, e.g., Section 106(3)) is the requirement that the acts constituting publication must be either by the copyright owner or under his authority.

By vesting copyright from the date a work, the subject matter of which is eligible for protection, is fixed in a "tangible medium of expression," the investitive role formerly played by publication no longer exists. We shall now turn to an examination of how other aspects of publication which were developed under the prior law have fared under the new act.

### "Limited" Versus "General" Publication

As under the 1909 Act, a publication without notice may, subject to curative steps (see Section 405(a)), result in loss of protection.[101] In order to prevent such forfeiture, courts construing the 1976 Act have continued the prior law's distinction between a "limited" and a "general" publication,[102] including the requirement for a limited publication that the distribution be for a limited purpose to a select group of persons. Thus, sale of a set of mailing labels for one-time use,[103] distribution of a computer program to licensees,[104] and distribution of a

---

[100]COMPENDIUM II OF COPYRIGHT OFFICE PRACTICES §906.01.

[101]*Shapiro & Son Bedspread Corp. v. Royal Mills Associates*, 764 F.2d 69, 72, 226 U.S.P.Q. 340, 342 (2d Cir. 1985) ("In general, publication of a work without proper notice of copyright affixed injects a work into the public domain"). *Cooling Systems & Flexibles, Inc. v. Stuart Radiator, Inc.*, 777 F.2d 485, 489, 228 U.S.P.Q. 275, 279 (9th Cir. 1985) ("Omitting the notice will invalidate the copyright unless one of the three exceptions [in §405] applies"). In *Campbell v. Mann, Inc.*, COPR. L. REP. ¶25,835 (S.D.N.Y. 1985), plaintiff shipped copies of the work from March 1981 to September 1984 without affixing a copyright notice. Sometime in September 1984 she began to affix a notice to copies of the work applied for registration the next month. The opinion is silent on the curative steps, if any, that were taken after omission of the notice was discovered. Based on omission of the notice over a three-year period, the court denied plaintiff's motion for a preliminary injunction. In a confusing passage the court seemingly took the position that plaintiff's works were in the public domain in this three-year period but were capable of being subsequently protected. See *id.*, at p. 19,803. This position has been superceded by the Second Circuit's subsequent decision in *Hasbro Bradley, Inc. v. Sparkle Toys, Inc.*, 780 F.2d 189, 193–194, 228 U.S.P.Q. 423, 426 (2d Cir. 1985), holding that the copyright owner possesses an incipient copyright in the period before curative steps are taken.

[102]The legislative reports indicate that

"[a] work is 'published' if one or more copies or phonorecords embodying it are distributed to the public—that is, generally to persons under no explicit or implicit restrictions with respect to its contents—without regard to the manner in which the copies or phonorecords changed hands."

H.R. REP. No. 94-1476, 94th Cong., 2d Sess. 138 (1976); S. REP. No. 94-473, 94th Cong., 1st Sess. 121 (1975). See also examples of public and private distribution given in COMPENDIUM II OF COPYRIGHT OFFICE PRACTICES §905.02.

[103]*National Research Bureau, Inc. v. Kucker*, 481 F. Supp. 612, 614–615, 204 U.S.P.Q. 938, 939–940 (S.D.N.Y. 1979); *Williams v. Arndt*, 227 U.S.P.Q. 615, 619 (D. Mass. 1985); *E. Harold Munn, Jr. & Associates, Inc. v. Minority Broadcasting of Midwest, Inc.*, Civ. No. 82-759 (N.D. Ill. filed Dec. 14, 1982).

[104]*Hubco Data Products Corp. v. Management Assistance Corp.*, 219 U.S.P.Q. 450 (D. Idaho 1983); *GCA Corp. v. Chance*, 217 U.S.P.Q. 718 (N.D. Cal. 1982), Query, if the source code and the object code are considered to be the same "work," as the *Chance* court indicated, whether an admitted general publication of the object code would not also result in a general publication of the source code.

business card to prospective employers[105] have been held to be limited publications.

## Publication by Exhibition

In an obvious reference to the *American Tobacco* decision and cases following it, the legislative reports accompanying the 1976 Act state:

"[U]nder the definition of 'publication' in section 101, there would no longer be any basis for holding, as a few court decisions have done in the past, that the public display of a work of art under some conditions (e.g., without restriction) would constitute publication of the work."[106]

The distribution of or offering to distribute copies of a work for purposes of public display does, however, constitute publication. The offering to distribute copies of a work for purposes of *private* display does not constitute publication, although the actual distribution of copies for purposes of private display does.[107]

## Publication by Performance

The definition of "publication" states in relevant part that "[a] public performance or display of a work of itself does not constitute publication."[108] The legislative reports amplify this by noting that "performances * * * on television * * * [are] not a publication no matter how many people are exposed to the work."[109] Regarding motion pictures, the Copyright Office has written that the above-quoted definition of publication

"is generally recognized as including motion picture distribution practices. Inherent within the definition as a whole is the presumption that copies are in existence and ready for distribution before a work can be published. Thus, offers in the form of advertising, and catalog or other distribution offers made before or during production of the motion picture, do not constitute publication."[110]

The offering by a film exchange to distribute prints of an existing motion picture for performance in theatres would be a publication.[111]

## Publication and Distribution of Sound Recordings

Contrary to prior law, under the 1976 Act the distribution of sound recordings does constitute a publication thereof (as well as of

---

[105] *Brewer v. Hustler Magazine, Inc.*, 749 F.2d 527, 224 U.S.P.Q. 550 (9th Cir. 1984).
[106] H.R. REP. No. 94-1476, 94th Cong., 2d Sess. 144 (1976); S. REP No. 94-473, 94th Cong., 1st Sess. 126–127 (1975).
[107] COMPENDIUM II OF COPYRIGHT OFFICE PRACTICES §907.
[108] 17 U.S.C. §101 (1978). See also *id.*, definition of "perform." A fortiori, a private performance does not constitute publication.
[109] H.R. REP. No. 94-1476, 94th Cong., 2d Sess. 138 (1976); S. REP. No. 94-473, 94th Cong., 1st Sess. 121 (1975).
[110] COMPENDIUM II OF COPYRIGHT OFFICE PRACTICES §§485.01; 906.01.
[111] *Id.* at §906.

the work recorded therein),[112] and as with other works, the offering to distribute a sound recording will not constitute publication unless it has been fixed.[113] Since distribution of sound recordings occurring on or after January 1, 1978, will result in a publication, sound recordings (or works fixed only in sound recordings) that were distributed both before and on or after that date are published as of the post-January 1, 1978, distribution.

## Notice Under the 1976 Act

### General Requirements: §401(a)

It should be noted that works published before January 1, 1978, but distributed after December 31, 1977, may comply with the notice provisions of *either* the 1909 Act or the 1976 Act.[114] The prescriptions of the 1976 Act are set forth in Sections 401 and 402, companion provisions governing, respectively, (1) notice on published *visually perceptible copies* and (2) notice on *phonorecords of sound recordings*.

Section 401(a) provides:

> "Whenever a work protected under this title is published in the United States or elsewhere by authority of the copyright owner, a notice of copyright as provided by this section shall be placed on all publicly distributed copies from which the work can be visually perceived, either directly or with the aid of a machine or device."

This makes it clear that (1) notice "shall" be used; i.e., despite curative provisions for omission of notice there is nothing permissive in the statutory language; (2) this basic requirement is not limited to the United States; (3) the requirement applies only to (a) visually perceptible copies (b) publicly distributed (c) pursuant to authorized publication.

When this requirement is read together with the definition of publication, we note that there can be publication, e.g., an unsuccessful "offering to distribute copies * * * ," which results in no publicly distributed copies and thus strictly speaking no requirement of a notice. Another example occurs with phonorecords. Here there is no requirement of notice pertaining to the work recorded (as opposed to the recorded performance) on the phonorecord since the recorded work is not visually perceptible.

---

[112]The definition of publication includes "copies or phonorecords." See 17 U.S.C. §101 (1978) (definitions of "phonorecords" and "sound recordings"). Sound recordings are fixed in "phonorecords," not in "copies."

[113]COMPENDIUM II OF COPYRIGHT OFFICE PRACTICES §906.01.

[114]TRANS. & SUPP. §108. But cf. 46 Fed. Reg. 58307 (Dec. 1, 1981) (Copyright Office Final Regulation on Methods of Affixation and Positions of the Copyright Notice) ("the [Copyright Office] retain[s] the point that the adequacy or legal sufficiency of the notice is governed by the law in effect at the time of first publication").

### Form and Position: §401(b)

The form of the notice prescribed in Section 401(b) follows substantially verbatim the formula of Section 19 of the 1909 law, namely: (1) ©, "Copyright," or "Copr."; (2) the year of first publication; and (3) the name of the owner of copyright. No order for these elements is specified, nor should one be implied or required. In 1981, the Copyright Office issued final regulations on methods of affixation and position of notice. Rejecting a request of a computer manufacturer that the regulations provide that an affixation consisting of "(c)" would constitute an acceptable substitute for the symbol "©" (owing to the inability of character matrix printers to print ©), the Office stated that it "has no authority to alter th[e] [Section 401(b)(1)] requirement."[115]

A decision from the District Court of Nevada, however, subsequently found that a notice consisting of a "c" surrounded by a hexagonal figure was an acceptable form of notice.[116] The phrase "copyright applied for" has, however, been held to be insufficient.[117]

### *Year Date*

As a general rule, the notice must include the year of first publication of the work. Where a compilation or derivative work incorporates previously published material, only the year date of first publication of such later work is needed (Section 401(b)(2)). The year date may be omitted "where a pictorial, graphic, or sculptural work, with accompanying text matter, if any, is reproduced in or on greeting cards, postcards, stationery, jewelry, dolls, toys, or any useful article." This provision represents a retrenchment from the 1909 Act, which required a year date only in the case of a "printed literary, musical, or dramatic work." In construing the 1976 Act provision, the Copyright Office has stated in section 1006 of *Compendium II of Copyright Office Practices*:

> "A label is not considered a useful article, from which the year date may be omitted. Those textiles and fabrics which are useful articles do not require a year date; however, where a copyright notice applicable to a textile or a fabric which is a useful article is contained on a label affixed to the textile or fabric, and the year date is omitted from the notice, such notice shall be acceptable insofar as it applies to the textile or fabric."

---

[115]But cf. COMPENDIUM II OF COPYRIGHT OFFICE PRACTICES §1005.01(c), which lists acceptable variants, including "(c)." See also *Shapiro & Son Bedspread Corp. v. Royal Mills Associates*, 764 F.2d 69, 72, 226 U.S.P.Q. 340, 342 (2d Cir. 1985) (words "Design Copyrighted" held deficient).

[116]*Videotronics, Inc. v. Bend Electronics*, 568 F. Supp. 478, 223 U.S.P.Q. 936 (D. Nev. 1984). Forfeiture of protection was found, however, due to the infrequent and random appearance of the notice, and failure to take the appropriate curative steps under §405. See also *Ronald Litoff, Ltd. v. American Express Co.*, 621 F. Supp. 981, 984, 228 U.S.P.Q. 739, 741 (S.D.N.Y. 1985) (argument that notice with a "c" not encircled was invalid rejected on motion for summary judgment).

[117]*M. Kramer Mfg. Co. v. Andrews*, 783 F. 2d 421, 443, 228 U.S.P.Q. 705, 720–721 (4th Cir. 1986).

The uncertainties of this provision would suggest a conservative inclusion of a year date, despite the disinclination of many marketers to appear to be selling "dated" merchandise. Moreover, the international ramifications of the year date also support its use. As noted earlier, the Universal Copyright Convention unequivocally prescribes for all works a notice consisting of ©, the name of the proprietor, and the year of first publication in order for a work to satisfy automatically any domestic formalities imposed in other countries. Although a number of countries do not impose such formalities, a number of them do (including the "formality" of domestic publication). In any event, any uncertainties in this respect on the international level can also be removed by use of a year date.

The year date is acceptable if represented in Arabic numerals (1986), abbreviations of Arabic numerals ('86), Roman numerals (MCMLXXXVI), or if spelled out in words.[118] A year date that is present but separated from the rest of the notice is acceptable "if it is an appropriate date and is reasonably identifiable as part of the notice."[119]

The omission of a year date where one is required will result in the work's being treated as if it had been published entirely without a notice.[120] Provisions with respect to an error in the year date are covered in Section 406(b):

> "When the year date in the notice on copies or phonorecords distributed by authority of the copyright owner is earlier than the year in which publication first occurred, any period computed from the year of first publication under section 302 is to be computed from the year in the notice. Where the year date is more than one year later than the year in which publication first occurred, the work is considered to have been published without any notice and is governed by the provisions of section 405."

*Name*

Section 401(b)(3) specifies that the notice must contain "the name of the owner of the copyright in the work, or an abbreviation by which the name can be recognized, or a generally known alternative designation of the owner."[121] A preliminary question raised by this provision is: Who is the owner of copyright? It will be recalled that the " '[c]opyright owner,' with respect to any one of the exclusive rights comprised in a copyright, refers to the owner of that particular

---

[118]Compendium II of Copyright Office Practices §1006.01.

[119]*Id.* at §1006.05. Examples of such acceptable notice placements are (1) a date that is the only date appearing on the same page as the other elements of the notice; and (2) a date prominently displayed elsewhere on the page, e.g., Library of Congress Card Catalogue Number or the year in the issuance date of a periodical. *Ibid.* The presence of intervening matter between the year date and the other elements of the notice does not "necessarily preclude considering a year date [as] part of the notice." *Ibid.* See also H.R. Rep. No. 94-1476, 94th Cong., 2d Sess. 150 (1976); S. Rep. No. 94-473, 94th Cong., 1st Sess. 133 (1975): "Unlike the present law, the bill contains no provision requiring the elements of the copyright notice to 'accompany' each other * * *."

[120]17 U.S.C. §406(c) (1978).

[121]*Ronald Litoff, Ltd. v. American Express Co.*, 621 F. Supp. 981, 984, 228 U.S.P.Q., 739, 741 (S.D.N.Y. 1985) (argument that "RL" inadequate rejected on motion for summary judgment).

right." There are thus as many possible "copyright owners" as there are exclusive rights that may be granted by the author.[122]

Section 406(a) contains a savings clause applicable to errors in name where there is an existing contractual relationship between the copyright owner and the person mistakenly named in the notice.[123] Such an error does not affect the validity and ownership of the copyright.[124] However, a complete defense to an action for infringement is given to persons who innocently begin an "undertaking" if they prove that they were misled by the notice and began the undertaking in good faith under a purported transfer or license from the person incorrectly named in the notice, unless: (1) registration had previously been made in the correct name of the copyright owner; or (2) "a document executed by the person named in the notice and showing the ownership of the copyright had been recorded."[125]

### *Position: §401(c)*

Section 401(c) follows the flexible approach of the Universal Copyright Convention by providing simply that the notice "shall be affixed to the copies in such manner and location as to give reasonable notice of the claim of copyright." The statute also directs the Register of Copyrights to prescribe by regulation examples of specific methods of affixation and positions that will satisfy the notice requirement, but adds that "these specifications shall not be considered exhaustive."[126] In 1981 the Register issued such regulations,[127] and these should be carefully consulted.[128]

---

[122]The notice provisions differ in this respect from the regulations governing registration, which permit only the author or person (or organization) owning *all* rights in the work to apply for registration. 37 C.F.R. §202.3(a)(3).

[123]H.R. REP. No. 94-1476, 94th Cong., 2d Sess. 149 (1976); S. REP. No. 94-473, 94th Cong., 1st Sess. 132 (1975). The licensee is liable to account to the copyright owner for receipts from all transfers or licenses purportedly made under the authority of the copyright owner. 17 U.S.C. §406(a) (1978).

[124]*Berger v. Computer Information Pub., Inc.*, COPR. L. REP. ¶25,681 (S.D.N.Y. 1984); *Arthur Retlaw & Associates, Inc. v. Travenol Laboratories, Inc.*, 582 F. Supp. 1010, 223 U.S.P.Q. 722 (N.D. Ill. 1984); *Fantastic Fakes, Inc. v. Pickwick Int'l, Inc.*, 661 F.2d 479, 212 U.S.P.Q. 727 (5th Cir. 1981) (dictum).

[125]17 U.S.C. §406(a)(2) (1978). See *Quinto v. Legal Times of Washington, Inc.*, 506 F. Supp. 554, 213 U.S.P.Q. 270 (D.D.C. 1981) (discussed in the text at notes 135–136, *infra*).

[126]17 U.S.C. §401(c)(2) (1978). See *Midway Mfg. Co. v. Dirkschneider*, 543 F. Supp. 466, 482, 214 U.S.P.Q. 417, 428 (D. Neb. 1981) ("the * * * regulations are not binding on the Court, [however], they do suggest a persuasive interpretation of the requirements of §401(c)"); *Ronald Litoff, Ltd. v. American Express Co.*, 621 F. Supp. 981, 984, 228 U.S.P.Q. 739, 741 (S.D.N.Y. 1985) (notice on jewelry pendants "although small and somewhat difficult to read, is sufficient to satisfy the statutory requirements"); *Dimitrakopoulus v. Flowers by Demetrios, Inc.*, COPR. L. REP. ¶25,551 (S.D.N.Y. 1983) (notice on flower sculptures affixed by jeweler's stamp "necessarily small" in light of size of work, but still held acceptable); *Wales Industrial, Inc. v. Hasbro Bradley, Inc.*, 612 F. Supp. 510, 518–519, 226 U.S.P.Q. 584, 590 (S.D.N.Y. 1985) (even though plaintiff obtained separate registrations for each "configuration" of a toy and notice contained on only one configuration, tradition of liberal construction of notice requirement led to conclusion that "reasonable notice" was given. Cf. *Kieselstein-Cord v. Accessories by Pearl, Inc.*, 206 U.S.P.Q. 439, 444 (S.D.N.Y.), *rev'd on other grounds*, 632 F.2d 989, 208 U.S.P.Q. 1 (2d Cir. 1980) (finding that notice on belt buckle that was "legible to the naked eye—at least that of someone with excellent vision" held to be a "reasonable" notice).

[127]37 C.F.R. §201.20. In issuing these regulations, the Copyright Office rejected a request to list the acceptable positions of the notice in descending order of preference, stating that it believed "ranking various positions in preferential order would be inconsistent with th[e] [§401(c)] mandate." 46 Fed. Reg. 58307 (Dec. 1, 1981).

[128]See also COMPENDIUM II OF COPYRIGHT OFFICE PRACTICES §1013.

### Notice on Phonorecords of Sound Recordings: §402

Section 402 contains a special notice provision for publicly distributed phonorecords of sound recordings.[129] The formula for notice on such works parallels the Section 401 requirements for "copies," with the following differences: (1) ℗ is the only acceptable designation of the claim; (2) the name requirement is satisfied by the appearance of the record producer's name on the label or container "if no other name appears in conjunction with the notice"; and (3) the notice may appear on the record itself, its label, or its container. It is important to bear in mind that these provisions have no application to the musical works embodied in the sound recording, which do not need a notice since they can not be visually perceived from the phonorecord and since phonorecords are not "copies" of the musical works.[130]

### Government Works: §403

Section 403 provides:

"Whenever a work is published in copies or phonorecords consisting preponderantly of one or more works of the United States Government, the notice of copyright provided by sections 401 and 402 shall also include a statement identifying, either affirmatively or negatively, those portions of the copies or phonorecords embodying any work or works protected under this title."[131]

This provision was added to prevent the practice of some publishers of adding an introduction, editorial revisions, or illustrations to a government work and placing a "general" copyright notice in the publisher's name on the work without indicating to the public that the rest of the work was in the public domain. The provision does not apply to unpublished works, and no guidance is given in determining when a published work consists "preponderantly" of one or more works of the U.S. government.[132] The omission of the identifying statement, where required, results in the work's being treated as if it were published without any notice.[133]

---

[129]See H.R. Rep. No. 94-1476, 94th Cong., 2d Sess. 145 (1976), and S. Rep. No. 94-473, 94th Cong., 1st Sess. 128 (1975), for an explanation of the reasons for this designation. But cf. Compendium II of Copyright Office Practices §1005.02, which lists acceptable and unacceptable variants of ℗. See also 17 U.S.C. §101 (1978) (definitions of "phonorecords" and "sound recordings").

[130]17 U.S.C. §401(a) (1978). See also *id.* at §101 (definitions of "copies" and "phonorecords").

[131]17 U.S.C. §403 (1978). See also *id.* at §101 (definition of "work of the United States Government"), §105 (prohibition on copyright in any work of U.S. government).

[132]But see *Stonehill Communications, Inc. v. Martuge*, 512 F. Supp. 349, 212 U.S.P.Q. 500 (S.D.N.Y. 1981), which construed the phrase "copies of a work consisting preponderantly of nondramatic literary material" in §601(a).

[133]H.R. Rep. No. 94-1476, 94th Cong., 2d Sess. 146 (1976); S. Rep. No. 94-473, 94th Cong., 1st Sess. 128 (1975).

## Collective Works

Section 404 of the Act permits a single contribution to a collective work to bear its own notice. A single notice applicable to the collective work as a whole is also sufficient to satisfy the provisions of Sections 401–403 except for advertisements inserted "on behalf of persons other than the owner of copyright in the collective work."[134] However, in view of the further provision in Section 404(b) that the absence of a separate notice on an individual contribution will result in the contribution being treated as if it had been published with the wrong name for purposes of innocent infringers qualifying under Section 406(a) (discussed below), it is advisable to affix a separate notice where applicable.

## Errors in Notice: §406

An error in the name of the copyright owner cannot affect the validity or ownership of the copyright. Section 406(a), however, provides a complete defense to an individual who "innocently begins an undertaking that infringes the copyright * * * if such person proves that he or she was misled by the notice and began the undertaking in good faith under a purported transfer or license from the person named therein" unless registration for the work has been made in the name of the copyright owner, or "a document executed by the person named in the notice and showing the ownership of the copyright" has been recorded in the Copyright Office.

In order to succeed in establishing a prima facie Section 406(a) defense, the individual must prove that

(1) he *innocently* began his infringing undertaking;
(2) he was *misled* by the affixation of the copyright notice with the name of a person other than the copyright owner;
(3) he began the undertaking in *good faith*; and
(4) under a purported transfer or license from the person named in the notice.

---

[134] 17 U.S.C. §404(a) (1978). See explanation of this exception in H.R. REP. No. 94-1476, 94th Cong., 2d Sess. 146 (1976), and S. REP. No. 94-473, 94th Cong., 1st Sess. 129 (1975). In *Canfield v. Ponchatoula Times*, 759 F.2d 493, 495–496, 226 U.S.P.Q. 112, 113–114 (5th Cir. 1985), the court construed the language in §404(a) "inserted on behalf of persons other than the owner of copyright in the collective work "to also include the situation where the advertisement is inserted on behalf of an advertiser but is owned (e.g., through a work-for-hire agreement) nevertheless by the newspaper in which it originally appears. In such a situation the court held that the general notice for the newspaper was insufficient to protect the advertisement, which was required to bear its own notice. Moreover, since the newspaper was the owner of the advertisement, §§404(b) and 406(a) were deemed inapplicable. See also *Evans & Associates, Inc. v. Continental Homes, Inc.*, 785 F.2d 897, 906–908, 229 U.S.P.Q. 321, 326–328 (11th Cir. 1986).

In *Southern Bell Tel. & Tel. Co. v. Associated Directory Pub.*, 756 F.2d 801, 225 U.S.P.Q. 899 (11th Cir. 1985), lack of a notice on each advertisement was found not to be a bar to a compilation infringement suit over copying of telephone yellow pages as a unit.

The "good faith" requirement of Section 406(a) was explored at length in *Quinto v. Legal Times of Washington, Inc.*, where defendant raised Section 406(a) as a defense to its reprinting of an article from a student legal periodical. In construing the term the court held that it "entails not only honesty in fact, but reasonableness as well."[135] Included within the ambit of reasonableness is a duty to inquire into ownership and perhaps to conduct a search of the Copyright Office records.

An omission of any name from the copyright notice will result in the work being treated as if it were published without any notice.[136] Antedated year notices are simply taken at their word—"any period computed from the year of first publication under Section 302(c) [i.e., anonymous and pseudonymous works, and works made for hire] is to be computed from the year in the notice."[137] Where the year date is postdated by more than one year from the date of first publication,[138] or is omitted entirely,[139] the work is treated as having been published without any notice. Where the year date is postdated by an amount up to and including one year from the date of first publication, the work is treated as having been published with a correct notice (assuming the other elements are also correct).

### Omission of Notice: §405

This brings us to the provision which has attracted much attention in early discussions of the new law—the provisions found in Section 405 governing omission of notice.

Since this section does contain curative provisions covering omissions of notice, it supports the notion that even as to published works protection under the 1976 Act is "automatic" and does not "require" a notice. It is true that, as a practical matter, a user can no longer generally rely on the absence of a notice on published copies as signifying that the work is in the public domain; the user copies at his or her peril, albeit a peril diminished by innocent infringement limitations on remedies.

Section 405(a) provides:

"Effect of Omission on Copyright.—The omission of the copyright notice prescribed by sections 401 through 403 from copies or phonorec-

---

[135]506 F. Supp. 554, 562, 213 U.S.P.Q. 270, 276 (D.D.C. 1981). See also *Vogel Music Co. v. Warner Bros., Inc.*, 535 F. Supp. 172, 219 U.S.P.Q. 58 (S.D.N.Y. 1982), which applied §406(a) to a case arising under the 1909 Act, and *Fantastic Fakes, Inc. v. Pickwick Int'l, Inc.*, 661 F.2d 479, 212 U.S.P.Q.727 (5th Cir. 1981).

Where the defense is established under §406(a)(2), the person named in the notice "is liable to account to the copyright owner for all receipts from transfers or licenses purportedly made under the copyright by the person named in the notice." Cf. *Wolfe v. United Artists Corp.*, 583 F. Supp. 52, 223 U.S.P.Q. 274 (E.D. Pa. 1983), which misconstrued §406(a) as referring to transfers or licenses of the copyright.

[136]17 U.S.C. §406(c) (1978).

[137]*Id.* at §406(b).

[138]*Ibid.*

[139]*Id.* at §406(c).

ords publicly distributed by authority of the copyright owner does not invalidate the copyright in a work if—

"(1) the notice has been omitted from no more than a relatively small number of copies or phonorecords distributed to the public; or

"(2) registration for the work has been made before or is made within five years after the publication without notice, and a reasonable effort is made to add notice to all copies or phonorecords that are distributed to the public in the United States after the omission has been discovered; or

"(3) the notice has been omitted in violation of an express requirement in writing that, as a condition of the copyright owner's authorization of the public distribution of copies or phonorecords, they bear the prescribed notice."[140]

The purpose of these provisions is forcefully set forth in the legislative reports:

---

[140] *Id.* at §405(a). Note that this provision includes the failure to state, as §403 directs, which portions of a work consist preponderantly of one or more works of the U.S. government.

It should not be overlooked that §401(a) requires a proper notice to be affixed where the work is "published in the United States *or elsewhere*," including countries which do not have notice requirements. Cf. *Midway Mfg. Co. v. Artic Int'l, Inc.*, 704 F.2d 1009, 1013, 218 U.S.P.Q. 791, 794 (7th Cir.), *cert. denied*, 464 U.S. 823, 220 U.S.P.Q. 480 (1983) (omission of notice from authorized copies in Japan excused under §405(a)(2) since all copies distributed in the United States contained notices); *Nintendo of America, Inc. v. Elcon Indus., Inc.*, 564 F. Supp. 937 (E.D. Mich. 1982) (omission of notice from authorized copies in Japan did not invalidate copyright); *Wales Industrial, Inc. v. Hasbro Bradley, Inc.*, 612 F. Supp. 507, 509 (S.D.N.Y. 1985); 612 F. Supp. 510, 519-520, 226 U.S.P.Q. 584, 590-591 (S.D.N.Y. 1985).

These decisions have correctly relied on §405(a)(2), which requires registration within five years after publication without notice and a reasonable effort to add notice to all copies distributed to the public *in the United States* after omission of the notice is discovered. However, to the extent that these decisions imply that notice need not be affixed to all copies subsequently manufactured and distributed overseas, they are erroneous. Whatever one may hope for by way of abolition of the archaic notice requirements, nevertheless at present there is a clear obligation to affix a notice on all copies "published in the United States *or elsewhere* by the authority of the copyright * * * ." §401(a). Section 405(a)(2) provides curative steps to remedy past sins; it does not release copyright owners from future obligations.

In *Hasbro Bradley, Inc., v. Sparkle Toys, Inc.*, 780 F.2d 189, 194 n. 7, 228 U.S.P.Q. 423, 426 n. 7 (2d Cir. 1985), the Second Circuit held that the omission of a notice by a foreign author in his country prior to assignment leaves the U.S. assignee with only an incipient copyright, subject to the curative provisions of §405(a)(2). In so doing, the court reviewed the above noted decisions, writing:

"To such extent as language in the three cases cited by Hasbro, *Wales Indus., Inc. v. Hasbro Bradley, Inc.*, 612 F. Supp. 510 (S.D.N.Y. 1985), *Nintendo of America, Inc. v. Elcon Indus., Inc.*, 564 F. Supp. 937 (E.D. Mich. 1982), and *Midway Mfg. Co. v. Artic Int'l, Inc.*, 547 F. Supp 999 (N.D. Ill. 1982), *aff'd*, 704 F.2d 1009 (7th Cir.), *cert. denied*, 464 U.S. 823, 220 U.S.P.Q. 480 (1983), may imply otherwise, we must respectfully disagree, although the results in the latter two cases may well be correct. The opinion of the Court of Appeals in *Midway*, as distinguished from that of the district court, 547 F. Supp. at 1008, can be read as resting on the basis that the plaintiff had affected a cure rather than on the theory that none was necessary. See 704 F.2d at 1013. *Nintendo* is inapposite on both its facts and its legal analysis, since there the publication without notice (by a licensee of the assignor), which took place in both Japan and the United States, occurred *after* assignment of the American copyright to the plaintiff, see 564 F. Supp. at 940, and was in violation of the licensing agreement, *id.* at 944."

In *Koontz v. Jaffarian*, 226 U.S.P.Q. 418 (E.D. Va. 1985), *aff'd*, 787 F.2d 906, 229 U.S.P.Q. 381 (4th Cir. 1986), the court adopted the "unit of publication" doctrine, under which "affixation of the copyright notice to one element of a publication containing various elements gives copyright protection to all elements of the publication." *Id.* at 420. In *Koontz* the omission of notice from a data base contained in a computer tape was excused since a manual used in conjunction with the data base did contain a notice and both were registered as a unit of publication. See also *Freedman v. Grolier Enters., Inc.*, 179 U.S.P.Q. 476 (S.D.N.Y. 1973) (notice on ace of spades in deck of cards sold as single commercial unit held sufficient) (1909 Act); 37 C.F.R. §202.19(b)(2); COMPENDIUM II OF COPYRIGHT OFFICE PRACTICES §910.07.

"The provisions of section 405(a) make clear that the notice require-ments of section 401, 402, and 403 are not absolute and that, unlike the law now in effect, the outright omission of a copyright notice does not automatically forfeit protection and throw the work into the public do-main. This not only represents a major change in the theoretical frame-work of American copyright law, but it also seems certain to have imme-diate practical consequences in a great many individual cases. Under the proposed law, a work published without any copyright notice will still be subject to statutory protection for at least 5 years, whether the omission was partial, or total, intentional or deliberate."[141]

In construing Section 405(a) the courts have had difficulty rec-onciling the statutory language with the above-quoted report lan-guage in at least two areas: (1) whether the word "discovered" in Sub-section (a)(2) includes deliberate omissions of notice; and (2) whether a copyright owner has a full five years to take the curative steps out-lined in Section 405(a) or whether a court may find the work to be in the public domain before the five-year period has expired on the basis of a conclusion, for example, that as of year four the copyright owner has failed to make a reasonable effort to add notice to all copies dis-tributed in the United States after "discovery" of the omission. Ad-ditionally, questions have arisen over the meaning of "no more than a relatively small number of copies" and a "reasonable effort" to add notice.

## Omission of Notices From a Relatively Small Number of Copies: §405(a)(1)

The legislative reports unfortunately do not provide any guid-ance in determining what a "relatively small number of copies" is, stating merely that the concept is "intended to be less restrictive than the phrase 'a particular copy or copies' now in section 21 of the [1909] law."[142] Case law has begun to gradually fill in the outlines of the concept, however. In *Flora Kung v. Items of California,*[143] omis-sion of notice from 9 percent of the copies was held to affect a rela-

---

[141]H.R. REP. No. 94-1476, 94th Cong., 2d Sess. 146–147 (1976); S. REP. No. 94–473, 94th Cong., 1st Sess. 129 (1975). See extended discussion of this lalguage in *Canfield v. Ponchatoula Times,* 759 F.2d 493, 497–500, 226 U.S.P.Q. 112, 115–116 (5th Cir. 1985).

[142]H.R. REP. No. 94-1476 at 147; S. REP. No. 94-473 at 130. A statement in the Register of Copyrights' *1965 Supplementary Report* that the phrase is "intended to establish that the num-ber must be small in an absolute sense and not merely in relation to the size of the entire edi-tion," COPYRIGHT LAW REVISION PART 6: SUPPLEMENTARY REPORT OF THE REGISTER OF COPY-RIGHTS ON THE GENERAL REVISION OF THE U.S. COPYRIGHT LAW, 89th Cong., 1st Sess. 106 (1965), has been criticized by Professor Nimmer. 2 NIMMER ON COPYRIGHT §7.13[A][1]. It should be noted that while §405(a) uses the phrase "omission of notice," the curative provisions of that section are equally applicable to situations where a notice is affixed but is defective. *Shapiro & Son Bedspread Corp. v. Royal Mills Associates,* 764 F.2d 69, 72, 226 U.S.P.Q. 340, 342 (2d Cir. 1985).

[143]Civ. No. 84-7851 (S.D.N.Y. filed Nov. 16, 1984). See also *Original Appalachian Artworks, Inc. v. Toy Loft, Inc.,* 684 F.2d 821, 215 U.S.P.Q. 745 (11th Cir. 1982) (omission from 1% of copies); *Berger v. Computer Information Pub., Inc.,* COPR. L. REP. ¶25,681 (S.D.N.Y. 1984) (omission from only copy of work); *Williams v. Arndt,* 227 U.S.P.Q. 615, 620 (D. Mass. 1985) (omission of 11 copies from indeterminate number of copies held to be a "relatively small num-ber of copies").

tively small number, while in *King v. Burnett*,[144] omission from 300 to 500 out of 1,335 copies was found to affect more than a relatively small number.

*Registration of Work Within Five Years of Publication Without Notice but With Reasonable Efforts to Add Notice After Omission Discovered: §405(a)(2)*

Section 405(a)(2) is an innovative provision that is expected to have broad application. It preserves copyright if registration is made no later than five years after publication without notice *and* "a reasonable effort is made to add notice to all copies * * * that are distributed to the public in the United States after the omission is discovered." While the above-quoted report language could be construed as indicating that no copyright may be forfeited until the full five years from publication without notice has elapsed (since the copyright owner may seek registration and make reasonable efforts to add notice at any time within that period), the courts have found copyrights to have been forfeited before the expiration of the five-year period.[145]

Whether Section 405(a)(2)[146] has any application to deliberate omissions of notice is a more difficult question, since the statutory language refers to a reasonable effort to add notice after the omission has been "discovered." This language may suggest that for the omission to have been "discovered," it must have been inadvertent. Yet the legislative reports state that the omission may be "intentional or unintentional," "unintentional or deliberate," and the history of the section reveals that a provision in an earlier draft bill containing an explicit reference to deliberate omissions[147] was deleted without any intent to limit the provision to inadvertent omissions.[148]

The first case to review this section, *O'Neill Developments, Inc. v. Galen Kilburn, Inc.*, found it to be "not a model of clarity, and espe-

---

[144]COPR. L. REP. ¶25,489 (D.D.C. 1982). See also *M. Kramer Mfg. Co. v. Andrews*, 783 F.2d 421, 443, 228 U.S.P.Q. 705, 720 (4th Cir. 1985) (omission from "several thousand" copies outside scope of §405(a)(1)). In *Florists' Transworld Delivery Ass'n v. Reliable Glassware & Pottery Co.*, 213 U.S.P.Q. 808 (N.D. Ill. 1981), omission from one million copies was understandably held to be more than a "relatively small number." Cf. *P. Kaufman, Inc. v. Rex Curtain Corp.*, 203 U.S.P.Q. 859 (S.D.N.Y. 1978) (2,700 copies distributed to one customer held to be relatively small number where notices subsequently affixed to copies); *Evans & Associates, Inc. v. Continental Homes, Inc.*, 785 F.2d 897, 909–910, 229 U.S.P.Q. 321, 329–330 (11th Cir. 1986).

[145]*Cooling Systems & Flexibles, Inc. v. Stuart Radiator, Inc.*, 777 F.2d 485, 487, 228 U.S.P.Q. 275, 277 (9th Cir. 1985); *Videotronics, Inc. v. Bend Electronics*, 568 F. Supp. 478, 223 U.S.P.Q. 936 (D. Nev. 1984) (two years); *Gemveto Jewelry Co. v. Jeff Cooper, Inc.*, 568 F. Supp. 319, 219 U.S.P.Q. 806 (S.D.N.Y. 1983) (same year); *King v. Burnett*, COPR. L. REP. ¶25,489 (D.D.C. 1982) (presumably same year).

[146]It is clear that under §405(a)(1) notice may be deliberately omitted from a relatively small number of copies. It has also been held that where defendant introduces a lawful copy of plaintiff's work that does not contain a copyright notice and alleges that a substantial number of other copies similarly did not bear a notice, plaintiff must introduce rebuttal evidence. *Cooling Systems & Flexibles, Inc. v. Stuart Radiator, Inc.*, supra note 145, 777 F.2d at 499, 228 U.S.P.Q. at 279.

[147]See PRELIMINARY DRAFT FOR REVISED U.S. COPYRIGHT LAW §27(a), *reproduced in* COPYRIGHT LAW REVISION PART 3 at 23–24 (1964).

[148]COPYRIGHT LAW REVISION PART 6: SUPPLEMENTARY REPORT OF THE REGISTER OF COPYRIGHTS ON THE GENERAL REVISION OF THE U.S. COPYRIGHT LAW, 86th Cong., 1st Sess. 105 (Comm. Print 1965). See also Patton and Hogan, *The Copyright Notice Requirement—Deliberate Omission of Notice*, 5 COMM/ENT L.J. 225 (1983).

cially in light of its legislative history * * * susceptible of two different interpretations * * * ."[149] The court nevertheless held that it applied to deliberate omissions. In *Innovative Concepts in Entertainment, Inc. v. Entertainment Enterprises, Ltd.*,[150] a deliberate omission based on a mistake of law[151] was excused where the other provisions of Section 405(a)(2) were complied with.

The most authoritative opinion on the question (and one which overruled lower court decisions to the contrary) is that of Judge Friendly in *Hasbro Bradley, Inc. v. Sparkle Toys, Inc.* Finding the language of Section 405(a)(2) "anything but 'plain,' " resort to the above-noted legislative history of the Act was made. Based on that history, and its revelation that the drafters of Section 405(a)(2) sought to avoid " 'the impossible problems of proof' relating to subjective intent," the Second Circuit panel held that omission of notice, even if deliberate, is subject to cure under Section 405(a)(2). In an intriguing passage, the court also wrote:

> "[N]o violence is done to the statutory language by saying that the omission, though deliberate on the part of the assignor or licensor, was 'discovered' by the person later attempting to cure it. Similarly, a deliberate omission at a lower level of a corporate hierarchy might well be 'discovered,' in realistic terms, by someone at a higher level."[152]

A number of decisions have reviewed the "reasonable effort to add notice" provision of Section 405(a)(2). Preliminarily, it should be noted that no effort need be made to add notices to copies already distributed to the public in the United States,[153] or to copies that are

---

[149]524 F. Supp. 710, 216 U.S.P.Q. 1123 (N.D. Ga. 1981). In *Williams v. Arndt*, 227 U.S.P.Q. 615 (D. Mass. 1985), the court suggested that where the copyright owner "did not become aware of, *or did not recall*" the distribution of copies without notice, §405(a)(2) applied.

[150]COPR. L. REP. ¶25,619 (E.D.N.Y. 1983). See also *Rodak v. Esprit Racing Team*, 227 U.S.P.Q. 239 (S.D. Ohio 1985), where the copyright owner omitted the notice under a mistake of law. Holding that there was evidence in the record that plaintiff had satisfied the requirements of §405(a)(2), the court denied defendant's motion for summary judgment.

In *Carol Barnhart, Inc. v. Economy Cover Corp.*, 773 F.2d 411, 414 n. 1, 228 U.S.P.Q. 385, 387 n. 1 (2d Cir. 1985), plaintiff failed to affix a copyright notice until 18 months after the initial distribution of its works. In finding this omission not fatal, the court noted plaintiff had registered its works within five years after publication without notice, had corresponded with customers advising them the notice had been inadvertently omitted, and had enclosed adhesive stickers bearing a proper copyright notice which it asked customers to affix to their inventory. The court further noted that "[a]t oral argument counsel for [plaintiff] maintained that Barnhart's President had made no affirmative decision not to copyright her [works] from the very beginning; rather she later discovered this omission and took steps to remedy it by corresponding with previous purchasers of the [works]." Since copyright subsists automatically upon creation of a copyrightable work (17 U.S.C. §102(a) (1978)) and the notice requirements of §401 are triggered automatically by publication of such a work, plaintiff's lack of an "affirmative decision not to copyright" her works would appear to be irrelevant. It seems likely that plaintiff was ignorant of the availability of copyright protection and that the "discovery" in *Barnhart*, as in *Innovative Concepts*, was the (potential) availability of copyright protection and not the omission of a copyright notice.

[151]The copyright owner and apparently its counsel were unaware that copyright protection was available.

[152]780 F.2d 189, 196, 228 U.S.P.Q. 423, 427 (2d Cir. 1985). This decision expressly rejected the lower court decision to the contrary in *Beacon Looms, Inc. v. S. Lichtenberg & Co.*, 552 F. Supp. 1305, 220 U.S.P.Q. 960 (S.D.N.Y 1983). See also *Shapiro & Son Bedspread Corp. v. Royal Mills Associates*, 568 F. Supp. 972, 977–978, 223 U.S.P.Q. 264, 268 (S.D.N.Y. 1983), *rev'd on other grounds*, 764 F.2d 69, 73 n. 5, 226 U.S.P.Q. 340, 343 n. 5 (2d Cir. 1985). Contra *Rachel v. Banana Republic, Inc.*, 228 U.S.P.Q. 416, 418 (N.D. Cal. 1985). Cf. *Evans & Associates, Inc. v. Continental Homes, Inc.*, 785 F.2d 897, 911 n. 22, 229 U.S.P.Q. 321, 330–331 n. 22 (11th Cir. 1986).

[153]H.R. REP. NO. 94-1476, 94th Cong., 2d Sess. 147 (1976); S. REP. NO. 94-473, 94th Cong.,

about to be distributed to the public overseas.[154] The duty arises only with respect to copies awaiting distribution to the public in the United States. As with Section 405(a)(1), "reasonable effort" has yet to be well defined. In *Videotronics, Inc. v. Bend Electronics, Inc.*, the court held that "[i]mplicit in the concept * * * is the expectation that an expenditure of time and money over and above that required in the normal course of business will be made."[155] Similarly, in *Beacon Looms, Inc. v. S. Lichtenberg & Co.*[156] the court found that the mailing of 50,000 labels to distributors with an offer to send additional labels "if needed" was not a reasonable effort since 900,000 copies were without notice.

By contrast, in *P. Kaufman, Inc. v. Rex Curtain Corp.*[157] prompt action to put a sticker containing the notice on a transparent wrapper was found to be a reasonable effort, and in *Innovative Concepts in Entertainment, Inc. v. Entertainment Enterprises, Ltd.*,[158] the court held that the mailing of stickers to distributors in an effort to affix them to copies already distributed was also sufficient.

The most extensive discussion on the question is found in the Second Circuit's decision in *Shapiro & Son Bedspread Corp. v. Royal Mills Associates*. In reversing the trial court's grant of summary judgment to defendant on the ground that plaintiff had made no effort to affix notices to copies in the hands of its distributors, Judge Pierce wrote:

> "Other district court cases that have considered whether efforts to add curative notice are 'reasonable' have also involved efforts to add notice to units no longer in their own possession. * * * We do not, however, believe that the mere consideration of this factor elevates it to the status of a statutory requirement under section 405. Although such a factor is clearly relevant, the fundamental inquiry remains whether the efforts undertaken in a given case, viewed as a whole, were 'reasonable.' "[159]

The court further held that where some effort is made, "the question whether it was 'reasonable' is one of fact." As the record was deemed inadequate to determine the reasonableness of the copyright owner's efforts, a remand was ordered for further proceedings. The

---

1st Sess. 130 (1975) ("copyright owner [is] to make a 'reasonable effort,' after discovering the error, to add the notice to copies * * * distributed thereafter").

[154] *Ibid.*

[155] 586 F. Supp. 478, 483, 223 U.S.P.Q. 936, 939 (D. Nev. 1984). See also *Canfield v. Ponchatoula Times*, 759 F.2d 493, 499, 226 U.S.P.Q. 112, 116–117 (5th Cir. 1985) ("What is considered a 'reasonable effort' under section 405(a)(2) will vary from case to case. * * * We merely point out that the record submitted on cross-motions for summary judgment is devoid of proof that *any* attempt whatsoever was made to add notice. [Plaintiff's] failure to allege or prove it made any attempt to add notice prevents it from qualifying under (a)(2)."); *Gemveto Jewelry Co. v. Jeff Cooper, Inc.*, 568 F. Supp. 319, 219 U.S.P.Q. 806 (S.D.N.Y. 1983); *King v. Burnett*, Copr. L. Rep. ¶25,489 (D.D.C. 1982). Cf. *M. Kramer Mfg. Co. v. Andrews*, 783 F.2d 421, 444, 228 U.S.P.Q. 705, 720–721 (4th Cir. 1986).

[156] 552 F. Supp. 1305, 220 U.S.P.Q. 960 (S.D.N.Y. 1982).

[157] 203 U.S.P.Q. 859 (S.D.N.Y. 1978).

[158] 546 F. Supp. 457, 221 U.S.P.Q. 376 (E.D.N.Y. 1983). Cf. *Florists' Transworld Delivery v. Reliable Glassware & Pottery Co.*, 213 U.S.P.Q. 208 (N.D. Ill. 1981) (court refusal to decide on motion for summary judgment whether mailing stickers containing notice to dealers for affixation on copies was reasonable effort).

[159] 764 F.2d 69, 75, 226 U.S.P.Q. 340, 343–344 (2d Cir. 1985). See also *M. Kramer Mfg. Co. v. Andrews*, 783 F.2d 421, 443–444, 228 U.S.P.Q. 705, 720–721 (4th Cir. 1986).

*Shapiro* decision nevertheless seems to have changed the atmosphere in the Second Circuit from that of cases like *Beacon Looms*.

## Notice Omitted in Violation of Agreement: §405(a)(3)

Section 401(a) requires a notice only where the work is published "by authority of the copyright owner." There is no necessity that the permission be in writing, and except as may be prohibited under state statute of fraud laws, an oral, nonexclusive license conditioned upon the affixing of notice is enforceable.

Section 405, on the other hand, presents curative steps that may be taken with respect to omission of notice from copies distributed by the authority of the copyright owner. It may be asked then why Section 405(a)(3), which concerns omissions of notice "in violation of an express requirement *in writing* that, as a condition of the copyright owner's authorization of the public distribution of copies * * * they bear the prescribed notice," is necessary; and, whether by including a requirement that the authorization be in writing, Section 405(a)(3) acts as a limitation on Section 401(a). The legislative history indicates that no such limitation was intended.[160]

## Effect of Omission on Innocent Infringers

The remedies against innocent infringers, "misled" by an absence of notice and without "actual notice" of registration, are sharply limited by Section 405(b), which provides:

> "Effect of Omission on Innocent Infringers.—Any person who innocently infringes a copyright, in reliance upon an authorized copy or phonorecord from which the copyright notice has been omitted, incurs no liability for actual or statutory damages under section 504 for any infringing acts committed before receiving actual notice that registration for the work has been made under section 408, if such person proves

---

[160]H.R. REP. No. 94-1476, 94th Cong., 2d Sess. 144, 148 (1976); S. REP. No. 94-473, 94th Cong., 1st Sess. 127, 130–131 (1975):
"The consequences of omissions or mistakes with respect to the notice are far less serious under the bill than under the present law, and section 405(a) makes doubly clear that a copyright owner may guard himself against errors or omissions by others if he makes use of the prescribed notice an express condition of his publishing licenses.
   * * *
"The basic notice requirements set forth in sections 401(a) and 402(a) are limited to cases where a work is published 'by authority of the copyright owner' and, in prescribing the effect of omission of notice, section 405(a) refers only to omission 'from copies or phonorecords publicly distributed by authority of the copyright owner.' The intention behind this language is that, where the copyright owner authorized publication of the work, the notice requirements would not be met if copies or phonorecords are publicly distributed without a notice, even if he expected a notice to be used. However, if the copyright owner authorized publication only on the express condition that all copies or phonorecords bear a prescribed notice, the provisions of section 401 or 402 and of section 405 would not apply since the publication itself would not be authorized. This principle is stated directly in section 405(a)(3)."
Although an implied condition of publication with notice may thus not be sufficient to render publication without notice unauthorized, cf. *Fantastic Fakes, Inc. v. Pickwick Int'l, Inc.*, 661 F.2d 479, 484 n. 3, 212 U.S.P.Q. 727, 731 n. 3 (5th Cir. 1981), the report language does not limit "express conditions" to those in writing.

that he or she was misled by the omission of notice. In a suit for infringement in such a case the court may allow or disallow recovery of any of the infringer's profits attributable to the infringement, and may enjoin the continuation of the infringing undertaking or may require, as a condition or [sic] permitting the continuation of the infringing undertaking, that the infringer pay the copyright owner a reasonable license fee in an amount and on terms fixed by the court."

Query whether under a system of "automatic copyright" one can be "misled" by the absence of a notice into believing a work is in the public domain. Indeed, the five-year registration requirement itself seems to make it unreasonable for a user to be "in reliance" on an authorized copy without a notice as contemplated by Section 405(b), unless indeed this provision puts a premium on *not* checking Copyright Office records. If a registration has been made, it might, on the other hand, be argued that one who does not search cannot be "innocent" or "misled."[161] In any event, the innocent infringer who satisfies the requirements of this subsection has four specified advantages: (1) complete insulation from statutory damages and (2) actual damages; (3) discretionary insulation from paying over profits; and (4) a discretionary judicial license to continue use upon payment of a reasonable license fee. The last advantage is arguably shared with any infringer if the court finds that equitable considerations so dictate. And although this section seems to have overlooked attorneys' fees, it is most unlikely that this discretionary award would be made against an innocent infringer meeting the requirements of Section 405(b).

## Removal of Notice Without Authority of the Copyright Owner: §405(c)

Where a notice has been properly affixed, its unauthorized removal, destruction, or obliteration will not affect protection[162] and, if done with fraudulent intent, will subject the unauthorized party so doing to a criminal penalty.[163]

---

[161]In *Quinto v. Legal Times of Washington, Inc.*, 506 F. Supp. 554, 562, 213 U.S.P.Q. 270, 275 (D.D.C. 1981), the court held in construing the relationship between §§404(b) and 406(a) that "even an innocent infringer who was misled by the copyright notice is not protected if a search of the Copyright Office records would have revealed that the owner was someone other than the person named in the notice"—reasoning that could be applied equally to the discovery of registration.

In *Canfield v. Ponchatoula Times*, 759 F.2d 493, 499, 226 U.S.P.Q. 112, 116 (5th Cir. 1985), the court held that "the good faith requirement raised by section 405(b) is triggered only in cases where a section 405(a) exception applies," and that where a copyright owner does not comply with any of the provisions of §405(a), "it may not invoke the good faith requirement of section 405(b) and [defendant] need not prove it acted in good faith, nor that it was misled by the omission." *Ibid.* See also *Williams v. Arndt*, 227 U.S.P.Q. 615, 622 (D. Mass. 1985) (defendant who had actual knowledge of plaintiff's claim of copyright held ineligible for §405(b) defense).

[162]17 U.S.C. §405(c) (1978).

[163]*Id.* at §506(d). In *Evans & Associates, Inc. v. Continental Homes, Inc.*, 785 F.2d 897, 912-913, 229 U.S.P.Q. 321, 332 (11th Cir. 1986), it was held that §506(c) does not give rise to a private cause of action.

# 6

# Registration and Deposit

Sections 407 through 412 of the 1976 Act provide a modernized administrative scheme with the dual purpose of enriching the resources of the Library of Congress and securing a comprehensive record of copyright claims. The former purpose is achieved in Section 407, which prescribes a mandatory system of deposit for published works and realistic sanctions for noncompliance (but not including forfeiture of copyright). The latter purpose is embodied in Section 408, which has been described as a "permissive" registration provision.

The Library deposit under Section 407 may do double duty as the deposit required for registration under Section 408.[1] Moreover, the incentives for registration are quite strong. Accordingly, the dichotomy between these two deposit provisions may not be quite as sharp as initially thought. When one considers the rarity of any actual forfeitures under Section 14 of the 1909 law, it would appear that the new law's "permissive" approach is not a significant innovation. The old system, which integrated deposit and registration, may indeed have been less "mandatory" in effect than the new registration system.

## Deposit for Library of Congress

The Section 407 deposit, which "shall" be made by "the owner of copyright or of the exclusive right of publication" within three months after publication with notice in the United States, is to consist of "two complete copies of the best edition" or, if the work is a

---

[1] 17 U.S.C. §408(b) (1978). See generally COMPENDIUM II OF COPYRIGHT OFFICE PRACTICES §600. In regulations issued on February 24, 1986, 51 Fed. Reg. 6402, the Copyright Office announced its intention to apply more strictly its requirement that the deposit be accompanied by the prescribed application and fee. See 37 C.F.R. §§202.19(f), 202.20(e).

sound recording, "two complete phonorecords of the best edition, together with all accompanying printed or visually perceptible material published with such phonorecords." The constitutionality of this provision was challenged in *Ladd v. Law & Technology Press*, in which the copyright owner claimed that the deposit requirements were a discriminatory tax upon those exercising First Amendment rights in written form, a taking of property without just compensation, and a violation of the equal protection clause (since the Copyright Office exempts selected works from the deposit requirements). These arguments were rejected without a written opinion by the district court. On appeal to the Ninth Circuit that court held that the deposit requirement was a "necessary and proper" exercise of Congress' authority under Article I, §8, clause 8; that the conditioning of the exercise of rights under a copyright upon deposit of the work "furthers the purpose of promoting arts and sciences by adding to the collection of our national library"; and that "[t]he first amendment does not protect the right to copyright, and therefore a condition on copyright protection does not implicate first amendment rights."[2]

The term "best edition" is defined in Section 101 as "the edition, published in the United States at any time before the date of deposit, that the Library of Congress determines to be most suitable for its purposes." Criteria for selection of the "best edition" from among two or more published editions of the same version of the work are set forth in a "Best Edition" statement published by the Copyright Office. See Appendix C, *infra*. Other criteria are set forth in regulations implementing the statute.[3]

The term "complete copy" is not defined in the statute but is said to include "all elements comprising the unit of publication of the best edition of the work, including elements that, if considered separately, would not be copyrightable subject matter or would otherwise be exempt from mandatory deposit requirements * * * ."[4] This definition thus includes material accompanying the copyrighted work if combined in a "unit of publication."[5]

The material for use or disposition of the Library of Congress under Section 407(b) is to be deposited in the Copyright Office. The Register of Copyrights is given authority to issue regulations exempting categories of material from the deposit requirements of this section, reducing the required number of copies or phonorecords to one or, in the case of certain pictorial, graphic, or sculptural works, providing

---

[2]762 F.2d 809, 226 U.S.P.Q. 774 (9th Cir. 1985). The court did note, though, that conditioning copyright on a work's not criticizing the government might be invalid. *Id.* at 815 n. 5, 226 U.S.P.Q at 779 n. 5.

[3]37 C.F.R. 202.19(b). See also Compendium II of Copyright Office Practices §805.03 and *id.* §486.04 (best edition for motion pictures).

[4]37 C.F.R. §202.19(b)(2).

[5]But see qualification on this in 37 C.F.R. §202.20(b)(ii) (registration). See also 33 Copyright Notices No. 2 at 3 (February 1985), which describes the Copyright Office position on this question. For an interesting application of the unit of publication concept to the notice requirements, see *Koontz v. Jaffarian*, 787 F.2d 906, 229 U.S.P.Q. 381 (4th Cir. 1986) (notice on manual held sufficient to protect copyright in data stored in accompanying computer tape).

for exemptions or alternative forms of deposit.[6] Twelve categories of works, including machine-readable computer programs and data bases, three-dimensional sculptural works, textiles, and other fabrics and packaging material, advertisements and literary, dramatic, or musical works embodied only in phonorecords, are among those exempt from the Section 407 deposit requirements.[7] In the case of any published work not exempt under the regulations, the Register may grant a petition for special relief either exempting the work or permitting the deposit of incomplete copies or identifying material.[8]

Pursuant to Section 407(e), the Register has issued regulations governing the Library of Congress' acquisition of technically unpublished radio and television programs (including through off-air taping).[9] The Librarian may also tape news broadcasts, under certain circumstances, as part of his or her duties to preserve programs under the American Television and Archives Act.[10]

## Copyright Registration

### Procedure

As noted above, if the Library deposit under Section 407 is accompanied by the prescribed application for registration and fee, it may be used to satisfy the separate deposit requirements of registration. However, because of the statutory language, the Copyright Office will generally no longer make registration if the application and fee do not "accompany" the deposit.[11]

Regulations implementing Section 408 permit the deposit of one copy instead of two in a great number of cases,[12] and actually require the deposit of identifying material in lieu of copies in others.[13] As

---

[6]See 37 C.F.R. §202.19(d)(2)(iv) (pictorial or graphic works published in less than 5 copies or offered for sale in a limited edition of no more than 300 numbered copies). The statutory authority to exempt works from the §407 requirements, or to permit the deposit of identifying material, is found in §407(c). Cf. §408(c).

[7]37 C.F.R. §202.19(c).

[8]*Id.* at §§202.19(e), 202.21. Under §202.19(d)(2)(ii), the Librarian of Congress has entered into a so-called "Motion Picture Agreement" permitting the return of deposits of published motion pictures subject to their recall at the Library's request. See also COMPENDIUM II OF COPYRIGHT OFFICE PRACTICES §807.

[9]37 C.F.R. §202.22.

[10]TRANS. & SUPPP. §113, 90 Stat. 2601.

[11]37 C.F.R. §202.20(e). In the past the Copyright Office had interpreted these provisions liberally where the deposit was accompanied by a "clear written request" that the deposit copy be held in connection with a subsequently submitted application or fee. Cf. discussion in note 1, *supra.*

[12]See 37 C.F.R. §§202.20(c)(2)(i), (ii), (v), (vi), (viii). Deposit of one copy is required. *Id.* at §§202.20(c)(1)(i), (iv).

[13]See *id.* at §§202.20(c)(2)(vii), (ix), (xi). Identifying material is permitted but not required, *id.* at §§202.20(c)(2)(iv), (x). The statutory authority to permit the deposit of identifying material or to require only one copy for deposit purposes is found in 17 U.S.C. §408(c). In *National Conference of Bar Examiners v. Multistate Legal Studies, Inc.,* 692 F.2d 478, 216 U.S.P.Q. 279 (7th Cir. 1982), *cert. denied,* 464 U.S. 814, 220 U.S.P.Q. 480 (1983), the provisions of 37 C.F.R. §§202.20(b)(4), (c)(2)(vi), which permit the deposit of identifying material of secure tests, were upheld against claims of unconstitutionality and alleged inconsistency with various sections of the Act.

with deposit requirements under Section 407, requests for special relief from deposit requirements of Section 408 may also be made.[14]

Registration under Section 408 differs from the Library deposit provision of Section 407 in the following respects: (1) it applies to unpublished as well as published works; (2) it includes works published abroad; (3) it may be made at any time during the subsistence of copyright; and (4) it can be a condition of preserving copyright if notice is omitted.[15] Section 408 applies to works of domestic and foreign authors equally.[16]

Section 408(c)(1) gives the Register of Copyrights authority to "specify by regulation the administrative classes into which works are to be placed for purposes of deposit and registration * * * ." This classification, however, "has no significance with respect to the subject matter of copyright or the exclusive rights provided by this title." The Register has created by the following four basic classifications: Class TX—Nondramatic Literary Works; Class PA—Works of the Performing Arts; Class VA—Works of the Visual Arts; Class SR—Sound Recordings.

Class TX includes works of fiction, nonfiction, poetry, textbooks, reference works, directories, catalogs, advertising copy, periodicals and serials, compilations of information, computer programs, and works that consist preponderantly of nondramatic literary material. Class PA includes works prepared "for the purpose of being performed directly before an audience or indirectly by means of a device or process," such as musical works (including any accompanying words), dramatic works (including any accompanying music), pantomimes and choreographic works, and motion pictures and other audiovisual works.[17] Class VA includes pictorial, graphic, and sculptural works, such as "[t]wo dimensional and three dimensional works of the fine, graphic, and applied arts, photographs, prints and art reproductions, maps, globes, charts, technical drawings, diagrams, models, and pictorial or graphic labels and advertisements."[18] Class SR includes not only sound recordings but, in certain circumstances, also literary, dramatic, and musical works embodied in phono-

---

[14]37 C.F.R. §§202.20(d), 202.21. The Copyright Office has stated a preference for source code deposits of computer programs, but will register, under its rule of doubt, deposits in object code form. See COPYRIGHT OFFICE GUIDE LETTER (Lit.) R-70 (July 1981). As an alternative to a rule of doubt registration, the Office will automatically accept, pursuant to a request for special relief, the following deposits:
  1. First and last 25 pages of source code with some portions blocked out. (Note: the blocked-out portions should be proportionately less than the material still remaining).
  2. At least the first and last 10 pages of source code alone with no blocked-out portions.
  3. First and last 25 pages of object code plus any 10 or more consecutive pages of source code with no blocked-out portions.
COMPENDIUM II OF COPYRIGHT OFFICE PRACTICES §324.05(a).

Deposits differing from these will be considered on a case-by-case basis. See also 37 C.F.R. §§202.20(c)(vii)–(viii), which specify identifying material for deposits of machine-readable works.
[15]17 U.S.C. §405(a)(2).
[16]Cf. 17 U.S.C. §215 (1909 *repealed* 1978).
[17]37 C.F.R. §202.3(b)(1)(ii).
[18]*Id.* at §202.3(b)(iii).

records.[19] Applications for sounds accompanying a motion picture may not be made on Form SR.[20]

Supplementary registration may be made (1) to correct information in a previous registration if the information was incorrect when given and the error is not one which the Copyright Office should itself have recognized,[21] or (2) to amplify the information in the registration to reflect (a) additional or clarifying information that could have been given but was omitted, or (b) changes in facts, other than those relating to transfer, license, or ownership rights in the work.[22] Supplementary registration is not appropriate

> "(A) as an amplification to reflect the ownership, division, allocation, licensing, or transfer of rights in a work, whether at the time basic registration was made or thereafter; or (B) to correct errors in statements or notices on the copies of phonorecords of a work, or to reflect changes in the content of a work."[23]

The information contained in the supplementary registration augments but does not supersede that contained in the earlier registration. (§408(d).)

Two additional forms have been issued to deal with works that are published on a frequent basis. Form SE is to be used for individual issues of serials, defined as "works issued or intended to be issued in successive parts bearing numerical or chronological designations and intended to be continued indefinitely."[24] Examples include periodicals, newspapers, magazines, bulletins, newsletters, annuals, journals, and proceedings of professional societies. Each serial issue is considered a separate work and must be registered separately. The claim extends not only to the serial as a collective work but to the individual contributions to the serial as well *if and only if* such individual contributions were created as works made for hire or "all

---

[19] *Id.* at §202.3(b)(1)(iv).
[20] *Id.* at §202.3(b)(2) n. 2.
[21] *Id.* at §201.5(b)(2)(i). The Register's authority to issue supplementary registrations is contained in 17 U.S.C. §408(d). A supplementary registration represents one of four exceptions to the general rule that only one registration can be made for the same version of a particular work. The other three exceptions are:
> "(i) Where a work has been registered as unpublished, another registration may be made for the first published edition of the work, even if it does not represent a new version:
> "(ii) Where someone other than the author is identified as copyright claimant in a registration, another registration for the same version may be made by the author in his or her own name as copyright claimant;[5]
> "(iii) Where an applicant for registration alleges that an earlier registration for the same version is unauthorized and legally invalid, a registration may be made by that applicant; * * *
> "[5]An 'author' includes an employer or other person for whom a work is 'made for hire' under 17 U.S.C. 101. This paragraph does not permit an employee or other person working 'for hire' under that section to make a later registration in his or her own name. In the case of authors of a joint work, this paragraph does not permit a later registration by one author in his or her own name as copyright claimant, where an earlier registration identifies only another author as claimant."
37 C.F.R. §§202.3(6)(i)–(iii).
[22] 37 C.F.R. §201.5(b)(2)(ii).
[23] *Id.* at §201.5(b)(2)(iii).
[24] Copyright Office Circular R62 at 3.

rights"[25] have been transferred by the contributor to the claimant in the serial issue as a whole.[26] If the individual contribution was not created as a work made for hire, or all rights have not been transferred, the contribution is not included in the claim being registered in the serial, but may be registered separately by the contributor.

Section 408(c)(2) requires the Register to establish regulations permitting a single registration for "a group of works by the same individual author, all first published as contributions to periodicals, including newspapers, within a 12-month period, on the basis of a single deposit, application and registration fee" if certain conditions are met.[27] Such registration, accomplished on Form GR/CP, differs from the Form SE registration by requiring, *inter alia*, that all works be by the same author, that the author not have created the works as works made for hire, and that each work has borne a separate copyright notice. (Forms for group renewal are also available.)

Registration is accomplished by submitting, in the same envelope, a properly filled out application accompanied by deposit copies or identifying material and the prescribed fee (currently $10).[28] By an amendment to Section 708(a) in 1982,[29] the fee is assessed for an *application* for registration and not, as under the Act as passed in 1976, for the registration. Thus, where a claimant fails to respond to Copyright Office inquiries within 120 days from the date a letter is sent from the Copyright Office, the file is closed, and the claimant is required to resubmit a new application, deposit, and fee.[30] The effective date of registration will then be based on the later submission. Similarly, where a check received in payment of the registration is returned for insufficient funds, or is otherwise uncollectible, the Copyright Office will cancel the registration for which the dishonored check was submitted, with the claimant being required to start afresh.[31]

In order to facilitate compliance with the general prerequisite of registration to institute an action for infringement (§411(a)), the Register has established a procedure for expedited processing, known as

---

[25]The term "all rights" is not defined or otherwise explained. Custom in the publishing industry is to allow the author of an individual contribution to make copies for personal or classroom use. Such "reservations of rights" should not be considered a failure to convey "all rights." See also 37 C.F.R. §202.3(ii).

[26]COPYRIGHT OFFICE CIRCULAR R62 at 5.

[27]17 U.S.C. §408(c)(2)(1978). The regulations are found at 37 C.F.R. §202.3(b)(5). Regulations for group registration of related works, to be contained *id.* at §202.3(b)(4), have yet to be issued. But cf. *Financial Information, Inc. v. Moody's Investors Service, Inc.*, 599 F. Supp. 994, 223 U.S.P.Q. 552 (S.D.N.Y. 1983), *rev'd and rem'd*, 751 F.2d 501, 224 U.S.P.Q. 632 (2d Cir. 1984), which, while noting that the regulations had not been issued, regarded daily bond cards as integral parts of a subsequently compiled and registered annual volume. On appeal, the factual basis for this holding was questioned, with the Second Circuit remanding for the taking of further evidence on the utility of the annually bound volume as compared to the daily cards.

[28]The schedule of fees for registration and other services is set forth in 17 U.S.C. §708(a).

[29]Act of Oct. 25, 1982, Pub. L. No. 97-366, 96 Stat. 1759.

[30]COPYRIGHT OFFICE ANNOUNCEMENT ML-245 (November 3, 1980); COPYRIGHT OFFICE CIRCULAR R7c. "Follow-up" letters will not be sent, contrary to prior practice. Published deposit copies are made available for the use or disposition of the Library of Congress. Unpublished deposit copies are returned to the claimant.

[31]*Notice of Policy Decision*, 46 Fed. Reg. 30221 (June 5, 1981).

"special handling." Requests for special handling are evaluated on an individual basis, and may be made in person or by mail to a designated address.[32] The current fee for special handling is $200 for each application (plus the $10 filing fee). Where a single deposit will satisfy the deposit requirements of multiple registrations and such multiple applications are also submitted for special handling, one fee of $200 is sufficient (although the $10 filing fee must be submitted for each application). Where such multiple applications do not require special handling, a fee of $50 per application will be assessed for the additional claims if included in the envelope with the request for special relief.

It should also be noted that, in response to a crisis in storage capacity, the Copyright Office no longer retains published materials deposited in connection with registration. Except for works of the visual arts, which are retained for at least 10 years, published copies are retained for no more than five years from the date of deposit, after which they are offered to the Library of Congress and regional library networks for their collections. In the event no library desires to add the work to its collection, it is destroyed. Copies of unpublished works are kept for the full term of copyright "unless a facsimile reproduction has been made."[33] The depositor may request so-called "full-term retention," defined as "a period of 75 years from the date of publication of the work identified by the particular copyright deposit which is retained."[34] If the request is granted by the Copyright Office, a fee of $135 for each deposit is required, payable within 60 days from the date of the Copyright Office's mailing of notification that the request was granted.[35]

## Register's Authority to Reject Applications for Registration: §410(b)

The 1976 Act expressly provides that the Register may refuse registration upon a determination that a claim is invalid.[36] Review of a refusal to register is available under the Administrative Procedure Act.[37] Contrary to practice under the 1909 Act, a mandamus action

---

[32]All mailed requests should be sent to: Library of Congress, Department D.S., Washington, D.C. 20540, Attn: Acquisitions and Processing Division. The transmittal envelope and letter should indicate that the request is one for special handling. The request must be accompanied by a properly filled out application, deposit copies or identifying material, and prescribed fee. See discussion in text at note 54, *infra*, for the effect of a registration obtained by special handling on the certificate's prima facie status under §410(c).

[33]*Policy Statement on Deposit Retention Schedule*, 48 Fed. Reg. 12862-12863 (March 28, 1983); 37 C.F.R. §202.23. See generally 17 U.S.C. §704. Under 17 U.S.C. §704(a), all copies and identifying material submitted in connection with claims (including those that are refused registration) are the property of the U.S. government.

[34]37 C.F.R. §202.23(a)(3).

[35]*Id.* at §202.23(e).

[36]17 U.S.C. §410(b) (1978).

[37]*Id.* at §710(d); *Nova Stylings, Inc. v. Ladd*, 695 F.2d 1179 (9th Cir. 1978). The APA is codified at 5 U.S.C. §101 *et seq.* (1946 and as amended).

under 28 U.S.C. §1361 to compel registration is not available.[38] The scope of review of the Register's determinations has been held to be "limited to whether the decision was 'arbitrary, capricious, an abuse of discretion, or otherwise not in accordance with law'."[39] Other courts, while noting they would not "simply accept the Register's decision without question,"[40] have nevertheless accorded the Register's determinations considerable deference, particularly in cases involving utilitarian articles.[41] This deference has been said to be based not on the Copyright Office's technical expertise but rather on its "expertise in the interpretation of the law and its application to the facts presented by the copyright application."[42]

## Registration as Prerequisite to Suit: §411(a)

Section 411(a) states a general rule that "no action for infringement of the copyright in any work shall be instituted until registration of the copyright claim has been made." It also provides, however, that where

> "[t]he deposit, application and fee required for registration have been delivered to the Copyright Office in proper form and registration has been refused, the applicant is entitled to institute an action for infringement if notice thereof, with a copy of the complaint, is served on the Register of Copyrights. The Register may, at his or her option, become a party to the action with respect to the registrability of the copyright claim by entering an appearance within sixty days after such service, but the Register's failure to become a party shall not deprive the court of jurisdiction to determine that issue."[43]

---

[38] *Nova Stylings, Inc. v. Ladd, supra* note 37. But compare *Esquire, Inc. v. Ringer,* 591 F.2d 796, 806 n. 28, 199 U.S.P.Q. 1, 8–9 n. 28 (D.C. Cir. 1978), and *id.* at 807–808, 199 U.S.P.Q. at 9–10 (concurring opinion of Judge Leventhal), which suggest in dicta that mandamus may still be available to review refusals made under the 1976 Act. The decision in *Techniques, Inc. v. Rohn,* 592 F. Supp. 1195, 1198, 225 U.S.P.Q. 741, 743 (S.D.N.Y. 1984), incorrectly ignored §411(a) and held that the copyright applicant must seek a writ of mandamus if registration is refused.

[39] *Gemveto Jewelry Co. v. Jeff Cooper, Inc.,* 568 F. Supp. 319, 330, 219 U.S.P.Q. 806, 814 (S.D.N.Y. 1983) (quoting 5 U.S.C. §706); *M. Kramer Mfg. Co. v. Andrews,* Civ. No. 83-1344-3 (D.S.C. filed May 29, 1984), *rev'd,* 783 F.2d 421, 228 U.S.P.Q. 705 (4th Cir. 1986).

[40] *Norris Indus., Inc. v. International Telephone & Telegraph Corp.,* 696 F.2d 918, 922, 217 U.S.P.Q. 226, 230 (9th Cir.), *cert. denied,* 464 U.S. 818, 220 U.S.P.Q. 385 (1983).

[41] *Norris Indus., supra* note 40; *Gemveto Jewelry Co. v. Jeff Cooper, Inc., supra* note 39; *Esquire, Inc. v. Ringer, supra* note 38; *Eltra Corp. v. Ringer,* 579 F.2d 294, 198 U.S.P.Q. 321 (4th Cir. 1978); *Mazer v. Stein,* 347 U.S. 201, 209, 100 U.S.P.Q. 325, 329 (1954) *Esquire* also rejected the trial court's suggestion that prior registration determinations create a form of "interpretative precedent." 591 F.2d at 802, 199 U.S.P.Q. at 2.

[42] *Norris Indus., Inc., supra* note 40, 696 F.2d at 922, 217 U.S.P.Q. at 229.

[43] 17 U.S.C. §411(a) (1978). This represents a deliberate change from the 1909 law, which had required actual registration, rather than mere application for registration. H.R. REP. No. 94-1476, 94th Cong., 2d Sess. 157 (1976); S. REP. No. 94-473, 94th Cong., 1st Sess. 139 (1975). Cf. *Vacheron & Constantin-LeCoultre Watches, Inc. v. Benrus Watch Co.,* 260 F.2d 637, 119 U.S.P.Q. 189 (2d Cir. 1958).

It should also be noted that the states may not impose conditions on corporations' standing to bring infringement actions. *BMI v. Lyndon Lanes, Inc.,* 227 U.S.P.Q. 731 (W.D. Ky. 1985) (failure of corporation to obtain a state certificate of authority under "door-closing" statute irrelevant where federal question jurisdiction exists). Decisions under the 1909 Act held that where the copyright owner of the original work and a derivative work based thereon were the

Section 411(a) has been held inapplicable where the claimant merely submitted the application,[44] and where the Copyright Office sought clarification from the claimant as to the nature and scope of the claim but had not "refused" registration.[45] The latter decision apparently contemplates exhaustion by claimants of administrative remedies—a slippery doctrine in this context owing to the lack of official administrative appellate procedures in the Copyright Office. In view of this, it would seem that receipt by a claimant of a letter from a Copyright Office examiner or other official indicating a refusal to register either immediately or upon the claimant's failure to take requested steps should be considered a refusal to register within the scope of Section 411(a) without the need to appeal that decision further within the Office.

---

same, and where defendant infringed material from the original work by copying it from the derivative work, plaintiff need only plead registration of the derivative work. See, e.g., *Williams Prods., Inc. v. Construction Gaskets, Inc.*, 206 U.S.P.Q. 622, 624 (E.D. Mich. 1977); *Rexnord, Inc. v. Modern Handling Systems, Inc.*, 379 F. Supp. 1190, 1198–1199, 183 U.S.P.Q. 413, 418–419 (D. Del. 1974). These decisions were based on the following language in §3 of the 1909 Act: "The copyright provided by this title shall protect all the copyrightable component parts of the work copyrighted, *and all matter therein in which copyright is already subsisting, but without extending the duration or scope of such copyright."* (Emphasis added).

Section 103(b) of the 1976, however, states:

"The copyright in a * * * derivative work extends only to the material contributed by the author of such work, as distinguished from any preexisting material employed in the work, and does not imply any exclusive right in the preexisting material. *The copyright in such work is independent of, and does not affect or enlarge * * * any copyright protection in the preexisting material."* (Emphasis added).

*Compendium II of Copyright Office Practices*, following §103(b), clearly limits the scope of a derivative work registration to the new material:

"Where part of the work was previously published or was covered by a previous registration, the copyright claim as reflected in the application should generally be limited to the new material covered by the claim being registered."

Compendium II of Copyright Office Practices §108.04. One decision under the 1976 Act, *Rand McNally & Co. v. Fleet Mgt. Systems, Inc.*, 591 F. Supp. 726, 733 n. 6, 221 U.S.P.Q. 827, 833 n. 6 (N.D. Ill. 1983), has continued the rule of the above-noted 1909 Act decisions. This position has, however, been rejected by another court. *M. Kramer Mfg. Co. v. Andrews*, Civ. No. 83-1344-3, slip opn. at 18–19, 23 (D.S.C. filed May 29, 1984). On appeal the Fourth Circuit, however, found it unnecessary to resolve the issue. 783 F.2d 421, 437 n. 17, 228 U.S.P.Q. 705, 716 n. 17 (4th Cir. 1986). See also *Cooling Systems & Flexibles, Inc. v. Stuart Radiator, Inc.*, 777 F.2d 485, 490, 228 U.S.P.Q. 275, 279 (9th Cir. 1985) (rejecting arguement that "the certificate of copyright in the [later] work—being a derivative work—preserved [plaintiff's] right to sue for infringement of both the new and underlying works"). Cf. 2 NIMMER ON COPYRIGHT §7.16[B][2].

[44] *International Trade Management, Inc. v. United States*, 553 F. Supp. 402 (Ct. Cl. 1982); *Strout Realty, Inc. v. Country 22 Real Estate Corp.*, 493 F. Supp. 997, 212 U.S.P.Q. 145 (W.D. Mo. 1980). But cf. *Frankel v. Stein & Day, Inc.*, 470 F. Supp. 209, 212 n. 2, 205 U.S.P.Q. 51, 53 n. 2 (S.D.N.Y. 1979), which permitted registration to be made subsequent to the filing of the suit where defendant did not object. See also *Conan Properties, Inc. v. Mattel, Inc.*, 601 F. Supp. 1179, 1182, 226 U.S.P.Q. 265, 267 (S.D.N.Y. 1984), which granted defendant's motion to dismiss because plaintiff failed to plead registration; *Gee v. CBS, Inc.*, 471 F. Supp. 600, 202 U.S.P.Q. 486 (E.D. Pa. 1979); *Burns v. Rockwood Distributing Co.*, 481 F. Supp. 841, 845, 209 U.S.P.Q. 713, 715 (N.D. Ill. 1979). The decision in *Apple Barrel Prods. v. Beard*, 730 F.2d 384, 386–387, 222 U.S.P.Q. 956, 957 (5th Cir. 1984), which held that the requirements of §411(a) were satisfied where the Copyright Office had merely received plaintiff's application for registration, fee, and deposit, is clearly erroneous and misconstrues §410(d) which is a housekeeping provision necessitated by the unavoidable delay between the Office's receipt of the application and eventual issuance of the certificate of registration. Indeed, the Copyright Office's procedure for special handling would be completely superfluous if the *Apple Barrel* court's interpretation of §411(a) were correct. (The special handling procedure is discussed in the text accompanying note 32, *supra.*)

[45] *Proulx v. Hennepin Technical Centers Dist. No. 287*, COPR. L. REP. ¶25,389 (D. Minn 1981).

**The Section 411(b) Exception**

Another exception to the requirement of registration as a prerequisite to suit is found in Section 411(b):

"In the case of a work consisting of sounds, images, or both, the first fixation of which is made simultaneously with its transmission, the copyright owner may, either before or after such fixation takes place, institute an action for infringement under Sections 502 through 506 and Sections 509 and 510, if, in accordance with requirements that the Register of Copyrights shall prescribe by regulation, the copyright owner—
  "(1) serves notice upon the infringer, not less than ten or more than thirty days before such fixation, identifying the work and the specific time and source of its first transmission, and declaring an intention to secure copyright in the work; and
  "(2) Makes registration for the work within three months after its first transmission."[46]

This extraordinary provision, which permits suits to be entertained and injunctive relief granted *before* the work is created, is designed to deal with "the special situation presented by works that are being transmitted 'live' at the same time they are being fixed in a tangible form for the first time."[47]

**Prima Facie Effect of Registration**

Although registration is permissive, the statute provides a number of inducements to copyright owners to register their works promptly. One such inducement is found in Section 410(c), which reads:

"In any judicial proceedings the certificate of a registration made before or within five years of first publication of the work shall constitute prima facie evidence of the validity of the copyright and of the facts stated in the certificate. The evidentiary weight to be accorded the certificate of a registration made thereafter shall be within the discretion of the court."

This provision is particularly useful where preliminary injunctive relief is sought, since both the originality of the copyright and plain-

---

[46]17 U.S.C. §411(b) (1978). The regulations implementing this section are found at 37 C.F.R. §201.22.

[47]H.R. REP. No. 94-1476, 94th Cong., 2d Sess. 157 (1976); S. REP. No. 94-473, 94th Cong., 1st Sess. 140 (1975). See *National Football League v. Cousin Hugo's*, 600 F. Supp. 84 (E.D. Mo. 1984), which granted a preliminary injunction against the unauthorized reception of an unfixed work. Cf. *Pacific & Southern Co. v. Duncan*, 572 F. Supp. 1186, 220 U.S.P.Q. 859 (N.D. Ga. 1983), *aff'd in part and rem'd on other grounds*, 744 F.2d 1490, 224 U.S.P.Q. 131 (11th Cir. 1984), *cert. denied*, 471 U.S. ____, *on remand*, 618 F. Supp. 469, 228 U.S.P.Q. 141 (N.D. Ga. 1985), which applied §411(b) to the question of statutory damages; *National Football League v. McBee & Bruno's*, 228 U.S.P.Q. 11 (E.D. Mo. 1985); *ESPN, Inc. v. Edinburg Community Hotel, Inc.*, 623 F. Supp. 647 (S.D. Tex. 1985). In *Production Contractors, Inc. v. WGN Continental Broadcasting Co.*, 622 F. Supp. 1500, 1504, 228 U.S.P.Q. 604, 606 (N.D. Ill. 1985), the court held that §411(b) did not apply to infringement of parade floats because they were fixed before the transmission and because "they are tangible objects not falling within the 'sounds' or 'images'" covered by the section.

tiff's title are given prima facie validity.[48] The certificate does not, however, create an irrebutable presumption of originality: "Where other evidence in the record casts doubt on the question, validity will not be assumed."[49] Examples of evidence that may be introduced to rebut the Section 410(c) presumption include evidence that the copyrighted work was copied from a public domain source[50] or from other copyrighted works,[51] evidence that defendant purchased a work identical to plaintiff's work several months before plaintiff's work was created,[52] and evidence that plaintiff's title is unclear.[53] One decision erroneously suggested that where registration is obtained through special handling

---

[48] *Carolina Enters., Inc. v. Coleco Indus.*, 211 U.S.P.Q. 479, 487 (D.N.J. 1981). It has been held that a certificate of registration obtained in compliance with §410(c) is not prima facie evidence that the notice requirements have been satisfied subsequent to registration. *Midway Mfg. Co. v. Dirkschneider*, 543 F. Supp. 466, 481, 214 U.S.P.Q. 417, 426 (D. Neb. 1981). For a decision reaching the same result under the 1909 Act, see *Krafft v. Cohen*, 117 F.2d 579, 48 U.S.P.Q. 401 (3d Cir. 1941).

[49] *Durham Indus., Inc. v. Tomy Corp.*, 630 F.2d 905, 908, 208 U.S.P.Q. 10, 13 (2d Cir. 1980); *Merritt Forbes & Co. v. Newman Investment Securities, Inc.*, 604 F. Supp. 943, 948, 225 U.S.P.Q. 1179, 1181 (S.D.N.Y. 1985); *Kenbrooke Fabrics, Inc. v. Material Things*, 223 U.S.P.Q. 1039 (S.D.N.Y. 1984); *Shapiro & Son Bedspread Corp. v. Royal Mills Associates*, 568 F. Supp. 972, 223 U.S.P.Q. 264 (S.D.N.Y. 1983), *rev'd*, 764 F.2d 69, 226 U.S.P.Q. 340 (2d Cir. 1985); *Childers v. High Society Magazine*, 557 F. Supp. 978, 217 U.S.P.Q. 1221 (S.D.N.Y. 1983). See also H.R. REP. No. 94-1476, 94th Cong., 2d Sess. 157 (1976); S. REP. No. 94-473, 94th Cong., 1st Sess. 139 (1975):

"The principle that a certificate [of registration] represents prima facie evidence of copyright validity has been established in a long line of court decisions, and it is a sound one. It is true that, unlike a patent claim, a claim to copyright is not examined for basic validity before a certificate is issued. On the other hand, endowing a copyright claimant who has obtained a certificate with a rebuttable presumption of the validity of the copyright does not deprive the defendant in an infringement suit of any rights; it merely orders the burdens of proof. The plaintiff should not ordinarily be forced in the first instance to prove all of the multitude of facts that underline the validity of the copyright unless the defendant, by effectively challenging them, shifts the burden of doing so to the plaintiff."

This passage is confusing at best. While it is true that copyright claims do not undergo the patent examination for prior art, novelty, or nonobviousness, it is inaccurate to state that the Copyright Office does not examine claims for "basic validity." See §410(a), which states:

"When, *after examination*, the Register of Copyrights determines that in accordance with the provisions of this title, the material deposited *constitutes copyrightable subject matter*, and that the other legal and formal requirements of this title have been met, the Register shall register the claim and issue to the applicant a certificate of registration." (Emphasis added).

Where plaintiff is an assignee of the copyright owner, it must independently prove title. *BMI v. Moor-Law*, 484 F. Supp. 357, 204 U.S.P.Q. 726 (D. Del. 1980). For a case discussing issuance of a certificate of registration to the defendant, see *Wallace Berrie & Co. v. Custom Styled Toys, Inc.*, 219 U.S.P.Q. 63 (E.D.N.Y. 1982).

Where registration has been obtained under the Copyright Office's "rule of doubt," it is unclear whether the certificate is accorded §410(c) prima facie status. Cf. *Ronald Litoff, Ltd. v. American Express Co.*, 621 F. Supp. 981, 983, 228 U.S.P.Q. 739, 740 (S.D.N.Y. 1985) (Copyright Office wrote plaintiff stating that it had "considerable doubt that there is any copyrightable authorship in [the work but] we have made the registration under the rule of doubt, for whatever the registrations may be worth"; court appeared to nevertheless accord the certificates prima facie status), with *In re Anderson*, 743 F.2d 1578, 1580, 223 U.S.P.Q. 378, 380 (Ct. App. Fed. Cir. 1984) (in patent case court held that statutory presumption of validity "does not embrace the rule of doubt").

[50] *Russ Berrie & Co. v. Jerry Elsner Co.*, 482 F. Supp. 980, 205 U.S.P.Q. 320 (S.D.N.Y. 1980), Cf. *Delman Fabrics, Inc. v. Holland Fabrics, Inc.*, 228 U.S.P.Q. 596 (S.D.N.Y. 1985) (defendant's claim rejected as based on "nothing but speculation").

[51] *Midway Mfg. Co. v. Bandai-America, Inc.*, 546 F. Supp. 125, 216 U.S.P.Q. 812 (D.N.J. 1982).

[52] *Delman Fabrics, Inc. v. Holland Fabrics, Inc.*, COPR. L. REP. ¶25,663 (S.D.N.Y. 1984). The existence of an earlier identical work would not preclude copyright protection for the later work if the later work was independently created.

[53] *SS Enters. v. India Sari Palace*, COPR. L. REP. ¶25,527 (S.D.N.Y. 1983).

"it is reasonable to infer that the Copyright Office deferred to the courts the consideration of the copyrightability question. Consequently, this Court does not consider the certificates of registration as insurmountable evidence of copyrightability. They are *prima facie* evidence that can be rebutted."[54]

The premise of this holding—that registrations obtained through special handling (in this case same day processing) are "an indication that the Copyright Office [did not] act[ ] with great deliberation and careful consideration"—is inaccurate. There appears to be no authority for a court to refuse to give prima facie effect to a certificate obtained in compliance with Section 410(c), regardless of whether the certificate was obtained by special handling. (To the extent that the court also suggested that, had it not been obtained through special handling, the certificate would have presented not just prima facie but "insurmountable" evidence of originality, the decision is erroneous as well.)

When the copyright owner produces a certificate of registration obtained before or within five years of first publication, "the burden of production shifts to the defendant to introduce evidence of invalidity."[55] If credible evidence of invalidity is introduced, the Section 410(c) presumption vanishes. Certificates of registration may also be

---

[54] *Carol Barnhart, Inc. v. Economy Cover Corp.*, 594 F. Supp. 364, 367 (E.D.N.Y. 1984), *aff'd*, 773 F.2d 411, 228 U.S.P.Q. 385 (2d Cir. 1985). The district court's conclusion that the Copyright Office had "deferred" on the issue of copyrightability is inconsistent with its subsequent statement that the certificate of registration nevertheless represented prima facie evidence of the works' originality. On appeal, the *Barnhart* court of appeals did not address the "deferral" issue, but held that

"Judge Wexler properly exercised the discretion conferred on him by 17 U.S.C. §410(c). Once defendant's response to plaintiff's claim put in issue whether the four Barnhart forms were copyrightable, he correctly reasoned that the 'mute testimony' of the forms put him in as good a position as the Copyright Office to decide the issue."

773 F.2d at 414, 228 U.S.P.Q. at 386.

This holding is troubling. The only discretion granted by the literal terms of the statute itself is with regard to certificates of registration obtained more than five years after first publication of the work—which was not the case in *Barnhart*. Assuming the certificate of registration is obtained within the statutory five-year period, the courts have no discretion to disregard the §410(c) grant of prima facie status to the certificate. It is true, though, as the legislative reports indicate (see note 49, *supra*), that where defendant *effectively* challenges plaintiff's certificate the burden of persuasion shifts back to plaintiff. What is disturbing about the *Barnhart* court of appeals opinion is its apparent holding that where defendant "put in issue" the copyrightability of the works, the "mute testimony of the works themselves" placed the trial judge in "as good a position as the Copyright Office to decide the issue." A mere challenge to copyrightability does not rise to an "effective challenge" and thus as a theoretical matter the *Barnhart* court is believed to have misstated the intent of §410(c). The court's reliance on the "mute testimony" of the works themselves appears to deny pictorial, graphic, and sculptural works (and perhaps all other "mute works," e.g., pantomimes and choreographic works) prima facie status under §410(c). As a factual matter, however, the defendant in *Barnhart* appears to have successfully mounted an "effective challenge" to copyrightability. Indeed, it ultimately prevailed. See discussion in the text at notes 113–114 in Chapter 2.

Cf. *Ace Novelty Co. v. Superior Toy & Novelty Co.*, 221 U.S.P.Q. 236, 238, 240 (N.D. Ill. 1983) (one-day special handling noted, but certificate of registration still given prima facie effect); *Midway Mfg. Co. v. Bandai-America, Inc.*, 546 F. Supp. 125, 143, 216 U.S.P.Q. 812, 824 (D.N.J. 1982), and cases cited therein (rejecting argument that §401(a) requires the Copyright Office to conduct a "substantive examination" for originality as "skirt[ing] the borders of bad faith").

[55] *Original Appalachian Artworks, Inc. v. Toy Loft, Inc.*, 489 F. Supp. 174, 179, 210 U.S.P.Q. 634, 637 (N.D. Ga. 1980), *aff'd*, 684 F.2d 821, 215 U.S.P.Q. 745 (11th Cir. 1982); *Durham Indus., Inc. v. Tomy Corp.*, 630 F.2d 905, 908, 208 U.S.P.Q. 10, 13 (2d Cir. 1980); *Midway Mfg. Co. v. Bandai-America, Inc.*, *supra* note 54; *Delman Fabrics, Inc. v. Holland Fabrics, Inc.*, COPR. L. REP. ¶25,663 (S.D.N.Y. 1984).

declared invalid where registration was obtained through fraud on the Copyright Office. In order to establish such fraud, it has been held that there must be a "knowing failure to advise the Copyright Office of facts which might have occasioned a rejection of the copyright * * * ."[56] This rule has been found to be particularly relevant to derivative works where the Copyright Office "did not have the opportunity to pass upon the question of originality in relation to a prior work because that work was not presented to that Office."[57] Immaterial errors will not result in invalidation of the registration.[58]

---

[56] *Russ Berrie & Co. v. Jerry Elsner Co.*, 482 F. Supp. 980, 988, 205 U.S.P.Q. 320, 328 (S.D.N.Y. 1980). Accord *M.S.R. Imports, Inc. v. R.E. Greenspan Co.*, 220 U.S.P.Q. 361 (E.D. Pa. 1983); *Original Appalachian Artworks, Inc. v. Toy Loft, Inc.*, supra note 54; *Knickerbocker Toy Co. v. Winterbrook Corp.*, 554 F. Supp. 1309, 216 U.S.P.Q. 621 (D.N.H. 1982). See also *Vogue Ring Creations, Inc. v. Hardman*, 410 F. Supp. 609, 190 U.S.P.Q. 329 (D.R.I. 1976) (1909 Act).

[57] *Knickerbocker Toy Co. v. Winterbrook Corp.*, 554 F. Supp. 1309, 1316, 216 U.S.P.Q. 621, 629 (D.N.H. 1982); *Russ Berrie & Co. v. Jerry Elsner Co.*, 482 F. Supp. 980, 988, 205 U.S.P.Q. 320, 328 (S.D.N.Y. 1980). But see discussion on this point in *Arc v. S.S. Sarna, Inc.*, 621 F. Supp. 916, 920–921, 229 U.S.P.Q. 25, 27–28 (E.D.N.Y. 1985) (noting technical nature of the term "derivative work"), and *Midway Mfg. Co. v. Bandai-America, Inc.*, 546 F. Supp. 125, 143 n. 14, 216 U.S.P.Q. 812, 824 n. 14 (D.N.J. 1982). *Original Appalachian Artworks, Inc. v. Toy Loft, Inc.*, 684 F.2d 821, 828, 215 U.S.P.Q. 745, 751 (11th Cir. 1982).

[58] *Cooling Systems & Flexibles, Inc. v. Stuart Radiator, Inc.*, 777 F.2d 485, 487, 228 U.S.P.Q. 275, 277 (9th Cir. 1985); *Arc v. S.S. Sarna, Inc.*, supra note 57, 621 F. Supp. at 921, 229 U.S.P.Q. at 28 ("The copyright law may be technical, but it is not so fragile that plaintiff's possible errors in its application will destroy its copyright protection in these works"); *Eckes v. Card Price Update*, 736 F.2d 859, 861–862, 222 U.S.P.Q. 762, 764 (2d Cir. 1984); *Harris v. Emus Records Corp.*, 734 F.2d 1329, 1335, 222 U.S.P.Q. 466, 470 (9th Cir. 1984); *Kenbrooke Fabrics, Inc. v. Holland Fabrics*, 602 F. Supp. 151, 153, 225 U.S.P.Q. 153 (S.D.N.Y. 1984); *Rand McNally & Co. v. Fleet Mgt. Systems, Inc.*, 591 F. Supp. 726, 736 n. 11, 221 U.S.P.Q. 827, 836 n. 11 (N.D. Ill. 1983); *Ace Novelty Co. v. Superior Toy & Novelty Co.*, 221 U.S.P.Q. 236, 240 (N.D. Ill. 1983); *Original Appalachian Artworks, Inc. v. Toy Loft, Inc.*, 684 F.2d 821, 828, 215 U.S.P.Q. 745, 749 (11th Cir. 1982); *Midway Mfg. Co. v. Bandai-America, Inc.*, 546 F. Supp. 125, 142–143, 216 U.S.P.Q. 812, 823 (D.N.J. 1982); *Testa v. Janssen*, 492 F. Supp. 198, 200, 208 U.S.P.Q. 213, 215 (W.D. Pa. 1980); *Urantia Foundation v. Burton*, 210 U.S.P.Q. 217, 221 (W.D. Mich. 1980).

There is no provision in the Copyright Act expressly permitting an individual to withdraw or request the Copyright Office to cancel a registration once it has been issued. As a general policy, the Copyright Office has stated it will cancel a registration only where:

"(1) It is clear that no registration should have been made because the work does not constitute copyrightable subject matter or fails to satisfy the other legal and formal requirements for obtaining copyright;

"(2) registration may be authorized but the application, deposit material, or fee does not meet the requirements of the law and Copyright Office regulations, and the Office is unable to get the defect corrected; or

"(3) an existing registration in the wrong class is to be replaced in the correct class."

37 C.F.R. §201.7(b).

When any of these circumstances are present, the claimant will be notified by correspondence of the proposed cancellation and the reasons therefor, and will be given 30 days from the date the letter is mailed to respond. A failure to respond (or to persuade the Office to change its position) will result in cancellation. 37 C.F.R. §§201.7(c)(1), (4).

A registration will also be cancelled where a check received in payment of the application fee is returned for insufficient funds, or is otherwise uncollectible. 37 C.F.R. §201.7(c)(2). The courts, of course, have the power to order the Copyright Office to cancel a registration. *Sargent v. American Greetings Corp.*, 588 F. Supp. 912, 925, 223 U.S.P.Q. 1327, 1337 (N.D. Ohio 1984).

The Copyright Office will also record an affidavit or other statement, signed by all the copyright owners, purporting to abandon the copyright, but will not express any opinion concerning the legal effect of such action. COMPENDIUM II OF COPYRIGHT OFFICE PRACTICES §1507.14.

# 7

# Rights Secured by Copyright and Infringement Thereof

Having passed through the various straits of copyrightability, duration, ownership, formalities, and registration, we come at last to the reward in the form of certain "exclusive" rights which are specified in Section 106 of the 1976 Act and then subjected to a remarkably detailed set of limitations contained in Sections 107 through 118. It should be noted that the Copyright Act does not define "infringement." In place of such a definition, Section 501(a) provides that infringement occurs when one or more of the copyright owner's Section 106 rights have been violated and there is no defense to the violation.

## Rights and Limitations: §§106–118

### The Right "To Reproduce the Copyrighted Work in Copies or Phonorecords": §106(1)

This right combines the basic right to "copy" under Section 1(a) of the 1909 law with the rather specialized right to mechanically record works under Sections 1(e) and 101(e) of that law. The special limitations of these latter sections have been modified in the new law (§115) and will be examined after a detailed review of the fundamental right to copy.

Since the right under the 1976 Act is to reproduce the work in copies or phonorecords, we must recall the expansive definitions of these terms in Section 101, which together cover all material objects "in which a work is fixed by any method now known or later developed, and from which the work can be perceived, reproduced, or otherwise communicated, either directly or with the aid of a machine or device." At the outset, it may be noted that this provision, coupled with the copyrightability of computer-readable material, removes any doubt that reproduction of copyrighted computer programs on electronic tape, so-called "floppy disks," or as embodied in a silicon chip, infringes the reproduction right.[1]

Just as a work must be "fixed" in order to qualify for protection, the legislative reports indicate that

> "[f]or a work to be 'reproduced,' its fixation in tangible form must be 'sufficiently permanent or stable to permit it to be perceived, reproduced, or otherwise communicated for a period of more than transitory duration.' * * *
> * * *
> "[T]he definition of 'fixation' [sic] would exclude from the concept purely evanescent or transient reproductions such as those projected briefly on a screen, shown electronically on a television or other cathode ray tube, or captured momentarily in the 'memory' of a computer."[2]

The operative phrase here, "communicated for a period of more than transitory duration," will no doubt thrust the judiciary into the intricacies of volatile and nonvolatile memory. One commentator has suggested that the loading of a copyrighted computer work into random access memory satisfies the fixation requirement.[3]

The legislative reports state that "since the mere scanning or manipulation of the contents of a work within the [computer] system would not involve a reproduction * * * it would be outside the scope of [Section 106(1)]."[4] If, however, the work were reproduced in any tangible medium of expression (punch cards, magnetic tape, disk) for input,[5] or were reproduced in substantial part as output, Section 106(1) would be violated.[6]

---

[1] *Apple Computer, Inc. v. Formula Int'l, Inc.*, 725 F.2d 521, 221 U.S.P.Q. 762 (9th Cir. 1984); *Apple Computer, Inc. v. Franklin Computer Corp.*, 714 F.2d 1240, 219 U.S.P.Q. 113 (3d Cir. 1983); *Williams Electronics, Inc. v. Artic Int'l*, 685 F.2d 870, 215 U.S.P.Q. 405 (3d Cir. 1982); *Midway Mfg. Co. v. Artic Int'l*, 704 F.2d 1009, 218 U.S.P.Q. 791 (7th Cir.), *cert denied*, 464 U.S. 823, 220 U.S.P.Q. 480 (1983).

[2] H.R. REP. No. 94-1476, 94th Cong., 2d Sess. 53, 62 (1976); S. REP. No. 94-473, 94th Cong., 1st Sess. 58 (1975). Such a showing may, however, nevertheless violate the performance or display rights granted, respectively, in §§106(4) and (5), since these rights are not dependent upon there being a fixation in a "copy." *Ibid.* See also the curious attack on the final paragraph in the quoted passage in the text in FINAL REPORT OF THE NATIONAL COMMISSION ON NEW TECHNOLOGICAL USES OF COPYRIGHTED WORKS 22 n. 111 (1978) and in Transcript of CONTU Meeting No. 19, Washington, D.C., Jan. 12-13, 1978) (NTIS no. PUB.-280-052) at 72.

[3] Grogan, *Decompilation and Disassembly: Undoing Software Protection*, 1 COMPUTER LAW. 1, 9-10 (1984).

[4] H.R. REP. No. 2237, 89th Cong., 2d Sess. 54 (1966); H.R. REP. No. 83, 90th Cong., 1st Sess. 25 (1967). In hearings on the recommendations of the National Commission on New Technological Uses of Copyrighted Works, the American Bar Association noted the absence of a specific "search" right and unsuccessfully argued for its inclusion. *Industrial Innovation and Patent and Copyright Law Amendments: Hearings on H.R. 6033 et al. Before the Subcomm. on Courts, Civil Liberties, and the Administration of Justice of the House Judiciary Comm.*, 96th Cong., 2d Sess. 685 (1980).

[5] See *Rand McNally & Co. v. Fleet Mgt. Systems, Inc.*, 600 F. Supp. 933, 223 U.S.P.Q. 1200 (N.D. Ill. 1984), which found that the inputting of a conventional work into a computer as a data base, and the subsequent output of parts thereof, violated §106(1); *Williams v. Arndt*, 227 U.S.P.Q. 615 (D. Mass. 1985) (computer formatting of printed futures trading manual); *West Pub. Co. v. Mead Data Central, Inc.*, 616 F. Supp. 1571, 227 U.S.P.Q. 631 (D. Minn. 1985) (computerized legal research service using "jump cites" to West Publishing Company's pagination of judicial opinions); *SAS Institute, Inc. v. S&H Computer Systems, Inc.*, 605 F. Supp. 816, 225

The standards for infringement and the burdens of persuasion remain unchanged under the 1976 Act:

> "As under the [1909 Act], a copyrighted work would be infringed by reproducing it in whole or in any substantial part, and by duplicating it exactly or by imitation or simulation. Wide departures or variations from the copyrighted work would still be an infringement as long as the author's 'expression' rather than merely the author's 'ideas' are taken."[7]

A copyright owner carries the initial burden of proving a prima facie case of infringement. This consists of (a) ownership of a valid copyright and (b) unauthorized copying of protected material by defendant that (c) goes so far as to constitute unlawful appropriation.[8] Where direct proof (such as an admission by defendant) is not available, plaintiff must prove copying by indirect or circumstantial evidence. Such evidence generally consists of (a) proof of access to the copyrighted work, as well as (b) similarities between the two works that are unlikely to have occurred in the absence of copying.

---

U.S.P.Q. 916 (M.D. Tenn. 1985) (unauthorized use of computer program for reverse engineering held infringement); *Hubco Data Products Corp. v. Management Assistance*, 219 U.S.P.Q. 450 (D. Idaho 1983) (infringement for unauthorized input for reverse engineering purposes). One potential defense applicable to input is found in 17 U.S.C. §117 (1980), discussed *infra* on pp. 210–213.

[6]The applicability of the fair use defense to the reproduction of "small excerpts or key words for purposes of input, and output of bibliographic lists or short summaries" was noted in early legislative reports. These reports also cautioned, however, that "because the potential capabilities of a computer system are vastly different from those of a mimeograph or photocopying machine, the factors to be considered in determining fair use would have to be weighed differently in each situation." H.R. REP. No. 2237, 89th Cong., 2d Sess. 64–65 (1966); H.R. REP. No. 83, 90th Cong., 1st Sess. 35–36 (1967). Compare also *id*, H.R. REP. No. 2237 at 54; H.R. REP. No. 83 at 25, which state that "reproduction of a work or substantial parts of it, in copies as the 'print-out' or output of the computer; preparation for input of an index or abstract of the work so complete and detailed that it would be considered a 'derivative work' would be an infringement *unless* fair use applied, with COPYRIGHT LAW REVISION PART 6: SUPPLEMENTARY REPORT OF THE REGISTER OF COPYRIGHTS ON THE GENERAL REVISION OF THE U.S. COPYRIGHT LAW: 1965 REVISION BILL, 89th Cong., 1st Sess. 19 (Comm. Print 1965): "An index or abstract so complete and detailed that it could replace the work on which it is based should probably be regarded as an 'abridgment' or 'condensation,' and hence a 'derivative work' covered by section 106(2)." This latter analysis seemingly adopts a fair use approach to the more preliminary finding of substantial similarity. See also *West Pub. Co. v. Mead Data Central, Inc.*, 616 F. Supp. 1571, 227 U.S.P.Q. 631 (D. Minn. 1985) (denying fair use for insertion of "jump cites" to West Reporter Systems' pagination of judicial opinions in the LEXIS computerized research service).

[7]H.R. REP. No. 94-1476, 94th Cong., 2d Sess. 61 (1976); S. REP. No. 94-473, 94th Cong., 1st Sess. 58 (1975). See also *Peter Pan Fabrics, Inc. v. Martin Weiner Corp.*, 274 F.2d 487, 124 U.S.P.Q. 154, 155 (2d Cir. 1960) (Learned Hand, J.):

> "[C]opyright extends beyond a photographic reproduction of the design, but one cannot say how far an imitator must depart from an undeviating reproduction to escape infringement. In deciding that question one should consider the uses for which the design is intended, especially the scrutiny that observers will give to it as used";

and *Nichols v. Universal Pictures Corp.*, 45 F.2d 119, 121, 7 U.S.P.Q. 84, 86 (2d Cir. 1930) (Learned Hand, J.), *cert. denied*, 282 U.S. 902 (1931) ("It is of course essential to any protection of literary property, whether at common law or under the statute, that the right cannot be limited literally to the text, else a plagiarist would escape by immaterial variations").

[8]*Arnstein v. Porter*, 154 F.2d 464, 468, 68 U.S.P.Q. 288, 293 (2d Cir. 1946), *cert. denied*, 330 U.S. 851, 73 U.S.P.Q. 550 (1947). See also *Scott v. WKJG, Inc.*, 376 F.2d 467, 469, 153 U.S.P.Q. 493, 495 (7th Cir. 1967); *Atari, Inc. v. North American Philips Consumer Electronics Corp.*, 672 F.2d 607, 614, 214 U.S.P.Q. 33, 38–39 (7th Cir.), *cert. denied*, 459 U.S. 880 (1982). Despite *Arnstein's* loss of authority on the correct standard for the granting of summary judgment, it is believed still to be the best guide to proving infringement. Judge Newman's opinion in *Warner Bros., Inc. v. ABC*, 720 F.2d 231, 222 U.S.P.Q. 101 (2d Cir. 1983), is particularly illuminating on both the summary judgment and infringement questions.

*Access*

Since direct proof of access is not always possible, the courts have held that plaintiff may indirectly prove access by demonstrating that defendant had a reasonable opportunity to view or copy plaintiff's work,[9] as, for example, where a copyrighted work has been widely disseminated,[10] where a third party with whom both plaintiff and defendant conducted business had possession of plaintiff's work,[11] or where the work was sent directly to defendant or to a close associate of his.[12]

Evidence that the copyrighted work was performed only locally,[13] sold in limited numbers in selected bookstores,[14] read by only one editor of defendant who did not show it to those responsible for the allegedly infringing work,[15] or that an unsolicited manuscript was not shown to decision-making or creative personnel,[16] has, however, been found insufficient to establish access.

*Copying*

Proof of access should not be confused with proof of copying. As noted by the Sixth Circuit in *Wickham v. Knoxville International Energy Exposition, Inc.*: "No amount of access will suffice to show

---

[9]*Selle v. Gibb*, 741 F.2d 896, 223 U.S.P.Q. 195 (7th Cir. 1983); *Arc v. S.S. Sarna, Inc.*, 621 F. Supp. 916, 921, 229 U.S.P.Q. 25, 28 (E.D.N.Y. 1985) ("Access is defined as a reasonable opportunity to copy plaintiff's work"); *Najarian v. Tobias*, COPR. L. REP. ¶25,595 (D. Mass. 1983); *M.S.R. Imports, Inc. v. R.E. Greenspan Co.*, 220 U.S.P.Q. 361 (E.D. Pa. 1983); *Kamar Int'l, Inc. v. Russ Berrie & Co.*, 657 F.2d 1059, 216 U.S.P.Q. 376 (9th Cir. 1981); *Testa v. Janssen*, 492 F. Supp. 198, 208 U.S.P.Q. 213 (W.D. Pa. 1980); *Ferguson v. NBC*, 584 F.2d 111, 200 U.S.P.Q. 65 (5th Cir. 1978); *R. Dakin & Co. v. A & L Novelty Co.*, 444 F. Supp. 1080, 196 U.S.P.Q. 746 (E.D.N.Y. 1978). Note that Judge Frank's use of the term "access" in *Arnstein, supra* note 8, does not distinguish between direct proof of defendant's actual contact with plaintiff's work and proof of a *potential* contact, i.e., opportunity to have seen or heard plaintiff's work.
[10]*ABKCO Music, Inc. v. Harrisongs, Ltd.*, 722 F.2d 988, 221 U.S.P.Q. 490 (2d Cir. 1983) (song was Number 1 and Number 12 on the charts in the United States and United Kingdom, respectively); *Arc v. S.S. Sarna, Inc., supra* note 9, 621 F. Supp. at 921, 229 U.S.P.Q. at 28 (plaintiff's works had been widely disseminated and were readily available in the market; plaintiff and defendant both participated in the same trade shows and had in the recent past maintained offices in the same building); *Midway Mfg. Co. v. Bandai-America, Inc.*, 546 F. Supp. 125, 216 U.S.P.Q. 812 (D.N.J. 1982) (popular electronic audiovisual game).
[11]*Kamar Int'l, Inc. v. Russ Berrie & Co.*, 657 F.2d 1059, 216 U.S.P.Q. 376 (9th Cir. 1981); *M.S.R. Imports, Inc. v. R.E. Greenspan Co.*, 220 U.S.P.Q. 361 (E.D. Pa. 1983). These cases come close to being examples of direct evidence of copying. Cf. *Thomas Wilson & Co. v. Irving J. Dorfman Co.*, 268 F. Supp. 711, 154 U.S.P.Q. 226 (S.D.N.Y. 1967), *aff'd*, 433 F.2d 409, 167 U.S.P.Q. 417 (2d Cir. 1970), *cert. denied*, 401 U.S. 977, 169 U.S.P.Q. 65 (1971), where a purchaser of plaintiff's lace fabric embodying a copyrighted design gave a sample thereof to defendant's vice-president, suggesting that defendant produce a design "which would have the look" of plaintiff's; and *Malden Mills, Inc. v. Regency Mills, Inc.*, 626 F.2d 1112, 207 U.S.P.Q. 87 (2d Cir. 1980).
[12]*Selle v. Gibb*, 741 F.2d 896, 902, 223 U.S.P.Q. 195, 198–199 (7th Cir. 1984).
[13]*Ibid.*
[14]*Jason v. Fonda*, 698 F.2d 966, 217 U.S.P.Q. 406 (9th Cir. 1983); *Najarian v. Tobias*, COPR. L. REP. ¶25,595 (D. Mass. 1983).
[15]*Najarian v. Tobias, supra* note 14.
[16]*Kornfield v. CBS, Inc.*, 226 U.S.P.Q. 1010 (C.D. Cal. 1985); *Vantage Point, Inc. v. Parker Bros.*, 529 F. Supp. 1204, 213 U.S.P.Q. 782 (E.D.N.Y. 1981). See especially the scholarly review of the case law in *Meta-Films Associates, Inc. v. MCA, Inc.*, 586 F. Supp. 1346, 222 U.S.P.Q. 211 (C.D. Cal. 1984).

copying if there are no similarities.''[17] The question thus arises, what type of similarities will suffice to demonstrate copying? As an initial matter, it must be stated that the question whether similarities are substantial and material enough to constitute unlawful appropriation, i.e., infringement, is entirely different from whether there are similarities sufficient to establish indirect proof of copying. Confusion on this point has occurred due to the unfortunate practice of some courts of using the short-hand term "substantial similarity" to connote both that type of similarity used to establish indirect proof of copying *and* that necessary to establish a prima facie case of infringement.[18]

Perhaps the word "substantial" should not be used at all in describing the similarity probative of copying rather than independent creation. The similarities *may* be substantial in quantity or they may be quite sparse but nevertheless clearly derived from plaintiff's work. Thus, the extent to which similarities are appropriate evidence of copying varies with the nature of the work, the subject with which it deals, and the attendant circumstances. A single verbatim sentence from a 1,000-page novel may, if unexplained, be more probative of copying than great similarity or even virtual identity between two maps, directories, or photographs. (If no more than one sentence is taken, this may, however, be excused as *de minimis* copying; see pp. 196–198, *infra.*)

Copying may also be established by proving that defendant appropriated uncopyrightable elements, or a number of elements which, either alone or in combination, may not be sufficient to support an ultimate finding of infringement but which nevertheless *are* sufficient to negate claims of independent creation and thus to justify the

---

[17]739 F.2d 1094, 1097, 222 U.S.P.Q. 778, 781 (6th Cir. 1984). See also Judge Frank's statement in *Arnstein v. Porter*, 154 F.2d 464, 468, 68 U.S.P.Q. 288, 293 (2d Cir. 1946), *cert. denied*, 330 U.S. 851, 73 U.S.P.Q. 550 (1947) ("if there are no similarities, no amount of evidence of access will suffice to prove copying").

[18]See, e.g., *Novelty Textile Mills, Inc. v. Joan Fabrics Corp.*, 558 F.2d 1090, 1092, 195 U.S.P.Q. 1, 2–3 (2d Cir. 1977):

"In order to prove infringement, a plaintiff must show ownership of a valid copyright and copying by defendant. * * * Since direct evidence of copying is rarely, if ever, available, a plaintiff may prove copying by showing access and 'substantial similarity of the two works' "

*Kamar Int'l, Inc. v. Russ Berrie & Co.*, 657 F.2d 1059, 1062–1063, 216 U.S.P.Q. 376, 379 (9th Cir. 1981); *Sid & Marty Krofft Television Prods. v. McDonald's Corp.*, 562 F.2d 1157, 1162, 196 U.S.P.Q. 97, 100–101 (9th Cir. 1977).

In *Universal Athletic Sales Co. v. Salkeld*, 511 F.2d 904, 907, 185 U.S.P.Q. 76, 78 (3d Cir. 1975), the Third Circuit correctly noted that "substantial similarity to show that the original work has been copied is not the same as substantial similarity to prove infringement," but little has been done to eliminate the confusion from the use of "substantial similarity" in both contexts. The confusion is aggravated when one of the uses is inaccurate. See also *Franklin Mint Corp. v. National Wildlife Art Exchange, Inc.*, 575 F.2d 62, 65–66, 197 U.S.P.Q. 721, 723–724 (3d Cir. 1978); *Klitzner Indus., Inc. v. H.K. James & Co.*, 535 F. Supp. 1249, 1253–1254, 216 U.S.P.Q. 73, 76 (E.D. Pa. 1982); *Midway Mfg. Co. v. Bandai-America, Inc.*, 546 F. Supp. 125, 138–139, 216 U.S.P.Q. 812, 820 (D.N.J. 1982); *Atari, Inc. v. North American Philips Consumer Electronics Corp.*, 672 F.2d 607, 614, 214 U.S.P.Q. 33, 38–39 (7th Cir.), *cert. denied*, 459 U.S. 880 (1982), which noted that "[s]ome courts have expressed the test of substantial similarity in two parts * * *."

inference that defendant copied plaintiff's work.[19] The fact of *any* copying has some evidentiary value in establishing the copying of other (and perhaps material) copyrighted elements of the same work.

A clear case of similarity which establishes copying occurs where defendant's work contains a "smoking gun" such as plaintiff's signature or copyright notice.[20] A related feature of similarity is the appearance of common errors in the two works.[21] There may, however, often be a difference of opinion as to whether both parties merely drew from common sources open to all or whether one of them resorted to "apt appropriation's artful aid" beyond the limits allowed by law. This is well illustrated in the case of dramas based upon the same conditions and modes of life or upon old narratives long since in the public domain. In *Simonton v. Gordon*,[22] Judge Winslow, on a preliminary motion, after reading plaintiff's novel "Hell's Playground" and defendant's play "White Cargo" (both dealing with life and customs in West Africa), reached the conclusion that the resemblances were only such as might naturally be expected, and refused to grant a preliminary injunction. The case came for final hearing before Judge Knox, who, on the other hand, after a careful analysis of both works, found sufficient evidence of deliberate piracy on the part of the author of "White Cargo" to justify the granting of an appropriate decree.[23]

In *Sheldon v. Metro-Goldwyn Pictures Corp.*,[24] the district court concluded that the photoplay "Letty Lynton" did not infringe plaintiff's drama "Dishonored Lady" (both based upon a famous Scottish murder trial of a bygone age). Upon appeal, however, the Court of

---

[19]See, e.g., *Heim v. Universal Pictures Corp.*, 154 F.2d 480, 488, 68 U.S.P.Q. 303, 311 (2d Cir. 1946) (Frank, J.) ("In an appropriate case, copying might be demonstrated, with no proof or weak proof of access, by showing that a single brief phrase, contained in both pieces, was so idiosyncratic in its treatment as to preclude coincidence"); *Concord Fabrics, Inc. v. Marcus Bros. Textile Corp.*, 409 F.2d 1315, 161 U.S.P.Q. 3 (2d Cir. 1969).

[20]*American Charm Corp. v. Omega Casting Corp.*, 211 U.S.P.Q. 635 (S.D.N.Y. 1979).

[21]*Oxford Book Co. v. College Entrance Book Co.*, 98 F.2d 688, 691, 39 U.S.P.Q. 7, 9–10 (2d Cir. 1938) (grammatical mistakes). The Supreme Court has stated that the appearance of common errors is one of the most significant types of evidence of copying. *Callaghan v. Meyers*, 128 U.S. 617, 662 (1888). Proof of common errors does not, however, obviate the need to prove substantial similarity in copyrightable expression. *Cooling Systems & Flexibles, Inc. v. Stuart Radiator, Inc.*, 777 F.2d 485, 492–493, 228 U.S.P.Q. 275, 281 (9th Cir. 1985).

Copyright owners sometimes purposely insert errors or fictitious elements in order to catch copying, a tactic frequently used with directories, maps, and other factual works. But cf. *Morrison v. Solomon*, 494 F. Supp. 218, 224, 210 U.S.P.Q. 121, 125 (S.D.N.Y. 1980) ("[t]he law of this Circuit casts considerable doubt upon the probative value of copied items as evidence of copyright violation"). *Morrison* arguably confuses evidence that proves copying with the quantum or quality of copying that will establish enough copying to constitute an unlawful appropriation.

See also *Camaro Headquarters, Inc. v. Bank*, 227 U.S.P.Q. 170, 171 (E.D. Pa. 1985) (same misspellings and typographical errors). In *Hassenfield Bros., Inc. v. Mego Corp.*, 150 U.S.P.Q. 786 (S.D.N.Y. 1966) (anatomical error appearing in both plaintiff's and defendant's dolls considered significant proof of copying); *Adventures in Good Eating v. Best Places to Eat*, 131 F.2d 809, 811, 56 U.S.P.Q. 242, 244–245 (7th Cir. 1942); *College Entrance Book Co. v. Amsco Book Co.*, 119 F.2d 874, 875, 49 U.S.P.Q. 517, 518–519 (2d Cir. 1941); *Rexnord, Inc. v. Modern Handling Systems, Inc.*, 379 F. Supp. 1190, 1194, 183 U.S.P.Q. 413, 415 (D. Del. 1974).

[22]297 F. 625 (S.D.N.Y. 1924).

[23]12 F.2d 116 (S.D.N.Y. 1925). Cf. *Granite Music Corp. v. United Artists Corp.*, 532 F.2d 718, 720–724, 189 U.S.P.Q. 406, 408–411 (9th Cir. 1976).

[24]7 F. Supp. 837 (S.D.N.Y. 1934).

Appeals for the Second Circuit[25] found evidence of unfair use of substantial parts of plaintiff's drama and reversed the decree.

In sum, "actual copying may be established by direct proof or by proof of access plus a demonstration of similarities *or other factors circumstantially evidencing copying.*"[26]

Copying (and indeed the ultimate question of infringement) may also be inferred, in appropriate circumstances, even in the absence of proof of access where the two works are found to be "strikingly similar." This type of similarity provides indirect proof of access, which in turn combines to provide indirect proof of copying.

A work is said to be "strikingly similar" where the similarities "are of a kind that can only be explained by copying, rather than coincidence, independent creation, or prior common source." Plaintiff's burden of proof regarding striking similarity is thus to demonstrate "similarity which reasonably precludes the possibility of any explanation other than that of copying."[27]

A finding of striking similarity is not, however, a complete substitute for proof of access. In affirming a district court's granting of defendant's motion for judgment notwithstanding the verdict in a case involving the popular musical group the "Bee Gees," the Seventh Circuit held:

> "[A]lthough it has frequently been written that striking similarity *alone* can establish access, the decided cases suggest that this circumstance would be most unusual. The plaintiff must always present sufficient evidence to support a reasonable possibility of access because the jury can not draw an inference of access based on speculation and conjecture alone."[28]

---

[25]81 F.2d 49 (2d Cir.), *cert. denied*, 298 U.S. 669 (1936).

[26]*Alexander v. Haley*, 460 F. Supp. 40, 43, 200 U.S.P.Q. 239, 240 (S.D.N.Y. 1978) (Emphasis added). See also *Kucker v. National Research Bureau, Inc.*, 204 U.S.P.Q. 938 (S.D.N.Y. 1979); *Soptra Fabrics Corp. v. Stafford Knitting Mills, Inc.*, 490 F.2d 1092, 1094, 180 U.S.P.Q. 545, 546 (2d Cir. 1974) ("The appearance in one of defendant's fabrics of colors identical to plaintiff's is additional evidence of copying * * *"); *E.F. Johnson Co. v. Uniden Corp. of America*, 623 F. Supp. 1485, 1497, 228 U.S.P.Q. 891, 899 (D. Minn. 1985) ("Verbatim copying of a computer manual is inferential evidence of pirating of the underlying software").

[27]*Testa v. Janssen*, 492 F. Supp. 198, 203, 208 U.S.P.Q. 213, 217 (W.D. Pa. 1980) (quoting *Stratchborneo v. Arc Music Corp.*, 357 F. Supp. 1393, 1403, 179 U.S.P.Q. 403, 410 (S.D.N.Y. 1973). But see discussion of *Stratchborneo* and criticism of *Testa* in Osterberg, *Striking Similarity and the Attempt to Prove Access in Music Plagiarism Cases*, 2 J. COPR., ENT. & SPORTS LAW 85, 87–90, 93–95 (1983). See also *Selle v. Gibb*, 741 F.2d 896, 904, 223 U.S.P.Q. 195, 201 (7th Cir. 1984) ("the similarities should appear in a sufficiently unique or complex context as to make it unlikely that both pieces were copied from a prior common source * * * or that the defendant was able to compose the accused work as a matter of independent creation"); *Price, Inc. v. Metzner*, 574 F. Supp. 281, 219 U.S.P.Q. 1092 (E.D. Pa. 1983); *M.S.R. Imports, Inc. v. R.E. Greenspan Co.*, 220 U.S.P.Q. 361 (E.D. Pa. 1983); *Russ Berrie & Co. v. Jerry Elsner Co.*, 482 F. Supp. 980, 205 U.S.P.Q. 320 (S.D.N.Y. 1980); *Arnstein v. Porter*, 154 F.2d 464, 468, 68 U.S.P.Q. 288, 293 (2d Cir. 1946), *cert. denied*, 330 U.S. 851, 73 U.S.P.Q. 550 (1947) ("In some cases, the similarities between the plaintiff's and defendant's work are so extensive and striking as, without more, both to justify an inference of copying and to prove improper appropriation"). But see Osterberg, *supra*, for criticism of *Arnstein* on this point.

The courts are split over whether expert testimony is required to prove striking similarity. Cf. *Testa v. Janssen*, *supra*, with *M.S.R. Imports, Inc. v. R.E. Greenspan Co.*, *supra*.

[28]*Selle v. Gibb*, 741 F.2d 896, 901, 223 U.S.P.Q. 195, 198 (7th Cir. 1984). See also *Jason v. Fonda*, 698 F.2d 966, 967, 217 U.S.P.Q. 406 (9th Cir. 1983); *Najarian v. Tobias*, COPR. L. REP. ¶25,595 (D. Mass. 1983); *M.S.R. Imports, Inc. v. R.E. Greenspan Co.*, *supra* note 27; *Ferguson v. NBC*, 584 F.2d 111, 113, 220 U.S.P.Q. 65, 66 (5th Cir. 1978) ("to support a finding of access

In short, in the absence of direct proof of copying, plaintiff must establish defendant had a reasonable opportunity to come into contact with his work and similarities between the works which, under the circumstances, make independent creation unlikely. Such similarities are not offered for their own sake in satisfaction of the *additional* requirement that defendant has taken a substantial and material amount of plaintiff's copyrightable expression so as to constitute infringement, but rather are offered as probative of the *act* of copying.

In attempting to establish copying, the courts have held that "analysis ('dissection') is relevant and the testimony of experts may be received to aid the trier of facts."[29] Such experts may, for example, show how particular passages are (or are not) common to the type of work at issue and whether seemingly dissimilar works are the result of "a crude effort to give the appearance of dissimilarity [which] is itself evidence of copying."[30]

## Substantial and Material Copying

Having succeeded in proving access and copying, plaintiff at the second stage of the infringement analysis must show (a) that the material allegedly infringed is protected by copyright and (b) that the infringement is substantial and material enough (either quantitatively or qualitatively[31]) to constitute an unlawful appropriation,[32]

---

there must be a reasonable possibility of access—not a bare possibility as we have in this case"). See also *Arnstein v. Porter, supra* note 27 ("If evidence of access is absent, the similarities must be so striking as to preclude the possibility that plaintiff and defendant independently arrived at the same result"). Cf. *Luecke v. G.P. Putnam's Sons*, 10 MEDIA L. REP. 1250, 1252 (S.D.N.Y. 1983) (characterizing *Arnstein's* statement as "dicta * * * which is not binding on this Court").

[29]*Arnstein v. Porter*, 154 F.2d 464, 468, 68 U.S.P.Q. 288, 293 (2d Cir. 1946), *cert. denied*, 330 U.S. 851, 73 U.S.P.Q. 550 (1947); *Heim v. Universal Pictures Corp.*, 154 F.2d 480, 68 U.S.P.Q. 303 (2d Cir. 1946); *Sid & Marty Krofft Television Prods. v. McDonald's Corp.*, 562 F.2d 1157, 1164, 196 U.S.P.Q. 97, 102 (9th Cir. 1977); *Universal Athletic Sales Co. v. Salkeld*, 511 F.2d 904, 185 U.S.P.Q. 76 (3d Cir. 1975); *Franklin Mint Corp. v. National Wildlife Art Exchange*, 575 F.2d 62, 197 U.S.P.Q. 721 (3d Cir. 1978); *Midway Mfg. Co. v. Bandai-America, Inc.*, 546 F. Supp. 125, 216 U.S.P.Q. 812 (D.N.J. 1982); *Atari, Inc. v. North American Philips Consumer Electronics Corp.*, 672 F.2d 607, 214 U.S.P.Q. 33 (7th Cir.), *cert. denied*, 459 U.S. 880 (1982).

In *Krofft, supra*, the Ninth Circuit created its own two-step infringement analysis purportedly based, in part, on that found in *Arnstein*, but in fact based on the (entirely different) idea-expression dichotomy. 562 F.2d at 1165, 196 U.S.P.Q. at 102–103. While the second prongs of the *Arnstein* and *Krofft* tests (involving substantial similarity) may approximate each other, the first prongs clearly do not. *Arnstein's* first prong focuses on copying versus independent creation; the *Krofft* first prong (called the "extrinsic test") focuses on the copying of ideas. As noted below in note 33, *Krofft* (and its progeny's) emphasis on the copying of ideas has led the Ninth Circuit to erroneously require that there be substantial similarity in both expression *and* ideas in order to establish infringement.

[30]*Joshua Meier Co. v. Albany Novelty Mfg. Co.*, 236 F.2d 144, 146, 111 U.S.P.Q. 197, 198 (2d Cir. 1956); *Concord Fabrics, Inc. v. Marcus Bros. Textile Corp.*, 409 F.2d 1315, 161 U.S.P.Q. 3 (2d Cir. 1969); *Scarves by Vera, Inc. v. United Merchants & Mfgrs., Inc.*, 173 F. Supp. 625, 121 U.S.P.Q. 578 (S.D.N.Y. 1959). See also *Investment Service Co. v. Fitch Pub. Co.*, 291 F. 1010 (7th Cir. 1923) (dissection revealed inversions, "tricks," and repetition of typographical errors in sufficient numbers to defeat theory of coincidence and to justify the inference that defendant copied more than the mistakes).

[31]See, e.g., *Harper & Row, Pub., Inc. v. Nation Enters.*, 471 U.S. ____, 225 U.S.P.Q. 1073 (1985) (300 words from 200,000-word manuscript); *WPOW, Inc. v. MRLJ Enters.*, 584 F. Supp. 132, 136, 222 U.S.P.Q. 502, 505 (D.D.C. 1984) ("Taking what is in essence the heart of the work is considered a taking of a substantial nature, even if what is actually taken is less than

i.e., that the works are "substantially similar." The first requisite illustrates the correlation between questions of copyrightability and infringement: defendant's taking of uncopyrightable material from plaintiff's work does not infringe. Thus, even though minute dissection of the works is inappropriate at the unlawful-appropriation stage of the infringement analysis, elements such as ideas and bare facts must be factored out of the substantial-similarity equation lest protection be inadvertently extended to uncopyrightable material. As one court wrote, "[t]he only similarity of significance in assessing claims of infringement is similarity of *expression.*"[33]

---

extensive"); *Wainwright Securities, Inc. v. Wall Street Transcript Corp.*, 418 F. Supp. 620, 194 U.S.P.Q. 328 (S.D.N.Y. 1976), *aff'd*, 558 F.2d 91, 194 U.S.P.Q. 401 (2d Cir. 1977), *cert. denied*, 434 U.S. 1014 (1978), and cases cited in W. PATRY, THE FAIR USE PRIVILEGE IN COPYRIGHT LAW 451–452 (BNA Books, 1985). Perhaps the most extreme example of a qualitatively substantial taking is found in *Dawn Associates, Inc. v. Links*, 203 U.S.P.Q. 831 (N.D. Ill. 1978), where the phrase "when there is no room in hell * * * the dead will walk the Earth," taken from a motion picture and its advertising, was held to be infringing. See also *Universal City Studios, Inc. v. Kamar Indus.*, 217 U.S.P.Q. 1162 (S.D. Tex. 1982) ("I Love you E.T."; "E.T. Phone Home" on consumer products held infringement of movie); *Henry Holt & Co. v. Liggett & Myers Tobacco Co.*, 23 F. Supp. 302, 37 U.S.P.Q. 449 (E.D. Pa. 1938) (fragments of three sentences from 242+-page book found to be infringement); *Higgins v. Baker*, 309 F. Supp. 635, 164 U.S.P.Q. 472 (S.D.N.Y. 1969) (0.8% appropriation found infringing).

Some decisions have erroneously held that the standard for substantial similarity is higher for nonfictional works than for fictional works. *Cooling Systems & Flexibles, Inc. v. Stuart Radiator, Inc.*, 777 F.2d 485, 491, 228 U.S.P.Q. 275, 280 (9th Cir. 1985); *Landsberg v. Scrabble Crossword Game Players, Inc.*, 736 F.2d 485, 221 U.S.P.Q. 1140 (9th Cir.), *cert. denied*, 469 U.S. 1037 (1984); *Hoehling v. Universal City Studios, Inc.*, 618 F.2d 972, 205 U.S.P.Q. 681 (2d Cir.), *cert. denied*, 449 U.S. 841, 207 U.S.P.Q. 1064 (1980); *Harper & Row, Pub., Inc. v. Nation Enters.*, 723 F.2d 195, 220 U.S.P.Q. 321 (2d Cir. 1983), *rev'd on other grounds*, 471 U.S. _____, 225 U.S.P.Q. 1073 (1985).

This higher standard is rationalized by: (1) an alleged need to construe copyrightability in order to allow "the free use of ideas," *Landsberg, supra*, 736 F.2d at 488, 221 U.S.P.Q. at 1142, or "access to that information which gives meaning to our society's highly valued freedom of expression," *Harper & Row, supra*, 723 F.2d at 202, 220 U.S.P.Q. at 328—goals that are fully accommodated by §102(b)'s *ab initio* denial of protection to ideas, facts, and information, and by the fair use privilege, where applicable; and (2) by a purportedly "narrow range of expression" available to "authors wishing to express the ideas contained in a factual work * * *," *Landsberg, supra*, 736 F.2d at 488, 221 U.S.P.Q. at 1143—a proposition that is wholly without support as applied to the broad class of all nonfictional works.

There is no reason, factual or legal, justifying the establishment of a different standard of substantial similarity for any class of work. It is noteworthy in this regard that in reversing the Second Circuit's decision in *Harper & Row, supra*, the Supreme Court held: "We agree with the Court of Appeals that copyright is intended to increase and not to impede the harvest of knowledge. But we believe the Second Circuit gave insufficient deference to the scheme established by the Copyright Act for fostering the original works that provide the seed and substance of this harvest." 471 U.S. at _____, 225 U.S.P.Q. at 1075. See also Patry, *Copyright in Collections of Facts: A Reply*, 6 COMM. AND THE LAW 11, 34–41 (1984).

[32]*Arnstein v. Porter*, 154 F.2d 464, 468, 68 U.S.P.Q. 288, 293 (2d Cir. 1946), *cert. denied*, 330 U.S. 851, 73 U.S.P.Q. 550 (1947); *Heim v. Universal Pictures Co.*, 154 F.2d 480, 68 U.S.P.Q. 303 (2d Cir. 1946); *Scott v. WKJG, Inc.*, 376 F.2d 467, 469, 153 U.S.P.Q. 493, 495 (7th Cir. 1967); *Atari, Inc. v. North American Philips Consumer Electronics Corp.*, 672 F.2d 607, 614, 214 U.S.P.Q. 33, 39 (7th Cir.), *cert. denied*, 459 U.S. 880 (1982).

[33]*Durham Indus., Inc. v. Tomy Corp.*, 630 F.2d 905, 912, 208 U.S.P.Q. 10, 17 (2d Cir. 1980); *Hoehling v. Universal City Studios, Inc.*, 618 F.2d 972, 977, 205 U.S.P.Q. 681, 685 (2d Cir.), *cert. denied*, 449 U.S. 841, 207 U.S.P.Q. 1064 (1980). See also *Warner Bros., Inc. v. ABC*, 530 F. Supp. 1187, 1190, 215 U.S.P.Q. 690, 691 (S.D.N.Y. 1982), *aff'd*, 720 F.2d 231, 222 U.S.P.Q. 101 (2d Cir. 1983) (courts must "distill the protected parts of a work from the unprotected"); *Mattel, Inc. v. Azrak-Hamway Int'l, Inc.*, 724 F.2d 357, 360, 221 U.S.P.Q. 302, 304 (2d Cir. 1983) (similarity in dolls' bodies attributed "to the fact that both are artists' renderings of the same unprotectable idea—a superhuman muscleman crouching in what since Neanderthal times has been a traditional fighting pose"). So-called merged expression—language that conveys an idea which "can be, or is typically expressed, in a limited number of stereotyped fashions," *Alexander v. Haley*, 460 F. Supp. 40, 46, 200 U.S.P.Q. 239, 243 (S.D.N.Y. 1978), is also factored out of the substantial similarity analysis. See discussion in the text at notes 70–74 in

In determining what elements are protectible, the courts have repeatedly relied on the opinions of Judge Learned Hand. In *Nichols v. Universal Pictures Corp.*, Judge Hand set forth what has become known as the "abstractions test":

> "[W]hen the plagiarist does not take out a block *in situ*, but an abstract of the whole, decision is more troublesome. Upon any work, and especially upon a play, a great number of patterns of increasing generality will fit equally well, as more and more of the incident is left out. The last may be no more than the most general statement of what the play is about, and at times might consist only of its title; but there is a point in a series of abstractions where they are no longer protected, since otherwise the playwright could prevent the use of his 'ideas,' to which apart from their expression, his property is never extended."[34]

On the question of how much taking is too much or how similar is too similar, Judge Hand's formulation in the context of textile designs is still the most authoritative guide:

> "No one disputes that the copyright extends beyond a photographic reproduction of the design, but one cannot say how far an imitator must depart from an undeviating reproduction to escape infringement. In deciding that question one should consider the uses for which the design is intended, especially the scrutiny that observers will give to it as used. In the case at bar we must try to estimate how far its overall appearance will determine its aesthetic appeal when the cloth is made into a garment. Both designs have the same general color, and the arches, scrolls, rows of symbols, etc. on one resemble those on the other though they are not identical. Moreover, the patterns in which these figures are distributed to make up the design as a whole are not identical. However, the ordinary observer, unless he set out to detect the disparities, would be disposed to overlook them, and regard their aesthetic appeal as the same. That is enough; and indeed, it is all that can be said, unless protection against infringement is to be denied because of variants irrelevant to the purpose for which the design is intended."[35]

---

Chapter 2, and the examples given by Judge Leval in *Amjon v. HBO*, 9 MEDIA L. REP. 1181, 1182 (S.D.N.Y. 1982).

In *Sid & Marty Krofft Television Prods. v. McDonald's Corp.*, 562 F.2d 1157, 1164, 196 U.S.P.Q. 97, 102 (9th Cir. 1977), and a number of cases following it, e.g., *Cooling Systems & Flexibles, Inc. v. Stuart Radiator, Inc.*, 777 F.2d 485, 491, 228 U.S.P.Q. 275, 280 (9th Cir. 1985), *Berkic v. Crichton*, 761 F.2d 1289, 226 U.S.P.Q. 787 (9th Cir.), *cert. denied*, 474 U.S. _____ (1985), *Litchfield v. Spielberg*, 736 F.2d 1352, 1356, 222 U.S.P.Q. 965, 967 (9th Cir. 1984), *cert. denied*, 470 U.S. _____ (1985), the Ninth Circuit has held that there must be substantial similarity of both expression *and* ideas in order for infringement to occur. While in most cases the underlying ideas of the works can be expected to be substantially similar if the expression is substantially similar, this need not always be the case. Since ideas are not protectible, 17 U.S.C. §102(b) (1978), the conditioning of defendant's copying of such unprotectible elements is contrary to the statute. Judge Newman's view in *Warner Bros., Inc. v. ABC*, 720 F.2d 231, 239, 222 U.S.P.Q. 101, 108 (2d Cir. 1983), represents the correct approach: "The similarity to be assessed must concern the expression of ideas, not the ideas themselves * * *."

[34]445 F.2d 119, 121, 7 U.S.P.Q. 84, 86 (2d Cir. 1930), cited with approval in *Sid & Marty Krofft Television Prods. v. McDonald's Corp.*, 562 F.2d 1157, 1163, 196 U.S.P.Q. 97, 102 (9th Cir. 1977). See also *Warner Bros., Inc. v. ABC*, 720 F.2d 231, 242, 222 U.S.P.Q. 101, 110 (2d Cir. 1983) ("Stirring one's memory of a copyrighted character is not the same as appearing to be substantially similar to that character, and only the latter is infringement"); Chafee, *Reflections on the Law of Copyright*, 45 COLUM. L. REV. 503, 513–514 (1945).

[35]*Peter Pan Fabrics, Inc. v. Martin Weiner Corp.*, 274 F.2d 487, 489, 124 U.S.P.Q. 154, 155 (2d Cir. 1960). See also Judge Frank's helpful analysis in *Arnstein v. Porter*, 154 F.2d 464, 468, 68 U.S.P.Q. 288, 293 (2d Cir. 1946), *cert. denied*, 330 U.S. 851, 73 U.S.P.Q. 550 (1947).

The essence of infringement thus "lies in taking not a general theme but its particular expression through similarities of treatment, details, scenes, events and characterization"[36] as viewed by the ordinary viewer of the subject matter.[37] The level of similarity which will be substantial enough to constitute unlawful appropriation hence depends initially on what is protected in plaintiff's work and then on the impression made by the protected material upon the "ordinary observer" for whose primary benefit the work has been created.

In *Arnstein v. Porter*, Judge Frank furnished a rare policy justification for using the ordinary observer (or ordinary listener in the case of *Arnstein*) at the unlawful-appropriation stage of the infringement analysis:

> "The proper criterion on this issue is not an analytic or other comparison of the respective musical compositions as they appear on paper or in the judgment of trained musicians. The plaintiff's legally protected interest is not, as such, his reputation as a musician but his interest in the potential financial returns from his compositions which derive from the lay public's approbation of his efforts. The question, therefore, is whether defendant took from plaintiff's work so much of what is pleasing to the ears of lay listeners, who comprise the audience for whom such popular music is composed, that defendant wrongfully appropriated something which belongs to the plaintiff."[38]

---

[36] *Reyher v. Children's Television Workshop*, 533 F.2d 87, 91, 190 U.S.P.Q. 387, 390–391 (2d Cir.), *cert. denied*, 429 U.S. 980, 192 U.S.P.Q. 64 (1976), cited with approval in *O'Neill v. Dell Pub. Co.*, 630 F.2d 685, 687, 208 U.S.P.Q. 705, 707 (1st Cir. 1980). It has been held, however, that this principle does not go so far as to permit a finding of infringement for the copying of a particular writing style. *McMahon v. Prentice-Hall, Inc.*, 486 F. Supp. 1296, 205 U.S.P.Q. 819 (E.D. Mo. 1980).

[37] See *Atari, Inc. v. North American Philips Consumer Electronics Corp.*, 672 F.2d 607, 619, 214 U.S.P.Q. 33, 42–43 (7th Cir.), *cert. denied*, 459 U.S. 880 (1982): "Video games, unlike an artist's painting or even other audiovisual works, appeal to an audience that is fairly undiscriminating insofar as their concern about more subtle differences in artistic expression"; *Sid & Marty Krofft Television Prods. v. McDonald's Corp.*, 562 F.2d 1157, 196 U.S.P.Q. 97 (9th Cir. 1977) (audience of young children). Compare the differing views of the majority and the dissent as applied to a toy snowman in *Eden Toys, Inc. v. Marshall Field & Co.*, 675 F.2d 498, 216 U.S.P.Q. 560 (2d Cir. 1982), and note the reversal of the district judge in *Sheldon v. Metro-Goldwyn Pictures Corp.*, 7 F. Supp. 837, 842 (S.D.N.Y. 1934), *rev'd*, 81 F.2d 49, 28 U.S.P.Q. 330 (2d Cir.), *cert. denied*, 298 U.S. 669 (1936), who had declared: "I must, as the trier of facts, have a more Olympian viewpoint than the average playgoer."

Although survey evidence of consumer confusion is permitted in trademark cases, the courts have disapproved of such evidence in establishing substantial similarity in copyright cases. See *Warner Bros., Inc. v. ABC*, 720 F.2d 231, 244–245, 222 U.S.P.Q. 101, 112 (2d Cir. 1983) (Newman, J.); *Original Appalachian Artworks, Inc. v. Blue Box Factory (USA) Ltd.*, 577 F. Supp. 625, 630–631, 222 U.S.P.Q. 593, 598 (S.D.N.Y. 1983). Cf. *Ideal Toy Corp. v. Kenner Products Division*, 443 F. Supp. 291, 197 U.S.P.Q. 738 (S.D.N.Y. 1977) (survey evidence presented); *Carol Barnhart, Inc. v. Economy Cover Corp.*, 773 F.2d 411, 423, 228 U.S.P.Q. 385, 394 (2d Cir. 1985) (Newman J., dissenting) (suggesting that survey evidence "ought generally to be received" in "determining whether the design of [a utilitarian] object engenders a separable concept of a work of art").

[38] 154 F.2d 464, 473, 68 U.S.P.Q. 288, 296–297 (2d Cir. 1946), *cert. denied*, 330 U.S. 851, 73 U.S.P.Q. 550 (1947). Cf. Judge Clark's dissent, *id.* at 475–480, 68 U.S.P.Q. at 302, which labeled the majority's approach as "anti-intellectual" and "book-burning." See also Judge Clark's similar dissent in *Heim v. Universal Pictures Co.*, 154 F.2d 480, 68 U.S.P.Q. 303 (2d Cir. 1946). Recent decisions using the ordinary-observer test include *Warner Bros., Inc. v. ABC*, 523 F. Supp. 611, 211 U.S.P.Q. 51 (S.D.N.Y.), *aff'd*, 654 F.2d 204, 211 U.S.P.Q. 97 (2d Cir. 1981) (on motion for preliminary injunction); 530 F. Supp. 1187, 215 U.S.P.Q. 690 (S.D.N.Y. 1982), *aff'd* 720 F.2d 231, 222 U.S.P.Q. 101 (2d Cir. 1983) (on motion for summary judgment) ("Superman"); *Twentieth Century-Fox Film Corp. v. MCA, Inc.*, 715 F.2d 1327, 217 U.S.P.Q. 611 (9th Cir. 1983) ("Star Wars"); *Litchfield v. Spielberg*, 736 F.2d 1352, 222 U.S.P.Q. 965 (9th Cir. 1984), *cert. denied*, 470 U.S. ____ (1985) ("E.T."); *Walker v. Time-Life Films, Inc.*, 615

Since the test of substantial similarity is that of the impression made on the ordinary observer, it has been held that "dissection" of the works and expert testimony are not relevant to this determination, despite their relevance to the earlier issue of copying.[39]

Of course, it is possible to envisage instances where the work is intended for an audience that is quite sophisticated, e.g., computer programs directing the reentry of space aircraft.

Not infrequently defendants seek to escape liability by emphasizing the differences between their work and the copyrighted work.[40] While it is clear that trivial or insubstantial differences are insufficient to avoid infringement,[41] it has been held that "the more numerous the differences between two works the less likely it is that they will create the same aesthetic impact so that one will appear to have

---

F. Supp. 430, 227 U.S.P.Q. 698 (S.D.N.Y. 1985), *aff'd,* 784 F.2d 44, 228 U.S.P.Q. 505 (2d Cir. 1986) ("Fort Apache, The Bronx"); *Universal City Studios, Inc. v. Film Ventures Int'l, Inc.,* 543 F. Supp. 1134, 214 U.S.P.Q. 865 (C.D. Cal. 1982) ("Jaws"); *Alexander v. Haley,* 460 F. Supp. 40, 200 U.S.P.Q. 239 (S.D.N.Y. 1978) ("Roots"); *Jason v. Fonda,* 698 F.2d 966, 217 U.S.P.Q. 406 (9th Cir. 1983) (Vietnam War); *Davis v. United Artists, Inc.,* 547 F. Supp. 722 (S.D.N.Y. 1982) (same); *Marshall v. Yates,* 223 U.S.P.Q. 453 (C.D. Cal. 1983) ("Frances"); *Smith v. Weinstein,* 578 F. Supp. 1297, 222 U.S.P.Q. 381 (S.D.N.Y.), *aff'd,* 738 F.2d 410 (2d Cir. 1984) ("Stir Crazy"); *Overman v. Universal City Studios, Inc.,* 224 U.S.P.Q. 838 (C.D. Cal. 1984), *aff'd, unpublished opn.* (9th Cir. filed July 2, 1985) ("Bustin Loose"); *Meta-Film Associates v. MCA, Inc.,* 586 F. Supp. 1346, 222 U.S.P.Q. 211 (C.D. Cal. 1984) ("Animal House"); *Anderson v. Paramount Pictures Corp.,* 226 U.S.P.Q. 131 (C.D. Cal. 1985) ("Trading Places").

[39] *Arnstein v. Porter,* 154 F.2d 464, 468, 68 U.S.P.Q. 288, 293 (2d Cir. 1946), *cert. denied,* 330 U.S. 851, 73 U.S.P.Q. 550 (1947); *Funkhouser v. Loew's, Inc.,* 208 F.2d 185, 99 U.S.P.Q. 448 (8th Cir. 1954); *Sid & Marty Krofft Television Prods. v. McDonald's Corp.,* 562 F.2d 1157, 1164–1166, 196 U.S.P.Q. 97, 102 (9th Cir. 1977) (so-called "intrinsic test"); *Litchfield v. Spielberg,* 736 F.2d 1352, 1357, 222 U.S.P.Q. 965, 967–968 (9th Cir. 1984), *cert. denied,* 470 U.S. ___ (1985); *Berkic v. Crichton,* 761 F.2d 1289, 226 U.S.P.Q. 787 (9th Cir.), *cert. denied,* 474 U.S. ___ (1985). See especially *Kamar Int'l, Inc. v. Russ Berrie & Co.,* 657 F.2d 1059, 1062–1063, 216 U.S.P.Q. 376, 380 (9th Cir. 1981), which expressly criticized the trial court for dissecting the works at the second stage (unlawful appropriation) of the infringement analysis. Cf. *Walker v. Time-Life Films, Inc.,* 784 F.2d 44, 51–52, 228 U.S.P.Q. 505, 510–511 (2d Cir. 1986) (affidavit of literary expert permitted); *E.F. Johnson Co. v. Uniden Corp. of America,* 623 F. Supp. 1485, 1493, 228 U.S.P.Q. 891, 897 (D. Minn. 1985) (experts permitted in software infringement analyses).

The decisions in *Ideal Toy Corp. v. Fab Lu Ltd.,* 360 F.2d 1021, 149 U.S.P.Q. 800 (2d Cir. 1966), *on remand,* 261 F. Supp. 238, 152 U.S.P.Q. 500 (S.D.N.Y. 1966), and *Ideal Toy Corp. v. Kenner Products Division,* 443 F. Supp. 291, 303 n. 11, 197 U.S.P.Q. 738, 748 n. 11 (S.D.N.Y. 1977), erroneously collapsed the two-step analysis of *Arnstein v. Porter* (i.e., establishing copying and then establishing unlawful appropriation) into a "single lay observer test for substantial similarity."

[40] In *Original Appalachian Artworks, Inc. v. Toy Loft, Inc.,* 684 F.2d 821, 829, 215 U.S.P.Q. 745, 751–752 (11th Cir. 1982), defendant argued that its works had as much originality as plaintiff's and "therefore cannot have infringed [plaintiff's] copyrights." The court correctly rejected the argument as "confus[ing] the standard of originality and substantial similarity."

[41] *Peter Pan Fabrics, Inc. v. Martin Weiner Corp.,* 274 F.2d 487, 489, 124 U.S.P.Q. 154, 155 (2d Cir. 1960); *Sheldon v. Metro-Goldwyn Pictures Corp.,* 81 F.2d 49, 56, 28 U.S.P.Q. 330, 337 (2d Cir.), *cert. denied,* 298 U.S. 669 (1936) (Learned Hand, J.) ("no plagiarist can excuse the wrong by showing how much of his work he did not pirate") (cited with approval in *Harper & Row, Pub., Inc. v. Nation Enters.,* 471 U.S. ___, ___, 225 U.S.P.Q. 1073, 1083 (1985)); *Concord Fabrics, Inc. v. Marcus Bros. Textile Corp.,* 409 F.2d 1315, 1316, 161 U.S.P.Q. 3 (2d Cir. 1969); *Tennessee Fabricating Co. v. Moultrie Mfg. Co.,* 421 F.2d 279, 164 U.S.P.Q. 481 (5th Cir.), *cert. denied,* 398 U.S. 928, 165 U.S.P.Q. 609 (1970); *Puddu v. Buonamici Statuary, Inc.,* 450 F.2d 401, 402, 171 U.S.P.Q. 709, 711 (2d Cir. 1971); *Soptra Fabrics Corp. v. Stafford Knitting Mills, Inc.,* 490 F.2d 1092, 1093, 180 U.S.P.Q. 545, 546 (2d Cir. 1974); *Novelty Textile Mills, Inc. v. Joan Fabrics Corp.,* 558 F.2d 1090, 1093 n. 4, 195 U.S.P.Q. 1, 3–4 n. 4 (2d Cir. 1977); *Durham Indus., Inc. v. Tomy Corp.,* 630 F.2d 905, 208 U.S.P.Q. 10 (2d Cir. 1980); *Atari, Inc. v. North American Philips Consumer Electronics Corp.,* 672 F.2d 607, 618, 214 U.S.P.Q. 33, 43 (7th Cir.), *cert. denied,* 459 U.S. 880 (1982).

been appropriated from the other";[42] and "[s]ignificant dissimilarities between two works * * * inevitably lessen the similarity that would exist between the total perceptions of the two works."[43]

Nevertheless, the *"sine qua non* of the ordinary observer test * * * is the overall similarities rather than the minute differences between the two works."[44] This in turn has led to disapproval of lists of similarities (and dissimilarities) as "inherently subjective and unreliable,"[45] and to adoption of what has become known as the "total concept and feel" test, in which the trier of fact determines whether the mood evoked by the total combination of elements in the allegedly infringing work is substantially similar to that of the copyrighted work.[46]

---

[42]*Durham Indus., Inc. v. Tomy Corp.*, 630 F.2d 905, 913, 208 U.S.P.Q. 10, 18 (2d Cir. 1980); *Herbert Rosenthal Jewelry Corp. v. Honora Jewelry Co.*, 509 F.2d 64, 65, 184 U.S.P.Q. 264, 264–265 (2d Cir. 1974). Where the defendant intentionally makes sufficient changes in his work to render it not substantially similar to plaintiff's, no infringement may be found. *Warner Bros., Inc. v. ABC*, 654 F.2d 204, 211, 211 U.S.P.Q. 97, 102 (2d Cir. 1981); 720 F.2d 231, 241, 222 U.S.P.Q. 101, 109 (2d Cir. 1983); *Eden Toys, Inc. v. Marshall Field & Co.*, 675 F.2d 498, 501, 216 U.S.P.Q. 560, 562 (2d Cir. 1982); *Durham Indus., Inc. v. Tomy Corp.*, 630 F.2d 905, 913 & *id.* at n. 11, 208 U.S.P.Q. 10, 18 n. 11 (2d Cir. 1980); *Perma Greetings, Inc. v. Russ Berrie & Co.*, 598 F. Supp. 445, 223 U.S.P.Q. 670 (E.D. Mo. 1984). Cf. *Arc v. S.S. Sarna, Inc.*, 621 F. Supp. 916, 923 n. 9, 229 U.S.P.Q. 25, 30 n. 9 (E.D.N.Y. 1985), which, while noting this principle, found defendants had not made sufficient changes to avoid infringement.

[43]*Warner Bros., Inc. v. ABC*, 720 F.2d 231, 241, 222 U.S.P.Q. 101, 109 (2d Cir. 1983).

[44]*Atari, Inc. v. North American Philips Consumer Corp.*, 672 F.2d 607, 618, 214 U.S.P.Q. 33, 42 (7th Cir.), *cert. denied*, 459 U.S. 880 (1982) (reversing district court that focused on dissimilarities); *Perma Greetings, Inc. v. Russ Berrie & Co.*, 598 F. Supp. 445, 449, 223 U.S.P.Q. 670, 673 (E.D. Mo. 1984); *Original Appalachian Artworks, Inc. v. Blue Box Factory (USA) Ltd.*, 577 F. Supp. 625, 631, 222 U.S.P.Q. 593, 598 (S.D.N.Y. 1983) (ordinary observer would not be disposed to overlook the dissimilarities); *Warner Bros., Inc. v. ABC*, 654 F.2d 204, 209–211, 211 U.S.P.Q. 97, 100–102 (2d Cir. 1981) ("Judge Motley's opinion indicates that she properly focused upon 'the similarities not the differences'"); *Malden Mills, Inc. v. Regency Mills, Inc.*, 626 F.2d 1112, 207 U.S.P.Q. 87 (2d Cir. 1980). See also *Animal Fair, Inc. v. Amfesco Indus., Inc.*, 620 F. Supp. 175, 188, 227 U.S.P.Q. 817, 826 (D. Minn. 1985) (minor differences between two novelty slippers in the shape of a bear's foot nevertheless not enough to negate "same overall impression to the casual observer"). See also the extensive analysis in *Arc v. S.S. Sarna, Inc.*, 621 F. Supp. 916, 229 U.S.P.Q. 25 (E.D.N.Y. 1985).

[45]*Litchfield v. Spielberg*, 736 F.2d 1352, 1356, 222 U.S.P.Q. 965, 967 (9th Cir. 1984), *cert. denied*, 470 U.S. ____ (1985). But cf. *Twentieth Century-Fox Film Corp. v. MCA, Inc.*, 715 F.2d 1327, 1329 n. 5, 217 U.S.P.Q. 611, 613 n. 5 (9th Cir. 1983), which "[f]or illustrative purposes only" listed 13 alleged similarities in reversing the trial court's grant of summary judgment of no infringement. See also *Sanford v. CBS, Inc.*, 225 U.S.P.Q. 136, 139 (N.D. Ill. 1984) ("[t]he cases do emphasize that the trier of fact should focus on the overall similarities between the works rather than on minute differences between them, but they do not suggest that the differences should be completely disregarded"); *Atari, Inc. v. Amusement World*, 547 F. Supp. 222, 215 U.S.P.Q. 929 (D. Md. 1981).

[46]*Roth Greeting Cards v. United Card Co.*, 429 F.2d 1106, 1109, 166 U.S.P.Q. 291, 294 (9th Cir. 1970); *Sid & Marty Krofft Television Prods. v. McDonald's Corp.*, 562 F.2d 1157, 1167, 196 U.S.P.Q. 97, 105 (9th Cir. 1977); *Berkic v. Crichton*, 761 F.2d 1289, 226 U.S.P.Q. 787 (9th Cir.), *cert. denied*, 474 U.S. ____ (1985). The total-concept-and-feel test was adopted by the Second Circuit in *Reyher v. Children's Television Workshop*, 533 F.2d 87, 91, 190 U.S.P.Q. 387, 390 (2d Cir.), *cert. denied*, 429 U.S. 980, 192 U.S.P.Q. 64 (1976); *Eden Toys, Inc. v. Marshall Field & Co.*, 675 F.2d 498, 500, 216 U.S.P.Q. 560, 562 (2d Cir. 1982); *Warner Bros., Inc. v. ABC*, 720 F.2d 231, 241, 222 U.S.P.Q. 101, 108–109 (2d Cir. 1983); *American Greetings Corp. v. Easter Unlimited, Inc.*, 579 F. Supp. 607, 615, 221 U.S.P.Q. 875, 881 (S.D.N.Y. 1983) (total concept and feel of plush toys different; but see subsequent entry of consent judgment, COPR. L. REP. ¶25,715 (S.D.N.Y. 1984)) and by the Seventh Circuit in *Atari, Inc. v. North American Philips Consumer Electronics Corp.*, 672 F.2d 607, 619–620, 214 U.S.P.Q. 33, 42–43 (7th Cir.), *cert. denied*, 459 U.S. 880 (1982). As a practical matter, it may be questioned whether the total-concept-and-feel test does not result in the trier of fact erroneously considering nonprotectible material in the infringement analysis. In *Cooling Systems & Flexibles, Inc. v. Stuart Radiator*,

In view of the necessarily subjective nature of infringement determinations, the philosophy of a reviewing court can be important. At times, appellate courts have left intact trial court findings not "clearly erroneous" under Rule 52 of the Federal Rules of Civil Procedure, a result seemingly dictated by the Supreme Court's decision in *Pullman-Standard v. Swint.*[47] At other times, appellate courts have reviewed the works *de novo* "where * * * the determination of similarity rests solely on a comparison of the works in issue rather than on the credibility of witnesses or other evidence only for the fact finder * * *."[48]

## Copying Versus Independent Creation; Subconscious Copying

Where it can be established that the work was independently created, substantial or even exact identity between the works will not result in infringement, for, unlike patent law, copyright law does not reach one who has independently arrived at the same result or even produced an identical work.[49] Although a plaintiff bears the burden

---

*Inc.*, 777 F.2d 485, 493, 228 U.S.P.Q. 275, 282 (9th Cir. 1985), the Ninth Circuit correctly cautioned against such an approach, writing: "What is important is not whether there is substantial similarity in the total concept and feel of the works but whether the very small protectible expression in [plaintiff's] catalog is substantially similar to the equivalent portions of [defendant's] catalog."

The taking may be by way of literal fragments or the pattern of the work. See 3 NIMMER ON COPYRIGHT §§13.03[A][1], [2] (discussing "nonliteral similarity" and "fragmented literal similarity"). In *Werlin v. Reader's Digest Ass'n*, 528 F. Supp. 451, 462, 213 U.S.P.Q. 1041, 1050 (S.D.N.Y. 1981), and *Walker v. Time-Life Films, Inc.*, 615 F. Supp. 430, 436, 227 U.S.P.Q. 698, 701 (S.D.N.Y. 1985), *aff'd*, 784 F.2d 44, 228 U.S.P.Q. 505 (2d Cir. 1986), this latter form of similarity was termed infringing the work's "fundamental essence."

A related question is whether plaintiff may demonstrate substantial similarity by comparing widely scattered passages. Although earlier decisions had held to the contrary, *McMahon v. Prentice-Hall, Inc.*, 486 F. Supp. 1296, 205 U.S.P.Q. 819 (E.D. Mo. 1980); *Funkhouser v. Loew's Inc.*, 208 F.2d 185, 188, 99 U.S.P.Q. 448, 450 (8th Cir. 1953); *Alexander v. Haley*, 460 F. Supp. 40, 200 U.S.P.Q. 239 (S.D.N.Y. 1978), the Supreme Court's decision in *Harper & Row, Pub., Inc. v. Nation Enters.*, 471 U.S. ___, 225 U.S.P.Q. 1073 (1985), which found infringement in defendant's verbatim copying of 300 words from disparate parts of a 200,000-word unpublished manuscript, would appear to be definitive on the issue.

[47]456 U.S. 273 (1982). See *Cooling Systems & Flexibles, Inc. v. Stuart Radiator, Inc.*, *supra* note 46, 777 F.2d at 492–493, 228 U.S.P.Q. at 281–282, and cases cited therein; *Original Appalachian Artworks, Inc. v. Toy Loft, Inc.*, 684 F.2d 821, 825 n. 4, 215 U.S.P.Q. 745, 748–749 n. 4 (11th Cir. 1982) (noting *Pullman-Standard*). But compare subsequent decision in *Sherry Mfg. Co. v. Towel King Co.*, 753 F.2d 1565, 1569 n. 6, 225 U.S.P.Q. 1005, 1008 n. 6 (11th Cir. 1985), which distinguished *Original Appalachian Artworks* as follows: "In cases such as this one, however, where the appellate court has the opportunity to view for itself the same tangible exhibits considered by the trial court, the rationale for applying the clearly erroneous standard disappears"; and *Franklin Mint Corp. v. National Wildlife Art Exchange, Inc.*, 575 F.2d 62, 66–67, 197 U.S.P.Q. 721, 725 (3d Cir. 1978), which limited its earlier decision in *Universal Athletic Sales Co. v. Salkeld*, 511 F.2d 904, 185 U.S.P.Q. 76 (3d Cir. 1975) (reviewing substantial similarity *de novo*), to situations where copying had been clearly established, or where there was no need for credibility determinations with respect to copying.

[48]*Durham Indus., Inc. v. Tomy Corp.*, 630 F.2d 905, 918, 208 U.S.P.Q. 10, 17 (2d Cir. 1980) (quoting *Reyher v. Children's Television Workshop*, 553 F.2d 87, 90, 190 U.S.P.Q. 387, 390 (2d Cir.), *cert. denied*, 429 U.S. 980, 192 U.S.P.Q. 64 (1976)). Accord *Malden Mills, Inc. v. Regency Mills, Inc.*, 626 F.2d 1112, 1113, 207 U.S.P.Q. 87, 88 (2d Cir. 1980); *Mount v. Viking Press, Inc.*, 204 U.S.P.Q. 353, 354 (2d Cir. 1979); *Concord Fabrics, Inc. v. Marcus Bros. Textile Corp.*, 409 F.2d 1315, 1317, 161 U.S.P.Q. 3 (2d Cir. 1969).

[49]*Fred Fisher Music Co. v. Dillingham*, 298 F. 145 (S.D.N.Y. 1924) (Learned Hand, J.); *Arnstein v. Edward B. Marks Music Corp.*, 82 F.2d 275, 28 U.S.P.Q. 426 (2d Cir. 1936); *Acuff-Rose Pub., Inc. v. Daniels*, Civ. No. 80-3729-N (M.D. Tenn. 1982) (independent-creation defense sustained even though plaintiff proved both access and strong similarity). Proof that defendant created his work before plaintiff disclosed his is persuasive proof of independent creation. *Her-*

of proving unlawful appropriation, where this is established the burden of proving independent creation shifts to defendant. This burden, like plaintiff's initial burden, is not one of "strong, convincing, and persuasive evidence," but rather the usual burden in civil cases, a preponderance of the evidence.[50]

The question arises, however, of how to determine what constitutes "independent creation." Must the defendant eschew all contact with the original work? This course was deemed necessary in *In Re Certain Personal Computers*, where the U.S. International Trade Commission held that "independent creation means creation without reference to the copyrighted work * * *."[51]

Claims of independent creation have been made where the copier earnestly contended that he or she did not consciously copy the work. Intent is not, however, an element of infringement,[52] although its presence[53] or absence[54] may affect the available remedies and may be

---

*bert v. Wicklund*, 744 F.2d 218 (1st Cir. 1984); *Pellegrino v. American Greetings Corp.*, 592 F. Supp. 459, 461–462, 224 U.S.P.Q. 181, 183 (S.D.N.Y. 1984); *Delman Fabrics, Inc. v. Holland Fabrics, Inc.*, COPR. L. REP. ¶25,663 (S.D.N.Y. 1984); 228 U.S.P.Q. 596 (S.D.N.Y. 1985) (defense rejected).

[50] *John L. Perry Studio, Inc. v. Wernick*, 597 F.2d 1308, 1310, 202 U.S.P.Q. 471, 472 (9th Cir. 1979). See also *Selle v. Gibb*, 741 F.2d 896, 223 U.S.P.Q. 195 (7th Cir. 1984); *Arc v. S.S. Sarna, Inc.*, 621 F. Supp. 916, 923, 229 U.S.P.Q. 25, 31 (E.D.N.Y. 1985); *American Greetings Corp. v. Easter Unlimited, Inc.*, 579 F. Supp. 607, 613, 221 U.S.P.Q. 875, 880 (S.D.N.Y. 1983); COPR. L. REP. ¶25,715 (S.D.N.Y. 1984) (consent judgment); *Kamar Int'l, Inc. v. Russ Berrie & Co.*, 657 F.2d 1059, 1062, 216 U.S.P.Q. 376, 379 (9th Cir. 1981); *Knickerbocker Toy Co. v. Genie Toys, Inc.*, 491 F. Supp. 526, 529, 211 U.S.P.Q. 461, 463 (E.D. Mo. 1980); *United Artists Corp. v. Ford Motor Co.*, 483 F. Supp. 89, 209 U.S.P.Q. 227 (S.D.N.Y. 1980); *Professional Systems & Supplies, Inc. v. Databank Supplies & Equipment Co.*, 202 U.S.P.Q. 693, 696 (W.D. Okla. 1979); *Novelty Textile Mills, Inc. v. Joan Fabrics Corp.*, 558 F.2d 1090, 1092 n. 2, 195 U.S.P.Q. 1, 3 n. 2 (2d Cir. 1977); *Sheldon v. Metro-Goldwyn Pictures Corp.*, 81 F.2d 49, 54, 28 U.S.P.Q. 330, 335–336 (2d Cir.), *cert. denied*, 298 U.S. 669 (1936). Evidence of independent creation need not be presented where plantiff fails to establish a prima facie case of infringement. *Eden Toys, Inc. v. Marshall Field & Co.*, 675 F.2d 498, 216 U.S.P.Q. 560 (2d Cir. 1982).

It has been held that "defendants' past record of copyright infringement indicates a practice of copying despite claims of independent creation. * * * This past record when considered with the remarkable similarity of the designs leads me to believe that 'no explanation other than copying is reasonably possible.'" *Pret-A-Printee, Ltd. v. Allton Knitting Mills, Inc.*, 218 U.S.P.Q. 150, 152 (S.D.N.Y. 1982) (quoting *Novelty Textile Mills, Inc. v. Joan Fabrics Corp.*, 558 F.2d 1090, 1092 n. 2, 195 U.S.P.Q. 1, 3 n. 2 (2d Cir. 1977)). See also *Roth Greeting Cards v. United Card Co.*, 429 F.2d 1106, 166 U.S.P.Q. 291 (9th Cir. 1970). Cf. *Greff Fabrics, Inc. v. Spectrum Fabrics Corp.*, 217 U.S.P.Q. 498 (S.D.N.Y. 1981); *Herbert Rosenthal Jewelry Corp. v. Honora Jewelry Co.*, 378 F. Supp. 485, 183 U.S.P.Q. 97 (S.D.N.Y.), *aff'd*, 509 F.2d 64, 184 U.S.P.Q. 264 (2d Cir. 1974).

[51] *In re Certain Personal Computers and Components*, Inv. No. 337-TA-140 (order filed March 9, 1984), opinion at 35, *reprinted* in COPR. L. REP. ¶25,651. See also *Miller v. Universal City Studios, Inc.*, 650 F.2d 1365, 1375, 212 U.S.P.Q. 345, 353 (5th Cir. 1981) (defendant can rebut prima facie showing of infringement by demonstrating that his work was "independently created without reference to the [copyrighted] work"). Cf. *United Artists Corp. v. Ford Motor Co.*, 483 F. Supp. 89, 209 U.S.P.Q. 227 (S.D.N.Y. 1980); *Mazer v. Stein*, 347 U.S. 201, 218, 100 U.S.P.Q. 325, 333 (1954).

Defendants frequently argue that the similarities between the works are also present in other works. It has been held, however, that "design aspects of another work are relevant * * * only if plaintiff or defendant copied from the work." *Animal Fair, Inc.v. Amfesco Indus., Inc.*, 620 F. Supp. 175, 188–189 n. 18, 227 U.S.P.Q. 817, 826 n. 18 (D. Minn. 1985).

[52] *ABKCO Music, Inc. v. Harrisongs, Ltd.*, 722 F.2d 988, 998, 221 U.S.P.Q. 490, 498 (2d Cir. 1983) (citing *Buck v. Jewell-LaSalle Realty Co.*, 283 U.S. 191, 198, 9 U.S.P.Q. 17, 18–19 (1931)).

[53] See 17 U.S.C. §504(c)(2) (1978) (statutory damages may be increased to $50,000 where infringement committed willfully).

[54] *Ibid.* (statutory damages may be reduced to $100 where infringer was not aware of and had no reason to believe his or her acts constituted infringement). See generally Latman & Tigar, *Liability of Innocent Infringers of Copyright*, COPYRIGHT OFFICE STUDY No. 25, 86th Cong., 2d Sess. (Comm. Print 1960) (surveying prior law).

an important factor in considering the weight of circumstantial evidence.[55]

The copying may be the result of subconscious memory derived from hearing, seeing, or reading the copyrighted work at some time in the past, and yet still be infringement.[56] Judge Learned Hand confronted this issue as a district judge[57] and again as a court of appeals judge,[58] writing in his inimitable style:

> "[I]n concluding as we do that the defendants used the play *pro tanto*, we need not charge their witnesses with perjury. With so many sources before them they might quite honestly forget what they took; nobody knows the origin of his inventions; memory and fancy merge even in adults; yet unconscious plagiarism is actionable quite as much as deliberate."[59]

Judge Hand's position has been followed in recent cases,[60] and in the face of a charge that permitting subconscious copying to be actionable brought the "law of copyright improperly close to patent law, which imposes a requirement of novelty."[61]

### Copying in a Different Medium

"That an infringing copy may be produced in a medium different than that of the protected work is not, in itself a bar to recovery * * *."[62] Common examples include a play or novel reproduced in substantial part in a motion picture,[63] and two-dimensional pictorial or graphic works reproduced in three-dimensional sculptural form.[64] The reverse, i.e., a two-dimensional pictorial representation of a three-dimensional sculptural work, may also result in infringement,[65]

---

[55] *Harold Lloyd Corp. v. Witwer*, 65 F.2d 1 (9th Cir. 1933).

[56] *Wihtol v. Wells*, 231 F.2d 550, 109 U.S.P.Q. 200 (7th Cir. 1956).

[57] *Fred Fisher Music Co. v. Dillingham*, 298 F. 145 (S.D.N.Y. 1924).

[58] *Sheldon v. Metro-Goldwyn Pictures Corp.*, 81 F.2d 49, 28 U.S.P.Q. 330 (2d Cir.), *cert. denied*, 298 U.S. 669 (1936).

[59] *Id.* at 54, 28 U.S.P.Q. at 335–336.

[60] *ABKCO Music, Inc. v. Harrisongs, Ltd.*, 722 F.2d 988, 221 U.S.P.Q. 490 (2d Cir. 1983); *Northern Music Corp. v. Pacemaker Music Co.*, 146 U.S.P.Q. 358 (S.D.N.Y. 1965). See also cases cited in note 49, *supra*.

[61] *ABKCO Music, Inc. v. Harrisongs, Ltd.*, *supra* note 60, 722 F.2d at 998, 221 U.S.P.Q. at 498.

[62] *Walker v. University Books, Inc.*, 602 F.2d 859, 864, 202 U.S.P.Q. 793, 797 (9th Cir. 1979). See also *Midway Mfg. Co. v. Bandai-America, Inc.*, 546 F. Supp. 125, 139, 216 U.S.P.Q. 812, 820–821 (D.N.J. 1982) ("It is clear that there can be substantial similarity and copyright infringement between works in different media"). It has been held that "[w]here defendant's work is adapted for use in a medium different than that of plaintiff's, the test for infringement remains the same." *Twentieth Century-Fox Film Corp. v. MCA, Inc.*, 715 F.2d 1327, 1329 n. 4, 217 U.S.P.Q. 611, 612 n. 4 (9th Cir. 1983).

[63] *Walco Products, Inc. v. Kittay & Blitz, Inc.*, 354 F. Supp. 121, 175 U.S.P.Q. 471 (S.D.N.Y. 1972).

[64] *Ideal Toy Corp. v. Kenner Products Division*, 443 F. Supp. 291, 197 U.S.P.Q. 738 (S.D.N.Y. 1977); *Fleischer Studios, Inc. v. Ralph A. Freundlich, Inc.*, 73 F.2d 276, 23 U.S.P.Q. 295 (2d Cir. 1934); *King Features Syndicate, Inc. v. Fleischer*, 299 F. 533 (2d Cir. 1924).

[65] *Ronald Litoff, Ltd. v. American Express Co.*, 621 F. Supp. 981, 228 U.S.P.Q. 739 (S.D.N.Y. 1985) (photograph of jewelry); *Original Appalachian Artworks, Inc. v. Cradle Creations, Inc.*, 223 U.S.P.Q. 80 (N.D. Ga. 1982); *Tennessee Fabricating Co. v. Moultrie Mfg. Co.*, 421 F.2d 279, 164 U.S.P.Q. 481 (5th Cir.), *cert. denied*, 398 U.S. 928, 165 U.S.P.Q. 609 (1970).

as may copying a two-dimensional work in one medium to a different two-dimensional medium.[66]

An interesting application of this principle as it pertains to characters may be seen in *DC Comics, Inc. v. Unlimited Monkey Business, Inc.*,[67] where the Superman and Wonder Woman characters were found infringed by defendant's "Super Stud" and "Wonder Wench" singing telegrams. As with copying in the same medium, the central question to be reached once the copyrighted work has been found to have been copied into a different medium is whether there is copying and "substantial similarity" between the works at issue.

## Compulsory License for Making and Distributing Phonorecords of Nondramatic Musical Works

The right to reproduce a dramatic or other literary work (e.g., a play—including a musical—speech, or poem) in phonorecords is as complete as the right to reproduce such works in copies. However, Section 115[68] of the 1976 Act provides that in the case of "nondramatic musical works, the exclusive rights provided by clauses (1) and (3) of Section 106, to make and to distribute phonorecords of such works, are subject to compulsory licensing under the conditions specified by this section." This limitation, by reason of the definition of "phonorecords," is inapplicable to fixed sounds "accompanying a motion picture or other audiovisual work."[69]

The concept of such a compulsory license was introduced into our copyright law in 1909. The Supreme Court had already decided in *White-Smith Music Publishing Co. v. Apollo Co.*[70] that piano rolls (and by analogy phonograph records and the like) did not embody a system of notation that could be read and hence were not "copies" of the musical composition within the meaning of the law, but constituted merely parts of devices for mechanically performing the music. The right of public performance already existed under the Act of

---

[66]See *Halbersham Plantation Corp. v. Country Concepts*, 209 U.S.P.Q. 711 (N.D. Ga. 1980); *Eden Toys, Inc. v. Floralee Undergarment Co.*, 697 F.2d 27, 217 U.S.P.Q. 201 (2d Cir. 1982); *Time, Inc. v. Bernard Geis Associates*, 293 F. Supp. 130, 144, 159 U.S.P.Q. 663, 673–674 (S.D.N.Y. 1968) (charcoal renderings of photographs).

[67]598 F. Supp. 110, 224 U.S.P.Q. 437 (N.D. Ga. 1984). See also *Atari, Inc. v. North American Philips Consumer Electronics Corp.*, 672 F.2d 607, 214 U.S.P.Q. 33 (7th Cir.), cert. denied, 459 U.S. 880 (1982) (PAC-MAN character); *West Pub. Co. v. Mead Data Central, Inc.*, 616 F. Supp. 1571, 227 U.S.P.Q. 631 (D. Minn. 1985) (copying judicial opinions in bound volumes into computer format); *Rand McNally & Co. v. Fleet Mgt. Systems, Inc.*, 600 F. Supp. 933, 223 U.S.P.Q. 1200 (N.D. Ill. 1984) (copying printed compilation into computer data base); *Williams v. Arndt*, 227 U.S.P.Q. 615 (D. Mass. 1985) (computer program held to be infringement of printed futures trading manual). In *Horgan v. MacMillan, Inc.*, 789 F.2d 157, ____, ____, 229 U.S.P.Q. 684, 686, 688 (2d Cir. 1986), the Second Circuit reversed a district court that held photographs of choreography noninfringing because "they do not, nor do they intend to, take or use the underlying choreography," holding "[w]hen the allegedly infringing material is in a different medium, as it is here, recreation of the original infringing material is unlikely if not impossible, but that is not a defense to infringement."

[68]17 U.S.C. §115 (1978).

[69]17 U.S.C. §101 (1978) (definition of "phonorecords").

[70]209 U.S. 1 (1908).

1897, and this undoubtedly included such *performance* by mechanical instruments. It was the right to *make* such devices that was lacking, and so Congress undertook to grant such right, but without intending to extend the right of copyright to the mechanical devices themselves.[71]

Because of what seemed at the time a well-grounded fear of monopolistic control of music for recording purposes, Congress qualified the right of mechanical control by providing in Subsection (e) of Section 1 that if the copyright proprietor himself used or sanctioned the use of his composition in this way, any other person was free to do so upon paying a royalty of two cents for each part (each roll or record) manufactured. A corresponding infringement provision was inserted in Section 101(e). Provisions were made for the filing of notices by the compulsory licensor (notice of use) and licensee (notice of intention to use).

These verbose and internally inconsistent provisions left many questions unanswered. However, the remarkable adjustment of the music industry to this unique provision perhaps contributed to its retention in 1976, but with changes designed to balance anew the competing interests and to answer some of the unanswered questions.

The "conditions specified by" Section 115 of the 1976 Act for enjoyment of the compulsory license may be summarized as follows:

(1) The compulsory license becomes available when phonorecords have been distributed to the public in the United States by authority of the copyright owner (§115(a)(1)).

This clarifies the status of the ubiquitous "demo," or demonstration record or tape, used to interest potential users in a work. The making of such a recording by a proprietor seemed to be within the literal language of Section 1(e) of the 1909 law; in other words, it was an authorized recording which theoretically should have triggered the compulsory license provision. But the industry never treated it as such, and the matter is put to rest by the requirement in the 1976 law of a public distribution authorized by the proprietor before the compulsory license provision becomes applicable. The requirement of a distribution in the United States is consistent with a decision finding such a limitation implicit in the 1909 Act.[72]

(2) A compulsory license is available only to someone primarily intending to distribute records to the public for private use, i.e., the usual record company, and not a producer for jukebox or background music use.

(3) A compulsory license is not available for use of the copyrighted musical work by means of duplicating, *without authorization*, someone else's sound recording of such work. This intersection of rights in the two kinds of works embodied in a record had caused a

---

[71]H.R. Rep. No. 2222, 60th Cong., 2d Sess. 9 (1909).
[72]*Beechwood Music Corp. v. Vee Jay Records, Inc.*, 328 F.2d 728, 140 U.S.P.Q. 499 (2d Cir. 1964).

good deal of litigation under the 1909 law, all of which ultimately resulted in the position adopted in this section: A compulsory license can be used only to produce an independent sound recording of a musical work and not to appropriate a third person's efforts in a recorded performance of the work without that person's permission.[73]

(4) The compulsory license obtained under Section 115 is not transferable.[74]

(5) A compulsory licensee's privilege to arrange the music for purposes of the recorded performance is constructed in Section 115(a)(2) as follows:

> "A compulsory license includes the privilege of making a musical arrangement of the work to the extent necessary to conform it to the style or manner of interpretation of the performance involved, but the arrangement shall not change the basic melody or fundamental character of the work, and shall not be subject to protection as a derivative work under this title, except with the express consent of the copyright owner."

This carries forward the hint given under the earlier law of some latitude for a compulsory licensee in preparing a recorded arrangement, *Edward B. Marks Music Corp. v. Foullon,*[75] but makes explicit a limitation against distortion, which is suggestive of moral right. Without the express denial of derivative-work protection, a compulsory licensee could qualify for protection under Section 103, since he is not using the musical work "unlawfully."[76]

(6) The compulsory licensee must serve a "Notice of Intention" on the copyright owner (or the Copyright Office, if its records fail to identify the owner or include his or her address) with respect to each nondramatic musical work embodied in or intended to be embodied in the phonorecord "before or within thirty days after making, and before distributing any phonorecords of the work."[77] Failure to do so forfeits the opportunity of securing a compulsory license and renders

---

[73]See, e.g., *United States v. Hellman,* 614 F.2d 1133, 205 U.S.P.Q. 201 (7th Cir. 1980); *Heilman v. Bell,* 583 F.2d 373, 199 U.S.P.Q. 321 (7th Cir. 1978), *cert. denied,* 440 U.S. 959, 201 U.S.P.Q. 960 (1979); *Fame Pub. Co. v. Alabama Custom Tape, Inc.,* 507 F.2d 667, 184 U.S.P.Q. 577 (5th Cir. 1975); *Edward B. Marks Music Corp. v. Colorado Magnetics, Inc.,* 497 F.2d 285, 181 U.S.P.Q. 129 (10th Cir.) (en banc), *cert. denied,* 419 U.S. 1120, 184 U.S.P.Q. 385 (1974); *Jondora Music Pub. Co. v. Melody Recordings, Inc.,* 506 F.2d 392, 184 U.S.P.Q. 326 (3d Cir. 1974), *cert. denied,* 421 U.S. 1012, 186 U.S.P.Q. 73 (1975); *Duchess Music Corp. v. Stern,* 458 F.2d 1305, 173 U.S.P.Q. 278 (9th Cir.), *cert. denied sub nom. Rosner v. Duchess Music Corp.,* 409 U.S. 847, 175 U.S.P.Q. 385 (1972).

[74]*Harris v. Emus Records Corp.,* 734 F.2d 1329, 222 U.S.P.Q. 466 (9th Cir. 1984).

[75]*Edward B. Marks Music Corp. v. Foullon,* 79 F. Supp. 664, 77 U.S.P.Q. 502 (S.D.N.Y. 1948), *aff'd,* 171 F.2d 905, 80 U.S.P.Q. 56 (2d Cir. 1949).

[76]H.R. REP. No. 94-1476, 94th Cong., 2d Sess. 58 (1976); S. REP. No. 94-473, 94th Cong., 1st Sess. 55 (1975).

[77]17 U.S.C. §115(b) (1978); 37 C.F.R. §201.18. The Copyright Office has also issued detailed regulations concerning the filing of Statements of Account accompanying §115 royalty payments. 37 C.F.R. §201.19. See generally Rosenlund, *Compulsory Licensing of Musical Compositions for Phonorecords Under the Copyright Act of 1976,* 30 HASTINGS L.J. 683 (1979). In practice, the compulsory-license rate frequently serves as a negotiating ceiling for licenses granted by the Harry Fox Agency, which serves as the agent for a large number of music publishers and copyright owners in granting not only mechanical rights but also synchronization rights for the reproduction of musical works in motion pictures and other audiovisual works— rights not subject to the §115 compulsory license.

the making and distribution of phonorecords actionable as acts of infringement fully subject to the remedies therefor (§115(b)(2)).

This provision cuts with a much sharper knife than the 1909 law. The required filing must be within the defined limits, i.e., within 30 days of the making of a recording *and* before any distribution; a late filing is presumably ineffectual.

The imposition of full remedies in the absence of compliance with the compulsory license provision is the final step in a long process. The 1909 law originally had special limitations on infringement of musical copyrights by mechanical reproduction. (Of course, prior to the proprietor's authorized recording, his or her rights against others were complete.) This essentially amounted to a discretionary trebling of the two-cent royalty, which was construed to mean six cents over and above the two-cent royalty.[78] Nevertheless, the insufficiency of this remedy led to a modification in 1971 whereby "the unauthorized manufacture, use or sale of such interchangeable parts (i.e., recordings) shall constitute an infringement of the copyrighted work rendering the infringer liable in accordance with all provisions of this title dealing with infringements of copyright."[79]

Even this amendment left open the argument that a compulsory licensee who insufficiently complied with the statutory provisions was nevertheless not engaging in "the unauthorized manufacture, use or sale of the work." This possible gap in the 1909 fabric is filled by Section 115(b)(2) and Section 115(c)(4) of the 1976 Act, the latter providing full infringement remedies against a compulsory licensee who, after a 30-day written notice, fails to render monthly payments, and monthly and annual accounts.

(7) The copyright owner is entitled to receive compulsory license royalties only on records "made and distributed after" he or she is identified in Copyright Office records. This identification replaces the formal notice of use under the 1909 law, but the owner must still file to be entitled to royalties.[80]

(8) The royalty payable for *each* work embodied in a phonorecord "made and distributed" has been set as follows by the Copyright Royalty Tribunal:

> "For every phonorecord made and distributed on or after January 1, 1986, the royalty payable with respect to each work embodied in the phonorecord shall be either 5 cents, or .95 cent per minute of playing time or fraction thereof, whichever amount is larger."[81]

---

[78]See, e.g., *ABC Music Corp. v. Janov*, 186 F. Supp. 443, 126 U.S.P.Q. 429 (S.D. Cal. 1960).
[79]Pub. L. No. 92-140, 85 Stat. 391.
[80]Cf. *Norbay Music, Inc. v. King Records, Inc.*, 290 F.2d 617, 129 U.S.P.Q. 336 (2d Cir. 1961) (failure to file timely notice of use bars suit for acts of infringement occurring prior to time notice filed, but not for acts occurring afterward).
[81]37 C.F.R. §§307.3(b) & (c). The validity of the CRT rate adjustments concerning §115 was upheld in *Recording Industry Association of America v. Copyright Royalty Tribunal*, 662 F.2d 1, 212 U.S.P.Q. 69 (D.C. Cir. 1981). But cf. *ACEMLA v. Copyright Royalty Tribunal*, 763 F.2d 101, 226 U.S.P.Q. 509 (2d Cir. 1985) (distribution of 1982 Jukebox Royalty Fund reversed and remanded); *on remand*, 50 Fed. Reg. 47577 (Nov. 19, 1985), *corrected*, 50 Fed. Reg. 50656 (Dec. 11, 1985). See also discussion of amendment to §115(c) accomplished by the Record Rental Amendment of 1984 in note 121, *infra*.

The exclusive right to make recordings is subjected to another limitation—indeed an exemption—in the specialized area of "ephemeral" recordings made by broadcasters holding performance licenses (§112). Moreover, public broadcasters and school districts have an additional recording exemption over and above the right to make "ephemeral recordings," subject to payment of a royalty fee privately negotiated or, failing such negotiation, determined by the Copyright Royalty Tribunal under Section 118. Since both of these recording rights are related to the Section 106(4) performance right, they will be dealt with after that complex subject has been reviewed.

## Sound Recordings

Throughout this volume, an effort has been made to emphasize the distinction between a recorded composition (usually musical) and the recorded performance of that composition. It is the latter—called a "sound recording"—that is the subject of a set of specialized provisions in the 1976 Act, e.g., Section 402 (notice), Section 407 (deposit). Before noting the specific limitations on the exclusive rights of such works, we should recall their history.

Until 1971, recorded performances were protected, if at all, by state law[82] preserved by *Goldstein v. California.*[83] In 1971, Public Law 92-140 offered federal protection for the first time to sound recordings provided that they were "fixed" between February 15, 1972, and December 31, 1974. The latter deadline was later removed.[84] The 1976 statute carries forward this protection.

Section 114 expressly limits the rights of the owner of a sound recording to protection against recordings "that directly or indirectly recapture the actual sounds fixed in the [protected] recording." The provision does not prevent a recording "that consists entirely of an independent fixation of other sounds, even though such sounds imitate or simulate those in the copyrighted sound recording."

While imitation through an independent recording is thus permitted, capturing the fixed sounds by re-recording—even with some technical changes—can still amount to infringement, as held in *United States v. Taxe.*[85] In construing the requirement that the protected work be "fixed" after February 15, 1972, the *Taxe* court held that where an album or a tape produced after that date contains some songs which were first recorded before 1972, the proprietor can nevertheless secure protection for the remaining songs which satisfy the statutory standard. The court also found that an unauthorized re-recording of the original album or tape could still constitute infringement under Section 1(f) of the prior law where superficial changes had

---

[82]See *Capitol Records, Inc. v. Mercury Records Corp.*, 221 F.2d 657, 105 U.S.P.Q. 163 (2d Cir. 1955).
[83]412 U.S. 546, 178 U.S.P.Q. 129 (1973).
[84]Pub. L. No. 93-573, 88 Stat. 1873 (1974).
[85]380 F. Supp. 1010, 184 U.S.P.Q. 5 (C.D. Cal. 1974), aff'd, 540 F.2d 961, 192 U.S.P.Q. 204 (9th Cir. 1976).

been made by speeding up or slowing down the recording, deleting certain frequencies and tones, or adding sounds from a "moog" synthesizer. The jury was instructed that it could convict the defendants of criminal infringement of a recording copyright under such circumstances as long as "the final product [is] 'recognizable' as the same performance as recorded in the original."[86]

It should be noted that pursuant to Section 114(a) sound recordings do not enjoy a separate performance right, i.e., the right to control or be compensated for broadcast or other public performance of a genuine sound recording, but the Register has recommended amendment of the statute in order to provide such a right.[87] Finally, the special exemption for educational television and radio use of sound recordings in Section 114(b) should be noted.

### The Right to Adapt a Computer Program and to Make an Archival Copy: §117

Section 117 of the 1976 Act was a holding action to enable the National Commission on New Technological Uses of Copyrighted Works (CONTU) to study and make recommendations concerning computer uses of copyrighted works, a category that included computer programs, electronic data bases, and "conventional" works that had not been formatted for computer uses.

In 1980 Congress enacted a new Section 117, which adopted, as revised, a number of CONTU's recommendations:

> "Notwithstanding the provisions of §106, it is not an infringement for the owner of a copy of a computer program to make or authorize the making of another copy or adaptation of that computer program provided:
> "(1) that such a new copy or adaptation is created as an essential step in the utilization of the computer program in conjunction with a machine and that it is used in no other manner, or
> "(2) that such new copy or adaptation is for archival purposes only and that all archival copies are destroyed in the event that continued possession of the computer program should cease to be rightful.
> "Any exact copies prepared in accordance with the provisions of this section may be leased, sold, or otherwise transferred, along with the copy from which such copies were prepared, only as part of the lease, sale, or other transfer of all rights in the program. Adaptations so prepared may be transferred only with the authorization of the copyright owner."[88]

The major change from the CONTU recommendations was the limitation of Section 117 privileges to lawful "owners" as opposed to

---

[86]380 F. Supp. at 1015, 184 U.S.P.Q. at 7.

[87]PERFORMANCE RIGHTS IN SOUND RECORDINGS, 95th Cong., 2d Sess. (June 1978) (House Judiciary Comm. Print No. 15); *Performance Rights in Sound Recordings: Hearings Before the Subcomm. on Courts, Civil Liberties, and the Administration of Justice of the House Judiciary Comm.*, 95th Cong., 2d Sess. (1978) (Serial No. 83).

[88]17 U.S.C. §117 (1980). Congress also added a definition of "computer program" to §101: "A set of statements or instructions to be used directly or indirectly in a computer in order to bring about a certain result."

licensees.[89] Aside from two laconic discussions of this change in the (single) legislative hearing on the CONTU recommendations,[90] the official legislative history of Section 117 is virtually nonexistent. In view of this deficiency, the courts have placed great emphasis on the CONTU Final Report.[91]

Section 117 creates two privileges: (1) to make an exact copy or adaptation of the original where this is done "as an essential step in the utilization of the computer program in conjunction with a machine * * *"; and (2) to make a new copy or adaptation of the original for archival purposes. Exact copies may be disposed of without the permission of the copyrighted owner,[92] while adaptations may be transferred only with the permission of the copyright owner. The right to make an exact copy was necessary since input of a work into a computer constitutes the reproduction of a copy within the meaning of Section 106(1).[93] Similarly, absent a statutory exemption, input and subsequent adaptation would also violate Section 106(3). It should be noted that Section 117 does *not* permit the reproduction for sale of adaptations,[94] and is limited to computer programs. Input of a conventional work is not exempt under Section 117 and if unauthorized will result in infringement absent other defenses.

As explained in the CONTU Final Report, the purpose of Section 117 was to allow the owner of a lawful copy of a work "to copy it to [the] extent that will permit its use by that [owner]. This would in-

---

[89] *GCA Corp. v. Chance*, 217 U.S.P.Q. 718, 720 (N.D. Cal. 1982).

[90] *Industrial Innovation and Patent and Copyright Law Amendments: Hearings on H.R. 6033 et al. Before the Subcomm. on Courts, Civil Liberties, and the Administration of Justice of the House Judiciary Comm.*, 96th Cong., 2d Sess. 645, 700–701 (1980). Cf. FINAL REPORT OF THE NATIONAL COMMISSION ON NEW TECHNOLOGICAL USES OF COPYRIGHTED WORKS (1979) ("CONTU FINAL REPORT"); and SALTMAN, COMPUTER SCIENCE AND TECHNOLOGY: COPYRIGHT IN COMPUTER-READABLE WORKS: POLICY IMPACTS OF TECHNOLOGICAL CHANGE (NBS Special Publication Oct. 1977) (National Science Foundation Report).

[91] *Micro-Sparc, Inc. v. Amtype Corp.*, 592 F. Supp. 33, 35, 223 U.S.P.Q. 1210, 1212 (D. Mass. 1984); *Apple Computer, Inc. v. Formula Int'l, Inc.*, 594 F. Supp. 617, 621, 224 U.S.P.Q. 560, 563 (C.D. Cal. 1984) (contempt proceeding); *Atari, Inc. v. JS&A Group, Inc.*, 597 F. Supp. 5, 9 (N.D. Ill. 1983); *Apple Computer, Inc. v. Franklin Computer Corp.*, 714 F.2d 1240, 1252, 219 U.S.P.Q. 113, 119 (3d Cir. 1983); *Midway Mfg. Co. v. Strohon*, 564 F. Supp. 741, 750 n. 6, 219 U.S.P.Q. 42, 50 n. 6 (N.D. Ill. 1983).

[92] By referring to "transfer of all rights in the *program*," it appears that Congress inadvertently confused the "copy" with the protected work of authorship embodied therein. So understood, the section may be construed in accordance with its intent: to permit the sale or other disposition of the copy lawfully made under §117 only when the "first" (i.e., lawfully purchased) copy is also sold or otherwise disposed of. Absent such a statutory limitation, the copy made under §117 could be sold or otherwise disposed of while the lawfully purchased copy was retained for use. Note in this connection that the preamble to §117 states that its privilege is granted "[n]otwithstanding the provisions of Section 106 * * *," and thus does not include the "first sale" provisions of §109. Cf. 2 NIMMER ON COPYRIGHT §8.08 n. 9.10.

[93] *Micro-Sparc, Inc. v. Amtype Corp.*, 592 F. Supp. 33, 233 U.S.P.Q. 1210 (D. Mass. 1984); *Rand McNally & Co. v. Fleet Mgt. Systems*, 591 F. Supp. 726, 221 U.S.P.Q. 827 (N.D. Ill. 1984); *Black's Guide, Inc. v. Real Estate Communications, Inc.*, No. CV 84-3526-CHH (C.D. Cal. filed June 29, 1984); CONTU FINAL REPORT, *supra* note 90, at 12, 39–40. This was also true under the prior §117. *Rand McNally & Co. v. Fleet Mgt. Systems*, COPR. L. REP. ¶25,711 (N.D. Ill. (1984).

[94] *Midway Mfg. Co. v. Strohon*, 564 F. Supp. 741, 745 n. 2, 219 U.S.P.Q. 42, 45 n. 2 (N.D. Ill. 1983). See extensive discussion of the adaptation right in Transcript of CONTU Meeting No. 20 at 104–122, in *Apple Computer, Inc. v. Formula Int'l, Inc.*, 594 F. Supp. 617, 224 U.S.P.Q. 560 (C.D. Cal. 1984) (contempt proceeding), and in CONTU FINAL REPORT, *supra* note 90, at 13. See also *Whelan Associates, Inc. v. Jaslow Dental Laboratory*, 609 F. Supp. 1307, 225 U.S.P.Q. 156 (E.D. Pa. 1985); *SAS Institute, Inc. v. S & H Computer Systems, Inc.*, 605 F. Supp. 816, 225 U.S.P.Q. 916 (M.D. Tenn. 1985).

clude the right to load it into a computer and to prepare archival copies of it to guard against destruction or damage by mechanical or electrical failure."[95] This privilege was not intended to allow the making of more than one copy[96] or the use of that copy seriatim on more than one machine,[97] e.g., in conjunction with a free-standing computer or a terminal linked through a network to a central computer. The adaptation right was added to take into account the lack of standardization among programming languages and computer hardware by allowing a lawful owner of a copy to "make those changes necessary to enable the use for which [the program] was both sold and purchased." This right was believed to be "more private in nature" than the right to make exact copies and "could only be exercised so long as [it] did not harm the interests of the copyright proprietor."[98]

Defendants raising the Section 117 privilege have been singularly unsuccessful. In *Atari, Inc. v. JS&A, Inc.* defendant marketed a device that allowed electronic audiovisual games contained in plastic cartridges to be copied. Such games embody two distinct works of authorship: the audiovisual work, and the underlying computer program.[99] Section 117 applies only to computer programs, and thus the decision arguably could have been rendered in plaintiff's favor on the ground that the primary purpose of defendant's machine was to copy the audiovisual work.[100] The court chose, however, to deny the Section 117 defense on the ground that

> "Congress did not enact a general rule that making back-up copies of copyrighted works would not infringe. Rather, according to the CONTU report, it limited its exception to computer programs which are subject to 'destruction or damage by mechanical or electrical failure.' Some media must be especially susceptible to this danger. JS&A has simply offered no evidence that a ROM [chip containing the computer program] in a * * * video game cartridge is such a medium."[101]

In *Apple Computer, Inc. v. Formula International, Inc.* defendant was held in contempt of court for violating the terms of a preliminary injunction prohibiting the reproduction of Apple's copyrighted computer programs and the selling of any computer components containing such programs. The contemptuous activity involved the sale of a "ROM Set" consisting, in relevant part, of silicon chips containing exact copies of Apple programs. Defendant argued that as it was the lawful owner of copies of the programs as embodied in a disk-

---

[95]CONTU FINAL REPORT, *supra* note 90, at 13.

[96]"[T]he owner of a computer program [may] make * * * *another* copy * * *." 17 U.S.C. §117 (1980) (emphasis added).

[97]"[P]rovided that such a * * * copy * * * is created as an essential step in the utilization of the computer program in conjunction with *a* machine * * * ." *Ibid.* (emphasis added).

[98]CONTU FINAL REPORT, *supra* note 90, at 13.

[99]See Patry, *Electronic Audiovisual Games: Navigating the Maze of Copyright*, 31 J. COPR. Soc'y 1 (1983).

[100]This ground was, in fact, extensively briefed and argued; however, the court did not address it in its opinion.

[101]597 F. Supp. 5, 9–10 (N.D. Ill. 1983).

ette it was permitted under Section 117 to put them on silicon chips "as an essential step in the utilization of the computer program in conjunction with" the Apple Computer. After reviewing the CONTU Final Report and related history, the court held:

> "1) Only an *owner-user* of a computer who rightfully owns a copy of a copyrighted program is authorized to make another copy of that program, and this copying must be necessary for him to be able to use the copyrighted program in *his* computer; 2) The copy authorized by Section 117 must be made only for the owner-user's internal use and must be destroyed when the original copyrighted work is resold; 3) The copy thus made by the owner-user cannot be made accessible to others."[102]

Defendant was found not to be an "owner-user," and the use in question was held to be "a *convenient* method of utilizing * * * a diskette, but * * * not 'essential.' 'Essential' means indispensable and necessary."[103] This emphasis on the ultimate consumer and disapproval of commercial intermediaries is also seen in *Micro-Sparc, Inc. v. Amtype Corp.*, in which plaintiff, a computer magazine, published 12 to 15 computer programs per issue and offered to sell diskettes containing the programs to its subscribers for a fee of $20–$30 per program. Defendant, a "typing service," offered to sell a disk containing all the programs in an issue for $7.50–$10.00, a substantial savings. This service was limited to lawful owners of copies of the programs as published in plaintiff's magazine.

In rejecting defendant's Section 117(1) and (2) arguments, the *Micro-Sparc* court, like the *Apple* court, limited the "essential step" privilege to the consumer, additionally finding that the program as published in the magazine was not subject to destruction or damage by mechanical or electrical failure, and thus the archival copy privilege was unavailable.[104] The court did hold, however, that if the subscribers had themselves typed the programs onto a "floppy disk" they could then make an archival copy of that disk since it would be susceptible to destruction or damage within the meaning of Section 117.

It may be argued that the *Micro-Sparc* court ignored the express language in Section 117 permitting the owner of a lawful copy to "make *or authorize* the making of another copy" and the CONTU Final Report, which, while characterizing the adaptation right as "more private in nature" and exercisable only "so long as [it] did not harm the interests of the copyright proprietor,"[105] contained no similar limitations on the making of exact copies. Whether future decisions will also construe the archival copying privileges to be a "personal right" is open to question.

---

[102]594 F. Supp. 617, 621–622, 224 U.S.P.Q. 560, 563 (C.D. Cal. 1984).
[103]*Ibid.*
[104]592 F. Supp. 33, 35, 223 U.S.P.Q. 1210, 1212 (D. Mass. 1984).
[105]CONTU FINAL REPORT, *supra* note 90, at 13.

## The Right "To Prepare Derivative Works Based Upon the Copyrighted Work": §106(2)

The right to prepare derivative works granted in Section 106(2) brings together a miscellany of rights of adaptation contained in Section 1(b) and sprinkled through other subdivisions of Section 1 of the 1909 law. Like the reproduction right set forth in Section 106(1) of the 1976 Act, it is applicable to all types of works. Unlike the reproduction right, however, but like the display and performance rights of Sections 106(4) and (5), infringement of Section 106(2) can take place without fixation of the infringing work in any tangible form. Notwithstanding the broad definition of "derivative work" in Section 101 (which includes specified examples and "any other form in which a work may be recast, transformed, or adapted"), an infringing work must be "based upon the copyrighted work"; i.e., it must "incorporate a portion of the copyrighted work in some form"[106] and be substantially similar to the original.[107]

The right to "arrange" or make new versions was frequently relied upon by copyright owners to avoid the limitations on the "right to vend" under the 1909 Act,[108] limitations carried over in the right to distribute copies of the work contained in Section 106(3) of the 1976 Act.

The right to prepare derivative works is becoming increasingly important for computer programs, and has been given a broad scope in a number of recent decisions.[109] Its importance to conventional

---

[106]H.R. REP. No. 94-1476, 94th Cong., 2d Sess. 62 (1976); S. REP. No. 94-473, 94th Cong., 1st Sess. 58 (1975).

[107]*Litchfield v. Spielberg*, 736 F.2d 1352, 222 U.S.P.Q. 965 (9th Cir. 1984), *cert. denied*, 470 U.S. ___ (1985). It should be noted, however, that the infringing derivative work need not itself be within one of the subject matter categories of protection. *Lone Ranger Television, Inc. v. Program Radio Corp.*, 740 F.2d 718, 223 U.S.P.Q. 112 (9th Cir. 1984). See H.R. REP. No. 94-1476, 94th Cong., 2d Sess. 62 (1976); S. REP. No. 94-473, 94th Cong., 1st Sess. 58 (1975):

"The exclusive right to prepare derivative works, specified separately in clause (2) of section 106, overlaps the exclusive right of reproduction [in §106(1)] to some extent. It is broader than that right, however, in the sense that reproduction requires fixation in copies or phonorecords, whereas the preparation of a derivative work, such as a ballet, pantomime, or improvised performance, may be an infringement even though nothing is even fixed in tangible form."

This intriguing statement seemingly refers not to any relaxation of the substantial similarity requirement for infringement, but solely to the lack of a requirement that the unauthorized (and substantially similar) derivative work be fixed in a tangible medium of expression. For a case in which the copyright of a literary work was held to have been infringed by a choreographic reproduction of the same original combinations or series of ideas or incidents which told the same story through the medium of action, see *Holland v. Vivian Van Damm Prods., Ltd.*, reported in MacGILLIVRAY'S COPYRIGHT CASES 69 (1936).

[108]See *National Geographic Society v. Classified Geographic, Inc.*, 27 F. Supp. 655, 41 U.S.P.Q. 719 (D. Mass. 1939) (rearranging for sale in book form of material removed from issues of copyrighted magazine purchased by defendant infringed plaintiff's right to publish and make compilations, adaptations, and arrangements implied in §§1(a) and 7). But cf. *Fawcett Pub., Inc. v. Elliot Pub. Co.*, 46 F. Supp. 717, 54 U.S.P.Q. 137 (S.D.N.Y. 1942) (combining two issues of plaintiff's comic books into a volume called "Double Comics" held not to constitute infringement).

[109]*Whelan Associates, Inc. v. Jaslow Dental Laboratory*, 609 F. Supp. 1307, 225 U.S.P.Q. 156 (E.D. Pa. 1985); *Hubco Data Products Corp. v. Management Assistance*, 219 U.S.P.Q. 450 (D. Idaho 1983); *Midway Mfg. Co. v. Artic Int'l, Inc.*, 704 F.2d 1009, 218 U.S.P.Q. 791 (7th Cir.), *cert. denied*, 464 U.S. 823, 220 U.S.P.Q. 480 (1983); *Midway Mfg. Co. v. Strohon*, 564 F. Supp. 741, 219 U.S.P.Q. 42 (N.D. Ill. 1983); *Williams v. Arndt*, 227 U.S.P.Q. 615 (D. Mass. 1985).

works, however, should not be overlooked,[110] including cases where the original is edited[111] and, perhaps less obviously, where additional material is added to a lawful copy of the original.[112]

## The Right "To Distribute Copies or Phonorecords of the Copyrighted Work to the Public by Sale or Other Transfer of Ownership or by Rental, Lease or Lending": §106(3)

The right to distribute the work must be contrasted with the other Section 106 rights. The former embraces the right to transfer *copies* of the work, as distinguished from the latter, which concern the continuing right to reproduce, display, or perform the work itself. While the terms of Section 106(3) seem plain enough, it should be noted that there is no definition of "distribute"—a deliberate omission:

> "The language of [Section 106(3)] is virtually identical with that in the definition of 'publication' in section 101, but for the sake of clarity, we have restated the concept here. And, lest there be any possible misunderstanding because of the language of the preceding clauses, the right of public distribution would apply to all types of copyrighted works, including derivative works."[113]

The definition of publication does, in fact, contain many of the terms found in Section 106(3) and begins by stating: "Publication is

---

[110]See, e.g., *MGM, Inc. v. Showcase Atlanta Cooperative Prods., Inc.*, 479 F. Supp. 351, 203 U.S.P.Q. 822 (N.D. Ga. 1979); 216 U.S.P.Q. 685, 217 U.S.P.Q. 857 (N.D. Ga. 1981), *aff'd*, 772 F.2d 740 (11th Cir. 1985) (dramatization of *Gone With The Wind*); *Harper & Row, Pub., Inc. v. Nation Enters.*, 471 U.S. ____, 225 U.S.P.Q. 1073 (1985) (magazine article based on unpublished autobiography). Cf. the following cases under the 1909 Act: *G. Ricordi & Co. v. Mason*, 201 F. 184 (S.D.N.Y. 1911), *aff'd*, 210 F. 277 (2d Cir. 1913) (booklet giving fragmentary description of the plot and characters of various operas held not to constitute "version" of operas within meaning of 1909 Act); *MacMillan Co. v. King*, 223 F. 862 (D. Mass. 1914) (teacher's lecture outline based on and using catchwords from plaintiff's textbooks held infringement).

Would a series of step-by-step solutions of problems contained in a copyrighted college physics textbook infringe the right to prepare derivative works under §106(2) of the 1976 Act? Such activities were held to infringe under the 1909 law, although the decision seemed to be based more on a violation of the basic right to copy than derivative work-type violations such as translations or other versions. *Addison-Wesley Pub. Co. v. Brown*, 223 F. Supp. 219, 139 U.S.P.Q. 47 (E.D.N.Y. 1963).

[111]*Gilliam v. ABC*, 538 F.2d 14, 192 U.S.P.Q. 1 (2d Cir. 1976). See also *Bobbs-Merrill Co. v. New American Library*, COPR. L. REP. ¶25,752 (S.D.N.Y. 1985) (selection of excerpts held infringement where licensee was authorized to make only a "condensation"); *WGN Continental Broadcasting Co. v. United Video, Inc.*, 693 F.2d 622, 216 U.S.P.Q. 97 (7th Cir. 1982) (deletion of teletext from cable retransmission of television programming).

[112]*WGN Continental Broadcasting Co. v. United Video, Inc.*, 693 F.2d 622, 626, 216 U.S.P.Q. 97, 101 (7th Cir. 1982) ("if the publisher of a book leaves the inside covers blank, the book seller [cannot] inscribe the Lord's Prayer on them in order to broaden the book's appeal"); *National Bank of Commerce v. Shaklee Corp.*, 503 F. Supp. 533, 207 U.S.P.Q. 1005 (W.D. Tex. 1980) (insertion of advertisements in book).

[113]COPYRIGHT LAW REVISION PART 6: SUPPLEMENTARY REPORT OF THE REGISTER OF COPYRIGHTS ON THE GENERAL REVISION OF THE U.S. COPYRIGHT LAW, 1965 REVISION BILL, 89th Cong., 1st Sess. 19 (Comm. Print 1965). The right of first publication featured heavily in *Harper & Row, Pub., Inc. v. Nation Enters.*, 471 U.S. ____, 225 U.S.P.Q. 1073 (1985), where the Court wrote: "The right of first publication implicates a threshold decision by the author whether and in what form to release his work. First publication is inherently different from other §106 rights in that only one person can be the first publisher * * * ." *Id.* at _____, 225 U.S.P.Q. at 1078.

the *distribution* of copies * * *."[114] The Section 106(3) right must also be related to Section 602(a), which characterizes unlawful importation as an "infringement of the exclusive right to distribute copies * * * under section 106, actionable under section 501."[115]

## The "First Sale" Limitation on the Distribution Right

The right to distribute copies or phonorecords is expressly limited by Section 109(a), which provides that "the owner of a particular copy or phonorecord *lawfully made* under this title * * * is entitled, without the authority of the copyright owner, to sell or otherwise dispose of the possession of that copy or phonorecord." The emphasis on ownership of copies is reinforced in Section 109(c), which states that the Section 109(a) privilege does not, "unless authorized by the copyright owner, extend to any person who has acquired possession of the copy * * * from the copyright owner, by rental, lease, loan, or otherwise, without acquiring ownership of it." Section 109(a) is thus said to embody the "first sale" or "exhaustion" doctrine. Under its provision, after the first sale of a lawfully made copy, the owner of that copy may "sell or otherwise dispose" of it, notwithstanding the copyright owner's exclusive distribution right.[116] In other terminology,

---

[114]17 U.S. §101 (1978) (definition of "publication"). See also *Wildlife Internationale, Inc. v. Clements*, 591 F. Supp. 1542, 223 U.S.P.Q. 806 (S.D. Ohio 1984), *aff'd on this point, remanded on other grounds*, Civ. Nos. 84-3828; 84-3834 (6th Cir. filed Dec. 3, 1985) (not for publication) (offering to distribute copies held infringement).

[115]17 U.S.C. §§602(a); 501(a) (1978) ("Anyone who * * * imports copies or phonorecords into the United States in violation of Section 602, is an infringer of the copyright"). See: *Cosmair, Inc. v. Dynamite Enters., Inc.*, 226 U.S.P.Q. 344 (S.D. Fla. 1985); *Selchow & Righter Co. v. Goldex Corp.*, 612 F. Supp. 19, 225 U.S.P.Q. 815 (S.D. Fla. 1985); *CBS, Inc. v. Scorpio Music Distributors, Inc.*, 569 F. Supp. 47, 222 U.S.P.Q. 975 (E.D. Pa. 1983), *aff'd mem.*, No. 83-1688 (3d Cir. filed June 21, 1984); *Nintendo of America, Inc. v. Elcon Indus., Inc.*, 564 F. Supp. 937 (E.D. Mich. 1982). See also *CBS, Inc. v. Important Record Distributors, Inc.*, COPR. L. REP. ¶25,446 (E.D.N.Y. 1982) (consent judgment); *CBS, Inc. v. Sutton*, COPR. L. REP. ¶25,559 (S.D.N.Y. 1983) (consent judgment).

[116]H.R. REP. No. 94-1476, 94th Cong., 2d Sess. 62 (1976); S. REP. No. 94-473, 94th Cong., 1st Sess. 58–59 (1975); H. R. REP. No. 98-987, 98th Cong., 2d Sess. 4 (1984); S. REP. No. 98-162, 98th Cong., 1st Sess. 3–4 (1983). The provisions of §109 were found inapplicable to video rental stores' rental of motion pictures for on-premises viewing in private booths in *Columbia Pictures Indus., Inc. v. Aveco, Inc.*, 612 F. Supp. 315, 227 U.S.P.Q. 397 (M.D. Pa. 1985), and in *Columbia Pictures Indus., Inc. v. Redd Horne, Inc.*, 749 F.2d 154, 224 U.S.P.Q. 641 (3d Cir. 1984). Cf, *Columbia Pictures Indus., Inc. v. Professional Real Estate Inv., Inc.*, 228 U.S.P.Q. 743 (C.D. Cal. 1986) (court erroneously injected right of privacy notions and ignored legislative history).

The most cogent explanation for not permitting the "first sale" provisions to act as an exception to the copyright owner's right of importation is found in a 1985 case from New Zealand, *Barson Computers (N.Z.) Ltd. v. John Gilbert & Co.*, FLEET STREET REP. 489, 493–494 (N.Z. High Ct.—Auckland Registry 1985):

"The object is to protect the interests of persons who own copyright in the country of importation. If, for example, a copyright owner licenses the making of copies of the original work in a foreign country and has no protection against importation of those copies into other countries where he owns the copyright the value of his copyright in the country of importation will be diminished. Foreign made copies could then be imported into the country where the copyright owner is domiciled and where he owns the copyright—possibly flooding the market with copies manufactured abroad far more cheaply than they can be made in the 'home' country. Or the foreign made copies might be imported into another overseas country to the detriment of an exclusive distributor or licensee appointed in that country by the copyright owner—and to the ultimate detriment of the copyright owner.

"Similarly, the unauthorized importation for resale of copies made, not by a licensee, but by the person who owns the copyright in the country of importation will have an adverse effect

the first-sale doctrine "exhausts" the exclusive distribution right and Section 109(a) embodies the "exhaustion doctrine."

In a case of first impression, *Columbia Broadcasting System, Inc. v. Scorpio Music Distributors, Inc.*, however, it was held that while Section 109(a) "grants first sale protection to the third party buyer of copies which have been legally manufactured and sold within the United States" it does not protect "purchasers of imports,"[117] thereby rendering the unauthorized importation of copies lawfully made abroad a violation of Section 106(3) (through Section 602(a)).[118]

In the case of domestic distribution, Section 109(a) is the cornerstone of both library lending and commercial rental stores. Section 109(b) was, however, amended in 1984 to prohibit owners of phonorecords, for purposes of direct or indirect commercial advantage, from disposing of, or authorizing the disposal of, phonorecords "by rental, lease, or any other act or practice in the nature of rental, lease or lending."[119] This limitation on Section 109(a) does not apply to the rental, lease, or lending for nonprofit purposes by a nonprofit library or other nonprofit educational institution.

The amendment was enacted in response to Congress' findings that "the nexus of commercial record rental and [unauthorized] duplication [of the rental] may directly and adversely affect the ability of copyright holders to exercise their reproduction and distribution rights under the Copyright Act,"[120] and that "litigation is not an ef-

---

on the business of any exclusive licensee or distributor in the country into which the copies are imported—and so deplete the royalties or other payments which the owner of the copyright can expect to receive."
See also discussion of the issue in A CHARTER OF RIGHTS FOR CREATORS: REPORT OF THE SUB-COMMITTEE ON THE REVISION OF COPYRIGHT, Standing Comm. on the Revision of Copyright, Standing Comm. on Communications and Culture, Canadian House of Commons at 18–20 (Oct. 1985) (noting that territorial divisibility of copyright is a "fundamental and necessary part of international copyright").
[117]569 F. Supp. 47, 49, 222 U.S.P.Q. 975, 977 (E.D. Pa. 1983), *aff'd mem.*, No. 83-1688 (3d Cir. filed June 21, 1984). See also *Cosmair, Inc. v. Dynamite Enters., Inc.*, 226 U.S.P.Q. 344 (S.D. Fla. 1985) (copies made in the United States, exported, and then imported; court questioned reasoning of *Scorpio* decision); *Selchow & Righter Co. v. Goldex Corp.*, 612 F. Supp. 19, 225 U.S.P.Q. 815 (S.D. Fla. 1985); *Nintendo of America, Inc. v. Elcon Indus., Inc.*, 564 F. Supp. 937 (E.D. Mich. 1982).
[118]17 U.S.C. §602(a) (1978): "Importation into the United States, without the authority of the owner of copyright under this title, of copies or phonorecords of a work that have been acquired outside the United States is an infringement of the exclusive right to distribute copies or phonorecords under section 106[3], actionable under section 501." Note that §§602(a)(1)–(3) contain certain exemptions which, where applicable, permit importation of copies or phonorecords without liability. Such copies must, of course, still have been lawfully made. See further discussion of the import provisions of the Act in Chapter 10.
[119]17 U.S.C. §109(b)(1) (1984), as codified by Pub. L. No. 98-450, 98 Stat. 1728. There is a five-year "sunset" provision in the amendment. A technical drafting error should be noted. In establishing new Subsections 109(b)(1)–(3), Subsections 109(b) and (c) as enacted in the 1976 Copyright Act were renumbered Subsections (c) and (d) respectively. In so doing, however, the language of "old" Subsection 109(c) (now Subsection 109(d)) that "[t]he privileges prescribed in subsections (a) and (b) * * * " should have been, but was not, amended to read "[t]he privileges prescribed in subsections (a) and (c) * * * ."
[120]H.R. REP. No. 98-987, 98th Cong., 2d Sess. 2 (1984).

fective solution to the pattern of rental-and-taping."[121] These same concerns are present perhaps to an even greater degree with computer programs, and thus it is possible that Section 109 will be subjected to further amendment.[122]

## The Right, "in the Case of Literary, Musical, Dramatic, and Choreographic Works, Pantomimes, and Motion Pictures and Other Audiovisual Works, to Perform the Copyrighted Work Publicly": §106(4)

The right of public performance, unlike the rights provided in Sections 106(1), (2), and (3), does not cover all works. Those classes *not* covered are pictorial, graphic, and sculptural works, which by their nature cannot be "performed" (the right to "display" such works publicly is protected by Section 106(5)), and sound recordings, which, as a matter of legislative policy thus far, are expressly denied a performing right. See Section 114(a).

Section 106(4) of the 1976 law does not distinguish between different classes of works that *are* covered by the performing right so as to limit the protection of any of them to public performance *for profit* as did the 1909 law. Compare Section 1(d) of 1909 law (public performance of dramas) with Sections 1(c) and (e) (public performance for profit of nondramatic literary works and musical compositions). Yet the 1976 Act does contain significant limitations on the performance rights of works, and these vary according to the type of work. For example, Section 110 contains a number of exemptions for the performance of nondramatic musical compositions which were generally covered by the "for profit" limitation under Section 1(e) of the 1909 law.[123] Of course, the shift to a broader prima facie right subject to detailed exemptions clearly has philosophical and practical consequences (e.g., burden of proof).

One must begin the analysis of Section 106(4) with the definitions in Section 101 of "perform" and "perform * * * a work publicly," as supplemented by the following key paragraphs in the legislative reports discussing these definitions:

> "Under the definitions of 'perform,' 'display,' 'publicly,' and 'transmit' in section 101, the concepts of public performance and public display cover not only the initial rendition or showing, but also any further

---

[121]S. Rep. No. 98-162, 98th Cong., 1st Sess. 4 (1983). Section 109(b)(3) prohibits imposition of criminal penalties for violations of the provisions of §109(b)(1). Cf. 130 Cong. Rec. S11673 (Sept. 21, 1984, daily ed.) (remarks of Sen. Mathias). Special problems relating to the burden of proof with regard to first sale are discussed in Chapter 8. Section 115 was amended at the same time by adding a Subsection 115(c)(3) (and by renumbering "old" Subsections (c)(3) and (4) as Subsections (4) and (5) respectively), which establishes a royalty mechanism for the rental, lease, or lending of phonorecords made pursuant to a compulsory license under §115(a). Under the provisions of §109(b), however, permission of the copyright owner is still required, and owing to the improbability that copyright owners will authorize such distribution, it is not believed that this provision will be used.

[122]See S. 3074, 98th Cong., 2d Sess. (1984).

[123]See H.R. Rep. No. 94-1476, 94th Cong., 2d Sess. 81 (1976).

act by which that rendition or showing is transmitted or communicated to the public. Thus, for example: a singer is performing when he or she sings a song; a broadcasting network is performing when it transmits his or her performance (whether simultaneously or from records); a local broadcaster is performing when it transmits the network broadcast; a cable television system is performing when it retransmits the broadcast to its subscribers; and any individual is performing whenever he or she plays a phonorecord embodying the performance or communicates the performance by turning on a receiving set. Although any act by which the initial performance or display is transmitted, repeated, or made to recur would itself be a 'performance' or 'display' under the bill, it would not be actionable as an infringement unless it were done 'publicly,' as defined in section 101. Certain other performances and displays, in addition to those that are 'private,' are exempted or given qualified copyright control under sections 107 through 118.

\* \* \*

"Under clause (1) of the definition of 'publicly' in section 101, a performance or display is 'public' if it takes place 'at a place open to the public or at any place where a substantial number of persons outside of a normal circle of a family and its social acquaintances is gathered.' One of the principal purposes of the definition was to make clear that, contrary to the decision in *Metro-Goldwyn-Mayer Distributing Corp. v. Wyatt*, 21 C.O. Bull. 203 (D. Md. 1932), performances in 'semi-public' places such as clubs, lodges, factories, summer camps and schools are 'public performances' subject to copyright control. The term 'a family' in this context would include an individual living alone, so that a gathering confined to the individual's social acquaintances would normally be regarded as private. Routine meetings of businesses and governmental personnel would be excluded because they do not represent the gathering of a 'substantial number of persons.'

"Clause (2) of the definition of 'publicly' in section 101 makes clear that the concepts of public performance and public display include not only performances and displays that occur initially in a public place, but also acts that transmit or otherwise communicate a performance or display of the work to the public by means of any device or process. The definition of 'transmit'—to communicate a performance or display 'by any device or process whereby images or sound are received beyond the place from which they are sent'—is broad enough to include all conceivable forms and combinations of wired or wireless communications media, including but by no means limited to radio and television broadcasting as we know them. Each and every method by which the images or sounds comprising a performance or display are picked up and conveyed is a 'transmission,' and if the transmission reaches the public in any form, the case comes within the scope of clauses (4) or (5) of section 106.

"Under the bill, as under the present law, a performance made available by transmission to the public at large is 'public' even though the recipients are not gathered in a single place, and even if there is no proof that any of the potential recipients was operating his receiving apparatus at the time of the transmission. The same principles apply whenever the potential recipients of the transmission represent a limited segment of the public, such as the occupants of hotel rooms or the subscribers of a cable television service. Clause (2) of the definition of 'publicly' is applicable 'whether the members of the public capable of receiving the performance or display receive it in the same place or in separate places and at the same time or at different times.' "[124]

---

[124] *Id.* at 63–65; S. REP. No. 94-473, 94th Cong., 1st Sess. 60–61 (1975). The statement that "routine" meetings of businesses and governmental bodies are outside of the provision "be-

*Performance*

The statutory definition of "performance" represents a reversal of two Supreme Court decisions regarding cable television retransmission[125] and disapproval of a third decision's[126] departure from a fourth (and much earlier) opinion[127] concerning performance of musical compositions by retail or other commercial establishments via passive radio broadcasts.

Under the 1976 Act, and unlike the 1909 Act as construed by the aforementioned decisions, retransmission to the public of copyrighted works by cable television systems is a "performance," which, absent a license from the copyright owner or other defense, will result in a violation of Section 106(4). The primary defense, that of the compulsory license provided for in Section 111, is discussed at pp. 229–235, *infra.* The scope of the Section 106(4) right reaches far beyond cable retransmission and covers "all transmission activity in its broad definition of transmit,"[128] including direct *and* indirect transmission[129] by microwave devices, satellites, so-called "earth station" dishes and other interception devices,[130] computers, and television

---

cause they do not represent a gathering of a 'substantial number of persons'" is at odds with the thrust of the rest of the discussion and appears in most cases to be factually erroneous. The passage was apparently inserted out of congressional concern that its own "performance" of works would be found to be covered under the definition; a concern that would be better addressed in a limited exemption than in report language distorting an important statutory definition.

In a case of first impression, *Hinton v. Mainlands of Tamarac*, 611 F. Supp. 494, 496, 228 U.S.P.Q. 379, 381 (S.D. Fla. 1985), the court found that a condominium association holding a dance in its members' clubhouse for the benefit of its members was ineligible for the "extended family exception" referred to in the above-quoted legislative report since there was "not the slightest impediment to the public attending the dance," and the association charged a $3.00 admission fee. The court, however, accepted the association's contention that "the clubhouse in a condominium association is an 'extension of the owner's living room' * * *."

[125] *Fortnightly Corp. v. United Artists Television, Inc.*, 392 U.S. 390, 158 U.S.P.Q. 1 (1968) (retransmission of local copyrighted television programs by community antenna television systems held not to result in a "performance" of the programs); *Teleprompter Corp. v. CBS*, 415 U.S. 394, 181 U.S.P.Q. 65 (1974) (extension of *Fortnightly* to cable retransmission of "distant signals," i.e., signals not ordinarily receivable by house-top antennas or both house-top and tower-mounted antennas).

[126] *Twentieth Century Music Corp. v. Aiken*, 422 U.S. 151, 186 U.S.P.Q. 65 (1975).

[127] *Buck v. Jewell-LaSalle Realty Co.*, 283 U.S. 191, 9 U.S.P.Q. 17 (1931).

[128] *Hubbard Broadcasting, Inc. v. Southern Satellite Systems, Inc.*, 593 F. Supp. 808, 812, 224 U.S.P.Q. 468, 470 (D. Minn. 1984), *aff'd*, 777 F.2d 393, 228 U.S.P.Q. 102 (8th Cir. 1985). The *Hubbard* district court erroneously stated that the infringing performance must be for profit. This position was correctly rejected in *LaSalle Music Pub., Inc. v. Highfill*, 622 F. Supp. 168, 228 U.S.P.Q. 63 (W.D. Mo. 1985).

[129] *WGN Continental Broadcasting Co. v. United Video, Inc.*, 685 F.2d 218 (7th Cir.), *on pet. for reh'g*, 693 F.2d 622, 216 U.S.P.Q. 97 (7th Cir. 1982); *Eastern Microwave, Inc. v. Doubleday Sports, Inc.*, 691 F.2d 125, 216 U.S.P.Q. 265 (2d Cir. 1982).

[130] *National Football League v. McBee & Bruno's*, 228 U.S.P.Q. 11 (E.D. Mo. 1985); *ESPN, Inc. v. Edinburg Community Hotel, Inc.*, 623 F. Supp. 647 (S.D. Tex. 1985); *National Football League v. Cousin Hugo's*, 600 F. Supp. 84 (E.D. Mo. 1984); *National Football League v. American Embassy, Inc.*, No. 83-0701 (S.D. Fla. filed March 25, 1983); *Rainbow Programming Services v. Patel*, No. PCA 82-6009 (N.D. Fla. filed Nov. 18, 1982).

As part of the Cable Telecommunications Act of 1984, Act of Oct. 30, 1984, Pub. L. No. 98-549, 98 Stat. 2779, the Communications Act was amended to permit individuals to intercept, for purposes of private viewing, unencrypted cable television programming transmitted via satellite signals primarily intended for direct reception by cable operators for their retransmission to cable television subscribers *if* a marketing system available to authorize such private viewing is not in place. 47 U.S.C. §705(b) (1984). Section 705(d) states, however, that "[n]othing in this section shall affect any right, obligation, or liability under title 17, United States Code * * *." See also 130 CONG. REC. S14284 (daily ed., Oct. 11, 1984) (remarks of Sen. Goldwater),

sets,[131] as well as renditions by live performances.[132] It is scarcely an exaggeration to state that the only limitation on the Section 106(4) right (other than limitations in different sections of the Act) is that the performance must be to the public.

## Public

The statutory definition of "public" performance in Section 101 recognizes that a performance can be to the "public" even though it is received at different times. This is consistent with determinations under the 1909 Act that a radio broadcast was to the "public."[133] In *Buck v. Jewell-La Salle Realty Co.*[134] the Supreme Court held that the act of a hotel proprietor of making available to its guests, by means of radio receivers and loudspeakers in public and private rooms, unauthorized reception of copyrighted music by a neighboring broadcast station was an infringing performance of the original program. The Court held further that foreknowledge of the selections to be played was immaterial, because intent to infringe is not essential under the Copyright Act, and that one who merely "tunes in" on his receiving set actually performs the work in the statutory sense of the term and therefore runs the risk of incurring a suit for infringement if he does so in public for the purpose of commercial profit. The court of appeals accordingly found on remand that the specific acts of the proprietor of the hotel constituted a public performance for profit.[135]

The *Buck* holdings were seriously eviscerated if not overruled in *Twentieth Century Music Corp. v. Aiken*,[136] where a fast-food shop using four ceiling-mounted speakers to transmit programs broadcast by a local radio station to customers and employees was sued for infringement of copyright in songs which were broadcast. The plaintiff argued that the case was governed by *Buck*, and the district court agreed. The Court of Appeals for the Third Circuit also agreed that *Aiken* was "on all fours" with *Buck* but nonetheless found for the defendant on the ground that *Buck* had been impliedly overruled by the intervening Supreme Court decisions in the *Fortnightly* and *Teleprompter* cable television cases.

---

and *id.* at S14287 (explanation of bill in document described as "Legislative History" of bill). For a decision under 47 U.S.C. §705(b), see *Air Capital Cable Television, Inc. v. Starlink Communications Group, Inc.*, 601 F. Supp. 1568 (D. Kan. 1985). But see discussion of this case in *National Football League v. McBee & Bruno's, supra.*

[131] *Sony Corp. v. Universal City Studios, Inc.*, 464 U.S. 417, 469, 220 U.S.P.Q. 665, 689 (1984) (Blackmun, J., dissenting).

[132] See *BMI v. L.R. Corp.*, COPR. L. REP. ¶25,741 (W.D. Ohio 1984); *BMI v. Abdalla*, COPR. L. REP. ¶25,690 (S.D. Ohio 1984); *BMI v. Club 30, Inc.*, 567 F. Supp. 36, 222 U.S.P.Q 140 (N.D. Ind. 1983). See also discussion of performers' rights in text at notes 39–41 in Chapter 3.

[133] See, e.g., *Jerome H. Remick & Co. v. American Automobile Accessories Co.*, 5 F.2d 411 (6th Cir.), *cert. denied*, 269 U.S. 556 (1925). See also *BMI v. Regal Broadcasting Corp.*, 212 U.S.P.Q. 624 (N.D.N.Y. 1980) (1976 Act); *Boz Scaggs Music v. KND Corp.*, 491 F. Supp. 908, 208 U.S.P.Q. 307 (D. Conn. 1980) (1976 Act); and *BMI v. CBS, Inc.*, 221 U.S.P.Q. 246 (S.D.N.Y. 1983) (performance of music by television network after expiration of license).

[134] 283 U.S. 191, 9 U.S.P.Q. 17 (1931).

[135] 51 F.2d 726, 10 U.S.P.Q. 70 (8th Cir. 1931).

[136] 422 U.S. 151, 186 U.S.P.Q. 65 (1975).

The Supreme Court affirmed, with Chief Justice Burger and Justice Douglas dissenting. The majority found that the Court's opinion in the *Fortnightly* case "could hardly be more explicitly dispositive of the question now before us."[137] In addition to relying on the broadcaster/viewer dichotomy of the cable television cases, the Court emphasized the negative aspects of a holding that Aiken's conduct amounted to infringement.

Although the majority purported not to overrule *Buck* but to distinguish it on the basis of the unauthorized initial broadcast, one can reasonably ask if anything remained of that case. *Aiken* was, however, itself "completely overruled by the [1976 Act] and its broad definition of 'perform' in section 101,"[138] and by the definition of "publicly perform," although the precise fact situation in *Aiken* is subject to an exemption in Section 110(5).

In interpreting the broad definition of "publicly perform" and the legislative history cited above,[139] the courts have held that

> "two categories of places can satisfy the definition of 'to perform a work publicly.' The first category is self-evident; it is a 'place open to the public.' The second category, commonly referred to as a semi-public place is determined by the size and composition of the audience.
>
> "* * * Clearly, if a place is public, the size and composition of the audience are irrelevant. However, if the place is not public, the size and composition of the audience will be determinative."[140]

In the cited case, defendant operated two retail video stores which, in addition to rental activity, featured 85 "private" viewing booths. Each booth was approximately four feet by six feet and contained a 19-inch color television set and an upholstered bench. Admission was limited to four people per booth. In affirming a district court finding that a public performance resulted from the viewing of rented films in the booths, the court of appeals held that

> "the transmission of a performance to members of the public, even in private settings such as hotels or [defendant's] viewing rooms, constitutes public performance. * * *
>
> "The relevant 'place' within the meaning of §101 is each of [defendant's] two stores, not each individual booth within each store. Simply

---

[137] *Id.* at 161, 186 U.S.P.Q. at 69.

[138] H.R. REP. No. 94-1476, 94th Cong., 2d Sess. 87 (1976).

[139] See text at note 124, *supra*.

[140] *Columbia Pictures Indus., Inc. v. Redd Horne, Inc.*, 749 F.2d 154, 158, 224 U.S.P.Q. 641, 643 (3d Cir. 1984). In *National Football League v. McBee & Bruno's*, 228 U.S.P.Q. 11 (E.D. Mo. 1985), interception and performance of a copyrighted football game telecast by a restaurant/bar was held not to be a public performance because the establishment was closed to the public on the day in question and the defendant-owner showed the work to only three of his friends. See also COPYRIGHT LAW REVISION PART 6: SUPPLEMENTARY REPORT OF THE REGISTER OF COPYRIGHTS ON THE GENERAL REVISION OF THE U.S. COPYRIGHT LAW, 89th Cong., 1st Sess. 16 (Comm. Print 1965):

> "Under the language of section 106 a copyright owner 'has the exclusive rights to do and to authorize' any of the activities specified in the five numbered clauses of subsection (a). The right to 'do' something is probably broad enough to include the right 'to authorize' that the thing be done, but we have added the phrase 'and to authorize' in order to avoid possible questions as to the liability of contributory infringers. One example cited was of a person who legally acquires an authorized print of a copyrighted motion picture but who then engages in the business of renting it to others for the purposes of unauthorized public performance. There should be no doubt that this kind of activity constitutes infringement."

because the cassettes can be viewed in private does not mitigate the essential fact that [defendant] is unquestionably open to the public."[141]

## Performing Rights Limitations

In establishing a broad definition of performance and in eliminating the for-profit limitations of the 1909 Act, the number of individuals and institutions liable for infringing performances was dramatically increased. In order to permit socially desirable uses of copyrighted works by educational or other nonprofit organizations, and to provide a substitute for individual licensing where such licensing was believed to be impractical owing to the large number of users or copyright owners, Congress provided a series of exemptions and compulsory licenses, to which we now turn.

*Instructional Performances: §§110(1) and (2).* Performances of copyrighted works for teaching purposes receive specialized treatment under the 1976 Act. Under specified conditions, an exemption is provided for such use of any work in face-to-face instruction (§110(1)) and of nondramatic literary and musical works in instructional broadcasting and other "transmissions" (§110(2)). (*Displays* of all works are also exempted under these provisions.)

Face-to-face teaching under Section 110(1) may include amplification or reproduction of sound or projection of images throughout a building (not broadcasting), but must be in "a classroom or similar place devoted to instruction," e.g., an auditorium only if used for *instruction.* Moreover, the performance must be "by instructors or pupils" in a nonprofit educational institution; this includes guest lecturers, but not outside performers.[142] Unlawful copies of audiovisual works may not be used for exempted performances by one with actual or constructive knowledge.

The instructional broadcasting exemption in Section 110(2) is more limited. The works affected exclude dramatic or dramatico-musical works and audiovisual works (where individual images are sequentially shown). Moreover, the performance, although not limited

---

[141] *Id.* at 159. In *Columbia Pictures Indus., Inc. v. Aveco, Inc.,* 612 F. Supp. 315, 227 U.S.P.Q. 397 (M.D. Pa. 1985), as in *Redd Horne,* defendant rented video cassettes and viewing rooms. Unlike *Redd Horne,* however, defendant in *Aveco* permitted its patrons to bring in their own video cassettes and/or video cassette players, and did not actually operate the players. Finding these differences legally insignificant, the court rejected defendant's argument that its customers (and not it) were performing the works. While stating in dictum that "[r]ental of videocassettes to members of the public who play the cassette at home does not constitute copyright infringement," *id.* at 319, 227 U.S.P.Q. at 400, the court found defendant guilty of contributory infringement by violating plaintiff's right to authorize public performances of their works. *Id.* at 319–320, 227 U.S.P.Q. at 400. Defendant's reliance on the so-called "first sale" doctrine (see 17 U.S.C. §109 (1978)) was also rejected.

An opinion by the Louisiana Attorney General, Op. No. 84-480 (Jan. 10, 1985), *reprinted in* COPR. L. REP. ¶25,833, came to the wholly erroneous conclusion that exhibition of rented videocassettes to inmates was not a performance to the "public." Cf. H.R. REP. No. 94-1476, 94th Cong., 2d Sess. 64 (1976); S. REP. No. 94-473, 94th Cong., 1st Sess. 60 (1975).

[142] H.R. Rep. No. 94-1476, 94th Cong., 2d Sess. 81–82 (1976); S. REP. No. 94-473, 94th Cong., 1st Sess. 74 (1975).

to instructors and pupils, must be "a regular part of the systematic instructional activities of a governmental body or a nonprofit educational institution." It must also be "directly related and of material assistance to the teaching content" of the program and primarily (though not necessarily solely) intended for classroom students, disabled persons, or others unable to attend school or government employees.

*Agricultural Fairs: §110(6).* Certain other nonprofit performances of nondramatic musical works are also exempted. Performances at annual agricultural or horticultural fairs are permitted without either direct or vicarious liability on the part of the governmental body or nonprofit organization conducting them (although concessionaires and others may be liable under Section 110(6)).[143]

*Religious Performances: §110(3).* Also exempt is the "performance of a nondramatic literary or musical work or of a dramatico-musical work of a religious nature, or display of a work, in the course of services at a place of worship or other religious assembly" (§110(3)). The location restriction precludes the use of this exemption for broadcast purposes. Although most religious performances would, despite the encouragement of contributions, probably be considered nonprofit, there does not appear to be any such requirement in order for the exemption to be enjoyed. One may wonder whether a specific exemption of religious uses from copyright royalties raises serious issues under the establishment clause of the First Amendment.

In any event, the 1976 Act singles out religious works more clearly than the 1909 Act. The latter, in addition to its general "for profit" limitation in Section 1(e), contained a curious proviso in Section 104: "That nothing in this title shall be so construed as to prevent the performance of religious or secular works such as oratorios, cantatas, masses, or octavo choruses by public schools, church choirs, or vocal societies, rented, borrowed, or obtained from some public library, public school, church choir, school choir, or vocal society, provided the performance is given for charitable or educational purposes and not for profit."

Long a source of confusion and considered by some redundant of the Section 1(e) limitation, it has been noted that Section 1(e) covered only musical works, and not dramatico-musical works; a nonprofit performance of the latter *could* thus have infringed but for the proviso in Section 104 which exempted performance of both classes. *The Robert Stigwood Group, Ltd. v. O'Reilly.*[144] The *Robert Stigwood*

---

[143]See *Mills Music, Inc. v. Arizona*, 187 U.S.P.Q. 22 (D. Ariz. 1975), *aff'd*, 591 F.2d 1278, 201 U.S.P.Q. 437 (9th Cir. 1979) (state held liable for arrangement and performance of song used to promote state fair).

[144]346 F. Supp. 376, 175 U.S.P.Q. 403 (D. Conn. 1972), *aff'd*, No. 72-1826 (2d Cir. filed May 30, 1973); *F.E.L. Pub., Inc. v. Catholic Bishop of Chicago*, 214 U.S.P.Q. 409 (7th Cir. 1982). See also Derenberg and Latman, *Copyright*, 1972/1973 ANN. SURVEY AM. L. 615, 621–622 (1973).

case involved the rock opera "Jesus Christ Superstar," an example of a work with "an underlying religious or philosophical theme" which would probably not be deemed to be a work "of a religious nature" within the meaning of the exemption.[145]

*Certain Other Nonprofit Performances: §110(4).* In addition to exemptions for teaching, including instructional broadcasting, state fairs, and religious services, the 1976 Act contains a catchall nonprofit exemption for performance of nondramatic literary and musical works under a somewhat complex provision with a unique feature. The exemption of performances of such works in Section 110(4) is inapplicable to broadcasts or other transmissions, and the performance must be "without any purpose of direct or indirect commercial advantage and without payment of any fee or other compensation for the performance to any of its performers, promoters, or organizers * * *." Performances satisfying these conditions *and* involving no direct or indirect admission charge are exempt. If there is a charge (such as at a benefit concert or fund-raising dinner), exemption is still possible if the net proceeds are used exclusively for educational, charitable, or religious purposes, but such a performance may be prohibited by the proprietor in a signed written notice, served at least seven days in advance (in a manner and form to be prescribed by regulation), stating reasons for the objection.[146] The statute is silent on the obligation, if any, of the fund-raising organization to give advance notice to the proprietor so that he or she might object, as well as on the relevance of the objections. The Copyright Office regulations grapple with, among other things, the resulting incomplete knowledge on the part of the copyright owner in many cases.[147]

In any event, the purpose of this provision is to avoid compelling owners to make "involuntary donations to the fund-raising activities of causes to which they are opposed."[148]

*Nonprofit Veterans and Fraternal Organizations: §110(10).* In 1982, for no apparent reason other than effective lobbying, Congress added a new exemption in Section 110(10) for certain nonprofit veterans and fraternal organizations:

> "[N]otwithstanding paragraph 4 [of Section 110] the following is not an infringement: performance of a nondramatic literary or musical work in the course of a social function which is organized and promoted by a nonprofit veterans' organization or a nonprofit fraternal organization to which the general public is not invited, but not including the invitees of the organizations, if the proceeds from the performance, after deducting the reasonable costs of producing the performance, are used exclusively

---

[145]H.R. REP. No. 94-1476, 94th Cong., 2d Sess. 84 (1976).

[146]See Louisiana Att'y Gen. Op. No. 79-1102 (Oct. 29, 1979), *reprinted in* COPR. L. REP. ¶25,136; Texas Att'y Gen. Op. No. H-1260 (Oct. 31, 1978), *reprinted in* COPR. L. REP. ¶25,048. Cf. Cal. Att'y Gen. Op. No. 81-503 (Feb. 5, 1982), *reprinted in* COPR. L. REP. ¶25,368, with La. Att'y Gen. Op. No. 84-480 (Jan. 10, 1985) (criticized in note 141, *supra*).

[147]37 C.R.F. §201.13.

[148]H.R. REP. No. 94-1476, 94th Cong., 2d Sess. 86 (1976).

for charitable purposes and not for financial gain. For purposes of this section the social functions of any college or university fraternity or sorority shall not be included unless the social function is held solely to raise funds for a specific charitable purpose."[149]

As the language of the provision makes clear, Congress' intent was not to exempt all performances by nonprofit and fraternal organizations, but only those where (a) the audience is limited to members of the organizations and their invitees, and (b) *all* of the "net" proceeds from the event are donated to charity. Where part of the donations go to charity and part to the general fund of the nonprofit organization, the exemption does not apply.

*Certain Communications of Broadcasts: §110(5).* The most troublesome limitation on performing rights has been a provision dealing with the nature of a "performance," rather than the contours of "for profit." Section 110(5) seeks to resolve the question of multiple performances of broadcasts—the *Buck* and *Aiken* problems discussed above.

Section 110(5) provides that the following is not an infringement:

> "communication of a transmission embodying a performance or display of a work by the public reception of the transmission on a single receiving apparatus of a kind commonly used in private homes, unless—
> "(A) a direct charge is made to see or hear the transmission; or
> "(B) the transmission thus received is further transmitted to the public * * *."

In passing the 1974 bill containing this provision (S.1361, 93d Cong.), the Senate construed it "to allow the use of ordinary radios and television sets for the incidental entertainment of patrons in small business or professional establishments such as taverns, lunch counters, hairdressers, dry cleaners, doctors offices and the like."[150] When the Senate repassed this bill as S.22 in 1976, the committee report noted the intervening *Aiken* decision and stated:

> "[T]his exemption would not apply where broadcasts are transmitted by means of loudspeakers or similar devices in such establishments as bus terminals, supermarkets, factories, and commercial offices, department and clothing stores, hotels, restaurants and quick-service food shops of the type involved in *Twentieth Century Music Corp. v. Aiken.*"[151]

The House committee also took note of the *Aiken* decision, found that its basis had been "completely overturned by the present bill and its broad definition of 'perform' in section 101," and proposed an amendment, adopted by the House, whereby the exemption was lost by further transmission "beyond the place where the receiving apparatus was located," rather than "to the public" as provided in the

---

[149]Act of Oct. 25, 1982, Pub. L. No. 97-366, sec. 3, 96 Stat. 1759. The amendment was effective on Nov. 24, 1982. See also 128 CONG. REC. S13155 (daily ed., Oct. 1, 1982), and *id.* at H8478 (Joint Explanatory Memorandum of the Committee of Conference); *To Amend The Copyright Act, S. 2082: Hearings Before the Subcomm. on Improvements in Judicial Machinery of the Senate Judiciary Comm.*, 96th Cong., 2d Sess. (1981).

[150]S. REP. NO. 93-983, 93d Cong., 2d Sess. 130 (1974).

[151]122 CONG. REC. S1546 (daily ed., Feb. 6, 1976).

Senate bill. The House Committee deemed the *Aiken* facts (1,055 square feet with a commercial area of 620 square feet open to the public, containing a radio connected to four ceiling speakers) the "outer limit of the exemption," stating:

> "Under the particular fact situation in the *Aiken* case, assuming a small commercial establishment and the use of a home receiver with four ordinary loudspeakers grouped within a relatively narrow circumference from the set, it is intended that the performances would be exempt under clause (5). However, the Committee considers this fact situation to represent the outer limit of the exemption, and believes that the line should be drawn at that point. Thus, the clause would exempt small commercial establishments whose proprietors merely bring onto their premises standard radio or television equipment and turn it on for their customers' enjoyment, but it would impose liability where the proprietor has a commercial 'sound system' installed or converts a standard home receiving apparatus (by augmenting it with sophisticated or extensive equipment) into the equivalent of a commercial sound system. Factors to consider in particular cases would include the size, physical arrangement, and noise level of the areas within the establishment where the transmissions are made audible or visible, and the extent to which the receiving apparatus is altered or augmented for the purpose of improving the aural or visual quality of the performance for individual members of the public using those areas."[152]

There are thus four factors to be considered in evaluating whether the Section 110(5) exemption applies: (1) physical *size* of the establishment (is the establishment within the outer limits of *Aiken*—1,055 square feet with a commercial area of 620 square feet open to the public?); (2) *physical arrangement* (are there more than four speakers, and are the speakers "grouped within a relatively narrow circumference from the [receiving] set"?); (3) *noise level of the areas within the establishment* (is it necessary to have extra speakers in order for the patrons to hear the broadcast?); and (4) *the sophistication of the system* (is the system a standard radio or television set or an augmentation thereof or a commercial sound system?).

The resolution of this issue in the conference committee was to adopt the Senate statutory language. The essence of the House report language was the following:

> "It is the intent of the conferees that a small commercial establishment of the type involved in *Twentieth Century Music Corp. v. Aiken*, 422 U.S. 151 (1975), which merely augmented a home-type receiver and which was not of sufficient size to justify, as a practical matter, a subscription to a commercial background music service, would be exempt. However, where the public communication was by means of something other than a home-type receiving apparatus, or where the establishment actually makes a further transmission to the public, the exemption would not apply."[153]

---

[152] H.R. REP. No. 94-1476, 94th Cong., 2d Sess. 87 (1976). See also Register of Copyrights Barbara Ringer's testimony in *Copyright Law Revision: Hearings Before the Subcomm. on Courts, Civil Liberties, and the Administration of Justice of the House Judiciary Comm.*, 94th Cong., 2d Sess. 1808–1812 (1975), for an enlightening review of the Senate report and §110(5).

[153] H.R. REP. No. 94-1733, 94th Cong., 2d Sess. 75 (1976). Query whether most of the difficulties of enforcement of §110(5) are attributable to the use of the House report language to interpret the much different Senate statutory language.

The contours of Section 110(5) have been tested in two appellate decisions, *Sailor Music v. Gap Stores*[154] and *BMI v. United States Shoe Corp.*[155] In *Sailor Music*, a chain of retail stores averaging 3,500 square feet claimed the exemption. Noting that the stores were more than three times larger than that in *Aiken*, and the House report's statement that the *Aiken* facts represented the outer limit of the Section 110(5) exemption, the Second Circuit affirmed a grant of summary judgment in plaintiff's favor, adding that the stores were of sufficient size to justify a subscription to a commercial background music service. The same result was reached in *United States Shoe*, where the Ninth Circuit focused not on the size of the store but on the type of sound equipment used—a "commercial monaural system, with widely separated speakers of a type not commonly found in private homes * * *."[156] These opinions suggest that Section 110(5) will be applied strictly both as to the size of the store and the nature of the equipment used.

*Certain Secondary Transmissions: §111(a)(1).* A related exemption is found in the "secondary transmission" section devoted generally, but not exclusively, to cable. Once again, the definition is indis-

---

[154]668 F.2d 84 (2d Cir.), *cert. denied*, 456 U.S. 945 (1982).

[155]678 F.2d 816, 217 U.S.P.Q. 224 (9th Cir. 1982). The decision in *Springsteen v. Plaza Roller Dome, Inc.*, 602 F. Supp. 1113, 225 U.S.P.Q. 1008 (M.D.N.C. 1985), which found defendant's miniature golf course to qualify for the §110(5) exemption is erroneous. Defendant operated the course in conjunction with an adjoining roller rink which did have a license. Plaintiffs asserted this license did not cover the golf course; defendant contented to the contrary. The disagreement ended in litigation, where the issue was framed as whether, wholly apart from the rink, the golf course required a license or instead qualified under §110(5). The golf course comprised an area of 7,500 square feet and utilized six separate speakers mounted on light poles distributed throughout the area. In holding that the §110(5) exemption applied, the court interjected a new factor: the quality of the sound emitted by the speakers, under the theory that the commercial sophistication of the sound system had a significant bearing on whether the receiving apparatus was one "not of a kind commonly used in private homes." The court dismissed the large size of the area and number of speakers as not being predominant factors in view of the lack of sophistication of the system and the relatively small size of defendant's operation. The court failed to consider the limitation on the placement of the speakers to a "relatively narrow circumference from the [receiving] set." This decision is contrary to the legislative history, which stated that the *Aiken* facts represented the "outer limits" of §110(5) and which did not contain any indication that an unsophisticated commercial system was any less one "not of a kind commonly used in private homes." Cf. *Lamminations Music v. P & X Markets*, COPR. L. REP. ¶25,790 (N.D. Cal. 1985); *Rodgers v. Eighty-Four Lumber Co.*, 617 F. Supp. 1021, 228 U.S.P.Q. 942 (W.D. Pa. 1985) (stores having public areas in excess of 10,000 square feet and equipped with radios and amplifiers wired to numerous separate speakers mounted throughout the interior of the store and on poles outside the store held ineligible for exemption. The court properly rejected defendant's argument that "since its primary purpose for using the music was to muffle industrial noise for the benefit of employees and not to attract the public to its stores" the exemption was applicable. *Id.* at 1022–1023); *St. Nicholas Music, Inc. v. D.V.W., Inc.*, Civ. No. C84-0307W (D. Utah filed Feb. 20, 1985) (club with 2,000–2,500 square feet with receiver hooked up to six ceiling speakers not eligible for §110(5) exemption); *Hampshire House Pub. Corp. v. Sal & Sam's Restaurant, Inc.*, Civ. No. 84-1296 (E.D. La. filed Feb. 8, 1985).

In *National Football League v. McBee & Bruno's*, 228 U.S.P.Q. 11, 15–16 (E.D. Mo. 1985), the court held that "earth stations" a/k/a satellite dishes were not receiving apparatuses of the kind commonly used in private homes and thus were ineligible for the §110(5) exemption. The court's decision was based on the relatively high costs of the dishes (compared to television sets) and the relatively small number in use in private homes (approximately one million according to the court). This case raises but does not answer the intriguing question of when a receiving apparatus becomes one "commonly used in private homes." (The court did find that another defendant came within the §110(5) exemption by virtue of its use of a TV antenna to receive and perform a broadcast from a television station located 100 miles away.) Accord *ESPN, Inc. v. Edinburg Community Hotel, Inc.*, 623 F. Supp. 647 (S.D. Tex. 1985).

[156]678 F.2d at 817, 217 U.S.P.Q. at 225.

pensable: "To 'transmit' a performance or display is to communicate it by any device or process whereby images or sounds are received beyond the place from which they are sent" (§101). Thus, transmissions can be by broadcasting, cable, or any other means. Section 111(a)(1) exempts from infringement a secondary transmission embodying a performance or display if: (1) the secondary transmission is *not* made by a cable system; (2) it consists entirely of the relaying, by the management of a hotel, apartment house, or similar establishment, of signals transmitted by a broadcast station licensed by the Federal Communications Commission, within the local service area of such station; (3) it is transmitted to the private lodgings of guests or residents of such establishments; and (4) no direct charge is made to see or hear the secondary transmission.

It may be recalled that the "transmission" in *Buck* was not only "to the private lodging of guests" but to the public rooms in the La-Salle Hotel as well; such a transmission would not be exempt by this provision. But *Buck* had been expanded in *Society of European Stage Authors & Composers, Inc. v. New York Hotel Statler Co.*,[157] where infringement was found in the transmission of broadcasts in guests' bedrooms subject to guests' turning on the set and selecting programs; the result of the *SESAC* case *would* be changed by Section 111(a)(1). The piping of the music from a central hotel receiver would seem to be indispensable to any finding of infringement, the committees having found that "[n]o special exception is needed to make clear that the mere placing of an ordinary radio or television set in a private hotel room does not constitute an infringement."[158]

*Other Exemptions: §§110(7), (8), and (9).* Before turning to the complex question of cable television and other "secondary transmissions," we may note several remaining limitations on performing rights. First, under Section 110(7) a retail record establishment open to the public without admission charge has the privilege of playing records for promotional purposes in its immediate sales area.[159] Second, certain nonprofit transmissions for handicapped persons of nondramatic literary works and (on a single occasion) of plays published at least 10 years earlier are exempt under Sections 110(8) and (9), respectively.

*Cable Television and Other "Secondary Transmissions": §111.* Perhaps the best known limitation on performing rights is the retransmission of copyrighted television programs by cable systems. It will be recalled that such retransmission, whether of local or distant signals, was held by the Supreme Court in *Fortnightly Corp. v. United Artists Television, Inc.* and *Teleprompter Corp. v. Columbia*

---

[157]19 F. Supp. 1, 34 U.S.P.Q. 6 (S.D.N.Y. 1937).
[158]H.R. REP. No. 94-1476, 94th Cong., 2d Sess. 92 (1976); S. REP. No. 94-473, 94th Cong., 1st Sess. 78 (1975).
[159]Cf. *Chappell & Co. v. Middletown Farmers & Auction Co.*, 334 F.2d 303, 142 U.S.P.Q. 54 (3d Cir. 1964).

*Broadcasting System, Inc.* not to constitute a performance at all. Statutory revision was significantly delayed as these cases worked their way through the courts and the contending parties adjusted their respective negotiating positions. It was apparently accepted for some time by the cable interests that, despite their judicial victories, some payment scheme was appropriate. The framework has finally been provided in one of the more complicated provisions of the 1976 Act—Section 111.

As already noted, this section deals principally, but not solely, with cable, covering other "secondary transmissions" as well. Secondary transmissions are generally the simultaneous retransmission of the signals of another, but also include nonsimultaneous retransmissions by offshore cable systems (§111(f)). An overview of the subsections reveals the following structure: (a) exemption from any copyright liability for certain secondary transmissions; (b) imposition of full copyright liability on a secondary transmission under certain circumstances; (c) provision for availability of a compulsory license for cable systems and prescription of disqualifying circumstances; (d) mechanics of the license, including filing requirements for cable systems and computation of payment and distribution of royalty fees; (e) specification of copyright liability consequences in situations involving nonsimultaneous secondary transmissions by offshore cable systems; and (f) definitions. We will now attempt to summarize the substance of each of these, discussing the definitions of Section 111(f) in the context of the other provisions.

(1) §111(a) / Exemptions. The statute provides for an exemption of hotels and apartment houses in relaying programs to the rooms of their guests or residents, but this is unavailable to cable systems. Such systems are also disqualified from other exemptions provided in favor of: (1) a governmental body or nonprofit organization, retransmitting on a cost basis, without any "purpose of direct or indirect commercial advantage," e.g., a nonprofit community "booster" or "translator" service (§111(a)(4)); and (2) a passive carrier which supplies wires, cables, etc., but has no control over content or recipients (§111(a)(3)).[160] A final exemption applies if "the secondary transmission is made solely for the purpose and under the conditions specified by clause (2) of section 110," i.e., instructional broadcasting, etc.

(2) §111(b) / Full Liability. A secondary transmission to the public by any means, including cable, is fully actionable as infringement "if the primary transmission [being carried by the secondary transmission] is not made for reception by the public at large but is con-

---

[160]Compare *Eastern Microwave, Inc. v. Doubleday Sports, Inc.*, 691 F.2d 125, 216 U.S.P.Q. 265 (2d Cir. 1982) (exemption held applicable); *Hubbard Broadcasting, Inc. v. Southern Satellite Systems, Inc.*, 593 F. Supp. 808, 224 U.S.P.Q. 468 (D. Minn. 1984), *aff'd*, 777 F.2d 393, 228 U.S.P.Q. 102 (8th Cir. 1985) (exemption available for satellite carrier), with *WGN Continental Broadcasting Co. v. United Video, Inc.*, 685 F.2d 218 (7th Cir.), *on pet. for reh'g*, 693 F.2d 622, 216 U.S.P.Q. 97 (7th Cir. 1982) (deletion of teletext from program rendered carrier an infringer). See discussion of the *Eastern Microwave* and *WGN* cases in Barnett, *From New Technology to Moral Rights*, 31 J. Copr. Soc'y 427 (1984).

trolled and limited to reception by particular members of the public." Thus, closed-circuit broadcasts, pay television, pay cable, and background music services are directed to controlled groups and may not be retransmitted. An exception is a secondary transmission, without alteration, *required* by the Federal Communications Commission, with respect to a primary transmission of one of its broadcast licensees. (As will be seen later, the FCC rules requiring that cable systems "must carry" certain broadcast signals have been held unconstitutional.) The prohibition of alterations means that the exception in no case permits the unscrambling of scrambled signals.[161]

(3) §111(c) / Compulsory License Availability. In discussing the compulsory license system for secondary transmissions of cable systems, we have been ignoring thus far the fact that cable systems also engage in some *primary* transmissions, i.e., origination of programming. In *Teleprompter Corp. v. Columbia Broadcasting System, Inc.*[162] this function was urged by plaintiff as a ground for distinguishing the *Fortnightly* case and imposing liability. The argument was rejected because this function, along with others, was not reflected in the particular copyrighted programs under consideration. In other words, the plaintiff was unsuccessful in arguing that *some* origination transformed *all* of a system's operations into that of a broadcaster. What was never doubted, however, was that a cable system using copyrighted material without permission for its originated programs would infringe under the 1909 law. The same result obtains under the 1976 Act by reason of the following syllogism: (1) a cable transmission is a performance; (2) the compulsory license applies only to *secondary* transmissions by cable; and (3) origination in a cable transmission is not a secondary transmission.

Turning to the availability of the compulsory license, the basic principle is to permit cable retransmission of signals of broadcast stations *licensed by the FCC* where such retransmission "is permissible under the rules, regulations, or authorizations of the Federal Communications Commission" (§111(c)(1)). The license is generally unavailable if the content of the program or of any accompanying commercials is "willfully altered by the cable system through changes, deletions, or additions" (§111(c)(3)). Special remedies are provided for such alteration under Section 510. Failure to comply with the reporting, payment, and other conditions of the compulsory license scheme can also result in liability for infringement in the case of "willful or repeated" transmissions (§111(c)(2)).

An unusual feature of this provision, emphasizing the increasingly international nature of copyright issues, was introduced in the final days of House consideration of the 1976 Act. Section 111(c)(3) basically extends the compulsory license to cable systems operating in specified zones near our borders, permitting the retransmission of

---

[161]H.R. REP. No. 94-1476, 94th Cong., 2d Sess. 92 (1976).
[162]415 U.S. 394, 405, 181 U.S.P.Q. 65, 68–69 (1974).

copyrighted material in the programs broadcast by stations licensed by the appropriate governmental authorities in Canada or Mexico (§111(c)(4)).

(4) §111(d) / Compulsory License System. In order to enjoy the license, a cable system must make an initial filing in the Copyright Office within one month before operation or by April 17, 1977, whichever is later, and a supplemental filing to reflect significant changes in such things as signals carried (§111(d)(1)), as well as semiannual statements of account and payments (§111(d)(2)). The schedule of fees begins with a minimum potential payment for so-called small systems depending on whether the actual gross receipts total $146,000 or less,[163] or are more than $146,000 but less than $292,000.[164]

Aside from these small systems which pay irrespective of the type of programming they carry, the basic percentage formula has two components. The first one is .893 of 1 percent of the gross receipts from subscribers "for the basic service of providing secondary transmissions of primary broadcast transmitters." (§111(d)(2)(B)(i)). This amount is paid, irrespective of what the system actually carries, "for the privilege of further transmitting any nonnetwork programming of a primary transmitter in whole or in part beyond the local service area of such primary transmitter." (*Ibid.*) The second component is a downward sliding scale determined by the number of "distant signal equivalents" ("dse") that the cable system carries, and is calculated as follows:[165] .893 of 1 per centum of subscribers' gross receipts for the first dse; .563 or 1 per centum of such receipts for each of the second, third, and fourth dses; and .265 of 1 per centum of such receipts for the fifth and each additional dse thereafter.[166]

These rates, adopted in the wake of the FCC's 1980 deregulation order abolishing its syndicated exclusivity rules and limitations on distant signal carriage,[167] proved highly controversial.[168] Section 111 itself has also raised a number of significant issues, including prora-

---

[163] 37 C.F.R. §308.2(b)(1).

[164] *Id.* at §308.2(b)(2). These rates reflect an agreed-to inflationary increase. See 50 Fed. Reg. 18480 (May, 1 1985).

[165] 37 C.F.R. §308.2(a).

[166] See also the syndicated exclusivity surcharges contained in 37 C.F.R. §308.2(d).

[167] 45 Fed. Reg. 60186 (Sept. 11, 1980). See *Malrite v. FCC*, 652 F.2d 1140 (2d Cir. 1981), *pet. for cert. denied sub nom. National Ass'n of Broadcasters v. FCC*, 454 U.S. 1143 (1982).

[168] See review of the rate adjustments in 49 Fed. Reg. 13029-13038 (April 2, 1984), and H.R. REP. No. 97-559 (Pt. 1), 97th Cong., 2d Sess. (1982); *Copyright Royalty Fees for Cable Systems: Hearings on H.R. 2902 and H.R. 3419 Before the Subcomm. on Courts, Civil Liberties, and the Administration of Justice of the House Judiciary Comm.*, 98th Cong., 1st & 2d Sess. (1983–1984); *Copyright/Cable Television: Hearings on H.R. 1805 et al. Before the Subcomm. on Courts, Civil Liberties, and the Administration of Justice of the House Judiciary Comm.*, 97th Cong., 1st & 2d Sess. (1981–1982); H.R. REP. No. 97-559 (Pt. 2), 97th Cong., 2d Sess. (1982); *Cable Copyright Legislation: Hearing on H.R. 5949 Before the Subcomm. on Telecommunications, Consumer Protection, and Finance of the House Energy & Commerce Comm.*, 97th Cong., 2d Sess. (1982); *Cable Copyright and Signal Carriage Act of 1982: Joint Hearing on H.R. 5949 Before the House Commerce, Science, and Transportation and Judiciary Comms.*, 97th Cong., 2d Sess. (1982); *Oversight of the Copyright Act of 1976 (Cable Television): Hearings Before the Senate Judiciary Comm.*, 97th Cong., 1st Sess. (1981); *Copyright Issues: Cable Television and Performance Rights: Hearings Before the Subcomm. on Courts, Civil Liberties, and the Administration of Justice of the House Judiciary Comm.*, 96th Cong., 1st Sess. (1979).

tion of distant signals, "tiering"[169] of basic services, and substitution for "grandfathered signals" at the nonadjusted rate,[170] with which the Copyright Office has attempted to deal in a series of interim and final regulations.[171]

The concept of "distant signal equivalent," defined in Section 111(f), must be related to the "local service area of a primary transmitter" (also defined in Section 111(f)), as the latter term "establishes the difference between 'local' and 'distant' signals and therefore the line between signals which are subject to payment under the compulsory license and those that are not."[172] The revision bill as it passed the Senate provided for a sliding scale related to the gross receipts of cable systems and did not exempt local retransmission of local signals from the calculation of those receipts. The House-passed version (the version that was ultimately enacted) chose instead to provide for no royalty fees for the retransmission of either "local" or "network" programming, but to compensate copyright owners for retransmission, into "local service areas," of "distant signals" based on the concept of "distant signal equivalents," computed on the basis of specified (and adjusted) percentages of the gross receipts received by the cable system from its subscribers for its basic service. Other receipts, such as those for pay-cable or installation charges, are not included in gross receipts.[173]

The rationale for distinguishing between retransmission of local and distant signals for royalty purposes is explained in the House report:

"The Committee determined * * * that there was no evidence that the retransmission of 'local' broadcast signals by a cable operator threatens the existing market for copyright program owners. Similarly, the retransmission of network programing, including network programing which is broadcast in 'distant' markets, does not injure the copyright owner. The copyright owner contracts with the network on the basis of his programing reaching all markets served by the network and is compensated accordingly.

"By contrast, the retransmission of distant non-network programing by cable systems causes damage to the copyright owner by distributing the program in an area beyond which it has been licensed. Such retransmission adversely affects the ability of the copyright owner to exploit the work in the distant market. It is also of direct benefit to the cable system by enhancing its ability to attract subscribers and increase revenues. For these reasons, the Committee has concluded that the

---

[169] 49 Fed. Reg. 13029, 13035 (April 2, 1984) (clarifying the definition of gross receipts for the "basic service of providing secondary transmissions of primary broadcast transmitters" in 37 C.F.R. §201.17(b)(1)) challenged in *NCTA v. Columbia Indus., Inc.*, Civ. No. 83-2785 (D.D.C. complaint filed Sept. 21, 1983). See also *Cablevision Systems Dev. v. MPAA*, Civ. No. 83-1655 (D.D.C. complaint filed June 8, 1983).

[170] 49 Fed. Reg. 26722-26727 (June 29, 1984), challenged in *Cox Cable Tucson, Inc. v. Ladd*, Civ. No. 84-534 TVC (D. Ariz. complaint filed July 18, 1984).

[171] See 37 C.F.R. §§201.11; 201.17; 43 Fed. Reg. 27827 (July 17, 1978); 45 Fed. Reg. 45270 (July 3, 1980); 48 Fed. Reg. 13166 (March 30, 1983) (letter of opinion); 49 Fed. Reg. 13029 (April 2, 1984); 49 Fed. Reg. 14944 (April 16, 1984); 50 Fed. Reg. 9270 (March 7, 1985) (affirming without modification 47 Fed. Reg. 21786 (May 20, 1982)); 50 Fed. Reg. 14725 (April 15, 1985).

[172] H.R. Rep. No. 94-1476, 94th Cong., 2d Sess. 99 (1976).

[173] *Id.* at 96.

copyright liability of cable television systems under the compulsory license should be limited to the retransmission of distant non-network programing."[174]

Collections of payments by the Register, after deduction of reasonable costs, are deposited in the Treasury for later distribution by the Copyright Royalty Tribunal. The distributees are copyright owners whose works were included in the transmission of a distant nonnetwork signal (or so listed in a special statement of account filed by the cable system) or in distant nonnetwork aural signals, e.g., FM programs picked up by a cable system (§111(d)(4)). Certain basic procedures for Tribunal distribution are outlined in the statute (§111(d)(5)), but they have been subsequently elaborated upon by Tribunal regulations.[175]

In order to ensure that subsequent FCC rule changes in the size of the "local service area of a primary transmitter" did not have an adverse effect for copyright purposes, Congress fixed the definition of that term as being, generally,[176] the area covered by the FCC's "must carry" rules in effect on April 15, 1976. This rigidity had unforeseen consequences when in 1982 the FCC authorized a new form of originating station, termed "low-power" television. These broadcast stations, which typically serve rural areas and have a limited signal strength, were not in existence as originating[177] stations on April 15, 1976, and could not, therefore, be must-carry stations.[178] Retransmission of low-power signals within the same geographic area as the local service area of a full-power station is, of course, "local" in the common-sense meaning of the term. However, due to the aforementioned definitional rigidity in Section 111(f), questions arose as to whether payment of royalties was required for "local" cable retransmission of "local" low-power television signals. On October 12, 1984, the Copyright Office held a public hearing on this and related issues. On December 4, 1984, the Office issued a Policy Decision stating that the question of whether royalty payments for such retransmission were required was ambiguous, and that accordingly, the Office would take a neutral position in processing Statements of Account reflect-

---

[174] *Id.* at 91.

[175] 37 C.F.R. §§301.40-301.77.

[176] Different rules apply in the case of television broadcast stations licensed by a governmental authority of Canada or Mexico. 17 U.S.C. §111(f) (1978).

[177] A number of these stations were, however, in existence as so-called nonoriginating "translator" stations.

[178] They were not accorded must-carry status by the FCC when the service was authorized, either. See 47 Fed. Reg. 21468 (1982), *on recon.* 48 Fed. Reg. 21478 (1983).

On July 30, 1985, Senator Mathias and Representative Kastenmeier introduced identical bills, S. 1526 and H.R. 3108, to amend the fourth paragraph of §111(f) as follows:

"In the case of a low power television station, as defined by the rules and regulations of the Federal Communications Commission, the local service area of a primary transmitter comprises the area within 35 miles of the transmitter site, except that in the case of such a station located in a standard metropolitan statistical area which has one of the 50 largest populations of all standard metropolitan statistical areas (based on the 1980 decennial census of population taken by the Secretary of Commerce), the number of miles shall be 20 miles."

This legislation stands an excellent chance of passage.

ing such retransmission but without payment therefor pending legislative clarification.[179]

In view of the FCC's repeal of its rules regarding syndicated exclusivity and the number of distant signals that may be imported into local markets, and the decision of the United States Court of Appeals for the District of Columbia declaring the FCC's must-carry rules unconstitutional,[180] it appears that many of the fundamental premises underlying Section 111 have been removed. When further considered in conjunction with the strong feelings of some members of Congress about the appropriateness of the Copyright Royalty Tribunal's rate adjustments and its overall performance, the time may be ripe for a serious reevaluation of continuing the present Section 111 compulsory licensing scheme.

*Jukebox Exemption: §116.* The 1909 law in its multifaceted Section 1(e) contained an express exception from liability for unauthorized performance of music by means of coin-operated machines where there was no admission fee to the place of performance. This provision was the notorious "jukebox exemption." Originally designed to insulate the "penny parlor," it was long attacked as an illogical historical relic but withstood numerous legislative attempts at repeal. It is only against this background that one can understand the accomplishments of Section 116, which might otherwise appear modest.

The section addresses itself to public performance of a nondramatic musical work "by means of a coin-operated phonorecord player." A detailed definition of such a machine, set forth in Section 116(e), includes an echo of the 1909 law in its limitation to machines located "in an establishment making no direct or indirect charge" for admission. In one of the few cases construing the 1909 law exemption, the court found it inapplicable because of a $1 admission charge, even though the charge was imposed for a live band performance and not for the offending jukebox, which was operated during band breaks.[181] This result was followed in a case arising under the 1976 Act.[182] An earlier decision under the 1909 Act involving the Section 1(e) exemption also construed it strictly in favor of the copyright proprietor by holding that the machine must be actually operated by the deposit of coins and not otherwise, as by disconnecting the wires and controlling the operation of the machine without coins.[183]

---

[179]49 Fed. Reg. 46829 (Nov. 28, 1984).

[180]*Quincy Cable TV, Inc. v. FCC*, 768 F.2d 1434 (D.C. Cir. 1985). This ruling has no effect, however, on the must-carry rules continuing to serve as "a convenient reference point for determining where a local signal ends and a distant signal begins" for copyright purposes. *Id.* at 1454 n. 42.

[181]*Quackenbush Music, Ltd. v. Wood*, 381 F. Supp. 904, 184 U.S.P.Q 210 (M.D. Tenn. 1974).

[182]*Stewart v. Southern Music Distributing Co.*, 503 F. Supp. 258, 213 U.S.P.Q. 277 (M.D. Fla. 1980). See also *BGO Music, Inc. v. Pee Bee Inv., Inc.*, 229 U.S.P.Q. 131 (4th Cir. 1986) (skating fee at roller rink constituted charge for admission).

[183]*Buck v. Kelly*, 7 U.S.P.Q. 164 (D. Mass. 1930).

If the machine qualifies, Section 116 accords the opportunity of a compulsory license to its "operator" (as defined in Section 116(f)) in return for a total payment of $50 per box per year. This rate is scheduled to be adjusted effective January 1, 1987, to take into account changes in the cost of living index, and is further subject to a voluntary agreement reached by the interested parties.[184] The proprietor of the location is broadly exempt from liability. The operator must file an application, pay the fee, and affix the certificate received to the player. Both the Copyright Office[185] and the Copyright Royalty Tribunal[186] have promulgated regulations implementing Section 116.

The failure to affix the certificate (or to obtain one) will result in an infringing public performance,[187] although an inadvertent failure may militate against a finding of willful infringement.[188] The requirement of affixation has been strictly construed, with the courts holding that mere application with the Copyright Office is insufficient to avoid liability.[189]

Section 116(c)(4) includes the first statutory recognition in this country of a "performing rights society," which is exemplified in its definition by ASCAP, BMI, and SESAC (§116(e)). Moreover, an express antitrust exemption is provided to claimants in order to encourage them to agree as to the proportionate distribution or common collection of fees (§116(c)(2)). Indeed, such cooperation would appear sorely needed if anything is to be economically recoverable after costs.

*Public Broadcasting: §118.* The final limitation on performing rights applies to published nondramatic musical, pictorial, graphic, and sculptural works performed or displayed on "a noncommercial educational broadcast station" (§118(d)) by a "public broadcasting entity" (§118(g)). In addition, such entities may record and distribute

---

[184] 37 C.F.R. §306.4. The $50 rate currently in effect was upheld against challenge in *AMOA v. Copyright Royalty Tribunal*, 676 F.2d 1144, 215 U.S.P.Q. 100 (7th Cir. 1982). See also *Coin-Operated Phonorecord Player Act of 1983: Hearing on S. 1734 Before the Subcomm. on Patents, Copyrights, and Trademarks of the Senate Judiciary Comm.*, 98th Cong., 2d Sess. (1984); ADMINISTRATIVE HISTORY: RECORDATION & CERTIFICATION OF COIN-OPERATED PHONORECORD PLAYERS (Copyright Office 1979).

On May 13, 1985, the music performing rights societies, ASCAP, BMI, and SESAC, and the AMOA (the principal representative of the jukebox owners) announced a voluntary agreement under which jukebox owners who have complied with the statutory and regulatory requirements of the Act may apply to the societies for a rebate from the CRT rate, provided the AMOA undertakes an extensive program of encouraging compliance with the applicable provisions and regulations of the Act and target numbers of jukebox owners in fact so comply.

[185] 37 C.F.R. §201.16.

[186] *Id.* at §§306.1–.4. See *AMOA v. Copyright Royalty Tribunal*, COPR. L. REP. ¶25,062 (D.D.C. 1979), *vacated and rem'd*, 636 F.2d 531, 207 U.S.P.Q. 374 (D.C. Cir. 1980), *cert. denied*, 450 U.S. 912, 211 U.S.P.Q. 400 (1981) (review of CRT regulation requiring jukebox owners to file list of locations of their machines).

[187] *BMI v. Allen-Genoa Road Drive-In, Inc.*, 598 F. Supp. 415, 223 U.S.P.Q. 574 (S.D. Tex. 1983); *BMI v. Fox Amusement Co.*, 551 F. Supp. 104, 219 U.S.P.Q. 874 (N.D. Ill. 1982).

[188] *BMI v. Wisconsin Novelty Co.*, COPR. L. REP. ¶25,718 (E.D. Wis. 1984).

[189] *BMI v. P & R Amusement, Inc.*, COPR. L. REP. ¶25,712 (S.D. Ind. 1984).

programs embodying such works for transmission by public broadcasting entities (§118(d)(2)). (They also enjoy under Section 114(b) the right to reproduce sound recordings in educational television and radio programs.) Provision is made for public schools and other nonprofit institutions to tape the broadcast of the specified works for nonprofit face-to-face instructional use within seven days.

The fees and other terms concerning such use are not set forth in the statute, but are set by the Copyright Royalty Tribunal[190] unless voluntary license agreements are entered into between the parties. At present, the Tribunal sets the rates for use of pictorial, graphic, and sculptural works, non-ASCAP, BMI, and SESAC covered works, and non-Harry Fox Agency synchronization rights.[191] Copyright Royalty Tribunal regulations require records of use (e.g., cue sheets) to be kept and furnished to copyright owners.[192]

*Ephemeral Recordings: §112.* For a number of years broadcasters, particularly in television, have recorded their programs as a convenience to their scheduling, rebroadcast arrangements, and the like. At times such recordings have been kept only temporarily and then discarded. Proprietors have generally ignored these "ephemeral" recordings, treating them as an adjunct to an authorized performance right rather than an infringement of the technically separate recording or synchronization right. This practice has been codified under limitations in Section 112 of the 1976 Act.

The provision covers all transmissions—broadcasting, closed circuit, background music, etc.—but not all classes of works; e.g., in no case are audiovisual works included. The number of copies or phonorecords permitted, the length of time they may be retained, and the use to which they may be put vary according to the four types of transmitting organizations covered, including nonprofit broadcasters or other transmitters of instructional material (30 copies for seven years under Section 112(b)), religious material (one copy for each transmitting organization for one year under Section 112(c)), and material designed for handicapped persons (10 copies under Section 112(d)). In addition, an authorized transmitter can make one copy to be used only by itself within its own local service area and to be destroyed within six months of performance unless "preserved exclusively for archival purposes" (§112(a)). As in the case of musical arrangements made pursuant to the compulsory license provision of Section 115, derivative work status is denied to programs embodied in ephemeral recordings made without express consent (§112(e)).

---

[190]See schedule of rates set forth in 37 C.F.R. §§304.7 & .8.

[191]37 C.F.R. §304.8.

[192]*Id. at* §§304.4(c), (e); 304.6(e); 304.7(e) (music); 308(d) (pictorial, graphic, and sculptural works). Under *id.* at §308(e), use reports of pictorial, graphic, and sculptural works are required to be filed with the CRT.

## The Right, "in the Case of Literary, Musical, Dramatic, and Choreographic Works, Pantomimes, and Pictorial, Graphic, or Sculptural Works, Including the Individual Images of a Motion Picture or Other Audiovisual Work, to Display the Copyrighted Work Publicly": §106(5)

Section 106(5) contains the first explicit statutory recognition in the United States copyright law of an exclusive right to display a copyrighted work, or an image of it, to the public. In common with the performance right in Section 106(4), the right of display is limited to "public" presentation, and thus one must consider the foregoing discussion as to what constitutes "public." Also in common with the performance right, the display right applies only to specified types of works; e.g., sound recordings are not covered, and audiovisual works are covered only to the extent of nonsequential presentation of individual images (a sequential presentation would amount to a "performance"). Moreover, the right to display is limited by the provisions of Section 109(b), whereby the owner of a lawfully made copy (or a person authorized by such an owner) may display it publicly to "viewers present at the place where the copy is located." Finally, the right to display published pictorial, graphic, and sculptural works is limited by the compulsory license granted to public broadcasters under Section 118. It should be noted, however, that, as with the performance right, the right to display is *not* dependent upon the work's being "reproduced" in a "copy."

The legislative history of Section 106(5) reveals that the primary impetus for its inclusion was the uncertainty of the existence and/or extent of such a right under prior law, and "the enormous potential importance of showing, rather than distributing, copies as a means of disseminating an author's work," particularly

> "use of closed- and open-circuit television for presenting images for graphic and textual material to large audiences * * * [use of] information storage and retrieval devices * * * linked together by communication satellites or other means * * * [to] provide libraries and individuals throughout the world with access to a single copy of a work by transmission of electronic images."[193]

---

[193] COPYRIGHT LAW REVISION PART 6: SUPPLEMENTARY REPORT OF THE REGISTER OF COPYRIGHTS ON THE GENERAL REVISION OF THE U.S. COPYRIGHT LAW: 1985 REVISION BILL, 89th Cong., 1st Sess. 20 (Comm. Print 1965). As noted, *ibid.*:
> "There is some authority for the existence of a right of exhibition under the existing [1909] law in the much-criticized decision of the Second Circuit Court of Appeals in *Patterson v. Century Productions, Inc.*, 93 F.2d 489 [35 U.S.P.Q. 471] (2d Cir. 1937), which suggests that, at least under the special circumstances in that case, the projection of the images of a motion picture on a screen constitutes a 'copying.' This view has little support and it is certainly arguable that, for example, the showing of a copyrighted photograph or musical score on television or a projector is not infringement today."
Cf. *Mura v. CBS, Inc.*, 245 F. Supp. 587, 147 U.S.P.Q. 38 (S.D.N.Y. 1965) (display of copyrighted hand puppets on "Captain Kangaroo" television show held not to result in "copying"; alternative finding of fair use). For decisions under the 1976 Act, see *Benwood Products Co. v. Marsel Mirror & Glass Products, Inc.*, 468 F. Supp. 1215 (N.D. Ill. 1979) (infringing display of wicker mirrors at trade show); *Streeter v. Rolfe*, 491 F. Supp. 416, 209 U.S.P.Q. 918 (W.D. La. 1980) (use of copyrighted turkey decoy in hunt did not result in a "public" display). In *Kirk-Brummel Associates, Inc. v. de Poortere Corp.*, 203 U.S.P.Q. 940, 942 (S.D.N.Y. 1979), the court

This concern was met through the broad definitions of "display" and "to transmit" in Section 101. The legislative reports make clear that these definitions were drafted with computer and advanced communications uses in mind:

> "In addition to the direct showings of a copy of a work, 'display' would include the projection of an image on a screen or other surface by any method, the transmission of an image by electronic or other means, and the showing of an image on a cathode ray tube, or similar viewing apparatus connected with any sort of information storage and retrieval system."[194]

The display right, as contemplated by the drafters of Section 106(5), has become an important focal point in copyright owners' efforts to control computer uses of their works, especially as regards the increasing utilization of multiple computers or computer terminals connected into a single system ("network"). As noted above, the concept of "public" includes recipients not gathered in a single place, and situations where such recipients receive the work at the same *or different* times. Thus, the computer transmission of a copyrighted work to multiple computers or computer terminals ("networking") will result in a "public display," and will fall outside the exemption in Section 109(b), since there is a projection of more than one image, regardless of whether the computers or terminals are located in the "same physical surroundings," including generally, a situation where "each person in a lecture hall has his own viewing apparatus in front of him,"[195] *even if* the viewers are "present at the place where the copy is located."

# Fair Use: §107

## The Statutory Setting

Most of the detailed statutory limitations imposed on exclusive rights in the 1976 Act pertain to particular rights, classes of works, or uses. We now turn to the most general limitation on rights—the principle of fair use embodied in Section 107.

Copyright statutes up through the 1909 law spoke in terms of "exclusive rights," but these were quite early subjected to a judge-made equitable rule of reason ultimately known as fair use. Devel-

---

refused to enjoin the sale of an allegedly infringing fabric design "[s]ince there are substantial dissimilarities between plaintiff's and defendant's designs when viewed in large samples," but did enjoin the *display* of the same design in showroom samples "[s]ince many of the differences in the fabrics' designs are not so apparent when the showroom samples are compared * * * ." See also H.R. REP. No. 94-1476, 94th Cong., 2d Sess. 63 (1976); S. REP. No. 94-473, 94th Cong., 1st Sess. 59 (1975).

[194]H.R. REP. No. 94-1476 at 64; S. REP. No. 94-473 at 60. See also *ibid.* for a discussion of the broad meaning of "to transmit."

[195]H.R. REP. No. 94-1476, 94th Cong., 2d Sess. 80 (1976); S. REP. No. 94-473, 94th Cong., 1st Sess. 72 (1975).

oped by the English equity and common law courts, the doctrine was adopted in the United States[196] and continued to be applied here without a statutory base until 1976, when it was codified in Section 107:

> "Notwithstanding the provisions of section 106, the fair use of a copyrighted work, including such use by reproduction in copies or phonorecords, or by any other means specified by that section, for purposes such as criticism, comment, news reporting, teaching (including multiple copies for classroom use), scholarship, or research, is not an infringement of copyright. In determining whether the use made of a work in any particular case is a fair use the factors to be considered shall include—
> "(1) the purpose and character of the use, including whether such use is of a commercial nature or is for nonprofit educational purposes;
> "(2) the nature of the copyrighted work;
> "(3) the amount and substantiality of the portion used in relation to the copyrighted work as a whole; and
> "(4) the effect of the use upon the potential market for or value of the copyrighted work."

The legislative reports reveal that the codification was designed to provide only general guidance to the courts:

> "The bill endorses the purpose and general scope of the judicial doctrine of fair use, but there is no disposition to freeze the doctrine in the statute, especially during a period of rapid technological change. Beyond a very broad statutory explanation of what fair use is and some of the criteria applicable to it, the courts must be free to adapt the doctrine to particular situations on a case-by-case basis. Section 107 is intended to restate the present judicial doctrine of fair use, not to change, narrow, or enlarge it in any way."[197]

Despite this intent not to change the doctrine, it has been held that by establishing a minimum of four factors that must be considered in all fair use determinations, Congress did alter fair use, since prior to 1978 the courts were free to reject fair use claims on the basis of any one or more of the factors.[198] It has also been suggested that Congress altered fair use by permitting so-called "passive uses" (e.g., uses such as photocopying that do not necessarily result in the creation of a second work of authorship) to be considered as a potential form of fair use. Previously, fair use was believed by most courts and commentators to be limited to so-called "productive uses"—the use

---

[196] *Gray v. Russell*, 10 F. Cas. 1035 (C.C.D. Mass. 1839) (No. 5,728); *Folsom v. Marsh*, 9 F. Cas. 342 (C.C.D. Mass. 1841) (No. 4,901).

[197] H.R. REP. No. 94-1476, 94th Cong., 2d Sess. 66 (1976); S. REP. No. 94-473, 94th Cong., 1st Sess. 62 (1975). In *DC Comics, Inc. v. Reel Fantasy, Inc.*, 696 F.2d 24, 27–28, 217 U.S.P.Q. 307, 309 (2d Cir. 1982), a panel of the Second Circuit erroneously held that §107 did not apply to works created before January 1, 1978, but allegedly infringed after that date.

[198] *Pacific & Southern Co. v. Duncan*, 744 F.2d 1490, 1495 n. 7, 224 U.S.P.Q. 131, 133 n. 7 (11th Cir. 1984), *cert. denied*, 471 U.S. ___, *on remand*, 618 F. Supp. 469, 228 U.S.P.Q. 141 (N.D. Ga. 1985). Courts may, however, consider factors in addition to those enumerated in the statute. See W. PATRY, THE FAIR USE PRIVILEGE IN COPYRIGHT LAW 363 (BNA Books 1985) ("PATRY").

by a second author of portions of a first author's work in the creation of a new work.[199] Regardless of the historical accuracy of this view, it is clear in light of the legislative history of the 1976 Act and the Supreme Court's decision in *Sony Corp. v. Universal City Studios, Inc.*,[200] which permitted private, noncommercial "time-shifting" of free broadcast television programming as fair use, that the defense is no longer strictly limited to use by one who is truly a second author (a concept characterized as "social productivity" by the *Sony* court).

A definitional analysis of Section 107 compels the same conclusion, for the section uses the terms "including" and "such as," terms defined in Section 101 as being illustrative and not limitative.[201] (E.g., "[n]otwithstanding the provisions of section 106, the fair use of a copyrighted work, *including* such use by reproduction in copies * * * for purposes *such as* * * *.")

The *Sony* court held that all the fair use factors are to be considered in an "equitable rule of reason" analysis, weighted by a preliminary determination of whether the use is for commercial or nonprofit purposes. If the use is for commercial purposes, it is presumptively not a fair use.[202] Harm to the potential market for the copyrighted work is then also presumed.[203] If the use is for nonprofit[204] purposes, *and* is favorably balanced under the first three factors, the copyright owner must shown some reasonable likelihood of potential (but not actual) harm to the work's market from the use.[205] There is no presumption that nonprofit (or any other) uses are fair uses, a point forcefully made by the Supreme Court in *Harper & Row, Publishers, Inc. v. Nation Enterprises*, where the Court held: "The drafters resisted pressures from special interest groups to create presumptive categories of fair use, but structured the provision as an affirmative defense requiring a case by case analysis."[206]

With these general rules in mind, we shall now turn to the specific types of uses and then examine the four statutory factors in greater detail.

---

[199]See PATRY, *supra* note 198, at ix.

[200]464 U.S. 417, 220 U.S.P.Q. 665 (1984).

[201]See 17 U.S.C. §101 (1978) (definitions of "including" and "such as"); PATRY, *supra* note 198, at 363; *Harper & Row, Pub., Inc. v. Nation Enters.*, 471 U.S. ____, ____, 225 U.S.P.Q. 1073, 1081 (1985).

[202]464 U.S. at 451, 220 U.S.P.Q. at 681.

[203]*Ibid*. See also *Pacific & Southern Co. v. Duncan*, 744 F.2d 1490, 224 U.S.P.Q. 131 (11th Cir. 1984), *cert. denied*, 471 U.S. ____, *on remand*, 618 F. Supp. 469, 228 U.S.P.Q. 141 (N.D. Ga. 1985); *Financial Information, Inc. v. Moody's Investors Serv.*, 751 F.2d 501, 224 U.S.P.Q. 632 (2d Cir. 1984).

[204]Although §107(1) refers to nonprofit *educational* use, the *Sony* majority referred broadly to nonprofit uses. Cf. 464 U.S. at 496, 220 U.S.P.Q. at 701 (dissent of Justice Blackmun).

[205]464 U.S. at 451, 220 U.S.P.Q. at 682.

[206]471 U.S. ____, ____, 225 U.S.P.Q. 1073, 1081 (1985) (citing PATRY, *supra* note 198, at 477 n. 4). Fair use is also a mixed question of law and fact, 471 U.S. at ____, 225 U.S.P.Q. at 1081, "that can be decided by an appellate court if the trial court has found facts sufficient to evaluate each of the four statutory factors." *Pacific & Southern Co. v. Duncan*, 744 F.2d 1490, 1495 n. 8, 224 U.S.P.Q. 131, 134 n. 8 (11th Cir. 1984), *cert. denied*, 471 U.S. ____, *on remand*, 618 F. Supp. 469, 228 U.S.P.Q. 141 (N.D. Ga. 1985).

## The Purposes of Fair Use

### Criticism, Comment, and Parody

The illustrative purposes and factors contained in the "preamble" to Section 107 emerged from the cases or assumptions under prior law. For example, fair use has traditionally been applicable to criticism and comment. The general rule with respect to such purposes was set forth in an 1807 English decision, *Roworth v. Wilkes*:

> "A review will not in general serve as a substitute for the book reviewed; and even there, if so much is extracted that it communicates the same knowledge with the original work, it is an actionable violation of literary property."[207]

The Second and Ninth Circuits[208] have indicated that greater leeway is to be allowed where verbatim excerpts are used in reviews and the like for purposes of accuracy or authenticity.

Parody is regarded as a form of criticism. The general rule with respect to such uses was set forth in *Columbia Pictures Corp. v. National Broadcasting Co.*, where the court held that the parodist could take enough of the work "to recall or conjure up the original" but that takings beyond that "run[ ] the calculated risk that on all the facts involved, a trier of fact may find the taking substantial."[209]

---

[207]1 Camp. 94, 98 (K.B. 1807).

[208]*Meeropol v. Nizer*, 560 F.2d 1061, 1071, 195 U.S.P.Q. 273, 279 (2d Cir.), *cert. denied*, 434 U.S. 1013, 196 U.S.P.Q. 592 (1977); *Walt Disney Prods. v. Air Pirates*, 581 F.2d 751, 758, 199 U.S.P.Q. 769, 774 (9th Cir.), *cert. denied*, 439 U.S. 1132 (1979). But cf. *Harper & Row, Pub., Inc. v. Nation Enters.*, 471 U.S. ___, 225 U.S.P.Q. 1073 (1985), which, while stating that "[t]he law generally recognizes a greater need to disseminate factual works than works of fiction or fantasy," *id.* at ___, 225 U.S.P.Q. at 1082, nevertheless rejected a fair use claim regarding 300 words from President Ford's 200,000-word then-unpublished autobiography, *A Time to Heal*, and *West Pub. Co. v. Mead Data Central, Inc.*, 616 F. Supp. 1571, 227 U.S.P.Q. 631 (D. Minn. 1985), which rejected LEXIS' fair use claim for use of "jump cites" to West's judicial reporters (e.g., Federal Supplement).

[209]137 F. Supp. 348, 350, 107 U.S.P.Q. 344 (S.D. Cal. 1955) (Carter, J.). Cf. *Loew's Inc. v. CBS, Inc.*, 131 F. Supp. 165, 105 U.S.P.Q. 302 (S.D. Cal. 1955) (Carter, J.), *aff'd sub nom. Benny v. Loew's Inc.*, 239 F.2d 532, 112 U.S.P.Q. 11 (9th Cir. 1956), *aff'd by an equally divided Court*, 356 U.S. 43, 116 U.S.P.Q. 479 (1958); *Berlin v. E.C. Pub., Inc.*, 219 F. Supp. 911 (S.D.N.Y. 1963), *aff'd*, 329 F.2d 541, 141 U.SP.Q. 1 (2d Cir.), *cert. denied*, 379 U.S. 822, 143 U.S.P.Q. 464 (1964); *Elsmere Music, Inc. v. NBC*, 482 F. Supp. 741, 206 U.S.P.Q. 913 (S.D.N.Y.) *aff'd*, 623 F.2d 252, 253 n. 1, 207 U.S.P.Q. 277, 277-278 n. 1 (2d Cir. 1980). See also Judge Newman's statement in *Warner Bros., Inc. v. ABC*, 720 F.2d 231, 242, 222 U.S.P.Q. 101, 110 (2d Cir. 1983): "Stirring one's memory of a copyright character is not the same as appearing to be substantially similar to that character, and only the latter is infringement." Under this analysis, the issue of fair use would not be reached, since fair use is an affirmative defense to a prima facie showing of infringement.

In *Elsmere, Inc. v. NBC*, *supra*, the court of appeals held:

"A parody is entitled to at least 'conjure up' the original. Even more extensive use would still be fair use, provided the parody builds upon the original as a known element of modern culture and contributing something new for humorous effect or commentary."

623 F.2d at 253 n. 1, 207 U.S.P.Q. at 278 n. 1. Apparently the Second Circuit later feared that this passage might signal the acceptance of "bodily appropriation" of copyrighted works under the guise of parody, for in *Warner Bros., Inc. v. ABC*, 654 F.2d 204, 211, 211 U.S.P.Q. 97, 103 (2d Cir. 1981), the court stated: "[W]e question whether the [parody] defense could be used to shield an entire work that is substantially similar to and in competition with the copyrighted work." See also *MCA, Inc. v. Wilson*, 677 F.2d 180, 185, 211 U.S.P.Q. 577, 581 (2d Cir. 1981) ("We are not prepared to hold that a commercial composer can plagiarize a competitor's copyrighted song, substitute dirty lyrics of his own, perform it for commercial gain, and then escape liability by calling the end result a parody or satire on the mores of society"); see also *DC Comics, Inc. v. Unlimited Monkey Business, Inc.*, 598 F. Supp. 110, 224 U.S.P.Q. 437 (N.D. Ga.

## Scholarship

Related to criticism is "scholarship," another enumerated "purpose" for fair use in Section 107, and a context in which fair use has also traditionally been important because of the frequent need of scholars to reproduce portions of earlier works. As Professor Chafee has noted: "The world goes ahead because each of us builds on the work of our predecessors. 'A dwarf standing on the shoulders of a giant can see farther than the giant himself.' "[210]

It has been emphasized in this connection that, while "the arts and sciences should be defined in their broadest terms," still "it is relevant whether the [copyrighted work] is used primarily for scholarly, historical reasons, or predominantly for commercial exploitation."[211]

Perhaps because of its essentially private nature, there have not been many cases involving scholarship outside of subsequent expression thereof in biographies and historical works. Legend to the contrary notwithstanding, there has never been a decision permitting, under the guise of fair use, a scholar's copying of an entire work by hand.

## Research

It is sometimes alleged that commercial entities such as drug, chemical, or manufacturing corporations are engaged in "research" within the meaning of Section 107. This argument, however correct colloquially, does fatal violence to the term as used in Section 107. Such entities are virtually always for-profit corporations seeking knowledge not for the immediate public good but to increase their profits. Under *Sony Corp. v. Universal City Studios, Inc.*, their use is presumptively not a fair use and presumptively results in harm to the market for the original.[212]

Copying for the purposes of medical research by the federal government's National Institutes of Health and National Library of

---

1984); cf. *Pillsbury Co. v. Milky Way Prods., Inc.*, 215 U.S.P.Q. 124, 131 (N.D. Ga. 1981) (rejecting pornographic nature of use as disqualifying defendant from fair use privilege); PATRY, *supra* note 198, at 168–169 (same).

[210]Chafee, *Reflections on the Law of Copyright*, 45 COLUM. L. REV. 503, 511 (1945). The "dwarf" quotation here may be traced to Plato's *Banquet*. See R. BURTON, THE ANATOMY OF MELANCHOLY, 25, 437 n. 4 (Jackson ed. 1977).

[211]*Meeropol v. Nizer*, 560 F.2d 1061, 1069, 195 U.S.P.Q. 273, 279 (2d Cir. 1977); *Rosemont Enters., Inc. v. Random House, Inc.*, 366 F.2d 303, 307, 150 U.S.P.Q. 715, 719 (2d Cir. 1966), *cert. denied*, 385 U.S. 1009, 152 U.S.P.Q. 844 (1967). Cf. *Thompson v. Gernsback*, 94 F. Supp. 453, 454, 87 U.S.P.Q. 238 (S.D.N.Y. 1950), in which defendant's magazine *Sexology* (labeled as a "Sex Magazine—Illustrated") was perceived by the court to be not even by the "remotest possibility * * * within the classification of a scientific document" and, generally, PATRY, *supra* note 198, at 65–91; 416–417.

[212]464 U.S. 417, 451, 220 U.S.P.Q. 665, 681 (1984). See also REPORT OF THE REGISTER OF COPYRIGHTS—LIBRARY REPRODUCTION OF COPYRIGHTED WORKS (17 U.S.C. 108) 85 (1983):

"[R]esearch in applied physics, for example, performed by an employee of an aerospace firm, and similar research by a graduate student in a university, may both involve photocopying of the same scholarly articles, but the copyright consequences are different; the former copying is of a clearly commercial nature, and less likely to be fair use."

Medicine was involved in *Williams & Wilkins Co. v. United States*, [213] designed to be a test case under the 1909 Act in the application of fair use to new technological developments. The Court of Claims, in a 4–3 reversal of a trial judge's decision, held that the government libraries' photocopying of journal articles from plaintiff's medical journals did not constitute infringement but was rather fair use. The court set forth the "core" of its rationale in three propositions: (1) plaintiff (together with "medical publishers generally") was not allegedly substantially harmed by the photocopying in question; (2) medicine and medical research would be injured by enjoining these particular practices; and (3) the problem of accommodating the competing interests involved called for legislative action, in the absence of which the courts should not place a risk of harm on science. In further support of its decision to apply the doctrine of fair use, the court emphasized the importance of several factors, including the nonprofit nature and scientific purpose of the libraries' activities, the single-copy-per-request policy of the libraries, the widespread use of library photocopying over several decades with apparent general acceptance, certain legislative comments in the course of the then-current general revision attempts, and, finally, provisions for photocopying in foreign statutes. Chief Judge Cowen argued in his dissent that there was clear and legally cognizable harm to plaintiff resulting from defendants' operation of "a reprint service which supplants the need for journal subscriptions" and operates "on a scale so vast that it dwarfs the output of many small publishing companies,"[214] and that the fair use doctrine in the field of science and scholarly works is designed to protect a new author's need to comment on and discuss earlier works in the same field, not to sanction "bare verbatim reproduction."

In a separate dissent, Judge Nichols stated that "the [majority] decision will be read, that a copyright holder has no rights a library is bound to respect" and that the majority was making "the Dred Scott decision of copyright law."[215]

The closeness of the vote and the far-reaching implications of this case of first impression created a sense of anticipation in the copyright and academic communities when the Supreme Court granted certiorari and then heard argument in December 1974. The result was anticlimactic. The Court split 4–4, with Justice Blackmun not participating in the decision. As is traditional in this situation, no opinions were filed and the votes of individual Justices were not disclosed; however, Justice Blackmun's subsequent dissent in *Sony* left no

---

[213] 487 F.2d 1345, 180 U.S.P.Q. 49 (Ct. Cl. 1973), *aff'd by an equally divided Court*, 420 U.S. 376, 184 U.S.P.Q. 705 (1975). Professor Latman represented the plaintiffs in this case.

[214] *Id.* at 1363–1364, 180 U.S.P.Q. at 62–63. Judge Cowen also noted that the Court of Claims had no power to issue injunctions and that plaintiff had, in any event, expressly stated it did not seek injunctive relief.

[215] *Id.* at 1386–1387, 180 U.S.P.Q. at 79. Judge Nichols also criticized the majority for altering the trial court's findings of fact. *Id.* at 1388–1389, 180 U.S.P.Q. at 80. For a further discussion of this case, see Patry, *supra* note 198, at 178–184.

doubt that he would have voted to reverse the decision of the Court of Claims in *Williams & Wilkins*. Whatever the merits of *Williams & Wilkins* under the 1909 Act, it has statutorily been reversed in the 1976 Act, which chose to treat the *Williams & Wilkins* type of activity as an infringement unless exempt under Section 108, an unlikely possibility, given Section 108(g)(2)'s prohibition on systematic reproduction.

## News Reporting

"News reporting," another "purpose" enumerated in Section 107, has traditionally been granted considerable latitude, beginning with recognition that "news" itself, i.e., the raw facts, is not subject to protection at all, although of course the form of expression of the news is. News reporting featured prominently in the Supreme Court's decision in *Harper & Row, Publishers, Inc. v. Nation Enterprises*, in which *The Nation* magazine asserted fair use for its unauthorized copying of excerpts of President Ford's then-unpublished autobiography, *A Time to Heal.* In rejecting this claim, the Court looked behind defendant's naked assertion of news reporting, writing "[t]he promise of copyright would be an empty one if it could be avoided by merely dubbing the infringement a fair use 'news report' of the book,"[216] and that "[i]n our haste to disseminate news, it should not be forgotten that the Framers [of the Constitution] intended copyright itself to be the engine of free expression."[217]

## Teaching

One of the most controversial purposes touched upon in Section 107 is "teaching." We have already examined a number of specific exemptions for educational uses sprinkled through the statute. (See, e.g., §§110(1), 110(2), and 112(b).) These partial limitations were enacted instead of the blanket exemption for teaching proposed by educational groups.[218]

An impetus for this proposal was *Wihtol v. Crow*,[219] which demonstrated that a teacher could be held liable for unauthorized arranging, duplicating, and performing of a musical work despite the absence of profit and a number of other circumstances seemingly favoring the defendant. The ultimate legislative response included

---

[216]471 U.S. ____, ____, 225 U.S.P.Q. 1073, 1079 (1985). See also *Radji v. Khakbaz*, 607 F. Supp. 1296, 226 U.S.P.Q. 610 (D.D.C. 1985); and *Wainwright Securities, Inc. v. Wall Street Transcript Corp.*, 418 F. Supp. 620, 194 U.S.P.Q. 328 (S.D.N.Y. 1976), aff'd, 558 F.2d 91, 194 U.S.P.Q. 401 (2d Cir. 1977), *cert. denied*, 434 U.S. 1014 (1978); *Time, Inc. v. Bernard Geis Associates, Inc.*, 293 F. Supp. 130, 159 U.S.P.Q. 663 (S.D.N.Y. 1968); *New York Tribune Co. v. Otis & Co.*, 39 F. Supp. 67, 49 U.S.P.Q. 361 (S.D.N.Y. 1941); *Chicago Record-Herald Co. v. Tribune Ass'n*, 275 F. 797 (7th Cir. 1921); and, generally, PATRY, *supra* note 198, at 410–412.

[217]471 U.S. at ____, 225 U.S.P.Q. at 1080.

[218]H.R. REP. No. 94-1476, 94th Cong., 2d Sess. 66–67 (1976). Cf. S. REP. No. 94-473, 94th Cong., 1st Sess. 63–65 (1975).

[219]309 F.2d 777, 135 U.S.P.Q. 385 (8th Cir. 1962).

express mention of "teaching (including multiple copies for classroom use)" as a "purpose" potentially leading to a fair use finding. But the legislators' principal response was a very lengthy discussion of the subject in the committee reports.[220]

Indeed, the six pages devoted to this subject in the 1976 House report led its drafters to warn both that "the concentrated attention given the fair use provision in the context of classroom teaching activities should not obscure its application in other areas" and that "the same general standards of fair use are applicable to all kinds of uses of copyrighted material, although the relative weight to be given them will differ from case to case."[221] Fair use outside the context of education is discussed, with illustrative examples given.[222] The committee discussions in 1966, 1967, 1975, and 1976 culminated in *Guidelines for Classroom Copying in Not-For-Profit Educational Institutions.*[223] The House committee, expressing the belief that these guidelines, formulated by educators, authors, and publishers at the request of the committee, "are a reasonable interpretation of the minimum standards of fair use,"[224] endorsed them "as part of their understanding of fair use."[225]

The guidelines seem to offer for the first time what users have long sought—some numerical guide to how much can be taken. And indeed their very purpose is to fulfill "the need for greater certainty and protection for teachers."[226]

The guidelines permit single copying for the teacher's personal scholarly or educational use of a chapter, article, and like small portions of a specified work. Multiple copies for distribution of no more than one copy per pupil are permitted under more stringent restrictions. They must meet defined tests of brevity, spontaneity, and cumulative effect, and include a notice of copyright. For example, a complete article of fewer than 2,500 words may be reproduced, as may "an excerpt from any prose work of not more than 1,000 words or 10% of the work, whichever is less, but in any event a minimum of 500 words." The timing of the copying must be such "that it would be unreasonable to expect a timely reply to a request for permission." No copying of any kind may "be repeated with respect to the same item by the same teacher from term to term." Copying for purposes

---

[220]S. Rep. No. 94-473, 94th Cong., 1st Sess. 63–65 (1975). Cf. H.R. Rep. No. 83, 90th Cong., 1st Sess. 32–35 (1967).
[221]H.R. Rep. No. 94-1476, 94th Cong., 2d Sess. 72 (1976).
[222]S. Rep. No. 94-473 at 61–62; H.R. Rep. No. 94-1476 at 72–74.
[223]H.R. Rep. No. 94-1476 at 68–71. See Appendix E.
[224]*Id.* at 72.
[225]122 Cong. Rec. H10727 (Sept. 21, 1976); 122 Cong. Rec. H10875 (Sept. 22, 1976).
[226]H.R. Rep. No. 94-1476 at 62. The guidelines also noted that
   "conditions determining the extent of permissible copying for educational purposes may change in the future; that certain types of copying permitted under these guidelines may not be permitted in the future; and conversely that in the future other types of copying not permitted under these guidelines may be permissible under revised guidelines."
*Id.* at 68. The applicability of the guidelines to a teacher's copying for classroom purposes was rejected in *Macus v. Rowley*, 695 F.2d 1171, 1178, 217 U.S.P.Q. 691, 695 (9th Cir. 1983).

of creating, replacing, or substituting for anthologies or avoiding the purchase of books, publishers' reprints, or periodicals is prohibited, as is copying directed by a higher authority and the copying of "consumables," such as workbooks, exercises, and the like.

A separate set of guidelines was developed at the same time for educational uses of music.[227] These guidelines permit, among other things, copying for academic purposes (other than performance) of excerpts of works that do not constitute a "performable unit," but in no case more than 10 percent of the whole work. Limited permission to edit or simplify a work is granted as well as the ability to make single recordings of performances by students for evaluation or rehearsal purposes.

One area expressly left unresolved by Congress in 1976 was the problem of off-air taping of television programming for nonprofit educational use. In 1981 a set of privately negotiated guidelines was agreed to and subsequently endorsed by the House Judiciary Committee.[228] The guidelines permit, generally, individual teachers to tape television programs broadcast for reception by the "general public" (a term that includes simultaneous cable retransmission but excludes pay cable) and to use the recording once in the course of relevant teaching activities within the first 10 consecutive school days following the taping. The recording may be retained for no more than 45 calendar days following the taping, after which time it must be erased or destroyed unless a license agreement or other permission is obtained from the copyright owner.

## The Criteria or Factors Governing Fair Use

In turning to the illustrative "factors" for fair use as set forth in Section 107, it will be recalled that Congress purported to be restating the then-existing judicial doctrine. It was recognized that "since the doctrine is an equitable rule of reason * * * each case raising the question must be decided on its own facts."[229] There was, however, a desire to provide some guidance, and thus the four factors specified in Subsections (1)–(4) were included. As noted above, although each of the four factors must be considered in all fair use determinations,[230] these factors are not exhaustive and, where applicable, the courts may supplement them.

---

[227]H.R. REP. No. 94-1476 at 70–71. See Appendix E.

[228]127 CONG. REC. E4751 (daily ed., Oct. 14, 1981); H.R. REP. No. 97-495, 97th Cong., 2d Sess. 6–7 (1982). See generally PATRY, *supra* note 198, at 354–358. The applicability of the guidelines to a particular defendant's use was rejected in *Encyclopaedia Britannica Educational Corp. v. Crooks*, 558 F. Supp. 1247, 1250, 219 U.S.P.Q. 612, 614 (W.D.N.Y. 1983).

[229]H.R. REP. No. 94-1476 at 65; S. REP. No. 94-473 at 62.

[230]*Pacific & Southern Co. v. Duncan*, 744 F.2d 1490, 1495, 224 U.S.P.Q. 131, 133 (11th Cir. 1984), *cert. denied*, 471 U.S. ____, *on remand*, 618 F. Supp. 469, 228 U.S.P.Q. 141 (N.D. Ga. 1985).

*"The Purpose and Character of the Use, Including Whether Such Use Is of a Commercial Nature or Is for Nonprofit Educational Purposes"*

The distinction between "commercial" and "nonprofit educational" purposes in Section 107(1) was added very late in the revision process,[231] but has taken on considerable importance owing to the presumptions created by the Supreme Court in *Sony Corp. v. Universal City Studios, Inc.*[232] These (rebuttable) presumptions are: (1) *every* commercial use is not a fair use; and (2) *every* commercial use results in harm to the potential market for the copyrighted work. They have been strictly applied in post-*Sony* decisions.[233] It has also been held that they apply where the use is partly for educational purposes but predominantly for commercial purposes.[234]

There is no similar presumption with respect to nonprofit uses, and, indeed, Congress expressly rejected attempts in this regard.[235] This refusal notwithstanding, a nonprofit purpose will weigh in defendant's favor in the application of the first factor.

In *Harper & Row, Publishers, Inc. v. Nation Enterprises*, the Supreme Court provided additional clarification of the *Sony* presumptions. In rejecting a claim that a for-profit magazine's unauthorized use of excerpts from an unpublished manuscript should not be considered a "commercial" use, the Court wrote:

> "In arguing that the purpose of news reporting is not purely commercial, The Nation misses the point entirely. The crux of the profit/non-

---

[231]See PATRY, *supra* note 198, at 304.

[232]464 U.S. 417, 451, 220 U.S.P.Q. 665, 681–682 (1984).

[233]*Harper & Row, Pub., Inc. v. Nation Enters.*, 471 U.S. ___, 225 U.S.P.Q. 1073 (1985); *Financial Information, Inc. v. Moody's Investors Serv.*, 751 F.2d 501, 224 U.S.P.Q. 632 (2d Cir. 1984); *Pacific & Southern Co. v. Duncan*, 744 F.2d 1490, 224 U.S.P.Q. 131 (11th Cir. 1984), *cert. denied*, 471 U.S. ___, *on remand*, 618 F. Supp. 469, 228 U.S.P.Q. 141 (N.D. Ga. 1985).

[234]*Horn Abbot, Ltd. v. Sarsaparilla, Ltd.*, 585 F. Supp. 975 (N.D. Ill. 1984). Cf. *Hustler Magazine, Inc. v. Moral Majority, Inc.*, 606 F. Supp. 1527, 226 U.S.P.Q. 721 (C.D. Cal. 1985), where the Reverend Jerry Falwell's reproduction of a copyrighted pornographic ad parodying him and his mother in numerous letters appealing for money for litigation expenses necessary for a lawsuit against *Hustler*, and for a "survival fund" to keep Falwell's broadcast stations on the air, was found to be fair use. The court noted that Falwell "obviously acted out of a variety of motivations," including "encouraging the faithful to donate money," *id.* at 1534, 226 U.S.P.Q. at 725, but that "[e]ven if Falwell's use had been purely commercial, the court would conclude that the [*Sony*] presumption of fairness had been rebutted in this case." *Id.* at 1534–1535, 226 U.S.P.Q. at 726. With respect to letters sent out following publication of the ad parody, beseeching contributions of funds for a lawsuit against *Hustler*, one may give the Reverend Falwell the benefit of the doubt and assume that a motive in reproducing the ad parody was to reply to its criticism. See *Avins v. Moll*, 610 F. Supp. 308, 325 (E.D. Pa. 1984); H.R. REP. No. 94-1476, 94th Cong., 2d Sess. 73 (1976); S. REP. No. 94-473, 94th Cong., 1st Sess. 66 (1975): "When a copyrighted work contains unfair, inaccurate, or derogatory information concerning an individual or institution, the individual or institution may copy and reproduce such parts of the work as are necessary to permit understandable comment on the statements made in the works." This passage does not, however, support using the work for fundraising purposes, but only for purposes of replying to the outrage. With respect to subsequent letters seeking money for the "survival fund" to continue Falwell's extensive television and radio network (an appeal that netted at least $672,000), it appears that Falwell's motive for the reproduction had nothing to do with responding to the ad, but was instead an opportunistic effort to make money. While the Reverend Falwell had every right to reproduce the work in his original letter in order to respond to its repulsive content, if applied to the "survival fund" letter (and arguably the "reply" letter as also containing requests for money), fair use becomes a mere handmaiden of fundraisers. Cf. 606 F. Supp. at 1534 n. 1, 226 U.S.P.Q. at 725–726 n. 1.

[235]PATRY, *supra* note 198, at 477 n. 4.

profit distinction is not whether the sole motive of the use is monetary gain but whether the user stands to profit from exploitation of the copyrighted material without paying the customary price."[236]

## *"The Nature of the Copyrighted Work"*

The second fair use factor requires the court to examine "the nature of the copyrighted work." The court of appeals in *Sony* stated regarding this factor that "[t]he legislative history and the case law dealing with this factor are sparse."[237] It is unfortunate that some of the cases, particularly those involving factual works, confuse the concept of copyrightability with that of fair use.[238] Works of an entertainment nature have traditionally been held to be less subject to fair use than factual works, although the reasoning behind this different treatment is unclear.[239]

It should also be noted that Congress has demonstrated special solicitude for a number of types of works, including independent newsletters, "consumables," tests, textbooks, and other material prepared for the school market, stating that these works should generally not be the subject of fair use.[240]

## *"The Amount and Substantiality of the Portion Used in Relation to the Copyrighted Work as a Whole"*

The use of the word "portion" in Section 107(3) supports the suggestion that "wholesale copying," i.e., the taking of an entire work or an unduly large portion thereof, should not be fair use. Prior to the Court of Claims' decision in *Williams & Wilkins Co. v. United States*, the courts had uniformly denied fair use for such extensive appropriation.[241] And, notwithstanding the notable (and unique) exception of the time shifting of entire works permitted by the Supreme Court in

---

[236]471 U.S. ____, ____, 225 U.S.P.Q. 1073, 1081 (1985). This passage also illustrates the role that custom can play in fair use determinations. See PATRY, *supra* note 198, at 363 n. 14; Latman, *Fair Use of Copyrighted Works*, COPYRIGHT OFFICE STUDY No. 14, 86th Cong., 2d Sess. 7 (Comm. Print 1960).

[237]659 F.2d 963, 972, 211 U.S.P.Q. 761, 771 (9th Cir. 1981), *rev'd*, 464 U.S. 417, 220 U.S.P.Q. 665 (1984). The *Sony* Supreme Court did not provide any further guidance, as it laconically remarked: "[M]oreover, when one considers the nature of a televised audiovisual work, see 17 U.S.C. §107(2) * * * ." But cf. the Eleventh Circuit's subsequent interpretation of this passage in *Pacific & Southern Co. v. Duncan*, 744 F.2d 1490, 1497 n. 12, 224 U.S.P.Q. 131, 135 n. 12 (1984), *cert. denied*, 471 U.S. ____, *on remand*, 618 F. Supp. 469, 228 U.S.P.Q. 141 (N.D. Ga. 1985). See also the Supreme Court's discussion of this factor in *Harper & Row, Pub., Inc. v. Nation Enters.*, 471 U.S. ____, ____, 225 U.S.P.Q. 1073, 1082 (1985).

[238]See PATRY, *supra* note 198, at 417–418. Compare Judge Sweet's illuminating decision in *Merritt Forbes & Co. v. Newman Investment Securities, Inc.*, 604 F. Supp. 943, 225 U.S.P.Q. 1179 (S.D.N.Y. 1985), with the bizarre interpretations of copyrightability and fair use in *West Pub. Co. v. Mead Data Central, Inc.*, 616 F. Supp. 1571, 227 U.S.P.Q. 631 (D. Minn. 1985). The latter case is criticized at note 246, *infra*, and at note 212 in Chapter 2, *supra*.

[239]See the Ninth Circuit's opinion in *Sony*, 659 F.2d at 972; *Diamond v. Am-Law Pub. Corp.*, 745 F.2d 142, 223 U.S.P.Q. 709 (2d Cir. 1984); *Rohauer v. Killiam Shows, Inc.*, 379 F. Supp. 723, 733, 183 U.S.P.Q. 592, 598 (S.D.N.Y. 1974), *rev'd on other grounds*, 551 F.2d 484, 192 U.S.P.Q. 545 (2d Cir.), *cert. denied*, 431 U.S. 949, 194 U.S.P.Q. 304 (1977).

[240]See PATRY, *supra* note 198, at 418–419.

[241]*Id.* at 449 n. 480.

*Sony Corp. v. Universal City Studios, Inc.*, this has continued to be the general rule, followed in post-*Sony* decisions.[242]

Questions of fair use (and infringement) do not always turn on quantitative assessments. As was appropriately noted in an 1836 English case:

> "When it comes to a question of quantity, it must be very vague. One writer might take all the vital part of another's book, though it might be but a small appropriation of the book in quantity. It is not only quantity but value that is always looked to. It is useless to refer to any particular cases as to quantity."[243]

## "The Effect of the Use Upon the Potential Market for or Value of the Copyrighted Work"

The least understood and, as a consequence, the most misapplied of the factors is the fourth, which the Supreme Court has described as "undoubtedly the single most important element of fair use."[244] As noted above, the Supreme Court in *Sony* created a bifurcated potential market inquiry, with the dividing line expressed in commercial versus noncommercial use terms. For commercial uses, the Court held that potential harm could be presumed. For noncommercial uses, if the use *otherwise qualifies* for fair use under the equitable balancing of the first three factors, the copyright owner is required to show "by a preponderance of the evidence that some meaningful likelihood of future harm exists."[245] The fair use analysis for noncommer-

---

[242] *Horn Abbot, Ltd. v. Sarsaparilla, Ltd.*, 585 F. Supp. 975 (N.D. Ill. 1984); *Financial Information, Inc. v. Moody's Investors Serv.*, 751 F.2d 501, 224 U.S.P.Q. 632 (2d Cir. 1984); *Pacific & Southern Co. v. Duncan*, 744 F.2d 1490, 224 U.S.P.Q. 131 (11th Cir. 1984), *cert. denied*, 471 U.S. ___, *on remand*, 618 F. Supp. 469, 228 U.S.P.Q. 141 (N.D. Ga. 1985). Indeed, the *Sony* court itself recognized this rule. 464 U.S. at 450, 220 U.S.P.Q. at 678–680.

[243] *Bramwell v. Halcomb*, 3 My. & Cr. (Ch.) 736, 738 (1836). See also *WPOW, Inc. v. MRL J Enters.*, 584 F. Supp. 132, 136, 222 U.S.P.Q. 502, 505 (D.D.C. 1984) ("Taking what is in essence the heart of the work is considered a taking of a substantial nature, even if what is actually taken is less than extensive"); PATRY, *supra* note 198, at 451–452. It should be noted that the 1976 Classroom Guidelines on fair use do contain and were specifically intended to have express quantitative figures.

Although §107(3) refers to the portion used in relation to the copyrighted work and not to defendant's work, the latter relationship is sometimes measured. See, e.g., *Harper & Row, Pub., Inc. v. Nation Enters.*, 471 U.S. ___, ___, 225 U.S.P.Q. 1073, 1083 (1985) (noting that the copyrighted material constituted 13% of defendant's work); *Henry Holt & Co. v. Liggett & Myers Tobacco Co.*, 23 F. Supp. 302, 37 U.S.P.Q. 449 (E.D. Pa. 1938) (court notes that three sentences constituted one twentieth of defendant's ad); *Meeropol v. Nizer*, 560 F.2d 1061, 195 U.S.P.Q. 273 (2d Cir.), *cert. denied*, 434 U.S. 1013, 196 U.S.P.Q. 592 (1977), *rev'g* 417 F. Supp. 1201, 191 U.S.P.Q. 346 (S.D.N.Y. 1976) (28 letters constituted 2.4% of copyrighted work and 0.85% of accused work); *Meredith Corp. v. Harper & Row, Pub., Inc.*, 192 U.S.P.Q. 92 (S.D.N.Y. 1974) (infringement went beyond direct appropriation amounting to 11% of defendant's work). Such an inquiry appears to relate to §107(1), i.e., whether defendant has made a productive use of the copyrighted work, or is instead engaged in "chiseling for personal profit."

[244] *Harper & Row, Pub., Inc. v. Nation Enters.*, 471 U.S. ___, ___, 225 U.S.P.Q. 1073, 1083 (1985).

[245] 464 U.S. 417, 451, 220 U.S.P.Q. 665, 682 (1984). In *Harper & Row, Pub., Inc. v. Nation Enters.*, 471 U.S. ___, 225 U.S.P.Q. 1073 (1985), the Court was faced with the question of whether actual harm resulted from the taking of copyrightable expression or from the mere act of unauthorized publication of the factual content of plaintiff's work. By analogy to §504(b), the Court held that "once a copyright owner establishes with reasonable probability the existence

cial uses thus does *not* begin with a presumption that the use is fair until the copyright owner proves harm to the potential market for the work. In *Harper & Row, Publishers, Inc. v. Nation Enterprises*, the Court rejected such an argument, noting that Congress had "resisted pressures from special interest groups * * * [and] structured the provision as an affirmative defense requiring a case by case analysis."[246]

The question thus becomes one of determining what "some meaningful likelihood of future harm is." Former Register of Copyrights David Ladd has written:

"While the 'value' of a copyrighted work obviously could include future uses, I believe the specific reference [in Section 107(4)] to 'potential' underscores the need to secure future markets from pre-emption, and leaves their exploitation to the designs of the copyright owner. The import is that potential markets may be as valuable as those presently exploited. Too narrow a view of adverse market impact may simply have the effect of destroying anticipated markets. Consequently, the concept of 'potential market' in 'fair use' should be as broad as the exclusive rights in §106 allow."[247]

The importance of potential markets was stressed by the Eleventh Circuit in *Pacific & Southern Co. v. Duncan*, which held:

"The fact that [the copyright owner] does not actively market copies of its [work] does not matter, for Section 107 looks to the 'potential market' in analyzing the effects of an alleged infringement. Copyrights protect owners who immediately market a work no more stringently than owners who delay before entering the market. [Defendant] sells a significant number of copies that [the copyright owner] could sell itself if it so desired; therefore, [defendant] competes with [the copyright owner] in a potential market and thereby injures [it.]"[248]

---

of a causal connection between the infringement and loss of revenue, the burden properly shifts to the infringer to show that this damage would have occurred had there been no taking of copyrighted expression." *Id.* at ____, 225 U.S.P.Q. at 1084. This passage does not require the copyright owner to prove actual harm where fair use is asserted as a defense, for *Sony* expressly holds to the contrary. 464 U.S. at 451, 220 U.S.P.Q. at 682. Rather, it holds that where actual harm *is* present *but* there exists a question of a causal relationship between that harm and defendant's taking of copyrighted expression, once the copyright owner has presented a prima facie case demonstrating such a causal relationship the burden shifts to the defendant to rebut the relationship.

[246] *West Pub. Co. v. Mead Data Central, Inc.*, 616 F. Supp. 1571, 227 U.S.P.Q. 631 (D. Minn. 1985), presents a situation where the harm to the market for plaintiff's product (bound reports of judicial opinions) due to defendant's appropriation was clearly evident but nevertheless was not legally cognizable since the portions appropriated (so-called "jump cites") were not copyrightable. Thus, defendant successfully rebutted the causal relationship under the *Harper & Row* test. Based, however, on its erroneous finding that the jump cites were protectible expression, the court held to the contrary, 616 F. Supp. at 1581, 227 U.S.P.Q. at 635–636; PATRY, *supra* note 198, at 455–456.

[247] Address by David Ladd to the Section of Patent, Trademark, and Copyright Law of the American Bar Association (Aug. 10, 1982), *reprinted in Audio and Video Rental: Hearing on S. 32 and S. 33 Before the Subcomm. on Patents, Copyrights, and Trademarks of the Senate Judiciary Comm.*, 98th Cong., 1st Sess. 45 (1983).

[248] 744 F.2d 1490, 1497, 224 U.S.P.Q. 131, 134 (11th Cir. 1984), *cert. denied*, 471 U.S. ____, *on remand*, 618 F. Supp. 469, 228 U.S.P.Q. 141 (N.D. Ga. 1985). See also *Harper & Row, Pub., Inc. v. Nation Enters.*, 471 U.S. ____, ____, 225 U.S.P.Q. 1073, 1084 (1985) ("This inquiry must take account not only of harm to the original but also of harm to the market for derivative works").

## Library Photocopying: §108

The shock waves sent through the educational community by *Wihtol v. Crow* were replicated in the library community by the commencement of the *Williams & Wilkins* case. Both educators and librarians came to feel uncertain in their reliance on general fair use principles and soon demanded a specific exemption with regard to their photocopying activities. After the *Williams & Wilkins* trial decision in favor of the publisher, librarians sought to broaden their exemption; the ultimate result of this quest is another fairly complex provision, which will now be examined.[249]

We may summarize the structure of Section 108 as follows: (1) It defines the coverage of works negatively through partial exclusions set forth in Section 108(h). The net result is that the section is most important with respect to books, periodicals, sound recordings, and television news programs (§108(f)(3)). (2) It sets forth general preconditions for library photocopying in Section 108(a) and (g). (3) It specifies in Section 108(b), (c), (d), and (e) the situations in which, under limitations and conditions over and above those in (a) and (g), works may be reproduced. (4) It covers miscellaneous matters in Section 108(f) and provides in Section 108(i) for a report from the Register in 1983 and at five-year intervals thereafter "setting forth the extent to which this section has achieved the intended statutory balancing of the rights of creators, and the needs of users."

To qualify, a library or archives need not be nonprofit or open to the public. It must, however, make the reproduction and distribution of material "without any purpose of direct or indirect commercial advantage" and, if not open to the public, be open at least to persons dong research in a specialized field who are not necessarily affiliated with the institution in question. The legislative interpretation of these requirements finally permitted libraries in for-profit organizations potentially to qualify, but subject to all the conditions and prohibitions of the section. For example, the collections must be open to the public and cannot be operated for direct or indirect commercial advantage. The latter requirement has caused considerable confusion, owing in part to conflicting legislative report language.[250]

---

[249]See PATRY, *supra* note 198, at 320–322; LIBRARY REPRODUCTION OF COPYRIGHTED WORKS (17 U.S.C. 108): REPORT OF THE REGISTER OF COPYRIGHTS (1983) ("REGISTER'S REPORT") for further discussion of §108.

[250]See REGISTER'S REPORT, *supra* note 249, at 79–84. Regardless of whether the collections are open to the public, §108(d)(1) permits copies to be made only if the library "has had no notice that the copy * * * [will] be used for any purpose other than *private* study, scholarship, or research." Corporate libraries making copies for the company's employees know the copies will be used, virtually always, for *corporate* and not "private" research purposes, and thus the library is not entitled to §108 privileges. See *Sony Corp. v. Universal City Studios, Inc.*, 459 U.S. 417, 469, 220 U.S.P.Q. 665, 689–690 (1984) (Blackmun, J., dissenting), noting that "a library can make a copy for a patron only for specific types of private use: 'private study, scholarship, or research'"; REGISTER'S REPORT, *supra* note 249, at 85 (rejecting assertion that employee of an aerospace company and graduate student at a university are both engaged in "research" within the meaning of §107; employee's conduct characterized as "of a clearly commercial nature * * * ").

Additionally, the reproduction must contain a notice of copyright, although the section does not expressly specify that this notice be identical to that set out in Sections 401–403. In his 1983 report on Section 108, the Register of Copyrights found that there was no conclusive congressional intent on this point but that, on balance, he believed the notice requirement of Section 108(a)(3) was substantially closer to the notice requirements of Sections 401–403 than the copyright "warning" advocated by librarians.[251]

The Section 108 privilege is to make "no more than one copy or phonorecord of a work." In his 1983 report, the Register wrote in this regard that "[h]owever complex, confusing, or troublesome are later provisions concerning supervised, related or concerted, or systematic photocopying, all §108 copying is governed by a clear, simple rule: no more than one copy at a time."[252] It should be noted that the "one copy at a time" rule does not mean that a single copy is always permissible. "Section 108(a) simply provides *only* that single copying is eligible for treatment under Section 108; whether such copying is authorized by that section will always depend on whether subsections (b) through (h) permit it."[253]

An important limitation on single copying is found in Section 108(g). Section 108(g)(1) prohibits copying where the library

"is aware or has substantial reason to believe that it is engaged in related or concerted reproduction or distribution of multiple copies or

---

[251]REGISTER'S REPORT, *supra* note 249, at 74.

[252]*Id.* at 66. In its version of the revision bill, the House added a proviso to §108(g)(2) concerning interlibrary loans. By its own terms, the proviso does not attempt to modify the language preceding it. See H.R. REP. No. 94-1476, 96th Cong., 2d Sess. 77–78 (1976). Cf. S. REP. No. 94-473, 94th Cong., 1st Sess. 70–71 (1975). This proviso was adopted by the conference committee. See H.R. REP. No. 94-1733, 94th Cong., 2d Sess. 71–72 (1976). Questions have subsequently arisen, however, over which legislative report is the authoritative source for the basic language in §108(g)(2) (viz., that preceding the proviso). On January 12, 1977, Senator McClellan, the Senate sponsor and floor manager of the Senate bill (S. 22) which became the Copyright Act of 1976, wrote the following letter to Townsend Hoopes, President of the Association of American Publishers on this question:

"Dear Mr. Hoopes:

"I have your letter of December 22nd concerning the legislative history of Public Law 94-553, which originated as my bill, S. 22. You state that certain suggestions have been made that the legislative history of the bill consists only of the House Committee Report and the Conference Report. I am not acquainted with the statements to which you make reference, but if they have been made they are clearly erroneous.

"The legislative history consists of the Committee Reports, of both the Senate and the House, the Conference Report and the Floor debates. Unless the Conference Report modified language in the Senate Bill or Report, the most authoritative expression of the intent of S. 22 would be the Report of the Senate Committee on the Judiciary. There are several sections of S. 22 where major changes were made by the House of Representatives and accepted in the Conference Committee. This, however, is not the situation with respect to the library photocopying provisions. Section 108 was principally developed in the Senate, and all the language of the Senate Bill was retained by the House of Representatives. The amendment made by the House to Section 108(g)(2) and accepted by the Senate managers of the bill incorporates in the statute the legislative intent of the Senate Report relating to 'systematic reproduction or distribution.'

"I have examined the Report of the House Committee on S. 22 and there is nothing contained in that document which in any way purports to modify the intent of the Senate language. Furthermore, it is significant that the Conference Report does not contain any language modifying the language of the Senate Report on 'systematic reproduction', although on other subjects the Conference Report does directly modify language in either the Senate or House Reports.

"I trust this information is responsive to your inquiry * * *."

[253]REGISTER'S REPORT, *supra* note 249, at 67.

phonorecords of the same material, whether made on one occasion or over a period of time, and whether intended for aggregate use by one or more individuals or for separate use by individual members of a group."

Another important limitation is contained in Section 108(g)(2), which denies the privilege to a library that

"engages in the systematic reproduction or distribution of single or multiple copies or phonorecords of material described in subsection (d): *Provided*, That nothing in this clause prevents a library from participating in interlibrary arrangements that do not have, as their purpose or effect, that the library or archives receiving such copies or phonorecords for distribution does so in such aggregate quantities as to substitute for a subscription to or purchase of the work."

This section proved to be a controversial provision. Guidance on its application in common situations was provided by the development of guidelines by the National Commission on New Technological Uses of Copyrighted Works (CONTU) in 1976, which were endorsed by the House and Senate conferees of the revision bill.[254] The basic CONTU formula used to warrant subscription to a given periodical is a group of requests "within any calendar year for a total of six or more copies of an article or articles published in such periodical within five years prior to the date of the request."

The result of this particular development is as follows: (a) A library whose requests exceed the number set forth in the guidelines is deemed to be substituting for subscription or purchase. Accordingly it does not come within the proviso to Section 108(g)(2). (b) That being the case, it may be deemed to be engaging in "systematic reproduction" within the meaning of Section 108(g)(2). (c) Such activity would disqualify it from the exemption in Section 108(d). Its only recourse, unless other parts of Section 108 apply, is to argue, citing Section 108(f)(4), that, despite the foregoing, it is still engaging in fair use within the meaning of Section 107.

This argument proved even more controversial than Section 108(g)(2) and is the subject of an extended discussion in the Register of Copyrights' 1983 report,[255] which summarized it as follows:

"To read §108(f)(4) as permitting 'post-108' reliance on fair use *as if no §108 copying had occurred* is to come dangerously close to reading §108 out of the statute. Since §108 was deemed necessary to exempt much library photocopying from copyright liability, and since Congress did not likely intend to construct the complex mechanisms in most of the section only to render them moot via (f)(4), that result is implausible. The better position is that library photocopying 'beyond' 108 may be fair use if *both*:

"(a) the transaction is of a *type* which could be fair use in the absence of §108, *and*

---

[254]H.R. Rep. No. 94-1733, 94th Cong., 2d Sess. 72–73 (1976).
[255]Register's Report, *supra* note 249, at 93–104. See also Patry, *supra* note 198, at 320–332.

"(b) the fair use analysis (conducted only if (a) applies) of *this* transaction takes into account the '108' copying which has already occurred."[256]

The Register's 1983 report made a number of recommendations, of both a statutory and a nonstatutory nature.[257]

It should be noted as well that libraries do not obtain the fair use privileges of their patrons, and that patrons (who conversely do not qualify for the Section 108 privilege) may be independently liable for infringement if their photocopying exceeds fair use.[258]

---

[256]REGISTER'S REPORT, *supra* note 249, at 98.
[257]*Id.* at xviii.
[258]*Id.* at xii.

# 8

# Remedies for Infringement

It was implicit in the 1909 Act that "infringement" of copyright meant the violation of one or more of the rights accorded the copyright owner.[1] In making this explicit, Section 501(a) of the 1976 Act also reminds us that such rights are shaped not only by the grants in Section 106 but by the limitations in Sections 107–118 as well.

It will be recalled that infringements committed prior to January 1, 1978, are governed by the 1909 Act,[2] and this provision covers remedies as well as defining the scope of rights. Our focus will be on the 1976 Act procedures, with comparison and contrast to those of the 1909 Act where appropriate.

Before examining the array of copyright remedies provided in Chapter 5 of the 1976 Act, we should note the provisions in the Judicial Code, Title 28 U.S.C., which cover jurisdiction and venue in copyright cases.

## Subject Matter Jurisdiction

### Actions "Arising Under" the Copyright Laws

Subject matter jurisdiction over statutory copyright is undoubtedly included in 28 U.S.C. §1331, which grants to the federal district courts "original jurisdiction of all civil actions * * * [which arise] under the Constitution, laws, or treaties of the United States." There has, however, long been in the Copyright Act a specific jurisdictional provision. This provision was transferred to the Judicial Code in 1948 and is now contained in Section 1338:

"(a) The district courts shall have original jurisdiction of any civil action arising under any Act of Congress relating to patents, plant vari-

---

[1]*Fortnightly Corp. v. United Artists Television, Inc.*, 392 U.S. 390, 158 U.S.P.Q. 1 (1968).
[2]TRANS. & SUPP. §112, 90 Stat. 2600. Cf. 17 U.S.C. §301(b)(2) (1978).

ety protection, copyrights and trademarks. Such jurisdiction shall be exclusive of the courts of the states in patent, plant variety protection and copyright cases."

The key terminology, "arising under," is less clear than it might facially appear. The need for reliable criteria in this area is particularly important because subject matter jurisdiction is, of course, a prerequisite to any federal court determination. Moreover, the absence of such jurisdiction is not waivable and can be the basis for collateral attack, even after a final appellate decision.[3]

The classic formulation of the general rule that jurisdiction over actions to enforce contracts relating to copyrights lies in state court was made by Judge Friendly in *T.B. Harms Co. v. Eliscu*:

> "Mindful of the hazards of formulation in this treacherous area, we think that an action 'arises under' the Copyright Act if and only if the complaint is for a remedy expressly granted by the Act, e.g., a suit for infringement or for the statutory royalties for record reproduction * * * or asserts a claim requiring construction of the Act * * * or, at the very least and perhaps more doubtfully, presents a case where a distinctive policy of the Act requires that federal principles control the disposition of the claim."[4]

The principal question in *Harms* was whether an assignment had been forged; indeed, a state court action raising the same issues had been commenced seven weeks earlier. In dismissing for lack of subject matter jurisdiction, Judge Friendly stated that "the general interest that copyrights, like other forms of property, should be enjoyed by their true owner is not enough to meet this last test," i.e., a distinctive federal policy. Similarly, a suit for "infringement" arising out of a failure to pay the agreed-upon consideration for an assignment of copyright has been held to be a matter of state and not federal law;[5] and the same result obtained in a complaint over inadequate consideration for renewal rights.[6]

Federal jurisdiction is exclusive in disputes over authorship,[7] since such disputes involve the construction of important terms of

---

[3]*Muse v. Mellin*, 212 F. Supp. 315, 136 U.S.P.Q. 297 (S.D.N.Y. 1962), *aff'd*, 339 F.2d 888, 144 U.S.P.Q. 114 (2d Cir. 1964). Cf. *RX Data Corp. v. Department of Social Services*, 684 F.2d 192, 216 U.S.P.Q. 69 (2d Cir. 1982).

[4]339 F.2d 823, 828, 144 U.S.P.Q. 46, 50 (2d Cir. 1964), *cert. denied*, 381 U.S. 915, 145 U.S.P.Q. 743 (1965). The reference in *Harms* to "statutory royalties for record royalties" did not concern claims for unpaid royalties due under a contract but rather the mechanical reproduction compulsory license fee. See *Hall v. Inner City Records*, 212 U.S.P.Q. 272, 273 n. 2 (S.D.N.Y. 1980). See also *Fantastic Fakes, Inc. v. Pickwick Int'l, Inc.*, 661 F.2d 479, 482–483, 212 U.S.P.Q. 727, 730 (5th Cir. 1981) (discussing relationship between state contract laws and federal copyright act); *Berger v. Simon & Schuster*, 631 F. Supp. 915 (S.D.N.Y. 1986); *Obolensky v. G. P. Putnam's Sons*, 628 F. Supp. 1552, 229 U.S.P.Q. 305 (S.D.N.Y. 1986).

[5]*Felix Cinematografica S.r.l. v. Penthouse Int'l Ltd.*, COPR. L. REP. ¶25,578 (S.D.N.Y. 1983).

[6]*Dolch v. United California Bank*, 702 F.2d 178, 218 U.S.P.Q. 916 (9th Cir. 1983).

[7]*RX Data Corp. v. Department of Social Services*, 684 F.2d 192, 196 n. 1, 216 U.S.P.Q. 69, 71 n. 1 (2d Cir. 1982) (work for hire); *Lieberman v. Chayefsky*, 535 F. Supp. 90, 215 U.S.P.Q. 741 (S.D.N.Y. 1982) (joint authorship). To the extent that the decisions in *Keith v. Scruggs*, 507 F. Supp. 968, 212 U.S.P.Q. 683 (S.D.N.Y. 1981), and *Newman v. Crowell*, 205 U.S.P.Q. 517 (S.D.N.Y. 1979), suggest to the contrary, they are believed to be erroneous.

The courts have held that failure to credit an author is not an act of infringement and, therefore, not cognizable under the Copyright Act. *Locke v. Times Mirror Magazine, Inc.*, COPR. L. REP. ¶25,750 (S.D.N.Y. 1985); *Wolfe v. United Artists Corp.*, 583 F. Supp. 52, 223 U.S.P.Q. 274 (E.D. Pa. 1984) (*Wolfe II*); *Wolfe v. United Artists Corp.*, 742 F.2d 1439 (2d Cir. 1983)

the Copyright Act. See, e.g., Sections 201(b) and 101 (definitions of "joint work," "work made for hire".) However, where the dispute regards title and not creation, the suit must generally be brought in state court.[8] Decision making in this area has proved difficult. Significant exceptions to the general rules have been found where defendant used the copyrighted work outside the terms of a contract or license,[9] where the author retained the copyright and the breach of contract or license was undisputed,[10] and where a breach of warranty of title is alleged in a factual setting where infringement must be determined in order to find such a breach.[11]

In *Kaholokula v. Hula Records, Inc.*, the Ninth Circuit, citing a "virtually unflagging obligation" to exercise federal statutory juris-

---

(*Wolfe I*). Such a failure may be actionable, though, under §43(a) of the Lanham Act. *Smith v. Montoro*, 648 F.2d 602, 211 U.S.P.Q. 775 (9th Cir. 1981); *Follett v. Arbor House Pub. Co.*, 497 F. Supp. 304, 208 U.S.P.Q. 597 (S.D.N.Y. 1980).

[8]*Cortner v. Israel*, 732 F.2d 267, 222 U.S.P.Q. 756 (2d Cir. 1984); *Motta v. Samuel Weiser, Inc.*, 768 F.2d 481, 226 U.S.P.Q. 934 (1st Cir. 1985); *Peay v. Morton*, 571 F. Supp. 108, 222 U.S.P.Q. 64 (M.D. Tenn. 1983); *Fantastic Fakes, Inc. v. Pickwick Int'l, Inc.*, 661 F.2d 479, 212 U.S.P.Q. 727 (5th Cir. 1981); *Rotardier v. Entertainment Co. Music Group*, 518 F. Supp. 919, 215 U.S.P.Q. 1078 (S.D.N.Y. 1981); *Stepdesign, Inc. v. Research Media, Inc.*, 442 F. Supp. 32, 200 U.S.P.Q. 77 (S.D.N.Y. 1977). Cf. *World Music Co. v. Adam R. Levy & Father Enters., Inc.*, 214 U.S.P.Q. 854 (S.D.N.Y. 1981).

[9]*Frank Music Corp. v. Metro-Goldwyn-Mayer, Inc.*, 772 F.2d 505, 512, 227 U.S.P.Q. 687, 689–690 (9th Cir. 1985); *Oddo v. Ries*, 743 F.2d 630, 634, 222 U.S.P.Q. 799, 801–802 (9th Cir. 1984); *Kamakazi Music Corp. v. Robbins Music Corp.*, 684 F.2d 228, 230 (2d Cir. 1982); *Costello Pub. Co. v. Rotelle*, 670 F.2d 1035, 1043, 212 U.S.P.Q. 811, 817–818 (D.C. Cir. 1981); *Fantastic Fakes, Inc. v. Pickwick Int'l, Inc.*, 661 F.2d 479, 483, 212 U.S.P.Q. 727, 731 (5th Cir. 1981); *Kanakos v. MX Trading Corp.*, 216 U.S.P.Q. 1030, 1032 (S.D.N.Y. 1981); *Power Lawn Mower Parts, Inc. v. Lawn Mower Parts, Inc.*, 217 U.S.P.Q. 636, 638 (W.D.N.Y. 1981) ("[d]efendants bear the burden of proving that their use of the infringing material was authorized by plaintiff"); *Gilliam v. ABC, Inc.*, 538 F.2d 14, 20, 192 U.S.P.Q. 1, 5 (2d Cir. 1976) ("[o]ne who obtains permission to use a copyrighted [work] * * * may not exceed the specific purpose for which permission was granted"); *Custom Imports, Inc. v. Hanmell Trading Co.*, 596 F. Supp. 1126 (S.D.N.Y. 1984); *Simon & Schuster, Inc. v. Cove Vitamin & Pharmaceutical, Inc.*, 211 F. Supp. 72, 136 U.S.P.Q. 32 (S.D.N.Y. 1962); *Southern Music Pub. Co. v. C&C Films, Inc.*, 171 F. Supp. 832, 833, 121 U.S.P.Q. 450, 450–451 (S.D.N.Y. 1959) (and cases cited therein); *MGM Distributing Corp. v. Bijou Theatre Co.*, 3 F. Supp. 66, 17 U.S.P.Q. 124 (D. Mass. 1933) (plaintiff may elect to sue for breach of contract or copyright infringement).

In *Burnett v. Warner Bros., Inc.*, 486 N.Y.S. 2d 613, 228 U.S.P.Q. 143 (N.Y. Sup. Ct. 1985), federal jurisdiction over a dispute between the authors of a work upon which the movie *Casablanca* was based was found to be exclusive notwithstanding the court's recognition that resolution of plaintiff's claim turned on whether certain rights had been contractually assigned. This decision was, however, modified on appeal, with the appellate court dismissing the suit on the ground that plaintiffs had assigned all their rights in the work. 493 N.Y.S. 2d 326 (N.Y. App. Div. 1st Dept. 1985).

Where the conduct that constitutes a material breach of the contract (and thereby revocation of the copyright license) does not violate any of the copyright owner's exclusive rights it is unclear whether an action for breach of contract only is available. The better view is that evisceration of the contract by any material breach deprives the licensee of its status as an authorized user, thereby rendering infringing any acts committed after the breach and permitted only by virtue of the contract. See *Costello Pub. Co. v. Rotelle*, 670 F.2d 1035, 1043, 212 U.S.P.Q. 811, 817–818 (D.C. Cir. 1981); *Fantastic Fakes, Inc. v. Pickwick Int'l, Inc.*, 661 F.2d 479, 483–484, 212 U.S.P.Q. 727, 730–731 (5th Cir. 1981) (discussion of effect of breach of condition versus breach of covenant); *Frank Music Corp. v. Metro-Goldwyn-Mayer, Inc.*, 772 F.2d 505, 512, 227 U.S.P.Q. 687, 690 (9th Cir. 1985) (holding that regardless of whether certain "visual representations" were copyrightable, defendant's utilization of such representations in breach of its license rendered it liable for infringement).

[10]*Frankel v. Stein & Day, Inc.*, 470 F. Supp. 209, 205 U.S.P.Q. 51 (S.D.N.Y. 1979), *aff'd without opinion*, 646 F.2d 560 (2d Cir. 1980).

[11]*Christopher v. Cavallo*, 218 U.S.P.Q. 396 (4th Cir. 1981). In an unusual factual twist, a state court passed on a fair use claim raised in a libel suit, the alleged libel being an act of infringement. *Mitcham v. Regents*, Copr. L. Rep. ¶25,667 (Tex. Civ. App. 1984).

diction, made a radical departure from prior decisions dismissing suits arising out of contract disputes over royalty payments, holding that where plaintiff seeks remedies available under the Copyright Act (e.g., statutory damages)

> "it would be inconsistent with the copyright statute to deny a federal forum to authors claiming infringement and invoking statutory remedies. * * * [W]here, as here, a plaintiff would be entitled, as a matter of law, to remedies granted by the copyright statute should the threshold issue of ownership be resolved in his favor, his complaint arises under the federal copyright law."[12]

While the Ninth Circuit's commitment to permitting liberal access to the federal courts and its apparent desire to avoid requiring deserving plaintiffs to litigate one dispute in two forums (i.e., a state court action to establish copyright ownership, and a subsequent federal copyright infringement suit) are certainly laudable, it remains to be seen whether other circuits will allow federal jurisdiction to be invoked by the mere artifice of including in the complaint a prayer for a remedy available under the Copyright Act. Indeed, it appears that the Ninth Circuit itself may have had misgivings about its opinion, as the court withdrew it from publication following a settlement by the parties.

## Federal Jurisdiction Over State Claims—Pendent Jurisdiction and 28 U.S.C. §1338(b)

It is frequently the case that activity giving rise to a claim of copyright infringement may also involve aspects actionable under state unfair competition laws. Federal courts have original jurisdiction for such state claims, under 28 U.S.C. §1338(b), "when joined with a substantial and related claim under the copyright * * * laws." As is the case with jurisdiction asserted under 28 U.S.C. §1338(a), the "law of pendent jurisdiction in copyright is in some disarray."[13] Guidance has, however, been supplied by the Supreme Court's decision in *United Mine Workers v. Gibbs*, where the court held:

---

[12]746 F.2d 583, 224 U.S.P.Q. 126 (9th Cir. 1984) (opinion withdrawn as reported in advance sheets following parties' settlement; see *id.* at 587 of bound volume). See also *Joseph J. Legat Architects, P.C. v. U.S. Dev. Corp.*, 601 F. Supp. 672, 676, 225 U.S.P.Q. 1176, 1178–1179 (N.D. Ill. 1985); 625 F. Supp. 293, 229 U.S.P.Q. 132 (N.D. Ill. 1985) (extending *Harms* to find that a suit for damages from copyright infringement is one "for a remedy expressly granted by the [Copyright] Act" and, while disagreeing that on the facts a contract dispute existed, nevertheless finding federal jurisdiction still present). Cf. *Peay v. Morton*, 571 F. Supp. 108, 222 U.S.P.Q. 64 (M.D. Tenn. 1983), and *Legat's* interpretation of it, 601 F. Supp. at 676–677, 225 U.S.P.Q. at 1179.

[13]*Lone Ranger Television, Inc. v. Program Radio Corp.*, 740 F.2d 718, 723, 223 U.S.P.Q. 112, 115 (9th Cir. 1984).

"[I]f, considered without regard to their federal or state character, a plaintiff's claims are such that he would ordinarily be expected to try them all in one judicial proceeding, then, assuming substantiality of the federal issues, there is *power* in federal courts to hear the whole."[14]

Even assuming a state law claim is joined with a substantial and related copyright claim, if the copyright claim is dismissed before trial the proper course is generally to dismiss the state law claim as well.[15]

## Personal Jurisdiction and Venue

Personal jurisdiction over defendants in copyright actions is governed by the rules applicable to federal civil actions generally, which have been fashioned in accordance with the due process requirements of minimum contacts set forth in *International Shoe Co. v. Washington.*[16] Necessary minimum contacts have been found in distribution of catalogs, fliers, or advertisements within the state,[17] distribution

---

[14]383 U.S. 715, 725 (1966). See also *Johnson v. University of Virginia*, 606 F. Supp. 321, 226 U.S.P.Q. 356 (W.D. Va. 1985); *Mister Vee Prods., Inc. v. Le Blanc*, 491 F. Supp. 493 (S.D.N.Y. 1980) (dismissing contention that claims arose out of a "common nucleus of operative fact" under *Gibbs* test). Cf. *Friedman, Eisenstein, Raemer & Schwartz v. Afterman*, 599 F. Supp. 902, 904 (N.D. Ill. 1984) (adopting "liberal" test for jurisdiction of unfair competition claim under 28 U.S.C. §1338(b)).

In *Angel Music, Inc. v. ABC Sports, Inc.*, Copr. L. Rep. ¶25,797 (S.D.N.Y. 1985), issues concerning pendent *party* jurisdiction were raised. In a scholarly and thoughtful opinion, Judge Sweet, following *Gibbs* and other Supreme Court decisions on the issue, held that so long as the claims against both the copyright defendant and the pendent party defendant derive from "a common nucleus of operative fact" the federal courts have the constitutional power to assert jurisdiction over the pendent party defendant.

[15]*Lone Ranger Television, Inc. v. Program Radio Corp.*, 740 F.2d 718, 223 U.S.P.Q. 112 (9th Cir. 1984); *Production Contractors, Inc. v. WGN Continental Broadcasting Co.*, 622 F. Supp. 1500, 228 U.S.P.Q. 604 (N.D. Ill. 1985); *Rokus v. ABC*, Copr. L. Rep. ¶25,726 (S.D.N.Y. 1984); *Calloway v. Marvel Entertainment Group*, Copr. L. Rep. ¶25,622 (S.D.N.Y. 1983). In *Walker v. Time-Life Films, Inc.*, 615 F. Supp. 430, 227 U.S.P.Q. 698 (S.D.N.Y. 1985), *aff'd*, 784 F.2d 44, 53, 228 U.S.P.Q. 505, 511–512 (2d Cir. 1986), the court granted defendant's motion for summary judgment on plaintiff's copyright infringement in what were described as "exceptional circumstances"—an earlier state court decision dismissing plaintiff's copyright claim, but nevertheless retained pendent jurisdiction over the state law claims infringement claim for lack of subject matter jurisdiction and dismissing the state law claims as "simply redundant and equivalent to the copyright claim and asserted for the purpose of avoiding federal preemption." Id. at 440, 227 U.S.P.Q. at 704. Where dismissal of the federal action will result in dismissal of a subsequent state suit on statute of limitations grounds, federal jurisdiction should be retained. *Overman v. Universal City Studios, Inc.*, 224 U.S.P.Q. 838 (C.D. Cal. 1984). Where the parties have agreed to arbitrate the state law claims, pendent jurisdiction must be declined. *Dean Witter Reynolds, Inc. v. Byrd*, 470 U.S. _____ (1985).

[16]326 U.S. 310 (1945). See also *Burger King Corp. v. Rudzewicz*, 471 U.S. _____ (1985); *Hall v. Helicopteros Nacionales de Columbia, S.A.*, 466 U.S. 408 (1984); *Calder v. Jones*, 465 U.S. 783 (1984); *Schaffer v. Heitner*, 433 U.S. 186 (1977).

[17]*Brandir Int'l, Inc. v. Cascade Pacific Lumber Co.*, Copr. L. Rep. ¶25,740 (S.D.N.Y. 1984); *Martin Luther King, Jr. Center for Social Change v. American Heritage Products*, 508 F. Supp. 854, 213 U.S.P.Q. 540 (N.D. Ga. 1981), *rev'd on other grounds*, 694 F.2d 674 (11th Cir. 1982). Cf. *Columbia Mint, Inc., v. Penn Estates*, Copr. L. Rep. ¶25,537 (E.D. Pa. 1983); *Keeton v. Hustler Magazine, Inc.*, 465 U.S. 770 (1984).

Defendant's use of advertising agencies located within the forum state as establishing the necessary minimum contacts for jurisdictional purposes has been the subject of different treatment. Compare *Arbitron Co. v. E.W. Scripps, Inc.*, 9 Media L. Rep. 1507 (S.D.N.Y. 1983), with *Katz v. Evening News*, 514 F. Supp. 423 (S.D.N.Y. 1981), *aff'd*, 705 F.2d 20, 23–25 (2d Cir. 1983).

of a limited number of allegedly infringing copies,[18] display at trade shows,[19] agreements to arbitrate in the forum state,[20] and sharing of performing rights royalties with a collective society or publisher operating within the forum state.[21]

Under the Federal Rules of Civil Procedure, state long-arm statutes may be used to obtain jurisdiction over out-of-state defendants.[22] Many states permit service of process on out-of-state defendants who commit torts outside the forum state that result in harmful effects within the forum state.[23] As long as such service of

---

[18]See especially Judge Leisure's scholarly opinion in *Mayer v. Josiah Wedgwood & Sons, Ltd.*, 601 F. Supp. 1523, 225 U.S.P.Q. 776 (S.D.N.Y. 1985), as well as *Vault Corp. v. Quaid Software Ltd.*, 228 U.S.P.Q. 139 (5th Cir. 1985); *Vallejo v. Webb*, COPR. L. REP. ¶25,751 (S.D.N.Y. 1985); *Pillsbury Co. v. Milky Way Prods., Inc.*, 204 U.S.P.Q. 106 (N.D. Ga. 1978); 215 U.S.P.Q. 124 (N.D. Ga. 1982); *Original Appalachian Artworks, Inc. v. Wormser*, 212 U.S.P.Q. 218 (N.D. Ga. 1980). Cf. *S.L. Kaye Co. v. Dulces Anahuac, S.A.*, 524 F. Supp. 17 (S.D.N.Y. 1981); *Universal City Studios, Inc. v. Photo-Lith Int'l*, 217 U.S.P.Q. 974 (S.D.N.Y. 1981); *Airola v. King*, 505 F. Supp. 30, 212 U.S.P.Q. 153 (D. Ariz. 1980); *JS&A Group, Inc. v. Braswell*, 205 U.S.P.Q. 965 (N.D. Ill. 1979); *Selle v. Gibb*, 567 F. Supp. 1173, 219 U.S.P.Q. 268 (N.D. Ill. 1979); *Children's Television Workshop v. Mary Maxim, Inc.*, 223 U.S.P.Q. 965 (S.D.N.Y. 1984); *Thomas Jackson Pub., Inc. v. Buckner*, 227 U.S.P.Q. 1048 (D. Neb. 1985).

[19]*Gallery House, Inc. v. Yi*, 582 F. Supp. 1294, 223 U.S.P.Q. 894; 587 F. Supp. 1036 (N.D. Ill. 1984). Defendant also sold a limited number of goods to retail outlets within the forum state.

[20]*John Wiley & Sons, Inc. v. Fuchs*, 217 U.S.P.Q. 741 (S.D.N.Y. 1981). See also *Burger King Corp. v. Rudzewicz*, 471 U.S. _____, _____ n. 14 (1985):

"We have noted that, because the personal jurisdiction requirement is a waivable right, there are a 'variety of legal arrangements' by which a litigant may give 'express or implied consent to the personal jurisdiction of the court.' * * * For example, particularly in the commercial context, parties frequently stipulate in advance to submit their controversies for resolution within a particular jurisdiction. * * * Where such forum-selection provisions have been obtained through 'freely negotiated' agreements and are not 'unreasonable and unjust,' * * * their enforcement does not offend due process."

[21]*Greenky v. Irving Music*, 217 U.S.P.Q. 750 (S.D.N.Y. 1981); *Testa v. Janssen*, 482 F. Supp. 1195, 209 U.S.P.Q. 534; 492 F. Supp. 198, 208 U.S.P.Q. 213 (W.D. Pa. 1980); *Donner v. Tams-Witmark Music Library*, 480 F. Supp. 1229, 208 U.S.P.Q. 367 (E.D. Pa. 1979). See also *Edy Clover Prods., Inc. v. NBC*, 572 F.2d 119, 120, 197 U.S.P.Q. 337 (3d Cir. 1978) (jurisdiction of U.S. District Court for New Jersey sustained in infringement suit brought by New Jersey residents against a California television producer, the court holding: "It is clear that a state has an interest in protecting its residents from interstate transmissions which infringe their copyrights").

[22]See *World-Wide Volkswagen Corp. v. Woodson*, 444 U.S. 826 (1980); *Vallejo v. Webb*, COPR. L. REP. ¶25,751 (S.D.N.Y. 1985); *Original Appalachian Artworks, Inc. v. Wormser*, 212 U.S.P.Q. 218 (N.D. Ga. 1980); *Testa v. Janssen,*, 482 F. Supp. 1195, 209 U.S.P.Q. 534 (W.D. Pa. 1980).

[23]*Burger King Corp. v. Rudzewicz*, 471 U.S. _____ (1985); *Calder v. Jones*, 465 U.S. 783 (1984); *Mayer v. Josiah Wedgwood & Sons, Ltd.*, 601 F. Supp. 1523, 1529, 225 U.S.P.Q. 776, 779 (S.D.N.Y. 1985); *Guccione v. Flynt*, COPR. L. REP. ¶25,654; ¶25,669 (S.D.N.Y. 1984); *Micromanipulator Co. v. Bough*, 558 F. Supp. 36, 222 U.S.P.Q. 733 (D. Nev. 1983); *Kinstler v. Saturday Evening Post*, 212 U.S.P.Q. 596 (S.D.N.Y. 1981). Cf. *Wood v. Santa Barbara Chamber of Commerce*, 507 F. Supp. 1128, 210 U.S.P.Q. 930 (D. Nev. 1980). Service of process is authorized under FED. R. CIV. P. 4(e). The amenability of foreign corporations to suit is determined by the law of the state in which the federal court sits. *Comptoir de l'Industrie Textile de France v. Fiorucci, Inc.*, 204 U.S.P.Q. 557 (S.D.N.Y. 1979); *Thomas Jackson Pub., Inc. v. Buckner*, 227 U.S.P.Q. 1048 (D. Neb. 1985).

In *Granada Television Int'l, Inc. v. Lorindy Pictures*, 224 U.S.P.Q. 505 (S.D.N.Y. 1984), plaintiffs sued under the Copyright Act for a declaration that its television series would not infringe defendant's rights and also complained that defendant's threats to institute litigation resulted in a business tort, to wit, "to knowingly claim a copyright which does not exist." The alleged tort consisted of defendant's California attorney mailing a letter to plaintiff's parent corporation in England indicating that defendant had acquired exclusive licensing rights to the Sherlock Holmes stories of Sir Arthur Conan Doyle and considered plaintiff's U.S. distribution of television shows based on certain of the stories to constitute a violation of U.S. copyright and trademark laws. It was not disputed that plaintiff's television shows were to be based only on stories for which U.S. copyright protection had expired. Plaintiffs alleged that since New York is the largest television market in the United States, defendant's threats would result in injury to them in New York, viz., their inability to sell the series to New York stations. The court agreed, holding that the jurisdictional requirements of N.Y. CPLR §302(a)(3) [governing the

process satisfies the federal constitutional requirements for personal jurisdiction, then valid service of process creates *in personam* jurisdiction in federal court. The courts are divided, however, on whether *in personam* jurisdiction over an individual officer of a corporation confers jurisdiction over the corporation.[24]

Intellectual property litigation frequently causes controversy over forum selection. A specific venue provision for copyright actions is contained in 28 U.S.C. §1400(a):

> "Civil actions, suits, or proceedings under any Act of Congress relating to copyrights may be instituted in the district in which the defendant or his agent resides or may be found."

It has been held that this provision, where applicable, controls over the general venue provision of 28 U.S.C. §1391(b).[25] The key word in the special venue provision, Section 1400(a), is "found." As with personal jurisdiction, it has been frequently held that "[a] defendant, whether an individual or entity is found wherever it may be validly served with process" and that "[i]f th[e] Court can constitution-

---

commission of tortious acts committed outside of New York causing injury to persons or property within the state] had been met. Cf. *Abitron Co. v. E.W. Scripps, Inc.*, 9 MEDIA L. REP. 1507, 1510 (S.D.N.Y. 1983) ("The only tie that the alleged tort in the present action has with New York is that the plaintiff resides here and that plaintiff claims to have suffered financial loss or loss of goodwill. These are inadequate links. Both would have been suffered by the plaintiff, if indeed they did occur, wherever it resided."), with *Guccione v. Flynt, supra,* which held that under *Calder v. Jones, supra,* knowledge that the infringing actions will injure plaintiff where plaintiff resides is a sufficient basis for *in personam* jurisdiction.

[24]Compare *Guccione v. Flynt,* COPR. L. REP. ¶25,654; ¶25,669 (S.D.N.Y. 1984), with *Vallejo v. Webb,* COPR. L. REP. ¶25,751 (S.D.N.Y. 1985); *Airola v. King,* 505 F. Supp. 30, 212 U.S.P.Q. 153 (D. Ariz. 1980). It has also been held that where the corporation can be held liable for infringement along with an individual officer, service of process on the officer as an individual rather than as an officer is sufficient to satisfy service of process on the corporation. *Warner Bros., Inc. v. O'Keefe,* 468 F. Supp. 16, 19, 202 U.S.P.Q. 735, 737 (S.D. Iowa 1978).

The reverse question from that posed in the text, viz., whether jurisdiction over a corporation confers jurisdiction over an officer thereof, was addressed by the Supreme Court in *Calder v. Jones,* 465 U.S. 783 (1984), which held that while officers' contacts with the forum state "are not to be judged according to their employer's activities [in the forum state] their status as employees does not somehow insulate them from jurisdiction. Each defendant's contacts with the forum State must be assessed individually." *Id.* at 790. *Calder* implicitly rejects the holding of *Testa v. Janssen,* 492 F. Supp. 198, 208 U.S.P.Q. 213 (W.D. Pa. 1980), that the individual officer's actions are relevant only if the officer acted in his personal capacity rather than on behalf of the corporation. See also *Keeton v. Hustler Magazine, Inc.,* 465 U.S. 770, 781 n. 13 (1984):

> "In *Calder v. Jones,* * * * we today reject the suggestion that employees who act in their official capacity are somehow shielded from suit in their individual capacity. But jurisdiction over an employee does not automatically follow from jurisdiction over the corporation which employs him; nor does jurisdiction over a parent corporation automatically establish jurisdiction over a wholly owned subsidiary. * * * Each defendant's contacts with the forum State must be assessed individually."

and *Kinstler v. Saturday Evening Post Co.,* 212 U.S.P.Q. 596 (S.D.N.Y. 1981) (jurisdiction over corporate officer found under long-arm statute).

[25]*Vallejo v. Webb,* COPR. L. REP. ¶25,751 (S.D.N.Y. 1985). Cf. *Micromanipulator Co. v. Bough,* 558 F. Supp. 36, 222 U.S.P.Q. 733 (D. Nev. 1983). Section 1391(b) allows an action to be brought in any district where the claim arose. The meaning of the term "where the claim arose" is extensively discussed in *Bastille Properties, Inc. v. Hometels of America, Inc.,* 476 F. Supp. 175, 178–182 (S.D.N.Y. 1979). In *Hester v. Tressard Fabrics, Inc.,* 203 U.S.P.Q. 817, 819 (C.D. Cal. 1978), the court raised, but did not answer, the question of whether 28 U.S.C. §1400(a) or §1391 governs actions for declaratory judgment of noninfringement of a copyrighted work.

See also Judge Sweet's opinion in *Children's Television Workshop v. Mary Maxim, Inc.,* 223 U.S.P.Q. 965 (S.D.N.Y. 1984), discussing the history and purpose of §1391(b), and which held that while for purposes of §1400(a) neither "mere shipment of merchandise into New York nor mere solicitation of business in New York constitutes transaction of business under [NYC-PLR] 302(a)(1) * * * solicitation plus shipment of a substantial quantity of goods does constitute transaction of business." *Id.* at 968.

ally exercise personal jurisdiction over defendants, then venue is proper * * *."[26] Under 28 U.S.C. §1391(c) a corporation is a resident of "any judicial district in which it is incorporated or licensed to do business or is doing business," and is "found" in any district in which personal jurisdiction may be obtained over it.[27]

Even when venue is proper in one district, transfer may be made to another district pursuant to 28 U.S.C. §1404(a) under the doctrine of *forum non conveniens*,[28] or the case may be dismissed without prejudice where jurisdiction cannot be obtained over an indispensable party.[29]

Since U.S. copyright law does not have extraterritorial effect, the courts have held that "at a minimum, an act of infringement within the United States is required to hold the defendant accountable for related and infringing acts occurring outside this country."[30] In con-

---

[26]*Vallejo v. Webb*, *supra* note 25; *Thomas Jackson Pub., Inc. v. Buckner*, 227 U.S.P.Q. 1048 (D. Neb. 1985); *Brandir Int'l, Inc. v. Cascade Pacific Lumber Co.*, COPR. L. REP. ¶25,740 (S.D.N.Y. 1984); *Mihalek Corp. v. Michigan*, 595 F. Supp. 903, 225 U.S.P.Q. 736 (E.D. Mich. 1984) (venue regarding state officials proper anywhere in state); *Burstein v. Inside-Outside Bodywear, Inc.*, COPR. L. REP. ¶25,488 (S.D.N.Y. 1983); *AED Research & Servs. Corp. v. International Equipment Exchange, Ltd.*, 223 U.S.P.Q. 457 (N.D. Ill. 1983); *Gallery House, Inc. v. Yi*, 582 F. Supp. 1294, 223 U.S.P.Q. 894; 587 F. Supp. 1036 (N.D. Ill. 1984); *Micromanipulator Co. v. Bough*, 558 F. Supp. 36, 222 U.S.P.Q. 733 (D. Nev. 1983); *Testa v. Janssen*, 482 F. Supp. 1195, 209 U.S.P.Q. 534; 492 F. Supp. 198, 208 U.S.P.Q. 213 (W.D. Pa. 1980); *Donner v. Tams-Witmark Music Library, Inc.*, 480 F. Supp. 1229, 208 U.S.P.Q. 367 (E.D. Pa. 1979).

[27]*Columbia Mint, Inc. v. Penn Estates*, COPR. L. REP. ¶25,537 (E.D. Pa. 1983); *Testa v. Janssen*, 482 F. Supp. 1195, 1197, 209 U.S.P.Q. 534, 535, (W.D. Pa. 1980) ("'[T]he reference in section 1400(a) to 'may be found' does not impose a greater finding of presence than is required to obtain jurisdiction over a corporate defendant. * * * Therefore, if a nonresident corporation is amenable to process under the forum's long-arm statute, *in personam* jurisdiction and venue are extant"); *Burstein v. Inside-Out Bodywear, Inc.*, CORP. L. REP. ¶25,488 (S.D.N.Y. 1983) (following *Testa*).

A defendant, of course, may always be found in the district where the allegedly infringing activity occurred. See *Geo-Physical Maps, Inc. v. Toycraft Corp.*, 162 F. Supp. 141, 146–147, 117 U.S.P.Q. 316, 319 (S.D.N.Y. 1958); *Mode Art Jewelers Co. v. Expansion Jewelry, Ltd.*, 409 F. Supp. 921, 193 U.S.P.Q. 48 (S.D.N.Y. 1976). Cf. *Manning v. Turf & Sport Int'l, Ltd.*, 5 MEDIA L. REP. 1299 (N.D.N.Y. 1979) (motion to dismiss for lack of personal jurisdiction and insufficiency of process granted due to lack of systematic and continuous activity).

[28]*Williams v. De Generes*, COPR. L. REP. ¶25,192 (S.D.N.Y. 1980); *Rootburst, Inc. v. Hustler Magazine, Inc.*, COPR. L. REP. ¶25,111 (D.D.C. 1979); *JS&A Group, Inc. v. Braswell*, 205 U.S.P.Q. 965 (N.D. Ill. 1979); *Schmitt & Stalb Juwelliere G.m.b.H v. Caleari, Teresa & Figil*, 201 U.S.P.Q. 794 (S.D.N.Y. 1978).

Where venue is improper, the suit may be transferred to an appropriate district under 28 U.S.C. §1406(a). *Universal City Studios, Inc. v. Photo-Lith Int'l*, 217 U.S.P.Q. 974 (S.D.N.Y. 1981); *Hester v. Tressard Fabrics, Inc.*, 205 U.S.P.Q. 817, 819 (C.D. Cal. 1978). It should be noted, however, that venue is not a jurisdictional requirement, and thus may be waived unless a timely objection is made. See 28 U.S.C. §1406(b); *Holloway v. Gunnell*, 685 F.2d 150 (5th Cir. 1982); *General Inv. Co. v. Lake Shore Ry. Co.*, 260 U.S. 261 (1922). An objection to improper venue is timely if made in a motion under Federal Rule of Civil Procedure 12(b) or if such a motion is not made, if made in defendant's answer.

[29]*Gallery House, Inc. v. Yi*, 582 F. Supp. 1294, 223 U.S.P.Q. 894; 587 F. Supp. 1036 (N.D. Ill. 1984); *Felix v. Cinemagrafica S.r.l. v. Penthouse Int'l Ltd.*, COPR. L. REP. ¶25,578 (S.D.N.Y. 1983); *Followay Prods., Inc. v. Maurer*, 603 F.2d 72, 203 U.S.P.Q. 76 (9th Cir. 1979). Cf. *Swarovski America Ltd. v. Silver Deer Ltd.*, 537 F. Supp. 1201, 218 U.S.P.Q. 599 (D. Colo 1982), and text at note 44, *infra*.

[30]*Ahbez v. Edwin H. Morris & Co.*, 548 F. Supp. 664, 667 (S.D.N.Y. 1982) (construing *Robert Stigwood Group Ltd. v. O'Reilly*, 530 F.2d 1096, 1100, 189 U.S.P.Q. 453, 457 (2d Cir.), *cert. denied*, 429 U.S. 848 (1976)). See also *Sheldon v. Metro-Goldwyn Pictures Corp.*, 106 F.2d 45, 52, 42 U.S.P.Q. 540, 545 (2d Cir. 1939), *aff'd*, 309 U.S. 390, 44 U.S.P.Q. 607 (1940); *Famous Music Corp. v. Seeco Records, Inc.*, 201 F. Supp. 560, 568–569, 132 U.S.P.Q. 342, 348–350 (S.D.N.Y. 1961). Cf. *Peter Starr Prod. Co. v. Twin Continental Films, Inc.*, 783 F.2d 1440, 229 U.S.P.Q. 127 (9th Cir. 1986) (execution of contract in United States which, without consent of copyright owner, authorized exhibition of motion picture overseas results in subject matter jurisdiction in U.S. court).

trast, the court in *London Film Productions v. Intercontinental Communications*[31] asserted diversity jurisdiction over an alleged infringement by a New York corporation of a British citizen's copyright occurring in Chile and other South American countries, based on the highly questionable theory that copyright infringement constitutes a "transitory cause of action, and hence may be adjudicated in the courts of a sovereign other than the one in which the cause of action arose,"[32] even though the works were in the public domain in the United States.

## Parties

### Plaintiffs

As noted in the discussion of ownership, the 1976 Act provides for a divisible copyright and divisible enforcement. Section 501(b) provides that "the legal or beneficial owner of an exclusive right under a copyright is entitled, subject to the requirements of sections 205(d) [recordation of transfers] and 411 [registration of claim to copyright], to institute an action for any infringement of that particular right committed while he or she is the owner of it."[33] This removes the bar to an exclusive licensee's bringing suit without the copyright owner's participation caused by the indivisibility of copyright under the 1909 law.[34] At a minimum, the licensee under the 1909 law had to join the "proprietor" as a party plaintiff or as a party defendant if he demurred or was himself an infringer. The same was true where an equitable owner sought to sue an infringer. Under the 1976 Act, the licensor of an exclusive right, while no longer the legal owner, is a "beneficial owner," especially if he or she retains a royalty interest.[35]

But Section 501(b)'s removal of obstacles to an exclusive licensee's bringing suit does not nullify the effect of Rule 19 of the Federal Rules of Civil Procedure, which in some circumstances may still

---

[31]580 F. Supp. 47, 223 U.S.P.Q. 381 (S.D.N.Y. 1984).

[32]*Id.* at 49, 223 U.S.P.Q. at 382.

[33]But see *Wildlife Internationale, Inc. v. Clements*, 591 F. Supp. 1542, 223 U.S.P.Q. 806 (S.D. Ohio 1984), *aff'd on this point, rem'd on other grounds*, Civ. Nos. 84-3828; 84-3834 (6th Cir. filed Dec. 3, 1985) (not for publication) (beneficial owners need not comply with §205(d) since they are not claiming ownership by virtue of a transfer).

[34]In *Comptoir de l'Industrie Textile de France v. Fiorucci, Inc.*, 204 U.S.P.Q. 557 (S.D.N.Y. 1979), the court denied standing to the exclusive distributor of works in the United States on the ground that the author "retained the copyright," and thus appears to have erroneously overlooked the change in the 1976 Act on this point. Cf. *Burns v. Rockwood Distributing Co.*, 481 F. Supp. 841, 209 U.S.P.Q. 713 (N.D. Ill. 1979) (exclusive distributor in Illinois given standing). See also discussion of divisability in text at notes 56–73 in Chapter 4.

[35]See, e.g., *Provident Tradesmens B&T Co. v. Patterson*, 390 U.S. 102 (1968); *Gilliam v. ABC*, 538 F.2d 14, 25–26, 192 U.S.P.Q. 1, 10 (2d Cir. 1976); *Defense Committee v. Tennessee Valley Authority*, 340 F. Supp. 408 (S.D.N.Y. 1971), *rev'd on other grounds*, 459 F.2d 255 (2d Cir. 1972); *Smith v. AFM*, 47 F.R.D. 152, 154–155 (S.D.N.Y. 1969). See also discussion in text at notes 72–75, *infra*, on the applicability of the Federal Rules of Civil Procedure to copyright actions.

Although not common, class action suits may be brought in copyright cases as in other civil litigation. See, e.g., *BMI v. CBS, Inc.*, 221 U.S.P.Q. 246, 252 (S.D.N.Y. 1983): "If the identity of the infringed works are difficult to ascertain and the copyright owners are so numerous as to become unwieldy, the inclusion in the complaint of one or more named copyright owners with a prayer for class certification under Rule 23, F.R. Civ. P., would seem appropriate."

require dismissal where an "indispensable" party plaintiff is not and cannot be brought within the court's jurisdiction. This problem is inherent in Rule 19. Although the rule embodies the desirable purpose of preventing multiple lawsuits involving the same subject matter and promoting judicial economy through a complete disposition of the dispute in one proceeding, the rule substantially fails to achieve this goal because its language is unworkable in a number of situations.[36]

The traditional notion that nonexclusive licensees are generally not proper party plaintiffs is also followed in the 1976 Act.[37] Nor may a copyright owner circumvent this rule by authorizing third parties to sue in its name, contrary to the practice permitted under Federal

---

[36]Compare the following 1909 Act cases: *Topolos v. Caldeway*, 698 F.2d 991, 217 U.S.P.Q. 715 (9th Cir. 1983); *National Bank of Commerce v. Shaklee Corp.*, 503 F. Supp. 533, 207 U.S.P.Q. 1005 (W.D. Tex. 1980); *Walker v. University Books, Inc.*, 602 F.2d 859, 202 U.S.P.Q. 793 (9th Cir. 1970), with the following cases under the 1976 Act: *Cortner v. Israel*, 732 F.2d 267, 222 U.S.P.Q. 756 (2d Cir. 1984) (insufficient interest; cf. concurring opinion of Judge Pierce and dissenting opinion of Judge Winter on the question of which act applied, *id.* at 272, 222 U.S.P.Q. at 760); *Hal Roach Studios, Inc. v. Richard Feiner & Co.*, COPR. L. REP. ¶25,709 (S.D.N.Y. 1984); *Wildlife Internationale, Inc. v. Clements*, 591 F. Supp. 1542, 223 U.S.P.Q. 806 (S.D. Ohio 1984), *aff'd on this point, rem'd on other grounds*, Civ. Nos. 84-3828; 84-3834 (6th Cir. filed Dec. 3, 1985) (not for publication); *Kamakazi Corp. v. Robbins Music Corp.*, 534 F. Supp. 69, 217 U.S.P.Q. 60 (S.D.N.Y. 1982); *Costello Pub. Co. v. Rotelle*, 670 F.2d 1035, 212 U.S.P.Q. 811 (D.C. Cir. 1981) (quoted in text at note 44, *infra*); *Dodd, Mead & Co. v. Lilienthal*, 495 F. Supp. 135 (S.D.N.Y. 1980); *Global Childcraft, Inc. v. Grolier, Inc.*, COPR L. REP. ¶25,224 (D. Conn. 1980); *Frankel v. Stein & Day, Inc.*, 470 F. Supp. 209, 205 U.S.P.Q. 51 (S.D.N.Y. 1979), *aff'd without opinion*, 646 F.2d 560 (2d Cir. 1980). See also H.R. REP. No. 94-1476, 94th Cong., 2d Sess. 159 (1976). A termination interest under §§203 or 304(c) suffices for standing as well. It has also been held that a nominal beneficial interest suffices for standing for state misappropriation claims. *Rossner v. CBS, Inc.*, 612 F. Supp. 334, 338, 226 U.S.P.Q. 593, 595 (S.D.N.Y. 1985).

Section 501(b) also provides that the court in its discretion may require joinder or that written notice of the action with a copy of the complaint be served upon any person shown by the records of the Copyright Office "or otherwise." H.R. REP. No. 94-1476 at 159; *Janus Films, Inc. v. Delta Communications*, Civ. No. 82-8653 (S.D.N.Y. filed Aug. 4, 1983); *Swarovski America Ltd. v. Silver Deer Ltd.*, 537 F. Supp. 1201, 1206, 218 U.S.P.Q. 599, 603 (D. Colo. 1982) ("the term 'interest' contained in §501(b) has the same meaning as in [Fed. R. Civ. P.] 19(a), namely 'a legally protected, not merely a financial interest or interest of convenience' "); *Skor-Mor Products, Inc. v. Sears, Roebuck & Co.*, COPR. L. REP. ¶25,591 (S.D.N.Y. 1983). Notice is required to be served upon any person whose interest is "likely to be affected by a decision in the case." Joinder of such persons is to be permitted.

In *Wales Industrial, Inc. v. Hasbro Bradley, Inc.*, 612 F. Supp. 510, 517, 226 U.S.P.Q. 584, 588 (S.D.N.Y. 1985), the court created the following rule regarding joinder:

"Absent special circumstances joinder should be required in cases challenging the validity of the copyright upon which rest the rights of the person to be joined and should not be required if the only issue is whether the defendant engaged in unlawful copying."

Joinder in *Wales* was found particularly appropriate since the license granted was for a three-year period and limited in geographical area, and defendant thus ran the risk of suits in other forums by the copyright owner-licensor.

What if the beneficial owner retains the right to have the legal title reassigned to it by its licensee; does the licensee still hold an "exclusive" license for §501(b) standing purposes? The courts have answered the question affirmatively. See *Bandai-America, Inc. v. Bally Midway Mfg. Co.*, 775 F.2d 70, 73-74, 227 U.S.P.Q. 716, 718-719 (3d Cir. 1985); *Williams & Wilkins Co. v. United States*, 172 U.S.P.Q. 670, 674-676 (Ct. Cl. 1972), *rev'd on other grounds*, 487 F.2d 1345, 180 U.S.P.Q. 49 (Ct. Cl. 1973), *aff'd by an equally divided Court*, 420 U.S. 376, 184 U.S.P.Q. 705 (1975).

[37]*Video Views, Inc. v. Kuhns*, No. C-84-1543 (N.D. Cal. 1984) (but cf. *Video Views, Inc. v. Alexander*, COPR. L. REP. ¶25,771 (D. Minn. 1985)); *BMI v. CBS, Inc.*, 221 U.S.P.Q. 246 (S.D.N.Y. 1983); *Eden Toys, Inc. v. Floralee Undergarment Co.*, 526 F. Supp. 1187, 1190, 217 U.S.P.Q. 163, 165 (S.D.N.Y. 1981), *rev'd and rem'd in part on other grounds, aff'd in part*, 697 F.2d 27, 217 U.S.P.Q. 201 (2d Cir. 1982). Cf. *BMI v. United States Shoe Corp.*, 678 F.2d 816, 217 U.S.P.Q. 224 (9th Cir. 1982); *BMI v. Moor-Law, Inc.*, 484 F. Supp. 357, 204 U.S.P.Q. 726 (D. Del. 1980). See also *Swarovski America Ltd. v. Silver Deer Ltd.*, 537 F. Supp. 1201, 218 U.S.P.Q. 599 (D. Colo. 1982) (questioning whether license was exclusive or nonexclusive).

Rule of Civil Procedure 17(a).[38] Nonexclusive licensees, among others, may sue in two situations involving infringement by cable (for which special remedies are provided in Section 510): (1) A local television licensee of copyrighted material may bring an action for the "willful or repeated" transmission of such material into its area against a cable operator who is not permitted by the Federal Communications Commission to do so or who has not made the prerequisite filings and payments (§§510(c), 111(c)).[39] (2) Any local broadcaster (with or without a license), as well as the primary transmitter, may sue for willful alteration of a primary transmission (§§501(d), 111(c)(3)).

A third exception, under the Universal Copyright Convention (UCC), was found where, upon compliance with the notice provisions of Article III (1) thereof (compliance with which excuses all formalities in the contracting State), a Canadian author was permitted to sue in the United States where authorized to do so under Canadian (but apparently not U.S.) law.[40]

Since Section 501(b) permits the legal (or beneficial) owner to institute an action for infringement of that right committed "while he or she is the owner of it," it may be asked whether a *nunc pro tunc* assignment is effective in the light of this statutory language and the general rule that assignment of copyright does not convey existing causes of action for infringement unless expressly included.[41] In *Co-Opportunities v. NBC*[42] the court held that a *nunc pro tunc* assignment of causes of action does relate back, despite concerns over manipulation of the statute of limitations.

### Defendants

It must always be remembered that copyright infringement is a tort.[43] Accordingly, all persons participating therein are liable. As noted in *Costello Publishing Co. v. Rotelle:*

---

[38]*Eden Toys, Inc. v. Floralee Undergarment Co.*, 697 F.2d 27, 32 n. 3, 217 U.S.P.Q. 201, 204–205 n. 3 (2d Cir. 1982). Cf. *Global Childcraft, Inc. v. Grolier, Inc.*, COPR. L. REP. ¶25,224 at p. 16,334 (D. Conn. 1980).

[39]See *Hubbard Broadcasting, Inc. v. Southern Satellite Systems, Inc.*, 593 F. Supp. 808, 224 U.S.P.Q. 468 (D. Minn. 1984), *aff'd*, 777 F.2d 393, 228 U.S.P.Q. 102 (8th Cir. 1985). The genesis of §501(c) appears to be broadcasters' concerns that their contracts with program syndicators or motion picture companies were not sufficiently "exclusive" for purposes of §501(b). See *Copyright Law Revision: Hearings on H.R. 4347 et al. Before Subcomm. No. 3 of the House Judiciary Comm.*, 89th Cong., 1st Sess. 1230, 1724 (1965); *Copyright Law Revision: Hearings on S. 1361 Before the Subcomm. on Patents, Trademarks, and Copyrights of the Senate Judiciary Comm.*, 93d Cong., 1st Sess. 626 (1973); *Copyright Law Revision: Hearings on H.R. 2223 Before the Subcomm. on Courts, Civil Liberties, and the Administration of Justice of the House Judiciary Comm.*, 94th Cong., 1st Sess. 784 (1975).

[40]*Dahinden v. Byrne*, COPR. L. REP. ¶25,564; 220 U.S.P.Q. 719 (D. Ore. 1982).

[41]*Skor-Mor Products, Inc. v. Sears, Roebuck & Co.*, COPR. L. REP. ¶25,397 (S.D.N.Y. 1982); COPR. L. REP. ¶25,591 (S.D.N.Y. 1983); *Co-Opportunities, Inc. v. NBC*, 510 F. Supp. 43 (N.D. Cal. 1981).

[42]510 F. Supp. 43 (N.D. Cal. 1981). Accord *Custom Decor, Inc. v. Nautical Crafts, Inc.*, 502 F. Supp. 154, 213 U.S.P.Q. 565 (E.D. Pa. 1980); *National Council of Young Israel, Inc. v. FEIT*, 347 F. Supp. 1293, 175 U.S.P.Q. 351 (S.D.N.Y. 1972).

[43]*DeGette v. Mine Co. Restaurant, Inc.*, 224 U.S.P.Q. 763, 765 (10th Cir. 1985).

"Courts have long held in patent, trademark, literary property, and copyright cases, that any member of the distribution claim can be sued as an alleged joint tort-feasor. * * * Since joint tort-feasors are jointly and severally liable, the victim of * * * infringement may sue as many or as few of the alleged wrongdoers as he chooses; those left out of the lawsuit, commentary underscores, are not indispensable parties."[44]

In a typical case, this may include the publisher, printer, and vendor.[45] But the net of liability may extend much further, to those having a less direct involvement in the infringement as well as to individuals perpetrating the infringing acts on behalf of a corporate employer. Although absence of knowledge or intention may affect the shaping of remedies,[46] it is not a defense.

Infringers are not merely those subject to rules of vicarious liability exemplified by the agency principle of *respondeat superior*;[47] the net also reaches those subsumed within the broad rubric of "contributory infringement."[48] In this regard, it has been held that

---

[44]670 F.2d 1035, 1043, 212 U.S.P.Q. 811, 816 (D.C. Cir. 1981) (quoting *Stabilierunfond Für Wien v. Kaiser Stuhl Wine Distrubuots Pyt, Ltd.*, 209 U.S.P.Q. 633, 639 (D.C. Cir. 1981). Cf. text at note 35, *supra*, and cases cited at note 35, *supra*. See also *Dixon v. Atlantic Recording Corp.*, 227 U.S.P.Q. 559 (S.D.N.Y. 1985) (motion of Harry Fox Agency for summary judgment on issue of vicarious liability for its granting of a mechanical license for allegedly infringing work denied). While there is joint and several liability for damages, there is only several liability for illegal profits. *Frank Music Corp. v. Metro-Goldwyn-Mayer, Inc.*, 772 F.2d 505, 519, 227 U.S.P.Q. 687, 696 (9th Cir. 1985) ("rule of several liability for profits applies, at least, where defendants do not act as partners, or 'practically partners' "); *Abeshouse v. Ultragraphics, Inc.*, 754 F.2d 467, 472 (2d Cir. 1985); *MCA, Inc. v. Wilson*, 677 F.2d 180, 186, 211 U.S.P.Q. 577, 582 (2d Cir. 1981).

[45]*American Code Co. v. Bensinger*, 282 F. 829 (2d Cir. 1922); *Gross v. Van Dyke Gravure Co.*, 230 F. 412 (2d Cir. 1916).

[46]See 17 U.S.C. §504(c)(2) (1978); *United Feature Syndicate, Inc. v. Powell*, COPR. L. REP. ¶25,508 at p. 18,001 (C.D. Cal. 1981) ("The term 'innocent infringement' * * * is an objective test which requires a person claiming innocence to establish more than a mere subjective intent not to infringe. A person who would fall within this provision must demonstrate that he or she had no means at his disposal by which he or she could have learned that his or her acts might infringe someone's copyrights."). For a review of these issues under the 1909 Act, see Latman and Tager, *Liability of Innocent Infringers of Copyright*, COPYRIGHT OFFICE STUDY No. 25, 86th Cong., 2d Sess. (Comm. Print 1960).

[47]H.R. REP. No. 94-1476, 94th Cong., 2d Sess. 129–130 (1976). The separate concepts of "vicarious" and "contributory" liability are frequently confused. Commentators have suggested that

"the fundamental difference between the two principles involves the power to police or control the activities and conduct of the primary infringer, which is necessary only to the imposition of liability for vicarious copyright infringement. In essence, the principle of vicarious copyright infringement is intended to *encourage* the exercise of any power a person may have to police or control the activities and conduct of a primary infringer, whereas the principle of contributory copyright infringement is intended to *discourage* all persons from aiding or furthering the activities and conduct of a primary infringer."

Gilburne and Meyer, *Liability for Copyright Infringement Committed by Third Parties or by Employees*, 2 COMPUTER LAWYER 1, 6 (1985). See also *Universal City Studios, Inc. v. Nintendo Co., Ltd.*, 615 F. Supp. 838, 860, 227 U.S.P.Q. 96, 112 (S.D.N.Y. 1985) (corporation that licensed infringing work to third party "with knowledge of the similarities and [which] induce[d] * * * the infringement through its license agreement" held liable for vicarious infringement); *F.E.L. Pub., Ltd. v. National Conference of Catholic Bishops*, 466 F. Supp. 1034, 1040, 200 U.S.P.Q. 301, 306 (N.D. Ill. 1978), and cases cited therein; *Warner Bros., Inc. v. O'Keefe*, 468 F. Supp. 16, 20, 202 U.S.P.Q. 735, 737–738 (S.D. Iowa 1978); *Famous Music Corp. v. Bay State Harness Horse Racing & Breeding Ass'n*, 423 F. Supp. 341, 342–343 (D. Mass. 1976), *aff'd*, 554 F.2d 1213, 194 U.S.P.Q. 177 (1st Cir. 1977); *Warner Bros.-Seven Arts, Inc. v. Kalantzakis*, 326 F. Supp. 80, 82, 170 U.S.P.Q. 228, 229 (S.D. Tex. 1971).

[48]Note that §106 gives the copyright owner exclusive power "to do *and to authorize*" the enumerated rights. This language was intended to continue the 1909 Act case law on contributory infringement. H.R. REP. No. 94-1476, 94th Cong., 2d Sess. 61 (1976); S. REP. No. 94-473, 94th Cong., 1st Sess. 57 (1975). See also 17 U.S.C. §108(f)(1) (library not liable "for the unsupervised use of reproducing equipment located on its premises," provided certain warnings are posted).

"[w]hether a participant in an infringing activity is classed as a contributory infringer does not depend upon his or her 'quantitive contribution' to the infringement. 'Rather, resolution of the issue * * * depends upon a determination of the function [the alleged infringer] plays in the total [reproduction] process.' "[49]

The emphasis here on the function of the alleged infringer raises the question of individual liability. In *Stygian Songs v. Patton*,[50] for example, the owner of a night club was held liable for the infringing performance of musical compositions despite an assertion that she had no control over what songs were performed. A similar result obtained in *Fourth Floor Music, Inc. v. Der Place Inc.*,[51] where the court held:

"[T]he fact that the compositions were performed by independent contractors is of no import, since the owner of the establishment has promoted the infringing acts, even if he/it has no knowledge that a copyright is being infringed."

Individual corporate officers have been held liable where they were personally involved in the infringing actions (and regardless of

[49]*RSO Records, Inc. v. Peri*, 596 F. Supp. 849, 853, 225 U.S.P.Q. 407, 409 (S.D.N.Y. 1984) (reproduction of color separations for graphics for counterfeit sound recordings held contributory infringement of sound recordings); *Southern Bell Tel. & Tel. Co. v. ATD Pub.*, 756 F.2d 801, 811, 225 U.S.P.Q. 899, 906 (11th Cir. 1985); *Original Appalachian Artworks, Inc. v. Cradle Creations, Inc.*, 223 U.S.P.Q. 80 (N.D. Ga. 1982) (publication of booklet containing instructions and patterns for making copyrighted "soft sculptures" held contributory infringement); *Telex Corp. v. IBM*, 367 F. Supp. 258, 332, 179 U.S.P.Q. 777, 794–795 (N.D. Okla. 1973) (infringing manuals used to "facilitate repair, preventive maintenance and operation" of computer for which defendant had exclusive marketing rights constituted sufficient interest to support finding of contributory infringement). Cf. *Vernon Music Corp. v. First Dev. Corp.*, Copr. L. Rep. ¶25,686 (D. Mass. 1984) ("mere" landlord relationship with tenant insufficient to establish liability), with *Gershwin Pub. Corp. v. Columbia Artists Mgt., Inc.*, 443 F.2d 1159, 1162, 170 U.S.P.Q. 182, 184–185 (2d Cir. 1971); *Shapiro, Bernstein & Co. v. H.L. Green Co.*, 316 F.2d 304, 307, 137 U.S.P.Q. 275, 277 (2d Cir. 1963).
[50]Copr. L. Rep. ¶25,539 (D. Kan. 1982).
[51]572 F. Supp. 41, 43, 223 U.S.P.Q. 900, 902 (D. Neb. 1983). See also *BMI v. Moor-Law, Inc.*, 612 F. Supp. 474, 227 U.S.P.Q. 829 (D. Del. 1985); *Columbia Pictures Indus., Inc. v. Aveco, Inc.*, 612 F. Supp. 315, 227 U.S.P.Q. 397 (M.D. Pa. 1985) (video rental store contributorily liable for on-premises "public" performances of motion pictures in private viewing booths); *Columbia Pictures Indus., Inc. v. Redd Horne, Inc.*, 749 F.2d 154, 224 U.S.P.Q. 641 (3d Cir. 1984) (same); *Sygma Photo News, Inc. v. High Society Magazine, Inc.*, 603 F. Supp. 829, 226 U.S.P.Q. 94 (S.D.N.Y.), *aff'd*, 778 F.2d 89, 92, 228 U.S.P.Q. 580, 582 (2d Cir. 1985) (corporations under common ownership and control); *Hal Roach Studios, Inc. v. Richard Feiner & Co.*, Copr. L. Rep. ¶25,709 (S.D.N.Y. 1984) (vicarious liability from inducing third-party infringement); *BMI v. Abdalla*, Copr. L. Rep. ¶25,690 (S.D. Ohio 1984) (music club); *BMI v. Terrose*, 223 U.S.P.Q. 137 (W.D.N.Y. 1983) (manager of club who had supervision over day-to-day operations held liable); *United Feature Syndicate, Inc. v. Powell*, Copr. L. Rep. ¶25,508 (C.D. Cal. 1981) (store owner selling infringing jewelry held liable).
These cases follow the so-called "dance hall," "ballroom," or related cases under the 1909 Act. See, e.g., *KECA Music, Inc. v. Dingus McGee's Co.*, 432 F. Supp. 72, 199 U.S.P.Q. 764 (W.D. Mo. 1977); *Famous Music Corp. v. Bay State Harness Horse Racing & Breeding Ass'n*, 554 F.2d 1213, 194 U.S.P.Q. 177 (1st Cir. 1977); *Gershwin Pub. Corp. v. Columbia Artists Mgt., Inc.*, 443 F.2d 1159, 170 U.S.P.Q. 182 (2d Cir. 1971); *Screen Gems–Columbia Music, Inc. v. Mark-Fi Records, Inc.*, 256 F. Supp. 399, 150 U.S.P.Q. 523 (S.D.N.Y. 1966); *Davis v. E.I. du Pont de Nemours & Co.*, 240 F. Supp. 612, 145 U.S.P.Q. 258 (S.D.N.Y. 1965); *Shapiro, Bernstein & Co. v. H.L. Green Co.*, 316 F.2d 304, 137 U.S.P.Q. 275 (2d Cir. 1963); *M. Witmark & Sons, Inc. v. Tremont Social & Athletic Club*, 188 F. Supp. 787, 127 U.S.P.Q. 447 (D. Mass. 1960); *Shapiro, Bernstein & Co. v. Veltin*, 47 F. Supp. 648, 55 U.S.P.Q. 335 (W.D. La. 1942); *Buck v. Jewell-La Salle Realty Co.*, 283 U.S. 191, 9 U.S.P.Q. 17 (1931); *Dreamland Ball Room, Inc. v. Shapiro, Bernstein & Co.*, 36 F.2d 354, 3 U.S.P.Q. 288 (7th Cir. 1929); *Herbert v. Shanley*, 242 U.S. 591 (1917). Cf. *Calloway v. Marvel Entertainment Group*, Copr. L. Rep. ¶25,622 (S.D.N.Y. 1983) (law firm that negotiated and drafted agreements between plaintiffs and alleged infringers could not be held contributorily liable).

whether they exceeded their corporate authority in so acting) or where they "had the right and ability to supervise them and had a financial stake in them."[52]

The extension of contributory liability for sale of machines capable of reproducing copyrighted works featured prominently in the Supreme Court's decision in *Sony Corp. v. Universal City Studios, Inc.*, where home taping of motion pictures on home video recorders was at issue. In adopting the patent law staple-article-of-commerce doctrine[53] into copyright law, the Court held that

> "the sale of copying equipment, like the sale of other articles of commerce, does not constitute contributory infringement, if the product is widely used for legitimate unobjectionable purposes. Indeed, it need merely be capable of substantial noninfringing uses."[54]

In examining the specific machine before it, however, the Court rephrased the inquiry by stating the question to be resolved as "whether the Betamax is capable of commercially significant noninfringing uses."[55] Since the Court expressly declined to "give precise content to the question of how much use is commercially significant,"[56] the lower courts will have to provide that content as well as determine whether there is a meaningful difference between the "substantial noninfringing use" and "commercially significant" tests outlined by the Court.

---

[52]*Columbia Pictures Indus., Inc. v. Redd Horne, Inc.*, 749 F.2d 154, 224 U.S.P.Q. 641 (3d Cir. 1984); *Warner Bros., Inc. v. Lobster Pot, Inc.*, 582 F. Supp. 478, 223 U.S.P.Q. 239 (N.D. Ohio 1984); *Kenbrooke Fabrics, Inc. v. Holland Fabrics, Inc.*, 602 F. Supp. 151, 225 U.S.P.Q. 153 (S.D.N.Y. 1984); *RSO Records, Inc. v. Peri*, 596 F. Supp. 849, 858, 225 U.S.P.Q. 407, 413 (S.D.N.Y. 1984); *United Feature Syndicate, Inc. v. Sunrise Mold Co.*, 569 F. Supp. 1475 (S.D. Fla. 1983); *Pret-A-Printee, Ltd. v. Allton Knitting Mills, Inc.*, 218 U.S.P.Q. 150 (S.D.N.Y. 1982); *United Feature Syndicate, Inc. v. Cornwall Indus.*, COPR. L. REP. ¶25,509 (C.D. Cal. 1981); *Rodgers v. Quests, Inc.*, 213 U.S.P.Q. 212 (N.D. Ohio 1981); *Lauratex Textile Corp. v. Allton Knitting Mills, Inc.*, 517 F. Supp. 900, 214 U.S.P.Q. 203; 519 F. Supp. 730, 215 U.S.P.Q. 521 (S.D.N.Y. 1981); COPR. L. REP. ¶25,360 (S.D.N.Y. 1982); *Boz Scaggs Music v. KND Corp.*, 491 F. Supp. 908, 208 U.S.P.Q. 307 (D. Conn. 1980). Cf. *Bourne Co. v. Khalil*, 611 F. Supp. 269, 271 (E.D. Mich. 1985) (status as sole shareholder and manager does not render individual "ipso facto liable for allegedly wrongful appropriation * * *"); *Donner v. Tams-Witmark Music Library*, 480 F. Supp. 1229, 1234 n. 4, 208 U.S.P.Q. 367, 370 n. 4 (E.D. Pa. 1979); and Judge Decker's thoughtful opinion in *Universal City Studios, Inc. v. American Invsco Mgt., Inc.*, 217 U.S.P.Q. 1076 (N.D. Ill. 1981). It has been held that "[a] parent corporation cannot be held liable for the infringing actions of its subsidiary unless there is a substantial and continuing connection with respect to the infringing acts." *Frank Music Corp. v. Metro-Goldwyn-Mayer, Inc.*, 772 F.2d 505, 519–520, 227 U.S.P.Q. 687, 696 (9th Cir. 1985).

[53]35 U.S.C. §271(c).

[54]464 U.S. 417, 442, 220 U.S.P.Q. 664, 678 (1984). For pre-*Sony* decisions on this point, see *Midway Mfg. Co. v. Artic Int'l, Inc.*, 704 F.2d 1009, 1013, 218 U.S.P.Q. 791, 794 (7th Cir.), *cert. denied*, 464 U.S. 823, 220 U.S.P.Q. 480 (1983) ("speed-up" kits for electronic audiovisual games; contributory infringement by sale of same); *Atari, Inc. v. JS&A Group*, 597 F. Supp. 5 (N.D. Ill. 1983) (electronic audiovisual game cartridge copying machine held not capable of substantial noninfringing uses); *Elektra Records Co. v. Gem Electronics Distributors, Inc.*, 360 F. Supp. 821, 179 U.S.P.Q. 617 (E.D.N.Y. 1973) ("Make-A-Tape" machine operated in conjunction with sale of blank tapes held infringement). Cf. *Midway Mfg. Co. v. Strohon*, 564 F. Supp. 741, 219 U.S.P.Q. 42 (N.D. Ill. 1983) (insufficient authority or control over purchasers for finding of contributory infringement).

[55]464 U.S. at 442, 220 U.S.P.Q. at 678. Aside from the question of substantial noninfringing uses, the *Sony* majority erected what may amount to an insurmountable standing hurdle by holding that "in an action for *contributory* infringement against the seller of copying equipment, the copyright holder may not prevail unless the relief that he seeks affects only his [works], or unless he speaks for virtually all copyright holders with an interest in the outcome." 464 U.S. at 446, 220 U.S.P.Q. at 680.

[56]464 U.S. at 442, 220 U.S.P.Q. at 678.

In *RCA Records v. All-Fast Systems, Inc.*, a post-*Sony* decision involving an audiocassette copying device, the court held that *Sony* "extends protection only to the manufacturer of the infringing machine, not to its operator."[57] As defendant, the owner of a retail copying service, was in a position to control the use of copyrighted works and had authorized the use without permission from the copyright owner,[58] the court issued a preliminary injunction prohibiting defendant from selling blank tapes which defendant knew or had reason to believe would be used in reproducing plaintiff's copyrighted works, and from using the copying machine for the purpose of reproducing plaintiff's works. Implicit in the court's ruling is a finding that the individual customers' conduct was infringing, since there can be no contributory infringement without direct infringement.[59]

It should be recalled that co-authors and co-owners cannot be infringers, and have an independent right to use or license the use of the copyrighted work, subject only to a duty to account to the other co-authors or co-owners for any profits earned thereby.[60]

## U.S. Government Liability

Section 8 of the 1909 Act expressly provided that U.S. government use of copyrighted material belonging to others would not transform the material into a government publication and thereby cause any loss of copyright; the proprietor maintained full rights against third persons who later used the material. The 1976 Act omits this savings clause as unnecessary, but with the clear intent not to change the result provided by the clause.[61]

An even more pressing problem was the liability of the government to the proprietor if its use was without consent. Until 1960, the doctrine of sovereign immunity seemed to preclude recovery. Relief under the Tucker Act[62] was apparently not available since the action would be one "sounding in tort."[63] Recovery under the Federal Tort Claims Act[64] probably would have been unsuccessful because of the supposition that the statute embraced only "common law" torts.

In view of the foregoing, on September 6, 1960, the President approved a measure rendering the government but not its employees

---

[57]594 F. Supp. 335, 339, 224 U.S.P.Q. 305, 308 (S.D.N.Y. 1984); Copr. L. Rep. ¶25,843 (S.D.N.Y. 1985).

[58]See also *Sony Corp. v. Universal City Studios, Inc.*, 464 U.S. 417, 437–438, 220 U.S.P.Q. 664, 676–677 (1984), where the Court emphasized defendant's lack of contact with the purchasers of its products.

[59]*Hubbard Broadcasting, Inc. v. Southern Satellite Systems, Inc.*, 593 F. Supp. 808, 823, 224 U.S.P.Q. 468, 479 (D. Minn. 1984), *aff'd*, 777 F.2d 393, 228 U.S.P.Q. 102 (8th Cir. 1985).

[60]*Oddo v. Ries*, 743 F.2d 630, 222 U.S.P.Q. 799 (9th Cir. 1984) (partners cannot be infringers); *Newman v. Crowell*, 205 U.S.P.Q. 517, 519 (S.D.N.Y. 1979).

[61]H.R. Rep. No. 94-1476, 94th Cong., 2d Sess. 60 (1976); S. Rep. No. 94-473, 94th Cong., 1st Sess. 57 (1975).

[62]28 U.S.C. §1346(a)(2).

[63]*Lanman v. United States*, 27 Ct. Cl. 260 (1892); *Turton v. United States*, 212 F.2d 354, 101 U.S.P.Q. 164 (6th Cir. 1954). See also *Curtis v. United States*, 168 F. Supp. 213, 216, 120 U.S.P.Q. 13, 15 (Ct. Cl. 1958), *cert. denied*, 361 U.S. 843 (1959).

[64]28 U.S.C. §§1346(b), 2671 *et seq.*

liable for copyright infringement.[65] Exemption of employees was deemed necessary because of prior authority to the effect that sovereign immunity of the government did not shield the employee performing the actual copying or other unauthorized use of protected material.[66] It should be noted that Section 1498(b) extends not only to the United States and to corporations owned or controlled by it, but to contractors, subcontractors, "or any person, firm or corporation acting for the Government and with the authorization or consent of the Government * * *."[67]

The sole remedy for violation of copyright by the United States or any other individual or organization covered in Section 1498(b) is recovery of "reasonable and entire compensation as damages for such infringement" (including minimum statutory damages) in an action in the U.S. Claims Court. No injunctive relief is available. Appeal is to the Court of Appeals for the Federal Circuit.

This statute has been remarkably underutilized, with the first case reaching substantive disposition 12 years after enactment.[68]

## State and Local Governments

Just as "[t]here appears to be no privilege for the United States to use copyrighted material without the consent of the owner,"[69] there is no similar privilege for states or their instrumentalities. As held by the Ninth Circuit in construing the 1909 Act:

> "[A] state may not, consistent with the Constitution, infringe the protected rights of the copyright holder, and thereafter avoid the federal system of statutory protection. The 'exclusive rights' of an author guaranteed under the Constitution and Copyright Act, would surely be illu-

---

[65]28 U.S.C. §1498(b). See S. REP. No. 1877, 86th Cong., 2d Sess. (1960); H.R. REP. No. 624, 86th Cong., 1st Sess. (1959); *Hearing on H.R. 4059 Before the Subcomm. on Patents, Trademarks, and Copyrights of the Senate Judiciary Comm.*, 86th Cong., 2d Sess. (1960).

[66]*Towle v. Ross*, 32 F. Supp. 125, 45 U.S.P.Q. 143 (D. Ore. 1940). See also *Belknap v. Schild*, 161 U.S. 10 (1896) (patent law).

[67]28 U.S.C. §1498(b) (see Appendix I); *Hearing on H.R. 4059 Before the Subcomm. on Patents, Trademarks, and Copyrights of the Senate Judiciary Comm.*, 86th Cong., 2d Sess. 6–7 (1960). But cf. *Combustion Engineering, Inc. v. Murray Tube Works, Inc.*, 222 U.S.P.Q. 239, 243 (E.D. Tenn. 1984) (suggesting that injunctive relief is available against a government contractor; noting that "[t]here is absolutely no indication that any infringing was done with the authorization or consent of the government as required by Section 1498(b)"); *Molinaro v. Watkins-Johnson CEI Division*, 359 F. Supp. 467, 470, 178 U.S.P.Q. 211, 212 (D. Md. 1973), noting that "there is authority that [implied consent by the government] is possible only where the Government contract requirement cannot be met without [committing] infringement." The suggestion made in *Molinaro* would appear to be the best approach: a government contractor's commission of copyright infringement in the course of fulfilling its contractual obligations will be "with the authorization or consent" of the government within the meaning of 28 U.S.C. §1498(b) if (1) the government expressly requires such infringement, or (2) the contract cannot be fulfilled without committing infringement. Where neither condition is met, the copyright owner is free to sue the contractor in federal district court and is entitled to the full panoply of remedies provided for in the Copyright Act.

[68]*Williams & Wilkins Co. v. United States*, 172 U.S.P.Q. 670 (Ct. Cl. 1972), *rev'd*, 487 F.2d 1345, 180 U.S.P.Q. 49 (Ct. Cl. 1973), *aff'd by an equally divided Court*, 420 U.S. 376, 184 U.S.P.Q. 705 (1975). See also *International Trade Mgt., Inc. v. United States*, 1 Cl. Ct. 39 (1982); *Shipkovitz v. United States*, 1 Cl. Ct. 400 (1983), *aff'd*, 732 F.2d 168 (Ct. App. Fed. Cir. 1984); *Lira v. United States*, No. 50-83 (Cl. Ct. bench opinion issued June 16, 1983), *aff'd*, Appeal No. 83-1620 (Ct. App. Fed. Cir. filed Feb. 2, 1984) (unpublished).

[69]*Time, Inc. v. Bernard Geis Associates*, 293 F. Supp. 130, 134, 159 U.S.P.Q. 663, 666 (S.D.N.Y. 1968).

sory were a state permitted to appropriate with impunity the rights of a lawful copyright holder. Accordingly, we conclude that the sovereign immunity does not permit a state to nullify the rights reserved and protected by Congress, acting pursuant to the Copyright and Patent Clause."[70]

---

[70]*Mills Music, Inc. v. Arizona*, 591 F.2d 1278, 201 U.S.P.Q. 437 (9th Cir. 1979). See also *Marcus v. Rowley*, 695 F.2d 1171, 217 U.S.P.Q. 691 (9th Cir. 1983) (damages ordered against individual teacher and school district); *Johnson v. University of Virginia*, 606 F. Supp. 321, 226 U.S.P.Q. 356 (W.D. Va. 1985) (following *Mills*; permitting award of monetary damages against state); *Association of American Medical Colleges v. Carey*, 482 F. Supp. 1358, 205 U.S.P.Q. 42 (N.D.N.Y. 1980) (suit for injunctive relief against state officials not barred by Eleventh Amendment); *Blackburn v. County of Ventura*, 362 F.2d 515, 150 U.S.P.Q. 160 (9th Cir. 1966); *Ohman v. City of New York*, 168 F. 953 (C.C.S.D.N.Y. 1909); *Howell v. Miller*, 91 F. 129 (6th Cir. 1898) (state officials acting on orders of state legislature not immune from suit under Eleventh Amendment); *Munsen v. Mayor, Aldermen, and Commonality of the City of New York*, 124 U.S. 601 (1888) (patent suit; patent held invalid for lack of novelty); Texas Att'y Gen. Opn. No. MW-307 (March 18, 1981), *reproduced in* COPR. L. REP. ¶25,247 ("state that infringes a copyright may be liable in damages to the holder"); Kansas Att'y Gen. Opn. No. 81-202 (Aug. 25, 1981), *reproduced in* COPR. L. REP. ¶25,331 (state department of education liable for infringement of musical compositions); California Att'y Gen. Opn. No. 81-503 (Feb. 5, 1982), *reproduced in* COPR. L. REP. ¶25,368 (performance of video tapes of copyrighted motion pictures by state prison would result in infringement). Cf. *Wihtol v. Crow*, 309 F.2d 777, 135 U.S.P.Q. 385 (8th Cir. 1962) (under Eleventh Amendment school district immune from suit for infringement); *Mihalek Corp. v. Michigan*, 595 F. Supp. 903, 225 U.S.P.Q. 736 (E.D. Mich. 1984) (state immune from damages under Eleventh Amendment); *Woelffer v. Happy States of America, Inc.*, 229 U.S.P.Q. 376 (N.D. Ill. 1985) (same).

The decision in *Wihtol v. Crow*, *supra*, finding, without discussion, a state school board district immune from an award of damages for infringement on the ground that it was an instrumentality of the state may be contrary to the Supreme Court's decision in *Lincoln County v. Luning*, 133 U.S. 529 (1890), which held that the Eleventh Amendment is *not* a bar to suits for monetary damages against such entities if the school district was, in fact, under *state law* comparable to a county or municipality. See especially Lee, *The Federal Courts and the Status of Municipalities: A Conceptual Challenge*, 62 BOSTON L. REV. 1, 24–32 (1982), for a comprehensive and searching study of the issue; *Mt. Healthy City School Dist. Bd. of Education v. Doyle*, 429 U.S. 274, 279–280 (1977); *Atascadero State Hospital v. Scanlon*, 473 U.S. ____, ____ n. 8 (1985) (Brennan, J., dissenting) ("the Eleventh Amendment is not a bar to suits against local governmental units," citing *Lincoln County*).

While the Supreme Court's decisions in *Ex Parte Young*, 209 U.S. 123 (1908); *Edelman v. Jordan*, 415 U.S. 651 (1974); and *Alabama v. Pugh*, 438 U.S. 781 (1978), permit injunctive relief against a state so long as plaintiff names the individual state officials as defendants rather than the state itself, there is a substantial unresolved question regarding whether the Copyright Act permits actions for damages against the state where the state has not waived its sovereign immunity. The decision in *Mills Music, Inc. v. Arizona*, *supra*, permitting such suits is believed to represent the correct position on this question. Contra *Mihalek Corp. v. Michigan*, *supra;* *Woelffer v. Happy States of America, Inc.*, *supra*.

In *Atascadero State Hospital v. Scanlon*, *supra*, the Supreme Court held that where a state has not waived its sovereign immunity "Congress may abrogate the States' constitutionally secured immunity from suit in federal court only by making its intention unmistakably clear in the language of the statute." 473 U.S. at ____. This holding, however, involving the Rehabilitation Act of 1973, was premised on the availability of *state* courts to entertain such suits. See *id.* at ____ n. 2: " '[T]he issue is not the general immunity of the States from private suit * * * but merely the susceptibility of the States to suit before *federal* tribunals.' It denigrates the judges who serve on the state courts to suggest that they will not enforce the supreme law of the land" (citing *Employees v. Missouri Public Health & Welfare Dep't*, 411 U.S. 279, 293–294 (1973) (Marshall, J., concurring in result), and *id.* at ____: "[A] State's constitutional interest in immunity encompasses not merely *whether* it may be sued but *where* it may be sued" (citing *Pennhurst State School & Hospital v. Halderman*, 465 U.S. 89 (1984)).

As noted in the text accompanying this note and in the text at notes 1–54 in Chapter 3, under §301 of the Copyright Act suits that involve the assertion of legal or equitable rights that are equivalent to any of the exclusive rights granted in §106 with respect to copyrighted works are preempted and may not be brought in state court, whether against the state or an individual. Applying the *Atascadero State Hospital* holding to a copyright suit against a state would thus result in *no* forum for infringement of a federal right. It should also be recognized that, unlike the Rehabilitation Act at issue in *Atascadero State Hospital*, copyright suits are based on a *constitutional* right (Article 1 §8 cl. 8), ceded by the states to the federal government and thus cannot be said to "implicate [ ] the fundamental constitutional balance between the Federal Government and the states * * *." *Atascadero State Hospital*, *supra*, 473 U.S. at ____. (*Quern v. Jordan*, 440 U.S. 332 (1976), is not to the contrary, since although it involved an attempt to enforce a federal statute (42 U.S.C. §1983) against a state in an area ceded by the

Furthermore, the Supreme Court's holding in *Goldstein v. California* that "[w]hen Congress grants an exclusive right or monopoly, its effects are pervasive; no citizen *or State* may escape its reach"[71] commands liability for unauthorized state or local government uses.

## Pleading

Undoubtedly, many members of the bar would be surprised to learn that the Federal Rules of Civil Procedure expressly do not apply to copyright proceedings. Federal Rule 81(a)(1) states: "These rules * * * do not apply to proceedings * * * in copyright under Title 17, U.S.C., except in so far as they may be made applicable thereto by rules promulgated by the Supreme Court of the United States." Although the Supreme Court issued rules governing impoundment under former 17 U.S.C. §101(c),[72] these rules were deleted in 1966[73] and do not apply to actions under the 1976 Act.[74]

The requirement of Rule 8(a) that "a short and plain statement of the claim" be made has, nevertheless, been held applicable to copyright proceedings, with the courts holding that infringing acts must be alleged with "some specificity."[75] The "notice" philosophy of pleading should permit a simple, clear complaint for a claim of copyright infringement with the following points covered: (1) ownership,

---

states to the federal government under the Fourteenth Amendment, concurrent jurisdiction with the state courts still existed.) Cf. *Fitzpatrick v. Bitzer*, 427 U.S. 445 (1976).

In any event, Justic Brennan's remark in *Atascadero State Hospital, supra*, 473 U.S. at \_\_\_\_\_, that the Supreme Court's current Eleventh Amendment doctrine "rests on flawed premises, misguided history, and an untenable vision of the needs of the federal system it purports to protect * * *" is well supported. See, e.g., *id.* at \_\_\_\_\_, and Judge Gibbons' monumental and enlightening study of the issue, *The Eleventh Amendment and State Sovereign Immunity: A Reinterpretation*, 83 COLUM. L. REV. 1889 (1983), and the other authorities cited in Justice Brennan's dissent in *Atascadero State Hospital, supra*, 473 U.S. at \_\_\_\_\_ n. 11, as well as Justice Stevens' dissent, *id.* at \_\_\_\_\_ (characterizing doctrine as "egregiously incorrect").

[71]412 U.S. 546, 560, 178 U.S.P.Q. 129, 135 (1973).

[72]214 U.S. 533 (1909), *as amended*, 307 U.S. 652 (1939). It should also be noted that the states may not impose rules interfering with the bringing of infringement actions. See *BMI v. Lyndon Lanes, Inc.*, 227 U.S.P.Q. 731 (W.D. Ky. 1985) (failure of a corporation to obtain a certificate of authority under a state "door-closing" statute held irrelevant where federal question jurisdiction exists).

[73]383 U.S. 1031, 1067 (1966).

[74]*WPOW, Inc. v. MRLJ Enters*, 584 F. Supp. 132, 222 U.S.P.Q. 502 (D.D.C. 1984). Cf. *RSO Records, Inc. v. Peri*, COPR. L. REP. ¶25,187 (S.D.N.Y. 1980); 596 F. Supp. 849, 225 U.S.P.Q. 407 (S.D.N.Y. 1984) (seizure according to §503(a) and old Supreme Court rules); H.R. REP. No. 94-1476, 94th Cong., 2d Sess. 160 (1976); S. REP. No. 94-473, 94th Cong., 1st Sess. 142 (1975) ("The present Supreme Court rules with respect to seizure and impounding were issued even though there is no specific provision authorizing them in the copyright statute, and there appears to be no need for including a special provision on the point in the bill"); *Nagler v. Admiral Corp.*, 248 F.2d 319, 322–323 (2d Cir. 1957) (Clark, J.) ("When the [federal] rules were adopted there was considerable pressure for separate provision in patent, copyright, and other allegedly special types of litigation. Such arguments did not prevail * * *").

[75]*Friedman, Eisenstein, Raemer & Schwartz v. Afterman*, 599 F. Supp. 902, 903–904 (N.D. Ill. 1984); *Calloway v. Marvel Entertainment Group*, COPR. L. REP. ¶25,570 (S.D.N.Y. 1983); *Gee v. CBS, Inc.*, 471 F. Supp. 600, 643–644, 202 U.S.P.Q. 486, 516 (E.D. Pa.), *aff'd*, 612 F.2d 572 (3d Cir. 1979). So long as the facts alleged and the claim asserted are sufficient to show federal jurisdiction, failure to plead the jurisdictional provision (28 U.S.C. §1338) is not fatal. *Schlesinger v. Councilman*, 420 U.S. 738 (1975).

by way of authorship, or a *recorded* assignment (§§201, 205(d)); (2) registration or other compliance with Section 411(a); (3) unauthorized activities that violate one or more of plaintiff's exclusive rights, with allegations of willfulness if appropriate (§504(c)) and, optionally in the case of uses covered by compulsory licenses, failure to comply with requirements for such a license (§§111, 115, 116, 118); (4) the activity engaged in occurred within the statute of limitations period (or if outside that period that the statute of limitations is tolled for specified reasons) (§507); (5) venue is proper; and (6) where required, compliance with the manufacturing clause (§601(e)).[76] Due lenience should be granted to *pro se* plaintiffs.

The normal rules apply to responsive pleadings such as answers and replies to counterclaims.[77] General denials will cover certain defenses such as lack of originality or noninfringement, though some lawyers plead them affirmatively. Fair use should be interposed as an affirmative defense.[78] It is also probably preferable for the defendant to plead affirmatively noncompliance with procedural formalities such as notice and registration, and the same applies to traditional affirmative defenses in areas outside copyright, such as license,[79] laches,[80] estoppel,[81] unclean hands,[82] abandonment,[83] and statute of limitations.[84]

---

[76]In *Conan Properties, Inc. v. Mattel, Inc.*, 601 F. Supp. 1179, 1182–1183, 226 U.S.P.Q. 265, 267 (S.D.N.Y. 1984), the court required plaintiff to plead the registration numbers of all copyrights allegedly infringed. While such a requirement may well be justified in individual cases, there is no statutory requirement that plaintiff do more than plead general compliance with §411. Since compliance with compulsory license provisions is an affirmative defense, plaintiff need not plead defendant's noncompliance.

[77]See FED. R. CIV. P. 9(c). Since the copyright owner is granted a bundle of exclusive rights in §106 subject only to certain privileges or exemptions in §§107–118 *where applicable* the copyright owner need not plead the absence of an available exemption. *LaSalle Music Pub., Inc. v. Highfill*, 622 F. Supp. 168, 228 U.S.P.Q. 63 (W.D. Mo. 1985).

[78]W. PATRY, THE FAIR USE PRIVILEGE IN COPYRIGHT LAW 477 (BNA Books, 1985) ("PATRY") (cited with approval in *Harper & Row, Pub., Inc. v. Nation Enters.*, 471 U.S. _____, _____, 225 U.S.P.Q. 1073, 1081 (1985).

[79]*Oddo v. Ries*, 743 F.2d 630, 634 n. 6, 222 U.S.P.Q. 799, 802 n. 6 (9th Cir. 1984).

[80]*Russell v. Price*, 612 F.2d 1123, 205 U.S.P.Q. 206 (9th Cir. 1979), *cert. denied*, 446 U.S. 952 (1980); *Hoste v. RCA Record Sales, Inc.*, 654 F.2d 11, 212 U.S.P.Q. 153 (6th Cir. 1981). In *Sherry Mfg. Co. v. Towel King of Florida, Inc.*, 220 U.S.P.Q. 855 (S.D. Fla. 1983), *rev'd on other grounds*, 753 F.2d 1565, 225 U.S.P.Q. 1005 (11th Cir. 1985), it was held that laches is unavailable to deliberate infringers. This principle has been criticized as ruling out the defense "[s]ince the great bulk of copyright infringement is deliberate * * *." *Eisenman Chemical Co. v. NL Indus., Inc.*, 595 F. Supp. 141, 147, 224 U.S.P.Q. 871, 875 (D. Nev. 1984). See also *Universal Pictures Co. v. Harold Lloyd Corp.*, 162 F.2d 354, 372, 73 U.S.P.Q. 317, 331 (9th Cir. 1947), and generally *Lemelson v. Carolina Enters., Inc.*, 541 F. Supp. 645, 657, 216 U.S.P.Q. 249, 258 (S.D.N.Y. 1982).

[81]*Schuchart & Associates v. Solo Serve Corp.*, 220 U.S.P.Q. 170, 184 (W.D. Tex. 1983); *National Business Lists, Inc. v. Dun & Bradstreet, Inc.*, 552 F. Supp. 89, 215 U.S.P.Q. 595 (N.D. Ill. 1982); *MGM v. Showcase Atlanta Cooperative Prods.*, 217 U.S.P.Q. 857 (N.D. Ga. 1981). See also *Blonder-Tongue Laboratories, Inc. v. University of Illinois Foundation*, 402 U.S. 313, 169 U.S.P.Q. 513 (1971) (patent case). A peculiar and highly questionable application of estoppel has been found where the copyright owner asserts or advertises his work to be factual in nature, but in a subsequent infringement action alleges it to be fictional. See *Houts v. Universal City Studios, Inc.*, 224 U.S.P.Q. 427 (C.D. Cal. 1984); *Marshall v. Yates*, 223 U.S.P.Q. (C.D. Cal. 1983); *Oliver v. St. Germain Foundation*, 41 F. Supp. 296, 51 U.S.P.Q. 20 (S.D. Cal. 1941). Where the work is obviously one of fiction (as in *Oliver*) there is no reason for the courts to blink at common sense. On the other hand, where the work covers an historical period and purports to tell the true "facts" about that period, plaintiff should be taken at his word. See *Mosley v. Follett*, 209 U.S.P.Q. 1109 (S.D.N.Y. 1980).

[82]*Mitchell Bros. Film Group v. Cinema Adult Theatre*, 604 F.2d 852, 203 U.S.P.Q. 1041 (5th Cir. 1979); *RSO Records, Inc. v. Peri*, COPR. L. REP. ¶25,187 (S.D.N.Y. 1980); 596 F. Supp. 849,

## Statute of Limitations

The 1976 and 1909 Acts each have three-year statutes of limitations. Both statutes require civil actions to be commenced "within three years after the claim accrued."[85] Although criminal proceedings have a limitation of the same length, the three years is measured from "the time the cause of action arose."[86] It is not believed that this slight variation in language is significant.[87] Its genesis would seem to be the historical anomaly that until 1957[88] there was no time limit prescribed in the 1909 Act for commencement of civil actions. The addition of such a provision in that year embodied the term "claim," which had been introduced by the Federal Rules of Civil Procedure in 1938. This language and the slightly inconsistent language which had been in the criminal provision were simply carried over into the 1976 statute.

There is some conflict between the courts on the application of the statutory three-year term to a series of infringements, viz., whether the limitation period runs from the last act of infringement. In *Hoste v. Radio Corp. of America*[89] the Sixth Circuit held that where the complaint was filed on March 9, 1978, all claims that had accrued prior to March 9, 1975, were barred. The greater weight of authority (and it is submitted the preferable view) holds that "[w]hen the final act of an unlawful course of conduct occurs within the statutory period * * * [the copyright owner may] reach back and get damages for the entire duration of the alleged violation."[90]

The statute of limitations may be tolled where there is fraudulent concealment of the infringement[91] and, under the better view, where "a reasonable man in [plaintiff's] shoes would [not] have discovered

---

225 U.S.P.Q. 407 (S.D.N.Y. 1984); *Schuchart & Associates v. Solo Serve Corp.*, 220 U.S.P.Q. 170, 184–185 (W.D. Tex. 1983).

[83]*Pacific & Southern Co. v. Duncan*, 744 F.2d 1490, 224 U.S.P.Q. 131 (11th Cir. 1984), *cert. denied*, 471 U.S. _____, *on remand*, 618 F. Supp. 469, 228 U.S.P.Q. 141 (N.D. Ga. 1985); *Goldsmith v. Max*, 213 U.S.P.Q. 1008, 1011 n. 3 (S.D.N.Y. 1981).

[84]*Wood v. Santa Barbara Chamber of Commerce*, 507 F. Supp. 1128, 210 U.S.P.Q. 930 (D. Nev. 1980). See also *Zenith Radio Corp. v. Hazeltine Research, Inc.*, 401 U.S. 321 (1971) (patent case).

[85]See §507(b) of the 1976 Act and §115(f) of the 1909 Act, and *Taylor v. Meirick*, 712 F.2d 1112, 219 U.S.P.Q. 420 (7th Cir. 1983), which held that there is no difference between the two acts on this point.

[86]17 U.S.C. §507(a) (1978).

[87]See *United States v. Shabazz*, 724 F.2d 1536 (11th Cir. 1984); H.R. Rep. No. 94-1476, 94th Cong., 2d Sess. 164 (1976).

[88]Act of Sept. 7, 1957, 71 Stat. 633.

[89]654 F.2d 11, 212 U.S.P.Q. 153 (6th Cir. 1981). See also *Hampton v. Paramount Pictures Corp.*, 279 F.2d 100, 125 U.S.P.Q. 623 (9th Cir.), *cert. denied*, 364 U.S. 882, 127 U.S.P.Q. 555 (1960).

[90]*Taylor v. Meirick*, 712 F.2d 1112, 1118–1119, 219 U.S.P.Q. 420, 423 (7th Cir. 1983) (copyright infringement treated as "continuing wrong"). Accord *Woods Hole Oceanographic Institution v. Goldman*, 228 U.S.P.Q. 874 (S.D.N.Y. 1985); *Eisenman Chemical Co. v. NL Indus., Inc.*, 595 F. Supp. 141, 224 U.S.P.Q. 871 (D. Nev. 1984); *United States v. Shabazz*, 724 F.2d 1536, 1540 (11th Cir. 1984) (criminal prosecution); *Baxter v. Curtis Indus., Inc.*, 201 F. Supp. 100, 133 U.S.P.Q. 78 (N.D. Ohio 1962); *Cain v. Universal Pictures Co.*, 47 F. Supp. 1013, 56 U.S.P.Q. 8 (S.D. Cal. 1942).

[91]*Taylor v. Meirick*, 712 F.2d 1112, 1118, 219 U.S.P.Q. 420, 423 (7th Cir. 1983); *Wood v. Santa Barbara Chamber of Commerce*, 705 F.2d 1515 (9th Cir. 1983).

the infringement," i.e., where even in the absence of active concealment the copyright owner "would have had no reason to suspect that
he was the victim of [infringement] \* \* \*."[92] With regard to the possibility of tolling the statute of limitations in specific cases, it has
been held that such tolling should be done on the basis of equitable
considerations "derived from general principles applicable to every
federal forum, not those peculiar to a local jurisdiction."[93]

## Injunctions

We finally turn to the remedies available to a successful copyright owner. A crucial one, that of injunctive relief, is grounded on
long-established principles of equity. Section 502(a) provides that except as to the U.S. government or its contractors a court "may \* \* \*
grant temporary and final injunctions on such terms as it may deem
reasonable to prevent or restrain infringement of a copyright." Section 502(b) provides for nationwide service of such injunctions and
certain mechanics for out-of-district enforcement.

The 1976 Act contains two provisions relating to injunctive relief
not found in the 1909 Act. Under Section 405(b), an innocent infringer misled by the absence of a notice from an authorized copy
may, in the court's discretion, be permitted to continue the "infringing undertaking" upon payment of a reasonable license fee. Under
Section 411(b), copyright owners of works consisting of sounds, images, or both whose first fixation is made simultaneously with their
transmission may, *before* fixation, institute an action for infringement and obtain injunctive relief for anticipatory infringement of the
unfixed work provided specified procedures are followed.[94]

Preliminary injunctions[95] have been most important in copyright
cases, as the grant or denial of such relief often effectively ends litiga-

---

[92]*Taylor v. Meirick, supra* note 91, 712 F.2d at 1117–1118, 219 U.S.P.Q. at 423. See also
*DeGette v. Mine Co. Restaurant, Inc.*, 224 U.S.P.Q. 763, 764–765 (10th Cir. 1985) ("discovery
rule" applied in action for common law copyright). In dictum, a Florida state court of appeals
wrote that "a contributory infringer may be rendered liable for his acts committed beyond the
period of statute of limitations if the acts of the primary infringer(s) are not yet barred by the
statute." *Van Dusen v. Southeast First National Bank of Miami*, 478 So. 2d 82, 88–89 n. 11, 228
U.S.P.Q. 19, 23–24 n. 11 (Fla. Dist. Ct. App. 1985).

[93]*Prather v. Neva Paperbacks, Inc.*, 446 F.2d 338, 340, 170 U.S.P.Q. 378, 379 (5th Cir. 1971).
See also *Charlotte Telecasters, Inc. v. Jefferson-Pilot Corp.*, 546 F.2d 570, 573–574 (4th Cir.
1976); and *Herald Square Music Co. v. Living Music, Inc.*, 205 U.S.P.Q. 1241, 1243 (S.D.N.Y.
1978) (defendant estopped from asserting statute-of-limitations defense where it misled plaintiffs into believing there was no need for litigation).

[94]*National Football League v. McBee & Bruno's*, 228 U.S.P.Q. 11 (E.D. Mo. 1985); *National
Football League v. Cousin Hugo's*, 600 F. Supp. 84 (E.D. Mo. 1984).

[95]Temporary restraining orders are, of course, also available under §502(a). See *Ascher v.
Saturday Review*, Civ. No. 84-7781 (S.D.N.Y. filed Oct. 29, 1984) (TRO against publication of
magazine containing allegedly infringing article).

Section 502 reasserts the discretionary power of courts to grant injunctions and restraining
orders, "whether 'preliminary,' 'temporary,' 'interlocutory,' 'permanent,' or 'final,' to prevent
or stop infringements of copyright." H.R. Rep. No. 94-1476, 94th Cong., 2d Sess. 160 (1976); S.
Rep. No. 94-473, 94th Cong., 1st Sess. 142 (1975). See also Strauss, *Remedies Other Than Damages for Copyright Infringement*, Copyright Office Study No. 24, 86th Cong., 2d Sess. 115-
121 (Comm. Print 1960), which traces the statutory provisions for injunctions to the Copyright

tion. As a discretionary remedy, the courts have developed quite a number of tests for granting preliminary injunctions,[96] drawing on Federal Rule of Civil Procedure 65 and standards set forth in court of appeals decisions.

While an evidentiary hearing of some kind is required under Federal Rule of Civil Procedure 65(a)(2), it is not clear what sort of evidence will suffice. In *Medco Security Locks, Inc. v. Swiderek* the Seventh Circuit wrote that "[i]t is well established that, in general, a motion for a preliminary injunction should not be resolved on the basis of affidavits alone. Normally, an evidentiary hearing is required to decide credibility issues."[97] The court vacated a preliminary injunction and ordered the taking of the testimony of live witnesses in a fact setting where the trial court had relied solely on an unverified complaint and deposition testimony. Other decisions have dispensed with hearings where the "taking of evidence would serve little purpose,"[98] or where the parties are "content to rely on affidavits, exhibits, briefs and oral arguments" so long as "the facts are clear and only the implications to be drawn from them are disputed."[99] Where material factual issues are in dispute, a hearing should be held.

Although not uniform, most courts evaluate a motion for temporary relief under a four-part test, which may be stated as follows:

(1) Is there a likelihood of success on the merits?
(2) Will the copyright owner suffer irreparable harm if relief is not granted?
(3) Will the harm to defendant if relief is granted significantly outweigh the harm to the copyright owner if relief is denied?
(4) Will the public interest be served by granting relief?[100]

---

Act of 1819 which permitted injunctions in copyright cases "according to the course and the principles of courts of equity, to prevent the violation of the rights of any authors or inventors * * * on such terms and conditions as the said courts may deem fit and reasonable." Every copyright statute since 1819 has included language to similar effect. See also *American Code Co. v. Bensinger*, 282 F. 829 (2d Cir. 1922) ("The remedy by injunction exists independently of express provision therefor in the copyright statutes; it being granted on the well established provision that a court of equity will protect a legal right where the remedy at law is inadequate").

[96]See the survey of these issue in Zelnick and Lynn, *Preliminary Injunctions in Copyright Infringement Cases, reprinted in* COPYRIGHT LITIGATION 61-142 (PLI Course Handbook G4-3732 1983) ("Zelnick and Lynn"). Courts may, of course, issue preliminary injunctions in circumstances where a grant of summary judgment would be inappropriate, e.g., where a material issue of fact or a plausible defense to a prima facie showing of infringement exists. *Midway Mfg. Co. v. Bandai-America, Inc.*, 546 F. Supp. 125, 141, 216 U.S.P.Q. 812, 822 (D.N.J. 1982).

[97]680 F.2d 37, 38, 216 U.S.P.Q. 577, 578 (7th Cir. 1981). See also *SEC v. Frank*, 388 F.2d 486 (2d Cir. 1968) (noncopyright case); *Ideal Toy Co. v. Sayco Doll Corp.*, 302 F.2d 623, 626, 133 U.S.P.Q. 104, 105 (2d Cir. 1962) (Clark, J., dissenting).

[98]*Herbert Rosenthal Jewelry Corp. v. Grossbardt*, 428 F.2d 551, 554–555, 166 U.S.P.Q. 65, 67 (2d Cir. 1970).

[99]Zelnick and Lynn, *supra* note 96, at 135 (citing *Russ Berrie & Co. v. Jerry Elsner Co.*, 482 F. Supp. 980, 205 U.S.P.Q. 320 (S.D.N.Y. 1980)). See also *id.* at 137.

[100]See *Apple Barrel Prods., Inc. v. Beard*, 730 F.2d 384, 222 U.S.P.Q. 956 (5th Cir. 1984); *Sargent v. American Greetings Corp.*, 588 F. Supp. 912, 223 U.S.P.Q. 1327 (N.D. Ohio 1984); *Price v. Metzner*, 574 F. Supp. 281, 219 U.S.P.Q. 1092 (E.D. Pa. 1983); *Atari, Inc. v. North American Philips Consumer Electronics Corp.*, 672 F.2d 607, 214 U.S.P.Q. 33 (7th Cir.), *cert. denied*, 459 U.S. 880 (1982); *Dataphase Systems, Inc. v. CL Systems, Inc.*, 640 F.2d 109, 114 (8th Cir. 1982); *Nintendo of America, Inc. v. Elcon Indus., Inc.*, 564 F. Supp. 937 (E.D. Mich. 1982); *Belushi v. Woodward*, 598 F. Supp. 36, 223 U.S.P.Q. 511 (D.D.C. 1984) (citing *WMATC v. Holiday Tours, Inc.*, 559 F.2d 841, 843 (D.C. Cir. 1977)); *Klitzner Indus., Inc. v. H.K. James &*

Other courts have either reduced or collapsed the inquiry. In the Second Circuit, for example, it has been held that the party seeking relief "must show both irreparable injury and either 1) a likelihood of success on the merits or 2) sufficiently serious questions going to the merits to make them a fair ground for litigation and a balance of hardships tipping decidedly in its favor."[101] This rule, applicable to cases in general, requires a showing of possible irreparable harm under the second prong of this test. Other courts have spoken of these two elements as "not separate tests but the 'outer reaches' of a single continuum: the greater the balance of hardships tip in favor of the moving party, the less likelihood of success on the merits must be shown,"[102] while yet others have limited such an inverse relationship standard to cases where the copyrighted work is not "central to the essence of the [copyright owner's] operation" and "where the injury from [infringement] can be fairly considered minimal, limited or conjectural."[103]

Likelihood of success on the merits is proved by establishing a prima facie case of infringement. A long-held view is that if plaintiff has established a prima facie case as to the validity of the copyright and its infringement, a preliminary injunction will generally be issued. The importance of a certificate of registration is strongly felt here since such a certificate is prima facie evidence of the facts stated therein and of the validity of the copyright.[104] Upon a showing of a likelihood of success on the merits, a presumption of irreparable harm is raised.[105] Detailed proof of actual damages is not necessary if infringement appears and damages may probably follow. This presumption is unique to copyright litigation. As held in *Wainwright Securities, Inc. v. Wall Street Transcript Corp.*:

---

*Co.*, 535 F. Supp. 1249, 216 U.S.P.Q. 73 (E.D. Pa. 1982); *Cassidy v. Bowlin*, 540 F. Supp. 901, 218 U.S.P.Q. 314 (W.D. Mo. 1982); *Clark Equipment Co. v. Harlan Corp.*, 539 F. Supp. 561, 215 U.S.P.Q. 1150 (D. Kan. 1982); *O'Neill Developments, Inc. v. Galen Kilburn*, 524 F. Supp. 710, 216 U.S.P.Q. 1123 (N.D. Ga. 1981); *Keep Thomson Governor v. Citizens for Gallen Committee*, 457 F. Supp. 957, 199 U.S.P.Q. 788 (D.N.H. 1978).

[101]*Consumers Union of the United States v. General Signal Corp.*, 730 F.2d 47 (2d Cir. 1983), *cert. denied*, 469 U.S. 823, 224 U.S.P.Q. 616 (1984); *Mattel, Inc. v. Azrak–Hamway Int'l, Inc.*, 724 F.2d 357, 221 U.S.P.Q. 302 (2d Cir. 1983); *Apple Computer, Inc. v. Formula Int'l, Inc.*, 725 F.2d 521, 221 U.S.P.Q. 762 (9th Cir. 1984); *Videotronics, Inc., v. Bend Electronics*, 568 F. Supp. 478, 223 U.S.P.Q. 936 (D. Nev. 1984).

In *Standard & Poor's Corp. v. Commodity Exchange, Inc.*, 683 F.2d 704, 711, 216 U.S.P.Q. 841, 846 (2d Cir. 1982), the Second Circuit noted:

"Although this Circuit's settled preliminary injunction standard does not explicitly mention the public interest, as do other Circuits' standards * * * we have recognized that, as a court of equity, we 'may go much further both to give or to withhold relief in furtherance of the public interest than where only private interests are involved.' "

[102]*Apple Computer, Inc. v. Formula Int'l, Inc.*, 562 F. Supp. 775, 783, 218 U.S.P.Q. 47, 53 (C.D. Cal. 1983), *aff'd*, 725 F.2d 521, 221 U.S.P.Q. 762 (9th Cir. 1984).

[103]*Apple Computer, Inc. v. Franklin Computer Corp.*, 714 F.2d 1240, 1254, 219 U.S.P.Q. 113, 125 (3d Cir. 1983).

[104]17 U.S.C. §410(c) (1978).

[105]*Apple Computer, Inc. v. Formula Int'l, Inc.*, *supra* note 102; *Wainwright Securities, Inc. v. Wall Street Transcript Corp.*, 558 F.2d 91, 94, 194 U.S.P.Q. 401, 402 (2d Cir. 1977), *cert. denied*, 434 U.S. 1014, 196 U.S.P.Q. 864 (1978); *American Metropolitan Enters. of New York, Inc. v. Warner Bros., Inc.*, 389 F.2d 903, 905, 157 U.S.P.Q. 69, 70 (2d Cir. 1968); *New Boston Tel., Inc. v. ESPN, Inc.*, 215 U.S.P.Q. 755 (D. Mass. 1981). Although some courts have suggested that the presumption is more applicable to certain categories of works than to others, see *Northwestern Bell Tel. Co. v. Bedco of Minnesota, Inc.*, 501 F. Supp. 299, 210 U.S.P.Q. 564 (D. Minn. 1980); *Dow Jones & Co. v. Board of Trade*, 546 F. Supp. 113, 217 U.S.P.Q. 901 (S.D.N.Y. 1982), these cases are submitted to be erroneous.

"In copyright cases * * * if probable success—a prima facie case of infringement—can be shown, the allegations of irreparable injury need not be very detailed, because such injury can normally be presumed when a copyright is infringed."[106]

Without detracting from the soundness of the foregoing, as a practical matter counsel would be ill-advised to rely entirely on the presumption and not present some evidence of harm.[107] Evidence that plaintiff would be deprived of its investment and competitive position is sufficient to prove irreparable harm,[108] as is loss of goodwill or reputation.[109]

Cases evaluating the third typical element of injunctive relief are, necessarily, ad hoc. However, as a general statement it appears that the more substantial a defendant's investment and ability to pay monetary damages, the greater chance it has to tip the balance in its favor,[110] although in *Apple Computer, Inc. v. Franklin Computer*

---

[106]558 F.2d 91, 94, 194 U.S.P.Q. 401, 402 (2d Cir. 1977), *cert. denied*, 434 U.S. 1014, 196 U.S.P.Q. 864 (1978). See also *Hasbro Bradley, Inc. v. Sparkle Toys, Inc.*, 780 F.2d 189, 192, 228 U.S.P.Q. 423, 424 (2d Cir. 1985); *Arc v. S.S. Sarna, Inc.*, 621 F. Supp. 916, 229 U.S.P.Q. 25 (E.D.N.Y. 1985); *Instant Fortunes, Inc. v. Strathmore Sales Enters.*, 201 U.S.P.Q. 754, 755 (S.D.N.Y. 1978).

[107]See, e.g., *Delman Fabrics, Inc. v. Holland Fabrics, Inc.*, COPR. L. REP. ¶25,663 (S.D.N.Y. 1984) (court held that record failed to establish any specific harm and that presumption rebutted where evidence tended to show that plaintiff and defendant sold to different markets, with plaintiff's sales not being directly affected by defendant's activities). Upon trial the court nevertheless issued a permanent injunction. 228 U.S.P.Q. 596 (S.D.N.Y. 1985). Cf. *Selchow & Righter Co. v. Book-of-the-Month Club*, 192 U.S.P.Q. 530, 533 (S.D.N.Y. 1976) (requiring at least a threshold showing of irreparable harm).

[108]*Arc v. S.S. Sarna, Inc.*, 621 F. Supp. 916, 924, 229 U.S.P.Q. 25, 31 (E.D.N.Y. 1985); *Apple Computer, Inc. v. Franklin Computer Corp.*, supra note 103; *Apple Computer, Inc. v. Formula Int'l, Inc.*, supra note 102; *Price v. Metzner*, 574 F. Supp. 281, 219 U.S.P.Q. 1092 (E.D. Pa. 1983); *Stern Electronics, Inc. v. Kaufman*, 669 F.2d 852, 213 U.S.P.Q. 443 (2d Cir. 1982); *DeMarco of California Fabrics, Inc. v. Block's Fashion Fabrics, Inc.*, COPR. L. REP. ¶25,416 (S.D.N.Y. 1982); *Custom Decor, Inc. v. Nautical Crafts, Inc.*, 502 F. Supp. 154, 213 U.S.P.Q. 565 (E.D. Pa. 1980); *MGM, Inc. v. Showcase Atlanta Cooperative Prods., Inc.*, 479 F. Supp. 351, 203 U.S.P.Q. 822 (N.D. Ga. 1979) (loss of derivative rights); *Universal City Studios, Inc. v. Kamar Indus.*, 217 U.S.P.Q. 1162 (S.D. Tex. 1982) (same).

[109]*Gallery House, Inc. v. Yi*, 582 F. Supp. 1294, 223 U.S.P.Q. 894 (N.D. Ill. 1984); *Price v. Metzner*, 574 F. Supp. 281, 219 U.S.P.Q. 1092 (E.D. Pa. 1983); *Midway Mfg. Co. v. Bandai-America, Inc.*, 546 F. Supp. 125, 216 U.S.P.Q. 812 (D.N.J. 1982); *Cassidy v. Bowlin*, 540 F. Supp. 901, 218 U.S.P.Q. 314 (W.D. Mo. 1982); *DC Comics, Inc. v. Crazy Eddie, Inc.*, 205 U.S.P.Q. 1117 (S.D.N.Y. 1979).

[110]See *King v. TJB, Inc.*, 227 U.S.P.Q. 575 (D.D.C. 1985) (defendant's use of copyrighted musical jingle in its advertising for two years and accompanying association of jingle with defendant, lead time necessary to create a new ad campaign, and availability of monetary damages resulted in denial of preliminary injunction); *American Chemical Society v. Dun-Donnelley Pub. Corp.*, 202 U.S.P.Q. 459, 462–463 (N.D. Ill. 1979) (denial of preliminary injunction where loss of defendant's good will in the eyes of its customers would result). Zelnick and Lynn, *supra* note 96, at 121–130; *Apple Barrel Prods., Inc. v. Beard*, 730 F.2d 384, 390–391, 222 U.S.P.Q. 956, 959–960 (5th Cir. 1984) (rejecting claim that third factor is presumed to be in plaintiff's favor after showing of substantial likelihood of success on merits). See also *Universal City Studios, Inc. v. Sony Corp.*, 659 F.2d 963, 976, 211 U.S.P.Q. 761, 775 (9th Cir. 1981), *rev'd on other grounds*, 464 U.S. 417, 220 U.S.P.Q. 665 (1984) ("In fashioning relief, the district court should not be overly concerned with the prospective harm to [defendant]. A defendant has no right to expect a return on investment from activities that violate the copyright laws. Once a determination has been made that an infringement is involved, the continued profitability of [defendant's] business is of secondary concern"); *Gilliam v. ABC*, 538 F.2d 14, 192 U.S.P.Q. 1 (2d Cir. 1976).

Preliminary injunctions have been denied when they were not applied for in a timely manner. *Citybank, N.A. v. Citytrust*, 756 F.2d 273, 275, 225 U.S.P.Q. 708, 710 (2d Cir. 1985); *Marjorica, S.A. v. R.H. Macy & Co.*, 762 F.2d 7, 8, 226 U.S.P.Q. 624 (2d Cir. 1985); *Wales Industrial, Inc. v. Hasbro Bradley, Inc.*, 612 F. Supp. 507 (S.D.N.Y. 1985). But cf. *Arc v. S.S. Sarna, Inc.*, 621 F. Supp. 916, 925, 229 U.S.P.Q. 25, 31 (E.D.N.Y. 1985) (plaintiff's conduct was "not so lax as to indicate a reduced need for immediate action"); *Wales Industrial, Inc. v. Hasbro Bradley, Inc.*, 612 F. Supp. 510, 520–522, 226 U.S.P.Q. 584, 591–592 (S.D.N.Y. 1985).

*Corp.* the Third Circuit sharply criticized the district court's emphasis on harm to the defendant, writing:

> "Nor can we accept the district court's explanation which stressed the 'devastating effect' of a preliminary injunction on Franklin's business. If that were the correct standard, then a knowing infringer would be permitted to construct its business around its infringement, a result we cannot condone. * * * The size of the infringer should not be determinative of the copyright holder's ability to get prompt judicial redress."[111]

The final factor, the public interest, is rarely a source of difficulty, since "it is virtually axiomatic that the public interest can only be served by upholding copyright protections and, correspondingly, preventing the misappropriation of the skills, creative energies, and resources which are invested in the protected work."[112] A few cases, however, have found a strong public interest weighing against the grant of preliminary relief.[113]

Section 502(a) also provides for permanent injunctions. Here the general rule is that where liability has been established and there is a threat of continuing violations, such relief will be ordered. Thus, injunctive relief has been denied where the infringement ceased and there was no likelihood of its resumption, although the court held that the plaintiff should not be forced to rely on the voluntary undertaking of the defendant not to resume infringement and is entitled to an injunction if there is any substantial risk of further infringement.[114] Permanent injunctive relief has been granted to protect works not yet created or registered where "the registered work and the future works are so closely related, part of a series of original works created with predictable regularity and similar format and function."[115]

---

[111]714 F.2d 1240, 1255, 219 U.S.P.Q. 113, 125 (3d Cir. 1983). See also 730 F.2d at 389 n. 11, 222 U.S.P.Q. at 960 n. 11, discussing "sliding scale" analysis.

[112]*Klitzner Indus., Inc. v. H.K. James & Co.*, 535 F. Supp. 1249, 1259–1260, 216 U.S.P.Q. 73, 80–81 (E.D. Pa. 1982), cited with approval in *Apple Computer, Inc. v. Franklin Computer Corp.*, 714 F.2d 1240, 1255, 219 U.S.P.Q. 113, 125 (3d Cir. 1983).

[113]*Belushi v. Woodward*, 598 F. Supp. 36, 223 U.S.P.Q. 511 (D.D.C. 1984); *Marino v. Josephson Bar Review Center*, Copr. L. Rep. ¶25,330 (S.D.N.Y. 1981). In reversing the trial court's refusal to issue a permanent injunction due to First Amendment concerns, the Eleventh Circuit held that "[t]he scope of liability affects First Amendment interests, but the choice of the form of relief in this case does not." *Pacific & Southern Co. v. Duncan*, 744 F.2d 1490, 1500, 224 U.S.P.Q. 131, 137 (11th Cir. 1984), *cert. denied*, 471 U.S. _____ (1985), *on remand*, 618 F. Supp. 469, 228 U.S.P.Q. 141 (N.D. Ga. 1985).

[114]*Sony Corp. v. Universal City Studios, Inc.*, 659 F.2d 963, 976, 211 U.S.P.Q. 761, 774–775 (9th Cir. 1981), *rev'd on other grounds*, 464 U.S. 417, 220 U.S.P.Q. 665 (1984); *Dowdey v. Phoenix Films, Inc.*, 199 U.S.P.Q. 579, 582 (S.D.N.Y. 1978); *Peter Pan Fabrics, Inc. v. Martin Weiner Corp.*, 173 F. Supp. 292, 121 U.S.P.Q. 81 (S.D.N.Y. 1959), *aff'd*, 274 F.2d 487, 124 U.S.P.Q. 154 (2d Cir. 1960); *Breffort v. The I Had a Ball Co.*, 271 F. Supp. 623, 155 U.S.P.Q. 391 (S.D.N.Y. 1967); *Trifari, Krussman & Fishel, Inc. v. B. Steinberg-Kaslo Co.*, 144 F. Supp. 577, 110 U.S.P.Q. 487 (S.D.N.Y. 1956).

Injunctions have also been issued prohibiting defendants from copying any of the plaintiff's material "whether copyrighted or uncopyrighted * * *." *Screw Machine Tool Co. v. Slater Tool & Engineering Corp.*, 683 F.2d 159, 163, 217 U.S.P.Q. 603, 606 (6th Cir. 1982); *Pacific & Southern Co. v. Duncan*, 618 F. Supp. 469, 228 U.S.P.Q. 141 (N.D. Ga. 1985).

[115]*Pacific & Southern Co. v. Duncan*, 744 F.2d 1490, 1499 n. 17, 224 U.S.P.Q. 131, 137 n. 17 (11th Cir. 1984), *cert. denied*, 471 U.S. _____, *on remand*, 618 F. Supp. 469, 228 U.S.P.Q. 141 (N.D. Ga. 1985). Accord *Orth-O-Vision, Inc. v. Home Box Office*, 474 F. Supp. 672, 685–686, 205 U.S.P.Q. 644, 655 (S.D.N.Y. 1979); *Encyclopaedia Britannica Educational Corp. v. Crooks*, 542 F. Supp. 1156, 1187–1188, 214 U.S.P.Q. 697, 721 (W.D.N.Y. 1982) (dictum); *Association of*

## Impoundment, Seizure, and Destruction

In addition to an injunction, other specific nonmonetary relief is available to a successful plaintiff. Under Subsections (c) and (d) of Section 101 of the 1909 law, a court might order impoundment of infringing articles during the pendency of the action and ultimate destruction of not only these articles but all means of making them. Since an unauthorized phonograph record, though not a "copy," is an infringing article, it was subject to these provisions.[116] In *Duchess Music Corp. v. Stern*, the Court of Appeals for the Ninth Circuit held blank tape and recording equipment used in a tape piracy operation to be included within this description, reversing the district court, which had limited seizure basically to material which "embodies a mechanical and/or electronic impression of plaintiff publishers' copyrighted works * * *."[117]

The seizure in *Duchess Music* was pursuant to a detailed procedure for impounding *pendente lite*, provided in Rules 3 through 13 of the copyright rules adopted by the Supreme Court.[118] These "no-knock" provisions required judicial intervention only in connection with the setting of a bond and were used principally against motion picture and record or tape piracy.

Section 503 of the 1976 Act expressly grants to the court discretionary power to impound, on reasonable terms, and later destroy infringing articles and the means of making them. Section 503(b) provides a new alternative to destruction, "other reasonable disposition," e.g., delivery to plaintiff or a charitable institution.[119]

The standard to be used in judging *ex parte* impoundment motions was addressed in *WPOW, Inc. v. MRLJ Enterprises*, in which the court, noting the discretionary nature of Section 503(b), found *Duchess Music* and the prior Supreme Court rules inapposite to

---

*American Medical Colleges v. Carey*, 482 F. Supp. 1358, 1364 n. 15, 205 U.S.P.Q. 42, 47 n. 15 (N.D.N.Y. 1980); *Breffort v. The I Had a Ball Co.*, 271 F. Supp. 623, 626, 155 U.S.P.Q. 391, 393 (S.D.N.Y. 1967).

[116]*Miller v. Goody*, 125 F. Supp. 348, 103 U.S.P.Q. 292 (S.D.N.Y. 1954).

The August 1, 1983, revision to Rule 11 of the Federal Rules of Civil Procedure requires the attorney or party signing a complaint to have conducted a "reasonable inquiry" into the basis for the suit. In an influential opinion construing the amendment, the Second Circuit held:

"[A] showing of subjective bad faith is no longer required to trigger the sanctions imposed by the rule. Rather, sanctions should be imposed against an attorney and/or his client when it appears that a pleading has been interposed for any improper purpose, or where after reasonable inquiry, a competent attorney could not form a reasonable belief that the pleading was well grounded in fact and is warranted by existing law or a good faith argument for the extension, modification or reversal of existing law."

*Eastway Construction Corp. v. City of New York*, 762 F.2d 243, 253–254 (2d Cir. 1985).

[117]458 F.2d 1305, 173 U.S.P.Q. 278 (9th Cir.), *cert. denied*, 409 U.S. 847, 175 U.S.P.Q. 385 (1972). But cf. *Elektra Records Co. v. Gem Electronic Distributors, Inc.*, 360 F. Supp. 821, 179 U.S.P.Q. 617 (E.D.N.Y. 1973).

[118]214 U.S. 533 (1909), *as amended*, 307 U.S. 652 (1959), *repealed*, 383 U.S. 1031 (1966).

[119]See *RSO Records, Inc. v. Peri*, 596 F. Supp. 849, 864, 225 U.S.P.Q. 407, 417 (S.D.N.Y. 1984); *Martin Luther King, Jr. Center for Social Change, Inc. v. American Heritage Products, Inc.*, 508 F. Supp. 854, 861, 213 U.S.P.Q. 540, 546 (N.D. Ga. 1981), *rev'd on other grounds*, 694 F.2d 674 (11th Cir. 1983). Cf. *M.S.R. Imports, Inc. v. R.E. Greenspan Co.*, 220 U.S.P.Q. 361, 375 (E.D. Pa. 1983), which, following the text, suggested that infringing toys be donated to a charitable institution.

actions under the 1976 statute, and then proceeded to hold that "a plaintiff seeking an impoundment must meet the requirements for permanent or preliminary injunctive relief."[120] The validity of this holding may be questioned in view of strong legislative history indicating that Congress intended to permit summary procedures.[121] This is not to say that in its discretion a court could (or should) not require a copyright owner to meet the burden required for a preliminary injunction; it is only to suggest that the burden is not required and may be inappropriate in particular cases. In this regard, it is perhaps significant that the chairman of the Senate Subcommittee on Patents, Copyrights, and Trademarks has expressed an opinion both that the *WPOW* type of standard is not required under the Copyright Act and that the courts have been too parsimonious in granting motions for *ex parte* impoundment orders.[122]

While it is clear that the courts have the discretionary power to order defendant to deliver up all infringing copies and all related devices used to create them, may a court order a defendant on pain of contempt to recreate the copyrighted work? This unusual scenario was presented in *Blue Pearl Music Corp. v. Bradford*, where the copyright owner (who had presumably lost all copies of the work), upon the entry of a default judgment against defendant, obtained an order directing her to "recreate [ ] all copyrightable material which were previously but are no longer in her possession and deliver same to plaintiff * * *."[123] In reversing this order, the Third Circuit nevertheless noted:

> "If * * * the record disclosed that the [defendant] had stolen the only copies of the musical works in question from the [plaintiff] and then destroyed them, and the record further disclosed that she had committed the works to memory, that she was technically competent to re-create them, and that she was the only person in the world who could re-create the lost material, then an order to 're-create' might arguably be permissible."[124]

---

[120]584 F. Supp. 132, 135, 222 U.S.P.Q. 502, 504 (D.D.C. 1984). See also *Clark Equipment Co. v. Harlan Corp.*, 539 F. Supp. 561, 215 U.S.P.Q. 1150 (D. Kan. 1982); *Munn v. Minority Broadcasting Co. of the Midwest*, Civ. No. 82-C-0759 (N.D. Ill. filed March 26, 1982); *Halbersham Plantation Corp. v. Country Concepts*, 209 U.S.P.Q. 711 (N.D. Ga. 1980). It has been held that as the issuance of an impoundment order is discretionary, vacation of such an order is discretionary and not subject to appellate review under the "collateral order" doctrine. *Midway Mfg. Co. v. Omni Video Games, Inc.*, 668 F.2d 70 (1st Cir. 1981). Query whether such an order is equivalent to the grant or denial of an interlocutory injunction reviewable under 28 U.S.C. §1292(a)(1).

[121]H.R. REP. No. 94-1476, 94th Cong., 2d Sess. 160 (1976); S. REP. No. 94-473, 94th Cong., 1st Sess. 142 (1975) ("[a]rticle may be impounded under [§503](a) 'at any time while an action under this title is pending,' thus permitting seizures of articles alleged to be infringing *as soon as suit is filed and without waiting for an injunction*") (emphasis added); see also COPYRIGHT LAW REVISION PART 6: SUPPLEMENTARY REPORT OF THE REGISTER OF COPYRIGHTS ON THE GENERAL REVISION OF THE U.S. COPYRIGHT LAW, 89th Cong., 1st Sess. 133 (Comm. Print 1965).

[122]*Civil and Criminal Enforcement of the Copyright Laws: Hearing Before the Subcomm. on Patents, Copyrights, and Trademarks of the Senate Judiciary Comm.*, 99th Cong., 1st Sess. 53 (1985).

[123]728 F.2d 603, 605, 221 U.S.P.Q. 1128, 1129 (3d Cir. 1984).

[124]*Id.* at 606 n. 4, 221 U.S.P.Q. at 1130 n. 4.

## Monetary Relief

Under the 1909 Act, the elements of potential monetary recovery were (1) actual damages suffered by the plaintiff; (2) actual profits enjoyed by the defendant; (3) "statutory" (also known as "in lieu") damages which were set within certain limits at the trier of fact's discretion without evidence of economic harm; (4) reasonable attorney's fees; and (5) costs. Confusion arose over whether recovery for actual damages and profits was cumulative, a point cleared up in the 1976 Act, which provides that recovery is cumulative only to the extent that profits have not already been taken into account in computing actual damages. The only other changes made by the 1976 Act are the amounts and limitations on statutory damages and the linking of awards of statutory damages, attorney's fees, and costs to registration. We will examine each of the above-mentioned five elements in turn.

### Actual Damages

It is generally agreed that actual damages are difficult to prove in copyright cases, and indeed this difficulty is the reason statutory damages are provided as an alternative remedy at the copyright owner's election. Nevertheless, uncertainty as to or the need for estimation of the amount of actual damages does not prevent a copyright owner from recovering his own lost profits. Once a copyright holder establishes with reasonable probability the existence of a causal connection between the infringement and a loss of revenue the burden shifts to the infringer to show that this damage would have occurred had there been no taking of copyrighted expression.[125] A primary problem in calculating damages is that "there is a distinction between proof of causation—meaning proof that defendant's acts caused any harm to plaintiff at all—and proof of the amount of dam-

---

[125]*Stevens Linen Associates, Inc. v. Mastercraft Corp.*, 656 F.2d 11, 210 U.S.P.Q. 865 (2d Cir. 1981). *Deltak, Inc. v. Advanced Systems, Inc.*, 767 F.2d 357, 226 U.S.P.Q. 919 (7th Cir. 1985); *Frank Music Corp. v. Metro-Goldwyn-Mayer, Inc.*, 772 F.2d 505, 513, 227 U.S.P.Q. 687, 691 (9th Cir. 1985) ("Although uncertainty as to the amount of damages will not preclude recovery, uncertainty as to the fact of damages may"). See *Rothschild v. Kisling*, 220 U.S.P.Q. 1010 (Fla. Dist. Ct. App. 1984), for an in-depth study of factors that may be considered in calculating actual damages).

The Ninth Circuit has held:

" 'Actual damages' are the extent to which the market value of a copyrighted work has been injured or destroyed by infringement. * * * In this circuit, we have stated the test of market value as 'what a willing buyer would have been reasonably required to pay to a willing seller for plaintiff's work.'

* * *

"The test is not what some buyer *was* willing to pay, but what a buyer *would have* been willing to pay for a use of a plaintiff's work similar to the defendant's use. In other words, the * * * test seeks to approximate what a reasonable market price would have been at the time of the infringement, not afterwards."

*Frank Music Corp., supra*, 772 F.2d at 513 n. 6, 227 U.S.P.Q. at 691 n. 6.

age,"[126] a problem felt most keenly in attempts to prove that sales made by defendant would have been made by plaintiff but for defendant's infringement.

A leading[127] decision on this question, *Stevens Linen Associates, Inc. v. Mastercraft Corp.*, created the following shifting burdens of proof on lost sales:

> "Although Stevens might not have made every one of Mastercraft's sales, we believe that once Stevens establishes that it had been damaged, and that its customers purchased both the infringed and the infringing products, the burden shifted to the infringer, Mastercraft, to prove that the customers * * * to whom it sold would not have acquired from Stevens alone all of the [copies] they purchased had there been no infringement."[128]

Aside from loss of sales, loss of licensing royalties is a particularly appropriate measure of damages,[129] including photocopying fees payable to copyright owners through the Copyright Clearance Center. It has also been held that "injury to business income includes any damage to * * * good will * * * although it does not extend to damage to reputation."[130] It should be noted that the Copyright Act does not permit an award of punitive damages for infringement;[131] however, they may be awarded on a pendent state claim.[132]

## Actual Profits

The obligation to account for the infringer's wrongfully obtained profits is enforced by the courts in a number of contexts. In copyright cases the most significant problems in determining defendant's profits have been (1) apportionment of profit to the infringing portion of defendant's work; and (2) the elements of cost properly deductible from sales receipts in arriving at profits.[133]

---

[126]*Stevens Linen Associates*, 656 F.2d at 14, 210 U.S.P.Q. at 867. The courts have held, however, that there is no presumption that actual damages result from unauthorized performances. See *Frank Music Corp. v. Metro-Goldwyn-Mayer, Inc.*, 772 F.2d 505, 514 n. 8, 227 U.S.P.Q. 687, 692 n. 8 (9th Cir. 1985). This must be contrasted with the presumption of irreparable harm for purposes of injunctive relief. See text at notes 105–106, *supra.*

[127]See also the Seventh Circuit's decisions in *Taylor v. Meirick*, 712 F.2d 1112, 219 U.S.P.Q. 420 (7th Cir. 1983), and *Deltak, Inc. v. Advanced Systems, Inc.*, 767 F.2d 357, 226 U.S.P.Q. 919 (7th Cir. 1985).

[128]656 F.2d at 15, 210 U.S.P.Q. at 867. See also *RSO Records, Inc. v. Peri*, 596 F. Supp. 849, 225 U.S.P.Q. 407 (S.D.N.Y. 1984).

[129]*Cream Records, Inc. v. Joseph Schlitz Brewing Co.*, 754 F.2d 826, 225 U.S.P.Q. 896 (9th Cir. 1985); *DC Comics, Inc. v. Reel Fantasy, Inc.*, 696 F.2d 24, 217 U.S.P.Q. 307 (2d Cir. 1982); *Encyclopaedia Britannica Educational Corp. v. Crooks*, 542 F. Supp. 1156, 214 U.S.P.Q. 697 (W.D.N.Y. 1982).

[130]*Mount v. Book-of-the-Month Club, Inc.*, COPR. L. REP. ¶25,010 at p. 15,058 (S.D.N.Y. 1978) (under 1909 Act).

[131]*Oboler v. Goldin*, 714 F.2d 211, 220 U.S.P.Q. 166 (2d Cir. 1983).

[132]*Stein & Day, Inc. v. Red Letter, Inc.*, COPR. L. REP. ¶25,728 (S.D.N.Y. 1984); *Roy Export Co. of Vaduz v. CBS*, 672 F.2d 1095, 215 U.S.P.Q. 289 (2d Cir.), *cert. denied*, 459 U.S. 826 (1982).

[133]It should be recalled here that while multiple defendants are jointly and severally liable for damages, there is only several liability for illegal profits. *Abeshouse v. Ultragraphics, Inc.*, 754 F.2d 467, 472 (2d Cir. 1985); *MCA, Inc. v. Wilson*, 677 F.2d 180, 186, 211 U.S.P.Q. 577, 582 (2d Cir. 1981); *Frank Music Corp. v. Metro-Goldwyn-Mayer, Inc.*, 772 F.2d 505, 227 U.S.P.Q. 687 (9th Cir. 1985) (where the defendants are partners or "practically partners," joint liability

Following decisions under the 1909 Act,[134] Section 504(b) of the 1976 Act expressly puts the burden of establishing the allocation of profits with respect to noninfringing elements on the defendant:

"In establishing the infringer's profits, the copyright owner is required to present proof only of the infringer's gross revenue, and the infringer is required to prove his or her deductible expense and the elements of profit attributable to factors other than the copyrighted work."[135]

The "gross revenue" referred to is gross revenue from the sale or use of the infringing work and not the defendant's total business gross revenue.[136] While this figure may be reasonably susceptible of calculation where defendant is engaged in head-to-head competition with the copyright owner for the sale of specific items, the task becomes difficult when the copyrighted work is merely one item in a package consisting of numerous items,[137] or when the copyrighted work is one element in an advertising campaign. In *Cream Records, Inc. v. Joseph Schlitz Brewing Co.,*[138] for example, plaintiff's copyrighted musical composition was infringed by its unauthorized use in a television commercial for malt liquor. Plaintiff argued that since the defendant's profit on malt liquor for the period in which the commercial ran was $4.876 million, it was entitled to recover $66,800 as defendant's profit attributable to the infringement (calculated as fol-

---

may be found). Factors to be considered in determining whether joint liability is appropriate include whether defendant received a fixed salary or percentage of the profits or bares any of the risks from the undertaking. *Id.* at 519, 227 U.S.P.Q. at 696.

[134]*Lottie Joplin Thomas Trust v. Crown Pub., Inc.*, 592 F.2d 651, 199 U.S.P.Q. 449 (2d Cir. 1978).

[135]17 U.S.C. §504(b) (1978); *Abeshouse v. Ultragraphics, Inc., supra* note 133; *Sygma Photo News, Inc. v. High Society Magazine, Inc.*, 603 F. Supp. 829, 226 U.S.P.Q. 94 (S.D.N.Y.), *aff'd as mod. and rem'd*, 778 F.2d 89, 228 U.S.P.Q. 580 (2d Cir. 1985); *Williams v. Arndt*, 227 U.S.P.Q. 615, 622 (D. Mass. 1985) (defendant's failure to keep credible records resulted in award of gross revenue from sale of infringing computer programs).

In *Deltak, Inc. v. Advanced Systems, Inc.*, 767 F.2d 357, 226 U.S.P.Q. 919 (7th Cir. 1985), *rev'g and rem'g* 574 F. Supp. 400, 221 U.S.P.Q. 716 (N.D. Ill. 1983) (Posner, J., sitting by designation), the district court was unable to determine what portion of defendant's gross revenues were attributable to its infringement and what portion was attributable to other factors such as lawful marketing methods. Despite evidence that defendant's revenues from customers who received its infringing work rose during the infringement period "to an extent not fully explained at trial," the district court held that "it would exceed the bounds of permissible speculation to base a damage award on the hypothesis that the infringing document boosted [defendant's] revenues." 574 F. Supp. at 411, 221 U.S.P.Q. at 725. This holding was criticized by the court of appeals as "seemingly plac[ing] the burden of distinguishing profits due to the infringement from 'the elements of profit attributable to factors other than the copyrighted work,' 17 U.S.C. §504(b), on the owner instead of the infringer." 767 F.2d at 360, 226 U.S.P.Q. at 920–921.

The legislative reports draw the following policy distinction between awards of damages and awards of an infringer's profits: "Damages are awarded to compensate the copyright owner for losses from the infringement, and profits are awarded to prevent the infringer from unfairly benefiting from a wrongful act." H.R. REP. No. 94-1476, 94th Cong., 2d Sess. 161 (1976); S. REP. No. 94-473, 94th Cong., 1st Sess. 143 (1975). See also *F.W. Woolworth Co. v. Contemporary Arts, Inc.*, 344 U.S. 228, 233, 95 U.S.P.Q. 396, 398 (1952) ("statutory rule, formulated after long experience, not merely compels restitution of profit and reparation for injury but is also designed to discourage wrongful conduct").

[136]*Taylor v. Meirick*, 712 F.2d 1112, 1122, 219 U.S.P.Q. 420, 426 (7th Cir. 1983): "If General Motors were to steal your copyright and put it in a sales brochure, you could not just put a copy of General Motors' corporate income tax return in the record and rest your case for an award of infringer's profits."

[137]*Deltak, Inc. v. Advanced Systems, Inc.*, 574 F. Supp. 400, 221 U.S.P.Q. 716 (N.D. Ill. 1983), *rev'd and rem'd*, 767 F.2d 357, 226 U.S.P.Q. 919 (7th Cir. 1985).

[138]754 F.2d 826, 225 U.S.P.Q. 896 (9th Cir. 1985).

lows: the infringing commercial constituted 13.7 percent of defendant's advertising budget for the year; the infringing music was responsible for 10 percent of the commercial's advertising "powers" and therefore equalled 1.37 percent of the profit on malt liquor).

The district court, finding that "the commercial was successful * * * and 'that the music had a portion of that,' "[139] calculated the amount of profit at one tenth of 1 percent of defendant's total profits, or $5,000. On appeal, the Ninth Circuit upheld the district court's decision on this point,[140] writing as follows:

> "Although the statute imposes upon the infringer the burden of showing 'the elements of profit attributable to the copyrighted work,' 17 U.S.C. §504(b), nonetheless where it is clear, as it is in this case, that not all of the profits are attributable to the infringing material, the copyright owner is not entitled to recover all of these profits merely because the infringer fails to establish with certainty the portion attributable to the non-infringing element. 'In cases such as this where an infringer's profits are not entirely due to the infringement, and the evidence suggests some division which may rationally be used as a springboard it is the duty of the court to make some apportionment.' "[141]

It has also been held that where revenue attributable to an advertising campaign cannot be reasonably determined but profits from the direct sale of infringing items can be, the latter should serve as the basis for the award.[142]

No definitive rule has been established specifying the deductions a defendant may properly claim as "deductible expenses." Although some older decisions permitted deduction of costs that would have been incurred even without the infringement, such as general overhead, the modern, and it is believed correct, rule is to allow only those expenses which actually assist in the infringement. As stated in *Kamar International, Inc. v. Russ Berrie & Co.*:

> "An award of infringer's profits is aimed in part at deterring infringements * * * and in part at appropriately compensating the copyright holder. These goals, we believe, can best be achieved by allowing a deduction for overhead only when the infringer can demonstrate it was of actual assistance in the production, distribution or sale of the infringing product."[143]

---

[139]*Id.* at 828, 225 U.S.P.Q. at 898.

[140]The court reversed the district court's inclusion in this figure of the profits made by a codefendant advertising agency. *Id.* at 828, 225 U.S.P.Q. at 899.

[141]*Id.* at 828–829, 225 U.S.P.Q. at 898 (citing *Orgel v. Clark Boardman Co.*, 301 F.2d 119, 121, 133 U.S.P.Q. 94, 96 (2d Cir. 1962)). Cf. *Deltak, Inc. v. Advanced Systems, Inc.*, 767 F.2d 357, 362–364, 226 U.S.P.Q. 919, 923–924 (7th Cir. 1985). See also *Frank Music Corp. v. Metro-Goldwyn-Mayer, Inc.*, 772 F.2d 505, 517–518, 227 U.S.P.Q. 687, 695–696 (9th Cir. 1985), and cases cited therein for an extended discussion of the question, and *Harper & Row, Pub., Inc. v. Nation Enters.*, 471 U.S. \_\_\_\_\_, \_\_\_\_\_, 225 U.S.P.Q. 1073, 1084 (1985).

[142]*Sid & Marty Krofft Television Prods., Inc. v. McDonald's Corp.*, 221 U.S.P.Q. 114, 117–120 (C.D. Cal. 1983) (statutory damages of $1,044,000 awarded under 1909 Act). An additional form of "profit," money saved by the infringer from having to create its own (noninfringing) work—termed "saved acquisition cost"—has also been awarded. See, e.g., *Deltak, Inc. v. Advanced Systems, Inc.*, 767 F.2d 357, 361–362, 226 U.S.P.Q. 919, 923–924 (7th Cir. 1985). See also discussion of awards of "indirect profits" in *Frank Music Corp. v. Metro-Goldwyn-Mayer, Inc.*, 772 F.2d 505, 517, 227 U.S.P.Q. 687, 694 (9th Cir. 1985).

[143]752 F.2d 1326, 1332, 224 U.S.P.Q. 674, 678 (9th Cir. 1984). Cf. *Frank Music Corp. v. Metro-Goldwyn-Mayer, Inc.*, 772 F.2d 505, 516, 227 U.S.P.Q. 687, 694 (9th Cir. 1985), rejecting

It has also been held that expense incurred to conceal infringement is not an expense "in the regular course of conventional business," and is, therefore, not deductible.[144]

## Actual Damages and Profits—Cumulative or Alternative?

Section 504(b) of the 1976 Act provides for the recovery of actual damages suffered by the copyright owner as a result of the infringement "and any profits of the infringer that are attributable to the infringement and are not taken into account in computing the actual damages." The intent of this provision is to recognize different elements of appropriate monetary relief, but to avoid recognizing the same element twice. Thus, if but for the infringement plaintiff would have made the profit defendant in fact did make, that profit may be recovered only once. On the other hand, where a plaintiff has, for example, lost the opportunity to license a novel for a motion picture because of defendant's infringing book, plaintiff has suffered damages not reflected in defendant's profits from book sales; he may thus recover both such damages and defendant's profits.[145] Where plaintiff's damages exceed defendant's profits, even an alternative remedy requires the infringer to do more than merely disgorge his profits.[146]

Section 504(b) seeks to resolve a conflict over the meaning of Section 101(b) in the 1909 law, which held an infringer liable "[t]o pay to the copyright proprietor such damages as the copyright proprietor may have suffered due to the infringement, as well as all the profits

---

defendants' argument that they met their burden of proof "when they introduced evidence of their total overhead costs allocated on a reasonable basis," holding that a "defendant additionally must show that the categories of overhead actually contributed to sales of the infringing work," and that "[a]ny doubt as to the computation of costs or profits is to be resolved in favor of the plaintiff. * * * If the infringing defendant does not meet its burden of proving costs, the gross figure stands as the defendant's profits." *Id.* at 516, 227 U.S.P.Q. at 692. The court also held, though, that an infringer need not prove his overhead expenses and their relationship to the infringing production in "minute detail," 772 F.2d at 516, 227 U.S.P.Q. at 694, and that because "a theoretically perfect allocation is impossible, we require only a 'reasonably acceptable formula.' " 772 F.2d at 516, 227 U.S.P.Q. at 693. See also *Taylor v. Meirick*, 712 F.2d 1112, 1121–1122, 219 U.S.P.Q. 420, 425–426 (7th Cir. 1983); *Sygma Photo News, Inc. v. High Society Magazine, Inc.*, 603 F. Supp. 829, 226 U.S.P.Q. 94 (S.D.N.Y.), *aff'd on this point, rem'd on other grounds*, 778 F.2d 89, 228 U.S.P.Q. 580 (2d Cir. 1985) (overhead expenses not shown to have been properly allocated to production of issue of magazine containing photograph); *Pret-A-Printee, Ltd. v. Allton Knitting Mills, Inc.*, 218 U.S.P.Q. 150 (S.D.N.Y. 1983). Cf. *Aitken, Hazen, Hoffman, & Miller, P.C. v. Empire Construction Co.*, 542 F. Supp. 252, 265, 218 U.S.P.Q. 409, 419–420 (D. Neb. 1982) (defendant not required to prove that "each item of overhead was used in connection with the infringing activity"), and the suggestion in *Frank Music Corp, supra*, 772 F.2d at 515, 227 U.S.P.Q. at 693, that deductions for overhead may be denied where the infringement was "willful, conscious, or deliberate."

[144]*Sygma Photo News, Inc. v. High Society Magazine, Inc.*, 603 F. Supp. 829, 831, 226 U.S.P.Q. 94, 94–95 (S.D.N.Y.), *aff'd as mod. and rem'd*, 778 F.2d 89, 228 U.S.P.Q. 580 (2d Cir. 1985). See also *Schnadig Corp. v. Gaines Mfg. Co.*, 620 F.2d 1166, 206 U.S.P.Q. 202 (6th Cir. 1980).

[145]H.R. REP. No. 94-1476, 94th Cong., 2d Sess. 161 (1976); S. REP. No. 94-473, 94th Cong., 1st Sess. 143 (1975). See the sophisticated analyses of this provision in *Abeshouse v. Ultragraphics, Inc.*, 754 F.2d 467 (2d Cir. 1985); *Taylor v. Meirick*, 712 F.2d 1112, 219 U.S.P.Q. 420 (7th Cir. 1983); and *Deltak, Inc. v. Advanced Systems, Inc.*, 767 F.2d 357, 226 U.S.P.Q. 919 (7th Cir. 1985).

[146]*Abeshouse v. Ultragraphics, Inc.*, *supra* note 145, 754 F.2d at 472.

which the infringer shall have made from such infringement
* * *."[147]

## Statutory Damages

It will be recalled that pursuant to Section 412 neither statutory damages nor attorney's fees are available for infringement "commenced" prior to registration, except for infringement of copyrights in published works registered within three months of publication, and in the case of works consisting of sounds, images, or both, the first fixation of which is made simultaneously with its transmission, where the copyright owner complies with regulations promulgated by the Copyright Office.[148]

A comprehensive revision and clarification of the confusing scheme for statutory damages under the 1909 Act is accomplished in Section 504(c) of the 1976 Act. This provision seeks to avoid troublesome questions raised under the 1909 Act by providing as follows:

(1) Statutory damages, "instead of actual damages and profits," are recoverable at the sole option of the copyright owner.[149] In establishing plaintiff's right of election, exercisable at any time before final judgment,[150] this section also implies that statutory damages are re-

---

[147]*F.W. Woolworth Co. v. Contemporary Arts, Inc.*, 344 U.S. 228, 234, 95 U.S.P.Q. 396, 398 (1952). Cf. *Sheldon v. Metro-Goldwyn Pictures Corp.*, 309 U.S. 390, 399, 44 U.S.P.Q. 607, 611 (1940); *Thomas Wilson & Co. v. Irving J. Dorfman Co.*, 433 F.2d 409, 167 U.S.P.Q. 417 (2d Cir. 1970), *cert. denied*, 401 U.S. 977, 169 U.S.P.Q. 65 (1971), with *Frank Music Corp. v. Metro-Goldwyn-Mayer, Inc.*, 772 F.2d 505, 512 n. 5, 227 U.S.P.Q. 687, 690 n. 5 (9th Cir. 1985); *Sid & Marty Krofft Television Prods., Inc. v. McDonald's Corp.*, 562 F.2d 1157, 196 U.S.P.Q. 97 (9th Cir. 1977); *Universal Pictures Corp. v. Harold Lloyd Corp.*, 162 F.2d 354, 376, 73 U.S.P.Q. 317, 334 (9th Cir. 1947); *Miller v. Universal City Studios, Inc.*, 650 F.2d 1365, 212 U.S.P.Q. 345 (5th Cir. 1981).

[148]*Harper & Row, Pubs., Inc. v. Nation Enters.*, 557 F. Supp. 1067, 220 U.S.P.Q. 210 (S.D.N.Y.), *rev'd on other grounds*, 723 F.2d 195, 220 U.S.P.Q. 321 (2d Cir. 1983), *rev'd*, 471 U.S. ____, 225 U.S.P.Q. 1073 (1985); *Taylor v. Meirick*, 712 F.2d 1112, 219 U.S.P.Q. 420 (7th Cir. 1983); *Schuchart & Associates v. Solo Serve Corp.*, 540 F. Supp. 928, 217 U.S.P.Q. 1227 (W.D. Tex. 1982); *Aitken, Hazen, Hoffman, & Miller, P.C. v. Empire Construction Co.*, 542 F. Supp. 252, 218 U.S.P.Q. 409 (D. Neb. 1982); *Pillsbury Co. v. Milky Way Prods., Inc.*, 215 U.S.P.Q. 124, 129 (N.D. Ga. 1982). This provision applies to foreign and domestic works alike. H.R. REP. No. 94-1476, 94th Cong., 2d Sess. 158 (1976); S. REP. No. 94-473, 94th Cong., 1st Sess. 140 (1975).

Neither the Act nor the legislative history provides guidance on the meaning of the term "commencement of infringement." In order to encourage prompt registration, the term has been interpreted as "the time when the first act of infringement in a series of on-going discrete infringements occurs (i.e., the first infringing sale in a series of on-going separate sales * * *"). *Whelan Associates, Inc. v. Jaslow Dental Laboratory, Inc.*, 609 F. Supp. 1325, 1331, 226 U.S.P.Q. 1013, 1017 (E.D. Pa. 1985). See also *Aitken, Hazen, Hoffman, & Miller, P.C. v. Empire Construction Co.*, 542 F. Supp. 252, 267–268, 218 U.S.P.Q. 409, 421–422 (D. Neb. 1982); *Streeter v. Rolfe*, 491 F. Supp. 416, 421–422, 209 U.S.P.Q. 918, 923 (W.D. La. 1980).

Where the work is an individual contribution to a collective or like work and that larger work (but not the individual contribution) has been registered prior to the commencement of the infringement, statutory damages and attorney's fees should be permitted. 17 U.S.C. 411(b) (1978); 37 C.F.R. §201.22.

[149]The decision in *Doehrer v. Caldwell*, 207 U.S.P.Q. 391 (N.D. Ill. 1980), which stated that statutory damages are recoverable under the 1976 Act only where there is insufficient proof of actual damages, is erroneous. Similarly, the decision in *National Football League v. McBee & Bruno's*, 228 U.S.P.Q. 11, 19 (E.D. Mo. 1985), which found infringement and compliance with §411(b) but refused to award statutory damages is clearly erroneous. See *Wildlife Internationale, Inc. v. Clements*, Civ. Nos. 84-3828; 84-3834 (6th Cir. filed Dec. 3, 1985) (not for publication) (remanding for award of statutory damages where infringement found).

[150]This includes an election made during the trial, H.R. REP. No. 94-1476, 94th Cong., 2d Sess. 162 (1976); S. REP. No. 94-473, 94th Cong., 1st Sess. 144 (1975), or even if not made at trial, if the judgment is vacated on appeal, at trial upon remand. *Oboler v. Goldin*, 714 F.2d 211, 213, 220 U.S.P.Q. 166, 167 (2d Cir. 1983).

coverable only upon such election; however, the better view is that where no election is made a court may fashion such relief.

(2) The schedule of amounts includes a basic set of awards modified by the principle that the courts should be given discretion to increase statutory damages in cases of willful infringement and to lower the minimum where the infringer is innocent. Awards within the prescribed limits are not subject to appellate review.[151] Accordingly: (a) The basic minimum remains at $250, as under the 1909 law, but the basic maximum is raised from $5,000 to $10,000.[152] Proof by plaintiff establishing willfullness permits a discretionary increase up to a maximum of $50,000.[153] (c) Proof by an infringer establishing

---

[151]*Harris v. Emus Records Corp.*, 734 F.2d 1329, 222 U.S.P.Q. 466 (9th Cir. 1984). Cf. *Morley Music Co. v. Dick Stacey's Plaza Motel*, 725 F.2d 1, 3, 222 U.S.P.Q. 751, 753 (1st Cir. 1983) ("[T]rial court is not left completely to its own devices in determining [statutory] damages. Although there need not be the kind of hearing required if actual damages were the issue * * * there must, we think, be either some hearing or sufficient affidavits to give the trial judge an adequate reference base for his judgment"). This holding is contrary to *Douglas v. Cunningham*, 294 U.S. 207, 210, 24 U.S.P.Q. 153, 154 (1935), which although decided under the 1909 Act is still believed to control on this point. See also *Frank Music Corp. v. Metro-Goldwyn-Mayer, Inc.*, 772 F.2d 505, 520, 227 U.S.P.Q. 687, 697 (9th Cir. 1985) (holding that in awarding statutory damages the trial court must keep in mind the purposes underlying the remedy provisions of the Copyright Act, i.e., "to provide adequate compensation to the copyright holder and to discourage wrongful conduct and deter infringements. * * * The $22,000 awarded by the district court obviously is too little to discourage wrongful conduct or to deter infringement").

[152]Some courts have held that "in the absence of a willful violation, an award of statutory damages should attempt to approximate the normal 'measure of damages' guide to compensation for the wrong done and the injury suffered by plaintiff." *M.S.R. Imports, Inc. v. R.E. Greenspan Co.*, 220 U.S.P.Q. 361, 373 (E.D. Pa. 1983). See also *Rare Blue Music, Inc. v. Guttadauro*, 227 U.S.P.Q. 325, 326 (D. Mass. 1985) ("Among the factors to be considered in awarding statutory damages are (1) expenses saved and profits reaped by defendants in connection with the infringement; (2) revenues lost by the plaintiffs; (3) whether the infringement was willful or knowing, or whether it was accidental and innocent"); *Milene Music, Inc. v. Gotauco*, 551 F. Supp. 1288, 1296, 220 U.S.P.Q. 880, 886 (D.R.I. 1982); *Quinto v. Legal Times of Washington, Inc.*, 511 F. Supp. 579, 214 U.S.P.Q. 668 (D.D.C. 1981); *Lauratex Textile Corp. v. Allton Knitting Mills, Inc.*, 519 F. Supp. 730, 215 U.S.P.Q. 521 (S.D.N.Y. 1981); *Boz Scaggs Music v. KND Corp.*, 491 F. Supp. 908, 914, 208 U.S.P.Q. 307, 311 (D. Conn. 1980). Cf. *RSO Records, Inc. v. Peri*, 596 F. Supp. 849, 862, 225 U.S.P.Q. 407, 416 (S.D.N.Y. 1984) ("Undoubtedly assessed statutory damages should bear some relation to actual damages suffered. Because statutory damages are often used in cases where actual damages cannot be precisely calculated, however, they cannot be expected to correlate exactly"). Other courts have looked to the size of defendant's business. *BMI v. P & R Amusement, Inc.*, COPR. L. REP. ¶25,712 (S.D. Ind. 1984).

[153]See *RCA Records v. All-Fast Systems, Inc.*, COPR. L. REP. ¶25,843 at p. 19,858 (S.D.N.Y. 1985) ([A]ward must be "of sufficient magnitude to act as an effective deterrent * * *. The degree to which an award of statutory damages 'smarts' the offender depends, in part, upon the offender's size and ability to absorb economic punishment"); *Delman Fabrics, Inc. v. Holland Fabrics, Inc.*, 228 U.S.P.Q. 596, 600 n. 4 (S.D.N.Y. 1985) (court notes defendant's involvement in 13 other infringement actions and awards the maximum of $50,000). *Kenbrooke Fabrics, Inc. v. Holland Fabrics*, 602 F. Supp. 151, 225 U.S.P.Q. 153 (S.D.N.Y. 1984) (maximum statutory damages awarded where defendant had been found guilty of previous infringements); *RSO Records, Inc. v. Peri*, 596 F. Supp. 849, 225 U.S.P.Q. 407 (S.D.N.Y. 1984) (statutory award of $1,450,000 permitted where defendant operated large-scale piracy business); *Bally/Midway Mfg. Co. v. American Postage Machine, Inc.*, COPR. L. REP. ¶25,601 (E.D.N.Y. 1983) (maximum award of $150,000 for infringement of three works in view of gaps in defendant's business records and evasive response of defendant's witness to discovery requests); *United Feature Syndicate, Inc. v. Sunrise Mold Co.*, 569 F. Supp. 1475 (S.D. Fla. 1983) ($275,000 in statutory damages for infringement of seven comic strip characters; purposes for damages said to include "restitution of wrongfully acquired gain to prevent unjust enrichment, reparation for injury done to plaintiff, and the deterrence of further wrongful conduct"); *Milene Music v. Gotauco*, 551 F. Supp. 1288, 1296, 220 U.S.P.Q. 880, 886 (D.R.I. 1982) ("Courts have * * * focused largely on the element of intent, and the per-infringement award tends understandably to escalate, in direct proportion to the blameworthiness of the infringing conduct"); *Hospital for Sick Children v. Melody Fare Dinner Theatre*, 516 F. Supp. 67, 72–73, 209 U.S.P.Q. 749, 753 (E.D. Va. 1980) (quadrupling amount of profits as award of statutory damages upon finding of willful infringement). See also *Fallaci v. New Gazette Literary Corp.*, 568 F. Supp. 1172, 1174 (S.D.N.Y. 1983) (doubling of republication fee—$10,000—called award of statutory damages for willful infringement).

The word "willful" is not defined in the statute. The better rule is that the word encom-

that such infringer "was not aware and had no reason to believe that his or her acts constituted an infringement of copyright" permits a discretionary decrease of the minimum to $100.[154] (d) A special provision in Section 504(c)(2) covering the activities of employees of nonprofit schools, libraries, and public broadcasting entities (infringing by broadcasting or recording published nondramatic literary works) remits statutory damages completely "in any case where an infringer believed and had reasonable grounds for believing that his or her use of the copyrighted work was a fair use under section 107 * * *." The legislative history indicates that the burden of proof as to defendant's lack of good faith in this situation is on plaintiff.[155]

(3) A minimum and a maximum amount apply (a) to each work, including all parts of a compilation or derivative work and irrespective of the number of copyrights or the number of copyright owners in the work, and (b) with respect to all infringements for which the infringers are individually or jointly liable. These limitations are addressed to the spectre of multiple infringements, with at least the mathematical possibility of parlaying statutory damage amounts to astronomical heights.[156] (Where the infringers are not jointly liable, an award of separate statutory damages for the same work is permitted.)

---

passes not only acts that defendant knows constitute copyright infringement but also instances where "defendant [ ] should have known (his) conduct was infringing or acted with reckless disregard of plaintiffs' rights." *Wow & Flutter Music v. Len's Tom Jones Tavern*, 606 F. Supp. 554, 556, 226 U.S.P.Q. 795, 797 (W.D.N.Y. 1985). Accordingly, a mere good faith belief on a defendant's part that his conduct does not constitute infringement does not bar a finding of willful infringement. See *Whelan Associates, Inc. v. Jaslow Dental Laboratory, Inc.*, 609 F. Supp. 1307, 1322; 609 F. Supp. 1325, 226 U.S.P.Q. 1013 (E.D. Pa. 1985) (reliance on advice of counsel and "sincere" belief that actions were noninfringing nevertheless resulted in finding of willful infringement).

A finding of willfulness has important consequences should the defendant file for bankruptcy after committing infringement, since a debt that arises from the willful and malicious conduct of the debtor is nondischargeable. See 11 U.S.C. §523(6); *BMI v. Gabaldon*, 227 U.S.P.Q. 163 (Bkr. Ct. N.M. 1985) (where performing rights society sent defendant correspondence advising him of his legal obligation to obtain a copyright license and defendant ignored the correspondence and subsequent cease and desist letters, the debt was found to be nondischargeable).

[154]The legislative reports state that this provision was designed "to protect against unwarranted liability in cases of occasional or isolated innocent infringement, and it offers adequate insulation to users, such as broadcasters and newspaper publishers, who are particularly vulnerable to this type of infringement suit. On the other hand, by establishing a realistic floor for liability, the provision preserves its intended deterrent effect; and it would not allow a defendant to escape simply because the plaintiff failed to disprove his claim of innocence." H.R. REP. No. 94-1476, 94th Cong., 2d Sess. 163 (1976); S. REP. No. 94-473, 94th Cong., 1st Sess. 145 (1975). Compare *Plymouth Music Co. v. Magnus Organ Corp.*, 456 F. Supp. 676, 203 U.S.P.Q. 268 (S.D.N.Y. 1978), with *BMI v. Coco's Dev. Corp.*, 212 U.S.P.Q. 714 (N.D.N.Y. 1981), and Professor Nimmer's criticism of the latter case. 3 NIMMER ON COPYRIGHT §14.04[B][2][a] at n. 17.1.

[155]See W. PATRY, THE FAIR USE PRIVILEGE IN COPYRIGHT LAW 479 (BNA Books, 1985).

[156]Under the 1909 Act, two tests—the "time" and "heterogeneity" tests—were used by some courts to judge whether an infringement was single or multiple. See *Iowa State University Research Foundation, Inc. v. ABC*, 475 F.2d 78, 82, 207 U.S.P.Q. 92, 95–96 (S.D.N.Y. 1979), *aff'd*, 621 F.2d 57, 207 U.S.P.Q. 97 (2d Cir. 1980); *MCA, Inc. v. Wilson*, 677 F.2d 180, 187, 211 U.S.P.Q. 577, 583 (2d Cir. 1981). Section 504(c) precludes application of these tests to actions arising under the 1976 Act. "A single infringer of a single work is liable for a single amount between $250 to $10,000, no matter how many acts of infringement are involved in the action and regardless of whether the acts were separate, isolated, or occurred in a related series." H.R. REP. No. 94-1476 at 162; S. REP. No. 94-473 at 144. But cf. 3 NIMMER ON COPYRIGHT §14.03[E][2]. Neither §504(c) nor *res judicata* is believed to prevent a copyright owner from bringing successive suits and thereby obtaining multiple awards of statutory damages for infringement of the same work by the same defendant.

(4) Infringement by a single defendant of multiple works owned by a single copyright owner will result in multiple awards (e.g., if a defendant infringed three separate works, the award must be at least $750 and may be up to $30,000, or $150,000 if willful).

(5) Infringement of multiple exclusive rights owned by a single copyright owner with respect to one work will result in a single award, regardless of whether the exclusive rights are owned by different individuals.[157]

## Costs and Attorney's Fees

Both costs and attorney's fees are discretionary under Section 505 of the 1976 Act, although registration is required for an award of attorney's fees (but not costs) for infringement of an unpublished work commenced before the effective date of its registration and for infringement of a published work commenced after first publication and before the effective date of its registration, unless such registration is made within three months after the first publication of the work.[158] Neither costs nor attorney's fees are, however, available to or against the government.[159]

The 1976 Act continues the language "prevailing party" to describe the potential recipient of an attorney fee award. This can sometimes be a troublesome definition.[160] There is no requirement that the

---

[157]H.R. REP. No. 94-1476 at 162; S. REP. No. 94-473 at 144. Professor Nimmer makes a very persuasive argument that this rule does not apply where there are several "works" based on the same original "work." 3 NIMMER ON COPYRIGHT §14.04[E][1].

[158]17 U.S.C. §412 (1978). Appellate review of awards of attorney's fees are made under an "abuse of discretion" standard. *Cooling Systems & Flexibles, Inc. v. Stuart Radiator, Inc.*, 777 F.2d 485, 487, 228 U.S.P.Q. 275, 277 (9th Cir. 1985), and cases cited therein. See note 148, *supra*, for a discussion of the meaning of the term "commencement of infringement." In *Sanford v. CBS*, 227 U.S.P.Q. 175, 176 (N.D. Ill. 1985), it was held that 17 U.S.C. §505 (1978) "overrides" Federal Rule of Civil Procedure 54(d) "at least insofar as costs relating to [a] copyright claim are concerned." The *Sanford* court denied costs to the prevailing defendant based on the hardship an award would impose on the unsuccessful plaintiff. See also *Pacific & Southern Co. v. Duncan*, 572 F. Supp. 1181, 1196, 220 U.S.P.Q. 859, 864 (N.D. Ga. 1983), *aff'd in part and rev'd on other grounds*, 744 F.2d 1490, 224 U.S.P.Q. 131 (11th Cir. 1984), *cert. denied*, 471 U.S. _____, *on remand*, 618 F. Supp. 469, 228 U.S.P.Q. 141 (N.D. Ga. 1985) (costs denied without explanation).

[159]H.R. REP. No. 94-1476, 94th Cong., 2d Sess. 163 (1976); S. REP. No. 94-473, 94th Cong., 1st Sess. 145 (1975).

[160]See *Shapiro, Bernstein & Co. v. 4636 S. Vermont Ave., Inc.*, 367 F.2d 236, 151 U.S.P.Q. 231 (9th Cir. 1966). See also *National Conference of Bar Examiners v. Multistate Legal Studies, Inc.*, 692 F.2d 478, 216 U.S.P.Q. 279 (7th Cir. 1982), *cert. denied*, 464 U.S. 814, 220 U.S.P.Q. 480 (1983) (voluntary dismissal by plaintiff did not make defendant "prevailing party"). Attorney's fees and costs have also been awarded to a "disinterested and innocent" stakeholder in an interpleader action concerning royalty payments, *Sparta Florida Music Group, Ltd. v. Chrysalis Records, Inc.*, 566 F. Supp. 321 (S.D.N.Y. 1983), although the opinion does not indicate that the award was made specifically pursuant to title 17. Attorney's fees have even been awarded to a plaintiff law student. *Quinto v. Legal Times of Washington, Inc.*, 511 F. Supp. 579, 214 U.S.P.Q. 668 (D.D.C. 1981).

An award of attorney's fees has been held to properly include time spent on unsuccessful claims, and discovery on actual damages where plaintiff subsequently sought and was awarded statutory damages, *M.S.R. Imports, Inc. v. R.E. Greenspan Co.*, 574 F. Supp. 31, 225 U.S.P.Q. 585 (E.D. Pa. 1983) (this decision also applied the "lodestar" formula for computing the amount of fees). Awards have also been made under the authority of state law. See *Roth v. Pritikin*, COPR. L. REP. ¶25,780 (S.D.N.Y. 1985) (award of attorney's fees to defendant under N.Y.C.P.L.R. §6212(e) where court determined that its previous order of attachment was improperly granted).

case be an "exceptional" one, and, indeed, the courts have correctly noted that awards of attorney's fees to the prevailing plaintiff are "routine,"[161] and particularly appropriate where plaintiff is a small business.[162] Although a few cases have stated that attorney's fees have "generally [been] * * * restricted to actions involving willful infringement,"[163] this characterization is erroneous. It is also noteworthy that the chairman of the Senate Subcommittee on Patents, Copyrights, and Trademarks has sharply criticized a statement that an attorney's fee generally will be awarded only "where there is some element of more blame against the losing party."[164] The courts have enumerated various factors to be applied in evaluating what constitutes a "reasonable" attorney's fee, including "the amount of work, the skill employed, damages at issue, and the result achieved * * *."[165]

Awards to prevailing defendants stand on a different footing and have been considered to "represent a penalty for the institution of a frivolous or bad faith suit."[166] The most extensive discussion on this point is found in the Second Circuit's decision in *Diamond v. Am-Law Publishing Corp.*:

"Because Section 505 is intended in part to encourage the assertion of colorable copyright claims and to deter infringement, fees are generally awarded to prevailing plaintiffs. * * * Fees to a prevailing defendant

---

[161]*Micromanipulator Co. v. Bough*, 779 F.2d 255, 259, 228 U.S.P.Q. 443, 446 (5th Cir. 1985); *BMI v. Lyndon Lanes, Inc.*, 227 U.S.P.Q. 731, 733 (W.D. Ky. 1985); *Warner Bros., Inc. v. Lobster Pot, Inc.*, 582 F. Supp. 478, 484, 223 U.S.P.Q. 239, 243 (N.D. Ohio 1984) (and cases cited therein). Cf. 35 U.S.C. §285, which limits awards to "exceptional" cases.

[162]*M.S.R. Imports, Inc. v. R.E. Greenspan Co., supra* note 160.

[163]*RSO Records, Inc. v. Peri*, 596 F. Supp. 849, 864, 225 U.S.P.Q. 407, 418 (S.D.N.Y. 1984). See also *Roth v. Pritikin*, 787 F.2d 54 (2d Cir. 1986). *Rare Blue Music, Inc. v. Guttadauro*, 227 U.S.P.Q. 325, 327 (D. Mass. 1985) (defendant's conduct said to be "sufficiently blameworthy" to justify an award of attorney's fees). Contra *Original Appalachian Artworks, Inc. v. Toy Loft, Inc.*, 684 F.2d 821, 832, 215 U.S.P.Q. 745, 755 (5th Cir. 1982); *Lieb v. D. Robbins & Co.*, 788 F.2d 151 (3d Cir. 1986). In the Ninth Circuit, an award of attorney's fees to the prevailing party requires a finding of bad faith or frivolity. *Cooling Systems & Flexibles, Inc. v. Stuart Radiator, Inc.*, 777 F.2d 485, 493, 228 U.S.P.Q. 275, 282 (9th Cir. 1985).

[164]*Civil and Criminal Enforcement of the Copyright Laws: Hearing Before the Subcomm. on Patents, Copyrights, and Trademarks of the Senate Judiciary Comm.*, 99th Cong., 1st Sess. 51 (1985).

Although it is sometimes argued that attorney's fees should be denied where the issues are complex or novel, *Williams v. Arndt*, 227 U.S.P.Q. 615, 623 (D. Mass. 1985) (suit said to be "sufficiently unusual"), this argument ignores the strong public interest in enforcing copyrights, *Apple Computer, Inc. v. Franklin Computer Corp.*, 714 F.2d 1240, 1254, 219 U.S.P.Q. 113, 124–125 (3d Cir. 1983), and the disincentive to bringing complex and novel copyright cases that such denial would entail.

[165]*Oboler v. Goldin*, 714 F.2d 211, 213, 220 U.S.P.Q. 166, 167 (2d Cir. 1983). See also *Southern Bell Tel. & Tel. Co. v. ATD Pub.*, 221 U.S.P.Q. 132 (N.D. Ga. 1983), *aff'd*, 756 F.2d 801, 225 U.S.P.Q. 899 (11th Cir. 1985); *Moorish Vanguard Concert v. Brown*, 498 F. Supp. 830, 212 U.S.P.Q. 479 (E.D. Pa. 1980). It has been held that a challenge to an award of attorney's fees cannot be made for the first time on appeal. *Herbert v. Wicklund*, 744 F.2d 218 (9th Cir. 1984). *Vy Pub., Inc. v. Hinish*, 212 U.S.P.Q. 185, 189 (D. Mass. 1980), which limited the amount of attorney's fees to three times the amount of minimum statutory damages, is contrary to the purposes of the Act and should not be followed. Cf. *Rockford Map Pub., Inc. v. Directory Service Co. of Colorado, Inc.*, 768 F.2d 145, 226 U.S.P.Q. 1025 (7th Cir. 1985) (upholding award of $22,000 in attorney's fees and costs where plaintiff recovered only $250 in statutory damages).

[166]*Jartech, Inc. v. Clancy*, 666 F.2d 403, 407, 213 U.S.P.Q. 1057, 1060 (9th Cir. 1982). Accord *Kenbrooke Fabrics, Inc. v. Material Things*, 223 U.S.P.Q. 1039 (S.D.N.Y. 1984); *Risdon v. Walt Disney Prods.*, Copr. L. Rep. ¶25,727 (S.D.N.Y. 1984); *Grossett & Dunlap, Inc. v. Gulf & Western Corp.*, 534 F. Supp. 606, 215 U.S.P.Q. 991 (S.D.N.Y. 1982); *Oakwood Mfg., Inc. v. Novi-American, Inc.*, 213 U.S.P.Q. 1014, 1023 (E.D. Mich. 1984). Contra *Williams Electronics, Inc. v. Bally Mfg. Corp.*, 568 F. Supp. 1274, 220 U.S.P.Q. 1091 (N.D. Ill. 1983).

should not be awarded when the plaintiff's claim is colorable since such awards would diminish the intended incentive to bring such claims. * * * When the plaintiff's claims are objectively without arguable merit, however, a prevailing defendant may recover attorney's fees under Section 505. * * * Because the award of fees has a statutory basis, a finding of subjective bad faith is not necessary * * * although the deliberate assertion of a meritless federal claim solely to obtain federal jurisdiction over a pendent state claim qualifies as bad faith no matter how meritorious the state claims."[167]

Section 505, as noted, also gives the court discretion to award "full costs." In *Stevens Linen Associates, Inc. v. Mastercraft Corp.*, the court rejected an argument that the word "full" permitted recovery of costs normally awarded to a prevailing party under 28 U.S.C. §1920, e.g., "disbursements for travel, telephone charges, duplicating, preparation of exhibits, meals of witnesses, and carfare to court."[168] The courts have permitted costs connected with the taking of depositions (including the costs of purchasing copies of transcripts thereof), and costs connected with expedited discovery.[169]

## Attachment of Copyright

Copyright is incorporeal and distinct from the material object embodying the work copyrighted. (§202 of 1976 law; §27 of 1909 law.) Accordingly, the "situs" of a copyright and the procedure for attaching or securing execution of copyright, if that is possible, are not clear. Seizure of the copies is certainly insufficient. So is a sheriff's sale of the certificate of registration.[170] What is required is personal jurisdiction over the copyright owner. See *Independent Film Distributors, Ltd. v. Chesapeake Industries, Inc.*[171] The splintering of copyright ownership under the 1976 Act presumably permits differing

---

[167]745 F.2d 142, 148, 223 U.S.P.Q. 709, 713 (2d Cir. 1984). See also *Roth v. Pritikin*, 787 F.2d 54 (2d Cir. 1986). The Second Circuit rule set forth in *Diamond* was subjected to vigorous criticism in *Cohen v. VEPCO*, 617 F. Supp. 619, 227 U.S.P.Q. 889 (E.D. Va. 1985), which characterized it as "the culmination of a long line of bootstrapping from nothing to something." *Id.* at 622, 227 U.S.P.Q. at 891. Based on the absence of any statutory language or legislative history indicating the courts are to apply a different standard for the awarding of attorney's fees to prevailing defendants than to prevailing plaintiffs, the *Cohen* court wrote that it cannot "be argued on any principled ground that society is better off when a plaintiff files and wins a copyright infringement suit than when a defendant defends and wins a copyright infringement suit." *Id.* at 623, 227 U.S.P.Q. at 891. Accord *Lieb v. D. Robbins & Co.*, 788 F.2d 151 (3d Cir. 1986).

[168]Copr. L. Rep. ¶25,229 (S.D.N.Y.), *mod. and rem'd on other grounds*, 656 F.2d 11, 210 U.S.P.Q. 865 (2d Cir. 1981). In *Williams Electronics, Inc. v. Bally Mfg. Corp., supra* note 166, costs for preparing exhibits were permitted. In *Quinto v. Legal Times of Washington, Inc.*, 511 F. Supp. 579, 214 U.S.P.Q. 668 (D.D.C. 1981), photocopying and postage fees were allowed in addition to filing and service of process fees. Costs have also been awarded to a prevailing defendant. *Kepner-Tregoe, Inc. v. Carabio*, 203 U.S.P.Q. 124 (E.D. Mich. 1979).

[169]*Williams Electronics, Inc. v. Bally Mfg. Corp., supra* note 166. Although no rationale is given, it has been stated that prejudgment interest is not "traditionally included in a copyright case." *Blackman v. Hustler Magazine, Inc.*, 620 F. Supp. 792, 802, 228 U.S.P.Q. 170, 177 (D.D.C. 1985).

[170]*Kingsrow Enters., Inc. v. Metromedia, Inc.*, 203 U.S.P.Q. 489, 492 (S.D.N.Y. 1978).

[171]148 F. Supp. 611, 112 U.S.P.Q. 380 (S.D.N.Y. 1957), *rev'd on other grounds*, 250 F.2d 951, 116 U.S.P.Q. 28 (2d Cir. 1958). Cf. *Stevens v. Cady*, 14 How. 528 (1852) (creditor's bill in equity compelling assignment was in conformity with copyright law).

procedures and more than one situs for attaching ownership interests.

The *Independent Film* case involved a lien on motion picture exhibition rights granted to film processors by a New York statute.[172] The district court raised the question "whether a copyright may be subjected to a lien otherwise than in the manner provided in 17 U.S.C.A. §28."[173] A proper relationship between state law and the federal statute would seem to suggest a negative answer.[174] Section 301 of the 1976 law may not be definitive since it is arguable that questions of ownership, as distinguished from infringement, are not necessarily preempted.

## Criminal Provisions

The 1970s and 1980s have seen a revolutionary upsurge in the use of criminal sanctions against copyright infringement. A concerted campaign by record and tape manufacturers resulted in enactment of criminal provisions against piracy of their products in almost all states.[175] Moreover, the criminal remedies against tape and motion picture piracy in the 1976 Copyright Act were stiffened in 1982 to include, for the first time, felony offenses, reflecting Congress' increased concern over the effects of piracy on copyright industries and the U.S. economy in general.[176]

There are four types of criminal offenses under the Copyright Act: willful infringement "for purposes of commercial advantage or private gain" (§506(a)); fraudulent use of a copyright notice (§506(c)); fraudulent removal of a copyright notice (§506(d)); and false representation in connection with a copyright application (§506(e)). The 1982 tape and motion picture amendments also provided substantial penalties for trafficking in counterfeit phonorecords and their labels, and copies of motion pictures and other audiovisual works.[177] In *Dowling v. United States*, however, the Supreme Court held that Congress' careful approach in imposing criminal penalties precluded use of the criminal provisions of the National Stolen Property Act to reach the interstate transportation of bootleg records that were " 'stolen, converted or taken by fraud' only in the sense that they were manufactured and distributed without the consent of the copyright owners of

---

[172]N.Y. LIEN LAW §188. Cf. N.J. STAT. ANN. 2A:44–69 through 173.

[173]148 F. Supp. at 615 n. 5, 112 U.S.P.Q. at 382 n. 5.

[174]But cf. *Republic Pictures Corp. v. Security-First National Bank of Los Angeles*, 197 F.2d 767, 94 U.S.P.Q. 291 (9th Cir. 1952) (no federal jurisdiction to foreclose mortgage of copyright).

[175]These statutes are reproduced in COPYRIGHT LAW REPORTER (CCH) VOL. 1 at ¶10,920–¶11,237. See also *State Antipiracy Legislation*, 23 BULL. COPR. SOC'Y 321, Item 335 (1976).

[176]Act of May 24, 1982, Pub. L. No. 97-180, §5, codified in 28 U.S.C. §2319. See Appendix I, *infra*. See *Piracy and Counterfeiting Amendments Act of 1981–S. 691: Hearing Before the Subcomm. on Criminal Law of the Senate Judiciary Comm.*, 97th Cong., 1st Sess. (1981); S. REP. No. 97-274, 97th Cong., 1st Sess. (1981).

[177]28 U.S.C. §2318 (1982). See *United States v. Steerwell Leisure Corp.*, 598 F. Supp. 171, 224 U.S.P.Q. 1059 (W.D.N.Y. 1985); *United States v. Gallo*, COPR. L. REP. ¶25,769 (W.D.N.Y. 1985) (probable cause said to be established under ordinary observer test if "a lay person's description of the shape of a game's figures, the pattern of play, the sounds that accompany the play of the games, the scoring, and other factors" are given).

the musical compositions performed on the records."[178] State prosecutions for criminal activity with respect to copyright infringement
are, of course, preempted,[179] except as regards pre-1972 sound
recordings.[180]

The burden of proving a willful infringement "for purposes of
commercial advantage or private financial gain" is on the government. However, it has been held that such advantage or gain need not
be personal; e.g., an individual engaging in such activity for the benefit of a corporation or third party will be criminally liable even if he
does not himself benefit.[181] The first-sale doctrine has played a role in
a number of criminal prosecutions, with defendants arguing that the
burden of proving the absence of a valid first sale rests with the government. In *United States v. Powell*, the Eighth Circuit enunciated
what is believed to be correct rule on this point:

> "Because there can be no lawful distribution of a bootleg record, the
> copyright holder cannot, by definition, part with legal title through a
> first sale.
> "Courts have applied the first sale doctrine only where the possibil-
> ity existed that the person possessing the copyrighted work obtained it
> lawfully in the first place."[182]

An unusual defense to a criminal action involving illegal distribution of motion pictures at overseas U.S. Army bases—that 28 U.S.C.
§1498(b) provided an exclusive (civil) remedy for monetary damages
in the U.S. Court of Claims—was rejected by the Ninth Circuit, which
stated that "[w]e publish this opinion not because the appellants'
principal argument has merit, but simply to insure that it will not be
repeated again."[183]

## Copyright Litigation—Miscellaneous Matters

Many aspects of pleading and practice in copyright actions are
similar to those in civil actions generally. Certain phases of the conduct of litigation in the copyright context not covered earlier will be
mentioned briefly.

Trial by jury has traditionally not been sought in copyright litigation; however, the incidence of copyright jury trials may be increasing. Where a jury demand is made, there is both a statutory and

---

[178]473 U.S. _____, _____, 226 U.S.P.Q. 529, _____ (1985). Dowling was also convicted of
criminal copyright infringement but did not appeal the conviction.
[179]*Crow v. Wainwright*, 720 F.2d 1224 (11th Cir. 1983), *cert. denied*, 469 U.S. 819 (1984);
*Massachusetts v. Rizzuto*, Copr. L. Rep. ¶25,233 (Sup. Ct. Mass. 1980); *People v. M&R
Records*, 212 U.S.P.Q. 797 (N.Y. Sup. Ct. 1980); *People v. Winley*, 211 U.S.P.Q. 455 (N.Y. Sup.
Ct. 1980).
[180]17 U.S.C. §301(c) (1978).
[181]*United States v. Stolon*, 555 F. Supp. 238, 240, 223 U.S.P.Q. 802, 803–804 (E.D.N.Y.
1983).
[182]701 F.2d 70, 73, 217 U.S.P.Q. 609, 611 (8th Cir. 1983). Accord *United States v. Steerwell
Leisure Corp., Inc.*, 598 F. Supp. 171, 224 U.S.P.Q. 1059 (W.D.N.Y. 1985); *United States v.
Gallo*, Copr. L. Rep. ¶25,769 (W.D.N.Y. 1985) (indictment also alleged criminal performance
and display of electronic video games; claim that alleged uncertain status of games as copyrightable subject matter required dismissal of charges rejected).
[183]*United States v. McCool*, 751 F.2d 1112, 1113, 225 U.S.P.Q. 393, 394 (9th Cir. 1985).

a constitutional right to a jury, even where only statutory damages are sought.[184] Although a number of courts have held to the contrary on this latter point, based on the language in Section 504(c) that statutory damages are to be awarded in a sum "as the court considers just," these decisions are flawed by their failure to trace both the nature of statutory damages and the history of the language in question and, in a recent case, *Oboler v. Goldin*,[185] by ignorance of an earlier decision[186] in the same circuit to the contrary.

In passing the Semiconductor Chip Protection Act of 1984, the House Judiciary Committee stated: "In using the term 'court' in Sections 911(b) and (c) it is the intent of the Committee, as under 17 U.S.C. §504(c), that there be a right to a jury where requested,"[187] thereby providing *post hoc* support for the position set forth herein.

While there is universal agreement that the question of substantial similarity is for the trier of fact, and that in a close case the court cannot substitute its judgment for that of the trier of fact,[188] there is less clarity as to the role of appellate courts in evaluating substantial similarity where the issue turns entirely on a visual (or aural) comparison of the two works,[189] and as to the appropriateness of summary judgment on the question. The Ninth Circuit has expressed its general disapproval of summary judgment in this context, writing:

> "Substantial similarity is usually an extremely close issue of fact and summary judgment has been disfavored in cases involving intellectual property. *Twentieth Century-Fox Film Corp. v. MCA, Inc.*, 715 F.2d 1327, 1330 n. 6, 217 U.S.P.Q. 611, 613 n. 6 (9th Cir. 1983). It is appropriate, however, if reasonable minds could not differ as to the absence of substantial similarity of expression. *See v. Durang*, 711 F.2d 141, 143, 219 U.S.P.Q. 771, 772 (9th Cir. 1983)."[190]

The Second Circuit has held that:

> "[A] court may determine non-infringement as a matter of law on a motion for summary judgment, either because the similarity between the two works concerns only '*non*-copyrightable elements of the plaintiff's

---

[184]Patry, *The Right to a Jury in Copyright Cases*, 29 J. COPR. SOC'Y 139 (1981).
[185]714 F.2d 211, 220 U.S.P.Q. 166 (2d Cir. 1983).
[186]*Mail & Express Co. v. Life Pub. Co.*, 192 F. 899 (2d Cir. 1912).
[187]H.R. REP. No. 97-781, 98th Cong., 2d Sess. 27 (1984) (Star Print).
[188]*Midway Mfg. Co. v. Bandai-America, Inc.*, 546 F. Supp. 125, 141, 216 U.S.P.Q. 812, 822 (D.N.J. 1982).
[189]See text at notes 68–69 in Chapter 7 and cases cited *id.*, notes 68–69.
[190]*Litchfield v. Spielberg*, 736 F.2d 1352, 1355–1366, 222 U.S.P.Q. 965, 967 (9th Cir. 1984), *cert. denied*, 470 U.S. _____ (1985). The court also held that it reviewed the propriety of summary judgment *de novo*. *Ibid. Twentieth Century-Fox Film Corp. v. MCA, Inc.*, 715 F.2d 1327, 1330, 217 U.S.P.Q. 611, 613 (9th Cir. 1983) (in reversing district court finding of no substantial similarity, the court of appeals stated: "Summary judgment is appropriate * * * where undisputed facts raise a complete defense as a matter of law. * * * A grant of summary judgment for plaintiff is proper where works are so overwhelmingly identical that the possibility of independent creation is precluded. * * * Similarly, summary judgment for defendant is appropriate where works are so dissimilar that a claim of infringement is without merit"); see also *Hollinger v. Wagner Min. Equipment Co.*, 667 F.2d 402, 405 (3d Cir. 1981). But cf. *Berkic v. Crichton*, 761 F.2d 1289, 1292, 226 U.S.P.Q. 787, 789 (9th Cir.), *cert. denied*, 474 U.S. _____ (1985): "[N]o special standard is employed in determining whether summary judgment is appropriate on the issue of substantial similarity in a copyright case" (quoting *See v. Durang*, 711 F.2d 141, 142, 219 U.S.P.Q. 771, 772 (9th Cir. 1983)); *Walker v. Time-Life Films, Inc.*, 615 F. Supp. 430, 227 U.S.P.Q. 698 (S.D.N.Y. 1985), *aff'd*, 784 F.2d 44, 228 U.S.P.Q. 505 (2d Cir. 1986); *Zambito v. Paramount Pictures Corp.*, 613 F. Supp. 1107, 227 U.S.P.Q. 649 (E.D.N.Y. 1985); *Smith v. Weinstein*, 578 F. Supp. 1297, 1302, 222 U.S.P.Q. 381, 384 (S.D.N.Y.), *aff'd mem.*, 738 F.2d 410 (2d Cir. 1984).

work,' * * * or because no reasonable jury, properly instructed, could find that the two works are substantially similar * * *
* * *
"* * * Courts have an important responsibility in copyright cases to monitor the outer limits within which juries may determine reasonably disputable issues of fact."[191]

Without detracting from the soundness of Judge Newman's analysis here, the application of the principles set forth is questionable in specific cases. For example, in *Hoehling v. Universal City Studios, Inc.*,[192] a different panel of the court of appeals affirmed a grant of summary judgment in defendant's favor by severely limiting the scope of protection for historical works. This limitation and the grant of summary judgment on the particular facts involved have properly been the subject of strong criticism.[193] Regardless of such individual misapplications, it must be recognized that there is an increasing willingness by the courts to set the "outer limits" of both copyright issues of fact and mixed questions of law and fact (e.g., fair use) in order to put a quick end to meritless litigation.

Discovery in copyright cases is accorded the broad scope envisioned by the federal rules, and the same penalties are provided for failure to comply with discovery requests and for abuse of the discovery process.[194]

---

[191]*Warner Bros., Inc. v. ABC*, 720 F.2d 231, 245, 222 U.S.P.Q. 101, 112 (2d Cir. 1983) (Newman, J.). See also *Walker v. Time-Life Films, Inc.*, 784 F.2d 44, 48, 228 U.S.P.Q. 505, 508 (2d Cir. 1986); *Alexander v. Haley*, 460 F. Supp. 40, 45, 200 U.S.P.Q. 239, 242 (S.D.N.Y. 1978); *Musto v. Meyer*, 434 F. Supp. 32, 36, 196 U.S.P.Q. 820, 823 (S.D.N.Y. 1977), *aff'd without opinion*, 598 F.2d 609 (2d Cir. 1979); *Fuld v. NBC*, 390 F. Supp. 877, 882, 185 U.S.P.Q. 460, 463 (S.D.N.Y. 1975); *Morrissey v. Procter & Gamble Co.*, 379 F.2d 675, 154 U.S.P.Q. 193 (1st Cir. 1967). Cf. *DC Comics, Inc. v. Reel Fantasy, Inc.*, 696 F.2d 24, 217 U.S.P.Q. 307 (2d Cir. 1982). See generally Hartnick, *Summary Judgment in Copyright: From Cole Porter to Superman*, 3 CARDOZO ARTS & ENT. 53 (1984).
   Summary judgment with respect to copyrightability has been found appropriate in a number of cases involving utilitarian works. See *Carol Barnhart, Inc. v. Economy Cover Corp.*, 773 F.2d 411, 228 U.S.P.Q. 385 (2d Cir. 1985); *Norris Indus., Inc. v. IT&T*, 696 F.2d 918, 217 U.S.P.Q. 226 (11th Cir.), *cert. denied*, 464 U.S. 818, 220 U.S.P.Q. 385 (1983); *Kieselstein-Cord v. Accessories by Pearl, Inc.*, 632 F.2d 989, 208 U.S.P.Q. 1 (2d Cir. 1980), but rejected in others, see *Poe v. Missing Persons*, 745 F.2d 1238, 223 U.S.P.Q. 1297 (9th Cir. 1985); *Trans-World Mfg. Corp. v. Nyman*, 218 U.S.P.Q. 208 (D. Del. 1982), and Judge Newman's dissent in *Carol Barnhart, Inc., supra*, 773 F.2d at 426, 228 U.S.P.Q. at 395.
   It has also been held that the trial court need not receive evidence on characteristics common to the subject matter of the works if those characteristics are generally known, i.e., are appropriate for judicial notice. *Eden Toys, Inc. v. Marshall Field & Co.*, 675 F.2d 498, 500 n. 1, 216 U.S.P.Q. 560, 562 n. 1 (2d Cir. 1982).
   Summary judgment was denied on the question of vicarious liability in *Dixon v. Atlantic Recording Corp.*, 227 U.S.P.Q. 559 (S.D.N.Y. 1985).
[192]618 F.2d 972, 205 U.S.P.Q. 681 (2d Cir.), *cert. denied*, 449 U.S. 841, 207 U.S.P.Q. 1064 (1980). See also *Knickerbocker Toy Co. v. Genie Toys, Inc.*, 491 F. Supp. 526, 529, 211 U.S.P.Q. 461, 463 (E.D. Mo. 1980) (mere denial of copying insufficient to overcome showing of striking similarity "even on a motion for summary judgment").
[193]See Ginsburg, *Copyright in Works of History*, 29 J. COPR. SOC'Y 647 (1982); Patry, *Copyright in Collections of Facts: A Reply*, 6 COMM. AND THE LAW 11 (1984).
[194]*Intersong USA, Inc. v. CBS, Inc.*, COPR. L. REP. ¶25,773 (S.D.N.Y. 1985); *Wood v. Santa Barbara Chamber of Commerce*, 705 F.2d 1515 (9th Cir. 1983); *Gero v. Seven-Up Co.*, 535 F. Supp. 212, 215 U.S.P.Q. 516 (E.D.N.Y. 1982); *Shipkovitz v. United States*, 732 F.2d 168 (Ct. App. Fed. Cir. 1983); *Mount v. Viking Press, Inc.*, COPR. L. REP. ¶25,134 (S.D.N.Y. 1980). See also *Seiler v. Lucasfilms, Ltd.*, 613 F. Supp. 1253 (N.D. Cal. 1985) (plaintiff was unable to produce original drawings allegedly infringed; court rejected secondary evidence offered under Federal Rules of Evidence 1004, 1008).
   Where plaintiff seeks only statutory damages, the court should generally deny a request for discovery into plaintiff's losses or harm, since plaintiff is not required to submit proof of same in order to receive statutory damages.

# 9

# The Copyright Office and the Copyright Royalty Tribunal

The last two chapters of the 1976 Act cover the specialized governmental bodies—both within the legislative branch—charged with responsibilities under the Act. Chapter 7 covers the Copyright Office, an agency which has been central in copyright matters in the United States since 1897. Chapter 8 creates a new agency embodying a new concept in this country—the Copyright Royalty Tribunal, which determines and/or adjusts royalty rates and provides for certain distributions under the four compulsory license systems contained in the Act.

## Copyright Office

The traditional role of the Copyright Office in registering claims to copyrights and renewals, recording assignments, etc., has been noted throughout this volume, as has the new regulatory authority given to the Office under the 1976 Act. (See Appendix C, *infra*, for text of Copyright Office regulations.) Mention may here be made of several other noteworthy activities of the Office found in Chapter 7 of the Act:

(1) The Office, though remaining in the Library of Congress, is made expressly subject to the provisions of the Administrative Procedure Act,[1] except that copies of deposited articles will be made available to the public only under conditions specified by regulations.

---

[1] 17 U.S.C. §§701(d), 706(b). It should be noted that the Copyright Office takes the following view of the application of the APA to its operations:

"The Copyright Office was not subject to the Administrative Procedure Act before 1978, and is now subject to it only in the areas specified by section 701(d) of the Copyright Act (i.e., 'all actions taken by the Register of Copyrights under this title [17],' except with respect to the making of copies of copyright deposits). (17 U.S.C. §706(b)). The Copyright

(2) Against a background of administrative flexibility, interest in maintaining full copyright records is demonstrated by the authorization to reproduce material before transfer to the Library of Congress or other disposition. Where material is not selected for preservation by the Library, retention of at least identifying portions of reproductions or deposited material is required "for the longest period considered practicable and desirable * * *." And for the first time depositors may request retention of deposits for such full term. (§704(e).) For unpublished works, retention of at least a facsimile reproduction of the entire deposit is required for the entire term of copyright. (§§704(c) and (d).)

(3) The basic fees are: (a) $10 for registration; (b) $6 for renewal under Section 304(a); (c) $10 minimum for recordation of transfers and statements concerning authors under Section 302(c) and (d); (d) $6 for notice of intention to make phonorecords under Section 115(b); and (e) $10 per hour for searches under Section 708.

In fiscal year 1984, the Copyright Office had a staff of 520 persons and processed 525,000 claims with respect to copyright.

## Copyright Royalty Tribunal

It is important to note that this is an independent agency contained in the legislative branch (§801(a)), even though supported by the Library of Congress, and performing functions which dovetail with those of the Copyright Office (e.g., §111(d)(2) and (3)). It consists of five full-time, high-level presidential appointees with seven-year terms. Its basic functions are to: (1) make periodic adjustments of the royalty rates provided in the statute with respect to (a) phonorecords of musical works under Section 115, (b) public performances of music on jukeboxes under Section 116, and (c) secondary transmissions by cable of all works under Section 111; (2) make the initial determination (as well as periodic adjustments), in the absence of voluntary agreements, of the rates and terms for broadcast and recording of published nondramatic musical works and published pictorial, graphic, and sculptural works by public broadcasting entities under Section 118; and (3) determine the distribution of royalties to claimants under the jukebox and cable provisions and resolve disputes over distribution. The criteria and timetables for royalty rate determinations differ, and the provisions of Chapter 8 and the Commis-

---

Act does not make the Office an 'agency' as defined in the Administrative Procedure Act. For example, personnel actions taken by the Office are not subject to APA–FOIA requirements."
50 Fed. Reg. 9272 n. 1 (March 7, 1985).
  The authority of the Register of Copyrights to issue regulations was upheld against a constitutional challenge in *Eltra Corp. v. Ringer*, 579 F.2d 294, 298–301, 198 U.S.P.Q. 321, 325–327 (4th Cir. 1978). Defendant's unsuccessful claim, based on *Buckley v. Valeo*, 424 U.S. 1 (1976), was that, as an officer of the legislative branch, she was prohibited from issuing what were described as executive rules and regulations.

sion's regulations (37 C.F.R. §§301–308) must be studied in detail for particular proceedings. (See Appendix D, *infra*, for text of Tribunal regulations.)

The criteria with respect to phonorecords and jukeboxes attempt to articulate objectives striking a general balance between fair return to the copyright owner and impact on the user. (§801(b)(1).) The House committee explained the lack of more specific standards by stating that "the Committee did not wish to limit the factors that the Commission [Tribunal] might consider in a world of constantly changing economics and technology."[2] The committee attributed the even more general statement of criteria regarding public broadcasting to "similar considerations."[3]

The rates for cable may be adjusted only to reflect inflation or deflation and certain changes in cable subscription rates. Reasonable additional rates may be provided to reflect such changes as were made by the Federal Communications Commission in 1980 with respect to deregulation of its syndicated exclusivity and distant carriage rules.

The early years of the Tribunal resembled those of the National Labor Relations Board; every action it took resulted in controversy and litigation.[4] Perhaps no action was more controversial than its November 19, 1982, rate adjustment regarding cable royalty fees imposed as a result of the aforementioned FCC deregulation.[5] Although generally affirming decisions of the Tribunal,[6] the courts have repeatedly stated concern over the quality of the Tribunal's decision making, and Congress has had second thoughts about the wisdom of continuing the Tribunal and the compulsory licensing scheme contained in various provisions of the Act. Indeed, at a 1981 oversight hearing, the then Chairman of the Tribunal testified in favor of its abolition.[7]

---

[2]H.R. REP. No. 94-1476, 94th Cong., 2d Sess. 173 (1976). See 17 U.S.C. §801(b)(1). See also Brennan, *Some Observations on the Revision of the Copyright Law From the Legislative Point of View*, 24 BULL. COPR. SOC'Y 151, 153 (1977):

> "A major policy objective of the bill—and one which I believe has been substantially accomplished—is to provide a flexible bare bones structure which can be accommodated to evolving technology. The Tribunal was conceived and structured to restore this flexibility in those sections of the bill where the compulsory license has introduced rigidity."

[3]H.R. REP. No. 94-1476 at 174.

[4]See Korman and Koenigsberg, *The First Proceeding Before the Copyright Royalty Tribunal: ASCAP and the Public Broadcasters*, 1 COMM. AND THE LAW 15 (1979), and cases cited in note 6, *infra*.

[5]47 Fed Reg. 52146.

[6]*Amusement & Music Operators Ass'n v. Copyright Royalty Tribunal*, 676 F.2d 1144, 215 U.S.P.Q. 100 (7th Cir.), *cert. denied*, 459 U.S. 907 (1982); *Amusement & Music Operators Ass'n v. Copyright Royalty Tribunal*, 636 F.2d 531, 207 U.S.P.Q. 374 (D.C. Cir. 1980), *cert. denied*, 450 U.S. 912, 211 U.S.P.Q. 400 (1981); *Christian Broadcasting Network, Inc. v. Copyright Royalty Tribunal*, COPR. L. REP. ¶25,415 (D.C. Cir. 1982); 720 F.2d 1295, 222 U.S.P.Q. 471 (D.C. Cir 1983); *National Ass'n of Broadcasters v. Copyright Royalty Tribunal*, COPR. L. REP. ¶25,153 (D.C. Cir. 1980); COPR. L. REP. ¶25,253 (D.C. Cir. 1981); 675 F.2d 367, 214 U.S.P.Q. 161 (D.C. Cir. 1982); COPR. L. REP. ¶25,444 (D.C. Cir. 1982); 772 F.2d 922, 227 U.S.P.Q. 203 (D.C. Cir. 1985); *National Cable Television Ass'n v. Copyright Royalty Tribunal*, 689 F.2d 1077, 217 U.S.P.Q. 323 (D.C. Cir. 1982); COPR. L. REP. ¶25,477 (D.C. Cir. 1982); 724 F.2d 176, 221 U.S.P.Q. 1044 (D.C. Cir. 1983); *Recording Industry Ass'n of America v. Copyright Royalty Tribunal*, 662 F.2d 1, 212 U.S.P.Q. 69 (D.C. Cir. 1981). Cf. *ACEMLA v. Copyright Royalty Tribunal*, 763 F.2d 101, 226 U.S.P.Q. 509 (2d Cir. 1985); *Old-Time Gospel Hour v. Copyright Royalty Tribunal*, COPR. L. REP. ¶25,655 (D.C. Cir. 1984).

[7]*Copyright Office, The U.S. Patent and Trademark Office, and the Copyright Royalty Tribunal: Oversight Hearings Before the Subcomm. on Courts, Civil Liberties, and the Administra-*

Many of the difficulties encountered by the Tribunal are due to the lack of an adequate (and experienced) staff and the lamentable practice of administrations of treating it, in the words of Senator Charles Mathias, chairman of the Senate Subcommittee on Patents, Copyrights, and Trademarks, as "a useful place to put otherwise embarrassing applicants for jobs."[8] Representative Robert Kastenmeier, chairman of the House Subcommittee on Courts, Civil Liberties, and the Administration of Justice, has also expressed concern over the qualifications of its members and has stated a belief that it is in dire need of reform.[9] It is hoped that that reform will be forthcoming.[10]

These sentiments notwithstanding, the support given to the Tribunal by the courts (by generally affirming its decisions) has had the salutary effect of forcing private sector interests into serious negotiations over voluntary rates. In the end perhaps the direct role of the Tribunal in rate setting will become less important as a result.

---

*tion of Justice of the House Judiciary Comm.*, 97th Cong., 1st Sess. 53 (1981). See also Ladd, Schrader, Leibowitz, and Oler, *Copyright, Cable, and the Compulsory License: A Second Chance*, 3 COMM. AND THE LAW 3 (1981).

[8]BROADCASTING, April 29, 1985, at p. 64 col. 3.

[9]*Oversight Hearing on the Copyright Royalty Tribunal and Copyright Office Before the Subcomm. on Courts, Civil Liberties, and the Administration of Justice of the House Judiciary Comm.*, 99th Cong., 1st Sess. (1985).

[10]The proposal of the Authors League of America, *ibid.*, suggesting that administrative law judges be used for purposes of conducting evidentiary hearings and making initial recommendations to the Tribunal, is particularly promising.

# 10

# International Copyright Matters

## Protection of Alien Authors: History and the 1976 Act

In 1961 the Register of Copyright recommended that all foreign and domestic works be protected on the same basis without regard to the nationality of the author (subject to restriction by presidential proclamation),[1] but this proposal never saw the legislative light of day. At least as to published works, the 1976 Act carries forward, though in liberalized form, the policy laid down in the Act of 1891 and followed in the 1909 Act. Under this policy, the United States demands a quid pro quo for the extension of the copyright privilege to the nationals of any foreign state or nation who are not domiciled here.[2] Absent treaty obligation, most foreign countries likewise condition copyright for nondomiciliary aliens on the existence of protection for their own nationals in the alien's country.[3]

The basic rule, both in the United States and abroad, is "national" rather than strictly "reciprocal" treatment; copyright is granted to an alien on the same terms that apply to a citizen and not on the terms of protection available in the alien's country. In other words, the alien is "assimilated" into the forum country.

In its coverage of all unpublished material (much of which had been protected by the common law), Section 104(a) of the 1976 Act adopts the common law rule of protection for unpublished works irre-

---

[1] REPORT OF THE REGISTER OF COPYRIGHTS ON THE GENERAL REVISION OF THE U.S. COPYRIGHT LAW, 87th Cong., 1st Sess. 119 (1961). For a more recent study of the issue by the Copyright Office, see TO SECURE INTELLECTUAL PROPERTY RIGHTS IN WORLD COMMERCE, *reprinted in Oversight on International Copyrights: Hearing Before the Subcomm. on Patents, Copyrights, and Trademarks of the Senate Judiciary Comm.*, 98th Cong., 2d Sess. 8–183 (1984).

[2] See Bogsch, *The Protection of Works of Foreign Origin*, COPYRIGHT OFFICE STUDY No. 32, 86th Cong., 2d Sess. 11 (Comm. Print 1961); Steup, *The Rule of National Treatment for Foreigners and Its Application to New Benefits for Authors*, 25 BULL. COPR. SOC'Y 279 (1978); Tannenbaum, *The Principle of "National Treatment," reprinted in* UNIVERSAL COPYRIGHT CONVENTION ANALYZED 13 (T. Kupferman & M. Foner, eds. 1955).

[3] E.g., United Kingdom Act of 1956, 4 & 5 ELIZ., c.74, §32(3).

spective of nationality or domicile. With respect to published works, however, protection is available under Section 104(b) only if at least one of the following four conditions is satisfied:

(1) one or more of the authors is, at the time of first publication, a national or domiciliary of:
   (a) the United States (§104(b)(1),
   (b) a country with which we have a copyright treaty, including the Universal Copyright Convention (or is the sovereign authority of such a country) (*id.*), or
   (c) no country, i.e., a stateless person (*id.*);[4]
(2) the work is first published in the United States or in a Universal Copyright Convention country (§104(b)(2));
(3) the work is first published by the United Nations (or any of its specialized agencies) or the Organization of American States (§104(b)(3)); or
(4) the work comes within the scope of a presidential proclamation finding that the author's country accords nondiscriminatory or national treatment to works of U.S. authorship or first publication (§104(b)(4)). Preexisting proclamations remain in force until further presidential action.[5]

In addition to its provision as to unpublished works, Section 104 liberalizes the requirements of Section 9 of the 1909 law by adding first publication in the United States as a basis for protection (§104(b)(2)) and also simplifies the presidential proclamation provision in Section 9 (which had covered countries according Americans reciprocal, rather than national, treatment and countries that were members of a convention "open" to the United States).

General proclamations have been issued in favor of more than 30 countries and their possessions. All have been on the basis of actual national or reciprocal treatment (rather than membership in an "open" convention). For the extension of mechanical music rights under Section 1(e) of the 1909 law, special proclamations were necessary, except where the original general proclamation expressly covered these rights.[6]

The President's power to issue proclamations in this area includes the granting of extensions to foreigners who are found to be prevented from complying with U.S. formalities because of the disruption or suspension of facilities essential for compliance. This power, added in 1941,[7] was exercised on a number of occasions as a result of World War II.[8]

---

[4]Cf. *Houghton-Mifflin Co. v. Stackpole Sons, Inc.*, 104 F.2d 306, 42 U.S.P.Q. 96 (2d Cir.), *cert. denied*, 308 U.S. 597, 43 U.S.P.Q. 521 (1939) (stateless persons protected under general grant of §9 of the 1909 Act, since only citizens of foreign states must meet the specified nationality requirements).
[5]TRANS. & SUPP. §104, 90 Stat. 2599. Under §405(b) of the Trade Act of 1974, 19 U.S.C. §2335(b)(5), bilateral trade agreements providing for most-favored-nation customs treatment may be authorized by the President for a country that is not a member of the Universal Copyright Convention only if the agreement "provides rights for United States nationals with respect to copyrights in such country not less than the rights specified in" the Universal Copyright Convention.
[6]29 Op. Att'y Gen. 64 (1911).
[7]55 Stat. 732.
[8]E.g., 25 Fed. Reg. 5373 (June 15, 1960) (Austria).

In determining the identity of an "author" for nationality purposes one must not neglect the special provisions of both the 1909 law and the 1976 law (§§101, 201(b)) which make an employee for hire an "author." Needless to say, any such relationship must be bona fide, even though motivated by nationality requirements, and not a sham attempt to create an employment relationship retroactively.[9]

Domicile within the meaning of this section is no different from the ordinary usage of this legal term. To acquire domicile there must be (1) residence in and (2) intention to remain in the United States, which may be inferred from various circumstances such as declarations, marriage to an American, payment of taxes, voting, establishment of a home, etc.[10]

Of course, aside from these specific provisions, another basis of protection is any treaty supplementing Title 17 of the U.S. Code as the copyright "law of the land." These bilateral treaties currently govern relations only with Taiwan and very few others.[11] Specific statutory enactments have also extended U.S. copyright to Guam, the U.S. Virgin Islands, and the Northern Mariana Islands.

## Universal Copyright Convention

The United States adhered to the Universal Copyright Convention in 1954, though its adherence did not become effective until September 16, 1955. The ramifications of this historical development bear significantly upon notice, the manufacturing clause, eligibility as an owner of copyright, and renewal.[12]

The essential feature of the Convention is nondiscrimination or national treatment. Under Article II, a member nation must accord works protected by the UCC the same protection as it grants to domestic works. Eligible for national treatment are works authored by a national of a UCC nation or first published there.

National treatment by the United States in and of itself would have given most foreign nationals no advantages not already enjoyed under bilateral treaties. National treatment for foreigners still would have included the same requirements of registration and domestic manufacturing as are imposed upon U.S. authors. The difficulties in meeting these requirements were hardly restricted to wartime conditions reflected in the proclamations mentioned above. Accordingly, the UCC excuses compliance with *all* domestic formalities with re-

---

[9]See *Olympia Press v. Lancer Books, Inc.*, 267 F. Supp. 920, 153 U.S.P.Q. 349 (S.D.N.Y. 1967).

[10]See *G. Ricordi & Co. v. Columbia Graphophone Co.*, 258 F. 72 (S.D.N.Y. 1919).

[11]See Copyright Office Circular R38a, International Copyright Relations of the United States.

[12]See generally A. Bogsch, The Universal Copyright Convention (1964); Universal Copyright Convention Analyzed (T. Kupferman & M. Foner, eds. 1955); Compendium II of Copyright Office Practices §1311.06(a). See Appendix F, *infra*, for text of convention.

spect to unpublished works and to published works which bear the prescribed notice. Such notice consists of

> "the symbol © accompanied by the name of the copyright proprietor and the year of first publication placed in such manner and location as to give reasonable notice of claim of copyright."[13]

In implementing the Convention, Congress took advantage of the restrictive option provided in Paragraph 2 of Article III: Formalities were not excused in the case of works first published in the United States (even if authored by a UCC national) and of works by U.S. nationals or residents (even if first published in a UCC country).[14]

"Publication" is defined in Article VI of the Convention as "the reproduction in tangible form and the general distribution to the public of copies of a work from which it can be read or otherwise visually perceived."

Several substantive provisions were originally attached to the national treatment principle of the UCC. A minimum has been provided with respect to term of protection: Duration must generally be at least 25 years after publication, prior registration, or death of the author.[15] In addition, a limited compulsory license scheme could be introduced under Article V with respect to the right of translation. This was supplemented in the Paris Revision of 1971 by a broader translation license,[16] as well as by a new compulsory license to publish protected works for instructional purposes[17] available under certain conditions to "developing countries."[18]

The 1971 revisions of the UCC (which did not enter into force until July 10, 1974) were an outgrowth of a movement, crystallized in Stockholm in 1967, whereby a number of developing countries sought to reduce their treaty obligations, particularly under the Berne Convention, to be discussed below. Along with broader translation and instructional use privileges in the UCC, the developing nations were given more latitude in withdrawing from Berne by the potential suspension of a clause found in Article XVII of the UCC designed to safeguard Berne Convention obligations. At the same time, the basic obligation under Article I of the UCC to provide "adequate and effective protection" for authors and other copyright proprietors was fleshed out to "include the basic rights ensuring the author's economic interests, including the exclusive right to authorize reproduction by any means, public performance and broadcasting."[19]

Because of the United States' withdrawal from UNESCO, the agency administering the UCC, calls have been made in some quar-

---

[13]Article III, para. 1.
[14]17 U.S.C. §9(c) (1909 *repealed* 1978).
[15]Article IV, para. 2.
[16]Article V*ter.*
[17]Article V*quater.*
[18]Article V*bis.*
[19]Article IV*bis.*

ters for U.S. adherence to the Berne Convention,[20] to which we now turn.

## Berne Convention

This convention originated in 1886 and has been revised six times. It extends copyright protection not only to authors of member countries but also to authors of nonmember countries (e.g., the United States) on the sole condition that they publish their works for the first time in a member country. This includes "simultaneous" publication elsewhere, which under the current revision of the Convention covers not only same-day publication but also publication in a Berne country within 30 days of first publication.[21] This "back door" to protection is open to an American author or publisher who effects such publication in any one of the countries adhering to this Convention (e.g., Canada or England); he or she thereby becomes assimilated to the status of a national of the country where the publication took place, and enjoys in other member countries all the rights accorded by the Convention.[22] It is to be noted that the Convention as amended in Brussels in 1948 defines "published works" for these purposes as works of which copies have been issued to the public and made available in sufficient quantities to meet the demand.[23]

Independent of the author's economic rights, "and even after the transfer of the said rights," Berne authors are accorded so-called "moral rights," including the right to claim authorship and to object to distortion, mutilation, or modification of the work or any other "derogatory action in relation to the said work which would be prejudicial to his honor or reputation." Article 6 *bis*.

Instead of adhering to Berne (a goal of many unsuccessful copyright law revision efforts during the 1920s and 1930s), the United States, several years after the Brussels revision, was to embark upon a new road that led to the formulation and ratification of the Universal Copyright Convention. Our 1976 domestic revision overcomes a number of obstacles to our joining Berne, but the requirement of Article V(2) of the Paris revision that enjoyment of rights "shall not be subject to any formality" would seem to require further revisions in U.S. law. Additional questions over, e.g., retroactivity, moral rights,

---

[20]See *United States Adherence to the Berne Convention: Hearings Before the Subcomm. on Patents, Copyrights, and Trademarks of the Senate Judiciary Comm.*, 99th Cong., 1st & 2d Sess. (1985 & 1986). See Appendix G, *infra*, for text of convention.

[21]Article 3(4).

[22]The efficacy of back-door protection may be questioned. In response to American efforts to use Canada as the "back door" country, Canada passed a law making illegal the importation into Canada of books within 14 days of their publication abroad. It should also be noted that a number of countries (including Canada) are not signatories to either the 1971 Paris or the 1948 Brussels text of Berne, which define "simultaneous publication" as publication in a second (Berne) country within 30 days of first publication (in a non-Berne country). The meaning of the term in non-Paris or Brussels text Berne countries is open to question.

[23]Article 3(3).

the manufacturing clause, and compulsory licensing may also pose problems.[24]

## Inter-American Relations

Prior to the consummation of the Universal Copyright Convention, the Pan-American Conventions were the nearest the United States came to reciprocity in the international copyright field. The first of these was the Mexico City Convention of 1902. This multilateral treaty was soon followed by the 1911 Buenos Aires Convention, ratified to date by 17 American countries, including the United States. (See Appendix F, *infra*.) El Salvador is the only Mexico City Convention adherent which has not also ratified the Buenos Aires Convention; however, it became a party to both the Geneva and Paris texts of the UCC, effective March 29, 1979. In addition to El Salvador, Cuba and Venezuela have not joined the Buenos Aires Convention. After a revision of the Buenos Aires Convention in Havana in 1928, ratified by only five countries, a more thoroughgoing revision was effected in Washington in 1946 but was never ratified by the United States.

The key provision of the Buenos Aires Convention, found in Article 3, is as follows:

> "The acknowledgement of a copyright obtained in one State, in conformity with its laws, shall produce its effects of full right in all the other States without the necessity of complying with any other formality, provided always there shall appear in the work a statement that indicates the reservation of the property right."

It is the law in force in the country of first publication in the Americas that determines what formalities, if any, must be complied with in the first instance. But upon such compliance the intention seems clearly to be that the work shall be automatically protected in all the other countries party to this Convention, without the need of complying with any additional requirements in such countries, provided the work bears notice of reservation of the property right. The words "Copyright Reserved," "All Rights Reserved," or the equivalent in any other language would seem sufficient to meet the requirement. Although a notice under the Universal Copyright Convention is arguably a notice of "the reservation of the property right,"[25] many conservative proprietors include both a UCC notice and "All Rights Reserved." Inconsistent with its treaty obligations, the United States will not accept a Buenos Aires notice as an acceptable notice for purposes of compliance with Sections 401 or 402.[26]

---

[24]See *Hearings, supra* note 20.

[25]The impact of the UCC on the inter-American copyright relations of the United States and the contracted scope of the Pan-American Conventions are surveyed in Rinaldo, *The Scope of Copyright Protection in the United States Under Existing Inter-American Relations*, 22 BULL. COPR. SOC'Y 417 (1975). See also COPYRIGHT PROTECTION IN THE AMERICAS (Pan American Union, 3d ed. 1962).

[26]COMPENDIUM II OF COPYRIGHT OFFICE PRACTICES §§1005.01(a), (b); 1104.02.

There is one important right, however, which this Convention does not expressly cover, namely, the right of mechanical musical reproduction by means of phonograph records, etc. In the case of *Todamerica Musica, Ltda. v. Radio Corp. of America*,[27] the court observed that Section 1(e) of the 1909 law denied this right unless substantially similar protection was accorded to citizens of the United States, and that the existence of the necessary reciprocal conditions must be signalized by a presidential proclamation.

## The Convention for the Protection of Producers of Phonograms Against Unauthorized Duplication of Their Phonograms

In 1971, the year the first federal copyright legislation protecting sound recordings was passed, an international convention for the protection of sound recordings (termed "phonograms") was opened for signature. (See Appendix F, *infra*.) The Senate ratified U.S. adherence to the convention on October 1, 1973, effective March 10, 1974.

Membership in the Convention has important consequences for national eligibility purposes, owing to the Copyright Office's position that the Universal Copyright Convention does not extend protection to sound recordings. Accordingly, foreign nationals may register sound recordings in the United States only if their country is (a) a member of the Phonograms Convention; (b) a signatory to a bilateral treaty with the United States that accords to U.S. sound recordings reciprocal protection or national treatment substantially equal to the protection secured by the foreign national here; or (c) the subject of a presidential proclamation signifying the protection in that country of sound recordings on substantially the same basis as that country accords the sound recordings of its own nationals and domiciliaries and to sound recordings first published in that country. (See 17 U.S.C. §104(b)(4) (1978).)

Unlike the Rome Convention of 1961 (see Appendix H, *infra*, for text of convention), of which the United States is not a signatory, the Convention for the Protection of Producers of Phonograms against Unauthorized Duplication of Their Phonograms does not accord performing rights, but rather gives protection against copying for purposes of public distribution (Article 2). The means for implementation of this protection are left up to the domestic law of the contracting states, save only for a requirement that the term of protection be at least 25 years from the date of either fixation or first publication, limitations on establishing compulsory licenses, and a provision stating that, where domestic law requires compliance with formalities as a condition of obtaining protection, a notice virtually identical to that found in 17 U.S.C. §402 shall fulfill all such formalities.

---

[27]171 F.2d 369, 79 U.S.P.Q 364 (2d Cir. 1948). Accord *Protuondo v. Columbia Phonograph Co.*, 81 F. Supp. 355, 36 U.S.P.Q. 104 (S.D.N.Y. 1937).

## The Brussels Satellite Convention

Owing to the lack of detailed provisions in the Universal Copyright Convention pertaining to satellite and broadcast (also called "rediffusion") rights, and uncertainty over the scope of the International Telecommunication Union Convention, negotiations were commenced in the 1960s because of a perceived international need to deal with unauthorized reception and distribution of program-carrying satellite signals. The result of these negotiations was the Convention Relating to the Distribution of Programme-Carrying Signals Transmitted by Satellite, better known as the Brussels Satellite Convention, signed by the United States on May 21, 1974, but not ratified by the Senate until 1984. (See Appendix F, *infra*.) The Federal Republic of Germany, Kenya, Mexico, Nicaragua, Austria, Italy, and Morocco are the only other signatories.

Contracting states pledge to take "adequate measures to prevent the distribution on or from [their] territory of any programme-carrying signal by a distributor for whom the signal emitted to or passing through the satellite is not intended." (Article 2(1).) The central feature of this provision (and of the Convention) is *distribution*; unauthorized *reception* for private viewing is not prohibited, a point reinforced in Article 3, which states that the terms of the Convention "shall not apply where the signals emitted by or on behalf of the originating organization are intended for direct reception from the satellite by the general public." (The reference to "originating organization" does, however, make it clear the *distribution* by a signal "poacher" via direct broadcast satellite will violate the Convention even though *reception* of signals from such a satellite is not within the scope of the Convention.)

As with the Phonogram Convention discussed immediately above, the Brussels Satellite Convention leaves the specific means of implementation of its terms up to each contracting country. It is the position of the United States that its existing copyright and communications laws provide a more than adequate basis to fulfill its obligations under the Convention, and thus no new implementing legislation was enacted upon U.S. adherence.

## Trade Legislation

As a result of U.S. balance-of-trade difficulties, and increased government awareness of the important role U.S. copyrighted works play in world markets, trade legislation was passed during the 98th Congress giving the U.S. government and copyright owners increased leverage in persuading foreign countries to make substantive and procedural improvements in their copyright and related laws. Favorable trade and tariff benefits were conditioned upon those countries providing adequate and effective protection to works of U.S. nationals. We shall examine each of the provisions in question separately.

### Generalized System of Preferences (GSP)

The GSP program, originally established in the Trade Act of 1974, offers duty-free entry into the United States to approximately 3,000 categories of products originating in 140 developing countries. The program was scheduled to expire on January 1, 1985, but was renewed on October 30, 1984, until July 4, 1993.[28] At the urging of copyright owners upset over the grant of special trade benefits to "advanced developing countries" such as Taiwan and Korea, where massive piracy of copyright occurs, Congress amended the GSP renewal so as to tie future duty-free import privileges to the country's providing "adequate and effective protection" to intellectual property of U.S. nationals.[29] Where a particular country either does not have or fails to enforce an adequate copyright law, the President may, under specified circumstances, refuse to designate a country a beneficiary under the program, remove it from the list of beneficiaries if it is already receiving benefits, or reduce its benefits.

In order to be initially designated a "beneficiary country," a country must meet certain "mandatory" criteria, three of which are that it has not

(1) "nationalized, expropriated or otherwise seized ownership or control of * * * copyrights, owned by a United States citizen or by a corporation, partnership or association which is 50 per cent or more beneficially owned by United States citizens;"

(2) "* * * taken steps to repudiate or nullify an existing contract or agreement with a United States citizen * * * the effect of which is to nationalize, expropriate, or otherwise seize ownership or control of * * * copyrights so owned;" or

(3) "* * * imposed or enforced taxes or other exactions, restrictive maintenance or operational conditions, or other measures with respect to property so owned, the effect of which is to nationalize, expropriate, or otherwise seize ownership or control of * * * copyrights."[30]

---

[28] Act of Oct. 30, 1984, Pub. L. No. 98-573, 98 Stat. 3018. See generally *Possible Renewal of the Generalized System of Preferences: Hearings Before the Subcomm. on Trade of the House Ways & Means Comm.*, 98th Cong., 1st & 2d Sess. (1983 & 1984); *Possible Renewal of the Generalized System of Preferences—1984: Hearing Before the Subcomm. on International Trade of the Senate Finance Comm.*, 98th Cong., 2d Sess. (1984); S. REP. No. 98-485, 98th Cong., 2d Sess. (1984); H.R. REP. No. 98-1090, 98th Cong., 2d Sess. (1984); H.R. REP. No. 98-1156, 98th Cong., 2d Sess. (1984) (conference report).

[29] The phrase "adequate and effective protection" found in 19 U.S.C. §2462(c)(5) was drafted to refer to the identical language contained in Article I of the Universal Copyright Convention and is intended to specify that the terms mean the ability "to secure," "to exercise," and "to enforce" exclusive rights, and to provide protection that goes beyond that generally required by the UCC. See text at note 32, *infra.*

[30] 19 U.S.C. §2462(b)(4) (1984). Since this section concerns the actions only of foreign governments and not of its nationals, and may be read to imply active participation, it may be questioned whether it covers the rampant piracy found in many developing countries. Cf. H.R. REP. No. 98-1090, 98th Cong., 2d Sess. 11 (1984), and statutory language quoted in the text at note 32, *infra.*

A country that engages in any of these three actions cannot be designated a beneficiary country unless the President determines that (1) prompt and adequate compensation has been paid, good faith negotiations are in progress, or arbitration has been commenced, or (2) that the failure to designate will be adverse to the national economic interests of the United States. This must be reported, with the reasons, to Congress.[31] Even where a country has met the mandatory criteria, the President, in considering so-called "discretionary" criteria, may refuse designation after taking account of "the extent to which such country is providing adequate and effective means under its laws for foreign nationals to secure, to exercise and to enforce exclusive rights in * * * copyrights."[32]

Procedures are established for suspending, terminating, or limiting benefits on a product-by-product basis and, in a positive vein, to waive mandatory reduction of benefits on a product exceeding defined "competitive need limits" where, among other factors, a country has succeeded in protecting U.S. intellectual property.[33] The United States Trade Representative (USTR) is instructed to file two studies, due respectively January 4, 1987, and January 4, 1988, directed at whether the competitive need limits for certain products should be halved and whether countries should be declared ineligible for benefits or duty-free treatment reduced by reason of their compliance with the discretionary criteria. In drafting these studies, USTR is to consult with, among others, the Copyright Office and the private sector.[34]

## The International Trade and Investment Act of 1984

The International Trade and Investment Act of 1984, passed as part of an omnibus trade bill that included the GSP renewal,[35] contains additional amendments to the 1974 Trade Act clarifying existing law and providing new authority in the President[36] to retaliate

---

[31]*Id.* at §2462(b)(4), (5). See also ANNUAL REPORT ON NATIONAL TRADE ESTIMATES 222–231 (1985) (report detailing trade barriers, including those regarding intellectual property).

[32]*Id.* at §2462(c)(5).

[33]*Id.* at §2462(c)(3)(A). See also *id.* at §2462(c)(3)(B)(ii).

[34]H.R. REP. No. 98-1090, 98th Cong., 2d Sess. 15 (1984); S. REP No. 98-485, 98th Cong., 2d Sess. 11 (1984).

[35]Act of Oct. 30, 1984, Pub. L. No. 98-573, 98 Stat. 3000. See generally UNFAIR FOREIGN TRADE PRACTICES: CRIMINAL COMPONENTS OF AMERICA'S TRADE. REPORT BY THE SUBCOMM. ON OVERSIGHT AND INVESTIGATIONS OF THE HOUSE ENERGY & COMMERCE COMM., 99th Cong., 1st Sess. (Comm. Print 99-H 1985); UNFAIR FOREIGN PRACTICES: STEALING AMERICAN INTELLECTUAL PROPERTY: IMITATION IS NOT FLATTERY. REPORT BY THE SUBCOMM. ON OVERSIGHT AND INVESTIGATIONS OF THE HOUSE ENERGY & COMMERCE COMM., 98th Cong., 2d Sess. (Comm. Print 98-V 1984); *Unfair Foreign Trade Practices: Hearings Before the Subcomm. on Oversight and Investigations of the House Energy & Commerce Comm.*, 98th Cong., 1st Sess. (1983); *Options to Improve the Trade Remedy Laws: Hearing Before the Subcomm. on Trade of the House Ways & Means Comm.*, 98th Cong., 1st Sess. (1983), the legislative reports cited in note 28, *supra*, and S. REP. No. 98-24, 98th Cong., 1st Sess. (1983).

[36]The U.S. Trade Representative is also directed to prepare for Congress annual trade estimates that include losses to U.S. intellectual property. See also THE PRESIDENT'S COMM'N ON INDUSTRIAL COMPETITIVENESS, GLOBAL COMPETITION: THE NEW REALITY (1985); TRADE BARRIERS TO U.S. MOTION PICTURE AND TELEVISION, PRERECORDED ENTERTAINMENT, PUBLISHING AND ADVERTISING INDUSTRIES (CBS, Inc. Sept. 1984).

against foreign countries that fail adequately to protect U.S. intellectual property. These amendments (1) define the failure to protect intellectual property as an "unreasonable" or "unjustifiable" act, policy, or practice;[37] (2) stipulate that the President's retaliatory authority is not restricted to the particular class of goods or services involved in the foreign country's unfair trade practice[38] (e.g., upon finding that country X is engaging in an "unreasonable" act with respect to U.S. sound recordings, the President may retaliate against the importation of prunes from country X); and (3) provide that the USTR can *sua sponte* initiate investigations of "unjustifiable" or "unreasonable" acts.[39]

"Unjustifiable" acts comprise those that are in violation of "international legal rights of the United States,"[40] thereby including any country's failure to live up to its obligation under the Universal Copyright Convention, among others, if it is also a party thereto. "Unreasonable" acts need not violate a treaty in order to be regarded as "unfair and inequitable."[41] This provision would appear to be applicable to piracy in many developing countries.

### The Caribbean Basin Economic Recovery Act

This legislation was signed into law on August 5, 1983,[42] and, although preceding the above-discussed revisions to the GSP, was modeled on the GSP program. It is designed to extend duty-free treatment to imports into the United States from designated Caribbean countries. As under the GSP, designation as a beneficiary country is conditioned upon that country's meeting both mandatory and discretionary criteria.

Two of the mandatory criteria expressly refer to intellectual property: Section 212(b)(2), which, as with the GSP, covers nationalization or government expropriation; and Section 212(b)(5), which prohibits designation where a "government owned entity * * * engages in the broadcast of copyrighted material, including films or television material belonging to United States copyright owners without their express consent." The discretionary criteria include a provision identical to that contained in the GSP concerning adequate and effective means for the protection of intellectual property.[43]

---

[37] 19 U.S.C. §2412(c)(3), (4) (1984).

[38] *Id.* at §2411(a)(2).

[39] *Id.* §2412(c). Petitions are filed by individuals under §301. Regulations regarding such petitions are found at 15 C.F.R. §2006.

[40] *Id.* at §2411(c)(4).

[41] *Id.* at §2411(c)(3).

[42] Act of Aug. 5, 1983, Pub. L. No. 98-67, 97 Stat. 384. See also H.R. REP. No. 98-266, 98th Cong., 1st Sess. (1983).

[43] See text at note 32, *supra.* The United States is also a member of the Florence Agreement. Pub. L. No. 89-634, 80 Stat. (1966), which provides for duty-free trade in specified categories of articles (e.g., literary works, audiovisual works, works of art) for educational, scientific, and cultural purposes.

## Manufacturing Clause[44]

### Historical and General Applicability

Our statutory scheme has long contained a unique provision emanating from international copyright relations and greatly complicating them—the so-called "manufacturing clause." This provision has linked full enjoyment of U.S. copyright to the "manufacture" of copies of certain works in this country and prohibited the importation, even by the copyright owner, of copies not so produced. It thus represents not only a trade barrier but a trap for authors and publishers.

Until 1891, copyright protection was extended only to citizens or residents of the United States. Indeed, Section 5 of the first copyright act expressly provided that that act did not "prohibit the importation, vending, reprinting or republishing within the United States, of any map, chart, book or books, written, printed, or published by any person not a citizen of the United States, in foreign parts or places without the jurisdiction of the United States," an approach which later led the Senate to characterize the United States as "the Barbary Coast of literature," and its citizens as "buccaneers of books."[45]

This picture changed in 1891 but with an unfortunate and indeed ironic catch exacted by the printing industry: Books, photographs, chromolithographs, and lithographs were required to be "printed from type set within the United States, or plates made therefrom, or from negatives, or drawings on stone made within the limits of the United States * * *."[46] The irony in this requirement is that it was against printers that the Statute of Anne (upon which our copyright law was based) was enacted in order to provide protection to authors. The manufacturing clause may thus be seen as a regression to the times of the Stationer's Company monopoly. Its continued existence is as lamentable as it is anachronistic.

In order to assuage concerns of foreign exhibitors at the Louisiana Purchase Exhibition of 1904, Congress for the first time provided for a temporary (known as "ad interim") copyright of two years, after which time protection could be extended to the full term if two copies of the original text or an English translation thereof "printed from

---

[44]For more detailed reviews of the manufacturing clause, see Reilly, *The Manufacturing Clause of the U.S. Copyright Law: A Critical Appraisal of Some Recent Studies*, 32 J. COPR. SOC'Y 109 (1984); REPORT OF THE REGISTER OF COPYRIGHTS ON THE LIKELY EFFECTS OF THE MANUFACTURING CLAUSE (July 22, 1981); Rembar, *Xenophilia in Congress: Ad Interim Copyright and the Manufacturing Clause*, 69 COLUM. L. REV. 770 (1969); Schrader, *Ad Interim Copyright and the Manufacturing Clause: Another View of the Candy Case*, 16 VILLANOVA L. REV. 215 (1970); McCannon, *The Manufacturing Clause of the U.S. Copyright Law*, COPYRIGHT OFFICE STUDY No. 35 (1963).

[45]S. REP. No. 622, 50th Cong., 1st Sess. 2 (1888).

[46]Act of March 3, 1891, §3, 26 Stat. 1106. See S. REP. No. 1188, 49th Cong., 1st Sess. (1886); S. REP. No. 622, 50th Cong., 1st Sess. (1888); H.R. REP. No. 2401, 51st Cong., 1st Sess. (1890). Protection was available on the basis of a presidential proclamation with respect to individual countries.

type set within the limits of the United States or from plates there-from" were deposited with the Library of Congress.[47] The following year, in response to threats by France and Germany to rescind copyright relations with the United States, ad interim protection for books in languages other than English was granted for one year if deposit of one copy was made within 30 days of first publication in a foreign country with notice of copyright. Upon expiration of the year, foreign authors were given an additional year to secure full-term protection by complying with the same manufacturing requirements as under the 1904 Act.[48]

The 1905 Act could hardly be considered a substantial improvement, and thus additional changes were sought and obtained in the general revision that culminated in the 1909 Act. Works of foreign authors in a language other than English were exempted from the manufacturing requirements, and ad interim protection was extended to cover English language works first published abroad. In a number of respects, however, the manufacturing clause provisions of the 1909 Act (contained in no fewer than nine sections—Sections 16–18, 22, 23, and 106–109) represented either no improvement or, even worse, a retrenchment.

First, whereas under prior acts only typesetting was required to be performed in the United States, Section 16 of the 1909 Act added printing and binding. Compliance with these requirements was, moreover, to be sworn to in an affidavit to be filed with the Copyright Office, with criminal penalties and forfeiture of copyright provided for the knowing submission of a false affidavit. The manufacturing requirements were also applicable to "illustrations within a book consisting of printed text and illustrations produced by lithographic process, or photoengraving process, and also to separate lithographic or photoengravings, except where in either case the subjects represented are located in a foreign country and illustrate a scientific work or reproduce a work of art."[49] Finally, the time periods for ad interim protection were shortened; deposits of an English language copy had to be made within 30 days of first publication abroad, with protection lasting only 30 days from such deposit unless all the manufacturing clause provisions were subsequently complied with.[50]

---

[47]Act of Jan. 7, 1904, 33 Stat. 4. See also the accompanying report, S. REP. No. 142, 58th Cong., 2d Sess. (1903), and Act of July 19, 1932, 47 Stat. 703 (ad interim protection granted to exhibitors at Chicago World's Fair).

[48]Act of March 3, 1905, 33 Stat. 1000. See also the accompanying reports, H.R. REP. No. 1287, 58th Cong., 2d Sess. (1904); S. REP. No. 3908, 58th Cong., 3d Sess. (1905). The Copyright Office took the position that the Act applied only to citizens of foreign countries and not to U.S. authors publishing in a foreign language, a problem continued in the 1909 Act. See COPYRIGHT OFFICE REGULATION 28 (1910).

[49]17 U.S.C. §16 (1909 *repealed* 1978).

[50]The manufacturing requirments of §16 of the 1909 Act purport to cover "all copies accorded protection under this title," thus suggesting that failure to comply could place a work in the public domain. Although this interpretation has been generally expressed, see, e.g., H. R. REP. No. 94-1476, 94th Cong., 2d Sess. 164 (1976), there are authorities suggesting that the effect of noncompliance is less drastic. See, e.g., *Bentley v. Tibbals*, 223 F. 247 (2d Cir. 1915); *Meccano, Ltd. v. Wagner*, 234 F. 912 (S. D. Ohio 1916), *mod. on other grounds*, 246 F. 603 (6th Cir. 1917); 28 Op. Att'y Gen. 150, 155 (1910). But cf. *Grove Press, Inc. v. Greenleaf Pub. Co.*,

Following both world wars, the coverage of the manufacturing clause gradually contracted and its requirements were relaxed. See p. 000, *supra*. By a curious twist of history, though, this provision, initially a protectionist shield, was transformed into a sword used only against U.S. authors. This ironic development began in 1954, when our law was amended to conform it with the Universal Copyright Convention. In order to comply with Article III of the Convention, which, *inter alia*, excuses manufacturing requirements upon affixation of a proper copyright notice, Congress amended Section 9 of the 1909 Act by adding a new subsection (c):

> "Upon the coming into force of the Universal Copyright Convention in a foreign state or nation as hereinbefore provided, every book or periodical of a citizen or subject thereof in which ad interim copyright was subsisting on the effective date of said coming into force shall have copyright for twenty-eight years from the date of first publication abroad without the necessity of complying with the further formalities specified in section 23 of this title."

This exemption did not, however, extend to "works of an author who is a citizen of, or domiciled in the United States * * * regardless of [the] place of first publication, or to works first published in the United States."[51]

### The 1976 Act

Despite a recommendation in 1961 by the Register of Copyrights that the manufacturing clause be omitted from the new act,[52] and considerable congressional doubt as to its efficacy,[53] Section 601 of the 1976 Act contains a manufacturing clause requirement, albeit in a considerably amended form. Although the requirement was statutorily scheduled to expire on July 1, 1982, and despite another recommendation by the Register of Copyrights in 1981 that the schedule be adhered to[54] and a veto by President Reagan of a bill to extend the

---

247 F. Supp. 518, 147 U.S.P.Q. 99 (E.D.N.Y. 1965) (failure to identify portions not complying with manufacturing clause excused infringement); *Hoffenberg v. Kaminstein*, 396 F.2d 684, 157 U.S.P.Q. 358 (D.C. Cir.), *cert. denied*, 393 U.S. 913, 159 U.S.P.Q. 799 (1968) (failure to comply justified refusal to register, but court did not reach issue of whether work was in public domain); *Imperial Toy Corp. v. Ringer*, 203 U.S.P.Q. 696 (C.D. Cal 1977) (same); *Storm v. Kennington, Ltd.*, 223 U.S.P.Q. 790 (N.D. Cal. 1984) (1909 Act). Where the work that violated the 1909 Act manufacturing clause was a derivative work, the underlying work was not thrown into the public domain where it was not subject to the clause. See *Grove Press, Inc. v. Greenleaf Pub. Co., supra*.

In 1949 §16 was liberalized to permit importation of up to 1,500 copies of English-language books or periodicals of foreign origin "where ad interim copyright was secured, with the term of such protection lasting for five years from first publication abroad." Ad interim copyright, however, had to be obtained within six months of such protection.

   [51] Act of Aug. 31, 1954, 68 Stat. 1030.
   [52] REPORT OF THE REGISTER OF COPYRIGHTS ON THE GENERAL REVISION OF THE U.S. COPYRIGHT LAW, 87th Cong., 1st Sess. 123 (Comm. Print 1961).
   [53] S. REP. No. 94-473, 94th Cong., 1st Sess. 148 (1975); H.R. REP. No. 94-1476, 94th Cong., 2d Sess. 166 (1976).
   [54] REPORT OF THE REGISTER OF COPYRIGHTS ON THE LIKELY EFFECTS OF THE EXPIRATION OF THE MANUFACTURING CLAUSE (July 22, 1981).

requirement,[55] Congress overrode the veto,[56] extending it until July 1, 1986.*

Following this extension, opposition to the manufacturing clause shifted to judicial fora. The European Economic Community instituted proceedings under the General Agreement on Tariffs and Trade (GATT)[57] claiming, *inter alia*, that the clause was a nontariff trade

---

[55]*Message to the House of Representatives Returning H.R. 6198 Without Approval*, 18 WEEKLY COMPILATION OF PRESIDENTIAL DOCUMENTS No. 27 (July 8, 1982).

[56]Act of July 13, 1982, Pub. L. No. 97-215, 96 Stat. 178. See *Extension of the Manufacturing Clause: Hearing Before the Subcomm. on Trade of the House Ways & Means Comm.*, 97th Cong., 2d Sess. (1982); *Copyright/Cable Television: Hearing Before the Subcomm, on Courts, Civil Liberties, and the Administration of Justice of the House Judiciary Comm.*, 97th Cong., 1st & 2d Sess. 1019–1264 (1981, 1982). Congress requested the U.S. International Trade Commission to prepare a report studying the economic effects of terminating the manufacturing clause. This report, released in July 1983, STUDY OF THE ECONOMIC EFFECTS OF TERMINATING THE MANUFACTURING CLAUSE—REPORT TO THE COMMITTEE ON WAYS AND MEANS, U.S. HOUSE OF REPRESENTATIVES ON INVESTIGATION NO. 332-145 UNDER SECTION 332 OF THE TARIFF ACT OF 1930 (USITC Pub. No. 1402), concluded that "the long-term effect of expiration of the manufacturing clause on conditions of competition between U.S. and foreign firms engaged in printing and related activities would be generally insignificant." *Id.* at xvi.

It appears that in overriding the presidential veto in 1982, Congress was influenced by a Department of Labor study which estimated a possible loss of 366,000 jobs in publishing, printing, and related industries from the elimination of the manufacturing clause. This study was both seriously flawed and misleading. See generally the criticism by the Copyright Office, reprinted in 27 PAT. TRADEMARK & COPYRIGHT J. (BNA) 288–289 (1981).

Footnotes to the Department's elaborate impact tables reveal that many of the estimated numbers were supplied by a report commissioned by a trade association, the Book Manufacturers' Institute. More important, as the Copyright Office observed in response to the study, the Department failed to tailor its review to those parts of the printing industry actually protected by the manufacturing clause. The only jobs potentially at issue were those relating to the printing of nondramatic literary works, half of whose surface area consisted of text, and for which copyright protection is claimed. In essence, this means books, newspapers, and periodicals lacking lavish illustration. The Labor Department, however, despite its acknowledgment of lack of information concerning how much material copyright is claimed in, went on to treat *all* categories of printed material as within the scope of the clause's protection.

This indiscriminate treatment of all categories of printed matter, for example, projected substantial job losses in the "sectors" of blank forms and greeting cards; subject matter whose paucity of text already exempts it from the clause, assuming, in the case of the forms, that they are copyrightable to begin with, a doubtful proposition. Similarly, the Labor Department failed to consider whether the time constraints of printing and distributing a daily newspaper or weekly periodical would render foreign printing unlikely, and in most cases, the Labor Department did not explain on what basis it reached its projected job-loss figures. Finally, the Labor Department failed to note that a large proportion of the material referred to in its study was also not subject to the Florence Agreement's limitation on the levy of duties for imported printed matter and thus relief in the form of tariff protection was (and remains) available to printers and book manufacturers. (In any event, a protocol to the Florence Agreement, inserted at the express request of the United States provides that material that *is* subject to the agreement may nevertheless be subject to tariff protection if a domestic industry is threatened with economic harm.) In short, the assumptions underlying the Labor Department study cannot withstand the scrutiny that too few legislators accorded them.

In a new study, requested by the Senate Subcommittee on Patents, Copyrights, and Trademarks, the Department revised its assumptions concerning displacement in the commercial printing sector and concluded that the sector would be only indirectly affected by termination of the manufacturing clause. See TERMINATION OF THE MANUFACTURING CLAUSE: AN ANALYSIS OF POTENTIAL EMPLOYMENT EFFECTS (Feb. 1986).

*As this book goes to press, a compromise, permanent manufacturing clause bill has been agreed to by the interested trade organizations and is working its way through Congress. A copy of this bill is reproduced in Appendix B immediately following existing §601. This bill would amend §601(a) of the Act in the following ways:

(1) the present Canadian exemption would expire on December 31, 1988; (2) manufacture in a "certified country" on or after July 1, 1988, would be permitted if the United States Trade Representative has certified to Congress that the country, inter alia, provides adequate and effective means under its laws for U.S. nationals to secure, exercise, and enforce exclusive rights under copyright, imposes neither material nontariff barriers to trade in printed material nor tariff barriers to trade in printed material that is materially inconsistent with certain tariff bindings, and the Secretary of Labor has certified to Congress that the country is taking or has taken steps to afford internationally recognized worker rights. Further exemptions are provided where the country is a member of the Florence Agreement or has in force a free trade agreement with the United States governing trade in printed material.

[57]55 U.N.T.S. 194; T.I.A.S. No. 1700.

barrier. In February 1984 a three-member GATT panel found the United States to be in violation of GATT and recommended its findings to the full GATT membership, which adopted them in May of the same year.

On August 30, 1982, the Authors League of America and its counsel filed suit to have the clause declared unconstitutional as a violation of the due process clause and the First Amendment, since only authors of specified nondramatic literary works are required to have their creations manufactured in the United States (or Canada). On October 8, 1985, Judge Goettel, of the Southern District of New York, granted the government's motion for summary judgment, holding:

> "Congress can create regulations and restrictions under the Copyright Act that apply to some materials, but not all, without violating the first amendment. Where, as here, a distinction is not content-based and is necessary for the accomplishment of a valid congressional purpose, it is lawful. * * *
>
> "In enacting the manufacturing clause, Congress was aiming to encourage and protect domestic printing and publishing. The distinctions embodied in the manufacturing clause are carefully suited to this legitimate congressional objective and are grounded in an explicit constitutional source of legislative authority."[58]

It appears that the court may have overlooked the more basic question: whether the objective of encouraging and protecting domestic printing and publishing through a manufacturing requirement is outside of Congress' limited authority under Article I §8 cl. 8 to promote the progress of science. The manufacturing clause cannot be said to promote that goal; indeed, in many cases it operates to its detriment by creating artificially high costs of production, thereby restricting access to works of authorship. In other cases, e.g., destruction of nonconforming copies (see Section 603(c)), the loss to both the copyright owner and the public is absolute.

The main provisions of Section 601 may be summarized as follows:

(1) The provision applies only to (a) "copies of a [copyrighted] work consisting preponderantly of nondramatic material" (b) "in the English language" (c) created by one or more American nationals (unless domiciled outside the United States continuously for at least a year immediately preceeding importation) or domiciliaries.

(2) This limited scope is further modified by exceptions in favor of braille works and governmental, scholarly, educational, religious, or personal use. Moreover, testing of the market is possible through an exemption permitting 2,000 copies of each work to be printed abroad and imported upon issuance of an import statement. 17 U.S.C. §§601(b)(2) and (6); 37 C.F.R. §201.8

(3) An exemption of great potential breadth, introduced at the request of the Authors League of America, permits individual au-

---

[58] *Authors League of America, Inc. v. Ladd*, 227 U.S.P.Q. 552, 559 (S.D.N.Y. 1985). This decision was affirmed on May 6, 1986. ____ F.2d ____ (2d Cir. 1986).

thors to arrange for first publication and manufacture abroad. §601(b)(7).

(4) If the manufacturing provision applies, only the portions consisting of nondramatic material must comply, i.e., be "manufactured" in either the United States or Canada. Importation of non-complying copies is prohibited (and subject to seizure, forfeiture, or destruction). §603.

(5) The troublesome question of what constitutes "manufacture" may perhaps best be summarized by the following quotation from the House report:

> "Under subsection (c) [of §601] the manufacturing requirement is confined to the following processes: (1) Typesetting and platemaking 'where the copies are printed directly from type that has been set, or directly from plates made from such type'; (2) the making of plates, 'where the making of plates by a lithographic or photoengraving process is a final or intermediate step preceding the printing of the copies'; and (3) in all cases, the 'printing or other final process of producing multiple copies and any binding of the copies.' Under the subsection there would be nothing to prevent the importation of reproduction proofs, however they were prepared, as long as the plates from which the copies are printed are made here and are not themselves imported. Similarly, the importation of computer tapes from which plates can be prepared here would be permitted. However, regardless of the process involved, the actual duplication of multiple copies, together with any binding, are required to be done in the United States or Canada."[59]

(6) A key means of implementing the manufacturing clause has been administrative enforcement of the prohibition of importation. What happens if copies are imported in violation of this prohibition? Section 601(d) expressly provides that such acts do not invalidate the copyright or affect the copyright owner's rights generally; but they may afford a defense to one who infringes by reproducing and distributing copies before registration of an authorized edition complying with the provision. (The application for registration under Section 409 will have to indicate compliance, as would a complaint for infringement; Section 601(e).) This defense applies to copying of illustrations or photographs (which do not themselves have to be domes-

---

[59]H.R. Rep. No. 94-1476, 94th Cong., 2d Sess. 168 (1976). Section 601(b)(1) provides that where a substantial part of the work is prepared as a work made for hire "for an employer or other person who is not a national or domiciliary of the United States or a domestic corporation or enterprise," the manufacturing clause requirement does not apply.

As might be expected, uncertainties regarding the proper interpretation of the so-called "first definition" of work made for hire in §101 of the Act (see notes 18–51 in Chapter 4) spill over into §601(b)(1). In *Cooling Systems & Flexibles, Inc. v. Stuart Radiator, Inc.*, 777 F.2d 485, 228 U.S.P.Q. 275 (9th Cir. 1985), the district court construed the words "prepared for" in §601(b)(1) as referring to "the nationality or domicile of the employer that actually *uses* the work." *Id.* at 488, 228 U.S.P.Q. at 278. (The work, a radiator catalogue, had been printed in Singapore by a Singaporean subsidiary for its California parent corporation.) In rejecting this view, the court of appeals, citing legislative history, found that

"the words 'prepared for' mean only that an employee created the work in the course of employment for his employer. The House Report on the Copyright Act of 1976 strongly suggests that 'prepared for' a foreign corporation means that a work is created by an employee, in the course and scope of his employment, for a foreign employer-corporation."

*Ibid.* (citing H.R. Rep. No. 94-1476, 94th Cong., 2d Sess. 167 (1976)).

For a decision questioning the bona fides of an employment relationship apparently designed to circumvent the manufacturing clause of the 1909 Act, see *Olympia Press v. Lancer Books, Inc.*, 267 F. Supp. 920, 153 U.S.P.Q. 349 (S.D.N.Y. 1967).

tically manufactured) contained in the nondramatic literary work subject to the clause but manufactured abroad, if but only if copyright in the illustration or photograph is also owned by the owner of copyright in the text.

The role of material not subject to the manufacturing clause was examined in *Stonehill Communications, Inc. v. Martuge*,[60] in which the meaning of the key adjective "preponderantly" in Section 601(a) was analyzed. Plaintiff, the publisher of *World Guide to Nude Beaches and Recreation*, a book written by an American author but printed in Italy, brought suit challenging the Customs Service's determination that the work (of which more than half consisted of photographs "depicting the life style at nude recreation areas in the United States and throughout the world") violated the manufacturing clause. Noting conflicting legislative history over whether a work is to be considered to consist "preponderantly" of nondramatic literary material according to a qualitative or quantitative standard,[61] the court expressed concern about "unfettered discretion on the part of the Customs Service to determine what is 'important' in a book," and the lack of an objective standard that could provide authors and publishers "with any realistic way of determining if a book will be subject to the clause * * *."[62] In order to provide such guidance, the court held that in the absence of other guidelines, a book constitutes preponderantly nondramatic literary material "when more than half of its surface area, exclusive of margins, consists of English language text."[63]

## Importation Provisions: §§602 and 603

In addition to relief in the federal courts, copyright owners seeking to prohibit unauthorized importation of their works may either request the Customs Service to seize infringing copies or have the U.S. International Trade Commission issue an exclusion order. We shall examine each of these alternative remedies separately.

### U.S. Customs Service

As indicated earlier, an innovation of the 1976 Act is an infringement-by-importation section, Section 602, which provides:

> "Importation into the United States, without the authority of the owner of copyright under this title, of copies or phonorecords of a work that have been acquired outside the United States is an infringement of the

---

[60]512 F. Supp. 349, 212 U.S.P.Q. 500 (S.D.N.Y. 1981).

[61]See *id.* at 351–352, 212 U.S.P.Q. at 501.

[62]*Id.* at 352, 212 U.S.P.Q. at 502.

[63]*Ibid.* In an unrelated subsequent action, individuals whose nude photographs were included in the book without their consent unsuccessfully sued the publisher for violation of §§50 and 51 of the New York Civil Rights Law. *Creel v. Crown Pub.*, 496 N.Y.S.2d 219 (App. Div. 1985).

exclusive right to distribute copies or phonorecords under section 106, actionable under section 501."

Exceptions similar to but somewhat broader than those to the manufacturing clause are provided. See, e.g., Section 602(a)(3) (important of up to five copies permitted for library lending unless in violation of "systematic reproduction or distribution" provision in Section 108(g)(2)).

Importation "without the authority of" the U.S. copyright owner is not limited to piratical copies; it can take place with authorized copies when contractual restrictions as to distribution are ignored (termed a "parallel import"). Making the latter situation an infringement seems to reflect a legislative decision contrary to the spirit of the "first sale" doctrine applicable to domestic distribution.[64]

Importation of copies in breach of contract, while amounting to infringement, may not be administratively barred.[65] Administrative enforcement of the prohibition of importation of copies produced in violation of the manufacturing clause has long been entrusted to the U.S. Customs Service. This agency (or its predecessor in the Treasury Department) was charged with excluding "piratical copies," which were prohibited from importation under Section 107 of the 1909 Act. These duties are carried over into the 1976 Act, but with regulatory authority given in Section 603 to solve serious administrative problems encountered by Customs throughout the years.

Copyright owners seeking to bar infringing copies must first record their certificate of registration with Customs.[66] Following recordation, Customs will seize allegedly piratical copies and notify the importer, who must file a statement within 30 days regarding the damage from exclusion and make a denial of infringement.[67] If a denial is filed, Customs will notify the copyright owner, who must either file a written demand for exclusion or post a bond in an amount set by Customs.[68] Upon submission of briefs and any relevant evidence, a determination is made as to whether the copies are, in fact, infringing.[69] If so, the copies may be destroyed. If there is no infringement, the copies are released and the bond forfeited to the importer. Because Customs has insufficient personnel and occasionally faces difficult questions concerning infringement, copyright owners should

---

[64]See *Cosmair, Inc. v. Dynamite Enters., Inc.*, 226 U.S.P.Q. 344 (S.D. Fla. 1985); *Selchow & Righter Co. v. Goldex Corp.*, 612 F. Supp. 19, 225 U.S.P.Q. 815 (S.D. Fla. 1985); *CBS, Inc. v. Scorpio Music Distributors, Inc.*, 569 F. Supp. 47, 222 U.S.P.Q. 975 (E.D. Pa. 1983), *aff'd mem.*, No. 83-1688 (3d Cir. filed June 21, 1984).

[65]The Customs Service is insulated from resolving contractual questions in this situation by the provision denying it authority to prevent infringing importation of copies which are "lawfully made," unless they are also in violation of the manufacturing clause. §602. See Feingold, *Parallel Imports Under the Copyright Act of 1976*, 32 J. COPR. SOC'Y 211 (1985).

[66]19 C.F.R. §133.33.

[67]*Id.* at §133.43(a).

[68]*Id.* at §133.43(b), (c).

[69]See *Schaper Mfg. Co. v. Regan*, COPR. L. REP. ¶25,581 (Ct. Int'l Trade 1983) (jurisdiction of Customs Service challenged).

take the initiative in assisting Customs in monitoring allegedly infringing imports.

## U. S. International Trade Commission (USITC)

Section 337 of the Tariff Act of 1930[70] prohibits the

"engagement in unfair acts and unfair methods of competition in the importation of articles into the U.S. or in their sale by the owner, importer, consignee, or agent of either, the effect or tendency of which is to substantially injure or destroy an industry, efficiently and economically operated, in the United States."

Complaints of violations of Section 337 are filed with the U. S. International Trade Commission, which has established detailed and expedited procedures for processing them.[71] Trial is before an administrative law judge, who files an "initial determination" that becomes a "final determination" unless an appeal is filed or the Commission itself does not grant review within 30 days of the initial determination.[72]

If a violation of Section 337 is found, an *in rem* exclusion order will be issued.

In view of the Customs Service's decision that it is without authority to bar importation of alleged contributorily infringing articles (such as so-called "ROM-less computers," i.e., computers with the infringing computer program embodied in the ROM chip removed from the computer for later insertion inside the United States),[73] the USITC has become an important forum for computer program copyright owners owing to the USITC's power to reach such conduct and to order Customs to bar such articles notwithstanding Customs' decision that it may not do so on its own.[74]

---

[70]19 U.S.C. §1337. See generally Lupo, *International Trade Commission Section 337 Proceedings and Their Applicability to Copyright Ownership*, 32 J. Copr. Soc'y 193 (1985).

[71]19 C.F.R. §210.20.

[72]Final review is made by the President, assisted by the U.S. Trade Representative. 19 U.S.C. §1337(g)(2).

[73]COP-2-03 CO:R:E:E 724225 KP (March 30, 1984).

[74]*In the Matter of Certain Personal Computers and Components Thereof*, Inv. No. 337-140 (USITC Notice of Issuance of Exclusion Order filed March 9, 1984); *In the Matter of Certain Coin-Operated Audiovisual Games and Components Thereof*, 214 U.S.P.Q. 217 (U.S.I.T.C. 1981); *Bally/Midway Mfg. Co. v. USITC*, 714 F.2d 1117, 219 U.S.P.Q. 97 (Ct. App. Fed. Cir. 1983). See generally *In the Matter of Certain Products With Gremlins Character Depictions*, Inv. No. 337-TA-140 (USITC Notice of Commission Decision to Reverse a Portion of Initial Determination; Termination of Investigation on the Basis of No Violation of Section 337 of the Tariff Act of 1930 filed Jan. 16, 1986).

# 11

# Taxation of Copyrights

The author or other copyright proprietor often attempts to take advantage of many of the same tax benefit provisions as do other taxpayers by (1) declaration of as much income as possible as capital gains; (2) assignments of property in order to shift income to family members in lower tax brackets; (3) exploitation of all or part of the author's creative efforts through a corporate entity; (4) use of deductions for depreciation or amortization; and (5) protection, upon death of an author, of his or her family from the double burden of an estate tax and an income tax on the residual income from the author's works. At the danger of oversimplification, let us proceed to summarize these and other principles of taxation as applied to copyrights.

## Exploitation of Copyright: Ordinary Income or Capital Gain?

A progressive tax imposed at the point of a sale or exchange disproportionately effects increases in the value of property that may have taken place over extended periods of time. The Internal Revenue Code has long attempted to reduce this impact through special low tax-rate treatment for gains from the sale or exchange of "capital assets" and of certain depreciable property used in a trade or business, if specified requirements have been met.[1] But by specific exclusion in Section 1221(3) (the statutory definition of the term "capital asset") these reduced effective rates of tax are not available for

> "a copyright, a literary, musical, or artistic composition, a letter or memorandum, or similar property, held by-(A) a taxpayer whose personal efforts created such property; (B) in the case of a letter, memorandum, or similar property, a taxpayer for whom such property was prepared or produced; or (C) a taxpayer in whose hands the basis of such property is determined, for purposes of determining gain from a sale or

---

[1] IRC §§1201, 1202, 1221, and 1231 (1954).

exchange, in whole or part by reference to the basis of such property in the hands of a taxpayer described in subparagraph (A) or (B)."

Subsection (A) prevents the author or other creative person from achieving a capital gain on the sale or exchange of his or her works. Subsection (B) applies the same restriction to the person for whom a letter or memorandum or similar property was prepared. Subsection (C) carries this result forward to a donee of the author or other creative person (or a donee of the person for whom a letter or memorandum was prepared), since a donee uses the same basis as the donor for purposes of computing gain.[2]

Prior to 1950 and the enactment of Section 1221(3), there was no specific exclusion of copyright or literary property in the Internal Revenue Code definition of the term "capital asset." The nonprofessional author or composer was able to treat gains from the exploitation of his or her works as capital gains if the sale or exchange and "holding period" requirements of the statute were met.[3] These requirements had their own built-in pitfalls, but at least there was hope for the amateur. The professional, even before 1950, was precluded from capital gain treatment on income from the exploitation of his or her works. Works created by a professional were considered held primarily for sale to customers in the ordinary course of business and thereby excluded from the definition of "capital asset" even prior to the 1950 amendment.[4]

The popular impetus for the enactment of Section 1221(3) of the Internal Revenue Code was the large capital gain achieved by President Eisenhower—an amateur author—on the publication of his memoirs. This event fanned the belief of the Internal Revenue Service and the tax law drafters in Congress that the work product of the author, composer, or creative person is integrally wound up in the performance of personal services.[5] Personal service income has traditionally been ordinary income not entitled to capital gain treatment.

It is an interesting commentary on the priorities of our times that the patented work product of the individual inventor is afforded special treatment under our tax laws, whereas the work product of the author, composer, or sculptor is subject to taxation at ordinary rates. If the individual inventor meets the requirements of IRC Section 1235 (1954), he or she may be entitled to report proceeds from the exploitation of the patented work product as long-term capital gains.

The Commissioner has taken an expansive view of what property is considered property similar to a copyright and excluded from the capital asset definition by Section 1221(3).[6] In *Cranford v. United States*,[7] the Court denied capital gain treatment to a sale by the au-

---

[2]See IRC §1015(a).
[3]See *Herwig v. United States*, 105 F. Supp. 384, 93 U.S.P.Q. 421 (Ct.Cl. 1952); *Richard W. Telinde*, 18 T.C. 91, 93 U.S.P.Q. 183 (1952).
[4]See the inventory exception of §117a of the 1939 Code, now §1221(1) of the 1954 Code.
[5]See H.R. REP. No. 2319, 81st Cong., 2d Sess., 1950-2 C.B. 380 at 421.
[6]See Treas. Reg. §1.1221-1.
[7]338 F.2d 379, 143 U.S.P.Q. 313 (Ct.Cl. 1964).

thor of the format for the radio program quiz show "Take It Or Leave It," even though the format was declared not to be subject to copyright by the Copyright Office. The basis for denying capital gain treatment was the nature of the author's input—personal services. In the Regulations other property similar to a copyright is defined to include

> "for example, such property as a draft of a speech, a manuscript, a research paper, an oral recording of any type, a transcript of an oral recording, a transcript of an oral interview or of dictation, a personal or business diary, a log or journal, a corporate archive, including a corporate charter, office correspondence, a financial record, a drawing, a photograph, or a dispatch. A letter, memorandum, or property similar to a letter or memorandum, addressed to a taxpayer shall be considered as prepared or produced for him. This subparagraph does not apply to property, such as a corporate archive, office correspondence, or a financial record, sold or disposed of as part of a going business if such property has no significant value separate and apart from its relation to and use in such business."[8]

Recognizing that the exclusion from capital gains of creative property sold by the creator was based upon the nature of the creator's input—personal services—the Commissioner has agreed to capital gain treatment on the sale of copyrighted motion picture films by a corporation producer. The Commissioner has stated:

> "Many corporations, including some whose stock is widely held and traded on established stock exchanges, create copyrights as well as other property described in paragraph (3) of section 1221. The property created by these corporations is not considered to be created by the personal efforts of a taxpayer where all of the costs and expenses are paid for by the corporation at the current going rate for the services rendered. The production of each of the films in the instant case involved a multiplicity of skills and abilities, the combined efforts of numerous individuals of various backgrounds and trades, and the use of substantial amounts of capital. Thus, no single individual may be said to have created by his personal efforts the films in question or a property in the films."[9]

This ruling is significant in that it recognizes that, at least in this instance of works made for hire, the corporate producer who uses input from several individuals may be able to achieve the capital gain benefits so elusive to the individual creative person if the other requirements for achieving capital gain are fulfilled.

For the copyright proprietor other than the author or those using the basis of the author for purposes of computing gain, capital gain is available if the other requirements of the Code are met, including the long-term capital gain holding period requirements. In *Richard W. Telinde*,[10] the then-required six-month "holding period" was held to begin on the completion of the manuscript. The long-standing re-

---

[8]Treas. Reg. §1.1221-1.

[9]Rev. Rul. 55-706, 1955-2 C.B. 300 (superseded on other grounds by Rev. Rul. 62-141, 1962-2 C.B. 182).

[10]18 T.C. 91, 93 U.S.P.Q. 183 (1952).

quirement that capital assets be held for six months in order to enjoy favorable long-term capital gain treatment was increased to nine and then 12 months by the Tax Reform Act of 1976, but has now been restored to six months.

It has already been noted that, in order for an asset to qualify for capital gain treatment, one must also avoid the IRC Section 1221(1) classification of "property of a kind which would properly be included in the inventory of the taxpayer if on hand at the close of the taxable year, or property held by the taxpayer primarily for sale to customers in the ordinary course of his trade or business."[11]

In Revenue Ruling 62-141[12] the Internal Revenue Service ruled that the purpose of holding motion picture and television films may change at some point. The films in the ruling were originally held for leasing and distribution rather than for sale and were thus depreciable property used in a trade or business (a classification allowing capital gain, IRC §1231(a)). But when later sold, they might be deemed held primarily for sale to customers in the ordinary course of the taxpayer's trade or business within the meaning of IRC Section 1231(b)(1)(B), in which case the gains or losses from their sale would be treated as ordinary gains or losses.[13]

For capital gain treatment, a transaction must qualify as a "sale or exchange" rather than a license. The sale or exchange requirement is one that has been relaxed over the years as it applies to copyright property. In Revenue Ruling 60-226[14] the Service held in part that amounts received by a proprietor of a copyright as consideration for the granting of the exclusive right to exploit the copyrighted work in a particular medium of publication throughout the life of the copyright should be treated as the proceeds of a sale of copyright, rather than ordinary royalty income. This applies even if the consideration received is measured by a percentage of the receipts from the sale, performance, exhibition, or publication of the copyrighted work, or if such receipts are payable over a period generally coterminous with the grantee's use of the copyrighted work. Thus, a copyright proprietor has for some time been able to satisfy the sale or exchange requirements without granting his or her entire bundle of rights in a transaction; sale of publishing rights to one purchaser qualifies as a sale or exchange even though other rights are retained for sale to a different purchaser or for exploitation by the copyright proprietor. Indeed, in Revenue Ruling 75-202[15] the possibility in a publishing agreement of a reversion outside the control of the transferor did not prevent the transaction from being considered a sale. In this respect

---

[11]See *Fields v. Commissioner*, 189 F.2d 950, 89 U.S.P.Q. 562 (2d Cir. 1951).

[12]1962-2 C.B. 182.

[13]But cf. Rev. Rul. 75-544, 1975-2 C.B. 343 (sale of motor vehicles by taxpayer primarily engaged in the business of leasing), and *Desilu Prods., Inc.*, 24 T.C. 307 (1955) (isolated forced sales of company in business to produce and hold films for licensing to television networks were not sales of property held primarily for sale in the ordinary course of business).

[14]1960-1 C.B. 26.

[15]1975-1 C.B. 170.

the tax law treated copyright as divisible before the copyright statute explicitly did so.

## Income Shifting by Assignment

A creative person may reduce the effective rate of tax on his or her income by transferring copyrights or qualified interests in copyrights to taxpayers who are taxed at the lower end of the graduated income tax rate table. The same reasoning should apply to the transfer of an undivided fractional interest in a work. An author who assigns all of his or her right, title, and interest in a manuscript prior to signing a publishing agreement should not realize income from the transferee's exploitation of the manuscript.[16]

In early years the government considered that a transfer of less than the entire copyright interest would not deflect income from the transferor for income tax purposes. This was an application of the "fruit and tree" doctrine to creative property.[17] Revenue Rulings 54-509 and 54-599[18] established the divisibility of copyright for income tax purposes and should allow a creative person to deflect income to a donee by transferring the exclusive right to exploit the copyrighted work throughout the life of the copyright in a medium of publication of expression. A completed gift of income-producing property should shift the income earned from the property subsequent to the completion of the gift and the resulting income tax liability to the donee of the gift. The donee who later enters into an agreement to exploit the rights in that medium should be taxed on the income from exploitation.

Where the author has previously entered into a publishing agreement, more difficult issues arise with respect to income previously earned and also with attempts to assign interests to future income from previously executed agreements. There appears to be a rationale that to shift the income tax there must be a transfer of control over the interest assigned. The complications present in this area are highlighted by comparing the Fourth Circuit decision in *Wodehouse v. Commissioner*[19] with the Second Circuit decision in *Wodehouse v. Commissioner.*[20] In Private Letter Ruling 8217037, which cannot be relied upon as authority, a husband and wife collaborated on a book and entered into a royalty contract with a publisher for payment of a royalty based upon sale of the book. The royalty contract assigned to the publisher publication rights throughout the world during the life of the copyright and any renewals. After entering into the publishing

---

[16]See Rev. Rul. 71-33, 1971-1 C.B. 30, dealing with the transfer of a manuscript prior to entering into a publishing agreement.

[17]See I.T. 2735, XII-2 C.B. 131 (1933).

[18]1954-2 C.B. 52.

[19]178 F.2d 987, 50-1 T.C. ¶9474 (4th Cir. 1949).

[20]177 F.2d 881 (2d Cir. 1949), *remanding* 8 T.C. 637 (1947). See also *Sax Rohmer*, 14 T.C. 1467 (1950).

agreement, the authors assigned the royalty contract to trusts established for their children. The royalties paid under the contract that accrued after the assignment were taxable to the trust and not the author–grantor. This is a difficult area, and in situations where the interest assigned may be of substantial value it would be prudent to consider requesting a private letter ruling from the Internal Revenue Service prior to the transaction.

## Corporate Techniques

The creative person may wish to reduce his or her tax burden by transferring creative properties to a controlled corporation. By interjecting a corporate entity to exploit copyright property, the effective rate of tax on income flowing from that property may be reduced. The maximum rate of federal tax for individuals is currently 50 percent. For unmarried individuals the 50-percent rate begins with taxable income in excess of $81,800. On the joint return of a husband and wife, the maximum rate begins with taxable income in excess of $162,400. The corporate taxpayer is subject to the following graduated rate table:

| Taxable income | Tax on column 1 | % on excess |
|---|---|---|
| $         0 | 0 | 15 |
| 25,000 | 3,750 | 18 |
| 50,000 | 8,250 | 30 |
| 75,000 | 15,750 | 40 |
| 100,000 | 25,750 | 46 |
| 1,100,000 | 439,750 | 51 |
| 1,405,000+ | 46% of taxable income | — |

As can be seen, a creative person whose income is in the highest bracket will pay a substantially lower effective rate of tax on the first $100,000 of income that is shifted to his or her controlled corporation. The income accumulated after paying lower corporate rates may be used to exploit creative properties further or for other business ventures.

Another advantage of the corporate form of doing business is the ability to maintain centralized control and management of copyright property while dispersing ownership by transferring minority interests in voting or nonvoting shares of the corporation. Upon death, if the shares of the corporation represent the required percentage of the value of the gross estate, the executors may elect to defer payment of estate tax.[21] The deferral can be of significant benefit to the estate of a creative person that is holding valuable but nonliquid interests in copyright property.

---

[21] See IRC §6166.

In prior years one of the major advantages of incorporating was the availability of a corporate retirement program into which much larger tax-deductible contributions could be made than were available in noncorporate form.[22] The Tax Equity and Fiscal Responsibility Act of 1982 (TEFRA)[23] removed many of the differences between corporate and noncorporate retirement plans and now generally places noncorporate plans on a par with those of partnerships and sole proprietors. For the most part retirement plan benefits should no longer be the substantial motivating factor for incorporation that they once were. Retirement plans remain an important method of accumulating wealth and deferring payment of taxes for creative people. Contributions made to qualified retirement plans are tax-deductible by the employer, income earned by the plan is accumulated tax-free, and the employee does not report income until such time as he or she receives payments under the plan.[24] At that time certain income tax benefits may be available, such as special 10-year averaging.[25] Among the fringe benefits for which tax deductions are available are medical insurance, group term life insurance, disability insurance, and accident and health benefits. Although self-employed individuals may qualify for the Internal Revenue Code exclusion from income for some benefits, corporate employees are generally eligible for a wider range of benefit exclusions from income.

The transfer of "property in exchange" for a controlling interest in the corporation's stock or securities would not be taxable under IRC Section 351.[26] When assigning intangible rights to a controlled corporation, retention of a substantial economic interest and the failure to assign substantially all rights in the property may cause the transaction to be treated as a license rather than the exchange necessary for Section 351.[27] In *E.I. du Pont de Nemours & Co. v. United States*[28] the court held that the exchange requirements of Section 351 are not tied to, nor as stringent as, the sale or exchange requirements of the capital gain provisions. Failure to satisfy Section 351 could result in substantial immediate tax cost; the transferor may realize gain equal to the difference between the value of the shares received and the tax basis of the property transferred to the corporation. The transfer to an existing corporation should also qualify under Section 351. It is not necessary that stock in a controlled corporation be received for each transfer of property.[29] In a transfer of copyrights to a controlled corporation in a transaction that qualifies under Section 351, the corporation would use the same basis as the creative person

---

[22]IRC §§401–409.
[23]Pub. L. No. 97-248.
[24]IRC §402(a)(1).
[25]IRC §402(e)(1).
[26]IRC §351, Treas. Reg. §1.351.1.
[27]See *A.E. Hickman*, 29 T.C. 864 (1958); *Magnus v. Commissioner*, 259 F.2d 893 (3d Cir. 1958).
[28]471 F.2d 1211, 31 A.F.T.R. 2d 614 (Ct.Cl. 1973).
[29]See Rev. Rul. 73-473.

for the transferred property increased in an amount equal to the gain recognized by the creative person on the transfer. This rule would also apply to transfers treated as capital contributions to the corporation.[30]

The Internal Revenue Service has a formidable array of tools to combat attempts by an author to use a corporate entity to reduce the effective rate of tax on ordinary income or to convert into capital gain income which would have been ordinary income had it been received by the creative person in his or her individual capacity. The collapsible corporation rules of Section 341 were enacted in response to a practice in the motion picture industry whereby producers, directors, and leading actors would organize a corporation for the production of a single motion picture.[31] With the key personnel working for modest salaries, the picture would be completed on a low cash budget. Upon completion of the motion picture, the corporation would be liquidated with the shareholders reporting as capital gain the difference between the value of the completed picture and their investment in the corporation's stock. The effect would be to convert the exhibition proceeds, which would have been reported as ordinary income by the corporation (or the shareholders had they operated in noncorporate form from the outset), into capital gain. Collapsible corporation rules tax a shareholder of a collapsible corporation at ordinary income rates on the proceeds of a sale, exchange, or liquidation of his or her shares.

The corporate entity may also run afoul of the personal holding company rules. Sections 541 through 547 impose an additional corporate tax at the rate of 50 percent (the highest rate charged individuals) on undistributed personal holding company income. The purpose is to discourage high-tax-bracket individuals from establishing corporate entities of a passive nature whose primary purpose is to receive and retain income at the lower corporate tax rates.

A personal holding company is defined in Section 542(a) as a corporation in which (1) more than 50 percent of stock ownership by value is in no more than five individuals and (2) at least 60 percent of gross income, with certain adjustments, fits into specified tainted categories—including copyright royalties. There are exceptions for copyright royalty income of active businesses engaged in copyright exploitation, but these exceptions are not available for shareholder-created works.[32] Rules covering collapsible corporations and personal holding company income are not the only obstacles to use of corporate techniques. The Commissioner may also attempt to use the provisions of Section 532(a), which impose a special tax on the accumulated earnings of any corporation formed, or availed of, for the purpose of avoiding the income tax on its shareholders by permitting its earnings and profits to accumulate instead of being distributed.

---

[30]See IRC §352(a).
[31]See *Pat O'Brien*, 25 T.C. 376 (1955).
[32]IRC §543(a)(4), (5).

Even if the hurdles are surmounted, the corporate setting is not necessarily the most advantageous for the creative person. Doing business in his or her individual capacity, the creative person is subject to one tax at the individual level on his or her income. In corporate form he or she is required to deal with the problems of a tax structure which taxes corporate income first at the corporate level and a second time when distributed to shareholders. A careful analysis must be made of each individual situation.

The right to terminate earlier transfers under Section 304(c) of the Copyright Act (see p. 109 et seq., *supra*) has afforded authors and certain heirs designated by the statute the opportunity to rethink the advisability of having a corporate entity receive income from copyright property. The authors or heirs who exercise their termination privileges may eliminate the double burdens of the corporate and individual income tax on income received from the exploitation of corporate-held copyright property. Whether this advantage is worthwhile and whether a new assignment—to the same corporation or someone else—should be made depend, of course, on the particular circumstances.

If the termination right is exercised, the reverted copyright or rights thereunder may be a capital asset for the designated heirs of a deceased author. If such is the case, a transfer by such heirs may give rise to tax-favored long-term capital gain. Query: Does the long-term capital gain holding period of the heirs commence upon the effective date of the termination (Copyright Law §304(c)(4)(A)) or upon the earlier service of the notice of termination (Copyright Law §304(c)(6)(B))? It would appear that the strongest argument can be made for the holding period's commencing on the date of the service of the notice of termination. Section 304(c)(6)(B) specifically states: "The future rights that will revert upon termination of the grant become vested on the date the notice of termination has been served as provided by clause (4) of this subsection."

## Depreciation

Section 167(a) of the Code allows as a deduction from gross income a reasonable depreciation allowance for (1) property used in the trade or business and (2) property held for the production of income. Copyright property may fall into either category. The first category would include manuscripts owned by a publisher and screenplays owned by a motion picture producer. The second category would include, for example, copyrights owned by the heir of (or purchaser from) a songwriter who owns copyright property and is receiving royalties in a passive capacity without engaging in the music business. The Commissioner's regulations recognize this and in pertinent part provide:

"If an intangible asset is known from experience or other factors to be of use in the business or in the production of income for only a limited period, the length of which can be estimated with reasonable accuracy, such an intangible asset may be the subject of a depreciation allowance. Examples are patents and copyrights."[33]

Before 1977, if the useful life of copyright property could not be determined, it was depreciated over the life of the original term of copyright, 28 years.[34] Because under the 1909 Act most copyrights were not renewed, a taxpayer would have been reasonably safe in using the original term of copyright as the starting point for determining useful life. If it could be established that the particular copyrighted work being depreciated was of such a nature that its useful life (generally the period it will be productive of income) was less than the original copyright term, that lesser period might be used for purposes of computing depreciation. Use of the initial term as the practical outside limit of useful life means that the extension of the renewal term to 47 years for pre-1978 copyrights will not be significant, except when depreciating additional capital costs incurred in the renewal term.

The copyright term for works created after 1978 is the life of the author (or the last surviving author in joint works) plus 50 years. For works made for hire created after 1977, the copyright term is 75 years from the date of first publication, or 100 years from creation, whichever expires first.[35] If the original copyright term is to remain the criterion, the useful life for depreciation purposes appears inordinately long. This is likely to place pressure on copyright proprietors to develop a reasonable basis to support a shorter commercially viable useful life that can be used for depreciation purposes.

Normally the method of depreciation would be "straight line," with the cost or basis of the copyright property, less its estimated salvage value, deductible in equal annual amounts over the period of the estimated useful life of the copyright property.[36] For motion picture films, television exhibition rights, and similar property, the Internal Revenue Service has approved the use of the "income forecast" method of depreciation.[37] This method is based on comparing projected net receipts for each year against total projected net receipts for the life of the property. In determining the projected receipts from a motion picture film, it may be necessary to include projected receipts from television distribution in addition to anticipated receipts from theatrical exhibition and other exploitation.[38] The theory of the income forecast method is that the owner of a motion picture, television film, taped show, or similar property should be able to

---

[33]Treas. Reg. §1.167(a)-(3).
[34]I.T. 1533, II-1 C.B. 101 (1923), Rev. Rul. 73-395, 1973-2 C.B. 87.
[35]17 U.S.C.A. §302(a).
[36]Treas. Reg. §1.167(b)-1, 1.167(c)-1.
[37]Rev. Rul. 60-358, 1960-2 C.B. 68, *as amplified by* Rev. Rul. 64-273, 1964-2 C.B. 62.
[38]Rev. Proc. 71-29, 1971-2 C.B. 568.

depreciate on the basis of the flow of income rather than the passage of time. Under the income forecast method, the forecast must be based on conditions existing at the end of each tax year. If, after the initial forecast has been made, it is found that projected net receipts were overestimated, the forecast should be revised for the purpose of computing later years' depreciation.[39]

For individual taxpayers, Subchapter S corporations, and personal holding companies, IRC Section 280 requires that the costs of producing books, films, and sound recordings be capitalized. The capitalized costs are deducted using a technique that is similar to the income forecast method of depreciation.[40] The amount deductible in a given year is arrived at by using the following formula:

$$\frac{\text{current year's income}}{\text{estimated total income}} \times \begin{array}{c}\text{production} \\ \text{costs}\end{array} = \begin{array}{c}\text{amount deductible} \\ \text{in tax year}\end{array}$$

Section 280 is applicable to production costs paid or incurred after December 31, 1975. An argument may be made that Section 280 was not intended to cover authors who develop their own work but was intended to apply only to investors as an attempt to curtail investment in tax shelters.[41] In *Faura v. Commissioner*[42] expenses incurred by an author in 1974 (prior to Section 280) in developing a manuscript were not required to be capitalized and were considered deductible under IRC Section 162.[43] *Encyclopaedia Britannica, Inc. v. Commissioner*[44] contains an analysis of the conflict between authors and the Internal Revenue Service on immediate deduction versus capitalization and deferred deduction of an author's expenses incurred to create a manuscript. In its analysis the court would allow an immediate deduction even though the asset created would produce income over an extended period of time only when the taxpayer is in the business of producing a series of assets so that a complex allocation would be necessary if the taxpayer had to capitalize the expenses of each of the works.

For the corporate taxpayer who does not elect to file as a Subchapter S corporation and is not within Section 280, the issue of current deduction of prepublication expenses is a muddled one. In

---

[39]See *Kiro, Inc.*, 51 T.C. 155 (1968) (use of sliding-scale method of depreciation); Rev. Rul. 60-358, *supra* note 37; *Inter-City Television Film Corp.*, 43 T.C. 270 (1964) (cost recovery method unacceptable for depreciation of television film and film rights).

[40]See IRC §280(b).

[41]S. REP. No. 938, 94th Cong., 2d Sess. 71-81 (1976).

[42]73 T.C. 849 (1980).

[43]See also *Stern v. United States*, 1971-1 T.C. ¶9375 (C.D. Cal. 1971) (travel expenses incurred while researching, writing, and arranging material for book held ordinary and necessary expenses of carrying on plaintiff's business of writer, hence deductible under IRC §162(a)(2)). Cf. Rev. Rul. 73-395, 1973-2, C.B. 87, specifically questioning the *Stern* decision in ruling that the costs incurred in writing, editing, design, and art work directly attributable to the development of textbooks and visual aids are not currently deductible but rather must be capitalized pursuant to §263 of the Code and depreciated under §167(a).

[44]T.C. Memo 1981-255, *rev'd and rem'd*, 685 F.2d 212 (7th Cir. 1982).

Revenue Ruling 73-395[45] the government took the position that expenditures directly attributable to producing and copyrighting the manuscript of a literary composition by the taxpayer that resulted in the creation of an asset having a useful life that will extend substantially beyond the close of the tax year are capital in nature and not immediately deductible for federal income tax purposes. The ruling stated that costs incurred in the publishing industry for writing, editing, compiling, illustrating, designing, developing, or improving a book were not currently deductible under IRC Section 174 or otherwise. The costs were to be capitalized under IRC Section 263 and written off over the life of the manuscript.[46] Section 2119 of the Tax Reform Act of 1976[47] suspended the applicability of Revenue Ruling 73-395 for corporate taxpayers until the government issues new regulations on prepublication expenses, and allowed taxpayers to treat prepublication expenses as they had done prior to the ruling. Until new regulations are issued, corporate taxpayers who had established contrary accounting methods prior to the ruling can disregard Revenue Ruling 73-395 and treat prepublication expenses in a manner consistent with their treatment prior to the ruling. See *Encyclopaedia Britannica v. Commissioner*,[48] where the taxpayer was not allowed to deduct in the current year prepublication expenses that did not meet the consistency requirements. The Seventh Circuit Court of Appeals reversed the Tax Court decision, which allowed the taxpayer to deduct currently prepublication expenses paid to a third-party subcontractor despite an inconsistency with prior years' treatment.

## Estate Considerations

The federal estate tax applies to the value of property or rights in property owned by a decedent at the time of death. IRC §2001; Treas. Reg. 20.0-1. Copyright property which has been productive of income, by direct exploitation or receipt of royalties, would normally be valued by capitalizing the property's future earning potential. Generally, earnings for the five-year period prior to death are averaged by weighting current years more heavily and multiplying the average by a factor approximately reflecting the proper capitalization.[49] If an estate owns copyright interests, the administrator should obtain the services of two qualified appraisers and also review the IRS manuals on valuation. In most situations, the extension of the term of copyright should not substantially affect valuation for estate tax purposes.

---

[45] 1973-2 C.B. 87.
[46] IRC §167.
[47] Pub. L. No. 94-455.
[48] T.C. Memo 1981-255, *rev'd and rem'd*, 685 F.2d 212 (7th Cir. 1982).
[49] See Rev. Ruls. 59-60, 1959-1 C.B. 237; 65-192, 1065-2 C.B. 259; 68-609, 1968-2 C.B. 327.

The federal estate tax marital deduction allows a deduction for qualified interests in the decedent's property that pass from the decedent to his or her surviving spouse.[50] An outright transfer of property to the surviving spouse would, of course, qualify for the marital deduction. A life estate to the surviving spouse qualifies the underlying property (the trust corpus) for the marital deduction if the surviving spouse is entitled to all the income from the property during his or her lifetime and, in addition, has the absolute right to appoint the remainder interest in his or her will.[51] The Economic Recovery Act of 1981 added the qualified terminable interest property or QTIP trust as a qualified marital deduction transfer.[52] In a QTIP trust, the decedent transfers a life income interest to his or her spouse but is not required to give the surviving spouse the right to appoint the remainder. The decedent can appoint the remainder following the death of the spouse. The QTIP is an elective provision so that the executors could be given the choice of whether to take advantage of the marital deduction or pass it up and pay the estate tax in the decedent's estate rather than the surviving spouse's estate.[53]

A copyright is considered a terminable interest.[54] The marital deduction is not available for a terminable interest (other than a qualified terminable interest under IRC Section 2056(b)(7)) if an interest in that property will pass from the decedent to any person other than the surviving spouse for less than full consideration.[55] The bequest of an interest in a copyright to one's spouse should qualify for the marital deduction if the decedent has not transferred an interest in the copyright to a third person for less than full consideration. The right of termination should not prevent a copyright in its initial term from qualifying for the marital deduction since no interest has passed from the decedent to a third person.

The estate and gift tax is a unified transfer tax that applies the same progressive rate of tax to estates of decedents dying and gifts made after 1976. There is a single unified credit that is applied against the gift and, to the extent not utilized during lifetime, the estate tax liability. The credit was equivalent to $400,000 in value of transfers in 1985 and will increase further to $500,000 in 1986 and $600,000 in 1987 and thereafter.[56]

Proper estate planning with the use of the marital deduction and a unified credit trust allows a husband and wife to pay no estate tax in the first estate and, conditioned upon survival to 1987, pass $1.2 million in value of property to their children or other beneficiaries free of estate or gift tax. Additional assets can be transferred to beneficiaries free of the estate or gift tax by use of lifetime gifts that qualify

---

[50]IRC §2056.
[51]IRC §2056(b)(5).
[52]IRC §2056(b)(7).
[53]IRC §2056(7)(B)(V).
[54]Treas. Reg. §20.2056(b)-1(b).
[55]See IRC §2056(b); Treas. Reg. §20.2056(b)-1(b), (c).
[56]IRC §2010.

for the gift tax annual exclusion of the first $10,000 ($20,000 with husband and wife gift splitting) of gifts of present interests in property to each donee.[57]

Income tax provisions have been developed to insure that the estate or beneficiary of a decedent reports any income to which the decedent was entitled, but which was not properly includible in computing taxable income during the decedent's lifetime. Such income is referred to as "income in respect of a decedent."[58] Examples are items of income accrued to, but not yet received by, a cash-basis taxpayer at the date of his death.[59] Even if the decedent does not have a legally enforceable right at the time of his or her death to receive the income, it may be considered income in respect of a decedent.[60] An example is the income receivable by the estate of a deceased actor who had performed in a motion picture and had part of his compensation based upon future receipts. After the production was completed, but before his receipt of all the future income, the actor died. In addition to the inclusion of the value of this right in the actor's gross estate for federal estate tax purposes, the income would be income in respect of a decedent and would be taxable as received to the recipient at ordinary income rates just as it would have been ordinary income if received by the actor during his lifetime.

Where the decedent, prior to death, licensed his interest in the copyright property in a transaction which is not considered a sale for tax purposes, royalty payments accrued after the date of death would not be considered income in respect of a decedent. If the transaction entered into by the decedent is considered a sale, then the decedent is considered to have earned, during his lifetime, the right to the periodic payments which continue to be paid after his death, and they would, therefore, be considered income in respect of a decedent to the recipient.[61]

Since the value of the right to receive income in the future represents a property right to be included in the decedent's estate for estate tax purposes, there is a double tax—an estate tax and an income tax. IRC Section 691(c) allows the recipient of income in respect of a decedent to take an income tax deduction for the federal estate tax attributable to the income in respect of the decedent. Since this is a deduction and not a credit, it does not completely alleviate the double tax burden. Property received by inheritance generally receives an increased or stepped-up basis equal to its fair market value as of the estate tax valuation date. IRC Section 1014(c) provides that there is no step-up in basis for items of income in respect of a decedent, so the recipient of income in respect of a decedent does not get an increased basis that can be offset against the future flow of income.

---

[57]IRC §2503.

[58]IRC §691.

[59]Treas. Reg. §1.691(b).

[60]Cf. *Latendresse v. Commissioner*, 243 F.2d 577 (7th Cir. 1957); *O'Daniel's Estate v. Commissioner*, 173 F.2d 966 (2d Cir. 1949).

[61]*Stephan H. Dorsey*, 49 T.C. 606 (1968). See also Rev. Rul. 60-227, 1960-1 C.B. 262, *clarifying* Rev. Rul. 57-544, 1957-2 C.B. 361.

# Appendix A

# The 1909 Copyright Act

*(Title 17 U.S.C., Revised to December 31, 1977)*

## Chapter 1—Registration of Copyrights

337

§ 1. EXCLUSIVE RIGHTS AS TO COPYRIGHTED WORKS—Any person entitled thereto, upon complying with the provisions of this title, shall have the exclusive right:

(a)  To print, reprint, publish, copy, and vend the copyrighted work;

(b)  To translate the copyrighted work into other languages or dialects, or make any other version thereof, if it be a literary work; to dramatize it if it be a nondramatic work; to convert it into a novel or other nondramatic work if it be a drama; to arrange or adapt it if it be a musical work; to complete, execute, and finish it if it be a model or design for a work of art;

(c)  To deliver, authorize the delivery of, read, or present the copyrighted work in public for profit if it be a lecture, sermon, address or similar production, or other nondramatic literary work; to make or procure the making of any transcription or record thereof by or from which, in whole or in part, it may in any manner or by any method be exhibited, delivered, presented, produced, or reproduced; and to play or perform it in public for profit, and to exhibit, represent, produce, or reproduce it in any manner or by any method whatsoever. The damages for the infringement by broadcast of any work referred to in this subsection shall not exceed the sum of $100 where the infringing broadcaster shows that he was not aware that he was infringing and that such infringement could not have been reasonably foreseen; and

(d)  To perform or represent the copyrighted work publicly if it be a drama or, if it be a dramatic work and not reproduced in copies for sale, to vend any manuscript or any record whatsoever thereof; to make or to procure the making of any transcription or record thereof by or from which, in whole or in part, it may in any manner or by any method be exhibited, performed, represented, produced, or reproduced; and to exhibit, perform, represent, produce, or reproduce it in any manner or by any method whatsoever; and

(e)  To perform the copyrighted work publicly for profit if it be a musical composition; and for the purpose of public performance for profit, and for the purposes set forth in subsection (a) hereof, to make any arrangement or setting of it or of the melody of it in any system of notation or any form of record in which the thought of an author may be recorded and from which it may be read or reproduced: *Provided,* That the provisions of this title, so far as they secure copyright controlling the parts of instruments serving to reproduce mechanically the musical work, shall include only compositions published and copyrighted after July 1, 1909, and shall not include the works of a foreign author or composer unless the foreign state or nation of which such author or composer is a citizen or subject grants, either by treaty, convention, agreement, or law, to citizens of the United States similar rights. And as a condition of extending the copyright control to such mechanical reproductions, that whenever the owner of a musical copyright has used or permitted or knowingly acquiesced in the use of the copyrighted work upon the parts of instruments serving to reproduce mechanically the musical work, any other person may make similar use of the copyrighted work upon the payment to the copyright proprietor of a royalty of 2 cents on each such part manufactured, to be paid by the manufacturer thereof; and the copyright proprietor may require, and if so the manufacturer shall furnish, a report under oath on the 20th day of each month on the number of parts of instruments manufactured during the previous month serving to reproduce mechanically said musical work, and royalties shall be due on the parts manufactured during any month upon the 20th of the next succeeding month. The payment of the royalty provided for by this section shall free the articles or devices for which such royalty has been paid from further contribution to the copyright except in case of public performance for profit. It shall be the duty of the copyright owner, if he uses the musical composition himself for the manufacture of parts of instruments serving to reproduce mechanically the musical work, or licenses others to do so, to file notice thereof, accompanied by a recording fee, in the copyright office, and any failure to file such notice shall be a complete defense to any suit, action, or proceeding for any infringement of such copyright.

In case of failure of such manufacturer to pay to the copyright proprietor within thirty days after demand in writing the full sum of royalties due at said rate at the date of such demand, the court may award taxable costs to the plaintiff and a reasonable counsel fee, and the court may, in its discretion, enter judgment therein for any sum in addition over the amount found to be due as royalty in accordance with the terms of this title, not exceeding three times such amount.

The reproduction or rendition of a musical composition by or upon coin-operated machines shall not be deemed a public performance for profit unless a fee is charged for admission to the place where such reproduction or rendition occurs.

(f)[1] To reproduce and distribute to the public by sale or other transfer of ownership, or by rental, lease, or lending, reproductions of the copyrighted work if it be a sound recording: *Provided*, That the exclusive right of the owner of a copyright in a sound recording to reproduce it is limited to the right to duplicate the sound recording in a tangible form that directly or indirectly recaptures the actual sounds fixed in the recording: *Provided further*, That this right does not extend to the making or duplication of another sound recording that is an independent fixation of other sounds, even though such sounds imitate or simulate those in the copyrighted sound recording; or to reproductions made by transmitting organizations exclusively for their own use.

§ 2. RIGHTS OF AUTHOR OR PROPRIETOR OF UNPUBLISHED WORK.—Nothing in this title shall be construed to annul or limit the right of the author or proprietor of an unpublished work, at common law or in equity, to prevent the copying, publication, or use of such unpublished work without his consent, and to obtain damages therefor.

§ 3. PROTECTION OF COMPONENT PARTS OF WORK COPYRIGHTED; COMPOSITE WORKS OR PERIODICALS.—The copyright provided by this title shall protect all the copyrightable component parts of the work copyrighted, and

---

[1]Section 1(f) was added by the Act of October 15, 1971, Pub. L. No. 92-140, 85 Stat. 391. This act also added section 5(n), added a sentence at the end of section 19, amended the first sentence of section 20, and added three sentences at the end of section 26. The Act specified that the provisions cited in this footnote shall take effect four months after its enactment, that these provisions "shall apply only to sound recordings fixed, published, and copyrighted on and after the effective date of this Act and before January 1, 1975," and that nothing in title 17, United States Code, as amended by these provisions "shall be applied retrospectively or be construed as affecting in any way rights with respect to sound recordings fixed before the effective date of this Act." The words "and before January 1, 1975" were stricken by the Act of December 31,1974, Pub. L. No. 93-573, 88 Stat. 1873, *infra.*

all matter therein in which copyright is already subsisting, but without extending the duration or scope of such copyright. The copyright upon composite works or periodicals shall give to the proprietor thereof all the rights in respect thereto which he would have if each part were individually copyrighted under this title.

§ 4. ALL WRITINGS OF AUTHOR INCLUDED.—The works for which copyright may be secured under this title shall include all the writings of an author.

§ 5. CLASSIFICATION OF WORKS FOR REGISTRATION.—The application for registration shall specify to which of the following classes the work in which copyright is claimed belongs:

  (a) Books, including composite and cyclopedic works, directories, gazetteers, and other compilations.
  (b) Periodicals, including newspapers.
  (c) Lectures, sermons, addresses (prepared for oral delivery).
  (d) Dramatic or dramatico-musical compositions.
  (e) Musical compositions.
  (f) Maps.
  (g) Works of art; models or designs for works of art.
  (h) Reproductions of a work of art.
  (i) Drawings or plastic works of a scientific or technical character.
  (j) Photographs.
  (k) Prints and pictorial illustrations including prints or labels used for articles of merchandise.
  (l) Motion-picture photoplays.
  (m) Motion pictures other than photoplays.
  (n)[2] Sound recordings.

The above specifications shall not be held to limit the subject matter of copyright as defined in section 4 of this title, nor shall any error in classification invalidate or impair the copyright protection secured under this title.

§ 6. REGISTRATION OF PRINTS AND LABELS.—Commencing July 1, 1940, the Register of Copyrights is charged with the registration of claims to copyright properly presented, in all prints and labels published in connection with the sale or advertisement of articles of merchandise, including all claims to copyright in prints and labels pending in the Patent Office and uncleared at the close of business June 30, 1940. There shall be paid for registering a claim of copyright in any such print or label not a trade-mark $6, which sum shall cover the expense of furnishing a certificate of such registration, under the seal of the Copyright Office, to the claimant of copyright.

§ 7. COPYRIGHT ON COMPILATIONS OF WORKS IN PUBLIC DOMAIN OR OF COPYRIGHTED WORKS; SUBSISTING COPYRIGHTS NOT AFFECTED.—Compilations or abridgments, adaptations, arrangements, dramatizations, translations, or other versions of works in the public domain or of copyrighted works when produced with the consent of the proprietor of the copyright in such works, or works republished with new matter, shall be regarded as new works subject to copyright under the provisions of this title; but the publication of any such new works shall not affect the force or validity of any subsisting copyright upon the matter employed or any part thereof, or be construed to imply an exclusive right to such use of the original works, or to secure or extend copyright in such original works.

---

[2]Section 5(n) was added by the Act of October 15, 1971, Pub. L. No. 92-140, 85 Stat. 391.

§ 8. COPYRIGHT NOT TO SUBSIST IN WORKS IN PUBLIC DOMAIN, OR PUB-
LISHED PRIOR TO JULY 1, 1909, AND NOT ALREADY COPYRIGHTED, OR GOV-
ERNMENT PUBLICATIONS; PUBLICATION BY GOVERNMENT OF COPYRIGHTED
MATERIAL.—No copyright shall subsist in the original text of any work
which is in the public domain, or in any work which was published in this
country or any foreign country prior to July 1, 1909, and has not been already copyrighted in the United States, or in any publication of the United
States Government, or any reprint, in whole or in part, thereof, except that
the Postmaster General may secure copyright on behalf of the United States
in the whole or any part of the publications authorized by section 2506 of
title 39.[3]

The publication or republication by the Government, either separately
or in a public document, of any material in which copyright is subsisting
shall not be taken to cause any abridgment or annulment of the copyright or
to authorize any use or appropriation of such copyright material without the
consent of the copyright proprietor.

§ 9. AUTHORS OR PROPRIETORS, ENTITLED: ALIENS.—The author or proprietor of any work made the subject of copyright by this title, or his executors, administrators, or assigns, shall have copyright for such work under
the conditions and for the terms specified in this title: *Provided, however,*
That the copyright secured by this title shall extend to the work of an author
or proprietor who is a citizen or subject of a foreign state or nation only under the conditions described in subsections (a), (b), or (c) below:

(a) When an alien author or proprietor shall be domiciled within the
United States at the time of the first publication of his work; or

(b) When the foreign state or nation of which such author or proprietor
is a citizen or subject grants, either by treaty, convention, agreement, or law,
to citizens of the United States the benefit of copyright on substantially the
same basis as to its own citizens, or copyright protection, substantially
equal to the protection secured to such foreign author under this title or by
treaty; or when such foreign state or nation is a party to an international
agreement which provides for reciprocity in the granting of copyright, by
the terms of which agreement the United States may, at its pleasure, become
a party thereto.

The existence of the reciprocal conditions aforesaid shall be determined
by the President of the United States, by proclamation made from time to
time, as the purposes of this title may require: *Provided,* That whenever the
President shall find that the authors, copyright owners, or proprietors of
works first produced or published abroad and subject to copyright or to renewal of copyright under the laws of the United States, including works subject to ad interim copyright, are or may have been temporarily unable to
comply with the conditions and formalities prescribed with respect to such
works by the copyright laws of the United States, because of the disruption
or suspension of facilities essential for such compliance, he may by proclamation grant such extension of time as he may deem appropriate for the fulfillment of such conditions or formalities by authors, copyright owners, or
proprietors who are citizens of the United States or who are nationals of

---

[3]A further exception was provided by a statute enacted in 1968, Pub. L. No. 90-396, 82
Stat. 339, 340, amending Title 15 of the United States Code (15 U.S.C. 272), authorizing the
Secretary of Commerce, at section 290(e), to secure copyright and renewal thereof on behalf of
the United States as author or proprietor "in all or any part of any standard reference data
which he prepares or makes available under this chapter."

countries which accord substantially equal treatment in this respect to authors, copyright owners, or proprietors who are citizens of the United States: *Provided further*, That no liability shall attach under this title for lawful uses made or acts done prior to the effective date of such proclamation in connection with such works, or in respect to the continuance for one year subsequent to such date of any business undertaking or enterprise lawfully undertaken prior to such date involving expenditure or contractual obligation in connection with the exploitation, production, reproduction, circulation, or performance of any such work.

The President may at any time terminate any proclamation authorized herein or any part thereof or suspend or extend its operation for such period or periods of time as in his judgment the interests of the United States may require.

(c) When the Universal Copyright Convention, signed at Geneva on September 6, 1952, shall be in force[4] between the United States of America and the foreign state or nation of which such author is a citizen or subject, or in which the work was first published. Any work to which copyright is extended pursuant to this subsection shall be exempt from the following provisions of this title: (1) The requirement in section 1 (e) that a foreign state or nation must grant to United States citizens mechanical reproduction rights similar to those specified therein; (2) the obligatory deposit requirements of the first sentence of section 13; (3) the provisions of sections 14, 16, 17, and 18; (4) the import prohibitions of section 107, to the extent that they are related to the manufacturing requirements of section 16; and (5) the requirements of sections 19 and 20: *Provided, however*, That such exemptions shall apply only if from the time of first publication all the copies of the work published with the authority of the author or other copyright proprietor shall bear the symbol © accompanied by the name of the copyright proprietor and the year of first publication placed in such manner and location as to give reasonable notice of claim of copyright.

Upon the coming into force of the Universal Copyright Convention in a foreign state or nation as hereinbefore provided, every book or periodical of a citizen or subject thereof in which ad interim copyright was subsisting on the effective date of said coming into force shall have copyright for twenty-eight years from the date of first publication abroad without the necessity of complying with the further formalities specified in section 23 of this title.

The provisions of this subsection shall not be extended to works of an author who is a citizen of, or domiciled in the United States of America regardless of place of first publication, or to works first published in the United States.

§ 10. PUBLICATION OF WORK WITH NOTICE.—Any person entitled thereto by this title may secure copyright for his work by publication thereof with the notice of copyright required by this title; and such notice shall be affixed to each copy thereof published or offered for sale in the United States by authority of the copyright proprietor, except in the case of books seeking ad interim protection under section 22 of this title.

§ 11. REGISTRATION OF CLAIM AND ISSUANCE OF CERTIFICATE.—Such person may obtain registration of his claim to copyright by complying with the provisions of this title, including the deposit of copies, and upon such

---

[4]The Universal Copyright Convention came into force with respect to the United States of America on September 16, 1955.

compliance the Register of Copyrights shall issue to him the certificates provided for in section 209 of this title.

§ 12. WORKS NOT REPRODUCED FOR SALE.—Copyright may also be had of the works of an author, of which copies are not reproduced for sale, by the deposit, with claim of copyright, of one complete copy of such work if it be a lecture or similar production or a dramatic, musical, or dramatico-musical composition; of a title and description, with one print taken from each scene or act, if the work be a motion-picture photoplay; of a photographic print if the work be a photograph; of a title and description, with not less than two prints taken from different sections of a complete motion picture, if the work be a motion picture other than a photoplay; or of a photograph or other identifying reproduction thereof, if it be a work of art or a plastic work or drawing. But the privilege of registration of copyright secured hereunder shall not exempt the copyright proprietor from the deposit of copies, under sections 13 and 14 of this title, where the work is later reproduced in copies for sale.

§ 13. DEPOSIT OF COPIES AFTER PUBLICATION; ACTION OR PROCEEDING FOR INFRINGEMENT.—After copyright has been secured by publication of the work with the notice of copyright as provided in section 10 of this title, there shall be promptly deposited in the Copyright Office or in the mail addressed to the Register of Copyrights, Washington, District of Columbia, two complete copies of the best edition thereof then published, or if the work is by an author who is a citizen or subject of a foreign state or nation and has been published in a foreign country, one complete copy of the best edition then published in such foreign country, which copies or copy, if the work be a book or periodical, shall have been produced in accordance with the manufacturing provisions specified in section 16 of this title; or if such work be a contribution to a periodical, for which contribution special registration is requested, one copy of the issue or issues containing such contribution; or if the work belongs to a class specified in subsections (g), (h), (i) or (k) of section 5 of this title, and if the Register of Copyrights determines that it is impracticable to deposit copies because of their size, weight, fragility, or monetary value he may permit the deposit of photographs or other identifying reproductions in lieu of copies of the work as published under such rules and regulations as he may prescribe with the approval of the Librarian of Congress; or if the work is not reproduced in copies for sale there shall be deposited the copy, print, photograph, or other identifying reproduction provided by section 12 of this title, such copies or copy, print, photograph, or other reproduction to be accompanied in each case by a claim of copyright. No action or proceeding shall be maintained for infringement of copyright in any work until the provisions of this title with respect to the deposit of copies and registration of such work shall have been complied with.

§ 14. SAME; FAILURE TO DEPOSIT; DEMAND; PENALTY.—Should the copies called for by section 13 of this title not be promptly deposited as provided in this title, the Register of Copyrights may at any time after the publication of the work, upon actual notice, require the proprietor of the copyright to deposit them, and after the said demand shall have been made, in default of the deposit of copies of the work within three months from any part of the United States, except an outlying territorial possession of the United States, or within six months from any outlying territorial possession of the United States, or from any foreign country, the proprietor of the copyright shall be liable to a fine of $100 and to pay to the Library of Congress twice the amount of the retail price of the best edition of the work, and the copyright shall become void.

§ 15. SAME; POSTMASTER'S RECEIPT; TRANSMISSION BY MAIL WITHOUT COST.—The postmaster to whom are delivered the articles deposited as provided in sections 12 and 13 of this title shall, if requested, give a receipt therefor and shall mail them to their destination without cost to the copyright claimant.

§ 16. MECHANICAL WORK TO BE DONE IN UNITED STATES.—Of the printed book or periodical specified in section 5, subsections (a) and (b), of this title, except the original text of a book or periodical of foreign origin in a language or languages other than English, the text of all copies accorded protection under this title, except as below provided, shall be printed from type set within the limits of the United States, either by hand or by the aid of any kind of typesetting machine, or from plates made within the limits of the United States from type set therein, or, if the text be produced by lithographic process, or photoengraving process, then by a process wholly performed within the limits of the United States, and the printing of the text and binding of the said book shall be performed within the limits of the United States; which requirements shall extend also to the illustrations within a book consisting of printed text and illustrations produced by lithographic process, or photoengraving process, and also to separate lithographs or photoengravings, except where in either case the subjects represented are located in a foreign country and illustrate a scientific work or reproduce a work of art: *Provided, however,* That said requirements shall not apply to works in raised characters for the use of the blind, or to books or periodicals of foreign origin in a language or languages other than English, or to works printed or produced in the United States by any other process than those above specified in this section, or to copies of books or periodicals, first published abroad in the English language, imported into the United States within five years after first publication in a foreign state or nation up to the number of fifteen hundred copies of each such book or periodical if said copies shall contain notice of copyright in accordance with sections 10, 19, and 20 of this title and if ad interim copyright in said work shall have been obtained pursuant to section 22 of this title prior to the importation into the United States of any copy except those permitted by the provisions of section 107 of this title: *Provided further,* That the provisions of this section shall not affect the right of importation under the provisions of section 107 of this title.

§ 17. AFFIDAVIT TO ACCOMPANY COPIES.—In the case of the book the copies so deposited shall be accompanied by an affidavit under the official seal of any officer authorized to administer oaths within the United States, duly made by the person claiming copyright or by his duly authorized agent or representative residing in the United States, or by the printer who has printed the book, setting forth that the copies deposited have been printed from type set within the limits of the United States or from plates made within the limits of the United States from type set therein; or, if the text be produced by lithographic process, or photoengraving process, that such process was wholly performed within the limits of the United States and that the printing of the text and binding of the said book have also been performed within the limits of the United States. Such affidavit shall state also the place where and the establishment or establishments in which such type was set or plates made or lithographic process, or photoengraving process or printing and binding were performed and the date of the completion of the printing of the book or the date of publication.

§ 18. MAKING FALSE AFFIDAVIT.—Any person who, for the purpose of obtaining registration of a claim to copyright, shall knowingly make a false affidavit as to his having complied with the above conditions shall be deemed guilty of a misdemeanor, and upon conviction thereof shall be punished by a fine of not more than $1,000, and all of his rights and privileges under said copyright shall thereafter be forfeited.

§ 19. NOTICE; FORM.[5]—The notice of copyright required by section 10 of this title shall consist either of the word "Copyright", the abbreviation "Copr.", or the symbol ©, accompanied by the name of the copyright proprietor, and if the work be a printed literary, musical, or dramatic work, the notice shall include also the year in which the copyright was secured by publication. In the case, however, of copies of works specified in subsections (f) to (k), inclusive, of section 5 of this title, the notice may consist of the letter C enclosed within a circle, thus ©, accompanied by the initials, monogram, mark, or symbol of the copyright proprietor: *Provided*, That on some accessible portion of such copies or of the margin, back, permanent base, or pedestal, or of the substance on which such copies shall be mounted, his name shall appear. But in the case of works in which copyright was subsisting on July 1, 1909, the notice of copyright may be either in one of the forms prescribed herein or may consist of the following words: "Entered according to Act of Congress, in the year ____, by A. B., in the office of the Librarian of Congress, at Washington, D.C.," or, at his option, the word "Copyright", together with the year the copyright was entered and the name of the party by whom it was taken out; thus, "Copyright, 19____, by A. B." In the case of reproductions of works specified in subsection (n) of section 5 of this title, the notice shall consist of the symbol ℗ (the letter P in a circle), the year of first publication of the sound recording, and the name of the owner of copyright in the sound recording, or an abbreviation by which the name can be recognized, or a generally known alternative designation of the owner: *Provided*, That if the producer of the sound recording is named on the labels or containers of the reproduction, and if no other name appears in conjunction with the notice, his name shall be considered a part of the notice.

§ 20. SAME; PLACE OF APPLICATION OF; ONE NOTICE IN EACH VOLUME OR NUMBER OF NEWSPAPER OR PERIODICAL.[6]—The notice of copyright shall be applied, in the case of a book or other printed publication, upon its title page or the page immediately following, or if a periodical either upon the title page or upon the first page of text of each separate number or under the title heading, or if a musical work either upon its title page or the first page of music, or if a sound recording on the surface of reproductions thereof or on the label or container in such manner and location as to give reasonable notice of the claim of copyright. One notice of copyright in each volume or in each number of a newspaper or periodical published shall suffice.

§ 21. SAME; EFFECT OF ACCIDENTAL OMISSION FROM COPY OR COPIES.— Where the copyright proprietor has sought to comply with the provisions of this title with respect to notice, the omission by accident or mistake of the

---

[5]The last sentence of section 19 was added by the Act of October 15, 1971, Pub. L. No. 92-140, 85 Stat. 391.

[6]The first sentence of section 20 was amended by the Act of October 15, 1971, Pub. L. No. 92-140, 85 Stat. 391.

prescribed notice from a particular copy or copies shall not invalidate the copyright or prevent recovery for infringement against any person who, after actual notice of the copyright, begins an undertaking to infringe it, but shall prevent the recovery of damages against an innocent infringer who has been misled by the omission of the notice; and in a suit for infringement no permanent injunction shall be had unless the copyright proprietor shall reimburse to the innocent infringer his reasonable outlay innocently incurred if the court, in its discretion, shall so direct.

§ 22. Ad Interim Protection of Book or Periodical Published Abroad.—In the case of a book or periodical first published abroad in the English language, the deposit in the Copyright Office, not later than six months after its publication abroad, of one complete copy of the foreign edition, with a request for the reservation of the copyright and a statement of the name and nationality of the author and of the copyright proprietor and of the date of publication of the said book or periodical, shall secure to the author or proprietor an ad interim copyright therein, which shall have all the force and effect given to copyright by this title, and shall endure until the expiration of five years after the date of first publication abroad.

§ 23. Same; Extension to Full Term.—Whenever within the period of such ad interim protection an authorized edition of such books or periodicals shall be published within the United States, in accordance with the manufacturing provisions specified in section 16 of this title, and whenever the provisions of this title as to deposit of copies, registration, filing of affidavits, and the printing of the copyright notice shall have been duly complied with, the copyright shall be extended to endure in such book or periodical for the term provided in this title.

§ 24. Duration; Renewal and Extension.[7]—The copyright secured by this title shall endure for twenty-eight years from the date of first publication, whether the copyrighted work bears the author's true name or is published anonymously or under an assumed name: *Provided,* That in the case of any posthumous work or of any periodical, cyclopedic, or other composite work upon which the copyright was originally secured by the proprietor thereof, or of any work copyrighted by a corporate body (otherwise than as assignee or licensee of the individual author) or by an employer for whom such work is made for hire, the proprietor of such copyright shall be entitled to a renewal and extension of the copyright in such work for the further term of twenty-eight years when application for such renewal and extension shall have been made to the copyright office and duly registered therein within one year prior to the expiration of the original term of copyright: *And provided further,* That in the case of any other copyrighted work, including a contribution by an individual author to a periodical or to a cyclopedic or other composite work, the author of such work, if still living, or the widow, widower, or children of the author, if the author be not living, or if such author, widow, widower, or children be not living, then the author's executors, or in the absence of a will, his next of kin shall be entitled to a renewal and extension of the copyright in such work for a further term of twenty-eight years when application for such renewal and extension shall have been made to the copyright office and duly registered therein within one year prior to

---

[7]Private Law 92-60, enacted December 15, 1971, provides specially for a term of 75 years from that date, or from the later date of first publication, for the various editions of "Science and Health" by Mary Baker Eddy.

the expiration of the original term of copyright:[8] *And provided further*, That in default of the registration of such application for renewal and extension, the copyright in any work shall terminate at the expiration of twenty-eight years from first publication.

§ 25. RENEWAL OF COPYRIGHTS REGISTERED IN PATENT OFFICE UNDER REPEALED LAW.—Subsisting copyrights originally registered in the Patent Office prior to July 1, 1940, under section 3 of the act of June 18, 1874, shall be subject to renewal on behalf of the proprietor upon application made to the Register of Copyrights within one year prior to the expiration of the original term of twenty-eight years.

§ 26. TERMS DEFINED.[9]—In the interpretation and construction of this title "the date of publication" shall in the case of a work of which copies are reproduced for sale or distribution be held to be the earliest date when copies of the first authorized edition were placed on sale, sold, or publicly distributed by the proprietor of the copyright or under his authority, and the word "author" shall include an employer in the case of works made for hire. For the purposes of this section and sections 10, 11, 13, 14, 21, 101, 106, 109, 209, 215, but not for any other purpose, a reproduction of a work described in subsection 5(n) shall be considered to be a copy thereof. "Sound recordings" are works that result from the fixation of a series of musical, spoken, or other sounds, but not including the sounds accompanying a motion picture. "Reproductions of sound recordings" are material objects in which sounds other than those accompanying a motion picture are fixed by any method now known or later developed, and from which the sounds can be perceived, reproduced, or otherwise communicated, either directly or with the aid of a machine or device, and include the "parts of instruments serving to reproduce mechanically the musical work", "mechanical reproductions", and "interchangeable parts, such as discs or tapes for use in mechanical music-producing machines" referred to in sections 1(e) and 101(e) of this title.

§ 27. COPYRIGHT DISTINCT FROM PROPERTY IN OBJECT COPYRIGHTED; EFFECT OF SALE OF OBJECT, AND OF ASSIGNMENT OF COPYRIGHT.—The copyright is distinct from the property in the material object copyrighted, and the sale or conveyance, by gift or otherwise, of the material object shall not of itself constitute a transfer of the copyright, nor shall the assignment of the copyright constitute a transfer of the title to the material object; but nothing in this title shall be deemed to forbid, prevent, or restrict the transfer of any copy of a copyrighted work the possession of which has been lawfully obtained.

§ 28. ASSIGNMENTS AND BEQUESTS.—Copyright secured under this title or previous copyright laws of the United States may be assigned, granted, or mortgaged by an instrument in writing signed by the proprietor of the copyright, or may be bequeathed by will.

§ 29. SAME; EXECUTED IN FOREIGN COUNTRY; ACKNOWLEDGMENT AND CERTIFICATE.—Every assignment of copyright executed in a foreign country shall be acknowledged by the assignor before a consular officer or secretary of legation of the United States authorized by law to administer oaths or

---

[8]A series of nine acts, the most recent being the Act of December 31, 1974, Pub. L. No. 93-573, 88 Stat. 1873, which cites the eight earlier acts, has extended until December 31, 1976, copyrights previously renewed in which the second term would otherwise have expired between September 19, 1962, and December 31, 1976.

[9]The last three sentences of section 26 were added by the Act of October 15, 1971, Pub. L. No. 92-140, 85 Stat. 391.

perform notarial acts. The certificate of such acknowledgment under the hand and official seal of such consular officer or secretary of legation shall be prima facie evidence of the execution of the instrument.

§ 30. SAME; RECORD.—Every assignment of copyright shall be recorded in the copyright office within three calendar months after its execution in the United States or within six calendar months after its execution without the limits of the United States, in default of which it shall be void as against any subsequent purchaser or mortgagee for a valuable consideration, without notice, whose assignment has been duly recorded.

§ 31. SAME; CERTIFICATE OF RECORD.—The Register of Copyrights shall, upon payment of the prescribed fee, record such assignment, and shall return it to the sender with a certificate of record attached under seal of the copyright office, and upon the payment of the fee prescribed by this title he shall furnish to any person requesting the same a certified copy thereof under the said seal.

§ 32. SAME; USE OF NAME OF ASSIGNEE IN NOTICE.—When an assignment of the copyright in a specified book or other work has been recorded the assignee may substitute his name for that of the assignor in the statutory notice of copyright prescribed by this title.

## Chapter 2—Infringement Proceedings[10]

§ 101. Infringement:
   (a) Injunction.
   (b) Damages and profits; amounts; other remedies.
   (c) Impounding during action.
   (d) Destruction of infringing copies and plates.
   (e) Interchangeable parts for use in mechanical music-producing machines.
§ 104. Willful infringement for profit.
§ 105. Fraudulent notice of copyright, or removal or alteration of notice.
§ 106. Importation of article bearing false notice or piratical copies of copyrighted work.
§ 107. Importation, during existence of copyright, of piratical copies, or of copies not produced in accordance with section 16 of this title.
§ 108. Forfeiture and destruction of articles prohibited importation.
§ 109. Importation of prohibited articles; regulations; proof of deposit of copies by complainants.
§ 112. Injunctions; service and enforcement.
§ 113. Transmission of certified copies of papers for enforcement of injunction by other court.
§ 114. Review of orders, judgments, or decrees.
§ 115. Limitations.
§ 116. Costs; attorney's fees

§ 101. INFRINGEMENT.—If any person shall infringe the copyright in any work protected under the copyright laws of the United States such person shall be liable:

(a) INJUNCTION.—To an injunction restraining such infringement;

(b) DAMAGES AND PROFITS; AMOUNT; OTHER REMEDIES.—To pay to the copyright proprietor such damages as the copyright proprietor may have suffered due to the infringement, as well as all the profits which the infringer shall have made from such infringement, and in proving profits the plaintiff shall be required to prove sales only, and the defendant shall be required to

---

[10]Sections 101(f), 102, 103, 110, and 111 were repealed by the Act of June 25, 1948, ch. 646, § 39, 62 Stat. 869, at 931, 936, and 996, effective September 1, 1948. However, see sections 1338, 1400, 1498, and 2072, Title 28, United States Code.

prove every element of cost which he claims, or in lieu of actual damages and profits, such damages as to the court shall appear to be just, and in assessing such damages the court may, in its discretion, allow the amounts as hereinafter stated, but in case of a newspaper reproduction of a copyrighted photograph, such damages shall not exceed the sum of $200 nor be less than the sum of $50, and in the case of the infringement of an undramatized or nondramatic work by means of motion pictures, where the infringer shall show that he was not aware that he was infringing, and that such infringement could not have been reasonably foreseen, such damages shall not exceed the sum of $100; and in the case of an infringement of a copyrighted dramatic or dramatico-musical work by a maker of motion pictures and his agencies for distribution thereof to exhibitors, where such infringer shows that he was not aware that he was infringing a copyrighted work, and that such infringements could not reasonably have been foreseen, the entire sum of such damages recoverable by the copyright proprietor from such infringing maker and his agencies for the distribution to exhibitors of such infringing motion picture shall not exceed the sum of $5,000 nor be less than $250, and such damages shall in no other case exceed the sum of $5,000 nor be less than the sum of $250, and shall not be regarded as a penalty. But the foregoing exceptions shall not deprive the copyright proprietor of any other remedy given him under this law, nor shall the limitation as to the amount of recovery apply to infringements occurring after the actual notice to a defendant, either by service of process in a suit or other written notice served upon him.

First. In the case of a painting, statue, or sculpture, $10 for every infringing copy made or sold by or found in the possession of the infringer or his agents or employees;

Second. In the case of any work enumerated in section 5 of this title, except a painting, statue, or sculpture, $1 for every infringing copy made or sold by or found in the possession of the infringer or his agents or employees;

Third. In the case of a lecture, sermon, or address, $50 for every infringing delivery;

Fourth. In the case of a dramatic or dramatico-musical or a choral or orchestral composition, $100 for the first and $50 for every subsequent infringing performance; in the case of other musical compositions $10 for every infringing performance;

(c) IMPOUNDING DURING ACTION.—To deliver up on oath, to be impounded during the pendency of the action, upon such terms and conditions as the court may prescribe, all articles alleged to infringe a copyright;

(d) DESTRUCTION OF INFRINGING COPIES AND PLATES.—To deliver up on oath for destruction all the infringing copies or devices, as well as all plates, molds, matrices, or other means for making such infringing copies as the court may order.

(e)[11] INTERCHANGEABLE PARTS FOR USE IN MECHANICAL MUSIC-PRODUCING MACHINES.—Interchangeable parts, such as discs or tapes for use in mechanical music-producing machines adapted to reproduce copyrighted musical works, shall be considered copies of the copyrighted musical works which they serve to reproduce mechanically for the purposes of this section 101 and sections 106 and 109 of this title, and the unauthorized manufacture, use, or sale of such interchangeable parts shall constitute an infringement of the

---

[11]The former section 101(e) was deleted in its entirety and the present language was substituted by the Act of October 15, 1971, Pub. L. No. 92-140, 85 Stat. 391, effective immediately upon enactment.

copyrighted work rendering the infringer liable in accordance with all provisions of this title dealing with infringements of copyright and, in a case of willful infringement for profit, to criminal prosecution pursuant to section 104 of this title. Whenever any person, in the absence of a license agreement, intends to use a copyrighted musical composition upon the parts of instruments serving to reproduce mechanically the musical work, relying upon the compulsory license provision of this title, he shall serve notice of such intention, by registered mail, upon the copyright proprietor at his last address disclosed by the records of the copyright office, sending to the copyright office a duplicate of such notice.

[(f) See footnote 10, p. 348, *supra.*]

[§ 102. See footnote 10, p. 348, *supra.*]

[§ 103. See footnote 10, p. 348, *supra.*]

§ 104.[12] WILLFUL INFRINGEMENT FOR PROFIT.—Any person who willfully and for profit shall infringe any copyright secured by this title, or who shall knowingly and willfully aid or abet such infringement, shall be deemed guilty of a misdemeanor, and upon conviction thereof shall be punished by imprisonment for not exceeding one year or by a fine of not less than $100 nor more than $1,000, or both, in the discretion of the court: *Provided, however,* That nothing in this title shall be so construed as to prevent the performance of religious or secular works such as oratorios, cantatas, masses, or octavo choruses by public schools, church choirs, or vocal societies, rented, borrowed, or obtained from some public library, public school, church choir, school choir, or vocal society, provided the performance is given for charitable or educational purposes and not for profit.

§ 105. FRAUDULENT NOTICE OF COPYRIGHT, OR REMOVAL OR ALTERATION OF NOTICE.—Any person who, with fraudulent intent, shall insert or impress any notice of copyright required by this title, or words of the same purport, in or upon any uncopyrighted article, or with fraudulent intent shall remove or alter the copyright notice upon any article duly copyrighted shall be guilty of a misdemeanor, punishable by a fine of not less than $100 and not more than $1,000. Any person who shall knowingly issue or sell any article bearing a notice of United States copyright which has not been copyrighted in this country, or who shall knowingly import any article bearing such notice or words of the same purport, which has not been copyrighted in this country, shall be liable to a fine of $100.

§ 106. IMPORTATION OF ARTICLE BEARING FALSE NOTICE OR PIRATICAL COPIES OF COPYRIGHTED WORK.—The importation into the United States of any article bearing a false notice of copyright when there is no existing copyright thereon in the United States, or of any piratical copies of any work copyrighted in the United States, is prohibited.

§ 107. IMPORTATION, DURING EXISTENCE OF COPYRIGHT, OF PIRATICAL COPIES, OR OF COPIES NOT PRODUCED IN ACCORDANCE WITH SECTION 16 OF THIS TITLE.—During the existence of the American copyright in any book the importation into the United States of any piratical copies thereof or of any copies thereof (although authorized by the author or proprietor) which have not been produced in accordance with the manufacturing provisions specified in section 16 of this title, or any plates of the same not made from type set within the limits of the United States, or any copies thereof pro-

---

[12]Amended. See Act of December 31, 1974, Pub. L. No. 93-573, 88 Stat. 1873.

duced by lithographic or photoengraving process not performed within the limits of the United States, in accordance with the provisions of section 16 of this title, is prohibited: *Provided, however*, That, except as regards piratical copies, such prohibition shall not apply:

(a) To works in raised characters for the use of the blind.

(b) To a foreign newspaper or magazine, although containing matter copyrighted in the United States printed or reprinted by authority of the copyright proprietor, unless such newspaper or magazine contains also copyright matter printed or reprinted without such authorization.

(c) To the authorized edition of a book in a foreign language or languages of which only a translation into English has been copyrighted in this country.

(d) To any book published abroad with the authorization of the author or copyright proprietor when imported under the circumstances stated in one of the four subdivisions following, that is to say:

First. When imported, not more than one copy at one time, for individual use and not for sale; but such privilege of importation shall not extend to a foreign reprint of a book by an American author copyrighted in the United States.

Second. When imported by the authority or for the use of the United States.

Third. When imported, for use and not for sale, not more than one copy of any such book in any one invoice, in good faith by or for any society or institution incorporated for educational, literary, philosophical, scientific, or religious purposes, or for the encouragement of the fine arts, or for any college, academy, school, or seminary of learning, or for any State, school, college, university, or free public library in the United States.

Fourth. When such books form parts of libraries or collections purchased en bloc for the use of societies, institutions, or libraries designated in the foregoing paragraph, or form parts of the libraries or personal baggage belonging to persons or families arriving from foreign countries and are not intended for sale: *Provided*, That copies imported as above may not lawfully be used in any way to violate the rights of the proprietor of the American copyright or annul or limit the copyright protection secured by this title, and such unlawful use shall be deemed an infringement of copyright.

§ 108. FORFEITURE AND DESTRUCTION OF ARTICLES PROHIBITED IMPORTATION.—Any and all articles prohibited importation by this title which are brought into the United States from any foreign country (except in the mails) shall be seized and forfeited by like proceedings as those provided by law for the seizure and condemnation of property imported into the United States in violation of the customs revenue laws. Such articles when forfeited shall be destroyed in such manner as the Secretary of the Treasury or the court, as the case may be, shall direct: *Provided, however*, That all copies of authorized editions of copyright books imported in the mails or otherwise in violation of the provisions of this title may be exported and returned to the country of export whenever it is shown to the satisfaction of the Secretary of the Treasury, in a written application, that such importation does not involve willful negligence or fraud.

§ 109. IMPORTATION OF PROHIBITED ARTICLES; REGULATIONS; PROOF OF DEPOSIT OF COPIES BY COMPLAINANTS.—The Secretary of the Treasury and the Postmaster General are hereby empowered and required to make and enforce individually or jointly such rules and regulations as shall prevent the importation into the United States of articles prohibited importation by this title, and may require, as conditions precedent to exclusion of any work in which copyright is claimed, the copyright proprietor or any person claiming actual or potential injury by reason of actual or contemplated importations of copies of such work to file with the Post Office Department or the Treasury Department a certificate of the Register of Copyrights that the provisions of section 13 of this title have been fully complied with, and to give notice of such compliance to postmasters or to customs officers at the ports of entry in the United States in such form and accompanied by such exhibits as may be deemed necessary for the practical and efficient administration and enforcement of the provisions of sections 106 and 107 of this title.

[§ 110.  See footnote 10, p. 348, *supra.*]
[§ 111.  See footnote 10, p. 348, *supra.*]

§ 112. INJUNCTIONS; SERVICE AND ENFORCEMENT.—Any court mentioned in section 1338 of Title 28 or judge thereof shall have power, upon complaint filed by any party aggrieved, to grant injunctions to prevent and restrain the violation of any right secured by this title, according to the course and principles of courts of equity, on such terms as said court or judge may deem reasonable. Any injunction that may be granted restraining and enjoining the doing of anything forbidden by this title may be served on the parties against whom such injunction may be granted anywhere in the United States, and shall be operative throughout the United States and be enforceable by proceedings in contempt or otherwise by any other court or judge possessing jurisdiction of the defendants.

§ 113. TRANSMISSION OF CERTIFIED COPIES OF PAPERS FOR ENFORCEMENT OF INJUNCTION BY OTHER COURT.—The clerk of the court or judge granting the injunction, shall, when required so to do by the court hearing the application to enforce said injunction, transmit without delay to said court a certified copy of all the papers in said cause that are on file in his office.

§ 114. REVIEW OF ORDERS, JUDGMENTS, OR DECREES.—The orders, judgments, or decrees of any court mentioned in section 1338 of Title 28 arising under the copyright laws of the United States may be reviewed on appeal in the manner and to the extent now provided by law for the review of cases determined in said courts, respectively.

§ 115. LIMITATIONS.—(a) CRIMINAL PROCEEDINGS.—No criminal proceedings shall be maintained under the provisions of this title unless the same is commenced within three years after the cause of action arose.

(b) CIVIL ACTIONS.—No civil action shall be maintained under the provisions of this title unless the same is commenced within three years after the claim accrued.

§ 116. COSTS; ATTORNEY'S FEES.—In all actions, suits, or proceedings under this title, except when brought by or against the United States or any officer thereof, full costs shall be allowed, and the court may award to the prevailing party a reasonable attorney's fee as part of the costs.

### Chapter 3—Copyright Office

§ 201.  Copyright office; preservation of records.
§ 202.  Register, assistant register, and subordinates.

§ 201. COPYRIGHT OFFICE; PRESERVATION OF RECORDS.—All records and other things relating to copyrights required by law to be preserved shall be kept and preserved in the copyright office, Library of Congress, District of Columbia, and shall be under the control of the register of copyrights, who shall, under the direction and supervision of the Librarian of Congress, perform all the duties relating to the registration of copyrights.

§ 202. REGISTER, ASSISTANT REGISTER, AND SUBORDINATES.—There shall be appointed by the Librarian of Congress a Register of Copyrights, and one Assistant Register of Copyrights, who shall have authority during the absence of the Register of Copyrights to attach the copyright office seal to all papers issued from the said office and to sign such certificates and other papers as may be necessary. There shall also be appointed by the Librarian such subordinate assistants to the register as may from time to time be authorized by law.

§ 203. SAME; DEPOSIT OF MONEYS RECEIVED; REPORTS.—The Register of Copyrights shall make daily deposits in some bank in the District of Columbia, designated for this purpose by the Secretary of the Treasury as a national depository, of all moneys received to be applied as copyright fees, and shall make weekly deposits with the Secretary of the Treasury, in such manner as the latter shall direct, of all copyright fees actually applied under the provisions of this title, and annual deposits of sums received which it has not been possible to apply as copyright fees or to return to the remitters, and shall also make monthly reports to the Secretary of the Treasury and to the Librarian of Congress of the applied copyright fees for each calendar month, together with a statement of all remittances received, trust funds on hand, moneys refunded, and unapplied balances.[13]

§ 204. SAME; BOND.—The Register of Copyrights shall give bond to the United States in the sum of $20,000, in form to be approved by the General Counsel for the Department of the Treasury and with sureties satisfactory to the Secretary of the Treasury, for the faithful discharge of his duties.

§ 205. SAME; ANNUAL REPORT.—The Register of Copyrights shall make an annual report to the Librarian of Congress, to be printed in the annual report on the Library of Congress, of all copyright business for the previous fiscal year, including the number and kind of works which have been deposited in the copyright office during the fiscal year, under the provisions of this title.

---

[13]"All moneys deposited with the Secretary of the Treasury under this section shall be credited to the appropriation for necessary expenses of the Copyright Office."

§ 206. SEAL OF COPYRIGHT OFFICE.—The seal used in the copyright office on July 1, 1909, shall be the seal of the copyright office, and by it all papers issued from the copyright office requiring authentication shall be authenticated.

§ 207. RULES FOR REGISTRATION OF CLAIMS.[14]—Subject to the approval of the Librarian of Congress, the Register of Copyrights shall be authorized to make rules and regulations for the registration of claims to copyright as provided by this title.

§ 208. RECORD BOOKS IN COPYRIGHT OFFICE.—The Register of Copyrights shall provide and keep such record books in the copyright office as are required to carry out the provisions of this title, and whenever deposit has been made in the copyright office of a copy of any work under the provisions of this title he shall make entry thereof.

§ 209. CERTIFICATE OF REGISTRATION; EFFECT AS EVIDENCE; RECEIPT FOR COPIES DEPOSITED.—In the case of each entry the person recorded as the claimant of the copyright shall be entitled to a certificate of registration under seal of the copyright office, to contain the name and address of said claimant, the name of the country of which the author of the work is a citizen or subject, and when an alien author domiciled in the United States at the time of said registration, then a statement of that fact, including his place of domicile, the name of the author (when the records of the copyright office shall show the same), the title of the work which is registered for which copyright is claimed, the date of the deposit of the copies of such work, the date of publication if the work has been reproduced in copies for sale, or publicly distributed, and such marks as to class designation and entry number as shall fully identify the entry. In the case of a book, the certificate shall also state the receipt of the affidavit, as provided by section 17 of this title, and the date of the completion of the printing, or the date of the publication of the book, as stated in the said affidavit. The Register of Copyrights shall prepare a printed form for the said certificate, to be filled out in each case as above provided for in the case of all registrations made after July 1, 1909, and in the case of all previous registrations so far as the copyright office record books shall show such facts, which certificate, sealed with the seal of the copyright office, shall, upon payment of the prescribed fee, be given to any person making application for the same. Said certificate shall be admitted in any court as prima facie evidence of the facts stated therein. In addition to such certificate the register of copyrights shall furnish, upon request, without additional fee, a receipt for the copies of the work deposited to complete the registration.

§ 210. CATALOG OF COPYRIGHT ENTRIES; EFFECT AS EVIDENCE.—The Register of Copyrights shall fully index all copyright registrations and assignments and shall print at periodic intervals a catalog of the titles of articles deposited and registered for copyright, together with suitable indexes, and at stated intervals shall print complete and indexed catalog for each class of copyright entries, and may thereupon, if expedient, destroy the original manuscript catalog cards containing the titles included in such printed volumes and representing the entries made during such intervals. The current catalog of copyright entries and the index volumes herein provided for shall be admitted in any court as prima facie evidence of the facts stated therein as regards any copyright registration.

---

[14]Published in the *Federal Register* and Title 37 of the *Code of Federal Regulations.*

§ 211. SAME; DISTRIBUTION AND SALE; DISPOSAL OF PROCEEDS.—The said printed current catalogs as they are issued shall be promptly distributed by the Superintendent of Documents to the collectors of customs of the United States and to the postmasters of all exchange offices of receipt of foreign mails, in accordance with revised list of such collectors of customs and postmasters prepared by the Secretary of the Treasury and the Postmaster General, and they shall also be furnished in whole or in part to all parties desiring them at a price to be determined by the Register of Copyrights for each part of the catalog not exceeding $75 for the complete yearly catalog of copyright entries. The consolidated catalogs and indexes shall also be supplied to all persons ordering them at such prices as may be fixed by the Register of Copyrights, and all subscriptions for the catalogs shall be received by the Superintendent of Documents, who shall forward the said publications; and the moneys thus received shall be paid into the Treasury of the United States and accounted for under such laws and Treasury regulations as shall be in force at the time.

§ 212. RECORDS AND WORKS DEPOSITED IN COPYRIGHT OFFICE OPEN TO PUBLIC INSPECTION; TAKING COPIES OF ENTRIES.—The record books of the copyright office, together with the indexes to such record books, and all works deposited and retained in the copyright office, shall be open to public inspection; and copies may be taken of the copyright entries actually made in such record books, subject to such safeguards and regulations as shall be prescribed by the Register of Copyrights and approved by the Librarian of Congress.

§ 213. DISPOSITION OF ARTICLES DEPOSITED IN OFFICE.—Of the articles deposited in the copyright office under the provisions of the copyright laws of the United States, the Librarian of Congress shall determine what books and other articles shall be transferred to the permanent collections of the Library of Congress, including the law library, and what other books or articles shall be placed in the reserve collections of the Library of Congress for sale or exchange, or be transferred to other governmental libraries in the District of Columbia for use therein.

§ 214. DESTRUCTION OF ARTICLES DEPOSITED IN OFFICE REMAINING UNDISPOSED OF; REMOVAL OF BY AUTHOR OR PROPRIETOR; MANUSCRIPTS OF UNPUBLISHED WORKS.—Of any articles undisposed of as above provided, together with all titles and correspondence relating thereto, the Librarian of Congress and the Register of Copyrights jointly shall, at suitable intervals, determine what of these received during any period of years it is desirable or useful to preserve in the permanent files of the copyright office, and, after due notice as hereinafter provided, may within their discretion cause the remaining articles and other things to be destroyed: *Provided*, That there shall be printed in the Catalog of Copyright Entries from February to November, inclusive, a statement of the years of receipt of such articles and a notice to permit any author, copyright proprietor, or other lawful claimant to claim and remove before the expiration of the month of December of that year anything found which relates to any of his productions deposited or registered for copyright within the period of years stated, not reserved or disposed of as provided for in this title. No manuscript of an unpublished work shall be destroyed during its term of copyright without specific notice to the copyright proprietor of record, permitting him to claim and remove it.

§ 215. FEES.—The Register of Copyrights shall receive, and the persons to whom the services designated are rendered shall pay, the following fees:

For the registration of a claim to copyright in any work, including a print or label used for articles of merchandise, $6; for the registration of a claim to renewal of copyright, $4; which fees shall include a certificate for each registration: *Provided*, That only one registration fee shall be required in the case of several volumes of the same book published and deposited at the same time: *And provided further*, That with respect to works of foreign origin, in lieu of payment of the copyright fee of $6 together with one copy of the work and application, the foreign author or proprietor may at any time within six months from the date of first publication abroad deposit in the Copyright Office an application for registration and two copies of the work which shall be accompanied by a catalog card in form and content satisfactory to the Register of Copyrights.

For every additional certificate of registration, $2.

For certifying a copy of an application for registration of copyright, and for all other certifications, $3.

For recording every assignment, agreement, power of attorney or other paper not exceeding six pages, $5; for each additional page or less, 50 cents; for each title over one in the paper recorded, 50 cents additional.

For recording a notice of use, or notice of intention to use, $3, for each notice of not more than five titles; and 50 cents for each additional title.

For any requested search of Copyright Office records, works deposited, or other available material, or services rendered in connection therewith, $5, for each hour of time consumed.

§ 216. WHEN THE DAY FOR TAKING ACTION FALLS ON SATURDAY, SUNDAY, OR A HOLIDAY.—When the last day for making any deposit or application, or for paying any fee, or for delivering any other material to the Copyright Office falls on Saturday, Sunday, or a holiday within the District of Columbia, such action may be taken on the next succeeding business day.

# Public Law 93–573, 93d Cong., December 31, 1974, 88 Stat. 1873 *et seq.*

## TITLE I—AMEND TITLE 17 UNITED STATES CODE, AND FOR OTHER PURPOSES

SEC. 101. Section 3 of the Act of October 15, 1971 (85 Stat. 391), is amended by striking out "and before January 1, 1975".

SEC. 102. Section 104 of title 17, United States Code, is amended—

(1) by striking out "Any person" and inserting in lieu thereof

"(a) Except as provided in subsection (b), any person"; and

(2) by adding at the end thereof the following new subsection:

"(b) Any person who willfully and for profit shall infringe any copyright provided by section 1(f) of this title, or who should knowingly and willfully aid or abet such infringement, shall be fined not more than $25,000 or imprisoned not more than one year, or both, for the first offense and shall be fined not more than $50,000 or imprisoned not more than two years, or both, for any subsequent offense."

SEC. 103. Section 2318 of title 18, United States Code, is amended by striking out all after "fined" and inserting in lieu thereof "not more than $25,000 or imprisoned for not more than one year, or both, for the first offense and shall be fined not more than $50,000 or imprisoned not more than two years, or both, for any subsequent offense."

SEC. 104. In any case in which the renewal term of copyright subsisting in any work on the date of approval of this bill, or the term thereof as extended by Public Law 87–668, by Public Law 89–142, by Public Law 90–141, by Public Law 90–416, by Public Law 91–147, by Public Law 91–555, by Public Law 92–170, or by Public Law 92–566 (or by all or certain of said laws), would expire prior to December 31, 1976, such term is hereby continued until December 31, 1976.

## TITLE II—NATIONAL COMMISSION ON NEW TECHNOLOGICAL USES OF COPYRIGHTED WORKS

### ESTABLISHMENT AND PURPOSE OF COMMISSION

SEC. 201. (a) There is hereby created in the Library of Congress a National Commission on New Technological Uses of Copyrighted Works (hereafter called the Commission).

(b) The purpose of the Commission is to study and compile data on:

(1) the reproduction and use of copyrighted works of authorship—

(A) in conjunction with automatic systems capable of storing, processing, retrieving, and transferring information, and

(B) by various forms of machine reproduction, not including reproduction by or at the request of instructors for use in face-to-face teaching activities; and

(2) the creation of new works by the application or intervention of such automatic systems or machine reproduction.

(c) The Commission shall make recommendations as to such changes in copyright law or procedures that may be necessary to assure for such purposes access to copyrighted works, and to provide recognition of the rights of copyright owners.

MEMBERSHIP OF THE COMMISSION

SEC. 202. (a) The Commission shall be composed of thirteen voting members, appointed as follows:

(1) Four members, to be appointed by the President, selected from authors and other copyright owners;

(2) Four members, to be appointed by the President, selected from users of copyright works;

(3) Four nongovernmental members to be appointed by the President, selected from the public generally, with at least one member selected from among experts in consumer protection affairs;

(4) The Librarian of Congress.

(b) The President shall appoint a Chairman, and a Vice Chairman who shall act as Chairman in the absence or disability of the Chairman or in the event of a vacancy in that office, from among the four members selected from the public generally, as provided by clause (3) of subsection (a). The Register of Copyrights shall serve ex officio as a nonvoting member of the Commission.

(c) Seven voting members of the Commission shall constitute a quorum.

(d) Any vacancy in the Commission shall not affect its powers and shall be filled in the same manner as the original appointment was made.

COMPENSATION OF MEMBERS OF COMMISSION

SEC. 203. (a) Members of the Commission, other than officers or employees of the Federal Government, shall receive compensation at the rate of $100 per day while engaged in the actual performance of Commission duties, plus reimbursement for travel, subsistence, and other necessary expenses in connection with such duties.

(b) Any members of the Commission who are officers or employees of the Federal Government shall serve on the Commission without compensation, but such members shall be reimbursed for travel, subsistence, and other necessary expenses in connection with the performance of their duties.

STAFF

SEC. 204. (a) To assist in its studies, the Commission may appoint a staff which shall be an administrative part of the Library of Congress. The staff shall be headed by an Executive Director, who shall be responsible to the Commission for the Administration of the duties entrusted to the staff.

(b) The Commission may procure temporary and intermittent services to the same extent as is authorized by section 3109 of title 5, United States Code, but at rates not to exceed $100 per day.

EXPENSES OF THE COMMISSION

SEC. 205. There are hereby authorized to be appropriated such sums as may be necessary to carry out the provisions of this title until June 30, 1976.

REPORTS

SEC. 206. (a) Within one year after the first meeting of the Commission it shall submit to the President and the Congress a preliminary report on its activities.

(b) Within three years after the enactment of this Act the Commission shall submit to the President and the Congress a final report on its study and investigation which shall include its recommendations and such proposals for legislation and administrative action as may be necessary to carry out its recommendations.

(c) In addition to the preliminary report and final report required by this section, the Commission may publish such interim reports as it may determine, including but not limited to consultant's reports, transcripts of testimony, seminar reports, and other Commission findings.

POWERS OF THE COMMISSION

SEC. 207. (a) The Commission or, with the authorization of the Commission, any three or more of its members, may, for the purpose of carrying out the provisions of this title, hold hearings, administer oaths, and require, by subpoena or otherwise, the attendance and testimony of witnesses and the production of documentary material.

(b) With the consent of the Commission, any of its members may hold any meetings, seminars, or conferences considered appropriate to provide a forum for discussion of the problems with which it is dealing.

TERMINATION

SEC. 208. On the sixtieth day after the date of the submission of its final report, the Commission shall terminate and all offices and employment under it shall expire.

Approved December 31, 1974.

# Appendix B

# The 1976 Copyright Act (With Amendments)
(*Title 17 U.S.C., 90 Stat. 2541 et seq., Public Law 94-553*)

### Title 1—General Revision of Copyright Law

SEC. 101. Title 17 of the United States Code, entitled "Copyrights," is hereby amended in its entirety to read as follows:

### Title 17—Copyrights

### Chapter 1—Subject Matter and Scope of Copyright

360

## § 101. Definitions

As used in this title, the following terms and their variant forms mean the following;

An "anonymous work" is a work on the copies or phonorecords of which no natural person is identified as author.

"Audiovisual works" are works that consist of a series of related images which are intrinsically intended to be shown by the use of machines or devices such as projectors, viewers, or electronic equipment, together with accompanying sounds, if any, regardless of the nature of the material objects, such as films or tapes, in which the works are embodied.

The "best edition" of a work is the edition, published in the United States at any time before the date of deposit, that the Library of Congress determines to be most suitable for its purposes.

A person's "children" are that person's immediate offspring, whether legitimate or not, and any children legally adopted by that person.

A "collective work" is a work, such as a periodical issue, anthology, or encyclopedia, in which a number of contributions, constituting separate and independent works in themselves, are assembled into a collective whole.

A "compilation" is a work formed by the collection and assembling of preexisting materials or of data that are selected, coordinated, or arranged in such a way that the resulting work as a whole constitutes an original work of authorship. The term "compilation" includes collective works.

"Copies" are material objects, other than phonorecords, in which a work is fixed by any method now known, or later developed, and from which the work can be perceived, reproduced, or otherwise communicated, either directly or with the aid of a machine or device. The term "copies" includes the material object, other than a phonorecord, in which the work is first fixed.

"Copyright owner," with respect to any one of the exclusive rights comprised in a copyright, refers to the owner of that particular right.

A work is "created" when it is fixed in a copy or phonorecord for the first time; where a work is prepared over a period of time, the portion of it that has been fixed at any particular time constitutes the work as of that time, and where the work has been prepared in different versions, each version constitutes a separate work.

A "derivative work" is a work based upon one or more preexisting works, such as a translation, musical arrangement, dramatization, fictionalization, motion picture version, sound recording, art reproduction, abridgment, condensation, or any other form in which a work may be recast, transformed, or adapted. A work consisting of editorial revisions, annotations, elaborations, or other modifications which, as a whole, represent an original work of authorship, is a "derivative work".

A "device", "machine", or "process" is one now known or later developed.

To "display" a work means to show a copy of it, either directly or by means of a film, slide, television image, or any other device or process or, in the case of a motion picture or other audiovisual work, to show individual images nonsequentially.

A work is "fixed" in a tangible medium of expression when its embodiment in a copy or phonorecord, by or under the authority of the author, is sufficiently permanent or stable to permit it to be perceived, reproduced, or otherwise communicated for a period of more than transitory duration. A work consisting of sounds, images, or both, that are being transmitted, is "fixed" for purposes of this title if a fixation of the work is being made simultaneously with its transmission.

The terms "including" and "such as" are illustrative and not limitative.

A "joint work" is a work prepared by two or more authors with the intention that their contributions be merged into inseparable or interdependent parts of a unitary whole.

"Literary works" are works, other than audiovisual works, expressed in words, numbers, or other verbal or numerical symbols or indicia, regardless of the nature of the material objects, such as books, periodicals, manuscripts, phonorecords, film, tapes, disks, or cards, in which they are embodied.

"Motion pictures" are audiovisual works consisting of a series of related images which, when shown in succession, impart an impression of motion, together with accompanying sounds, if any.

To "perform" a work means to recite, render, play, dance, or act it, either directly or be means of any device or process or, in the case of a motion picture or other audiovisual work, to show its images in any sequence or to make the sounds accompanying it audible.

"Phonorecords" are material objects in which sounds, other than those accompanying a motion picture or other audiovisual work, are fixed by any method now known or later developed, and from which the sounds can be perceived, reproduced, or otherwise communicated, either directly or with the aid of a machine or device. The term "phonorecords" includes the material object in which the sounds are first fixed.

"Pictorial, graphic, and sculptural works" include two-dimensional and three-dimensional works of fine, graphic, and applied art, photographs, prints and art reproductions, maps, globes, charts, technical drawings, diagrams, and models. Such works shall include works of artistic craftsmanship insofar as their form but not their mechanical or utilitarian aspects are concerned; the design of a useful article, as defined in this section, shall be considered a pictorial, graphic, or sculptural work only if, and only to the extent that, such design incorporates pictorial, graphic, or sculptural features that can be identified separately from, and are capable of existing independently of, the utilitarian aspects of the article.

A "pseudonymous work" is a work or the copies or phonorecords of which the author is identified under a fictitious name.

"Publication" is the distribution of copies or phonorecords of a work to the public by sale or other transfer of ownership, or by rental, lease, or lending. The offering to distribute copies or phonorecords to a group of persons for purposes of further distribution, public performance, or public display, constitutes publication. A public performance or display of a work does not of itself constitute publication.

To perform or display a work "publicly" means—

(1) to perform or display it at a place open to the public or at any place where a substantial number of persons outside of a normal circle of a family and its social acquaintances is gathered; or

(2) to transmit or otherwise communicate a performance or display of the work to a place specified by clause (1) or to the public, by means of any device or process, whether the members of the public capable of receiving the performance or display receive it in the same place or in separate places and at the same time or at different times.

"Sound recordings" are works that result from the fixation of a series of musical, spoken, or other sounds, but not including the sounds accompanying a motion picture or other audiovisual work, regardless of the nature of the material objects, such as disks, tapes, or other phonorecords, in which they are embodied.

"State" includes the District of Columbia and the Commonwealth of Puerto Rico, and any territories to which this title is made applicable by an Act of Congress.

A "transfer of copyright ownership" is an assignment, mortgage, exclusive license, or any other conveyance, alienation, or hypothecation of a copyright or of any of the exclusive rights comprised in a copyright, whether or not it is limited in time or place of effect, but not including a nonexclusive license.

A "transmission program" is a body of material that, as an aggregate, has been produced for the sole purpose of transmission to the public in sequence and as a unit.

To "transmit" a performance or display is to communicate it by any device or process whereby images or sounds are received beyond the place from which they are sent.

The "United States," when used in a geographical sense, comprises the several States, the District of Columbia and the Commonwealth of Puerto Rico, and the organized territories under the jurisdiction of the United States Government.

A "useful article" is an article having an intrinsic utilitarian function that is not merely to portray the appearance of the article or to convey information. An article that is normally a part of a useful article is considered a "useful article."

The author's "widow" or "widower" is the author's surviving spouse under the law of the author's domicile at the time of his or her death, whether or not the spouse has later remarried.

A "work of the United States Government" is a work prepared by an officer or employee of the United States Government as part of that person's official duties.

A "work made for hire" is—

(1) a work prepared by an employee within the scope of his or her employment; or

(2) a work specially ordered or commissioned for use as a contribution to a collective work, as a part of a motion picture or other audiovisual work, as a translation, as a supplementary work, as a

compilation, as an instructional text, as a test, as answer material for a test, or as an atlas, if the parties expressly agree in a written instrument signed by them that the work shall be considered a work made for hire. For the purpose of the foregoing sentence, a "supplementary work" is a work prepared for publication as a secondary adjunct to a work by another author for the purpose of introducing, concluding, illustrating, explaining, revising, commenting upon, or assisting in the use of the other work, such as forewords, afterwords, pictorial illustrations, maps, charts, tables, editorial notes, musical arrangements, answer material for tests, bibliographies, appendixes, and indexes, and an "instructional text" is a literary, pictorial, or graphic work prepared for publication and with the purpose of use in systematic instructional activities.

A "computer program" is a set of statements or instructions to be used directly or indirectly in a computer in order to bring about a certain result.*

## § 102. Subject matter of copyright: In general

(a) Copyright protection subsists, in accordance with this title, in original works of authorship fixed in any tangible medium of expression, now known or later developed, from which they can be perceived, reproduced, or otherwise communicated, either directly or with the aid of a machine or device. Works of authorship include the following categories:

(1) literary works;
(2) musical works, including any accompanying words;
(3) dramatic works, including any accompanying music;
(4) pantomimes and choreographic works;
(5) pictorial, graphic, and sculptural works;
(6) motion pictures and other audiovisual works; and
(7) sound recordings.

(b) In no case does copyright protection for an original work of authorship extend to any idea, procedure, process, system, method of operation, concept, principle, or discovery, regardless of the form in which it is described, explained, illustrated, or embodied in such work.

## § 103. Subject matter of copyright: Compilations and derivative works

(a) The subject matter of copyright as specified by section 102 includes compilations and derivative works, but protection for a work employing preexisting material in which copyright subsists does not extend to any part of the work in which such material has been used unlawfully.

(b) The copyright in a compilation or derivative work extends only to the material contributed by the author of such work, as distinguished from the preexisting material employed in the work, and does not imply any exclusive right in the preexisting material. The copyright in such work is independent of, and does not affect or enlarge the scope, duration, ownership, or subsistence of, and copyright protection in the preexisting material.

---

*Added by Pub. L. No. 96-517, December 12, 1980.

### § 104. Subject matter of copyright: National origin

(a) UNPUBLISHED WORKS.—The works specified by sections 102 and 103, while unpublished, are subject to protection under this title without regard to the nationality or domicile of the author.

(b) PUBLISHED WORKS.—The works specified by sections 102 and 103, when published, are subject to protection under this title if—

(1) on the date of first publication, one or more of the authors is a national or domiciliary of the United States, or is a national, domiciliary, or sovereign authority of a foreign nation that is a party to a copyright treaty to which the United States is also a party, or is a stateless person, wherever that person may be domiciled; or

(2) the work is first published in the United States or in a foreign nation that, on the date of first publication, is a party to the Universal Copyright Convention; or

(3) the work is first published by the United Nations or any of its specialized agencies, or by the Organization of American States; or

(4) the work comes within the scope of a Presidential proclamation. Whenever the President finds that a particular foreign nation extends, to works by authors who are nationals or domiciliaries of the United States or to works that are first published in the United States, copyright protection on substantially the same basis as that on which the foreign nation extends protection to works of its own nationals and domiciliaries and works first published in that nation, the President may by proclamation extend protection under this title to works of which one or more of the authors is, on the date of first publication, a national, domiciliary, or sovereign authority of that nation, or which was first published in that nation. The President may revise, suspend, or revoke any such proclamation or impose any conditions or limitations on protection under a proclamation.

### § 105. Subject matter of copyright: United States Government works

Copyright protection under this title is not available for any work of the United States Government, but the United States Government is not precluded from receiving and holding copyrights transferred to it by assignment, bequest, or otherwise.

### § 106. Exclusive rights in copyrighted works

Subject to sections 107 through 118, the owner of copyright under this title has the exclusive rights to do and to authorize any of the following:

(1) to reproduce the copyrighted work in copies or phonorecords;

(2) to prepare derivative works based upon the copyrighted work;

(3) to distribute copies or phonorecords of the copyrighted work to the public by sale or other transfer of ownership, or by rental, lease, or lending;

(4) in the case of literary, musical, dramatic, and choreographic works, pantomimes, and motion pictures and other audiovisual works, to perform the copyrighted work publicly; and

(5) in the case of literary, musical, dramatic, and choreographic works, pantomimes, and pictorial, graphic, or sculptural works, including the individual images of a motion picture or other audiovisual work, to display the copyrighted work publicly.

## § 107. Limitations on exclusive rights: Fair use

Notwithstanding the provisions of section 106, the fair use of a copyrighted work, including such use by reproduction in copies or phonorecords or by any other means specified by that section, for purposes such as criticism, comment, news reporting, teaching (including multiple copies for classroom use), scholarship, or research, is not an infringement of copyright. In determining whether the use made of a work in any particular case is a fair use the factors to be considered shall include—

(1) the purpose and character of the use, including whether such use is of a commercial nature or is for nonprofit educational purposes;

(2) the nature of the copyrighted work;

(3) the amount and substantiality of the portion used in relation to the copyright work as a whole; and

(4) the effect of the use upon the potential market for or value of the copyrighted work.

## § 108. Limitations on exclusive rights: Reproduction by libraries and archives

(a) Notwithstanding the provisions of section 106, it is not an infringement of copyright for a library or archives, or any of its employees acting within the scope of their employment, to reproduce no more than one copy or phonorecord of a work, or to distribute such copy or phonorecord, under the conditions specified by this section, if—

(1) the reproduction or distribution is made without any purpose of direct or indirect commercial advantage;

(2) the collections of the library or archives are (i) open to the public, or (ii) available not only to researchers affiliated with the library or archives or with the institution of which it is a part, but also to other persons doing research in a specialized field; and

(3) the reproduction or distribution of the work includes a notice of copyright.

(b) The rights of reproduction and distribution under this section apply to a copy or phonorecord of an unpublished work duplicated in facsimile form solely for purposes of preservation and security or for deposit for research use in another library or archives of the type described by clause (2) of subsection (a), if the copy or phonorecord reproduced is currently in the collections of the library or archives.

(c) The right of reproduction under this section applies to a copy or phonorecord of a published work duplicated in facsimile form solely for the purpose of replacement of a copy or phonorecord that is damaged, deteriorating, lost, or stolen, if the library or archives has, after a reasonable effort, determined that an unused replacement cannot be obtained at a fair price.

(d) The rights of reproduction and distribution under this section apply to a copy, made from the collection of a library or archives where the user makes his or her request or from that of another library or archives, of no more than one article or other contribution to a copyrighted collection or periodical issue, or to a copy or phonorecord of a small part of any other copyrighted work, if—

(1) the copy or phonorecord becomes the property of the user, and the library or archives has had no notice that the copy or phonorecord would be used for any purpose other than private study, scholarship, or research; and

(2) the library or archives displays prominently, at the place where orders are accepted, and includes on its order form, a warning of copyright in accordance with requirements that the Register of Copyrights shall prescribe by regulation.

(e) The rights of reproduction and distribution under this section apply to the entire work, or to a substantial part of it, made from the collection of a library or archives where the user makes his or her request or from that of another library or archives, if the library or archives has first determined, on the basis of a reasonable investigation, that a copy or phonorecord of the copyrighted work cannot be obtained at a fair price, if—

(1) the copy or phonorecord becomes the property of the user, and the library or archives has had no notice that the copy or phonorecord would be used for any purpose other than private study, scholarship, or research; and

(2) the library or archives displays prominently, at the place where orders are accepted, and includes on its order form, a warning of copyright in accordance with requirements that the Register of Copyrights shall prescribe by regulation.

(f) Nothing in this section—

(1) shall be construed to impose liability for copyright infringement upon a library or archives or its employees for the unsupervised use of reproducing equipment located on its premises: *Provided*, That such equipment displays a notice that the making of a copy may be subject to the copyright law;

(2) excuses a person who uses such reproducing equipment or who requests a copy or phonorecord under subsection (d) from liability for copyright infringement for any such act, or for any later use of such copy or phonorecord, if it exceeds fair use as provided by section 107;

(3) shall be construed to limit the reproduction and distribution by lending of a limited number of copies and excerpts by a library or archives of an audiovisual news program, subject to clauses (1), (2), and (3) of subsection (a); or

(4) in any way affects the right of fair use as provided by section 107, or any contractual obligations assumed at any time by the library or archives when it obtained a copy or phonorecord of a work in its collections.

(g) The rights of reproduction and distribution under this section extend to the isolated and unrelated reproduction or distribution of a single copy or phonorecord of the same material on separate occasions, but do not extend to cases where the library or archives, or its employee—

(1) is aware or has substantial reason to believe that it is engaging in the related or concerted reproduction or distribution of multiple copies or phonorecords of the same material, whether made on one occasion or over a period of time, and whether intended for aggregate use by one or more individuals or for separate use by the individual members of a group; or

(2) engages in the systematic reproduction or distribution of single or multiple copies or phonorecords of material described in subsection (d): *Provided*, That nothing in this clause prevents a library or archives from participating in interlibrary arrangements that do not have, as their purpose or effect, that the library or archives receiving such copies or phonorecords for distribution does so in such aggregate quantities as to substitute for a subscription to or purchase of such work.

(h) The rights of reproduction and distribution under this section do not apply to a musical work, a pictorial, graphic or sculptural work, or a motion picture or other audiovisual work other than an audiovisual work dealing with news, except that no such limitation shall apply with respect to rights granted by subsections (b) and (c), or with respect to pictorial or graphic works published as illustrations, diagrams, or similar adjuncts to works of which copies are reproduced or distributed in accordance with subsections (d) and (e).

(i) Five years from the effective date of this Act, and at five-year intervals thereafter, the Register of Copyrights, after consulting with representatives of authors, book and periodical publishers, and other owners of copyrighted materials, and with representatives of library users and librarians, shall submit to the Congress a report setting forth the extent to which this section has achieved the intended statutory balancing of the rights of creators, and the needs of users. The report should also describe any problems that may have arisen, and present legislative or other recommendations, if warranted.

## § 109. Limitations on exclusive rights: Effect of transfer of particular copy or phonorecord

(a) Notwithstanding the provisions of section 106(3), the owner of a particular copy or phonorecord lawfully made under this title, or any person authorized by such owner, is entitled, without the authority of the copyright owner, to sell or otherwise dispose of the possession of that copy or phonorecord.

(b)(1) *Notwithstanding the provisions of subsection (a), unless authorized by the owners of copyright in the sound recording and in the musical

---

*Subsections (b) and (c) of § 109 as originally enacted in 1976 were later redesignated as subsections (c) and (d), and subsection (b) was added, by the "Record Rental Amendment of 1984," which was § 2 of Pub. L. No. 98-450, 98 Stat. 1728, effective Oct. 4, 1984. In addition, § 4 of Pub. L. No. 98-450 provided that "(b) The provisions of section 109(b) of title 17, United States Code, as added by section 2 of this Act, shall not affect the right of an owner of a particular phonorecord of a sound recording, who acquired such ownership before the date of the enact-

works embodied therein, the owners of a particular phonorecord may not, for purposes of direct or indirect commercial advantage, dispose of, or authorize the disposal of, the possession of that phonorecord by rental, lease, or lending, or by any other act or practice in the nature of rental, lease, or lending. Nothing in the preceding sentence shall apply to the rental, lease, or lending of a phonorecord for nonprofit purposes by a nonprofit library or nonprofit education institution.

(2) Nothing in this subsection shall affect any provision of the antitrust laws. For purposes of the preceding sentence, "antitrust laws" has the meaning given that term in the first section of the Clayton Act and includes section 5 of the Federal Trade Commission Act to the extent that section relates to unfair methods of competition.

(3) Any person who distributes a phonorecord in violation of clause (1) is an infringer of copyright under section 501 of this title and is subject to the remedies set forth in sections 502, 503, 504, 505, and 509. Such violation shall not be a criminal offense under section 506 or cause such person to be subject to the criminal penalties set forth in section 2319 of title 18.

(c) Notwithstanding the provisions of section 106(5), the owner of a particular copy lawfully made under this title, or any person authorized by such owner, is entitled, without the authority of the copyright owner, to display that copy publicly, either directly or by the projection of no more than one image at a time, to viewers present at the place where the copy is located.

(d) The privileges prescribed by subsections (a) and (c) do not, unless authorized by the copyright owner, extend to any person who has acquired possession of the copy or phonorecord from the copyright owner, by rental, lease, loan, or otherwise, without acquiring ownership of it.

## § 110. Limitations on exclusive rights: Exemption of certain performances and displays

Notwithstanding the provisions of section 106, the following are not infringements of copyright:

(1) performance or display of a work by instructors or pupils in the course of face-to-face teaching activities of a nonprofit educational institution, in a classroom or similar place devoted to instruction, unless, in the case of a motion picture or other audiovisual work, the performance, or the display of individual images, is given by means of a copy that was not lawfully made under this title, and that the person responsible for the performance knew or had reason to believe was not lawfully made;

(2) performance of a nondramatic literary or musical work or display of a work, by or in the course of a transmission, if—

(A) the performance or display is a regular part of the systematic instructional activities of a governmental body or a nonprofit educational institution; and

---

ment of this Act, to dispose of the possession of that particular phonorecord on or after such date of enactment in any manner permitted by section 109 of title 17, United States Code, as in effect on the day before the date of the enactment of this Act. (c) The amendments made by this Act shall not apply to rentals, leasings, lendings (or acts or practices in the nature of rentals, leasings, or lendings) occurring after the date which is five years after the date of the enactment of this Act."

(B) the performance or display is directly related and of material assistance to the teaching content of the transmission; and
(C) the transmission is made primarily for—
(i) reception in classrooms or similar places normally devoted to instruction, or
(ii) reception by persons to whom the transmission is directed because their disabilities or other special circumstances prevent their attendance in classrooms or similar places normally devoted to instruction, or
(iii) reception by officers or employees of governmental bodies as a part of their official duties or employment;
(3) performance of a nondramatic literary or musical work or of a dramatico-musical work of a religious nature, or display of a work, in the course of services at a place of worship or other religious assembly;
(4) performance of a nondramatic literary or musical work otherwise than in a transmission to the public, without any purpose of direct or indirect commercial advantage and without payment of any fee or other compensation for the performance to any of its performers, promoters, or organizers, if—
(A) there is no direct or indirect admission charge; or
(B) the proceeds, after deducting the reasonable costs of producing the performance, are used exclusively for educational, religious, or charitable purposes and not for private financial gain, except where the copyright owner has served notice of objection to the performance under the following conditions;
(i) the notice shall be in writing and signed by the copyright owner or such owner's duly authorized agent; and
(ii) the notice shall be served on the person responsible for the performance at least seven days before the date of the performance, and shall state the reasons for the objection; and
(iii) the notice shall comply, in form, content, and manner of service, with requirements that the Register of Copyrights shall prescribe by regulation;
(5) communication of a transmission embodying a performance or display of a work by the public reception of the transmission on a single receiving apparatus of a kind commonly used in private homes, unless—
(A) a direct charge is made to see or hear the transmission; or
(B) the transmission thus received is further transmitted to the public;
(6) performance of a nondramatic musical work by a governmental body or a nonprofit agricultural or horticultural organization, in the course of an annual agricultural or horticultural fair or exhibition conducted by such body or organization; the exemption provided by this clause shall extend to any liability for copyright in infringement that would otherwise be imposed on such body or organization, under doctrines of vicarious liability or related infringement, for a performance by a concessionnaire, business establishment, or other person at such fair or exhibition, but shall not excuse any such person from liability for the performance;
(7) performance of a nondramatic musical work by a vending establishment open to the public at large without any direct or indirect admission charge, where the sole purpose of the performance is to promote the retail sale of copies or phonorecords of the work, and the performance is

not transmitted beyond the place where the establishment is located and is within the immediate area where the sale is occurring;

(8) performance of a nondramatic literary work, by or in the course of a transmission specifically designed for and primarily directed to blind or other handicapped persons who are unable to read normal printed material as a result of their handicap, or deaf or other handicapped persons who are unable to hear the aural signals accompanying a transmission of visual signals, if the performance is made without any purpose of direct or indirect commercial advantage and its transmission is made through the facilities of: (i) a governmental body; or (ii) a noncommercial educational broadcast station (as defined in section 397 of title 47); or (iii) a radio subcarrier authorization (as defined in 47 CFR 73.293–73.295 and 73.593–73.595); or (iv) a cable system (as defined in section 111(f)).

(9) performance on a single occasion of a dramatic literary work published at least ten years before the date of the performance, by or in the course of a transmission specifically designed for and primarily directed to blind or other handicapped persons who are unable to read normal printed material as a result of their handicap, if the performance is made without any purpose or direct or indirect commercial advantage and its transmission is made through the facilities of a radio subcarrier authorization referred to in clause (8)(iii), *Provided*, That the provisions of this clause shall not be applicable to more than one performance of the same work by the same performers or under the auspices of the same organization.

(10) notwithstanding paragraph 4 above, the following is not an infringement of copyright: performance of a nondramatic literary or musical work in the course of a social function which is organized and promoted by a nonprofit veterans' organization or a nonprofit fraternal organization to which the general public is not invited, but not including the invitees of the organizations, if the proceeds from the performance, after deducting the reasonable costs of producing the performance, are used exclusively for charitable purposes and not for financial gain. For purposes of this section the social functions of any college or university fraternity or sorority shall not be included unless the social function is held solely to raise funds for a specific charitable purpose.

## § 111. Limitations on exclusive rights: Secondary transmissions

(a) CERTAIN SECONDARY TRANSMISSIONS EXEMPTED.—The secondary transmission of a primary transmission embodying a performance or display of a work is not an infringement of copyright if—

(1) the secondary transmission is not made by a cable system, and consists entirely of the relaying, by the management of a hotel, apartment house, or similar establishment, of signals transmitted by a broadcast station licensed by the Federal Communications Commission, within the local service area of such station, to the private lodgings of guests or residents of such establishment, and no direct charge is made to see or hear the secondary transmission; or

(2) the secondary transmission is made solely for the purpose and under the conditions specified by clause (2) of section 110; or

(3) the secondary transmission is made by any carrier who has no direct or indirect control over the content or selection of the primary transmission or over the particular recipients of the secondary transmission, and whose activities with respect to the secondary transmission consist solely of providing wires, cables, or other communications channels for the use of others: *Provided,* That the provisions of this clause extend only to the activities of said carrier with respect to secondary transmissions and do not exempt from liability the activities of others with respect to their own primary or secondary transmissions; or

(4) the secondary transmission is not made by a cable system but is made by a governmental body, or other nonprofit organization, without any purpose of direct or indirect commercial advantage, and without charge to the recipients of the secondary transmission other than assessments necessary to defray the actual and reasonable costs of maintaining and operating the secondary transmission service.

(b) SECONDARY TRANSMISSION OF PRIMARY TRANSMISSION TO CONTROLLED GROUP.—Notwithstanding the provisions of subsections (a) and (c), the secondary transmission to the public of a primary transmission embodying a performance or display of a work is actionable as an act of infringement under section 501, and is fully subject to the remedies provided by sections 502 through 506 and 509; if the primary transmission is not made for reception by the public at large but is controlled and limited to reception by particular members of the public: *Provided,* however, That such secondary transmission is not actionable as an act of infringement if—

(1) the primary transmission is made by a broadcast station licensed by the Federal Communications Commission; and

(2) the carriage of the signals comprising the secondary transmission is required under the rules, regulations, or authorizations of the Federal Communications Commission; and

(3) the signal of the primary transmitter is not altered or changed in any way by the secondary transmitter.

(c) SECONDARY TRANSMISSIONS BY CABLE SYSTEMS.—

(1) Subject to the provisions of clauses (2), (3), and (4) of this subsection, secondary transmissions to the public by a cable system of a primary transmission made by a broadcast station licensed by the Federal Communications Commission or by an appropriate governmental authority of Canada or Mexico and embodying a performance or display of a work shall be subject to compulsory licensing upon compliance with the requirements of subsection (d) where the carriage of the signals comprising the secondary transmissions is permissible under the rules, regulations, or authorizations of the Federal Communications Commission.

(2) Notwithstanding the provisions of clause (1) of this subsection, the willful or repeated secondary transmission to the public by a cable system of a primary transmission made by a broadcast station licensed by the Federal Communications Commission or by an appropriate governmental authority of Canada or Mexico and embodying a performance or display of a work is actionable as an act of infringement under section 501, and is fully subject to the remedies provided by sections 502 through 506 and 509, in the following cases:

(A) where the carriage of the signals comprising the secondary transmission is not permissible under the rules, regulations, or authorizations of the Federal Communications Commission; or

(B) where the cable system has not recorded the notice specified by subsection (d) and deposited the statement of account and royalty fee required by subsection (d).

(3) Notwithstanding the provisions of clause (1) of this subsection and subject to the provisions of subsection (e) of this section, the secondary transmission to the public by a cable system of a primary transmission made by a broadcast station licensed by the Federal Communications Commission or by an appropriate governmental authority of Canada or Mexico and embodying a performance or display of a work is actionable as an act of infringement under section 501, and is fully subject to the remedies provided by sections 502 through 506 and sections 509 and 510, if the content of the particular program in which the performance or display is embodied, or any commercial advertising or station announcements transmitted by the primary transmitter during, or immediately before or after, the transmission of such program, is in any way willfully altered by the cable system through changes, deletions, or additions, except for the alteration, deletion, or substitution of commercial advertisements performed by those engaged in television commercial advertising market research: *Provided*, That the research company has obtained the prior consent of the advertiser who has purchased the original commercial advertisement, the television station broadcasting that commercial advertisement, and the cable system performing the secondary transmission: *And provided further*, That such commercial alteration, deletion, or substitution is not performed for the purpose of deriving income from the sale of that commercial time.

(4) Notwithstanding the provisions of clause (1) of this subsection, the secondary transmission to the public by a cable system of a primary transmission made by a broadcast station licensed by an appropriate governmental authority of Canada or Mexico and embodying a performance or display of a work is actionable as an act of infringement under section 501, and is fully subject to the remedies provided by sections 502 through 506 and section 509, if (A) with respect to Canadian signals, the community of the cable system is located more than 150 miles from the United States-Canadian border and is also located south of the forty-second parallel of latitude, or (B) with respect to Mexican signals, the secondary transmission is made by a cable system which received the primary transmission by means other than direct interception of a free space radio wave emitted by such broadcast television station, unless prior to April 15, 1976, such cable system was actually carrying, or was specifically authorized to carry, the signal of such foreign station on the system pursuant to the rules, regulations, or authorizations of the Federal Communications Commission.

(d) COMPULSORY LICENSE FOR SECONDARY TRANSMISSIONS BY CABLE SYSTEMS.—

(1) For any secondary transmission to be subject to compulsory licensing under subsection (c), the cable system shall, at least one month before the date of the commencement of operations of the cable system or within one hundred and eighty days after the enactment of this Act, whichever is later, and thereafter within thirty days after each occasion on which the ownership or control or the signal carriage complement of the cable system changes, record in the Copyright Office a notice including a statement of the identity and address of the person who owns or operates the secondary transmission service or has power to exercise

primary control over it, together with the name and location of the primary transmitter or primary transmitters whose signals are regularly carried by the cable system, and thereafter, from time to time, such further information as the Register of Copyrights, after consultation with the Copyright Royalty Tribunal (if and when the Tribunal has been constituted), shall prescribe by regulation to carry out the purpose of this clause.

(2) A cable system whose secondary transmissions have been subject to compulsory licensing under subsection (c) shall, on a semiannual basis, deposit with the Register of Copyrights, in accordance with requirements that the Register shall, after consultation with the Copyright Royalty Tribunal (if and when the Tribunal has been constituted), prescribe by regulation—

(A) a statement of account, covering the six months next preceding, specifying the number of channels on which the cable system made secondary transmissions to its subscribers, the names and locations of all primary transmitters whose transmissions were further transmitted by the cable system, the total number of subscribers, the gross amounts paid to the cable system for the basic service of providing secondary transmissions of primary broadcast transmitters, and such other data as the Register of Copyrights may, after consultation with the Copyright Royalty Tribunal (if and when the Tribunal has been constituted), from time to time prescribe by regulation. Such statement shall also include a special statement of account covering any nonnetwork television programming that was carried by the cable system in whole or in part beyond the local service area of the primary transmitter, under rules, regulations, or authorizations of the Federal Communications Commission permitting the substitution or addition of signals under certain circumstances, together with logs showing the times, dates, stations, and programs involved in such substituted or added carriage; and

(B) except in the case of a cable system whose royalty is specified in subclause (C) or (D), a total royalty fee for the period covered by the statement, computed on the basis of specified percentages of the gross receipts from subscribers to the cable service during said period for the basic service of providing secondary transmissions of primary broadcast transmitters, as follows:*

(i) 0.893 of 1 per centum of such gross receipts for the privilege of further transmitting any nonnetwork programming of a primary transmitter in whole or in part beyond the local service area of such primary transmitter, such amount to be applied against the fee, if any, payable pursuant to paragraphs (ii) through (iv);

(ii) 0.893 of 1 per centum of such gross receipts for the first distant signal equivalent;

(iii) 0.563 of 1 per centum of such gross receipts for each of the second, third, and fourth distant signal equivalents;

---

*The fees specified here reflect the adjustments made by the Copyright Royalty Tribunal as of May 1, 1985. See 37 C.F.R. § 308.2. See also additional syndicated exclusivity surcharges established in 37 C.F.R. § 308.2(d).

(iv) 0.265 of 1 per centum of such gross receipts for the fifth distant signal equivalent and each additional distant signal equivalent thereafter; and in computing the amounts payable under paragraph (ii) through (iv), above, any fraction of a distant signal equivalent shall be computed at its fractional value and, in the case of any cable system located partly within and partly without the local service area of a primary transmitter, gross receipts shall be limited to those gross receipts derived from subscribers located without the local service area of such primary transmitter; and

(C) if the actual gross receipts paid by subscribers to a cable system for the period covered by the statement for the basic service of providing secondary transmissions of primary broadcast transmitters total $146,000 or less, gross receipts of the cable system for the purpose of this subclause shall be computed by subtracting from such actual gross receipts the amount by which $146,000 exceeds such actual gross receipts, except that in no case shall a cable system's gross receipts be reduced to less than $5,600. The royalty fee payable under this subclause shall be 0.5 of 1 per centum, regardless of the number of distant signal equivalents, if any; and

(D) if the actual gross receipts paid by subscribers to a cable system for the period covered by the statement, for the basic service of providing secondary transmissions of primary broadcast transmitters, are more than $146,000 but less than $292,000, the royalty fee payable under this subclause shall be (i) 0.5 of 1 per centum of any gross receipts up to $146,000; and (ii) 1 per centum of any gross receipts in excess of $146,000 but less than $292,000, regardless of the number of distant signal equivalents, if any.

(3) The Register of Copyrights shall receive all fees deposited under this section and, after deducting the reasonable costs incurred by the Copyright Office under this section, shall deposit the balance in the Treasury of the United States, in such manner as the Secretary of the Treasury directs. All funds held by the Secretary of the Treasury shall be invested in interest-bearing United States securities for later distribution with interest by the Copyright Royalty Tribunal as provided by this title. The Register shall submit to the Copyright Royalty Tribunal, on a semiannual basis, a compilation of all statements of account covering the relevant six-month period provided by clause (2) of this subsection.

(4) The royalty fees thus deposited shall, in accordance with the procedures provided by clause (5), be distributed to those among the following copyright owners who claim that their works were the subject of secondary transmissions by cable systems during the relevant semiannual period:

(A) any such owner whose work was included in a secondary transmission made by a cable system of a nonnetwork television program in whole or in part beyond the local service area of the primary transmitter; and

(B) any such owner whose work was included in a secondary transmission identified in a special statement of account deposited under clause (2)(A); and

(C) any such owner whose work was included in nonnetwork programming consisting exclusively of aural signals carried by a cable system in whole or in part beyond the local service area of the primary transmitter of such programs.

(5) The royalty fees thus deposited shall be distributed in accordance with the following procedures:

(A) During the month of July in each year, every person claiming to be entitled to compulsory license fees for secondary transmissions shall file a claim with the Copyright Royalty Tribunal, in accordance with requirements that the Tribunal shall prescribe by regulation. Notwithstanding any provisions of the antitrust laws, for purposes of this clause any claimants may agree among themselves as to the proportionate division of compulsory licensing fees among them, may lump their claims together and file them jointly or as a single claim, or may designate a common agent to receive payment on their behalf.

(B) After the first day of August of each year, the Copyright Royalty Tribunal shall determine whether there exists a controversy concerning the distribution of royalty fees. If the Tribunal determines that no such controversy exists, it shall, after deducting its reasonable administrative costs under this section, distribute such fees to the copyright owners entitled, or to their designated agents. If the Tribunal finds the existence of a controversy, it shall, pursuant to chapter 8 of this title, conduct a proceeding to determine the distribution of royalty fees.

(C) During the pendency of any proceeding under this subsection, the Copyright Royalty Tribunal shall withhold from distribution an amount sufficient to satisfy all claims with respect to which a controversy exists, but shall have discretion to proceed to distribute any amounts that are not in controversy.

(e) NONSIMULTANEOUS SECONDARY TRANSMISSIONS BY CABLE SYSTEMS.—

(1) Notwithstanding those provisions of the second paragraph of subsection (f) relating to nonsimultaneous secondary transmissions by a cable system, any such transmissions are actionable as an act of infringement under section 501, and are fully subject to the remedies provided by sections 502 through 506 and sections 509 and 510, unless—

(A) the program on the videotape is transmitted no more than one time to the cable system's subscribers; and

(B) the copyrighted program, episode, or motion picture videotape, including the commercials contained within such program, episode, or picture, is transmitted without deletion or editing; and

(C) an owner or officer of the cable system (i) prevents the duplication of the videotape while in the possession of the system, (ii) prevents unauthorized duplication while in the possession of the facility making the videotape for the system if the system owns or controls the facility, or takes reasonable precautions to prevent such duplication if it does not own or control the facility, (iii) takes adequate precautions to prevent duplication while the tape is being transported, and (iv) subject to clause (2), erases or destroys, or causes the erasure or destruction of, the videotape; and

(D) within forty-five days after the end of each calendar quarter, an owner or officer of the cable system executes an affidavit attesting (i) to the steps and precautions taken to prevent duplication of the videotape, and (ii) subject to clause (2), to the erasure or destruction of all videotapes made or used during such quarter; and

(E) such owner or officer places or causes each such affidavit, and affidavits received pursuant to clause (2)(C), to be placed in a file, open to public inspection, at such system's main office in the community where the transmission is made or in the nearest community where such system maintains an office; and

(F) the nonsimultaneous transmission is one that the cable system would be authorized to transmit under the rules, regulations, and authorizations of the Federal Communications Commission in effect at the time of the nonsimultaneous transmission if the transmission had been made simultaneously, except that this subclause shall not apply to inadvertent or accidental transmissions.

(2) If a cable system transfers to any person a videotape of a program nonsimultaneously transmitted by it, such transfer is actionable as an act of infringement under section 501, and is fully subject to the remedies provided by sections 502 through 506 and 509, except that, pursuant to a written, nonprofit contract providing for the equitable sharing of the costs of such videotape and its transfer, a videotape nonsimultaneously transmitted by it, in accordance with clause (1), may be transferred by one cable system in Alaska to another system in Alaska, by one cable system in Hawaii permitted to make such nonsimultaneous transmissions to another such cable system in Hawaii, or by one cable system in Guam, the Northern Mariana Islands, or the Trust Territory of the Pacific Islands, to another cable system in any of those three territories, if—

(A) each such contract is available for public inspection in the offices of the cable systems involved, and a copy of such contract is filed, within thirty days after such contract is entered into, with the Copyright Office (which Office shall make each such contract available for public inspection); and

(B) the cable system to which the videotape is transferred complies with clause (1)(A), (B), (C)(i), (iii), and (iv), and (D) through (F); and

(C) such system provides a copy of the affidavit required to be made in accordance with clause (1)(D) to each cable system making a previous nonsimultaneous transmission of the same videotape.

(3) This subsection shall not be construed to supersede the exclusivity protection provisions of any existing agreement, or any such agreement hereafter entered into, between a cable system and a television broadcast station in the area in which the cable system is located, or a network with which such station is affiliated.

(4) As used in this subsection, the term "videotape," and each of its variant forms, means the reproduction of the images and sounds of a program or programs broadcast by a television broadcast station licensed by the Federal Communications Commission, regardless of the nature of the material objects, such as tapes or films, in which the reproduction is embodied.

(f) DEFINITIONS.—As used in this section, the following terms and their variant forms mean the following:

A "primary transmission" is a transmission made to the public by the transmitting facility whose signals are being received and further transmitted by the secondary transmission service, regardless of where or when the performance or display was first transmitted.

A "secondary transmission" is the further transmitting of a primary transmission simultaneously with the primary transmission, or nonsimultaneously with the primary transmission if by a "cable system" not located in whole or in part within the boundary of the forty-eight contiguous States, Hawaii, or Puerto Rico: *Provided, however,* That a nonsimultaneous further transmission by a cable system located in Hawaii of a primary transmission shall be deemed to be a secondary transmission if the carriage of the television broadcast signal comprising such further transmission is permissible under the rules, regulations, or authorizations of the Federal Communications Commission.

A "cable system" is a facility, located in any State, Territory, Trust Territory, or Possession, that in whole or in part receives signals transmitted or programs broadcast by one or more television broadcast stations licensed by the Federal Communications Commission, and makes secondary transmissions of such signals or programs by wires, cables, or other communications channels to subscribing members of the public who pay for such service. For purposes of determining the royalty fee under subsection (d)(2), two or more cable systems in contiguous communities under common ownership or control or operating from one head-end shall be considered as one system.

The "local service area of a primary transmitter," in the case of a television broadcast station, comprises the area in which such station is entitled to insist upon its signal being retransmitted by a cable system pursuant to the rules, regulations, and authorizations of the Federal Communications Commission in effect on April 15, 1976, or in the case of a television broadcast station licensed by an appropriate governmental authority of Canada or Mexico, the area in which it would be entitled to insist upon its signal being retransmitted if it were a television broadcast station subject to such rules, regulations, and authorizations. The "local service area of a primary transmitter," in the case of a radio broadcast station, comprises the primary service area of such station, pursuant to the rules and regulations of the Federal Communications Commission.

A "distant signal equivalent" is the value assigned to the secondary transmission of any nonnetwork television programming carried by a cable system in whole or in part beyond the local service area of the primary transmitter of such programming. It is computed by assigning a value of one to each independent station and a value of one-quarter to each network station and noncommercial educational station for the nonnetwork programming so carried pursuant to the rules, regulations, and authorizations of the Federal Communications Commission. The foregoing values for independent, network, and noncommercial educational stations are subject, however, to the following exceptions and limitations. Where the rules and regulations of the Federal Communications Commission require a cable system to omit the further transmission of a particular program and such rules and regulations also permit the substitution of another program embodying a performance or display of a work in place of the omitted transmission, or where such rules and regulations in effect on the date of enactment of this Act permit a cable system, at its election, to effect such deletion and substitution of a nonlive program or to carry additional programs not transmitted by primary transmitters within whose local service area the cable system is located, no value shall be assigned for the substituted or additional program; where the rules, regulations, or authorizations of the Federal Communications Commission in effect on the date of enactment of this Act permit a cable system, at its election, to omit the further transmission of a particular program and such rules, regulations, or authorizations also permit the substitution of another program embodying a performance or display of a work in place of the omitted transmission, the value assigned for the substituted or additional program shall be, in the case of a live program, the value of one full distant signal equivalent multiplied by a fraction that has as its numerator the number of days in the year in which such substitution occurs and as its denominator the number of days in the year. In the case of a station carried pursuant to the late-night or specialty programming rules of the Federal Communications Commission, or a station carried on a part-time basis where full-time carriage is not possible because the cable system lacks the activated channel capacity to retransmit on a full-time basis all signals which it is authorized to carry, the values for independent, network, and noncommercial educational stations set forth above, as the case may be, shall be multiplied by a fraction which is equal to the ratio of the broadcast hours of such station carried by the cable system to the total broadcast hours of the station.

A "network station" is a television broadcast station that is owned or operated by, or affiliated with, one or more of the television networks in the United States providing nationwide transmissions, and that transmits a substantial part of the programming supplied by such networks for a substantial part of that station's typical broadcast day.

An "independent station" is a commercial television broadcast station other than a network station.

A "noncommercial educational station" is a television station that is a noncommercial educational broadcast station as defined in section 397 of title 47.

## § 112. Limitations on exclusive rights: Ephemeral recordings

(a) Notwithstanding the provisions of section 106, and except in the case of a motion picture or other audiovisual work, it is not an infringement of copyright for a transmitting organization entitled to transmit to the public a performance or display of a work, under a license or transfer of the copyright or under the limitations on exclusive rights in sound recordings specified by section 114(a), to make no more than one copy or phonorecord of a particular transmission program embodying the performance or display, if—

(1) the copy or phonorecord is retained and used solely by the transmitting organization that made it, and no further copies or phonorecords are reproduced from it; and

(2) the copy or phonorecord is used solely for the transmitting organization's own transmissions within its local service area, or for purposes of archival preservation or security; and

(3) unless preserved exclusively for archival purposes, the copy or phonorecord is destroyed within six months from the date the transmission program was first transmitted to the public.

(b) Notwithstanding the provisions of section 106, it is not an infringement of copyright for a governmental body or other nonprofit organization entitled to transmit a performance or display of a work, under section 110(2) or under the limitations on exclusive rights in sound recordings specified by section 114(a), to make no more than thirty copies or phonorecords of a particular transmission program embodying the performance or display, if—

(1) no further copies or phonorecords are reproduced from the copies or phonorecords made under this clause; and

(2) except for one copy or phonorecord that may be preserved exclusively for archival purposes, the copies or phonorecords are destroyed within seven years from the date the transmission program was first transmitted to the public.

(c) Notwithstanding the provisions of section 106, it is not an infringement of copyright for a governmental body or other nonprofit organization to make for distribution no more than one copy or phonorecord, for each transmitting organization specified in clause (2) of this subsection, of a particular transmission program embodying a performance of a nondramatic musical work of a religious nature, or of a sound recording of such a musical work, if—

(1) there is no direct or indirect change for making or distributing any such copies or phonorecords; and

(2) none of such copies or phonorecords is used for any performance other than a single transmission to the public by a transmitting organization entitled to transmit to the public a performance of the work under a license or transfer of the copyright; and

(3) except for one copy or phonorecord that may be preserved exclusively for archival purposes, the copies or phonorecords are all destroyed within one year from the date the transmission program was first transmitted to the public.

(d) Notwithstanding the provisions of section 106, it is not an infringement of copyright for a governmental body or other nonprofit organization entitled to transmit a performance of a work under section 110(8) to make no more than ten copies or phonorecords embodying the performance, or to permit the use of any such copy or phonorecord by any governmental body or nonprofit organization entitled to transmit a performance of a work under section 110(8), if—

(1) any such copy or phonorecord is retained and used solely by the organization that made it, or by a governmental body or nonprofit organization entitled to transmit a performance of a work under section 110(8), and no further copies or phonorecords are reproduced from it; and

(2) any such copy or phonorecord is used solely for transmissions authorized under section 110(8), or for purposes of archival preservation or security; and

(3) the governmental body or nonprofit organization permitting any use of any such copy or phonorecord by any governmental body or nonprofit organization under this subsection does not make any charge for such use.

(e) The transmission program embodied in a copy or phonorecord made under this section is not subject to protection as a derivative work under this title except with the express consent of the owners of copyright in the preexisting works employed in the program.

### § 113. Scope of exclusive rights in pictorial, graphic, and sculptural works

(a) Subject to the provisions of subsections (b) and (c) of this section, the exclusive right to reproduce a copyrighted pictorial, graphic, or sculptural work in copies under section 106 includes the right to reproduce the work in or on any kind of article, whether useful or otherwise.

(b) This title does not afford, to the owner of copyright in a work that portrays a useful article as such, any greater or lesser rights with respect to the making, distribution, or display of the useful article so portrayed than those afforded to such works under the law, whether title 17 or the common law or statutes of a State, in effect on December 31, 1977, as held applicable and construed by a court in an action brought under this title.

(c) In the case of a work lawfully reproduced in useful articles that have been offered for sale or other distribution to the public, copyright does not include any right to prevent the making, distribution, or display of pictures or photographs of such articles in connection with advertisements or commentaries related to the distribution or display of such articles, or in connection with news reports.

### § 114. Scope of exclusive rights in sound recordings

(a) The exclusive rights of the owner of copyright in a sound recording are limited to the rights specified by clauses (1), (2), and (3) of section 106, and do not include any right of performance under section 106(4).

(b) The exclusive right of the owner of copyright in a sound recording under clause (1) of section 106 is limited to the right to duplicate the sound recording in the form of phonorecords, or of copies of motion pictures and other audiovisual works, that directly or indirectly recapture the actual sounds fixed in the recording. The exclusive right of the owner of copyright in a sound recording under clause (2) of section 106 is limited to the right to prepare a derivative work in which the actual sounds fixed in the sound recording are rearranged, remixed, or otherwise altered in sequence or quality. The exclusive rights of the owner of copyright in a sound recording under clauses (1) and (2) of section 106 do not extend to the making or duplication of another sound recording that consists entirely of an independent fixation of other sounds, even though such sounds imitate or simulate those in the copyrighted sound recording. The exclusive rights of the owner of copyright in a sound recording under clauses (1), (2), and (3) of section 106 do not apply to sound recordings included in educational television and radio programs (as defined in section 397 of title 47) distributed or transmitted by or through public broadcasting entities (as defined by section 118(g)): *Provided*, That copies or phonorecords of said programs are not commercially distributed by or through public broadcasting entities to the general public.

(c) This section does not limit or impair the exclusive right to perform publicly, by means of a phonorecord, any of the works specified by section 106(4).

(d) On January 3, 1978, the Register of Copyrights, after consulting with representatives of owners of copyrighted materials, representatives of the broadcasting, recording, motion picture, entertainment industries, and arts organizations, representatives of organized labor and performers of copyrighted materials, shall submit to the Congress a report setting forth recommendations as to whether this section should be amended to provide for performers and copyright owners of copyrighted material any performance rights in such material. The report should describe the status of such rights in foreign countries, the views of major interested parties, and specific legislative or other recommendations, if any.

### § 115. Scope of exclusive rights in nondramatic musical works: Compulsory license for making and distributing phonorecords

In the case of nondramatic musical works, the exclusive rights provided by clauses (1) and (3) of section 106, to make and to distribute phonorecords of such works, are subject to compulsory licensing under the conditions specified by this section.

(a) AVAILABILITY AND SCOPE OF COMPULSORY LICENSE.—

(1) When phonorecords of a nondramatic musical work have been distributed to the public in the United States under the authority of the copyright owner, any other person may, by complying with the provisions of this section, obtain a compulsory license to make and distribute phonorecords of the work. A person may obtain a compulsory license only if his or her primary purpose in making phonorecords is to distribute them to the public for private use. A person may not obtain a compulsory license for use of the work in the making of phonorecords duplicating a sound recording fixed by another, unless: (i) such sound recording was fixed lawfully; and (ii) the making of the phonorecords was authorized by the owner of copyright in the sound recording or, if the sound recording was fixed before February 15, 1972, by any person who fixed the sound recording pursuant to an express license from the owner of the copyright in the musical work or pursuant to a valid compulsory license for use of such work in a sound recording.

(2) A compulsory license includes the privilege of making a musical arrangement of the work to the extent necessary to conform it to the style or manner of interpretation of the performance involved, but the arrangement shall not change the basic melody or fundamental character of the work, and shall not be subject to protection as a derivative work under this title, except with the express consent of the copyright owner.

(b) NOTICE OF INTENTION TO OBTAIN COMPULSORY LICENSE—

(1) Any person who wishes to obtain a compulsory license under this section shall, before or within thirty days after making, and before distributing any phonorecords of the work, serve notice of intention to do so on the copyright owner. If the registration or other public records of the Copyright Office do not identify the copyright owner and include an address at which notice can be served, it shall be sufficient to file the notice of intention in the Copyright Office. The notice shall comply, in form, content, and manner of service, with requirements that the Register of Copyrights shall prescribe by regulation.

(2) Failure to serve or file the notice required by clause (1) forecloses the possibility of a compulsory license and, in the absence of a negotiated license, renders the making and distribution of phonorecords actionable as acts of infringement under section 501 and fully subject to the remedies provided by sections 502 through 506 and 509.

(c) ROYALTY PAYABLE UNDER COMPULSORY LICENSE.—

(1) To be entitled to receive royalties under a compulsory license, the copyright owner must be identified in the registration or other public records of the Copyright Office. The owner is entitled to royalties for phonorecords made and distributed after being so identified, but is not entitled to recover for any phonorecords previously made and distributed.

(2) Except as provided by clause (1), the royalty under a compulsory license shall be payable for every phonorecord made and distributed in accordance with the license. For this purpose, a phonorecord is considered "distributed" if the person exercising the compulsory license has voluntarily and permanently parted with its possession. With respect to each work embodied in the phonorecord, the royalty shall be either five cents, or 0.95 cent per minute of playing time or fraction thereof, whichever amount is larger.*

(3) **A compulsory license under this section includes the right of the maker of a phonorecord of a nondramatic musical work under subsection (a)(1) to distribute or authorize distribution of such phonorecord by rental, lease, or lending (or by acts or practices in the nature of rental, lease, or lending). In addition to any royalty payable under clause (2) and chapter 8 of this title, a royalty shall be payable by the compulsory licensee for every act of distribution of a phonorecord by or in the nature of rental, lease, or lending, by or under the authority of the compulsory licensee. With respect to each nondramatic, musical work embodied in the phonorecord, the royalty shall be a proportion of the revenue received by the compulsory licensee from every such act of distribution of the phonorecord under this clause equal to the proportion of the revenue received by the compulsory licensee from distribution of the phonorecord under clause (2) that is payable by a compulsory licensee under that clause and under chapter 8. The Register of Copyrights shall issue regulations to carry out the purpose of this clause.

(4) Royalty payments shall be made on or before the twentieth day of each month and shall include all royalties for the month next preceding. Each monthly payment shall be made under oath and shall comply with requirements that the Register of Copyrights shall prescribe by regulation. The Register shall also prescribe regulations under which detailed cumulative annual statements of account, certified by a certified public accountant, shall be filed for every compulsory license under this

---

*The fees specified here reflect the adjustments made by the Copyright Royalty Tribunal. See 37 C.F.R. § 307.3.

**Paragraphs (3) and (4) of § 115(c) as originally enacted were redesignated as paragraphs (4) and (5), and paragraph (3) was added, by section 3 of Pub. L. No. 98-450, 98 Stat. 1727, the "Record Rental Amendment of 1984," effective Oct. 4, 1984. In addition, § 4 of Pub. L. No. 98-450, provided that "(c) The amendments made by this Act shall not apply to rentals, leasings, lendings (or acts or practices in the nature of rentals, leasings, or lendings) occurring after the date which is five years after the date of the enactment of this Act."

section. The regulations covering both the monthly and the annual statements of account shall prescribe the form, content, and manner of certification with respect to the number of records made and the number of records distributed.

(5) If the copyright owner does not receive the monthly payment and the monthly and annual statements of account when due, the owner may give written notice to the licensee that, unless the default is remedied within thirty days from the date of the notice, the compulsory license will be automatically terminated. Such termination renders either the making or the distribution, or both, of all phonorecords for which the royalty had not been paid, actionable as acts of infringement under section 501 and fully subject to the remedies provided by sections 502 through 506 and 509.

### § 116. Scope of exclusive rights in nondramatic musical works: Public performances by means of coin-operated phonorecord players

(a) LIMITATION ON EXCLUSIVE RIGHT.—In the case of a nondramatic musical work embodied in a phonorecord, the exclusive right under clause (4) of section 106 to perform the work publicly by means of a coin-operated phonorecord player is limited as follows:

(1) The proprietor of the establishment in which the public performance takes place is not liable for infringement with respect to such public performance unless—

(A)  such proprietor is the operator of the phonorecord player; or

(B)  such proprietor refuses or fails, within one month after receipt by registered or certified mail of a request, at a time during which the certificate required by clause (1)(C) of subsection (b) is not affixed to the phonorecord player, by the copyright owner, to make full disclosure, by registered or certified mail, of the identity of the operator of the phonorecord player.

(2) The operator of the coin-operated phonorecord player may obtain a compulsory license to perform the work publicly on that phonorecord player by filing the application, affixing the certificate, and paying the royalties provided by subsection (b).

(b) RECORDATION OF COIN-OPERATED PLAYER, AFFIXATION OF CERTIFICATE, AND ROYALTY PAYABLE UNDER COMPULSORY LICENSE.—

(1) Any operator who wishes to obtain a compulsory license for the public performance of works on a coin-operated phonorecord player shall fulfill the following requirements:

(A) Before or within one month after such performances are made available on a particular phonorecord player, and during the month of January in each succeeding year that such performances are made available on that particular phonorecord player, the operator shall file in the Copyright Office, in accordance with requirements that the Register of Copyrights, after consultation with the Copyright Royalty Tribunal (if and when the Tribunal has been constituted), shall prescribe by regulation, an application containing the name and address of the operator of the phonorecord player and the manufacturer and serial number or other explicit identification of the phonorecord player, and deposit with the Register of Copyrights a royalty fee for the current calendar year of $50 for that particular phonorecord player.* If such performances are made available on a particular phonorecord player for the first time after July 1 of any year, the compulsory license fee shall be one half of the annual rate.**

(B) Within twenty days of receipt of an application and a royalty fee pursuant to subclause (A), the Register of Copyrights shall issue to the applicant a certificate for the phonorecord player.

(C) On or before March 1 of the year in which the certificate prescribed by subclause (B) of this clause is issued, or within ten days after the date of issue of the certificate, the operator shall affix to the particular phonorecord player, in a position where it can be readily examined by the public, the certificate, issued by the Register of Copyrights under subclause (B), of the latest application made by such operator under subclause (A) of this clause with respect to that phonorecord player.

(2) Failure to file the application, to affix the certificate, or to pay the royalty required by clause (1) of this subsection renders the public performance actionable as an act of infringement under section 501 and fully subject to the remedies provided by sections 502 through 506 and 509.

(c) DISTRIBUTION OF ROYALTIES.—

(1) The Register of Copyrights shall receive all fees deposited under this section and, after deducting the reasonable costs incurred by the Copyright Office under this section, shall deposit the balance in the Treasury of the United States, in such manner as the Secretary of the Treasury directs. All funds held by the Secretary of the Treasury shall be invested in interest-bearing United States securities for later distribution with interest by the Copyright Royalty Tribunal as provided by this title. The Register shall submit to the Copyright Royalty Tribunal, on an annual basis, a detailed statement of account covering all fees received for the relevant period provided by subsection (b).

(2) During the month of January in each year, every person claiming to be entitled to compulsory license fees under this section for performances during the preceding twelve-month period shall file a claim with the Copyright Royalty Tribunal, in accordance with requirements that the Tribunal shall prescribe by regulation. Such claim shall include an agreement to accept as final, except as provided in section 810 of this title, the determination of the Copyright Royalty Tribunal in any controversy concerning the distribution of royalty fees deposited under subclause (A) of subsection (b)(1) of this section to which the claimant is a party. Notwithstanding any provisions of the antitrust laws, for purposes of this subsection any claimants may agree among themselves as to the proportionate division of compulsory licensing fees among them,

---

*The fee specified here reflects the adjustment made by the Copyright Royalty Tribunal. See 37 C.F.R. § 306.3.

**The concluding portion of this sentence has been altered by the author to conform it with the adjustment made by the Copyright Royalty Tribunal. See 37 C.F.R. § 306.3(c).

may lump their claims together and file them jointly or as a single claim, or may designate a common agent to receive payment on their behalf.

(3) After the first day of October of each year, the Copyright Royalty Tribunal shall determine whether there exists a controversy concerning the distribution of royalty fees deposited under subclause (A) of subsection (b)(1). If the Tribunal determines that no such controversy exists, it shall, after deducting its reasonable administrative costs under this section, distribute such fees to the copyright owners entitled, or to their designated agents. If it finds that such a controversy exists, it shall, pursuant to chapter 8 of this title, conduct a proceeding to determine the distribution of royalty fees.

(4) The fees to be distributed shall be divided as follows:

(A) to every copyright owner not affiliated with a performing rights society, the pro rata share of the fees to be distributed to which such copyright owner proves entitlement.

(B) to the performing rights societies, the remainder of the fees to be distributed in such pro rata shares as they shall by agreement stipulate among themselves, or, if they fail to agree, the pro rata share to which such performing rights societies prove entitlement.

(C) during the pendency of any proceeding under this section, the Copyright Royalty Tribunal shall withhold from distribution an amount sufficient to satisfy all claims with respect to which a controversy exists, but shall have discretion to proceed to distribute any amounts that are not in controversy.

(5) The Copyright Royalty Tribunal shall promulgate regulations under which persons who can reasonably be expected to have claims may, during the year in which performances take place, without expense to or harassment of operators or proprietors of establishments in which phonorecord players are located, have such access to such establishments and to the phonorecord players located therein and such opportunity to obtain information with respect thereto as may be reasonably necessary to determine, by sampling procedures or otherwise, the proportion of contribution of the musical works of each such person to the earnings of the phonorecord players for which fees shall have been deposited. Any person who alleges that he or she has been denied the access permitted under the regulations prescribed by the Copyright Royalty Tribunal may bring an action in the United States District Court for the District of Columbia for the cancellation of the compulsory license of the phonorecord player to which such access has been denied, and the court shall have the power to declare the compulsory license thereof invalid from the date of issue thereof.

(d) CRIMINAL PENALTIES.—Any person who knowingly makes a false representation of a material fact in an application filed under clause (1)(A) of subsection (b), or who knowingly alters a certificate issued under clause (1)(B) of subsection (b) or knowingly affixes such a certificate to a phonorecord player other than the one it covers, shall be fined not more than $2,500.

(e) DEFINITIONS.—As used in this section, the following terms and their variant forms mean the following:

(1) A "coin-operated phonorecord player" is a machine or device that—

(A) is employed solely for the performance of nondramatic musical works by means of phonorecords upon being activated by insertion of coins, currency, tokens, or other monetary units or their equivalent;

(B) is located in an establishment making no direct or indirect charge for admission;

(C) is accompanied by a list of the titles of all the musical works available for performance on it, which list is affixed to the phonorecord player or posted in the establishment in a prominent position where it can be readily examined by the public; and

(D) affords a choice of works available for performance and permits the choice to be made by the patrons of the establishment in which it is located.

(2) An "operator" is any person who, alone or jointly with others:

(A) owns a coin-operated phonorecord player; or

(B) has the power to make a coin-operated phonorecord player available for placement in an establishment for purposes of public performance; or

(C) has the power to exercise primary control over the selection of the musical works made available for public performance on a coin-operated phonorecord player.

(3) A "performing rights society" is an association or corporation that licenses the public performance of nondramatic musical works on behalf of the copyright owners, such as the American Society of Composers, Authors and Publishers, Broadcast Music, Inc., and SESAC, Inc.

## § 117. Limitations on exclusive rights: Computer programs*

Notwithstanding the provisions of section 106, it is not an infringement for the owner of a copy of a computer program to make or authorize the making of another copy or adaptation of that computer program provided:

(1) that such a new copy or adaptation is created as an essential step in the utilization of the computer program in conjunction with a machine and that it is used in no other manner, or

(2) that such new copy or adaptation is for archival purposes only and that all archival copies are destroyed in the event that continued possession of the computer program should cease to be rightful.

Any exact copies prepared in accordance with the provisions of this section may be leased, sold, or otherwise transferred, along with the copy from which such copies were prepared, only as part of the lease, sale, or other transfer of all rights in the program. Adaptations so prepared may be transferred only with the authorization of the copyright owner.

---

*This section reads as amended by Pub. L. No. 96-517, § 10, 94 Stat. 3028, Dec. 12, 1980. As originally enacted in 1976, the section had read as follows: "Notwithstanding the provisions of sections 106 through 116 and 118, this title does not afford to the owner of copyright in a work any greater or lesser rights with respect to the use of the work in conjunction with automatic systems capable of storing, processing, retrieving, or transferring information, or in conjunction with any similar device, machine, or process, than those afforded to works under the law, whether title 17 of the common law or statutes of a State, in effect on December 31, 1977, as held applicable and construed by a court in an action brought under this title."

## § 118. Scope of exclusive rights: Use of certain works in connection with noncommercial broadcasting

(a) The exclusive rights provided by section 106 shall, with respect to the works specified by subsection (b) and the activities specified by subsection (d), be subject to the conditions and limitations prescribed by this section.

(b) Not later than thirty days after the Copyright Royalty Tribunal has been constituted in accordance with section 802, the Chairman of the Tribunal shall cause notice to be published in the Federal Register of the initiation of proceedings for the purpose of determining reasonable terms and rates of royalty payments for the activities specified by subsection (d) with respect to published nondramatic musical works and published pictorial, graphic, and sculptural works during a period beginning as provided in clause (3) of this subsection and ending on December 31, 1982. Copyright owners and public broadcasting entities shall negotiate in good faith and cooperate fully with the Tribunal in an effort to reach reasonable and expeditious results. Notwithstanding any provision of the antitrust laws, any owners of copyright in works specified by this subsection and any public broadcasting entities, respectively, may negotiate and agree upon the terms and rates of royalty payments and the proportionate division of fees paid among various copyright owners, and may designate common agents to negotiate, agree to, pay, or receive payments.

(1) Any owner of copyright in a work specified in this subsection or any public broadcasting entity may, within one hundred and twenty days after publication of the notice specified in this subsection, submit to the Copyright Royalty Tribunal proposed licenses covering such activities with respect to such works. The Copyright Royalty Tribunal shall proceed on the basis of the proposals submitted to it as well as any other relevant information. The Copyright Royalty Tribunal shall permit any interested party to submit information relevant to such proceedings.

(2) License agreements voluntarily negotiated at any time between one or more copyright owners and one or more public broadcasting entities shall be given effect in lieu of any determination by the Tribunal: *Provided*, That copies of such agreements are filed in the Copyright Office within thirty days of execution in accordance with regulations that the Register of Copyrights shall prescribe.

(3) Within six months, but not earlier than one hundred and twenty days, from the date of publication of the notice specified in this subsection the Copyright Royalty Tribunal shall make a determination and publish in the Federal Register a schedule of rates and terms which, subject to clause (2) of this subsection, shall be binding on all owners of copyright in works specified by this subsection and public broadcasting entities, regardless of whether or not such copyright owners and public broadcasting entities have submitted proposals to the Tribunal. In establishing such rates and terms the Copyright Royalty Tribunal may consider the rates for comparable circumstances under voluntary license agreements negotiated as provided in clause (2) of this subsection. The Copyright Royalty Tribunal shall also establish requirements by which copyright owners may receive reasonable notice of the use of their works under this section, and under which records of such use shall be kept by public broadcasting entities.

(4) With respect to the period beginning on the effective date of this title and ending on the date of publication of such rates and terms, this title shall not afford to owners of copyright or public broadcasting entities any greater or lesser rights with respect to the activities specified in subsection (d) as applied to works specified in this subsection than those afforded under the law in effect on December 31, 1977, as held applicable and construed by a court in an action brought under this title.

(c) The initial procedure specified in subsection (b) shall be repeated and concluded between June 30 and December 31, 1982, and at five-year intervals thereafter, in accordance with regulations that the Copyright Royalty Tribunal shall prescribe.

(d) Subject to the transitional provisions of subsection (b)(4), and to the terms of any voluntary license agreements that have been negotiated as provided by subsection (b)(2), a public broadcasting entity may, upon compliance with the provisions of this section, including the rates and terms established by the Copyright Royalty Tribunal under subsection (b)(3), engage in the following activities with respect to published nondramatic musical works and published pictorial, graphic, and sculptural works:

(1) performance or display of a work by or in the course of a transmission made by a noncommercial educational broadcast station referred to in subsection (g); and

(2) production of a transmission program, reproduction of copies or phonorecords of such a transmission program, and distribution of such copies or phonorecords, where such production, reproduction, or distribution is made by a nonprofit institution or organization solely for the purpose of transmissions specified in clause (1); and

(3) the making of reproductions by a governmental body or a nonprofit institution of a transmission program simultaneously with its transmission as specified in clause (1), and the performance or display of the contents of such program under the conditions specified by clause (1) of section 110, but only if the reproductions are used for performances or displays for a period of no more than seven days from the date of the transmission specified in clause (1), and are destroyed before or at the end of such period. No person supplying, in accordance with clause (2), a reproduction of a transmission program to governmental bodies or nonprofit institutions under this clause shall have any liability as a result of failure of such body or institution to destroy such reproduction: *Provided*, That it shall have notified such body or institution of the requirement for such destruction pursuant to this clause: *And provided further*, That if such body or institution itself fails to destroy such reproduction it shall be deemed to have infringed.

(e) Except as expressly provided in this subsection, this section shall have no applicability to works other than those specified in subsection (b).

(1) Owners of copyright in nondramatic literary works and public broadcasting entities may, during the course of voluntary negotiations, agree among themselves, respectively, as the terms and rates of royalty payments without liability under the antitrust laws. Any such terms and rates of royalty payments shall be effective upon filing in the Copyright Office, in accordance with regulations that the Register of Copyrights shall prescribe.

(2) On January 3, 1980, the Register of Copyrights, after consulting with authors and other owners of copyright in nondramatic literary works and their representatives, and with public broadcasting entities and their representatives, shall submit to the Congress a report setting forth the extent to which voluntary licensing arrangements have been reached with respect to the use of nondramatic literary works by such broadcast stations. The report should also describe any problems that may have arisen, and present legislative or other recommendations, if warranted.

(f) Nothing in this section shall be construed to permit, beyond the limits of fair use as provided by section 107, the unauthorized dramatization of a nondramatic musical work, the production of a transmission program drawn to any substantial extent from a published compilation of pictorial, graphic, or sculptural works, or the unauthorized use of any portion of an audiovisual work.

(g) As used in this section, the term "public broadcasting entity" means a noncommercial educational broadcast station as defined in section 397 of title 47 and any nonprofit institution or organization engaged in the activities described in clause (2) of subsection (d).

## Chapter 2—Copyright Ownership and Transfer

## § 201. Ownership of copyright

(a) INITIAL OWNERSHIP.—Copyright in a work protected under this title vests initially in the author or authors of the work. The authors of a joint work are coowners of copyright in the work.

(b) WORKS MADE FOR HIRE.—In the case of a work made for hire, the employer or other person for whom the work was prepared is considered the author for purposes of this title, and, unless the parties have expressly agreed otherwise in a written instrument signed by them, owns all of the rights comprised in the copyright.

(c) CONTRIBUTIONS TO COLLECTIVE WORKS.—Copyright in each separate contribution to a collective work is distinct from copyright in the collective work as a whole, and vests initially in the author of the contribution. In the absence of an express transfer of the copyright or of any rights under it, the owner of copyright in the collective work is presumed to have acquired only the privilege of reproducing and distributing the contribution as part of that particular collective work, any revision of that collective work, and any later collective work in the same series.

(d) TRANSFER OF OWNERSHIP.—

(1) The ownership of a copyright may be transferred in whole or in part by any means of conveyance or by operation of law, and may be

bequeathed by will or pass as personal property by the applicable laws of intestate succession.

(2) Any of the exclusive rights comprised in a copyright, including any subdivision of any of the rights specified by section 106, may be transferred as provided by clause (1) and owned separately. The owner of any particular exclusive right is entitled, to the extent of that right, to all of the protection and remedies accorded to the copyright owner by this title.

(e) INVOLUNTARY TRANSFER.—When an individual author's ownership of a copyright, or of any of the exclusive rights under a copyright, has not previously been transferred voluntarily by that individual author, no action by any governmental body or other official or organization purporting to seize, expropriate, transfer, or exercise rights of ownership with respect to the copyright, or any of the exclusive rights under a copyright, shall be given effect under this title except as provided under Title 11.*

## § 202. Ownership of copyright as distinct from ownership of material object

Ownership of a copyright, or of any of the exclusive rights under a copyright, is distinct from ownership of any material object in which the work is embodied. Transfer of ownership of any material object, including the copy or phonorecord in which the work is first fixed, does not of itself convey any rights in the copyrighted work embodied in the object; nor, in the absence of an agreement, does transfer of ownership of a copyright or of any exclusive rights under a copyright convey property rights in any material object.

## § 203. Termination of transfers and licenses granted by the author

(a) CONDITIONS FOR TERMINATION.—In the case of any work other than a work made for hire, the exclusive or nonexclusive grant of a transfer or license of copyright or of any right under a copyright, executed by the author on or after January 1, 1978, otherwise than by will, is subject to termination under the following conditions:

(1) In the case of a grant executed by one author, termination of the grant may be effected by that author or, if the author is dead, by the person or persons who, under clause (2) of this subsection, own and are entitled to exercise a total of more than one-half of that author's termination interest. In the case of a grant executed by two or more authors of a joint work, termination of the grant may be effected by a majority of the authors who executed it; if any of such authors is dead, the termination interest of any such author may be exercised as a unit by the person or persons who, under clause (2) of this subsection, own and are entitled to exercise a total of more than one-half of that author's interest.

(2) Where an author is dead, his or her termination interest is owned, and may be exercised, by his widow or her widower and his or her children or grandchildren as follows:

---

*The phrase "except as provided under Title 11" was added to the end of the sentence by § 313 of Pub. L. No. 95-598 in 1978.

(A) the widow or widower owns the author's entire termination interest unless there are any surviving children or grandchildren of the author, in which case the widow or widower owns one-half of the author's interest;

(B) the author's surviving children, and the surviving children of any dead child of the author, own the author's entire termination interest unless there is a widow or widower, in which case the ownership of one-half of the author's interest is divided among them;

(C) the rights of the author's children and grandchildren are in all cases divided among them and exercised on a per stirpes basis according to the number of such author's children represented; the share of the children of a dead child in a termination interest can be exercised only by the action of a majority of them.

(3) Termination of the grant may be effected at any time during a period of five years beginning at the end of thirty-five years from the date of execution of the grant; or, if the grant covers the right of publication of the work, the period begins at the end of thirty-five years from the date of publication of the work under the grant or at the end of forty years from the date of execution of the grant, whichever term ends earlier.

(4) The termination shall be effected by serving an advance notice in writing, signed by the number and proportion of owners of termination interests required under clauses (1) and (2) of this subsection, or by their duly authorized agents, upon the grantee or the grantee's successor in title.

(A) The notice shall state the effective date of the termination, which shall fall within the five-year period specified by clause (3) of this subsection, and the notice shall be served not less than two or more than ten years before that date. A copy of the notice shall be recorded in the Copyright Office before the effective date of termination, as a condition to its taking effect.

(B) The notice shall comply, in form, content, and manner of service, with requirements that the Register of Copyrights shall prescribe by regulation.

(5) Termination of the grant may be effected notwithstanding any agreement to the contrary, including an agreement to make a will or to make any future grant.

(b) EFFECT OF TERMINATION.—Upon the effective date of termination, all rights under this title that were covered by the terminated grants revert to the author, authors, and other persons owning termination interests under clauses (1) and (2) of subsection (a), including those owners who did not join in signing the notice of termination under clause (4) of subsection (a), but with the following limitations:

(1) A derivative work prepared under authority of the grant before its termination may continue to be utilized under the terms of the grant after its termination, but this privilege does not extend to the preparation after the termination of other derivative works based upon the copyrighted work covered by the terminated grant.

(2) The future rights that will revert upon termination of the grant become vested on the date the notice of termination has been served as provided by clause (4) of subsection (a). The rights vest in the author,

authors, and other persons named in, and in the proportionate shares provided by, clauses (1) and (2) of subsection (a).

(3) Subject to the provisions of clause (4) of this subsection, a further grant, or agreement to make a further grant, of any right covered by a terminated grant is valid only if it is signed by the same number and proportion of the owners, in whom the right has vested under clause (2) of this subsection, as are required to terminate the grant under clauses (1) and (2) of subsection (a). Such further grant or agreement is effective with respect to all of the persons in whom the right it covers has vested under clause (2) of this subsection, including those who did not join in signing it. If any person dies after rights under a terminated grant have vested in him or her, that person's legal representatives, legatees, or heirs at law represent him or her for purposes of this clause.

(4) A further grant, or agreement to make a further grant, of any right covered by a terminated grant is valid only if it is made after the effective date of the termination. As an exception, however, an agreement for such a further grant may be made between the persons provided by clause (3) of this subsection and the original grantee or such grantee's successor in title, after the notice of termination has been served as provided by clause (4) of subsection (a).

(5) Termination of a grant under this section affects only those rights covered by the grants that arise under this title, and in no way affects rights arising under any other Federal, State, or foreign laws.

(6) Unless and until termination is effected under this section, the grant, if it does not provide otherwise, continues in effect for the term of copyright provided by this title.

## § 204. Execution of transfers of copyright ownership

(a) A transfer of copyright ownership, other than by operation of law, is not valid unless an instrument of conveyance, or a note or memorandum of the transfer, is in writing and signed by the owner of the rights conveyed or such owner's duly authorized agent.

(b) A certificate of acknowledgement is not required for the validity of a transfer, but is prima facie evidence of the execution of the transfer if—

(1) in the case of a transfer executed in the United States, the certificate is issued by a person authorized to administer oaths within the United States; or

(2) in the case of a transfer executed in a foreign country, the certificate is issued by a diplomatic or consular officer of the United States, or by a person authorized to administer oaths whose authority is proved by a certificate of such an officer.

## § 205. Recordation of transfers and other documents

(a) CONDITIONS FOR RECORDATION.—Any transfer of copyright ownership or other document pertaining to a copyright may be recorded in the Copyright Office if the document filed for recordation bears the actual signature of the person who executed it, or if it is accompanied by a sworn official certification that it is a true copy of the original, signed document.

(b) CERTIFICATE OF RECORDATION.—The Register of Copyrights shall, upon receipt of a document as provided by subsection (a) and of the fee provided by section 708, record the document and return it with a certificate of recordation.

(c) RECORDATION AS CONSTRUCTIVE NOTICE.—Recordation of a document in the Copyright Office gives all persons constructive notice of the facts stated in the recorded document, but only if—

(1) the document, or material attached to it, specifically identifies the work to which it pertains so that, after the document is indexed by the Register of Copyrights, it would be revealed by a reasonable search under the title or registration number of the work; and

(2) registration has been made for the work.

(d) RECORDATION AS PREREQUISITE TO INFRINGEMENT SUIT.—No person claiming by virtue of a transfer to be the owner of copyright or of any exclusive right under a copyright is entitled to institute an infringement action under this title until the instrument of transfer under which such person claims has been recorded in the Copyright Office, but suit may be instituted after such recordation on a cause of action that arose before recordation.

(e) PRIORITY BETWEEN CONFLICTING TRANSFERS.—As between two conflicting transfers, the one executed first prevails if it is recorded, in the manner required to give constructive notice under subsection (c), within one month after its execution in the United States or within two months after its execution outside the United States, or at any time before recordation in such manner of the later transfer. Otherwise the later transfer prevails if recorded first in such manner, and if taken in good faith, for valuable consideration or on the basis of a binding promise to pay royalties, and without notice of the earlier transfer.

(f) PRIORITY BETWEEN CONFLICTING TRANSFER OF OWNERSHIP AND NON-EXCLUSIVE LICENSE.—A nonexclusive license, whether recorded or not, prevails over a conflicting transfer of copyright ownership if the license is evidenced by a written instrument signed by the owner of the rights licensed or such owner's duly authorized agent, and if—

(1) the license was taken before execution of the transfer; or

(2) the license was taken in good faith before recordation of the transfer and without notice of it.

## Chapter 3—Duration of Copyright

## § 301. Preemption with respect to other laws

(a) On and after January 1, 1978, all legal or equitable rights that are equivalent to any of the exclusive rights within the general scope of copyright as specified by section 106 in works of authorship that are fixed in a tangible medium of expression and come within the subject matter of copyright as specified by sections 102 and 103, whether created before or after that date and whether published or unpublished, are governed exclusively by this title. Thereafter, no person is entitled to any such right or equivalent right in any such work under the common law or statutes of any State.

(b) Nothing in this title annuls or limits any rights or remedies under the common law or statutes of any State with respect to—

(1) subject matter that does not come within the subject matter of copyright as specified by sections 102 and 103, including works of authorship not fixed in any tangible medium of expression; or

(2) any cause of action arising from undertakings commenced before January 1, 1978; or

(3) activities violating legal or equitable rights that are not equivalent to any of the exclusive rights within the general scope of copyright as specified by section 106.

(c) With respect to sound recordings fixed before February 15, 1972, any rights or remedies under the common law or statutes of any State shall not be annulled or limited by this title until February 15, 2047. The preemptive provisions of subsection (a) shall apply to any such rights and remedies pertaining to any cause of action arising from undertakings commenced on and after February 15, 2047. Notwithstanding the provisions of section 303, no sound recording fixed before February 15, 1972, shall be subject to copyright under this title before, on, or after February 15, 2047.

(d) Nothing in this title annuls or limits any rights to remedies under any other Federal statute.

## § 302. Duration of copyright: Works created on or after January 1, 1978

(a) IN GENERAL.—Copyright in a work created on or after January 1, 1978, subsists from its creation and, except as provided by the following subsections, endures for a term consisting of the life of the author and fifty years after the author's death.

(b) JOINT WORKS.—In the case of a joint work prepared by two or more authors who did not work for hire, the copyright endures for a term consisting of the life of the last surviving author and fifty years after such last surviving author's death.

(c) ANONYMOUS WORKS, PSEUDONYMOUS WORKS, AND WORKS MADE FOR HIRE.—In the case of an anonymous work, a pseudonymous work, or a work made for hire, the copyright endures for a term of seventy-five years from the year of its first publication, or a term of one hundred years from the year of its creation, whichever expires first. If, before the end of such term, the identity of one or more of the authors of an anonymous or pseudonymous work is revealed in the records of a registration made for that work under subsections (a) or (d) of section 408, or in the records provided by this subsection, the copyright in the work endures for the term specified by subsection (a) or (b), based on the life of the author or authors whose identity has been revealed. Any person having an interest in the copyright in an anonymous or pseudonymous work may at any time record, in records to be maintained by the Copyright Office for that purpose, a statement identifying one or more authors of the work; the statement shall also identify the person filing it, the nature of that person's interest, the source of the information recorded, and the particular work affected, and shall comply in form and content with requirements that the Register of Copyrights shall prescribe by regulation.

(d) RECORDS RELATING TO DEATH OF AUTHORS.—Any person having an interest in a copyright may at any time record in the Copyright Office a statement of the date of death of the author of the copyrighted work, or a statement that the author is still living on a particular date. The statement shall identify the person filing it, the nature of that person's interest, and the source of the information recorded, and shall comply in form and content with requirements that the Register of Copyrights shall prescribe by regulation. The Register shall maintain current records of information relating to the death of authors of copyrighted works, based on such recorded statements and, to the extent the Register considers practicable, on data contained in any of the records of the Copyright Office of in other reference sources.

(e) PRESUMPTION AS TO AUTHOR'S DEATH.—After a period of seventy-five years from the year of first publication of a work, or a period of one hundred years from the year of its creation, which ever expires first, any person who obtains from the Copyright Office a certified report that the records provided by subsection (d) disclose nothing to indicate that the author of the work is living, or died less than fifty years before, is entitled to the benefit of a presumption that the author has been dead for at least fifty years. Reliance in good faith upon this presumption shall be a complete defense to any action for infringement under this title.

### § 303. Duration of copyright: Works created but not published or copyrighted before January 1, 1978

Copyright in a work created before January 1, 1978, but not theretofore in the public domain or copyrighted, subsists from January 1, 1978, and endures for the term provided by section 302. In no case, however, shall the term of copyright in such a work expire before December 31, 2002; and, if the work is published on or before December 31, 2002, the term of copyright shall not expire before December 31, 2027.

### § 304. Duration of copyright: Subsisting copyrights

(a) COPYRIGHTS IN THEIR FIRST TERM ON JANUARY 1, 1978.—Any copyright, the first term of which is subsisting on January 1, 1978, shall endure for twenty-eight years from the date it was originally secured: *Provided,* That in the case of any posthumous work or of any periodical, cyclopedic, or other composite work upon which the copyright was originally secured by the proprietor thereof, or of any work copyrighted by a corporate body (otherwise than as assignee or licensee of the individual author) or by an employer for whom such work is made for hire, the proprietor of such copyright shall be entitled to a renewal and extension of the copyright in such work for the further term of forty-seven years when application for such renewal and extension shall have been made to the Copyright Office and duly registered therein within one year prior to the expiration of the original term of copyright: *And provided further,* That in the case of any other copyrighted work, including a contribution by an individual author to a periodical or to a cyclopedic or other composite work, the author of such work, if still living, or the widow, widower, or children of the author, if the author be not living, or if such author, widow, widower, or children be not living, then the author's executors, or in the absence of a will, his or her next of kin shall be entitled to a renewal and extension of the copyright in such work for a further term of forty-seven years when application for such renewal and extension shall have been made to the Copyright Office and duly registered therein within one year prior to the expiration of the original term of copyright: *And provided further*, That in default of the registration of such application for renewal and extension, the copyright in any work shall terminate at the expiration of twenty-eight years from the date copyright was originally secured.

(b) COPYRIGHTS IN THEIR RENEWAL TERM OR REGISTERED FOR RENEWAL BEFORE JANUARY 1, 1978.—The duration of any copyright, the renewal term of which is subsisting at any time between December 31, 1976, and December 31, 1977, inclusive, or for which renewal registration is made between December 31, 1976, and December 31, 1977, inclusive, is extended to endure for a term of seventy-five years from the date copyright was originally secured.

(c) TERMINATION OF TRANSFERS AND LICENSES COVERING EXTENDED RENEWAL TERM.—In the case of any copyright subsisting in either its first or renewal term on January 1, 1978, other than a copyright in a work made for hire, the exclusive or nonexclusive grant of a transfer or license of the renewal copyright or any right under it, executed before January 1, 1978, by any of the persons designated by the second proviso of subsection (a) of this section, otherwise than by will, is subject to termination under the following conditions:

(1) In the case of a grant executed by a person or persons other than the author, termination of the grant may be effected by the surviving person or persons who executed it. In the case of a grant executed by one or more of the authors of the work, termination of the grant may be effected, to the extent of a particular author's share in the ownership of the renewal copyright, by the author who executed it or, if such author is dead, by the person or persons who, under clause (2) of this subsection, own and are entitled to exercise a total of more than one-half of that author's termination interest.

(2) Where an author is dead, his or her termination interest is owned, and may be exercised, by his widow or her widower and his or her children or grandchildren as follows:

(A) the widow or widower owns the author's entire termination interest unless there are any surviving children or grandchildren of the author, in which case the widow or widower owns one-half of the author's interest;

(B) the author's surviving children, and the surviving children of any dead child of the author, own the author's entire termination interest unless there is a widow or widower, in which case the ownership of one-half of the author's interest is divided among them;

(C) the rights of the author's children and grandchildren are in all cases divided among them and exercised on a per stirpes basis according to the number of such author's children represented; the share of the children of a dead child in a termination interest can be exercised only by the action of a majority of them.

(3) Termination of the grant may be effected at any time during a period of five years beginning at the end of fifty-six years from the date

copyright was originally secured, or beginning on January 1, 1978, whichever is later.

(4) The termination shall be effected by serving an advance notice in writing upon the grantee or the grantee's successor in title. In the case of a grant executed by a person or persons other than the author, the notice shall be signed by all of those entitled to terminate the grant under clause (1) of this subsection, or by their duly authorized agents. In the case of a grant executed by one or more of the authors of the work, the notice as to any one author's share shall be signed by that author or his or her duly authorized agent or, if that author is dead, by the number and proportion of the owners of his or her termination interest required under clauses (1) and (2) of this subsection, or by their duly authorized agents.

(A) The notice shall state the effective date of the termination, which shall fall within the five-year period specified by clause (3) of this subsection, and the notice shall be served not less than two or more than ten years before that date. A copy of the notice shall be recorded in the Copyright Office before the effective date of termination, as a condition to its taking effect.

(B) The notice shall comply, in form, content, and manner of service, with requirements that the Register of Copyrights shall prescribe by regulation.

(5) Termination of the grant may be effected notwithstanding any agreement to the contrary, including an agreement to make a will or to make any future grant.

(6) In the case of a grant executed by a person or persons other than the author, all rights under this title that were covered by the terminated grant revert, upon the effective date of termination, to all of those entitled to terminate the grant under clause (1) of this subsection. In the case of a grant executed by one or more of the authors of the work, all of a particular author's rights under this title that were covered by the terminated grant revert, upon the effective date of termination, to that author or, if that author is dead, to the persons owning his or her termination interest under clause (2) of this subsection, including those owners who did not join in signing the notice of termination under clause (4) of this subsection. In all cases the reversion of rights is subject to the following limitations:

(A) A derivative work prepared under authority of the grant before its termination may continue to be utilized under the terms of the grant after its termination, but this privilege does not extend to the preparation after the termination of other derivative works based upon the copyrighted work covered by the terminated grant.

(B) The future rights that will revert upon termination of the grant become vested on the date the notice of termination has been served as provided by clause (4) of this subsection.

(C) Where the author's rights revert to two or more persons under clause (2) of this subsection, they shall vest in those persons in the proportionate shares provided by that clause. In such a case, and subject to the provisions of subclause (D) of this clause, a further grant, or agreement to make a further grant, of a particular author's share with respect to any right covered by a terminated grant is valid only if it is signed by the same number and proportion of the owners, in whom the right has vested under this clause, as are required to terminate the grant under clause (2) of this subsection. Such further grant or agreement is effective with respect to all of the persons in whom the right it covers has vested under this subclause, including those who did not join in signing it. If any person dies after rights under a terminated grant have vested in him or her, that person's legal representatives, legatees, or heirs at law represent him or her for purposes of this subclause.

(D) A further grant, or agreement to make a further grant, of any right covered by a terminated grant is valid only if it is made after the effective date of the termination. As an exception, however, an agreement for such a further grant may be made between the author or any of the persons provided by the first sentence of clause (6) of this subsection, or between the persons provided by subclause (C) of this clause, and the original grantee or such grantee's successor in title, after the notice of termination has been served as provided by clause (4) of this subsection.

(E) Termination of a grant under this subsection affects only those rights covered by the grant that arise under this title, and in no way affects rights arising under any other Federal, State, or foreign laws.

(F) Unless and until termination is effected under this subsection, the grant, if it does not provide otherwise, continues in effect for the remainder of the extended renewal term.

## § 305. Duration of copyright: Terminal date

All terms of copyright provided by sections 302 through 304 run to the end of the calendar year in which they would otherwise expire.

## Chapter 4—Copyright Notice, Deposit, and Registration

## § 401. Notice of copyright: Visually perceptible copies

(a) GENERAL REQUIREMENT.—Whenever a work protected under this title is published in the United States or elsewhere by authority of the copyright owner, a notice of copyright as provided by this section shall be placed on all publicly distributed copies from which the work can be visually perceived, either directly or with the aid of a machine or device.

(b) FORM OF NOTICE.—The notice appearing on the copies shall consist of the following three elements:

(1) the symbol © (the letter C in a circle), or the word "Copyright", or the abbreviation "Copr."; and

(2) the year of first publication of the work; in the case of compilations or derivative works incorporating previously published material, the year date of first publication of the compilation or derivative work is sufficient. The year date may be omitted where a pictorial, graphic, or sculptural work, with accompanying text matter, if any, is reproduced in or on greeting cards, postcards, stationery, jewelry, dolls, toys, or any useful articles; and

(3) the name of the owner of copyright in the work, or an abbreviation by which the name can be recognized, or a generally known alternative designation of the owner.

(c) POSITION OF NOTICE.—The notice shall be affixed to the copies in such manner and location as to give reasonable notice of the claim of copyright. The Register of Copyrights shall prescribe by regulation, as examples, specific methods of affixation and positions of the notice on various types of works that will satisfy this requirement, but these specifications shall not be considered exhaustive.

### § 402. Notice of copyright: Phonorecords of sound recordings

(a) GENERAL REQUIREMENT.—Whenever a sound recording protected under this title is published in the United States or elsewhere by authority of the copyright owner, a notice of copyright as provided by this section shall be placed on all publicly distributed phonorecords of the sound recording.

(b) FORM OF NOTICE.—The notice appearing on the phonorecords shall consist of the following three elements:

(1) the symbol ℗ (the letter P in a circle); and

(2) the year of first publication of the sound recording; and

(3) the name of the owner of copyright in the sound recording, or an abbreviation by which the name can be recognized, or a generally known alternative designation of the owner; if the producer of the sound recording is named on the phonorecord labels or containers, and if no other name appears in conjunction with the notice, the producer's name shall be considered a part of the notice.

(c) POSITION OF NOTICE.—The notice shall be placed on the surface of the phonorecord, or on the phonorecord label or container, in such manner and location as to give reasonable notice of the claim of copyright.

### § 403. Notice of copyright: Publications incorporating United States Government works

Whenever a work is published in copies or phonorecords consisting preponderantly of one or more works of the United States Government, the notice of copyright provided by sections 401 or 402 shall also include a statement identifying, either affirmatively or negatively, those portions of the copies or phonorecords embodying any work or works protected under this title.

## § 404. Notice of copyright: Contributions to collective works

(a) A separate contribution to a collective work may bear its own notice of copyright, as provided by sections 401 through 403. However, a single notice applicable to the collective work as a whole is sufficient to satisfy the requirements of sections 401 through 403 with respect to the separate contributions it contains (not including advertisements inserted on behalf of persons other than the owner of copyright in the collective work), regardless of the ownership of copyright in the contributions and whether or not they have been previously published.

(b) Where the person named in a single notice applicable to a collective work as a whole is not the owner of copyright in a separate contribution that does not bear its own notice, the case is governed by the provisions of section 406(a).

## § 405. Notice of copyright: Omission of notice

(a) EFFECT OF OMISSION ON COPYRIGHT.—The omission of the copyright notice prescribed by sections 401 through 403 from copies or phonorecords publicly distributed by authority of the copyright owner does not invalidate the copyright in a work if—

> (1) the notice has been omitted from no more than a relatively small number of copies or phonorecords distributed to the public; or
> (2) registration for the work has been made before or is made within five years after the publication without notice, and a reasonable effort is made to add notice to all copies or phonorecords that are distributed to the public in the United States after the omission has been discovered; or
> (3) the notice has been omitted in violation of an express requirement in writing that, as a condition of the copyright owner's authorization of the public distribution of copies or phonorecords, they bear the prescribed notice.

(b) EFFECT OF OMISSION ON INNOCENT INFRINGERS.—Any person who innocently infringes a copyright, in reliance upon an authorized copy or phonorecord from which the copyright notice has been omitted, incurs no liability for actual or statutory damages under section 504 for any infringing acts committed before receiving actual notice that registration for the work has been made under section 408, if such person proves that he or she was misled by the omission of notice. In a suit for infringement in such a case the court may allow or disallow recovery of any of the infringer's profits attributable to the infringement, and may enjoin the continuation of the infringing undertaking or may require, as a condition or [*sic*] permitting the continuation of the infringing undertaking, that the infringer pay the copyright owner a reasonable license fee in an amount and on terms fixed by the court.

(c) REMOVAL OF NOTICE.—Protection under this title is not affected by the removal, destruction, or obliteration of the notice, without the authorization of the copyright owner, from any publicly distributed copies or phono-records.

### § 406. Notice of copyright: Error in name or date

(a) ERROR IN NAME.—Where the person named in the copyright notice on copies or phonorecords publicly distributed by authority of the copyright owner is not the owner of copyright, the validity and ownership of the copyright are not affected. In such a case, however, any person who innocently begins an undertaking that infringes the copyright has a complete defense to any action for such infringement if such person proves that he or she was misled by the notice and began the undertaking in good faith under a purported transfer or license from the person named therein, unless before the undertaking was begun—

(1) registration for the work had been made in the name of the owner of copyright; or
(2) a document executed by the person named in the notice and showing the ownership of the copyright had been recorded.

The person named in the notice is liable to account to the copyright owner for all receipts from transfers or licenses purportedly made under the copyright by the person named in the notice.

(b) ERROR IN DATE.—When the year date in the notice on copies or phonorecords distributed by authority of the copyright owner is earlier than the year in which publication first occurred, any period computed from the year of first publication under section 302 is to be computed from the year in the notice. Where the year date is more than one year later than the year in which publication first occurred, the work is considered to have been published without any notice and is governed by the provisions of section 405.

(c) OMISSION OF NAME OR DATE.—Where copies or phonorecords publicly distributed by authority of the copyright owner contain no name or no date that could reasonably be considered a part of the notice, the work is considered to have been published without any notice and is governed by the provisions of section 405.

### § 407. Deposit of copies or phonorecords for Library of Congress

(a) Except as provided by subsection (c), and subject to the provisions of subsection (e), the owner of copyright or of the exclusive right of publication in a work published with notice of copyright in the United States shall deposit, within three months after the date of such publication—

(1) two complete copies of the best edition; or
(2) if the work is a sound recording, two complete phonorecords of the best edition, together with any printed or other visually perceptible material published with such phonorecords.

Neither the deposit requirements of this subsection nor the acquisition provisions of subsection (e) are conditions of copyright protection.

(b) The required copies or phonorecords shall be deposited in the Copyright Office for the use or disposition of the Library of Congress. The Register of Copyrights shall, when requested by the depositor and upon payment of the fee prescribed by section 708, issue a receipt for the deposit.

(c) The Register of Copyrights may by regulation exempt any categories of material from the deposit requirements of this section, or require deposit of only one copy or phonorecord with respect to any categories. Such regulations shall provide either for complete exemption from the deposit requirements of this section, or for alternative forms of deposit aimed at providing a satisfactory archival record of a work without imposing practical or financial hardships on the depositor, where the individual author is the owner of copyright in a pictorial, graphic, or sculptural work and (i) less than five copies of the work have been published, or (ii) the work has been published in a limited edition consisting of numbered copies, the monetary value of which would make the mandatory deposit of two copies of the best edition of the work burdensome, unfair, or unreasonable.

(d) At any time after publication of a work as provided by subsection (a), the Register of Copyrights may make written demand for the required deposit on any of the persons obligated to make the deposit under subsection (a). Unless deposit is made within three months after the demand is received, the person or persons on whom the demand was made are liable—

(1) to a fine of not more than $250 for each work; and

(2) to pay into a specially designated fund in the Library of Congress the total retail price of the copies or phonorecords demanded, or, if no retail price has been fixed, the reasonable cost of the Library of Congress of acquiring them; and

(3) to pay a fine of $2,500, in addition to any fine or liability imposed under clauses (1) and (2), if such person willfully or repeatedly fails or refuses to comply with such a demand.

(e) With respect to transmission programs that have been fixed and transmitted to the public in the United States but have not been published, the Register of Copyrights shall, after consulting with the Librarian of Congress and other interested organizations and officials, establish regulations governing the acquisition, through deposit or otherwise, of copies or phonorecords of such programs for the collections of the Library of Congress.

(1) The Librarian of Congress shall be permitted, under the standards and conditions set forth in such regulations, to make a fixation of a transmission program directly from a transmission to the public, and to reproduce one copy or phonorecord from such fixation for archival purposes.

(2) Such regulations shall also provide standards and procedures by which the Register of Copyrights may make written demand, upon the owner of the right of transmission in the United States, for the deposit of a copy or phonorecord of a specific transmission program. Such deposit may, at the option of the owner of the right of transmission in the United States, be accomplished by gift, by loan for purposes of reproduction, or by sale at a price not to exceed the cost of reproducing and supplying the copy or phonorecord. The regulations established under this clause shall provide reasonable periods of not less than three months for compliance with a demand, and shall allow for extensions of such periods and adjustments in the scope of the demand or the methods for fulfilling it, as reasonably warranted by the circumstances. Willful

failure or refusal to comply with the conditions prescribed by such regulations shall subject the owner of the right of transmission in the United States to liability for an amount, not to exceed the cost of reproducing and supplying the copy or phonorecord in question, to be paid into a specially designated fund in the Library of Congress.

(3) Nothing in this subsection shall be construed to require the making or retention, for purposes of deposit, of any copy or phonorecord of an unpublished transmission program, the transmission of which occurs before the receipt of a specific written demand as provided by clause (2).

(4) No activity undertaken in compliance with regulations prescribed under clauses (1) or (2) of this subsection shall result in liability if intended solely to assist in the acquisition of copies or phonorecords under this subsection.

### §408. Copyright registration in general

(a) REGISTRATION PERMISSIVE.—At any time during the subsistence of copyright in any published or unpublished work, the owner of copyright or of any exclusive right in the work may obtain registration of the copyright claim by delivering to the Copyright Office the deposit specified by this section, together with the application and fee specified by sections 409 and 708. Subject to the provisions of section 405(a), such registration is not a condition of copyright protection.

(b) DEPOSIT FOR COPYRIGHT REGISTRATION.—Except as provided by subsection (c), the material deposited for registration shall include—

(1) in the case of an unpublished work, one complete copy or phonorecord;

(2) in the case of a published work, two complete copies or phonorecords of the best edition;

(3) in the case of a work first published outside the United States, one complete copy or phonorecord as so published;

(4) in the case of a contribution to a collective work, one complete copy or phonorecord of the best edition of the collective work.

Copies or phonorecords deposited for the Library of Congress under section 407 may be used to satisfy the deposit provisions of this section, if they are accompanied by the prescribed application and fee, and by any additional identifying material that the Register may, by regulation, require. The Register shall also prescribe regulations establishing requirements under which copies or phonorecords acquired for the Library of Congress under subsection (e) of section 407, otherwise than by deposit, may be used to satisfy the deposit provisions of this section.

(c) ADMINISTRATIVE CLASSIFICATION AND OPTIONAL DEPOSIT.—

(1) The Register of Copyrights is authorized to specify by regulation the administrative classes into which works are to be placed for purposes of deposit and registration, and the nature of the copies or phonorecords to be deposited in the various classes specified. The regulations may require or permit, for particular classes, the deposit of identifying material instead of copies or phonorecords, the deposit of only one copy or phonorecord where two would normally be required, or a single registration for a group of related works. This administrative classification of works has no significance with respect to the subject matter of copyright or the exclusive rights provided by this title.

(2) Without prejudice to the general authority provided under clause (1), the Register of Copyrights shall establish regulations specifically permitting a single registration for a group of works by the same individual author, all first published as contributions to periodicals, including newspapers, within a twelve-month period, on the basis of a single deposit, application, and registration fee, under all of the following conditions—

(A) if each of the works as first published bore a separate copyright notice, and the name of the owner of copyright in the work, or an abbreviation by which the name can be recognized, or a generally known alternative designation of the owner was the same in each notice; and

(B) if the deposit consists of one copy of the entire issue of the periodical, or of the entire section in the case of a newspaper, in which each contribution was first published; and

(C) if the application identifies each work separately, including the periodical containing it and its date of first publication.

(3) As an alternative to separate renewal registrations under subsection (a) of section 304, a single renewal registration may be made for a group of works by the same individual author, all first published as contributions to periodicals, including newspapers, upon the filing of a single application and fee, under all of the following conditions:

(A) the renewal claimant or claimants, and the basis of claim or claims under section 304(a), is the same for each of the works; and

(B) the works were all copyrighted upon their first publication, either through separate copyright notice and registration or by virtue of a general copyright notice in the periodical issue as a whole; and

(C) the renewal application and fee are received not more than twenty-eight or less than twenty-seven years after the thirty-first day of December of the calendar year in which all of the works were first published; and

(D) the renewal application identifies each work separately, including the periodical containing it and its date of first publication.

(d) CORRECTIONS AND AMPLIFICATIONS.—The Register may also establish, by regulation, formal procedures for the filing of an application for supplementary registration, to correct an error in a copyright registration or to amplify the information given in a registration. Such application shall be accompanied by the fee provided by section 708, and shall clearly identify the registration to be corrected or amplified. The information contained in a supplementary registration augments but does not supersede that contained in the earlier registration.

(e) PUBLISHED EDITION OF PREVIOUSLY REGISTERED WORK.—Registration for the first published edition of a work previously registered in unpublished form may be made even though the work as published is substantially the same as the unpublished version.

## § 409. Application for copyright registration

The application for copyright registration shall be made on a form prescribed by the Register of Copyrights and shall include—

(1) the name and address of the copyright claimant;

(2) in the case of a work other than an anonymous or pseudonymous work, the name and nationality or domicile of the author or authors, and, if one or more of the authors is dead, the dates of their deaths;

(3) if the work is anonymous or pseudonymous, the nationality or domicile of the author or authors;

(4) in the case of a work made for hire, a statement to this effect;

(5) if the copyright claimant is not the author, a brief statement of how the claimant obtained ownership of the copyright;

(6) the title of the work, together with any previous or alternative titles under which the work can be identified;

(7) the year in which creation of the work was completed;

(8) if the work has been published, the date and nation of its first publication;

(9) in the case of a compilation or derivative work, an identification of any preexisting work or works that it is based on or incorporates, and a brief, general statement of the additional material covered by the copyright claim being registered;

(10) in the case of a published work containing material of which copies are required by section 601 to be manufactured in the United States, the names of the persons or organizations who performed the processes specified by subsection (c) of section 601 with respect to that material, and the places where those processes were performed; and

(11) any other information regarded by the Register of Copyrights as bearing upon the preparation or identification of the work or the existence, ownership, or duration of the copyright.

### § 410. Registration of claim and issuance of certificate

(a) When after examination, the Register of Copyrights determines that, in accordance with the provisions of this title, the material deposited constitutes copyrighted subject matter and that the other legal and formal requirements of this title have been met, the Register shall register the claim and issue to the applicant a certificate of registration under the seal of the Copyright Office. The certificate shall contain the information given in the application, together with the number and effective date of the registration.

(b) In any case in which the Register of Copyrights determines that, in accordance with the provisions of this title, the material deposited does not constitute copyrightable subject matter or that the claim is invalid for any other reason, the Register shall refuse registration and shall notify the applicant in writing of the reasons for such refusal.

(c) In any judicial proceedings the certificate of a registration made before or within five years after first publication of the work shall constitute prima facie evidence of the validity of the copyright and of the facts stated in the certificate. The evidentiary weight to be accorded the certificate of a registration made thereafter shall be within the discretion of the court.

(d) The effective date of a copyright registration is the day on which an application, deposit, and fee, which are later determined by the Register of Copyrights or by a court of competent jurisdiction to be acceptable for registration, have all been received in the Copyright Office.

## § 411. Registration as prerequisite to infringement suit

(a) Subject to the provisions of subsection (b), no action for infringement of the copyright in any work shall be instituted until registration of the copyright claim has been made in accordance with this title. In any case, however, where the deposit, application, and fee required for registration have been delivered to the Copyright Office in proper form and registration has been refused, the applicant is entitled to institute an action for infringement if notice thereof, with a copy of the complaint, is served on the Register of Copyrights. The Register may, at his or her option, become a party to the action with respect to the issue of registrability of the copyright claim by entering an appearance within sixty days after such service, but the Register's failure to become a party shall not deprive the court of jurisdiction to determine that issue.

(b) In the case of a work consisting of sounds, images, or both, the first fixation of which is made simultaneously with its transmission, the copyright owner may, either before or after such fixation takes place, institute an action for infringement under section 501, fully subject to the remedies provided by sections 502 through 506 and sections 509 and 510, if, in accordance with requirements that the Register of Copyrights shall prescribe by regulation, the copyright owner—

(1) serves notice upon the infringer, not less than ten or more than thirty days before such fixation, identifying the work and the specific time and source of its first transmission, and declaring an intention to secure copyright in the work; and

(2) makes registration for the work within three months after its first transmission.

## § 412. Registration as prerequisite to certain remedies for infringement

In any action under this title, other than an action instituted under section 411(b), no award of statutory damages or of attorney's fees, as provided by sections 504 and 505, shall be made for—

(1) any infringement of copyright in an unpublished work commenced before the effective date of its registration; or

(2) any infringement of copyright commenced after first publication of the work and before the effective date of its registration, unless such registration is made within three months after the first publication of the work.

### Chapter 5—Copyright Infringement and Remedies

## § 501. Infringement of copyright

(a) Anyone who violates any of the exclusive rights of the copyright owner as provided by sections 106 through 118, or who imports copies or phonorecords into the United States in violation of section 602, is an infringer of the copyright.

(b) The legal or beneficial owner of an exclusive right under a copyright is entitled, subject to the requirements of sections 205(d) and 411, to institute an action for any infringement of that particular right committed while he or she is the owner of it. The court may require such owner to serve written notice of the action with a copy of the complaint upon any person shown, by the records of the Copyright Office or otherwise, to have or claim an interest in the copyright, and shall require that such notice be served upon any person whose interest is likely to be affected by a decision in the case. The court may require the joinder, and shall permit the intervention, of any person having or claiming an interest in the copyright.

(c) For any secondary transmission by a cable system that embodies a performance or a display of a work which is actionable as an act of infringement under subsection (c) of section 111, a television broadcast station holding a copyright or other license to transmit or perform the same version of that work shall, for purposes of subsection (b) of this section, be treated as a legal or beneficial owner if such secondary transmission occurs within the local service area of that television station.

(d) For any secondary transmission by a cable system that is actionable as an act of infringement pursuant to section 111(c)(3), the following shall also have standing to sue: (i) the primary transmitter whose transmission has been altered by the cable system; and (ii) any broadcast station within whose local service area the secondary transmission occurs.

## § 502. Remedies for infringement: Injunctions

(a) Any court having jurisdiction of a civil action arising under this title may, subject to the provisions of section 1498 of title 28, grant temporary and final injunctions on such terms as it may deem reasonable to prevent or restrain infringement of a copyright.

(b) Any such injunction may be served anywhere in the United States on the person enjoined; it shall be operative throughout the United States and shall be enforceable, by proceedings in contempt or otherwise, by any United States court having jurisdiction of that person. The clerk of the court granting the injunction shall, when requested by any other court in which enforcement of the injunction is sought, transmit promptly to the other court a certified copy of all the papers in the case on file in such clerk's office.

## § 503. Remedies for infringement: Impounding and disposition of infringing articles

(a) At any time while an action under this title is pending, the court may order the impounding, on such terms as it may deem reasonable, of all copies or phonorecords claimed to have been made or used in violation of the copy-right owner's exclusive rights, and of all plates, molds, matrices, masters, tapes, film negatives, or other articles by means of which such copies or phonorecords may be reproduced.

(b) As part of a final judgment or decree, the court may order the de-struction or other reasonable disposition of all copies or phonorecords found to have been made or used in violation of the copyright owner's exclusive rights, and of all plates, molds, matrices, masters, tapes, film negatives, or other articles by means of which such copies or phonorecords may be reproduced.

## § 504. Remedies for infringement: Damages and profits

(a) IN GENERAL.—Except as otherwise provided by this title, an in-fringer of copyright is liable for either—

(1) the copyright owner's actual damages and any additional profits of the infringer, as provided by subsection (b); or

(2) statutory damages, as provided by subsection (c).

(b) ACTUAL DAMAGES AND PROFITS.—The copyright owner is entitled to recover the actual damages suffered by him or her as a result of the infringe-ment, and any profits of the infringer that are attributable to the infringe-ment and are not taken into account in computing the actual damages. In establishing the infringer's profits, the copyright owner is required to present proof only of the infringer's gross revenue, and the infringer is re-quired to prove his or her deductible expenses and the elements of profit at-tributable to factors other than the copyrighted work.

(c) STATUTORY DAMAGES.—

(1) Except as provided by clause (2) of this subsection, the copy-right owner may elect, at any time before final judgment is rendered, to recover, instead of actual damages and profits, an award of statutory damages for all infringements involved in the action, with respect to any one work for which any one infringer is liable individually, or for which any two ore more infringers are liable jointly and severally, in a sum of not less than $250 or more than $10,000 as the court considers just. For the purposes of this subsection, all the parts of a compilation of deriva-tive work constitute one work.

(2) In a case where the copyright owner sustains the burden of prov-ing, and the court finds, that infringement was committed willfully, the court in its discretion may increase the award of statutory damages to a sum of not more than $50,000. In a case where the infringer sustains the burden of proving, and the court finds, that such infringer was not aware and had no reason to believe that his or her acts constituted an infringe-ment of copyright, the court in its discretion may reduce the award of statutory damages to a sum of not less than $100. The court shall remit statutory damages in any case where an infringer believed and had rea-sonable grounds for believing that his or her use of the copyrighted work was fair use under section 107, if the infringer was: (i) an employee or agent of a nonprofit educational institution, library, or archives acting within the scope of his or her employment who, or such institution, li-brary, or archives itself, which infringed by reproducing the work in cop-ies or phonorecords; or (ii) a public broadcasting entity which or a person

who, as a regular part of the nonprofit activities of a public broadcasting entity (as defined in subsection (g) of section 118) infringed by performing a published nondramatic literary work or by reproducing a transmission program embodying a performance of such a work.

## § 505.  Remedies for infringement: Costs and attorney's fees

In any civil action under this title, the court in its discretion may allow the recovery of full costs by or against any party other than the United States or an officer thereof. Except as otherwise provided by this title, the court may also award a reasonable attorney's fee to the prevailing party as part of the costs.

## § 506.  Criminal offenses*

(a) CRIMINAL INFRINGEMENT.—Any person who infringes a copyright willfully and for purposes of commercial advantage or private financial gain shall be punished as provided in section 2319 of title 18.

(b) FORFEITURE AND DESTRUCTION.—When any person is convicted of any violation of subsection (a), the court in its judgment of conviction shall, in addition to the penalty therein prescribed, order the forfeiture and destruction or other disposition of all infringing copies or phonorecords and all implements, devices, or equipment used in the manufacture of such infringing copies or phonorecords.

(c) FRAUDULENT COPYRIGHT NOTICE.—Any person who, with fraudulent intent, places on any article a notice of copyright or words of the same purport that such person knows to be false, or who, with fraudulent intent, publicly distributes or imports for public distribution any article bearing such notice or words that such person knows to be false, shall be fined not more than $2,500.

(d) FRAUDULENT REMOVAL OF COPYRIGHT NOTICE.—Any person who, with fraudulent intent, removes or alters any notice of copyright appearing on a copy of a copyrighted work shall be fined not more than $2,500.

(e) FALSE REPRESENTATION.—Any person who knowingly makes a false representation of a material fact in the application for copyright registration provided for by section 409, or in any written statement filed in connection with the application, shall be fined not more than $2,500.

## § 507.  Limitations on actions

(a) CRIMINAL PROCEEDINGS.—No criminal proceeding shall be maintained under the provisions of this title unless it is commenced within three years after the cause of action arose.

(b) CIVIL ACTIONS.—No civil action shall be maintained under the provisions of this title unless it is commenced within three years after the claim accrued.

---

*As amended by Pub. L. No. 97-180, § 5, 96 Stat. 91, May 24, 1982.

## § 508. Notification of filing and determination of actions

(a) Within one month after the filing of any action under this title, the clerks of the courts of the United States shall send written notification to the Register of Copyrights setting forth, as far as is shown by the property filed in the court, the names and addresses for the parties and the title, author, and registration number of each work involved in the action. If any other copyrighted work is later included in the action by amendment, answer, or other pleading, the clerk shall also send a notification concerning it to the Register within one month after the pleading is filed.

(b) Within one month after any final order or judgment is issued in the case, the clerk of the court shall notify the Register of it, sending with the notification a copy of the order or judgment together with the written opinion, if any, of the court.

(c) Upon receiving the notifications specified in this section, the Register shall make them a part of the public records of the Copyright Office.

## § 509. Seizure and forfeiture

(a) All copies or phonorecords manufactured, reproduced, distributed, sold, or otherwise used, intended for use, or possessed with intent to use in violation of section 506(a), and all plates, molds, matrices, masters, tapes, film negatives, or other articles by means of which such copies or phonorecords may be reproduced, and all electronic, mechanical, or other devices for manufacturing, reproducing, or assembling such copies or phonorecords may be seized and forfeited to the United States.

(b) The applicable procedures relating to (i) the seizure, summary and judicial forfeiture, and condemnation of vessels, vehicles, merchandise, and baggage for violations of the customs laws contained in title 19, (ii) the disposition of such vessels, vehicles, merchandise, and baggage or the proceeds from the sale thereof, (iii) the remission or mitigation of such forfeiture, (iv) the compromise of claims, and (v) the award of compensation to informers in respect of such forfeitures, shall apply to seizures and forfeitures incurred, or alleged to have been incurred, under the provisions of this section, insofar as applicable and not inconsistent with the provisions of this section; except that such duties as are imposed upon any officer or employee of the Treasury Department or any other person with respect to the seizure and forfeiture of vessels, vehicles, merchandise; and baggage under the provisions of the customs laws contained in title 19 shall be performed with respect to seizure and forfeiture of all articles described in subsection (a) by such officers, agents, or other persons as may be authorized or designated for that purpose by the Attorney General.

## § 510. Remedies for alteration of programming by cable systems

(a) In any action filed pursuant to section 111(c)(3), the following remedies shall be available:

(1) Where an action is brought by a party identified in subsections (b) or (c) of section 501, the remedies provided by sections 502 through 505, and the remedy provided by subsection (b) of this section; and

(2)  When an action is brought by a party identified in subsection (d) of section 501, the remedies provided by sections 502 and 505, together with any actual damages suffered by such party as a result of the infringement, and the remedy provided by subsection (b) of this section.

(b)  In any action filed pursuant to section 111(c)(3), the court may decree that, for a period not to exceed thirty days, the cable system shall be deprived of the benefit of a compulsory license for one or more distant signals carried by such cable system.

## Chapter 6—Manufacturing Requirement and Importation

## § 601.  Manufacture, importation, and public distribution of certain copies

(a)  Prior to July 1, 1986,* and except as provided by subsection (b), the importation into or public distribution in the United States of copies of a work consisting preponderantly of nondramatic literary material that is in the English language and is protected under this title is prohibited unless the portions consisting of such material have been manufactured in the United States or Canada.

(b)  The provisions of subsection (a) do not apply—

(1)  where, on the date when importation is sought or public distribution in the United States is made, the author of any substantial part of such material is neither a national nor a domiciliary of the United States or, if such author is a national of the United States, he or she has been domiciled outside the United States for a continuous period of at least one year immediately preceding that date; in the case of a work made for hire, the exemption provided by this clause does not apply unless a substantial part of the work was prepared for an employer or other person who is not a national or domiciliary of the United States or a domestic corporation or enterprise;

(2)  where the United States Customs Service is presented with an import statement issued under the seal of the Copyright Office, in which case a total of no more than two thousand copies of any one such work shall be allowed entry; the import statement shall be issued upon request to the copyright owner or to a person designated by such owner at the time of registration for the work under section 408 or at any time thereafter;

(3)  where importation is sought under the authority or for the use, other than in schools, of the Government of the United States or of any State or political subdivision of a State;

(4)  where importation, for use and not for sale, is sought—

---

*Pub. L. No. 97-215, 96 Stat. 178, July 13, 1982, substituted "1986" for "1982."

(A)  by any person with respect to no more than one copy of any work at any one time;

(B)  by any person arriving from outside the United States, with respect to copies forming part of such person's personal baggage; or

(C)  by an organization operated for scholarly, educational, or religious purposes and not for private gain, with respect to copies intended to form a part of its library;

(5)  where the copies are reproduced in raised characters for the use of the blind; or

(6)  where, in addition to copies imported under clauses (3) and (4) of this subsection, no more than two thousand copies of any one such work, which have not been manufactured in the United States or Canada, are publicly distributed in the United States; or

(7)  where, on the date when importation is sought or public distribution in the United States is made—

(A)  the author of any substantial part of such material is an individual and receives compensation for the transfer or license of the right to distribute the work in the United States; and

(B)  the first publication of the work has previously taken place outside the United States under a transfer or license granted by such author to a transferee or licensee who was not a national or domiciliary of the United States or a domestic corporation or enterprise; and

(C)  there has been no publication of an authorized edition of the work of which the copies were manufactured in the United States; and

(D)  the copies were reproduced under a transfer or license granted by such author or by the transferee or licensee of the right of first publication as mentioned in subclause (B), and the transferee or the licensee of the right of reproduction was not a national or domiciliary of the United States or a domestic corporation or enterprise.

(c)  The requirement of this section that copies be manufactured in the United States or Canada is satisfied if—

(1)  in the case where the copies are printed directly from type that has been set, or directly from plates made from such type, the setting of the type and the making of the plates have been performed in the United States or Canada; or

(2)  in the case where the making of plates by a lithographic or photoengraving process is a final or intermediate step preceding the printing of the copies, the making of the plates has been performed in the United States or Canada; and

(3)  in any case, the printing or other final process of producing multiple copies and any binding of the copies have been performed in the United States or Canada.

(d)  Importation or public distribution of copies in violation of this section does not invalidate protection for a work under this title. However, in any civil action or criminal proceeding for infringement of the exclusive rights to reproduce and distribute copies of the work, the infringer has a complete defense with respect to all of the nondramatic literary material comprised in the work and any other parts of the work in which the exclusive rights to reproduce and distribute copies are owned by the same person who owns such exclusive rights in the nondramatic literary material, if the infringer proves—

(1) that copies of the work have been imported into or publicly distributed in the United States in violation of this section by or with the authority of the owner of such exclusive rights; and

(2) that the infringing copies were manufactured in the United States or Canada in accordance with the provisions of subsection (c); and

(3) that the infringement was commenced before the effective date of registration for an authorized edition of the work, the copies of which have been manufactured in the United States or Canada in accordance with the provisions of subsection (c).

(e) In any action for infringement of the exclusive rights to reproduce and distribute copies of a work containing material required by this section to be manufactured in the United States or Canada, the copyright owner shall set forth in the complaint the names of the persons or organizations who performed the processes specified by subsection (c) with respect to that material, and the places where those processes were performed.

## Effective July 1, 1986*

### § 601. Manufacture, importation, and public distribution of certain copies

(a) Except as provided by subsection (b), the importation into or public distribution in the United States of copies of a work consisting preponderantly of nondramatic literary material that is in the English language and is protected under this title is prohibited unless the portions consisting of such material have been manufactured in the United States or unless the portions consisting of such material have been—

(1) manufactured in Canada prior to January 1, 1989; or

(2) manufactured in a certified country on or after July 1, 1988. For the purpose of this section, a 'certified country' means a country, territory, possession, or other jurisdiction which—

(A) the United States Trade Representative has certified to the Congress—

(i) as providing adequate and effective means under its laws for U.S. nationals to secure, exercise, and enforce exclusive rights under copyright; and

(ii) either

(I) as imposing no material nontariff barriers to trade in printed material; as imposing no tariff barriers to trade in printed material that is materially inconsistent with tariff bindings, if any, entered into by such jurisdiction with the United States; and as being an adherent to the Agreement on the Importation of Educational, Scientific and Cultural Material of 1950 (the Florence Agreement), or with respect to printed books, newspapers and periodicals, and catalogues of books and publications identified in items (i), (ii), and (viii) of Annex A to such Agreement, as imposing no

---

*As proposed by S. 1822. See S. REP. No. 99-303, 99th Cong., 2d Sess. (1986).

tariff barrier materially inconsistent with the provisions of Article I of such Agreement if such jurisdiction is not an adherent to such Agreement; or

(II) as having in force a free trade agreement with the United States governing trade in printed material and as being an adherent to the Agreement on the Importation of Educational, Scientific and Cultural Material of 1950 (the Florence Agreement) or, with respect to printed books, newspapers and periodicals, and catalogues of books and publications identified in items (i), (ii), and (viii) of Annex A to such Agreement, as imposing no tariff barrier materially inconsistent with the provisions of Article I of such Agreement if such jurisdiction is not an adherent to such Agreement and regardless of whether such tariff is permitted under the pertinent trade agreement; and

(B) the Secretary of Labor has certified to the Congress as taking or having taken steps to afford internationally recognized worker rights, in section 502(a)(4) of the Trade Act of 1974 (19 U.S.C. 2462(a)(4)) to its workers, except that such certification by the Secretary of Labor may be waived if the President determines that such waiver is in the national economic interest of the United States.

(b) The provisions of subsection (a) do not apply—

(1) where, on the date when importation is sought or public distribution in the United States is made, the author of any substantial part of such material is neither a national nor a domiciliary of the United States or, if such author is a national of the United States, he or she has been domiciled outside the United States for a continuous period of at least one year immediately preceding that date; in the case of a work made for hire, the exemption provided by this clause does not apply unless a substantial part of the work was prepared for an employer or other person who is not a national or domiciliary of the United States or a domestic corporation or enterprise;

(2) where the United States Customs Service is presented with an import statement issued under the seal of the Copyright Office, in which case a total of no more than two thousand copies of any one such work shall be allowed entry; the import statement shall be issued upon request to the copyright owner or to a person designated by such owner at the time of registration for the work under section 408 or at any time thereafter;

(3) where importation is sought under the authority or for the use, other than in schools, of the Government of the United States or of any State or political subdivision of a State;

(4) where importation, for use and not for sale, is sought—

(A) by any person with respect to no more than one copy of any work at any one time;

(B) by any person arriving from outside the United States, with respect to copies forming part of such person's personal baggage; or

(C) by an organization operated for scholarly, educational, or religious purposes and not for private gain, with respect to copies intended to form a part of its library;

(5) where the copies are reproduced in raised characters for the use of the blind; or

(6) where, in addition to copies imported under clauses (3) and (4) of this subsection, no more than two thousand copies of any one such work, which have not been manufactured in the United States or Canada, are publicly distributed in the United States; or

(7) where, on the date when importation is sought or public distribution in the United States is made—

(A) the author of any substantial part of such material is an individual and receives compensation for the transfer or license of the right to distribute the work in the United States; and

(B) the first publication of the work has previously taken place outside the United States under a transfer or license granted by such author to a transferee or licensee who was not a national or domiciliary of the United States or a domestic corporation or enterprise; and

(C) there has been no publication of an authorized edition of the work of which the copies were manufactured in the United States; and

(D) the copies were reproduced under a transfer or license granted by such author or by the transferee or licensee of the right of first publication as mentioned in subclause (B), and the transferee or the licensee of the right of reproduction was not a national or domiciliary of the United States or a domestic corporation or enterprise.

(c) The requirement of this section that copies be manufactured in the United States or, during the applicable period, Canada or a certified country is satisfied if—

(1) in the case where the copies are printed directly from type that has been set, or directly from plates made from such type, the setting of the type and the making of the plates have been performed in the United States or, during the applicable period, Canada or a certified country; or

(2) in the case where the making of plates by a lithographic or photoengraving process is a final or intermediate step preceding the printing of the copies, the making of the plates has been performed in the United States or, during the applicable period, Canada or a certified country; and

(3) in any case, the printing or other final process of producing multiple copies and any binding of the copies have been performed in the United States or, during the applicable period, Canada or a certified country.

(d) Importation or public distribution of copies in violation of this section does not invalidate protection for a work under this title. However, in any civil action or criminal proceeding for infringement of the exclusive rights to reproduce and distribute copies of the work, the infringer has a complete defense with respect to all of the nondramatic literary material comprised in the work and any other parts of the work in which the exclusive rights to reproduce and distribute copies are owned by the same person who owns such exclusive rights in the nondramatic literary material, if the infringer proves—

(1) that copies of the work have been imported into or publicly distributed in the United States in violation of this section by or with the authority of the owner of such exclusive rights; and

(2) that the infringing copies were manufactured in the United States in accordance with the provisions of subsection (c); and

(3) that the infringement was commenced before the effective date of registration for an authorized edition of the work, the copies of which have been manufactured in the United States, Canada or a certified country in accordance with the provisions of subsection (c).

(e) In any action for infringement of the exclusive rights to reproduce and distribute copies of a work containing material required by this section to be manufactured in the United State or Canada, the copyright owner shall set forth in the complaint the names of the persons or organizations who performed the processes specified by subsection (c) with respect to that material, and the places where those processes were performed.

(f)(1) The certification referred to in subsection (a) shall be commenced upon the initiative of the United States Trade Representative or upon petition to the United States Trade Representative by any jurisdiction or interested party. Such proceedings may be commenced on or after January 1, 1987, and final certifications may be published at any time thereafter pursuant to the terms of this section: *Provided,* That no certification shall permit the importation, under clause (2) of subsection (a), of materials subject to this section manufactured prior to July 1, 1988.

(2) Any certification made pursuant to subsection (a) shall be withdrawn by notification to the Congress given by the United States Trade Representative if the United States Trade Representative shall find that the criteria of subsection (a)(2)(A) are no longer met, or by the Secretary of Labor if such Secretary finds that the criteria of subsection (a)(2)(B) are no longer met: *Provided, however,* That no such withdrawal, no expiration, termination, or other cancellation of any trade agreement referred to in subsection (a)(2)(A) and no other provision of this section shall prevent the importation or distribution of any copies manufactured prior to the effective date of such withdrawal or cancellation, or the importation or distribution of any copies manufactured following such effective date in a country referred to in subsection (a) pursuant to any contract, agreement, or understanding entered into, or reasonable expectation relied upon, prior to such effective date and imported during a period of 24 months following such date. The terms of the foregoing proviso shall apply equally to the importation and distribution on or after January 1, 1989 of copies manufactured in Canada, in the event that on such date Canada is not a certified country.

(3) Any proposed certification, or notification of withdrawal made pursuant to this section shall be published promptly in the Federal Register by the United States Trade Representative and opportunity for public comment shall be afforded to interested parties. For purposes of this section, interested parties shall not necessarily be limited to parties with a material interest in the certification or notification of withdrawal of a jurisdiction. No certification or notification of withdrawal shall become final until at least 30 days following publication of such notice in the Federal Register.

## § 602. Infringing importation of copies or phonorecords

(a) Importation into the United States, without the authority of the owner of copyright under this title, of copies or phonorecords of a work that have been acquired outside the United States is an infringement of the exclusive right to distribute copies or phonorecords under section 106, actionable under section 501. This subsection does not apply to—

(1) importation of copies or phonorecords under the authority or for the use of the Government of the United States or of any State or political subdivision of a State, but not including copies or phonorecords for use in schools, or copies of any audiovisual work imported for purposes other than archival use;

(2) importation, for the private use of the importer and not for distribution, by any person with respect to no more than one copy or phonorecord of any one work at any one time, or by any person arriving from outside the United States with respect to copies or phonorecords forming part of such person's personal baggage; or

(3) importation by or for an organization operated for scholarly, educational, or religious purposes and not for private gains, with respect to no more than one copy of an audiovisual work solely for its archival purposes, and no more than five copies or phonorecords of any other work for its library lending or archival purposes, unless the importation of such copies or phonorecords is part of an activity consisting of systematic reproduction or distribution, engaged in by such organization in violation of the provisions of section 108(g)(2).

(b) In a case where the making of the copies or phonorecords would have constituted an infringement of copyright if this title had been applicable, their importation is prohibited. In a case where the copies or phonorecords were lawfully made, the United States Customs Service has no authority to prevent their importation unless the provisions of section 601 are applicable. In either case, the Secretary of the Treasury is authorized to prescribe, by regulation, a procedure under which any person claiming an interest in the copyright in a particular work may, upon payment of a specified fee, be entitled to notification by the Customs Service of the importation of articles that appear to be copies or phonorecords of the work.

### § 603. Importation prohibitions: Enforcement and disposition of excluded articles

(a) The Secretary of the Treasury and the United States Postal Service shall separately or jointly make regulations for the enforcement of the provisions of this title prohibiting importation.

(b) These regulations may require, as a condition for the exclusion of articles under section 602—

(1) that the person seeking exclusion obtain a court order enjoining importation of the articles; or

(2) that the person seeking exclusion furnish proof, of a specified nature and in accordance with prescribed procedures, that the copyright in which such person claims an interest is valid and that the importation would violate the prohibition in section 602; the person seeking exclusion may also be required to post a surety bond for any injury that may result if the detention or exclusion of the articles proves to be unjustified.

(c) Articles imported in violation of the importation prohibitions of this title are subject to seizure and forfeiture in the same manner as property imported in violation of the customs revenue laws. Forfeited articles shall be destroyed as directed by the Secretary of the Treasury or the court, as the case may be; however, the articles may be returned to the country of export whenever it is shown to the satisfaction of the Secretary of the Treasury that the importer had no reasonable grounds for believing that his or her acts constituted a violation of law.

## Chapter 7—Copyright Office

## § 701. The Copyright Office: General responsibilities and organization

(a) All administrative functions and duties under this title, except as otherwise specified, are the responsibility of the Register of Copyrights as director of the Copyright Office of the Library of Congress. The Register of Copyrights, together with the subordinate officers and employees of the Copyright Office, shall be appointed by the Librarian of Congress, and shall act under the Librarian's general direction and supervision.

(b) The Register of Copyrights shall adopt a seal to be used on and after January 1, 1978, to authenticate all certified documents issued by the Copyright Office.

(c) The Register of Copyrights shall make an annual report to the Librarian of Congress of the work and accomplishments of the Copyright Office during the previous fiscal year. The annual report of the Register of Copyrights shall be published separately and as a part of the annual report of the Librarian of Congress.

(d) Except as provided by section 706(b) and the regulations issued thereunder, all actions taken by the Register of Copyrights under this title are subject to the provisions of the Administrative Procedure Act of June 11, 1946, as amended (c. 324, 60 Stat. 237, title 5, United States Code, Chapter 5, Subchapter II and Chapter 7).

## § 702. Copyright Office regulations

The Register of Copyrights is authorized to establish regulations not inconsistent with law for the administration of the functions and duties made the responsibility of the Register under this title. All regulations established by the Register under this title are subject to the approval of the Librarian of Congress.

### § 703.  Effective date of actions in Copyright Office

In any case in which time limits are prescribed under this title for the performance of an action in the Copyright Office, and in which the last day of the prescribed period falls on a Saturday, Sunday, holiday, or other nonbusiness day within the District of Columbia or the Federal Government, the action may be taken on the next succeeding business day, and is effective as of the date when the period expired.

### § 704.  Retention and disposition of articles deposited in Copyright Office

(a)  Upon their deposit in the Copyright Office under sections 407 and 408, all copies, phonorecords, and identifying material, including those deposited in connection with claims that have been refused registration, are the property of the United States Government.

(b)  In the case of published works, all copies, phonorecords, and identifying material deposited are available to the Library of Congress for its collections, or for exchange or transfer to any other library. In the case of unpublished works, the Library is entitled, under regulations that the Register of Copyrights shall prescribe, to select any deposits for its collections or for transfer to the National Archives of the United States or to a Federal records center, as defined in section 2901 of title 44.

(c)  The Register of Copyrights is authorized, for specific or general categories of works, to make a facsimile reproduction of all or any part of the material deposited under section 408, and to make such reproduction a part of the Copyright Office records of the registration, before transferring such material to the Library of Congress as provided by subsection (b), or before destroying or otherwise disposing of such material as provided by subsection (d).

(d)  Deposits not selected by the Library under subsection (b), or identifying portions or reproductions of them, shall be retained under the control of the Copyright Office, including retention in Government storage facilities, for the longest period considered practicable and desirable by the Register of Copyrights and the Librarian of Congress. After that period it is within the joint discretion of the Register and the Librarian to order their destruction or other disposition; but, in the case of unpublished works, no deposit shall be knowingly or intentionally destroyed or otherwise disposed of during its term of copyright unless a facsimile reproduction of the entire deposit has been made a part of the Copyright Office records as provided by subsection (c).

(e)  The depositor of copies, phonorecords, or identifying material under section 408, or the copyright owner of record, may request retention, under the control of the Copyright Office, of one or more of such articles for the full term of copyright in the work. The Register of Copyrights shall prescribe, by regulation, the conditions under which such requests are to be made and granted, and shall fix the fee to be charged under section 708(a)(11) if the request is granted.

## § 705. Copyright Office records: Preparation, maintenance, public inspection, and searching

(a) The Register of Copyrights shall provide and keep in the Copyright Office records of all deposits, registrations, recordations, and other actions taken under this title, and shall prepare indexes of all such records.

(b) Such records and indexes as well as the articles deposited in connection with completed copyright registrations and retained under the control of the Copyright Office, shall be open to public inspection.

(c) Upon request and payment of the fee specified by section 708, the Copyright Office shall make a search of its public records, indexes, and deposits, and shall furnish a report of the information they disclose with respect to any particular deposits, registrations, or recorded documents.

## § 706. Copies of Copyright Office records

(a) Copies may be made of any public records or indexes of the Copyright Office; additional certificates of copyright registration and copies of any public records or indexes may be furnished upon request and payment of the fees specified by section 708.

(b) Copies or reproductions of deposited articles retained under the control of the Copyright Office shall be authorized or furnished only under the conditions specified by the Copyright Office regulations.

## § 707. Copyright Office forms and publications

(a) CATALOG OF COPYRIGHT ENTRIES.—The Register of Copyrights shall compile and publish at periodic intervals catalogs of all copyright registrations. These catalogs shall be divided into parts in accordance with the various classes of works, and the Register has discretion to determine, on the basis of practicability and usefulness, the form and frequency of publication of each particular part.

(b) OTHER PUBLICATIONS.—The Register shall furnish, free of charge upon request, application forms for copyright registration and general informational material in connection with the functions of the Copyright Office. The Register also has the authority to publish compilations of information, bibliographies, and other material he or she considers to be of value to the public.

(c) DISTRIBUTION OF PUBLICATIONS.—All publications of the Copyright Office shall be furnished to depository libraries as specified under section 1905 of title 44, and, aside from those furnished free of charge, shall be offered for sale to the public at prices based on the cost of reproduction and distribution.

## § 708. Copyright Office fees

(a) The following fees shall be paid to the Register of Copyrights:

(1) for the registration of a copyright claim or a supplementary registration under section 408, including the issuance of a certificate of registration, $10;

(2) for the registration of a claim to renewal of a subsisting copy-right in its first term under section 304(a), including the issuance of a certificate of registration, $6;

(3) for the issuance of a receipt for a deposit under section 407, $2;

(4) for the recordation, as provided by section 205, of a transfer of copyright ownership or other document of six pages or less, covering no more than one title, $10; for each page over six and each title over one, 50 cents additional;

(5) for the filing, under section 115(b), of a notice of intention to make phonorecords, $6;

(6) for the recordation, under section 302(c), of a statement reveal-ing the identity of an author of an anonymous or pseudonymous work, or for the recordation, under section 302(d), of a statement relating to the death of an author, $10 for a document of six pages or less, covering no more than one title; for each page over six and for each title over one, $1 additional;

(7) for the issuance, under section 601, of an import statement, $3;

(8) for the issuance, under section 706, of an additional certificate of registration, $4;

(9) for the issuance of any other certification, $4; the Register of Copyrights has discretion, on the basis of their costs, to fix the fees for preparing copies of Copyright Office records, whether they are to be cer-tified or not;

(10) for the making and reporting of a search as provided by section 705, and for any related services, $10 for each hour or fraction of an hour consumed;

(11) for any other special services requiring a substantial amount of time or expense, such fees as the Register of Copyrights may fix on the basis of the cost of providing the service.

(b) The fees prescribed by or under this section are applicable to the United States Government and any of its agencies, employees, or officers, but the Register of Copyrights has discretion to waive the requirement of this subsection in occasional or isolated cases involving relatively small amounts.

(c) All fees received under this section shall be deposited by the Register of Copyrights in the Treasury of the United States and shall be credited to the appropriation for necessary expenses of the Copyright Office. The Regis-ter may, in accordance with regulations that he or she shall prescribe, refund any sum paid by mistake or in excess of the fee required by this section; however, before making a refund in any case involving a refusal to register a claim under section 410(b), the Register may deduct all or any part of the prescribed registration fee to cover the reasonable administrative costs of processing the claim.

### § 709. Delay in delivery caused by disruption of postal or other services

In any case in which the Register of Copyrights determines, on the basis of such evidence as the Register may by regulation require, that a deposit, application, fee, or any other material to be delivered to the Copyright Office by a particular date, would have been received in the Copyright Office in due time except for a general disruption or suspension of postal or other transportation or communications services, the actual receipt of such material in the Copyright Office within one month after the date on which the Register determines that the disruption or suspension of such services has terminated, shall be considered timely.

## § 710. Reproductions for use of the blind and physically handicapped: Voluntary licensing forms and procedures

The Register of Copyrights shall, after consultation with the Chief of the Division for the Blind and Physically Handicapped and other appropriate officials of the Library of Congress, establish by regulation standardized forms and procedures by which, at the time applications covering certain specified categories of nondramatic literary works are submitted for registration under section 408 of this title, the copyright owner may voluntarily grant to the Library of Congress a license to reproduce the copyrighted work by means of Braille or similar tactile symbols, or by fixation of a reading of the work in a phonorecord, or both, and to distribute the resulting copies or phonorecords solely for the use of the blind and physically handicapped and under limited conditions to be specified in the standardized forms.

## Chapter 8—Copyright Royalty Tribunal

## § 801. Copyright Royalty Tribunal: Establishment and purpose

(a) There is hereby created an independent Copyright Royalty Tribunal in the legislative branch.

(b) Subject to the provisions of this chapter, the purposes of the Tribunal shall be—

(1) to make determinations concerning the adjustment of reasonable copyright royalty rates as provided in sections 115 and 116, and to make determinations as to reasonable terms and rates of royalty payments as provided in section 118. The rates applicable under sections 115 and 116 shall be calculated to achieve the following objectives:

(A) To maximize the availability of creative works to the public;

(B) To afford the copyright owner a fair return for his creative work and the copyright user a fair income under existing economic conditions;

(C) To reflect the relative roles of the copyright owner and the copyright user in the product made available to the public with respect to relative creative contribution, technological contribution, capital investment, cost, risk, and contribution to the opening of new markets for creative expression and media for their communication;

(D) To minimize any disruptive impact on the structure of the industries involved and on generally prevailing industry practices.

(2) to make determinations concerning the adjustment of the copyright royalty rates in section 111 solely in accordance with the following provisions:

(A) The rates established by section 111(d)(B) may be adjusted to reflect (i) national monetary inflation or deflation or (ii) changes in the average rates charged cable subscribers for the basic service of providing secondary transmissions to maintain the real constant dollar level of the royalty fee per subscriber which existed as of the date of enactment of this Act: *Provided*, That if the average rates charged cable system subscribers for the basic service of providing secondary transmissions are changed so that the average rates exceed national monetary inflation, no change in the rates established by section 111(d)(2)(B) shall be permitted: *And provided further*, That no increase in the royalty fee shall be permitted based on any reduction in the average number of distant signal equivalents per subscriber. The Commission may consider all factors relating to the maintenance of such level of payments including, as an extenuating factor, whether the cable industry has been restrained by subscriber rate regulating authorities from increasing the rates for the basic service of providing secondary transmissions.

(B) In the event that the rules and regulations of the Federal Communications Commission are amended at any time after April 15, 1976, to permit the carriage by cable systems of additional television broadcast signals beyond the local service area of the primary transmitters of such signals, the royalty rates established by section 111(d)(2)(B) may be adjusted to insure that the rates for the additional distant signal equivalents resulting from such carriage are reasonable in the light of the changes effected by the amendment to such rules and regulations. In determining the reasonableness of rates proposed following an amendment of Federal Communications Commission rules and regulations, the Copyright Royalty Tribunal shall consider, among other factors, the economic impact on copyright owners and users: *Provided*, That no adjustment in royalty rates shall be made under this subclause with respect to any distant signal equivalent or fraction thereof represented by (i) carriage of any signal permitted under the rules and regulations of the Federal Communications Commission in effect on April 15, 1976, or the carriage of a signal of the same type (that is, independent, network, or noncommercial educational) substituted for such permitted signal, or (ii) a television broadcast signal first carried after April 15, 1976, pursuant to an individual waiver of the rules and regulations of the Federal Communications Commission, as such rules and regulations were in effect on April 15, 1976.

(C) In the event of any change in the rules and regulations of the Federal Communications Commission with respect to syndicated and sports program exclusivity after April 15, 1976, the rates established by section 111(d)(2)(B) may be adjusted to assure that such rates are reasonable in light of the changes to such rules and regulations, but any such adjustment shall apply only to the affected television broadcast signals carried on those systems affected by the change.

(D) The gross receipts limitations established by section 111(d)(2)(C) and (D) shall be adjusted to reflect national monetary inflation or deflation or changes in the average rates charged cable system subscribers for the basic service of providing secondary transmissions to maintain the real constant dollar value of the exemption provided by such section; and the royalty rate specified therein shall not be subject to adjustment; and

(3) to distribute royalty fees deposited with the Register of Copyrights under sections 111 and 116, and to determine, in cases where controversy exists, the distribution of such fees.

(c) As soon as possible after the date of enactment of this Act, and no later than six months following such date, the President shall publish a notice announcing the initial appointments provided in section 802, and shall designate an order of seniority among the initially appointed commissioners for purposes of section 802(b).

### § 802. Membership of the Tribunal

(a) The Tribunal shall be composed of five commissioners appointed by the President with the advice and consent of the Senate for a term of seven years each; of the first five members appointed, three shall be designated to serve for seven years from the date of the notice specified in section 801(c), and two shall be designated to serve for five years from such date, respectively. Commissioners shall be compensated at the highest rate now or hereafter prescribe[d] for grade 18 of the General Schedule pay rates (5 U.S.C. 5332).

(b) Upon convening the commissioners shall elect a chairman from among the commissioners appointed for a full seven-year term. Such chairman shall serve for a term of one year. Thereafter, the most senior commissioner who has not previously served as chairman shall serve as chairman for a period of one year, except that, if all commissioners have served a full term as chairman, the most senior commissioner who has served the least number of terms as chairman shall be designated as chairman.

(c) Any vacancy in the Tribunal shall not affect its powers and shall be filed, for the unexpired term of the appointment, in the same manner as the original appointment was made.

### § 803. Procedures of the Tribunal

(a) The Tribunal shall adopt regulations, not inconsistent with law, governing its procedure and methods of operation. Except as otherwise provided in this chapter, the Tribunal shall be subject to the provisions of the Administrative Procedure Act of June 11, 1946, as amended (c. 324, 60 Stat. 237, title 5, United States Code, chapter 5, subchapter II and chapter 7).

(b) Every final determination of the Tribunal shall be published in the Federal Register. It shall state in detail the criteria that the Tribunal determined to be applicable to the particular proceeding, the various facts that it found relevant to its determination in that proceeding, and the specific reasons for its determination.

### § 804. Institution and conclusion of proceedings

(a) With respect to proceedings under section 801(b)(1) concerning the adjustment of royalty rates as provided in sections 115 and 116, and with respect to proceedings under section 801(b)(2)(A) and (D)—

(1) on January 1, 1980, the Chairman of the Tribunal shall cause to be published in the Federal Register notice of commencement of proceedings under this chapter; and

(2) during the calendar years specified in the following schedule, any owner or user of a copyrighted work whose royalty rates are specified by this title, or by a rate established by the Tribunal, may file a petition with the Tribunal declaring that the petitioner requests an adjustment of the rate. The Tribunal shall make a determination as to whether the applicant has a significant interest in the royalty rate in which an adjustment is requested. If the Tribunal determines that the petitioner has a significant interest, the Chairman shall cause notice of this determination, with the reasons therefor, to be published in the Federal Register, together with notice of commencement of proceedings under this chapter.

(A) In proceedings under section 801(b)(2)(A) and (D), such petition may be filed during 1985 and in each subsequent fifth calendar year.

(B) In proceedings under section 801(b)(1) concerning the adjustment of royalty rates as provided in section 115, such petition may be filed in 1987 and in each subsequent tenth calendar year.

(C) In proceedings under section 801(b)(1) concerning the adjustment of royalty rates under section 116, such petition may be filed in 1990 and in each subsequent tenth calendar year.

(b) With respect to proceedings under subclause (B) or (C) of section 801(b)(2), following an event described in either of those subsections, any owner or user of a copyrighted work whose royalty rates are specified by section 111, or by a rate established by the Tribunal, may, within twelve months, file a petition with the Tribunal declaring that the petitioner requests an adjustment of the rate. In this event the Tribunal shall proceed as in subsection (a)(2), above. Any change in royalty rates made by the Tribunal pursuant to this subsection may be reconsidered in 1980, 1985, and each fifth calendar year thereafter, in accordance with the provisions in section 801(b)(2)(B) or (C), as the case may be.

(c) With respect to proceedings under section 801(b)(1), concerning the determination of reasonable terms and rates of royalty payments as provided in section 118, the Tribunal shall proceed when and as provided by that section.

(d) With respect to proceedings under section 801(b)(3), concerning the distribution of royalty fees in certain circumstances under sections 111 or 116, the Chairman of the Tribunal shall, upon determination by the Tribunal that a controversy exists concerning such distribution, cause to be published in the Federal Register notice of commencement of proceedings under this chapter.

(e) All proceedings under this chapter shall be initiated without delay following publication of the notice specified in this section, and the Tribunal shall render its final decision in any such proceeding within one year from the date of such publication.

### § 805. Staff of the Tribunal

(a) The Tribunal is authorized to appoint and fix the compensation of such employees as may be necessary to carry out the provisions of this chapter, and to prescribe their functions and duties.

(b) The Tribunal may procure temporary and intermittent services to the same extent as is authorized by section 3109 of title 5.

### § 806. Administrative support of the Tribunal

(a) The Library of Congress shall provide the Tribunal with necessary administrative services, including those related to budgeting, accounting, financial reporting, travel, personnel, and procurement. The Tribunal shall pay the Library for such services, either in advance or by reimbursement from the funds of the Tribunal, at amounts to be agreed upon between the Librarian and the Tribunal.

(b) The Library of Congress is authorized to disburse funds for the Tribunal, under regulations prescribed jointly by the Librarian of Congress and the Tribunal and approved by the Comptroller General. Such regulations shall establish requirements and procedures under which every voucher certified for payment by the Library of Congress under this chapter shall be supported with a certification by a duly authorized officer or employee of the Tribunal, and shall prescribe the responsibilities and accountability of said officers and employees of the Tribunal with respect to such certifications.

### § 807. Deduction of costs of proceedings

Before any funds are distributed pursuant to a final decision in a proceeding involving distribution of royalty fees, the Tribunal shall assess the reasonable costs of such proceeding.

### § 808. Reports

In addition to its publication of the reports of all final determinations as provided in section 803(b), the Tribunal shall make an annual report to the President and the Congress concerning the Tribunal's work during the preceding fiscal year, including a detailed fiscal statement of account.

### § 809. Effective date of final determinations

Any final determination by the Tribunal under this chapter shall become effective thirty days following its publication in the Federal Register as provided in section 803(b), unless prior to that time an appeal has been filed pursuant to section 810, to vacate, modify, or correct such determination, and notice of such appeal has been served on all parties who appeared before the Tribunal in the proceeding in question. Where the proceeding involves the distribution of royalty fees under sections 111 or 116, the Tribunal shall, upon the expiration of such thirty-day period, distribute any royalty fees not subject to an appeal filed pursuant to section 810.

### § 810. Judicial review

Any final decision of the Tribunal in a proceeding under section 801(b) may be appealed to the United States Court of Appeals, within thirty days after its publication in the Federal Register by an aggrieved party. The judicial review of the decision shall be had, in accordance with chapter 7 of title 5, on the basis of the record before the Tribunal. No court shall have jurisdiction to review a final decision of the Tribunal except as provided in this section.

## Transitional and Supplementary Provisions

SEC. 102. This Act becomes effective on January 1, 1978, except [as] otherwise expressly provided by this Act, including provisions of the first section of this Act. The provisions of sections 118, 304(b), and chapter 8 of title 17, as amended by the first section of this Act, take effect upon enactment of this Act.

SEC. 103. This Act does not provide copyright protection for any work that goes into the public domain before January 1, 1978. The exclusive rights, as provided by section 106 of title 17 as amended by the first section of this Act, to reproduce a work in phonorecords and to distribute phonorecords of the work, do not extend to any nondramatic musical work copyrighted before July 1, 1909.

SEC. 104. All proclamations issued by the President under section 1(e) or 9(b) of title 17 as it existed on December 31, 1977, or under previous copyright statutes of the United States, shall continue in force until terminated, suspended, or revised by the President.

SEC. 105. (a)(1) Section 505 of title 44 is amended to read as follows:

### "§ 505. Sale of duplicate plates

"The Public Printer shall sell, under regulations of the Joint Committee on Printing to persons who may apply, additional or duplicate stereotype or electrotype plates from which a Government publication is printed, at a price not to exceed the cost of composition, the metal, and making to the Government, plus 10 per centum, and the full amount of the price shall be paid when the order is filed.".

(2) The item relating to section 505 in the sectional analysis at the beginning of chapter 5 of title 44, is amended to read as follows:

### "505. Sale of duplicate plates.".

(b) Section 2113 of title 44 is amended to read as follows:

**"§ 2113. Limitation on liability**

"When letters and other intellectual productions (exclusive of patented material, published works under copyright protection, and unpublished works for which copyright registration has been made) come into the custody or possession of the Administrator of General Services, the United States or its agents are not liable for infringement of copyright or analogous rights arising out of use of the materials for display, inspection, research, reproduction, or other purposes.".

(c) In section 1498(b) of title 28, the phrase "section 101(b) of title 17" is amended to read "section 504(c) of title 17."

(d) Section 543(a)(4) of the Internal Revenue Code of 1954, as amended, is amended by striking out "(other than by reason of section 2 or 6 thereof)."

(e) Section 3202(a) of title 39 is amended by striking out clause (5). Section 3206 of title 39 is amended by deleting the words "subsections (b) and (c)" and inserting "subsection (b)" in subsection (a), and by deleting subsection (c). Section 3206(d) is renumbered (c).

(f) Subsection (a) of section 290(e) of title 15 is amended by deleting the phrase "section 8" and inserting in lieu thereof the phrase "section 105."

(g) Section 131 of title 2 is amended by deleting the phrase "deposit to secure copyright," and inserting in lieu thereof the phrase "acquisition of material under the copyright law,".

SEC. 106. In any case where, before January 1, 1978, a person has lawfully made parts of instruments serving to reproduce mechanically a copyrighted work under the compulsory license provisions of section 1(e) of title 17 as it existed on December 31, 1977, such person may continue to make and distribute such parts embodying the same mechanical reproduction without obtaining a new compulsory license under the terms of section 115 of title 17 as amended by the first section of this Act. However, such parts made on or after January 1, 1978, constitute phonorecords and are otherwise subject to the provisions of said section 115.

SEC. 107. In the case of any work in which an ad interim copyright is subsisting or is capable of being secured on December 31, 1977, under section 22 of title 17 as it existed on that date, copyright protection is hereby extended to endure for the term or terms provided by section 304 of title 17 as amended by the first section of this Act.

SEC. 108. The notice provisions of sections 401 through 403 of title 17 as amended by the first section of this Act apply to all copies or phonorecords publicly distributed on or after January 1, 1978. However, in the case of a work published before January 1, 1978, compliance with the notice provisions of title 17 either as it existed on December 31, 1977, or as amended by the first section of this Act, is adequate with respect to copies publicly distributed after December 31, 1977.

SEC. 109. The registration of claims to copyright for which the required deposit, application, and fee were received in the Copyright Office before January 1, 1978, and the recordation of assignments of copyright or other instruments received in the Copyright Office before January 1, 1978, shall be made in accordance with title 17 as it existed on December 31, 1977.

SEC. 110. The demand and penalty provisions of section 14 of title 17 as it existed on December 31, 1977, apply to any work in which copyright has been secured by publication with notice of copyright on or before that date, but any deposit and registration made after that date in response to a demand under that section shall be made in accordance with the provisions of title 17 as amended by the first section of this Act.

SEC. 111. Section 2318 of title 18 of the United States Code is amended to read as follows:

## "§ 2318. Transportation, sale or receipt of phonograph records bearing forged or counterfeit labels

"(a) Whoever knowingly and with fraudulent intent transports, causes to be transported, receives, sells, or offers for sale in interstate or foreign commerce any phonograph record, disk, wire, tape, film, or other article on which sounds are recorded, to which or upon which is stamped, pasted, or affixed any forged or counterfeited label, knowing the label to have been falsely made, forged, or counterfeited shall be fined not more than $10,000 or imprisoned for not more than one year, or both, for the first such offense and shall be fined not more than $25,000 or imprisoned for not more than two years, or both, for any subsequent offense.

"(b) When any person is convicted of any violation of subsection (a), the court in its judgment of conviction shall, in addition to the penalty therein prescribed, order the forfeiture and destruction or other disposition of all counterfeit labels and all articles to which counterfeit labels have been affixed or which were intended to have had such labels affixed.

"(c) Except to the extent they are inconsistent with the provisions of this title, all provisions of section 509, title 17, United States Code, are applicable to violations of subsection (a)."

SEC. 112. All causes of action that arose under title 17 before January 1, 1978, shall be governed by title 17 as it existed when the cause of action arose.

SEC. 113. (a) The Librarian of Congress (hereinafter referred to as the "Librarian") shall establish and maintain in the Library of Congress a library to be known as the American Television and Radio Archives (hereinafter referred to as the "Archives"). The purpose of the Archives shall be to preserve a permanent record of the television and radio programs which are the heritage of the people of the United States and to provide access to such programs to historians and scholars without encouraging or causing copyright infringement.

(1) The Librarian, after consultation with interested organizations and individuals, shall determine and place in the Archives such copies and phonorecords of television and radio programs transmitted to the public in the United States and in other countries which are of present or potential public or cultural interest, historical significance, cognitive value, or otherwise worthy of preservation, including copies and phonorecords of published and unpublished transmission programs—

(A) acquired in accordance with sections 407 and 408 of title 17 as amended by the first section of this Act; and
(B) transferred from the existing collections of the Library of Congress; and
(C) given to or exchanged with the Archives by other libraries, archives, organizations, and individuals; and
(D) purchased from the owner thereof.
(2) The Librarian shall maintain and publish appropriate catalogs and indexes of the collections of the Archives, and shall make such col-

lections available for study and research under the conditions prescribed under this section.

(b) Notwithstanding the provisions of section 106 of title 17 as amended by the first section of this Act, the Librarian is authorized with respect to a transmission program which consists of a regularly scheduled newscast or on-the-spot coverage of news events and, under standards and conditions that the Librarian shall prescribe by regulation—

(1) to reproduce a fixation of such a program, in the same or another tangible form, for the purposes of preservation or security or for distribution under the conditions of clause (3) of this subsection; and

(2) to compile, without abridgment or any other editing, portions of such fixations according to subject matter, and to reproduce such compilations for the purpose of clause (1) of this subsection; and

(3) to distribute a reproduction made under clause (1) or (2) of this subsection—

(A) by loan to a person engaged in research; and

(B) for deposit in a library or archives which meets the requirements of section 108(a) of title 17 as amended by the first section of this Act, in either case for use only in research and not for further reproduction or performance.

(c) The Librarian or any employee of the Library who is acting under the authority of this section shall not be liable in any action for copyright infringement committed by any other person unless the Librarian or such employee knowingly participated in the act of infringement committed by such person. Nothing in this section shall be construed to excuse or limit liability under title 17 as amended by the first section of this Act for any act not authorized by that title or this section, or for any act performed by a person not authorized to act under that title or this section.

(d) This section may be cited as the "American Television and Radio Archives Act".

SEC. 114. There are hereby authorized to be appropriated such funds as may be necessary to carry out the purposes of this Act.

SEC. 115. If any provision of title 17, as amended by the first section of this Act, is declared unconstitutional, the validity of the remainder of this title is not affected.

Approved October 19, 1976.

# Appendix C

# Copyright Office Regulations*

## PART 201—GENERAL PROVISIONS

Sec.

AUTHORITY: Sec. 207, 61 Stat. 666; 17 U.S.C. 207, unless otherwise noted.

---

*The Copyright Office was not subject to the Administrative Procedure Act before 1978, and it is now subject to it only in areas specified by section 701(d) of the Copyright Act (i.e., "all actions taken by the Register of Copyrights under this title [17]," except with respect to the making of copies of copyright deposits). [17 U.S.C. 706(b)]. The Copyright Act does not make the Office an "agency" as defined in the Administrative Procedure Act. For example, personnel actions taken by the Office are not subject to APA-FOIA requirements.

432

## § 201.1 Communications with the Copyright Office.

(a) *In general.* Mail and other communications shall be addressed to the Register of Copyrights, Library of Congress, Washington, D.C. 20559.

(b) *Inquiries to Licensing Division.* Inquiries about filings related to the four compulsory licenses (17 U.S.C. 111, 115, 116, and 118) should be addressed to the Licensing Division, LM-454, Copyright Office, Library of Congress, Washington, D.C. 20557.

(c) *Copies of records or deposits.* Requests for copies of records or deposits should be addressed to the Certifications and Documents Section, LM-402, Copyright Office, Library of Congress, Washington, D.C. 20559.

(d) *Search of records.* Requests for searches of registrations and recordations in the completed catalogs, indexes, and other records of the Copyright Office should be addressed to the Reference and Bibliography, Section LM-450, Copyright Office, Library of Congress, Washington, D.C. 20559.

## § 201.2 Information given by the Copyright Office.

(a) *In general.* (1) Information relative to the operations of the Copyright Office is supplied without charge. A search of the records, indexes, and deposits will be made for such information as they may contain relative to copyright claims upon application and payment of the statutory fee. The Copyright Office, however, does not undertake the making of comparisons of copyright deposits to determine similarity between works.

(2) The Copyright Office does not furnish the names of copyright attorneys, publishers, agents, or other similar information.

(3) In the administration of the Copyright Act in general, the Copyright Office interprets the Act. The Copyright Office, however, does not give specific legal advice on the rights of persons, whether in connection with particular uses of copyrighted works, cases of alleged foreign or domestic copyright infringement, contracts between authors and publishers, or other matters of a similar nature.

(b) *Inspection and copying of records.* (1) Inspection and copying of completed records and indexes relating to a registration or a recorded document, and inspection of copies or identifying material deposited in connection with a completed copyright registration may be undertaken in the Certifications and Documents Section. Since some of these materials are not stored on the immediate premises of the Copyright Office, it is advisable to consult the Certifications and Documents Section to determine the length of time necessary to produce the requested materials.

(2) It is the general policy of the Copyright Office to deny direct public access to in-process files and to any work (or other) areas where they are kept. Likewise, direct public use of computer terminal intended to access the automated equivalents of these files is not permitted.

(3) Information contained in Copyright Office in-process files may be obtained by anyone upon payment of applicable fees and request to the Information and Reference Division, in accordance with the following procedures:

(i) In general, all requests by the public for information in the in-process and open unfinished business files should be made to the Certifications and Documents Section, which upon receipts of applicable fees will give a report that provides the following for each request:

(A) the date(s) of receipt of: (1) The application(s) for registration that may have been submitted and is (are) in process; (2) the document(s) that may have been submitted for recordation and is (are) in process; (3) the copy or copies (or phonorecords) that may have been submitted; (B) the title of the work(s); and (C) the name of the remitter.

(ii) Such searches of the in-process files will be given priority to the extent permitted by the demands of normal work flow of the affected sections of the Copyright Office.

(4) Access will be afforded as follows to pending applications for registration, the deposit material accompanying them, and pending documents for recordation that were submitted within the twelve month period immediately preceding the request for access: (i) in the case of applications for registration and deposits accompanying them, upon the request of the copyright claimant or his/her authorized representative, and (ii) in the case of documents, upon the request of at least one of the persons who executed the document or by an authorized representative of that person. These requests should be made to the Public Information Office, and the review of the materials will be permitted there. No charge will be made for this service.

(5) In exceptional circumstances, the Register of Copyrights may allow inspection of pending applications and open correspondence files by someone other than the copyright claimant, upon submission of a written request which is deemed by the Register to show good cause for such access and establishes that the person making the request is one properly and directly concerned. The written request should be addressed to the General Counsel of the Copyright Office, Department DS, Washington, D.C. 20540.

(6) In no case will direct public access be permitted to any financial or accounting records.

(7) The Copyright Office maintains administrative staff manuals referred to as its "Compendium of Office Practices I" and "Compendium of Office Practices II" for the general guidance of its staff in making registrations and recording documents. The manuals, as amended and supplemented from time to time, are available for purchase from the National Technical Information Service (Compendium I) and the Government Printing Office (Compendium II). They are also available for public inspection and copying in the Certifications and Documents Section.

(c) *Correspondence*. (1) Official correspondence, including preliminary applications, between copyright claimants or their agents and the Copyright Office, and directly relating to a completed registration, a recorded document, a rejected application for registration, or a document for which recordation was refused is available for public inspection. Requests for reproductions of the correspondence shall be made pursuant to paragraph (d) of this section.

(2) Correspondence, application forms, and any accompanying material forming a part of a pending application are considered in-process files and access to them is governed by paragraph (b) of this section.

(3) Correspondence, memoranda, reports, opinions, and similar material relating to internal matters of personnel and procedures, office administration, security matters, and internal consideration of policy and decisional matters including the work product of an attorney, are not open to public inspection.

(4) The Copyright Office will return unanswered any abusive or scurrilous correspondence.

(d) *Requests for copies*. (1) Requests for copies of records should include the following:

(i) A clear identification of the type of records desired (for example, additional certificates of registration, copies of correspondence, copies of deposits).

(ii) A specification of whether the copies are to be certified or uncertified.

(iii) A clear identification of the specific records to be copied. Requests should include the following specific information, if possible: (A) the type of work involved (for example, novel, lyrics, photograph); (B) the registration number; (C) the year date or approximate year date of registration; (D) the complete title of the work; (E) the author(s) including any pseudonym by which the author may be known; and (F) the claimant(s); and (G) if the requested copy is of an assignment license, contract, or other recorded document, the volume and page number of the recorded document.

(iv) If the copy requested is an additional certificate of registration, include the fee. The Certifications and Documents Section will review requests for copies of other records and quote fees for each.

(v) The telephone number and address of the requestor.

(2) Requests for certified or uncertified reproductions of the copies, phonorecords, or identifying material deposited in connection with a copyright registra-

tion of published or unpublished works in the custody of the Copyright Office will be granted only when one of the following three conditions has been met:

(i) The Copyright Office receives written authorization from the copyright claimant of record or his or her designated agent, or from the owner of any of the exclusive rights in the copyright as long as this ownership can be demonstrated by written documentation of the transfer of ownership.

(ii) The Copyright Office receives a written request from an attorney on behalf of either the plaintiff or defendant in connection with litigation, actual or prospective, involving the copyrighted work. The following information must be included in such a request: (A) The names of all the parties involved and the nature of the controversy; (B) the name of the court in which the actual case is pending or, in the case of a prospective proceeding, a full statement of the facts of the controversy in which the copyrighted work is involved; and (C) satisfactory assurance that the requested reproduction will be used only in connection with the specified litigation.

(iii) The Copyright Office receives a court order for reproduction of the deposited copies, phonorecords, or identifying material of a registered work which is the subject of litigation. The order must be issued by a court having jurisdiction of the case in which the reproduction is to be submitted as evidence.

(3) When a request is made for a reproduction of a phonorecord, such as an audiotape or cassette, in which either a sound recording or the underlying musical, dramatic, or literary work is embodied, the Copyright Office will provide proximate reproduction. The Copyright's Office reserves the right to substitute a monaural reproduction for a stereo, quadraphonic, or any other type of fixation of the work accepted for deposit.

## § 201.3 [Reserved]

## § 201.4 Recordation of transfers and certain other documents.

(a) *General.* (1) This section prescribes conditions for the recordation of transfers of copyright ownership and other documents pertaining to a copyright under section 205 of Title 17 of the United States Code, as amended by Pub. L. 94–553. The filing or recordation of the following documents is not within the provisions of this section:

(i) Certain contracts entered into by cable systems located outside of the 48 contiguous States (17 U.S.C. 111(e); see 37 CFR 201.12);

(ii) Notices of identity and signal carriage complement, and statements of account, of cable systems (17 U.S.C. 111(d); see 37 CFR 201.11; 201.17);

(iii) Original, signed notices of intention to obtain compulsory license to make and distribute phonorecords of nondramatic musical works (17 U.S.C. 115(b); see 37 CFR 201.18);

(iv) License agreements, and terms and rates of royalty payments, voluntarily negotiated between one or more public broadcasting entities and certain owners of copyright (17 U.S.C. 118; see 37 CFR 201.9);

(v) Notices of termination (17 U.S.C. 203, 304(c); see 37 CFR 201.10); and

(vi) Statements regarding the identity of authors of anonymous and pseudonymous works, and statements relating to the death of authors (17 U.S.C. 302).

(2) A "transfer of copyright ownership" has the meaning set forth in section 101 of Title 17 of the United States Code, as amended by Pub. L. 94-553. A document shall be considered to "pertain to a copyright" if it has a direct or indirect relationship to the existence, scope, duration, or identification of a copyright, or to the ownership, division, allocation, licensing, transfer, or exercise of rights under a copyright. That relationship may be past, present, future, or potential.

(3) For purposes of this section:

(i) A "sworn certification" is an affidavit under the official seal of any officer authorized to administer oaths within the United States, or if the original is located outside of the United States, under the official seal of any diplomatic or consular officer of the United States or of a person authorized to administer oaths whose authority is proved by the certificate of such an officer, or a statement in accordance with section 1746 of Title 28 of the United States Code; and

(ii) An "official certification" is a certification, by the appropriate Government official, that the original of the document is on file in a public office and that the reproduction is a true copy or the original.

(b) *Forms.* The Copyright Office does not provide forms for the use of persons recording documents.

(c) *Recordable documents.* Any transfer of copyright ownership (including any instrument of conveyance, or note or memorandum of the transfer), or any other document pertaining to a copyright, may be recorded in the Copyright Office if it is accompanied by the fee set forth in paragraph (d) of this section, and if the requirements of this paragraph with respect to signatures, completeness, and legibility are met.

(1) To be recordable, the document must bear the actual signature or signatures of the person or persons who executed it. Alternatively, the document may be recorded if it is a legible photocopy or other full-size facsimile reproduction of the signed document, accompanied by a sworn certification or an official certification that the reproduction is a true copy of the signed document. Any sworn certification accompanying a reproduction shall be signed by at least one of the persons who executed the document, or by an authorized representative of that person.

(2) To be recordable, the document must be complete by its own terms. (i) A document that contains a reference to any schedule, appendix, exhibit, addendum, or other material as being attached to the document or made a part of it shall be recordable only if the attachment is also submitted for recordation with the document or if the reference is deleted by the parties to the document. If a document has been submitted for recordation and has been returned by the Copyright Office at the request of the sender for deletion of the reference to an attachment, the document will be recorded only if the deletion is signed or initialed by the persons who executed the document or by their authorized representatives. In exceptional cases a document containing a reference to an attachment will be recorded without the attached material and without deletion of the reference if the person seeking recordation submits a written request specifically asserting that: (A) The attachment is completely unavailable for recordation; and (B) the attachment is not essential to the identification of the subject matter of the document; and (C) it would be impossible or wholly impracticable to have the parties to the document sign or initial a deletion of the reference. In such exceptional cases, the Copyright Office records of the document will be annotated to show that recordation was made in response to a specific request under this paragraph.

(ii) If a document otherwise recordable under this indicates on its face that it is a self-contained part of a larger instrument (for example: if it is designated "Attachment A" or "Exhibit B"), the Copyright Office will raise the question of completeness, but will record the document if the person requesting recordation asserts that the document is sufficiently complete as it stands.

(iii) When the document submitted for recordation merely identifies or incorporates by reference another document, or certain terms of another document, the Copyright Office will raise no question of completeness, and will not require recordation of the other document.

(3) To be recordable, the document must be legible and capable of being reproduced in legible microform copies.

(d) *Fee.* For a document consisting of six pages or less covering no more than one title, the basic recording fee is $10. An additional charge of 50 cents is made for each page over six and each title over one. For these purposes:

(1) A fee is required for each separate transfer or other document, even if two or more documents appear on the same page;

(2) The term "title" generally denotes "appellation" or "denomination" rather than "registration," "work," or "copyright"; and

(3) In determining the number of pages in a document, each side of a leaf bearing textual matter is regarded as a "page."

(e) *Recordation*. The date of recordation is the date when a proper document under paragraph (c) of this section and a proper fee under paragraph (d) of this section are all received in the Copyright Office. After recordation the document is returned to the sender with a certificate of record.

(17 U.S.C. 205, 702, 708)
[43 FR 36044, Aug. 8, 1978]

## § 201.5 Corrections and amplifications of copyright registration; applications for supplementary registration.

(a) *General*. (1) This section prescribes conditions relating to the filing of an application for supplementary registration, to correct an error in a copyright registration or to amplify the information given in a registration, under section 408(d) of Title 17 of the United States Code, as amended by Pub. L. 94-553. For the purposes of this section:

(i) A "basic registration" means any of the following: (A) A copyright registration made under sections 408, 409, and 410 of the Title 17 of the United States Code, as amended by Pub. L. 94-553; (B) a renewal registration made under section 304 of Title 17 of the United States Code, as so amended; (C) a registration of claim to copyright made under Title 17 of the United States Code as it existed before January 1, 1978; or (D) a renewal registration made under Title 17 of the United States Code as it existed before January 1, 1978; and

(ii) A "supplementary registration" means a registration made upon application under section 408(d) of Title 17 of the United States Code, as amended by Pub. L. 94-553, and the provisions of this section.

(2) No correction or amplification of the information in a basic registration will be made except pursuant to the provisions of this § 201.5. As an exception, where it is discovered that the record of a basic registration contains an error that the Copyright Office itself should have recognized at the time registration was made, the Office will take appropriate measures to rectify its error.

(b) *Persons entitled to file an application for supplementary registration; grounds of application*. (1) Supplementary registration can be made only if a basic copyright registration for the same work has already been completed. After a basic registration has been completed, any author or other copyright claimant of the work, or the owner of any exclusive right in the work, or the duly authorized agent of any such author, other claimant, or owner, who wishes to correct or amplify the information given in the basic registration for the work may file an application for supplementary registration.[1]

(2) Supplementary registration may be made either to correct or to amplify the information in a basic registration. For the purposes of this section:

(i) A "correction" is appropriate if information in the basic registration was incorrect at the time that basic registration was made, and the error is not one that the Copyright Office itself should have recognized;

(ii) An "amplification" is appropriate: (A) To reflect additional information that could have been given, but was omitted, at the time basic registration was made; or (B) to reflect changes in facts, other than those relating to transfer, license, or ownership of rights in the work, that have occurred since the basic registration was made; or (C) to clarify information given in the basic registration;

---

[1] If the person who, or on whose behalf, an application for supplementary registration is submitted is the same as the person identified as the copyright claimant in the basic registration, the Copyright Office will place a note referring to the supplementary registration on its records of the basic registration.

(iii) Supplementary registration is not appropriate: (A) As an amplification, to reflect the ownership, division, allocation, licensing, or transfer of rights in a work, whether at the time basic registration was made or thereafter; or (B) to correct errors in statements or notices on the copies of phonorecords of a work, or to reflect changes in the content of a work; and

(iv) Supplementary registration to correct a renewal claimant or basis of claim in a basic renewal registration may be made only if the application for supplementary registration and fee are received in the Copyright Office within the statutory time limits for renewal. If the error or omission in a basic renewal registration is extremely minor, and does not involve the identity of the renewal claimant or the legal basis of the claim, supplementary registration may be made at any time. Supplementary registration is not appropriate to add a renewal claimant.

(c) *Form and content of application for supplementary registration.* (1) An application for supplementary registration shall be made on a form prescribed by the Copyright Office shall be accompanied by a fee of $10,[2] and shall contain the following information:

(i) The title of the work as it appears in the basic registration, including previous or alternative titles, if they appear;

(ii) The registration number of the basic registration;

(iii) The year when the basic registration was completed;

(iv) The name or names of the author or authors of the work, and the copyright claimant or claimants in the work, as they appear in the basic registration;

(v) In the case of a correction: (A) The line number and heading or description of the part of the basic registration where the error occurred; (B) a transcription of the erroneous information as it appears in the basic registration; (C) a statement of the correct information as it should have appeared; and (D) if desired, an explanation of the error or its correction;

(vi) In the case of an amplification: (A) The line number and heading or description of the part of the basic registration where the information to be amplified appears; (B) a clear and succinct statement of the information to be added; and (C) if desired, an explanation of the amplification;

(vii) The name and address: (A) To which correspondence concerning the application should be sent; and (B) to which the certificate of supplementary registration should be mailed; and

(viii) A certification. The certification shall consist of: (A) The handwritten signature of the author, other copyright claimant, or owner of exclusive right(s) in the work, or of the duly authorized agent of such author, other claimant or owner (who shall also be identified); (B) the typed or printed name of the person whose signature appears, and the date of signature; and (C) a statement that the person signing the application is the author, other copyright claimant or owner of exclusive right(s) in the work, or the authorized agent of such author, other claimant, or owner, and that the statements made in the application are correct to the best of that person's knowledge.

(2) The form prescribed by the Copyright Office for the foregoing purposes is designated "Application for Supplementary Copyright Registration (Form CA)." Copies of the form are available free upon request to the Public Information Office, United States Copyright Office, Library of Congress, Washington, D.C. 20559.

(3) Copies, phonorecords or supporting documents cannot be made part of the record of a supplementary registration and should not be submitted with the application.

(d) *Effect of supplementary registration.* (1) When a supplementary registration is completed, the Copyright Office will assign it a new registration number if the

---

[2]The $10 fee applies to all applications for supplementary registration, including those made to correct or amplify the information in a renewal registration.

appropriate class, and issue a certificate of supplementary registration under that number.

(2) As provided in section 408(d) of Title 17, the information contained in a supplementary registration augments but does not supersede that contained in the basic registration. The basic registration will not be expunged or cancelled.

(Pub. L. 94-553; 17 U.S.C. 205, 408(d), 601(b), 702, 708)
[43 FR 773, Jan. 4, 1978]

## § 201.6 Payment and refund of Copyright Office fees.

(a) *In general.* All fees sent to the Copyright Office should be in the form of a money order, check or bank draft payable to the Register of Copyrights. Coin or currency sent to the Office in letters or packages will be at the remitter's risk. Remittances from foreign countries should be in the form of an International Money Order or Bank Draft payable and immediately negotiable in the United States for the full amount of the fee required. Uncertified checks are accepted subject to collection. Where the statutory fee is submitted in the form of a check, the registration of the copyright claim or other record made by the Office is provisional until payment in money is received. In the event the fee is not paid, the registration or other record shall be expunged.

(b) *Deposit accounts.* Persons or firms having a considerable amount of business with the Copyright Office may, for their own convenience, prepay copyright expenses by establishing a Deposit Account.

(c) *Refunds.* Money remitted to the Copyright Office for original, basic, supplementary or renewal registration will not be refunded if the claim is rejected because the material deposited does not constitute copyrightable subject matter or because the claim is invalid for any other reason. Payments made by mistake or in excess of the statutory fee will be refunded, but amounts of $5 or less will not be refunded unless specifically requested, and refunds of less than $1 may be made in postage stamps.

(d) *Return of deposit copies.* Copies of works deposited in the Copyright Office pursuant to law are either retained in the Copyright Office, transferred for the permanent collections or other uses of the Library of Congress, or disposed of according to law. When an application is rejected, the Copyright Office reserves the right to retain the deposited copies.

(17 U.S.C. 702, 708(c))
[24 FR 4955, June 18, 1959, as amended at 46 FR 25442, May 7, 1981]

## § 201.7 Cancellation of completed registrations.

(a) *Definition.* Cancellation is an action taken by the Copyright Office whereby either the registration is eliminated on the ground that the registration is invalid under the applicable law and regulations, or the registration number is eliminated and a new registration is made under a different class and number.

(b) *General policy.* The Copyright Office will cancel a completed registration only in those cases where: (1) it is clear that no registration should have been made because the work does not constitute copyrightable subject matter or fails to satisfy the other legal and formal requirements for obtaining copyright; (2) registration may be authorized but the application, deposit material, or fee does not meet the requirements of the law and Copyright Office regulations, and the Office is unable to get the defect corrected; or (3) an existing registration in the wrong class is to be replaced by a new registration in the correct class.

(c) *Circumstances under which a registration will be cancelled.* (1) Where the Copyright Office becomes aware after registration that a work is not copyrightable, either because the authorship is de minimis or the work does not contain authorship subject to copyright, the registration will be cancelled. The copyright claimant will be notified by correspondence of the proposed cancellation and the reasons therefor, and be given 30 days, from the date the Copyright Office letter is mailed, to show cause in writing why the cancellation should not be made. If the claimant fails to respond within the 30 day period, or if the Office after considering the response, determines that the registration was made in error and not in accordance with Title 17 U.S.C., Chapters 1 through 8, the registration will be cancelled.

(2) When a check received in payment of a registration fee is returned to the Copyright Office marked "insufficient funds" or is otherwise uncollectible the Copyright Office will immediately cancel any registration(s) for which the dishonored check was submitted and will notify the remitter the registration has been cancelled because the check was returned as uncollectible.

(3) Where registration is made in the wrong class, the Copyright Office will cancel the first registration, replace it with a new registration in the correct class, and issue a corrected certificate.

(4) Where registration has been made for a work which appears to be copyrightable but after registration the Copyright Office becomes aware that, on the administrative record before the Office, the statutory requirements have apparently not been satisfied, or that information essential to registration has been omitted entirely from the application or is questionable, or correct deposit material has not been deposited, the Office will correspond with the copyright claimant in an attempt to secure the required information or deposit material or to clarify the information previously given on the application. If the Copyright Office receives no reply to its correspondence within 30 days of the date the letter is mailed, or the response does not resolve the substantive defect, the registration will be cancelled. The correspondence will include the reason for the cancellation. The following are instances where a completed registration will be cancelled unless the substantive defect in the registration can be cured:

(i) Eligibility for registration has not been established;

(ii) A work was registered more than 5 years after the date of first publication and the deposit copy or phonorecord does not contain a statutory copyright notice;

(iii) The deposit copies or phonorecords of a work published before January 1, 1978 do not contain a copyright notice or the notice is defective;

(iv) A renewal claim was registered after the statutory time limits for registration had apparently expired;

(v) The application and copy(s) or phonorecord(s) do not match each other and the Office cannot locate a copy of phonorecord as described in the application elsewhere in the Copyright Office of the Library of Congress;

(vi) The application for registration does not identify a copyright claimant or it appears from the transfer statement on the application or elsewhere that the "claimant" named in the application does not have the right to claim copyright;

(vii) A claim to copyright is based on material added to a preexisting work and a reading of the application in its totality indicates that there is no copyrightable new material on which to base a claim;

(viii) A work subject to the manufacturing provisions of the Act of 1909 was apparently published in violation of those provisions;

(ix) For a work published after January 1, 1978 the only claimant given on the application was deceased on the date the application was certified;

(x) A work is not anonymous or pseudonymous and statements on the application and/or copy vary so much that the author cannot be identified; and

(xi) Statements on the application conflict or are so unclear that the claimant cannot be adequately identified.

(d) *Minor substantive errors.* Where a registration includes minor substantive errors or omissions which would generally have been rectified before registration, the Copyright Office will attempt to rectify the error through correspondence with the remitter. Except in those cases enumerated in paragraph (c) of this section, if the Office is unable for any reason to obtain the correct information or deposit copy the registration record will be annotated to state the nature of the informality and show that the Copyright Office attempted to correct the registration.

(17 U.S.C. 406, 409, 410, 702)
[50 FR 40833, Oct. 7, 1985]


§ 201.8 Import statements.

(a) *General.* (1) Upon receipt of a proper request under paragraph (b) of this section, and a fee of $3, the Copyright Office will issue an initial import statement for a work consisting preponderantly of nondramatic literary material that is in the English language, copies of which are to be imported into the United States under section 601(b)(2) of Title 17 of the United States Code, as amended by Pub. L. 94-553, whether registration has been made for the work before, on, or after January 1, 1978, provided no import statement has been issued previously for the same version of the work.

(2) After the issuance of an initial import statement for a work in accordance with a request made under paragraph (b) of this section, and upon receipt of a statement from an appropriate official of the United States Customs Service showing importation of less than two thousand copies of a work, the Copyright Office will issue an additional import statement permitting importation of the number of copies representing the difference between the number of copies already imported and two thousand copies. Additional import statements under paragraph (a)(2) will be issued without request and shall not require payment of a fee.

(3) Any import statement issued by the Copyright Office before January 1, 1978 shall remain valid to permit the importation of the number of copies stated therein. In the case of a work under copyright on December 31, 1977, an additional import statement permitting the importation of the number of copies representing the difference between the number of copies already imported under an import statement issued before January 1, 1978 and two thousand copies will be issued by the Copyright Office:

(i) Without request or payment of a fee, if a statement from an appropriate official of the United States Customs Service showing importation of fifteen-hundred or less copies is received after the effective date of this regulation; and

(ii) Upon the request of the copyright owner, as defined in paragraph (b)(2) of this section, and without payment of a fee, if a statement from an appropriate official of the United States Custom Service showing importation of fifteen-hundred or less copies is received before the effective date of this regulation.

(4) Except as provided by paragraph (a)(5) of this section, the Copyright Office will not issue an import statement where a work is eligible under section 601 of Title 17 of the United States Code, as amended by Pub. L. 94-553, for importation in an unlimited number of copies. A work may be eligible for such importation if it is either:

(i) Outside the scope of the manufacturing requirements of section 601 of Title 17 of the United States Code, as amended by Pub. L. 94-553; or

(ii) Exempted by section 601(b) of Title 17 of the United States Code, as amended by Pub. L. 94-553 from the importation prohibition of paragraph (a) of the same section 601; or

(iii) Unprotected by Title 17 of the United States Code, as amended by Pub. L. 94-553.

(5) In case of a dispute between the United States Customs Service and the copyright owner, as defined in paragraph (b)(2) of this section, regarding eligibility of the work for unlimited importation of copies under section 601 of Title 17 of the United States Code, as amended by Pub. L. 94-553, the Copyright Office will issue an import statement, upon request of the copyright owner, to permit the entry into

the United States of no more than two thousand copies of any work identified in paragraph (a)(4)(i) and (ii) of this section.

(b) *Requests for Import Statement and Issuance.* (1) Import statements will not be issued until after the effective date of registration for the work. However, a request for an import statement may be submitted simultaneously with an application for registration.

(2) Requests for import statements shall be made by the copyright owner of the work as shown in the records of the Copyright Office, or by the duly authorized agent of such owner. For the purpose of this section, the "copyright owner" is a person or organization that owns the exclusive right to import copies of the work into the United States at the time the request is made. The "copyright owner" may be either:

(i) The author of the work (including, in the case of a work made for hire, the employer or other person for whom the work was prepared); or

(ii) A claimant, other than the author, identified in the registration for the work; or

(iii) A person or organization that has obtained ownership of one or more exclusive rights, initially owned by the author, including the exclusive right to import copies into the United States.

(3) Requests for import statements shall be made on a form prescribed by the Copyright Office, and shall contain the following information:

(i) The title of the work;

(ii) The name or names of the author or authors of the work;

(iii) The name or names of the copyright claimants in the work;

(iv) The registration number, if registration has already been made for the work:

(v) The full name, mailing address, and telephone number of an individual person who may be contacted if further information is needed;

(vi) The full name and mailing address of the person or entity to whom or which the statement is to be issued; and

(vii) A certification of the request. The certification shall consist of: (A) The handwritten signature of the copyright owner of the work as shown in the records of the Copyright Office, or the duly authorized agent of such copyright owner (whose identity shall also be given); (B) the typewritten or printed name and address of such copyright owner or agent; (C) the date of signature; and (D) a statement that the person signing the request is the copyright owner or a duly authorized agent of the copyright owner, and that the Copyright Office is authorized to issue an import statement to the name and address given under paragraph (b)(3)(vi) of this section.

(4) The form prescribed by the Copyright Office for the foregoing purposes is designated "Request for Issuance of an Import Statement under sec. 601 of the U.S. Copyright Law (Form IS)." Copies of the form are available free upon request to the Public Information Office, United States Copyright Office, Washington, D.C. 20559.

(5) After the effective date of registration for the work named in the request, the Copyright Office will issue an import statement permitting the importation of two thousand copies of the work to the name and address given under paragraph (b)(3)(vi) of this section.

(17 U.S.C. 601(b); 702)
[46 FR 12704, Feb. 18, 1981]

## § 201.9 Recordation of agreements between copyright owners and public broadcasting entities.

(a) License agreements voluntarily negotiated between one or more owners of copyright in published nondramatic musical works and published pictorial, graphic, and sculptural works, and one or more public broadcasting entities, and terms and rates of royalty payments agreed to among owners of copyright in nondramatic literary works and public broadcasting entities will be filed in the Copyright Office by recordation upon payment of the fee prescribed by this section. The document submitted for recordation shall meet the following requirements:

(1) It shall be an original instrument of agreement; or it shall be a legible photocopy or other full-size facsimile reproduction of an original, accompanied by a certification signed by at least one of the parties to the agreement, or an authorized representative of that party, that the reproduction is a true copy;

(2) It shall bear the signatures of all persons identified as parties to the agreement, or of their authorized agents or representatives;

(3) It shall be complete on its face, and shall include any schedules, appendixes, or other attachments referred to in the instrument as being part of it; and

(4) It shall be clearly identified, in its body or a covering transmittal letter, as being submitted for recordation under 17 U.S.C. 118.

(b) For a document consisting of six pages or less covering no more than one title, the basic recordation fee is $10; an additional charge of 50 cents is made for each page over six and each title over one.

(c) The date of recordation is the date when all of the elements required for recordation, including the prescribed fee, have been received in the Copyright Office. A document is filed in the Copyright Office, and a filing in the Copyright Office takes place on the date of recordation. After recordation the document is returned to the sender with a certificate of record.

(17 U.S.C. 207 and 17 U.S.C. 118, 702, 708(11), as amended by Pub. L. 94-553)
[42 FR 16777, Mar. 30, 1977, as amended at 46 FR 33249, June 29, 1981]

## § 201.10 Notices of termination of transfers and licenses covering extended renewal term.

(a) *Form.* The Copyright Office does not provide printed forms for the use of persons serving notices of termination.

(b) *Contents.* (1) A notice of termination must include a clear identification of each of the following:

(i) The name of each grantee whose rights are being terminated, or the grantee's successor in title, and each address at which service of the notice is being made;

(ii) The title and the name of at least one author of, and the date copyright was originally secured in, each work to which the notice of termination applies; and, if possible and practicable, the original copyright registration number;

(iii) A brief statement reasonably identifying the grant to which the notice of termination applies;

(iv) The effective date of termination; and

(v) In the case of a termination of a grant executed by a person or persons other than the author, a listing of the surviving person or persons who executed the grant. In the case of a termination of a grant executed by one or more of the authors of the work where the termination is exercised by the successors of a deceased author, a listing of the names and relationships to that deceased author of all of the following, together with specific indication of the person or persons executing the notice who constitute more than one-half of that author's termination interest: That author's surviving widow or widower; and all of that author's surviving children; and, where any of that author's children are dead, all of the surviving children of any such deceased child of that author; however, instead of the information required by this paragraph (v), the notice may contain both of the following: (A) A statement of as much of such information as is currently available to the person or persons signing the notice, with a brief explanation of the reasons why full information is or may be lacking; together with (B) a statement that, to the best knowledge and belief of the person or persons signing the notice, the notice has been signed by all persons whose signature is necessary to terminate the grant under section 304(c) of Title 17 U.S.C., or by their duly authorized agents.

(2) Clear identification of the information specified by paragraph (b)(1) of this section requires a complete and unambiguous statement of facts in the notice itself, without incorporation by reference of information in other documents or records.

(c) *Signature.* (1) In the case of a termination of a grant executed by a person or persons other than the author, the notice shall be signed by all of the surviving person or persons who executed the grant, or by their duly authorized agents.

(2) In the case of a termination of a grant executed by one or more of the authors of the work, the notice as to any one author's share shall be signed by that author or by his or her duly authorized agent. If that author is dead, the notice shall be signed by the number and proportion of the owners of that author's termination interest required under clauses (1) and (2) of section 304(c) of Title 17, U.S.C., or by their duly authorized agents, and shall contain a brief statement of their relationship or relationships to that author.

(3) Where a signature is by a duly authorized agent, it shall clearly identify the person or persons on whose behalf the agent is acting.

(4) The handwritten signature of each person effecting the termination shall either be accompanied by a statement of the full name and address of that person, typewritten or printed legibly by hand, or shall clearly correspond to such a statement elsewhere in the notice.

(d) *Service.* (1) The notice of notice of termination shall be served upon each grantee whose rights are being terminated, or the grantee's successor in title, by personal service, or by first-class mail sent to an address which, after a reasonable investigation, is found to be the last known address of the grantee or successor in title.

(2) The service provision of section 304(c)(4) of Title 17, U.S. C., will be satisfied if, before the notice of termination is served, a reasonable investigation is made by the person or persons executing the notice as to the current ownership of the rights being terminated, and based on such investigation: (i) If there is no reason to believe that such rights have been transferred by the grantee to a successor in title, the notice is served on the grantee; or (ii) if there is reason to believe that such rights have been transferred by the grantee to a particular successor in title, the notice is served on such successor in title.

(3) For purposes of paragraph (d)(2) of this section, a "reasonable investigation" includes, but is not limited to, a search of the records in the Copyright Office; in the case of a musical composition with respect to which performing rights are licensed by a performing rights society, as defined by section 116(e)(3) of Title 17, U.S.C., a "reasonable investigation" also includes a report from that performing rights society identifying the person or persons claiming current ownership of the rights being terminated.

(4) Compliance with the provisions of clauses (2) and (3) of this paragraph (d) will satisfy the service requirements of section 304(c)(4) of Title 17, U.S.C. However, as long as the statutory requirements have been met, the failure to comply with the regulatory provisions of paragraph (d)(2) or (3) of this section will not affect the validity of the service.

(e) *Harmless errors.* (1) Harmless errors in a notice that do not materially affect the adequacy of the information required to serve the purposes of section 304(c) of Title 17, U.S.C., shall not render the notice invalid.

(2) Without prejudice to the general rule provided by paragraph (e)(1) of this section (e), errors made in giving the date or registration number referred to in paragraph (b)(1)(ii) of this section, or in complying with the provisions of paragraph (b)(1)(v) of this section, or in describing the precise relationships under clause (2) of paragraph (c) of this section, shall not affect the validity of the notice if the errors were made in good faith and without any intention to deceive, mislead, or conceal relevant information.

(f) *Recordation.* (1) A copy of the notice of termination will be recorded in the Copyright Office upon payment of the fee prescribed by paragraph (2) of this paragraph (f) and upon compliance with the following provisions:

(i) The copy submitted for recordation shall be a complete and exact duplicate of the notice of termination as served and shall include the actual signature or signatures, or a reproduction of the actual signature or signatures, appearing on the notice; where separate copies of the same notice were served on more than one grantee or successor in title, only one copy need be submitted for recordation; and

(ii) The copy submitted for recordation shall be accompanied by a statement setting forth the date on which the notice was served and the manner of service, unless such information is contained in the notice.

(2) For a document consisting of six pages or less, covering no more than one title, the basic recordation fee is $5 if recorded before January 1, 1978, and $10 if recorded after December 31, 1977; in either case an additional charge of 50 cents is made for each page over six and each title over one. The statement referred to in paragraph (f)(1)(ii) of this section will be considered a part of the document for this purpose.

(3) The date of recordation is the date when all of the elements required for recordation, including the prescribed fee and, if required, the statement referred to in paragraph (f)(1)(ii) of this section, have been received in the Copyright Office. After recordation the document, including any accompanying statement, is returned to the sender with a certificate of record.

(4) Recordation of a notice of termination by the Copyright Office is without prejudice to any party claiming that the legal and formal requirements for issuing a valid notice have not been met.

(Pub. L. 94-553: 17 U.S.C. 304(c), 702, 708(11))
[42 FR 45920, Sept. 13, 1977]

## § 201.11 Notices of identity and signal carriage complement of cable systems.

(a) *Definitions.* (1) An "Initial Notice of Identity and Signal Carriage Complement" or "Initial Notice" is a notice under section 111(d)(1) of Title 17 of the United States Code as amended by Pub. L. 94-553 and required by that section to be recorded in the Copyright Office "at least one month before the date of commencement of operations of the cable system or within one hundred and eighty days after (October 19, 1976), whichever is later," for any secondary transmission by the cable system to be subject to compulsory licensing.

(2) A "Notice of Change of Identity or Signal Carriage Complement" or "Notice of Change" is a notice under section 111(d)(1) of Title 17 of the United States Code as amended by Pub. L. 94-553 and required by that section to be recorded in the Copyright Office "within thirty days after each occasion on which the ownership or control or signal carriage complement of the cable system changes" for any secondary transmission by the cable system to be subject to compulsory licensing.

(3) A "cable system" is a facility, located in any State, Territory, Trust Territory, or Possession, that in whole or in part receives signals transmitted or programs broadcast by one or more television broadcast stations licensed by the Federal Communications Commission, and makes secondary transmissions of such signals or programs by wires, cables, or other communications channels to subscribing members of the public who pay for such service. A system that meets this definition is considered a "cable system" for copyright purposes, even if the FCC excludes it from being considered a "cable system" because of the number or nature of its subscribers or the nature of its secondary transmissions. The Notices required to be recorded by this section, and the statements of account and royalty fees to be deposited under § 201.17 of these regulations, shall be recorded and deposited by each individual cable system desiring its secondary transmissions to be subject to compulsory licensing. For these purposes, and the purposes of § 201.17 of these regulations, an "individual" cable system is each cable system recognized as a distinct

entity under the rules, regulations, and practices of the Federal Communications Commission in effect: (i) On the date of recordation with the Copyright Office, in the case of the preparation and filing of an Initial Notice of Identity and Signal Carriage Complement or Notice of Change of Identity or Signal Carriage Complement; or (ii) on the last day of the accounting period covered by a Statement of Account, in the case of the preparation and deposit of a Statement of Account and copyright royalty fee. For these purposes, two or more cable facilities are considered as one individual cable system if the facilities are either: (A) In contiguous communities under common ownership or control or (B) operating from one headend.

(4) In the case of cable systems which make secondary transmissions of all available FM radio signals, which signals are not electronically processed by the system as separate and discrete signals, an FM radio signal is "generally receivable" if: (i) It is usually carried by the system whenever it is received at the system's headend, and (ii) as a result of monitoring at reasonable times and intervals, it can be expected to be received at the system's headend, with the system's FM antenna, at least three consecutive hours each day at the same time each day, five or more days a week, for four or more weeks during any calendar quarter, with a strength of not less than fifty microvolts per meter measured at the foot of the tower or pole to which the antenna is attached.

(5) The signals of a primary transmitter are "regularly carried" if they are carried by the cable system for at least one hour each week for thirteen or more consecutive weeks, or if, in the cases described in paragraph (a)(4) of this section, they comprise generally receivable FM radio signals.

(b) *Forms.* The Copyright Office does not provide printed forms for the use of persons recording Initial Notices or Notices of Change.

(c) *Initial notices.* (1) An Initial Notice of Identity and Signal Carriage Complement shall be identified as such by prominent caption or heading, and shall include the following:

(i) The designation "Owner," followed by: (A) The full legal name of the owner of the cable system. If the owner is a partnership, the name of the partnership is to be followed by the name of at least one individual partner; (B) any other name or names under which the owner conducts or proposes to conduct the business of the cable system; and (C) the full mailing address of the owner. Ownership, other names under which the owner conducts the business of the cable system, and the owner's mailing address shall reflect facts existing on the day the Notice is signed.

(ii) The designation "System," followed by: (A) Any business or trade names used to identify the business and operation of the cable system, unless these names have already been given under the designation "Owner"; and (B) the full mailing address of the system, unless such address is the same as the address given under the designation "Owner." Business or trade names used to identify the business and operation of the system, and the system's mailing address, shall reflect the facts existing on the day the Notice is signed.

(iii) The designation "Area Served," followed by the name of the community or communities served by the system. For this purpose a "community" is the same as a "community unit" as defined in FCC rules and regulations.

(iv) The designation "Signal Carriage Complement," followed by the name and location of the primary transmitter or primary transmitters whose signals are, or are expected to be, regularly carried by the cable system. Carriage of a primary transmitter under FCC rules and regulations in effect on October 19, 1976, which permitted carriage of specific network programs on a part-time basis in certain circumstances (former 47 CFR 76.59(d)(2) and (4); 76.61(e)(2) and (4); and 76.63, referring to § 76.61(e)(2) and (4), all of which were deleted June 25, 1981) need not be reported.

(A) The "name" of the primary transmitter(s) shall be given by station call sign, accompanied by a brief statement of the type of signal carried (for example, "TV," "FM," or "AM"). The "location" of the primary transmitter(s) shall be given as the name of the community to which the transmitter is licensed by the Federal Communications Commission (in the case of domestic signals) or with which the transmitter is identified (in the case of foreign signals).

(B) In the case of cable systems which make secondary transmissions of all available FM radio signals, which signals are not electronically processed by the system as separate and discrete signals, the Notice shall identify that portion of its signal carriage as "all-band FM" or the like, and shall separately identify the name and location of each primary transmitter of such signals whose signals are generally receivable by the system. In any case where such generally receivable FM signals cannot be determined at the time of recording of the initial Notice, they shall be subsequently identified in a Special Amendment recorded in compliance with paragraph (e)(2) of this section.

(v) The individual signature of: (A) The owner of the cable system or of a duly authorized agent of the owner, if the owner is not a partnership or a corporation; or (B) a partner, if the owner is a partnership; or (C) an officer of the corporation, if the owner is a corporation. The signature shall be accompanied by the printed or typewritten name of the person signing the Notice, by the date of signature and, if the owner of the cable system is a partnership or corporation, by the title or official position held in the partnership or corporation by the person signing the Notice.

(d) *Notices of change.* (1) A Notice of Change of Identity or Signal Carriage Complement shall be identified as such by prominent caption or heading, and shall include the following:

(i) In the case of a change of ownership: (A) The designation "Former Owner," followed by the full legal name of the owner of the cable system as given in the Initial Notice recorded by the cable system, or, if an earlier Notice of Change affecting ownership has been recorded by the cable system, as given in the last such Notice;[3] (B) the designation "New Owner," followed by: (*1*) The full legal name of the person who, or partnership or corporation which, now owns the cable system. If the new owner is a partnership, the name of the partnership is to be followed by the name of at least one individual partner; (*2*) any other name or names under which the new owner conducts, or proposes to conduct, the business of the cable system; and (*3*) the full mailing address of the new owner; (C) the designation "System," followed by the information required by paragraph (c)(1)(ii) of this section; and (D) the effective date of the change of ownership.

(ii) In the case of a change of signal carriage complement: (A) The designation "Owner," followed by the information called for by paragraph (c)(1)(i) or (d)(1)(i)(B) of this section, as given in the Initial Notice recorded by the cable system or, if an earlier Notice of Change affecting ownership has been recorded by the cable system, as given in the last such Notice;[4] (B) the designation "System," followed by the information required by paragraph (c)(1)(ii) of this section; (C) the names and locations of the primary transmitter or primary transmitters whose signals have been added to or deleted (as shall be stated in the Notice) from the system's signal carriage complement, given as set forth in paragraphs (c)(1)(iv) (A) and (B) of this section; and (D) the approximate date of each such addition or deletion.

(iii) In the case of either a change in ownership or in signal carriage complement, the Notice of Change shall be signed and dated in accordance with paragraph (c)(1)(v) of this section.

(2) Unless accompanying a change in ownership and required to be given by paragraph (d)(1)(i) of this section, a Notice of Change is not required to be recorded to

---

[3]In the case of a change of ownership: (i) for which a Notice of Change was not recorded before February 10, 1978 and (ii) which involves a cable system that recorded an Initial Notice or Notice of Change before February 10, 1978 without identifying the owner of the system, the designation "Former Owner" shall be followed by the name of the person who, or entity which, was given as the operator or person or entity exercising primary control in the Initial Notice or last Notice of Change.

[4]In the case of a change of signal carriage complement: (i) for which a Notice of Change was not recorded before February 10, 1978 and (ii) which involves a cable system that recorded an Initial Notice or Notice of Change before February 10, 1978 without identifying the owner of the system, the designation "Owner" shall be followed by the name of the person who, or entity which, was given as the operator or person or entity exercising primary control in the Initial Notice or last Notice of Change.

reflect changes occurring on or after February 10, 1978, in: (i) Fictitious or assumed names used by the owner of a cable system for the purpose of conducting the business of the cable system; (ii) trade or business names or styles used to identify the business and operation of the cable system; (iii) mailing addresses of the owner of the cable system or of the system; (iv) the name of the operator of the cable system; or (v) the name of the person or entity exercising primary control over the system. A Notice of Change is not required to be recorded to reflect changes in, or in the names of, the community or communities served by the cable system.

(3) In the case of cable systems which make secondary transmissions of all available FM radio signals, which signals are not electronically processed by the system as separate and discrete signals, and which have not recorded an Initial Notice identifying the primary transmitters of FM signals generally receivable by the system, a Notice of Change shall not be required to be recorded to reflect changes in the complement of such signals until the expiration of one hundred and twenty days from the date of recordation of a Special Amendment under paragraph (e)(2) or (e)(3) of this section.

(4) Notice of change in ownership and in signal carriage complement may be combined in one Notice of Change, if the information required under paragraph (d)(1) of this section is given for each change.

(e) *Amendment of notices—*(1) *General (permissive) amendments to correct errors or omissions.* The Copyright Office will record amendments to Initial Notices or Notices of Change submitted to correct an error or omission in the information given in the earlier document. An amendment is not appropriate to reflect developments or changes in facts occurring after the date of signature of an Initial Notice or Notice of Change. An amendment shall: (i) Be clearly and prominently identified as an "Amendment to Initial Notice of Identity and Signal Carriage Complement" or "Amendment to Notice of Change of Identity or Signal Carriage Complement"; (ii) identify the specific Notice intended to be amended so that it may be readily located in the records of the Copyright Office; (iii) clearly specify the nature of the amendment to be made; and (iv) be signed and dated in accordance with paragraph (c)(1)(v) of this section. The signature shall be accompanied by the printed or typewritten name of the owner of the system as given in the Notice sought to be amended. The recordation of an amendment under this paragraph shall have only such effect as may be attributed to it by a court of competent jurisdiction.

(2) *Special (Required) Amendments for Certain Cable Systems.* Any cable system which records an Initial Notice of Identity and Signal Carriage Complement and is required by the last sentence of paragraph (c)(1)(iv)(B) of this section to record a special amendment shall, no later than one hundred and twenty days after recordation of the Initial Notice, record an amendment to that Notice identifying the primary transmitter or primary transmitters of FM signals generally receivable by the system as of the date of the amendment in accordance with paragraphs (c)(1)(iv) (A) and (B) of this section. Such amendment shall: (i) Be clearly and prominently identified as an "Amendment to Initial Notice of Identity and Signal Carriage Complement"; (ii) specifically identify the Initial Notice intended to be amended so that it may be readily located in the records of the Copyright Office; and (iii) be signed and dated in accordance with paragraph (c)(1)(v) of this section. The signature shall be accompanied by the printed or typewritten name of the owner of the system as given in the Notice sought to be amended.

(f) *Recordation.* (1) The Copyright Office will record the Notices and amendments described in this section by placing them in the appropriate public files of the Office. The Copyright Office will advise cable systems of errors or omissions appearing on the face of documents submitted to it, and will require that any such obvious errors or omissions be corrected before the documents will be recorded. However, recordation by the Copyright Office shall establish only the fact and date thereof; such recordation shall in no case be considered a determination that the document

---

[5] [Reserved]

was, in fact, properly prepared or that all of the requirements to qualify for a compulsory license have been satisfied.

(2) No fee shall be required for the recording of Initial Notices, Notices of Change, or the Special Amendments identified in paragraphs (e)(2) and (e)(3) of this section. A fee of $10 shall accompany any General Amendment permitted by paragraph (e)(1) of this section.

(3) Upon request and payment of a fee of $3, the Copyright Office will furnish a certified receipt for any Notice or amendment recorded under this section.

(17 U.S.C. 111, 702)
[43 FR 27830, June 27, 1978, as amended at 47 FR 21789, May 20, 1982; 49 FR 13037, Apr. 2, 1984]

## § 201.12 Recordation of certain contracts by cable systems located outside of the forty-eight contiguous states.

(a) Written, nonprofit contracts providing for the equitable sharing of costs of videotapes and their transfer, as identified in section 111(e)(2) of Title 17 of the United States Code as amended by Pub. L. 94-553, will be filed in the Copyright Office by recordation upon payment of the fee prescribed by this section. The document submitted for recordation shall meet the following requirements:

(1) It shall be an original instrument of contract; or it shall be a legible photocopy or other full-size facsimile reproduction of an original, accompanied by a certification signed by at least one of the parties to the contract, or an authorized representative of that party, that the reproduction is a true copy;

(2) It shall bear the signatures of all persons identified as parties to the contract, or of their authorized agents or representatives;

(3) It shall be complete on its face, and shall include any schedules, appendixes, or other attachments referred to in the instrument as being part of it; and

(4) It shall be clearly identified, in its body or a covering transmittal letter, as being submitted for recordation under 17 U.S.C. 111(e).

(b) For a document consisting of six pages or less the recordation fee is $10; an additional charge of 50 cents is made for each page over six. If titles of works are specified in the contract, an additional charge of 50 cents is made for each title over one.

(c) The date of recordation is the date when all of the elements required for recordation, including the prescribed fee, have been received in the Copyright Office. A document is filed in the Copyright Office and a filing in the Copyright Office takes place on the date of recordation. After recordation the document is returned to the sender with a certificate of record.

(Pub. L. 94-553; 17 U.S.C. 111, 702, 708(11))
[42 FR 53961, Oct. 4, 1977]

## § 201.13 Notices of objection to certain noncommercial performances of nondramatic literary or musical works.

(a) *Definitions.* (1) A "Notice of Objection" is a notice, as required by section 110(4) of Title 17 of the United States Code as amended by Pub. L. 94-553, to be served as a condition of preventing the noncommercial performance of a nondramatic literary or musical work under certain circumstances.

(2) For purposes of this section, the "copyright owner" of a nondramatic literary or musical work is the author of the work (including, in the case of a work made for hire, the employer or other person for whom the work was prepared), or a person or organization that has obtained ownership of the exclusive right, initially owned by the author of performance of the type referred to in 17 U.S.C. 110(4). If the other

requirements of this section are met, a Notice of Objection may cover the works of more than one copyright owner.

(b) *Form.* The Copyright Office does not provide printed forms for the use of persons serving Notices of Objection.

(c) *Contents.* (1) A Notice of Objection must clearly state that the copyright owner objects to the performance, and must include all of the following:

(i) Reference to the statutory authority on which the Notice of Objection is based, either by citation of 17 U.S.C. 110(4) or by a more general characterization or description of that statutory provision.

(ii) The date and place of the performance to which an objection is being made; however, if the exact date or place of a particular performance, or both, are not known to the copyright owner, it is sufficient if the Notice describes whatever information the copyright owner has about the date and place of a particular performance, and the source of that information unless the source was considered private or confidential;

(iii) Clear identification, by title and at least one author, of the particular nondramatic literary or musical work or works, to the performance of which the copyright owner thereof is lodging objection; a Notice may cover any number of separately identified copyrighted works owned by the copyright owner or owners serving the objection. Alternatively, a blanket notice, with or without separate identification of certain copyrighted works, and purporting to cover one or more groups of copyrighted works not separately identified by title and author, shall have effect if the conditions specified in paragraph (c)(2) of this section are met; and

(iv) A concise statement of the reasons for the objection.

(2) A blanket notice purporting to cover one or more groups of copyrighted works not separately identified by title and author shall be valid only if all of the following conditions are met:

(i) The Notice shall identify each group of works covered by the blanket notice by a description of any common characteristics distinguishing them from other copyrighted works, such as common author, common copyright owner, common publisher, or common licensing agent;

(ii) The Notice shall identify a particular individual whom the person responsible for the performance can contact for more detailed information about the works covered by the blanket notice and to determine whether a particular work planned for performance is in fact covered by the Notice. Such identification shall include the full name and business and residence addresses of the individual, telephone numbers at which the individual can be reached throughout the period between service of the notice and the performance, and name, addresses, and telephone numbers of another individual to contact during that period in case the first cannot be reached.

(iii) If the copyright owner or owners of all works covered by the blanket notice is not identified in the Notice, the Notice shall include an offer to identify, by name and last known address, the owner or owners of any and all such works, upon request made to the individual referred to in paragraph (c)(2)(ii) of this section.

(3) A Notice of Objection must also include clear and prominent statements explaining that:

(i) A failure to exclude the works identified in the Notice from the performance in question may subject the person responsible for the performance to liability for copyright infringement; and

(ii) The objection is without legal effect if there is no direct or indirect admission charge for the performance, and if the other conditions of 17 U.S.C. 110(4) are met.

(d) *Signature and identification.* (1) A Notice of Objection shall be in writing and signed by each copyright owner, or such owner's duly authorized agent, as required by 17 U.S.C. 110(4)(B)(i).

(2) The signature of each owner or agent shall be an actual handwritten signature of an individual, accompanied by the date of signature and the full name, address, and telephone number of that person, typewritten or printed legibly by hand.

(3) If a Notice of Objection is initially served in the form of a telegram or similar communication, as provided by paragraph (e) of this section, the requirement for an

individual's handwritten signature shall be considered waived if the further conditions of said paragraph (e) are met.

(e) *Service.* (1) A Notice of Objection shall be served on the person responsible for the performance at least seven days before the date of the performance, as provided by 17 U.S.C. 110 (4)(B)(ii).

(2) Service of the Notice may be effected by any of the following methods:

(i) Personal service;

(ii) First-class mail;

(iii) Telegram, cablegram, or similar form of communication, if: (A) The Notice meets all of the other conditions provided by this section; and (B) before the performance takes place, the person responsible for the performance receives written confirmation of the Notice, bearing the actual handwritten signature of each copyright owner or duly authorized agent.

(3) The date of service is the date the Notice of Objection is received by the person responsible for the performance or any agent or employee of that person.

(Pub. L. 94-553; 17 U.S.C. 110(4), 702)
[42 FR 64684, Dec. 28, 1977]

## § 201.14 Warnings of copyright for use by certain libraries and archives.

(a) *Definitions.* (1) A "Display Warning of Copyright" is a notice under paragraphs (d)(2) and (e)(2) of section 108 of title 17 of the United States Code as amended by Pub. L. 94-553. As required by those sections the "Display Warning of Copyright" is to be displayed at the place where orders for copies or phonorecords are accepted by certain libraries and archives.

(2) An "Order Warning of Copyright" is a notice under paragraphs (d)(2) and (e)(2) of section 108 of Title 17 of the United States Code as amended by Pub. L. 94-553. As required by those sections the "Order Warning of Copyright" is to be included on printed forms supplied by certain libraries and archives and used by their patrons for ordering copies or phonorecords.

(b) *Contents.* A Display Warning of Copyright and an Order Warning of Copyright shall consist of a verbatim reproduction of the following notice, printed in such size and form and displayed in such manner as to comply with paragraph (c) of this section:

NOTICE WARNING CONCERNING COPYRIGHT RESTRICTIONS

The copyright law of the United States (Title 17, United States Code) governs the making of photocopies or other reproductions of copyrighted material.

Under certain conditions specified in the law, libraries and archives are authorized to furnish a photocopy or other reproduction. One of these specific conditions is that the photocopy or reproduction is not to be "used for any purpose other than private study, scholarship, or research." If a user makes a request for, or later uses, a photocopy or reproduction for purposes in excess of "fair use," that user may be liable for copyright infringement.

This institution reserves the right to refuse to accept a copying order if, in its judgment, fulfillment of the order would involve violation of copyright law.

(c) *Form and manner of use.* (1) A Display Warning of Copyright shall be printed on heavy paper or other durable material in type at least 18 points in size, and shall be displayed prominently, in such manner and location as to be clearly visible, legible, and comprehensible to a casual observer within the immediate vicinity of the place where orders are accepted.

(2) An Order Warning of Copyright shall be printed within a box located prominently on the order form itself, either on the front side of the form or immediately adjacent to the space calling for the name or signature of the person using the form. The notice shall be printed in type size no smaller than that used predominantly throughout the form, and in no case shall the type size be smaller than 8 points. The

notice shall be printed in such manner as to be clearly legible, comprehensible, and readily apparent to a casual reader of the form.

(Pub. L. 94-553; 17 U.S.C. 108, 702)
[42 FR 59265, Nov. 16, 1977]

## § 201.15  Voluntary license to permit reproduction of nondramatic literary works solely for use of the blind and physically handicapped.

(a) *General.* (1) The "blind and physically handicapped" are persons eligible for special loan services of the Library of Congress, as designated by section 135a of Title 2 of the United States Code as amended by Pub. L. 89-552 and regulations of the Library of Congress issued under that section.

(2) This section, and any license granted or exercised under this section, applies only to nondramatic literary works that have previously been published with the consent of the copyright owner.

(b) *Form.* The Copyright Office provides the following form as part of the applications for registration of claims to copyright in nondramatic literary works (Form TX):

REPRODUCTION FOR USE OF BLIND OR PHYSICALLY HANDICAPPED PERSONS

Signature of this form at space 10, and a check in one of the boxes here in space 8, constitutes a nonexclusive grant of permission to the Library of Congress to reproduce and distribute solely for the blind and physically handicapped and under the conditions and limitations prescribed by the regulations of the Copyright Office: (1) copies of the work identified in space 1 of this application in Braille (or similar tactile symbols); or (2) phonorecords embodying a fixation of a reading of that work; or (3) both.

a ☐ Copies and phonorecords; b ☐ Copies only; c ☐ Phonorecords only.

(c) *Terms and conditions.* A copyright owner who consents to the use of a copyrighted work by the Library of Congress for the use of the blind and physically handicapped may accomplish this purpose by checking the appropriate box on the application form, by signing the application form as a whole, and by submitting the application for copyright registration to the Copyright Office. The copyright owner thereby grants a nonexclusive license to the Library of Congress with respect to the work identified in the application under the terms and conditions set forth in this section.

(1) The work may be reproduced only by or on behalf of the Library of Congress.

(2) The work may not be reproduced in any other form than Braille (or similar tactile symbols), or by a fixation of a reading of the work in phonorecords specifically designed for use of the blind and physically handicapped, or both, as designated by the copyright owner on the application form.

(3) Such copies and phonorecords of the work may be distributed by the Library of Congress solely for the use of the blind and physically handicapped under conditions and guidelines provided by the National Library Service for the Blind and Physically Handicapped of the Library of Congress.

(4) In the case of any conflict with any other right or license given by the copyright owner to the Library of Congress pertaining to the work, the terms and conditions most favorable to the Library of Congress for the benefit of the blind and physically handicapped shall govern.

(5) Copies and phonorecords reproduced and distributed under this license will contain identification of the author and publisher of the work, and copyright notice, as they appear on the copies or phonorecords deposited with the application.

(6) This license is nonexclusive, and the copyright owner is in no way precluded from granting other nonexclusive licenses with respect to reproduction for the use of the blind and physically handicapped, or exclusive licenses for the same purpose on condition they are subject to the nonexclusive license granted to the Library of Con-

gress, or other exclusive or nonexclusive licenses or transfers with respect to reproduction or distribution for other purposes.

(7) All responsibility for the clearing and exercise of the rights granted is that of the Library of Congress.

(d) *Duration of license.* (1) The license is effective upon the effective date of registration for the work and, subject to the conditions and procedures stated in paragraph (d)(2) of this section, continues for the full term of copyright in the work provided in section 302 of Title 17 of the United States Code as amended by Pub. L. 94-553.

(2) Termination of the license may be accomplished by the copyright owner at any time by submitting a written statement of intent to terminate, signed by the copyright owner or by the duly authorized agent of the copyright owner, to the National Library Service for the Blind and Physically Handicapped of the Library of Congress. Termination will become effective 90 days after receipt of the written statement, or at a later time set forth in the statement. Upon the effective date of termination the Library of Congress will be prohibited from reproducing additional copies or phonorecords of the work, or both, without the consent of the copyright owner, but copies or phonorecords, or both, reproduced under authority of the license before the effective date of termination may continue to be utilized and distributed under the terms of the license after its termination.

(17 U.S.C. 408, 702, 710)
[45 FR 13073, Feb. 28, 1980]

## § 201.16 Recordation and certification of coin-operated phonorecord players.

(a) *General.* This regulation prescribes the procedures to be followed by operators of coin-operated phonorecord players who wish to obtain a compulsory license for the public performance of nondramatic musical works, and by the Copyright Office in issuing certificates, under section 116 of Title 17 of the United States Code as amended by Pub. L. 94-553. The terms "operator" and "coin-operated phonorecord player" have the meanings given to them by paragraph (e) of that section.

(b) *Form and content of application.* (1) Each application for a compulsory license under this section shall be on a form prescribed by the Copyright Office and shall contain the following information:

(i) The legal name of the operator, together with any fictitious or assumed name used by the operator for the purpose of conducting the business relating to the coin-operated phonorecord player for which the application is made. If the operator is a partnership, the name of at least one individual partner shall also be given;

(ii) The full address of the operator's place of business, including a specific number and street name or rural route. A post office box number or similar designation will not generally be accepted. The Copyright Office will accept a post office box number or similar designation in special cases if, after consulting with officials of the U.S. Postal Service, the Office concludes that no better address for the operator's place of business is possible.

(iii) The name or a specified designation of the manufacturer of the coin-operated phonorecord player for which the application is made;

(iv) The serial number on the coin-operated phonorecord player for which the application is made. If a serial number does not appear on that player, all the information required by paragraph (b)(2) of this section shall be given;

(v) The name, address, and telephone number of an individual who may be contacted by the Copyright Office fur further information about the application; and

(vi) The handwritten signature of the operator or the duly authorized agent of the operator. If a business entity is identified as the operator, the signature should be that of an officer if the entity is a corporation or of a partner if the entity is a partnership. The signature shall be accompanied by: (A) A certification that the statements made in the application are correct to the best of the signing person's knowledge; (B) the typed or printed name (and title if the operator is a corporation or partnership) of that person; and (C) the date of signature.

(2) If a serial number is not present on the coin-operated phonorecord player for which the application is made, the application shall also contain the following information for that player:

(i) Its model number if known;

(ii) Its model year and name, if known;

(iii) Whether the sound system employed in the player at the time the application is signed is monaural, stereophonic, quadraphonic, or other;

(iv) The maximum number of phonorecords it is capable of holding; and

(v) The charge to the public for each play at the time the application is signed.

(3) Each application shall be accompanied by a fee in the form of a certified check, cashier's check, or money order, in the following amount:

(i) $25 per player per year in 1982 and 1983;

(ii) $50 per player per year in 1984, 1985, and 1986;

(iii) $50 per player per year in 1987 and each year thereafter, subject to a cost of living adjustment as determined by the Copyright Royalty Tribunal;

(iv) One-half the applicable annual rate for each player on which performances of nondramatic musical works were made available for the first time after July 1 of any year.

(4) A single application may be submitted for multiple players owned or controlled by a particular operator if all the identifying information is given for each player and the proper aggregate fee is submitted for all players covered by the application. However, separate applications must be filed for players covered by the full-year fee and players covered by the half-year fee.

(5) The form prescribed by the Copyright Office for the foregoing purposes is designated "Application for Recordation of Coin-Operated Phonorecord Players (Form JB)." Copies of the form are available free upon request to the Licensing Division, United States Copyright Office, Library of Congress, Washington, D.C. 20557.

(6)(i) Where an operator has recorded one or more players in the Copyright Office during a particular year, the Copyright Office will, during the month of December of that year, send to the operator, at the operator's last address shown in the records of the Licensing Division, a "Renewable Application for Recordation of Coin-Operated Phonorecord Players (Form JB/R)." The renewal application will be accompanied by a list of the players recorded by the operator in the Copyright Office earlier during that year; such list will contain the information provided by the operator in its earlier application or applications, and will be based on the assumption that such players were properly identified in the earlier application or applications. The renewal application may be used during the month of January of the immediately succeeding year, in lieu of an application on Form JB, to apply for a compulsory license to cover: (A) Players recorded during the previous year, and (B) any other players operated by the applicant. A renewal application on Form JB/R shall comply with paragraphs (b)(1) through (b)(4) of this section and the instructions accompanying the form; however, a renewal application on Form JB/R may not be used for players covered by a half-year fee.

(ii) Nothing in this paragraph (b)(6) shall be considered to relieve an operator from its obligation to file an application for a compulsory license in compliance with, and within the time periods set forth in, section 116 of Title 17 of the United States Code. In particular, and without limiting the foregoing: (A) The receipt of a renewal application form by an operator does not relieve the operator from its obligation to complete and file the application in the Copyright Office; (B) failure to receive a renewal application form from the Copyright Office or the late arrival of such form does not relieve the operator from its obligation to file an application in the Copyright Office within the statutory time periods;[6] (C) neither the receipt of a renewal

---

[6]If an operator does not receive a renewal application form (Form JB/R) in time to file it within the statutory time periods, an "Application for Recordation of Coin-Operated Phonorecord Players" shall be filed on Form JB in compliance with paragraphs (b)(1) through (b)(5) of this section.

application form nor the filing of a renewal application shall relieve the operator from its obligation to identify its players fully and accurately in compliance with this section; and (D) the filing of a renewal application does not relieve the operator from its obligation to file an application to cover any players not included in the renewal application as filed.[7]

(c) *Certificate.* (1) After receipt of the prescribed form and fee, the Copyright Office will issue a certificate containing the information set forth in paragraphs (b)(1)(i) and (ii) of this section, together with a unique licensing number, the date of issuance of the certificate and the date of expiration of the license. The date of expiration of the license will be December 31st of the year in which the certificate is issued. Certificates issued upon payment of a half-year fee will be valid only after July 1 of the year in which they are issued and will be so identified.

(2) The certificate may be affixed in the record selection (title strip) panel of a player or in another position on the player where it can be readily examined by the public, but in any case it must be clearly visible.

(3) A certificate issued for a player with auxiliary selectors (wall boxes) shall be affixed to the master control player if the certificate, when so affixed, can be readily examined by the public. If a certificate affixed to the master control player cannot be readily examined by the public, it shall be affixed to one of the auxiliary selectors in a position where it can be so examined.

(4) The Copyright Office will advise jukebox operators of errors or omissions appearing on the face of forms submitted to it, and will require that any such obvious errors or omissions (including errors in the calculation of fees) be corrected before certificates will be issued. However, the issuance of a certificate by the Copyright Office shall establish only the fact, date of issuance, and date of expiration of the certificate; it shall in no case be considered a determination that the application form was properly prepared or that all of the requirements to qualify for a compulsory license have been satisfied.

(d) *Replacement certificates.* In the case of the loss or destruction of a certificate issued for a particular coin-operated phonorecord player, a replacement certificate may be obtained upon submission of a fee of $4 in the form of a certified check, cashier's check or money order, and an affidavit under the official seal of any officer authorized to administer oaths within the United States, or a statement in accordance with section 1746 of Title 28 of the United States Code, made and signed by an operator or agent in accordance with paragraph (b)(1)(vi) of this section. The affidavit or statement shall describe the circumstances of the loss or destruction and give all the information required by paragraphs (b)(1)(i) through (v) and (b)(2) of this section pertaining to the player for which a replacement certificate is desired. A replacement certificate will be identified by an asterisk following the name of the manufacturer.

(e) *Sale or transfers.* The sale or transfer of a coin-operated phonorecord player during a period for which the certificate has been issued will not require a new application.

(f) *Time limitations.* (1) The Copyright Office may, when it considers it reasonable and appropriate, advise applicants of the time limitations governing the filing of applications and amount of royalty fees as set forth in 17 U.S.C. 116. However, except as set forth in paragraph (f)(2) of this section, the Office will normally not inquire into the date on which performances were actually made available on particular phonorecord players identified in the application or whether such players were previously recorded in the Copyright Office. In the following cases, the Office's acceptance of the application and issuance of a certificate is not to be considered as relieving the operator from any legal consequences arising from the late filing, and shall have only such effect as may be attributed to it by a court of competent jurisdiction: (i) Where, on the date the application covering a particular phonorecord player was received in the Copyright Office, performances had been first made avail-

---

[7]Application for recordation of players not included on the renewal application as filed shall be made on Form JB ("Application for Recordation of Coin-Operated Phonorecord Players") in compliance with paragraphs (b)(1) through (b)(5) of this section.

able on that player more than 1 month earlier; and (ii) where, in 1979 and thereafter, a particular phonorecord player had been recorded in the Copyright Office during the previous calendar year, but the application is received after January 31 of the year in question.

(2) In the case of an application that is received in the Copyright Office before June 1 of a particular year, and that is accompanied by a half-year fee for each player identified in the application, the Copyright Office will not issue certificates unless the application is accompanied or supplemented by a statement that performances will not be made available on such players until after July 1 of that year. The statement shall be in the form of a letter addressed to the Licensing Division of the Copyright Office, and shall be signed by the operator named in the application or the duly authorized agent of that operator. If a business entity is the operator, the signature or name shall be that of an officer if the entity is a corporation, or a partner if the entity is a partnership, and shall be accompanied by the organizational title of that person. The statement shall, for all purposes including section 116 (b)(1)(B) of Title 17 of the United States Code, be considered a part of the application. The statement described in this paragraph shall not be required in the case of applications covering a particular year received in the Copyright Office after June 1 of that year. In any case, if performances are actually made available for the first time on any players covered by half-year fees on or before July 1 of that year, the Office's acceptance of the application and issuance of a certificate is not to be considered as relieving the operator from any legal consequences arising from the failure to pay the correct fee, and shall have only such effect as may be attributed to it by a court of competent jurisdiction.

(3) If an application received in the Copyright Office after July 1 of any year is accompanied by the prescribed full-year royalty fee for each player identified, the Copyright Office will assume without further inquiry that the application pertains to players on which performances were made available for the first time on or before July 1 of that year.

(g) *Corrections and refunds.* (1) Upon compliance with the procedures and within the time limits set forth in paragraph (g)(3) of this section, corrections to applications for recordation of coin-operated phonorecord players will be made, and corrected certificates and refunds will be issued, in the following cases:

(i) Where the same player, identified by the same serial number or other identifying information is listed more than once in the same application, or in two or more applications filed during the same year by or on behalf of the same operator. In these cases the operator named in the application shall be entitled to a refund of any duplicate fee paid;

(ii) Where any of the following information was incorrect at the time the application was signed: (A) The operator's name or address; (B) the serial number or name of the manufacturer of a player; or (C) the identifying information requested by paragraph (b)(2) of this section. In any such case the Copyright Office will issue a new certificate containing the correct information. Each corrected certificate will be identified by a double asterisk following the name of the manufacturer.

(iii) Where an application contains information that was correct at the time the application was signed but, as the result of Copyright Office error, the certificate contains incorrect information. In this case the Copyright Office will issue a new certificate containing the correct information; and

(iv) Where an application was accompanied by payment of the prescribed yearly fee for each phonorecord listed but, with respect to one or more such players, performances were actually made available for the first time after July 1 of the year in which the application was filed. In this case the operator named in the application shall be entitled to a refund of any excess fee paid and the Copyright Office will issue a new certificate for each player subject to the half-year fee.

(2) Corrected certificates or refunds will not be issued after the issuance of original certificates in the following cases;

(i) Where the application was correct on the date on which the application was signed, but changes (for example, a change in the operator's name or address, or the sale of destruction of a player) took place later;

(ii) Where the application identified one or more players that the operator named in the application never owned or operated, or did not own or operate at the time the application was signed, or where, before the application was signed, an identified player had been destroyed or otherwise rendered permanently incapable of being repaired; or

(iii) In any other case not specifically mentioned in paragraph (g)(1) of this section.

(3) Requests for corrections and refunds in the cases mentioned in paragraph (g)(1) of this section shall be made to the Licensing Division of the Copyright Office, and shall meet the following conditions:

(i) The request must be in writing, must be clearly identifiable as a request for a correction or refund, and except in the cases described in paragraph (g)(1)(iii) of this section, must be received in the Copyright Office with the appropriate fee, certificate or certificates, and affidavit (where required) before the expiration of 30 days from the date on which the original certificate was issued by the Copyright Office. A request made by telephone or by telegraphic or similar unsigned communication, will be considered to meet this requirement, if it clearly identifies the basis of the request, if it is received in the Copyright Office within the required 30-day period, and if a written request meeting all the conditions of this paragraph (g)(3) of this section is also received in the Copyright Office within 14 days after the end of such 30-day period.

(ii) The original application pertaining to each correction must be sufficiently identified in the request so that it can be readily located in the records of the Copyright Office.

(iii) The original certificate pertaining to each correction or refund must be returned to the Copyright Office within the time period prescribed by paragraph (g)(3)(i) of this section. No request will be processed until the applicable certificate is returned; and

(iv) The request must contain a clear statement of the facts on which it is based, in accordance with the following requirements:

(A) In the case of duplicate listings (paragraph (g)(1)(i)) a precise and accurate identification of the particular player or players must be given.

(B) In the case of incorrect information given in the application (paragraph (g)(1)(ii) of this section) the request must clearly identify the erroneous information and provide the correct information.

(C) In the case of a certificate that contains erroneous information resulting from Copyright Office error (paragraph (g)(1)(iii) of this section) the error must be clearly indicated.

(D) In the case of overpayment within the meaning of paragraph (g)(1)(iv) of this section, the request must be accompanied by an affidavit under the official seal of any officer authorized to administer oaths within the United States, or a statement in accordance with section 1746 of Title 28 of the United States Code, made and signed by the operator named in the application or the duly authorized agent of that operator in accordance with paragraph (b)(1)(vi) of this section. The affidavit or statement shall: aver that performances of nondramatic musical works were actually made available on the particular phonorecord player(s) for the first time after July 1 of the year covered by the application; give the exact date, including month, day, and year on which such performances were first made available and the location where that event took place; specifically identify the particular phonorecord player(s) involved by the same identifying information as given in the application; and include a brief explanation of the reason for the original submission of a full-year fee for those players.

(v) In those cases where corrections or refunds are to be made under paragraph (g)(1) of this section, the request must be accompanied by a certified check, cashier's check, or money order in the following amount: (A) In the case of a duplicate listing (paragraph (g)(1)(i) of this section): $4 for each application involved; (B) in the case of an error in the operator's name or address (paragraph (g)(1)(ii)(A)) or overpayment within the meaning of paragraph (g)(1)(iv) of this section: $4 for each separate original application pertaining to the certificates to be corrected; and (C) in the case of an error in the serial number or name of the manufacturer of the player, or other identifying information (paragraph (g)(1)(ii) (B) and (C) of this section): $4 for each separate certificate to be corrected. No request will be processed until the appropriate fee is received; and

(vi) The request must be signed by the operator named in the application, or the duly authorized agent of the operator, in accordance with paragraph (b)(1)(vi) of this section.

(4) Each request for correction or refund will be made part of the original application in the records of the Copyright Office. Nothing contained in this paragraph (g) shall be considered to relieve the operator from its full obligations under Title 17 of the United States Code, including penalties for affixing a certificate to a player other than the one it covers.

(h) *Supplemental certificates for 1982.* (1) In all cases, new supplemental certificates for 1982 must replace those issued prior to June 15, 1982. The Copyright Office will attempt to notify all jukebox operators who recorded a player in 1982 of the need to obtain supplemental certificates. Jukebox operators who for any reason are not notified are not relieved of their obligation to obtain supplemental certificates.

(i) Jukebox operators who were previously issued certificates for 1982 at the $8 rate must apply for supplemental certificates on a form prescribed by the Copyright Office and pay an additional $17 per player on or before July 15, 1982. The form shall be signed in the manner designated in paragraph (b)(vi) of this § 201.16 for original certificates. Copies of the form are free upon request to the Licensing Division, United States Copyright Office, Library of Congress, Washington, D.C. 20557.

(ii) Jukebox operators who have already submitted $25 fee should notify the Copyright Office to provide them with a supplemental certificate at no additional cost.

(2) Supplemental certificates must be affixed to each player within 10 days after the certificate is issued.

(3) Acceptance by the Copyright Office of applications for supplemental certificates after July 15, 1982, and issuance of corresponding certificates, is not to be considered as relieving the operator from any legal consequences arising from the late filing, and shall have only such effect as may be attributed to it by a court of competent jurisdiction.

(Pub. L. 94-553, 17 U.S.C. 116, 702, 708(11))

[42 FR 63780, Dec. 20, 1977, as amended at 43 FR 50679, Oct. 31, 1978; 43 FR 59379, Dec. 20, 1978; 47 FR 25005, June 9, 1982]

## § 201.17 Statement of Account covering compulsory licenses for secondary transmissions by cable systems.

(a) *General.* This section prescribes rules pertaining to the deposit of Statements of Account and royalty fees in the Copyright Office as required by section 111(d)(2) of Title 17 of the United States Code, as amended by Pub. L. 94-553, in order for secondary transmissions of cable systems to be subject to compulsory licensing.

(b) *Definitions.* (1) Gross receipts for the "basic service of providing secondary transmissions of primary broadcast transmitters" include the full amount of monthly (or other periodic) service fees for any and all service or tiers of services which include one or more secondary transmissions of television or radio broadcast signals, for additional set fees, and for converter fees. All such gross receipts shall be aggregated and the DSE calculations shall be made against the aggregated amount. Gross receipts for secondary transmission services do not include installation (including connection, relocation, disconnection, or reconnection) fees, separate charges for security, alarm or facsimile services, charges for late payments, or charges for pay cable or other program origination services: *Provided* That, the origination services are not offered in combination with secondary transmission service for a single fee.

(2) A "cable system" and "individual cable system" have the meanings set forth in § 201.11(a)(3) of these regulations.

(3) "FCC" means the Federal Communications Commission.

(4) In the case of cable systems which make secondary transmissions of all available FM radio signals, which signals are not electronically processed by the system as separate and discrete signals, an FM radio signal is "generally receivable" under the conditions set forth in § 201.11(a)(4) of these regulations.

(5) The terms "primary transmission," "secondary transmission," "local service area of a primary transmitter," "distant signal equivalent," "network station," "independent station," and "noncommercial educational station" have the meanings set forth in section 111(f) of Title 17 of the United States Code, as amended by Pub. L. 94-553.

(6) A primary transmitter is a "distant" station, for purposes of this section, if the programming of such transmitter is carried by the cable system in whole or in part beyond the local service area of such primary transmitter.

(7) A translator station is, with respect to programs both originally transmitted and retransmitted by it, a primary transmitter for the purposes of this section and § 201.11 of these regulations. A translator station which retransmits the programs of a network station will be considered a network station; a translator station which retransmits the programs of an independent station shall be considered an independent station; and a translator station which retransmits the programs of a noncommercial educational station shall be considered a noncommercial educational station. The determination of whether a translator station should be identified as a "distant" station depends on the local service area of the translator station.

(8) For purposes of this section, the "rules and regulations of the FCC in effect on October 19, 1976," which permitted a cable system, at its election, to omit the retransmission of a particular program and substitute another program in its place, refers to that portion of former 47 CFR 76.61(b)(2), revised June 25, 1981, and § 76.63 (referring to § 76.61(b)(2)), deleted June 25, 1981, concerning the substitution of a program that is primarily of local interest to the distant community (e.g., a local news or public affairs program).

(9) For purposes of this section, the "rules and regulations of the FCC," which require a cable system to omit the retransmission of a particular program and substitute another program in its place, refers to 47 CFR 76.67.

(10) For purposes of this section, a cable system "lacks the activated channel capacity to retransmit on a full-time basis all signals which it is authorized to carry" only if: (i) All of its activated television channels are used exclusively for the secondary transmission of television signals; and (ii) the number of primary television transmitters secondarily transmitted by the cable system exceeds the number of its activated television channels.

(c) *Accounting periods and deposit.* (1) Statements of Account shall cover semi-annual accounting periods of (i) January 1 through June 30, and (ii) July 1 through December 31, and shall be deposited in the Copyright Office, together with the total royalty fee for such accounting periods as prescribed by section 111(d)(2) (B), (C), or (D) of Title 17, by not later than the immediately following August 29, if the Statement of Account covers the January 1 through June 30 accounting period, and by not later than the immediately following March 1, if the Statement of Account covers the July 1 through December 31 accounting period.

(2) Upon receiving a Statement of Account and royalty fee, the Copyright Office will make an official record of the actual date when such Statement and fee were physically received in the Copyright Office. Thereafter, the Office will examine the Statement and fee for obvious errors or omissions appearing on the face of the documents, and will require that any such obvious errors or omissions be corrected before final processing of the documents is completed. If, as the result of communications between the Copyright Office and the cable system, an additional fee is deposited or changes or additions are made in the Statement of Account, the date that additional deposit or information was actually received in the Office will be added to the official record of the case. However, completion by the Copyright Office of the final processing of a Statement of Account and royalty fee deposit shall establish only the fact of

such completion and the date or dates of receipt shown in the official record. It shall in no case be considered a determination that the Statement of Account was, in fact, properly prepared and accurate, that the correct amount of the royalty fee had been deposited, that the statutory time limits for filing had been met, or that any other requirements to qualify for a compulsory license have been satisfied.

(3) Statements of Account and royalty fees received before the end of the particular accounting period they purport to cover will not be processed by the Copyright Office. Statements of Account and royalty fees received after the filing deadlines of August 29 or March 1, respectively, will be accepted for whatever legal effect they may have, if any.

(d) *Forms.* (1) Each Statement of Account shall be furnished on an appropriate form prescribed by the Copyright Office, and shall contain the information required by that form and its accompanying instructions. Computation of distant signal equivalents and the copyright royalty fee shall be in accordance with the procedures set forth in the forms. Copies of Statement of Account forms are available free upon request to the Licensing Division, United States Copyright Office, Library of Congress, Washington, D.C. 20557.

(2) The forms prescribed by the Copyright Office are designated "Statement of Account for Secondary Transmissions By Cable Systems":

(i) Form CS/SA-1—"Short Form" for use by cable systems whose semiannual gross receipts for secondary transmissions total $41,500 or less;

(ii) Form CS/SA-2—"Intermediate Form" for use by cable systems whose semi-annual gross receipts for secondary transmissions total between $41,500 and $160,000; and

(iii) Form CS/SA-3—"Long Form" for use by cable systems whose semiannual gross receipts for secondary transmissions total $160,000 or more.

(e) *Contents.* Each Statement of Account shall contain the following information:

(1) A clear designation of the accounting period covered by the Statement.

(2) The designation "Owner," followed by: (i) The full legal name of the owner of the cable system. If the owner is a partnership, the name of the partnership is to be followed by the name of at least one individual partner; (ii) any other name or names under which the owner conducts the business of the cable system; and (iii) the full mailing address of the owner. Ownership, other names under which the owner conducts the business of the cable system, and the owner's mailing address shall reflect facts existing on the last day of the accounting period covered by the Statement of Account.[8]

(3) The designation "System," followed by: (i) Any business or trade names used to identify the business and operation of the system, unless these names have already been given under the designation "Owner"; and (ii) the full mailing address of the system, unless such address is the same as the address given under the designation "Owner." Business or trade names used to identify the business and operation of the system, and the system's mailing address, shall reflect the facts existing on the last day of the accounting period covered by the Statement of Account.

(4) The designation of "Area Served," followed by the name of the community or communities served by the system. For his purpose a "community" is the same as a "community unit" as defined in FCC rules and regulations.

(5) The designation "Channels," followed by: (i) The number of channels on which the cable system made secondary transmissions to its subscribers, and (ii) the cable system's total activated channel capacity, in each case during the period covered by the Statement.

---

[8]In the case of the first Statement of Account deposited by a cable system which has not earlier filed an Initial Notice or Notice of Change under § 201.11 of these regulations identifying the owner of the system, that Statement of Account shall also give the name of the person who, or entity which, was given as the operator or person or entity exercising primary control in the Initial Notice or last Notice of Change.

(6) The designation "Secondary Transmission Service: Subscribers and Rates," followed by: (i) A brief description of each subscriber category for which a charge is made by the cable system for the basic service of providing secondary transmissions of primary broadcast transmitters; (ii) the number of subscribers to the cable system in each such subscriber category; and (iii) the charge or charges made per subscriber to each such subscriber category for the basic service of providing such secondary transmissions. Standard rate variations within a particular category should be summarized; discounts allowed for advance payment should not be included. For these purposes: (A) The description, the number of subscribers, and the charge or charges made shall reflect the facts existing on the last day of the period covered by the Statement; and (B) each entity (for example, the owner of a private home, the resident of an apartment, the owner of a motel, or the owner of an apartment house) which is charged by the cable system for the basic service of providing secondary transmissions shall be considered one subscriber.

(7) The designation "Gross Receipts," followed by the gross amount paid to the cable system by subscribers for the basic service of providing secondary transmissions of primary broadcast transmissions during the period covered by the Statement of Account. If the cable system maintains its revenue accounts on an accrual basis, gross receipts for any accounting period includes all such amounts accrued for secondary transmission service furnished during that period, regardless of when accrued: (i) Less the amount of any bad debts actually written-off during that accounting period, excluding bad debts for secondary transmission service furnished before January 1, 1978; (ii) plus the amount of any previously written-off bad debts for secondary transmission service which were actually recovered during that accounting period excluding bad debt recoveries for secondary transmission service furnished before January 1, 1978. If the cable system maintains its revenue accounts on a cash basis, gross receipts for any accounting period includes all such amounts actually received by the cable system during that accounting period, excluding amounts paid for secondary transmission service furnished before January 1, 1978; however, amounts received before January 1, 1978, for secondary transmission service furnished after that date, are to be considered as if they had been received during the accounting period in which the service covered by such payments was furnished.

(8) The designation "Services Other Than Secondary Transmissions: Rates," followed by a description of each package of service which consists solely of services other than secondary transmission services, for which a separate charge was made or established, and which the cable system furnished or made available to subscribers during the period covered by the Statement of Account, together with the amount of such charge. However, no information need be given concerning services furnished at cost. Specific amounts charged for pay cable programming need not be given if the rates are on a variable, per-program basis. (The fact of such variable charge shall be indicated.)

(9) The designation "Primary Transmitters: Television," followed by an identification of all primary television transmitters whose signals were carried by the cable system during the period covered by the Statement of Account, other than primary transmitters of programs carried by the cable system exclusively pursuant to rules, regulations, or authorizations of the FCC in effect on October 19, 1976, permitting the substitution of signals under certain circumstances, and required to be specially identified by paragraph (e)(11) of this section, together with the information listed below:

(i) The station call sign of the primary transmitter.

(ii) The name of the community to which that primary transmitter is licensed by the FCC (in the case of domestic signals) or with which that primary transmitter is identified (in the case of foreign signals).

(iii) The number of the channel upon which that primary transmitter broadcasts in the community to which that primary transmitter is licensed by the FCC (in the case of domestic signals) or with which that primary transmitter is identified (in the case of foreign signals).

(iv) A designation as to whether that primary transmitter is a "network station," an "independent station," or a "noncommercial educational station."

(v) A designation as to whether that primary transmitter is a "distant" station.

(vi) If that primary transmitter is a "distant" station, a specification of whether the signals of that primary transmitter are carried: (A) On a part-time basis where full-time carriage is not possible because the cable system lacks the activated channel capacity to retransmit on a full-time basis all signals which it is authorized to carry; or (B) on any other basis. If the signals of that primary transmitter are carried on a part-time basis because of lack of activated channel capacity, the Statement shall also include a log showing the dates on which such carriage occurred, and the hours during which such carriage occurred on those dates. Hours of carriage shall be accurate to the nearest quarter-hour, except that, in any case where such part-time carriage extends to the end of the broadcast day of the primary transmitter, an approximate ending hour may be given if it is indicated as an estimate.

(vii) The information indicated by paragraph (e)(9), subclauses (v) and (vi) of this section, is not required to be given by any cable system that appropriately completed Form CS/SA-1 or Form CS/SA-2 for the period covered by the Statement.

(viii) Notwithstanding the requirements of this section, where a cable system carried a distant primary transmitter under FCC rules and regulations in effect on October 19, 1976 which permitted carriage of specific network programs on a part-time basis in certain circumstances (former 47 CFR 76.59(d)(2) and (4), 76.61(e)(2) and (4), and 76.63, referring to § 76.61(e)(2) and (4), all of which were deleted June 25, 1981), carriage of that primary transmitter on that basis need not be reported in computing the distant signal equivalent of that primary transmitter.

(10) The designation "Primary Transmitters: Radio," followed by an identification of primary radio transmitters whose signals were carried by the cable system during the period covered by the Statement of Account, together with the information listed below:

(i) A designation as to whether each primary transmitter was electronically processed by the system as a separate and discrete signal.

(ii) The station call sign of each:

(A) AM primary transmitter;

(B) FM primary transmitter, the signals of which were electronically processed by the system as separate and discrete signals; and

(C) FM primary transmitter carried on an all-band retransmission basis, the signals of which were generally receivable by the system.

(iii) A designation as to whether the primary transmitter is AM or FM.

(iv) The name of the community to which that primary transmitter is licensed by the FCC (in the case of domestic signals) or with which that primary transmitter is identified (in the case of foreign signals).

(11) A special statement and program log, which shall consist of the information indicated below for all nonnetwork television programming that, during the period covered by the Statement, was carried in whole or in part beyond the local service area of the primary transmitter of such programming under (i) rules or regulations of the FCC requiring a cable system to omit the further transmission of a particular program and permitting the substitution of another program in place of the omitted transmission; or (ii) rules, regulations, or authorizations of the FCC in effect on October 19, 1976, permitting a cable system, at its election, to omit the further transmission of a particular program and permitting the substitution of another program in place of the omitted transmission:

(A) The name or title of the substitute program.

(B) Whether the substitute program was transmitted live by its primary transmitter.

(C) The station call sign of the primary transmitter of the substitute program.

(D) The name of the community to which the primary transmitter of the substitute program is licensed by the FCC (in the case of domestic signals) or with which that primary transmitter is identified (in the case of foreign signals).

(E) The date when the secondary transmission of the substitute program occurred, and the hours during which such secondary transmission occurred on that date accurate to the nearest 5 minutes.

(F) A designation as to whether deletion of the omitted program was permitted by the rules, regulations, or authorizations of the FCC in effect on October 19, 1976, or was required by the rules, regulations, or authorizations of the FCC.

(12) A statement of the total royalty fee payable for the period covered by the Statement of Account, together with a royalty fee analysis which gives a clear, complete, and detailed presentation of the determination of such fee. This analysis shall present in appropriate sequence all facts, figures, and mathematical processes used in determining such fee, and shall do so in such manner as required in the appropriate form so as to permit the Copyright Office to verify readily, from the face of the Statement of Account, the accuracy of such determination and fee. The royalty fee analysis is not required to be given by any cable system whose gross receipts from subscribers for the period covered by the Statement of Account, for the basic service of providing secondary transmissions of primary broadcast transmissions, total $41,500 or less.

(13) The name, address, and telephone number of an individual who may be contacted by the Copyright Office for further information about the Statement of Account.

(14) The handwritten signature of: (i) The owner of the cable system or a duly authorized agent of the owner, if the owner is not a partnership or a corporation; or (ii) a partner, if the owner is a partnership; or (iii) an officer of the corporation, if the owner is a corporation. The signature shall be accompanied by: (A) The printed or typewritten name of the person signing the Statement of Account; (B) the date of signature; (C) if the owner of the cable system is a partnership or a corporation, by the title or official position held in the partnership or corporation by the person signing the Statement of Account; (D) a certification of the capacity of the person signing; and (E) the following statement:

I certify that I have examined this Statement of Account and that all statements of fact contained herein are true, complete, and correct to the best of my knowledge, information, and belief, and are made in good faith.

(f) *Computation of distant signal equivalents.* (1) A cable system that elects to delete a particular television program and substitute for that program another television program ("substitute program") under rules, regulations, or authorizations of the FCC in effect on October 19, 1976, which permit a cable system, at its election, to omit the retransmission of a particular program and substitute another program in its place shall compute the distant signal equivalent ("DSE") of each primary transmitter that broadcasts one or more substitute programs by dividing: (i) The number of the primary transmitter's live, nonnetwork, substitute programs that were carried by the cable system, during the period covered by the Statement of Account, in substitution for programs deleted at the option of the system; by (ii) the number of days in the year in which the substitution occurred.

(2)(i) Where a cable system carries a primary transmitter on a full-time basis during any portion of an accounting period, the system shall compute a DSE for that primary transmitter as if it was carried full-time during the entire accounting period.

(ii) Where a cable system carries a primary transmitter solely on a substitute or part-time basis, in accordance with subparagraph (3) of this paragraph (f), the system shall compute a DSE for that primary transmitter based on its cumulative carriage on a substitute or part-time basis. If that primary transmitter is carried on a full-time basis as well as on a substitute or part-time basis, the full DSE for that primary transmitter shall be the full DSE type value for that primary transmitter, for the entire accounting period.

(3)(i) In computing the DSE of a primary transmitter in a particular case of carriage before July 1, 1981, the cable system may make no prorated adjustments other than those specified as permissible "exceptions and limitations" in the definition of "distant signal equivalent" in the fifth paragraph of section 111(f) of Title 17 of the United States Code, as amended by Pub. L. 94-553. Four prorated adjustments, as prescribed in the fourth and fifth sentences of said definition, are permitted under certain conditions where:

(A) A station is carried pursuant to the late-night programming rules of the Federal Communications Commission in effect on the date of carriage;

(B) A station is carried pursuant to the specialty programming rules of the Federal Communications Commission in effect on the date of carriage;

(C) A station is carried on a part-time basis where full-time carriage is not possible because the cable system lacks the activated channel capacity to retransmit on a full-time basis all signals which it is authorized to carry; and

(D) A station is carried on a "substitute" basis under rules, regulations, or authorizations of the Federal Communications Commission in effect on October 19, 1976.

(ii) In computing the DSE of a primary transmitter in a particular case of carriage on or after July 1, 1981, the cable system may make no prorated adjustments other than those specified as permissible "exceptions and limitations" in the definition of "distant signal equivalent" in the fifth paragraph of Section 111(f) of Title 17 of the United States Code, as amended by Pub. L. 94-553, and which remain in force under that provision. Two prorated adjustments, as prescribed in the fourth and fifth sentences of said definition, are permitted under certain conditions where:

(A) A station is carried on a part-time basis where full-time carriage is not possible because the cable system lacks the activated channel capacity to retransmit on a full-time basis all signals which it is authorized to carry; and

(B) A station is carried on a "substitute" basis under rules, regulations, or authorizations of the Federal Communications Commission in effect on October 19, 1976, which permitted a cable system, at its election, to omit the retransmission of a particular program and substitute another program in its place.

(4) In computing a DSE, a cable system may round off to the third decimal point. If a DSE is rounded off in any case in a Statement of Account, it must be rounded off throughout the Statement. Where a cable system has chosen to round off, and the fourth decimal point for a particular DSE value would, without rounding off, have been 1, 2, 3, or 4, the third decimal point remains unchanged; if, in such a case, the fourth decimal point would, without rounding off, be 5, 6, 7, 8, or 9, the third decimal point must be rounded off the next higher number.

(5) For the purposes of computing DSE values, specialty primary television transmitters in the United States and all Canadian and Mexican primary television transmitters shall be assigned a value of one.

(g) *Computation of the copyright royalty fee: Partially distant stations.* A cable system located partly within and partly without the local service area of a primary television transmitter ("partially distant station") computes the royalty fee specified in section 111(d)(2)(B)(ii), (iii), and (iv) of the Copyright Act ("DSE fee") by excluding gross receipts from subscribers located within that station's local service area from total gross receipts. A cable system which carries two or more partially distant stations with local service areas that do not exactly coincide shall compute a separate DSE fee for each group of subscribers who are located outside of the local service areas of exactly the same complement of distant stations. Computation of the DSE fee for each subscriber group is to be based on: (1) The total distant signal equivalents of that group's complement of distant stations, and (2) the total gross receipts from that group of subscribers. The copyright royalty fee for that cable system is: (i) the total of the subscriber group royalty fees thus computed, or (ii) 0.799 of 1 percent of the system's gross receipts from all subscribers, whichever is larger.

(h) *Computation of the copyright royalty fee pursuant to the 1982 cable rate adjustment.* (1) For the purposes of this paragraph, in addition to the definitions of paragraph (b) of this section, the following definitions shall also apply:

(i) "Current base rate" means the applicable royalty rates in effect on December 31, 1982, as reflected in 37 CFR 308.2(a).

(ii) "Surcharge" means the applicable syndicated exclusivity surcharge established by 37 CFR 308.2(d), in effect on January 1, 1983.

(iii) The "3.75% rate" means the rate established by 37 CFR 308.2(c), in effect on March 15, 1983.

(iv) "Top 100 television market" means a television market defined or interpreted as being within either the "top 50 television markets" or "second 50 television markets" in accordance with 47 CFR 76.51, in effect on June 24, 1981.

(v) The "1982 cable rate adjustment" means the rate adjustment adopted by the Copyright Royalty Tribunal on October 20, 1982 (CRT Docket No. 81-2, 47 FR 52146, November 19, 1982).

(vi) The terms "DSE" or "DSE's" mean "distant signal equivalent(s)" as defined in 17 U.S.C. 111(f) and any fraction thereof.

(2) A cable system whose semiannual gross receipts for secondary transmissions total $214,000 or more shall compute its royalty fee for carriage after June 30, 1983, in the following manner:

(i) The cable system shall first determine those DSE's to which the 3.75% rate established by 37 CFR 308.2(c) applies.

(ii) If the 3.75% rate does not apply to certain DSE's, in the case of a cable system located wholly or in part within a top 100 television market, the current base rate together with the surcharge shall apply. However, the surcharge shall not apply for carriage of a particular signal first carried prior to March 31, 1972.

(iii) If the 3.75% rate does not apply to certain DSE's, in the case of a cable system located wholly outside a top 100 television market, the current base rate shall apply.

(3) A cable system whose semiannual gross receipts for secondary transmissions total $214,000 or more shall compute its royalty fee for carriage during the period January 1, 1983, through June 30, 1983, in the following manner:

(i) Copyright royalty fees must be paid on the basis of carriage for the entire accounting period except where proration of the DSE is permitted as described in paragraph (f)(3) of this section.

(ii) Where a distant signal was carried at any time only between January 1, 1983, and March 14, 1983;

(A) In the case of a cable system located wholly or in part within a top 100 television market, the current base rate, together with the surcharge shall apply. However, the surcharge shall not apply for carriage of a particular signal first carried prior to March 31, 1972.

(B) In case of a cable system located wholly outside a top 100 television market, the current base rate shall apply.

(iii) Where a distant signal was carried at any time after March 14, 1983;

(A) The cable system shall first determine those DSE's to which the 3.75% rate established by 37 CFR 308.2(c) applies.

(B) If the 3.75% rate is applicable to a particular DSE, it shall be applied against the per centum .5967 (representing the number of days from March 15, 1983, through June 30, 1983, inclusive, in relation to the entire accounting period); and either

(1) In the case of cable system located wholly or in part within a top 100 television market, the current base rate, together with the surcharge, applied against the per centum .4033 (representing the number of days from January 1, 1983, through March 14, 1983, inclusive, in relation to the entire accounting period); however, the surcharge shall not apply for carriage of a particular signal first carried prior to March 31, 1972; or

(2) In the case of a cable system located wholly outside a top 100 television market, the current base rate applied against the per centum .4033.

(C) If the 3.75% rate does not apply to certain DSE's, in the case of a cable system located wholly or in part within a top 100 television market, the current base rate together with the surcharge shall apply. However, the surcharge shall not apply for carriage of a particular signal first carried prior to March 3, 1972.

(D) If the 3.75% rate does not apply to certain DSE's, in the case of a cable system located wholly outside a top 100 television market, the current base rate shall apply.

(4)(i) Separate Supplement DSE Schedules as prescribed by the Copyright Office shall be completed and filed by a cable system affected by the 1982 cable rate adjustment for the accounting periods January 1, 1983, through June 30, 1983 (83-1), and July 1, 1983, through December 31, 1983 (83-2). Each Supplemental DSE schedule shall contain the information required by that form and its accompanying instructions.

(ii) The Supplemental DSE Schedule will be mailed to all cable systems whose gross receipts for secondary transmissions total $214,000 or more either for accounting period 83-1 or for 83-2, and shall be completed and returned to the Copyright Office with the supplemental royalty fee due, if any, within sixty-five (65) days from the date of mailing by the Copyright Office.

(iii) Cable systems located wholly outside all major and smaller television markets as defined by the FCC are not affected by the 1982 cable rate adjustment. Such systems shall complete a certifying statement provided in the Supplemental DSE Schedule and return it within sixty-five days from the date of mailing by the Copyright Office.

(iv) Revised Statement of Account form CS/SA-3 shall be completed and filed for the accounting periods January 1, 1984, through June 30, 1984 *et seq.*, by a cable system whose semiannual gross receipts for secondary transmissions total $214,000 or more in accordance with paragraph (c) of this section. The Statement shall contain the information required by that form and its accompanying instructions.

(5)(i) It shall be presumed that the 3.75% rate of 37 CFR 308.2(c) applies to DSE's accruing from newly added distant signals, carried for the first time by a cable system after June 24, 1981.

(ii) The presumption of paragraph (h)(5)(i) of this section can be rebutted in whole or in part:

(A) By actual carriage of a particular distant signal prior to June 25, 1981, as reported in Statements of Account duly filed with the Copyright Office ("actual carriage"), unless the prior carriage was not permitted by the FCC; or

(B) By carriage of no more than the number of distant signals which was or would have been allotted to the cable system under the FCC's quota for importation of network and nonspecialty independent stations [47 CFR 76.59(b), 76.61(b) and (c) and 76.63, referring to 76.61(b) and (c), in effect on June 24, 1981].

(6) To qualify as an FCC-permitted signal on the ground of individual waiver of the FCC rules (47 CFR 76.7 in effect on June 24, 1981), the waiver must have actually been granted by the FCC, and the signal must have been first carried by the cable system after April 15, 1976.

(7) Expanded geographic carriage after June 24, 1981, of a signal previously carried within only certain parts of a cable system is governed by the current base rate and the surcharge, if applicable.

(8) In cases of expended temporal carriage of the same signal, previously carried pursuant to the FCC's former part-time or substitute carriage rules [47 CFR 76.61(b)(2), 76.61(e)(1) and (e)(3), and 76.63, referring to 76.61(e)(1) and (e)(3), in effect on June 24, 1981], the 3.75% rate shall be applied to any additional fraction of a DSE accruing from the expanded temporal carriage of that signal. To identify such additional DSE's, a comparison shall be made of DSE's reported for that signal in any single accounting period prior to the July 1, 1981, to December 31, 1981, period (81-2), as designated by the cable system, with the DSE's for that same signal reported in the current relevant accounting period.

(9) Substitution of like signals pursuant to 37 CFR 308(c)(2) is possible at the relevant non-3.75% rate (the surcharge together with the current base rate or the current base rate alone) only if the substitution does not exceed the number of distant signals which was or would have been allotted to the cable system under FCC's television market quota for importation of network and nonspecialty independent

stations (47 CFR 76.59(b), 76.61(b) and (c), and 76.63, referring to 76.61(b) and (c), in effect on June 24, 1981.

(i) *Royalty fee payment.* The royalty fee payable for the period covered by the Statement of Account shall accompany that Statement of Account, and shall be deposited at the Copyright Office with it. Payment must be in the form of a certified check, cashier's check, or money order, payable to: Register of Copyrights.

(j) *Corrections, supplemental payments, and refunds.* (1) Upon compliance with the procedures and within the time limits set forth in paragraph (j)(3) of this section, corrections to Statements of Account will be placed on record, supplemental royalty fee payments will be received for deposit, or refunds will be issued, in the following cases:

(i) Where, with respect to the accounting period covered by a Statement of Account, any of the information given in the Statement filed in the Copyright Office is incorrect or incomplete;

(ii) Where, for any reason except that mentioned in paragraph (j)(1)(ii) of this section, calculation of the royalty fee payable for a particular accounting period was incorrect, and the amount deposited in the Copyright Office for that period was either too high or too low; or

(iii) Where, for the semiannual accounting period of January 1, 1978, through June 30, 1978, the total royalty fee deposited was incorrect because the cable operator failed to compute royalties attributable to carriage of late-night, specialty, or part-time programming between January 1, 1978, and February 9, 1978.

(2) Corrections to Statements of Account will not be placed on record, supplemental royalty fee payments will not be received for deposit, and refunds will not be issued, where the information in the Statements of Account, the royalty fee calculations, or the payments were correct as of the date on which the accounting period ended, but changes (for example, addition or deletion of a distant signal) took place later.

(3) Requests that corrections to a Statement of Account be placed on record, that fee payments be accepted or requests for the issuance of refunds, shall be made only in the cases mentioned in paragraph (j)(1) of this section. Such requests shall be addressed to the Licensing Division of the Copyright Office, and shall meet the following conditions:

(i) The request must be in writing, must clearly identify its purpose, and in the case of a request for a refund, must be received in the Copyright Office before the expiration of 60 days from the last day of the applicable Statement of Account filing period, as provided for in paragraph (c)(1) of this section, or before September 1, 1980, whichever is later. A request made by telephone or by telegraphic or similar unsigned communication, will be considered to meet this requirement if it clearly identifies the basis of the request, if it is received in the Copyright Office within the required 60-day period, and if a written request meeting all the conditions of this paragraph (j)(3) is also received in the Copyright Office within 14 days after the end of such 60-day period;

(ii) The Statement of Account to which the request pertains must be sufficiently identified in the request (by inclusion of the name of the owner of the cable system, the community or communities served, and the accounting period in question) so that it can be readily located in the records of the Copyright Office;

(iii) The request must contain a clear statement of the facts on which it is based, in accordance with the following requirements:

(A) In the case of a request filed under paragraph (j)(1)(i) of this section, where the information given in the Statement of Account is incorrect or incomplete, the request must clearly identify the erroneous or incomplete information and provide the correct or additional information;

(B) In the case of a request filed under paragraph (j)(1)(ii) of this section, where the royalty fee was miscalculated and the amount deposited in the Copyright Office was either too high or too low, the request must be accompanied by an affidavit under the official seal of any officer authorized to administer oaths within the United

States, or a statement in accordance with section 1746 of Title 28 of the United States Code, made and signed in accordance with paragraph (e)(14) of this section. The affidavit or statement shall describe the reasons why the royalty fee was improperly calculated and include a detailed analysis of the proper royalty calculations:

(C) In the case of a request filed under paragraph (j)(1)(iii) of this section, the request shall be identified as "Transitional and Supplemental Royalty Fee Payment" and include a detailed analysis of the proper royalty calculations;

(iv)(A) All requests filed under this paragraph (j) (except those filed under subparagraph (1)(iii) of this paragraph) must be accompanied by a filing fee in the amount of $15 for each Statement of Account involved. Payment of this fee may be in the form of a personal or company check, or of a certified check, cashier's check or money order, payable to: Register of Copyrights. No request will be processed until the appropriate filing fees are received.

(B) All requests that a supplemental royalty fee payment be received for deposit under this paragraph (j), must be accompanied by a remittance in the full amount of such fee. Payment of the supplemental royalty fee must be in the form of a certified check, cashier's check, or money order, payable to: Register of Copyrights. No such request will be processed until an acceptable remittance in the full amount of the supplemental royalty fee has been received.

(v) All requests submitted under this paragraph (j) must be signed by the cable system owner named in the Statement of Account, or the duly authorized agent of the owner, in accordance with paragraph (e)(14) of this section.

(vi) A request for a refund is not necessary where the Licensing Division during its examination of a Statement of Account or related document, discovers an error that has resulted in a royalty overpayment. In this case, the Licensing Division will forward the royalty refund to the cable system owner named in the Statement of Account without regard to the time limitations provided for in paragraph (j)(3)(i) of this section.

(4) Following final processing, all requests submitted under this paragraph (j) will be filed with the original Statement of Account in the records of the Copyright Office. Nothing contained in this paragraph shall be considered to relieve cable systems from their full obligations under Title 17 of the United States Code, and the filing of a correction or supplemental payment shall have only such effect as may be attributed to it by a court of compentent jurisdiction.

(5) In the case of Forms CS/SA-3 for the accounting period ending June 30, 1984 and of the Supplemental DSE Schedules for 1983, a period of 120 days shall apply in lieu of the 60 day period specified by this paragraph (j)(3)(i).

(17 U.S.C. 111, 702, 708)
[43 FR 27832, June 27, 1978, as amended at 45 FR 45274, July 3, 1980; 47 FR 21789, May 20, 1982; 49 FR 13037, Apr. 2, 1984; 49 FR 26726, June 29, 1984; 49 FR 33017, Aug. 20, 1984]

## § 201.18 Notice of intention to obtain a compulsory license for making and distributing phonorecords of nondramatic musical works.

(a) *General.* (1) A "Notice of Intention" is a notice identified in section 115(b) of Title 17 of the United States Code, as amended by Pub. L. 94-553, and required by that section to be served on a copyright owner, or in certain cases to be filed in the Copyright Office, to obtain a compulsory license to make and distribute phonorecords of nondramatic musical works.

(2) A separate Notice of Intention shall be served or filed for each nondramatic musical work embodied, or intended to be embodied, in phonorecords made under the compulsory license.

(3) For the purposes of this section, the term "copyright owner," in the case of any work having more than one copyright owner, means any one of the coowners. In

such cases, the service of a Notice of Intention on any one of the coowners under paragraph (e)(2) of this section shall be sufficient with respect to all coowners.

(b) *Form.* The Copyright Office does not provide printed forms for the use of persons serving or filing Notices of Intention.

(c) *Content.* (1) A Notice of Intention shall be clearly and prominently designated, at the head of the notice, as a "Notice of Intention to Obtain a Compulsory License for Making and Distributing Phonorecords," and shall include a clear statement of the following information:

(i) The full legal name of the person or entity intending to obtain the compulsory license, together with all fictitious or assumed names used by such person or entity for the purpose of conducting the business of making and distributing phonorecords;

(ii) The full address, including a specific number and street name or rural route of the place of business of the person or entity intending to obtain the compulsory license. A post office box or similar designation will not be sufficient for this purpose except where it is the only address that can be used in that geographic location;

(iii) A statement of the nature of each and every business organization that the person or entity intending to obtain the compulsory license will use for the purpose of conducting the business of making and distributing phonorecords under the license (for example, a corporation, a partnership, or an individual proprietorship); additionally:

(A) If the person or entity intending to obtain the compulsory license is a corporation registered with the Securities and Exchange Commission under section 12 of the Securities and Exchange Act of 1934, the Notice shall so state.

(B) If the person or entity intending to obtain the compulsory license is a corporation that is not registered with the Securities and Exchange Commission under section 12 of the Securities and Exchange Act of 1934, the Notice shall include a list of the names of the corporation's directors and officers, and the names of each beneficial owner of twenty-five percent (25%) or more of the outstanding securities of the corporation.

(C) In all other cases, the Notice shall include the names of each entity or individual owning a beneficial interest of twenty-five percent (25%) or more in the entity intending to exercise the compulsory license. If a corporate entity is named in response to this paragraph (C), then: If that corporation is registered with the Securities and Exchange Commission under section 12 of the Securities and Exchange Act of 1934, the Notice shall so state; if that corporation is not so registered, the Notice shall include a list of the names of the corporation's directors and officers, and the names of each beneficial owner of twenty-five percent (25%) or more of the outstanding securities of that corporation;

(iv) The fiscal year of the person or entity intending to obtain the compulsory license. If that fiscal year is a calendar year, the Notice shall state that this is the case;

(v) The title of the nondramatic musical work embodied or intended to be embodied in phonorecords made under the compulsory license, and the names of the author or authors of such work if known;

(vi) The types of all phonorecord configurations already made (if any) and expected to be made under the compulsory license (for example: Single disk, long-playing disk, cassette, cartridge, reel-to-reel, or a combination of them);

(vii) The expected date of initial distribution of phonorecords already made (if any) or expected to be made under the compulsory license;

(viii) The name of the principal recording artist or group actually engaged or expected to be engaged in rendering the performances fixed on phonorecords already made (if any) or expected to be made under the compulsory license;

(ix) The catalog number or numbers, and label name or names, used or expected to be used on phonorecords already made (if any) or expected to be made under the compulsory license; and

(x) In the case of phonorecords already made (if any) under the compulsory license, the date or dates of such manufacture.

(2) A "clear statement" of the information listed in paragraph (c)(1) of this section requires a clearly intelligible, legible, and unambiguous statement in the Notice itself and (subject to paragraph (c)(1)(iii)(A) of this section) without incorporation by reference of facts or information contained in other documents or records.

(3) Where information is required to be given by paragraph (c)(1) of this section "if known" or as "expected," such information shall be given in good faith and on the basis of the best knowledge, information, and belief of the person signing the Notice. If so given, later developments affecting the accuracy of such information shall not affect the validity of the Notice.

(d) *Signature.* The Notice shall be signed by the person or entity intending to obtain the compulsory license. If that person or entity is a corporation, the signature shall be that of a duly authorized officer of the corporation; if that person or entity is a partnership, the signature shall be that of a partner. The signature shall be accompanied by the printed or typewritten name of the person signing the Notice, and by the date of signature.

(e) *Filing and service.* (1) If, with respect to the nondramatic musical work named in the Notice of Intention, the registration or other public records of the Copyright Office do not identify the copyright owner of such work and include an address for such owner, the Notice shall be filed in the Copyright Office. Notices of Intention submitted for filing shall be accompanied by a fee of $6.00. Notices of Intention will be filed by being placed in the appropriate public records of the Licensing Division of the Copyright Office. The date of filing will be the date when a proper Notice and fee are both received in the Copyright Office. A written acknowledgment of receipt and filing will be provided to the sender. Upon request and payment of an additional fee of $4.00, a Certificate of Filing will be provided to the sender.

(2) If the registration or other public records of the Copyright Office do identify the copyright owner of the nondramatic musical work named in the Notice of Intention and include an address for such owner, the Notice shall be served on such owner by certified mail or by registered mail sent to the last address for such owner shown by the records of the Office; it shall not be necessary to file a copy of the Notice in the Copyright Office in this case.

(3) If the Notice is sent by certified or registered mail to the last address for the copyright owner shown by the records of the Copyright Office and is returned to the sender because the copyright owner is no longer located at the address or has refused to accept delivery, the original Notice as sent shall be filed in the Copyright Office. Notices of Intention submitted for filing under this paragraph (e)(3) shall be submitted to the Licensing Division of the Copyright Office, and shall be accompanied by a brief statement that the Notice was sent to the last address for the copyright owner shown by the records of the Copyright Office but was returned, and by appropriate evidence that it was sent by certified or registered mail to that address. In these cases, the Copyright Office will specially mark its records to consider the date the original Notice was mailed, as shown by the evidence mentioned above, as the date of filing. A written acknowledgment of receipt and filing will be provided to the sender. No filing fee will be required in the case of Notices filed under this paragraph (e)(3). Upon request and payment of a fee of $4.00, a Certificate of Filing will be provided to the sender.

(17 U.S.C. 115, 702, 708)
[45 FR 79045, Nov. 28, 1980]

## § 201.19 Royalties and statements of account under compulsory license for making and distributing phonorecords of nondramatic musical works.

(a) *Definitions.* (1) A "Monthly Statement of Account" is a statement accompanying monthly royalty payments identified in section 115(c)(3) of Title 17 of the United States Code, as amended by Pub. L. 94-553, and required by that section to be made under the compulsory license to make and distribute phonorecords of nondramatic musical works.

(2) An "Annual Statement of Account" is a statement identified in section 115(c)(3) of Title 17 of the United States Code, as amended by Pub. L. 94-553, and required by that section to be filed for every compulsory license to make and distribute phonorecords of nondramatic musical works.

(3) For the purposes of this section, the term "copyright owner," in the case of any work having more than one copyright owner means any one of the coowners. In such cases, the service of a Statement of Account, on one coowner under paragraph (e)(7) or (f)(7) of this section shall be sufficient with respect to all coowners.

(4) For the purposes of this section, a "compulsory licensee" is a person or entity exercising the compulsory license to make and distribute phonorecords of nondramatic musical works as provided under section 115 of Title 17 of the United States Code, as amended by Pub. L. 94-553.

(5) A phonorecord is considered "voluntarily distributed" if the compulsory licensee has voluntarily and permanently parted with possession of the phonorecord. For this purpose, and subject to the provisions of paragraph (d) of this section, a compulsory licensee shall be considered to have "permanently parted with possession" of a phonorecord made under the license:

(i) In the case of phonorecords relinquished from possession for purposes other than sale, at the time at which the compulsory licensee actually first parts with possession;

(ii) In the case of phonorecords relinquished from possession for purposes of sale without a privilege of returning unsold phonorecords for credit or exchange, at the time at which the compulsory licensee actually first parts with possession;

(iii) In the case of phonorecords relinquished from possession for purposes of sale accompanied by a privilege of returning unsold phonorecords for credit or exchange: (A) At the time when revenue from a sale of the phonorecord is "recognized" by the compulsory licensee; or (B) nine months from the month in which the compulsory licensee actually first parted with possession, whichever occurs first. For these purposes, a compulsory licensee shall be considered to "recognize" revenue from the sale of a phonorecord when sales revenue would be recognized in accordance with generally accepted accounting principles as expressed by the American Institute of Certified Public Accountants or the Financial Accounting Standards Board, whichever would cause sales revenue to be recognized first.

(6) A "phonorecord reserve" comprises the number of phonorecords, if any, that have been relinquished from possession for purposes of sale in a given month accompanied by a privilege of return, as described in paragraph (a)(5)(iii) of this section, and that have not been considered voluntarily distributed during the month in which the compulsory licensee actually first parted with their possession. The initial number of phonorecords comprising a phonorecord reserve shall be determined in accordance with generally accepted accounting principles as expressed by the American Institute of Certified Public Accountants or the Financial Accounting Standards Board.

(7) A "negative reserve balance" comprises the aggregate number of phonorecords, if any, that have been relinquished from possession for purposes of sale accompanied by a privilege of return, as described in paragraph (a)(5)(iii) of this section, and that have been returned to the compulsory licensee, but because all available phonorecord reserves have been eliminated, have not been used to reduce a phonorecord reserve.

(b) *Accounting requirements where sales revenue is "recognized."* Where under paragraph (a)(5)(iii)(A) of this section, revenue from the sale of phonorecords is "recognized" during any month after the month in which the compulsory licensee actually first parted with their possession, said compulsory licensee shall reduce particular phonorecord reserves by the number of phonorecords for which revenue is being "recognized," as follows:

(1) If the number of phonorecords for which revenue is being "recognized" is smaller than the number of phonorecords comprising the earliest eligible phonorecord reserve, this phonorecord reserve shall be reduced by the number of phonorecords for which revenue is being "recognized." Subject to the time limitations of subparagraph (B) of this § 201.19(a)(5)(iii), the number of phonorecords remaining in this reserve shall be available for use in subsequent months.

(2) If the number of phonorecords for which revenue is being "recognized" is greater than the number of phonorecords comprising the earliest eligible phonorecord reserve but less than the total number of phonorecords comprising all eligible phonorecord reserves, the compulsory licensee shall first eliminate those phonorecord reserves, beginning with the earliest eligible phonorecord reserve and continuing to the next succeeding phonorecord reserves, that are completely offset by phonorecords for which revenue is being "recognized." Said licensee shall then reduce the next succeeding phonorecord reserve by the number of phonorecords for which revenue is being "recognized" that have not been used to eliminate a phonorecord reserve. Subject to the time limitations of subparagraph (B) of § 201.19(a)(5)(iii), the number of phonorecords remaining in this reserve shall be available for use in subsequent months.

(3) If the number of phonorecords for which revenue is being "recognized" equals the number of phonorecords comprising all eligible phonorecord reserves, the person or entity exercising the compulsory license shall eliminate all of the phonorecord reserves.

(c) *Accounting requirements for offsetting phonorecord reserves with returned phonorecords.* (1) In the case of a phonorecord that has been relinquished from possession for purposes of sale accompanied by a privilege of return, as described in paragraph (a)(5)(iii) of this section, where the phonorecord is returned to the compulsory licensee for credit or exchange before said compulsory licensee is considered to have "permanently parted with possession" of the phonorecord under paragraph (a)(5) of this section, the compulsory licensee may use such phonorecord to reduce a "phonorecord reserve," as defined in paragraph (a)(6) of this section.

(2) In such cases, the compulsory licensee shall reduce particular phonorecord reserves by the number of phonorecords that are returned during the month covered by the Monthly Statement of Account in the following manner:

(i) If the number of phonorecords that are returned during the month covered by the Monthly Statement is smaller than the number comprising the earliest eligible phonorecord reserve, the compulsory licensee shall reduce this phonorecord reserve by the total number of returned phonorecords. Subject to the time limitations of paragraph (B) of § 201.19(a)(5)(iii), the number of phonorecords remaining in this reserve shall be available for use in subsequent months.

(ii) If the number of phonorecords that are returned during the month covered by the Monthly Statement is greater than the number of phonorecords comprising the earliest eligible phonorecord reserve but less than the total number of phonorecords comprising all eligible phonorecord reserves, the compulsory licensee shall first eliminate those phonorecord reserves, beginning with the earliest eligible phonorecord reserve, and continuing to the next succeeding phonorecord reserves, that are completely offset by returned phonorecords. Said licensee shall then reduce the next succeeding phonorecord reserve by the number of returned phonorecords that have not been used to eliminate a phonorecord reserve. Subject to the time limitations of paragraph (B) of § 201.19(a)(5)(iii), the number of phonorecords remaining in this reserve shall be available for use in subsequent months.

(iii) If the number of phonorecords that are returned during the month covered by the Monthly Statement is equal to or is greater than the total number of phonorecords comprising all eligible phonorecord reserves, the compulsory licensee shall eliminate all eligible phonorecord reserves. Where said number is greater than the total number of phonorecords comprising all eligible phonorecord reserves, said compulsory licensee shall establish a "negative reserve balance," as defined in paragraph (a)(7) of this section.

(3) Except where a negative reserve balance exists, a separate and distinct phonorecord reserve shall be established for each month during which the compulsory licensee relinquishes phonorecords from possession for purposes of sale accompanied by a privilege of return, as described in paragraph (a)(5)(iii) of this section. In accordance with paragraph (B) of § 201.19(a)(5)(iii), any phonorecord remaining in a particular phonorecord reserve nine months from the month in which the particular reserve was established shall be considered "voluntarily distributed"; at that point,

the particular monthly phonorecord reserve shall lapse and royalties for the phonorecord remaining in it shall be paid as provided in paragraph (e)(4)(ii) of this section.

(4) Where a negative reserve balance exists, the aggregate total of phonorecords comprising it shall be accumulated into a single balance rather than being separated into distinct monthly balances. Following the establishment of a negative reserve balance, any phonorecords relinquished from possession by the compulsory licensee for purposes of sale or otherwise, shall be credited against such negative balance, and the negative reserve balance shall be reduced accordingly. The nine month limit provided by paragraph (B) of § 201.19(a)(5)(iii) shall have no effect upon a negative reserve balance; where a negative reserve balance exists, relinquishment from possession of a phonorecord by the compulsory licensee at any time shall be used to reduce such balance, and shall not be considered a "voluntary distribution" within the meaning of paragraph (a)(5) of this section.

(5) In no case shall a phonorecord reserve be established while a negative reserve balance is in existence; conversely, in no case shall a negative reserve balance be established before all available phonorecord reserves have been eliminated.

(d) *Situations in which a compulsory licensee is barred from maintaining reserves.* Notwithstanding any other provisions of this section, in any case where, within three years before the phonorecord was relinquished from possession, the compulsory licensee has had final judgment entered against it for failure to pay royalties for the reproduction of copyrighted music on phonorecords, or within such period has been definitively found in any proceeding involving bankruptcy, insolvency, receivership, assignment for the benefit of creditors, or similar action, to have failed to pay such royalties, that compulsory licensee shall be considered to have "Permanently parted with possession" of a phonorecord made under the license at the time at which that licensee actually first parts with possession. For these purposes the "compulsory licensee," as defined in § 201.19(a)(4), shall include:

(1) In the case of any corporation, the corporation or any director, officer, or beneficial owner of twenty-five percent (25%) or more of the outstanding securities of the corporation;

(2) In all other cases, any entity or individual owing a beneficial interest of twenty-five percent (25%) or more in the entity exercising the compulsory license.

(e) *Monthly statements of account.* (1) *Forms.* The Copyright Office does not provide printed forms for the use of persons serving Monthly Statements of Account.

(2) *General content.* A Monthly Statement of Account shall be clearly and prominently identified as a "Monthly Statement of Account Under Compulsory License for Making and Distributing Phonorecords," and shall include a clear statement of the following information:

(i) The period (month and year) covered by the Monthly Statement;

(ii) The full legal name of the compulsory licensee, together with all fictitious or assumed names used by such person or entity for the purpose of conducting the business of making and distributing phonorecords;

(iii) The full address, including a specific number and street name or rural route, of the place of business of the compulsory licensee. A post office box or similar designation will not be sufficient for this purpose, except where it is the only address that can be used in that geographic location;

(iv) The title or titles of the nondramatic musical work or works embodied in phonorecords made under the compulsory license and owned by the copyright owner being served with the Monthly Statement and the name of the author or authors of such work or works, if known;

(v) For each nondramatic musical work that is owned by the same copyright owner being served with the Monthly Statement and that is embodied in phonorecords covered by the compulsory license, a detailed statement of all of the information called for in paragraph (e)(3) of this section;

(vi) The total royalty payable for the month covered by the Monthly Statement, computed in accordance with the requirements of this section and the formula specified in paragraph (e)(4) of this section, together with a statement of account showing in detail how the royalty was computed; and

(vii) In any case where the compulsory licensee falls within the provisions of paragraph (d) of this section, a clear description of the action or proceeding involved, including the date of the final judgment or definitive finding described in that paragraph.

(3) *Specific content of monthly statements: Identification and accounting of phonorecords.* (i) The information called for by paragraph (e)(2)(v) of this section shall, with respect to each nondramatic musical work include a separate listing of each of the following items of information:

(A) The number of phonorecords made during the month covered by the Monthly Statement;

(B) The number of phonorecords that, during the month covered by the Monthly Statement and regardless of when made, were either:

Relinquished from possession for purposes other than sale;

Relinquished from possession for purposes of sale without any privilege of returning unsold phonorecords for credit or exchange;

Relinquished from possession for purposes of sale accompanied by a privilege of returning unsold phonorecords for credit or exchange;

Returned to the compulsory licensee for credit or exchange; or

Placed in a phonorecord reserve (except that if a negative reserve balance exists give either the number of phonorecords added to the negative reserve balance, or the number of phonorecords relinquished from possession that have been used to reduce the negative reserve balance);

(C) The number of phonorecords, regardless of when made, that were relinquished from possession during a month earlier than the month covered by the Monthly Statement but that, during the month covered by the Monthly Statement either have had revenue from their sale "recognized" under paragraph (a)(5)(iii) of this section, or were comprised in a phonorecord reserve that lapsed after nine months under paragraph (B) of § 201.19(a)(5)(iii).

(ii) Each of the items of information called for by paragraph (e)(3)(i) of this section shall also include, and if necessary shall be broken down to identify separately, the following:

(A) The catalog number or numbers and label name or names, used on the phonorecords;

(B) The names of the principal recording artist or group engaged in rendering the performances fixed on the phonorecords;

(C) The playing time on the phonorecords of each nondramatic musical work covered by the statement; and

(D) Each phonorecord configuration involved (for example: single disk, long-playing disk, cartridge, cassette, reel-to-reel).

(4) *Royalty payment and accounting.* (i) The total royalty called for by paragraph (e)(2)(vi) of this section shall, as specified in section 115(c)(2) of Title 17 of the United States Code, as amended by Pub. L. 94-553, be payable for every phonorecord "voluntarily distributed" during the month covered by the Monthly Statement.

(ii) The amount of royalty payment shall be calculated in accordance with the following formula:

*Step 1. Compute the number of phonorecords shipped for sale with a privilege of return.* This is the total of phonorecords that, during the month covered by the Monthly Statement, were relinquished from possession by the compulsory licensee, accompanied by the privilege of returning unsold phonorecords to the compulsory licensee for credit or exchange. This total does *not* include: (1) Any phonorecords relinquished from possession by the compulsory licensee for purposes of sale without the privilege of return; and (2) any phonorecords relinquished from possession for purposes other than sale.

*Step 2: Subtract the number of phonorecords reserved.* This involves deducting, from the subtotal arrived at in Step 1, the number of phonorecords that have been placed in the phonorecord reserve for the month covered by the Monthly Statement. The number of phonorecords reserved is determined by multiplying the subtotal from Step 1 by the percentage reserve level established under GAAP. This step should be skipped by a compulsory licensee barred from maintaining reserves under paragraph (d) of this section.

*Step 3: Add the total of all phonorecords that were shipped during the month and were not counted in Step 1.* This total is the sum of two figures: (1) The number of phonorecords that, during the month covered by the Monthly Statement, were relinquished from possession by the compulsory licensee for purposes of sale, without the privilege of returning unsold phonorecords to the compulsory licensee for credit or exchange; and (2) the number of phonorecords relinquished from possession by the compulsory licensee, during the month covered by the Monthly Statement, for purposes other than sale.

*Step 4: Make any necessary adjustments for sales revenue "recognized," lapsed reserves, or reduction of negative reserve balance during the month.* If necessary, this step involves adding to or subtracting from the subtotal arrived at in Step 3 on the basis of three possible types of adjustments:

*(a) Sales revenue "recognized."* If, in the month covered by the Monthly Statement, the compulsory licensee "recognized" revenue from the sale of phonorecords that had been relinquished from possession in an earlier month, the number of such phonorecords is *added* to the Step 3 subtotal;

*(b) Lapsed reserves.* If, in the month covered by the Monthly Statement, there are any phonorecords remaining in the phonorecord reserve for the ninth previous month (that is, any phonorecord reserves from the ninth previous month that have not been offset under FOFI, the first-out-first-in accounting convention, by actual returns during the intervening months), the reserve lapses and the number of phonorecords in it is *added* to the Step 3 subtotal.

*(c) Reduction of negative reserve balance.* If, in the month covered by the Monthly Statement, the aggregate reserve balance for all previous months is a negative amount, the number of phonorecords relinquished from possession by the compulsory licensee during that month and used to reduce the negative reserve balance is *subtracted* from the Step 3 subtotal.

*Step 5: Multiply by the statutory royalty rate.* The total monthly royalty payment is obtained by multiplying the subtotal from Step 3, as adjusted if necessary by Step 4, by the statutory royalty rate of 2¾ cents or ½ cent per minute or fraction of playing time, whichever is larger.

(iii) Each step in computing the monthly payment, including the arithmetical calculations involved in each step, shall be set out in detail in the Monthly Statement.

(5) *Clear statements.* The information required by paragraphs (e)(2) and (3) of this section involves intelligible, legible, and unambiguous statements in the Monthly Statements of Account itself and without incorporation of facts or information contained in other documents or records.

(6) *Oath and signature.* Each Monthly Statement of Account shall include the handwritten signature of the compulsory licensee. If that compulsory licensee is a corporation, the signature shall be that of a duly authorized officer of the corporation; if that compulsory licensee is a partnership, the signature shall be that of a partner. The signature shall be accompanied by: (i) The printed or typewritten name of the person signing the Monthly Statement of Account; (ii) the date of signature; (iii) if the compulsory licensee is a partnership or a corporation, by the title or official position held in the partnership or corporation by the person signing the Monthly Statement of Account; (iv) a certification of the capacity of the person signing; and (v) the following statement:

I certify that I have examined this Monthly Statement of Account and that all statements of fact contained herein are true, complete, and correct to the best of my knowledge, information, and belief, and are made in good faith.

(7) *Service.* (i) Each Monthly Statement of Account shall be served on the copyright owner to whom or which it is directed, together with the total royalty for the month covered by the Monthly Statement, by certified mail, or by registered mail on or before the 20th day of the immediately succeeding month. It shall not be necessary to file a copy of the Monthly Statement in the Copyright Office.

(ii) (A) In any case where a Monthly Statement of Account is sent by certified mail or registered mail and is returned to the sender because the copyright owner is not located at that address or has refused to accept delivery, or in any case where an address for the copyright owner is not known, the Monthly Statement of Account, together with any evidence of mailing, may be filed in the Licensing Division of the Copyright Office. Any Monthly Statement of Account submitted for filing in the Copyright Office shall be accompanied by a brief statement of the reason why it was not served on the copyright owner. A written acknowledgment of receipt and filing will be provided to the sender.

(B) The Copyright Office will not accept any royalty fees submitted with Monthly Statements of Account under § 202.19(e)(7)(ii).

(C) Neither the filing of a Monthly Statement of Account in the Copyright Office, nor the failure to file such Monthly Statement, shall have effect other than that which may be attributed to it by a court of competent jurisdiction.

(D) No filing fee will be required in the case of Monthly Statements of Account submitted to the Copyright Office under this § 201.19(e)(7)(ii). Upon request and payment of a fee of $4.00, a Certificate of Filing will be provided to the sender.

(iii) A separate Monthly Statement of Account shall be served for each month during which there is any activity relevant to the payment of royalties under section 115 of Title 17, United States Code, as amended by Pub. L. 94-553, and under this section. The Annual Statement of Account identified in paragraph (f) of this section does not replace any Monthly Statement of Account.

(f) *Annual statements of account*—(1) *Forms.* The Copyright Office does not provide printed forms for the use of persons serving Annual Statements of Account.

(2) *Annual period.* Any Annual Statement of Account shall cover the full fiscal year of the compulsory licensee.

(3) *General content.* An Annual Statement of Account shall be clearly and prominently identified as an "Annual Statement of Account Under Compulsory License for Making and Distributing Phonorecords," and shall include a clear statement of the following information:

(i) The fiscal year covered by the Annual Statement;

(ii) The full legal name of the compulsory licensee, together with all fictitious or assumed names used by such person or entity for the purpose of conducting the business of making and distributing phonorecords;

(iii) A statement of the nature of the business organization used by the compulsory licensee in connection with the making and distribution of phonorecords (for example, a corporation, a partnership, or an individual proprietorship); additionally:

(A) If the compulsory licensee is a corporation registered with the Securities and Exchange Commission under section 12 of the Securities and Exchange Act of 1934, the Annual Statement shall state that this is the case.

(B) If the compulsory licensee is a corporation that is not registered with the Securities and Exchange Commission under section 12 of the Securities and Exchange Act of 1934, the Annual Statement shall include a list of the names of the corporation's directors and officers, and the names of each beneficial owner of twenty-five percent (25%) or more of the outstanding securities of the corporation.

(C) In all other cases, the Annual Statement shall include the names of each entity or individual owing a beneficial interest of twenty-five percent (25%) or more in the entity exercising the compulsory license. If a corporate entity is named in response to this paragraph (C), then: If that corporation is registered with the Securities and Exchange Commission under section 12 of the Securities and Exchange Act of 1934, the Annual Statement shall so state; if that corporation is not so registered, the Annual Statement shall include a list of the corporation's directors and officers, and the names of each beneficial owner of twenty-five percent (25%) or more of the outstanding securities of that corporation;

(iv) The full address, including a specific number and street name or rural route, or the place of business of the compulsory licensee. A post office box or similar designation will not be sufficient for this purpose except where it is the only address that can be used in that geographic location;

(v) The title or titles of the nondramatic musical work or works embodied in phonorecords made under the compulsory license and owned by the copyright owner being served with the Annual Statement and the name of the author or authors of such work or works, if known;

(vi) The playing time of each nondramatic musical work on such phonorecords;

(vii) For each nondramatic musical work that is owned by the same copyright owner being served with the Annual Statement and that is embodied in phonorecords covered by the compulsory license, a detailed statement of all of the information called for in paragraph (f)(4) of this section;

(viii) The total royalty payable for the fiscal year covered by the Annual Statement computed in accordance with the requirements of this section, together with a statement of account showing in detail how the royalty was computed. For these purposes, the applicable royalty as specified in section 115(c)(2) of Title 17 of the United States Code, as amended by Pub. L. 94-553, shall be payable for every phonorecord "voluntarily distributed" during the fiscal year covered by the Annual Statement;

(ix) The total sum paid under Monthly Statements of Account by the compulsory licensee to the copyright owner being served with the Annual Statement during the fiscal year covered by the Annual Statement; and

(x) In any case where the compulsory license falls within the provisions of paragraph (d) of this section, a clear description of the action or proceeding involved, including the date of the final judgment or definitive finding described in that paragraph.

(4) *Specific content of annual statements: Identification and accounting of phonorecords.* (i) The information called for by paragraph (f)(3)(vii) of this section shall, with respect to each nondramatic musical work, include a separate listing of each of the following items of information separately stated and identified for each phonorecord configuration (for example, single disk, long playing disk, cartridge, cassette, or reel-to-reel) made:

(A) The number of phonorecords made through the end of the fiscal year covered by the Annual Statement, including any made during earlier years;

(B) The number of phonorecords which have never been relinquished from possession of the compulsory licensee through the end of the fiscal year covered by the Annual Statement;

(C) The number of phonorecords involuntarily relinquished from possession (as through fire or theft) of the compulsory licensee during the fiscal year covered by the Annual Statement and any earlier years, together with a description of the facts of such involuntary relinquishment;

(D) The number of phonorecords "voluntarily distributed" by the compulsory licensee during all years before the fiscal year covered by the Annual Statement;

(E) The number of phonorecords relinquished from possession of the compulsory licensee for purposes of sale during the fiscal year covered by the Annual Statement accompanied by a privilege of returning unsold records for credit or exchange, but not "voluntarily distributed" by the end of that year;

(F) The number of phonorecords "voluntarily distributed" by the compulsory licensee during the fiscal year covered by the Annual Statement, together with: (*1*) The catalog number or numbers, and label name or names, used on such phonorecords; and (*2*) the names of the principal recording artists or groups engaged in rendering the performances fixed on such phonorecords.

(ii) If the information given under paragraphs (A) through (F) of this § 201.19(f)(4)(i) does not reconcile, the Annual Statement shall also include a clear and detailed explanation of the difference. For these purposes, the information given under such paragraphs shall be considered not to reconcile if, after the number of phonorecords given under paragraphs (B), (C), (D), and (E) are added together and that sum is deducted from the number of phonorecords given under paragraph (A), the result is different from the amount given under paragraph (F).

(5) *Clear statement.* The information required by paragraph (f)(3) of this section involves intelligible, legible, and unambiguous statements in the Annual Statement of Account itself and [subject to paragraph (f)(3)(iii)(A)] without incorporation by reference of facts or information contained in other documents or records.

(6) *Signature and certification.* (i) Each Annual Statement of Account shall include the handwritten signature of the compulsory licensee. If that compulsory licensee is a corporation, the signature shall be that of a duly authorized officer of the corporation; if that compulsory licensee is a partnership, the signature shall be that of a partner. The signature shall be accompanied by: (A) The printed or typewritten name of the person signing the Annual Statement of Account; (B) the date of signature; (C) if the compulsory licensee is a partnership or a corporation, by the title or official position held in the partnership or corporation by the person signing the Annual Statement of Account; and (D) a certification of the capacity of the person signing.

(ii)(A) Each Annual Statement of Account shall also be certified by a licensed Certified Public Accountant. Such certification shall consist of the following statement:

We have examined the attached "Annual Statement of Account Under Compulsory License For Making and Distributing Phonorecords" for the fiscal year ended (date) of (name of the compulsory licensee) applicable to phonorecords embodying (title or titles of nondramatic musical works embodied in phonorecords made under the compulsory license) made under the provisions of section 115 of Title 17 of the United States Code, as amended by Pub. L. 94-553, and applicable regulations of the United States Copyright Office. Our examination was made in accordance with generally accepted auditing standards and accordingly, included tests of the accounting records and such other auditing procedures as we considered necessary in the circumstances.

In our opinion the Annual Statement of Account referred to above presents fairly the number of phonorecords embodying each of the above-identified nondramatic musical works made under compulsory license and voluntarily distributed by (name of the compulsory licensee) during the fiscal year ending (date), and the amount of royalties applicable thereto under such compulsory license, on a consistent basis and in accordance with the above cited law and applicable regulations published thereunder.

_____

(City and State of Execution)

_____

(Signature of Certified Public Accountant or CPA Firm)

_____

Certificate Number

_____

Jurisdiction of Certificate

_____

(Date of Opinion)

(B) The certificate shall be signed by an individual, or in the name of a partnership or a professional corporation with two or more shareholders. The certificate number and jurisdiction are not required if the certificate is signed in the name of a partnership or a professional corporation with two or more shareholders.

(7) *Service.* (i) Each Annual Statement of Account shall be served on the copyright owner to whom or which it is directed by certified mail or by registered mail on or before the twentieth day of the third month following the end of the fiscal year covered by the Annual Statement. It shall not be necessary to file a copy of the Annual Statement in the Copyright Office. An Annual Statement of Account shall be served for each fiscal year during which at least one Monthly Statement of Account was required to have been served under paragraph (e)(7) of this section.

(ii) In any case where the amount required to be stated in the Annual Statement of Account under paragraph (f)(3)(viii) of this section is greater than the amount stated in that Annual Statement under paragraph (f)(3)(ix) of this section, the difference between such amounts shall be delivered to the copyright owner together with the service of the Annual Statement. The delivery of such sum does not require the copyright owner to accept such sum, or to forego any right, relief, or remedy which may be available under law.

(iii)(A) In any case where an Annual Statement of Account is sent by certified mail or registered mail and is returned to the sender because the copyright owner is not located at that address or has refused to accept delivery, or in any case where an address for the copyright owner is not known, the Annual Statement of Account, together with any evidence of mailing, may be filed in the Licensing Division of the Copyright Office. Any Annual Statement of Account submitted for filing shall be accompanied by a brief statement of the reason why it was not served on the copyright owner. A written acknowledgment of receipt and filing will be provided to the sender.

(B) The Copyright Office will not accept any royalty fees submitted with Annual Statements of Account under § 202.19(f)(7)(iii).

(C) Neither the filing of an Annual Statement of Account in the Copyright Office, nor the failure to file such Annual Statement, shall have any effect other than that which may be attributed to it by a court of competent jurisdiction.

(D) No filing fee will be required in the case of Annual Statements of Account submitted to the Copyright Office under this § 201.19(f)(7)(iii). Upon request and payment of a fee of $4, a Certificate of Filing will be provided to the sender.

(g) *Documentation.* All compulsory licensees shall, for a period of at least three years from the date of service of an Annual Statement of Account, keep and retain in their possession all records and documents necessary and appropriate to support fully the information set forth in such Annual Statement and in Monthly Statements served during the fiscal year covered by such Annual Statement.

(17 U.S.C. 115, 702, 708)
[45 FR 79046, Nov. 28, 1980]

# § 201.20 Methods of affixation and positions of the copyright notice on various types of works.

(a) *General,* (1) This section specifies examples of methods of affixation and positions of the copyright notice on various types of works that will satisfy the notice requirement of section 401(c) of Title 17 of the United States Code, as amended by Pub. L. 94-553. A notice considered "acceptable" under this regulation shall be considered to satisfy the requirement of that section that it be "affixed to the copies in such manner and location as to give reasonable notice of the claim of copyright." As provided by that section, the examples specified in this regulation shall not be considered exhaustive of methods of affixation and positions giving reasonable notice of the claim of copyright.

(2) The provisions of this section are applicable to copies publicly distributed on or after December 1, 1981. This section does not establish any rules concerning the form of the notice or the legal sufficiency of particular notices, except with respect to methods of affixation and positions of notice. The adequacy or legal sufficiency of a copyright notice is determined by the law in effect at the time of first publication of the work.

(b) *Definitions.* For the purposes of this section:

(1) The terms "audiovisual works," "collective works," "copies," "device," "fixed," "machine," "motion picture," "pictorial, graphic, and sculptural works," and their variant forms, have the meanings given to them in section 101 of Title 17.

(2) "Title 17" means Title 17 of the United States Code, as amended by Pub. L. 94-553.

(3) In the case of a work consisting preponderantly of leaves on which the work is printed or otherwise reproduced on both sides, a "page" is one side of a leaf; where the preponderance of the leaves are printed on one side only, the terms "page" and "leaf" mean the same.

(4) A work is published in "book form" if the copies embodying it consist of multiple leaves bound, fastened or assembled in a predetermined order, as for example, a volume, booklet, pamphlet, or multipage folder. For the purpose of this section, a work need not consist of textual matter in order to be considered published in "book form."

(5) A "title page" is a page, or two consecutive pages facing each other, appearing at or near the front of the copies of a work published in book form, on which the complete title of the work is prominently stated and on which the names of the author or authors, the names of the publisher, the place of publication, or some combination of them, are given.

(6) The meaning of the terms "front," "back," "first," and "following," when used in connection with works published in book form, will vary in relation to the physical form of the copies, depending upon the particular language in which the work is written.

(7) In the case of a work published in book form with a hard or soft cover, the "front page" and "back page" of the copies are the outsides of the front and back covers; where there is no cover, the "front page" and "back page" are the pages visible at the front and back of the copies before they are opened.

(8) A "masthead" is a body of information appearing in approximately the same location in most issues of a newspaper, magazine, journal, review, or other periodical or serial, typically containing the title of the periodical or serial, information about the staff, periodicity of issues, operation, and subscription and editorial policies, of the publication.

(9) A "single-leaf work" is a work published in copies consisting of a single leaf, including copies on which the work is printed or otherwise reproduced on either one side or on both sides of the leaf, and also folders which, without cutting or tearing the copies, can be opened out to form a single leaf. For the purpose of this section, a work need not consist of textual matter in order to be considered a "single-leaf work."

(c) *Manner of affixation and position generally.* (1) In all cases dealt with in this section, the acceptability of a notice depends upon its being permanently legible to an ordinary user of the work under normal conditions of use, and affixed to the copies in such manner and position that, when affixed, it is not concealed from view upon reasonable examination.

(2) Where, in a particular case, a notice does not appear in one of the precise locations prescribed in this section but a person looking in one of those locations would be reasonably certain to find a notice in another somewhat different location, that notice will be acceptable under this section.

(d) *Works published in book form.* In the case of works published in book form, a notice reproduced on the copies in any of the following positions is acceptable:

(1) The title page, if any;

(2) The page immediately following the title page, if any;

(3) Either side of the front cover, if any; or, if there is no front cover, either side of the front leaf of the copies:

(4) Either side of the back cover, if any; or, if there is no back cover, either side of the back leaf of the copies;

(5) The first page of the main body of the work;

(6) The last page of the main body of the work;

(7) Any page between the front page and the first page of the main body of the work, if: (i) There are no more than ten pages between the front page and the first page of the main body of the work; and (ii) the notice is reproduced prominently and is set apart from other matter on the page where it appears;

(8) Any page between the last page of the main body of the work and back page, if: (i) There are no more than ten pages between the last page of the main body of the work and the back page; and (ii) the notice is reproduced prominently and is set apart from the other matter of the page when it appears.

(9) In the case of a work published as an issue of a periodical or serial, in addition to any of the locations listed in paragraphs (d)(1) through (8) of this section, a notice is acceptable if it is located: (i) As a part of, or adjacent to, the masthead; (ii) on the page containing the masthead if the notice is reproduced prominently and is set apart from the other matter appearing on the page; or (iii) adjacent to a prominent heading, appearing at or near the front of the issue, containing the title of the periodical or serial and any combination of the volume and issue number and date of the issue.

(10) In the case of a musical work, in addition to any of the locations listed in paragraphs (d)(1) through (9) of this section, a notice is acceptable if it is located on the first page of music.

(e) *Single-leaf works.* In the case of single-leaf works, a notice reproduced on the copies anywhere on the front or back of the leaf is acceptable.

(f) *Contributions to collective works.* For a separate contribution to a collective work to be considered to "bear its own notice of copyright," as provided by 17 U.S.C. 404, a notice reproduced on the copies in any of the following positions is acceptable:

(1) Where the separate contribution is reproduced on a single page, a notice is acceptable if it appears: (i) Under the title of the contribution on that page: (ii) adjacent to the contribution; or (iii) on the same page if, through format, wording, or both, the application of the notice to the particular contribution is made clear;

(2) Where the separate contribution is reproduced on more than one page of the collective work, a notice is acceptable if it appears: (i) Under a title appearing at or near the beginning of the contribution; (ii) on the first page of the main body of the contribution; (iii) immediately following the end of the contribution; or (iv) on any of the pages where the contribution appears, if: (A) The contribution is reproduced on no more than twenty pages of the collective work; (B) the notice is reproduced prominently and is set apart from other matter on the page where it appears; and (C) through format, wording, or both, the application of the notice to the particular contribution is made clear;

(3) Where the separate contribution is a musical work, in addition to any of the locations listed in paragraphs (f)(1) and (2) of this section, a notice is acceptable if it is located on the first page of music of the contribution.

(4) As an alternative to placing the notice on one of the pages where a separate contribution itself appears, the contribution is considered to "bear its own notice" if the notice appears clearly in juxtaposition with a separate listing of the contribution by title, or if the contribution is untitled, by a description reasonably identifying the contribution: (i) On the page bearing the copyright notice for the collective work as a whole, if any; or (ii) in a clearly identified and readily accessible table of contents or listing of acknowledgements appearing near the front or back of the collective work as a whole.

(g) *Works reproduced in machine-readable copies.* For works reproduced in machine-readable copies (such as magnetic tapes or disks, punched cards, or the like), from which the work cannot ordinarily be visually perceived except with the aid of a machine or device,[1] each of the following constitute examples of acceptable methods of affixation and position of notice:

(1) A notice embodied in the copies in machine-readable form in such a manner that on visually perceptible printouts it appears either with or near the title, or at the end of the work;

(2) A notice that is displayed at the user's terminal at sign on;

(3) A notice that is continuously on terminal display; or

(4) A legible notice reproduced durably, so as to withstand normal use, on a gummed or other label securely affixed to the copies or to a box, reel, cartridge, cassette, or other container used as a permanent receptacle for the copies.

(h) *Motion pictures and other audiovisual works.* (1) The following constitute examples of acceptable methods of affixation and positions of the copyright notice on motion pictures and other audiovisual works: A notice that is embodied in the copies by a photomechanical or electronic process, in such a position that it ordinarily would appear whenever the work is performed in its entirety, and that is located: (i) With or near the title; (ii) with the cast, credits, and similar information; (iii) at or immediately following the beginning of the work; or (iv) at or immediately preceding the end of the work.

(2) In the case of an untitled motion picture or other audiovisual work whose duration is sixty seconds or less, in addition to any of the locations listed in paragraph (h)(1) of this section, a notice that is embodied in the copies by a photomechanical or electronic process, in such a position that it ordinarily would appear to the projectionist or broadcaster when preparing the work for performance, is acceptable if it is located on the leader of the film or tape immediately preceding the beginning of the work.

(3) In the case of a motion picture or other audiovisual work that is distributed to the public for private use, the notice may be affixed, in addition to the locations specified in paragraph (b)(1) of this section, on the housing or container, if it is a permanent receptacle for the work.

(i) *Pictorial, graphic, and sculptural works.* The following constitute examples of acceptable methods of affixation and positions of the copyright notice on various forms of pictorial, graphic, and sculptural works:

(1) Where a work is reproduced in two-dimensional copies, a notice affixed directly or by means of a label cemented, sewn, or otherwise attached durably, so as to withstand normal use, of the front or back of the copies, or to any backing, mounting, matting, framing, or other material to which the copies are durably attached, so as to withstand normal use, or in which they are permanently housed, is acceptable.

(2) Where a work is reproduced in three-dimensional copies, a notice affixed directly or by means of a label cemented, sewn, or otherwise attached durably, so as to withstand normal use, to any visible portion of the work, or to any base, mounting, framing, or other material on which the copies are durably attached, so as to withstand normal use, or in which they are permanently housed, is acceptable.

(3) Where, because of the size or physical characteristics of the material in which the work is reproduced in copies, it is impossible or extremely impracticable to affix a notice to the copies directly or by means of a durable label, a notice is acceptable if it appears on a tag that is of durable material, so as to withstand normal use, and that is attached to the copy with sufficient durability that it will remain with the copy while it is passing through its normal channels of commerce.

(4) Where a work is reproduced in copies consisting of sheet-like or strip material bearing multiple or continuous reproductions of the work, the notice may be applied: (i) To the reproduction itself; (ii) to the margin, selvage, or reverse side of the material at frequent and regular intervals; or (iii) if the material contains neither a

---

[1]Works published in a form requiring the use of a machine or device for purposes of optical enlargement (such as film, filmstrips, slide films, and works published in any variety of microform) and works published in visually perceptible form but used in connection with optical scanning devices, are not within this category.

selvage nor a reverse side, to tags or labels, attached to the copies and to any spools, reels, or containers housing them in such a way that a notice is visible while the copies are passing through their normal channels of commerce.

(5) If the work is permanently housed in a container, such as a game or puzzle box, a notice reproduced on the permanent container is acceptable.

(17 U.S.C. 401, 702)
[46 FR 58312, Dec. 1, 1981]

## § 201.21 [Reserved]

## § 201.22 Advance notices of potential infringement of works consisting of sounds, images, or both.

(a) *Definitions.* (1) An "Advance Notice of Potential Infringement" is a notice which, if served in accordance with section 411(b) of Title 17 of the United States Code, and in accordance with the provisions of this section, enables a copyright owner to institute an action for copyright infringement either before or after the first fixation of a work consisting of sounds, images, or both that is first fixed simultaneously with its transmission, and to enjoy the full remedies of said Title 17 for copyright infringement, provided registration for the work is made within three months after its first transmission.

(2) For purposes of this section, the "copyright owner" of a work consisting of sounds, images, or both, the first fixation of which is made simultaneously with its transmission, is the person or entity that will be considered the author of the work upon its fixation (including, in the case of a work made for hire, the employer or other person or entity for whom the work was prepared), or a person or organization that has obtained ownership of an exclusive right, initially owned by the person or entity that will be considered the author of the work upon its fixation.

(3) A "transmission program" is a body of material that, as an aggregate, has been produced for the sole purpose of transmission to the public in sequence and as a unit.

(b) *Form.* The Copyright Office does not provide printed forms for the use of persons serving Advance Notices of Potential Infringement.

(c) *Contents.* (1) An Advance Notice of Potential Infringement shall be clearly and prominently captioned "ADVANCE NOTICE OF POTENTIAL INFRINGEMENT" and must clearly state that the copyright owner objects to the relevant activities of the person responsible for the potential infringement, and must include all of the following:

(i) Reference to Title 17 U.S.C. section 411(b) as the statutory authority on which the Advance Notice of Potential Infringement is based;

(ii) The date, specific time, and expected duration of the intended first transmission of the work or works contained in the specific transmission program;

(iii) The source of the intended first transmission of the work or works;

(iv) Clear identification, by title, of the work or works. A single Advance Notice of Potential Infringement may cover all of the works of the copyright owner embodied in a specific transmission program. If any work is untitled, the Advance Notice of Potential Infringement shall include a detailed description of that work.

(v) The name of at least one person or entity that will be considered the author of the work upon its fixation;

(vi) The identity of the copyright owner, as defined in paragraph (a)(2) of this section. If the copyright owner is not the person or entity that will be considered the author of the work upon its fixation, the Advance Notice of Potential Infringement also shall include a brief, general statement summarizing the means by which the copyright owner obtained ownership of the copyright and the particular rights that are owned; and

(vii) A description of the relevant activities of the person responsible for the potential infringement which would, if carried out, result in an infringement of the copyright.

(2) An Advance Notice of Potential Infringement must also include clear and prominent statements:

(i) Explaining that the relevant activities may, if carried out, subject the person responsible to liability for copyright infringement; and

(ii) Declaring that the copyright owner intends to secure copyright in the work upon its fixation.

(d) *Signature and identification.* (1) An Advance Notice of Potential Infringement shall be in writing and signed by the copyright owner, or such owner's duly authorized agent.

(2) The signature of the owner or agent shall be an actual handwritten signature of an individual, accompanied by the date of signature and the full name, address, and telephone number of that person, typewritten or printed legibly by hand.

(3) If an Advanced Notice of Potential Infringement is initially served in the form of a telegram or similar communication, as provided by paragraph (e)(2)(iii) of this section, the requirement for an individual's handwritten signature shall be considered waived if the further conditions of said paragraph (e) are met.

(e) *Service.* (1) An Advance Notice of Potential Infringement shall be served on the person responsible for the potential infringement at least ten days but not more than thirty days before the first fixation and simultaneous transmission of the work as provided by 17 U.S.C. 411(b)(1).

(2) Service of the Advance Notice may be effected by any of the following methods:

(i) Personal service;

(ii) First-class mail; or

(iii) Telegram, cablegram, or similar form of communication, if: (A) The Advance Notice meets all of the other conditions provided by this section; and (B) before the first fixation and simultaneous transmission take place, the person responsible for the potential infringement receives written confirmation of the Advance Notice, bearing the actual handwritten signature of the copyright owner or duly authorized agent.

(3) The date of service is the date the Advance Notice of Potential Infringement is received by the person responsible for the potential infringement or by any agent or employee of that person.

(17 U.S.C. 411, 702)
[46 FR 28849, May 29, 1981]

## § 201.23 Transfer of unpublished copyright deposits to the Library of Congress.

(a) *General.* This section prescribes rules governing the transfer of unpublished copyright deposits in the custody of the Copyright Office to the Library of Congress. The copyright deposits may consist of copies, phonorecords, or identifying material deposited in connection with registration of claims to copyright under section 408 of Title 17 of the United States Code, as amended by Pub. L. 94-553, 90 Stat. 2541, effective January 1, 1978. These rules establish the conditions under which the Library of Congress is entitled to select deposits of unpublished works for its collections or for permanent transfer to the National Archives of the United States or to a Federal records center in accordance with section 704(b) of Title 17 of the United States Code, as amended by Pub. L. 94-553.

(b) *Selection by the Library of Congress.* The Library of Congress may select any deposits of unpublished works for the purposes stated in paragraph (a) of this section at the time of registration or at any time thereafter; *Provided,* That:

(1) A facsimile reproduction of the entire copyrightable content of the deposit shall be made a part of the Copyright Office records before transfer to the Library of

Congress as provided by section 704(c) of Title 17 of the United States Code, as amended by Pub. L. 94-553, unless, within the discretion of the Register of Copyrights, it is considered impractical or too expensive to make the reproduction;

(2) All unpublished copyright deposits retained by the Library of Congress in its collections shall be maintained under the control of the Library of Congress with appropriate safeguards against unauthorized copying or other unauthorized use of the deposits which would be contrary to the rights of the copyright owner in the work under Title 17 of the United States Code, as amended by Pub. L. 94-553; and

(3) At the time selection is made a request for full term retention of the deposit under the control of the Copyright Office has not been granted by the Register of Copyrights, in accordance with section 704(e) of Title 17 of the United States Code, as amended by Pub. L. 94-553.

(17 U.S.C. 702, 704)
[45 FR 41414, June 19, 1980]

# PART 202—REGISTRATION OF CLAIMS TO COPYRIGHT

AUTHORITY: Sec. 207, 61 Stat. 666; 17 U.S.C. 207, unless otherwise noted.

## § 202.1 Material not subject to copyright.

The following are examples of works not subject to copyright and applications for registration of such works cannot be entertained:

(a) Words and short phrases such as names, titles, and slogans; familiar symbols or designs; mere variations of typographic ornamentation, lettering or coloring; mere listing of ingredients or contents;

(b) Ideas, plans, methods, systems, or devices, as distinguished from the particular manner in which they are expressed or described in a writing;

(c) Blank forms, such as time cards, graph paper, account books, diaries, bank checks, scorecards, address books, report forms, order forms and the like, which are designed for recording information and do not in themselves convey information;

(d) Works consisting entirely of information that is common property containing no original authorship, such as, for example: Standard calendars, height and weight charts, tape measures and rulers, schedules of sporting events, and lists of tables taken from public documents or other common sources.

[24 FR 4956, June 18, 1959, as amended at 38 FR 3045, Feb. 1, 1973]

## § 202.2 Copyright notice.

(a) *General.* (1) With respect to a work published before January 1, 1978, copyright was secured, or the right to secure it was lost, except for works seeking ad interim copyright, at the date of publication, i.e., the date on which copies are first placed on sale, sold, or publicly distributed, depending upon the adequacy of the notice of copyright on the work at that time. The adequacy of the copyright notice for such a work is determined by the copyright statute as it existed on the date of first publication.

(2) If before January 1, 1978, publication occurred by distribution of copies or in some other manner, without the statutory notice or with an inadequate notice, as determined by the copyright statute as it existed on the date of first publication, the right to secure copyright was lost. In such cases, copyright cannot be secured by adding the notice to copies distributed at a later date.

(3) Works first published abroad before January 1, 1978, other than works for which ad interim copyright has been obtained, must have borne an adequate copyright notice. The adequacy of the copyright notice for such works is determined by the copyright statute as it existed on the date of first publication abroad.

(b) *Defects in notice.* Where the copyright notice on a work published before January 1, 1978, does not meet the requirements of Title 17 of the United States Code as it existed on December 31, 1977, the Copyright Office will reject an application for copyright registration. Common defects in the notice include, among others the following:

(1) The notice lacks one or more of the necessary elements (i.e., the word "Copyright," the abbreviation "Copr.," or the symbol ©, or, in the case of a sound recording, the symbol ○; the name of the copyright proprietor, or, in the case of a sound recording, the name, a recognizable abbreviation of the name, or a generally known alternative designation, of the copyright owner; and, when required, the year date of publication);

(2) The elements of the notice are so dispersed that a necessary element is not identified as a part of the notice; in the case of a sound recording, however, if the producer is named on the label or container, and if no other name appears in conjunction with the notice, his name will be considered a part of the notice;

(3) The notice is not in one of the positions prescribed by law;

(4) The notice is in a foreign language;

(5) The name in the notice is that of someone who had no authority to secure copyright in his name;

(6) The year date in the copyright notice is later than the date of the year in which copyright was actually secured, including the following cases:

(i) Where the year date in the notice is later than the date of actual publication;

(ii) Where copyright was first secured by registration of a work in unpublished form, and copies of the same work as later published without change in substance bear a copyright notice containing a year date later than the year of unpublished registration;

(iii) Where a book or periodical published abroad, for which ad interim copyright has been obtained, is later published in the United States without change in substance and contains a year date in the copyright notice later than the year of first publication abroad:

*Provided, however,* That in each of the three foregoing types of cases, if the copyright was actually secured not more than one year earlier than the year date in the notice, registration may be considered as a doubtful case.

(7) A notice is permanently covered so that it cannot be seen without tearing the work apart;

(8) A notice is illegible or so small that it cannot be read without the aid of a magnifying glass: *Provided, however,* That where the work itself requires magnification for its ordinary use (e.g., a microfilm, microcard or motion picture) a notice which will be readable when so magnified, will not constitute a reason for rejection of the claim;

(9) A notice is on a detachable tag and will eventually be detached and discarded when the work is put in use;

(10) A notice is on the wrapper or container which is not a part of the work and which will eventually be removed and discarded when the work is put to use; the notice may be on a container which is designed and can be expected to remain with the work;

(11) The notice is restricted or limited exclusively to an uncopyrightable element, either by virtue of its position on the work, by the use of asterisks, or by other means.

[24 FR 4956, June 18, 1959; 24 FR 6163, July 31, 1959, as amended at 37 FR 3055, Feb. 11, 1972; 46 FR 33249, June 29, 2981; 46 FR 34329, July 1, 1981]

## § 202.3 Registration of copyright.

(a) *General.* (1) This section prescribes conditions for the registration of copyright, and the application to be made for registration under sections 408 and 409 of Title 17 of the United States Code, as amended by Pub. L. 94-553.

(2) For the purposes of this section, the terms "audiovisual work," "compilation," "copy," "derivative work," "device," "fixation," "literary work," "motion picture," "phonorecord," "pictorial, graphic and sculptural works," "process," "sound recording," and their variant forms, have the meanings set forth in section 101 of Title 17. The term "author" includes an employer or other person for whom a work is "made for hire" under section 101 of Title 17.

(3) For the purpose of this section, a copyright "claimant" is either:

(i) The author of a work;

(ii) A person or organization that has obtained ownership of all rights under the copyright initially belonging to the author.[1]

(b) *Administrative classification and application forms*—(1) *Classes of works.* For the purpose of registration, the Register of Copyrights has prescribed four classes of works in which copyright may be claimed. These classes, and examples of works which they include, are as follows:

(i) *Class TX: Nondramatic literary works.* This class includes all published and unpublished nondramatic literary works. Examples: Fiction; nonfiction; poetry; textbooks; reference works; directories; catalogs; advertising copy; periodicals and serials; and compilations of information.

(ii) *Class PA: Works of the performing arts.* This class includes all published and unpublished works prepared for the purpose of being performed directly before an audience or indirectly by means of a device or process. Examples: Musical works, including any accompanying words; dramatic works, including any accompanying music; pantomimes and choreographic works; and motion pictures and other audiovisual works.

(iii) *Class VA: Works of the visual arts.* This class includes all published and unpublished pictorial, graphic, and sculptural works. Examples: Two dimensional and three dimensional works of the fine, graphic, and applied arts; photographs; prints and art reproductions; maps, globes, and charts; technical drawings, diagrams, and models; and pictorial or graphic labels and advertisements.

(iv) *Class SR: Sound recordings.* This class includes all published and unpublished sound recordings fixed on and after February 15, 1972. Claims to copyright in literary, dramatic, and musical works embodied in phonorecords may also be registered in this class under paragraph (b)(3) of this section if: (A) Registration is sought on the same application for both a recorded literary dramatic or musical work and a sound recording; (B) the recorded literary dramatic or musical work and the sound

---

[1]This category includes a person or organization that has obtained, from the author or from an entity that has obtained ownership of all rights under the copyright initially belonging to the author, the contractual right to claim legal title to the copyright in an application for copyright registration.

recording are embodied in the same phonorecord; and (C) the same claimant is seeking registration of both the recorded literary, dramatic, or musical work and the sound recording.

(2) *Application forms.* For the purpose of registration, The Register of Copyrights has prescribed four basic forms to be used for all applications submitted on and after January 1, 1978. Each form corresponds to a class set forth in paragraph (b)(1) of this section and is so designated ("Form TX"; "Form PA"; "Form VA"; and "Form SR"). Copies of the forms are available free upon request to the Public Information Office, United States Copyright Office, Library of Congress, Washington, D.C. 20559. Applications should be submitted in the class most appropriate to the nature of the authorship in which copyright is claimed. In the case of contributions to collective works, applications should be submitted in the class representing the copyrightable authorship in the contribution. In the case of derivative works, applications should be submitted in the class most appropriately representing the copyrightable authorship involved in recasting, transforming, adapting, or otherwise modifying the preexisting work. In cases where a work contains elements of authorship in which copyright is claimed which fall into two or more classes, the application should be submitted in the class most appropriate to the type of authorship that predominates in the work as a whole. However, in any case where registration is sought for a work consisting of or including a sound recording in which copyright is claimed[2] the application shall be submitted on Form SR.

(3) *Registration as a single work.* (1) For the purpose of registration on a single application and upon payment of a single registration fee, the following shall be considered a single work:

(A) In the case of published works: All copyrightable elements that are otherwise recognizable as self-contained works, that are included in a single unit of publication, and in which the copyright claimant is the same; and

(B) In the case of unpublished works: all copyrightable elements that are otherwise recognizable as self-contained works, and are combined in a single unpublished "collection." For these purposes, a combination of such elements shall be considered a "collection" if (*1*) The elements are assembled in an orderly form; (*2*) the combined elements bear a single title identifying the collection as a whole; (*3*) the copyright claimant in all of the elements, and in the collection as a whole, is the same; and (*4*) all of the elements are by the same author, or, if they are by different authors, at least one of the authors has contributed copyrightable authorship to each element. Registration of an unpublished "collection" extends to each copyrightable element in the collection and to the authorship, if any, involved in selecting and assembling the collection.

(ii) In the case of applications for registration made under paragraphs (b)(3) and (b)(5) of this section, the "year in which creation of this work was completed," as called for by the application, means the latest year in which the creation of any copyrightable element was completed.

(4) *Group registration of related works.* [Reserved]

(5) *Group registration of contributions to periodicals.* (i) As provided by section 408(c)(2) of Title 17 of the United States Code, as amended by Pub. L. 94-553, a single registration, on the basis of a single application, deposit, and registration fee, may be made for a group of works if all of the following conditions are met:

(A) All of the works are by the same author;

(B) The author of each work is an individual, and not an employer or other person for whom the work was made for hire;

---

[2] A "sound recording" does not include the sounds accompanying a motion picture or other audiovisual work (17 U.S.C. 101). For this purpose, "accompanying" does not require physical integration in the same copy. Accordingly, registration may be made for a motion picture or audiovisual kit in Class PA and that registration will cover the sounds embodied in the "sound track" of the motion picture or on disks, tapes, or the like included in the kit. Separate application in Class SR is not appropriate for these elements.

(C) Each of the works first published as a contribution to a periodical (including newspapers) within a twelve-month period;[3]

(D) Each of the works as first published bore a separate copyright notice, and the name of the owner of copyright in each work (or an abbreviation by which the name can be recognized, or a generally known alternative designation of the owner) was the same in each notice; and

(E) The deposit accompanying the application consists of one copy of the entire issue of the periodical, or of the entire section in the case of a newspaper, in which each contribution was first published.

(ii) An application for group registration under section 408(c)(2) of Title 17 and this § 202.3(b)(5) shall consist of: (A) A basic application for registration on Form TX, Form PA, or Form VA,[4] which shall contain the information required by the form and its accompanying instructions; (B) an adjunct form prescribed by the Copyright Office and designated "Adjunct Application for Copyright Registration for a Group of Contributions to Periodicals) Form GR/CP," which shall contain the information required by the form and its accompanying instructions; and (C) a fee of $10 and the deposit required by paragraph (b)(5)(i)(E) of this section.

(6) *One registration per work.* As a general rule only one copyright registration can be made for the same version of a particular work. However:

(i) Where a work has been registered as unpublished, another registration may be made for the first published edition of the work, even if it does not represent a new version;

(ii) Where someone other than the author is identified as copyright claimant in a registration, another registration for the same version may be made by the author in his or her own name as copyright claimant;[5]

(iii) Where an applicant for registration alleges that an earlier registration for the same version is unauthorized and legally invalid, a registration may be made by that applicant; and

(iv) Supplementary registrations may be made, under the conditions of § 201.5 of these regulations, to correct or amplify the information in a registration made under this section.

(c) *Application for registration.* (1) An application for copyright registration may be submitted by any author or other copyright claimant of a work, or the owner of any exclusive right in a work, or the duly authorized agent of any such author, other claimant, or owner.

(2) An application for copyright registration shall be submitted on the appropriate form prescribed by the Register of Copyrights under paragraph (b) of this section, and shall be accompanied by a fee of $10 and the deposit required under 17 U.S.C. 408 and § 202.20 of these regulations.[6] The application shall contain the information required by the form and its accompanying instructions, and shall include a certification. The certification shall consist of: (i) A designation of whether the applicant is the author of, or other copyright claimant or owner of exclusive rights in, the

---

[3]This does not require that each of the works must have been first published during the same calendar year; it does require that, to be grouped in a single application, the earliest and latest contributions must not have been first published more than twelve months apart.

[4]The basic application should be filed in the class appropriate to the nature of authorship in the majority of the contributions. However, if any of the contributions consists preponderantly of nondramatic literary material that is in the English language, the basic application for the entire group should be submitted on Form TX.

[5]An "author" includes an employer or other person for whom a work is "made for hire" under 17 U.S.C. 101. This paragraph does not permit an employee or other person working "for hire" under that section to make a later registration in his or her own name. In the case of authors of a joint work, this paragraph does permit a later registration by one author in his or her own name as copyright claimant, where an earlier registration identifies only another as claimant.

[6]In the case of applications for group registration of contributions to periodicals under paragraph (b)(5) of this section, the deposit shall comply with paragraph (b)(5)(i)(E). Only one $10 fee is required in such cases.

work, or the duly authorized agent of such author, other claimant, or owner (whose identity shall also be given); (ii) the handwritten signature of such author, other claimant, owner, or agent, accompanied by the typed or printed name of that person; (iii) a declaration that the statements made in the application are correct to the best of that person's knowledge; and (iv) the date of certification. An application for registration of a published work will not be accepted if the date of certification is earlier than the date of publication given in the application.

(Pub. L. 94-553; secs. 408, 409, 410, 702)
[43 FR 966, Jan. 5, 1978]

## §§ 202.4–202.9 [Reserved]

## § 202.10 Pictorial, graphic, and sculptural works.

(a) In order to be acceptable as a pictorial, graphic, or sculptural work, the work must embody some creative authorship in its delineation or form. The registrability of such a work is not affected by the intention of the author as to the use of the work or the number of copies reproduced. The potential availability of protection under the design patent law will not affect the registrability of a pictorial, graphic, or sculptural work, but a copyright claim in a patented design or in the drawings or photographs in a patent application will not be registered after the patent has been issued.

(b) A claim to copyright in a scientific or technical drawing, otherwise registrable as a pictorial, graphic, or sculptural work, will not be refused registration solely by reason of the fact that it is known to form a part of a pending patent application. Where the patent has been issued, however, the claim to copyright in the drawing will be denied copyright registration.

(c) A claim to copyright cannot be registered in a print or label consisting solely of trademark subject matter and lacking copyrightable matter. While the Copyright Office will not investigate whether the matter has been or can be registered at the Patent and Trademark Office, it will register a properly filed copyright claim in a print or label that contains the requisite qualifications for copyright even though there is a trademark on it. However, registration of a claim to copyright does not give the claimant rights available by trademark registrations at the Patent and Trademark Office.

[46 FR 3329, June 29, 1981]

## §§ 202.11–202.16 [Reserved]

## § 202.17 Renewals.

(a) *General.* This section prescribes rules pertaining to the application for renewal copyright under section 304(a) of title 17 of the United States Code, as amended by Pub. L. 94-553.

(b) *Definition.* For purposes of this section, the term "posthumous work" means a work that was unpublished on the date of the death of the author and with respect to which no copyright assignment or other contract for exploitation of the work occurred during the author's lifetime.

(c) *Renewal time-limits.* (1) For works originally copyrighted between January 1, 1950 and December 31, 1977, claims to renewal copyright must be registered within the last year of the original copyright term, which begins on December 31 of the 27th year of the copyright, and runs through December 31, of the 28th year of the copyright. The original copyright term for a published work is computed from the date of first publication; the term for a work originally registered in unpublished form is computed from the date of registration in the Copyright Office. Unless the required application and fee are received in the Copyright Office during the prescribed period before the first term of copyright expires, the copyright in the unrenewed work terminates at the expiration of twenty-eight years from the end of the calendar year in which copyright was originally secured. The Copyright Office has no discretion to extend the renewal time limits.

(2) The provisions of paragraph (c)(1) of this section are subject to the following qualification: In any case where the year date in the notice on copies distributed by authority of the copyright owner is earlier than the year of first publication, claims to renewal copyright must be registered within the last year of the original copyright term, which begins on December 31 of the 27th year from the year contained in the notice, and runs through December 31 of the 28th year from the year contained in the notice.

(3) Whenever a renewal applicant has cause to believe that a formal application for renewal (Form RE), and in the case of works under paragraph (d)(2) of this section, an accompanying affidavit and submission relating to the subsistence of first-term copyright, if sent to the Copyright Office by mail, might not be received in the Copyright Office before expiration of the time limits provided by 17 U.S.C., section 304(a), he or she may apply for renewal registration by telegraphic or similar unsigned written communication. An application made by this method only will be accepted if: (i) The message is received in the Copyright Office within the specified time limits; (ii) the applicant adequately identifies the work involved, the date of first publication or original registration, the name and address of the renewal claimant, and the statutory basis of the renewal claim; (iii) the fee for renewal registration, if not already on deposit, is received in the Copyright Office before the time for renewal registration has expired; and (iv) a formal application for renewal (Form RE), and in the case of works under paragraph (d)(2) of this section, an accompanying affidavit and submission relating to subsistence of the first-term copyright are also received in the Copyright Office before February 1 of the following year.

(d) *Original registration.* (1) Except as provided by paragraph (d)(2) of this section, copyright in a work will not be registered for a renewal term unless an original registration for the work has been made in the Copyright Office.

(2) An original registration in the Copyright Office is not a condition precedent for renewal registration in the case of a work in which United States copyright subsists by virtue of section 9(c) of title 17 of the United States Code, in effect on December 31, 1977 (which implemented the Universal Copyright Convention) provided, however, that the application for renewal registration is accompanied by:

(i) An affidavit identified as "Renewal Affidavit for a U.C.C. Work" and containing the following information:

(A) The date of first publication of the work;

(B) The place of first publication of the work;

(C) The citizenship of the author on the date of first publication of the work;

(D) The domicile of the author on the date of first publication of the work;

(E) An averment that, at the time of first publication, all the copies of the work published under the authority of the author or other copyright proprietor bore the symbol © accompanied by the name of the copyright proprietor and the year of first publication, and that United States copyright subsists in the work;

(F) The handwritten signature of the renewal claimant or the duly authorized agent of the renewal claimant. The signature shall (*1*) be accompanied by the printed or typewritten name of the person signing the affidavit and by the date of the signature; and (*2*) shall be immediately preceded by the following printed or typewritten statement in accordance with section 1746 of title 18 of the United States Code: I certify under penalty of perjury under the laws of the United States of America that the foregoing is true and correct.

(ii) A submission relating to the notice of copyright and copyrightable content which shall be, in descending order of preference, comprised of:

(A) One complete copy of the work as first published; or

(B)(*1*)  A photocopy of the title page of the work as first published, and

(*2*)  A photocopy of the page of the work as first published bearing the copyright notice, and

(*3*)  A specification as to the location, relative to each other, of the title and notice pages of the work as first published, if the pages are different, and

(*4*)  A brief description of the copyrightable content of the work, and

(*5*)  An explanation of the inability to submit one complete copy of the work as first publicized; or

(C)  A statement describing the position and contents of the copyright notice as it appeared on the work as first published, and a brief description of the copyrightable content. The statement shall be made and signed in accordance with paragraph (d)(2)(i)(F) of this section and shall also include an explanation of the inability to submit either one complete copy of the work as first published or photocopies of the title and notice pages of the work as first published.

(e)  *Application for renewal registration.* (1) Each application for renewal registration submitted on or after January 1, 1978 shall be furnished on Form RE. Copies of Form RE are available free upon request to the Public Information Office, United States Copyright Office, Library of Congress, Washington, D.C. 20559.

(2)(i)  An application for renewal registration may be submitted by any eligible renewal claimant as specified in paragraph (f) of this section or by the duly authorized agent of any such claimant.

(ii)  An application for renewal registration shall be accompanied by a fee of $6. The application shall contain the information required by the form and its accompanying instructions, and shall include a certification. The certification shall consist of: (A) a designation of whether the applicant is the renewal claimant, or the duly authorized agent of such claimant (whose identity shall also be given); (B) the handwritten signature of such claimant or agent, accompanied by the typewritten or printed name of that person; (C) a declaration that the statements made in the application are correct to the best of that person's knowledge; and (D) the date of certification.

(iii)  In the case of an application for renewal registration for a foreign work protected under the U.C.C. which has not been the subject of an original copyright registration, the application shall be accompanied by a "Renewal Affidavit for a U.C.C. Work" and a submission relating to the notice of copyright and the copyrightable content in accordance with paragraph (d)(2) of this section.

(3)  Once a renewal registration has been made, the Copyright Office will not accept a duplicate application for renewal registration on behalf of the same renewal claimant.

(f)  *Renewal claimants.* (1) Except as otherwise provided by paragraphs (f)(2) and (3) of this section, renewal claims may be registered only in the name(s) of the eligible person(s) falling within one of the following classes of renewal claimants specified in section 304(a) of the copyright law. If the work was a new version of a previous work, renewal may be claimed only in the new matter.

(i)  In the case of any posthumous work or of any periodical, cyclopedic, or other composite work upon which the copyright was originally secured by the proprietor thereof, the renewal claim may be registered in the name of the proprietor;

(ii)  In the case of any work copyrighted by a corporate body (otherwise than as assignees or licensees of the individual author) or by an employer for whom such work is made for hire, the renewal claim may be registered in the name of the proprietor; and

(iii)  In the case of any other copyrighted work, including a contribution by an individual author to a periodical or to a cyclopedic or other composite work, the renewal claim may be registered in the name(s) of the following person(s) in descending order of eligibility:

(A)  The author of the work, if still living;

(B)  The widow, widower, or children of the author, if the author is not living;

(C)  The author's executors, if there is a will and neither the author nor any widow, widower, or child of the author is living;

(D) The author's next of kin, in the absence of a will and if neither the author nor any widow, widower, or child of the author is living.

(2) The provisions of paragraph (f)(1) are subject to the following qualification: Notwithstanding the definition of "posthumous work" in paragraph (b) of this section, a renewal claim may be registered in the name of the proprietor of the work, as well as in the name of the appropriate claimant under paragraph (f)(1)(iii), in any case where a contract for exploitation of the work but no copyright assignment in the work has occurred during the author's lifetime. However, registration by the Copyright Office in this case should not be interpreted as evidencing the validity of the claim.

(3) The provisions of paragraphs (f)(1)(iii)(C) and (D) of this section are subject to the following qualifications:

(i) In any case where: (A) The author has left a will which names no executor; (B) the author has left a will which names an executor who cannot or will not serve in that capacity; or (C) the author has left a will which names an executor who has been discharged upon settlement of the estate or removed before the estate has been completely administered, the renewal claim may be registered either in the name of an administrator cum testamento annexo (administrator c.t.a.) or an administrator de bonis non cum testamento annexo (administrator d.b.n.c.t.a.) so appointed by a court of competent jurisdiction;

(ii) In any case described in paragraph (f)(3)(i) of this section, except in the case where the author has left a will without naming an executor and a court appointed administrator c.t.a. or administrator d.b.n.c.t.a. is in existence at the time of renewal registration, the renewal claim also may be registered in the name of the author's next of kin. However, registration by the Copyright Office of the conflicting renewal claims in these cases should not be interpreted as evidencing the validity of either claim.

(17 U.S.C. 304, 205, 702, and 708)
[46 FR 58671, Dec. 3, 1981]

## § 202.18 [Reserved]

## § 202.19 Deposit of published copies or phonorecords for the Library of Congress.

(a) *General.* This section prescribes rules pertaining to the deposit of copies and phonorecords of published works for the Library of Congress under section 407 of title 17 of the United States Code, as amended by Pub. L. 94-553. The provisions of this section are not applicable to the deposit of copies and phonorecords for purposes of copyright registration under section 408 of title 17, except as expressly adopted in § 202.20 of these regulations.

(b) *Definitions.* For the purposes of this section:

(1)(i) The "best edition" of a work is the edition, published in the United States at any time before the date of deposit, that the Library of Congress determines to be most suitable for its purposes.

(ii) Criteria for selection of the "best edition" from among two or more published editions of the same version of the same work are set forth in the statement entitled "Best Edition of Published Copyrighted Works for the Collections of the Library of Congress" (hereafter referred to as the "Best Edition Statement") in effect at the time of deposit. Copies of the Best Edition Statement are available upon request made to the Deposits and Acquisitions Division of the Copyright Office.

(iii) Where no specific criteria for the selection of the "best edition" are established in the Best Edition Statement, that edition which, in the judgment of the Library of Congress, represents the highest quality for its purposes shall be considered the "best edition." In such cases:

(A) When the Copyright Office is aware that two or more editions of a work have been published it will consult with other appropriate officials of the Library of Congress to obtain instructions as to the "best edition" and (except in cases for which special relief is granted) will require deposit of that edition; and

(B) When a potential depositor is uncertain which of two or more published editions comprises the "best edition," inquiry should be made to the Deposits and Acquisitions Division of the Copyright Office.

(iv) Where differences between two or more "editions" of a work represent variations in copyrightable content, each edition is considered a separate version, and hence a different work, for the purpose of this section, and criteria of "best edition" based on such differences do not apply.

(2) A "complete" copy includes all elements comprising the unit of publication of the best edition of the work, including elements that, if considered separately, would not be copyrightable subject matter or would otherwise be exempt from mandatory deposit requirements under paragraph (c) of this section. In the case of sound recordings, a "complete" phonorecord includes the phonorecord, together with any printed or other visually perceptible material published with such phonorecord (such as textual or pictorial matter appearing on record sleeves or album covers, or embodied in leaflets or booklets included in a sleeve, album, or other container). In the case of a musical composition published in copies only, or in both copies and phonorecords:

(i) If the only publication of copies in the United States took place by the rental, lease, or lending of a full score and parts, a full score is a "complete" copy; and

(ii) If the only publication of copies in the United States took place by the rental, lease, or lending of a conductor's score and parts, a conductor's score is a "complete" copy.

In the case of a motion picture, a copy is "complete" if the reproduction of all of the visual and aural elements comprising the copyrightable subject matter in the work is clean, undamaged, undeteriorated, and free of splices, and if the copy itself and its physical housing are free of any defects that would interfere with the performance of the work or that would cause mechanical, visual, or audible defects or distortions.

(3) The terms "copies," "collective work," "device," "fixed," "literary work," "machine," "motion picture," "phonorecord," "publication," "sound recording," and "useful article," and their variant forms, have the meanings given to them in section 101 of title 17.

(4) "Title 17" means title 17 of the United States Code, as amended by Pub. L. 94-553.

(c) *Exemptions from deposit requirements.* The following categories of material are exempt from the deposit requirements of section 407(a) of title 17:

(1) Diagrams and models illustrating scientific or technical works or formulating scientific or technical information in linear or three-dimensional form, such as an architectural or engineering blueprint, plan, or design, a mechanical drawing, or an anatomical model.

(2) Greeting cards, picture postcards, and stationery.

(3) Lectures, sermons, speeches, and addresses when published individually and not as a collection of the works of one or more authors.

(4) Literary, dramatic, and musical works published only as embodied in phonorecords. This category does not exempt the owner of copyright, or of the exclusive right of publication, in a sound recording resulting from the fixation of such works in a phonorecord from the applicable deposit requirements for the sound recording.

(5) Literary works, including computer programs and automated databases, published in the United States only in the form of machine-readable copies (such as magnetic tape or disks, punched cards, or the like) from which the work cannot ordinarily be visually perceived except with the aid of a machine or device. Works published in a form requiring the use of a machine or device for purposes of optical enlargement (such as film, filmstrips, slide films and works published in any variety of microform), and works published in visually perceivable form but used in connection

with optical scanning devices, are not within this category and are subject to the applicable deposit requirements.

(6) Three-dimensional sculptural works, and any works published only as reproduced in or on jewelry, dolls, toys, games, plaques, floor coverings, wallpaper and similar commercial wall coverings, textiles and other fabrics, packaging material, or any useful article. Globes, relief models, and similar cartographic representations of area are not within this category and are subject to the applicable deposit requirements.

(7) Prints, labels, and other advertising matter, including catalogs, published in connection with the rental lease, lending, licensing, or sale of articles of merchandise, works of authorship, or services.

(8) Tests, and answer material for tests when published separately from other literary works.

(9) Works first published as individual contributions to collective works. This category does not exempt the owner of copyright, or of the exclusive right of publication, in the collective work as a whole, from the applicable deposit requirements for the collective work.

(10) Works first published outside the United States and later published in the United States without change in copyrightable content, if:

(i) Registration for the work was made under 17 U.S.C. 408 before the work was published in the United States; or

(ii) registration for the work was made under 17 U.S.C. 408 after the work was published in the United States but before a demand for deposit is made under 17 U.S.C. 407(d).

(11) Works published only as embodied in a soundtrack that is an integral part of a motion picture. This category does not exempt the owner of copyright, or of the exclusive right of publication, in the motion picture, from the applicable deposit requirements for the motion picture.

(12) Motion pictures that consist of television transmission programs and that have been published, if at all, only by reason of a license or other grant to a nonprofit institution of the right to make a fixation of such programs directly from a transmission to the public, with or without the right to make further uses of such fixations.

(d) *Nature of required deposit.* (1) Subject to the provisions of paragraph (d)(2) of this section, the deposit required to satisfy the provisions of section 407(a) of title 17 shall consist of:

(i) In the case of published works other than sound recordings, two complete copies of the best edition; and

(ii) In the case of published sound recordings, two complete phonorecords of the best edition.

(2) In the case of certain published works not exempt from deposit requirements under paragraph (c) of this section, the following special provisions shall apply:

(i) In the case of published three-dimensional cartographic representations of area, such as globes and relief models, the deposit of one complete copy of the best edition of the work will suffice in lieu of the two copies required by paragraph (d)(1) of this section.

(ii) In the case of published motion pictures, the deposit of one complete copy of the best edition of the work will suffice in lieu of the two copies required by paragraph (d)(1) of this section. Any deposit of a published motion picture must be accompanied by a separate description of its contents, such as a continuity, pressbook, or synopsis. The Library of Congress may, at its sole discretion, enter into an agreement permitting the return of copies of published motion pictures to the depositor under certain conditions and establishing certain rights and obligations of the Library with respect to such copies. In the event of termination of such an agreement by the Library it shall not be subject to reinstatement, nor shall the depositor or any successor in interest of the depositor be entitled to any similar or subsequent agreement with the Library, unless at the sole discretion of the Library it would be in the best interests of the Library to reinstate the agreement or enter into a new agreement.

(iii) In the case of any published work deposited in the form of hologram, the deposit shall be accompanied by: (A) Two sets of precise instructions for displaying the image fixed in the hologram; and (B) two sets of identifying material in compliance with § 202.21 of these regulations and clearly showing the displayed image.

(iv) In any case where an individual author is the owner of copyright in a published pictorial or graphic work and (A) less than five copies of the work have been published, or (B) the work has been published and sold or offered for sale in a limited edition consisting of no more than three hundred numbered copies, the deposit of one complete copy of the best edition of the work or, alternatively, the deposit of photographs or other identifying material in compliance with § 202.21 of these regulations, will suffice in lieu of the two copies required by paragraph (d)(1) of this section.

(v) In the case of a musical composition published in copies only, or in both copies and phonorecords, if the only publication of copies in the United States took place by rental, lease, or lending, the deposit of one complete copy of the best edition will suffice in lieu of the two copies required by paragraph (d)(1) of this section.

(vi) In the case of published multimedia kits, that include literary works, audiovisual works, sound recordings, or any combination of such works, the deposit of one complete copy of the best edition will suffice in lieu of the two copies required by paragraph (d)(1) of this section.

(e) *Special relief.* (1) In the case of any published work not exempt from deposit under paragraph (c) of this section, the Register of Copyrights may, after consultation with other appropriate officials of the Library of Congress and upon such conditions as the Register may determine after such consultation:

(i) Grant an exemption from the deposit requirements of section 407(a) of title 17 on an individual basis for single works or series or groups of works; or

(ii) permit the deposit of one copy or phonorecord, or alternative identifying material, in lieu of the two copies or phonorecords required by paragraph (d)(1) of this section; or

(iii) permit the deposit of incomplete copies or phonorecords, or copies or phonorecords other than those normally comprising the best edition; or

(iv) permit the deposit of identifying material which does not comply with § 202.21 of these regulations.

(2) Any decision as to whether to grant such special relief, and the conditions under which special relief is to be granted, shall be made by the Register of Copyrights after consultation with other appropriate officials of the Library of Congress, and shall be based upon the acquisition policies of the Library of Congress then in force.

(3) Requests for special relief under this paragraph shall be made in writing to the Chief, Deposits and Acquisitions Division of the Copyright Office, shall be signed by or on behalf of the owner of copyright or of the exclusive right of publication in the work, and shall set forth specific reasons why the request should be granted.

(4) The Register of Copyrights may, after consultation with other appropriate officials of the Library of Congress, terminate any ongoing or continuous grant of special relief. Notice of termination shall be given in writing and shall be sent to the individual person or organization to whom the grant of special relief had been given, at the last address shown in the records of the Copyright Office. A notice of termination may be given at any time, but it shall state a specific date of termination that is at least 30 days later than the date the notice is mailed. Termination shall not affect the validity of any deposit made earlier under the grant of special relief.

(f) *Submission and receipt of copies and phonorecords.* (1) All copies and phonorecords deposited in the Copyright Office will be considered to be deposited only in compliance with section 407 of title 17 unless they are accompanied by an application for registration of a claim to copyright in the work represented by the deposit, and either a registration fee or a deposit account number on the application. Copies or phonorecords deposited without such an accompanying application and either a fee or a deposit account notation will not be connected with or held for receipt of separate applications, and will not satisfy the deposit provisions of section 408 of title 17 or § 202.20 of these regulations.

(2) All copies and phonorecords deposited in the Copyright Office under section 407 of title 17, unless accompanied by written instructions to the contrary, will be considered to be deposited by the person or persons named in the copyright notice on the work.

(3) Upon request by the depositor made at the time of the deposit, the Copyright Office will issue a certificate of receipt for the deposit of copies or phonorecords of a work under this section. Certificates of receipt will be issued in response to requests made after the date of deposit only if the requesting party is identified in the records of the Copyright Office as having made the deposit. In either case, requests for a certificate of receipt must be in writing and accompanied by a fee of $2. A certificate of receipt will include identification of the depositor, the work deposited, and the nature and format of the copy or phonorecord deposited, together with the date of receipt.

(17 U.S.C. 407, 408, 702)
[51 FR 6402, Feb. 24, 1986]

---

# "Best Edition" of Published Copyrighted Works for the Collections of the Library of Congress

The Copyright Law (Title 17, United States Code) requires that copies or phonorecords deposited in the Copyright Office be of the "best edition" of the work. The law states that "The 'best edition' of work is the edition, published in the United States at any time before the date of deposit, that the Library of Congress determines to be most suitable for its purposes."

When two or more editions of the same version of a work have been published, the one of the highest quality is generally considered to be the best edition. In judging quality, the Library of Congress will adhere to the criteria set forth below in all but exceptional circumstances.

Where differences between editions represent variations in copyrightable content, each edition is a separate version and "best edition" standards based on such differences do not apply. Each such version is a separate work for the purposes of the Copyright Law.

Appearing below are lists of criteria to be applied in determining the best edition of each of several types of material. The criteria are listed in descending order of importance. In deciding between two editions, a criterion-by-criterion comparison should be made. The edition which first fails to satisfy a criterion is to be considered of inferior quality and will not be an acceptable deposit. For example, if a comparison is made between two hardbound editions of a book, one a trade edition printed on acid-free paper and the other a specially bound edition printed on average paper, the former will be the best edition because the type of paper is a more important criterion than the binding.

Under regulations of the Copyright Office, potential depositors may request authorization to deposit copies or phonorecords of other than the best edition of a specific work (e.g., a microform rather than a printed edition of a serial).

### I. PRINTED TEXTUAL MATTER

A. *Paper, Binding, and Packaging:*
   1. Archival-quality rather than less-permanent paper.
   2. Hard cover rather than soft cover.
   3. Library binding rather than commercial binding.
   4. Trade edition rather than book club edition.
   5. Sewn rather than glue-only binding.

6. Sewn or glued rather than stapled or spiral-bound.

7. Stapled rather than spiral-bound or plastic-bound.

8. Bound rather than looseleaf, except when future looseleaf insertions are to be issued.

9. Slipcased rather than nonslipcased.

10. With protective folders rather than without (for broadsides).

11. Rolled rather than folded (for broadsides).

12. With protective coatings rather than without (except broadsides, which should not be coated).

B. *Rarity:*

1. Special limited edition having the greatest number of special features.

2. Other limited edition rather than trade edition.

3. Special binding rather than trade binding.

C. *Illustrations:*

1. Illustrated rather than unillustrated.

2. Illustrations in color rather than black and white.

D. *Special Features:*

1. With thumb notches or index tabs rather than without.

2. With aids to use such as overlays and magnifiers rather than without.

E. *Size:*

1. Larger rather than smaller sizes. (Except that large-type editions for the partially-sighted are not required in place of editions employing type of more conventional size.)

## II. PHOTOGRAPHS

A. Size and finish, in descending order of preference:

1. The most widely distributed edition.

2. 8 × 10-inch glossy print.

3. Other size or finish.

B. Unmounted rather than mounted.

C. Archival-quality rather than less-permanent paper stock or printing process.

## III. MOTION PICTURES

A. Film rather than another medium. Film editions are listed below in descending order of preference.

1. Preprint material, by special arrangement.

2. Film gauge in which most widely distributed.

3. 35 mm rather than 16 mm.

4. 16 mm rather than 8 mm.

5. Special formats (e.g., 65 mm) only in exceptional cases.

6. Open reel rather than cartridge or cassette.

B. Videotape rather than videodisc. Videotape editions are listed below in descending order of preference.

1. Tape gauge in which most widely distributed.

2. Two-inch tape.

3. One-inch tape.

4. Three-quarter-inch tape cassette.

5. One-half-inch tape cassette.

## IV. OTHER GRAPHIC MATTER

A. *Paper and Printing:*

1. Archival-quality rather than less-permanent paper.

2. Color rather than black and white.

B. *Size and Content:*
    1. Larger rather than smaller size.
    2. In the case of cartographic works, editions with the greatest amount of information rather than those with less detail.
C. *Rarity:*
    1. The most widely distributed edition rather than one of limited distribution.
    2. In the case of a work published only in a limited, numbered edition, one copy outside the numbered series but otherwise identical.
    3. A photographic reproduction of the original, by special arrangement only.
D. *Text and Other Materials:* 1. Works with annotations, accompanying tabular or textual matter, or other interpretative aids rather than those without them.
E. *Binding and Packaging:*
    1. Bound rather than unbound.
    2. If editions have different binding, apply the criteria in I.A.2-I.A.7 above.
    3. Rolled rather than folded.
    4. With protective coatings rather than without.

### V. PHONORECORDS

A. Disc rather than tape.
B. With special enclosures rather than without.
C. Open-reel rather than cartridge.
D. Cartridge rather than cassette.
E. Quadraphonic rather than stereophonic.
F. True stereophonic rather than monaural.
G. Monaural rather than electronically rechanneled stereo.

### VI. MUSICAL COMPOSITIONS

A. *Fullness of Score:* 1. *Vocal music:* a. With orchestral accompaniment—
    i. Full score and parts, if any, rather than conductor's score and parts, if any. (In cases of compositions published only by rental, lease, or lending, this requirement is reduced to full score only.)
    ii. Conductor's score and parts, if any, rather than condensed score and parts, if any. (In cases of compositions published only by rental, lease, or lending, this requirement is reduced to conductor's score only.)
    b. Unaccompanied: Open score (each part on separate staff) rather than closed score (all parts condensed to two staves).
    2. *Instrumental music:*
    a. Full score and parts, if any, rather than conductor's score and parts, if any. (In cases of compositions published only by rental, lease, or lending, this requirement is reduced to full score only.)
    b. Conductor's score and parts, if any, rather than condensed score and parts, if any. (In cases of compositions published only by rental, lease, or lending, this requirement is reduced to conductor's score only.)
B. *Printing and Paper:* 1. Archival-quality rather than less-permanent paper.
C. *Binding and Packaging:*
    1. Special limited editions rather than trade editions.
    2. Bound rather than unbound.
    3. If editions have different binding, apply the criteria in I.A.2-I.A.12 above.
    4. With protective folders rather than without.

### VII. MICROFORMS

A. *Related Materials:* 1. With indexes, study guides, or other printed matter rather than without.

B. *Permanence and Appearance:*
   1. Silver halide rather than any other emulsion.
   2. Positive rather than negative.
   3. Color rather than black and white.
C. *Format (newspapers and newspaper-formatted serials):* 1. Reel microfilm rather than any other microform.
D. *Format (all other materials):*
   1. Microfiche rather than reel microfilm.
   2. Reel microfilm rather than microform cassettes.
   3. Microfilm cassettes rather than micro-opaque prints.
E. *Size:* 1.35 mm rather than 16 mm.

### VIII. WORKS EXISTING IN MORE THAN ONE MEDIUM

Editions are listed below in descending order of preference.
A. Newspapers, dissertations and theses, newspaper-formatted serials:
   1. Microform.
   2. Printed matter.
B. All other materials:
   1. Printed matter.
   2. Microform.
   3. Phonorecord.

[43 FR 766, Jan. 4, 1978]

---

## § 202.20 Deposit of copies and phonorecords for copyright registration.

(a) *General.* This section prescribes rules pertaining to the deposit of copies and phonorecords of published and unpublished works for the purpose of copyright registration under section 408 of title 17 of the United States Code, as amended by Pub. L. 94-553. The provisions of this section are not applicable to the deposit of copies and phonorecords for the Library of Congress under section 407 of title 17, except as expressly adopted in § 202.19 of these regulations.

(b) *Definitions.* For the purposes of this section:

(1) The "best edition" of a work has the meaning set forth § 202.19(b)(1) of these regulations.

(2) A "complete" copy or phonorecord means the following:

(i) *Unpublished works.* Subject to the requirements of paragraph (b)(2)(vi) of this section, a "complete" copy or phonorecord of an unpublished work is a copy or phonorecord representing the entire copyrightable content of the work for which registration is sought;

(ii) *Published works.* Subject to the requirements of paragraphs (b)(2)(iii) through (vi) of this section, a "complete" copy or phonorecord of a published work includes all elements comprising the applicable unit of publication of the work, including elements that, if considered separately, would not be copyrightable subject matter. However, even where certain physically separable elements included in the applicable unit of publication are missing from the deposit, a copy or phonorecord will be considered "complete" for purposes of registration where:

(A) The copy or phonorecord deposited contains all parts of the work for which copyright registration is sought; and

(B) The removal of the missing elements did not physically damage the copy or phonorecord or garble its contents; and

(C) The work is exempt from the mandatory deposit requirements under section 407 of title 17 of the United States Code and § 202.19(c) of these regulations, or the copy deposited consists entirely of a container, wrapper, or holder, such as an envelope, sleeve, jacket, slipcase, box, bag, folder, binder, or other receptacle acceptable for deposit under paragraph (c)(2) of this section;

(iii) *Contribution to collective works.* In the case of a published contribution to a collective work, a "complete" copy or phonorecord is the entire collective work including the contribution or, in the case of a newspaper, the entire section including the contribution;

(iv) *Sound recordings.* In the case of published sound recordings, a "complete" phonorecord has the meaning set forth in § 202.19(b)(2) of these regulations;

(v) *Musical scores.* In the case of a musical composition published in copies only, or in both copies and phonorecords:

(A) If the only publication of copies took place by the rental, lease, or lending of a full score and parts, a full score is a "complete" copy; and

(B) If the only publication of copies took place by the rental, lease, or lending of a conductor's score and parts, a conductor's score is a "complete" copy;

(vi) *Motion pictures.* In the case of a published or unpublished motion picture, a copy is "complete" if the reproduction of all of the visual and aural elements comprising the copyrightable subject matter in the work is clean, undamaged, undeteriorated, and free of splices, and if the copy itself and its physical housing are free of any defects that would interfere with the performance of the work or that would cause mechanical, visual, or audible defects or distortions.

(3) The terms "copy," "collective work," "device," "fixed," "literary work," "machine," "motion picture," "phonorecord," "publication," "sound recording," "transmission program," and "useful article," and their variant forms, have the meanings given to them in section 101 of title 17.

(4) A "secure test" is a nonmarketed test administered under supervision at specified centers on specific dates, all copies of which are accounted for and either destroyed or returned to restricted locked storage following each administration. For these purposes a test is not marketed if copies are not sold but it is distributed and used in such a manner that ownership and control of copies remain with the test sponsor or publisher.

(5) "Title 17" means title 17 of the United States Code, as amended by Pub. L. 94-553.

(6) For the purposes of determining the applicable deposit requirements under this § 202.20 only, the following shall be considered as unpublished motion pictures: motion pictures that consist of television transmission programs and that have been published, if at all, only by reason of a license or other grant to a nonprofit institution of the right to make a fixation of such programs directly from a transmission to the public, with or without the right to make further uses of such fixations.

(c) *Nature of required deposit.* (1) Subject to the provisions of paragraph (c)(2) of this section, the deposit required to accompany an application for registration of claim to copyright under section 408 of title 17 shall consist of:

(i) In the case of unpublished works, one complete copy or phonorecord.

(ii) In the case of works first published in the United States before January 1, 1978, two complete copies or phonorecords of the work as first published.

(iii) In the case of works first published in the United States on or after January 1, 1978, two complete copies or phonorecords of the best edition.

(iv) In the case of works first published outside of the United States, whenever published, one complete copy or phonorecord of the work as first published. For the purposes of this section, any works simultaneously first published within and outside of the United States shall be considered to be first published in the United States.

(2) In the case of certain works, the special provisions set forth in this clause shall apply. In any case where this clause specifies that one copy or phonorecord may be submitted, that copy or phonorecord shall represent the best edition, or the work as first published, as set forth in paragraph (c)(1) of this section.

(i) *General.* In the following cases the deposit of one complete copy or phonorecord will suffice in lieu of two copies or phonorecords:

(A) Published three-dimensional cartographic representations of area, such as globes and relief models;

(B) Published diagrams illustrating scientific or technical works or formulating scientific or technical information in linear or other two-dimensional form, such as an architectural or engineering blueprint, or a mechanical drawing;

(C) Published greeting cards, picture postcards, and stationery;

(D) Lectures, sermons, speeches, and addresses published individually and not as a collection of the works of one or more authors;

(E) Musical compositions published in copies only, or in both copies and phonorecords, if the only publication of copies took place by rental, lease, or lending;

(F) Published multimedia kits or any part thereof;

(G) Works exempted from the requirement of depositing identifying material under paragraph (c)(2)(xi)(B)(5) of this section;

(H) Literary, dramatic, and musical works published only as embodied in phonorecords, although this category does not exempt the owner of copyright in a sound recording;

(I) Choreographic works, pantomimes, literary, dramatic, and musical works published only as embodied in motion pictures;

(J) Published works in the form of two-dimensional games, decals, fabric patches or emblems, calendars, instructions for needle work, needle work and craft kits; and

(K) Works reproduced on three-dimensional containers such as boxes, cases, and cartons.

(ii) *Motion pictures.* In the case of published or unpublished motion pictures, the deposit of one complete copy will suffice. The deposit of a copy or copies for any published or unpublished motion picture must be accompanied by a separate description of its contents, such as a continuity, pressbook, or synopsis. In any case where the deposit copy or copies required for registration of a motion picture cannot be viewed for examining purposes or equipment in the Examining Division of the Copyright Office, the description accompanying the deposit must comply with § 202.21(b) of these regulations. The Library of Congress may, at its sole discretion, enter into an agreement permitting the return of copies of published motion pictures to the depositor under certain conditions and establishing certain rights and obligations of the Library of Congress with respect to such copies. In the event of termination of such an agreement by the Library, it shall not be subject to reinstatement, nor shall the depositor or any successor in interest of the depositor be entitled to any similar or subsequent agreement with the Library, unless at the sole discretion of the Library it would be in the best interests of the Library to reinstate the agreement or enter into a new agreement. In the case of unpublished motion pictures (including television transmission programs that have been fixed and transmitted to the public, but have not been published), the deposit of identifying material in compliance with § 202.21 of these regulations may be made and will suffice in lieu of an actual copy.

(iii) *Holograms.* In the case of any work deposited in the form of a three-dimensional hologram, the copy or copies shall be accompanied by:

(A) Precise instructions for displaying the image fixed in the hologram; and

(B) Photographs or other identifying material complying with § 202.21 of these regulations and clearly showing the displayed image.

The number of sets of instructions and identifying material shall be the same as the number of copies required. In the case of a work in the form of a two-dimensional hologram, the image of which is visible without the use of a machine or device, one actual copy of the work shall be deposited.

(iv) *Certain pictorial and graphic works.* In the case of any unpublished pictorial or graphic work, deposit of identifying material in compliance with § 202.21 of these regulations may be made and will suffice in lieu of deposit of an actual copy. In the case of a published pictorial or graphic work, deposit of one complete copy, or of identifying material in compliance with § 202.21 of these regulations, may be made and will suffice in lieu of deposit of two actual copies where an individual author is the owner of copyright, and either:

(A) Less than five copies of the work have been published; or

(B) The work has been published and sold or offered for sale in a limited edition consisting of no more than 300 numbered copies.

(v) *Commercial prints and labels.* In the case of prints, labels, and other advertising matter, including catalogs, published in connection with the rental, lease, lending, licensing, or sale of articles of merchandise, works of authorship, or services, the deposit of one complete copy will suffice in lieu of two copies. Where the print or label is published in a larger work, such as a newspaper or other periodical, one copy of the entire page or pages upon which it appears may be submitted in lieu of the entire larger work. In the case of prints or labels physically inseparable from a three-dimensional object, identifying material complying with § 202.21 of these regulations must be submitted rather than an actual copy or copies except under the conditions of paragraph (c)(2)(xi)(B)(4) of this section.

(vi) *Tests.* In the case of tests, and answer material for tests, published separately from other literary works, the deposit of one complete copy will suffice in lieu of two copies. In the case of any secure test the Copyright Office will return the deposit to the applicant promptly after examination: Provided, That sufficient portions, description, or the like are retained so as to constitute a sufficient archival record of the deposit.

(vii) *Computer programs and databases embodied in machine-readable copies.* In cases where a computer program, database, compilation, statistical compendium or the like, if unpublished is fixed, or if published is published only in the form of machine-readable copies (such as magnetic tape or disks, punched cards, semiconductor chip products, or the like) from which the work cannot ordinarily be perceived except with the aid of a machine or device, the deposit shall consist of: (A) For published or unpublished computer programs, one copy of identifying portions of the program, reproduced in a form visually perceptible without the aid of a machine or device, either on paper or in microform. For these purposes, "identifying portions" shall mean either the first and last 25 pages or equivalent units of the program if reproduced on paper, or at least the first and last 25 pages or equivalent units of the program if reproduced in microform, together with the page or equivalent unit containing the copyright notice, if any. If the program is 50 pages or less, the required deposit will be the entire work. In the case of revised versions of such works, if the revisions occur throughout the entire computer program, the deposit of the first and last 25 pages will suffice; if the revisions are not contained in the first and last 25 pages, the deposit should consist of any 50 pages representative of the revised material.

(B) For published and unpublished automated databases, compilations, statistical compendia, and other literary works so fixed or published, one copy of identifying portions of the work, reproduced in a form visually perceptible without the aid of a machine or device, either on paper or in microform. For these purposes: (*1*) "identifying portions" shall mean either the first and last 25 pages or equivalent units of the work if reproduced on paper, or at least the first and last 25 pages or equivalent units of work if reproduced in microform, or, in the case of automated databases comprising separate and distinct data files, representative portions of each separate data file consisting of either 50 complete data records from each file or the entire file, whichever is less; and (*2*) "data file" and "file" mean a group of data records pertaining to a common subject matter, regardless of the physical size of the records or the number of data items included in them. (In the case of revised versions of such databases, the portions deposited must contain representative data records which have been added or modified.) In any case where the deposit comprises representative portions of each separate file of an automated database as indicated above, it shall be accompanied by a typed or printed descriptive statement containing: The title of the database; the name and address of the copyright claimant; the name and content of each separate file within the database, including the subject matter involved, the origin(s) of the data, and the approximate number of individual records within the file; and a description of the exact contents of any machine-readable copyright notice employed in or with the work and the manner and frequency with which it is displayed (e.g., at user's terminal only at sign-on, or continuously on terminal display, or on printouts, etc.). If a visually perceptible copyright notice is placed on any copies of the work (such as magnetic tape reels or their container) a sample of such notice must also accompany the statement.

(viii) *Machine-readable copies of works other than computer programs and databases.* Where a literary, musical, pictorial, graphic, or audiovisual work, or a sound recording, except for literary works which are computer programs, databases, compilations, statistical compendia or the like, if unpublished has been fixed or, if published, has been published only in machine-readable form, the deposit must consist of identifying material. The type of identifying material submitted should generally be appropriate to the type of work embodied in machine-readable form, but in all cases should be that which best represents the copyrightable content of the work. In all cases the identifying material must include the title of the work. A synopsis may also be requested in addition to the other deposit materials as appropriate in the discretion of the Copyright Office. In the case of any published work subject to this section, the identifying material must include a representation of the copyright notice, if one exists. Identifying material requirements for certain types of works are specified below. In the case of the types of works listed below, the requirements specified shall apply except that, in any case where the specific requirements are not appropriate for a given work the form of the identifying material required will be determined by the Copyright Office in consultation with the applicant, but the Copyright Office will make the final determination of the acceptability of the identifying material.

(A) For pictorial or graphic works, the deposit shall consist of identifying material in compliance with § 202.21 of these regulations;

(B) For audiovisual works, the deposit shall consist of either a videotape of the work depicting representative portions of the copyrightable content, or a series of photographs or drawings, depicting representative portions of the work, plus in all cases a separate synopsis of the work;

(C) For musical compositions, the deposit shall consist of a transcription of the entire work such as a score, or a reprodution of the entire work on an audiocassette or other phonorecord;

(D) For sound recordings, the deposit shall consist of a reproduction of the entire work on an audiocassette or other phonorecord;

(E) For literary works, the deposit shall consist of a transcription of representative portions of the work including the first and last 25 pages or equivalent units, and five or more pages indicative of the remainder.

(ix) *Copies containing both visually perceptible and machine-readable material.* Where a published literary work is embodied in copies containing both visually perceptible and machine-readable material, the deposit shall consist of the visually perceptible material and identifying portions of the machine-readable material.

(x) *Works reproduced in or on sheetlike materials.* In the case of any unpublished work that is fixed, or any published work that is published, only in the form of a two-dimensional reproduction on sheetlike materials such as textiles and other fabrics, wallpaper and similar commercial wall coverings, carpeting, floor tile, and similar commercial floor coverings, and wrapping paper and similar packaging material, the deposit shall consist of one copy in the form of an actual swatch or piece of such material sufficient to show all elements of the work in which copyright is claimed and the copyright notice appearing on the work, if any. If the work consists of a repeated pictorial or graphic design, the complete design and at least part of one repetition must be shown. If the sheetlike material in or on which a published work has been reproduced has been embodied in or attached to a three-dimensional object, such as furniture, or any other three-dimensional manufactured article, and the work has been published only in that form, the deposit must consist of identifying material complying with § 202.21 of these regulations instead of a copy. If the sheetlike material in or on which a published work has been reproduced has been embodied in or attached to a two-dimensional object such as wearing apparel, bed linen, or a similar item, and the work has been published only in that form, the deposit must consist of identifying material complying with § 202.21 of these regulations instead of a copy unless the copy can be folded for storage in a form that does not exceed four inches in thickness.

(xi) *Works reproduced in or on three-dimensional objects.* (A) In the following cases the deposit must consist of identifying material complying with § 202.21 of these regulations instead of a copy or copies:

(*1*) Any three-dimensional sculptural work, including any illustration or formulation of artistic expression or information in three-dimensional form. Examples of such works include statues, carvings, ceramics, moldings, constructions, models, and maquettes; and

(*2*) Any two-dimensional or three-dimensional work that, if unpublished, has been fixed, or, if published, has been published only in or on jewelry, dolls, toys, games, except as provided in paragraph (c)(2)(xi)(B)(*3*) below, or any three-dimensional useful article.

(B) In the following cases the requirements of paragraph (c)(2)(xi)(A) of this section for the deposit of identifying material shall not apply:

(*1*) Three-dimensional cartographic representations of area, such as globes and relief models;

(*2*) Works that have been fixed or published in or on a useful article that comprises one of the elements of the unit of publication of an educational or instructional kit which also includes a literary or audiovisual work, a sound recording, or any combination of such works;

(*3*) Published games consisting of multiple parts that are packaged and published in a box or similar container with flat sides and with dimensions of no more than 12×24×6 inches;

(*4*) Works reproduced on three-dimensional containers or holders such as boxes, cases, and cartons, where the container or holder can be readily opened out, unfolded, slit at the corners, or in some other way made adaptable for flat storage, and the copy, when flattened, does not exceed 96 inches in any dimension; or

(*5*) Any three-dimensional sculptural work that, if unpublished, has been fixed, or, if published, has been published only in the form of jewelry cast in base metal which does not exceed four inches in any dimension.

(xii) *Soundtracks.* For separate registration of an unpublished work that is fixed, or a published work that is published, only as embodied in a soundtrack that is an integral part of a motion picture, the deposit of identifying material in compliance with § 202.21 of these regulations will suffice in lieu of an actual copy of the motion picture.

(xiii) *Oversize deposits.* In any case where the deposit otherwise required by this section exceeds 96 inches in any dimension, identifying material complying with § 202.21 of these regulations must be submitted instead of an actual copy or copies.

(xiv) *Pictorial advertising material.* In the case of published pictorial advertising material, except for advertising material published in connection with motion pictures, the deposit of either one copy as published or prepublication material consisting of camera-ready copy is acceptable.

(xv) *Contributions to collective works.* In the case of published contributions to collective works, the deposit of either one complete copy of the best edition of the entire collective work, the complete section containing the contribution if published in a newspaper, the entire page containing the contribution, the contribution cut from the paper in which it appeared, or a photocopy of the contribution itself as it was published in the collective work, will suffice in lieu of two complete copies of the entire collective work.

(xvi) *Phonorecords.* In any case where the deposit phonorecord or phonorecords submitted for registration of a claim to copyright is inaudible on audio playback devices in the Examining Division of the Copyright Office, the Office will seek an appropriate deposit in accordance with paragraph (d) of this section.

(d) *Special relief.* (1) In any case the Register of Copyrights may, after consultation with other appropriate officials of the Library of Congress and upon such conditions as the Register may determine after such consultation:

(i) Permit the deposit of one copy or phonorecord, or alternative identifying material, in lieu of the one or two copies or phonorecords otherwise required by paragraph (c)(1) of this section;

(ii) Permit the deposit of incomplete copies or phonorecords, or copies or phonorecords other than those normally comprising the best edition; or

(iii) Permit the deposit of an actual copy or copies, in lieu of the identifying material otherwise required by this section; or

(iv) Permit the deposit of identifying material which does not comply with § 202.21 of these regulations.

(2) Any decision as to whether to grant such special relief, and the conditions under which special relief is to be granted, shall be made by the Register of Copyrights after consultation with other appropriate officials of the Library of Congress, and shall be based upon the acquisition policies of the Library of Congress then in force and the archival and examining requirements of the Copyright Office.

(3) Requests for special relief under this paragraph may be combined with requests for special relief under § 202.19(e) of these regulations. Whether so combined or made solely under this paragraph, such requests shall be made in writing to the Chief, Examining Division of the Copyright Office, shall be signed by or on behalf of the person signing the application for registration, and shall set forth specific reasons why the request should be granted.

(4) The Register of Copyrights may, after consultation with other appropriate officials of the Library of Congress, terminate any ongoing or continuous grant of special relief. Notice of termination shall be given in writing and shall be sent to the individual person or organization to whom the grant of special relief had been given, at the last address shown in the records of the Copyright Office. A notice of termination may be given at any time, but it shall state a specific date of termination that is at least 30 days later than the date the notice is mailed. Termination shall not affect the validity of any deposit or registration made earlier under the grant of special relief.

(e) *Use of copies and phonorecords deposited for the Library of Congress.* Copies and phonorecords deposited for the Library of Congress under section 407 of title 17 and § 202.19 of these regulations may be used to satisfy the deposit provisions of this section if they are accompanied by an application for registration of claim to copyright in the work represented by the deposit, and either a registration fee or a deposit account number on the application.

(17 U.S.C. 407, 408, 702)
[51 FR 6402, Feb. 24, 1986]


## § 202.21 Deposit of identifying material instead of copies.

(a) *General.* Subject to the specific provisions of paragraphs (f) and (g) of this section, and to §§ 202.19(e)(1)(iv) and 202.20(d)(1)(iv), in any case where the deposit of identifying material is permitted or required under § 202.19 or § 202.20 of these regulations for published or unpublished works, the material shall consist of photographic prints, transparencies, photostats, drawings, or similar two-dimensional reproductions or renderings of the work, in a form visually perceivable without the aid of a machine or device. In the case of pictorial or graphic works, such material should reproduce the actual colors employed in the work. In all other cases, such material may be in black and white or may consist of a reproduction of the actual colors.

(b) *Completeness; number of sets.* As many pieces of identifying material as are necessary to show the entire copyrightable content in the ordinary case, but in no case less than an adequate representation of such content, of the work for which deposit is being made, or for which registration is being sought shall be submitted.

Except in cases falling under the provisions of § 202.19(d)(2)(iii) or § 202.20(c)(2)(iii) with respect to holograms, only one set of such complete identifying material is required.

(c) *Size.* Photographic transparencies must be at least 35mm in size and, if such transparencies are $3 \times 3$ inches or less, must be fixed in cardboard, plastic, or similar mounts to facilitate identification, handling, and storage. The Copyright Office prefers that transparencies larger than $3 \times 3$ inches be mounted in a way that facilitate their handling and preservation, and reserves the right to require such mounting in particular cases. All types of identifying material other than photographic transparencies must be not less than $3 \times 3$ inches and not more than $9 \times 12$ inches, but preferably $8 \times 10$ inches. Except in the case of transparencies, the image of the work must be either lifesize or larger, or if less than lifesize must be large enough to show clearly the entire copyrightable content of the work.

(d) *Title and dimensions.* At least one piece of identifying material must, on its front, back, or mount, indicate the title of the work; and the indication of an exact measurement of one or more dimensions of the work is preferred.

(e) *Copyright notice.* In the case of works published with notice of copyright, the notice and its position on the work must be clearly shown on at least one piece of identifying material. Where necessary because of the size or position of the notice, a separate drawing or similar reproduction shall be submitted. Such reproduction shall be no smaller than $3 \times 3$ inches and no larger than $9 \times 12$ inches, and shall show the exact appearance and content of the notice, and its specific position on the work.

(f) For separate registration of an unpublished work that is fixed, or a published work that is published, only as embodied as a soundtrack that is an integral part of a motion picture, identifying material deposited in lieu of an actual copy of the motion picture shall consist of:

(1) A transcription of the entire work, or a reproduction of the entire work on a phonorecord; and

(2) Photographs or other reproductions from the motion picture showing the title of the motion picture, the soundtrack credits, and the copyright notice for the soundtrack, if any.

The provisions of paragraphs (b), (c), (d), and (e) of this section do not apply to identifying material deposited under this paragraph (f).

(g)(1) In the case of unpublished motion pictures (including transmission programs that have been fixed and transmitted to the public, but have not been published), identifying material deposited in lieu of an actual copy shall consist of either:

(i) An audio cassette or other phonorecord reproducing the entire soundtrack or other sound portion of the motion picture, and description of the motion picture; or

(ii) A set consisting of one frame enlargement or similar visual reproduction from each 10-minute segment of the motion picture, and a description of the motion picture.

(2) In either case the "description" may be a continuity, a pressbook, or a synopsis but in all cases it must include:

(i) The title or continuing title of the work, and the episode title, if any;

(ii) The nature and general content of the program;

(iii) The date when the work was first fixed and whether or not fixation was simultaneous with first transmission;

(iv) The date of first transmission, if any;

(v) The running time; and

(vi) The credits appearing on the work, if any.

(3) The provisions of paragraphs (b), (c), (d), and (e) of this section do not apply to identifying material submitted under this paragraph (g).

(h) In the case where the deposit copy or copies of a motion picture cannot be viewed for examining purposes on equipment in the Examining Division of the Copyright Office, the "description" required by § 202.20(c)(2)(ii) of these regulations may be a continuity, a pressbook, a synopsis, or a final shooting script but in all cases must be sufficient to indicate the copyrightable material in the work and include:

508   *Latman's The Copyright Law*

(1) The continuing title of the work and the episode title, if any;

(2) The nature and general content of the program and of its dialogue or narration, if any;

(3) The running time; and

(4) All credits appearing on the work including the copyright notice, if any. The provisions of paragraphs (b), (c), and (d) of this section do not apply to identifying material submitted under this paragraph (h).

(17 U.S.C. 407, 408, 702)
[51 FR 6402, Feb. 24, 1986]

### § 202.22 Acquisition and deposit of unpublished television transmission programs.

(a) *General.* This section prescribes rules pertaining to the acquisition of copies of unpublished television transmission programs by the Library of Congress under section 407(e) of Title 17 of the United States Code, as amended by Pub. L. 94-553. It also prescribes rules pertaining to the use of such copies in the registration of claims to copyright, under section 408(b)(2).

(b) *Definitions.* For purposes of this section:

(1) The terms "copies," "fixed," "publication," and "transmission program" and their variant forms, have the meanings given to them in section 101 of Title 17. The term "network station" has the meaning given it in section 111(f) of Title 17.

(2) "Title 17" means Title of the United States Code, as amended by Pub. L. 94-553.

(c) *Off-the-air copying.* (1) Library of Congress employees acting under the general authority of the Librarian of Congress may make a fixation of an unpublished television transmission program directly from a transmission to the public in the United States, in accordance with section 407(e)(1) and (4) of Title 17 of the United States Code. The choice of programs selected for fixation shall be based on the Library of Congress acquisition policies in effect at the time of fixation. Specific notice of an intent to copy a transmission program off-the-air will ordinarily not be given. In general, the Library of Congress will seek to copy off-the-air a substantial portion of the programming transmitted by noncommercial educational broadcast stations as defined in section 397 of Title 47 of the United States Code, and will copy off-the-air selected programming transmitted by commercial broadcast stations, both network and independent.

(2) Upon written request addressed to the Chief, Motion Picture, Broadcasting and Recorded Sound Division by a broadcast station or other owner of the right of transmission, the Library of Congress will inform the requestor whether a particular transmission program has been copied off-the-air by the Library.

(3) The Library of Congress will not knowingly copy off-the-air any unfixed or published television transmission program under the copying authority of section 407(e) of Title 17 of the United States Code.

(4) The Library of Congress is entitled under this paragraph (c) to presume that a television program transmitted to the public in the United States by a noncommercial educational broadcast station as defined in section 397 of Title 47 of the United States Code has been fixed but not published.

(5) The presumption established by paragraph (c)(4) of this section may be overcome by written declaration and submission of appropriate documentary evidence to the Chief, Motion Picture, Broadcasting and Recorded Sound Division, either before or after off-the-air copying of the particular transmission program by the Library of Congress. Such written submission shall contain:

(i) The identification, by title and time of broadcast, of the transmission program in question;

(ii) A brief statement declaring either that the program was not fixed or that it was published at the time of transmission;

(iii) If it is declared that the program was published at the time of transmission, a brief statement of the facts of publication, including the date and place thereof, the method of publication, the name of the owner of the right of first publication, and whether the work was published in the United States with a notice of copyright; and

(iv) The actual handwritten signature of an officer or other duly authorized agent of the organization which transmitted the program in question.

(6) A declaration that the program was unfixed at the time of transmission shall be accepted by the Library of Congress, unless the Library can cite evidence to the contrary, and the off-the-air copy will either be

(i) Erased; or

(ii) Retained, if requested by the owner of copyright or of any exclusive right, to satisfy the deposit provision of section 408 of Title 17 of the United States Code.

(7) If it is declared that the program was published at the time of transmission, the Library of Congress is entitled under this section to retain the copy to satisfy the deposit requirement of section 407(a) of Title 17 of the United States Code, unless the Library is notified in writing by the owner of copyright or of the exclusive right of publication that the work has never been published in the United States with notice of copyright.

(8) The Library of Congress in making fixations of unpublished transmission programs transmitted by commercial broadcast stations shall not do so without notifying the transmitting organization or its agent that such activity is taking place. In the case of network stations, the notification will be sent to the particular network. In the case of any other commercial broadcasting station, the notification will be sent to the particular broadcast station that has transmitted, or will transmit, the program. Such notice shall, if possible, be given to the Library of Congress prior to the time of broadcast. In every case, the Library of Congress shall transmit such notice no later than fourteen days after such fixation has occurred. Such notice shall contain:

(i) The identification, by title and time of broadcast, of the transmission program in question;

(ii) A brief statement asserting the Library of Congress' belief that the transmission program has been, or will be by the date of transmission, fixed and is unpublished, together with language converting the notice to a demand for deposit under section 407(a) and (b) of Title 17 of the United States Code, if the transmission program has been published in the United States with notice of copyright.

(9) The notice required by paragraph (c)(8) of this section shall not cover more than one transmission program except that the notice may cover up to thirteen episodes of one title if such episodes are generally scheduled to be broadcast at the same time period on a regular basis, or may cover all the episodes comprising the title if they are scheduled to be broadcast within a period of not more than two months.

(d) *Demands for deposit of a television transmission program.* (1) The Register of Copyrights may make a written demand upon the owner of the right of transmission in the United States to deposit a copy of a specific transmission program for the benefit of the Library of Congress under the authority of section 407(e)(2) of Title 17 of the United States Code.

(2) The Register of Copyrights is entitled to presume, unless clear evidence to the contrary is proffered, that the transmitting organization is the owner of the United States transmission right.

(3) Notices of demand shall be in writing and shall contain:

(i) The identification by title and time of broadcast, of the work in question;

(ii) An explanation of the optional forms of compliance, including transfer of ownership of a copy to the Library, lending a copy to the Library for reproduction, or selling a copy to the Library at a price not to exceed the cost of reproducing and supplying the copy;

(iii) A ninety-day deadline by which time either compliance or a request for an extension of a request to adjust the scope of the demand or the method for fulfilling it shall have been received by the Registered Copyrights;

(iv) A brief description of the controls which are placed on the copies' use;

(v) A statement concerning the Register's perception of the publication status of the program, together with language converting this demand to a demand for a deposit, under 17 U.S.C. 407(a) and (c), if the recipient takes the position that the work is published; and

(vi) A statement that a "compliance copy" must be made and retained if the notice is received prior to transmission.

(4) With respect to paragraph (d)(3)(ii) of this section, the sale of a copy in compliance with a demand of this nature shall be at a price not to exceed the cost to the Library of reproducing and supplying the copy. The notice of demand should therefore inform the recipient of that cost and set that cost, plus reasonable shipping charges, as the maximum price for such a sale.

(5) Copies transferred, lent, or sold under paragraph (d) of this section shall be of sound physical condition as described in Appendix A to this section.

(6) *Special relief.* In the case of any demand made under paragraph (d) of this section the Register of Copyrights may, after consultation with other appropriate officials of the Library of Congress and upon such conditions as the Register may determine after such consultation,

(i) Extend the time period provided in subparagraph (d)(3)(iii);

(ii) Make adjustments in the scope of the demand; or

(iii) Make adjustments in the method of fulfilling the demand. Any decision as to whether to allow such extension or adjustments shall be made by the Register of Copyrights after consulting with other appropriate officials of the Library of Congress and shall be made as reasonably warranted by the circumstances. Requests for special relief under paragraph (d) of this section shall be made in writing to the Chief, Acquisitions and Processing Division of the Copyright Office, shall be signed by or on behalf of the owner of the right of transmission in the United States and shall set forth the specific reasons why the request shall be granted.

(e) *Disposition and use of copies.* (1) All copies acquired under this section shall be maintained by the Motion Picture, Broadcasting and Recorded Sound Division of the Library of Congress. The Library may make one archival copy of a program which it has fixed under the provisions of section 407(e)(1) of Title 17 of the United States Code and paragraph (c) of this section.

(2) All copies acquired or made under this section, except copies of transmission programs consisting of a regularly scheduled newscast or on-the-spot coverage of news events, shall be subject to the restrictions concerning copying and access found in Library of Congress Regulation 818-17, *Policies Governing the Use and Availability of Motion Pictures and Other Audiovisual Works in the Collections of the Library of Congress,* or its successors. Copies of transmission programs consisting of regularly scheduled newscasts or on-the-spot coverage of news events are subject to the provisions of the "American Television and Radio Archives Act" (section 170 of Title 2 of the United States Code) and such regulations as the Librarian of Congress shall prescribe.

(f) *Registration of claims to copyright.* (1) Copies fixed by the Library of Congress under the provisions of paragraph (c) of this section may be used as the deposit for copyright registration provided that:

(i) The application and fee, in a form acceptable for registration, is received by the Copyright Office not later than ninety days after transmission of the program, and

(ii) Correspondence received by the Copyright Office in the envelope containing the application and fee states that a fixation of the instant work was made by the Library of Congress and requests that the copy so fixed be used to satisfy the registration deposit provisions.

(2) Copies transferred, lent, or sold to the Library of Congress under the provisions of paragraph (d) of this section may be used as the deposit for copyright registration purposes only when the application and fee, in a form acceptable for registration, accompany, in the same container, the copy lent, transferred, or sold, and there is an explanation that the copy is intended to satisfy both the demand issued under

section 407(e)(2) of Title 17 of the United States Code and the registration deposit provisions.

(g) *Agreements modifying the terms of this section.* (1) The Library of Congress may, at its sole discretion, enter into an agreement whereby the provision of copies of unpublished television transmission programs on terms different from those contained in this section is authorized.

(2) Any such agreement may be terminated without notice by the Library of Congress.

(17 U.S.C. 407, 408, 702)
[48 FR 37208, Aug. 17, 1983]

## § 202.23 Full-term retention of copyright deposits.

(a) *General.* (1) This section prescribes conditions under which a request for full term retention, under the control of the Copyright Office, of copyright deposits (copies, phonorecords, or identifying material) of published works may be made and granted or denied pursuant to section 704(e) of Title 17 of the United States Code. Only copies, phonorecords, or identifying material deposited in connection with registration of a claim to copyright under Title 17 of the United States Code are within the provisions of this section. Only the depositor or the copyright owner of record of the work identified by the copyright deposit, or a duly authorized agent of the depositor or copyright owner, may request full term retention. A fee for this service is fixed by this section pursuant to section 708(a)(11) of Title 17 of the United States Code.

(2) For purposes of this section, "under the control of the Copyright Office" shall mean within the confines of Copyright Office buildings and under the control of Copyright Office employees, including retention in a Federal records center, but does not include transfer to the Library of Congress collections.

(3) For purposes of this section, "full term retention" means retention for a period of 75 years from the date of publication of the work identified by the particular copyright deposit which is retained.

(4) For purposes of this section, "copyright deposit" or its plural means the copy, phonorecord, or identifying material submitted to the Copyright Office in connection with a published work that is subsequently registered and made part of the records of the Office.

(b) *Form and content of request for full term retention*—(1) *Forms.* The Copyright Office does not provide printed forms for the use of persons requesting full term retention of copyright deposits.

(2) Requests for full term retention must be made in writing, addressed to the Chief, Records Management Division of the Copyright Office, and shall: (i) Be signed by or on behalf of the depositor or the copyright owner of record, and (ii) clearly indicate that full term retention is desired.

(3) The request for full term retention must adequately identify the particular copyright deposit to be retained, preferably by including the title used in the registration application, the name of the depositor or copyright owner of record, the publication date, and, if registration was completed earlier, the registration number.

(c) *Conditions under which requests will be granted or denied*—(1) *General.* A request that meets the requirements of subsection (b) will generally be granted if the copyright deposit for which full term retention is requested has been continuously in the custody of the Copyright Office and the Library of Congress has not, by the date of the request, selected the copyright deposit for its collections.

(2) *Time of request.* The request for full term retention of a particular copyright deposit may be made at the time of deposit or at any time thereafter; however, the request will be granted only if at least one copy, phonorecord, or set of identifying materials is in the custody of the Copyright Office at the time of the request. Where

the request is made concurrent with the initial deposit of the work for registration, the requestor must submit one copy or phonorecord more than the number specified in § 202.20 of 37 CFR for the particular work.

(3) *One deposit retained.* The Copyright Office will retain no more than one copy, phonorecord, or set of identifying material for a given registered work.

(4) *Denial of request for full term retention.* The Copyright Office reserves the right to deny the request for full term retention where: (i) The excessive size, fragility, or weight of the deposit would, in the sole discretion of the Register of Copyrights, constitute an unreasonable storage burden. The request may nevertheless be granted if, within 60 calendar days of the original denial of the request, the requestor pays the reasonable administrative costs, as fixed in the particular case by the Register of Copyrights, of preparing acceptable identifying materials for retention in lieu of the actual copyright deposit;

(ii) The Library of Congress has selected for its collections the single copyright deposit, or both, if two copies or phonorecords were deposited; or

(iii) Retention would result in a health or safety hazard, in the sole judgment of the Register of Copyrights. The request may nevertheless be granted if, within 60 calendar days of the original denial of the request, the requestor pays the reasonable administrative costs, as fixed in the particular case by the Register of Copyrights, of preparing acceptable identifying materials for retention in lieu of the actual copyright deposit.

(d) *Form of copyright deposit.* If full term retention is granted, the Copyright Office will retain under its control the particular copyright deposit used to make registration for the work. Any deposit made on or after September 19, 1978 shall satisfy the requirements of 37 CFR 202.20 and 202.21.

(e) *Fee for full term retention.* (1) Pursuant to section 708(a)(11) of Title 17 of the United States Code, the Register of Copyrights has fixed the fee for full term retention at $135.00 for each copyright deposit granted full term retention.

(2) A check or money order in the amount of $135.00 payable to the Register of Copyrights, must be received in the Copyright Office within 60 calendar days from the date of mailing of the Copyright Office's notification to the requestor that full term retention has been granted for a particular copyright deposit.

(3) The Copyright Office will issue a receipt acknowledging payment of the fee and identifying the copyright deposit for which full term retention has been granted.

(f) *Selection by Library of Congress*—(1) *General.* All published copyrighted deposits are available for selection by the Library of Congress until the Copyright Office has formally granted a request for full term retention. Unless the requestor has deposited the additional copy or phonorecord specified by paragraph (c)(2) of this section, the Copyright Office will not process a request for full term retention submitted concurrent with a copyright registration application and deposit, until the Library of Congress has had a reasonable amount of time to make its selection determination.

(2) A request for full term retention made at the time of deposit of a published work does not affect the right of the Library to select one or both of the copyright deposits.

(3) If one copyright deposit is selected, the second deposit, if any, will be used for full term retention.

(4) If both copyright deposits are selected, or, in the case where the single deposit made is selected, full term retention will be granted only if the additional copy or phonorecord specified by paragraph (c)(2) of this section was deposited.

(g) *Termination of full term storage.* Full term storage will cease 75 years after the date of publication of the work identified by the copyright deposit retained, and the copyright deposit will be disposed of in accordance with section 704, paragraph (b) through (d), of Title 17 of the United States Code.

(17 U.S.C. 408, 702, 704, and 708)
[48 FR 32777, July 19, 1983]

APPENDIX A—TECHNICAL GUIDELINES REGARDING SOUND PHYSICAL CONDITION

To be considered a copy "of sound physical condition" within the meaning of 37 CFR 202.22(d)(5), a copy shall conform to all the technical guidelines set out in this Appendix.

A. *Physical Condition.* All portions of the copy that reproduce the transmission program must be:

1. *Clean:* Free from dirt, marks, spots, fungus, or other smudges, blotches, blemishes, or distortions;

2. *Undamaged:* Free from burns, blisters, tears, cuts, scratches, breaks, erasure, or other physical damage. The copies must also be free from:

(i) Any damage that interferes with performance from the tape or other reproduction, including physical damage resulting from earlier mechanical difficulties such as cassette jamming, breaks, tangles, or tape overflow; and

(ii) Any erasures, damage causing visual or audible defects or distortions or any material remaining from incomplete erasure of previously recorded works.

3. *Unspliced:* Free from splices in any part of the copy reproducing the transmission program, regardless of whether the splice involves the addition or deletion of material or is intended to repair a break or cut.

4. *Undeteriorated:* Free from any visual or aural deterioration resulting from aging or exposure to climatic, atmospheric, or other chemical or physical conditions, including heat, cold, humidity, electromagnetic fields, or radiation. The copy shall also be free from excessive brittleness or stretching from any visible flaking of oxide from the tape base or other medium, and from other visible signs of physical deterioration or excessive wear.

B. *Physical Appurtenances of Deposit Copy.*

1. *Physical Housing of Video Tape Copy.* (a) In the case of video tape reproduced for reel-to-reel performance, the deposit copy shall consist of reels of uniform size and length. The length of the reels will depend on both the size of the tape and its running time (the last reel may be shorter). (b) In the case of video tape reproduced for cassette, cartridge, or similar performance, the tape drive mechanism shall be fully operable and free from any mechanical defects.

2. *"Leader" or Equivalent.* The copy, whether housed in reels, cassettes, or cartridges, shall have a leader segment both preceding the beginning and following the end of the recording.

C. *Visual and Aural Quality of Copy.*

1. *Visual Quality.* The copy should be equivalent to an evaluated first generation copy from an edited master tape and must reproduce a flawless and consistent electronic signal that meets industry standards for television screening.

2. *Aural Quality.* The sound channels or other portions must reproduce a flawless and consistent electronic signal without any audible defects.

(17 U.S.C. 407, 408, 702)
[48 FR 37209, Aug. 17, 1983]

## PART 203—FREEDOM OF INFORMATION ACT: POLICIES AND PROCEDURES

ORGANIZATION

AUTHORITY: Copyright Act, Pub. L. 94-553; 90 Stat. 2541-2602 (17 U.S.C. 101-710).

SOURCE: 43 FR 774, Jan. 4, 1978, unless otherwise noted.

## ORGANIZATION

### § 203.1  General.

This information is furnished for the guidance of the public and in compliance with the requirements of section 552 of Title 5, United States Code as amended.

### § 203.2  Authority and functions.

(a)  The administration of the copyright law was entrusted to the Library of Congress by an act of Congress in 1870, and the Copyright Office has been a separate department of the Library since 1897. The statutory functions of the Copyright Office are contained in and carried out in accordance with the Copyright Act, Pub. L. 94-553 (90 Stat. 2541-2602), 17 U.S.C. 101-710.

### § 203.3  Organization.

(a)  *In general.* The organization of the Copyright Office consists of the Office of the Register of Copyrights and six operating divisions. The Office of the Register of Copyrights includes the Register of Copyrights, the Associate Registers, the Assistant Register, the International Copyright Officer, the Executive Officer, and the Administrative Officer. The Register of Copyrights provides overall direction of the work of the Copyright Office. The Register is assisted by the Associate Registers of Copyright and other Officers, who have delegated responsibilities for particular aspects of the activities of the Copyright Office.

(b)  The Associate Register of Copyrights serves as a deputy to the Register of Copyrights and has oversight of the operating divisions of the Copyright Office. The operating divisions are:

(1)  The Acquisitions and Processing Division, which receives incoming materials, dispatches outgoing materials, establishes control over fiscal accounts and controls over materials acquired for the collections of the Library of Congress under the deposit requirements of the copyright statute.

(2)  The Examining Division, which examines all applications and material presented to the Copyright Office for registration of original and renewal copyright claims and for recordation of documents, and which determines whether the materials deposited constitute copyrightable subject matter and whether the other legal and formal requirements of Title 17 have been met.

(3)  The Cataloging Division, which prepares the bibliographic description of all copyrighted works registered in the Copyright Office, including the recording of le-

gal facts of copyright pertaining to each work, and creates a data base from which catalog cards and the Catalog of Copyright Entries are produced.

(4) The Information and Reference Division, which provides a national copyright information service through the public information office, educates staff and the public on the copyright law, issues and distributes information materials, responds to reference requests regarding copyright matters, prepares search reports based upon copyright records, certifies copies of legal documents concerned with copyright, and maintains liaison with the United States Customs Service, the Department of the Treasury, and the United States Postal Service on certain matters.

(5) The Licensing Division, which implements the sections of the Copyright Act dealing with secondary transmissions of radio and television programs, compulsory licenses for making and distributing phonorecords of nondramatic musical works, public performances through coin-operated phonorecord players, and use of published nondramatic musical, pictorial, graphic, and sculptural works in connection with noncommercial broadcasting.

(6) The Records Management Division, which develops, services, stores, and preserves the official records and catalogs of the Copyright Office, including applications for registration, historical records, and materials deposited for copyright registration that are not selected by the Library of Congress for addition to its collections.

(c) The Associate Register of Copyrights for Legal Affairs and Copyright General Counsel is the principal legal officer of the Office. The General Counsel has overall supervisory responsibility for the legal staff and primary responsibility for providing liaison on legal matters between the Office and the Congress, the Department of Justice and other agencies of Government, the courts, the legal community, and a wide range of interests affected by the copyright law.

(d) The Associate Register of Copyrights for Special Programs is primarily responsible for initiating, planning, developing, and implementing projects and activities covering the broad range of legal, international, and scholarly matters with which the Copyright Office deals.

(e) The Office has no field organization.

(f) The Office is located in The James Madison Memorial Building of the Library of Congress, 1st and Independence Avenue, S.E., Washington, D.C. 20559. The Public Information Office is located in Room LM-401. Its hours are 8:30 a.m. to 5 p.m., Monday through Friday except legal holidays. The phone number of the Public Information Office is (202) 287-8700. Informational material regarding the copyright law, the registration process, fees, and related information about the Copyright Office and its functions may be obtained free of charge from the Public Information Office upon request.

(g) All Copyright Office forms may be obtained free of charge from the Public Information Office.

[47 FR 36820, Aug. 24, 1982]

PROCEDURES

## § 203.4 Methods of operation.

(a) In accordance with section 552(a)(2) of the Freedom of Information Act, the Copyright Office makes available for public inspection and copying records of copyright registrations and of final refusals to register claims to copyright; statements of policy and interpretations which have been adopted but are not published in the FEDERAL REGISTER; and administrative staff manuals and instructions to the staff that affect a member of the public.

(b) The Copyright Office also maintains and makes available for public inspection and copying current indexes providing identifying information as to matters issued, adopted, or promulgated after July 4, 1967, that are within the scope of 5 U.S.C. 552(a)(2). The Copyright Office has determined that publication of these indexes is unnecessary and impractical. Copies of the indexes will be provided to any member of the public upon request at the cost of reproduction.

(c) The material and indexes referred to in paragraphs (a) and (b) of this section are available for public inspection and copying at the Public Information Office of the Copyright Office, Room LM-401, The James Madison Memorial Building of the Library of Congress, 1st and Independence Avenue, S.E., Washington, D.C., between the hours of 8:30 a.m. and 5 p.m. Monday through Friday except legal holidays.

(d) The Supervisory Copyright Information Specialist is responsible for responding to all initial requests submitted under the Freedom of Information Act. Individuals desiring to obtain access to Copyright Office information under the Act should make a written request to that effect either by mail to the Supervisory Copyright Information Specialist, Information and Publications Section, Information and Reference Division, Copyright Office, Library of Congress, Washington, D.C. 20559, or in person between the hours of 8:30 a.m. and 5 p.m. on any working day except legal holidays at Room LM-401, The James Madison Memorial Building, 1st and Independence Avenue, SE., Washington, D.C.

If a request is made by mail, both the request and the envelope carrying it should be plainly marked Freedom of Information Act Request. Failure to so mark a mailed request may delay the Office response.

(e) Records must be reasonably described. A request reasonably describes records if it enables the Office to identify the records requested by any process that is not unreasonably burdensome or disruptive of Office operations. The Supervisory Copyright Information Specialist will, upon request, aid members of the public to formulate their requests in such a manner as to enable the Office to respond effectively and reduce search costs for the requester.

(f) The Office will respond to all properly marked mailed requests and all personally delivered requests within 10 working days of receipt by the Supervisory Copyright Information Specialist. The Office response will notify the requester whether or not the request will be granted. If the request is denied, the written notification will include the basis for the denial and also include the names of all individuals who participated in the determination and a description of procedures available to appeal the determination.

(g) In the event a request is denied and that denial is appealed, the Supervisory Copyright Information Specialist will refer the appeal to the General Counsel. Appeals shall be set forth in writing and addressed to the Supervisory Copyright Information Specialist at the address listed in paragraph (d) of this section. The appeal shall include a statement explaining the basis for the appeal. Determinations of appeals will be set forth in writing and signed by the General Counsel or his or her delegate within 20 working days. If, on appeal, the denial is in whole or in part upheld, the written determination will include the basis for the appeal denial and will also contain a notification of the provisions for judicial review and the names of the persons who participated in the determination.

(h) In unusual circumstances, the General Counsel may extend the time limits prescribed in paragraphs (f) and (g) of this section for not more than 10 working days. The extension period may be split between the initial request and the appeal but the total period of extension shall not exceed 10 working days. Extensions will be by written notice to the person making the request. The Copyright Office will advise the requester of the reasons for the extension and the date the determination is expected. As used in this paragraph "unusual circumstances" means:

(1) The need to search for and collect the requested records from establishments that are physically separate from the office processing the request;

(2) The need to search for, collect, and examine a voluminous amount of separate and district records which are demanded in a single request; or

(3) The need for consultation, which shall be conducted with all practical speed, with another agency having a substantial interest in the determination of the re-

quest or among two or more components of the Copyright Office which have a substantial subject matter interest therein.

[43 FR 774, Jan. 4, 1978, as amended at 47 FR 36820, Aug. 24, 1982]

AVAILABILITY OF INFORMATION

## § 203.5 Inspection and copying.

(a) When a request for information has been approved, the person making the request may make an appointment to inspect or copy the materials requested during regular business hours by writing or telephoning the Supervisory Copyright Information Specialist at the address or telephone number listed in § 203.4(d). Such material may be copied manually without charge, and reasonable facilities are available in the Public Information Office for that purpose. Also, copies of individual pages of such materials will be made available at the price per page specified in paragraphs (a) and (b) of § 203.6.

CHARGES FOR SEARCH FOR REPRODUCTION

## § 203.6 Schedule of fees and method of payment for services rendered.

(a) Fees shall be charged according to the schedule in paragraph (b) of this section for services rendered in responding to requests for Copyright Office records under this section. The Copyright Office will furnish the documents without charge or at a reduced charge where the Office determines that waiver or reduction of the fee is in the public interest because furnishing the information can be considered as primarily benefiting the general public or where the requester claims indigency. When the request is for a copy of a record for which a specific fee is required under section 708 of Pub. L. 94-553, that fee shall be charged. Copies of Copyright Office publications are offered for sale to the public at prices based on the cost of reproduction and distribution, as required under section 707 of Pub. L. 94-553.

(b) The following charges will be assessed for the services listed:

(1) For copies of certificates of copyright registration, $4,

(2) For copies of all other Copyright Office records not otherwise provided for in this section $.45 per page for 24 pages or less, and $.40 per page for 25 pages or more, with a minimum fee of $6.00.

(3) For each hour or fraction of an hour spent in searching for a requested record, $10,

(4) For certification of each document, $4,

(5) Other costs incurred by the Copyright Office in fulfilling a request will be chargeable at the actual cost to the Office.

(c) No charge will be made for time spent in resolving legal or policy issues affecting access to Office records. No charge will be made for the time involved in examining records to determine whether some or all such records may or will be withheld. Normally, no charge will be made if the records requested are not found. However, if the time expended in processing the request is substantial, and if the requester has been notified in advance that the Copyright Office cannot determine if the requested record exists or can be located fees may be charged.

(d) Where it is anticipated that the fees chargeable under this section will amount to more than $50.00, and the requester has not indicated in advance willingness to pay fees as high as are anticipated, the Copyright Office shall furnish the requester an estimate of the anticipated fee. In such cases, a request will not be deemed to have been received until the requester is notified of the anticipated fee and agrees to bear it. Such a notification will be transmitted as soon as possible, but in any event, within five working days after the receipt of the initial request. The Supervisory Copyright Information Specialist will, when appropriate, consult with the requester in an effort to formulate the request so as to reduce the total fees chargeable.

(e) Payment should be made by check or money order payable to the Register of Copyrights.

[43 FR 774, Jan. 4, 1978, as amended at 47 FR 36820, Aug. 24, 1982]

## PART 204—PRIVACY ACT, POLICIES AND PROCEDURES

AUTHORITY: Copyright Act, Pub. L. 94-553; 90 Stat. 2541-2602 (17 U.S.C. 101-710).

SOURCE: 43 FR 776, Jan. 4, 1978, unless otherwise noted.

### § 204.1  Purposes and scope.

The purposes of these regulations are:

(a) The establishment of procedures by which an individual can determine if the Copyright Office maintains a system of records in which there is a record pertaining to the individual; and

(b) The establishment of procedures by which an individual may gain access to a record or information maintained on that individual and have such record or information disclosed for the purpose of review, copying, correction, or amendment.

### § 204.2  Definitions.

For purposes of this part:

(a) The term "individual" means a citizen of the United States or an alien lawfully admitted for permanent residence;

(b) The term "maintain" includes maintain, collect, use, or disseminate;

(c) The term "record" means any item, collection, or grouping of information about an individual that is maintained by an agency, including, but not limited to, his education, financial transactions, medical history, and criminal or employment history, and that contains his or her name, or the identifying number, symbol, or other identifying particular assigned to the individual, such as a finger or voice print or a photograph;

(d) The term "system of records" means a group of any records under the control of any agency from which information is retrieved by the name of the individual; and

(e) The term "routine use" means, with respect to the disclosure of a record the use of such record for a purpose which is compatible with the purpose for which it was collected.

## § 204.3 General policy.

The Copyright Office serves primarily as an office of public record. Section 705 of Title 17, United States Code, requires the Copyright Office to open for public inspection all records of copyright deposits, registrations, recordations, and other actions taken under Title 17. Therefore, a routine use of all Copyright Office systems of records created under section 705 of Title 17 is disclosure to the public. All Copyright Office systems of records created under section 705 of Title 17 are also available for public copying as required by section 706(a), with the exception of copyright deposits, whose reproduction is governed by section 706(b) and the regulations issued under that section. In addition to the records mandated by section 705 of Title 17, the Copyright Office maintains other systems of records which are necessary for the Office effectively to carry out its mission. These systems of records are routinely consulted and otherwise used by Copyright Office employees in the performance of their duties. The Copyright Office will not sell, rent, or otherwise make publicly available any mailing list prepared by the Office.

[47 FR 36821, Aug. 24, 1982]

## § 204.4 Procedure for notification of the existence of records pertaining to individuals.

(a) The Copyright Office will publish annually in the FEDERAL REGISTER notices of all Copyright Office systems of records subject to the Privacy Act. Individuals desiring to know if a Copyright Office system of records contains a record pertaining to them should submit a written request to that effect either by mail to the Supervisory Copyright Information Specialist, Information and Publications Section, Information and Reference Division, Copyright Office, Library of Congress, Washington, D.C., 20559, or in person between the hours of 8:30 a.m. and 5 p.m. on any working day except legal holidays at Room LM-401, The James Madison Memorial Building, 1st and Independence Avenue, S.E., Washington, D.C.

(b) The written request should identify clearly the system of records which is the subject of inquiry, by reference, whenever possible, to the system number and title as given in the notices of systems of records in the FEDERAL REGISTER. Both the written request and the envelope carrying it should be plainly marked "Privacy Act Request." Failure to so mark the request may delay the Office response.

(c) The Office will acknowledge all properly marked requests within ten working days of receipt and will notify the requester within 30 working days of receipt of the existence or non-existence of records pertaining to the requester.

(d) Since all Copyright Office Records created under section 705 of Title 17 are open to public inspection, no identity verification is necessary for individuals who wish to know whether a system of records created under section 705 pertains to them.

[43 FR 776, Jan. 4, 1978, as amended at 47 FR 36821, Aug. 24, 1982]

## § 204.5 Procedures for requesting access to records.

(a) Individuals desiring to obtain access to Copyright Office information pertaining to them in a system of records other than those created under section 705 of Title 17 should make a written request, signed by themselves or their duly authorized agent, to that effect either by mail to the Supervisory Copyright Information Specialist, Information and Publications Section, Information and Reference Division, Copyright Office, Library of Congress, Washington, D.C. 20559, or in person between the hours of 8:30 a.m. and 5 p.m. on any working day except legal holidays at Room LM-401, The James Madison Memorial Building, 1st and Independence Avenue, S.E., Washington, D.C.

(b) The written request should identify clearly the system of records which is the subject of inquiry, by reference, whenever possible, to the system number and title as given in the notices of systems of records in the FEDERAL REGISTER. Both the written request and the envelope carrying it should be plainly marked "Privacy Act Request." Failure to so mark the request may delay the Office response.

(c) The Office will acknowledge all properly marked requests within ten working days of receipt; and will notify the requester within 30 working days of receipt when and where access to the record will be granted. If the individual requested a copy of the record, the copy will accompany such notification.

[43 FR 776, Jan. 4, 1978, as amended at 47 FR 36821, Aug. 24, 1982]

## § 204.6 Fees.

(a) The Copyright Office will provide, free of charge, one copy to an individual of any record pertaining to that individual contained in a Copyright Office system of records, except where the request is for a copy of a record for which a specific fee is required under section 708 of Title 17 of the United States Code, in which case that fee shall be charged. For additional copies of records not covered by section 708 the fee will be computed at the rate of $.45 per page for 24 pages or less, and $.40 per page for 25 pages or more with a minimum fee of $6.00. The Office will require prepayment of fees estimated to exceed $25.00 and will remit any excess paid or bill an additional amount according to the differences between the final fee charged and the amount prepaid. When prepayment is required, a request is not deemed "received" until prepayment has been made.

(b) The Copyright Office may waive the fee requirement whenever it determines that such waiver would be in the public interest.

[43 FR 776, Jan. 4, 1978, as amended at 47 FR 36821, Aug. 24, 1872]

## § 204.7 Request for correction or amendment of records.

(a) Any individual may request the correction or amendment of a record pertaining to her or him. With respect to an error in a copyright registration the procedure for correction and fee chargeable is governed by section 408(d) of Title 17 of the United States Code, and the regulations issued as authorized by that section. With respect to an error in any other record, the request shall be in writing and delivered either by mail addressed to the Supervisory Copyright Information Specialist, Information and Publications Section, Information and Reference Division, Copyright Office, Library of Congress, Washington, D.C. 20559, or in person between the hours of 8:30 a.m. and 5 p.m. on any working day except legal holidays, at Room LM-401, The James Madison Memorial Building, 1st and Independence Avenue, S.E., Washington, D.C. The request shall explain why the individual believes the record to be incomplete, inaccurate, irrelevant, or untimely.

(b) With respect to an error in a copyright registration, the time limit for Office response to requests for correction is governed by section 408(d) of Pub. L. 94-553, and the regulations issued as authorized by that section. With respect to other requests for correction or amendment of records, the Office will respond within 10 working days indicating to the requester that the requested correction or amendment has been made or that it has been refused. If the requested correction or amendment is refused, the Office response will indicate the reason for the refusal and the procedure available to the individual to appeal the refusal.

[43 FR 776, Jan. 4, 1978, as amended at 47 FR 36821, Aug. 24, 1982]

## § 204.8 Appeal of refusal to correct or amend an individual's record.

(a) An individual has 90 calendar days from receipt of the Copyright Office's response to appeal the refusal to correct or amend a record pertaining to the individual. The individual should submit a written appeal to the Register of Copyright, Copyright Office, Library of Congress, Washington, D.C. 20559 for the final administrative determination. Appeals, and the envelopes carrying them, should be plainly marked "Privacy Act Appeal." Failure to so mark the appeal may delay the Register's response. An appeal should contain a copy of the request for amendment or correction and a copy of the record alleged to be untimely, inaccurate, incomplete or irrelevant.

(b) The Register will issue a written decision granting or denying the appeal within 30 working days after receipt of the appeal unless, after showing good cause, the Register extends the 30 day period. If the appeal is granted, the requested amendment or correction will be made promptly. If the appeal is denied, in whole or part, the Register's decision will set forth reasons for the denial. Additionally, the decision will advise the requester that he or she has the right to file with the Copyright Office a concise statement of his or her reasons for disagreeing with the refusal to amend the record and that such statement will be attached to the requester's record and included in any future disclosure of such record.

## § 204.9 Judicial review.

Within two years of the receipt of a final adverse administrative determination, an individual may seek judicial review of that determination as provided in 5 U.S.C. 552a(g)(1).

## PARTS 205–210—RESERVED

# Appendix D

# Copyright Royalty Tribunal Regulations

## PART 301—COPYRIGHT ROYALTY TRIBUNAL RULES OF PROCEDURE

### Subpart A—Organization

### Subpart B—Public Access to Tribunal Meetings

### Subpart C—Public Access to and Inspection of Records

### Subpart D—Equal Employment Opportunity

AUTHORITY: 17 U.S.C. 803(a).

SOURCE: 43 FR 53719, Nov. 17, 1978, unless otherwise noted.

## Subpart A—Organization

## § 301.1 Purpose.

The Copyright Royalty Tribunal (Tribunal) is an independent agency in the Legislative Branch, created by Pub. L. 94-553 of October 19, 1976.

The Tribunal's statutory responsibilities are:

(a) To make determinations concerning copyright royalty rates in the areas of cable television covered by 17 U.S.C. 111.

(b) To make determinations concerning copyright royalty rates for phono-records (17 U.S.C. 115) and for coin-operated phonorecord players (jukeboxes) (17 U.S.C. 116).

(c) To establish and later make determinations concerning royalty rates and terms for non-commercial broadcasting (17 U.S.C. 118).

(d) To distribute cable television and jukebox royalties under 17 U.S.C. 111 and 17 U.S.C. 116 deposited with the Register of Copyrights.

## § 301.2  Address for information.

The official address of the Copyright Royalty Tribunal is 1111 20th Street NW, Suite 450, Washington, DC 20036. Office hours are Monday through Friday, 9:00 a.m. to 5:00 p.m., excluding legal holidays.

[49 FR 49092, Dec. 18, 1984]

## § 301.3  Composition of the Tribunal.

The Tribunal is composed of five members appointed by the President with the advice and consent of the Senate.

## § 301.4  The Chairman.

(a) On December 1st of each year the Chairman will be designated for a term of 1 year from the most senior Commissioner who has not yet previously served as Chairman, or, if all the Commissioners have served, the most senior Commissioner who has served the least number of terms will be designated Chairman.

(b) The responsibilities of the Chairman are, first, to preside at meetings and hearings of the Tribunal, and second, to represent the Tribunal officially in all external matters. In matters of legislation and legislative reports, the Chairman will represent the majority opinion of the Tribunal; however, any Commissioner with a minority or supplemental opinion may have that opinion represented also. The Chairman is the initial authority for all communications with other government officials or agencies and is the contracting officer; however, another Commissioner or subordinate official may be designated to act in his stead. The Chairman shall convene a meeting of the Tribunal upon the request of a majority of the Commissioners.

## § 301.5  Standing committee.

The Tribunal may establish standing or temporary committees to act in whatever capacity the Tribunal feels is appropriate. Said committees are authorized, in the areas of their jurisdiction, to conduct hearings, meetings, and other proceedings, but no such subdivision shall be authorized to act on behalf of the agency as a whole within the official meeting of 5 U.S.C. 552(a)(1).

## § 301.6  Administration of the Tribunal.

The administration of the Tribunal denotes chiefly the maintenance of the Tribunal records and the custodianship of Tribunal property. The records to be maintained include legal and public records, a current index of opinions, orders, policy statements, procedures, and rules of practice, and instructions that affect the public. Also, announcements of Tribunal actions must be published in the FEDERAL REGISTER as required, and the observance by the Tribunal of appropriate administrative procedure must be supervised, as well as the disposition of Tribunal correspondence. From time to time other administrative responsibilities may emerge. To manage the above, the Tribunal may choose to install an Administrative Officer; however, if not, it will be the Chairman's duty to see that these responsibilities are met.

### § 301.7 Proceedings.

(a) *Location*. The Tribunal will normally hold all proceedings at its principal office, except under exceptional circumstances, in which case the Tribunal may perform its duties anywhere in the United States. The Tribunal's proceedings will all be public, except as exempted in § 301.15.

(b) *Quorum*. A majority of the members of the Tribunal constitutes a quorum.

(c) *Voting*. Each Commissioner's vote shall be recorded separately, and the votes of the Commissioners shall be taken in order of their seniority, except that the Chairman shall vote last. No proxy votes will be recorded.

### Subpart B—Public Access to Tribunal Meetings

### § 301.11 Open meetings.

(a) The purpose of this chapter is to comply with the Government in the Sunshine Act, Pub. L. 94-409; 90 Stat. 1241 *et seq.*, 5 U.S.C. 522(b), and insure that all Tribunal meetings shall be open to the public. The conditions under which meetings, as an exception, may be closed, are listed in § 301.13.

(b) Each meeting announcement by the Tribunal shall be made at least 7 calendar days in advance in the FEDERAL REGISTER and shall state the time and place of the meeting, the subject to be discussed, whether the meeting is to be open or closed, and the name and telephone number of the person to contact for further information.

(c) If amendments are made to the original announcement, they must be placed in the FEDERAL REGISTER as soon as practicable. Changes in time and place may be made simply by making such an announcement, but a change in subject matter requires a recorded vote by Commissioners, with the results of that vote appearing in the announcement of the amendment.

(d) If it is decided that a meeting must be held on shorter notice than 7 days, that decision must be made by recorded vote of Commissioners and included in the announcement.

### § 301.12 Conduct of open meetings.

(a) Meetings of the Tribunal will be conducted in a manner to insure both the public's right to observe and the ability of the Tribunal to conduct its business properly. The Chairman or presiding officer will take whatever measures he feels necessary to achieve this.

(b) The right of the public to be present does not include the right to participate or make comments.

(c) Reasonable access for news media will be provided at all public sessions provided that it does not interfere with the comfort of Commissioners, staff, or witnesses. Cameras will be admitted only on the authorization of the Chairman, and no witness may be photographed or have his testimony recorded for broadcast if he objects.

## § 301.13  Closed meetings.

In the following circumstances (as per 5 U.S.C. 552(c), 1–10) the Tribunal may close its meetings or withhold information from the public.

(a) If the matter to be discussed has been specifically authorized to be kept secret by Executive order, in the interests of national defense or foreign policy;

(b) If the matter relates solely to the internal personnel rules and practices of the Tribunal;

(c) If the matter has been specifically exempted from disclosure by statute (other than 5 U.S.C. 552) and there is no discretion on the issue;

(d) If the matter involves privileged or confidential trade secrets or financial information;

(e) If the result might be to accuse any person of a crime or formally censure him;

(f) If there would be a clearly unwarranted invasion of personal privacy;

(g) If there would be disclosure of investigatory records compiled for law enforcement, or information which if written would be contained in such records, and to the extent disclosure would (1) interfere with enforcement proceedings, (2) deprive a person of the right to a fair trial or impartial adjudication, (3) constitute an unwarranted invasion of personal privacy, (4) disclose the identity of a confidential source or, in the case of a criminal investigation or a national security intelligence investigation, confidential information furnished only by a confidential source, (5) disclose investigative techniques and procedures, or (6) endanger the life or safety of law enforcement personnel.

(h) If premature disclosure of the information would frustrate the Tribunal's action, unless the Tribunal has already disclosed the concept or nature of the proposed action, or is required by law to make disclosure before taking final action.

(i) If the matter concerns the Tribunal's participation in a civil action or proceeding or in an action in a foreign court or international tribunal, or an arbitration, or a particular case of formal agency adjudication pursuant to 5 U.S.C. 554, or otherwise involving a determination on the record after opportunity for a hearing.

## § 301.14  Procedure for closing meetings.

(a) Meetings may be closed, or information withheld from the public, only by a recorded vote of a majority of the Commissioners. Each question, either to close a meeting or withhold information, must be voted on separately, unless a series of meetings is involved, in which case the Tribunal may vote to keep the discussions closed for 30 days, starting from the first meetings. If the Tribunal feels that information about a closed meeting must be withheld, the decision to do so must also be the subject of a recorded vote.

(b) Before a discussion to close a meeting or withhold information, the Chairman must certify that, in his opinion, such a step is permissible, and he shall cite the appropriate exemption under § 301.13. This certification shall be included in the announcement of the meeting and be maintained as part of the Tribunal's records.

(c) Following such a vote, and by the end of the working day, the Chairman must transmit the following information to the FEDERAL REGISTER for publication:

(1) The vote of each Commissioner;

(2) The appropriate exemption under § 301.13;

(3) A list of all persons expected to attend the meeting and their affiliation.

## § 301.15  Transcripts of closed meetings.

(a) All meetings closed to the public shall be subject to either a complete transcript or, in the case of § 301.13(i) and at the Tribunal's discretion, detailed minutes. Detailed minutes shall describe all matters discussed, identify all documents considered, summarize action taken as well as the reasons for it, and record all rollcall votes as well as any views expressed.

(b) Such transcripts or minutes shall be kept by the Tribunal for 2 years or 1 year after the conclusion of the proceedings, whichever is later. Any portion of transcripts of meetings which the Chairman does not feel is exempt from disclosure under § 301.13 will ordinarily be available to the public within 20 working days of the meeting. Transcripts or minutes of closed meetings will be reviewed by the Chairman at the end of each calendar year and if he feels they may at that time be disclosed, he will resubmit the question to the Tribunal to gain authorization for their disclosure.

## § 301.16  Requests to open or close meetings.

(a) Any person may request the Tribunal to open or close a meeting or disclose or withhold information. Such a request must be captioned "Request to Open" or "Close" a meeting on a specific date concerning a specific subject. The requester must state his or her reasons and include name and address, and desirably, telephone number.

(b) In the case of a request to open a meeting the Tribunal has previously voted closed, the Tribunal must receive the request within 3 working days of the meeting's announcement. If not, it will not be heeded and the requester will be so notified. Requests are desired in seven copies.

(c) For the Tribunal to act on a request to open or close a meeting, the question must be brought to a vote before the Tribunal by one of the Commissioners. If the request is granted, an amended meeting announcement will be issued immediately and the requester notified. If a vote is not taken, or if after a vote the request is denied, the requester will also be notified promptly.

## § 301.17  Ex parte communication.

(a) No person not employed by the Tribunal and no employee of the Tribunal who performs any investigative function in connection with a Tribunal proceeding shall communicate, directly or indirectly, with any member of the Tribunal or with any employee involved in the decisions of the proceeding, with respect to the merits of any proceeding before the Tribunal or of a factually related proceeding.

(b) No member of the Tribunal and no employee involved in the decision of a proceeding shall communicate, directly or indirectly, with any person not employed by the Tribunal or with any employee of the Tribunal who performs an investigative function in connection with the proceeding, with respect to the merit of any proceeding before the Tribunal or of a factually related proceeding.

(c) If an *ex parte* communication is made to or by any member of the Tribunal or employee involved in the decision of the proceeding, in violation of paragraph (a) or (b) of this section, such member or employee shall promptly inform the Tribunal of the substance of such communication and of the circumstance surrounding it. The Tribunal shall then take such action it considers appropriate; provided that any written *ex parte* communication and a summary of any oral *ex parte* communication shall be made part of the public records of the Tribunal, but shall not be considered part of the record for the purposes of decision unless introduced into evidence by one of the parties.

(d) A request for information with respect to the status of proceeding shall not be considered an *ex parte* communication prohibited by this section.

## Subpart C—Public Access To and Inspection of Records

The following is the manner in which Tribunal opinions, recommended decisions, public reports and records shall be made available to the public.

## § 301.21  Public records.

(a) Final official determinations of the Tribunal will be published in the FEDERAL REGISTER and include the relevant facts and the reasons for those determinations.

(b) An annual report, required of the Tribunal to be presented to the President and Congress each fiscal year, along with a detailed fiscal statement of account, will be available both for inspection at the Tribunal and for purchase from the Superintendent of Documents, U.S. Government Printing Office, Washington, DC 20402.

(c) All other Tribunal records are available, for inspection or copying at the Tribunal, except:

(1) Records that relate solely to the internal personnel rules and practices of the Tribunal;

(2) Records exempted by statute from disclosure;

(3) Interoffice memoranda or correspondence not available by law except to a party in litigation with the Tribunal;

(4) Personnel, medical, or similar files whose disclosure would be an invasion of personal privacy;

(5) Communications among Commissioners concerning the drafting of decisions, opinions, reports, and findings on any Tribunal matter or proceeding;

(6) Offers of settlement which have not been accepted unless they have been made public by the offerer;

(7) Records not herein listed but which may be withheld as "exempted" if the Tribunal finds compelling reasons exist.

## § 301.22  Public access.

(a) Information may be required from the Tribunal in person, by telephone, or by mail.

(b) If the material sought is not a Tribunal record, is exempted, or for some reason is unavailable, the person requesting it will be so informed and in the case of an "exempted record," will be explained the reason for the exemption and the procedure for appeal under the Freedom of Information Act, § 301.13.

(c) Fees for copies of Tribunal records are: $.15 per page; $10 for each hour or fraction thereof spent searching for records; $4 for certification of each document; and the actual cost to the Tribunal for any other costs incurred.

[43 FR 53719, Nov. 11, 1978, as amended at 44 FR 53161, Sept. 13, 1979]

## § 301.23  Freedom of Information Act.

(a) If a request is made under the Freedom of Information Act (5 U.S.C. 552), it must be in writing, be captioned "Freedom of Information Act Request," and identify as accurately as possible, the information desired.

(c) Within 10 working days after the Tribunal has received such a request the Chairman shall inform the requester how the records may be inspected or copied and the cost (as under § 301.22) of copying. The Chairman may, however, extend this time limit up to 10 working days if:

(1) Records must be located or transferred;

(2) Voluminous material must be examined;

(3) Other agencies with substantial interest in the matter must be consulted or other elements of the Tribunal must be consulted.

In this case the requester shall be notified in accordance with 5 U.S.C. 552(a)(6)(B).

(c) If the request is denied, the Chairman shall so inform the requester in writing, citing the exemption authorizing the denial and informing the requester that he or she may appeal the denial to the Tribunal within 20 working days. Appeals must be in writing and must be acted on by the Tribunal within 20 working days of their receipt. If the appeal is rejected, the requester must be so notified immediately and informed of the provisions for judicial review under 5 U.S.C. 552(a)(4).

## § 301.24 Privacy Act.

(a) The Privacy Act of 1974 (Pub. L. 93-579) 5 U.S.C. 552(a), concerns only requests which contain personal information retrievable by a person identified. This section does not apply to personnel records located in Government-wide systems elsewhere.

The purpose of the Privacy Act is to enable individuals to:
(1) Learn if the Tribunal maintains records concerning them;
(2) Have access to such records;
(3) Learn if and to whom the Tribunal has disclosed such records; and
(4) Amend such records.

The Tribunal, in compliance with paragraph (a)(4) of this section, will record the disclosures of all records, their dates, the material disclosed, and to whom the material has been disclosed.

(b) A request made under the Privacy Act must be in writing, captioned "Privacy Act Request," and identify as accurately as possible the records in question and the nature of the information desired. This section is not to be construed as allowing an individual access to information compiled in reasonable anticipation of a civil action or proceeding.

(c) The request must be signed by the person making it, and such signature will be considered certification that the person signing is either the individual involved or that person's guardian. If the Chairman considers it necessary, he may require additional verification. Section 552(a)(i)(3) of the Privacy Act; 5 U.S.C. 552(a)(i)(3), states the penalties for false representation.

(d) If a medical record is involved and the Chairman feels that its disclosure might adversely affect the individual, he shall require that person to designate a medical doctor to whom the record will be transmitted.

(e) Within 10 working days after the Tribunal has received such a request, the Chairman shall acknowledge its receipt to the requester and within 30 days shall inform the requester how the records may be inspected and the cost for copying, unless the records are exempted under § 301.21(c).

(f) If an individual who has obtained access to personal records wishes to have those records amended, he or she must make such a request in writing, state the nature of the information desired amended, and cite the reasons. Within 10 working days after the Tribunal has received such a request, the Chairman shall acknowledge its receipt and inform the requester whether or not the request has been granted. If the request is denied, the Chairman shall explain why and inform the requester of the right to appeal the denial to the Tribunal. All appeals must be in writing, with the caption "Privacy Act Appeal," and the Chairman will inform the requester of their disposition within 30 working days, unless there is good cause for the time to be extended. If the appeal is denied the requester will be notified of the provision for judicial review under 5 U.S.C. 552(b).

(g) Exempt from this section is all investigatory material compiled for law enforcement purposes as stipulated in 5 U.S.C. 552(k)(2).

## Subpart D—Equal Employment Opportunity

## § 301.31 Purpose.

(a) This section sets forth the Tribunal's policy concerning Equal Employment Opportunity and the complaint procedures in the case of discrimination.

(b) The policy of the Tribunal is to oppose discrimination in all areas of job application, employment, and promotion on the basis of race, religion, sex, national origin, age, or physical handicap; this is because such a policy is right and any other would be morally indefensible. This policy will be pursued actively and affirmatively.

### § 301.32  Recruitment and hiring.

(a) Except in the case of the personal staffs of Commissioners, responsibility for equal employment opportunity is the Tribunal's as a whole; however, the authority to execute this policy may be delegated to a Personnel Committee.

(b) All hiring will be done on the basis of individual qualifications, without discrimination. The criteria of who is best qualified to fill a vacancy rests with the Tribunal, but there will be no criteria which discriminates in the areas covered by § 301.31(b).

(c) In soliciting job applicants, systematic efforts will be made to locate and encourage qualified minority and women candidates. Where appropriate, the positions will be advertised in publications with primarily minority and women readership and announced through organizations or groups with high minority and women representation.

(d) Applicants for the same position will be required to have the same skills and to provide the same background information. The total number of applicants considered must reflect the proportion of minorities and women reasonably available for such a position. The criteria by which applicants are screened and selected shall be job related.

### § 301.33  Complaint procedures.

(a) Any person who believes that he or she has been discriminated against on the basis of race, religion, sex, national origin, age, or physical handicap, must first resolve such a complaint through the following procedure before taking civil action. Before a complaint may be presented formally the procedures for resolving it informally must be exhausted.

(1) *Informal complaint procedures.* (i) Within 30 days of an alleged discriminatory act, or in the case of a personnel action, within 30 days of its effective date, the complainant must contact the Chairman of the Personnel Committee and explain the case for the complaint. In case the complaint is against the Chairman of the Personnel Committee, it will be made to the Chairman of the Tribunal. The complainant may be accompanied or represented by any person of his or her choosing.

(ii) The Chairman of the Personnel Committee, or the Chairman of the Tribunal, or a Commissioner designated by the Chairman, shall then make whatever inquiry seems necessary into the circumstances surrounding the complaint and shall attempt to resolve it informally through counseling. Such counseling shall be completed within twenty-one (21) days of the date on which the complaint was first brought, and written record will be kept. If an informal resolution is reached, its terms will be in writing. The identity of the complainant at this stage, however, will at no time be revealed unless he or she specifically authorizes it.

(iii) If an informal resolution is not reached, the complainant will be advised that he or she may then file a formal complaint.

(2) *Formal complaint procedure.* (i) Within 15 days of the final counseling session under the informal procedure above, and if no resolution has been reached, the complainant may file a formal written complaint addressed to the Chairman of the Tribunal, signed by the complainant, and specifying all the details surrounding the complaint.

(ii) On receipt of the complaint, the Chairman shall request an investigation by the Chairman of the Personnel Committee and two Commissioners not on the Committee. This investigation will review thoroughly all the circumstances surrounding the alleged discrimination and analyze the treatment of the complainant as compared with others in the same situation. The results shall be in writing and a copy sent to the complainant. The complainant shall then be given the opportunity to meet with the Commissioners who prepared this report to try to reach an adjustment of the complaint. The complainant may be accompanied or represented by a person of his or her own choosing. If the complainant is an employee of the Tribunal, he or she shall be allowed sufficient official time to present the complaint. If the complainant has designated another Tribunal employee to advise or represent him, that person shall be allowed sufficient official time to perform the appropriate duties.

(iii) If an adjustment is reached at this point, it must be signed by the complainant and shall serve to terminate the matter. If an adjustment is not reached, the investigative report will be transmitted to the Chairman of the Tribunal, and the Tribunal shall make a disposition of the complaint to take affect within 15 days. This disposition will be relayed to the complainant in writing immediately. The complainant shall also be advised of his or her right to file a civil action, or in the case of an employee of the Tribunal to demand a hearing.

(iv) Within 15 days of the announcement of the Tribunal's proposed disposition, a complainant who is an employee of the Tribunal may request a hearing. Upon receipt of such a request, the Chairman shall request from another Federal agency, a qualified Hearing Examiner who has been certified to hear Equal Employment Opportunity complaints.

(v) The Hearing Examiner, within 21 days, shall conduct a hearing. Witnesses will be allowed to testify, but their testimony must relate only to the complaint; information will be admitted into evidence, but only information having a direct bearing on the complaint. Both parties to the complaint shall have the opportunity to cross-examine. The hearing shall be recorded, and the transcript as well as the findings and recommendations of the Hearing Examiner shall be transmitted to the Tribunal for a final decision.

(vi) The Tribunal will give special consideration to the recommendations of the Hearing Examiner, and if he wishes to reject or modify those recommendations, the Tribunal must accompany such a decision with a letter detailing his reasons. The Tribunal's final decision will be accompanied by a copy of the Hearing Examiner's findings and recommendations and a transcript of the hearing.

(vii) After the decision has been issued, the complainant shall be advised immediately that he or she has the right to file a civil action in the appropriate District Court within 30 days.

(viii) If within one hundred eighty (180) days from the date the complainant first brought the complaint, the Tribunal has failed to issue a decision, the complainant will also have the right to file a civil action.

(ix) Where discrimination is found, the Tribunal shall review the matter which gave rise to the complaint and determine whether or not disciplinary action is necessary. The basis for this action shall be in writing, but not included in the complaint file.

## § 301.34 Third party allegation of discrimination.

Organizations or third parties may bring allegations of discrimination against the Tribunal in areas unrelated to individual complaints, but such allegations must be in writing, and in sufficient detail for the Tribunal to investigate them. The Tribunal may order an investigation, and the party bringing the allegations will be informed of its results as well as of any decision by the Tribunal and corrective action.

## § 301.35 Business relations.

Business contracts entered into by the Tribunal shall stipulate that all contractors, subcontractors, and suppliers to the Tribunal conform in their own policies with the substance of the Tribunal's Equal Employment Opportunity Policy.

## Subpart E—Procedures and Regulations

### § 301.40  Scope.

All Tribunal proceedings will be governed by the procedures of this subpart. This subpart does not apply to general statements of policy or to rules of agency organization, procedure, or practice.

### § 301.41  Formal hearings.

(a) The formal hearings which will be conducted pursuant to the rules of this subpart are rate adjustment proceedings, royalty fee distribution proceedings, and all rulemaking proceedings in which it has been determined to conduct a hearing. The Tribunal may also, on its own motion or on the petition of an interested party, hold other proceedings it deems necessary on any matter it has the authority to investigate, in order to obtain information in determining its policies, in exercising its duties, or in formulating or amending its rules and regulations. Such proceedings also will be subject to the rules of this subpart.

(b) Studies or conferences the Tribunal may hold in carrying out its statutory responsibilities may be conducted in whole or in part under the provisions of this subpart, depending upon the discretion of the Tribunal.

### § 301.42  Suspension, amendment, or waiver of rules.

(a) The provisions of this subpart may be suspended, revoked, amended, or waived, in whole or in part, at any time by the Tribunal for good cause shown, subject to the provisions of the Administrative Procedure Act. Where procedures have not been specifically prescribed in this subpart, the Tribunal shall follow those which in its opinion will best serve the purposes of a proceeding.

### § 301.43  Notice of proposed rulemaking.

(a) *General notice.* Public notice for rate adjustment and royalty distribution proceedings is covered in Subparts F and G of this part. Before the adoption of any rule of general applicability, or the commencement of any hearing on any proposed rulemaking the Tribunal shall publish a general notice in the FEDERAL REGISTER, such notice to be published not less than 30 days prior to the date on which the proposed rules may be considered by the Tribunal, or the date of any hearing on such proposed rules. However, where the Tribunal, for good cause, finds it impracticable, unnecessary, or contrary to the public interest to give such notice, it may adopt the rules without notice by incorporating a finding to such effect and a concise statement of the reasons therefor in the notice.

(b) *Notice.* A rule proceeding shall commence with a notice of proposed rulemaking. Such notice shall be published in the FEDERAL REGISTER, and to the extent practicable, otherwise made available to interested persons. The notice shall include: (1) The terms or substance of the proposed rule or a description of the subjects and issues involved; (2) reference to the legal authority under which the rule is proposed; (3) a statement describing the particular reason for the rule; and (4) an invitation to all interested persons to comment.

(c) *Hearing notice.* A hearing notice of proposed rulemaking shall be published in the FEDERAL REGISTER, and to the extent practicable, otherwise made available to interested persons. The hearing notice shall include: (1) Designated issues which are to be considered; (2) the time and place of hearing, and (3) instructions to interested persons seeking to make oral presentation.

## § 301.44  Conduct of proceedings.

(a)  At the opening of the proceeding the Chairman shall announce the subject under consideration.

(b)  Only Commissioners of the Tribunal, authorized Tribunal staff, or counsel as provided in this chapter shall question witnesses.

(c)  Subject to the approval of the Tribunal, the Chairman will have the responsibility for:

(1)  Setting the order of presentation of evidence and appearance of witnesses;

(2)  Ruling on objections and motions;

(3)  Administering oaths and affirmations to all witnesses;

(4)  Making all rulings with respect to introducing or excluding documentary or other evidence;

(5)  Regulating the course of the proceedings and the decorum of the parties and their counsel, and insuring that the procedures are fair and impartial;

(6)  Announcing the schedule of subsequent hearing;

(7)  Taking any other action which is consistent with this chapter and which has been authorized by the Tribunal.

(d)  With all due regard for the convenience of witnesses, proceedings shall be conducted as expeditiously as possible.

(e)  Following the opening statement, the Tribunal may convene first in executive session if such is the requirement of a statute or rule.

## § 301.45  Declaratory rulings.

In accordance with 5 U.S.C. 554(e) the Tribunal may on motion of its own, or on motion of an interested party, issue a declaratory ruling in order to terminate a controversy or remove uncertainty.

## § 301.46  Testimony under oath or affirmation.

All witnesses at Tribunal proceedings shall be required to take an oath or affirmation before testifying; however, attorneys who do not appear as witnesses shall not be required to do so.

## § 301.47  Transcript and record.

(a)  An official reporter for the recording and transcribing of hearings will be designated by the Tribunal from time to time. Anyone wishing to inspect the transcript of any hearing may do so at the Tribunal; however, anyone wishing a copy must purchase it from the official reporter.

(b)  After the close of the hearing, the complete transcript of testimony together with all exhibits shall be certified as to identity by the Chairman and filed in the offices of the Tribunal.

(c)  The transcript of testimony and all exhibits, papers, and requests filed in the proceedings, shall constitute the exclusive record or decision. Any decision resting on official notice of a material fact not appearing in the record shall automatically afford any party on timely request, to have an opportunity to show the contrary.

## § 301.48  Closing the hearing.

To close the record of hearing, the Chairman shall make an announcement that the taking of testimony has concluded. In its discretion the Tribunal may close the record as of a future specified date, and allow time for exhibits yet to be prepared to be admitted: *Provided*, That the parties to the proceeding stipulate on the record that they waive the opportunity to cross-examine or present evidence with respect to such exhibits. The record in any hearing which has been recessed may not be closed by the Chairman prior to the day on which the hearing is to resume, except upon 10 days' notice to all parties.

## § 301.49  Documents.

(a) *Copies of documents*. The original and 15 copies of every document filed and served in proceedings before the Tribunal shall be furnished for the Tribunal's use, except exhibits made a part of the record.

(b) *Subscription and verification*. (1) The original of all documents filed by any party represented by counsel shall be signed by at least one attorney of record and list his address and telephone number. All copies shall be confirmed. Except when otherwise specifically provided, documents signed by the attorney for a party need not be verified or accompanied by an affidavit. The signature of an attorney constitutes certification by him that he has read the document, that to the best of his knowledge and belief there is good ground to support it, and that it has not been interposed for delay.

(2) The original of all documents filed by a party not represented by counsel shall be both signed and verified by that party and list the party's address and telephone number.

(3) The original of a document that is not signed, or is signed with intent to defeat the purpose this section, may be stricken as sham and false and the matter proceed as though the document had not been filed.

## § 301.50  Reopening of proceedings, modification or setting.

(a) *Condition for reopening*. (1) Except in the case of rate adjustment proceedings and distribution proceedings the Tribunal may, upon petition or its own motion, reopen any proceeding, after reasonable notice, for the purpose of rehearing arguments or reconsideration.

(2) After granting an opportunity to be heard, the Tribunal may alter, modify or set aside in whole or in part, the report of its finding or order if it finds such action required by changed conditions, by material mistake of fact or law, or by the public interest.

(b) *Petition for reopening*. A petition for reopening shall be made in writing and shall state its grounds. If it is a petition to take further evidence, the nature and purpose of the new evidence to be adduced shall be stated briefly, and an explanation given for why such evidence was not available at the time of the prior hearing. If it is a petition for reargument or reconsideration, the matter that is claimed to have been erroneously decided shall be specified and the alleged errors outlined briefly. Copies of the petition shall be furnished to all participants or their counsel.

(c) *Stay of rule or order*. No petition for reopening nor permission for reopening shall constitute a stay of any Tribunal rule or order; except that the Tribunal may postpone the effective date of any action taken by it pending judicial review and if, in the Tribunal's opinion, justice so requires.

## § 301.51  Rules of evidence.

(a) *Admissibility*. In any public hearing before the Tribunal, evidence which is not unduly repetitious or cumulative and is relevant and material shall be admissible. The testimony of any witness will not be considered evidence in a proceeding unless the witness has been sworn.

(b) *Documentary evidence*. Evidence which is submitted in the form of documents or detailed data and information shall be presented as exhibits. Relevant and material matter embraced in a document containing other matter not material or relevant or not intended as evidence must be plainly designated as the matter offered in evidence, and the immaterial or irrelevant parts shall be marked clearly so as to show they are not intended as evidence. A document in which material and relevant matter occurs which is of such bulk that it would unnecessarily encumber the record, may instead be marked for identification, and the relevant and material parts, once properly authenticated, may be read into the record. If the Tribunal desires, a true copy of the material and relevant matter may be presented in extract and submitted as evidence. Anyone presenting documents as evidence must present copies of all other participants at the hearing or their attorneys, and afford them an opportunity to examine the documents in their entirety and offer any other portion in evidence which may be felt material and relevant.

(c) *Documents filed with the Tribunal*. If the matter offered in evidence is contained in documents already on file with the Tribunal, the documents themselves need not be produced, but may instead be referred to according to how they have been filed with the Tribunal.

(d) *Public documents*. If a public document is offered in evidence either in whole or in part, such as an official report, decision, opinion or published scientific or economic data, and the document has been issued by an Executive Department, a legislative agency or committee, or a Federal administrative agency (Government-owned corporations included), and is proved by the party offering it to be reasonably available to the public, the document need not be produced physically, but may be offered instead by identifying the document and signaling the relevant parts.

(e) *Copies to participants*. Copies of all prepared testimony and exhibits must be distributed to the Tribunal and to other participants or their counsel at a hearing, unless the Chairman directs otherwise. For its use the number of copies the Tribunal requires is seven.

(f) *Reception and ruling*. Any ruling on the admissibility of evidence will be made by the Chairman, and he shall control the reception of evidence and insure that it confines itself to the issues of the proceeding.

(g) *Offers of proof.* If the Chairman rejects or excludes proposed oral testimony and an offer of proof is made, the offer of proof shall consist of a statement of the substance of the evidence which it is contended would have been adduced. In the case of documentary or written evidence, a copy of such evidence shall be marked for identification and shall constitute the offer of proof.

(h) *Introduction of studies and analysis*. If studies or analysis are offered in evidence, they shall state clearly the study plan, all relevant assumptions, the techniques of data collection, and the techniques of estimation and testing. The facts and judgments upon which conclusions are based shall be stated clearly, together with any alternative courses of action considered. If requested, tabulations of input data shall be made available to the Tribunal.

(i) *Statistical studies*. Statistical studies offered in evidence shall be accompanied by a summary of their assumptions, their study plans, and their procedures. Supplementary details shall be added in appendices. For each of the following types of statistical studies the following should be furnished:

(1) *Sample surveys*. (i) A clear description of the survey design, the definition of the universe under consideration, the sampling frame and units, the validity and confidence limits on major estimates; and

(ii) An explanation of the method of selecting the sample and of which characteristics were measured or counted.

(2) *Econometric investigations*. (i) A complete description of the econometric model, the reasons for each assumption, and the reasons for the statistical specification;

(ii) A clear statement of how any changes in the assumptions might affect the final result; and

(iii) Any available alternative studies, if requested, which employ alternatively models and variables.

(3) *Experimental analysis.* (i) A complete description of the design, the controlled conditions, and the implementation of controls; and

(ii) A complete description of the methods of observation and adjustment of observation.

(4) *Studies involving statistical methodology.* (i) The formula used for statistical estimates;

(ii) The standard error for each component;

(iii) The test statistics, the description of how the tests were conducted, related computations, computer programs, and all final results; and

(iv) Summarized descriptions of input data and, if requested, the input data itself.

(j) *Cumulative evidence.* Cumulative evidence will be discouraged by the Tribunal and the Tribunal may limit the number of witnesses that may be heard in behalf of any one party on any one issue.

(k) *Further evidence.* At any stage of a hearing the Chairman may call upon any party to furnish further evidence upon any issue.

(1) *Rights of parties as to presentation of evidence.* Every participant shall have the right to present his case by oral or documentary evidence, to submit rebuttal evidence, and to conduct such cross-examinations as may be necessary to disclose the facts fully and truthfully. The Chairman, however, may limit introduction of evidence, examination, and cross-examination if in his judgment this evidence or examination would be cumulative or cause undue delay.

## § 301.52 Participation in any proceeding.

Interested persons will be afforded an opportunity to participate in any proceeding and submit written data, views, or arguments, with or without the opportunity to present the same orally. If proposed rules are required by statute to be made on the record after opportunity for a hearing, such a hearing shall be conducted pursuant to 5 U.S.C., Subchapter II, and 7 U.S.C., and the procedure will be the same as in § 301.55 herein.

## § 301.53 Examination, cross-examination, and rebuttal.

(a) Each Commissioner may examine any witness at any time.

(b) Examination, cross-examination, and rebuttals relevant to the issues under consideration, shall be allowed by the Chairman, but only to the extent they are necessary for a full and true disclosure of the facts.

(c) *Selection of representatives for cross-examination.* The Tribunal will encourage individuals or groups with the same or similar interests in a proceeding to select a single representative to conduct their examination and cross-examination for them. However, if there is no agreement on the selection of a representative, then each individual or group will be allowed to conduct his own examination and cross-examination, but only issues affecting his particular interest.

## § 301.54 Proposed findings and conclusions.

(a) Any party to the proceeding may file proposed findings of fact and conclusions, briefs, or memoranda of law, or may be directed by the Chairman so to file, such filings to take place within 20 days after the record has been closed, unless additional time is granted.

(b) Failure to file when directed to so do may be considered a waiver of the right to participate further in the proceeding, unless good cause is shown.

(c) Proposed findings of fact shall be numbered by paragraph and include all basic evidentiary facts developed on the record used to support proposed conclusions and cite appropriately the record for each evidentiary fact. Proposed conclusions shall be stated separately. Proposed findings submitted by someone other than an applicant in a proceeding shall be restricted to those issues which specifically affect that person.

(d) Proof of service upon all other counsel or parties in a proceeding must accompany pleadings and all other papers filed under this section.

## § 301.55 Promulgation of rules or orders.

(a) In adopting a rule or order the Tribunal will consider all relevant matters of fact, law, and policy, and all relevant matters which have been presented by interested persons, and will exercise due discretion. Together with a concise general statement of its basis and purpose and any necessary findings, the rule or order will be published in the FEDERAL REGISTER, and if any other public notice is necessary that will be made also.

(b) The effective date of any rule, or its amendment, suspension, or repeal, will be at least 30 days after it is published in the FEDERAL REGISTER, unless good cause has been shown and is published with the rule.

## § 301.56 Public suggestions and comments.

(a) The Tribunal encourages the public, not just those persons subject to its regulations, to submit suggestions and proposals concerning any substantial question before it, when that question will have substantial impact either upon those directly regulated by the Tribunal or upon others. It is in the best interests of both the Tribunal and the public at large that the Tribunal be advised on issues and problems that are potentially significant to it. This will permit the Tribunal to consider policy questions and administrative reforms early enough so that they may be viewed in a general context and not in the detailed application of a particular proceeding.

(b) Upon receiving such suggestions or proposals, the Tribunal shall review them and take whatever action seems necessary. Further information may be requested from the party submitting the suggestion or proposals, and the Tribunal staff may be asked to make a study or an informal public conference may be held. Conferences or procedures undertaken pursuant to this section shall not be deemed subject to the Administrative Procedure Act with respect to notice of rulemaking. They are intended by the Tribunal simply as a means of determining the need for Tribunal action, prior to issuing a notice of proposed rulemaking.

(c) Such suggestions or proposals, however, shall be filed in accordance with the Tribunal's rules.

(d) This policy may not be used to advocate ex parte a position in a pending proceeding. Suggestions or proposals offered must relate to general conditions, such as conditions in industry, the public interest, or the policies of the Tribunal.

## Subpart F—Rate Adjustment Proceedings

## § 301.60 Scope.

This chapter governs only those proceedings dealing with royalty rate adjustments affecting cable television (17 U.S.C. 111), the production of phonorecords (17 U.S.C. 115), coin-operated phonorecord players (jukeboxes) (17 U.S.C. 116), and noncommercial broadcasting (17 U.S.C. 118). It does not govern unrelated rulemaking proceedings. Those provisions of Subpart E generally regulating the conduct of proceedings shall apply to rate adjustment proceedings, unless they are inconsistent with the specific provisions of this subpart.

## § 301.61 Commencement of adjustment proceedings.

(a) In the case of cable television, phonorecords, and coin-operated phonorecord players (jukeboxes) rate adjustment proceedings will commence by the publication of a notice to that effect in the FEDERAL REGISTER on January 1, 1980, pursuant to 17 U.S.C. 804(a)(1). In the case of non-commercial broadcasting the notice will be published on June 30, 1982 and at 5-year intervals thereafter, pursuant 10 U.S.C. 118(c). The notice shall, to the extent feasible, describe the general structure and schedule of the proceeding.

(b) Initially, as outlined in paragraph (a) of this section a petition from an interested party is not necessary to commence proceedings. Thereafter, however, for rate adjustment proceedings to commence, a petition must be filed by an interested party according to the following schedule:

(1) Cable Television: During 1985 and each subsequent fifth calendar year.

(2) Phonorecords: During 1987 and each subsequent 10th calendar year.

(3) Coin-operated phonorecord players (jukeboxes): During 1990 and each subsequent 10th calendar year.

(c) Cable television rate adjustment proceedings may also be commenced by the filing of a petition, according to 17 U.S.C. 801(b)(2) (B) and (C), if the Federal Communications Commission amends certain of its rules concerning the carriage by cable of broadcast signals, or with respect to syndicated and sports program exclusivity.

(d) In the case of non-commercial broadcasting, a petition is not necessary for the commencement of proceedings. They commence automatically according to paragraph (a) of this section.

## § 301.62 Content of petition.

(a) The petition shall detail the petitioner's interest in the royalty rate sufficiently to permit the Tribunal to determine whether the petitioner has "significant interest" in the matter. The petition must also identify the extent to which the petitioner's interest is shared by other owners or users, and owners or users with similar interests may file a petition jointly.

(b) In the case of a petition for rate adjustment as the result of a Federal Communications Commission rule change, the petition shall also set forth the action of the Federal Communications Commission which the party filing the petition feels authorizes a rate adjustment proceeding.

## § 301.63 Consideration of petition.

The Tribunal shall not start to consider any petition before the expiration of 90 days from the start of the calendar year specified in § 301.61(b) or 90 days from the effective date of the Federal Communications Commission action mentioned in § 301.62(c). Similar petitions may be joined together by the Tribunal for the purpose of determining "significant interest," and the Tribunal may permit written comments or a hearing on pending petitions.

## § 301.64 Disposition of petition.

At the end of the 90-day period, the Tribunal shall determine as expeditiously as possible if one or more petitioner's interest is "significant," and shall publish in the FEDERAL REGISTER a notice of its determination and the reasons therefor, together with a notice of the commencement of proceedings if it has been determined to commence a proceeding. Any commencement notice shall, to the extent feasible, describe the general structure and schedule of the proceeding.

## § 301.65  Rate adjustment proceedings.

In any rate adjustment proceeding, all interested persons shall have the opportunity to present written comments and oral testimony, subject to the general provisions of Subpart E.

## § 301.66  Publication of proposed rate determination.

(a) Following the conclusion of the hearings, the Tribunal shall publish as soon as possible in the FEDERAL REGISTER, a notice of its proposed findings and conclusions in the rate adjustment proceeding. The Tribunal shall afford all parties a reasonable opportunity to submit written comments on the proposed determination. The Tribunal may, if necessary, conduct additional hearings.

(b) A proposed determination will not be published if, in the Tribunal's judgment, a final determination cannot feasibly be rendered before the year's end as required by 17 U.S.C. 118(c) and 17 U.S.C. 804(e) concerning the termination of proceedings.

## § 301.67  Final determination.

Upon the conclusion of the procedures for proposed determinations described in § 301.66, or upon the conclusion of the rate adjustment proceedings provided in § 301.65, if the publication of a proposed rate determination is not feasible because of the requirements to reach a final determination before the end of the year (17 U.S.C. 118(c) and 17 U.S.C. 804(e)), the Tribunal shall publish in the FEDERAL REGISTER a written opinion stating in detail the criteria it found applicable, the facts found relevant, and the specific reasons for its determination.

## § 301.68  Reopening of proceedings.

Following the publication of a final determination in the FEDERAL REGISTER the Tribunal shall not reopen or conduct any further proceedings.

## § 301.69  Effective date of final determination.

A final determination by the Tribunal shall become effective thirty days following its publication in the FEDERAL REGISTER, unless an appeal has been filed prior to that time pursuant to 17 U.S.C. 810 to vacate, modify or correct a determination, and notice of the appeal has been served on all parties who appeared in the proceeding.

## Subpart G—Royalty Fees Distribution Proceedings

## § 301.70  Scope.

This subpart governs only those proceedings dealing with the distribution of compulsory cable television and coin-operated phonorecord player (jukebox) royalties deposited with the Register of Copyrights, according to the terms of 17 U.S.C.,

111(d)(5) and 116(c). It does not govern unrelated rulemaking proceedings. Those provisions of Subpart E generally regulating the conduct of proceedings shall apply to royalty fee distribution proceedings, unless they are inconsistent with the specific provisions of this subpart.

## § 301.71  Commencement proceedings.

(a) *Cable television.* In the case of compulsory royalty fees for secondary transmissions by cable television, any person claiming to be entitled to such fees must file a claim with the Tribunal during the month of July each year in accordance with Tribunal regulations.

(b) *Coin-operated phonorecord players.* In the case of compulsory royalty fees for the use of nondramatic musical works by coin-operated phonorecord players (jukeboxes) any person claiming to be entitled to such fees must file a claim with the Tribunal during the month of January each year in accordance with Tribunal regulations.

## § 301.72  Determination of controversy.

(a) *Cable television.* After the first day of August each year, the Tribunal shall determine whether a controversy exists among the claimants of cable television compulsory royalty fees. In order to determine whether a controversy exists, the Tribunal may conduct whatever proceedings it feels necessary, subject to the procedures and regulations of Subpart E. The results of this determination shall be announced in the FEDERAL REGISTER. If the Tribunal decides that a controversy exists, the FEDERAL REGISTER notice shall also announce the commencement of the royalty distribution proceeding, and shall, to the extent feasible, describe the general structure and schedule of the proceeding.

(b) *Coin-operated phonorecord players.* After the first day of October each year, the Tribunal shall determine whether a controversy exists among the claimants of coin-operated phonorecord player (jukebox) compulsory royalty fees. In order to determine whether a controversy exists the Tribunal may conduct whatever proceedings it feels necessary, subject to the procedures and regulations of Subpart E. The results of this determination shall be announced in the FEDERAL REGISTER. If the Tribunal decides that a controversy exists, the FEDERAL REGISTER notice shall also announce the commencement of the royalty distribution proceeding, and shall, to the extent feasible, describe the general structure and schedule of the proceeding.

## § 301.73  Royalty distribution proceedings.

In any royalty distribution proceeding all interested claimants shall have the opportunity to present written comments and oral testimony, subject to the general provisions of Subpart E.

## § 301.74  Publication of proposed royalty distribution determination.

(a) Following the conclusion of the hearings, the Tribunal shall publish, as soon as possible, in the FEDERAL REGISTER, a notice of its proposed findings and conclusion in the royalty distribution proceeding. The Tribunal shall afford all claimants a reasonable opportunity to submit written comments on the proposed determination. The Tribunal may, if necessary, conduct additional hearings.

(b) A proposed determination will not be published if, in the Tribunal's judgment, a final determination cannot feasibly be rendered before the year's end, as required by 17 U.S.C. 804(e) concerning the termination of proceedings.

## § 301.75  Final determination.

Upon the conclusion of the procedures for proposed determination described in § 301.74, or upon the conclusion of the royalty distribution proceedings provided in § 301.73, if the publication of a proposed royalty distribution determination is not feasible because of the requirements to reach a final determination before the end of the year (17 U.S.C. 804(e)), the Tribunal shall publish in the FEDERAL REGISTER a written opinion stating in detail the criteria it found applicable, the facts found relevant, and the specific reasons for its determination.

## § 301.76  Reopening of proceedings.

Following the publication of a final determination in the FEDERAL REGISTER, the Tribunal shall not reopen or conduct any further proceedings.

## § 301.77  Effective date of final determination.

A final determination of the Tribunal shall become effective thirty days following its publication in the FEDERAL REGISTER, unless an appeal has been filed prior to that time pursuant to 17 U.S.C. 810 to vacate, modify, or correct a determination, and notice of the appeal has been served on all parties who appeared in the proceeding.

# PART 302—FILING OF CLAIMS TO CABLE ROYALTY FEES

Sec.
302.1  General.
302.2  Filing of claims to cable royalty fees for secondary transmissions during the period January 1 through June 30, 1979.
302.3  Content of claims.
302.4  Forms.
302.6  Filing of claims to cable royalty fees for secondary transmissions during the period July 1 through December 31, 1978.
302.7  Filing of claims to cable royalty fees for secondary transmissions during calendar year 1979 and subsequent calendar years.
302.8  Compliance with statutory dates.
302.9  Proof of fixation of works.
302.10  Deduction of costs of distribution proceedings.

AUTHORITY: 17 U.S.C. 111(d)(5)(A).

SOURCE: 43 FR 24528, June 6, 1978, unless otherwise noted.

## § 302.1  General.

This regulation prescribes procedures pursuant to 17 U.S.C. 111(d)(5)(A), whereby persons claiming to be entitled to compulsory license fees for secondary transmissions by cable systems shall file claims with the Copyright Royalty Tribunal (CRT).

## § 302.2  Filing of claims to cable royalty fees for secondary transmissions during the period January 1 through June 30, 1979.

Every person claiming to be entitled to compulsory license fees for secondary transmissions by cable systems during the period January 1 through June 30, 1978, shall file in the office of the Copyright Royalty Tribunal a claim to such fee during the calendar month of July 1978 or July 1979. Any claimant so filing shall be considered as having filed a claim for the period January 1 through June 30, 1978. For purposes of this clause claimants may file claims jointly or as a single claim. A joint claim shall include a concise statement of the authorizations for the filing of the joint claim.

[44 FR 60727, Oct. 22, 1979]

### § 302.3  Content of claims.

The claims filed pursuant to § 302.2 shall include the following information:
(a) The full legal name of the person or entity claiming compulsory license fees.
(b) The full address, including a specific number and street name or rural route, of the place of business of the person or entity.
(c) A general statement of the nature of the copyrighted works, whose secondary transmission provides the basis of the claim.
(d) Identification of at least one secondary transmission establishing a basis for the claim.

### §  302.4  Forms.

The Copyright Royalty Tribunal does not provide printed forms for the filing of claims.

### § 302.6  Filing of claims to cable royalty fees for secondary transmissions during the period July 1 through December 31, 1978.

(a) During the month of July 1979, every person claiming to be entitled to compulsory license fees for secondary transmissions during the period July 1 through December 31, 1978, shall file in the office of the Copyright Royalty Tribunal a claim to such fees. Any claimant so filing shall be considered as having filed a claim for the period July 1 through December 31, 1978.
(b) Every person who filed in the office of the Copyright Royalty Tribunal during the calendar month of July, 1979, claiming to be entitled to compulsory license fees for secondary transmissions by cable systems during the period July 1 through December 31, 1978, but who did not file a claim for the period January 1 through June 30, 1978, shall be considered as having filed a claim for the period of January 1 through June 30, 1978.
(c) For the purpose of this clause claimants may file claims jointly or as a single claim.

[44 FR 60727, Oct. 22, 1979]

### § 302.7  Filing of claims to cable royalty fees for secondary transmissions during calendar year 1979 and subsequent calendar years.

(a) During the month of July 1980 and in July of each succeeding year, every person claiming to be entitled to compulsory license fees for secondary transmissions during the preceding calendar year shall file a claim to such fees in the office of the Copyright Royalty Tribunal. No royalty fees shall be distributed to copyright owners for secondary transmissions during the specified period unless such owner has filed a claim to such fees during the following calendar month of July. For purposes of this clause claimants may file claims jointly or as a single claim. Such filing shall include such information as the Copyright Royalty Tribunal may require. A joint claim shall include a concise statement of the authorization for the filing of the joint claim.

(b) Claims filed during the month of July 1980 shall include the following information:

(1) The full legal name of the person or entity claiming compulsory license fees.

(2) The full address, including a specific number and street name or rural route, of the place of business of the person or entity.

(3) A general statement of the nature of the copyrighted works, whose secondary transmission provides the basis of the claim.

(4) Identification of at least one secondary transmission establishing a basis for the claim.

[45 FR 26959, Apr. 22, 1980]

## § 302.8 Compliance with statutory dates.

For purposes of 17 U.S.C. (d)(5)(A), claims required to be filed with the Copyright Royalty Tribunal during the month of July shall be considered as timely filed if: (a) They are addressed to the Copyright Royalty Tribunal, 1111 20th Street N.W., Washington, D.C. 20036, and deposited with the U.S. Postal Service with sufficient postage as first class mail prior to the expiration of the statutory period, and (b) they are accompanied by a certificate stating the date of deposit. The persons signing the certificate should have reasonable basis to expect that the correspondence would be mailed on or before the date indicated.

## § 302.9 Proof of fixation of works.

The Copyright Royalty Tribunal shall not require in any proceeding for the distribution of cable royalty fees the filing by claimants of tangible fixations of works in whole or in part. In the event of a controversy concerning the actual fixation of a work in a tangible medium as required by the Copyright Act, the Copyright Royalty Tribunal shall resolve such controversy for purposes of the distribution proceeding solely on the basis of affidavits by appropriate operational personnel and other appropriate documentary evidence, and such oral testimony as the Copyright Royalty Tribunal may deem necessary. Affidavits submitted by claimants should establish that the work for which the claim is submitted was fixed in its entirety, and should state the nature of the work, the title of the program, the duration of the program, and the date of fixation. No such affidavits need be filed with the Copyright Royalty Tribunal unless requested by the Tribunal.

[43 FR 40225, Sept. 11, 1978]

## § 302.10 Deduction of costs of distribution proceedings.

In compliance with 17 U.S.C. 111(d)(5)(c) and 17 U.S.C. 807, before any distributions are made pursuant to 17 U.S.C. 111, the Copyright Royalty Tribunal will deduct all costs which would not have been incurred by the Tribunal but for the distribution proceeding.

[44 FR 29894, May 23, 1979]

## PART 303—ACCESS TO PHONORECORD PLAYERS (JUKEBOXES)

Sec.
303.1 General.
303.2 Access to establishment and phonorecord players.

## § 303.1 General.

This regulation prescribes the procedures pursuant to 17 U.S.C. 116 by which persons who can reasonably be expected to have claims to royalty fees paid by the operators of coin-operated phonorecord players under the compulsory license established by 17 U.S.C. 116 may have access to the establishments in which such phonorecord players are located and to the phonorecord players located therein to obtain information which may be reasonably necessary to determine the proportion of contribution of the musical works of each such person to the earnings of the phonorecord players for which fees shall have been deposited. The terms "operator" and "coin-operated phonorecord player" have the meanings given to them by paragraph (3) of section 116 of Title 17.

(17 U.S.C. 116(c)(5); 17 U.S.C. 801(b))
[43 FR 40500, Sept. 12, 1978]

## § 303.2 Access to establishments and phonorecord players.

A person, or authorized representatives of such person, who can reasonably be expected to have claims to royalty fees paid by the operators of phonorecord players shall have access to the establishments in which such phonorecord players are located during customary business hours on regular business days. Such access shall be only for the purpose of obtaining information concerning the performance of musical works by the phonorecord players. The right of access shall be exercised in such a manner as not to cause any significant interference with the normal functioning of an establishment.

(17 U.S.C. 116(c)(5); 17 U.S.C. 801(b))
[43 FR 40500, Sept. 12, 1978]

## PART 304—USE OF CERTAIN COPYRIGHTED WORKS IN CONNECTION WITH NONCOMMERCIAL BROADCASTING

AUTHORITY: Pub. L. 94-553, unless otherwise noted.

SOURCE: 47 FR 57925, Dec. 29, 1982, unless otherwise noted.

## § 304.1 General.

This Part 304 establishes terms and rates of royalty payments for certain activities using published nondramatic musical works and published pictorial, graphic, and sculptural works during a period beginning on January 1, 1983 and ending on December 31, 1987. Upon compliance with 17 U.S.C. 118, and the terms and rates of this part, a public broadcasting entity may engage in the activities with respect to such works set forth in 17 U.S.C. 118(d).

## § 304.2 Definition of public broadcasting entity.

As used in this part, the term "public broadcasting entity" means a noncommercial educational broadcast station as defined in section 397 of Title 47 and any nonprofit institution or organization engaged in the activities described in 17 U.S.C. 118(d)(2).

## § 304.3 [Reserved]

## § 304.4 Performance of musical compositions by PBS, NPR and other public broadcasting entities engaged in the activities set forth in 17 U.S.C. 118(d).

The following schedule of rates and terms shall apply to the performance by PBS, NPR and other public broadcasting entities (other than those covered by §§ 304.5 and 304.6) engaged in the activities set forth in 17 U.S.C. 118(d), of copyrighted published nondramatic musical compositions, other than such compositions subject to the provisions of 17 U.S.C. 118(b)(2).

(a) *Determination of royalty rate.*

For the performance of such a work in a feature presentation of PBS:

| 1983–1984 | 1985–1986 | 1987 |
|-----------|-----------|----------|
| $140.00 | $148.00 | $157.00 |

For the performance of such a work as background or theme music in a PBS program:

| 1983–1984 | 1985–1986 | 1987 |
|-----------|-----------|----------|
| $35.00 | $37.30 | $39.65 |

For the performance of such a work in a feature presentation of a station of PBS:

| 1983–1984 | 1985–1986 | 1987 |
|-----------|-----------|----------|
| $10.00 | $12.00 | $13.00 |

For the performance of such a work as background or theme music in a program of a station of PBS:

| 1983–1984 | 1985–1986 | 1987 |
| --- | --- | --- |
| $2.50 | $2.70 | $2.85 |

For the performance of such a work in a feature presentation of NPR:

| 1983–1984 | 1985–1986 | 1987 |
| --- | --- | --- |
| $14.00 | $14.90 | $15.85 |

For the performance of such a work as background or theme music in an NPR program:

| 1983–1984 | 1985–1986 | 1987 |
| --- | --- | --- |
| $3.50 | $3.70 | $3.90 |

For the performance of such a work in a feature presentation of a station of NPR:

| 1983–1984 | 1985–1986 | 1987 |
| --- | --- | --- |
| $1.00 | $1.10 | $1.15 |

For the performance of such a work as background or theme music in a program of a station of NPR:

| 1983–1984 | 1985–1986 | 1987 |
| --- | --- | --- |
| $0.25 | $0.30 | $0.35 |

For the purpose of this schedule the rate for the performance of theme music in an entire series shall be double the single program theme rate.

In the event the work is first performed in a program of a station of PBS or NPR, and such program is subsequently distributed by PBS or NPR, an additional royalty payment shall be made equal to the difference between the rate specified in this section for a program of a station of PBS or NPR, respectively and the rate specified in this section for PBS or NPR program, respectively.

(b) *Payment of royalty rate.* The required royalty rate shall be paid to each known copyright owner not later than July 31 of each calendar year for uses during the first six months of that calendar year, and not later than January 31 for uses during the last six months of the preceding calendar year.

(c) *Records of use.* PBS and NPR shall, upon the request of a copyright owner of a published musical work who believes a musical composition of such owner has been performed under the terms of this schedule, permit such copyright owner a reasonable opportunity to examine their standard cue sheets listing the nondramatic performances of musical compositions on PBS and NPR programs. Any local PBS and NPR station that is required by paragraph 4b of the PBS/NPR/ASCAP license agreement dated October 28, 1982 to prepare a music use report shall, upon request of a copyright owner who believes a musical composition of such owner has been performed under the terms of this schedule, permit such copyright owner to examine the report.

(d) *Terms of use.* The applicable fee in this schedule shall be the fee for the time period during which the first performance in a program occurred, and shall cover performances of such work in such program for a period of three years following the fist performance.

## § 304.5 Performance of musical compositions by public broadcasting entities licensed to colleges or universities.

(a) *Scope.* This section applies to the performance of copyrighted published nondramatic musical compositions by nonprofit radio stations which are licensed to colleges, universities, or other nonprofit educational institutions and which are not affiliated with National Public Radio.

(b) *Voluntary license agreements.* Notwithstanding the schedule of rates and terms established by this section, the rates and terms of any license agreements entered into by copyright owners and colleges, universities, and other nonprofit educational institutions concerning the performance of copyrighted musical compositions, including performances by nonprofit radio stations, shall apply in lieu of the rates and terms of this section.

(c) *Royalty rate.* A public broadcasting entity within the scope of this section may perform published nondramatic music compositions subject to the following schedule of royalty rates:

For all such compositions in the repertory of ASCAP annually. . . . . . . . . . . . . $149  
For all such compositions in the repertory of BMI annually . . . . . . . . . . . . . . 149  
For all such compositions in the repertory of SESAC annually . . . . . . . . . . . . 33  
For the performances of any other such composition . . . . . . . . . . . . . . . . . . . . 1

(d) *Payment of royalty rate.* The public broadcasting entity shall pay the required royalty rate to ASCAP, BMI and SESAC, not later than January 31 of each year.

(e) *Records of use.* A public broadcasting entity subject to this section shall furnish to ASCAP, BMI, and SESAC upon request, a music use report during one week of each calendar year. ASCAP, BMI and SESAC shall not in any one calendar year request more than 10 stations to furnish such reports.

[47 FR 57925, Dec. 29, 1982, as amended at 49 FR 47488, Dec. 5, 1984]

## § 304.6 Performance of musical compositions by other public broadcasting entities.

(a) *Scope.* This section applies to the performance of copyrighted published nondramatic musical compositions by radio stations not licensed to college, universities or other nonprofit educational institutions.

(b) *Voluntary license agreements.* Notwithstanding the schedule of rates and terms established in this section, the rates and terms of any license agreements entered into by copyright owners and nonprofit radio stations within the scope of this section concerning the performance of copyrighted musical compositions, including performances by nonprofit radio stations, shall apply in lieu of the rates and terms of this section.

(c) *Royalty rate.* A public broadcasting entity within the scope of this section may perform published nondramatic musical compositions subject to the following schedule of royalty rates:

For all such compositions in the repertory of ASCAP,
    in 1983, $180;
    in 1984, $190;
    in 1985, $200;
    in 1986, $210;
    in 1987, $220

For all such compositions in the repertory of BMI,
    in 1983, $180;
    in 1984, $190;
    in 1985, $200;
    in 1986, $210;
    in 1987, $220

For all such compositions in the repertory of SESAC,
    in 1983, $40;
    in 1984, $42;
    in 1985, $44;
    in 1986, $46;
    in 1987, $48

For the performance of any other such composition, in 1983 through 1987, $1.

(d) *Payment of royalty rate.* The public broadcasting entity shall pay the required royalty rate to ASCAP, BMI, and SESAC not later than July 31, 1983, for the calendar year 1983, and not later than January 31 for each calendar year thereafter.

(e) *Records of use.* A public broadcasting entity subject to this section shall furnish to ASCAP, BMI, and SESAC, upon request, a music use report during one week of each calendar year. ASCAP, BMI, and SESAC each shall not in any one calendar year request more than 5 stations to furnish such reports.

[47 FR 57925, Dec. 29, 1982, as amended at 48 FR 22716, May 20, 1983]

## § 304.7  Recording rights, rates and terms.

(a) *Scope.* This section establishes rates and terms for the recording of nondramatic performances and displays of musical works on and for the radio and television programs of public broadcasting entities, whether or not in synchronization or timed relationship with the visual or aural content, and for the making, reproduction, and distribution of copies and phonorecords of public broadcasting programs containing such recorded nondramatic performances and displays of musical works solely for the purpose of transmission by public broadcasting entities, as defined in 17 U.S.C. 118(g). The rates and terms established in this schedule include the making of the reproductions described in 17 U.S.C. 118(d)(3).

(b) *Royalty rate.* (1) For uses described in subsection (a) of a musical work in a PBS-distributed program:

| | 1983–1984 | 1985–1986 | 1987 |
|---|---|---|---|
| Feature | $75.00 | $80.00 | $85.00 |
| Concert feature (per minute) | 22.25 | 23.75 | 25.25 |
| Background | 37.50 | 40.00 | 42.50 |
| Theme: | | | |
| Single program or first series program | 37.50 | 40.00 | 42.50 |
| Other series program | 15.25 | 16.25 | 17.25 |

For such use other than in a PBS-distributed television program:

| | 1983–1984 | 1985–1986 | 1987 |
|---|---|---|---|
| Feature | $5.00 | $5.35 | $6.00 |
| Concert feature (per minute) | 1.50 | 1.60 | 1.70 |
| Background | 2.50 | 2.70 | 2.85 |
| Theme: | | | |
| Single program or first series program | 2.50 | 2.70 | 2.85 |
| Other series program | 1.00 | 1.10 | 1.15 |

In the event the work is first recorded other than in a PBS-distributed program, and such program is subsequently distributed by PBS, an additional royalty payment shall be made equal to the difference between the rate specified in this section for other than a PBS-distributed program and the rate specified in this section for a PBS-distributed program.

(2) For uses licensed herein of a musical work in a NPR program, the royalty fees shall be calculated by multiplying the following per-composition rates by the number of different compositions in any NPR program distributed by NPR. For purposes of this schedule "National Public Radio" programs includes all programs produced in whole or in part by NPR, or by any NPR station or organization under contract with NPR.

| | 1983–1984 | 1985–1986 | 1987 |
|---|---|---|---|
| Feature | $7.50 | $8.00 | $8.50 |
| Concert feature (per half hour) | 11.00 | 11.00 | 12.00 |
| Background | 3.75 | 4.00 | 4.25 |
| Theme: | | | |
| Single program or first series program | 3.75 | 4.00 | 4.25 |
| Other series program | 1.50 | 1.60 | 1.70 |

(3) For the purposes of this schedule, a "Concert Feature" shall be deemed to be the nondramatic presentation of all or part of a symphony, concerto, or other serious work originally written for concert or opera performance.

(4) For such uses other than in a NPR-produced radio program:

| | |
|---|---|
| Feature | $.50 |
| Feature (concert) (per ½ hour) | $1.00 |
| Background | $.25 |

(5) The schedule of fees covers broadcast use for a period of three years following the first broadcast. Succeeding broadcast use periods will require the following additional payment: second three-year period—50 percent; each three-year period thereafter—25 percent; provided that a 100 percent additional payment prior to the expiration of the first three-year period will cover broadcast use periods without limitation. Such succeeding uses which are subsequent to December 31, 1987 shall be subject to the rates established in this schedule.

(c) *Payment of royalty rates.* PBS, NPR, or other television public broadcasting entity shall pay the required royalty fees to each copyright owner not later than July 31 of each calendar year for uses during the first six months of that calendar year, and not later than January 31 for uses during the last six months of the preceding calendar year.

(d) *Records of use.* (1) Maintenance of cue sheets. PBS and its stations, NPR or other television public broadcasting entity shall maintain and furnish to copyright owners whose musical works are recorded pursuant to this schedule copies of their standard cue sheets or summaries of same listing the recording of the musical works of such copyright owners. Such cue sheets or summaries shall be furnished not later than July 31 of each calendar year for recording the first six months of the calendar year, and not later than January 31 of each calendar year for recordings during the second six months of the preceding calendar year.

(2) Content of cue sheets or summaries. Such cue sheets or summaries shall include:

(i) The title, composer and author to the extent such information is reasonably obtainable.

(ii) The type of use and manner of performance thereof in each case.

(iii) For Concert Feature music, the actual recorded time period on the program, plus all distribution and broadcast information available to the public broadcasting entity.

(e) *Filing of use reports with the Copyright Royalty Tribunal (CRT).* (1) Deposit of cue sheets or summaries. PBS and its stations, NPR, or other television public broadcasting entity shall deposit with the CRT copies of their standard music cue sheets or summaries of same (which may be in the form of hard copy of computerized reports) listing the recording pursuant to this schedule of the musical works of copyright owners. Such cue sheets or summaries shall be deposited not later than July 31 of each calendar year for recordings during the first six months of the calendar year, and not later than January 31 of each calendar year for recordings during the second six months of the preceding calendar year. PBS and NPR shall maintain at their offices copies of all standard music sheets from which such music use reports are prepared. Such music cue sheets shall be furnished to the Copyright Royalty Tribunal upon its request and also shall be available during regular business hours at the offices of PBS or NPR for examination by a copyright owner who believes a musical composition of such owner has been recorded pursuant to this schedule.

## § 304.8 Terms and rates of royalty payments for the use of published pictorial, graphic, and sculptural works.

(a) *Scope.* This section establishes rates and terms for the use of published pictorial, graphic, and sculptural works by public broadcasting entities for the activities described in 17 U.S.C. 118. The rates and terms established in this schedule include the making of the reproductions described in 17 U.S.C. 118(d)(3).

(b) *Royalty rate.* (1) The following schedule of rates shall apply to the use of works within the scope of this section:

For such uses in a PBS-distributed program:

For a featured display of a work.

| 1983–1984 | 1985–1986 | 1987 |
|-----------|-----------|------|
| $45.75 | $49.00 | $52.00 |

For background and montage display.

| 1983–1984 | 1985–1986 | 1987 |
|-----------|-----------|------|
| $22.25 | $23.75 | $25.25 |

For use of a work for program identification or for thematic use.

| 1983–1984 | 1985–1986 | 1987 |
|-----------|-----------|------|
| $90.25 | $96.25 | $102.25 |

For the display of an art reproduction copyrighted separately from the work of fine art from which the work was reproduced, irrespective of whether the reproduced work of fine art is copyrighted so as to be subject also to payment of a display fee under the terms of this schedule.

| 1983–1984 | 1985–1986 | 1987 |
|-----------|-----------|------|
| $29.50 | $31.50 | $33.50 |

For such uses in other than PBS-distributed programs:
For a featured display of a work.

| 1983–1984 | 1985–1986 | 1987 |
|-----------|-----------|------|
| $29.50 | $31.50 | $33.50 |

For background and montage display.

| 1983–1984 | 1985–1986 | 1987 |
|-----------|-----------|------|
| $15.25 | $16.25 | $17.25 |

For use of a work for program identification or for thematic use.

| 1983–1984 | 1985–1986 | 1987 |
|-----------|-----------|------|
| $60.75 | $64.75 | $68.75 |

For the display of an art reproduction copyrighted separately from the work of fine art from which the work was reproduced, irrespective of whether the reproduced work of fine art is copyrighted so as to be subject also to payment of a display fee under the terms of schedule.

| 1983–1984 | 1985–1986 | 1987 |
| --- | --- | --- |
| $15.25 | $16.25 | $17.25 |

For the purposes of this schedule the rate for the thematic use of a work in an entire series shall be double the single program theme rate.

In the event the work is first used other than in a PBS-distributed program, and such program is subsequently distributed by PBS, an additional royalty payment shall be made equal to the difference between the rate specified in this section for other than a PBS-distributed program and the rate specified in this section for a PBS-distributed program.

(2) "Featured display" for purposes of this schedule means a full-screen or substantially full-screen display *appearing on the screen for more than three seconds.* Any display less than full-screen or substantially full-screen, or *full-screen for three seconds or less,* is deemed to be a "background or montage display."

(3) "Thematic use" is the utilization of the work of one or more artists where the works constitute the central theme of the program or convey a story line.

(4) "Display of an art reproduction copyrighted separately from the work of fine art from which the work was reproduced" means a transparency or other reproduction of an underlying work of fine art.

(c) *Payment of royalty rate.* PBS or other public broadcasting entity shall pay the required royalty fees to each copyright owner not later than July 31 of each calendar year for uses during the first six months of the calendar year, and not later than January 31 for uses during the last six months of the preceding calendar year.

(d) *Records of use.* (1) PBS and its stations or other public broadcasting entity shall maintain and furnish either to copyright owners, or to the offices of generally recognized organizations representing the copyright owners of pictorial, graphic, and sculptural works, copies of their standard lists containing the pictorial, graphic, and sculptural works displayed on their programs. Such notice shall include the name of the copyright owner, if known, the specific source from which the work was taken, a description of the work used, the title of the program on which the work was used, and the date of the original broadcast of the program.

(2) Such listings shall be furnished not later than July 31 of each calendar year for displays during the first six months of the calendar year, and not later than January 31 of each calendar year for displays during the second six months of the preceding calendar year.

(e) *Filing of use reports with the CRT.* (1) PBS and its stations or other public broadcasting entity shall deposit with the CRT copies of their standard lists containing the pictorial, graphic, and sculptural works displayed on their programs. Such notice shall include the name of the copyright owner, if known, the specific source from which the work was taken, a description of the work used, the title of the program on which the work was used, and the date of the original broadcast of the program.

(2) Such listings shall be furnished not later than July 31 of each calendar year for displays during the first six months of the calendar year, and not later than January 31 of each calendar year for displays during the second six months of the preceding calendar year.

(f) *Terms of use.* The rates of this schedule are for unlimited broadcast use for a period of three years from the date of the first broadcast use of the work under this schedule. Succeeding broadcast use periods will require the following additional payment: second three-year period—50 percent; each three-year period thereafter—25 percent; provided that a 100 percent additional payment prior to the expiration of the first three-year period will cover broadcast use during all subsequent broadcast use periods without limitation. Such succeeding uses which are subsequent to December 31, 1987 shall be subject to the rates established in this schedule.

(2) Pursuant to the provisions of 17 U.S.C. 118(f), nothing in this schedule shall be construed to permit, beyond the limits of fair use as provided in 17 U.S.C. 107, the production of a transmission program drawn to any substantial extent from a published compilation of pictorial, graphic, or sculptural works.

### § 304.9  Unknown copyright owners.

If PBS and its stations, NPR and its stations, or other public broadcasting entity is not aware of the identity of, or unable to locate, a copyright owner who is entitled to receive a royalty payment under this Part, they shall retain the required fee in a segregated trust account for a period of three years from the date of the required payment. No claim to such royalty fees shall be valid after the expiration of the three year period. Public broadcasting entities may establish a joint trust fund for the purposes of this section. Public broadcasting entities shall make available to the CRT, upon request, information concerning fees deposited in trust funds.

### § 304.10  Cost of living adjustment.

(a) On December 1, 1983 the CRT shall publish in the FEDERAL REGISTER a notice of the change in the cost of living as determined by the Consumer Price Index (all urban consumers, all items) from the May, 1982 to the last Index published prior to December 1, 1983. On each December 1 thereafter the CRT shall publish a notice of the change in the cost of living during the period from the first Index published subsequent to the previous notice, to the last index published prior to December 1 of that year.

(b) On the same date of the notices published pursuant to paragraph (a) of this section, the CRT shall publish in the FEDERAL REGISTER a revised schedule of rates for § 304.5, alone, which shall adjust those royalty amounts established in dollar amounts according to the change in the cost of living determined as provided in paragraph (a) of this section. Such royalty rates shall be fixed at the nearest dollar.

(c) The adjusted schedule of rates for § 304.5, alone, shall become effective thirty days after publication in the FEDERAL REGISTER.

### § 304.11  Notice of restrictions on use of reproductions of transmission programs.

Any public broadcasting entity which, pursuant to 17 U.S.C. 118, supplies a reproduction of a transmission program to governmental bodies or nonprofit institutions shall include with each copy of the reproduction a warning notice stating in substance that the reproductions may be used for a period of no more than seven days from the specified date of transmission, that the reproductions must be destroyed by the user before or at the end of such period, and that a failure to fully comply with these terms shall subject the body or institution to the remedies for infringement of copyright.

### § 304.12  Amendment of certain regulations.

Subject to 17 U.S.C. 118, the Administrative Procedure Act and the Rules of Procedure of the Copyright Royalty Tribunal, the CRT may at any time amend, modify or repeal regulations in this part adopted pursuant to 17 U.S.C. 118(b)(3) by which "copyright owners may receive reasonable notice of the use of their works" and "under which records of such use shall be kept by public broadcasting entities."

### § 304.13 Issuance of interpretative regulations.

Subject to 17 U.S.C. 118, the Administrative Procedure Act and the Rules of Procedure of the Copyright Royalty Tribunal, the CRT may at any time, either on its own motion or the motion of a person having a significant interest in the subject matter, issue such interpretative regulations as may be necessary or useful [for] the implementation of this part. Such regulations may not prior to January 1, 1988, alter the schedule of rates and terms of royalty payments by this part.

## PART 305—CLAIMS TO PHONORECORD PLAYER (JUKEBOX) ROYALTY FEES

Sec.
305.1 General.
305.2 Time of filing.
305.3 Content of claims.
305.4 Justification of claims.
305.5 Forms.

AUTHORITY: 17 U.S.C. 116(c)(2).

SOURCE: 43 FR 40501, Sept. 12, 1978, unless otherwise noted.

### § 305.1 General.

This regulation prescribes procedures pursuant to 17 U.S.C. 116(c)(2), whereby persons claiming to be entitled to compulsory license fees for public performances of nondramatic musical works by means of coin-operated phonorecord players shall file claims with the Copyright Royalty Tribunal.

### § 305.2 Time of filing.

During the month of January in each year every person claiming to be entitled to phonorecord player fees for performances of nondramatic musical works during the preceding calendar year shall file a claim with the Copyright Royalty Tribunal. Claimants may file jointly or as a single claim. A performing rights society shall not be required to obtain from its members or affiliates separate authorizations, apart from their standard membership or affiliation agreements, for purposes of this filing and fee distribution.

### § 305.3 Content of claims.

The claims filed shall include the following information:
(a) The full legal name of the person or entity claiming compulsory license fees. Performing rights societies are not required to include lists of members or affiliates to whom distributions would be made by such societies.
(b) The full address, including a specific number and street name or rural route, of the place of business of the person or entity.

(c) A specific agreement to accept as final the determination of the Copyright Royalty Tribunal in any controversy concerning the distribution of royalty fees, except for the judicial review provided in 17 U.S.C. 116.

## § 305.4 Justification of claims.

(a) Not later than the first day of November of each year, every person or entity which has filed a claim pursuant to § 305.2 shall file with the Copyright Royalty Tribunal a statement claiming the proportionate share of compulsory license fees to which such person or entity believes it is entitled. The statement shall include a detailed justification for the requested entitlement and shall also include such specific information as the Copyright Royalty Tribunal may require by regulation or order.

(b) The entitlement justification statement required by paragraph (a) need not be filed with the Copyright Royalty Tribunal if it has been determined by the Tribunal that there is no controversy as to the distribution of royalty fees.

## § 305.5 Forms.

The Copyright Royalty Tribunal does not provide printed forms for the filing of claims.

## PART 306—ADJUSTMENT OF ROYALTY RATE FOR COIN-OPERATED PHONORECORD PLAYERS

Sec.
306.1 General.
306.2 Definition of coin-operated phonorecord player.
306.3 Compulsory license fees for coin-operated phonorecord players.
306.4 Cost of living adjustment.

AUTHORITY: 17 U.S.C. 801(b)(1) and 804(e).

SOURCE: 45 FR 890, Jan. 5, 1981 unless otherwise noted.

## § 306.1 General.

This Part 306 establishes the compulsory license fees for coin-operated phonorecord players beginning on January 1, 1982, in accordance with the provisions of 17 U.S.C. 116 and 804(a).

## § 306.2 Definition of coin-operated phonorecord player.

As used in this part, the term "coin-operated phonorecord player" shall have the same meaning as set forth in 17 U.S.C. 116(e)(1).

## § 306.3 Compulsory license fees for coin-operated phonorecord players.

(a) Commencing on January 1, 1982 the annual compulsory license fee for a coin-operated phonorecord player, as set forth in 17 U.S.C. 116(b)(1)(A), shall be $25.

(b) Commencing on January 1, 1984 the annual compulsory license fee for a coin-operated phonorecord player, as set forth in 17 U.S.C. 116(b)(1)(A), shall be $50, subject to adjustment in accordance with § 306.4 hereof.

(c) In accordance with 17 U.S.C. 116(b)(1)(A), if performances are made available on a particular phonorecord player for the first time after July 1 of any year, the compulsory license fee for the remainder of that year shall be one half of the annual rate of (a) or (b) of this section, subject to adjustment in accordance with § 306.4 hereof.

## § 306.4  Cost of living adjustment.

(a) On August 1, 1986 the Copyright Royalty Tribunal (CRT) shall publish in the FEDERAL REGISTER a notice of the change in the cost of living as determined by the Consumer Price Index (all urban consumers, all items) from the first Index published subsequent to February 1, 1981 to the last Index published prior to August 1, 1986.

(b) On the same date as the notices published pursuant to paragraph (a), the CRT shall publish in the FEDERAL REGISTER a revised schedule of the compulsory license fee which shall adjust the dollar amount set forth in § 306.3(b) according to the change in the cost of living determined as provided in paragraph (a). Such compulsory license fees shall be fixed at the nearest dollar.

(c) The adjusted schedule for the compulsory license fee shall become effective on January 1, 1987.

### PART 307—ADJUSTMENT OF ROYALTY PAYABLE UNDER COMPULSORY LICENSE FOR MAKING AND DISTRIBUTING PHONORECORDS

Sec.
307.1  General.
307.2  Royalty payable under compulsory license.
307.3  Adjustment of royalty rate.

AUTHORITY: 17 U.S.C. 801(b)(1) and 804.

## § 307.1  General.

This Part 307 adjusts the rates of royalty payable under compulsory license for making and distributing phonorecords embodying nondramatic musical works, under 17 U.S.C. 115.

[46 FR 891, Jan. 5, 1981]

## § 307.2  Royalty payable under compulsory license.

With respect to each work embodied in the phonorecord, the royalty payable shall be either four cents, or three-quarters of one cent per minute of playing time or fraction thereof, whichever amount is larger, for every phonorecord made and distributed on or after July 1, 1981, subject to adjustment pursuant to § 307.3.

[46 FR 891, Jan. 5, 1981, as amended at 46 FR 62268, Dec. 23, 1981]

## § 307.3  Adjustment of royalty rate.

(a) For every phonorecord made and distributed on or after January 1, 1983, the royalty payable with respect to each work embodied in the phonorecord shall be either 4.25 cents, or .8 cent per minute of playing time or fraction thereof, whichever amount is larger, subject to further adjustment pursuant to paragraphs (b) and (c) of this section.

(b) For every phonorecord made and distributed on or after July 1, 1984, the royalty payable with respect to each work embodied in the phonorecord shall be either 4.5 cents, or .85 cent per minute of playing time or fraction thereof, which every amount is larger, subject to further adjustment pursuant to paragraph (c) of this section.

(c) For every phonorecord made and distributed on or after January 1, 1986, the royalty payable with respect to each work embodied in the phonorecord shall be either 5 cents, or .95 cent per minute of playing time or fraction thereof, whichever amount is larger.

[46 FR 62268, Dec. 23, 1981]

# PART 308—ADJUSTMENT OF ROYALTY FEE FOR COMPULSORY LICENSE FOR SECONDARY TRANSMISSION BY CABLE SYSTEM

Sec.
308.1 General.
308.2 Royalty fee for compulsory license for secondary transmission by cable systems.

## § 308.1 General.

This part establishes adjusted terms and rates or royalty payments in accordance with the provisions of 17 U.S.C. 111 and 801(b)(2)(A), (B), (C), and (D). Upon compliance with 17 U.S.C. 111 and the terms and rates of this part, a cable system entity may engage in the activities set forth in 17 U.S.C. 111.

(17 U.S.C. 801(b)(2)(A) and (D))
[47 FR 52159, Nov. 19, 1982]

## § 308.2 Royalty fee for compulsory license for secondary transmission by cable systems.

(a) Commencing with the first semiannual accounting period of 1985 and for each semiannual accounting period thereafter, the royalty rates established by 17 U.S.C. 111(d)(2)(B) shall be as follows:

(1) .893 of 1 per centum of such gross receipts for the privilege of further transmitting any nonnetwork programming of a primary transmitter in whole or in part beyond the local service area of such primary transmitter, such amount to be applied against the fee, if any, payable pursuant to paragraphs (a)(2) through (4);

(2) .893 of 1 per centum of such gross receipts for the first distant signal equivalent;

(3) .563 of 1 per centum of such gross receipts for each of the second, third and fourth distant signal equivalents; and

(4) .265 of 1 per centum of such gross receipts for the fifth distant signal equivalent and each additional distant signal equivalent thereafter.

(b) Commencing with the first semiannual accounting period of 1985 and for each semiannual accounting period thereafter, the gross receipts limitations established by 17 U.S.C. 111(d)(2)(C) and (D) shall be adjusted as follows:

(1) If the actual gross receipts paid by subscribers to a cable system for the period covered by the statement for the basic service of providing secondary transmission of primary broadcast transmitters total $146,000 or less, gross receipts of the cable system for the purpose of this paragraph shall be computed by subtracting

from such actual gross receipts the amount by which $146,000 exceeds such actual gross receipts, except that in no case shall a cable system's gross receipts be reduced to less than $5,600. The royalty fee payable under this paragraph shall be 0.5 of 1 per centum regardless of the number of distant signal equivalents, if any; and

(2) If the actual gross receipts paid by the subscribers to a cable system for the period covered by the statement, for the basic service of providing secondary transmissions of primary broadcast transmitters, are more than $146,000 but less than $292,000, the royalty fee payable under this paragraph shall be: (i) 0.5 of 1 per centum of any gross receipts up to $146,000 and (ii) 1 per centum of any gross receipts in excess of $146,000 but less than $292,000, regardless of the number of distant signal equivalents, if any.

(c) Notwithstanding paragraphs (a) and (d) of this section, commencing with the first accounting period of 1983 and for each semiannual accounting period thereafter, for each distant signal equivalent or fraction thereof not represented by the carriage of:

(1) Any signal which was permitted (or, in the case of cable systems commencing operations after June 24, 1981, which would have been permitted) under the rules and regulations of the Federal Communications Commission in effect on June 24, 1981, or

(2) A signal of the same type (that is, independent, network, or non-commercial educational) substituted for such permitted signal, or

(3) A signal which was carried pursuant to an individual waiver of the rules and regulations of the Federal Communications Commission, as such rules were in effect on June 24, 1981;

the royalty rate shall be, in lieu of the royalty rates specified in paragraphs (a) and (d) of this section, 3.75 per centum of the gross receipts of the cable systems for each distant signal equivalent; any fraction of a distant signal equivalent shall be computed at its fractional value.

(d) Commencing with the first accounting period of 1983 and for each semiannual accounting period thereafter, for each distant signal equivalent or fraction thereof represented by the carriage of any signal which was subject (or, in the case of cable systems commencing operations after June 24, 1981, which would have been subject) to the FCC's syndicated exclusivity rules in effect on June 24, 1981 (former 47 CFR 76.151 3et seq.), the royalty rate shall be, in addition to the amount specified in paragraph (a) of this section,

(1) For cable systems located wholly or in part within a top 50 television market,

(i) .599 per centum of such gross for the first distant signal equivalent;

(ii) .377 per centum of such gross receipts for each of the second, third, and fourth distant signal equivalents;

(iii) .178 of 1 per centum for the fifth distant signal equivalent and each additional distant signal equivalent thereafter;

(2) For cable systems located wholly or in part within a second 50 television market,

(i) .300 per centum of such gross receipts for the first distant signal equivalent;

(ii) .189 of 1 per centum of such gross receipts for each of the second, third, and fourth distant signal equivalents; and

(iii) .089 of 1 per centum for the fifth distant signal equivalent and each additional distant signal equivalent thereafter;

(3) For purposes of this section "top 50 television markets" and "second 50 television markets" shall be defined as the comparable terms are defined or interpreted in accordance with 47 CFR 76.51, as effective June 24, 1981.

(17 U.S.C. 801(b)(2)(A) and (D))
[47 FR 52159, Nov. 19, 1982, as amended at 50 FR 18481, May 1, 1985]

# Appendix E

# Fair Use Guidelines

In a joint letter to Chairman Kastenmeier, dated March 19, 1976, the representatives of the Ad Hoc Committee of Educational Institutions and Organizations on Copyright Law Revision, and of the Authors League of America, Inc., and the Association of American Publishers, Inc., stated:

"You may remember that in our letter of March 8, 1976 we told you that the negotiating teams representing authors and publishers and the Ad Hoc Group had reached tentative agreement on guidelines to insert in the Committee Report covering educational copying from books and periodicals under Section 107 of H.R. 2223 and S. 22, and that as part of that tentative agreement each side would accept the amendments to Sections 107 and 504 which were adopted by your Subcommittee on March 3, 1976.

"We are now happy to tell you that the agreement has been approved by the principals and we enclose a copy herewith. We had originally intended to translate the agreement into language suitable for inclusion in the legislative report dealing with Section 107, but we have since been advised by committee staff that this will not be necessary.

"As stated above, the agreement refers only to copying from books and periodicals, and it is not intended to apply to musical or audiovisual works."

The full text of the agreement is as follows:

"Agreement on Guidelines for Classroom Copying in Not-For-Profit Educational Institutions

"with respect to books and periodicals

"The purpose of the following guidelines is to state the minimum and not the maximum standards of educational fair use under Section 107 of H.R. 2223. The parties agree that the conditions determining the extent of permissible copying for educational purposes may change in the future; that certain types of copying permitted under these guidelines may not be permissible in the future; and conversely that in the future other types of copying not permitted under these guidelines may be permissible under revised guidelines.

"Moreover, the following statement of guidelines is not intended to limit the types of copying permitted under the standards of fair use under judicial decision and which are stated in Section 107 of the Copyright Revision Bill. There may be instances in which copying which does not fall within the guidelines stated below may nonetheless be permitted under the criteria of fair use.

"GUIDELINES

"I. *Single Copying for Teachers*

"A single copy may be made of any of the following by or for a teacher at his or her individual request for his or her scholarly research or use in teaching or preparation to teach a class:

A.  A chapter from a book;

B.  An article from a periodical or newspaper;

C.  A short story, short essay or short poem, whether or not from a collective work;

D.  A chart, graph, diagram, drawing, cartoon or picture from a book, periodical, or newspaper;

"II. *Multiple Copies for Classroom Use*

"Multiple copies (not to exceed in any event more than one copy per pupil in a course) may be made by or for the teacher giving the course for classroom use or discussion; *provided that:*

A.  The copying meets the tests of brevity and spontaneity as defined below; *and,*

B.  Meets the cumulative effect test as defined below; *and,*

C.  Each copy includes a notice of copyright

"*Definitions*

"*Brevity*

"(*i*)  Poetry: (a) A complete poem if less than 250 words and if printed on not more than two pages or, (b) from a longer poem, an excerpt of not more than 250 words.

"(*ii*)  Prose: (a) Either a complete article, story or essay of less than 2,500 words, or (b) an excerpt from any prose work of not more than 1,000 words or 10% of the work, whichever is less, but in any event a minimum of 500 words.

"[Each of the numerical limits stated in 'i' and 'ii' above may be expanded to permit the completion of an unfinished line of a poem or of an unfinished prose paragraph.]

"(*iii*)  Illustration: One chart, graph, diagram, drawing, cartoon or picture per book or per periodical issue.

"(*iv*)  'Special' works: Certain works in poetry, prose or in 'poetic prose' which often combine language with illustrations and which are intended sometimes for children and at other times for a more general audience fall short of 2,500 words in their entirety. Paragraph 'ii' above notwithstanding such 'special works' may not be reproduced in their entirety; however, an excerpt comprising not more than two of the published pages of such special work and containing not more than 10% of the words found in the text thereof, may be reproduced.

"*Spontaneity*

"(*i*) The copying is at the instance and inspiration of the individual teacher, and

"(*ii*) The inspiration and decision to use the work and the moment of its use for maximum teaching effectiveness are so close in time that it would be unreasonable to expect a timely reply to a request for permission.

"*Cumulative Effect*

"(*i*) The copying of the material is for only one course in the school in which the copies are made.

"(*ii*) Not more than one short poem, article, story, essay or two excerpts may be copied from the same author, nor more than three from the same collective work or periodical volume during one class term.

"(*iii*) There shall not be more than nine instances of such multiple copying for one course during one class term.

"[The limitations stated in 'ii' and 'iii' above shall not apply to current news periodicals and newspapers and current news sections of other periodicals.]

"III. *Prohibitions as to I and II Above*

"Notwithstanding any of the above, the following shall be prohibited:

"(A) Copying shall not be used to create or to replace or substitute for anthologies, compilations or collective works. Such replacement or substitution may occur whether copies of various works or excerpts therefrom are accumulated or reproduced and used separately.

"(B) There shall be no copying of or from works intended to be 'consumable' in the course of study or of teaching. These include workbooks, exercises, standardized tests and test booklets and answer sheets and like consumable material.

"(C) Copying shall not:

(a) substitute for the purchase of books, publishers' reprints or periodicals;

(b) be directed by higher authority;

(c) be repeated with respect to the same item by the same teacher from term to term.

"(D) No charge shall be made to the student beyond the actual cost of the photocopying.

"Agreed March 19, 1976.

Ad Hoc Committee on Copyright Law Revision:

"By SHELDON ELLIOTT STEINBACH.

"AUTHOR-PUBLISHER GROUP:

AUTHORS LEAGUE OF AMERICA:

"By IRWIN KARP, *Counsel.*

"Association of American Publishers, Inc.:

"By ALEXANDER C. HOFFMAN,
*Chairman, Copyright Committee.*"

In a joint letter dated April 30, 1976, representatives of the Music Publishers' Association of the United States, Inc., the National Music Publishers' Association, Inc., the Music Teachers National Association, the Music Educators National Conference, the National Association of Schools of Music, and the Ad Hoc Committee on Copyright Law Revision, wrote to Chairman Kastenmeier as follows:

"During the hearings on H.R. 2223 in June 1975, you and several of your subcommittee members suggested that concerned groups should work together in developing guidelines which would be helpful to clarify Section 107 of the bill.

"Representatives of music educators and music publishers delayed their meetings until guidelines had been developed relative to books and periodicals. Shortly after that work was completed and those guidelines were forwarded to your subcommittee, representatives of the undersigned music organizations met together with representatives of the Ad Hoc Committee on Copyright Law Revision to draft guidelines relative to music.

"We are very pleased to inform you that the discussions thus have been fruitful on the guidelines which have been developed. Since private music teachers are an important factor in music education, due consideration has been given to the concerns of that group.

"We trust that this will be helpful in the report on the bill to clarify Fair Use as it applies to music."

The text of the guidelines accompanying this letter is as follows:

"GUIDELINES FOR EDUCATIONAL USES OF MUSIC

"The purpose of the following guidelines is to state the minimum and not the maximum standards of educational fair use under Section 107 of H.R. 2223. The parties agree that the conditions determining the extent of permissible copying for educational purposes may change in the future; that certain types of copying permitted under these guidelines may not be permissible in the future, and conversely that in the future other types of copying not permitted under these guidelines may be permissible under revised guidelines.

"Moreover, the following statement of guidelines is not intended to limit the types of copying permitted under the standards of fair use under judicial decision and which are stated in Section 107 of the Copyright Revision Bill. There may be instances in which copying which does not fall within the guidelines stated below may nonetheless be permitted under the criteria of fair use.

"*A. Permissible Uses*

"1. Emergency copying to replace purchased copies which for any reason are not available for an imminent performance provided purchased replacement copies shall be substituted in due course.

"2. For academic purposes other than performance, single or multiple copies of excerpts of works may be made, provided that the excerpts do not comprise a part of the whole which would constitute a performable unit such as a section,* movement or aria, but in no case more than 10 percent of the whole work. The number of copies shall not exceed one copy per pupil.**

---

*Corrected from *Congressional Record.*

**Editor's Note:* As reprinted in the House Report, subsection A.2 of the Music Guidelines had consisted of two separate paragraphs, one dealing with multiple copies and a second dealing with single copies. In his introductory remarks during the House debates on S.22, the Chairman of the House Judiciary Subcommittee, Mr. Kastenmeier, announced that "the report, as printed, does not reflect a subsequent change in the joint guidelines which was described in a subsequent letter to me from a representative of [the signatory organizations]," and provided the revised text of subsection A.2. (122 CONG. REC. H. 10875, Sept. 22, 1976). The text reprinted here is the revised text.

"3. Printed copies which have been purchased may be edited or simplified provided that the fundamental character of the work is not distorted or the lyrics, if any, altered or lyrics added if none exist.

"4. A single copy of recordings of performances by students may be made for evaluation or rehearsal purposes and may be retained by the educational institution or individual teacher.

"5. A single copy of a sound recording (such as a tape, disc or cassette) of copyrighted music may be made from sound recordings owned by an educational institution or an individual teacher for the purpose of constructing aural exercises or examinations and may be retained by the educational institution or individual teacher. (This pertains only to the copyright of the music itself and not to any copyright which may exist in the sound recording.)

*"B. Prohibitions*

"1. Copying to create or replace or substitute for anthologies, compilations or collective works.

"2. Copying of or from works intended to be 'consumable' in the course of study or of teaching such as workbooks, exercises, standardized tests and answer sheets and like material.

"3. Copying for the purpose of performance, except as in A(1) above.

"4. Copying for the purpose of substituting for the purchase of music, except as in A(1) and A(2) above.

"5. Copying without inclusion of the copyright notice which appears on the printed copy."

## THE 1981 GUIDELINES FOR OFF-AIR TAPING OF COPYRIGHTED WORKS FOR EDUCATIONAL USE*

The Committee has been involved in a review of the 1976 Copyright Act and has been studying several issues in addition to the piracy and counterfeiting issues addressed in H.R. 3530. For example: the Committee has recently approved H.R. 5949 which addresses the copyright liability of cable television; legislation to provide a performance right in sound recordings has been considered; bills which address the issues raised by the home video-recording litigation are currently under review; also, H.R. 4441 which permits a greater retention of copyright registration fees has recently been approved by the Committee. Many of these issues were ones which were initially addressed in the 1976 Act and have required adjustment given changing times. Some are new issues. The Committee remains hopeful there will be an equitable resolution of each of these controversies. The Committee calls upon each of the interested parties in these issues to remain open to compromise. The most notable feature of the 15-year effort to revise the Nation's copyright laws, which was largely completed in 1976, was the cooperative nature of that effort.

Of course, there were fierce struggles over particular issues. However, in the last analysis, almost every affected group desired that the revision effort succeed, and contributed to that success by modifying and compromising their initial positions.

---

*H.R. REP. No. 97-495, 97th Cong., 2d Sess. 6-11 (1982).

The spirit of cooperation was expressed most visibly in efforts on the part of proprietors and users in working out a series of guidelines defining fair use in certain situations. Three sets of guidelines were ultimately agreed upon and were published as part of the official legislative history of the act.

These guidelines covered classroom copying of books and periodicals in nonprofit educational institutions, educational uses of music and photocopying by libraries.

One area in which parties had been negotiating, but in which guidelines were not forthcoming, was off-the-air taping of copyrighted broadcast programs for educational purposes.

The Committee is pleased to include in this official Committee report a new set of guidelines negotiated by a committee of interested parties for use by copyright owners and educators which will go a long way toward resolving the lingering problems associated with off-air video-taping of copyrighted works for educational purposes.

The Committee is pleased to endorse these guidelines and include them here as part of the legislative history of our Nation's copyright law.

### TEXT OF GUIDELINES FOR OFF-AIR RECORDING OF BROADCAST PROGRAMMING FOR EDUCATIONAL PURPOSES

AUGUST 31, 1981.

Hon. ROBERT W. KASTENMEIER,
*Chairman, Subcommittee on Courts, Civil Liberties and Administration of Justice, Committee on the Judiciary, U.S. House of Representatives, Washington, D.C.*

DEAR CONGRESSMAN KASTENMEIER: We are forwarding herewith the "Guidelines for Off-Air Recording of Broadcast Programming for Educational Purposes," developed by the Negotiating Committee appointed by your subcommittee.

The Negotiating Committee has concurred that these guidelines reach an appropriate balance between the proprietary rights of copyright owners and the instructional needs of educational institutions. The Negotiating Committee recognized that beyond these guidelines, specific licenses or permissions from copyright proprietors may be required under the Copyright Law. The Committee believes that these guidelines should be reviewed periodically at reasonable intervals.

In accordance with what we believe was your intent, the Negotiating Committee had limited its discussion to nonprofit educational institutions and to television programs broadcast for reception by the general public without charge. Within the guidelines, the Negotiating Committee does not intend that off-air recordings by teachers under fair use be permitted to be intentionally substituted in the school curriculum for a standard practice of purchase or license of the same educational material by the institution concerned.

Sincerely,

EILEEN D. COOKE,
*Co-Chairman.*
LEONARD WASSER,
*Co-Chairman.*

MEMBERS OF THE NEGOTIATING TEAM

Eugene Aleinkoff, Agency for Instructional Television.
Joseph Bellon, CBS.
Ivan Bender, Association of Media Producers.[1]
James Bouras, Motion Picture Association of America.[2]
Eileen D. Cooke, American Library Association.
Bernard Freitag, National Education Association.
Howard Hitchens, Association for Educational Communications and Technology.
Irwin Karp, Authors League of America.
John McGuire, Screen Actors Guild.
Frank Norwood, Joint Council on Educational Communications.
Ernest Ricca, Directors Guild of America.
Carol Risher, Association of American Publishers.
James Popham, National Association of Broadcasters.
Judith Bresler, ABC.
Eric H. Smith, Public Broadcasting Service.
Sheldon Steinbach, American Council on Education.
August W. Steinhilber, National School Boards Association.
Leonard Wasser, Writers Guild of America, East.
Sanford Wolff, American Federation of Television and Radio Artists.[3]

GUIDELINES FOR OFF-AIR RECORDING OF BROADCAST PROGRAMMING FOR
EDUCATIONAL PURPOSES

In March of 1979, Congressman Robert Kastenmeier, Chairman of the House Subcommittee on Courts, Civil Liberties and Administration of Justice, appointed a Negotiating Committee consisting of representatives of education organizations, copyright proprietors, and creative guilds and unions. The following guidelines reflect the Negotiating Committee's consensus as to the application of "fair use" to the recording, retention and use of television broadcast programs for educational purposes. They specify periods of retention and use of such off-air recordings in classrooms and similar places devoted to instruction and for homebound instruction. The purpose of establishing these guidelines is to provide standards for both owners and users of copyrighted television programs.

1. The guidelines were developed to apply only to off-air recording by non-profit educational institutions.

2. A broadcast program may be recorded off-air simultaneously with broadcast tranmission (including simultaneous cable retransmission) and retained by a non-profit educational institution for a period not to exceed the first forty-five (45) consecutive calendar days after date of recording. Upon conclusion of such retention period, all off-air recordings must be erased or destroyed immediately. "Broadcast programs," are television programs

---

[1] See attached letters from Association of Media Producers and Films, Inc.
[2] See attached letter.
[3] As a result of a summer hiatus, the guidelines have not yet been submitted to the AFTRA National Governing Board.

transmitted by television stations for reception by the general public without charge.

3. Off-air recordings may be used once by individual teachers in the course of relevant teaching activities, and repeated once only when instructional reinforcement is necessary, in classrooms and similar places devoted to instruction within a single building, cluster or campus, as well as in the homes of students receiving formalized home instruction, during the first ten (10) consecutive school days in the forty-five (45) day calendar day retention period. "School days" are school session days—not counting weekends, holidays, vacations, examination periods, or other scheduled interruptions—within the forty-five (45) calendar day retention period.

4. Off-air recordings may be made only at the request of and used by individual teachers, and may not be regularly recorded in anticipation of requests. No broadcast program may be recorded off-air more than once at the request of the same teacher, regardless of the number of times the program may be broadcast.

5. A limited number of copies may be reproduced from each off-air recording to meet the legitimate needs of teachers under these guidelines. Each such additional copy shall be subject to all provisions governing the original recording.

6. After the first ten (10) consecutive school days, off-air recordings may be used up to the end of the forty-five (45) calendar day retention period only for teacher evaluation purposes, i.e., to determine whether or not to include the broadcast program in the teaching curriculum, and may not be used in the recording institution for student exhibition or any other non-evaluation purpose without authorization.

7. Off-air recordings need not be used in their entirety, but the recorded programs may not be altered from their original content. Off-air recordings may not be physically or electronically combined or merged to constitute teaching anthologies or compilations.

8. All copies of off-air recordings must include the copyright notice on the broadcast program as recorded.

9. Educational institutions are expected to establish appropriate control procedures to maintain the integrity of these guidelines.

MOTION PICTURE ASSOCIATION OF AMERICA, INC.,
*New York, N.Y., August 24, 1981.*

Re Guidelines for Off-Air Recording of Broadcast Programming for Educational Purposes.

Mr. LEONARD WASSER
*Writers Guild of America, East, Inc.,*
*New York, N.Y.*

DEAR LEN: This is to advise you that, although we were a party to the discussions which led to their formulation, the Motion Picture Association of America, as such will take no position on the above-style guidelines.

However, we are authorized to advise you that the following individual MPAA member companies assent to the guidelines:

Avco Embassy Pictures Corp.
Columbia Pictures Industries, Inc.
Filmways Pictures, Inc.

Metro-Goldwyn-Mayer Film Co.
Paramount Pictures Corp.
Twentieth Century-Fox Film Corp.
Universal Pictures, a division of Universal City Studios, Inc.

I would appreciate it if a copy of this letter could be included in any transmittal which you and Eileen Cooke make to Congressman Kastenmeier so that it is made part of the record.

Kindest regards.

Very truly yours,
JAMES BOURAS.

ASSOCIATION OF MEDIA PRODUCERS,
*Washington, D.C., September 17, 1981.*

Hon. ROBERT C. KASTENMEIER,
*Chairman, Subcommittee on Courts, Civil Liberties and the Administration of Justice, U.S. House of Representatives, Washington, D.C.*

DEAR CONGRESSMAN KASTENMEIER: The Association of Media Producers, the national trade association representing the producers and distributors of educational media materials, has appreciated the opportunity to participate as a member of the Negotiating Committee to establish guidelines for off-air taping of copyrighted works.

This is to advise you the AMP Board of Directors recently voted not to endorse the "Guidelines for Off-Air Recording of Broadcast Programming for Educational Purposes," now being submitted to the Committee on Courts, Civil Liberties and the Administration of Justice.

The guidelines are not in keeping with the principal objectives of our industry, and we are fearful that they may seriously jeopardize the future well-being of the small but vital educational media industry, its market, and the availability of a broad variety of instructional materials essential to maintaining quality educational programs.

Sincerely,

GORDON L. NELSON,
*President.*

FILMS, INC.,
*Wilmette, Ill., September 15, 1981.*

Mr. GORDON NELSON,
*President, Association of Media Producers, 1101 Connecticut Avenue, Washington, D.C.*

DEAR GORDON: As you know since approximately January 1, 1980, I have represented the Association of Media Producers on the Committee to Negotiate Fair-use Guidelines for Off-air Videotaping For Educational Uses. At that time James LeMay, formerly of Coronet Instructional Media, also represented AMP. Prior to the time I began serving on the committee Mr. Gale Livengood of Films Inc. was in that capacity.

I have steadfastly recommended adoption of the guidelines to the Board of Directors of AMP and since becoming a member of the Board earlier this year, continued to take that position. I believe that adoption of the guidelines would be a positive development in the educational audio-visual industry. My recommendation to the Board also reflects the overwhelming opinion throughout my company on this issue.

As you also know, my recommendation was continually made during the actual voting by the Board on this matter but that in spite of my recommendation and vote in favor of adoption of the guidelines, the question was narrowly defeated.

I wish to have this letter become a part of the materials you transmit to Eileen Cooke of the American Library Association regarding AMP's decision. You should also know that Films Inc. intends to transmit its own views on this issue directly to Congressman Robert Kastenmeier.

Sincerely yours,

IVAN R. BENDER.
*Vice President and General Counsel.*

# Appendix F

# International Copyright Conventions to Which the United States Is a Party

## Universal Copyright Convention as Revised at Paris, 1971

*Convention and protocols done at Paris July 24, 1971;*
*Ratification advised by the Senate of the United States of America August 14, 1972;*
*Ratified by the President of the United States of America August 28, 1972;*
*Ratification of the United States of America deposited with the Director-General of*
  *the United Nations Educational, Scientific and Cultural Organization Septem-*
  *ber 18, 1972;*
*Proclaimed by the President of the United States of America July 18, 1974;*
*Entered into force July 10, 1974.*

---

BY THE PRESIDENT OF THE UNITED STATES OF AMERICA

A PROCLAMATION

CONSIDERING THAT:

The Universal Copyright Conventions as revised at Paris on July 24, 1971, together with two related protocols, the text of which, as certified by the Director, Office of International Standards and Legal Affairs, United Nations Educational, Scientific and Cultural Organization, in the French, English and Spanish languages, is hereto annexed;

The Senate of the United States of America by its resolution of August 14, 1972, two-thirds of the Senators present concurring therein, gave its advice and consent to ratification of the Convention as revised, together with the two related protocols;

The President of the United States of America ratified the Convention as revised, together with the two related protocols on August 28, 1972, in pursuance of the advice and consent of the Senate;

The instrument of ratification by the United States of America was deposited with the Director-General of the United Nations Educational, Scientific and Cultural Organization on September 18, 1972, in accordance with paragraph 3 of Article VIII of the Convention as revised;

It is provided in paragraph 1 of Article IX of the Convention as revised that it shall come into force three months after the deposit of twelve instruments of ratification, acceptance or accession;

It is provided in paragraph 2(b) of each of the protocols that it shall enter into force in respect of each State on the date of deposit of the instrument of ratification, acceptance or accession of the State concerned or on the date of entry into force of the 1971 Convention with respect to such State, whichever is the later; and

Pursuant to the provisions of paragraph 1 of Article IX of the Convention as revised and paragraph 2(b) of each of the two related protocols, the Convention as revised, together with the two related protocols, entered into force on July 10, 1974.

NOW, THEREFORE, be it known that I, Richard Nixon, President of the United States of America, proclaim and make public the Convention as revised, together with the two related protocols, to the end that they shall be observed and fulfilled with good faith by the United States of America and by the citizens of the United States of America and all other persons subject to the jurisdiction thereof.

IN TESTIMONY WHEREOF, I have signed this proclamation and caused the Seal of the United States of America to be affixed.

DONE at the city of Washington this eighteenth day of July in the year of our Lord one thousand nine hundred seventy-four and of the Independence of the United States of America the one hundred ninety-ninth.


[SEAL]

By the President

RICHARD NIXON




HENRY A. KISSINGER
*Secretary of State*

The Contracting States.

Moved by the desire to ensure in all countries copyright protection of literary, scientific and artistic works,

Convinced that a system of copyright protection appropriate to all nations of the world and expressed in a universal convention, additional to, and without impairing international systems already in force, will ensure respect for the rights of the individual and encourage the development of literature, the sciences and the arts,

Persuaded that such a universal copyright system will facilitate a wider dissemination of works of the human mind and increase international understanding,

Have resolved to revise the Universal Copyright Convention as signed at Geneva on 6 September 1952 (hereinafter called "the 1952 Convention"), and consequently,

Have agreed as follows:


ARTICLE I

Each Contracting State undertakes to provide for the adequate and effective protection of the rights of authors and other copyright proprietors in literary, scientific and artistic works, including writings, musical, dramatic and cinematographic works, and paintings, engravings and sculpture.

## ARTICLE II

1. Published works of nationals of any Contracting State and works first published in that State shall enjoy in each other Contracting State the same protection as that other State accords to works of its nationals first published in its own territory, as well as the protection specially granted by the Convention.

2. Unpublished works of nationals of each Contracting State shall enjoy in each other Contracting State the same protection as that other State accords to unpublished works of its own nationals, as well as the protection specially granted by this Convention.

(3) For the purpose of this Convention any Contracting State may, by domestic legislation, assimilate to its own nationals any person domiciled in that State.

## ARTICLE III

1. Any Contracting State which, under its domestic law, requires as a condition of copyright, compliance with formalities such as deposit, registration, notice, notarial certificates, payment of fees or manufacture or publication in that Contracting State, shall regard these requirements as satisfied with respect to all works protected in accordance with this Convention and first published outside its territory and the author of which is not one of its nations, if from the time of the first publication all the copies of the work published with the authority of the author or other copyright proprietor bear the symbol © accompanied by the name of the copyright proprietor and the year of first publication placed in such manner and location as to give reasonable notice of claim of copyright.

2. The provisions of paragraph 1 shall not preclude any Contracting State from requiring formalities or other conditions for the acquisition and enjoyment of copyright in respect of works first published in its territory or works of its nationals wherever published.

3. The provisions of paragraph 1 shall not preclude any Contracting State from providing that a person seeking judicial relief must, in bringing the action, comply with procedural requirements, such as that the complainant must appear through domestic counsel or that the complainant must deposit with the court of an administrative office, or both, a copy of the work involved in the litigation; provided that failure to comply with such requirements shall not affect the validity of the copyright, nor shall any such requirement be imposed upon a national of another Contracting State if such requirement is not imposed on nationals of the State in which protection is claimed.

(4) In each Contracting State there shall be legal means of protection without formalities the unpublished works of nationals of other Contracting States.

(5) If a Contracting State grants protection for more than one term of copyright and the first term is for a period longer than one of the minimum periods prescribed in Article IV, such State shall not be required to comply with the provisions of paragraph 1 of this Article in respect of the second or any subsequent term of copyright.

## ARTICLE IV

1. The duration of protection of a work shall be governed, in accordance with the provisions of Article II and this Article, by the law of the Contracting State in which protection is claimed.

2. (a) The term of protection for works protected under this Convention shall not be less than the life of the author and twenty-five years after his death. However, any Contracting State which, on the effective date of this Convention in that State, has limited this term for certain classes of works to a period computed from the first publication of the work, shall be entitled to maintain these exceptions and to extend

them to other classes of works. For all these classes the term of protection shall not be less than twenty-five years from the date of first publication.

(b) Any Contracting State which, upon the effective date of this Convention in that State, does not compute the term of protection upon the basis of the life of the author, shall be entitled to compute the term of protection from the date of the first publication of the work or from its registration prior to publication, as the case may be, provided the term of protection shall not be less than twenty-five years from the date of first publication or from its registration prior to publication, as the case may be.

(c) If the legislation of a Contracting State grants two or more successive terms of protection, the duration of the first term shall not be less than one of the minimum periods specified in subparagraphs (a) and (b).

3. The provisions of paragraph 2 shall not apply to photographic works or to works of applied art; provided, however, that the term of protection in those Contracting States which protect photographic works, or works of applied art in so far as they are protected as artistic works, shall not be less than ten years for each of said classes of works.

(4) (a) No Contracting State shall be obliged to grant protection to a work for a period longer than that fixed for the class of works to which the work in question belongs, in the case of unpublished works by the law of the Contracting State of which the author is a national, and in the case of published works by the law of the Contracting State in which the work has been first published.

(b) For the purposes of the application of subparagraph (a), if the law of any Contracting State grants two or more successive terms of protection, the period of protection of that State shall be considered to be the aggregate of those terms. However, if a specified work is not protected by such State during the second or any subsequent term for any reason, the other Contracting States shall not be obliged to protect it during the second or any subsequent term.

(5) For the purposes of the application of paragraph 4, the work of a national of a Contracting State, first published in a non-Contracting State, shall be treated as though first published in the Contracting State of which the author is a national.

(6) For the purpose of the application of paragraph 4, in case of simultaneous publication in two or more Contracting States, the work shall be treated as though first published in the State which affords the shortest term; any work published in two or more Contracting States within thirty days of its first publication shall be considered as having been published simultaneously in said Contracting States.

## ARTICLE IV*bis*

1. The rights referred to in Article I shall include the basic rights ensuring the author's economic interests, including the exclusive right to authorize reproduction by any means, public performance and broadcasting. The provisions of this Article shall extend to works protected under this Convention either in their original form or in any form recognizably derived from the original.

2. However, any Contracting State may, by its domestic legislation, make exceptions that do not conflict with the spirit and provisions of this Convention, to the rights mentioned in paragraph 1 of this Article. Any State whose legislation so provides, shall nevertheless accord a reasonable degree of effective protection to each of the rights to which exception has been made.

## ARTICLE V

1. The rights referred to in Article I shall include the exclusive right of the author to make, publish and authorize the making and publication of translations of works protected under this Convention.

2. However, any Contracting State may, by its domestic legislation, restrict the right of translation of writings, but only subject to the following provisions:

(a) If, after the expiration of a period of seven years from the date of the first publication of a writing, a translation of such writing has not been published in a language in general use in the Contracting State, by the owner of the right of translation or with his authorization, any national of such Contracting State may obtain a non-exclusive licence from the competent authority thereof to translate the work into that language and publish the work so translated.

(b) Such national shall in accordance with the procedure of the State concerned, establish either that he has requested, and been denied, authorization by the proprietor of the right to make and publish the translation, or that, after due diligence on his part, he was unable to find the owner of the right. A licence may also be granted on the same conditions if all previous editions of a translation in a language in general use in the Contracting State are out of print.

(c) If the owner of the right of translation cannot be found, then the applicant for a licence shall send copies of his application to the publisher whose name appears on the work and, if the nationality of the owner of the right of translation is known, to the diplomatic or consular representative of the State of which such owner is a national, or to the organization which may have been designated by the government of that State. The license shall not be granted before the expiration of a period of two months from the date of the dispatch of the copies of the application.

(d) Due provision shall be made by domestic legislation to ensure to the owner of the right of translation a compensation which is just and conforms to international standards, to ensure payment and transmittal of such compensation, and to ensure a correct translation of the work.

(e) The original title and the name of the author of the work shall be printed on all copies of the published translation. The license shall be valid only for publication of the translation in the territory of the Contracting State where it has been applied for. Copies so published may be imported and sold in another Contracting State if a language in general use in such other State is the same language as that into which the work has been so translated, and if the domestic law in such other State makes provision for such licences and does not prohibit such importation and sale. Where the foregoing conditions do not exist, the importation and sale of such copies in a Contracting State shall be governed by its domestic law and its agreements. The licence shall not be transferred by the licensee.

(f) The licence shall not be granted when the author has withdrawn from circulation all copies of the work.

## ARTICLE V*bis*

1. Any Contracting State regarded as a developing county in conformity with the established practice of the General Assembly of the United Nations may, by a notification deposited with the Director-General of the United Nations Educational, Scientific and Cultural Organization (hereinafter called "the Director-General") at the time of its ratification, acceptance or accession or thereafter, avail itself of any or all of the exceptions provided for in Articles V*ter* and V*quater*.

2. Any such notification shall be effective for ten years from the date of coming into force of this Convention, or for such a part of that ten-year period as remains at the date of deposit of the notification, and may be renewed in whole or in part for further periods of ten years each if, not more than fifteen or less than three months before the expiration of the relevant ten-year period, the contracting State deposits a further notification with the Director-General. Initial notifications may also be made during these further periods of ten years in accordance with the provisions of this Article.

3. Notwithstanding the provisions of paragraph 2, a Contracting State that has ceased to be regarded as a developing country as referred to in paragraph 1 shall no

longer be entitled to renew its notification made under the provisions of paragraph 1 or 2, and whether or not it formally withdraws the notification such State shall be precluded from availing itself of the exceptions provided for in Articles V*ter* and V*quater* at the end of the current ten-year period, or at the end of three years after it has ceased to be regarded as a developing country, whichever period expires later.

4. Any copies of a work already made under the exceptions provided for in Articles V*ter* and V*quater* may continue to be distributed after the expiration of the period for which notifications under this Article were effective until their stock is exhausted.

5. Any Contracting State that has deposited a notification in accordance with Article XIII with respect to the application of this Convention to a particular country or territory, the situation of which can be regarded as analagous to that of the States referred to in paragraph 1 of this Article, may also deposit notifications and renew them in accordance with the provisions of this Article with respect to any such country or territory. During the effective period of such notifications, the provisions of Articles V*ter* and V*quater* may be applied with respect to such country or territory. The sending of copies from the country or territory to the Contracting State shall be considered as export within the meaning of Articles V*ter* and V*quater*.

ARTICLE V*ter*

1. (a) Any Contracting State to which Article V*bis* (1) applies may substitute for the period of seven years provided for in Article V(2) a period of three years or any longer period prescribed by its legislation. However, in the case of a translation into a language not in general use in one or more developed countries that are party to this Convention or only the 1952 Convention, the period shall be one year instead of three.

(b) A Contracting State to which Article V*bis*(1) applies may, with the unanimous agreement of the developed countries party to this Convention or only the 1952 Convention and in which the same language is in general use, substitute, in the case of translation into that language, for the period of three years provided for in sub-paragraph (a) another period as determined by such agreement but not shorter than one year. However, the sub-paragraph shall not apply where the language in question is English, French or Spanish. Notification of any such agreement shall be made to the Director-General.

(c) The licence may only be granted if the applicant, in accordance with the procedure of the State concerned, establishes either that he has requested, and been denied, authorization by the owner of the right of translation, or that, after due diligence on his part, he was unable to find the owner of the right. At the same time as he makes his request he shall inform either the International Copyright Information Centre established by the United Nations Educational, Scientific and Cultural Organization or any national or regional information centre which may have been designated in a notification to that effect deposited with the Director-General by the government of the State in which the publisher is believed to have his principal place of business.

(d) If the owner of the right of translation cannot be found, the applicant for a licence shall send, by registered airmail, copies of his application to the publisher whose name appears on the work and to any national or regional information centre as mentioned in sub-paragraph (c). If no such centre is notified he shall also send a copy to the international copyright information centre established by the United Nations Educational, Scientific and Cultural Organization.

2. (a) Licences obtainable after three years shall not be granted under this Article until a further period of six months has elapsed and licences obtainable after one year until a further period of nine months has elapsed. The further period shall begin either from the date of the request for permission to translate mentioned in paragraph 1(c) or, if the identity or address of the owner of the right of translation is not

known, from the date of dispatch of the copies of the application for a licence mentioned in paragraph 1(d).

(b) Licences shall not be granted if a translation has been published by the owner of the right of translation or with his authorization during the said period of six or nine months.

3. Any licence under this Article shall be granted only for the purpose of teaching, scholarship or research.

4. (a) Any licence granted under this Article shall not extend to the export of copies and shall be valid only for publication in the territory of the Contracting State where it has been applied for.

(b) Any copy published in accordance with a licence granted under this Article shall bear a notice in the appropriate language stating that the copy is available for distribution only in the Contracting State granting the licence. If the writing bears the notice specified in Article III(1) the copies shall bear the same notice.

(c) The prohibition of export provided for in sub-paragraph (a) shall not apply where a governmental or other public entity of a State which has granted a licence under this Article to translate a work into a language other than English, French or Spanish sends copies of a translation prepared under such licence to another country if:

(i) the recipients are individuals who are nationals of the Contracting State granting the licence, or organizations grouping such individuals;

(ii) the copies are to be used only for the purpose of teaching, scholarship or research;

(iii) the sending of the copies and their subsequent distribution to recipients is without the object of commercial purpose; and

(iv) the country to which the copies have been sent has agreed with the Contracting State to allow the receipt, distribution or both and the Director-General has been notified of such agreement by any one of the governments which have concluded it.

5. Due provision shall be made at the national level to ensure:

(a) that the licence provides for just compensation that is consistent with standards of royalties normally operating in the case of licences freely negotiated between persons in the two countries concerned; and

(b) payment and transmittal of the compensation; however, should national currency regulations intervene, the competent authority shall make all efforts, by the use of international machinery, to ensure transmittal in internationally convertible currency or its equivalent.

6. Any licence granted by a Contracting State under this Article shall terminate if a translation of the work in the same language with substantially the same content as the edition in respect of which the licence was granted is published in the said State by the owner of the right of translation or with his authorization, at a price reasonably related to that normally charged in the same State for comparable works. Any copies already made before the licence is terminated may continue to be distributed until their stock is exhausted.

7. For works which are composed mainly of illustrations a licence to translate the text and to reproduce the illustrations may be granted only if the conditions of Article V*quater* are also fulfilled.

(8) (a) A licence to translate a work protected under this Convention, published in printed or analogous forms of reproduction, may also be granted to a broadcasting organization having its headquarters in a Contracting State to which Article V*bis* (1) applies, upon an application made in that State by the said organization under the following conditions:

(i) the translation is made from a copy made and acquired in accordance with the laws of the Contracting State;

(ii) the translation is for use only in broadcasts intended exclusively for teaching or for the dissemination of the results of specialized technical or scientific research to experts in a particular profession;

(iii) the translation is used exclusively for the purposes set out in condition (ii), through broadcasts lawfully made which are intended for recipients on the territory of the Contracting State, including broadcasts made through the medium of sound or visual recordings lawfully and exclusively made for the purpose of such broadcasts;

(iv) sound or visual recordings of the translation may be exchanged only between broadcasting organizations having their headquarters in the Contracting State granting the licence; and

(v) all uses made of the translation are without any commercial purpose.

(b) Provided all of the criteria and conditions set out in sub-paragraph (a) are met, a licence may also be granted to a broadcasting organization to translate any text incorporated in an audio-visual fixation which was itself prepared and published for the sole purpose of being used in connection with systematic instructional activities.

(c) Subject to sub-paragraphs (a) and (b), the other provisions of this Article shall apply to the grant and exercise of the licence.

9. Subject to the provisions of this Article, any licence granted under this Article shall be governed by the provisions of Article V, and shall continue to be governed by the provisions of Article V and of this Article, even after the seven-year period provided for in Article V(2) has expired. However, after the said period has expired, the licensee shall be free to request that the said licence be replaced by a new licence governed exclusively by the provisions of Article V.

## ARTICLE V*quater*

1. Any Contracting State to which Article V*bis* (1) applies may adopt the following provisions:

(a) If, after the expiration of (i) the relevant period specified in sub-paragraph (c) commencing from the date of first publication of a particular edition of a literary, scientific or artistic work referred to in paragraph 3, or (ii) any longer period determined by national legislation of the State, copies of such edition have not been distributed in that State to the general public or in connection with systematic instructional activities at a price reasonably related to that normally charged in the State for comparable works, by the owner of the right of reproduction or with his authorization, any national of such State may obtain a non-exclusive licence from the competent authority to publish such edition at that or a lower price for use in connection with systematic instructional activities. The licence may only be granted if such national, in accordance with the procedure of the State concerned, establishes either that he has requested, and been denied, authorization by the proprietor of the right to publish such work, or that, after due diligence on his part, he was unable to find the owner of the right. At the same time as he makes his request he shall inform either the international copyright information centre established by the United Nations Educational, Scientific and Cultural Organization or any national or regional information centre referred to in sub-paragraph (d).

(b) A licence may also be granted on the same conditions if, for a period of six months, no authorized copies of the edition in question have been on sale in the State concerned to the general public or in connection with systematic instructional activities at a price reasonably related to that normally charged in the State for comparable works.

(c) The period referred to in sub-paragraph (a) shall be five years except that:

(i) for works of the natural and physical sciences, including mathematics, and of technology, the period shall be three years;

(ii) for works of fiction, poetry, drama and music, and for art books, the period shall be seven years.

(d) If the owner of the right of reproduction cannot be found, the applicant for a licence shall send, by registered air mail, copies of his application to the publisher whose name appears on the work and to any national or regional information centre identified as such in a notification deposited with the Director-General by the State in which the publisher is believed to have his principal place of business. In the absence of any such notification, he shall also send a copy to the international copyright information centre established by the United Nations Educational, Scientific and Cultural Organization. The licence shall not be granted before the expiration of a period of three months from the date of dispatch of the copies of the application.

(e) Licences obtained after three years shall not be granted under this Article:

(i) until a period of six months has elapsed from the date of the request for permission referred to in sub-paragraph (a) or, if the identity or address of the owner of the right of reproduction is unknown, from the date of the dispatch of the copies of the application for a licence referred to in sub-paragraph (d);

(ii) if any such distribution of copies of the edition as is mentioned in sub-paragraph (a) has taken place during that period.

(f) The name of the author and the title of the particular edition of the work shall be printed on all copies of the published reproduction. The licence shall not extend to the export of copies and shall be valid only for publication in the territory of the Contracting State where it has been applied for. The licence shall not be transferable by the licensee.

g. Due provision shall be made by domestic legislation to ensure an accurate reproduction of the particular edition in question.

(h) A licence to reproduce and publish a translation of a work shall not be granted under this Article in the following cases:

(i) where the translation was not published by the owner of the right of translation or with his authorization;

(ii) where the translation is not in a language in general use in the State with power to grant the licence.

2. The exceptions provided for in paragraph 1 are subject to the following additional provisions:

(a) Any copy published in accordance with a licence granted under this Article shall bear a notice in the appropriate language stating that the copy is available for distribution only in the Contracting State to which the said licence applies. If the edition bears the notice specified in Article III(1), the copies shall bear the same notice.

(b) Due provision shall be made at the national level to ensure:

(i) that the license provides for just compensation that is consistent with standards of royalties normally operating in the case of licences freely negotiated between persons in the two countries concerned; and

(ii) payment and transmittal of the compensation; however, should national currency regulations intervene, the competent authority shall make all efforts, by the use of international machinery, to ensure transmittal in international convertible currency or its equivalent.

(c) Whenever copies of an edition of a work are distributed in the Contracting State to the general public or in connection with systematic instructional activities, by the owner of the right of reproduction or with his authorization, at a price reasonably related to that normally charged in the State for comparable works, any licence granted under this Article shall terminate if such edition is in the same language and is substantially the same in content as the edition published under the licence. Any copies already made before the licence is terminated may continue to be distributed until their stock is exhausted.

(d) No licence shall be granted when the author has withdrawn from circulation all copies of the edition in question.

(3) (a) Subject to sub-paragraph (b), the literary, scientific or artistic works to which the Article applies shall be limited to works published in printed or analogous forms of reproduction.

(b) The provisions of this Article shall also apply to reproduction in audio-visual form of lawfully made audio-visual fixations including any protected works incorporated therein and to the translation of any incorporated text into a language in general use in the State with power to grant the licence; always provided that the audio-visual fixations in question were prepared and published for the sole purpose of being used in connection with systematic instructional activities.

## ARTICLE VI

"Publication," as used in this Convention, means the reproduction in tangible form and the general distribution to the public of copies of a work from which it can be read or otherwise visually perceived.

## ARTICLE VII

This Convention shall not apply to works or rights in works which, at the effective date of this Convention in a Contracting State where protection is claimed, are permanently in the public domain in the said Contracting State.

## ARTICLE VIII

1. This Convention, which shall bear the date of 24 July 1971, shall be deposited with the Director-General and shall remain open for signature by all States party to the 1952 Convention for a period of 120 days after the date of this Convention. It shall be subject to ratification or acceptance by the signatory States.
2. Any State which has not signed this Convention may accede thereto.
3. Ratification, acceptance or accession shall be effected by the deposit of an instrument to that effect with the Director-General.

## ARTICLE IX

1. This Convention shall come into force three months after the deposit of twelve instruments of ratification, acceptance or accession.
2. Subsequently, this Convention shall come into force in respect of each State three months after that State has deposited its instrument of ratification, acceptance or accession.
3. Accession to this Convention by a State not party to the 1952 Convention shall also constitute accession to that Convention; however, if its instrument of accession is deposited before this Convention comes into force, such State may make its accession to the 1952 Convention conditional upon the coming into force of this Convention. After the coming into force of this Convention, no State may accede solely to the 1952 Convention.
4. Relations between States party to this Convention and States that are party only to the 1952 Convention, shall be governed by the 1952 Convention. However, any State party only to the 1952 Convention may, by a notification deposited with the Director-General, declare that it will admit the application of the 1971 Convention to works of its nationals or works first published in its territory by all States party to this Convention.

## ARTICLE X

1. Each Contracting State undertakes to adopt, in accordance with its Constitution, such measures as are necessary to ensure the application of this Convention.

2. It is understood that at the date this Convention comes into force in respect of any State, that State must be in a position under its domestic law to give effect to the terms of this Convention.

## ARTICLE XI

1. An Intergovernmental Committee is hereby established with the following duties:
(a) to study the problems concerning the application and operation of the Universal Copyright Convention;
(b) to make preparation for periodic revisions of this Convention;
(c) to study any other problems concerning the international protection of copyright, in co-operation with the various interested international organizations, such as the United Nations Educational, Scientific and Cultural Organization, the International Union for the Protection of Literary and Artistic Works and the Organization of American States;
(d) to inform States party to the Universal Copyright Convention as to its activities.
2. The Committee shall consist of the representatives of eighteen States party to this Convention or only to the 1952 Convention.
3. The Committee shall be selected with due consideration to a fair balance of national interests on the basis of geographical location, population, languages and stage of development.
4. The Director-General of the United Nations Educational, Scientific and Cultural Organization, the Director-General of the World Intellectual Property Organization and the Secretary-General of the Organization of American States, or their representatives, may attend meetings of the Committee in an advisory capacity.

## ARTICLE XII

The Intergovernmental Committee shall convene a conference for revision whenever it deems necessary, or at the request of at least ten States party to this Convention.

## ARTICLE XIII

1. Any Contracting State may, at the time of deposit of its instrument of ratification, acceptance or accession, or at any time thereafter, declare by notification addressed to the Director-General that this Convention shall apply to all or any of the countries or territories for the international relations of which it is responsible and this Convention shall thereupon apply to the countries or territories named in such notification after the expiration of the term of three months provided for in Article IX. In the absence of such notification, this Convention shall not apply to any such country or territory.
2. However, nothing in this Article shall be understood as implying the recognition or tacit acceptance by a Contracting State of the factual situation concerning a country or territory to which this Convention is made applicable by another Contracting State in accordance with the provisions of this Article.

## ARTICLE XIV

1. Any Contracting State may denounce this Convention in its own name or on behalf of all or any of the countries of territories with respect to which a notification has been given under Article XIII. The denunciation shall be made by notification

addressed to the Director-General. Such denunciation shall also constitute denunciation of the 1952 Convention.

2. Such denunciation shall operate only in respect of the State or of the country or territory on whose behalf it was made and shall not take effect until twelve months after the date of receipt of the notification.

## ARTICLE XV

A dispute between two or more Contracting States concerning the interpretation or application of this Convention, not settled by negotiation, shall, unless the States concerned agree on some other method of settlement, be brought before the International Court of Justice for determination by it.

## ARTICLE XVI

1. This Convention shall be established in English, French, and Spanish. The three texts shall be signed and shall be equally authoritative.

2. Official texts of this Convention shall be established by the Director-General, after consultation with the governments concerned, in Arabic, German, Italian and Portuguese.

3. Any Contracting State or group of Contracting States shall be entitled to have established by the Director-General other texts in the language of its choice by arrangement with the Director-General.

4. All such texts shall be annexed to the signed texts of this Convention.

## ARTICLE XVII

1. This Convention shall not in any way affect the provisions of the Berne Convention for the Protection of Literary and Artistic Works or membership in the Union created by that Convention.

2. In application of the foregoing paragraph, a declaration has been annexed to the present Article. This declaration is an integral part of this Convention for the States bound by the Berne Convention on 1 January 1951, or which have or may become bound to it at a later date. The signature of this Convention by such States shall also constitute signature of the said declaration, and ratification, acceptance or accession by such States shall include the declaration, as well as this Convention.

## ARTICLE XVIII

This Convention shall not abrogate multilateral or bilateral copyright conventions or arrangements that are or may be in effect exclusively between two or more American Republics. In the event of any difference either between the provisions of such existing conventions or arrangements and the provisions of this Convention, or between the provisions of this Convention and those of any new convention or arrangement which may be formulated between two or more American Republics after this Convention comes into force, the convention or arrangement most recently formulated shall prevail between the parties thereto. Rights in works acquired in any Contracting State under existing conventions or arrangements before the date this Convention comes into force in such State shall not be affected.

## ARTICLE XIX

This Convention shall not abrogate multilateral or bilateral conventions or arrangements in effect between two or more Contracting States. In the event of any difference between the provisions of such existing conventions or arrangements and the provisions of this Convention, the provisions of this Convention shall prevail. Rights in works acquired in any Contracting State under existing conventions or arrangements before the date on which this Convention comes into force in such State shall not be affected. Nothing in this Article shall affect the provisions of Articles XVII and XVIII.

## ARTICLE XX

Reservations to this Convention shall not be permitted.

## ARTICLE XXI

1. The Director-General shall send duly certified copies of this Convention to the States interested and to the Secretary-General of the United Nations for registration by him.

2. He shall also inform all interested States of the ratifications, acceptances and accessions which have been deposited, the date on which this Convention comes into force, the notifications under this Convention and denunciations under Article XIV.

## APPENDIX DECLARATION RELATING TO ARTICLE XVII

The States which are members of the International Union for the Protection of Literary and Artistic Works (hereinafter called "the Berne Union") and which are signatories to this Convention,

Desiring to reinforce their mutual relations on the basis of the said Union and to avoid any conflict which might result from the coexistence of the Berne Convention and the Universal Copyright Convention,

Recognizing the temporary need of some States to adjust their level of copyright protection in accordance with their stage of cultural, social and economic development.

Have, by common agreement, accepted the terms of the following declaration:

(a) Except as provided by paragraph (b), works which, according to the Berne Convention, have as their country of origin a country which has withdrawn from the Berne Union after 1 January 1951, shall not be protected by the Universal Copyright Convention in the countries of the Berne Union;

(b) Where a Contracting State is regarded as a developing country in conformity with the established practice of the General Assembly of the United Nations, and has deposited with the Director-General of the United Nations Educational, Scientific and Cultural Organization, at the time of its withdrawal from the Berne Union, a notification to the effect that it regards itself as a developing country, the provision of paragraph (a) shall not be applicable as long as such State may avail itself of the exceptions provided for by this Convention in accordance with Article V*bis*;

(c) The Universal Copyright Convention shall not be applicable to the relationships among countries of the Berne Union in so far as it relates to the protection of works having as their country of origin, within the meaning of the Berne Convention, a country of the Berne Union.

## RESOLUTION CONCERNING ARTICLE XI

The Conference for Revision of the Universal Copyright Convention,

Having considered the problems relating to the Intergovernmental Committee provided for in Article XI of this Convention, to which this resolution is annexed,

Resolves that:

1. At its inception, the Committee shall include representatives of the twelve States members of the Intergovernmental Committee established under Article XI of the 1952 Convention and the resolution annexed to it, and, in addition, representatives of the following States: Algeria, Australia, Japan, Mexico, Senegal and Yugoslavia.

2. Any States that are not party to the 1952 Convention and have not acceded to this Convention before the first ordinary session of the Committee following the entry into force of this Convention shall be replaced by other States to be selected by the Committee at its first ordinary session in conformity with the provisions of Article XI(2) and (3).

3. As soon as the Convention comes into force the Committee as provided for in paragraph 1 shall be deemed to be constituted in accordance with Article XI of this Convention.

4. A session of the Committee shall take place within one year after the coming into force of this Convention; thereafter the Committee shall meet in ordinary session at intervals of not more than two years.

5. The Committee shall elect its Chairman and two Vice-Chairmen. It shall establish its Rules of Procedure having regard to the following principles:

(a) The normal duration of the term of office of the members represented on the Committee shall be six years with one-third retiring every two years, it being however understood that, of the original terms of office, one-third shall expire at the end of the Committee's second ordinary session which will follow the entry into force of this Convention, a further third at the end of its third ordinary session, and the remaining third at the end of its fourth ordinary session.

(b) The rules governing the procedure whereby the Committee shall fill vacancies, the order in which terms of membership expire, eligibility for re-election, and election procedures, shall be based upon a balancing of the needs for continuity of membership and rotation of representation, as well as the considerations set out in Article XI(3).

Expresses the wish that the United Nations Educational, Scientific and Cultural Organization provide its Secretariat.

In faith whereof the undersigned, having deposited their respective full powers, have signed this Convention.

DONE at Paris, this twenty-fourth day of July 1971, in a single copy.


## PROTOCOL 1

**Annexed to the Universal Copyright Convention as revised at Paris on 24 July 1971 concerning the application of that Convention to works of Stateless persons and refugees**

The States party hereto, being also party to the University Copyright Convention as revised at Paris on 24 July 1971 (hereinafter called "the 1971 Convention"),

Have accepted the following provisions:

1. Stateless persons and refugees who have their habitual residence in a State party to this Protocol shall, for the purpose of the 1971 Convention, be assimilated to the nationals of that State.

2. (a) This Protocol shall be signed and shall be subject to ratification or acceptance, or may be acceded to, as if the provisions of Article VIII of the 1971 Convention applied hereto.

(b) This Protocol shall enter into force in respect of each State, on the date of deposit of the instrument of ratification, acceptance or accession of the State concerned or on the date of entry into force of the 1971 Convention with respect to such State, whichever is the later.

(c) On the entry into force of this Protocol in respect of a State not party to Protocol 1 annexed to the 1952 Convention, the latter Protocol shall be deemed to enter into force in respect of such State.

In faith whereof the undersigned, being duly authorized thereto, have signed this Protocol.

Done at Paris this twenty-fourth day of July 1971, in the English, French and Spanish languages, the three texts being equally authoritative, in a single copy which shall be deposited with the Director-General of the United Nations Educational, Scientific and Cultural Organization. The Director-General shall send certified copies to the signatory States, and to the Secretary-General of the United Nations for registration.

## PROTOCOL 2

**Annexed to the Universal Copyright Convention as revised at Paris on 24 July 1971 concerning the application of that Convention to the works of certain international organizations**

The States party hereto, being also party to the Universal Copyright Convention as revised at Paris on 24 July 1971 (hereinafter called "the 1971 Convention"),

Have accepted the following provisions:

1. (a) The protection provided for in Article II (1) of the 1971 Convention shall apply to works published for the first time by the United Nations, by the Specialized Agencies in Relationship therewith, or by the Organization of American States.

(b) Similarly, Article II(2) of the 1971 Convention shall apply to the said organization or agencies.

2. (a) This protocol shall be signed and shall be subject to ratification or acceptance, or may be acceded to, as if the provisions of Article VIII of the 1971 Convention applied hereto.

(b) This Protocol shall enter into force for each State on the date of deposit of the instrument of ratification, acceptance or accession of the State concerned or on the date of entry into force of the 1971 Convention with respect to such State, whichever is the later.

In faith whereof the undersigned, being duly authorized thereto, have signed this Protocol.

Done at Paris, this twenty-fourth day of July 1971, in the English, French and Spanish languages, the three texts being equally authoritative, in a single copy which shall be deposited with the Director-General of the United Nations Educational, Scientific and Cultural Organization. The Director-General shall send certified copies to the signatory States, and to the Secretary-General of the United Nations for registration.

Certified a true and complete copy of the original of the Universal Copyright Convention as revised at Paris on 24 July 1971, of the Protocol 1 annexed to the Universal Copyright Convention as revised at Paris on 24 July 1971 concerning the application of that Convention to works of Stateless persons and refugees and of the Protocol 2 annexed to the Universal Copyright Convention as revised at Paris on 24 July 1971 concerning the application of that Convention to the works of certain international organizations.

Paris, 24. 12. 1971 Claude Lussier.

Director, Office of International Standards and Legal Affairs, United Nations Educational, Scientific and Cultural Organization

# Universal Copyright Convention—
# Geneva, 1952

*Convention and protocols dated at Geneva September 6, 1952;*
*Ratification advised by the Senate of the United States of America June 25, 1954;*
*Ratified by the President of the United States of America November 5, 1954;*
*Ratification of the United States of America deposited with the United Nations Educational, Scientific and Cultural Organization December 6, 1954;*
*Proclaimed by the President of the United States of America August 5, 1955;*
*Convention and protocols 1 and 2 entered into force September 16, 1955;*
*Protocol 3 entered into force with respect to the United States of America December 6, 1954.*

---

### BY THE PRESIDENT OF THE UNITED STATES OF AMERICA

#### A PROCLAMATION

WHEREAS a universal copyright convention, together with three related protocols, was signed at Geneva under date of September 6, 1952, on behalf of the United States of America and certain other states;

WHEREAS the texts of the said convention and protocols, in the English, French, and Spanish languages, are word for word as follows:
The Contracting States,

Moved by the desire to assure in all countries copyright protection of literary, scientific and artistic works,

Convinced that a system of copyright protection appropriate to all nations of the world and expressed in a universal convention, additional to, and without impairing international systems already in force, will ensure respect for the rights of the individual and encourage the development of literature, the sciences and the arts,

Persuaded that such a universal copyright system will facilitate a wider dissemination of works of the human mind and increase international understanding.

Have agreed as follows:

### ARTICLE I

Each Contracting State undertakes to provide for the adequate and effective protection of the rights of authors and other copyright proprietors in literary, scientific and artistic works, including writings, musical, dramatic and cinematographic works, and paintings, engravings and sculpture.

### ARTICLE II

1. Published works of nationals of any Contracting State and works first published in that Sate shall enjoy in each other Contracting State the same protection as that other State accords to works of the nationals first published in its own territory.

2. Unpublished works of nationals of each Contracting State shall enjoy in each other Contracting State the same protection as that other State accords to unpublished works of its own nationals.

3. For the purpose of this Convention any Contracting State may, by domestic legislation, assimilate to its own nationals any person domiciled in that State.

## ARTICLE III

1. Any Contracting State which, under its domestic law, requires as a condition of copyright, compliance with formalities such as deposit, registration, notice, notarial certificates, payment of fees or manufacture or publication in that Contracting State, shall regard these requirements as satisfied with respect to all works protected in accordance with this Convention and first published outside its territory and the author of which is not one of its nationals, if from the time of the first publication all the copies of the work published with the authority of the author or other copyright proprietor bear the symbol © accompanied by the name of the copyright proprietor and the year of first publication placed in such manner and location as to give reasonable notice of claim of copyright.

2. The provisions of paragraph 1 of this Article shall not preclude any Contracting State from requiring formalities or other conditions for the acquisition and enjoyment of copyright in respect of works first published in its territory or works of its nationals wherever published.

3. The provisions of paragraph 1 of this Article shall not preclude any Contracting State from providing that a person seeking judicial relief must, in bringing the action, comply with procedural requirements, such as that the complainant must appear through domestic counsel or that the complainant must deposit with the court or an administrative office, or both, a copy of the work involved in the litigation; provided that failure to comply with such requirements shall not affect the validity of the copyright, nor shall any such requirement be imposed upon a national of another Contracting State if such requirement is not imposed on nationals of the State in which protection is claimed.

4. In each Contracting State there shall be legal means of protecting without formalities the unpublished works of nationals of other Contracting States.

5. If a Contracting State grants protection for more than one term of copyright and the first term is for a period longer than one of the minimum periods prescribed in Article IV, such State shall not be required to comply with the provisions of paragraph 1 of this Article III in respect of the second or any subsequent term of copyright.

## ARTICLE IV

1. The duration of protection of a work shall be governed, in accordance with the provisions of Article II and this Article, by the law of the Contracting State in which protection is claimed.

2. The term of protection for works protected under this Convention shall not be less than the life of the author and 25 years after his death.

However, any Contracting State which, on the effective date of this Convention in that State, has limited this term for certain classes of works to a period computed from the first publication of the work, shall be entitled to maintain these exceptions and to extend them to other classes of works. For all these classes the term of protection shall not be less than 25 years from the date of first publication.

Any Contracting State which, upon the effective date of this Convention in that State, does not compute the term of protection upon the basis of the life of the author, shall be entitled to compute the term of protection from the date of the first publication of the work or from its registration prior to publication, as the case may be, provided the term of protection shall not be less than 25 years from the date of first publication or from its registration prior to publication, as the case may be.

If the legislation of a Contracting State grants two or more successive terms of protection, the duration of the first term shall not be less than one of the minimum periods specified above.

3. The provisions of paragraph 2 of this Article shall not apply to photographic works or to works of applied art; provided, however, that the term of protection in those Contracting States which protect photographic works, or works of applied art in so far as they are protected as artistic works, shall not be less than ten years for each of said classes of works.

4. No Contracting State shall be obliged to grant protection to a work for a period longer than that fixed for the class of works to which the work in question belongs, in the case of unpublished works by the law of the Contracting State of which the author is a national, and in the case of published works by the law of the Contracting State in which the work has been first published.

For the purposes of the application of the preceding provision, if the law of any Contracting State grants two or more successive terms of protection, the period of protection of that State shall be considered to be the aggregate of those terms. However, if a specified work is not protected by such State during the second or any subsequent term for any reason, the other Contracting States shall not be obliged to protect it during the second or any subsequent term.

5. For the purposes of the application of paragraph 4 of this Article, the work of a national of a Contracting State, first published in a non-Contracting State, shall be treated as though first published in the Contracting State of which the author is a national.

6. For the purposes of the application of paragraph 4 of this Article, in case of simultaneous publication in two or more Contracting States, the work shall be treated as though first published in the State which affords the shortest term; any work published in two or more Contracting States within thirty days of its first publication shall be considered as having been published simultaneously in said Contracting States.

## ARTICLE V

1. Copyright shall include the exclusive right of the author to make, publish, and authorize the making and publication of translations of works protected under this Convention.

2. However, any Contracting State may, by its domestic legislation, restrict the right of translation of writings, but only subject to the following provisions:

If, after the expiration of a period of seven years from the date of the first publication of a writing, a translation of such writing has not been published in the national language or languages, as the case may be, of the Contracting State, by the owner of the right of translation or with his authorization, any national of such Contracting State may obtain a non-exclusive licence from the competent authority thereof to translate the work and publish the work so translated in any of the national languages in which it has not been published; provided that such national, in accordance with the procedure of the State concerned, establishes either that he has requested, and been denied, authorization by the proprietor of the right to make and publish the translation, or that, after due diligence on his part, he was unable to find the owner of the right. A licence may also be granted on the same conditions if all previous editions of a translation in such language are out of print.

If the owner of the right of translation cannot be found, then the applicant for a licence shall send copies of his application to the publisher whose name appears on the work and, if the nationality of the owner of the right of translation is known, to the diplomatic or consular representative of the State of which such owner is a national, or to the organization which may have been designated by the government of that State. The licence shall not be granted before the expiration of a period of two months from the date of the dispatch of the copies of the application.

Due provision shall be made by domestic legislation to assure to the owner of the right of translation a compensation which is just and conforms to international standards, to assure payment and transmittal of such compensation, and to assure a correct translation of the work.

The original title and the name of the author of the work shall be printed on all copies of the published translation. The licence shall be valid only for publication of the translation in the territory of the Contracting State where it has been applied for. Copies so published may be imported and sold in another Contracting State if one of the national languages of such other State is the same language as that into which the work has been so translated, and if the domestic law in such other State makes provision for such licences and does not prohibit such importation and sale. Where the foregoing conditions do not exist, the importation and sale of such copies in a Contracting State shall be governed by its domestic law and its agreements. The licence shall not be transferred by the licencee.

The licence shall not be granted when the author has withdrawn from circulation all copies of the work.

## ARTICLE VI

"Publication," as used in this Convention, means the reproduction in tangible form and the general distribution to the public of copies of a work from which it can be read or otherwise visually perceived.

## ARTICLE VII

This Convention shall not apply to works or rights in works which, at the effective date of the Convention in a Contracting State where protection is claimed, are permanently in the public domain in the said Contracting State.

## ARTICLE VIII

1. This Convention, which shall bear the date of 6 September 1952, shall be deposited with the Director-General of the United Nations Educational, Scientific and Cultural Organization and shall remain open for signature by all States for a period of 120 days after that date. It shall be subject to ratification or acceptance by the signatory States.

2. Any State which has not signed this Convention may accede thereto.

3. Ratification, acceptance or accession shall be effected by the deposit of an instrument to that effect with the Director-General of the United Nations Educational, Scientific and Cultural Organization.

## ARTICLE IX

1. This Convention shall come into force three months after the deposit of twelve instruments of ratification, acceptance or accession, among which there shall be those of four States which are not members of the International Union for the Protection of Literary and Artistic Works.

2. Subsequently, this Convention shall come into force in respect of each State three months after that State has deposited its instrument of ratification, acceptance or accession.

## ARTICLE X

1. Each State party to this Convention undertakes to adopt, in accordance with its Constitution, such measures as are necessary to ensure the application of this Convention.

2. It is understood, however, that at the time an instrument of ratification, acceptance or accession is deposited on behalf of any State, such State must be in a position under its domestic law to give effect to the terms of this Convention.

## ARTICLE XI

1. An Inter-governmental Committee is hereby established with the following duties:
   (a) to study the problems concerning the application and operation of this Convention;
   (b) to make preparation for periodic revisions of this Convention;
   (c) to study any other problems concerning the international protection of copyright, in co-operation with the various interested international organizations, such as the United Nations Educational, Scientific and Cultural Organization, the International Union for the Protection of Literary and Artistic Works and the Organization of American States;
   (d) to inform the Contracting States as to its activities.

2. The Committee shall consist of the representatives of twelve Contracting States to be selected with due consideration to fair geographical representation and in conformity with the Resolution relating to this article, annexed to this Convention.

The Director-General of the United Nations Educational, Scientific and Cultural Organization, the Director of the Bureau of the International Union for the Protection of Literary and Artistic Works and the Secretary-General of the Organization of American States, or their representatives, may attend meetings of the Committee in an advisory capacity.

## ARTICLE XII

The Inter-governmental Committee shall convene a conference for revision of this Convention whenever it deems necessary, or at the request of at least ten Contracting States, or of a majority of the Contracting States if there are less than twenty Contracting States.

## ARTICLE XIII

Any Contracting State may, at the time of deposit of its instrument of ratification or accession, or at any time thereafter declare by notification addressed to the Director-General of the United Nations Educational, Scientific and Cultural Organization that this Convention shall apply to all or any of the countries or territories for the international relations of which it is responsible and this Convention shall thereupon apply to the countries or territories named in such notification after the expiration of the term of three months provided for in Article IX. In the absence of such notification, this Convention shall not apply to any such country or territory.

## ARTICLE XIV

1. Any Contracting State may denounce this Convention in its own name or on behalf of all or any of the countries or territories as to which a notification has been

given under Article XIII. The denunciation shall be made by notification addressed to the Director-General of the United Nations Educational, Scientific and Cultural Organization.

2. Such denunciation shall operate only in respect of the State or of the country or territory on whose behalf it was made and shall not take effect until twelve months after the date of receipt of the notification.

## ARTICLE XV

A dispute between two or more Contracting States concerning the interpretation or application of this Convention, not settled by negotiation, shall, unless the States concerned agree on some other method of settlement, be brought before the International Court of Justice for determination by it.

## ARTICLE XVI

1. This Convention shall be established in English, French and Spanish. The three texts shall be signed and shall be equally authoritative.

2. Official texts of this Convention shall be established in German, Italian and Portuguese.

Any Contracting State or group of Contracting States shall be entitled to have established by the Director-General of the United Nations Educational, Scientific and Cultural Organization other texts in the language of its choice by arrangement with the Director-General.

All such texts shall be annexed to the signed texts of this Convention.

## ARTICLE XVII

1. This Convention shall not in any way affect the provisions of the Berne Convention for the Protection of Literary and Artistic Works or membership in the Union created by that Convention.

2. In application of the foregoing paragraph, a Declaration has been annexed to the present article. This Declaration is an integral part of this Convention for the States bound by the Berne Convention on January 1, 1951, or which have or may become bound to it at a later date. The signature of this Convention by such States shall also constitute signature of the said Declaration, and ratification, acceptance or accession by such States shall include the Declaration as well as the Convention.

## ARTICLE XVIII

This Convention shall not abrogate multilateral or bilateral copyright conventions or arrangements that are or may be in effect exclusively between two or more American Republics. In the event of any difference either between the provisions of such existing conventions or arrangements and the provisions of this Convention, or between the provisions of this Convention and those of any new convention or arrangement which may be formulated between two or more American Republics after this Convention comes into force, the convention or arrangement most recently formulated shall prevail between the parties thereto. Rights in works acquired in any Contracting State under existing conventions or arrangements before the date this Convention comes into force in such State shall not be affected.

## ARTICLE XIX

This Convention shall not abrogate multilateral or bilateral conventions or arrangements in effect between two or more Contracting States. In the event of any difference between the provisions of such existing conventions or arrangements and the provisions of this Convention, the provisions of this Convention shall prevail. Rights in works acquired in any Contracting State under existing conventions or arrangements before the date on which this Convention comes into force in such State shall shall not be affected. Nothing in this article shall affect the provisions of Articles XVII and XVII of this Convention.

## ARTICLE XX

Reservations to this Convention shall not be permitted.

## ARTICLE XXI

The Director-General of the United Nations Educational, Scientific and Cultural Organization shall send duly certified copies of this Convention to the States interested, to the Swiss Federal Council and to the Secretary-General of the United Nations for registration by him.

He shall also inform all interested States of the ratifications, acceptances and accessions which have been deposited, the date on which this Convention comes into force, the notifications under Article XIII of this Convention, and denunciations under Article XIV.

## APPENDIX DECLARATION

### *relating to Article XVII*

The States which are members of the International Union for the Protection of Literary and Artistic Works, and which are signatories to the Universal Copyright Convention,

Desiring to reinforce their mutual relations on the basis of the said Union and to avoid any conflict which might result from the co-existence of the Convention of Berne and the Universal Convention,

Have, by common agreement, accepted the terms of the following declaration:
  (a) Works which, according to the Berne Convention, have as their country of origin a country which has withdrawn from the International Union created by the said Convention, after January 1, 1951, shall not be protected by the Universal Copyright Convention in the countries of the Berne Union;
  (b) The Universal Copyright Convention shall not be applicable to the relationships among countries of the Berne Union insofar as it relates to the protection of works having as their country of origin, within the meaning of the Berne Convention, a country of the International Union created by the said Convention.

## RESOLUTION CONCERNING ARTICLE XI

### The Inter-governmental Copyright Conference
Having considered the problems relating to the Inter-governmental Committee provided for in Article XI of the Universal Copyright Convention,

resolves

1. The first members of the Committee shall be representatives of the following twelve States, each of those States designating one representative and an alternate: Argentina, Brazil, France, Germany, India, Italy, Japan, Mexico, Spain, Switzerland, United Kingdom, and United States of America.

2. The Committee shall be constituted as soon as the Convention comes into force in accordance with Article XI of this Convention;

3. The Committee shall elect its chairman and one vice-chairman. It shall establish its rules of procedure having regard to the following principles:

(a) the normal duration of the term of office of the representatives shall be six years; with one-third retiring every two years;

(b) before the expiration of the term of office of any members, the Committee shall decide which States shall cease to be represented on it and which States shall be called upon to designate representatives; the representatives of those States which have not ratified, accepted or acceded shall be the first to retire;

(c) the different parts of the world shall be fairly represented;

and expresses the wish

that the United Nations Educational, Scientific and Cultural Organization provide its Secretariat.

In faith whereof the undersigned, having deposited their respective full powers, have signed this Convention.

Done at Geneva, this sixth day of September, 1952 in a single copy.

**Protocol 1 annexed to the Universal Copyright Convention concerning the application of that Convention to the works of stateless persons and refugees**

The States parties hereto, being also parties to the Universal Copyright Convention (hereinafter referred to as the "Convention") have accepted the following provisions:

1. Stateless persons and refugees who have their habitual residence in a State party to this Protocol shall, for the purposes of the Convention, be assimilated to the nationals of the State.

2. (a) This Protocol shall be signed and shall be subject to ratification or acceptance, or may be acceded to, as if the provisions of Article VII of the Convention applied hereto.

(b) This Protocol shall enter into force in respect of each State, on the date of deposit of the instrument of ratification, acceptance or accession of the State concerned or on the date of entry into force of the Convention with respect to such State, whichever is the later.

In faith whereof the undersigned, being duly authorized thereto, have signed this Protocol.

Done at Geneva this sixth day of September, 1952, in the English, French and Spanish languages, the three texts being equally authoritative, in a single copy which shall be deposited with the Director-General of Unesco. The Director-General shall send certified copies to the signatory States, to the Swiss Federal Council and to the Secretary-General of the United Nations for registration.

**Protocol 2 annexed to the Universal Copyright Convention, concerning the application of that Convention to the works of certain international organizations**

The States parties hereto, being also parties to the Universal Copyright Convention (hereinafter referred to as the "Convention"),

Have accepted the following provisions:

1. (a) The protection provided for in Article II(1) of the Convention shall apply to works published for the first time by the United Nations, by the Specialized Agencies in relationship therewith, or by the Organization of American States;

(b) Similarly, Article II(2) of the Convention shall apply to the said organization or agencies.

2. (a) This Protocol shall be signed and shall be subject to ratification or acceptance, or may be acceded to, as if the provisions of Article VIII of the Convention applied hereto.

(b) This Protocol shall enter into force for each State on the date of deposit of the instrument of ratification, acceptance or accession of the State concerned or on the date of entry into force of the Convention with respect to such State, whichever is the later.

In faith whereof the undesigned, being duly authorized thereto, have signed this Protocol.

Done at Geneva, this sixth day of September, 1952, in the English, French and Spanish languages, the three texts being equally authoritative, in a single copy which shall be deposited with the Director-General of Unesco.

The Director-General shall send certified copies to the signatory States, to the Swiss Federal Council, and to the Secretary-General of the United Nations for registration.

**Protocol 3 annexed to the Universal Copyright Convention concerning the effective date of instruments of ratification or acceptance of or accession to that Convention**

States parties hereto,

Recognizing that the application of the Universal Copyright Convention (hereinafter referred to as the "Convention") to States participating in all the international copyright systems already in force will contribute greatly to the value of the Convention;

Have agreed as follows:

1. Any State party hereto may, on depositing its instrument of ratification or acceptance of or accession to the Convention, notify the Director-General of the United Nations Educational, Scientific and Cultural Organization (hereinafter referred to as "Director-General") that that instrument shall not take effect for the purposes of Article IX of the Convention until any other State named in such notification shall have deposited its instrument.

2. The notification referred to in paragraph 1 above shall accompany the instrument to which it relates.

3. The Director-General shall inform all States signatory or which have then acceded to the Convention of any notifications received in accordance with this Protocol.

4. This Protocol shall bear the same date and shall remain open for signature for the same period as the Convention.

5. It shall be subject to ratification or acceptance by the signatory States. Any State which has not signed this Protocol may accede thereto.

6. (a) Ratification or acceptance or accession shall be affected by the deposit of an instrument to that effect with the Director-General.

(b) This Protocol shall enter into force on the date of deposit of not less than four instruments of ratification or acceptance or accession. The Director-General shall inform all interested States of this date. Instruments deposited after such date shall take effect on the date of their deposit.

In faith whereof the undersigned, being duly authorized thereto, have signed this Protocol.

Done at Geneva, the sixth day of September 1952, in the English, French and Spanish languages, the three texts being equally authoritative, in a single copy which shall be annexed to the original copy of the Convention. The Director-General shall send certified copies to the signatory States, to the Swiss Federal Council, and to the Secretary-General of the United Nations for registration.

WHEREAS the Senate of the United States of America by their resolution of June 25, 1954, two-thirds of the Senators present concurring therein, did advise and consent to the ratification of the said convention, together with the three related protocols;

WHEREAS the said convention and the three related protocols were duly ratified by the President of the United States of America on November 5, 1954, in pursuance of the aforesaid advice and consent of the Senate;

WHEREAS it is provided in paragraph 1 of Article IX of the said convention that it shall come into force three months after the deposit of twelve instruments of ratification, acceptance or accession, among which there shall be those of four states which are not members of the International Union for the Protection of Literary and Artistic Works;

WHEREAS instruments of ratification or accession were, by June 16, 1955, deposited by the following twelve states, including seven which are not members of the International Union for the Protection of Literary and Artistic Works: Andorra, Cambodia, Pakistan, Laos, Haiti, Spain, United States of America, Costa Rica, Chile, Israel, German Federal Republic and Monaco;

WHEREAS, pursuant to the aforesaid provision of paragraph 1 of Article IX of the said convention, the convention will come into force on September 16, 1955, three months after June 16, 1955, the date of deposit of the twelfth instrument;

WHEREAS it is provided in paragraph 2 b) of protocol 1 annexed to the universal copyright convention, concerning the application of that convention to the works of stateless persons and refugees, and in paragraph 2 b) of protocol 2 annexed to the universal copyright convention, concerning the application of that convention to the works of certain international organizations, that the respective protocols shall enter into force for each state on the date of deposit of the instrument of ratification, acceptance or accession of the state concerned or on the date of entry into force of the convention with respect to such state, whichever is the later;

WHEREAS instruments of ratification or accession with respect to the said protocol 1 were deposited by the following states: Andorra, Cambodia, Pakistan, Laos, Haiti, United States of America, Costa Rica, Israel, German Federal Republic and Monaco;

WHEREAS instruments of ratification or accession with respect to the said protocol 2 were deposited by the following states: Andorra, Cambodia, Pakistan, Laos, Haiti, Spain, United States of America, Costa Rica, Chile, Israel, German Federal Republic and Monaco;

WHEREAS, pursuant to the aforesaid provision in paragraph 2 b) of the said protocol 1 and protocol 2, the protocols will enter into force on September 16, 1955, the date of entry into force of the convention;

WHEREAS it is provided in paragraph 6 b) of protocol 3 annexed to the universal copyright convention, concerning the effective date of instruments of ratification or acceptance of or accession to that convention, that the protocol shall enter into force on the date of deposit of not less than four instruments of ratification or acceptance or accession and that instruments deposited after such date shall take effect on the date of their deposit;

WHEREAS, pursuant to the aforesaid provision in paragraph 6 b) of the said protocol 3, the protocol entered into force on August 19, 1954, the date of deposit of the fourth instrument, and entered into force with respect to the United States of America on December 6, 1954, the date of deposit of its instrument:

NOW, THEREFORE, be it known that I, Dwight D. Eisenhower, President of the United States of America, do hereby proclaim and make public the said convention and the said protocols 1, 2 and 3, to the end that the same and every article and clause thereof shall be observed and fulfilled with good faith, on and after September 16, 1955 with respect to the said convention and protocols 1 and 2, and on and after

December 6, 1954 with respect to the said protocol 3, by the United States of America and by the citizens of the United States of America and all other persons subject to the jurisdiction thereof.

IN TESTIMONY WHEREOF, I have hereunto set my hand and caused the Seal of the United States of America to be affixed.

By the President:
JOHN FOSTER DULLES
*Secretary of State*

DONE at the city of Washington this fifth day of August in the year of our Lord one thousand nine hundred fifty-five and of the Independence of the United States of America the one hundred eightieth.

DWIGHT D. EISENHOWER

# Convention for the Protection of Producers of Phonograms Against Unauthorized Duplication of Their Phonograms

*Done at Geneva October 29, 1971;*
*Ratification advised by the Senate of the United States of America October 1, 1973;*
*Ratified by the President of the United States of America November 9, 1973;*
*Ratification of the United States of America deposited with the Secretary-General of*
*the United Nations November 26, 1973;*
*Proclaimed by the President of the United States of America April 17, 1974;*
*Entered into force with respect to the United States of America March 10, 1974.*

---

BY THE PRESIDENT OF THE UNITED STATES OF AMERICA

A PROCLAMATION

CONSIDERING THAT:

The Convention for the Protection of Producers of Phonograms Against Unauthorized Duplication of their Phonograms was opened for signature at Geneva October 29, 1971;

The Senate of the United States of America by its resolution of October 1, 1973, two-thirds of the Senators present concurring therein, gave its advice and consent to ratification of the Convention;

The President of the United States of America ratified the Convention on November 9, 1973, in pursuance of the advice and consent of the Senate;

The United Sates of America deposited its instrument of ratification on November 26, 1973 with the Secretary General of the United Nations, and on December 10, 1973 the Director General of the World Intellectual Property Organization informed the States indicated in the Convention of such deposit;

Pursuant to the provisions of paragraph (2) of Article 11 of the Convention, the Convention entered into force for the United States of America on March 10, 1974;

NOW, THEREFORE, I, Richard Nixon, President of the United States of America, proclaim and make public the said Convention to the end that it shall be observed and fulfilled with good faith by the United States of America and by the citizens of the United States of America and all other persons subject to the jurisdiction thereof.

IN TESTIMONY WHEREOF, I have signed this proclamation and caused the Seal of the United States of American to be affixed.

DONE at the city of Washington this seventeenth day of April in the year of our Lord one thousand nine hundred seventy-four and of the Independence of the United States of America the one hundred ninety-eighth.

RICHARD NIXON

[SEAL]

By the President:

HENRY A. KISSINGER
*Secretary of State*

The Contracting States,

concerned at the widespread and increasing unauthorized duplication of phonograms and the damage this is occasioning to the interests of authors, performers and producers of phonograms;

convinced that the protection of producers of phonograms against such acts will also benefit the performers whose performances, and the authors whose works, are recorded on the said phonograms;

recognizing the value of the work undertaken in this field by the United Nations Educational, Scientific and Cultural Organization and the World Intellectual Property Organization;

anxious not to impair in any way international agreements already in force and in particular in no way to prejudice wider acceptance of the Rome Convention of October 26, 1961, which affords protection to performers and to broadcasting organizations as well as to producers of phonograms;

have agreed as follows:

## Article 1

For the purposes of this Convention:

(a) "phonogram" means any exclusively aural fixation of sounds of a performance or of other sounds;

(b) "producer of phonograms" means the person who, or the legal entity which, first fixes the sounds of a performance or other sounds;

(c) "duplicate" means an article which contains sounds taken directly or indirectly from a phonogram and which embodies all or a substantial part of the sounds fixed in that phonogram;

(d) "distribution to the public" means any act by which duplicates of a phonogram are offered, directly or indirectly, to the general public or any section thereof.

## Article 2

Each Contracting State shall protect producers of phonograms who are nationals of other Contracting States against the making of duplicates without the consent of the producer and against the importation of such duplicates, provided that any such making or importation is for the purpose of distribution to the public, and against the distribution of such duplicates to the public.

## Article 3

The mans by which this Convention is implemented shall be a matter for the domestic law of each Contracting State and shall include one or more of the following: protection by means of the grant of a copyright or other specific right; protection by means of the law relating to unfair competition; protection by means of penal sanctions.

## Article 4

The duration of the protection given shall be a matter for the domestic law of each Contracting State. However, if the domestic law prescribes a specific duration for the protection, that duration shall not be less than twenty years from the end either of the year in which the sounds embodied in the phonogram were first fixed or of the year in which the phonogram was first published.

## Article 5

If, as a condition of protecting the producers of phonograms, a Contracting State, under its domestic law, requires compliance with formalities, these shall be considered as fulfilled if all the authorized duplicates of the phonogram distributed to the public or their containers bear a notice consisting other symbol ℗, accompanied by the year date of the first publication, placed in such manner as to give reasonable notice of claim of protection; and, if the duplicates or their containers do not identify the producer, his successor in title or the exclusive licensee (by carrying his name, trademark or other appropriate designation), the notice shall also include the name of the producer, his successor in title or the exclusive licensee.

## Article 6

Any Contracting State which affords protection by means of copyright or other specific right, or protection by means of penal sanctions, may in its domestic law provide, with regard to the protection of producers of phonograms, the same kinds of limitations as are permitted with respect to the protection of authors of literary and artistic works. However, no compulsory licenses may be permitted unless all of the following conditions are met:

(a) the duplication is for use solely for the purpose of teaching or scientific research;

(b) the license shall be valid for duplication only within the territory of the Contracting State whose competent authority has granted the license and shall not extend to the export of duplicates;

(c) the duplication made under the license gives rise to an equitable remuneration fixed by the said authority taking into account, *inter alia*, the number of duplicates which will be made.

## Article 7

(1) This Convention shall in no way be interpreted to limit or prejudice the protection otherwise secured to authors, to performers, to producers of phonograms or to broadcasting organizations under any domestic law or international agreement.

(2) It shall be a matter for the domestic law of each Contracting State to determine the extent, if any, to which performers whose performances are fixed in a phonogram are entitled to enjoy protection and the conditions for enjoying any such protection.

(3) No Contracting State shall be required to apply the provisions of this Convention to any phonogram fixed before this Convention entered into force with respect to that State.

(4) Any Contracting State which, on October 29, 1971, affords protection to producers of phonograms solely on the basis of the place of first fixation may, by a notification deposited with the Director General of the World Intellectual Property Organization, declare that it will apply this criterion instead of the criterion of the nationality of the producer.

## Article 8

(1) The International Bureau of the World Intellectual Property Organization shall assemble and publish information concerning the protection of phonograms. Each Contracting State shall promptly communicate to the International Bureau all new laws and official texts on this subject.

(2) The International Bureau shall, on request, furnish information to any Contracting State on matters concerning this Convention, and shall conduct studies and provide services designed to facilitate the protection provided for therein.

(3) The International Bureau shall exercise the functions enumerated in paragraphs (1) and (2) above in cooperation, for matters within their respective competence, with the United Nations Educational, Scientific and Cultural Organization and the International Labour Organisation.

### Article 9

(1) This Convention shall be deposited with the Secretary-General of the United Nations. It shall be open until April 30, 1972, for signature by any State that is a member of the United Nations, any of the Specialized Agencies brought into relationship with the United Nations, or the International Atomic Energy Agency, or is a party to the Statute of the International Court of Justice.

(2) This Convention shall be subject to ratification or acceptance by the signatory States. It shall be open for accession by any State referred to in paragraph (1) of this Article.

(3) Instruments of ratification, acceptance or accession shall be deposited with the Secretary-General of the United Nations.

(4) It is understood that, at the time a State becomes bound by this Convention, it will be in a position in accordance with its domestic law to give effect to the provisions of the Convention.

### Article 10

No reservations to this Convention as permitted.

### Article 11

(1) This Convention shall enter into force three months after deposit of the fifth instrument of ratification, acceptance or accession.

(2) For each State ratifying, accepting or acceding to this Convention after the deposit of the fifth instrument of ratification, acceptance or accession, the Convention shall enter into force three months after the date on which the Director General of the World Intellectual Property Organization informs the States, in accordance with Article 13, paragraph (4), of the deposit of its instrument.

(3) Any State may, at the time of ratification, acceptance or accession or at any later date, declare by notification addressed to the Secretary-General of the United Nations that this Convention shall apply to all or any one of the territories for whose international affairs it is responsible. This notification will take effect three months after the date on which it is received.

(4) However, the preceding paragraph may in no way be understood as implying the recognition or tacit acceptance by a Contracting State of the factual situation concerning a territory to which this Convention is made applicable by another Contracting State by virtue of the said paragraph.

### Article 12

(1) Any Contracting State may denounce this Convention, on its own behalf or on behalf of any of the territories referred to in Article 11, paragraph (3), by written notification addressed to the Secretary-General of the United Nations.

(2) Denunciation shall take effect twelve months after the date on which the Secretary-General of the United Nations has received the notification.

## Article 13

(1) This Convention shall be signed in a single copy in English, French, Russian and Spanish, the four texts being equally authentic.

(2) Official texts shall be established by the Director General of the World Intellectual Property Organization, after consultation with the interested Governments, in the Arabic, Dutch, German, Italian and Portuguese languages.

(3) The Secretary-General of the United Nations shall notify the Director General of the World Intellectual Property Organization, the Director-General of the United Nations Educational, Scientific and Cultural Organization and the Director-General of the International Labour Office of:

*(a)* signatures to this Convention;

*(b)* the deposit of instruments of ratification, acceptance or accession;

*(c)* the date of entry into force of this Convention;

*(d)* any declaration notified pursuant to Article 11, paragraph (3);

*(e)* the receipt of notifications of denunciation.

(4) The Director General of the World Intellectual Property Organization shall inform the States referred to in Article 9, paragraph (1), of the notifications received pursuant to the preceding paragraph and of any declarations made under Article 7, paragraph (4). He shall also notify the Director-General of the United Nations Educational, Scientific and Cultural Organization and the Director-General of the International Labour Office of such declarations.

(5) The Secretary-General of the United Nations shall transmit two certified copies of this Convention to the States referred to in Article 9, paragraph (1).

IN WITNESS WHEREOF, the undersigned, being duly authorized, have signed this Convention.

DONE at Geneva, this twenty-ninth day of October, 1971.

# Copyright Convention Between the United States and Other American Republics— Buenos Aires, 1910

## BY THE PRESIDENT OF THE UNITED STATES OF AMERICA

### A PROCLAMATION

Whereas, a Convention on Literary and Artistic Copyright between the United States of America and the Argentine Republic, Brazil, Chile, Colombia, Costa Rica, Cuba, Dominican Republic, Ecuador, Guatemala, Haiti, Honduras, Mexico, Nicaragua, Panama, Paraguay, Peru, Salvador, Uruguay, and Venezuela was concluded and signed by their respective Plenipotentiaries at Buenos Aires on the eleventh day of August, one thousand nine hundred and ten, the original of which Convention, being in the Spanish, English, Portuguese and French languages, is word for word as follows:

## FOURTH INTERNATIONAL AMERICAN CONVENTION
## LITERARY AND ARTISTIC COPYRIGHT

Their Excellencies the Presidents of the United States of America, the Argentine Republic, Brazil, Chile, Colombia, Costa Rica, Cuba, Dominican Republic, Ecuador, Guatemala, Haiti, Honduras, Mexico, Nicaragua, Panama, Paraguay, Peru, Salvador, Uruguay and Venezuela;

Being desirous that their respective countries may be represented at the Fourth International American Conference, have sent thereto the following Delegates duly authorized to approve the recommendations, resolutions, conventions and treaties which they might deem advantageous to the interests of America:

[Here follow the names of the respective delegates, omitted.]

Who, after having presented their credentials and the same having been found in due and proper form, have agreed upon the following Convention on Literary and Artistic Copyright.

ARTICLE 1. The signatory States acknowledge and protect the rights of Literary and Artistic Property in conformity with the stipulations of the present convention.

ARTICLE 2. In the expression "Literary and Artistic Works" are included books, writings, pamphlets of all kinds, whatever may be the subject of which they treat, and whatever the number of their pages; dramatic or dramatico-musical works; choreographic and musical compositions with or without words; drawings, paintings, sculpture, engravings; photographic works; astronomical or geographic globes; plans, sketches or plastic works relating to geography, geology or topography, architecture or any other science, and, finally, all productions that can be published by any means of impression or reproduction.

ARTICLE 3. The acknowledgement of a copyright obtained in one State, in conformity with its laws, shall produce its effects of full right in all the other States without the necessity of complying with any other formality, provided always there shall appear in the work a statement that indicates the reservation of the property right.

600

ARTICLE 4. The copyright of a literary or artistic work, includes for its author or assigns the exclusive power of disposing of the same, of publishing, assigning, translating or authorizing its translation and reproducing it in any form whether wholly or in part.

ARTICLE 5. The author of a protected work, except in case of proof to the contrary, shall be considered the person whose name or well known nom de plume is indicated therein; consequently suit brought by such author or his representative against counterfeiters or violators, shall be admitted by the Courts of the Signatory States.

ARTICLE 6. The authors or their assigns, citizens or domiciled foreigners, shall enjoy in the signatory countries the rights that the respective laws accord, without those rights being allowed to exceed the term of protection granted in the country of origin.

For works comprising several volumes that are not published simultaneously, as well as for bulletins, or parts, or periodical publications, the term of the copyright will commence to run, with respect to each volume, bulletin, part, or periodical publication, from the respective date of its publication.

ARTICLE 7. The country of origin of a work will be deemed that of its first publication in America, and if it shall have appeared simultaneously in several of the signatory countries, that which fixes the shortest period of protection.

ARTICLE 8. A work which was not originally copyrighted shall not be entitled to copyright in subsequent editions.

ARTICLE 9. Authorised translations shall be protected in the same manner as original works.

Translators of works concerning which no right of guaranteed property exists, or the guaranteed copyright of which may have been extinguished, may obtain for their translations the rights of property set forth in Article 3rd but they shall not prevent the publication of other translations of the same work.

ARTICLE 10. Addresses or discourses delivered or read before deliberative assemblies, Courts of Justice, or at public meeting, may be printed in the daily press without the necessity of any authorization, with due regard, however, to the provisions of the domestic legislation of each nation.

ARTICLE 11. Literary, scientific or artistic writings, whatever may be their subjects, published in newspapers or magazines, in any one of the countries of the Union, shall not be reproduced in the other countries without the consent of the authors. With the exception of the works mentioned, any article in a newspaper may be reprinted by others, if it has not been expressly prohibited, but in every case, the source from which it is taken must be cited.

News and miscellaneous items published merely for general information, do not enjoy protection under this Convention.

ARTICLE 12. The reproduction of extracts from literary or artistic publications for the purpose of instruction or chrestomathy, does not confer any right of property, and may, therefore, be freely made in all the signatory countries.

ARTICLE 13. The indirect appropriation of unauthorized parts of a literary or artistic work, having no original character, shall be deemed an illicit reproduction, in so far as affects civil liability.

The reproduction in any form of an entire work, or of the greater part thereof, accompanied by notes or commentaries under the pretext of literary criticism or amplification, or supplement to the original work, shall also be considered illicit.

ARTICLE 14. Every publication infringing a copyright may be confiscated in the signatory countries in which the original work had the right to be legally protected, without prejudice to the indemnities or penalties which the counterfeiters may have incurred according to the laws of the country in which the fraud may have been committed.

ARTICLE 15. Each of the Governments of the signatory countries, shall retain the right to permit, inspect, or prohibit the circulation, representation or exhibition of works or productions, concerning which the proper authority may have to exercise that right.

ARTICLE 16. The present Convention shall become operative between the Signatory States which ratify it, three months after they shall have communicated their ratification to the Argentine Government, and it shall remain in force among them until a year after the date when it may be denounced. This denunciation shall be addressed to the Argentine Government and shall be without force except with respect to the country making it.

IN WITNESS WHEREOF, the Plenipotentiaries have signed the present treaty and affixed thereto the Seal of the Fourth International American Conference.

Made and signed in the City of Buenos Aires on the eleventh day of August in the year one thousand nine hundred and ten, in Spanish, English, Portuguese and French, and deposited in the Ministry of Foreign Affairs of the Argentine Republic, in order that certified copies be made for transmission to each one of the signatory nations through the appropriate diplomatic channels.

[Here follow the signatures (omitted) of the delegates of the United States of America and the other nineteen contracting states: Argentine Republic, Brazil, Chile, Colombia, Costa Rica, Cuba, Dominican Republic, Ecuador, Guatemala, Haiti, Honduras, Mexico, Nicaragua, Panama, Paraguay, Peru, Salvador, Uruguay, Venezuela.]

And whereas, the said Convention has been ratified by the Government of the United States, by and with the advice and consent of the Senate thereof, and by the Governments of the Dominican Republic, Guatemala, Honduras, Panama, Nicaragua, and Ecuador, and the ratification of the said Governments were, by the provisions of Article 16 of the said Convention, deposited by their respective Plenipotentiaries with the Government of the Argentine Republic;

Now, therefore, be it known that I, Woodrow Wilson, President of the United States of America, have caused the said Convention to be made public, to the end that the same and every article and clause thereof may be observed and fulfilled with good faith by the United States and the citizens thereof.

In testimony whereof, I have hereunto set may hand and caused the seal of the United States to be affixed.

Done at the City of Washington this thirteenth day of July in the year of our Lord one thousand nine hundred and fourteen, and of the Independence of the United States of America the one hundred and thirty-ninth.

[SEAL]

WOODROW WILSON
By the President:
W. J. BRYAN
**Secretary of State**

# Convention Relating to the Distribution of Programme-Carrying Signals Transmitted by Satellite

The Contracting States,

*Aware* that the use of satellites for the distribution of programme-carrying signals is rapidly growing both in volume and geographical coverage;

*Concerned* that there is no world-wide system to prevent distributors from distributing programme-carrying signals transmitted by satellite which were not intended for those distributors, and that this lack is likely to hamper the use of satellite communications;

*Recognizing*, in this respect, the importance of the interests of authors, performers, producers of phonograms and broadcasting organizations;

*Convinced* that an international system should be established under which measures would be provided to prevent distributors from distributing programme-carrying signals transmitted by satellite which were not intended for those distributors;

*Conscious* of the need not to impair in any way international agreements already in force, including the International Telecommunication Convention and the Radio Regulations annexed to that Convention, and in particular in no way to prejudice wider acceptance of the Rome Convention of October 26, 1961, which affords protection to performers, producers of phonograms and broadcasting organizations,

Have agreed as follows:

## Article 1

For the purposes of this Convention:
  (i) "signal" is an electronically-generated carrier capable of transmitting programmes;
  (ii) "programme" is a body of live or recorded material consisting of images, sounds or both, embodied in signals emitted for the purpose of ultimate distribution;
  (iii) "satellite" is any device in extraterrestrial space capable of transmitting signals;
  (iv) "emitted signal" or "signal emitted" is any programme-carrying signal that goes to or passes through a statellite;
  (v) "derived signal" is a signal obtained by modifying the technical characteristics of the emitted signal, whether or not there have been one or more intervening fixations;
  (vi) "originating organization" is the person or legal entity that decides what programme the emitted signals will carry;

(vii) "distributor" is the person or legal entity that decides that the transmission of the derived signals to the general public or any section thereof should take place;

(viii) "distribution" is the operation by which a distributor transmits derived signals to the general public or any section thereof.

## Article 2

(1) Each Contracting State undertakes to take adequate measures to prevent the distribution on or from its territory of any programme-carrying signal by an distributor for whom the signal emitted to or passing through the satellite is not intended. This obligation shall apply where the originating organization is a national of another Contracting State and where the signal distributed is a derived signal.

(2) In any Contracting State in which the application of the measures referred to in paragraph (1) is limited in time, the duration thereof shall be fixed by its domestic law. The Secretary-General of the United Nations shall be notified in writing of such duration at the time of ratification, acceptance or accession, or if the domestic law comes into force or is changed thereafter, within six months of the coming into force of that law or of its modification.

(3) The obligation provided for in paragraph (1) shall not apply to the distribution of derived signals taken from signals which have already been distributed by a distributor for whom the emitted signals were intended.

## Article 3

This Convention shall not apply where the signals emitted by or on behalf of the originating organization are intended for direct reception from the satellite by the general public.

## Article 4

No Contracting State shall be required to apply the measures referred to in Article 2(1) where the signal distributed on its territory by a distributor for whom the emitted signal is not intended

(i) carries short excerpts of the programme carried by the emitted signal, consisting of reports of current events, but only to the extent justified by the informatory purpose of such excerpts, or

(ii) carries, as quotations, short excerpts of the programme carried by the emitted signal, provided that such quotations are compatible with fair practice and are justified by the information purpose of such quotations, or

(iii) carries, where the said territory is that of a Contracting State regarded as a developing country in conformity with the established practice of the General Assembly of the United Nations, a programme carried by the emitted signal, provided that the distribution is solely for the purpose of teaching, including teaching in the framework of adult education, or scientific research.

## Article 5

No Contracting State shall be required to apply this Convention with respect to any signal emitted before this Convention entered into force for that State.

## Article 6

This Convention shall in no way be interpreted to limit or prejudice the protection secured to authors, performers, producers of phonograms, or broadcasting organizations, under any domestic law or international agreement.

## Article 7

This Convention shall in no way be interpreted as limiting the right of any Contracting State to apply its domestic law in order to prevent abuses of monopoly.

## Article 8

(1) Subject to paragraph (2) and (3), no reservation to this Convention shall be permitted.

(2) Any Contracting State whose domestic law, on May 21, 1974, so provides may, by a written notification deposited with the Secretary-General of the United Nations, declare that, for its purposes, the words "where the originating organization is a national of another Contracting State" appearing in Article 2(1) shall be considered as if they were replaced by the words "where the signal is emitted from the territory of another Contracting State."

(3) *(a)* Any Contracting State which, on May 21, 1974, limits or denies protection with respect to the distribution of programme-carrying signals by means of wires, cable or other similar communications channels to subscribing members of the public may, by a written notification deposited with the Secretary-General of the United Nations, declare that, to the extent that and as long as its domestic law limits or denies protection, it will not apply this Convention to such distributions.

*(b)* Any State that has deposited a notification in accordance with subparagraph *(a)* shall notify the Secretary-General of the United Nations in writing, within six months of their coming into force, of any changes in its domestic law whereby the reservation under that subparagraph becomes inapplicable or more limited in scope.

## Article 9

(1) This Convention shall be deposited with the Secretary-General of the United Nations. It shall be open until March 31, 1975, for signature by any State that is a member of the United Nations, any of the Specialized Agencies brought into relationship with the United Nations, or the International Atomic Energy Agency, or is a party to the Statute of the International Court of Justice.

(2) This Convention shall be subject to ratification or acceptance by the signatory States. It shall be open for accession by any State referred to in paragraph (1).

(3) Instruments of ratification, acceptance or accession shall be deposited with the Secretary-General of the United Nations.

(4) It is understood that, at the time a State becomes bound by this Convention, it will be in a position in accordance with its domestic law to give effect to the provisions of the Convention.

## Article 10

(1) This convention shall enter into force three months after the deposit of the fifth instrument of ratification, acceptance or accession.

(2) For each State ratifying, accepting or acceding to this Convention after the deposit of the fifth instrument of ratification, acceptance or accession, this Convention shall enter into force three months after the deposit of its instrument.

## Article 11

(1) Any Contracting State may denounce this Convention by written notification deposited with the Secretary-General of the United Nations.

(2) Denunciation shall take effect twelve months after the date on which the notification referred to in paragraph (1) is received.

## Article 12

(1) This Convention shall be signed in a single copy in English, French, Russian and Spanish, the four texts being equally authentic.

(2) Official texts shall be established by the Director-General of the United Nations Educational, Scientific and Cultural Organization and the Director General of the World Intellectual Property Organization, after consultation with the interested Governments, in the Arabic, Dutch, German, Italian and Portuguese languages.

(3) The Secretary-General of the United Nations shall notify the States referred to in Article 9(1), as well as the Director-General of the United Nations Educational, Scientific and Cultural Organization, the Director General of the World Intellectual Property Organization, the Director-General of the International Labour Office and the Secretary-General of the International Telecommunication Union, of

    (i) signatures to this Convention:

    (ii) the deposit of instruments of ratification, acceptance or accession;

    (iii) the date of entry into force of this Convention under Article 10(1);

    (iv) the deposit of any notification relating to Article 2(2) or Article 8(2) or (3), together with its text;

    (v) the receipt of notifications of denunciation.

(4) The Secretary-General of the United Nations shall transmit two certified copies of this Convention to all States referred to in Article 9(1).

# Appendix G

# Berne Convention for the Protection of Literary and Artistic Works

*(Paris Act of July 24, 1971)*

The countries of the Union, being equally animated by the desire to protect, in as effective and uniform a manner as possible, the rights of authors in their literary and artistic works,

Recognizing the importance of the work of the Revision Conference held at Stockholm in 1967,

Have resolved to revise the Act adopted by the Stockholm Conference, while maintaining without change Articles 1 to 20 and 22 to 26 of that Act.

Consequently, the undersigned Plenipotentiaries, having presented their full powers, recognized as in good and due form, have agreed as follows:

### Article 1

The countries to which this Convention applies constitute a Union for the protection of the rights of authors in their literary and artistic works.

### Article 2

(1) The expression "literary and artistic works" shall include every production in the literary, scientific and artistic domain, whatever may be the mode or form of its expression, such as books, pamphlets and other writings; lectures, addresses, sermons and other works of the same nature; dramatic or dramatico-musical works; choreographic works and entertainments in dumb show; musical compositions with or without words; cinematographic works to which are assimilated works expressed by a process analogous to cinematography; works of drawing, painting, architecture, sculpture, engraving and lithography; photographic works to which are assimilated works expressed by a process analogous to photography; works of applied art; illustrations, maps, plans, sketches and three-dimensional works relative to geography, topography, architecture or science.

(2) It shall, however, be a matter for legislation in the countries of the Union to prescribe that works in general or any specified categories of works shall not be protected unless they have been fixed in some material form.

(3) Translations, adaptations, arrangements of music and other alterations of a literary or artistic work shall be protected as original works without prejudice to the copyright in the original work.

(4) It shall be a matter for legislation in the countries of the Union to determine the protection to be granted to official texts of a legislative, administrative and legal nature, and to official translations of such texts.

(5) Collections of literary or artistic works such as encyclopaedias and anthologies which, by reason of the selection and arrangement of their contents, constitute intellectual creations shall be protected as such, without prejudice to the copyright in each of the works forming part of such collections.

(6) The works mentioned in this Article shall enjoy protection in all countries of the Union. This protection shall operate for the benefit of the author and his successors in title.

(7) Subject to the provisions of Article 7(4) of this Convention, it shall be a matter for legislation in the countries of the Union to determine the extent of the application of their laws to works of applied art and industrial designs and models, as well as the conditions under which such works, designs and models shall be protected. Works protected in the country of origin solely as designs and models shall be entitled in another country of the Union only to such special protection as is granted in that country to designs and models; however, if no such special protection is granted in that country, such works shall be protected as artistic works.

(8) The protection of this Convention shall not apply to news of the day or to miscellaneous facts having the character of mere items of press information.

## Article 2[bis]

(1) It shall be a matter for legislation in the countries of the Union to exclude, wholly or in part, from the protection provided by the preceding Article political speeches and speeches delivered in the course of legal proceedings.

(2) It shall also be a matter for legislation in the countries of the Union to determine the conditions under which lectures, addresses and other works of the same nature which are delivered in public may be reproduced by the press, broadcast, communicated to the public by wire and made the subject of public communication as envisaged in Article 11[bis](1) of this Convention, when such use is justified by the informatory purpose.

(3) Nevertheless, the author shall enjoy the exclusive right of making a collection of his works mentioned in the preceding paragraphs.

## Article 3

(1) The protection of this Convention shall apply to:
*(a)* authors who are nationals of one of the countries of the Union, for their works, whether published or not;

*(b)* authors who are not nationals of one of the countries of the Union, for their works first published in one of those countries, or simultaneously in a country outside the Union and in a country of the Union.

(2) Authors who are not nationals of one of the countries of the Union but who have their habitual residence in one of them shall, for the purposes of this Convention, be assimilated to nationals of that country.

(3) The expression "published works" means works published with the consent of their authors, whatever may be the means of manufacture of the copies, provided that the availability of such copies has been such as to satisfy the reasonable requirements of the public, having regard to the nature of the work. The performance of a dramatic, dramatico-musical, cinematographic or musical work, the public recitation of a literary work, the communication by wire or the broadcasting of literary or artistic works, the exhibition of a work of art and the construction of a work of architecture shall not constitute publication.

(4) A work shall be considered as having been published simultaneously in several countries if it has been published in two or more countries within thirty days of its first publication.

## Article 4

The protection of this Convention shall apply, even if the conditions of Article 3 are not fulfilled, to:
*(a)* authors of cinematographic works the maker of which has his headquarters or habitual residence in one of the countries of the Union;
*(b)* authors of works of architecture erected in a country of the Union or of other artistic works incorporated in a building or other structure located in a country of the Union.

## Article 5

(1) Authors shall enjoy, in respect of works for which they are protected under this Convention, in countries of the Union other than the country of origin, the rights which their respective laws do now or may hereafter grant to their nationals, as well as the rights specially granted by this Convention.

(2) The enjoyment and the exercise of these rights shall not be subject to any formality; such enjoyment and such exercise shall be independent of the existence of protection in the country of origin of the work. Consequently, apart from the provisions of this Convention, the extent of protection, as well as the means of redress afforded to the author to protect his rights, shall be governed exclusively by the laws of the country where protection is claimed.

(3) Protection in the country of origin is governed by domestic law. However, when the author is not a national of the country of origin of the work for which he is protected under this Convention, he shall enjoy in that country the same rights as national authors.

(4) The country of origin shall be considered to be:
*(a)* in the case of works first published in a country of the Union, that country; in the case of works published simultaneously in several countries of the Union which grant different terms of protection, the country whose legislation grants the shortest term of protection;

*(b)* in the case of works published simultaneously in a country outside the Union and in a country of the Union, the latter country;

*(c)* in the case of unpublished works or of works first published in a country outside the Union, without simultaneous publication in a country of the Union, the country of the Union of which the author is a national, provided that:

  (i) when these are cinematographic works the maker of which has his headquarters or his habitual residence in a country of the Union, the country of origin shall be that country, and

  (ii) when these are works of architecture erected in a country of the Union or other artistic works incorporated in a building or other structure located in a country of the Union, the country of origin shall be that country.

## Article 6

(1) Where any country outside the Union fails to protect in an adequate manner the works of authors who are nationals of one of the countries of the Union, the latter country may restrict the protection given to the works of authors who are, at the date of the first publication thereof, nationals of the other country and are not habitually resident in one of the countries of the Union. If the country of first publication avails itself of this right, the other countries of the Union shall not be required to grant to works thus subjected to special treatment a wider protection than that granted to them in the country of first publication.

(2) No restrictions introduced by virtue of the preceding paragraph shall affect the rights which an author may have acquired in respect of a work published in a country of the Union before such restrictions were put into force.

(3) The countries of the Union which restrict the grant of copyright in accordance with this Article shall give notice thereof to the Director General of the World Intellectual Property Organization (hereinafter designated as "the Director General") by a written declaration specifying the countries in regard to which protection is restricted, and the restrictions to which rights of authors who are nationals of those countries are subjected. The Director General shall immediately communicate this declaration to all the countries of the Union.

## Article 6$^{bis}$

(1) Independently of the author's economic rights, and even after the transfer of the said rights, the author shall have the right to claim authorship of the work and to object to any distortion, mutilation or other modification of, or other derogatory action in relation to, the said work, which would be prejudicial to his honor or reputation.

(2) The rights granted to the author in accordance with the preceding paragraph shall, after his death, be maintained, at least until the expiry of the economic rights, and shall be exercisable by the persons or institutions authorized by the legislation of the country where protection is claimed. However, those countries whose legislation, at the moment of their ratification of or accession to this Act, does not provide for the protection after the death of the author of all the rights set out in the preceding paragraph

may provide that some of these rights may, after his death, cease to be maintained.

(3) The means of redress for safeguarding the rights granted by this Article shall be governed by the legislation of the country where protection is claimed.

## Article 7

(1) The term of protection granted by this Convention shall be the life of the author and fifty years after his death.

(2) However, in the case of cinematographic works, the countries of the Union may provide that the term of protection shall expire fifty years after the work has been made available to the public with the consent of the author, or, failing such an event within fifty years from the making of such a work, fifty years after the making.

(3) In the case of anonymous or pseudonymous works, the term of protection granted by this Convention shall expire fifty years after the work has been lawfully made available to the public. However, when the pseudonym adopted by the author leaves no doubt as to his identity, the term of protection shall be that provided in paragraph (1). If the author of an anonymous or pseudonymous work discloses his identity during the above-mentioned period, the term of protection applicable shall be that provided in paragraph (1). The countries of the Union shall not be required to protect anonymous or pseudonymous works in respect of which it is reasonable to presume that their author has been dead for fifty years.

(4) It shall be a matter for legislation in the countries of the Union to determine the term of protection of photographic works and that of works of applied art in so far as they are protected as artistic works; however, this term shall last at least until the end of a period of twenty-five years from the making of such a work.

(5) The term of protection subsequent to the death of the author and the terms provided by paragraphs (2), (3) and (4) shall run from the date of death or of the event referred to in those paragraphs, but such terms shall always be deemed to begin on the first of January of the year following the death or such event.

(6) The countries of the Union may grant a term of protection in excess of those provided by the preceding paragraphs.

(7) Those countries of the Union bound by the Rome Act of this Convention which grant, in their national legislation in force at the time of signature of the present Act, shorter terms of protection than those provided for in the preceding paragraphs shall have the right to maintain such terms when ratifying or acceding to the present Act.

(8) In any case, the term shall be governed by the legislation of the country where protection is claimed; however, unless the legislation of that country otherwise provides, the term shall not exceed the term fixed in the country of origin of the work.

## Article 7[bis]

The provisions of the preceding Article shall also apply in the case of a work of joint authorship, provided that the terms measured from the death of the author shall be calculated from the death of the last surviving author.

## Article 8

Authors of literary and artistic works protected by this Convention shall enjoy the exclusive right of making and of authorizing the translation of their works throughout the term of protection of their rights in the original works.

## Article 9

(1) Authors of literary and artistic works protected by this Convention shall have the exclusive rights of authorizing the reproduction of these works, in any manner or form.

(2) It shall be a matter for legislation in the countries of the Union to permit the reproduction of such works in certain special cases, provided that such reproduction does not conflict with a normal exploitation of the work and does not unreasonably prejudice the legitimate interests of the author.

(3) Any sound or visual recording shall be considered as a reproduction for the purposes of this Convention.

## Article 10

(1) It shall be permissible to make quotations from a work which has already been lawfully made available to the public, provided that their making is compatible with fair practice, and their extent does not exceed that justified by the purpose, including quotations from newspaper articles and periodicals in the form of press summaries.

(2) It shall be a matter for legislation in the countries of the Union, and for special agreements existing or to be concluded between them, to permit the utilization, to the extent justified by the purpose, of literary or artistic works by way of illustration in publications, broadcasts or sound or visual recordings for teaching, provided such utilization is compatible with fair practice.

(3) Where use is made of works in accordance with the preceding paragraphs of this Article, mention shall be made of the source, and of the name of the author if it appears thereon.

## Article 10bis

(1) It shall be a matter for legislation in the countries of the Union to permit the reproduction by the press, the broadcasting or the communication to the public by wire of articles published in newspapers or periodicals on current economic, political or religious topics, and of broadcast works of the same character, in cases in which the reproduction, broadcasting or such communication thereof is not expressly reserved. Nevertheless, the source must always be clearly indicated; the legal consequences of a breach of this obligation shall be determined by the legislation of the country where protection is claimed.

(2) It shall also be a matter for legislation in the countries of the Union to determine the conditions under which, for the purpose of reporting current events by means of photography, cinematography, broadcasting or

communication to the public by wire, literary or artistic works seen or heard in the course of the event may, to the extent justified by the informatory purpose, be reproduced and made available to the public.

## Article 11

(1) Authors of dramatic, dramatico-musical and musical works shall enjoy the exclusive right of authorizing;
    (i) the public performance of their works, including such public performance by any means or process;
    (ii) any communication to the public of the performance of their works.

(2) Authors of dramatic or dramatico-musical works shall enjoy, during the full term of their rights in the original works, the same rights with respect to translations thereof.

## Article 11bis

(1) Authors of literary and artistic works shall enjoy the exclusive right of authorizing:
    (i) the broadcasting of their works or the communication thereof to the public by any other means of wireless diffusion of signs, sounds or images;
    (ii) any communication to the public by wire or by rebroadcasting of the broadcast of the work, when this communication is made by an organization other than the original one;
    (iii) the public communication by loudspeaker or any other analogous instrument transmitting, by signs, sounds or images, the broadcast of the work.

(2) It shall be a matter for legislation in the countries of the Union to determine the conditions under which the rights mentioned in the preceding paragraph may be exercised, but these conditions shall apply only in the countries where they have been prescribed. They shall not in any circumstances be prejudicial to the moral rights of the author, nor to his right to obtain equitable remuneration which, in the absence of agreement, shall be fixed by competent authority.

(3) In the absence of any contrary stipulation, permission granted in accordance with paragraph (1) of this Article shall not imply permission to record, by means of instruments recording sounds or images, the work broadcast. It shall, however, be a matter for legislation in the countries of the Union to determine the regulations for ephemeral recordings made by a broadcasting organization by means of its own facilities and used for its own broadcasts. The preservation of these recordings in official archives may, on the ground of their exceptional documentary character, be authorized by such legislation.

## Article 11ter

(1) Authors of literary works shall enjoy the exclusive right of authorizing:
    (i) the public recitation of their works, including such public recitation by any means or process;

(ii) any communication to the public of the recitation of their works.

(2) Authors of literary works shall enjoy, during the full term of their rights in the original works, the same rights with respect to translations thereof.

## Article 12

Authors of literary or artistic works shall enjoy the exclusive right of authorizing adaptations, arrangements and other alterations of their works.

## Article 13

(1) Each country of the Union may impose for itself reservations and conditions on the exclusive right granted to the author of a musical work and to the author of any words, the recording of which together with the musical work has already been authorized by the latter, to authorize the sound recording of that musical work, together with such words, if any; but all such reservations and conditions shall apply only in the countries which have imposed them and shall not, in any circumstances, be prejudicial to the rights of these authors to obtain equitable remuneration which, in the absence of agreement, shall be fixed by competent authority.

(2) Recordings of musical works made in a country of the Union in accordance with Article 13(3) of the Conventions signed at Rome on June 2, 1928, and at Brussels on June 26, 1948, may be reproduced in that country without the permission of the author of the musical work until a date two years after that country becomes bound by this Act.

(3) Recordings made in accordance with paragraphs (1) and (2) of this Article and imported without permission from the parties concerned into a country where they are treated as infringing recordings shall be liable to seizure.

## Article 14

(1) Authors of literary or artistic works shall have the exclusive right of authorizing:
  (i) the cinematographic adaptation and reproduction of these works, and the distribution of the works thus adapted or reproduced;
  (ii) the public performance and communication to the public by wire of the works thus adapted or reproduced.

(2) The adaptation into any other artistic form of a cinematographic production derived from literary or artistic works shall, without prejudice to the authorization of the author of the cinematographic production, remain subject to the authorization of the authors of the original works.

(3) The provisions of Article 13(1) shall not apply.

## Article 14bis

(1) Without prejudice to the copyright in any work which may have been adapted or reproduced, a cinematographic work shall be protected as an original work. The owner of copyright in a cinematographic work shall

enjoy the same rights as the author of an original work, including the rights referred to in the preceding Article.

(2) *(a)* Ownership of copyright in a cinematographic work shall be a matter for legislation in the country where protection is claimed.

*(b)* However, in the countries of the Union which, by legislation, include among the owners of copyright in a cinematographic work authors who have brought contributions to the making of the work, such authors, if they have undertaken to bring such contributions, may not, in the absence of any contrary or special stipulation, object to the reproduction, distribution, public performance, communication to the public by wire, broadcasting or any other communication to the public, or to the subtitling or dubbing of texts, of the work.

*(c)* The question whether or not the form of the undertaking referred to above should, for the application of the preceding subparagraph *(b)*, be in a written agreement or a written act of the same effect shall be a matter for the legislation of the country where the maker of the cinematographic work has his headquarters or habitual residence. However, it shall be a matter for the legislation of the country of the Union where protection is claimed to provide that the said undertaking shall be in a written agreement or a written act of the same effect. The countries whose legislation so provides shall notify the Director General by means of a written declaration, which will be immediately communicated by him to all the other countries of the Union.

*(d)* By "contrary or special stipulation" is meant any restrictive condition which is relevant to the aforesaid undertaking.

(3) Unless the national legislation provides to the contrary, the provisions of paragraph (2)*(b)* above shall not be applicable to authors of scenarios, dialogues and musical works created for the making of the cinematographic work, or to the principal director thereof. However, those countries of the Union whose legislation does not contain rules providing for the application of the said paragraph (2)*(b)* to such director shall notify the Director General by means of a written declaration, which will be immediately communicated by him to all the other countries of the Union.

### Article 14<sup>ter</sup>

(1) The author, or after his death the persons or institutions authorized by national legislation, shall, with respect to original works of art and original manuscripts of writers and composers, enjoy the inalienable right to an interest in any sale of the work subsequent to the first transfer by the author of the work.

(2) The protection provided by the preceding paragraph may be claimed in a country of the Union only if legislation in the country to which the author belongs so permits, and to the extent permitted by the country where this protection is claimed.

(3) The procedure for collection and the amounts shall be matters for determination by national legislation.

### Article 15

(1) In order that the author of a literary or artistic work protected by this Convention shall, in the absence of proof to the contrary, be regarded as

such, and consequently be entitled to institute infringement proceedings in the countries of the Union, it shall be sufficient for his name to appear on the work in the usual manner. This paragraph shall be applicable even if this name is a pseudonym, where the pseudonym adopted by the author leaves no doubt as to his identity.

(2) The person or body corporate whose name appears on a cinematographic work in the usual manner shall, in the absence of proof to the contrary, be presumed to be the maker of the said work.

(3) In the case of anonymous and pseudonymous works, other than those referred to in paragraph (1) above, the publisher whose name appears on the work shall, in the absence of proof to the contrary, be deemed to represent the author, and in this capacity he shall be entitled to protect and enforce the author's rights. The provisions of this paragraph shall cease to apply when the author reveals his identity and establishes his claim to authorship of the work.

(4) *(a)* In the case of unpublished works where the identity of the author is unknown, but where there is every ground to presume that he is a national of a country of the Union, it shall be a matter for legislation in that country to designate the competent authority which shall represent the author and shall be entitled to protect and enforce his rights in the countries of the Union.

*(b)* Countries of the Union which made such designation under the terms of this provision shall notify the Director General by means of a written declaration giving full information concerning the authority thus designated. The Director General shall at once communicate this declaration to all other countries of the Union.

## Article 16

(1) Infringing copies of a work shall be liable to seizure in any country of the Union where the work enjoys legal protection.

(2) The provisions of the preceding paragraph shall also apply to reproductions coming from a country where the work is not protected, or has ceased to be protected.

(3) The seizure shall take place in accordance with the legislation of each country.

## Article 17

The provisions of this Convention cannot in any way affect the right of the Government of each country of the Union to permit, to control, or to prohibit, by legislation or regulation, the circulation, presentation, or exhibition of any work or production in regard to which the competent authority may find it necessary to exercise that right.

## Article 18

(1) This Convention shall apply to all works which, at the moment of its coming into force, have not yet fallen into the public domain in the country of origin through the expiry of the term of protection.

(2) If, however, through the expiry of the term of protection which was previously granted, a work has fallen into the public domain of the country where protection is claimed, that work shall not be protected anew.

(3) The application of this principle shall be subject to any provisions contained in special conventions to that effect existing or to be concluded between countries of the Union. In the absence of such provisions, the respective countries shall determine, each in so far as it is concerned, the conditions of application of this principle.

(4) The preceding provisions shall also apply in the case of new accessions to the Union and to cases in which protection is extended by the application of Article 7 or by the abandonment of reservations.

## Article 19

The provisions of this Convention shall not preclude the making of a claim to the benefit of any greater protection which may be granted by legislation in a country of the Union.

## Article 20

The Governments of the countries of the Union reserve the right to enter into special agreements among themselves, in so far as such agreements grant to authors more extensive rights than those granted by the Convention, or contain other provisions not contrary to this Convention. The provisions of existing agreements which satisfy these conditions shall remain applicable.

## Article 21

(1) Special provisions regarding developing countries are included in the Appendix.

(2) Subject to the provisions of Article 28(1)*(b)*, the Appendix forms an integral part of this Act.

## Article 22

(1) *(a)* The Union shall have an Assembly consisting of those countries of the Union which are bound by Articles 22 to 26.

*(b)* The Government of each country shall be represented by one delegate, who may be assisted by alternate delegates, advisors, and experts.

*(c)* The expenses of each delegation shall be borne by the Government which has appointed it.

(2) *(a)* The Assembly shall:
    (i) deal with all matters concerning the maintenance and development of the Union and the implementation of this Convention;
    (ii) give directions concerning the preparation for conferences of revision to the International Bureau of Intellectual Property (hereinafter designated as "the International Bureau") referred to in the Convention Establishing the World Intellectual Property Organi-

zation (hereinafter designated as "the Organization"), due account being taken of any comments made by those countries of the Union which are not bound by Articles 22 to 26;

(iii) review and approve the reports and activities of the Director General of the Organization concerning the Union, and give him all necessary instructions concerning matters within the competence of the Union;

(iv) elect the members of the Executive Committee of the Assembly;

(v) review and approve the reports and activities of its Executive Committee, and give instructions to such Committee;

(vi) determine the program and adopt the triennial budget of the Union, and approve its final accounts;

(vii) adopt the financial regulations of the Union;

(viii) establish such committees of experts and working groups as may be necessary for the work of the Union;

(ix) determine which countries not members of the Union and which intergovernmental and international non-governmental organizations shall be admitted to its meetings as observers;

(x) adopt amendments to Articles 22 to 26;

(xi) take any other appropriate action designed to further the objectives of the Union;

(xii) exercise such other functions as are appropriate under this Convention;

(xiii) subject to its acceptance, exercise such rights as are given to it in the Convention establishing the Organization.

*(b)* With respect to matters which are of interest also to other Unions administered by the Organization, the Assembly shall make its decisions after having heard the advice of the Coordination Committee of the Organization.

(3) *(a)* Each country member of the Assembly shall have one vote.

*(b)* One-half of the countries members of the Assembly shall constitute a quorum.

*(c)* Notwithstanding the provisions of subparagraph *(b)*, if, in any session, the number of countries represented is less than one-half but equal to or more than one-third of the countries members of the Assembly, the Assembly may make decisions but, with the exception of decisions concerning its own procedure, all such decisions shall take effect only if the following conditions are fulfilled. The International Bureau shall communicate the said decisions to the countries members of the Assembly which were not represented and shall invite them to express in writing their vote or abstention within a period of three months from the date of the communication. If, at the expiration of this period, the number of countries having thus expressed their vote or abstention attains the number of countries which was lacking for attaining the quorum in the session itself, such decisions shall take effect provided that at the same time the required majority still obtains.

*(d)* Subject to the provisions of Article 26(2), the decisions of the Assembly shall require two-thirds of the votes cast.

*(e)* Abstentions shall not be considered as votes.

*(f)* A delegate may represent, and vote in the name of, one country only.

*(g)* Countries of the Union not members of the Assembly shall be admitted to its meetings as observers.

(4) *(a)* The Assembly shall meet once in every third calendar year in ordinary session upon convocation by the Director General and, in the absence

of exceptional circumstances, during the same period and at the same places as the General Assembly of the Organization.

*(b)* The Assembly shall meet in extraordinary session upon convocation by the Director General, at the request of the Executive Committee or at the request of one-fourth of the countries members of the Assembly.

(5) The Assembly shall adopt its own rules of procedure.

## Article 23

(1) The Assembly shall have an Executive Committee.

(2) *(a)* The Executive Committee shall consist of countries elected by the Assembly from among countries members of the Assembly. Furthermore, the country on whose territory the Organization has its headquarters shall, subject to the provisions of Article 25(7)*(b)*, have an *ex officio* seat on the Committee.

*(b)* The Government of each country member of the Executive Committee shall be represented by one delegate, who may be assisted by alternate delegates, advisors, and experts.

*(c)* The expenses of each delegation shall be borne by the Government which has appointed it.

(3) The number of countries members of the Executive Committee shall correspond to one-fourth of the number of countries members of the Assembly. In establishing the number of seats to be filled, remainders after division by four shall be disregarded.

(4) In electing the members of the Executive Committee, the Assembly shall have due regard to an equitable geographical distribution and to the need for countries party to the Special Agreements which might be established in relation with the Union to be among the countries constituting the Executive Committee.

(5) *(a)* Each member of the Executive Committee shall serve from the close of the session of the Assembly which elected it to the close of the next ordinary session of the Assembly.

*(b)* Members of the Executive Committee may be re-elected, but not m e than two-thirds of them.

*(c)* The Assembly shall establish the details of the rules governing the election and possible re-election of the members of the Executive Committee.

(6) *(a)* The Executive Committee shall:
  (i) prepare the draft agenda of the Assembly;
  (ii) submit proposals to the Assembly respecting the draft program and triennial budget of the Union prepared by the Director General;
  (iii) approve, within the limits of the program and the triennial budget, the specific yearly budgets and programs prepared by the Director General;
  (iv) submit, with appropriate comments, to the Assembly the periodical reports of the Director General and the yearly audit reports on the accounts;
  (v) in accordance with the decisions of the Assembly and having regard to circumstances arising between two ordinary sessions of the Assembly, take all necessary measures to ensure the execution of the program of the Union by the Director General;

(vi) perform such other functions as are allocated to it under this Convention.

*(b)* With respect to matters which are of interest also to other Unions administered by the Organization, the Executive Committee shall make its decisions after having heard the advice of the Coordination Committee of the Organization.

(7) *(a)* The Executive Committee shall meet once a year in ordinary session upon convocation by the Director General, preferably during the same period and at the same place as the Coordination Committee of the Organization.

*(b)* The Executive Committee shall meet in extraordinary session upon convocation by the Director General, either on his own initiative, or at the request of its Chairman or one-fourth of its members.

(8) *(a)* Each country member of the Executive Committee shall have one vote.

*(b)* One-half of the members of the Executive Committee shall constitute a quorum.

*(c)* Decisions shall be made by a simple majority of the votes cast.

*(d)* Abstentions shall not be considered as votes.

*(e)* A delegate may represent, and vote in the name of, one country only.

(9) Countries of the Union not members of the Executive Committee shall be admitted to its meetings as observers.

(10) The Executive Committee shall adopt its own rules of procedure.


### Article 24

(1) *(a)* The administrative tasks with respect to the Union shall be performed by the International Bureau, which is a continuation of the Bureau of the Union united with the Bureau of the Union established by the International Convention for the Protection of Industrial Property.

*(b)* In particular, the International Bureau shall provide the secretariat of the various organs of the Union.

*(c)* The Director General of the Organization shall be the chief executive of the Union and shall represent the Union.

(2) The International Bureau shall assemble and publish information concerning the protection of copyright. Each country of the Union shall promptly communicate to the International Bureau all new laws and official texts concerning the protection of copyright.

(3) The International Bureau shall publish a monthly periodical.

(4) The International Bureau shall, on request, furnish information to any country of the Union on matters concerning the protection of copyright.

(5) The International Bureau shall conduct studies, and shall provide services, designed to facilitate the protection of copyright.

(6) The Director General and any staff member designated by him shall participate, without the right to vote, in all meetings of the Assembly, the Executive Committee and any other committee of experts or working group. The Director General, or a staff member designated by him, shall be *ex officio* secretary of these bodies.

(7) *(a)* The International Bureau shall, in accordance with the directions of the Assembly and in cooperation with the Executive Committee, make the preparations for the conferences of revision of the provisions of the Convention other than Articles 22 to 26.

*(b)* The International Bureau may consult with intergovernmental and international non-governmental organizations concerning preparations for conferences of revision.

*(c)* The Director General and persons designated by him shall take part, without the right to vote, in the discussions at these conferences.

(8) The International Bureau shall carry out any other tasks assigned to it.

## Article 25

(1) *(a)* The Union shall have a budget.

*(b)* The budget of the Union shall include the income and expenses proper to the Union, its contribution to the budget of expenses common to the Unions, and, where applicable, the sum made available to the budget of the Conference of the Organization.

*(c)* Expenses not attributable exclusively to the Union but also to one or more other Unions administered by the Organization shall be considered as expenses common to the Unions. The share of the Union in such common expenses shall be in proportion to the interest the Union has in them.

(2) The budget of the Union shall be established with due regard to the requirements of coordination with the budgets of the other Unions administered by the Organization.

(3) The budget of the Union shall be financed from the following sources:

(i) contributions of the countries of the Union;

(ii) fees and charges due for services performed by the International Bureau in relation to the Union;

(iii) sale of, or royalties on, the publications of the International Bureau concerning the Union;

(iv) gifts, bequests, and subventions;

(v) rents, interests, and other miscellaneous income.

(4) *(a)* For the purpose of establishing its contribution towards the budget, each country of the Union shall belong to a class, and shall pay its annual contributions on the basis of a number of units fixed as follows:

| | |
|---|---|
| Class I | .... 25 |
| Class II | .... 20 |
| Class III | .... 15 |
| Class IV | .... 10 |
| Class V | .... 5 |
| Class VI | .... 3 |
| Class VII | .... 1 |

*(b)* Unless it has already done so, each country shall indicate, concurrently with depositing its instrument of ratification or accession, the class to which it wishes to belong. Any country may change class. If it chooses a lower class, the country must announce it to the Assembly at one of its ordinary sessions. Any such change shall take effect at the beginning of the calendar year following the session.

*(c)* The annual contribution of each country shall be an amount in the same proportion to the total sum to be contributed to the annual budget of the Union by all countries as the number of its units is to the total of the units of all contributing countries.

*(d)* Contributions shall become due on the first of January of each year.

*(e)* A country which is in arrears in the payment of its contributions shall have no vote in any of the organs of the Union of which it is a member if the amount of its arrears equals or exceeds the amount of the contributions due from it for the preceding two full years. However, any organ of the Union may allow such a country to continue to exercise its vote in that organ if, and as long as, it is satisfied that the delay in payment is due to exceptional and unavoidable circumstances.

*(f)* If the budget is not adopted before the beginning of a new financial period, it shall be at the same level as the budget of the previous year, in accordance with the financial regulations.

(5) The amount of the fees and charges due for services rendered by the International Bureau in relation to the Union shall be established, and shall be reported to the Assembly and the Executive Committee, by the Director General.

(6) *(a)* The Union shall have a working capital fund which shall be constituted by a single payment made by each country of the Union. If the fund becomes insufficient, an increase shall be decided by the Assembly.

*(b)* The amount of the initial payment of each country to the said fund or of its participation in the increase thereof shall be a proportion of the contribution of that country for the year in which the fund is established or the increase decided.

*(c)* The proportion and the terms of payment shall be fixed by the Assembly on the proposal of the Director General and after it has heard the advice of the Coordination Committee of the Organization.

(7) *(a)* In the headquarters agreement concluded with the country on the territory of which the Organization has its headquarters, it shall be provided that, whenever the working capital fund is insufficient, such country shall grant advances. The amount of these advances and the conditions on which they are granted shall be the subject of separate agreements, in each case, between such country and the Organization. As long as it remains under the obligation to grant advances, such country shall have *ex officio* seat on the Executive Committee.

*(b)* The country referred to in subparagraph *(a)* and the Organization shall each have the right to denounce the obligation to grant advances, by written notification. Denunciation shall take effect three years after the end of the year in which it has been notified.

(8) The auditing of the accounts shall be effected by one or more of the countries of the Union or by external auditors, as provided in the financial regulations. They shall be designated, with their agreement, by the Assembly.

## Article 26

(1) Proposals for the amendment of Articles 22, 23, 24, 25, and the present Article, may be initiated by any country member of the Assembly, by the Executive Committee, or by the Director General. Such proposals shall be communicated by the Director General to the member countries of the Assembly at least six months in advance of their consideration by the Assembly.

(2) Amendments to the Articles referred to in paragraph (1) shall be adopted by the Assembly. Adoption shall require three-fourths of the votes

cast, provided that any amendment of Article 22, and of the present paragraph, shall require four-fifths of the votes cast.

(3) Any amendment to the Articles referred to in paragraph (1) shall enter into force one month after written notifications of acceptance, effected in accordance with their respective constitutional processes, have been received by the Director General from three-fourths of the countries members of the Assembly at the time it adopted the amendment. Any amendment to the said Articles thus accepted shall bind all the countries which are members of the Assembly at the time the amendment enters into force, or which become members thereof at a subsequent date, provided that any amendment increasing the financial obligations of countries of the Union shall bind only those countries which have notified their acceptance of such amendment.

## Article 27

(1) This Convention shall be submitted to revision with a view to the introduction of amendments designed to improve the system of the Union.

(2) For this purpose, conferences shall be held successively in one of the countries of the Union among the delegates of the said countries.

(3) Subject to the provisions of Article 26 which apply to the amendment of Articles 22 to 26, any revision of this Act, including the Appendix, shall require the unanimity of the votes cast.

## Article 28

(1) *(a)* Any country of the Union which has signed this Act may ratify it, and, if it has not signed it, may accede to it. Instruments of ratification or accession shall be deposited with the Director General.

*(b)* Any country of the Union may declare in its instrument of ratification or accession that its ratification or accession shall not apply to Articles 1 to 21 and the Appendix, provided that, if such country has previously made a declaration under Article VI(1) of the Appendix, then it may declare in the said instrument only that its ratification or accession shall not apply to Articles 1 to 20.

*(c)* Any country of the Union which, in accordance with subparagraph *(b)*, has excluded provisions therein referred to from the effects of its ratification or accession may at any later time declare that it extends the effect of its ratification or accession to those provisions. Such declaration shall be deposited with the Director General.

(2) *(a)* Articles 1 to 21 and the Appendix shall enter into force three months after both of the following two conditions are fulfilled:

(i) at least five countries of the Union have ratified or acceded to this Act without making a declaration under paragraph (1)*(b)*,

(ii) France, Spain, the United Kingdom of Great Britain and Northern Ireland, and the United States of America, have become bound by the Universal Copyright Convention as revised at Paris on July 24, 1971.

*(b)* The entry into force referred to in subparagraph *(a)* shall apply to those countries of the Union which, at least three months before the said entry into force, have deposited instruments of ratification or accession not containing a declaration under paragraph (1)*(b)*.

*(c)* With respect to any country of the Union not covered by subparagraph *(b)* and which ratifies or accedes to this Act without making a declaration under paragraph (1)*(b)*, Articles 1 to 21 and the Appendix shall enter into force three months after the date on which the Director General has notified the deposit of the relevant instrument of ratification or accession, unless a subsequent date has been indicated in the instrument deposited. In the latter case, Articles 1 to 21 and the Appendix shall enter into force with respect to that country on the date thus indicated.

*(d)* The provisions of subparagraphs *(a)* to *(c)* do not affect the application of Article VI of the Appendix.

(3)  With respect to any country of the Union which ratifies or accedes to this Act with or without a declaration made under paragraph (1)*(b)*, Articles 22 to 38 shall enter into force three months after the date on which the Director General has notified the deposit of the relevant instrument of ratification or accession, unless a subsequent date has been indicated in the instrument deposited. In the latter case, Articles 22 to 38 shall enter into force with respect to that country on the date thus indicated.

## Article 29

(1)  Any country outside the Union may accede to this Act and thereby become party to this Convention and a member of the Union. Instruments of accession shall be deposited with the Director General.

(2)  *(a)* Subject to subparagraph *(b)*, this Convention shall enter into force with respect to any country outside the Union three months after the date on which the Director General has notified the deposit of its instrument of accession, unless a subsequent date has been indicated in the instrument deposited. In the latter case, this Convention shall enter into force with respect to that country on the date thus indicated.

*(b)* If the entry into force according to subparagraph *(a)* precedes the entry into force of Articles 1 to 21 and the Appendix according to Article 28(2)*(a)*, the said country shall, in the meantime, be bound, instead of by Articles 1 to 21 and the Appendix, by Articles 1 to 20 of the Brussels Act of this Convention.

## Article 29<sup>bis</sup>

Ratification of or accession to this Act by any country not bound by Articles 22 to 38 of the Stockholm Act of this Convention shall, for the sole purposes of Article 14(2) of the Convention establishing the Organization, amount to ratification of or accession to the said Stockholm Act with the limitation set forth in Article 28(1)*(b)*(i) thereof.

## Article 30

(1)  Subject to the exceptions permitted by paragraph (2) of this Article, by Article 28(1)*(b)*, by Article 33(2), and by the Appendix, ratification or accession shall automatically entail acceptance of all the provisions and admission to all the advantages of this Convention.

(2)  *(a)* Any country of the Union ratifying or acceding to this Act may, subject to Article V(2) of the Appendix, retain the benefit of the reservations

it has previously formulated on condition that it makes a declaration to that effect at the time of the deposit of its instrument of ratification or accession.

*(b)* Any country outside the Union may declare, in acceding to this Convention and subject to Article V(2) of the Appendix, that it intends to substitute, temporarily at least, for Article 8 of this Act concerning the right of translation, the provisions of Article 5 of the Union Convention of 1886, as completed at Paris in 1896, on the clear understanding that the said provisions are applicable only to translations into a language in general use in the said country. Subject to Article I(6)*(b)* of the Appendix, any country has the right to apply, in relation to the right of translation of works whose country of origins is a country availing itself of such a reservation, a protection which is equivalent to the protection granted by the latter country.

*(c)* Any country may withdraw such reservations at any time by notification addressed to the Director General.

## Article 31

(1) Any country may declare in its instrument of ratification or accession, or may inform the Director General by written notification at any time thereafter, that this Convention shall be applicable to all or part of those territories, designated in the declaration or notification, for the external relations of which it is responsible.

(2) Any country which has made such a declaration or given such a notification may, at any time, notify the Director General that this Convention shall cease to be applicable to all or part of such territories.

(3) *(a)* Any declaration made under paragraph (1) shall take effect on the same date as the ratification or accession in which it was included, and any notification given under that paragraph shall take effect three months after its notification by the Director General.

(b) Any notification given under paragraph (2) shall take effect twelve months after its receipt by the Director General.

(4) This Article shall in no way be understood as implying the recognition or tacit acceptance by a country of the Union of the factual situation concerning a territory to which this Convention is made applicable by another country of the Union by virtue of a declaration under paragraph (1).

## Article 32

(1) This Act shall, as regards relations between the countries of the Union, and to the extent that it applies, replace the Berne Convention of September 9, 1886, and the subsequent Acts of revision. The Acts previously in force shall continue to be applicable, in their entirety or to the extent that this Act does not replace them by virtue of the preceding sentence, in relations with countries of the Union which do not ratify or accede to this Act.

(2) Countries outside the Union which become party to this Act shall, subject to paragraph (3), apply it with respect to any country of the Union not bound by this Act or which, although bound by this Act, has made a declaration pursuant to Article 28(1)*(b)*. Such countries recognize that the said country of the Union, in its relations with them:

  (i) may apply the provisions of the most recent Act by which it is bound, and

(ii) subject to Article I(6) of the Appendix, has the right to adapt the protection to the level provided for by this Act.

(3) Any country which has availed itself of any of the faculties provided for in the Appendix may apply the provisions of the Appendix relating to the faculty or faculties of which it has availed itself in its relations with any other country of the Union which is not bound by this Act, provided that the latter country has accepted the application of the said provisions.

## Article 33

(1) Any dispute between two or more countries of the Union concerning the interpretation or application of this Convention, not settled by negotiation, may, by any one of the countries concerned, be brought before the International Court of Justice by application in conformity with the Statute of the Court, unless the countries concerned agree on some other method of settlement. The country bringing the dispute before the Court shall inform the International Bureau; the International Bureau shall bring the matter to the attention of the other countries of the Union.

(2) Each country may, at the time it signs this Act or deposits its instrument of ratification or accession, declare that it does not consider itself bound by the provisions of paragraph (1). With regard to any dispute between such country and any other country of the Union, the provisions of paragraph (1) shall not apply.

(3) Any country having made a declaration in accordance with the provisions of paragraph (2) may, at any time, withdraw its declaration by notification addressed to the Director General.

## Article 34

(1) Subject to Article 29[bis], no country may ratify or accede to earlier Acts of this Convention once Articles 1 to 21 and the Appendix have entered into force.

(2) Once Articles 1 to 21 and the Appendix have entered into force, no country may make a declaration under Article 5 of the Protocol Regarding Developing Countries attached to the Stockholm Act.

## Article 35

(1) This Convention shall remain in force without limitation as to time.

(2) Any country may denounce this Act by notification addressed to the Director General. Such denunciation shall constitute also denunciation of all earlier Acts and shall affect only the country making it, the Convention remaining in full force and effect as regards the other countries of the Union.

(3) Denunciation shall take effect one year after the day on which the Director General has received the notification.

(4) The right of denunciation provided by this Article shall not be exercised by any country before the expiration of five years from the date upon which it becomes a member of the Union.

## Article 36

(1) Any country party to this Convention undertakes to adopt, in accordance with its constitution, the measures necessary to ensure the application of this Convention.

(2) It is understood that, at the time a country becomes bound by this Convention, it will be in a position under its domestic law to give effect to the provisions of this Convention.

## Article 37

(1) *(a)* This Act shall be signed in a single copy in the French and English languages and, subject to paragraph (2), shall be deposited with the Director General.

*(b)* Official texts shall be established by the Director General, after consultation with the interested Governments, in the Arabic, German, Italian, Portuguese and Spanish languages, and such other languages as the Assembly may designate.

*(c)* In case of differences of opinions on the interpretation of the various texts, the French text shall prevail.

(2) This Act shall remain open for signature until January 31, 1972. Until that date, the copy referred to in paragraph (1) *(a)* shall be deposited with the Government of the French Republic.

(3) The Director General shall certify and transmit two copies of the signed text of this Act to the Governments of all countries of the Union and, on request, to the Government of any other country.

(4) The Director General shall register this Act with the Secretariat of the United Nations.

(5) The Director General shall notify the Governments of all countries of the Union of signatures, deposits of instruments of ratification or accession and any declarations included in such instruments or made pursuant to Articles 28(1)*(c)*, 30(2)*(a)* and *(b)*, and 33(2), entry into force of any provisions of this Act, notifications of denunciation, and notifications pursuant to Articles 30(2)*(c)*, 31(1) and (2), 33(3), and 38(1), as well as the Appendix.

## Article 38

(1) Countries of the Union which have not ratified or acceded to this Act and which are not bound by Articles 22 to 26 of the Stockholm Act of this Convention may, until April 26, 1975, exercise, if they so desire, the rights provided under the said Articles as if they were bound by them. Any country desiring to exercise such rights shall give written notification to this effect to the Director General; this notification shall be effective on the date of its receipt. Such countries shall be deemed to be members of the Assembly until the said date.

(2) As long as all the countries of the Union have not become Members of the Organization, the International Bureau of the Organization shall also function as the Bureau of the Union, and the Director General as the Director of the said Bureau.

(3) Once all the countries of the Union have become Members of the Organization, the rights, obligations, and property, of the Bureau of the Union shall devolve on the International Bureau of the Organization.

## APPENDIX

### Article I

(1) Any country regarded as a developing country in conformity with the established practice of the General Assembly of the United Nations which ratifies or accedes to this Act, of which this Appendix forms an integral part, and which, having regard to its economic situation and its social or cultural needs, does not consist itself immediately in a position to make provision for the protection of all the rights as provided for this Act, may, by a notification deposited with the Director General at the time of depositing its instrument of ratification or accession or, subject to Article V(1)*(c)*, at any time thereafter, declare that it will avail itself of the faculty provided for in Article II, or of the faculty provided for in Article III, or both of those faculties. It may, instead of availing itself of the faculty provided for in Article II, make a declaration according to Article V(1)*(a)*.

(2) *(a)* Any declaration under paragraph (1) notified before the expiration of the period of ten years from the entry into force of Articles 1 to 21 and this Appendix according to Article 28(2) shall be effective until the expiration of the said period. Any such declaration may be renewed in whole or in part for periods of ten years each by a notification deposited with the Director General not more than fifteen months and not less than three months before the expiration of the ten-year period then running.

*(b)* Any declaration under paragraph (1) notified after the expiration of the period of ten years from the entry into force of Articles 1 to 21 and this Appendix according to Article 28(2) shall be effective until the expiration of the ten-year period then running. Any such declaration may be renewed as provided for in the second sentence of subparagraph *(a)*.

(3) Any country of the Union which has ceased to be regarded as a developing country as referred to in paragraph (1) shall no longer be entitled to renew its declaration as provided in paragraph (2), and, whether or not it formally withdraws its declaration, such country shall be precluded from availing itself of the faculties referred to in paragraph (1) from the expiration of the ten-year period then running or from the expiration of a period of three years after it has ceased to be regarded as a developing country, whichever period expires later.

(4) Where, at the time when the declaration made under paragraph (1) or (2) ceases to be effective, there are copies in stock which were made under a license granted by virtue of this Appendix, such copies may continue to be distributed until their stock is exhausted.

(5) Any country which is bound by the provisions of this Act and which has deposited a declaration or a notification in accordance with Article 31(1) with respect to the application of this Act to a particular territory, the situation of which can be regarded as analogous to that of the countries referred to in paragraph (1), may, in respect of such territory, make the declaration referred to in paragraph (1) and the notification of renewal referred to in paragraph (2). As long as such declaration or notification remains in effect, the

provisions of this Appendix shall be applicable to the territory in respect of which it was made.

(6) *(a)* The fact that a country avails itself of any of the faculties referred to in paragraph (1) does not permit another country to give less protection to works of which the country of origin is the former country than it is obliged to grant under Articles 1 to 20.

*(b)* The right to apply reciprocal treatment provided for in Article 30(2)*(b)*, second sentence, shall not, until the date on which the period applicable under Article I(3) expires, be exercised in respect of works the country of origin of which is a country which has made a declaration according to Article V(1)*(a)*.

## Article II

(1) Any country which has declared that it will avail itself of the faculty provided for in this Article shall be entitled, so far as works published in printed or analogous forms of reproduction are concerned, to substitute for the exclusive right of translation provided for in Article 8 a system of non-exclusive and non-transferable licenses, granted by the competent authority under the following conditions and subject to Article IV.

(2) *(a)* Subject to paragraph (3), if, after the expiration of a period of three years, or of any longer period determined by the national legislation of the said country, commencing on the date of the first publication of the work, a translation of such work has not been published in a language in general use in that country by the owner of the right of translation, or with his authorization, any national of such country may obtain a license to make a translation of the work in the said language and publish the translation in printed or analogous forms of reproduction.

*(b)* A license under the conditions provided for in this Article may also be granted if all the editions of the translation published in the language concerned are out of print.

(3) *(a)* In the case of translations into a language which is not in general use in one or more developed countries which are members of the Union, a period of one year shall be substituted for the period of three years referred to in paragraph (2)*(a)*.

*(b)* Any country referred to in paragraph (1) may, with the unanimous agreement of the developed countries which are members of the Union and in which the same language is in general use, substitute, in the case of translations into that language, for the period of three years referred to in paragraph (2)*(a)* a shorter period as determined by such agreement but not less than one year. However, the provisions of the foregoing sentence shall not apply where the language in question is English, French or Spanish. The Director General shall be notified of any such agreement by the Governments which have concluded it.

(4) *(a)* No license obtainable after three years shall be granted under this Article until a further period of six months has elapsed, and no license obtainable after one year shall be granted under this Article until a further period of nine months has elapsed

    (i) from the date on which the applicant complies with the requirements mentioned in Article IV(1), or

    (ii) where the identity or the address of the owner of the right of translation is unknown, from the date on which the applicant sends, as provided for in Article IV(2), copies of his application submitted to the authority competent to grant the license.

(b) If, during the said period of six or nine months, a translation in the language in respect of which the application was made is published by the owner of the right of translation or with his authorization, no license under this Article shall be granted.

(5) Any license under this Article shall be granted only for the purpose of teaching, scholarship or research.

(6) If a translation of a work is published by the owner of the right of translation or with his authorization at a price reasonably related to that normally charged in the country for comparable works, any license granted under this Article shall terminate if such translation is in the same language and with substantially the same content as the translation published under the license. Any copies already made before the license terminates may continue to be distributed until their stock is exhausted.

(7) For works which are composed mainly of illustrations, a license to make and publish a translation of the text and to reproduce and publish the illustrations may be granted only if the conditions of Article III are also fulfilled.

(8) No license shall be granted under this Article when the author has withdrawn from circulation all copies of his work.

(9) (a) A license to make a translation of a work which has been published in printed or analogous forms of reproduction may also be granted to any broadcasting organization having its headquarters in a country referred to in paragraph (1), upon an application made to the competent authority of that country by the said organization, provided that all of the following conditions are met:

  (i) the translation is made from a copy made and acquired in accordance with the laws of the said country;

  (ii) the translation is only for use in broadcasts intended exclusively for teaching or for the dissemination of the results of specialized technical or scientific research to experts in a particular profession;

  (iii) the translation is used exclusively for the purposes referred to in condition (ii) through broadcasts made lawfully and intended for recipients on the territory of the said country, including broadcasts made through the medium of sound or visual recordings lawfully and exclusively made for the purpose of such broadcasts;

  (iv) all uses made of the translations are without any commercial purpose.

(b) Sound or visual recordings of a translation which was made by a broadcasting organization under a license granted by virtue of this paragraph may, for the purposes and subject to the conditions referred to in subparagraph (a) and with the agreement of that organization, also be used by any other broadcasting organization having its headquarters in the country whose competent authority granted the license in question.

(c) Provided that all of the criteria and conditions set out in subparagraph (a) are met, a license may also be granted to a broadcasting organization to translate any text incorporated in an audio-visual fixation where such fixation was itself prepared and published for the sole purpose of being used in connection with systematic instructional activities.

(b) Subject to paragraphs (a) to (c), the provisions of the preceding paragraphs shall apply to the grant and exercise of any license granted under this paragraph.

## Article III

(1) Any country which has declared that it will avail itself of the faculty provided for in this Article shall be entitled to substitute for the exclusive right of reproduction provided for in Article 9 a system of non-exclusive and non-transferable licenses, granted by the competent authority under the following conditions and subject to Article IV.

(2) *(a)* If, in relation to a work to which this Article applies by virtue of paragraph (7), after the expiration of

  (i) the relevant period specified in paragraph (3), commencing on the date of first publication of a particular edition of the work, or

  (ii) any longer period determined by national legislation of the country referred to in paragraph (1), commencing on the same date,

copies of such edition have not been distributed in that country to the general public or in connection with systematic instructional activities, by the owner of the right of reproduction or with his authorization, at a price reasonably related to that normally charged in the country for comparable works, any national of such country may obtain a license to reproduce and publish such edition at that or a lower price for use in connection with systematic instructional activities.

  *(b)* A license to reproduce and publish an edition which has been distributed as described in subparagraph *(a)* may also be granted under the conditions provided for in this Article if, after the expiration of the applicable period, no authorized copies of that edition have been on sale for a period of six months in the country concerned to the general public or in connection with systematic instructional activities at a price reasonably related to that normally charged in the country for comparable works.

(3) The period referred to in paragraph (2)*(a)*(i) shall be five years, except that

  (i) for works of the natural and physical sciences, including mathematics, and of technology, the period shall be three years;

  (ii) for works of fiction, poetry, drama and music, and for art books, the period shall be seven years.

(4) *(a)* No license obtainable after three years shall be granted under this Article until a period of six months has elapsed

  (i) from the date on which the applicant complies with the requirements mentioned in Article IV(1), or

  (ii) where the identity or the address of the owner of the right of reproduction is unknown, from the date on which the applicant sends, as provided for in Article IV(2), copies of his application submitted to the authority competent to grant the license.

  *(b)* Where licenses are obtainable after other periods and Article IV(2) is applicable, no license shall be granted until a period of three months has elapsed from the date of the dispatch of the copies of the application.

  *(c)* If, during the period of six or three months referred to in subparagraphs *(a)* and *(b)*, a distribution as described in paragraph (2)*(a)* has taken place, no license shall be granted under this Article.

  *(d)* No license shall be granted if the author has withdrawn from circulation all copies of the edition for the reproduction and publication of which the license has been applied for.

(5) A license to reproduce and publish a translation of a work shall not be granted under this Article in the following cases:

(i) where the translation was not published by the owner of the right of translation or with his authorization, or

(ii) where the translation is not in a language in general use in the country in which the license is applied for.

(6) If copies of an edition of a work are distributed in the country referred to in paragraph (1) to the general public or in connection with systematic instructional activities, by the owner of the right of reproduction or with his authorization, at a price reasonably related to that normally charged in the country for comparable works, any license granted under this Article shall terminate of such edition is in the same language and with substantially the same content as the edition which was published under the said license. Any copies already made before the license terminates may continue to be distributed until their stock is exhausted.

(7) *(a)* Subject to paragraph *(b)*, the works to which this Article applies shall be limited to works published in printed or analogous forms of reproduction.

*(b)* This Article shall also apply to the reproduction in audio-visual form of lawfully made audio-visual fixations including any protected works incorporated therein and to the translation of any incorporated text into a language in general use in the country in which the license is applied for, always provided that the audio-visual fixations in question were prepared and published for the sole purpose of being used in connection with systematic instructional activities.

### Article IV

(1) A license under Article II or Article III may be granted only if the applicant, in accordance with the procedure of the country concerned, establishes either that he has requested, and has been denied, authorization by the owner of the right to make and publish the translation or to reproduce and publish the edition, as the case may be, or that, after due diligence on his part, he was unable to find the owner of the right. At the same time as making the request, the applicant shall inform any national or international information center referred to in paragraph (2).

(2) If the owner of the right cannot be found, the applicant for a license shall send, by registered airmail, copies of his application, submitted to the authority competent to grant the license, to the publisher whose name appears on the work and to any national or international information center which may have been designated, in a notification to that effect deposited with the Director General, by the Government of the country in which the publisher is believed to have his principal place of business.

(3) The name of the author shall be indicated on all copies of the translation or reproduction published under a license granted under Article II or Article III. The title of the work shall appear on all such copies. In the case of a translation, the original title of the work shall appear in any case on all the said copies.

(4) *(a)* No license granted under Article II or Article III shall extend to the export of copies, and any such license shall be valid only for publication of the translation or of the reproduction, as the case may be, in the territory of the country in which it has been applied for.

*(b)* For the purpose of subparagraph *(a)*, the notion of export shall include the sending of copies from any territory to the country which, in respect of that territory, has made a declaration under Article I(5).

*(c)* Where a governmental or other public entity of a country which has granted a license to make a translation under Article II into a language other than English, French or Spanish sends copies of a translation published under such license to another country, such sending of copies shall not, for the purpose of subparagraph *(a)*, be considered to constitute export if all of the following conditions are met:

    (i)  the recipients are individuals who are nationals of the country whose competent authority has granted the license, or organizations grouping such individuals;

    (ii)  the copies are to be used only for the purpose of teaching, scholarship or research;

    (iii)  the sending of the copies and their subsequent distribution to recipients is without any commercial purpose; and

    (iv)  the country to which the copies have been sent has agreed with the country whose competent authority has granted the license to allow the receipt, or distribution, or both, and the Director General has been notified of the agreement by the Government of the country in which the license has been granted.

(5)  All copies published under a license granted by virtue of Article II or Article III shall bear a notice in the appropriate language stating that the copies are available for distribution only in the country or territory to which the said license applies.

(6)  *(a)* Due provision shall be made at the national level to ensure

    (i)  that the license provides, in favour of the owner of the right of translation or of reproduction, as the case may be, for just compensation that is consistent with standards of royalties normally operating on licenses freely negotiated between persons in the two countries concerned, and

    (ii)  payment and transmittal of the compensation: should national currency regulations intervene, the competent authority shall make all efforts, by the use of international machinery, to ensure transmittal in internationally convertible currency or its equivalent.

*(b)* Due provision shall be made by national legislation to ensure a correct translation of the work, or an accurate reproduction of the particular edition, as the case may be.

### Article V

(1)  *(a)* Any country entitled to make a declaration that it will avail itself of the faculty provided for in Article II may, instead, at the time of ratifying or acceding to this Act:

    (i)  if it is a country to which Article 30(2)*(a)* applies, make a declaration under that provision as far as the right of translation is concerned;

    (ii)  if it is a country to which Article 30(2)*(a)* does not apply, and even if it is not a country outside the Union, make a declaration as provided for in Article 30(2)*(b)*, first sentence.

*(b)* In the case of a country which ceases to be regarded as a developing country as referred to in Article I(1), a declaration made according to this paragraph shall be effective until the date on which the period applicable under Article I(3) expires.

*(C)* Any country which has made a declaration according to this paragraph may not subsequently avail itself of the faculty provided for in Article II even if it withdraws the said declaration.

(2) Subject to paragraph (3), any country which has availed itself of the faculty provided for in Article II may not subsequently make a declaration according to paragraph (1).

(3) Any country which has ceased to be regarded as a developing country as referred to in Article I(1) may, not later than two years prior to the expiration of the period applicable under Article I(3), make a declaration to the effect provided for in Article 30(2)*(b)*, first sentence, notwithstanding the fact that it is not a country outside the Union. Such declaration shall take effect at the date on which the period applicable under Article I(3) expires.

## Article VI

(1) Any country of the Union may declare, as from the date of this Act, and at any time before becoming bound by Articles 1 to 21 and this Appendix:

  (i) if it is a country which, were it bound by Articles 1 to 21 and this Appendix, would be entitled to avail itself of the faculties referred to in Article I(1), that it will apply the provisions of Article II or of Article III or of both to works whose country of origin is a country which, pursuant to (ii) below, admits the application of those Articles to such works, or which is bound by Articles 1 to 21 and this Appendix; such declaration may, instead of referring to Article II, refer to Article V;

  (ii) that it admits the application of this Appendix to works of which it is the country of origin by countries which have made a declaration under (i) above or a notification under Article I.

(2) Any declaration made under paragraph (1) shall be in writing and shall be deposited with the Director General. The declaration shall become effective from the date of its deposit.

# Appendix H

# Rome Convention, 1961

International Convention for the Protection of Performers, Producers of Phonograms and Broadcasting Organizations

The Contracting States, moved by the desire to protect the rights of performers, producers of phonograms, and broadcasting organizations,
Have agreed as follows:

### Article 1

Protection granted under this Convention shall leave intact and shall in no way affect the protection of copyright in literary and artistic works. Consequently, no provision of this Convention may be interpreted as prejudicing such protection.

### Article 2

1. For the purposes of this Convention, national treatment shall mean the treatment accorded by the domestic law of the Contracting State in which protection is claimed:
   *(a)* to performers who are its nationals, as regards performances taking place, broadcast, or first fixed, on its territory;
   *(b)* to producers of phonograms who are its nationals, as regards phonograms first fixed or first published on its territory;
   *(c)* to broadcasting organizations which have their headquarters on its territory, as regards broadcasts transmitted from transmitters situated on its territory.
2. National treatment shall be subject to the protection specifically guaranteed, and the limitations specifically provided for, in this Convention.

### Article 3

For the purposes of this Convention:
*(a)* "performers" means actors, singers, musicians, dancers, and other persons who act, sing, deliver, declaim, play in, or otherwise perform literary or artistic works;

635

(b) "phonogram" means any exclusively aural fixation of sounds of a performance or of other sounds;

(c) "producer of phonograms" means the person who, or the legal entity which, first fixes the sounds of a performance or other sounds;

(d) "publication" means the offering of copies of a phonogram to the public in reasonable quantity;

(e) "reproduction" means the making of a copy or copies of a fixation;

(f) "rebroadcasting" means the transmission by wireless means for public reception of sounds or of images and sounds;

(g) "rebroadcasting" means the simultaneous broadcasting by one broadcasting organization of the broadcast of another broadcasting organization.

## Article 4

Each Contracting State shall grant national treatment to performers if any of the following conditions is met:

(a) the performance takes place in another Contracting State;

(b) the performance is incorporated in a phonogram which is protected under Article 5 of this Convention;

(c) the performance, not being fixed on a phonogram, is carried by a broadcast which is protected by Article 6 of this Convention.

## Article 5

1. Each Contracting State shall grant national treatment to producers of phonograms if any of the following conditions is met:

(a) the producer of the phonogram is a national of another Contracting State (criterion of nationality);

(b) the first fixation of the sound was made in another Contracting State (criterion of fixation);

(c) the phonogram was first published in another Contracting State (criterion of publication).

2. If a phonogram was first published in a non-contracting State but if it was also published, within thirty days of its first publication, in a Contracting State (simultaneous publication), it shall be considered as first published in the Contracting State.

3. By means of a notification deposited with the Secretary-General of the United Nations, any Contracting State may declare that it will not apply the criterion of publication or, alternatively, the criterion of fixation. Such notification may be deposited at the time of ratification, acceptance or accession, or at any time thereafter; in the last case, it shall become effective six months after it has been deposited.

## Article 6

1. Each Contracting State shall grant national treatment to broadcasting organizations if either of the following conditions is met:

*(a)* the headquarters of the broadcasting organization is situated in another Contracting State;

*(b)* the broadcast was transmitted from a transmitter situated in another Contracting State.

2. By means of a notification deposited with the Secretary-General of
the United Nations, any Contracting State may declare that it will protect
broadcasts only if the headquarters of the broadcasting organization is situated in another Contracting State and the broadcast was transmitted from a
transmitter situated in the same Contracting State. Such notification may
be deposited at the time of ratification, acceptance or accession, or at any
time thereafter; in the last case, it shall become effective six months after it
has been deposited.

### Article 7

1. The protection provided for performers by this Convention shall include the possibility of preventing:

*(a)* the broadcasting and the communication to the public, without their
consent, of their performance, except where the performance used in the
broadcasting or the public communication is itself already a broadcast performance or is made from a fixation;

*(b)* the fixation, without their consent, of their unfixed performance;

*(c)* the reproduction, without their consent, of a fixation of their
performance:

> (i) if the original fixation itself was made without their consent;
>
> (ii) if the reproduction is made for purposes different from those for
> which the performers gave their consent;
>
> (iii) if the original fixation was made in accordance with the provisions
> of Article 15, and the reproduction is made for purposes different
> from those referred to in those provisions.

2. (1) If broadcasting was consented to by the performers, it shall be a
matter for the domestic law of the Contracting State where protection is
claimed to regulate the protection against rebroadcasting, fixation for
broadcasting purposes and the reproduction of such fixation for broadcasting purposes.

(2) The terms and conditions governing the use by broadcasting organizations of fixations made for broadcasting purposes shall be determined in
accordance with the domestic law of the Contracting State where protection
is claimed.

(3) However, the domestic law referred to in sub-paragraphs (1) and (2)
of this paragraph shall not operate to deprive performers of the ability to
control, by contract, their relations with broadcasting organizations.

### Article 8

Any Contracting State may, by its domestic laws and regulations, specify the manner in which performers will be represented in connection
with the exercise of their rights if several of them participate in the same
performance.

## Article 9

Any Contracting State may, by its domestic laws and regulations, extend the protection provided for in this Convention to artists who do not perform literary or artistic works.

## Article 10

Producers of phonograms shall enjoy the right to authorize or prohibit the direct or indirect reproduction of their phonograms.

## Article 11

If, as a condition of protecting the rights of producers of phonograms, or of performers, or both, in relation to phonograms, a Contracting State, under its domestic law, requires compliance with formalities, these shall be considered as fulfilled if all the copies in commerce of the published phonogram of their containers bear a notice consisting of the symbol ℗, accompanied by the year date of the first publication, placed in such a manner as to give reasonable notice of claim of protection; and if the copies or their containers do not identify the producer or the licensee of the producer (by carrying his name, trade mark or other appropriate designation), the notice shall also include the name of the owner of the rights of the producer; and, furthermore, if the copies or their containers do not identify the principal performers, the notice shall also include the name of the person who, in the country in which the fixation was effected, owns the rights of such performers.

## Article 12

If a phonogram published for commercial purposes, or a reproduction of such phonogram, is used directly for broadcasting or for any communication to the public, a single equitable remuneration shall be paid by the user to the performers, or to the producers of the phonograms, or to both. Domestic law may, in the absence of agreement between these parties, lay down the conditions as to the sharing of the remuneration.

## Article 13

Broadcasting organizations shall enjoy the right to authorize or prohibit:
  *(a)* the rebroadcasting of their broadcasts;
  *(b)* the fixation of their broadcasts;
  *(c)* the reproduction:
  (i) of fixations, made without their consent, of their broadcasts;
  (ii) of fixations, made in accordance with the provisions of Article 15, of their broadcasts, if the reproduction is made for purposes different from those referred to in those provisions;
  *(d)* the communication to the public of their television broadcasts if such communication is made in places accessible to the public against payment of

an entrance fee; it shall be a matter for the domestic law of the State where protection of this right is claimed to determine the conditions under which it may be exercised.

## Article 14

The term of protection to be granted under this Convention shall last at least until the end of a period of twenty years computed from the end of the year in which:

*(a)* the fixation was made—for phonograms and for performances incorporated therein;

*(b)* the performance took place—for performances not incorporated in phonograms;

*(c)* the broadcast took place—for broadcasts.

## Article 15

1. Any Contracting State may, in its domestic laws and regulations, provide for exceptions to the protection guaranteed by this Convention as regards:

*(a)* private use;

*(b)* use of short excerpts in connection with the reporting of current events;

*(c)* ephemeral fixation by a broadcasting organization by means of its own facilities and for its own broadcasts;

*(d)* use solely for the purpose of teaching or scientific research.

2. Irrespective of paragraph 1 of this Article, any contracting State may, in its domestic laws and regulations, provide for the same kinds of limitations with regard to the protection of performers, producers of phonograms and broadcasting organizations, as it provides for, in its domestic laws and regulations, in connection with the protection of copyright in literary and artistic works. However, compulsory licenses may be provided for only to the extent to which they are compatible with the Convention.

## Article 16

1. Any State, upon becoming party to this Convention, shall be bound by all the obligations and shall enjoy all the benefits thereof. However, a State may at any time, in a notification deposited with the Secretary-General of the United Nations, declare that:

*(a)* as regards Article 12:

(i) it will not apply the provisions of that Article;

(ii) it will not apply the provisions of that Article in respect of certain uses;

(iv) as regards phonograms the producer of which is not a national of another Contracting State, it will not apply that Article;

(iv) as regards phonograms the producer of which is a national of another Contracting State, it will limit the protection provided for by that Article to the extent to which, and to the term for which, the latter State grants protection to phonograms first fixed by a national of the State making the declaration; however, the fact that the Contracting State of which the producer is a national does not grant the protection to the same beneficiary or beneficiaries as the State making the declaration shall not be considered as a difference in the extent of the protection;

*(b)* as regards Article 13, it will not apply item *(d)* of that Article; if a Contracting State makes such a declaration, the other Contracting States shall not be obliged to grant the right referred to in Article 13, item *(d)*, to broadcasting organizations whose headquarters are in that State.

2. If the notification referred to in paragraph 1 of this Article is made after the date of the deposit of the instrument of ratification, acceptance or accession, the declaration will become effective six months after it has been deposited.

## Article 17

Any State which, on October 26, 1961, grants protection to producers of phonograms solely on the basis of the criterion of fixation may, by a notification deposited with the Secretary-General of the United Nations at the time of ratification, acceptance or accession, declare that it will apply, for the purposes of Article 5, the criterion of fixation alone and, for the purposes of paragraph 1 *(a)* (iii) and (iv) of Article 16, the criterion of fixation instead of the criterion of nationality.

## Article 18

Any State which has deposited a notification under paragraph 3 of Article 5, paragraph 2 of Article 6, paragraph 1 of Article 16 or Article 17, may, by a further notification deposited with the Secretary-General of the United Nations, reduce its scope or withdraw it.

## Article 19

Notwithstanding anything in this Convention, once a performer has consented to the incorporation of his performance in a visual or audio-visual fixation, Article 7 shall have no further application.

## Article 20

1. This Convention shall not prejudice rights acquired in any Contracting State before the date of coming into force of this Convention for that State.

2. No Contracting State shall be bound to apply the provisions of this Convention to performances or broadcasts which took place, or to phonograms which were fixed, before the date of coming into force of this Convention for that State.

## Article 21

The protection provided for in this Convention shall not prejudice any protection otherwise secured to performers, producers of phonograms and broadcasting organizations.

## Article 22

Contracting States reserve the right to enter into special agreements among themselves in so far as such agreements grant to performers, producers of phonograms or broadcasting organizations more extensive rights than those granted by this Convention or contain other provisions not contrary to this Convention.

## Article 23

This Convention shall be deposited with the Secretary-General of the United Nations. It shall be open until June 30, 1962, for signature by any State invited to the Diplomatic Conference on the International Protection of Performers, Producers of Phonograms and Broadcasting Organizations which is a party to the Universal Copyright Convention or a member of the International Union for the Protection of Literary and Artistic Works.

## Article 24

1. This Convention shall be subject to ratification or acceptance by the signatory States.
2. This Convention shall be open for accession by any State invited to the Conference referred to in Article 23, and by any State Member of the United Nations, provided that in either case such State is a party to the Universal Copyright Convention or a member of the International Union for the Protection of Literary and Artistic Works.
3. Ratification, acceptance or accession shall be effected by the deposit of an instrument to that effect with the Secretary-General of the United Nations.

## Article 25

1. This Convention shall come into force three months after the date of deposit of the sixth instrument of ratification, acceptance or accession.
2. Subsequently, this Convention shall come into force in respect of each State three months after the date of deposit of its instrument of ratification, acceptance or accession.

## Article 26

1. Each Contracting State undertakes to adopt, in accordance with its Constitution, the measures necessary to ensure the application of this Convention.

2. At the time of deposit of its instrument of ratification, acceptance or accession, each State must be in a position under its domestic law to give effect to the terms of this Convention.

## Article 27

1. Any State may, at the time of ratification, acceptance or accession, or at any time thereafter, declare by notification addressed to the Secretary-General of the United Nations that this Convention shall extend to all or any of the territories for whose international relations it is responsible, provided that the Universal Copyright Convention or the International Convention for the Protection of Literary and Artistic Works applies to the territory or territories concerned. This notification shall take effect three months after the date of its receipt.

2. The notifications referred to in paragraph 3 of Article 5, paragraph 2 of Article 6, paragraph 1 of Article 16 and Articles 17 and 18, may be extended to cover all or any of the territories referred to in paragraph 1 of this Article.

## Article 28

1. Any Contracting State may denounce this Convention, on its own behalf or on behalf of all or any of the territories referred to in Article 27.

2. The denunciation shall be effected by a notification addressed to the Secretary-General of the United Nations and shall take effect twelve months after the date of receipt of the notification.

3. The right of denunciation shall not be exercised by a Contracting State before the expiry of a period of five years from the date on which the Convention came into force with respect to that State.

4. A Contracting State shall cease to be a party to this Convention from that time when it is neither a party to the Universal Copyright Convention nor a member of the International Union for the Protection of Literary and Artistic Works.

5. This Convention shall cease to apply to any territory referred to in Article 27 from that time when neither the Universal Copyright Convention nor the International Convention for the Protection of Literary and Artistic Works applies to that territory.

## Article 29

1. After this Convention has been in force for five years, any Contracting State may, by notification addressed to the Secretary-General of the United Nations, request that a conference be convened for the purpose of revising the Convention. The Secretary-General shall notify all Contracting States of this request. If, within a period of six months following the date of notification by the Secretary-General of the United Nations, not less than one half of the Contracting States notify him of their occurrence with the request, the Secretary-General shall inform the Director-General of the International Labour Office, the Director-General of the United Nations Edu-

cational, Scientific and Cultural Organization and the Director of the Bureau of the International Union for the Protection of Literary and Artistic Works, who shall convene a revision conference in co-operation with the Intergovernmental Committee provided for in Article 32.

2. The adoption of any revision of this Convention shall require an affir-mative vote by two-thirds of the States attending the revision conference, provided that this majority includes two-thirds of the States which, at the time of the revision conference, are parties to the Convention.

3. In the event of adoption of a Convention revising this Convention in whole or in part, and unless the revising Convention provides otherwise:

*(a)* this Convention shall cease to be open to ratification, acceptance or accession as from the date of entry into force of the revising Convention;

*(b)* this Convention shall remain in force as regards relations between or with Contracting States which have not become parties to the revising Convention.

## Article 30

Any dispute which may arise between two or more Contracting States concerning the interpretation or application of this Convention and which is not settled by negotiation shall, at the request of any one of the parties to the dispute, be referred to the International Court of Justice for decision, unless they agree to another mode of settlement.

## Article 31

Without prejudice to the provisions of paragraph 3 of Article 5, para-graph 2 of Article 6, paragraph 1 of Article 16 and Article 17, no reservation may be made to this Convention.

## Article 32

1. An Intergovernmental Committee is hereby established with the following duties:

*(a)* to study questions concerning the application and operation of this Convention; and

*(b)* to collect proposals and to prepare documentation for possible revision of this Convention.

2. The Committee shall consist of representatives of the Contracting States, chosen with due regard to equitable geographical distribution. The number of members shall be six if there are twelve Contracting States or less, nine if there are thirteen to eighteen Contracting States and twelve if there are more than eighteen Contracting States.

3. The Committee shall be constituted twelve months after the Convention comes into force by an election organized among the Contracting States, each of which shall have one vote, by the Director-General of the International Labour Office, the Director-General of the United Nations Educational, Scientific and Cultural Organization and the Director of the Bureau of the International Union for the Protection of Literary and Artistic Works,

in accordance with rules previously approved by a majority of all Contracting States.

4. The Committee shall elect its Chairman and officers. It shall establish its own rules of procedure. These rules shall in particular provide for the future operation of the Committee and for a method of selecting its members for the future in such a way as to ensure rotation among the various Contracting States.

5. Officials of the International Labour Office, the United Nations Educational, Scientific and Cultural Organization and the Bureau of the International Union for the Protection of Literary and Artistic Works, designated by the Directors-General and the Director thereof, shall constitute the Secretariat of the Committee.

6. Meetings of the Committee, which shall be convened whenever a majority of its members deems it necessary, shall be held successively at the headquarters of the International Labour Office, the United Nations Educational, Scientific and Cultural Organization and the Bureau of the International Union for the Protection of Literary and Artistic Works.

7. Expenses of members of the Committee shall be borne by their respective Governments.

## Article 33

1. The present Convention is drawn up in English, French and Spanish, the three texts being equally authentic.

2. In addition, official texts of the present Convention shall be drawn up in German, Italian and Portuguese.

## Article 34

1. The Secretary-General of the United Nations shall notify the States invited to the Conference referred to in Article 23 and every State Member of the United Nations, as well as the Director-General of the International Labour Office, the Director-General of the United Nations Educational, Scientific and Cultural Organization and the Director of the Bureau of the International Union for the Protection of Literary and Artistic Works:

*(a)* of the deposit of each instrument of ratification, acceptance or accession;

*(b)* of the date of entry into force of the Convention;

*(c)* of all notifications, declarations or communications provided for in this Convention;

*(d)* if any of the situations referred to in paragraphs 4 and 5 of Article 28 arise.

2. The Secretary-General of the United Nations shall also notify the Director-General of the International Labour Office, the Director-General of the United Nations Educational, Scientific and Cultural Organization and the Director of the Bureau of the International Union for the Protection of Literary and Artistic Works of the requests communicated to him in accordance with Article 29, as well as of any communication received from the Contracting States concerning the revision of the Convention.

IN FAITH WHEREOF, the undersigned, being duly authorized thereto, have signed this Convention.

DONE at Rome, this twenty-sixth day of October 1961, in a single copy in the English, French and Spanish languages. Certified true copies shall be delivered by the Secretary-General of the United Nations to all the States invited to the Conference referred to in Article 23 and to every State Member of the United Nations, as well as to the Director-General of the International Labour Office, the Director-General of the United Nations Educational, Scientific and Cultural Organization and the Director of the Bureau of the International Union for the Protection of Literary and Artistic Works.

# Appendix I

# United States Code Sections

## Sections 2318 and 2319 of Title 18, United States Code

**§ 2318. Trafficking in counterfeit labels for phonorecords, and copies of motion pictures or other audiovisual works**

(a) Whoever, in any of the circumstances described in subsection (c) of this section, knowingly traffics in a counterfeit label affixed or designed to be affixed to a phonorecord, or a copy of a motion picture or other audiovisual work, shall be fined not more than $250,000 or imprisoned for not more than five years, or both.

(b) As used in this section—

(1) the term "counterfeit label" means an identifying label or container that appears to be genuine, but is not;

(2) the term "traffic" means to transport, transfer or otherwise dispose of, to another, as consideration for anything of value or to make or obtain control of with intent to so transport, transfer or dispose of; and

(3) the terms "copy", "phonorecord", motion picture", and "audiovisual work" have, respectively, the meanings given those terms in section 101 (relating to definitions) of title 17.

(c) The circumstances referred to in subsection (a) of this section are—

(1) the offense is committed within the special maritime and territorial jurisdiction of the United States; or within the special aircraft jurisdiction of the United States (as defined in section 101 of the Federal Aviation Act of 1958);

(2) the mail or a facility of interstate or foreign commerce is used or intended to be used in the commission of the offense; or

(3) the counterfeit label is affixed to or encloses, or is designed to be affixed to or enclose, a copyrighted motion picture or other audiovisual work, or a phonorecord of a copyrighted sound recording.

(d) When any person is convicted of any violation of subsection (a), the court in its judgment of conviction shall in addition to the penalty therein prescribed, order the forfeiture and destruction or other disposition of all counterfeit labels and all articles to which counterfeit labels have been affixed or which were intended to have had such labels affixed.

(e) Except to the extent they are inconsistent with the provisions of this title, all provisions of section 509, title 17, United States Code, are applicable to violations of subsection (a).

### § 2319. Criminal infringement of a copyright

(a) Whoever violates section 506(a) (relating to criminal offenses) of title 17 shall be punished as provided in subsection (b) of this section and such penalties shall be in addition to any other provisions of title 17 or any other law.

(b) Any person who commits an offense under subsection (a) of this section—

(1) shall be fined not more than $250,000 or imprisoned for not more than five years, or both, if the offense—

(A) involves the reproduction or distribution, during any one-hundred-and-eighty-day period, of at least one thousand phonorecords or copies infringing the copyright in one or more sound recordings;

(B) involves the reproduction or distribution, during any one-hundred-and-eighty-day period, of at least sixty-five copies infringing the copyright in one or more motion pictures or other audiovisual works; or

(C) is a second or subsequent offense under either of subsection (b)(1) or (b)(2) of this section, where a prior offense involved a sound recording, or a motion picture or other audiovisual work;

(2) shall be fined not more than $250,000 or imprisoned for not more than two years, or both, if the offense—

(A) involves the reproduction or distribution, during any one-hundred-and-eighty-day period, of more than one hundred but less than one thousand phonorecords or copies infringing the copyright in one or more sound recordings; or

(B) involves the reproduction or distribution, during any one-hundred-and-eighty-day period, of more than seven but less than sixty-five copies infringing the copyright in one or more motion pictures or other audiovisual works; and

(3) shall be fined not more than $25,000 or imprisoned for not more than one year, or both, in any other case.

(c) As used in this section—

(1) the terms "sound recording", "motion picture", "audiovisual work", "phonorecord", and "copies" have, respectively, the meanings set forth in section 101 (relating to definitions) of title 17; and

(2) the terms "reproduction" and "distribution" refer to the exclusive rights of a copyright owner under clauses (1) and (3) respectively of section 106 (relating to exclusive rights in copyrighted works), as limited by sections 107 through 118, of title 17.

# Sections 1338, 1400(a), and 1498(b) of Title 28, United States Code

### § 1338. Patents, plant variety protection, copyrights, trade-marks, and unfair competition

(a) The district courts shall have original jurisdiction of any civil action arising under any Act of Congress relating to patents, plant variety protection, copyrights and trade-marks. Such jurisdiction shall be exclusive of the courts of the states in patent, plant variety protection and copyright cases.

(b) The district courts shall have original jurisdiction of any civil action asserting a claim of unfair competition when joined with a substantial and related claim under the copyright, patent, plant variety protection or trade-mark laws.

### § 1400(a). Patents and copyrights

(a) Civil actions, suits, or proceedings arising under any Act of Congress relating to copyrights may be instituted in the district in which the defendant or his agent resides or may be found.

### § 1498(b). Patents and copyrights

Hereafter, whenever the copyright in any work protected under the copyright laws of the United States shall be infringed by the United States, by a corporation owned or controlled by the United States, or by a contractor, subcontractor, or any person, firm, or corporation acting for the Government and with the authorization or consent of the Government, the exclusive remedy of the owner of such copyright shall be by action against the United States in the Claims Court for the recovery of his reasonable and entire compensation as damages for such infringement, including the minimum statutory damages as set forth in section 504(c), of title 17, United States Code: *Provided,* That a Government employee shall have a right of action against the Government under this subsection except where he was in a position to order, influence, or induce use of the copyrighted work by the Government: *Provided, however,* That this subsection shall not confer a right of action on any copyright owner or any assignee of such owner with respect to any copyrighted work prepared by a person while in the employment of service of the United States, where the copyrighted work was prepared as a part of the official functions of the employee, or in the preparation of which Government time, material, or facilities were used: *And provided further,* That before such action against the United States has been instituted the appropriate corporation owned or controlled by the United States or the head of the appropriate department or agency of the Government, as the case may be, is authorized to enter into an agreement with the copyright owner in full settlement and compromise for the damages accruing to him by reason of such infringement and to settle the claim administratively out of available appropriations.

Except as otherwise provided by law, no recovery shall be had for any infringement of a copyright covered by this subsection committed more than three years prior to filing of the complaint or counterclaim for infringement in the action, except that the period between the date of receipt of a written claim for compensation by the Department or agency of the Government or corporation owned or controlled by the United States, as the case may be, having authority to settle such claim and the date of mailing by the Government of a notice to the claimant that his claim has been denied shall not be counted as a part of the three years, unless suit is brought before the last-mentioned date.

# Table of Cases

American Vitagraph, Inc. v. Levy, 659 F.2d 1023, 213 USPQ 31 (9th Cir. 1981); 1095 (2d Cir.), *cert. denied*, 459 U.S. 826 (1982)　140, 143

Amjon v. HBO, 9 MEDIA L. REP. 1181 (S.D.N.Y. 1982)　198

AMOA v. Copyright Royalty Tribunal, COPR. L. REP. ¶25,062 (D.D.C. 1979), *vacated and rem'd*, 636 F.2d 531, 207 USPQ 374 (D.C. Cir. 1980), *cert. denied*, 450 U.S. 912, 211 USPQ 400 (1981)　236

Amplex Mfg. Co. v. ABC Plastic Fabricators, 184 F. Supp. 285 (E.D. Pa. 1960)　79

Amsterdam v. Triangle Publications, 189 F.2d 104, 89 USPQ 468 (3d Cir. 1951)　70

Amusement & Music Operators Ass'n v. Copyright Royalty Tribunal, 676 F.2d 1144, 215 USPQ 100 (7th Cir.), *cert. denied*, 459 U.S. 907 (1982)　300

—636 F.2d 531, 207 USPQ 374 (D.C. Cir. 1980), *cert. denied*, 450 U.S. 912, 211 USPQ 400 (1981)　300

Andersen, Walter, In Re Successor in Interest to, 743 F.2d 1578, 223 USPQ 378 (Ct. App. Fed. Cir. 1984)　60, 186

Anderson v. Paramount Pictures Corp., 226 USPQ 131 (C.D. Cal. 1985)　200

Angel Music, Inc. v. ABC Sports, Inc., COPR. L. REP. ¶25,797 (S.D.N.Y. 1985)　260

Animal Fair, Inc. v. Amfesco Indus., Inc., 620 F. Supp. 175, 227 USPQ 817 (D. Minn. 1985), *aff'd*, No. 85-5260 (8th Cir. filed April 9, 1986)　32, 41, 42, 43, 154, 201, 203

Apple Barrel Prods., Inc. v. Beard, 730 F.2d 384, 222 USPQ 956 (5th Cir. 1984)　63, 184, 277, 279

Apple Computer, Inc. v. Formula Int'l, Inc., 562 F. Supp. 775, 218 USPQ 47 (C.D. Cal. 1983), *aff'd*, 725 F.2d 521, 221 USPQ 762 (9th Cir. 1984)　19, 33, 60, 190, 278, 279

—594 F. Supp. 617, 224 USPQ 560 (C.D. Cal. 1984)　211, 212-213

Apple Computer, Inc. v. Franklin Computer Corp., 714 F.2d 1240, 219 USPQ 113 (3d Cir. 1983)　19, 29, 33, 60-61, 190, 211, 278, 279-280, 292

April Prods., Inc. v. G. Schirmer, Inc., 308 N.Y. 366, 105 USPQ 286 (1955)　127

Arbitron Co. v. E.W. Scripps, Inc., 9 MEDIA L. REP. 1507 (S.D.N.Y. 1983)　260, 262

Arc v. S. S. Sarna, Inc., 621 F. Supp. 916, 229 USPQ 25 (E.D.N.Y. 1985)　24, 25, 32, 124, 188, 192, 201, 203, 279

Arnold, Ted, Ltd. v. Silvercraft Co., 259 F. Supp. 733, 151 USPQ 286 (S.D.N.Y. 1966)　37, 155

Arnstein v. Edward B. Marks Music Corp., 82 F.2d 275, 28 USPQ 426 (2d Cir. 1936)　202

Arnstein v. Porter, 154 F.2d 464, 68 USPQ 288 (2d Cir. 1946), *cert. denied*, 330 U.S. 851, 73 USPQ 550 (1947)　45, 191, 192, 193, 195, 196, 197, 198, 199, 200

Aronson v. Quick Point Pencil, 440 U.S. 257, 201 USPQ 1 (1979)　35

Ascher v. Saturday Review, Civ. No. 84-7781 (S.D.N.Y. filed Oct. 29, 1984)　276

Associated Film Dist. Corp. v. Thornburgh, 520 F. Supp. 971, 214 USPQ 742 (E.D. Pa. 1981), *rev'd and rem'd*, 683 F.2d 808, 216 USPQ 184 (3d Cir. 1982), *on remand*, 227 USPQ 184 (E.D. Pa. 1985)　89, 90

Association of American Medical Colleges v. Carey, 482 F. Supp. 1358, 205 USPQ 42 (N.D.N.Y. 1980)　272, 280-281

Astor-Honor, Inc. v. Grosset & Dunlap, Inc., 441 F.2d 627, 170 USPQ 65 (2d Cir. 1971)　85

Atari, Inc. v. Amusement World, Inc., 547 F. Supp. 222, 215 USPQ 929 (D. Md. 1981)　31, 201

Atari, Inc. v. JS&A Group, Inc., 597 F. Supp. 5 (N.D. Ill. 1983)　211, 212, 269

Atari, Inc. v. North American Philips Consumer Electronics Corp., 672 F.2d 607, 214 USPQ 33 (7th Cir.), *cert. denied*, 459 U.S. 880 (1982)　29, 31, 47, 48, 191, 193, 196, 197, 199, 200, 201, 205

Atascadero State Hospital v. Scanlon, 473 U.S. ＿＿ (1985)　272-273

Atlantic Monthly Co. v. Post Pub. Co., 27 F.2d 556 (D. Mass. 1928)　142

Authors League of America, Inc. v. Ladd, 227 USPQ 552 (S.D.N.Y. 1985), *aff'd sub nom.* Authors League of America, Inc. v. Oman, 790 F.2d 220, 229 USPQ 724 (2d Cir. 1986)　16, 317

Authors League of America, Inc. v. Oman (*see* Authors League of America, Inc. v. Ladd)

Avco Corp. v. Precision Air Parts, Inc., 210 USPQ 894 (M.D. Ala. 1980), *aff'd*, 676 F.2d 494, 216 USPQ 1086 (11th Cir.), *cert. denied*, 459 U.S. 1037 (1982)　86

Avins v. Moll, 610 F. Supp. 308 (E.D. Pa. 1984)　248

**B**

Bailey v. Logan Typographics, 441 F.2d 47 (7th Cir. 1971)　79

Bailie v. Fisher, 258 F.2d 425, 117 USPQ 334 (D.C. Cir. 1958)　29, 56

Baker v. Libbie, 210 Mass. 599, 97 N.E. 109 (1912)　130

Baker v. Selden, 101 U.S. 99 (1879)　23, 29, 30

Baker v. Taylor, 2 F. Cas. 478 (C.C.S.D.N.Y. 1848)　151

Baldwin Cooke Co. v. Keith Clarke, Inc., 383 F. Supp. 650, 183 USPQ 209 (N.D. Ill.), *aff'd per curiam*, 505 F.2d 1250, 183 USPQ 769 (7th Cir. 1974)　29

Baldwin County Welcome Center v. Brown, 466 U.S. 147 (1984)　136

Ballas, George P., Buick-GMC, Inc. v. Taylor Buick, Inc., 5 Ohio Misc. 2d 16, 449 N.E.2d 805 (C.P. Lucas County 1981),

—v. Allen-Genoa Road Drive-In, Inc., 598 F. Supp. 415, 223 USPQ 574 (S.D. Tex. 1983) 236

—v. CBS, Inc., 221 USPQ 246 (S.D.N.Y. 1983) 221, 264, 265

—v. Club 30, Inc., 567 F. Supp. 36, 222 USPQ 140 (N.D. Ind. 1983) 221

—v. Coco's Dev. Corp., 212 USPQ 714 (N.D.N.Y. 1981) 290

—v. Fox Amusement Co., 551 F. Supp. 104, 219 USPQ 874 (N.D. Ill. 1982) 236

—v. Gabaldon, 227 USPQ 163 (Bkr. Ct. N.M. 1985) 290

—v. L.R. Corp., Copr. L. Rep. ¶25,741 (W.D. Ohio 1984) 221

—v. Lyndon Lanes, Inc., 227 USPQ 731 (W.D. Ky. 1985) 183, 273, 292

—v. Moor-Law, 484 F. Supp. 357, 204 USPQ 726 (D. Del. 1980) 186, 265

—v. Moor-Law, 612 F. Supp. 474, 227 USPQ 829 (D. Del. 1985) 268

—v. P&R Amusement, Inc., Copr. L. Rep. ¶25,712 (S.D. Ind. 1984) 236, 289

—v. Regal Broadcasting Corp., 212 USPQ 624 (N.D.N.Y. 1980) 221

—v. Terrose, 223 USPQ 137 (W.D.N.Y. 1983) 268

—v. United States Shoe Corp., 678 F.2d 816, 217 USPQ 224 (9th Cir. 1982) 228, 265

—v. Wisconsin Novelty Co., Copr. L. Rep. ¶25,718 (E.D. Wis. 1984) 236

Board of Trade v. Dow Jones & Co., 96 Ill. 2d 109, 256 N.E.2d 84 (1983) 85

Bobbs-Merrill Co. v. New American Library, Copr. L. Rep. ¶25,752 (S.D.N.Y. 1985) 215

Booth v. Colgate-Palmolive Co., 362 F. Supp. 343, 179 USPQ 819 (S.D.N.Y. 1973) 88

Bourne Co. v. Khalil, 611 F. Supp. 269 (E.D. Mich. 1985) 269

Bouvé v. Twentieth Century-Fox Film Corp., 122 F.2d 51, 50 USPQ 338 (D.C. Cir. 1941) 142

Boz Scaggs Music v. KND Corp., 491 F. Supp. 908, 208 USPQ 307 (D. Conn. 1980) 221, 269, 289

BPI Systems, Inc. v. Leith, 532 F. Supp. 209 (W.D. Tex. 1981) 86, 123

Brady v. Daly, 175 U.S. 148 (1899) 8

Bramwell v. Halcomb, 2 My. & Cr. (Ch.) 736 (1836) 250

Brandir Int'l, Inc. v. Cascade Pacific Lumber Co., Copr. L. Rep. ¶25,740 (S.D.N.Y. 1984) 260, 263

Brandon v. Regents, 441 F. Supp. 1086, 196 USPQ 163 (D. Mass. 1977) 46

Brattleboro Pub. Co. v. Winmill Pub. Co., 369 F.2d 565, 151 USPQ 666 (2d Cir. 1966) 105

Breffort v. The I Had a Ball Co., 271 F. Supp. 623, 155 USPQ 391 (S.D.N.Y. 1967) 280, 281

Brewer v. Hustler Magazine, Inc., 749 F.2d 527, 224 USPQ 550 (9th Cir. 1984) 161

Broder v. Zeno Mauvais Music, 88 F. 74 (C.C.N.D. Cal. 1898) 50

Bromhall v. Rorvik, 478 F. Supp. 361, 203 USPQ 774 (E.D. Pa. 1979) 35, 79–80, 90

Brown v. Select Theatres Corp., 56 F. Supp. 438, 62 USPQ 240 (D. Mass. 1944) 141

Brown v. Tabb, 714 F.2d 1088, 220 USPQ 21 (11th Cir. 1983) 143

Brown Instruments Co. v. Warner, 161 F.2d 910, 73 USPQ 427 (D.C. Cir. 1947) 29

Brunswick Beacon, Inc. v. Schock-Hopchas Pub. Co., 84-40-CIV-7 (E.D.C. filed March 11, 1985) 122

Bryce, M., & Associates, Inc. v. Gladstone, 107 Wisc. 2d 241, 319 N.W.2d 907, 215 USPQ 81 (Ct. App.), *cert. denied*, 459 U.S. 944 (1982) 35, 84, 86

Buck v. Jewell-LaSalle Realty Co., 283 U.S. 191, 9 USPQ 17 (1931) 203, 220, 221– 222, 226, 229, 268

Buck v. Kelly, 7 USPQ 164 (D. Mass. 1930) 235

Buck v. Lester, 24 F.2d 877 (E.D.S.C. 1928) 145

Buckley v. Valeo, 424 U.S. 1 (1976) 299

Building Officials & Code Administrators v. Code Technology, Inc., 628 F.2d 730, 207 USPQ 81 (1st Cir.), *on remand*, 210 USPQ 289 (D. Mass. 1980) 38, 53, 55

Burger King Corp. v. Rudzewicz, 471 U.S. ____ (1985) 260, 261

Burke v. Medical Economics Co., 219 USPQ 139 (D.N.J. 1982) 118

Burke v. NBC, 598 F.2d 688, 202 USPQ 531 (1st Cir.), *cert. denied*, 444 U.S. 869, 203 USPQ 640 (1979) 90, 143, 144

Burnett v. Warner Bros., Inc., 486 N.Y.S.2d 613, 228 USPQ 143 (Sup. Ct.), *modified and dismissed*, 493 N.Y.S.2d 326 (App. Div. 1st Dept. 1985) 258

Burns v. Rockwood Distributing Co., 481 F. Supp. 841, 209 USPQ 713 (N.D. Ill. 1979) 136, 184, 264

Burroughs v. MGM, Inc., 491 F. Supp. 1320, 210 USPQ 579 (S.D.N.Y. 1980) 111–112

—519 F. Supp. 388, 215 USPQ 37 (S.D.N.Y. 1981), *aff'd*, 683 F.2d 610, 215 USPQ 495 (2d Cir. 1982) 47, 49, 111–112

Burroughs, Edgar Rice, Inc. v. Charlton Pub., Inc., 243 F. Supp. 731, 145 USPQ 655 (S.D.N.Y. 1965) 46

Burroughs, Edgar Rice, Inc. v. High Society Magazine, Inc., 7 Media L. Rep. 1863 (S.D.N.Y. 1981) 49

Burrow-Giles Lithographic Co. v. Sarony, 111 U.S. 53 (1884) 18, 69

Burstein v. Inside-Outside Bodywear, Inc., Copr. L. Rep. ¶25,488 (S.D.N.Y. 1983) 263

## C

Cablevision Systems Dev. v. MPAA, Civ. No. 83-1655 (D.D.C. complaint filed June 8, 1983) 233

## V

Vacheron & Constantin-Le Coultre Watches, Inc. v. Benrus Watch Co., 155 F. Supp. 932, 115 USPQ 115 (S.D.N.Y. 1957), *rev'd*, 260 F.2d 637, 119 USPQ 189 (2d Cir. 1958)   37, 183

Vallejo v. Webb, COPR. L. REP. ¶25,751 (S.D.N.Y. 1985)   261, 262, 263

Van Dusen v. Southeast First National Bank of Miami, 478 So. 2d 82, 228 USPQ 19 (D. Ct. App. Fla. 1985)   78, 90, 130, 139, 142, 159, 276

Vantage Point, Inc. v. Parker Bros., 529 F. Supp. 1204, 213 USPQ 782 (E.D.N.Y. 1981)   192

Varon v. Santa Fe Reporter, Inc., 218 USPQ 716 (D.N.M. 1982)   118

Vault Corp. v. Quaid Software Ltd., 228 USPQ 139 (5th Cir. 1985)   261

Venus Music Corp. v. Mills Music, Inc., 261 F.2d 577, 119 USPQ 360 (2d Cir. 1958)   106

Vermont Castings, Inc. v. Evans Prod. Co., 215 USPQ 758 (D. Vt. 1981)   41, 58, 81

Vernon Music Corp. v. First Dev. Corp., COPR. L. REP. ¶25,686 (D. Mass. 1984)   268

Videotronics Inc. v. Bend Electronics, 564 F. Supp. 1471, 223 USPQ 296 (D. Nev. 1983)   35, 86

—568 F. Supp. 478, 223 USPQ 936 (D. Nev. 1984)   163, 171, 173, 278

Video Views, Inc. v. Alexander, COPR. L. REP. ¶25,771 (D. Minn. 1985)   265

Video Views, Inc. v. Kuhns, No. C-84-1543 (N.D. Cal. 1984)   265

Vogel, Jerry, Music Co. v. Warner Bros., Inc., 535 F. Supp. 172, 219 USPQ 58 (S.D.N.Y. 1982)   139, 168

Vogue Ring Creations, Inc. v. Hardman, 410 F. Supp. 609, 190 USPQ 329 (D.R.I. 1976)   188

Vy Pub., Inc. v. Hinish, 212 USPQ 185 (D. Mass. 1980)   292

## W

Wainwright Securities, Inc. v. Wall Street Transcript Corp., 418 F. Supp. 620, 194 USPQ 328 (S.D.N.Y. 1976), *aff'd*, 558 F.2d 91, 194 USPQ 401 (2d Cir. 1977), *cert. denied*, 434 U.S. 1014 (1978)   197, 245, 278–279

Walco Products, Inc. v. Kittay & Blitz, Inc., 354 F. Supp. 121, 175 USPQ 471 (S.D.N.Y. 1972)   204

Wales Industrial, Inc. v. Hasbro Bradley, Inc., 612 F. Supp. 507 (S.D.N.Y. 1985)   279

—612 F. Supp. 510, 226 USPQ 584 (S.D.N.Y. 1985)   128, 129, 136, 165, 169, 265

Walker v. Time-Life Films, Inc., COPR. L. REP. ¶25,554 (N.Y. Sup. Ct. 1983)   78

—615 F. Supp. 430, 227 USPQ 698 (S.D.N.Y. 1985), *aff'd*, 784 F.2d 44, 228 USPQ 505 (2d Cir. 1986)   31, 84, 85, 86, 199–200, 202, 260, 296, 297

Walker v. University Books, Inc., 602 F.2d 859, 202 USPQ 793 (9th Cir. 1979)   148, 204, 265

Walt Disney Prods. v. Air Pirates, 345 F. Supp. 108, 174 USPQ 463 (N.D. Cal. 1972), *aff'd*, 581 F.2d 751, 199 USPQ 769 (9th Cir. 1978), *cert. denied*, 439 U.S. 1132 (1979)   49, 242

Waring v. Dunlea, 26 F. Supp. 338, 41 USPQ 201 (D.N.C. 1939)   88

Waring v. WDAS Broadcasting Station, Inc., 327 Pa. 433, 194 P. 631, 35 USPQ 272 (Sup. Ct. 1937)   88

Warne, Frederick, & Co., In re, 218 USPQ 345 (Pat. & Trademark Off. TTAB 1983)   49

Warne, Frederick, & Co. v. Book Sales, Inc., 481 F. Supp. 1191, 205 USPQ 444 (S.D.N.Y. 1979)   49

Warner Bros., Inc. v. ABC, 523 F. Supp. 611, 211 USPQ 51 (S.D.N.Y.), *aff'd*, 654 F.2d 204, 211 USPQ 97 (2d Cir. 1981)   31, 47, 48, 199, 201, 242

—530 F. Supp. 1187, 215 USPQ 690 (S.D.N.Y. 1982), *aff'd*, 720 F.2d 231, 222 USPQ 101 (2d Cir. 1983)   31, 47, 48, 49, 50, 84, 85, 191, 197, 198, 199, 201, 242, 297

Warner Bros., Inc. v. Lobster Pot, Inc., 582 F. Supp. 478, 223 USPQ 239 (N.D. Ohio 1984)   269, 292

Warner Bros., Inc. v. O'Keefe, 202 USPQ 735 (S.D. Iowa 1978)   262, 267

Warner Bros., Inc. v. Wilkinson, 533 F. Supp. 105, 216 USPQ 837 (D. Utah 1981)   89

Warner Bros. Pictures, Inc. v. Columbia Broadcasting System, Inc., 216 F.2d 945, 104 USPQ 103 (9th Cir. 1954), *cert. denied*, 348 U.S. 971, 105 USPQ 518 (1955)   49

Warner Bros. Pictures, Inc. v. Majestic Pictures Corp., 70 F.2d 310, 21 USPQ 405 (2d Cir. 1934)   46

Warner Bros.-Seven Arts, Inc. v. Kalantzakis, 326 F. Supp. 80, 170 USPQ 228 (S.D. Tex. 1971)   267

Warrington Associates, Inc. v. Real-Time Engineering Systems, Inc., 522 F. Supp. 367, 216 USPQ 1024 (N.D. Ill. 1981)   35, 59, 79, 86

Werlin v. Reader's Digest Ass'n, 528 F. Supp. 451, 213 USPQ 1041 (S.D.N.Y. 1981)   85, 202

West Pub. Co. v. Mead Data Central, Inc., 616 F. Supp. 1571, 227 USPQ 631 (D. Minn. 1985)   62, 63–64, 190–191, 205, 242, 249, 251

WGN Continental Broadcasting Co. v. United Video, Inc., 685 F.2d 218 (7th Cir.), *on pet. for reh'g*, 693 F.2d 622, 216 USPQ 97 (7th Cir. 1982)   73, 215, 220, 230

# Index

# About the Author

William F. Patry is an attorney with the law firm of Paskus, Gordon & Mandel in New York City, where he specializes in copyright law. He is the Editor of the Journal of the Copyright Society of the U.S.A. and is on the Advisory Board of BNA's *Patent, Trademark and Copyright Journal*.

Mr. Patry is the author of *The Fair Use Privilege in Copyright Law* (BNA Books 1985) and has published numerous law review articles on copyright law.